D1297208

Sloinnte Ʒaeꝺeal ıꞃ Ʒall
IRISH NAMES AND SURNAMES

COLLECTED AND EDITED
WITH
EXPLANATORY AND HISTORICAL NOTES

BY

REV. PATRICK WOULFE

Priest of the Diocese of Limerick
Member of the Council, National Academy of Ireland

₤

Originally published: Dublin, 1923
Reprinted 1967, 1969, 1993, 2007
by Genealogical Publishing Company
3600 Clipper Mill Rd., Suite 260
Baltimore, MD 21211-1953
Library of Congress Catalogue Card Number 67-27570
ISBN-10: 0-8063-0381-6
ISBN-13: 978-0-8063-0381-9
Made in the United States of America

PREFACE

It is now nearly twenty-five years since I began to collect Irish names in one of the large towns of Lancashire. At that time there was still, in most of the industrial districts of England, a good sprinkling of Irish speakers, exiles of the famine years half a century before. Of those I met nearly all were from the West of Ireland. Not one of them, I am sure, is now living. In the course of two or three years I took down from them most of the names westward of a line drawn from Limerick to Sligo.

Those were the early days of the Irish Language Movement, when there was a great demand on the part of students for the Irish forms of their names, and I was urged to bring out in book form the names I had collected. My collection was, however, far too embryonic to admit of publication at that stage, and I decided before going to press to tap such remaining sources of information, oral and written, as were then accessible to me. My position as assistant chaplain to the Limerick Workhouse enabled me to get a good number of names from different parts of Munster, and my annual holidays for some years were spent in the same quest. In the autumn of 1905 I made an excursion to the Highlands of Scotland, where I became acquainted with Scottish Gaelic names. At the same time I sought, and in most instances received, lists of names from Irish scholars living in the various Irish-speaking districts, and the lists sent in for the Oireachtas prize (1901) were placed at my disposal by the Publication Committee of the Gaelic League. The result of seven or eight years' research was published in 1906, and though still far from complete, was exceedingly well received. A new edition was published in the spring of last year, enlarged by about sixty pages.

It was my intention from the beginning to add a second part containing explanatory and historical notes, but pressure of other work and the outbreak of the European

War, coupled with the difficulties of the task itself, delayed its publication until now. That the book has not suffered by the delay, I am confident. Long and patient study was required to strip our present English names of the various corruptions that in course of time had fastened upon them, trace them back to older forms, and bring to light and identify with them their Irish originals. That study I can now claim to have given to the subject. Whether I have been successful or not, it is for others to judge. I do not say that the book is free from error in every detail —that would be a rash thing to say—but I can honestly claim to have left nothing undone to make it as complete and reliable as possible.

On one point alone must I speak with considerable diffidence. Investigation into the meaning of ancient personal names is, in the most favourable circumstances, surrounded with great difficulty, but in the case of Irish names the task is rendered well-nigh impossible for want of a dictionary of Old and Middle Irish. To deal adequately with this portion of the work would require another volume as large as the present, but it cannot be satisfactorily undertaken until the publication of the Royal Irish Academy Dictionary is complete.

To give anything like a detailed history of the various families would be manifestly impossible within the compass of a single volume. Books as bulky as the present have been written on the history of more than one Irish family, and there are hundreds more whose history would supply material for a nice monograph. My aim has been rather to compress within the limits of a single volume such information as would be of interest to the ordinary Irish citizen.

To the gentlemen, clerical and lay, who sent me lists of names, I am deeply indebted, but above all I owe grateful acknowledgments to my friend, Riſceáṙo Ó Foṫlaṫa, whose invaluable assistance I had in reading the proofs.

páoraiz oe ḃulḃ.

Kilmallock, May 18, 1923.

CONTENTS

ABBREVIATIONS

acc.—accusative.
adj.—adjectival.
angl.—anglice, anglicised.
Ang.-Sax.—Anglo-Saxon.
Celt.—Celtic.
Cf., cf.—compare.
comp.—compound.
dat.—dative.
der., deriv.—derivative.
des.—descendant.
dess.—descendants.
dim.—diminutive.
Eng.—English.
fem.—feminine.
Fr.—French.
Frank.—Frankish.
g., gen.—genitive.
Gen.—Genesis, Genealogies.
Ger.—German.
Gr.—Greek.
Heb.—Hebrew.

ibid.—ibidem, in the same place.
id.—idem, the same.
i.e.—id est, that is.
Ir.—Irish.
Lat.—Latin, latinised.
masc.—masculine.
Mid. Eng.—Middle English.
Mid. Ir.—Middle Irish.
mod. Fr.—modern French.
Nom.—nominative.
Nor.—Norman.
Nor. Fr.—Norman French.
Old Eng.—Old English.
O. Fr., Old Fr.—Old French.
Old Ir.—Old Irish.
q.v.—which see.
Teut.—Teutonic.
V., v.—see.
var.—variant, variants.
voc.—vocative.

N.B.—Special Abbreviations employed in the lists in Part I
are given at pp. 42-5.

INTRODUCTION

In early times, when the population of Ireland was small and scattered, one name generally sufficed to designate each individual, and one name, as a rule, is all that we find. A man was known to his neighbours as Ꭺꞃꞇ, or Conn, or ꞅiꞏꞇᴌᴌ, and as long as there was no one else of the same name in the locality nothing more was required to complete the identification. Personal names were, of course, far more numerous then than now, and it was by no means difficult for each individual in an average Irish community to have a distinct name all to himself. But surnames or family names, as we understand them, were unknown. The Irish had, indeed, from a remote period a well-established system of clan-names, formed from the names of distinguished ancestors, as : Ui ꞃéιᴌᴌ, descendants of Niall of the Nine Hostages, in Meath and Ulster ; Ui Ꝺꞃúiꞏn, descendants of his brother Brian (or Brion), in Connacht and Breifney ; eoᵹꞏnꞏꞇ and Ꝺꞏᴌ ᵹCꞏꞁꞃ, descendants of Eoghan Mor and Cormac Cas respectively, in Munster ; but these names were ordinarily used in the plural and as a common designation of the whole clan. For the individual the single name was the rule.

Nor was this peculiar to Ireland. The Bible is, of course, our oldest record of human nomenclature. There all the names, at least in the earlier books, are single appellations—Abraham, Isaac, Jacob, Joseph, David— given for the most part from some circumstance of birth or as an expression of some religious sentiment. Among the Greeks, too, and the early Romans, the same practice prevailed. The use of the single name was, in fact, universal among the nations of antiquity.

That personal names were originally all significant, there can be no doubt. In the earliest times it must have been so, for without a pre-existing stock to draw from, names, if given at all, could only be given out of the spoken language of the people by whom they were first imposed. The same is true of primitive peoples everywhere. As a matter of fact, the use of proper names only becomes general in a more or less advanced stage of civilisation, when the spoken tongue has drifted away from its primitive form, and intercourse with foreign nations makes possible the use of archaic and exotic words, the meaning of which is commonly unknown. Among the negroes of certain African tribes there are no proper names, nor is the need for them felt, their want being fully supplied by the general use of nicknames. The difference between these two classes of appellations is this : a proper name is given, altogether independently of its meaning, for the sole purpose of distinguishing him on whom it is bestowed from all others ; while a nickname is given precisely because of its signification and as a description of him on whom it is imposed, who is thereby marked off from others by some personal characteristic which distinguishes him being brought into prominence. When, therefore, a name is given because of its signification, it is a nickname ; when given independently of its signification, it is a proper name. All personal names were originally nicknames, in the sense that they were significant and descriptive.

The facility with which nicknames lose their descriptive character tends to convert them rapidly into proper names. Take, for example, the Irish name Ꝺuḃᵹiolla, meaning ' black youth.' As originally employed, it was without doubt a nickname descriptive of the person on whom it was first imposed. But if Ꝺuḃᵹiolla lived long enough, there came a time when he was no longer a ' black youth,' but a grey-haired old man. The name had thus already ceased to be descriptive. Suppose Ꝺuḃᵹiolla had a grandson called after him, but who was not black like his grandfather but fair, here the name would be no longer descriptive, would not even be given because of its signification, but rather quite independently of it—would, in fact, have already become a proper name. And once a name got adopted into a family, the tendency was to perpetuate it and pass it on from one generation to another independently of its original signification.

Few, if any, of our present names have a meaning for the unlearned. Most of them are archaic words which were once part and parcel of the common speech of our ancestors, but now discharge no other function but that of distinguishing between persons. Others are borrowed names that had each a meaning in the original language to which it belonged ; but unlike common words which when translated bring their meaning with them, proper names, having no need of a meaning to serve their purpose, lose whatever meaning they had when taken from their original language. There is scarcely a civilised people but has some names which have no meaning, or of which the meaning has so far remained a mystery. Some of these have come down from ancient languages now lost ; others are exotic words which have undergone such changes that it is impossible to trace their roots. Proper names, too, are in a special way exposed to corrupting influences which tend to disfigure their form and hide their original meaning. Not the least important of these is the practice of forming ' pet ' names, which in turn become the starting point of new names bearing often not the slightest resemblance to the original.

The main sources from which names were originally derived may be enumerated under the following heads : religion and mythology ; circumstances connected with the birth ; physical, mental, or moral qualities or defects ; animal characteristics ; dress ; rank, occupation, office ; trees, fruits, flowers ; weapons ; abstract ideas.

The dithemetic character of the Aryan or Indo-European system of name-giving, which was common to all the Aryan races with the striking exception of the Romans, is well exemplified in the case of many of our Irish names. The Aryan name in full was a compound of two elements placed side by side without anything to show their gram-

matical relationship. The elements are usually epithets
drawn from the strenuous and warlike aspects of life.
Animal names may form one of the elements, the wolf
and the bear being prominent. Religion naturally enters
largely into these compounds. Some nations, like the
Greeks and Anglo-Saxons, made the name show descent
from father or grandfather, and, according to Professor
Weekley, a very common practice was to compound the
name from that of the father and mother, somewhat after
the practice followed by modern racehorse owners. As a
consequence of this genealogical practice, the meanings
of dithemetic names are not always consistent, and in
interpreting them one can only indicate the general idea
which each part expressed.

The single-name system, which, as I have said, was
universal in the beginning, after a time broke down. With
the growth of population, or as one name outstripped
others in popularity, difficulties of identification arose.
Namesakes were necessarily multiplied and the single
name was no longer sufficient in many cases to particularise
the individual, with the result that a further distinction
became a necessity.

From an early period we find the patronymic in use for
this purpose. Irish patronymics were formed by prefixing
mac to the genitive case of the father's name, or ua (or ó)
to that of the grandfather, and the Irish Annals are full
of designations of this character. Copmac macaipc
(Cormac, son of Art) and Laoġaipe macnéill (Leary, son
of Niall), among the names of our early kings, are examples. In addition to this there were descriptive epithets
of various kinds. Some personal characteristic, physical,
mental, or moral, complimentary or the reverse, the trade
one followed, or the place where he was born, or was
fostered, or lived ; one or other of these—it mattered not
which—gave rise to a sobriquet which attached itself to
the name and like the patronymic served to give increased
individuality to the bearer. Epithets denoting age, size,
shape, peculiarities of complexion, existed in endless variety,
and instances of their use are to be found in every page

of the Annals. This system of distinguishing between namesakes was extremely common at every period of Irish history and still survives in a modified form in Irish-speaking and semi-Irish-speaking districts, especially where the same surname largely prevails.

Nor, any more than in the case of the single name, was it peculiar to Ireland. As long as men are living in small and isolated communities there is little danger of confusion in the use of single names, especially when the stock of names is very large ; but when people congregate together in a town or city, with the same name common to several individuals, difficulties of identification must necessarily at once arise. As Canon Bardsley observes, we cannot imagine to ourselves how such a population as that of Manchester or Birmingham could possibly get on with but single appellations. It is no wonder then that in the later books of Moses we should find the Israelites falling back on the patronymic as a means of identifying the individual. ' Joshua, son of Nun ' is a type of name of frequent occurrence ; and in the New Testament we have not only ' Simon Barjonas,' that is, Simon, son of Jonas, but also ' Simon Zelotes ' and ' Simon the Leper ' and ' Simon of Cyrene.' Among the Greeks and Romans the same custom prevailed, since there was the same need.

Of all ancient peoples, the Roman patricians had the most precise and elaborate system of nomenclature, a system which had already reached its full development at the dawn of history. The few facts which have reached us from times anterior to the taking of Rome by the Gauls are traditional and so far conjectural, but there is every reason to believe that the early Romans, like all other ancient peoples, were called by single names, with the occasional addition of a distinguishing epithet. Within historical times, however, while the slave was still known by a single name indicative of his place of origin or some other characteristic, the freeman had three names, the *praenomen*, or forename, corresponding to our baptismal name, the *nomen*, or name of his *gens*, what we might term his clan-name, and the *cognomen*, or family name, which corresponded to our present surname. ' Marcus Tullius Cicero ' and ' Caius Julius Caesar ' are examples of the type of name ordinarily borne by a Roman citizen. In addition to these, some persons had what was called an *agnomen*, or an appendage to the name proper, as Publius Cornelius Scipio Africanus. With the overthrow of the Empire this system was lost ; the patricians who bore these names fled or were exterminated ; and there remained only the common people who, like the barbarians themselves, had been content with single names.

The Celts of Gaul, before the conquest of their country by the Romans, were called each by a proper name, to which was added, when there was need to avoid confusion, either an epithet implying personal description or the name of the father in the genitive case followed by the word *cnos* (son), as Atengnatos Druti-cnos (Atengnatos, son of Drutos), Andecamulos Toutissi-cnos (Andecamulos, son of Toutissus).* Similarly, the Anglo-Saxons used *ing* as a termination to express sonship, as Baducing (son of Baduc), Cidding (son of Cidda or Cydda).

After the fall of the Western Empire the loss of hereditary names was in part supplied by the use of patronymics. These, which were general among all the Latin peoples, were formed from the genitive case of the father's name preceded by the word *filius* (son), expressed or understood, as Petrus filius Martini, or simply Petrus Martini (Peter, son of Martin). Among the Normans, who borrowed it from the French, *filius* was represented by the corrupt form *fitz*, as fitzGerald, fitzSimon. But in the spoken language everywhere the prefix was soon dropped ; among the French, even the genitive termination fell off and the patronymic finally came to be merely the father's name in its simple and unaltered form such as we now see it in so many surnames of Norman origin. Among the Spaniards, filiation was shown by the ending -ez, as in Rodriguez (son of Rodrigo or Roderick), Gonzalez (son of

---

*This word, *cnos*, is now represented by the diminutive termination -án, found in so many Irish names, as Conán, Ɔallán, &c.

Gonzalo), Fernandez (son of Fernando).* The Basques
employed for the same purpose the ending -ana or -ena, as
Lorenzana (son of Lorenzo or Laurence), Juanena (son of
Juan or John), Michelena (son of Michael).
Welsh patronymics were formed by prefixing Mab or
Map (son), shortened to ab or ap, as ab Evan, now Bevan,
ab Owen, now Bowen, ap Howel, now Howel and Powell.
Among the Teutonic races the patronymic ending was
-son, or its cognates -shon, -sen, -zon, as English : Williamson, Richardson ; German : Mendelsshon, Davidshon ;
Danish : Andersen, Jansen ; Dutch : Janzon or Jantzon ;
Swedish and Norwegian : Olsen, Petersen, Magnussen ;
and among the Slavonic races, -vich, -evich, -wicz, -ich,
-vitch, -evitch, -itch, -off and -eff, so common in Russian
and Polish names. The Polish -ski is an adjectival suffix,
like the Irish -ᴀċ, which is added to place-names to form
surnames ; with names of women it becomes -ska.
In the early Middle Ages the use of epithets or nicknames for the purpose of distinguishing individuals of the
same name was also very common throughout Western
Europe. As in the case of the patronymic, it was probably
a result of the loss of hereditary names in the barbarian
invasions. Many of these epithets have come down to
our own time in the form of surnames. Thus arose in
France such surnames as ' le Grand,' ' le Fort,' ' le Bon,'
and in Germany ' Roth,' ' Weiss,' ' Schwarz,' ' Schneider,'
&c. Designations derived from place of birth or residence
were very frequent. In France and Spain these were
characterised by the use of the preposition ' de ' ; in Italy,
of ' di ' and ' da ' ; in Germany, of ' von ' ; in Holland,
of ' van,' corresponding to the English ' of.'

*The origin of this Spanish name-genitive in -ez has been much
discussed. Harrison does not think there is any doubt that it is
the old Teutonic genitive suffix -es (Gothic -is), though he quotes
a German writer on nomenclature who affirmed that it represented
the Latin -icius. Letelier, the Spanish writer, also says it was a
Latin ending. In documents of date prior to the 10th century it
was written -izi, as Federnandizi, Roderizi, &c. ; in those immediately after, Federnandiz, Roderiz, &c. ; while from the 11th
century onwards, the modern form -ez was gradually substituted.

These second designations were not, however, surnames in the modern sense of that term. They were not fixed or hereditary, nor common to all the members of a family. The adjunct, whether descriptive or patronymic, was purely personal and ceased with him whom it described and to whose name it was attached. The son in due course got a designation of his own, but this again was no more hereditary than his father's before him. And so things went on for several centuries, only as population grew and the number of namesakes increased the difficulties of identification became every day greater, until at length individuals could only be described by a complete string of patronymics or by a number of epithets and patronymics combined.*

Surnames in the modern sense are the growth of the 10th and three succeeding centuries. During that period the patronymic, which before was purely personal and changed with each generation, gradually became fixed, like the clan-names centuries before, and began to assume the permanent and hereditary character of a family name. Canon Bardsley writes : " By a silent and unpremeditated movement over the whole of the more populated and civilised European societies, nomenclature began to assume a solid lasting basis. It was the result, in fact, of an insensibly growing necessity. Population was on the increase, commerce was spreading, and society was fast becoming corporate. With all this arose difficulties of individualisation. Is was impossible, without some further distinction, to maintain the current identity. Hence what had been but an occasional and irregular custom became a fixed and general practice—the distinguishing sobriquet, not, as I say of premeditation, but by a silent compact, became part and parcel of a man's pro-

---

*The father of Saul is described in the First Book of Kings (IX, 1) as " Cis, son of Abiel, son of Seror, son of Bechorath, son of Aphia, son of a man of Jemini." As an example of a Welsh patronymic, the following has often been quoted : " Jenkin ap Griffith ap Robin ap William ap Rees ap Evan." With these we may compare many entries in the Irish Annals of the 9th and 10th century.

perty, and passed on with his other possessions to his direct descendants."*

The period at which this change began can only be determined approximately. It is stated by Keating and others, and the statement has been adopted by O'Curry, that surnames first became fixed in the reign of Brian Boru (A.D. 1002-1014) and in obedience to an ordinance of that monarch. O'Curry's words are :—

" Previous to the time of Brian Boroimhe (about the year 1000), there was no general system of family names in Erinn ; but every man took the name either of his father or his grandfather for a surname. Brian, however, established a new and most convenient arrangement, namely, that families in the future should take permanent names, either those of their immediate fathers, or of any person more remote in their line of pedigree."†

Now, if this were true, Brian himself, as the originator of the system, should have been the first to set the example of obedience to his own laws. But Brian never adopted a hereditary surname. Nor did his sons. It was only in the time of his grandsons that the surname Ó bṙiain (O'Brien) first came into existence. It is clear that the new system was of gradual growth and that it arose, as Bardsley remarks, out of the necessity of the time, rather than as part of a settled policy or according to any pre-arranged plan. Apart from the fact that royal ordinances of the kind described by O'Curry were unknown in Ireland before the Anglo-Norman invasion, and in the best of times would be difficult, if not impossible, to enforce, it can be shown from the Irish Annals that fixed surnames were already in process of formation before Brian was born and that the process was not complete until nearly two centuries after his death.

Ó Cléiriġ (O'Clery) was probably a fixed surname as early as the beginning of the 10th century, for we find the death of Tigearnaċ Ua Cléiriġ, lord of Aidhne, recorded in the Annals of the Four Masters at the year 916, and that

*English Surnames, p. 6.   †MS. Materials,p. 214.

of his brother ꝼlᴀnn Uᴀ Cléiꝛig, lord of South Connacht, who was slain by the men of Munster, at the year 950. I doubt if we have any older surname in Europe. Ó Cᴀnᴀnnáin of Tirconaill is mentioned at 941 ; Ɗoṁnᴀll Uᴀ Néill, the first of the O'Neills of Ulster, at 943 ; Uᴀ Ruᴀiꝛc of Breifney and Uᴀ Ciᴀꝛɗᴀ (O'Keary) of Cairbre, at 952 ; Mᴀg ᴀongusᴀ (Maguiness) at 956 ; while Ó Mᴀolɗoꝛᴀiɗ (O'Muldory) of Tirconaill, Ó Ɗuɓɗᴀ (O'Dowd) of Tireragh, Ó Ceᴀllᴀig (O'Kelly) of Ui Maine, and many others were firmly established as surnames before the end of the century.

With a view to showing that the statement of Keating and others just referred to was more rhetorical than correct, Dr. O'Donovan drew up a list of the progenitors of various important Irish families, showing the periods at which, according to the Irish Annals, they flourished or died, the dates being taken for the most part from the Annals of Ulster or the Four Masters. This list, which cannot fail to be of interest to Irish readers, is here subjoined :

> Fox (Sionnach) of Teffia, slain 1084.
> MacCarthy of Desmond, slain 1043.
> MacEgan of Ui Maine, flourished 940.
> MacEochy, or Keogh, of Ui Maine, 1290.
> MacGillapatrick of Ossory, slain 995.
> MacMurrough of Leinster, died 1070.
> MacNamara of Thomond, flourished 1074.
> O'Boyle of Tirconnell, flourished 900.
> O'Brien of Thomond, died 1014.
> O'Byrne of Leinster, died 1050.
> O'Cahill of Ui Fiachrach, flourished 900.
> O'Callaghan of Desmond, flourished 1092.
> O'Canannan of Tirconnell, flourished 950.
> O'Clery of South Ui Fiachrach, flourished 850.
> O'Conor of Connacht, died 974.
> O'Connor of Corcomruadh, died 1002.
> O'Connor of Offaly, died 977.
> O'Dea of Thomond, flourished 1014.
> O'Doherty of Tirconnell, flourished 901.

O'Donnell of Corca Bhaiscinn, slain 1014.
O'Donnell of Ui Maine, flourished 960.
O'Donnell of Tirconnell, flourished 950.
O'Donoghue of Desmond, flourished 1030.
O'Donovan, slain 976.
O'Dowda of Tireragh, flourished 876.
O'Dugan of Fermoy, flourished 1050.
O'Faelain of Decies, flourished 970.
O'Flaherty of Iar-Connacht, flourished 970.
O'Gallagher of Tirconnell, flourished 950.
O'Heyne of Ui Fiachrach, flourished 950.
O'Keeffe of Desmond, flourished 950.
O'Kelly of Ui Maine, flourished 874.
O'Kevan of Ui Fiachrach, flourished 876.
O'Loughlin of Burren, died 983.
O'Madden of Ui Maine, flourished 1009.
O'Mahony of Desmond, slain 1014.
O'Melaghlen of Meath, died 1022.
O'Molloy of Feara Ceall, slain 1019.
O'Muldory of Tirconnell, flourished 870.
O'Neill of Ulster, slain 919.
O'Quin of Thomond, flourished 970
O'Ruairc of Breifny, died 893.
O'Scanlan of Ui Fiachrach, flourished 946.
O'Shaughnessy of Ui Fiachrach, flourished 1100
O'Sullivan of Desmond, flourished 950.
O'Tuathail or O'Toole of Leinster, died 950.

From this list it will be seen that the ancestors of the most distinguished Irish families, whose names have been preserved in the surnames of their descendants, flourished at some period between the middle of the 9th and the end of the 13th century. In the case of families whose eponymous ancestor flourished in the 9th century, as O'Clery, O'Dowd, O'Kelly of Ui Maine, O'Kevan of Ui Fiachrach, O'Muldory of Tirconaill and O Ruairc of Breifney, the date when the surname became fixed cannot have been much later than the beginning of the 10th century, though it may not appear in the Annals until a considerable time after.

The date, at most, cannot have been more than sixty
years from the period when the ancestor flourished or
died ; but, indeed, there is no reason why the surname
might not have become fixed even in his lifetime, as seems
to have happened in the case of the family of Ó Canannáin
of Tirconaill, where the surname is mentioned in the
Annals at the year 941, while the *floruit* of the ancestor
is set down at 950. The surname O'Neill of Ulster, which
was taken from Niall Glundubh, Monarch of Ireland,
slain in 919, appears in the Annals at the year 943. Instances where the ancestor flourished or died in the first
half of the 10th century are numerous, as, besides those
just mentioned, MacEgan, O'Cahill of Ui Fiachrach,
O'Doherty, O'Donnell of Tirconaill, O'Gallagher, O'Heyne,
O'Keeffe, O'Scanlan of Ui Fiachrach, O'Sullivan and
O'Toole. All these must have been fixed surnames before
Brian Boru began his reign and became such independently
of any royal ordinance.

On the other hand, many surnames only came into
existence long after Brian's time. Surnames like Mac-
Giollapatrick (Fitzpatrick) of Ossory, O'Connor of Connacht, O'Connor of Offaly, O'Donovan, O'Phelan of
Decies, O'Flaherty of Connacht, O'Loughlin of Burren,
and O'Quin of Thomond, must have been already fixed in
the early part of the 11th century ; but many others, as
MacCarthy of Desmond, MacMurrough of Leinster, Mac-
Namara of Thomond, O'Byrne, O'Callaghan, O'Dea,
O'Donoghue of Desmond, O'Dugan of Fermoy, O'Melaghlen
of Meath, O'Molloy of Feara Ceall and O'Shaughnessy,
cannot have become fixed until long after Brian had been
laid to rest at Armagh.

But while it cannot be admitted that our surnames owe
their existence to any ordinance of Brian Boru, still many
of them arose in his time. The 11th and 12th centuries
must, however, be assigned as the period within which
the great bulk of our Irish patronymics became fixed and
began to assume the hereditary character of family names.
The practice of forming surnames with ua (or Ó) had
almost certainly ceased before the coming of the English,

and I doubt if we have any Ó-surname that can be shown to have arisen at a later date. Mac-surnames are, generally speaking, of later date than Ó-surnames ; still I think it must be admitted that by the end of the 12th century surnames were universal among Irish families. It is true, indeed, that they were not all at first of a lasting character, and in some instances were laid aside after a generation or two in favour of new surnames taken from less remote ancestors. Thus Ó Roḃuiḃ was replaced by Maʒ Oineaċċaiʒ (Mageraghty), Ó Maolnuanaiḋ (O'Mulrooney), originally a branch of the O'Connors, by Mac Dianmaḋa (MacDermott), Ó héoċaḋa (O'Heochy) by Mac Duinnḟléiḃe (MacDunlevy), Ó ʒéanaḋáin (O'Geran) by Maʒ ḟionnḃainn (Gaynor). It is also true that many Mac-surnames of purely Irish origin are of later date than the Anglo-Norman invasion, but this was due to the breaking up of the old surnames into septs and the assumption of new surnames in Mac by branches that had separated from the parent stock. After the Anglo-Norman invasion, many of the great families began to split up into septs, some of which took distinct surnames from the names of their founders, even at a comparatively late period. The instances are numerous. Thus the MacSweenys are, according to MacFirbis, a branch of the O'Neills of Ulster ; the MacMahons of Thomond, the MacConsidines and the MacLysaghts, of the O'Briens ; the MacGoldricks of the O'Rourkes ; the MacAuliffes of the MacCarthys ; the Mac-Crohans and MacGillicudys, of the O'Sullivans ; the Mac-Eochys, or Keoghs, of Connacht, of the O'Kellys of Ui Maine ; the MacDermotts and MacManuses of Connacht, of the O'Connors ; the MacDonoughs of Sligo, of the Mac-Dermotts ; the MacGillykellys, or Kilkellys, of the O'Clerys ; the MacDunlevys, of the O'Heochys of Ulidia ; the Mac-Gilhoolys, of the O'Mulveys ; the MacSheedys and Mac-Clancys of Thomond, of the MacNamaras ; the MacClos-keys and MacAvenues, of the O'Kanes ; the MacDevitts and MacConnellogues, of the O'Dohertys ; the MacCaffreys, MacAwleys and MacManuses of Fermanagh, of the Ma-guires ; and so on. At what period this practice ceased it is impossible to say with any degree of certainty, but it is well known that some of the foregoing sur-names cannot be allowed a higher antiquity than the 13th or 14th century. I think we have a few surnames that originated only in the 16th.

It is a remarkable fact, though so far as I am aware hitherto unnoticed, that Ireland was the first country after the fall of the Western Empire to adopt hereditary surnames. I have already mentioned Ó Cléiṗiṡ as our oldest Irish surname ; and several others, as I have shown, were already fixed by the end of the 10th century. All these must be older than any other existing surnames in Europe. The oldest surnames on the Continent are those of France and Italy, especially the Province of Venice, but the earliest date assigned to them is the 11th century. Among the common people hereditary surnames were not universal until more than two or three centuries later.

Of surnames in England, William Camden, the oldest authority on the subject, in his ' Remaines concerning Britaine,' writes :

" As for my self, I never hitherto found any hereditary surname before the Conquest (1066), neither any that I know ; and yet both I my self and divers whom I know, have pored and pusled upon many an old Record and evidence to satisfie our selves herein ; and for my part I will acknowledge my self greatly indebted to them that will clear this doubt."

Freeman, in his History of the Norman Conquest of England, states that " in England before the Conquest there is no ascertained case of a strictly hereditary sur-name." " If the Norman Conquest had never happened," he writes, " it is almost certain we should have formed for ourselves a system of hereditary surnames. Still, as a matter of fact, the use of hereditary surnames begins in England with the Conquest, and it may be set down as one of its results."

The late Isaac Taylor, author of the celebrated ' Words and Places ' and ' Names and their Histories,' in a con-tribution to ' Notes and Queries ' (2nd Feb., 1901), writes :

" Surnames grew out of descriptive appellations, and the date at which they originated varied according to the locality and the person's rank in life. In the South we find them at the beginning of the 12th century. In the Northern counties they were not universal at the end of the 14th ; and in remote parts of Wales, in the mining districts, and in the slums of Glasgow they are still unknown. They were first used by the barons and franklins, then by the tradesmen and artisans, and lastly by the labourers."*

The approximate date of the introduction of surnames in France is given by Camden as 1000, and that he was not much out in his calculation appears when comparison is made with the investigations of modern scholars. Monsieur H. de Gallier, in an essay on the origin of proper names in ' La Revue,' Paris, 1901, shows that the heredity of names was not evident in France before the 11th century, and then was confined to the nobility.†

Freeman writes : " At the time of the Norman invasion of England, the practice of hereditary surnames seems still to have been a novelty in Normandy, but a novelty that was fast taking root. The members of the great Norman houses already bore surnames, sometimes territorial, sometimes patronymic, of which the former class easily became hereditary."‡

In the Lowland Scottish towns the use of surnames began in the 12th century. The oldest Highland surnames, Mac Oubȝaill and Mac Oomnaill (MacDougall and MacDonald), only date from the 13th century. Oubȝaill, who was son of Somerled, flourished about 1200 ; Oomnaill, who was grandson of Somerled, about 1250. The surname Campbell is recorded somewhat later in the same century. Surnames were rare in the Highlands until the 16th and 17th centuries. Manx Gaelic surnames appear to have been formed about the same time as Scottish Gaelic surnames.

*Quoted by Harrison, Surnames of the United Kingdom, II, p. ii.
†Ibid. p. iii.
‡History of the Norman Conquest of England.

In regard to Wales, it is stated in the 16th Annual Report of the Registrar-General for England and Wales (1853) that "hereditary surnames were not in use even among the gentry of Wales until the time of Henry VIII, nor were they generally established until a much later period ; indeed, at the present day they can scarcely be said to be adopted among the lower classes in the wilder districts, where, as the marriage registers show, the Christian name of the father still frequently becomes the patronymic of the son."

In Scandinavian countries, as in Wales, surnames were of comparatively late introduction. Of Iceland, Baring-Gould, in his 'Family Names and their Story' (1910) says that "to this day there does not exist a family name in the island pertaining to a native. Every man is known by his personal designation, and as the son of his father."*

Of surnames in Germany it has been said : "Family names did not come into general employ until late in the Middle Ages. First of all, the nobility in the 12th century called themselves after their ancestral seats, as Conrad von Wettin, Rudolf von Hapsburg ; then among the citizens they were adopted in the 14th century, but did not become general until the 16th century."†

Surnames were not general in Spain at the time of the discovery of the New World.

So tenaciously did the Jews stick to their single Hebrew names that it was only in the 18th and 19th century that they were forced by governmental action in Austria, Germany and France to adopt hereditary surnames.

Strictly speaking, all our Irish surnames are of patronymic origin, that is to say, formed from the names or other designations of ancestors by prefixing ᵯᴀc or Ó, and in that respect they differ most from English surnames in which the descriptive and local elements predominate. There are, however, some apparent exceptions. In districts where the same surname largely prevailed, epithets,

* p. 40.   †Ibid. p. 21.

or, as we should now call them, nicknames, continued to be used, as indeed they do to the present day, for the purpose of distinguishing persons of the same name and surname, and in some instances these in course of time supplanted the real surnames. Strangers, too, were often called by names indicative of their place of origin, as in the case of the celebrated family of MacDunlevy, members of which were known all over Ireland by the sobriquet of ultac in reference to their Ulidian origin. Similarly we had muimneac (Munsterman), laiġneac (Leinsterman), Déireac (Decian, native of the Decies of Waterford), &c. All these families had, however, originally distinct surnames in mac or Ó, but owing to constant disuse these were in course of time forgotten and the epithet had thenceforward to do duty instead. The distinctive mark, therefore, of a real Irish surname is mac or Ó, according to the well-known lines :

> Per Mac atque O, tu veros cognoscis Hibernos ;
> His duobus demptis, nullus Hibernus adest ;

which have been translated :

> By Mac and O
> You'll always know
>   True Irishmen, they say ;
> But if they lack
> Both O and Mac,
>   No Irishmen are they.

But as we shall see in a moment, many surnames in Ó and mac are of foreign origin.

The only difference between a surname commencing with mac and one commencing with Ó is that the former was taken from the name of the father and the latter from that of the grandfather of the first person who bore the surname. Dr. O'Donovan thought it " perhaps not improbable " that at the period when surnames first became hereditary some families went back several generations to select an illustrious ancestor from whom to take a surname, but though his conjecture is supported by O'Curry, it seems to me altogether groundless, for the simple reason that surnames arose naturally without premeditation, and were given rather than taken. The idea certainly was that all the members of a family derived their origin from the ancestor whose name they bore in their surname; but not all families of the same name are of the same origin. Every Murphy, for instance, is proclaimed by his surname to be descended from an ancestor named Mu̱p̱c̱a̱ꝺ, but not all the Murphys are descended from one original Muꝑc̱a̱ꝺ, nor all the Caseys from one original Ca̱ṯa̱p̱a̱c̱.

Instead of Ó or Ṁac, ní, a contraction of in̄s̄ean, daughter, was used in the surnames of women, as Ṁáip̱e ní Ḃꝑia̱in (Mary O'Brien), and this is still the practice when speaking Irish. (See p. 27).

Let us now consider the effect of the invasions of the Norsemen and Anglo-Normans on our name-system.

It may be stated at once that we have no distinct class of surnames that can properly be termed Norse or Danish,* and that beyond the introduction of a certain number of new names the Norse invasions do not seem to have materially influenced our nomenclature. At the period of the Norse invasions, hereditary surnames, it will be remembered, were not yet in vogue, and whatever surnames were adopted at a later period by the Norsemen who settled down in Ireland were formed after the Irish fashion by prefixing Ó or Ṁac to the names or other designations of their ancestors. Meanwhile through intermarriages and other alliances of friendship with the Irish, they had been adopting Irish personal names. The

*The viking-settlements in Ireland, and particularly the kingdom of Dublin, were Norwegian, not Danish. This, of course, does not exclude the possibility that many Danes also lived in Ireland, just as in the Danish settlement Danelage in England, there was a considerable number of Norwegians. But the bulk of the people was Norwegian, and likewise the royal race of Dublin came from Norway.—Contributions to the History of the Norsemen in Ireland, by Dr. Alexander Bugge, 1900.

Landnámabók, which contain an account of the settlements
in Iceland from the 9th century to the middle of the 13th,
has a good number of Irish names which the invaders who
returned took back with them to their homes in the North ;
and even within the last century Finn Magnussen, or, as
we should call him in Irish, ꝼıonn mᴀcmᴀᵹnuıꝛ, a native
of Iceland, was the chief authority for Scandinavian
antiquities. Moreover, some of the Norsemen had, in
addition to their native names, names of a descriptive
character bestowed on them by the Irish, and were thus
known to the Irish by Irish names. Ꝺuꝩᴄeᴀnn and
Cúᴀꞁꞁᴀıꝺ, the names of two of the sons of Ivar of Limerick,
were not Norse, but Irish, meaning respectively ' black-
head ' and ' wild-dog ' or ' wolf.' The Irish, in like manner,
borrowed names from the Norsemen, and some of the
names thus introduced have been popular ever since. As
a consequence of this interchange of names between the
two nations, a name, whether Norse or Irish, was, at the
period when surnames were being formed, no sure indication of nationality, and for the same reason it is now
impossible to say, judging merely from the surname,
whether a family is of Irish or Norse descent. A Norse
eponym, generally speaking, merely indicates a Norse
strain in the family, Norse names having been adopted by
the Irish mostly through intermarriages.

It is not, at the same time, an improbable conjecture
that Ó Ꝺuꝩᵹᴀıꞁꞁ (O'Doyle), Ó nᴀꝛᴀıꞁꞇ (O'Harold), Ó
neᴀnꝛᴀıc (O'Henrick), Ó nıomᴀıꝛ (O'Hure or Howard),
mᴀc Oıꞇıꝛ (MacCotter), and some few other surnames
represent Norse or Danish families. The Irish distinguished between two nations of the Northmen, the Fionn-
Ghaill, or fair strangers, and the Dubhghaill, or black
strangers, Norwegians and Danes respectively. The individual of the latter nation was known as Ꝺuꝩᵹᴀꞁꞁ, the
black-stranger, or Dane. This in course of time became
a personal name ; Ꝺuꝩᵹᴀꞁꞁ, for instance, was the name of
one of the Danish leaders who fell at Clontarf. Ó Ꝺuꝩᵹᴀıꞁꞁ (O'Doyle) is ' grandson of Ꝺuꝩᵹᴀıꞁꞁ,' the black
stranger. The family, as I have said, is probably of

Danish or Norse race, for while there are O'Doyles in all parts of Ireland, it will be remarked that they are most numerous in the maritime counties of Leinster and Munster, and in the neighbourhood of the old Norse or Danish settlements. Ó hﺩpﺩ1lc (O'Harold) is a surname that almost certainly originated at Limerick, and ﺩpﺩlc, as we know, was one of the sons of Ivar, king of the Norsemen of Limerick. Ivar himself has left us his name in the Thomond surname Ó hﺍoﺍﺩﺍp, now generally anglicised Howard. Ó heﺩnpﺩɩc (O'Henrick) is a surname of Norse origin in Waterford or Wexford. ﺍﺩc Oɩcɩp (MacCotter, Cotter) is an unmistakably Norse surname and the family is almost certainly of Norse descent. More than one leader named Oɩcɩp is mentioned among the invaders. In 916, the Earl, Oɩcɩp Ouﬡ, or Oitir the Black, arrived at Waterford in one hundred ships and plundered all Munster. Another Oɩcɩp Ouﬡ, probably his grandson, is mentioned among the leaders of the Norsemen at Clontarf.

On the other hand, many families bearing surnames formed from a Norse eponym are of purely Irish descent. The MacDugalds of Scotland, for instance, are of the same stock as the MacDonalds, who claim to be Gaels and descendants of Colla Uais, King of Ireland. So also are the MacSorleys, from the Norse Soﺍﺩɩple (or Somerled), and some of the MacRorys. The MacAuliffes and MacAwleys, the MacManuses and MacCaffreys, are, as we have seen, branches of some of our chief Irish families. Ó Sɩocﬤpﺩﬡﺩ (Segrue) comes from a famous Norse name, Sigefrid, but the family so called is said to be a branch of the O'Sullivans. Upuﺩﬡﺩp, whence the well-known surname Ó Upuﺩﬡﺩɩp, is commonly regarded as Danish and identical with the name of the Dane who slew King Brian at Clontarf. The difficulty is that it seems to occur too early. The Norse invasions began in 795, but for many years after the inland parts of the country were unmolested. The Annals of the Four Masters, however, record under the year 809 (*recte* 814) the death of Upuﺩﬡﺩp, lord of Ui Fidhgheinte, the present Co. Limerick, who must have got his name some considerable time previous to the first appearance of the invaders. But though this seems to prove that bʀuᴀoᴀʀ is not of Norse origin, yet it is just possible that a Norse name may have been introduced through commercial intercourse with that people prior to the period of the warlike invasions. bʀuᴀoᴀʀ certainly became common as a personal name only during the period of the Norse invasions, and this seems to lend colour to the theory of its Norse origin. There is no reason, however, for thinking that any of the several families of Ó bʀuᴀoᴀıʀ in Ireland is of Norse descent. Coıʀoeᴀlbᴀċ, anglice Turlough, was a famous name among the O'Briens, who got it from their ancestor, Coıʀoeᴀlbᴀċ, who was son of Cᴀċᴀl, King of Munster in the early part of the 7th century. It occurs too early to be Norse ; Cᴀċᴀl, the father of Coıʀoeᴀlbᴀċ, died in 620. Still, it appears to have its root in a Norse word. Thor was the Jupiter of the North. We have his name in the word Thursday, and it is the root of many personal names. Coıʀoeᴀlbᴀċ is 'Thor-shaped,' shaped like the god Thor. Oıʀoeᴀlbᴀċ, whence the surname Mᴀc Oıʀoeᴀlbᴀıᵹ (Costelloe), is of exactly similar formation and import, meaning 'god-shaped,' or shaped like the god Os. I have already mentioned MacManus as the name of two families of Irish descent. Mᴀᵹnuʀ was the Latin Magnus borne by a son of St. Olave of Norway and introduced by the Norsemen into Ireland. Ó Comnᴀıʀ (O'Toner) comes from a famous Norse name, but the family is a branch of Cineal Eoghain. The Annals of Ulster, under the year 874, record the slaying of Oıʀċín, son of Amlᴀoıb, king of the Norsemen. Oıʀċín is the source of the surname Ó hOıʀċín, borne by a Connacht family who were followers of the MacDermotts of Moylurg and apparently of purely Irish descent.

The Anglo-Norman invasion, unlike that of the Norsemen, profoundly influenced our Irish system of momenclature. Not only was an entirely new set of Christian names introduced, and a type of surname previously unknown, but the continuous existence side by side for centuries of two peoples speaking different languages

necessitated a bilingual nomenclature, to meet the needs
of which each name and surname had to appear in both
a native and a foreign dress.

The old Irish system of nomenclature was a very marked
one. Down to the Anglo-Norman invasion, the personal
names in use in Ireland were almost purely Celtic. The
Irish had been very slow in adopting either Scriptural
names or the Latin and Greek names of saints. The few
Norse names that had come in as a result of the invasions
of the Northmen scarcely affected the Celtic character of
our nomenclature. The nomenclature of the Anglo-
Normans, on the other hand, was partly Teutonic, partly
Scriptural and saintly. The most popular names were
those Germanic names which the Franks had brought
across the Rhine and which ultimately found their way
into every corner of Europe. Of names common to the
Irish and Anglo-Normans, there were none. To take a
name that afterwards found favour with both peoples, we
had no Patricks except among the Norsemen in the cities.
So that at the period of the invasion and for several centuries after a man's name was an absolute guide to his
nationality. Every Donald, every Dermott, was an Irishman ; every Robert, every William, a Norman or Englishman. In England after the Conquest it was different.
There the use of Norman names at once became the fashion.
In a short time the great mass of Anglo-Saxon names were
driven out, a few only excepted which were favoured by
special circumstances. " The Englishman," says Freeman,
" whose child was held at the font by a Norman gossip,
the Englishman who lived on friendly terms with his
Norman lord or his Norman neighbour, nay the Englishman who simply thought it fine to call his children after
the reigning king or queen, cast aside his own name and
the names of his parents, to give his sons and daughters
names after the new foreign pattern. . . . In every
list of names throughout the 11th and 12th centuries we
find the habit spreading. The name of the father is
English ; the name of the son is Norman. This is a point
of far more importance than anything in the mere history

of nomenclature. It helps to disguise one side of the fusion between Normans and Englishmen. Many a man who bears a Norman name, many a Richard or Gilbert whose parentage does not happen to be recorded, must have been as good an Englishman as if he had been called Ealdred or Æthelwulf. No one would have dreamed that Robert, the most daring of knights, was of other than of Norman descent, if the English name of his father had not by good luck been preserved."* But unlike the English, the Irish for centuries clung to their ancient names. Here and there, indeed, a Norman name was borrowed, but down to the end of the reign of Elizabeth, in every Irish family without exception, the bulk of the names were Celtic ; and in those cases where the surname left it doubtful, it was possible to judge, with tolerable accuracy, a man's nationality from the name he bore. But ever since the Irish power was broken at Kinsale, Irish names have been falling into decay and their places taken by names of Norman origin. In the long run, what happened in England after the Conquest was sure, unless arrested, to happen in Ireland. Already eighty per cent of the names borne by Irishmen and ninety per cent of those borne by Irishwomen are of foreign origin. The rarer names were the first to die out. Those which still survive are names which were too frequent and too widespread to be killed off in the space that has elapsed since the fashion of taking foreign names began.

Besides the introduction of a new set of Christian names, the Anglo-Norman invasion brought with it also a new type of surname. Irish surnames were, as I have said, all patronymic, the only exceptions being those descriptive epithets which at a later period supplanted the real surnames. At the time of the Norman Conquest, hereditary surnames had not yet arisen in England. Even in Normandy they were still a novelty, but, as Freeman says, a novelty which was fast taking root. Members of the great Norman houses already bore surnames, sometimes patronymic, sometimes territorial. Many of these were

*The History of the Norman Conquest of England, Chap. XXV.

brought into England by the Conqueror and his followers, thus setting the example of hereditary surnames. And besides patronymics and local surnames, those distinctive epithets indicative of the bearer's calling or descriptive of his person, which were already common everywhere on the Continent, also came in and took root in England as hereditary surnames. Englishmen took surnames after the Norman fashion, patronymic, local, occupative and descriptive ; and surnames of all these types were introduced into Ireland by the Anglo-Normans, and all except the first were new.

The character of the surnames borne by the Anglo-Norman invaders will be best illustrated by examples taken from our oldest Anglo-Irish records : (1) patronymics, with fitz, as Maurice fitz Gerald, Meiler fitz Henry, Adam fitz Simon ; or the ancestor's name appears in its simple and unaltered form, without any prefix, as : John Jordan, Robert Wallerond, Adam Fraunceis, William Matheu, John Herberd, Robert Bryan ; (2) local, with de, as Richard de Burgo, William de Barri, William de Freynes, John de Hynteberge, Henry de Maundeville, Philip de Stauntoun, Adam de Keusaac, Roger de Hyda, Hugh de Lacy, John de Verdune, John de Cogan, John de Kent, John de Andoun, Walter de Lecton, Robert de Stapiltoun, Maurice de Rochfort, David de Cauntetoun, Richard de Val ; (3) occupative, with le, as : Thomas le Clerc, Philip le Harpur, Michael le Fireter, Henry le Marescal, Richard le Archer ; (4) descriptive, with le (sometimes corrupted to de), as : Fromund le Brun, Richard le Blake, Geoffrey le Hore, John de Long, William le Graunt, John le Fort, Maurice le Wolf, William le Poer, Thomas le Engleys, Rys le Waleys, Milo de Bret, Adam le Flemyng, Robert le Deveneys.

At the period of the invasion, surnames were still far from universal in England, and many of the first settlers came to this country with only single names. Some of these took surnames on Irish soil, after the Norman fashion, from the places where they settled, as : John de Athy, Richard de Fineglas, Adam de Trim. Others were sur-

named from the places abroad whence they set forth, or
from the trades they followed, as : Jordan de Anglia
(England), Peter de Birmegham, William de London,
Walter le Tailur ; but these, except the first, cannot be
distinguished from other Anglo-Norman surnames of the
same period.

A further effect of the Anglo-Norman invasion on our
name-system was the introduction of bilingualism, as a
result of which most of our names and surnames have two
forms, one Irish and the other English. Ever since the
coming of the Anglo-Normans, a contest for supremacy
has been going on between the two races that inhabit this
island ; and English policy once deemed it of such political
importance to force Irishmen to conform to English ways
and adopt English surnames, that the matter was thought
worthy of special legislation. Accordingly it was enacted
by the Statute of 5 Edward IV (1465), that every Irishman
dwelling within the Pale, which then comprised the
counties of Dublin, Meath, Louth and Kildare, should
take an English surname. This Act which curiously
illustrates the history of Irish family names contained the
following provision, namely : that every Irishman dwelling
among the English in the counties mentioned shall " take
to him an English surname of one towne, as Sutton, Ches-
ter, Trym, Skryne, Corke, Kinsale ; or colour, as white,
blacke, browne ; or art or science, as smith or carpenter ;
or office, as cooke, butler ; and that he and his issue shall
use this name under payne of forfeyting of his goods
yearely till the premises be done, to be levied two times
by the yeare to the king's warres, according to the dis-
cretion of the lieutenant of the king or his deputy."*
This Statute, though it did not, to any great extent, pro-
duce the desired effect, caused some of the Irish families
of the Pale to translate their surnames or assimilate them
to English ones. They must, however, have been very
few ; for about a century later, we find the poet Spenser

---

*5 Edward IV, c, 3. Statutes at Large, Ireland, vol. I, p. 29,
quoted by O'Donovan, Top. Poems, Introduction, p. 26.

recommending a revival of the Statute, inasmuch as the Irish were then as Irish as ever.*

Meanwhile, the descendants of the Anglo-Norman invaders were being gradually absorbed into the Irish nation. They had in many places laid aside entirely their Norman-French dialect and were speaking the Irish language. This necessitated an Irish form of their names. The Norman Fitz was replaced by mac. Other forms of surname were either hibernicised or the families who bore them took patronymic surnames after the Irish fashion by prefixing mac to the Christian names of their ancestors. Thus the Birminghams took the surname of mac ḟeóṙair, from an ancestor named Piers or Peter de Bermingham ; the Stauntons, that of mac an ṁileaḋa (MacEvilly), from an ancestor named Milo de Staunton ; the de Exeters, that of mac Ṡiúrtáin, from Jordan de Exeter, the founder of the family.

Like the great Irish families, some of the Anglo-Norman families also split up into septs which adopted distinct surnames of their own. Thus the MacDavids, the Mac-Philbins, the MacKeoneens, the MacGibbons, the Mac-Walters and MacRedmonds of Connacht are all said to be branches of the great Anglo-Irish family of de Burgo or Burke.

It was only after the defeat of the Irish at Kinsale that what the Statute of 5 Edward IV aimed at really began to be accomplished. Then set in the fashion of changing Irish into English surnames ; and it continued all through the century, until, after the fall of Limerick, the Irish people were brought completely into subjection. Thenceforward an Ó or mac to a man's name was no recommendation in the eyes of the powers that ruled the country. The people were taught or forced to believe that they

*The following appeared in the *Cork Examiner* of 2nd Feb., 1921 : " Miss Abina Corkery, MacCurtain St., Macroom, trading in the name of her deceased father, was obliged to remove from the facia board over the shop window the Gaelic characters ' Séamur Ó Corcora.' She was informed by the authorities that failure to comply with the order within seven days would result in the burning down of the premises. The Irish inscription has been painted over."

must have an English surname, or at least an English version of their Irish surname. Hence the almost wholesale rejection of the Ó and mᴀc during the long night of slavery and oppression through which Ireland passed in the century of the penal laws. To reduce one's name as much as possible to the level of English pronunciation, to give it an English appearance, to modify it in some way and to some degree, was almost a condition of life. Fortunately, however, the original surname continued to live on, unaffected by any changes in the English form, wherever the Irish language continued to be spoken, and thus we are able to recover the Irish form of many surnames that otherwise would have long since disappeared for ever.

BIBLIOGRAPHY

Barber H. *British Family Names.* London, 1894.

Bardsley, C. W. *A Dictionary of English and Welsh Surnames.* London, 1901.

——*English Surnames.* London, 1906.

Baring-Gould, S. *Family Names and their Story.* London, 1910.

Camden, W. *Remaines concerning Britaine.* London, 1605.

Foerstemann, E. W. *Altdeutsches Namenbuch.* Bonn, 1900.

Fumagalli, G. *Piccolo Dizionario dei nomi italiani di persone.* Genova, 1901.

Harrison, H. *Surnames of the United Kingdom.* London, 1912-1918. 2 vols.

Heintze, A. *Die deutschen Familiennamen.* Halle, 1903.

Kleinpaul, R. *Die deutschen Personennamen.* Leipsig, 1909.

Letelier, V. *Ensayo de Onomatologia ó estudio de los Nombres Propios y Hereditarios.* Madrid, 1906.

Long, H. A. *The Names we Bear.* Glasgow. n.d.

Lower, M. A. *English Surnames.* London, 1849. 2 vols.

Macbain, A. *Personal Names and Surnames of the Town of Inverness.* Inverness, 1895.

Moody, S. *What is Your Name?* London, 1863.

Moore, A. W. *Manx Names.* London, 1903.

Pianigiani, O. *Che cosa significa il mio nome?* Lucca, 1911.

Poma, C. *Saggio di onomastica italiana.* Torino, 1911.

Stolfi, N. *I Segni di distinzione personali.* Napoli, 1905.

Toro y Gisbert, M. de. *Ortologia castellana des nombres propios.* 1911.

Trauzzi, A. *Attraverso l'onomastica del medio evo in Italia.* Rocca S. Casciano, 1911.

Weekley, E. *The Romance of Names.* London, 1914.

——*Surnames.* London, 1916.

Weidenhan, J. L. *Baptismal Names.* Washington, D.C. 1919.

Yonge, Charlotte M. *History of Christian Names.* London, 1884.

Brash, R. R. *The Ogam Inscribed Monuments of the Gaedhil.* London, 1879.

Colgan, John. *Acta Sanctorum Hiberniae.* Louvain. 1645.

Dunn, Joseph. *The Ancient Irish Epic Tale Táin Bó Cúilnge.* London, 1914.

Ellis, H. *General Introduction to Domesday Book.* London, 1833. 2 vols.

Farley, A. *Domesday Book.* London, 1783. 2 vols.

Giles, J. A. *The Venerable Bede's Ecclesiastical History of England.* London, 1859.

Hennessy, W. H. *Chronicum Scotorum—A Chronicle of Irish Affairs.* London, 1866.

——*The Annals of Loch Cé. A Chronicle of Irish Affairs from A.D. 1014 to A.D. 1590.* London, 1871. 2 vols.

——& MacCarthy, B. *Annals of Ulster.* Dublin, 1887-1901. 4 vols.

Hogan, E. *Cath Ruis na Rig for Bóinn.* Dublin, 1892.

——*Onomasticon Goedelicum Locorum et Tribuum Hiberniae et Scotiae.* Dublin, 1910.

Jónsson, Finnur. *Landnámabók.* Kobenhavn, 1900.

Joyce, P. W. *Irish Names of Places.* Dublin, 1883-1913. 3 vols.

Kelly, M. *The Martyrology of Tallaght.* Dublin, 1857.

MacAlister, R. A. S. *Studies in Irish Epigraphy.* London, 1897-1907.

Mac Firbhisigh, Dubhaltach. *Genealogical Manuscript in the Royal Irish Academy.*

——*Annals of Ireland. Three Fragments* (edited by O'Donovan). Dublin, 1860

MacNeill, John. *Notes on the Distribution, History, Grammar, and Import of the Irish Ogham Inscriptions* (R.I.A. Proc., vol. XXVII, Sect. C.).

——*Early Irish Population Groups : Their Nomenclature, Classification and*

Chronology (R.I.A. Proc., vol. XXIX, Sect, C).

Moran, P. F. *Irish Saints in Great Britain.* Dublin, 1879.

Murphy, D. *The Annals of Clonmacnoise.* Dublin, 1896.

Ó Cléiɼiȝ, Luȝaiꝺ. ꝺeaċa Aoꝺa Ruaiꝺ uí ꝺomnaill. Dublin, 1893.

O'Conor, C. *Annales Buellani (in Rerum Hibernicarum Scriptores,* Tom. II). Buckinghamiae, 1825.

——*Annales Inisfalenses (in Rerum Hibernicarum Scriptores,* Tom. II). Buckinghamiae, 1825.

——*Annales Tigernachi abbatis Cluanensis (in Rerum Hibernicarum Scriptores,* Tom. II). Buckinghamiae 1825.

O'Curry, E. *Lectures on the Manuscript Materials of Ancient Irish History.* Dublin, 1878.

O'Donovan, John. *The Circuit of Ireland by Muircheartach Mac Neill.* Dublin, 1841.

——*The Banquet of Dun na n-Gedh and the Battle of Magh Rath.* Dublin, 1842.

——*The Tribes and Customs of Hy-Many.* Dublin, 1843.

——*The Genealogies, Tribes, and Customs of Hy-Fiachrach.* Dublin, 1844.

——*Leabhar na gCeart or the Book of Rights.* Dublin, 1847.

——*Miscellany of the Celtic Society.* Dublin, 1849.

——*Ann ls of the Kingdom of Ireland by the Four Masters.* Dublin, 1851. 7 vols.

——*The Tribes of Ireland* by Aenghus O'Daly. Dublin, 1852.

——*The Topographical Poems of John O'Dubhagain and Giolla na Naomh O'Huidhrin.* Dublin, 1862.

O'Donnell, Manus. *Betha Colaim Chille—Life of Columcille* (edited by A. O'Kelleher and G. Schoepperle). Chicago, 1918.

O'Hanlon, John. *Lives of the Irish Saints.* Dublin. 9 vols.

Plummer, C. *Bethada Naem nErenn : Lives of Irish Saints.* Oxford, 1922. 2 vols.

Petrie, George. *Christian Inscriptions in the Irish Language.* Dublin, 1872.

Power, P. *The Place-Names of Decies.* London, 1907.

Reeves, W. *Vita Sancti Columbae, auctore Adamnano.* Dublin, 1857.

Searle, W. G. *Onomasticon Anglo - Saxonicum.* Cambridge, 1897.

Todd, J. H. *Cogadh Gaedhel re Gallaibh—The War of the Gaedhil with the Gaill.* London, 1867.

Thorpe, B. *The Anglo-Saxon Chronicle.* London, 1861. 2 vols.

Ua Ɗuinnín, p. me Ꞡuıƌıp ꝼeapmanaċ : *The Maguires of Fermanagh.* baıle Áċa Clıaċ, 1917.

Walsh, Paul. *The Place-Names of Westmeath.* Dublin, 1915.

——*The Flight of the Earls.* Dublin. 1916.

Williams Ab Ithel, John. *Brut y Tywysogion ; or The Chronicle of the Princes.* London, 1860.

Bibliography of Irish Philology and of Printed Irish Literature. Dublin, 1913.

Islands Landnamabok, Hoc est : Liber Originum Islandiae. Havniae, 1774.

Martyrologium Romanum. Romae. MDCCCCXIII.

The Martyrology of Donegal. Dublin, 1864.

The Miscellany of the Irish Archaelogical Society. Vol. I. Dublin, 1846.

Conán maol. mac ꝼínꞡín ƌuƀ. baıle Áċa Clıaċ. 1903.

Hyde, D. *The Religious Songs of Connacht.* Dublin and London. 2 vols.

MacNeill, John. *Clare Island Survey : Place-Names and Family Names* (R.I.A. Proc., Vol. XXXI).

Meehan, C. P. *The Poets and Poetry of Munster.* Fourth Edition.

O Flannghaile, Tomas. *For the Tongue of the Gael.* London, 1896.

Ó Sıoċꝼpaƌa, páƌpaıꞡ. An baıle Seo 'Ꞡaınne. baıle Áċa Clıaċ. 1916.

Ua Ɗuƀꞡaıll, Séamuр. beıpc ꝼeap ó'n ƌCuaıċ. baıle-Áċa Clıaċ. 1903.

——ppácaí miċíl ċaıƌꞡ. baıle Áċa Clıaċ. 1904.

——muınnċeap na ċuaċa. baıle Áċa Clıaċ. 1921.

Ua Ɗuınnín, p. Ampáın Seaꞡáın Clápaıꞡ mıc Ɗomnaıll baıle Áċa Clıaċ. 1902.

——Ɗánca Séappaıƌ uí Ɗonn caƌa an Ꞡleanna. baıle Áċa Clıaċ. 1902.

——Aṁráin Eoġain Ruaió uí
Súilleabáin. baile Áta
Cliat. 1901.
——Filióe na máiġe. baile
Áta Cliat. 1906.
ua Laoġaire, peaoar. mo
sġéal féin. baile Áta
Cliat. 1915.
——Ṡuaire. baile Áta Cliat.
1915.
The Gaelic Journal. Dublin,
1882-1909. 19 vols.
Proceedings of the Oireachtas,
1899-1901.

Bosworth, Rev. Joseph. *A
Compendious Anglo-Saxon
and English Dictionary.*
London, 1887.
Dinneen, P. S. foclóir ġaeó-
ilġe aġur béarla, an Irish-
English Dictionary. Dublin
and London, 1904.
Halliwell, J. O. *Dictionary of
Archaic and Provincial
Words.* London, 1847. 2
vols.
Kelham, R. *A Dictionary of
the Norman or Old French
Language.* London, 17 . .
(date obliterated).
Liddell & Scott. *Greek-English
Lexicon.*
Macbain, Alexander. *An Ety-
mological Dictionary of the
Gaelic Language.* Stirling,
1911.
——*Etymology of the Principal
Gaelic National Names,
Personal Names and Sur-
names.* Stirling, 1911.
mac ġiolla eáin, e. C. oánta
aṁráin ir Caointe Seat-
rúin Céitinn. baile Áta
Cliat. 1900.
Marstrander, Carl J. S. *Dic-
tionary of the Irish Language*
Dublin, 1913.

Meyer, Kuno. *Contributions to
Irish Lexicography.* Halle
a S., 1906.
O'Brien, J. *Focalóir Gaoid-
hilge-Sax-Bhéarla or an
Irish-English Dictionary.*
Paris, 1768.
O'Connell, F. W. *A Grammar
of Old Irish.* Belfast and
London, 1912.
Ó oonncaóa, Caóġ. oánta
Seáin uí murcaóa na
Ráitíneac. Dublin, 1907.
——Saotar filióeacta an Ataṙ
páoraiġín haicéao. baile
Áta Cliat. 1916.
O'Donovan, John. *A Grammar
of the Irish Language.*
Dublin, 1845.
Ó flannġaile, Comár. eactra
ġiolla an Amaráin : The
Adventures of a Luckless
Fellow. Dublin, 1897.
Ó foġluóa, R. Aṁráin piar-
air mic ġearailt. Dublin,
1905.
——Cúirt an meaóon Oióce.
Dublin, 1912.
O'Kelly, J. J. leabar na
Laoiteaó : A Collection of
Ossianic Poems. Dublin,
1911.
O'Rahilly, T. F. *Gadelica.*
Dublin, 1912-1913.
O'Reilly, Edward. *Irish-Eng-
lish Dictionary.* Dublin,
1817.
Pokorny, J. *A Concise Old
Irish Grammar and Reader.*
Halle a S. and Dublin,
1914.
Stokes, W. *Three Irish Glos-
saries.* London, 1862.
——*On the Calendar of Oengus.*
Dublin, 1880.
——*Saltair na Rann.* Oxford,
1883.
——*The Old-Irish Glosses at*

Wurzburg and Carlsruhe.
Hertford, 1887.
——*Urkeltischer Sprachschatz.*
Gottingen, 1894.
——and Meyer, K. *Archiv für Celtische Lexikographie.*
Halle a S. and London, 1907.
——and Strachan, J. *Thesaurus Palaeohibernicus.*
Cambridge, 1901-1903. 2 vols.
Uᴀ Ꝺuɪnnín, ᵽ. Ꝺᴀnᴄᴀ ᵽɪᴀᵽᴀɪᵲ ꝼeɪᵽɪᴄéᵲ. Dublin, 1900.
Uᴀ Lᴀoᵹᴀɪᵽe, ᵽeᴀ́ᴅᴀᵲ. Luᵹᴀɪᴅ mᴀc Con. bᴀɪle Áᴄᴀ Clɪᴀᴄ. 1914.
——bᵲɪcᵽɪú. bᴀɪle Áᴄᴀ Clɪᴀᴄ 1915.
Windisch, E. *A Concise Irish Grammar.* Cambridge, 1882.
——*Compendium of Irish Grammar.* Dublin, 1883.
Wright, Thomas. *Dictionary of Obsolete and Provincial English.* London, 1857. 2 vols.
Zeuss, J. C. *Grammatica Celtica.* Lipsiae, 1853. 2 vols.
Eriu. *Dublin.* Dublin, 1904.
Irish Texts Society Publications. London, 1898-1920. 22 vols.
Revue Celtique. Paris, 1870-.
Welsh Dictionary.

Begley, J. *The Diocese of Limerick, Ancient and Mediaeval.* Dublin, 1905.
Berry, H. F. *Ancient Charters in the Liber Albus Ossoriensis* (R.I.A. Proc., vol. XXVII, Sect. C).
Brady, W. Maziere. *The Episcopal Succession in England, Scotland and Ireland, A.D. 1400 to 1875.* Rome, 1876.

Burke, W. P. *Irish Priests in the Penal Times.* Waterford, 1914.
Butler, R. *Registrum Prioratus Omnium Sanctorum juxta Dublin.* Dublin, 1845.
Costello, A. *De Annatis Hiberniae* (A.D. 1400-1535). Vol. I. Dublin, 1912.
Gilbert, John T. *Historic and Municipal Documents of Ireland,* A.D. 1172-1320. London, 1870.
——*A Contemporary History of Affairs in Ireland from 1641 to 1652.* Dublin, 1879-1880. 6 vols.
——*History of the Irish Confederation and War in Ireland, 1641-1649.* Dublin, 1882-1891. 7 vols.
——" *Crede Mihi.*"--*The Most Ancient Register Book of the Archbishops of Dublin before the Reformation.* Dublin, 1897.
Grace, James. *Annales Hiberniae.* Dublin, 1842.
Hogan, E. *Description of Ireland in* 1598. Dublin, 1878.
Laffan, T. *Tipperary Hearth Records.*
Lawlor, H. J. *A Calendar of the Liber Niger and Liber Albus of Christ Church, Dublin* (R.I.A., Proc., Vol. XXVII, Sect. C).
——*Calendar of the Liber Ruber of the Diocese of Ossory* (R.I.A. Proc., Vol. XXVII, Sect. C).
——*A Calendar of the Register of Archbishop Sweteman* (R.I.A. Proc., Vol. XXIX, Sect. C).
MacCaffrey, J. *The Black Book of Limerick.* Dublin, 1907.

Matheson, R. E. *Varieties and Synonymes of Surnames and Christian Names in Ireland.* Dublin, 1901.
——*Special Report on Surnames in Ireland.* Dublin, 1909.
Meillet, A. *Introduction a l'Étude Comparative des Langues Indo-Européennes.* Paris, 1912.
Mills, James. *Calendar of Justiciary Rolls, Ireland, temp. Edward I.* Part I, Dublin, 1905 ; Part II, London, 1914.
——*Justiciary Rolls, Ireland,* 1295-1303. London, 1906.
Morrin J. *Calendar of the Patent and Close Rolls of Chancery in Ireland, of the reigns of Henry VIII, Edward VI, Mary, and Elizabeth.* Dublin, 1861-1862. 2 vols.
——*Calendar of the Patent and Close Rolls of Chancery in Ireland, of the reign of Charles I.* London, 1863.
Murphy, D. *Triumphalia Chronologica Monasterii Sanctae Crucis in Hibernia.* Dublin, 1891.
O'Grady, S. *Pacata Hibernia.* London, 1896. 2 vols.
Reeves, W. *Ecclesiastical Antiquities of Down, Connor, and Dromore.* Dublin, 1847.
Sweetman, H. S. *Calendar of Documents relating to Ireland* (A.D. 1171-1307). London, 1875-1886. 5 vols.
Calendar of State Papers, Ireland. Henry VIII, Edward VI, Mary, Elizabeth, and James I. 1860-1912. 16 vols.

Calendar of Papal Registers, 1198—1435. London, 1894-1915. 10 vols.
Irish Patent Rolls of James I.
Reports of the Deputy Keeper of the Public Records in Ireland (1 to 47).
Report of the Franciscan Manuscripts. Dublin, 1906.
Rotuli Hundredorum temp. Henry III & Edward I (1273). Vol. I (1812). Vol. II (1818).
Rotuloroum Patentium et Clausorum Cancellariae Hiberniae Calendarium. Vol. I, Part I, Henry II—Henry VII. 1828.
Transactions of the Ossory Archaeological Society. Kilkenny, 1879.

Bugge, A. *Contributions to the History of the Norsemen in Ireland.* Christiania, 1900.
——*On the Fomorians and Norsemen by Duald Mac Firbis.* Christiania, 1905.
Connellan, Owen. *The Annals of Ireland by the Four Masters.* Dublin, 1847.
D'Alton, John. *Illustrations, Historical and Genealogical, of King James' Irish Army List.* Dublin, 1855.
Frost, J. *The History and Topography of the County of Clare.* Dublin, 1893.
Haliday, C. *The Scandinavian Kingdom of Dublin.* Dublin, 1884.
Hardiman, James. *The History of Town and County of the Town of Galway.* Dublin, 1820.
Harris, Walter. *The Works of Sir James Ware concerning*

Ireland. Dublin, 1739-1746. 4 vols.

Healy, W. *History and Antiquities of Kilkenny.* Kilkenny, 1893.

Hogan, E. *Distinguished Irishmen of the Sixteenth century.* London, 1894.

Hyde, D. *A Literary History of Ireland.* London, 1906.

Johnston, W. & A. K. *The Scottish Clans and Their Tartans.* 5th edition. Edinburgh & London.

Kelly, M. *Cambrensis Eversus.* Dublin, 1848-1852. 3 vols.

Lenihan, M. *Limerick; its History and Antiquities.* Dublin, 1866.

Mageoghegan, Abbe. *History of Ireland.*

Meehan, C. P. *The Rise, Increase, and Exit of the Geraldines.* Dublin. Third Edition.

Mitchell, Dugald. *A Popular History of the Highlands and Gaelic Scotland.* Paisley, 1900.

Morley, H. *Ireland under Elizabeth and James I.* London, 1890.

O'Callaghan, J. C. *History of the Irish Brigades in the Service of France.* Glasgow, 1870.

O'Connell, Mrs. M. J. *The Last Colonel of the Irish Brigade.* London, 1892. 2 vols.

O'Conor Don, C. O. *The O'Conors of Connaught.* Dublin, 1891.

O'Flaherty, R. *Ogygia.*
——*A Chronological Description of West or H-Iar-Connaught.* Dublin, 1846.

O'Hanlon & O'Leary. *History of the Queen's County.* Dublin, 1907.

O'Laverty, J. *An Historical Account of the Diocese of Down and Connor.* Dublin, 1880. 2 vols.

O'Mahony, John. *History of Ireland by Geoffrey Keating.*

O'Rorke, T. *The History of Sligo.* Dublin. 2 vols.

O'Sullevan, Philip. *Historiae Catholicae Iberniae Compendium.* Dublinii, 1850.

O'Toole, P. L. *History of the Clan O'Toole and other Leinster Septs.* Dublin, 1890

Prendergast, J. P. *The Cromwellian Settlement of Ireland.* London, 1870.

Skene, W. F. *The Highlanders of Scotland.* Stirling, 1902.

Stuart, James. *Historical Memoirs of the City of Armagh.* Dublin, 1900.

Webb, Alfred. *A Compendium of Irish Biography.* Dublin, 1878.

White, P. *History of Clare and the Dalcassian Clans.* Dublin, 1893.

Archivium Hibernicum. Dublin, 1912-1916. 5 vols.

Proceedings and Transactions of the Kilkenny and South-East of Ireland Archaeological Society. 10 vols.

The Celtic Review. Edinburgh, 1904-1914. 10 vols.

The Irish Ecclesiastical Record (1864-1916).

Bourke, U. J. *The Aryan Origin of the Gaelic Race and Language.* London, 1875.

Freeman, Edward A. *The History of the Norman Conquest of England.*

Gougaud, Louis. *Les Chrétientes Celtiques.* Paris, 1911.

Green, Alice Stopford. *The Making of Ireland and its Undoing.* London, 1908.

Healy, J. *Insula Sanctorum et Doctorum ; or Ireland's Ancient Schools and Scholars.* Dublin, 1893.

Hull, E. *A Text Book of Irish Literature.* Dublin and London, 1906.

Johnson, A. H. *The Normans in Europe.* London, 1877.

Joyce, P. W. *Old Celtic Romances.* London, 1907.

Lanigan, John. *An Ecclesiastical History of Ireland.* Dublin, 1829. 4 vols.

MacNeill, Eoin. *Phases of Irish History.* Dublin, 1919.

——*Celtic Ireland.* Dublin and London, 1921.

Perry, Walter C. *The Franks.* London, 1857.

Taylor, Isaac. *Words and Places.* London, n.d.

Baudrand, Michel - Antoine. *Dictionaire Geographique et Historique.* Paris, 1705.

Biblia Sacra.

Butler, Alban. *Lives of the Saints.* Dublin, 1872. 12 vols.

Gazetteer of the United Kingdom.

General Topographical Index of Ireland. Dublin, 1904.

Journal of the Ivernian Society. 7 vols.

Proceedings of the Royal Irish Academy. Vol. XXVII-XXXI.

The Catholic Encyclopedia.

The New Ireland Review.

TABLE OF THE VALUES OF IRISH LETTERS

(For the use of readers unacquainted with Irish.)

The vowels in Irish are of two kinds, *broad* and *slender*. The broad vowels are ᴀ, o, u ; and the slender e, ɪ. Each vowel, whether broad or slender, has two sounds, a *long* sound and a *short* sound. Long vowels are marked by an acute accent, as á, é, í, ó, ú ; short vowels have no mark. After accented syllables the short vowels have an obscure sound, like *a* in the word *tolerable*. Final vowels are usually pronounced with a short or obscure sound. The consonants are also divided into *broad* and *slender*. A consonant is said to be broad when the vowel next to it in the same word is broad ; and slender when the vowel next to it is slender. Most of the consonants, whether broad or slender, are subject to 'aspiration,' which changes their radical sound. Aspiration is shown by a dot placed over the consonant, as ḃ, ċ, ḋ, &c. When Roman type is used in the printing of Irish the aspiration is shown by inserting an h after the aspirated consonant. The following Table shows approximately the values of the Irish letters and the various combinations of vowels and consonants :—

A.—SINGLE LETTERS.

Irish Letters			Equivalent in Roman Letters	sounds like	in the word
Á á			A a	a	call, or mar
ᴀ ᴀ				a	that, or fat
b b	broad		B b	b	bad, been
b b	slender				
ḃ ḃ	broad		Bh bh	v	vote,
				or w	wool, power
ḃ ḃ	slender			v	van
c c	broad		C c	c	cool
c c	slender			k	king
ċ ċ	broad		Ch ch	gh	lough
ċ ċ	slender			h	hill
d d	broad		D d	th	though
d d	slender			d	duke, radiant
ḋ ḋ	broad		Dh dh	gh	lough
ḋ ḋ	slender			y	year

Irish Letters			Equivalent in Roman Letters			sounds like	in the word
é	é		E	e		e	where, there
e	e					e	met
ꝼ	ꝼ	broad	F	f		f	fall
ꝼ	ꝼ	slender				f	fill
ḟ	ḟ	broad	Fh	fh			silent
ḟ	ḟ	slender					
ᵹ	ᵹ	broad	G	g		g	gall
ᵹ	ᵹ	slender				g	give
ġ	ġ	broad	Gh	gh		gh	lough, sight
ġ	ġ	slender				y	year
h	h		H	h		h	hat, hit
í	í		I	i		ee	feel
ı	ı					i	mill
l	l	broad	L	l		l	law
l	l	slender				ll	million
m	m	broad	M	m		m	man, mill
m	m	slender					
ṁ	ṁ	broad	Mh	mh		v, *or* w	vain, or win
ṁ	ṁ	slender				v	vile
n	n	broad	N	n		nh	
n	n	slender				n	new
ó	ó		O	o		o	more, or lord. or
o	o					o	other, or lot [move
p	p	broad	P	p		p	past
p	p	slender				p	pet
ṗ	ṗ	broad	Ph	ph			
ṗ	ṗ	slender				ph *or* f in English	
ꞃ	ꞃ	broad	R	r		r	raw
ꞃ	ꞃ	slender				rr	carrion
s	ꞅ	broad	S	s		s	son
s	ꞅ	slender				sh	shun
ś	ṡ	broad	Sh	sh		h	hall, hill
ś	ṡ	slender					
ꞇ	ꞇ	broad	T	t		th	thaw
ꞇ	ꞇ	slender				t	tune
ṫ	ṫ	broad	Th	th		h	hall, hill
ṫ	ṫ	slender					
ú	ú		U	u		u	rule
u	u					u	full

B.—DIPHTHONGS AND TRIPHTHONGS.

		sounds like	in the word
ᴀe		ay	mayor
ᴀ́ı		awi	drawing
ᴀı	{ or	a i	art. plaid king
ᴀo	in Munster in Connacht in Ulster	ay uee ooi	mayor queen wooing
ᴀoı		uee	queen
éᴀ		ea	swear, or fear
eᴀ		ea	heart
eᴀ́		a	father
eᴀ́ı		awi	gnawing
éı		ei	reign
eı		e	ferry
eó	{ in Ulster	oa aw	shoal shawl
eo	{ in Ulster	u o	just mock
eóı	{ in Ulster	owi awi	owing gnawing
ıᴀ		ea	fear
ıᴀı		ei	being
ío		ee	see
ıo		io	motion
ıú		ew	few
ıúı		ewi	chewing
ıu		oo	good
óı	{ in Ulster	oi awi	going drawing
oı	{ or or	u e i	shut let hit
uᴀ		ooe	wooer
uᴀı		ooi	wooing
úı		ui	ruin
uı		ui	guilt

C.—COMBINATIONS OF CONSONANTS.

	sounds like			sounds like
ḃḟ	f	lp	sometimes	rr
ḃḟ	f	ṁc		f or v
bp	b	nd		nn
ḃc	f or v	nl		ll
cṁ	f	ċḃ		f or v
dl	ll	ċṁ		f or v
ꞡc	g	cs		t

D.—COMBINATIONS OF VOWELS AND CONSONANTS.

	in	final	syllable of a name	sounds like	in the word
ᚐıᛟ, ᚐıᚷ		,,	,, ,,	y	trusty
ᚐıᛟe, ᚐıᚷe		,,	,, ,,	ee	trustee
ᚐıᛟín		,,	,, ,,	ueen	queen
ᚐoıᛟ	first	,,	,,	uee	queen
eᚐᛟ, eᚐᚷ		,,	,, ,,	a	father
eoᛟ, eoᚷ		,,	,, ,,	oa	shoal
ıᚐᛟ		,,	,, ,,	ea	fear
ıᛟ, ıᚷ	first	,,	,,	ee	feel
	final	,,	,,	y	trusty
ıᛟe, ıᚷe	first	,,	,,	ee	feel
	final	,,	,,	ee	trustee
ıoᛟ, ıoᚷ	first	,,	,,	ee	feel
oıᛟe		,,	,, ,,	ee	feel
uᚐıᛟ	any	,,	,,	ooi	wooing
uıᛟ	first	,,	,,	uee	queen
uıᛟe, uıᚷe	final	,,	,,	uee	queen

E.—IRREGULAR SOUNDS OF VOWELS AND CONSONANTS

ᚐᛒ, in the combinations ᚐᛒᚐ, ᚐᛒl ᚐᛒř, forming the first syllable of a name, is pronounced in Munster and Connacht like *ou* in *ounee*, but in Ulster like ó. In any other syllable it is pronounced like ú, or *oo* in *tocl*.

ᚐᛟ and ᚐᚷ in an accented syllable, when followed immediately by a broad vowel or one of the consonants c, ᚷ, are generally pronounced like *i* in *high*, but in North Ulster like *uee* in *queen*, and in South Ulster and parts of Connacht and Thomond like *ay* in *may* ř. When followed by l, m, n, or ř, they are generally pronounced like *i* in *high*, but in Connacht generally like á, or *aw* in *saw*. ᚐᛟ, final, is sounded like *a* in *tolerable*.

ᚐᛟᚐ, in the termination of surnames sounds like ú.

ᚐıᛟ and ᚐıᚷ in an accented syllable, when followed by a vowel or one of the consonants l, m, n, ř, ᚷ, ᚷ, ċ, are pronounced in Munster and Connacht like *oi* in *toil*, but in Ulster like *ai* in *main*.

ᚐıᛒ and ᚐıṁ in an accented syllable, when followed by a vowel, or l, n, or ř, are pronounced in Munster like *oi* in *toil*.

ᚐı in monosyllabic names ending in ll, m, nn, nc, and in the accented syllable of dissyllabic names when followed by ll, m, nn, and another consonant, is pronounced in Munster like *oi* in *toil* or like *uee* in *queen*.

ᚐ in similar circumstances is pronounced in Munster like *ou* in *ounce*.

ᚐṁ, in the combinations ᚐṁᚐ, ᚐṁl, ᚐṁn, ᚐṁř, forming the first syllable of a name, is pronounced in Munster and Connacht like *ou* in *ounce*, but in any other syllable like *oo* in *tool*.

ᴀoʊ́ and ᴀoᵹ are sometimes pronounced like *oo* in *tool*, sometimes like *oi* in *toil*.

ʙ, in the combinations lʙᴀ, nʙᴀ, ꞃʙᴀ, generally sounds like ú. ʙ, final, after l and ꞃ is sometimes pronounced ú. -ıʙe in the termination of surnames in Ulster is sometimes pronounced ıú.

ċ, broad, is sometimes pronounced like c, sometimes like ᵹ, frequently like ꞅ, and in the combination -ᴀċᴅ in South Ulster is silent.

ʊ́ᴀ, in the termination of names, is generally pronounced like ᴀ, but sometimes like ᵹᴀ.

ᴀʊ́ᴀċ, in the termination of names, is pronounced like ıᴀċ.

ᴀʊ́ᴀıᵹ, in the termination of names, is generally pronounced like ᴀıʊ́e, or *ee* in *trustee*, sometimes corrupted to uıᵹċe, sometimes to ᴀċᴀıᵹ, ᴀᵹᴀıᵹ. Similarly, eᴀʊ́ᴀıᵹ is pronounced like ıʊ́e, or *ee* in *trustee*, sometimes corrupted to ıᵹċe.

ᴀʊ́, medial, is sometimes pronounced like ᴀċ.

ʊ́, broad and slender, is sometimes pronounced like ʙ ; as also ᵹ, broad.

eᴀʊ́ᴀ, in the termination of surnames, is sounded like í, oı *ee* in *trustee*.

eᴀʊ́, in the termination of surnames, is pronounced in Ulster like ıu.

eᴀ, in the combinations eᴀʙᴀ, eᴀṁ, is pronounced like ᴀʙ above.

eᴀnnꞃ is pronounced like *our*.

eıʙ, in an accented syllable, followed by a vowel or l, m, n, or ꞃ, is pronounced in Munster like *ei* in *height*. eıṁ in similar circumstances is pronounced sometimes like *ei* in *height*, sometimes *ee* in *feel*.

eıʊ́ and eıᵹ, in an accented syllable, are pronounced like *ei* in *height*.

ᵹ, final, is sometimes pronounced in Munster like ᵹ.

ᵹᴀıl and ᵹᴀıle, in the final syllable of surnames, are pronounced respectively ᴀoıl, úıl, and ᴀoıle, úıle.

ᵹuıꞅ and ᵹuꞃᴀ, in the same position, are pronounced ᴀoıꞅ and ᴀoꞃᴀ.

ı, followed by ll or nn, in monosyllabic names, is pronounced in Munster sometimes like *ee* in *feel*, sometimes like *i* in *high*.

ıo, in similar circumstances, is pronounced like ıú.

ṁ, in the combinations lṁᴀ, nṁᴀ, ꞃṁᴀ, generally sounds like ú.

nn, slender, sometimes sounds like nᵹ.

o in the combinations oʙ and oṁ sounds like ó.

oʊ́ and oᵹ, in names of two syllables, are pronounced in Munster like *ou* in *ounce*, but in Connacht and Ulster like ó.

oı, followed by ll or nn, in monosyllabic names, is pronounced in Munster sometimes like *uee* in *queen*, sometimes like *oi* in *toil*.

ċ, broad, in the middle of a name is sometimes pronounced like ċ, and sometimes is silent.

u, followed by ʙ or ᵹ is pronounced ú.

uı, followed by ll or nn, in monosyllabic names, is pronounced in Munster like *uee* in *queen* or like *oi* in *toil*.

uıʙ, uıʊ́, uıᵹ and uıṁ, in an accented syllable, when followed by a vowel, or n, are similarly pronounced.

I

THE IRISH NAME--SYSTEM

CHAPTER I—PERSONAL NAMES

§ 1—Native Names

The Ancient Irish, like the Greeks and Hebrews, were called by only one name, as Aonʒuſ, Ⅾiaſimaiⅾ, Ⅾoṁ-nall, &c. ; but, for the sake of distinction, a cognomen derived from some personal peculiarity, or a patronymic formed by prefixing mac to the genitive case of the father's name, or ó to that of the grandfather, was sometimes added. Surnames in the modern sense were unknown in Ireland before the tenth century.

This usage necessitated a large number of names and led to the formation of a very varied and interesting Gaelic personal nomenclature. The Annals of the Four Masters alone contain nearly two thousand names, and perhaps as many more might be collected from genealogical books and other sources.

Some of these names, no doubt, lived only for a short time and have long since entirely disappeared ; but we have names, like Aoⅾ, Aſit, Cian, Conċoḃaſi, Ⅾiaſimaiⅾ, Ⅾoṁnall, Ⅾonnċaⅾ, Eoċaiⅾ, Eoʒan, &c., which have been in uninterrupted use from the earliest period of which we have any record down to the present day ; while many others, though long obsolete as Christian names, are still preserved in our surnames.

§ 2—CLASSIFICATION OF IRISH NAMES

Irish personal names may be divided according to form into several classes :

1. The first and oldest class consists of names formed by the union of two independent elements or themes,* both nouns and generally monosyllables, as :

Aon-ġuṙ †(one-choice),
Uláċ-ṁac (blossom-son),
Uṙan-ġal (raven-valour),
Caiċ-nia (battle-hero),
Caċ-al (battle-ruler),
Faol-ċaṁ (wolf-warrior),
Flaiċ-ġeaṙ (dominion-choice),
Leaṙ-ġuṙ (sea-choice),

Maon-ġal (gift-valour),
Muġ-ṗón (slave-seal),
Muiṙ-ġeaṙ (sea-choice),
Muṙ-ċaṁ (sea-warrior),
Muṙ-ġal (sea-valour),
Niall-ġuṙ (champion-choice),
Cuaċ-al (people-ruler),
Cuaċ-ġal (people-valour).

2. The second class comprises names formed by the union of two nouns, the first of which governs the second in the genitive case, as :

Cú-ċaċa (hound of battle),
Cú-maṙa (hound of the sea),
Uonnṙléiḃe (Brown-man‡ of the mountain),
Uuḃ-eaṁna (Black-man of Eaṁain),
Uuḃ-ṙíte (Black-man of peace),
Maol-anṙaiṁ (chief of the storm).

The second noun sometimes takes the article, as .

Cú-an-aonaiġ (hound of the fair),
Ġiolla na naoṁ (servant of the saints).

A large number of names of this class are compounds of Maol, or Ġiolla, and the name of God or a saint, as ꞉

Maolḃṙíġṁe (servant of St. Brigid),
Maolṗáṁṙaiġ (servant of St. Patrick),
Ġiolla Cṙíoṙc (servant of Christ)
Ġiolla Ṁé (servant of God).

---

*Such names are termed dithematic. The first element is called the prototheme, the second the deuterotheme. Some themes are exclusively protothemes, others exclusively deuterothemes; while others can be either protothemes or deuterothemes. Names containing only one element are termed monothematic.
† In order to show more clearly the composition of the names, the themes are separated by a hyphen.
‡Or Lord of the mountain.

Céile was used in the same way, as :

Céile Críort (spouse of Christ),
Céile Peavair (spouse of Peter).

Oub is frequently compounded with a word, or place-name, preceded by the numeral vá, two, as :

Oub-vá-boipeann (Black of the two Burrens),
Oub-vá-críoc (Black of the two territories),
Oub-vá-inbeap (Black of the two river mouths),
Oub-vá-leite (Black of the two sides, or halves).

feap was similarly used, as :

feap-vá-críoc (man of the two territories),

Cú, a hound, and figuratively a warrior or chieftain, enters largely into the composition of names of this class.

3. The third class, which comprises only a few names, consists of names formed from two nouns connected by a conjunctive particle, as :

Cú-ʒan-mátaip (motherless hound),
Oál-pe-vocaip (difficult division).
feap-ʒan-ainm (nameless).

4. The fourth class, which is very numerous, comprises names formed by the union of a noun and a qualifying adjective, as :

Ápv-ʒal (high valour),   Oub-cú (black hound),
Ciap-mac (black son),   Oub-ʒiolla (black lad),
Oonn-ceann (brown head),   fionn-bapp (fair head),
Oub-ceann (black head),   flann-cav (ruddy warrior).

Or the adjective may follow the noun, as :

Oaipp-fionn (fair head),   Cú-vub (black hound),
Opan-vub (black raven),   ʒiolla-vub (black lad),
Ceann-vub (black head),   maol-caoin (gentle chief).

5. The fifth class comprises " pet" names,* or shortened forms of the dithematic names already described, as :

Oaippe, Oáipe, Oappa for Oaippfionn or fionnbapp :
fionna, fionnu, finnia for fionnbapp, or some other name commencing with fionn-.

---

* Ordinary "pet" names are : Pat and Paddy for Patrick, Tom and Tommy for Thomas, Will and Willie for William.

Sometimes no trace of the second element remains, and the " pet" name is then undistinguishable from a monothematic name (next class below). Thus, for instance, Ꝺoꝺ may be a shortened form of Ꝺeꝺ̇ein, Ꝺoꝺ̇ᴀl, or Ꝺoꝺ̇luᵹ, or it may be a monothematic name and originally bestowed directly.   Besides, the " pet" name may be either the prototheme or the deuterotheme.   bꝼᴀn, for instance, may be short for bꝼᴀncú or bꝼᴀnᵹᴀl, or for Ꝺꝑꞇbꝼᴀn or ꝼᴀolbꝼᴀn or ᵐᴀllbꝼᴀn ; or it may be a monothematic name.   " Pet " names are usually found with a diminutive termination, especially -ᴀ́n.   (See below, Class 8).

6.   The sixth class consists of monothematic names, that is, names which contain only a single element and at the same time are not reduced forms of dithematic names, as :

bꝼeᴀc (speckled, spotted),	Ꝣuᴀiꝑe (noble, generous),
bꝼoc (a badger),	Reᴀnn (a spear),
Cᴀꝺ̇lᴀ (fair, beautiful),	Seᴀꝑꝼᴀc̣ (a foal, flighty),
Cᴀoṁ (gentle, loveable),	Síoꝺᴀ (silk, silken),
Colm (a dove),	Ceiṁeᴀn (dark grey).

7.   The seventh class comprises derivatives, that is, names formed from other names, and from nouns and adjectives, by the aid of prefixes and suffixes, as :

Prefixes :

Ꝺin-éiꝼliꝼ
Ꝺin-ᵹein
Ꝺin-ṁiꝼe,
Ꝺic̣-ᵹein,
Ꝺn-ᵹᴀl,
Ꝺn-luᴀn,
Coṁ-ᵹᴀn,
Coṁ-ᵹᴀll,
Ꝺío-c̣ú,
Ꝺío-mᴀꝼᴀc̣,
Ꝺo-c̣ᴀꝼꞇᴀc̣,
éiᵹ-ceᴀꝼꞇᴀc̣,
eo-ᵹᴀn,
ꝼᴀiꝼ-c̣eᴀllᴀc̣,
Ró-bᴀꝼꞇᴀc̣,
So-c̣ᴀꝼꞇᴀc̣,
Su-ibne,

Suffixes :

Cᴀc̣-ᴀc̣
Ꝺúnᴀꝺ-ᴀc̣,
bloꝼc-ᴀꝺ,
Lᴀbꝼ-ᴀiꝺ*,
Ꝺoꝼc̣-ᴀiꝺe,
Scol-ᴀiᵹe,
Lᴀoᵹ-ᴀiꝼe,
Ciᴀꝼ-ꝺᴀ,
Ꝺub-ꝺᴀ,
bꝼuᴀiꝺ-eᴀꝺ,
Riṁ-eᴀꝺ,
Ꝣlᴀiꝼ-ne,
Coin-neᴀc̣,
Cnᴀ́iṁ-ꝼeᴀc̣,
Colꝑ-c̣ᴀ,
Ꝺub-c̣ᴀc̣,
Cꝼoiᵹ-c̣eᴀc̣.

*When the suffix is added to a dissyllabic name or word, contraction usually takes place.

8. The eighth class consists of diminutives. These are formed by the addition of the following terminations, viz. : -án* (eán), -agán† (·eagán), -éin, -ín, and -óg(-eóg), as :

Ailgeanán,	bradagán,	Cróinín,	maoóg,
Ceallacán,	eocagán,	Ouibín,	gormóg,
ionṁaineán,	muipeagán,	Finnéin,	muineóg.

The same root word, or " pet" or monothematic name, has often several diminutive forms. Thus many have diminutives in -án and -agán, as :

Apc ,	Apcán,‡	Apcagán,
bran,	branán,	branagán,
fionn,	fionnán,	fionnagán,
flann,	flannán,	flannagán,
niall,	niallán,	niallagán ;

some in -án and -ín as :

Car,	Carán,	Cairín,
Crón,	Crónán,	Cróinín,
glar,	glarán,	glairín,
Or,	Orán,	Oirín ;

and a few in -án and -óg as :

Caoṁ,	Caoṁán,	Caoṁóg,
Colm,	Colmán,	mocolmóg.

A large number have three forms of diminutive, viz. : in -án, -ín, and -agán, as :

Ciar,	Ciarán,	Céirín,	Ciaragán,
Oonn,	Oonnán,	Ouinnín,	Oonnagán,
Oub,	Oubán,	Ouibín,	Oubagán,
Oóar,	Oórán,	Uiórín,	Oóragán ;

---

*-án had originally the force of a patronymic, like the Greek -ides, and meant " son of."

† -agán is a double diminutive from -óg and -án.

‡Many of these diminutives are "pet" names. Thus Anfaóán (little storm) is best explained as a pet diminutive of maolanfaió (chief of the storm) ; gaoicín of maolgaoice (chief of the wind) ; sléibín of Oonnṛléibe (Lord of the mountain) ; Cogaóán of Cú cogaió (hound of war) ; naoṁán (little saint) of giolla na naoṁ (servant of the saints).

also in -án, -ós, and -asán, as :

| Aoú, | Aoúán, | Maoúós,* | Aoúasán, |
| Sorm, | Sormán, | Sormós, | Sormasán ; |

and in -án, -ín, and -ós, as :

| earna, | earnán, | eirnín, | mearnós. |

There is also a diminutive form in -nac (modern -naic) used in the names of females and corresponding to -án in names of males.

Examples :

Male.	Female.
Aoúán,	Aoúnac,
Cianán,	Ciannac,
Daṁán,	Daṁnac,
Sobán,	Sobnac,
Oúrán,	Oúarnac,
Orán,	Ornac,
Rónán,	Rónnac.

Some names take the article, as : An Calbac, An Cornaṁac, An Dubalcac, An feardorca, An Siolla dub, &c.

§ 3—FOREIGN NAMES IN IRELAND

Probably all the names in use in Ireland before the fifth century were of Gaelic, or at least Celtic, origin ; but from that period onwards foreign names have been borrowed from time to time from the various nations with which Ireland was brought into contact, directly or indirectly, in the course of her history.

A number of names of Latin, Greek, and Hebrew origin came in with Christianity. They were almost exclusively Biblical names and the Greek and Latin

---

*The names of saints are sometimes preceded by mo, my, a term of endearment, and at the same time take the diminutive termination -ós as : mocaoṁós moceallós, mocolmós. When the name begins with a vowel, the o of mo is elided and the m incorporated with the name, as maoúós, foe, &c.

names of saints ; but, strange to say, they were not adopted, to any considerable extent, as Christian names by our Gaelic ancestors. The few instances of their use recorded in the Annals and elsewhere show that they were, for the most part, borne only by monks and ecclesiastics, who had, we may not doubt, taken them at their monastic profession or ordination.

Adam must have been in use and, in its diminutive form, Adamnan, was borne by the celebrated Abbot of Iona. Abel was somewhat of a favourite, and we have several instances of its use in the Annals. Noe gave name to two Irish saints. Joseph occurs once, as do Aaron and David. Of the names of the prophets, Daniel is of rather frequent occurrence ; and we had also Abdias and Habacuc.*

New Testament names are represented by John, for John the Baptist, always a favourite baptismal name among Christian nations, and an occasional Philip and Thomas. Of saintly names, we had Augustine, Donat, Hilary, Januarius, Liber, Martin, Natal, &c., all exceedingly rare.

John (eóin) is apparently the only one of all these names that attained permanency. Patrick, the name of the national apostle, came into general use only at a comparatively late period, and its adoption even then was due to Danish and English influence. It is only in the thirteenth century that we first find it in use among Irishmen. Michael, another name of the same class, which now bids fair to rival in popularity the name of the national saint, was until a few centuries ago extremely rare in Ireland. Mary, the name of the Blessed Virgin, was not used at all until long after the Anglo-Norman invasion. Martha occurs once, in the eighth century, as the name of an Abbess of Kildare.

---

*See Annals of the Four Masters at the year 539 where a strange story is told of an Irishman of this name, which is scarcely surpassed by the adventure of his Hebrew namesake, as related in Daniel, XIV., 32 et seqq.

Strange as it may appear. it was the very reverence in which these names were held that prevented their more widespread adoption, our ancestors preferring to be known as the servants, rather than the namesakes, of the saintly men and women who bore them. Hence, instead of directly adopting the name of the saint, they formed from it a new name by prefixing to it the word maoɫ* or ʒ1oɫɫa† signifying servant or devotee, and names so formed were common in Ireland—those formed with maoɫ from early Christian times. The following is a list of such names: ‡

> maoɫ ƀeanóin (servant of Benignus),
> maoɫ eóin (servant of John),
> maoɫ íora (servant of Jesus),
> maoɫ ʒ1ric (servant of Cyriacus),
> maoɫ máptain (servant of Martin),
> maoɫ mícíl (servant of Michael),
> maoɫ muipe (servant of Mary),
> maoɫ pápraiʒ (servant of Patrick),
> maoɫ peaoaip (servant of Peter),
> maoɫ póiɫ (servant of Paul),
> maoɫ Seaclainn (servant of Secundinus),
> ʒ1oɫɫa Aoamnáin (servant of Adamnan),
> ʒ1oɫɫa eóin (servant of John),
> ʒ1oɫɫa íora (servant of Jesus),
> ʒ1oɫɫa Steapáin (servant of Stephen),
> ʒ1oɫɫa máptain (servant of Martin).
> ʒ1oɫɫa mícíl (servant of Michael),
> ʒ1oɫɫa muipe (servant of Mary),
> ʒ1oɫɫa pápraiʒ (servant of Patrick),
> ʒ1oɫɫa peaoaip (servant of Peter),
> ʒ1oɫɫa póiɫ (servant of Paul),
> ʒ1oɫɫa Seaclainn (servant of Secundinus),

---

*maoɫ originally meant bald, hence tonsured, and when prefixed to the name of a saint, the tonsured servant or devotee of that saint. It is now confused with the old word máɫ (Old Celtic maglos), a chief, and consequently has sometimes also that meaning, as in maoɫanraio, chief of the storm, maoɫcaoin, gentle chief &c.

† ʒ1oɫɫa is probably derived from the Norse " gisl," a pledge or hostage. It only became common during the Danish period when it was largely used by the Northmen, on their conversion to Christianity, to form Christian names. In this connection it signifies servant or devotee. At other times it has

Many of these scriptural and saintly names, and others of the same origin, were again introduced as a later period by the Normans, when they passed into more general use. Hence, names of this class have sometimes two forms in Irish, according to the date and channel of introduction, the older form being used exclusively for the saint, and the more modern one for ordinary individuals of the name. Examples:

	Older Form.	Later Form.
Adam,	Áóaṁ,	Áoam,
Mary,	muiṗe,	máiṗe,
John,	eóin,	Seán, Seón,
Andrew,	Ainoṗéaṗ,	Ainoṗiú,
Stephen,	Steaṗán,	Stiaḃna,
Martin,	máṗtan,	máiṗtín, &c.

The British missionaries who accompanied St. Patrick to Ireland, and the Saxon saints and students who frequented the Irish schools, have left us a few names; but probably the only one that still survives as a Christian name is that of St. Beircheart (anglice Benjamin) of Tullylease.

Owing to intermarriage, and other alliances of friendship, many Danish and Norse names passed into Irish families during the ninth, tenth and eleventh centuries, and some of them became very popular. A few still survive as Christian names, and they have left us

___

to be translated youth, boy, lad, &c., as Ꞁ ᵹiollaouḃ, the black youth, ᵹiollaṗuaó, the red-haired lad, ᵹiolla na neaċ, the horse-boy, &c.

‡ In the case of names like the present, in which the second element is a proper name, the initial letter of the second part may be a capital, or it may be written small and the second part itself joined on to the first, as ᵹiolla ṗáoṗaiᵹ or ᵹiollaṗáoṗaiᵹ, maol ṁuiṗe or maolṁuiṗe. After ᵹiolla it is better to separate the second part when it commences with a vowel, as ᵹiolla íoṗa, ᵹiolla iaṗaċta. Similarly Cú Ulaó, but genitive Conulaó.

several important surnames.   The following are the
principal names of this class :

Aṁlaoiḃ,	Maġnur.
Apalt	Oirtín.
Ḃruaḋaṗ,	Oitiṗ,
Caṗluṗ,	Raġnall,
Ɗuḃġall,	Ruaiṫṗí,
Eanṗac,	Ruaṫṗac,
Ʒoṫṗaiṫ,	Siocḟṗaiṫ,
Ioṁaṗ,	Sitṗeac,
Loċlainn,	Soṁaiṗle, &c.

In the same manner Norman and English names
became current in Irish families during the thirteenth
and subsequent centuries.   These have now almost
completely supplanted the old Gaelic names.

The names borne by the Normans and by them
introduced into Ireland were of three kinds : (1) names
of Scandinavian origin which their ancestors had
carried with them to Normandy ; (2) names of Germanic
origin which the Frankish conquerors had brought
across the Rhine and which had ousted the old Celtic
and Latin names from France ; and (3) Biblical names
and Latin and Greek names of saints, which the Normans
began to adopt about the beginning of the eleventh
century.

Together with these came in a few Celtic names from
Brittany, a small number of Anglo-Saxon names, some
Danish and Norse names from England, and one or
two British or Welsh names.   These were nearly all
very rare and most of them soon died out.   Of the
Anglo-Saxon names, only two, Edmund and Edward,
and these owing to special circumstances, survived.
Alfred has been revived in recent times.

At the period of the Invasion, Frankish names were
by far the most popular among the Normans, but
Biblical and saintly names were coming rapidly into
favour.   The following is a list, in order of frequency,

of the more common names borne by the early Anglo-Norman invaders, the Biblical and saintly names of Latin and Greek origin being printed in italics :
William, Robert, Richard, *John*, Walter, Roger, Ralph, *Adam*, Hugh, Henry, *Thomas*, *Nicholas*, Gilbert, Geoffrey, *Elias*, *Peter* (*Piers*), Osbert, Reginald, *Jordan*, *Simon*, Alan, *Stephen*, *Philip*, *David*, Arnold, *Alexander*, *Laurence*, Baldwin, Herbert, *Martin*, *Maurice*, Godfrey, *Andrew*, Alfred, *James*, *Samson*, Turstein, Warin, Ailward, *Daniel*, Edward, *Gregory*, Bernard, *Benedict*, Hamon, *Matthias*, *Michael*, Gerard, Gervase, Lambert, Wilkin, *Patrick*, Edmund, Edwin, Hubert, Ivor, *Joseph*, Oliver, *Mark*.

The following in alphabetical order were all very rare : *Abraham*, Adelard, Ailmer, *Antony*, *Augustine*, Brian, *Clement*, *Constantine*, Estmund, *Eustace*, Everard, Gocelin, *Isaac*, Leonard, *Luke*, *Matthew*, *Miles*, *Milo*, Odo, Osbern, Osmund, Pagan, *Ponce*, Randulf, Redmund Rodulf, *Silvester*, Turold, Ulf, *Vincent*.

The following names only came in, or at least became popular, at a later period : *Bartholomew*, *Christopher*, *Francis*, Gerald, *George*, *Paul*, Roland, Theobald.

Women's names among the Normans were all, or nearly all, of the Biblical or saintly class, as :
Agnes, Alice, Amelina, Anastasia, Annabella, Catherine, Cecily, Christina, Dorothy, Egidia, Eleanor, Evelyn, Frances, Honora, Isabella, Johanna, Matilda, Margaret, Susanna. The name Mary does not seem to have come into use in Ireland before the end of the 16th century. Brigid only began to be used about the same period.

The Anglo-Normans had several diminutive suffixes, viz. : -el, -et, -ot, (-at), -in, -on, (-en), -oc, -uc, -kin, and -cock. These were generally added to the shortened or " pet" form of the name, as : Martel, dim. of Martin ; Benet, dim. of Benedict ; Davet, dim. of David ; Adamot, dim. of Adam ; Milot, dim. of Miles ; Baldin, dim. of Baldwin ; Dobin, dim. of Dob (Robert) ;

Baldon, dim .of Baldwin; Gibbon, dim. of Gilbert; Paton, dim. of Patrick; Davoc, dim. of David; Jonoc, dim. of John; Mayoc, dim. of Matthew; Aduc, dim. of Adam; Hobuc, dim. of Hob (Robert); Philbuc, dim. of Philip; Robuc, dim. of Robert; Tomuc, dim. of Thomas; Adkin, dim. of Adam; Baldkin, dim. of Baldwin; Hobkin, dim. of Hob; Hodgkin, dim. of Hodge, Roger; Tomkin, dim. of Thomas; Alcoc, dim. of Alan; Simcoc, dim. of Simon, &c.

Not infrequently we find a double diminutive suffix, as:—-elin, -elet, -inet, -elot, sometimes contracted to -lin, -let, -net, -lot, &c. Examples:—Gocelin, Hughelin, Hughelet, Hughelot, Hamelin, Hamelet, Hamlet, Robinet, Robnet, Tomelin, Tomlin, &c.

Religious motives have frequently led to the introduction of names of foreign saints. The Spanish name Iago (James) was brought to Ireland in the thirteenth or fourteenth century by pilgrims from the shrine of St. James at Compostella, and other names of foreign saints, as Aloysius, Alphonsus, Dominic, Agatha, Monica, Teresa, &c., have been adopted from time to time from similar motives. In England, a large number of new names from Holy Scripture was introduced by the Puritans, and some of these have found their way into Ireland.

It may be remarked that many foreign names found at present in Ireland are merely modern substitutes for Irish names which they are supposed to translate, but with which they have often little or no connection, as Cornelius for Conċoḃar, Denis for Donnċaḋ, Daniel for Domnall, Eneas for Aonġus, Eugene for Eoġan, Hugh for Aoḋ, Humphrey for Amlaoiḃ, Jeremiah and Jerome for Diarmaiḋ, Malachy for Maol Seaċlainn, Justin for Saerḃreaċaċ, Mortimer for Muirċearṫaċ, Moses for Maoḋóg, Myles for Maolmuire and Maolmórḋa, Roger for Ruaiḋrí, Terence for Toirḋealḃaċ, Timothy for Taḋg and Tomaltaċ, etc. Charles was

an extremely rare name in Ireland until the early part
of the 17th century when it began to be substituted
in honour of Charles I., for several Irish names, such as
Cᴀᴛᴀʟ, Cᴀᴛᴀoιρ, Coρmᴀc, etc.   Similarly, in the case
of women's names, we have Abigail and Deborah for
Ꝿoꝃnᴀιᴛ, Agnes for Móρ and Únᴀ, Dorothy for Ꝺoιρeᴀnn,
Gertrude and Grace for Ꝿρáιnne, Mabel for meᴀꝺꝃ,
Penelope for ꝼιonnꝿuᴀʟᴀ, Sarah for Soρċᴀ and Sᴀꝺꝃ,
Winefred for Únᴀ, etc.

§ 4-–Cognomina

A cognomen, or epithet, was frequently added to a
name to distinguish different individuals of the same
name.   These cognomina were of three kinds :—

1. An adjective conveying personal description,
   as Coρmᴀc Cᴀρ, Ꝺoṁnᴀʟʟ ꝃán, eoꝿᴀn Ruᴀꝺ.

2. A substantive in -ᴀċ, denoting place of birth,
   residence, fosterage, etc., Aoꝺ muιṁneᴀċ,
   Ꝺoṁnᴀʟʟ Cᴀoṁánᴀċ, eóιn Cᴀᴛánᴀċ.

3. A noun in the genitive case, usually with the
   article, signifying place of origin, residence,
   or some other connection, as ꝃριᴀn ᴀn ꝺoιρe,
   Cᴀꝺꝿ ᴀn ᴛρʟéιꝃe, Conn nᴀ mꝃoċᴛ.

§ 5—Interchange of Names

A marked feature of our Irish name-system was the
frequent interchange of names of the same or similar
meaning.   This was doubtless due to the fact that our
ancestors paid attention to the meaning no less than
to the form of their names.

The following classes of names are to a greater or less extent interchangeable :—

(1) Variants of the same name, as ᴀodán and ᴍᴀodóᵹ, Colmán and ᴍoċolmóᵹ, ſde and ᴍíde

(2) A name and its diminutives, and the various diminutive forms among themselves, as : ſionnḃᴀſſ and ſionnᴄán, ſiᴀċán and ſeiċín.

(3) Names of the same signification, though differing in form, as : ḃᴀiſſſionn and ſionnḃᴀſſ.

(4) Different names used for the same individual, as : Cáſᴄᴀċ and ᴍoċuᴅᴀ.

§ 6—Declension of Names

The declension of names follows the ordinary rules for common nouns. The following points may, however, be noted :—

1. Many names belong to more than one declension.

2. A few names have in the course of time changed their declension.

3. Names of the fifth declension which form their genitive case by adding ċ or n, generally drop these letters in the spoken language.

4. Diminutives in -óᵹ are masculine and invariable.

5. In the case of compound names, the part to be inflected depends on the nature of the compound. Sometimes both parts are inflected, as Cú ᴅuḃ, gen. Conᴅuiḃ ; sometimes the second only, as ᴅuḃċú, gen. ᴅuḃċon. When the second part is already in the genitive case the first alone changes, as Cú Ulᴀḋ, gen. Con Ulᴀḋ, Conulᴀḋ.

6. The nominative case is sometimes used for the genitive, and *vice versa*.

A perusal of the list of surnames will show the genitive form of most names.

CHAPTER II—SURNAMES

§ 1—Gaelic Surnames

Gaelic surnames comprise surnames of Irish, Scottish-Gaelic, and Manx origin.

Irish surnames came into use gradually from about the middle of the tenth to the end of the thirteenth century, and were formed from the genitive case of the names of ancestors who flourished within that period, by prefixing Ó (also written Ua) or Mac (sometimes written Mag*), as :

Ó Briain,	Mac Aoḋaġáin,
Ó hAoḋa,	Mac Cárċaiġ,
Ó néill,	Mag Uiḋir.

Ó literally signifies *a grandson*, and Mac *a son* : but in the wider sense which they have acquired in surnames both now mean any male descendant. The only difference between a surname commencing with Mac and one commencing with Ó is that the former was taken from the name of the father and the latter from that of the grandfather of the first person who bore the surname. Mac-surnames are, generally speaking, of later formation than Ó-surnames.

Surnames were frequently formed, not from the real name of the ancestor, but from some other designation, as rank, trade, occupation, etc., as :

Ó ṡoḃann (descendant of the smith),
Ó híceaḋa (descendant of the healer),
Mac an Ḃáirv (son of the bard),
Mac an tSaoir (son of the craftsman).

The Gaels of Scotland belonged by race and language to the Irish nation, bore the same or similar personal names, and formed their surnames in the same manner as the Irish from the names or designations of their

---

*Mag is used before vowels, the consonants c, ṡ, l, n, and R, and the aspirated consonants ḃ, ḋ, ḟ, ṁ, ṡ, and ċ, but not always even before these.

ancestors. Scottish-Gaelic surnames are, however, of much later date than Irish surnames. The instances of the use of Ó are very rare.*

The Manx language is closely allied to the Irish and Scottish-Gaelic. Manx surnames were formed in the same manner as Irish surnames, by prefixing mac. Ó, however, was not used. The modern spelling is very corrupt, mac being generally represented by an initial C or K.

The Danes and Norsemen who settled in Ireland in the ninth and tenth centuries took surnames after the Irish fashion, by prefixing Ó or mac to the genitive case of the names of their ancestors; but the surnames so formed are in nowise distinguishable from the surnames adopted about the same time by Irish families. What are called Danish surnames are merely surnames formed from a Danish eponym, which, however, owing to the interchange of names, was, at the period when surnames were formed, no longer a sure indication of nationality. The following are examples of this class of surname :

Ó hᴀrᴀilt,	mᴀc ᴀṁlᴀoiḃ,
Ó ḃrуᴀoᴀir,	mᴀc íoṁᴀir,
Ó ᴅuḃġᴀill,	mᴀc Oitir.

Many Scottish and **Manx** surnames are of this hybrid class.

---

*Down to the eighteenth century, the Irish and the Scottish Gaels had a common literary language, though the spoken tongues had diverged considerably. In that century Scottish Gaelic broke completely with the Irish and began a literary career of its own. The spelling of surnames in modern Scottish Gaelic is consequently somewhat different from what it would be in Irish. The Scottish surnames included in this book are given in the Irish spelling.

§ 2—SURNAMES OF THE SEAN-GAILL

The surnames brought into Ireland by the Anglo-Normans were of four kinds :—

1. Patronymic.   3. Occupative.
2. Local.   4. Descriptive.

1. The Norman patronymic was formed by prefixing Fitz (a corruption of the French " fils," Latin " filius"), denoting " son of," as Fitz-Gerald, Fitz-Gibbon, Fitz-Herbert, Fitz-Simon. The English added " -son," as Richardson, Williamson ; or merely the genitive suffix " -s," as Richards, Williams. Welsh patronymics were formed by prefixing " ap" or " ab," from older " Map," cognate with the Irish mac, which, when it came before a name beginning with a vowel or h, was in many instances incorporated with it, as Ab Evan, now Bevan ; Ab Owen, now Bowen ; Ap Howel, now Howell and Powell.

English surnames in " -s" and " -son," and Welsh surnames in " Ap" were, however, at first extremely rare ; they became common only at a much later date.* The type of patronymic most common among the Anglo-Normans was that in which the father's name appears in its simple and unaltered form, without prefix or desinence. Fitz seems to have been dropped early.† The great bulk of Anglo-Norman patronymic surnames are of this type.

---

*The early Anglo-Norman invaders, coming as they did from Wales, were called bρeatnaiġ, or Welshmen, by the Irish ; but Welshmen they certainly were not, at least to any appreciable extent, as the almost complete absence of Welsh Christian names from among them amply proves. English surnames in " s " and " son " were peculiar to the Danish districts in the North of England, from which few, if any, of the early invaders came.

† Nothing is more common at the present day in certain parts of the country than to hear a man designated. no matter what his surname, as Maurice William or John James, meaning Maurice, son of William, or John, son of James. This is but a survival of the Norman practice.

The names from which these patronymic surnames were formed were of Norman, Anglo-Saxon, Norse, Danish, Flemish, Breton, Welsh, and even Irish origin.*

2. Local surnames were taken either from specific place names, or common local designations, or some local landmark ; and the language in which they occur may be either Norman-French or English. If the surname was from a specific place name and the language Norman-French, the local element was preceded by " de " ; if English, by " of," familiarly pronounced " a," as : Robert de Arcy, David de Barri, Torkaill of Kardif, Samsun of Stanlega. The local element may be the name of a country, province, county, city, town, village, or even farmstead. Surnames derived from places in Normandy alone denote Norman origin.

When the source of the surname was a common local designation, or mere landmark, the Normans prefixed " de la," " del," or " du " ; the English " atte," which became " atten " before a vowel, as Henry de la Chapelle, Richard de la Felda, John de la Hyde. Robert del Bois (du Bois), Robert atte Brigge, Gilbert atte Wode, Walter atten Angle, Simon atten Ashe. The local element may be either Norman-French or English or Welsh. †

3. Occupative surnames are those derived from office, profession, trade, or occupation generally. They were originally all common nouns, and usually Norman-French. The definite article " le," the English " the," was generally, but not always, prefixed, as : le Archer, le Baillif, le Botiller, le Boucher, le Erchedecne, le Marescall, the Miller.

4. Descriptive surnames are those which convey

---

* The name Colman which occurs in Domesday Book is an instance.

†A small number of surnames—perhaps not more than thirty—are formed after the Norman fashion from Irish place-names. These, however, were not brought in by the invaders, but taken by them from places where they settled in Ireland.

personal description, and they are of various kinds according to the different ways in which a person can be described. They are generally Norman-French or English, but we have a few surnames formed from Welsh and Anglo-Saxon nouns and adjectives.

Physical peculiarities are represented by "le Gras," "le Grant," "le Petit," "le Brun," "le White," "the Black"; mental and moral by "le Prut," "le Curteis," "le Salvage," "l'Enfant," "the Babe"; animal characteristics by "le Bacoun," le Veel," "le Wolf," "the Fox"; nationality by "l'Engleys," "le Fleming," "le Lombard," le Waleys."

Many of the early Anglo-Norman families assumed surnames after the Irish fashion by prefixing mac to the names or other designations of their ancestors, as :

mac Feórair,   mac an mileaóa
mac Seóinín,   mac an Rioise ;

but most of them retained their original surname in an hibernicised form, as : Oalacún for Dalton, Réamonn for Redmond, hoipeabápo for Herbert, etc. The Norman Fitz was replaced by mac, as mac Seapailc, mac Siomúin for FitzGerald, FitzSimon. English surnames ending in -s and son are similarly hibernicised ; but Anglo-Norman patronymic surnames which had neither prefix nor filial desinence have the same form in Irish as the Christian name. The diminutive suffixes -el, -et, -ot, -in, -on, -oc, -uc, -kin, and -cock are represented in Irish by -éil,* -éio, -óio, -ín, -ún, -oc (óg), -uc (ac), -cín, and -cóc respectively.

The prefix " de " of Norman surnames is represented in Irish by " oe," as oe búpc for de Burgh, oe Léip for de Laci, etc. oe is sometimes incorporated with the local part of the surname, as Oácún for de Autun, Oéabpúp for d'Evereux, etc. oe also sometimes stands for " de la," as oe múpa for " de la Mor ; or perhaps its English equivalent " atte Mor." " de la "

---

* Or éal. The usage is not uniform.

itself, in the few instances in which it survives, is incorporated with the second part of the surname, as Ɗᴀʟᴀɪᴄɪꝺ for " de la Hyde," Ɗᴀʟᴀᴍᴀꝼᴀ for " de la Mare." ꝺe, pronounced ꝺo, is possibly for the Norman " du," the equivalent before masculine nouns of " de la." The English " of" is, of course, represented by " ᴀ" in Irish, but " ᴀ" is sometimes a worn down " ꝺe," as in ᴀ ɓʟᴀc, ᴀ ꜰᴏꝼᴀ. The English " atte," or " at the," is also represented in Irish by ꝺe, as ꝺe ɓᴏɪꝺ for " atte Wode," at the wood. The n of the extended form, " atten," is attracted over to the second part of the name, as ꝺe ꝼᴏ̵ᴦʟᴀ for " atten Angle," at the corner ; ꝺe ꝼᴀɪꝼ for " atten Ashe," at the ash.

The Norman definite article " le" and the English " the," used with occupative and descriptive surnames, are both represented in Irish by ꝺe, " le" having apparently been translated into its English equivalent " the" before the surname was hibernicised, as ꝺe ꝼᴀᴏɪᴄ for " le Whyte," the White, ꝺe ɓʟᴀcᴀ for " the Blake," the Black, ꝺe ɓᴏꝼc for " the Fox," ꝺe ɓuʟɓ for " le Wolf," the wolf, ꝺe ɓᴀɪʟᴇ̵ɪꝼ, ꝺe ɓᴀɪʟɪꝼ for, " le Waleys," the Welshman, etc.

There was, almost from the first, a strong tendency to drop all these enclitic particles, and in many instances they had actually been dropped before the surnames to which they had been attached attained an Irish form ; hence many of these surnames have no prefix in Irish.* Norman diminutives, it should be remarked, like Blanchet, Porcel, Russel, never took the article and consequently never take " ꝺe" in Irish.

---

*This is true of nearly all English surnames which came in after the fifteenth century. In my list I have inserted ꝺe in every instance where I had the authority of old Anglo-Irish records or the present spoken language for its use. ꝺe should not be used before surnames derived from personal names. Norman diminutives, or Anglo-Saxon or Welsh nouns or adjectives.

§ 3—Cognomina used as Surnames

A small number of surnames are substantives in -aċ, -eaċ, indicative of nationality, place of origin, fosterage, etc., as Breaṫnaċ, Caoṁánaċ, Déiseaċ, Muiṁneaċ, Ultaċ.

A few are descriptive adjectives, as Bán, Beag, Glas, Liaṫ, Uaiṫne, etc.

We have also a few surnames derived from place of residence, as an Ṁaċaire, na Bríġde.

These three classes of surnames are merely cognomina substituted for the real surnames which are now lost or forgotten. Families bearing these surnames may be of either Irish or English origin.

§ 4—Alternative Form of Surnames

Most of the patronymic surnames given above (§§ 1-2) have a second form obtained by dropping Ó or Mac and postfixing -aċ (-eaċ) to the nominative case of the name of the ancestor,* as Ó Briain or Brianaċ, Ó Broin or Branaċ, Ó Nualláin or Nuallánaċ, Mac Suiḃne or Suiḃneaċ.

This form is also used in the case of surnames of foreign origin, as Céitinn or Céitinneaċ (Céitneaċ), Dairsiġ or Dairsiġeaċ, Dalatún or Dalatúnaċ, Peitíd or Peitídeaċ. The prefix de is dropped when -aċ is postfixed, as de Búrc or Búrcaċ, de Róiste or Róisteaċ. Surnames ending in -éil and éir change these terminations into -éal and -éar before -aċ is added.

The foregoing forms when standing alone have an indefinite signification and cannot, unless defined by

---

*When the name of the ancestor already ends in -aċ (-eaċ) the termination is not repeated, as Ó Ceallaiġ or Ceallaċ, Ó Cinnsealaġ or Cinnsealaċ.

the context, be used to indicate a particular individual.*
To make them definite they must be preceded by the
Christian name or a title, or turned into one of the
forms mentioned in the remaining paragraphs of this
section, as: Oomnall Ó Briain, Cormac Mac Cárcaig,
Pádraig Conoún, Éamonn de Búrc, Ualtar Caománac,
An tearprog Ó Oomnaill, An Ooctúir Ó Loingrig

The forms in -ac may also be made definite by prefixing the article and can then be used for a particular
individual without the Christian name or title †   The
form has then the force of the English Mr. when the
Christian name is not expressed, as an barrac, Mr.
Barry ; an búrcac, Mr. Burke ; an brianac, Mr.
O'Brien ; an Suibneac, Mr. MacSweeny.

Another way of indicating a particular individual,
without using the Christian name, is to prefix Mac
to the genitive case of the surname, as Mac Uí Briain,
Mr. O'Brien, Mac Uí Caoim, Mr. O'Keeffe, Mac mic
an Báird, Mr. Ward.   In this construction surnames
commencing with Mac are sometimes treated as if
they commenced with Ó, as : Mac Uí Gearailt, Mr.
Fitzgerald, Mac Uí Suibne, Mr. MacSweeny.

We have also corresponding forms of -ac-surnames
with the article, as : Mac an Breatnaig, Mr Walsh,
Mac an Búrcaig, Mr. Burke ; Mac an Róirtig, Mr.
Roche.

---

*In the case of surnames in Ó and Mac, the name alone was
formerly used as the title of the chief of the name, as Ó Néill,
(The) O'Neill, Ó Oomnaill, (The) O Donnell ; and it is still
used as an honorary title in some families, as Ó Concobair
Oonn, The O'Conor Don, Mac Oiarmada, The MacDermott.

†This -ac form with the article was formerly used, in the case
of surnames of foreign origin, to signify the chief of an Anglo-
Irish family, and corresponded to the use of the surname alone
in the case of native Irish chiefs.

§ 5—Synopsis of Types of Surnames

It will be convenient to summarize here under different types the surnames of which we have so far treated.

Type I.	Ó briain. Ó haoḋa. Ó néill.	**XI.**	De Bál. De búrc. Céitinn. Conḋún.
II.	Ó bruaḋair. Ó Duḃġaill. Ó haṁailt.		
III.	Ó ġoḃann. Ó hiceaḋa.	**XII.**	De Bailéir. De Borc. De faoit. aingléir. airréir. Laiġléir.
IV.	mac aoḋaġáin. mac cárṫaiġ. maġ uiḋir.		
V.	mac íoṁair. mac maġnuir. mac feórair. mac Seóinín.	**XIII.**	an ṁaċaire. na briġḋe.
VI.	a paol. a prír.	**XIV.**	brianaċ. búrcaċ. Róirteaċ.
VII.	mac an ḃáirḋ. mac an tSaoir. mac an ṁileaḋa. mac an Riḋire.	**XV.**	an brianaċ. an búrcaċ. an Róirteaċ.
VIII.	báróiḋ. mirtéil. Réamonn.	**XVI.**	mac uí briain. mac uí Caoiṁ. mac ṁic an ḃáirḋ mac uí ġearailt. mac uí Suiḃne. mac an breatnaiġ mac an búrcaiġ mac an Róirtiġ.
IX.	bán. beaġ. liaṫ.		
X.	breatnaċ. caoṁánaċ. ultaċ.		

§ 6—Declension of Surnames

In surnames of Types I, II, III, IV, V, and VII, the name or designation of the ancestor is in the genitive case and remains unchanged in the declension of the surname, except that its initial letter is sometimes aspirated or eclipsed, if a consonant, or has h or n prefixed, if a vowel. With this exception ṁac and Ó alone change.

Ó, or ua, and ṁac are thus declined :—

	Singular.		Plural.	
Nom. and acc.	Ó	ua	í	uí
gen.	í	uí	ó	ua
dat.	ó	ua	íb	uíb
voc.	a	uí	a	uí.

Nom. and acc.	ṁac		ṁic, ṁeic, ṁaca	
gen.	ṁic, ṁeic		ṁac	
dat.	ṁac		ṁacaib	
voc.	a ṁic		a ṁaca.	

Ó, is the usual form in the nominative case, uí in the genitive. When the name of the ancestor begins with a vowel, h is prefixed after Ó in the nominative case singular,* and n in the genitive plural. Ó sometimes aspirates ʄ in the nominative case singular, and always eclipses in the gen. plural, if the name commences with an eclipsable consonant. Uí causes aspiration in the singular. Ṁac sometimes aspirates the initial consonant of the name in the nominative case singular. The ṁ of ṁac is itself frequently aspirated in the nom. case singular after the Christian name ; always in the genitive case, and sometimes in the dative.

---

*There are a few exceptions.

EXAMPLES :

(a) Ḃꞃıⱥn Ó hⱥıꞃꞇ

Nom. and acc.		Ḃꞃıⱥn Ó hⱥıꞃꞇ
gen.	ⱥınm	Ḃꞃıⱥın Uí ⱥıꞃꞇ
dat.	ⱥꞅ	Ḃꞃıⱥn { Ó hⱥıꞃꞇ / Ó ⱥıꞃꞇ
Voc.	ⱥ	Ḃꞃıⱥın Uí ⱥıꞃꞇ.

(b) Ḃꞃıⱥn Ó Ḋoṁnⱥıll.

Nom. and acc.		Ḃꞃıⱥn Ó Ḋoṁnⱥıll
gen.	ⱥınm	Ḃꞃıⱥın Uí Ḋoṁnⱥıll
dat.	ⱥꞅ	Ḃꞃıⱥn Ó Ḋoṁnⱥıll
voc.	ⱥ	Ḃꞃıⱥın Uí Ḋoṁnⱥıll.

(c) Ḃꞃıⱥn Mⱥc Ḋoṁnⱥıll.

Nom. and acc.		Ḃꞃıⱥn Mⱥc Ḋoṁnⱥıll
gen.	ⱥınm	Ḃꞃıⱥın Ṁıc Ḋoṁnⱥıll
dat.	ⱥꞅ	Ḃꞃıⱥn Mⱥc Ḋoṁnⱥıll
voc.	ⱥ	Ḃꞃıⱥın Ṁıc Ḋoṁnⱥıll.

The plural forms of Ó and Mⱥc are now met with only in place-names derived from clan or family names, as : Uı Cınnꞃeⱥlⱥıʓ, Uı Ḋꞃóⱥ, Cúıl Ó ḃFınn, Mⱥınıꞃꞇıꞃ Ó ꞇⱦóꞃnⱥ, ı nUıḃ Lⱥoʓⱥıꞃe. The modern collective plural of surnames of these types is formed by prefixing Muınnꞇeⱥꞃ, Clⱥnn, or Síol* to the genitive case of the name of the ancestor, as :

> Muınnꞇeⱥꞃ Ḃⱥoıʓıll, the O'Boyles ;
> Muınnꞇeⱥꞃ Éılıⱦe, the O'Healys ;
> Muınnꞇeⱥꞃ Rⱥʓⱥllⱥıʓ, the O'Reillys ;
> Muınnꞇeⱥꞃ Ruⱥıꞃc, the O'Rourkes ;
> Clⱥnn Aṁlⱥoıḃ, the MacAuliffes ;
> Clⱥnn ⱥn Ḃⱥıꞃⱦ, the MacWards ;
> Clⱥnn Ḋıⱥꞃmⱥⱦⱥ, the MacDermotts ;
> Clⱥnn ꞇSíꞇıʓ, the MacSheehys ;
> Síol mḂꞃıⱥın, the O'Briens ;
> Síol ʓCeⱥllⱥıʓ, the O'Kellys ꞇ
> Síol Móꞃⱦⱥ, the O'Mores ;
> Síol Uıⱦıꞃ, the Maguires.

Muınnꞇeⱥꞃ is used in the case of Ó-surnames ; Clⱥnn, with a few exceptions, is confined to Mⱥc-surnames.

---

*Muınnꞇeⱥꞃ and Clⱥnn cause aspiration, Síol eclipsis.

Síol is now used only in literature. Muinnteaṗ and
Clann are sometimes prefixed to the gen. case of the
surname, as: Muinnteaṗ Uı Ċeallaċáın, the
O'Callaghans; Clann Ṁıc Conmaṗa, the MacNamaras.

The following examples show the declension of surnames in -aċ (Types X, XIV, XV): —

(a) An Caoṁánaċ.

	Singular.	Plural.
Nom. and acc.	an Caoṁánaċ	na Caoṁánaıg
gen.	an Ċaoṁánaıg	na gCaoṁánaċ
dat.	leıṗ an gCaoṁánaċ	leıṗ na Caoṁánċaıḃ
voc.	a Ċaoṁánaıg	a Ċaoṁánċa.

(b) An tiúṗtáṗaċ.

Nom. and acc.	an tiúṗtáṗaċ	na hiúṗtáṗaıg
gen.	an iúṗtáṗaıg	na niúṗtáṗaċ
dat.	leıṗ an iúṗtáṗaċ	leıṗ na hiúṗtáṗċaıḃ
voc.	a iúṗtáṗaıg	a iúṗtáṗċa.

(c) An Sáḃaoıṗeaċ.

Nom. and acc.	an Sáḃaoıṗeaċ	na Sáḃaoıṗıg
gen.	an tSáḃaoıṗıg	na Sáḃaoıṗeaċ
dat.	{ oo'n tSáḃaoıṗeaċ { leıṗ an Sáḃaoıṗeaċ	leıṗ na Sáḃaoıṗeaċaıḃ,
voc.	a Śáḃaoıṗıg	a Śáḃao ṗeaċa

Surnames of Types VI, VIII, XI, XII are not declined. All these surnames form their collective
plurals like surnames in -aċ, as: na Baṗóıoıt, the
Barretts; teaċ na mBúṗcaċ, the house of the Burkes.

Surnames of Type IX follow the rule of adjectives.
They form their plural like surnames in -aċ.

Surnames of Type XIII are invariable. The plural
is formed by prefixing Muinnteaṗ.

In surnames of Type XVI., Mac alone changes.

A personal epithet, or cognomen, comes between the Christian name and the surname, and, if an adjective, agrees in case with the Christian name, as : Domnall bán Ó bμιαιη, do Domnaill báιη Uí bμιαιη.

Sometimes the father's name, in the genitive case with Mac prefixed, is inserted in the same position to distinguish persons of the same name and surname, as : Domnall mac Donncada Ó bμιαιη ; or the patronymic may follow the surname, as : Domnall Ó bμιαιη mac Donncada. Mac always aspirates in this case. The mac is now usually dropped, but the aspiration remains, as : Páμαιζ Caдóζ Óιζ Ó Conaill.

When two Christian names are used, the second is put in the gen. case, with its initial letter aspirated, —mac being understood if the father's name, and ζιοlla if the name of a saint, as : Seán Peaдαιμ Ó Néill, John Peter O'Neill.*

In the case of a double surname in English, as Patrick Sarsfield O'Donnell, Hugh O'Neill Flanagan, the first surname assumes the -ac termination, thus : Páμαιζ Sáιμμέαλαc Ó Domnaill, Aoд Niallac Ó Flannagáin.

When a personal cognomen of the ancestor appears in the surname, it agrees in case with the name of the ancestor, as : Seán Mac Muιμιμ Ruaд, Caдóζ Mac Conaill Óιζ.

An agnomen used to distinguish different branches of the same family agrees in case with the surname ; in other words, it is in the same case as Mac or Ó, as : Magnuμ Mac Diaμmaдα Ruaд, Ó Concoδαιμ Donn.

§ 7—Surnames of Females

Instead of Ó and Mac, Ní and Nic respectively are used after names of females in surnames of Types I, II, III, IV, V and VII. Ní is an abbreviation of ní

---

* This rule is not always observed by present-day Irish speakers.

(from ınʒeᴧn, a daughter) and í or Uı (genitive case of
Ó or Uᴧ) ; and ᵰıc of ᵰı ᵯıc.

Examples :—

{ pᴀopᴧıʒ Ó ᴅoᵯnᴧıll, Patrick O'Donnell
{ mᴀıᵽe ᵰí ᴅoᵯnᴧıll, Mary O'Donnell

{ seᴀn Ó hÓʒᴧın, John Hogan
{ eıᵬlín ᵰí Óʒᴧın, Ellen Hogan.

{ séᴧmuᵽ mᴧc Seóınín, James Jennings
{ cᴀıc ᵰíc Seóınín, Kate Jennings.

{ pᴀopᴧıʒ mᴧc ᴧn ʒoıll, Patrick Gill
{ mᴀıᵽe ᵰíc ᴧn ʒoıll, Mary Gill.

{ eoʒᴧn mᴧc ᴧoᴅᴧʒᴧın, Owen Egan
{ mᴀıᵽe ᵰíc ᴧoᴅᴧʒᴧın, Mary Egan.

The unabbreviated form ᵰı ᵯıc is used in some
places, as :

{ seᴀn mᴧc ᴧn Ბᴀıᵽᴅ, John Ward
{ mᴀıᵽe ᵰí ᵯıc ᴧn Ბᴀıᵽᴅ, Mary Ward.

ᵰıʒ is the form corresponding to mᴧʒ, as :

{ concoᵬᴧᵽ mᴧʒ Uıᴅıᵽ, Connor Maguire
{ Soᵽcᴧ ᵰıʒ Uıᴅıᵽ, Sarah Maguire.

Surnames of females are sometimes, like those of
males, formed directly from the name of the ancestor,
as :

cᴀıc ᵰí cSeóınín, Kate Jennings
Ბᵽíʒıᴅ ᵰí cSuıᵬne, Brigid MacSweeny
mᴀıᵽe ᵰí ᵽᴧᵽcᴧlᴧın, Mary MacPartland.

It will be seen from the foregoing examples that in
the surnames of females, except those formed directly
from the name of the ancestor, the part of the
surname following ᵰı or ᵰıc is in all cases the same
as that after Uı or ᵯıc in the surnames of males. The
reason of this is obvious, ᵰı and ᵰıc being contractions
of ᵰí Uı and ᵰí ᵯıc respectively.*

*Hence eıᵬlín ᵰí Óʒᴧın, not eıᵬlín ᵰí hÓʒᴧın, is the correct
form.

In surnames of Types VI, VIII, XI, XII and XIII.,
the form of the surname after names of females is the
same as after those of males, as :

{ Seán Ḃáróiᴅ, John Barrett
{ Peig Ḃáróiᴅ, Peg Barrett.
{ Seán Ḃrún, John Brown
{ Máire Ḃrún, Mary Brown.
{ Réamonn ᴅe Róiſte, Redmund Roche.
{ Máire ᴅe Róiſte, Mary Roche.
{ Éamonn na Ḃríᵹᴅe, Edmond Bride
{ Eiḃlín na Ḃríᵹᴅe, Ellen Bride.

Surnames of Type IX, being adjectives, are aspirated
in the nominative case, as : Máire Ᵹlar, Mary Green.

Surnames of Types X and XIV, that is, all surnames
ending in -ać, may be either substantives or adjectives,
When the surname is an adjective, its initial letter is
aspirated in the nominative case after names of females,
as :

{ Seán Ḃreaċnać, John Walsh
{ Cáit Ḃreaċnać, Kate Walsh.
{ Seán Cáṙċać, John MacCarthy
{ Sioḃán Ċáṙċać, Joan MacCarthy.*

The following forms corresponding to Type XVI may
be used as equivalent to the English *Miss* when the
Christian name is omitted :—

Inᵹean Uí Ḃriain, Miss O'Brien.
Inᵹean an Cáṙċaiᵹ, Miss MacCarthy.
Inᵹean Ṁic an Ḃáirᴅ, Miss Ward.
Inᵹean an Ᵹearalⱅaiᵹ, Miss Fitzgerald.
Inᵹean an Ḃúrcaiᵹ, Miss Burke.
Inᵹean an Róiṙⱅiᵹ, Miss Roche.†

*This was first pointed out to me by the late Canon O'Leary
(An ⱅAċair Peaᴅaſ), who, when the first edition of this book
was passing through the press, kindly sent me the following
note on the Introductory Chapters which he had read :
" I have just one remark to make. In the case of women's
names I have heard ' Sioḃán Ċáṙċać, not ' Sioḃán Cáṙċać,' and
' Cáit Ḃreaċnać,' not 'Cáit Ḃreaċnać.' That is to say,
when the surname is an *adjective* it agrees with the noun like any
adjective. When the surname is not an adjective I have heard
exactly what you say, *i.e.*, ' Peig Ḃáróiᴅ,' not ' Peig Ḃáróiᴅ.'
Instead of ' Máire Ḃreaċnać' I have heard ' Máire an Ḃreaċ-
naiᵹ,' where the surname is treated as a definite noun."
†But not Inᵹean ᴅe Ḃúrc, Inᵹean ᴅe Róiſte, &c.

The same construction may be used to express *Miss* with the Christian name, as :

máⱜe, 1ⁿᵹeaⁿ uí Ḃⱜaⁱⁿ, Miss Mary O'Brien.
eⁱḃlíⁿ, 1ⁿᵹeaⁿ aⁿ Ḃúⱜcaⁱᵹ, Miss Eileen Burke.

Mrs. may be similarly expressed, as :

beaⁿ uí Ḃⱜaⁱⁿ, Mrs. O'Brien.
beaⁿ aⁿ Ḃúⱜcaⁱᵹ, Mrs. Burke.
beaⁿ ṁⁱc aⁿ Ḃáⱜ♂, Mrs. Ward.
beaⁿ Śeáⁱⁿ uí Ḃⱜaⁱⁿ, Mrs. John O'Brien.
beaⁿ Ċaⁱóᵹ ṁⁱc aⁿ Ḃáⱜ♂, Mrs. T. Ward.
beaⁿ Éamuⁱⁿⁿ ♂e Róⱜce, Mrs. Edmund Roche.
máⱜe, beaⁿ ṁⁱc aⁿ Ḃáⱜ♂, Mrs. Mary Ward.
Cáⁱc, beaⁿ Śeáⁱⁿ ♂e búⱜc, Mrs. Kate Burke, or Mrs. John Burke.*

In the case of a widow, baⁱⁿcⱜeaċ (baⁱⁿcⱜeaḃaċ) is to be used instead of beaⁿ, as :

baⁱⁿcⱜeaċ Śeáⁱⁿ uí Ḃⱜaⁱⁿ, Mrs. John O'Brien.
baⁱⁿcⱜeaċ Éamuⁱⁿⁿ ♂e búⱜc, Mrs. Edmund Burke.
baⁱⁿcⱜeaċ aⁿ Ḃⱜeaċⁿaⁱᵹ, Mrs. Walsh.
máⱜe, baⁱⁿcⱜeaċ aⁿ Róⱜcⁱᵹ, Mrs. Mary Roche.

Married women retain their maiden name in Irish. We may therefore say : máⱜe ⁿí Ḃⱜaⁱⁿ, beaⁿ Śeáⁱⁿ ♂e búⱜc, Mrs. John Burke, née Mary O'Brien.

ⁿí and ⁿⁱc do not change in the genitive case.

§ 8—Surnames in the Spoken Language

Surnames are variously corrupted in the spoken language, and deviate in many important respects from the standard or literary form, but it would be impossible within the limits of a short introduction to deal with this aspect of the subject in detail. The corruptions and variations of Ó and Mac, as they affect

*But not beaⁿ Ḃⱜeaċⁿaċ, beaⁿ ♂e búⱜc, beaⁿ ♂e Róⱜce, &c. which are incorrect.

a large number of surnames, may however be briefly noted.

Ó, or Uᴀ, is corrupted as follows :

1. Sometimes shortened to ᴀ,·as : ᴀ Oeópáin for
   Ó Oeópáin, ᴀ ȝnim for Ó ȝnim.
2. Sometimes altogether dropped, as : Cᴀomáin
   for Ó Cᴀomáin, Cᴀcᴀpᴀiȝ for Ó Cᴀcᴀpᴀiȝ.
3. Sometimes replaced by the gen. case Uí, as : Uí
   ḟloinn for Ó ḟloinn, Uí Lᴀoȝᴀipe for Ó
   Lᴀoȝᴀipe.
4. Sometimes prefixed to surnames to which it
   does not properly belong, as: Ó Oíolúin for
   Oíolúin, Ó ȝoȝáin for ȝoȝán, Ó Róipce for
   Oe Róipce.

The following are the corruptions and variations of
Mᴀc and Mᴀȝ :—

1. c or ȝ attracted over to the name of the ancestor.
   This happens when the name of the ancestor
   commences with a vowel or h or with l, n,
   or R, or with a consonant aspirated after Mᴀc
   or Mᴀȝ. The name of the ancestor is then
   treated in all the forms of the surname as if it
   commenced with C or ȝ. Examples:—

   > Mᴀc Cᴀpcáin for Mᴀc ᴀpcáin
   > Mᴀc Ceoȝᴀin for Mᴀc eoȝᴀin
   > Mᴀc Coicip for Mᴀc Oicip
   > Mᴀc ȝpᴀic for Mᴀȝ Rᴀic.

   Hence such forms as : báp ᴀn Coicipiȝ for
   báp ᴀn Oicpiȝ ; ᴀn Ceoȝnᴀc for ᴀn ceoȝnᴀc ;
   nᴀ Ceoȝnᴀiȝ for nᴀ heoȝnᴀiȝ.

2. M in some places always aspirated after the
   Christian name, as : eoȝᴀn Mᴀȝ ᴀoᴅᴀ,
   Séᴀmup Mᴀȝ ḟloinn, Oomnᴀll Mᴀc Suibne ;
   and sometimes entirely dropped, as : Séᴀmup
   'ᴀc Conpᴀoi. The c of Mᴀc is also very
   frequently aspirated, as éᴀmonn 'ᴀc Sícȝ.

3. Sometimes takes the form ṁ, ṁ, ṁé, the
c or ᵹ being attracted over as above, as : ṁ
ᵹloinn for ṁᵹ floinn, ṁ ᵹionnáin for
ṁᵹ fionnáin, ṁ ᵹuiḋiṗ for ṁᵹ uiḋiṗ,
ṁ ᵹṗaiċ for ṁᵹ Raiċ, ṁé ᵹuḃáin for ṁᵹ
Ḋuḃáin.

4. Takes the form ᴀ when ṁ is dropped and c or
ᵹ attracted over, as : Tᴀḋᵹ ᴀ Cionnṗáċtaiᵹ
for Tᴀḋᵹ ṁᴀc Ionnṗáċtaiᵹ.

5. Sometimes c or ᵹ alone retained, as Caiḃiṗtin
for ṁᴀc Aiḃiṗtin, Cuilcin for ṁᴀc Uilcin,
ᵹionnᵹaile for ṁᵹ fionnᵹaile.

6. Sometimes made ṁáᵹ, ṁáᵹ, as : ṁáᵹ Coċláin,
ṁáᵹ ᵹaṗaiḋ.

7. Sometimes ṁóc, ṁóᵹ, and then, by the dropping of the initial ṁ, óc, óᵹ, uᴀc, uᴀᵹ. When
in this case c or ᵹ is attracted over, the final
form is the same as in Ó surnames. Examples :—

    Ó Caċṁaoil for ṁᴀc Caċṁaoil.
    Ó Ceaċṁaṗcaiᵹ for ṁᴀc eaċṁaṗcaiᵹ
    Ó Ceóinín for ṁᴀc Seóinín.
    Ó Ciúṗtáin for ṁᴀc Siúṗtáin.
    Ó Coṁnaill for ṁᴀc Ḋoṁnaill
    Ó Connċaḋa for ṁᴀc Ḋonnċaḋa.
    Ó Cuṗtáin for ṁᴀc Cuṗtáin.
    Ó ᵹṗiaḋa for ṁᵹ Riaḋa.
    Ó ᵹṗuaiṗc for ṁᵹ Ruaiṗc.
    Ó ᵹuḃáin for ṁᵹ Ḋuḃáin.
    Uᴀ Coiḃicín for ṁᴀc hoiḃicín.
    Uᴀ ᵹoiṗeaċtaiᵹ for ṁᵹ Oiṗeaċtaiᵹ.

8. In a few instances simply replaced by Ó, as :
Ó filiḃín for ṁᴀc filiḃín, Ó Siúṗtáin for
ṁᴀc Siúṗtáin, Ó Suiḃne for ṁᴀc Suiḃne.

9. Frequently replaced by the genitive case ṁic
or 'ic, as : Séamuṗ ṁic Seóinín for Séamuṗ
ṁᴀc Seóinín, Séamuṗ 'ic an fṗanncaiᵹ for
Séamuṗ ṁᴀc an fṗanncaiᵹ.

10. In Omeath, ṁᴀc ᵹiolla is corrupted to ṁᴀ'l,
as ṁᴀ'l ṗáḋṗaiᵹ for ṁᴀc ᵹiolla ṗáḋṗaiᵹ,
ṁᴀ'l Coille for ṁᴀc ᵹiolla coille.

Corruptions and variations of individual surnames, especially when they are reflected in the anglicised form, are noted as they occur in the lists.

§ 9.—INTERCHANGE OF SURNAMES.

1. Some Irish families have two surnames, each derived from a different ancestor, or one derived from the name and another from a designation of the same ancestor, as :—

> Ó maolṗuanaḋa and mac Ḋiaꞃmaḋa,
> mac Conmaꞃa and mac Síoḋa,
> mac ᵹiolla ṗáḋꞃaiᵹ and mac Séaꞃċa,
> mac Síomoinn and mac an Ríoꞃꞃe.

2. Some families of foreign origin have two Irish surnames, one an hibernicised form of the foreign name and the other a patronymic formed from the name or a designation of the ancestor, as :—

> Conḋún and mac máiᵹeóc,
> Ḋalamaꞃa and mac hoiꞃeabáiꞃḋ,
> ḋe Búꞃc and mac Uilliam,
> Sconḋún and mac an míleaḋa.

3. Nearly a dozen families have two surnames one commencing with Ó and another with mac, followed by the same ancestral name ; but whether both surnames are derived from the same ancestor, or from two different ancestors of the same name, it is impossible to say. Examples :—

> Ó Caoċáin and mac Caoċáin,
> Ó Coḋlaċáin and mac Coḋlaċáin,
> Ó ᵹeaꞃᵹáin and mac ᵹeaꞃᵹáin.

4. A few families have besides their surname a cognomen which is sometimes used instead, as :—

> Ó Ḋuinnꞃléiḃe and Ulṫaċ.

All these double surnames were used interchangeably, so that the same person might be called indifferently

by ᴜne or the other, irrespective of the anglicised form.
In the majority of cases only one surname is now
retained ; but as the anglicised form is, in many instances, derived from the one that has become obselete,
there is often apparently no connection between the
anglicised form and its present Irish equivalent. Thus
the surname Fitzpatrick is derived from Ⅿ⒜ᴄ Ꙅɪ⒪ᴌᴌ⒜
Ⅾ⒜⒪⒫⒜ɪꙅ, but the present Irish equivalent of Fitzpatrick in many parts of the South of Ireland is Ⅿ⒜ᴄ
Ꙅé⒜⒫ᴛ⒜ or Ⅿ⒜ᴄ Ꙅé⒜ᴄⱤ⒜, a new surname which the
Fitzpatricks took from an ancestor named Geoffrey
or Ꙅé⒜⒫ᴛ⒜ Ⅿ⒜ᴄ Ꙅɪ⒪ᴌᴌ⒜ Ⅾ⒜⒪⒫⒜ɪꙅ. Similarly the Birminghams are called in Irish Ⅿ⒜ᴄ ꝼé⒪⒫⒜ɪⱤ from an
ancestor named Piers de Bermingham.

Besides the interchange of totally distinct surnames, our Irish name system admitted, with considerable latitude, of the substitution one for another
of different forms of the same surname, and even of
different surnames of the same or somewhat similar
meaning. Hence we find the following classes and
variants of surnames sometimes interchanged :—

1. Surnames of the same signification though
   differing in form, as :

Ⅿ⒜ᴄ Ᏸ⒜⒫ᴌⒶɪⱤ and Ⅿ⒜ᴄ Ᏸ⒜ᴛ⒜ɪᴌ (Ᏸ⒜⒫ᴌⒶⱤ and Ᏸ⒜ᴛ⒜ᴌ, each⸗
Charles).
Ⅿ⒜ᴄ ⒜ɴ Ⅿ⒜⒪⒜ɪⱱ and Ó Ⅿ⒜⒪⒜ɪⱱíɴ (both from Ⅿ⒜⒪⒜ⱱ, a dog).

2. A surname and its diminutive, as :

Ⅿ⒜ᴄ ᏸⱤⱴ⒜ɪⱱⱸ⒜⒪⒜ and Ⅿ⒜ᴄ ᏸⱤⱴ⒜ɪⱱíɴ.
Ó ᴌ⒜ᴄᴛⱸ⒜ and Ó ᴌ⒜ᴄᴛⱸáɪɴ.
Ó Ꙅᴄ⒜ɴɴ⒜ɪᴌ and Ó Ꙅᴄ⒜ɴɴᴌáɪɴ.

3. Surnames derived from different diminutives of
   the same root, as :

Ó ᏸⱤ⒜ɴáɪɴ and Ó ᏸⱤ⒜ɴ⒜Ᏸáɪɴ,
Ó ᴄɪ⒜⒫áɪɴ and Ó ᴄɪ⒜⒫⒜Ᏸáɪɴ,
Ó Ⱝⱴ⒜ᏸáɪɴ and Ó Ⱝⱴɪᏸíɴ,
Ó ꝼɪ⒜ᴄáɪɴ and Ó ꝼⱸɪᴄíɴ.

4. Surnames derived from different genitive forms
of the same name, as :

Ó ₣eₐₙ₃uₚₐ and Ó ₣eₐₙ₃uiₚ.
Ó ₣iₐiċ and Ó ₣éiċ.
mₐc ₐn Ḃₑₙċeₐṁₐn and mₐc ₐn Ḃₑₙċiṁ.

5. Variants of the same surname owing to aspiration, attenuation, and interchange of letters, as :

mₐc Ḋoṁnₐill and mₐc Ḋoṁnₐill.
Ó Ḃₙolċáin and Ó Ḃₙoileₐċáin.
Ó Ḋeₐₚáin and Ó Ḋioₚáin.
Ó mₐċáin and Ó moċáin.

6. A standard or literary form and a corrupt or
spoken form, as

Ó muiₙ₃eₐₚáin and Ó bₙíoₚáin.
Ó Cₐoinḋeₐlḃáin and Ó Cₐoinliobáin.
Ó heiₒiₚₚceóil and Ó Ḋuₚceóil.

7. An older form and a more modern one, as :—

mₐc ₐn ₐiₚċinni₃ and mₐc ₐn Oiₚċinni₃.
mₐ₃ ₐiₚeₐċcₐi₃ and mₐ₃ Oiₚeₐċcₐi₃.

A discrepancy (similar to that mentioned above)
between the anglicised form and its present-day Irish
equivalent often results from the interchange of these
forms

§ 10.—ANGLICISATION OF SURNAMES

The various ways in which Irish surnames have been
anglicised may be enumerated under the following
heads :

1. Phonetically.
2. By translation.
3. By attraction.
4. By assimilation.
5. By substitution.

1. *Phonetically.*—This was the method almost exclusively adopted when surnames were first anglicised.* The surname was written down more or less as it was pronounced, but without any regard to the Irish spelling, as :

> O'Brien for Ó Dṁiain,
> O'Callaghan for Ó Ceallacáin,
> O'Donoghue for Ó Donncaḋa,
> O'Flanagan for Ó Flannagáin,
> O'Neill for Ó néill.†

The same Irish surname often gives several very different anglicised forms owing to dialectical variations and the vagaries of the phonetic system employed to represent them, as :

> Ó Coḃṫaiġ, Coffey, Cowie, Cowhey, Cowhig, &c.,
> Ó Duḃṫaiġ, Duffy, Dowie, Dooey, Duhig, &c.

On the other hand, very different Irish surnames have sometimes the same anglicised form, as :

> Coffey for Ó Coḃṫaiġ, Ó Caṫḃaḋa, Ó Caṫḃuaḋaiġ, Ó Caṫmoġa.

In many instances the anglicised form has in course of time been contracted, as : O'Hare for O'Hehir, O'Kane for O'Cahan ; and not unfrequently only a part of the original form is retained, as Ryan for O'Mulryan. Most surnames have been mutilated by dropping Mac or O', and Mac when retained in usually, but improperly, written Mc or M'.

---

*Most Irish surnames were anglicised during the second half of the 16th century (1550-1600), and appear for the first time in in an English dress in the State documents of that period. The anglicisation seems to have been the work of Anglo-Irish government officials possessing, in some instances at least, a knowledge of the Irish language. The present anglicised forms, generally speaking, date from that period.

† It may be remarked that the anglicised form was in most instances originally much nearer the Irish pronounciation than at present, owing partly to a change in the sound of the English letters, and partly to the corruption of the Irish forms. Thus O'Brien and O'Neill were originally pronounced O'Breen and O'Nail.

2. *Translation.*—During the last and the preceding century, many families rejected the old phonetic rendering of their surnames and adopted instead an English surname which was supposed to be a translation of the Irish surname. These " translations" are, in most instances, incorrect. The following are examples of translated surnames :—

Ó bruic	translated	Badger,
Ó bruacáin	,,	Banks,
Ó Cavain	,,	Barnacle,
Ó maoilbeannacta	,,	Blessing,
Ó marcaiġ	,,	Ryder,
Ó bravain	,,	Salmon and Fisher,
mac an tSaoir	,,	Carpenter, Freeman
mac Conraoi	,,	King,
mac Conrnáma	,,	Forde,
mac Seáin	,,	Johnson.

The translated form sometimes takes an English termination, as :

Ó Oraiġneáin	translated	Thornton,
Ó Ṡaoitín	,,	Wyndham.

3. *Attraction.*—A surname of comparatively rare occurrence is often attracted to, and confounded with, a better known surname of somewhat similar sound existing in the same locality, and instead of its proper anglicised form assumes that of the better known or more numerous surname. The following are examples :

	Anglicised	attracted to
Ó blácṁaic,	Blawick, Blowick,	Blake,
Ó braoin,	O'Breen, Breen,	O'Brien,
Ó Ouibóíorma,	O'Dughierma, Dooyearma,	MacDermott,
Ó heocaġáin,	O'Hoghegan,	Mageoghegan,
Ó maoil Seáclainn,	O'Melaghlin,	MacLoughlin.

It must be remembered that a surname of comparatively rare occurrence in one district may be quite common in another, and *vice versa*, and that consequently the attracting surname in one locality may be itself attracted in another.

4. The custom of assimilating Irish to foreign names is old in Ireland. During the Middle Ages Irish scholars writing in Latin, instead of latinising the Irish names with which they had to deal, often simply substituted for them well-known Latin names of somewhat similar sound or meaning. Hence we find such substitution as Cornelius for Conóobaρ, Eugenius for eoξan, Thaddaeus for Caóg, Virgilius for ſeaρξaι, etc. This practice was well known in the sixteenth century, and was frequently followed in the anglicisation of Irish Christian names. Nearly all the anglicised forms of this kind existing at present were already in use in the time of Elizabeth, the only important exceptions being Jeremiah for Oιaρmaιo, and Timothy for Caóg, which only came into use about half a century later.

The extension of the practice to surnames is of still later date, few traces of such anglicisation being found earlier than the middle of the seventeenth century. The principal cause of the change of these names, according to O'Donovan, was the ridicule thrown upon them by English magistrates and lawyers, who were ignorant of the Irish language; but an anxiety on the part of the people themselves to get rid of uneuphonious or otherwise undesirable surnames doubtless operated in the same direction. The following are examples of surnames anglicised in this way :

Broderick for Ó bρuaoaιρ,
Carleton for Ó Caιρeaλλáιn,
Harrington for Ó haρρaċτáιn and Ó hιonξaρoaιλ,
Reddington for Ó Roιoeaċáιn,
Summerville for Ó Somaċáιn.

In a few instances the assimilation is to a French surname, as :

De Lapp for Ó Lapáιn,
De Moleyns for Ó maoλáιn,
D'Ermott for Ó Ouιoóιoρma.

5. *Substitution.*—Substitution differs from assimilation only in degree. The similarity between the Irish surname and its English equivalent is in this case much more remote ; very often there is no connection whatsoever. The following are examples :

> Clifford for Ó Clúmáin,
> Fenton for Ó Fiannacta,
> Loftus for Ó Lactnáin,
> Neville for Ó Niaḋ,
> Newcombe for Ó Niaḋóg.

It sometimes happens that the natural phonetic rendering of an Irish surname has, when Ó or Mac is dropped, the same form as an English surname, as : Ó Beargá, Barry ; Mac an Ḃáiṙo, Ward ; Ó Buacalla, Buckley.

EXPLANATORY NOTE.

Lists of Christian Names.—The names contained in these lists are of three kinds, viz. : (1) names at present in use, of whatever origin, but well-known abbreviations and pet names are not always included ; (2) names which, though now obsolete, were at one time in use under an anglicised form and which it may be considered well to revive ; and (3) names of Irish saints taken from the Martyrology of Donegal. These have not been in use as Christian names within English-speaking times, but they might now under the influence of the Gaelic revival very appropriately be given as baptismal names to Irish children. Every name on these lists is, therefore, a genuine Christian name, either in use at the present time or at some period in the past.

List of Surnames.—We have unfortunately no complete list of Irish surnames. The present one is compiled from two imperfect lists published by the late Registrar-General, supplemented from such addtional sources as newspaper reports, personal observation, lists received from different parts of the country, the writings of Dr. O'Donovan and Father O'Growney, etc. All the more common varieties of the anglicised forms are included. Mac is written—as it should be—in full, not contracted to M' or Mc.

The Irish Forms.—The arrangement is the same for both Christian names and surnames. The English or anglicised name or surname is followed by the Irish form. Variants of the latter are separated only by commas, as :

Andrew, ᴀ᎐ᴅᴏᴩéᴀᴩ, ᴀ᎐ᴅᴏᴩᴌᴀᴩ, ᴀ᎐ᴅᴏᴩᴌú.
O'Brallaghan, Ó ᴆᴩᴏʟᴄáᴌ᎐, Ó ᴆᴩᴏʟᴀᴄáᴌ᎐, Ó ᴆᴩᴏᴌᴄᴀᴄáᴌ᎐.

Distinct names or surnames, when there are two or more corresponding to the same English or anglicised name or surname, are separated by semicolons, as :

Ferdinand, ᴘᴇᴀᴩᴏᴏᴩᴄᴀ ; ᴘᴇᴀᴩᴈᴀ᎐ᴀᴌ᎐ᴍ ; ᴘᴇᴀᴩᴀᴏᴀᴄ ; ᴘᴇᴀᴩᴈᴜᴩ.

The locality in which each of the Irish forms is found is usually indicated by a number placed after the name or surname, as :

Barry*, ḃᴀᵱᵱᴀ 7 ; ḃeᴀᵱᴀċ 9.

O'Brien, Ó ḃᵱiᴀin 12 ; Ó ḃᵱᴀoin 15.

Single forms are marked only for some special reason.   In the case of names and surnames used everywhere interchangeably there is no need of localisation ; but variants, or distinct forms, used interchangeably only in certain places are localised.   It is not necessary in every case, nor is it possible, to localise the Christian names.

In some cases the different forms can be distinguished, if at all, only by reference to origin or nationality.   This is indicated by the letters I, E, or S placed after the name or surname, and meaning respectively Irish, English, and Scottish.   When in the case of foreign surnames no Irish form has been ascertained to exist, the letter E or S is inserted instead.

The relation between different Irish names or surnames having the same English or anglicised form, that is, whether they are synonyms, or distinct names used interchangeably, or the one an older form, or a spoken form, of the other, is indicated by letters placed in brackets between the two forms. In order to avoid confusion it will often be necessary to use the spoken form in preference to the literary or standard form. Hence the spoken form is frequently the one given, the literary form being generally placed after it with the letters (o.f.) prefixed.

The initials of authorities quoted are placed in brackets after the name.

When two or more surnames have the same anglicised form in the same locality, whether owing to attraction or otherwise, local knowledge is necessary to determine the correct Irish form in each case.   The older spelling of the anglicised form will ofter throw light on it, or recourse may be had to the local ᵱeᴀnċᴀiṫe.   In cities and large towns it will generally have to be determined by the part of the country from which the family originally came.   Thus in the City of Limerick the name Mannix is both Ó muineóᵹ and Ó mᴀinċín, the former family coming from Co. Clare and the latter from Co. Limerick.

In case of doubt the form phonetically nearest the anglicised form is the one to be used.

---

* Christian name.

LIST OF ABBREVIATIONS

(a) LOCATION.

1—Usual form in any part of Ireland.
2—Some parts of Ireland.
3—Leaṫ Cuinn—the northern half of Ireland.
4—Leaṫ Ṁoḡa—the southern half of Ireland.
5—The Midland Counties.
6—Ulster.
7—Munster.
8—Leinster.
9—Connacht.
10—Usual form, except in the district or districts to which another name is assigned.
11—Usual form, including places to which other forms are assigned.   There are in this case two or more names or surnames similarly anglicised in the same locality.
12—Usual form, but only rarely met with in the district or districts in which another name or surname is stated to be similarly anglicised.
13—Armagh.
14—Kildare.
15—Westmeath.
16—Donegal.
17—Limerick.
18—Co. Dublin.
19—Mayo.
20—Some parts of Ireland, but not met with in the district or districts for which another name is given as similarly anglicised.
21—Some parts of Ireland, including places to which other forms are assigned.
22—Some parts of Ireland, but only rarely met with in those places to which other forms are assigned.
23—Fermanagh.
24—Kilkenny.
25—Offaly—King's County.
26—Derry.
27—Tipperary.
28—Wexford.
29—Sligo.

30—leaċ Cuınn, but not those parts of it for which other forms
are given.
31—Usual form in leaċ Cuınn, including the parts of it to
which other names or surnames are assigned.
32—Some parts of leaċ Cuınn.
33—Tyrone.
34—Roscommon.
35—Monaghan.
36—Antrim.
37—Louth.
38—Down.
39 —Leitrim.
40—leaċ moġa, but not those parts of it for which other forms
are given.
41—Usual form in leaċ moġa, including the parts of it to
which other names or surnames are assigned.
42—Some parts of leaċ moġa.
43—Meath.
44—Carlow.
45—Leix—Queen's County.
46—Clare.
47—Waterford.
48—Wicklow.
49—Kerry.
50—The Midland Counties, but not in the district or districts
for which other forms are given.
51—Usual form in the Midland Counties, including the district
or districts to which other names or surnames are assigned.
52—Some of the Midland Counties.
53—North Longford, North Westmeath, South Leitrim, and
West Cavan.
54—South Longford, West Westmeath, and East Roscommon.
55—Longford.
56—Leitrim and Cavan.
57—Westmeath and Roscommon.
58—Westmeath and Cavan.
59—Roscommon and Longford.
60—Ulster, but not those parts of it for which other forms are
given.
61—Usual form in Ulster, including the parts of it to which
other names or surnames are assigned.
62—Some parts of Ulster.
63—Donegal, Derry, Tyrone, and Antrim.
64—Louth, Armagh, Monaghan, and Fermanagh.
65—Tyrone, Armagh, Monaghan, and Fermanagh.
66—Donegal, Derry and Antrim.
67—Cavan.
68—Antrim and Down.

69—Donegal, Tyrone, and Fermanagh.
70—Munster, but not those parts of it for which other forms are given.
71—Usual form in Munster, including the parts of it to which other names or surnames are assigned.
72—Some parts of Munster.
73—Clare, Limerick, North Kerry, and North Tipperary.
74—Cork, Waterford, South Kerry, and South Tipperary.
75—East Limerick, North East Cork, and South West Tipperary.
76—Clare, North East Limerick, and North Tipperary.
77—Cork.
78—Tipperary, Kilkenny, and Waterford.
79—Kerry, West Limerick, and West Cork.
79a—Kerry, Cork, and Limerick.
80—Leinster, but not those parts of it for which other forms are given.
81—Usual form in Leinster, including the parts of it to which other names or surnames are assigned.
82—Some parts of Leinster.
83—Meath, Louth, and Co. Dublin.
84—Wicklow, Wexford, and Carlow.
85—Kildare, Leix, and Offaly.
86—Meath and Louth.
87—Carlow and Wexford.
88—Co. Dublin and Wicklow.
89—Longford, Westmeath and Offaly.
90—Connacht, but not those parts of it for which other forms are given.
91—Usual form in Connacht, including the parts of it to which other names or surnames are assigned.
93—Mayo, Sligo, and Leitrim.
94—Galway and Roscommon.
95—North Galway, East Mayo, and West Roscommon.
96—Sligo, Mayo, North Leitrim, and North Roscommon.
97—Galway.
98—Roscommon and South Leitrim.
99—West Mayo and West Galway.
When the location mark consists of three figures, the first two have the same signification as above. The third varies or modifies the meaning as in the following examples :
191—Usual form in Mayo, including the parts of it to which other names or surnames are assigned.
192—Some parts of Mayo.
273—The northern half of Tipperary.
274—The southern half of Tipperary.
775—Mid-Cork.
976—North Galway.
977—South Galway.

978—East Galway.

979—West Galway.

N.B.—A location mark refers not only to the form immediately preceding it, but to all the forms preceding it, back to the last one numbered or to the last semicolon.

(b) RELATION.

The relation between different names or surnames having the same anglicised form is sometimes indicated by the following letters placed in brackets between the different forms :—

(s.)—Synonym, that is, the second name or surname has the same signification as the one immediately preceding and is on that account sometimes used interchangeably with it ;

(s.s.)—Second surname, that is, there are two surnames in the same family.

(G.p.)—Gaelic patronymic surname taken by a family of foreign origin ;

(o.s.)—Older surname, now obsolete ;

(o.f.)—Older form of the present surname ;

(s.l.)—Form in the spoken language of the name or surname immediately preceding.

N.B.—A relation mark refers not only to the name or surname immediately following, but to all the forms following it, on to the next one *similarly* marked, or to the next semicolon.

(c) AUTHORITIES QUOTED.

The intials of authorities quoted are placed in brackets after the name, thus :—

(G.J.)—The Gaelic Journal.

(K.)—Keating.

(O'C.)—O'Curry.

(O'D.)—O'Donovan.

(O'G.)—O'Growney.

(O'M.)—O'Mahony in his Edition of Keating's History.

(S.L.)—Spoken Language.   The spoken language is in this case the only authority for the name.   The spelling, therefore, may not always be etymologically correct.

(d) OTHER ABBREVIATIONS.

I.—Irish origin.

E.—English or foreign origin.

S.—Scottish origin.

NAMES OF MEN

ENGLISH—IRISH

Abban, ⱥbbán.
Abraham, ⱥbⱥaⱨam.
Adam, ⱥóaṁ, ⱥoam.
Aedan, ⱥoóán.
Aeneas, ⱥonġuⱡ 1 ; eiⱡneaċán
eiⱡneaċán, 16.
Affy, ⱥiⱡiⱡcín.
Aghy, eaċaió.
Aidan, ⱥoóán 11, (s.) maoóóⱡ
28.
Alban, ⱥlbán.
Albert, Alby, ⱥilbe.
Alex, Alexander, ⱥlⱡanoaⱡ,
ⱥlⱡaⱡⱡann, ⱥlaⱡⱡom, ⱥlaⱡ-
ⱡaⱡ.
Alfons, v. Alphonsus.
Alfred, ⱥilⱡⱡió.
Alick, v. Alexander.
Allen, ⱥilín.
Allister, ⱥlaⱡⱡaⱡ.
Aloysius, ⱥlaⱡaoiⱡ ; luⱡaió.
Alphonsus, ⱥlⱡonⱡuⱡ, ⱥlⱡon-
ⱡuⱡ 1 ; ⱥnniuan 49.
Alvy, ⱥilbe.
Ambrose, ⱥmⱡⱡóⱡ, ⱥmⱡⱡuⱡ 1 ;
ⱥnmċaó 978.
Andrew, ⱥinoⱡéaⱡ, ⱥinoⱡiaⱡ,
ⱥinoⱡⱡú.
Aneslis, ⱥinéiⱡⱡiⱡ.
Angus, ⱥonġuⱡ.
Anlou, ⱥnniuan.
Anthin, ⱥnnⱡoin.
Anthony, Antony, ⱥnⱡoine, ⱥn-
ⱡoin, ⱥnnⱡoin 1 ; uaiⱡne
8, 72.

Archibald, ⱡiolla eaⱡⱡuiⱡ.
Ardal, Arnold, ⱥⱡoⱡal.
Art, ⱥⱡⱡ.
Arthur, ⱥⱡⱡúⱡ ; ⱥⱡⱡ.
Augustin, Augustine, ⱥⱡuiⱡⱡín,
ⱥⱡuiⱡⱡín, ⱥⱡuiⱡⱡín, ⱥiⱡiⱡⱡín.
Auliffe, ⱥṁlaoiⱡ.
Austin, ⱥiⱡiⱡⱡín, oiⱡⱡín. V.
Augustine.
Avvy, ⱥiⱡiⱡⱡín.

Barclay, Barkley, paⱡⱡlón. V.
Bartholomew.
Barnaby, Barney, bⱡian.
Barry, baⱡⱡa 7 ; beaⱡaċ 9.
Bartel, v. Bartley and Bartholo-
mew.
Bartholomew, paⱡⱡⱥlán, páⱡ-
ⱡⱥlán, 11, páⱡⱡlán 72, paⱡⱡ-
lón 26, 62, páⱡⱡlán 92,
páⱡⱡnán 72.
Bartlemy, páⱡⱡnán. V. Bar-
tholomew.
Bartley, beaⱡⱡlaió. V. Bar-
tholomew.
Basil, bⱡeaⱡal.
Bat, Batt, paⱡⱡⱥlán, páⱡⱡlán.
Becan, beaⱡán.
Ben, beiⱡċeaⱡⱡ.
Benedict, maolbeannaċⱡa.
Benen, Benignus, beineán,
beineón, beanón, bineán.
Benjamin, beiⱡċeaⱡⱡ.
Bercan, beaⱡⱡán.

Berkley, Pαɾτlón. V. Bartholomew.

Bernard, bεαɾnáɾo ; bɾιαn 11 ; bειɾċεαɾτ 272.

Bertie, bειɾċεαɾτ ; αιlbε.

Boetius, bαοτ̇αlαċ ; buαϋαċ 49.

Bowes, bαοτ̇αlαċ.

Bran, bɾαn.

Brasil, bɾεαɾαl.

Brendan, bɾéαnαιnn, bɾεαnϋán, bɾεαnnϋán.

Brian, Brien, Brine, Bryan, bɾιαn.

Buagh, buαϋαċ.

Caffar, Cατ̇bαɾɾ.

Cahal, Cαċαl.

Cahir, Cαċαοιɾ, Cαċαιɾ.

Cain, Cιαn.

Callaghan, Cεαllαċán.

Calvagh, αn Cαlbαċ, Cαlbαċ.

Canice, Cαιnnεαċ, Cοιnnεαċ.

Carbry, Cαιɾbɾε.

Carroll, Cεαɾbαll.

Cartagh, Cartage, Cáɾċαċ.

Celsus, Cεαllαċ.

Charles, Séαɾlαɾ, Séαɾluɾ, Cαɾluɾ ; Cαċαl 7, 9 ; Coɾmαc 7, 64 ; Cεαɾbαll 72 ; Cαċαοιɾ 8, 72 ; αn Cαlbαċ, Cαlbαċ, 8, 9 ; Sαɱαιɾlε, Soɱαιɾlε 36 ; Cοιɾϋεαlbαċ 16.

Christian, ʒιοllα Ċɾíoɾτ.

Christopher, Christy, Cɾíoɾτóιɾ 1, Cɾιoɾταl 33.

Cole, Coɱ̇αll.

Colin, Cοιlín, Cοιlεán 1 ; Cαιlεαn S.

Colla, Cοllα.

Colm, Colm.

Colman, Colmán 11, Cóιlín 99.

Colum, Columba, Colm, Colum.

Columban, Colmán.

Coman, Comán.

Comyn, Cuιmín.

Con, Conn 1 ; Conċobαɾ 7, Conall, Conαll.

Conan, Conán.

Conary, Conαιɾε.

Conleth, Conley, Connlαοϋ, Connlαοτ̇.

Conn, Oonn.

Connell, Conαll.

Connor, Conor, Conċobαɾ.

Constantine, Conɾαιoín 7 ; Conn 26, 33 ; Cú Connαċτ 23.

Cooey, Cúɱαιʒε.

Cooley, Cú υlαϋ.

Cormac, Coɾmαc.

Cornelius, Corney, Conċobαɾ.

Covey, Cúɱεαϋα.

Cowan, Coɱϋαn, Coɱ̇án.

Crevan, Cɾιoɱċαnn.

Crohan, Cɾóċán.

Cronan, Cɾónán.

Cuan, Cuαn.

Cullo, Cú υlαϋ.

Cumin, Cuιmín.

Cyril, Coιɾεαll.

Dahy, Oáιċι.

Daniel, Ooɱnαll.

Darby, Oιαɾmαιϋ.

Dary, Oáιɾε.

David, Oáιϋιϋ, Oáιϋιϋ, Oαιϋéιϋ, Oáιċí.

Davy, Oáιτí, Oáċ, Oáιċ, Oáιċín.

Declan, Oéαʒlán.

Denis, Denny, Oonnċαϋ.

Dermod, Dermot, Oιαɾmαιϋ.

Desmond, Oεαɾɱuɱnαċ.

Dominic, Dominick, Oοιmιnιc 1, Oαɱínαιc, Oαɱlαιc 26.

Donaghy, Oonnċαϋ.

Donall, Donald, Ooɱnαll.

Donat, Oonnċαϋ.

Donn, Oonn.

Donnan, Oonnán.

Donogh, Donough, Oonnċαϋ.

Douglas, Oubʒlαɾ.

Dowan, Oubán.

Duald, Dualtagh, Oubαlταċ.

Dudley, Oubϋáleιċε, 34 ; Oubαlταċ 3 ; Oubϋαɾαċ, Oubϋαɾα 99.

Dugald, Ɗuḃġall.
Duncan, Ɗonnċaḋ.

Ea, Aoḋ.
Eamon, Éamonn.
Eber, Éiḃeaɼ.
Edan, Aoḋán.
Eddie, Edmond, Edmund,
  Éamonn.
Edward, Éaḋḃárͻ; Éamonn.
Egan, Aoḋaġán.
Enan, Éanán.
Enda, Éanna.
Eneas, Aonġuɼ 1; Éiġneaċán,
  eiɼneaċán, 16.
Eny, Éanna.
Eoghan, Eoġan.
Eoin, Eóin.
Ercan, Erkan, Eaɼcán.
Erevan, Eiɼeaṁón.
Ernan, Ernest, Eaɼnán.
Ernin, Eiɼnín.
Eugene, Eoġan.
Eunan, Aḋaṁnán.
Eustace, Iúɼtáɼ.
Euston, Úiɼteaɼn.
Eveny, Aiḃne.
Ever, Éiḃeaɼ, Éiṁeaɼ.
Evin, Éiṁín.

Fachnan, Faċtna.
Falvy, Fáilḃe.
Farrell, Feaɼġal.
Farry, Feaɼaḋaċ.
Feagh, Fiaċa.
Feary, Fiaċɼa.
Fehin, Feiċín
Felan, Faolán
Felimy, Feiḋlimiḋ.
Felix, Feiḋlimiḋ, Feiḋlim.
Ferdinand, Feaɼḋoɼċa; Feaɼ-
  ġanainm; Feaɼaḋaċ; Feaɼ-
  ġuɼ.
Fergal, Feaɼġal.
Fergus, Feaɼġuɼ.
Festus, Feiċín 11; Faċtna 97.
Fiachra, Fiaċɼa.
Finan, Fionnán.

Fineen, Finġin.
Finian, Finnian; Finġin.
Finn, Fionn.
Finbar, Fionnḃaɼɼ.
Finneen, Finnin, Finġin.
Fionan, Fionnán, Fionán.
Fintan, Fionntán.
Flan, Flann.
Flannan, Flannán.
Florence, Florry, Flaitɼí 9;
  Finġin 7; Flann 92; Fiteal
  92.
Foulk, Folc.
Francis, Pɼóinɼiaɼ, Pɼoinnɼiaɼ,
  Pɼoinnɼeaɼ.
Frank, Fɼainc 7; Pɼeannͻaiġ
  64.
Frederick, Feaɼͻoɼċa.
Fursey, Fuɼɼa.

Garrett, Ʒeaɼóiͻ, Ʒioɼóiͻ.
Garvan, Ʒaɼḃán.
Geoffrey, Seaɼɼaiḋ, Sioɼɼaiḋ,
  Séaɼɼa, Séaċɼa, Séaɼċa,
  Séaċɼún, Seaċɼún, Seaɼċún,
  &c.
George, Seóiɼɼe.
Gerald, Ʒeaɼalt, Ʒeaɼóiͻ.
Gerard, Ʒeaɼáɼͻ, Ʒioɼáɼͻ,
  Ʒeaɼóiͻ, Ʒioɼóiͻ.
Gibbon, Ʒioḃún.
Gilbert, Ʒiliḃeaɼt.
Gilbride, Ʒiolla Ḃɼíġͻe.
Gildea, Ʒiolla Ꝺé.
Gill, Gillesa, Gillisa, Ʒiolla
  Íoɼa.
Gilvarry, Ʒiolla Ḃeaɼaiġ.
Glasny, Ʒlaiɼne.
Godfrey, Ʒoċɼɼaiḋ, Ʒoċɼaiḋ.
Gordon, Ʒoɼͻan.
Gorry, Ʒoċɼaiḋ.
Gregory, Ʒɼéaġóiɼ.

Harold, Aɼalt.
Harry, v. Henry.
Heber, Éiḃeaɼ, Éiṁeaɼ.
Hector, Eaċtaiɼ.; Eaċann 68.

Henry, Éinrí, Annraoi,
   hanraoi.
Herbert, hoireabaro.
Heremon, Hermon, eireamón.
Hewney, Uaitne.
Hubert, hoibearo.
Hugh, Aoḋ 11; hoibearo.
   92.
Hughey, Hughie, Aoḋaiġ 26;
   Cúṁaiġe 64.
Hugony, úġaine.
Humphrey, Unfraiḋ; Aṁlaoiḃ
   79.

Ignatius, eiġneacán, éiġneacán.
Irial, Irial.
Irving, eireamón.
Isaac, Iorac, Ioróc, Ioróg.
Ivor, Ioṁar 1; Éiḃear, Éiṁear
   64.

James, Séamur.
Jarlath, Iarflaiṫ.
Jarmy, Diarmaiḋ.
Jasper, Searpar.
Jeffrey, v. Geoffrey.
Jeremiah, Jerome, Jerry, Diar-
   maiḋ.
Jimmy, Simiḋ, Siomaiḋ,
   Séamuirín.
John, Eóin, Seaġán, Seán,
   Seón.
John Baptist, Eóin Dairte.
Joseph, Ióref, Ióreḃ, Seórap,
   Seórap, Seóraṁ.
Justin, Saerḃreasac 7.

Kealan, Kelan, Caolán.
Kean, Cian.
Kellagh, Ceallac.
Kenan, Cianán.
Kennedy, Cinnéioiḋ, Cinnéioiġ
Kenny, Coinneac.
Kerill, Coireall.
Kevan, Caoṁán.
Kevin, Caoiṁġin.
Kian, Cian,
Kienan, Cianán.

Kieran, Ciarán.
Killian, Cillín, Cillian.

Laserian, Lairrian.
Laughlin, Leaclainn, (o.f.)
   mael Seaclainn; Loclainn,
   Loclann.
Laurence, Laḃrár; Lorcán.
Leo, León.
Lewis, Lewy, Luġaiḋ 1;
   Laoiġreac, Laoireac 2.
Loman, Lomán.
Lonan, Lonán.
Lorcan, Lorcán.
Loughlin, Loclainn, Loclann.
   V. Laughlin.
Louis, Laoiġreac, Laoireac;
   Luġaiḋ.
Lucan, Lúcán.
Lucius, Laoiġreac, Laoireac;
   Lactna.
Luke, Lúcár, 1, Laḃcár 9.
Lysagh, Laoiġeac, Laoireac.

Maelisa, mael Iora.
Mahon, Matġaṁain.
Malachy, mael Seaclainn;
   maol ṁaoḋóg*.
Malcolm, mael Coluim, mael
   Colm.
Manasses, maġnur.
Mantan, manntán.
Manus, maġnur, máġnur.
Marcus, Mark, Marcur.
Martin, Mártan, Mártain,
   Máirtín.
Mat, mait, maitín.
Matthew, mata, maitiú;
   matġaṁain.
Matthias, maitiar, maitiar.
Maurice, muirir; muirġear.
Melaghlin, mael Seaclainn.
Melchor, meilreóir.
Meldan, Mellan, meallán.
Melrone, maol Ruaḋáin.
Meyler, maoilir; maol muire.
Michael, míceál, míceál.

* The name of St. Malachy of Armagh.

Miles, Milo, maol muipe;
maolmópóa : mael Seáċ-
lainn 26
Mogue, maoóóg.
Morgan, mupċaó 1. (s.l.)
bpoċaó 99.
Mortimer, muipċeaptaċ.
Moses, maoóóg.
Munchin, maincín.
Mundy, Réamonn.
Murrough, mupċaó.
Murry, muipeaóaċ.
Murtough, Murty, muipċeaptaċ
Myles, maol muipe; maol-
mópóa.

Naugher, Noghor, Nohor, Con-
ċoḃap.
Neal, Neale, niall 11, néill 62.
Neece, Neese, naop. (o.f.)
aongup.
Nehemiah, giolla na naoṁ.
Neil, néill, 6 ; Conċoḃap 7.
Nessan, neapán.
Nevan, naoṁán.
Niall, niall
Niallan, niallán
Nicholas, nioclár 11 ; naop 62,
Nicol, niocol
Niece, naop, (o.f.) aongup.

Oghie, eoċaió.
Oisin, Oipín.
Olave, aṁlaoiḃ.
Oliver, Oiliḃéap.
Oney, uaiċne.
Oran, Oópán.
Oscar, Orcap.
Ossian, Oipín.
Owen, eoġan 1 ; eóin 99.
Owney, uaiċne.
Oynie, eoġainín ; uaiċne.

Padden, páivín.
Paddy, páivín, paivi, paúpa,
pappa.
Parlan, papċalán, pápċalán,
pápċlán.

Pat, páiv.
Patrick, páopaig, páopaic,
páopaig, páopaic &c.
Paul, pól.
Peregrine, cúċoigcpíċe, cú-
ċpíċe.
Peter, peavap, peavaip.
Phelim, Phelimy, feivlimió,
feivlim.
Philip, pilib, filib 11 ; feiv-
limió, feivlim 62.
Pierce, piapap, feópap.
Pius, píup.

Quintin, Quinton, cúṁaiġe.

Ralph, Ráóulḃ ; Roóulḃ.
Randal, Raġnall, Ráġnall.
Randulph, Rannulḃ ; Raġnall.
Raymond, Redmond, Réamonn.
Reginald, Raġnall.
Revelin, Raiḃilín, Roiḃilín,
Ruiḃilín.
Richard, Rickard, Ripteápo,
Riocápo, Riocapo.
Robert, Riobápo, Riobapt,
Roibeápo, Roibeapo, Ri-
beapo, Ribeapt, Ribipt.
Robin, Roiḃín, Roibean.
Roddy, v. Rory.
Roderick, Roger, Ruaiópí 1,
(s.l.) Raiópí 2, Reiópí 7.
Roland, Roólann 1, Roólaióe 2
Ronald, Raġnall.
Ronan, Rónán.
Rory, Ruaiópí 1, (s.l.) Raiópí 2.
Reiópí 7.
Ross, Rop.
Rowan, Ruaóán.
Rowland, Roólann 1, Roólaióe
2 ; Roiḃilín, Ruiḃilín 64.

Samuel, Soṁaiple.
Senan, Seanán.
Shane, Scaġán, Seán.
Sheary, Séaċpa, Séa .
Geoffrey
Shemus, Séamup

Sheron, Seaċṙún, Séaċṙún.
Shiel, Siaḃal, Siaġal.
Sidney, Séaḋna.
Simon, Síomonn, Síomón,
　Síomún ; Suiḃne 2.
Sinan, Sinon, Sionán, Seanán.
Sivnev, Suiḃne.
Solomon, Solaṁ.
Sorlev, Soṁairle.
Standish, Stanislaus, Ainéirlir.
Stephen, Steaṙán, Stioṙán,
　Stiaḃán, Stiaḃna, Stiana,
　Stiḃin, Steiṁin.
Sylvester, Sailbeartar.
Synan, Seanán, Sionán.

Teague, Teige, Taḋg.
Terence, Terry, Toirḋealḃaċ.
Thaddaeus, Thaddeus, Thady,
　Taḋg.
Theobald, Tiobóid, Teabóid.
Theodore, Téaḋóir.
Thomas, Tomár.
Tibbot, Tiobóid, Teabóid.
Tiernan, Tiġearnán.
Tierney, Tiġearnaċ.

Tim, Taḋg, Taiḋġín.
Timothy, Tiomóid 19; Taḋg 1 ;
　Tomaltaċ 34.
Toal, Tuaċal.
Tobias, Tiobóid, Teabóid.
Tomaltagh, Tomaltaċ.
Tommy, Tomáirín.
Tully, Tuaċal.
Tumelty, Tomaltaċ.
Turlough, Toirḋealḃaċ, (s.l.)
　Traelaċ, Tarla.

Ulick, Uillioc, Uileóg.
Ultan, Ultán.
Ulysses, Uillioc, Uilleac,
　Uileóg.

Val, Ḃail.
Valentine, Ḃailintín.
Victor, Ḃuaḃaċ.
Vincent, Uinrionn, Uinreann.

Walter, Ualtar, Uaitéir.
Wilfrid, Uilṙriḋ.
William, Willie, Uilliam, Liam.

NAMES OF WOMEN

ENGLISH—IRISH

Abbie, Abby, v. Abigail.
Abigail, Abaigeal, Abaig 26, 64 ; Gobnaic 7, 9.
Abina, Gobnaic.
Afric, Africa, Aippic.
Agatba, Agaca.
Agnes, Aignéip : Úna ; Mór 92.
Aileen, Aibilín, eiblín.
Alastrina, Alexandra, Alarcríona.
Alice, Alicia, Ailir, Ailír, Ailíre, Ailre, eilír, eilíre.
Alley, Ailiò, Alaiò.
Allison, Allrún.
Alvy, Ailbe
Amelina, Aimilíona
Anastasia, Annrcár, Scéire.
Angela, Aingeal.
Anna, Ánna, Anna ; Áine.
Annabel, Annabella, Annábla, náible ; Iribéal, Sibéal 26.
Anne, Áine ; Ánna, Anna ; neanr, nainreaò.
Annie, eicne. V. Anne.
Apbria, Aippic.
Arabella, v. Annabella.
Attracta, Acracc.
Atty, Aicce.
Aylce, v. Alice.

Bab, Baibín.
Babe, Báb.
Barbara, Barbary, Bairbre, Báirbre 1, Baibín 99 ; Goirmflaic 2.
Beesy, Brígiò, Bríguín.
Bella, v. Annabella.

Benvon, Bean múman.
Benvy, Bean míuòe.
Bessie, Betsey, Betty, v. Elizabeth.
Bevin, Béuinn.
Bidelia, Bidina, Birdie, Brígiò, Bríguín,
Blanche, Bluinre ; Blinne 64.
Breeda, Bride, Bridget, Brigid, Brígiò 1, Brígue 2.

Catherine, Caicríona, Cacraoine, Caicrín, Caiclín.
Cecelia, Cecily, Celia, Sirile, Síle.
Charlotte, Séarlaic.
Christina, Cjurcíona. Cjurcín.

Daisey, nóirín nóinín
Debby, Deborah Gobnaic
Delia, Brígiò Bríguín.
Derval, Dervilia Dearbáil.
Devnet, Damnaic.
Dillie, Dina, Brígiò, Bríguín.
Dolly, Dorothy, Dorren, Doireann.
Downet, Dymphna, Damnaic.

Eavan, Aoibeann.
Edwina, Éavaoin.
Eileen, eiblín.
Eithne, eicne.
Eleanor, Eleanora, eilíonóir, eileanóra 1, léan 49.
Eliza, Elizabeth, eilír, eilíre 1 ; Ireabal, Iribéal, Sibéal 2.

Ellen, Ellie, Cibdlín.
Elsha, Ailſe.
Elva, Ailbe, Oilbe.
Emily, eimíle.
Enat, Ena, Eny, Aoúnait.
Ernet, eaｉnait.
Esther, eiｉtiｉ; Airlinn,
　Aіｉling 64.
Ethna, Etney, eitne.
Eva, Aoiｉe.
Eveleen, Evelyn, Aibilín,
　eibilín, eiblín.

Fanny, Fainｃe; pｉoinnｉéaｉ.
Feena, Feenat, Fiaúnait.
Finola, Fionnｇuala.
Flora, blát; Fionnｇuala.
Florence, blátnaiｄ.
Frances, pｉoinnｉéaｉ, pｉóin
　ｉéaｉ.

Gertrude, Gertie, Ｚｉáinne.
Gobinet, Gobnet, Ｚobnait.
Gormlaith, Gormley, Ｚoｉm
　 Flait.
Grace, Ｚｉáinne.
Gubby, Ｚobnait.

Hannah, Siobán, Siubán, Siob
　áinín, Siubáinín 1; Onóｉa,
　nóｉa 16, 26.
Helen, eiblín.
Hilda, Hildy, hilｄe.
Honor, Honora, Onóｉa, 1ｉoｉｉ

Ida, íｄe.
Ina, Aｇna.
Ita, íｄe.
Isabella, 1ｉibéal, 1ｉeabal,
　Sibéal.

Jane, Jannet, Jenny, Sinéaｄ í,
　Sineaiｄ, Sine 26.
Joan, Johanna, Siobán, Siubán.
Josephine, Seóｉaiｍtín; Sio
　báinín, Siubáinín.
Jude, Judith, Judy, Síle 11;
　Siobán, Siubán. 3.

Julia, July, Síle 1; Siubán,
　Siobán 9.

Kate, Cáit.
Kathleen, Caitilín, Caitlín.
Katie, Cáitín, Tｉíona, Tｉaoine.
Katty, Caiti, Cáitín.
Keavy, Caoiｍe.
Keelin, Caoilｉionn.
Keenet, Kinnat, Ciannait.

Lassarina, Laｉaiｉｉiona.
Lelia, líle.
Lena, eiblín.
Lily, Lil, líle.
Lizzie, eilíｉ. V. Elizabeth.
Louisa, Labaoiｉe.
Lucy, Luiｇｉeáć.

Mabbina, meaｄb, meiｉбín.
Mabel, máible; nábla; meaｄb
Madeline, máiｇｄlín, maｄail
　éin.
Madge, meaｄb 6; niaiｇｉéaｄ
　70; muｉainn 499.
Marcella, maiｉｉil, maiｉｉile.
Maggie, v. Margaret.
Margaret, máiｉｇｉéaｄ, maiｉ
　ｇｉéaｄ, muiｉｇéaｄ, niaiｇｉéaｄ,
　máiｉéaｄ. maiｉéaｄ, muiｉ
　éaｄ, máｉaoｄ, muｉáiｄ.
Margery, meaｄб; máille,
　máilｉe, máilti.
Maria, máiｉe.
Marjory, v. Margery.
Marion, muiｉeann, muiｉｉnn,
　muｉainn.
Martha, maｉta; móｉ.
Mary, muiｉe*, máiｉe; móｉ 2;
　méaｉｉ 492.
Matilda, maitilｄe.
Matty, maiti.
Maud, máｄa; meaｄb.
Maureen, May, máiｉín.
Meave, meaｄб.
Meeda, míｄe.
Mella, mealla.
Moira, máiｉe.

* The name of the Blessed Virgin Mary.

Molly, Máirín; mallaiḋ, máille, máilre, máilti.
Mona, Monat, muaḋnaic.
Monica, moncá.
More, móp.
Moreen, móipín.
Morrin, muipeann, muipinn, mupainn.
Murel, muipġeal.

Nabla, nábla, náible.
Nan, Nance, Nancy, neanp, nainpeaḋ.
Nanno, nópá.
Nappy, nuala, pionnġuala.
Nell, Nellie, neill, neilli, eiḃlín.
Nessa, neapa.
Nonie, nóipín 1 ; Sioḃán 499.
Nora, Norah, Onópá, nópá.
Nuala, nuala.

Olive, Oilḃe.
Orlaith, Ópḟlaiċ.
Orna, Ornat, Oḋaipnaic.

Peg, Peggy, peig, peigí.
Penelope, Penny, pionnġuala, nuala.
Poll, Polly, pal, pailp, paili.

Regina, Ríoġnaċ.
Renny, Raċnaic.

Richella, Riċeal.
Rose, Róip, Róipe, Róipín.

Sabia, Saḃḃ.
Sabina, Saiḃḃín 1 · Síle 19, 97.
Sally, Sopċa 1 ; Saḃḃ (Saḃa) 99 ; Síle 192.
Sarah, Sopċa 1 : Saḃḃ 16, 64.
Selia, Sheela, Sheila, Síle.
Sibby, Síle ; Siḃéal, Sibi, S·obaiġ.
Sive. Saḃḃ.
Slany, Sláine.
Sophia, Sophy, Saḃḃ, Saḃḃa 16, 26.
Susan, Susanna, Sópanna, Sópaiḋ, Siúi ; Sioḃán, Siuḃán 3, 469.
Sybil, Siḃéal.

Teresa, Tessie, toipéapa, Tpeapa, Tpeipe.
Tilda, Cilḋe.
Trina, Tpiona, Tpaoine.

Una, Unity, Uny, úna.
Ursula, Uppula.

Vivian, Béḃinn.

Webbie, ġobnaic.
Whiltierna, paoilciġeapna.
Winefred, Winifred, Winnie, Winny, úna.

SURNAMES

ENGLISH—IRISH

Abbott, Abbóıd.
Abraham, Ábраһam.
Adair, Ó Ɗáıpe.
Adams, mac Áɗaım, mac
Aɗaım 1 ; mac Aɗamóıɗ 99 ;
mac Conｒnáṁa 197.
Adamson, mac Áɗaım, mac
Aɗaım.
Addley, Addly, Ó hÁɗɫaıᵹ.
Addy, mac Áɗaıɗ.
Adkins, Adkinson, Adkisson,
mac Aıoᵹcín.
Adorian, Ó Ɗeóｒaɗáın, Ó
Ɗeóｒáın.
Adrian, Adrien, Ó Ɗｒeáın.
Agar, éıᵹeaｒ.
Agarty, Ó hÁᵹaｒtaıᵹ.
Aghoon, Ó heacóuɗáın.
Agnew, Ó ᵹníṁ.
Ahearn, Ahearne, v. Ahern.
Aher, Ó h aıcıｒ.
Aheran, Aherin, Ahern, Aherne,
Aheron, Ó heacċıᵹeıｒn, Ó
eacċıᵹeıｒn, &c.
Ahessy, Ó hÁıceaｒa.
Aiken, v. Eakin.
Ailward, v. Aylward.
Airey, Áıｒıᵹ.
Aison, mac Aoɗa.
Alcock, Aɫcóc.
Alexander, Aɫｒanɗaıｒ 1 ; mac
Aɫｒanɗaıｒ 2, mac Aɫaｒ-
cｒaınn 2, mac Aɫaｒcｒuım 2.
Allan, Ó hAɫɫaṁaın 197. V.
Allen.

Allen, Ó hAıɫín, Ó hAıɫlín 1 ;
mac Aıɫín 8 ; Aıɫín 2 ;
Aıɫéın 82 ; Ó hAɫɫaṁaın 197.
Alleine, Alleyne, Aıɫéın.
Allin v. Allen.
Allman, Aɫamán.
Alton, Aɫcún.
Alyward, v. Aylward.
Ambrose, Ambｒóｒ, Ampóｒ,
Ampuｒ.
Anbora, Anborough, v. Hanbury.
Anders, mac Aınɗｒıú.
Anderson, mac Aınɗｒıú 11 ;
mac ᵹıoɫɫa Aınɗｒéıｒ 36 ;
Anɗｒaoｒán 192.
Andrew, Aınɗｒıú.
Andrews, Andrewson, mac
Aınɗｒıú.
Angland, Aınᵹɫeonc.
Anglim, Ó hAnᵹɫuınn, (s.l.) Ó
hAnᵹɫuım 179.
Anglin, Ó hAnᵹɫuınn.
Angus, mac Aonᵹuıｒ.
Anketell, Ankethill, Ancoıcıɫ.
Ankland, v. Angland.
Ankle, v. Anketell.
Ansberry, Ansboro, Ó haın-
ṁıｒeac, (s.l.) Ó hAınmｒeac,
Ó Aınmneac 97.
Anthony, Antony, Ancóıｒ,
Ancoıne 2 ; mac Ancoıne 2.
Archabald, Archbald, Archbold,
Áıｒｒeabóıɗ 1 ; Áıｒｒıbáﬁﬂ 19.
Archdeacon, Áıｒｒɗéıcın, Áıｒ-
céıcın ; (G.p.) mac Óɗa.

Archer, Áirréin, Áiréin 4;
mac Arcail 83.
Archfield, Áirréil;
Archibald Archibold Áirreabóro 1, Áirríbéal 6
Ardagh Ároaca.
Arkins ó hOrcáin.
Armstrong, Tréanlámac 1;
Ó Labraóa Tréan 68.
Arnold, Arnott, Arnóio.
Arthur, Arthurs, mac Artúir
2; Artúir 2.
Ashe, Air, 1, Ágar, Átarac
172, 499.
Asken, Askin, v. Heskin.
Aspel, Aspell, Áireabóro.
Aspig, Earpog 2; mac Giolla
earpuig 2; mac an earpuig 2.
Aspill, v. Aspell.
Asping v. Aspig.
Aspol, v. Aspell.
Atamney, mac an Tiompánaig.
Atasney, mac an tSaranaig.
Athy, Átaoi.
Atkins, Atkinson, mac Aioicín.
Aughney, mac Factna.
Auher, Áiréir.
Aungier, Óinréir.
Aurachaun ó hannracáin.
Austen, Austin, Oirtín 1; mac
Aibirtín 9.
Aylmar, Aylmer, Aiglmear.
Aylward, Aigleart.
Ayres, ó hiarrac (S.L.) 469.

Babe, báb.
Bacon, ve bacún, bacún.
Badger, ó bruic.
Bagley, v. Begley.
Bagnall, Bagnell, bagnal 11;
ó beigléiginn 43.
Baggot,   Baggott,   Bagot,
Bagott, bagóio.
Bailey, Bailie, Baillie, Baily,
báille.
Bain, bán.
Baird, mac an báiro.
Baith, v. Bath.

Baker, báicéir, bácaeir.
Bakey, ó béice.
Baldin, Baldoon, bároún.
Baldwin, bároún, bárouing 1;
ó maolagáin 16 (O'D).
Balfe, balb.
Ball, bál.
Ballantine. bailintín.
Ballard, balláro.
Ballesty, bailirte.
Ballevan, ó balbáin.
Ballinger, bailinréir.
Ballon, báróun.
Banan, v. Bannon.
Banane, ó banáin 1; buinneán
49.
Banahan, ó beannacáin
Bane, bán.
Banfell, Banfield, v. Bonfield.
Banigan, ó banagáin.
Banim, Banin, ó banáin.
Banks, ó bruacóg 19, ó
bruacáin 45.
Bannan, Bannen, Bannin, ó
banáin.
Bannigan, ó banagáin.
Bannon, Banon, ó banáin 11,
(s.l.) ó bionáin 2.
Banvill, Banville, v. Bonfield.
Baragrey, v. Barragry.
Bardan, Barden, Bardon, ó
báróáin.
Bargrey, v. Barragry.
Barker, barcar.
Barnacle, ó Caváin.
Barnane, ó beannáin.
Barnard, beannáro 11; ó
beannáin 779.
Barnavill, v. Barnwell.
Barnes, beannair 1; ó beanáin
92, ó bionáin 19.
Barnewall, Barnwell, ve
beannabál, beannabál.
Baron, barún.
Barr, ó bairr.
Barragry, mac beantagra
Barratt, Barrett, báióro,
baróro 7; bairéiv 9.

Barrie, v. Barry.
Barrington, E. 1 ; Ó beaṗáin 46.
Barron, bapún 78 ; Ó beaṗáin 16, 46.
Barry, ve bappa 11 ; Ó báiṗe 772, 492 ; Ó beaṗġa 172.
Bartholomew, Bartley, mac Ṗaṙċaláin.
Barton, ve baṙcún, baṙcún.
Baskin, Ó baiṙcinn.
Basnet, baiṙnéiv.
Bass, ve baṙ.
Bassett, baiṙéiv.
Bastable, Bastible, ve baṙ- tábla.
Baston, beaṙcún.
Bates, Bath, ve báċ, báċ.
Battle, Battles, mac Conċaċa.
Baun, bán.
Baun-Lavery, Ó labṙaóa bán.
Bawn, bán.
Bayley, Bayly, báille.
Bayne, Baynes, bán.
Beaghan, Beahan, Ó beaċáin.
Beaky, Ó béice.
Bean Beane, Ó beaċáin.
Bearkery, v. Berkery.
Bearnes, v. Barnes.
Beary, Ó béaṙa.
Beasley, béaṙlaiġ béaṙlaoi.
Beasty, Ó biaṙca.
Beatagh, Beattie, Beatty, biaóċaċ, (s.l.) Ó biaóa 979
Beaumont, ve buamonn, bua monn.
Beausang, Ṗṙanncaċ.
Beck, ve beic 11 ; Ó béice 2 (O'D).
Beegan, Ó beaċáin.
Begane, Ó beaġáin.
Begg, Ó beiġ 2 ; beaġ 2
Beggan, Ó beaġáin.
Beggs, Ó beiġ 2 ; beaġ 2.
Beglan, Ó beiġléiġinn, Ó biġléiġinn.
Begley, Ó beaġlaoiċ.
Beglin, v. Beglan.
Behan, Behane, Ó beaċáin.

Beirne, Beirnes, Ó beiṙn, Ó biṙn.
Bell, ve beil 1 ; mac ġiolla an Ċloiġ 19.
Bellew, beilliú, beille.
Bellingham, beilleaġam.
Belton, ve béalacún, béalacún.
Benan, v. Bannon.
Bennett, beinéiv, binéiv, bionóiv 1 ; buinneán 496.
Benson mac binéiv 11 ; mac ġiollaóé 39; Ó manaċáin 19.
Bera, Ó béaṙa.
Berachry, v. Berkerry.
Beresford, Ṿúinṙméaṙaċ.
Bergan, Bergen, Bergin, Berigin, Ó haimiṙġin, Ó haimeiṙġin, (s.l.) Ó beiṙġin.
Berkerry, berkery, mac bioṙcaġṙa, mac beaṙcaġṙa.
Bermingham, mac Ṗeóṙaiṙ, mac Ṗeóṗuiṙ, maġ Ṗeóṙaiṙ, maġ Ṗeóṗuiṙ, (s.l.) a Ceóṗaiṙ, &c.
Bernard, beaṙnáṗv 1 ; Ó beaṙnáin 779.
Berne, v. Beirne.
Berney, v. Birney.
Bernwell, v. Barnwell.
Berocry, v. Berkerry.
Berrall, v. Berrill.
Berrane, Ó beaṙáin. Ó bioṙáin.
Berreen, Ó biṙín.
Berrigan v. Bergan.
Berrill, boiṙéil.
Berry, Ó béaṙa.
Berth, beiṙc.
Bertram, beaṙcṙam.
Beston, beaṙcún.
Betagh, Betty, biaóċaċ.
Bex, ve beic.
Biern, Bierne, v. Beirne.
Bigam, Biggam, v. Bingham.
Biggane, Ó biġeáin, Ó beaġáin.
Biggar, Bigger, biġeaṙ.
Biggin, Biggins, Ó biġín, Ó beiġín.
Biggs, v. Beggs.

Biggy, Ó biʒiʒ.
Bigham, v. Bingham.
Bigly, v. Begley
Bignel, v. Bagnall.
Binchy, binnre.
Binane, buinneán.
Bingham, bionʒam, binʒeam.
Biracrea, Biracree, v. Berkerry.
Bird, E. 1; ó héanna, ó
  héinne 19; ó héiniʒ 2; ó
  héanacáin, ó héineacáin 19,
  97; mac Conʒonaiʒ, (s.l.)
  mac an éanaiʒ 35, 43.
Birmingham, v. Bermingham.
Birne, Birnes, v. Byrne.
Birney, mac biorna.
Birrane, ó bioráin.
Birrell, boiréil.
Bishop, earpoʒ 1; mac an ear-
  puic 2; mac ʒiolla erpuiʒ 2.
Bissett, biréiv; (G.p) mac eóin.
Blacagh, blácac.
Black, ó vuib 2; mac vuib 2;
  mac ʒiolla vuib 2; ó
  vubtaiʒ 62.
Blackhall, ve blácál 1; ó vub-
  ʒaill 469.
Blackham, ve blácam.
Blackwood, coillvub.
Blake, ve bláca, ve blác 11;
  ó blátmaic 192.
Blanchfield, Blanchville, ve
  bluinnríol, (s.l.) bluinnrín.
Blaney, bléine.
Blawick, ó blátmaic.
Blayney, bléine.
Bleheen. ó blicín.
Blessing, ó maoilbeannacta.
Blewett, blaov, bliúit.
Bligh, Blighe, ó bliʒe.
Bloomer, ó ʒoirmrleaʒaiʒ, 6.
Blouk, Blowick, ó blátmaic.
Bluett, Blute, blaov, bliúit.
Bly, v. Blighe.
Blythe, ve blaʒv.
Boag, v. Bogue.
Boal, Boale, Boales, v. Bole, Boles
Bockley, ó baclaiʒ.

Bodan, Boden, bóvún 14,
  bóvín 82; ó buaváin 24, 45.
Bodkin, bóvoicín.
Bogan, Boggan, ó boʒáin.
Bogue, ó buavaiʒ.
Bohan, ó buavácáin.
Bohanan, ó buavácáin 469.
Bohane,* ó buavácáin.
Bohig, ó buavaiʒ.
Bohill, ó baotʒalaiʒ 6.
Boice, v. Boyce.
Boil, Boile, v. Boyle.
Bolan, Boland, ó beólláin 11;
  ó breólláin 192.
Bole, Boles, (?) ó baoiʒill.
Bolger, ó bolʒuivír.
Bollard, ballápv.
Bolton, ve bolltún, bóltún.
Bonar, ó cnáimríʒe, (s.l.) ó
  cráimríʒe.
Bond, Bonde, ve bonv.
Bone, ve botún.
Boner, v. Bonar.
Bones, mac cnáim 19, mac
  cnámaiʒ 192.
Bonfield, ve buinbíol.
Bonin, buinneán.
Bonner, v. Bonar.
Boohan, ó buavácáin.
Boran, ó bovráin.
Borris, v. Burris.
Borroughs, Borrowes, ve bruʒa.
Borthwick, bórtuic.
Bosher, v. Busher.
Bostick, Bostock, ve bortóc.
Boucher, Bouchier, búiréir.
Boughan, ó buavácáin.
Boughla, ó buacalla.
Bouhan, ó buavácáin.
Boulger, v. Bolger.
Bourke, ve búrc, ve búrca.
Bowden, v. Boden.
Bowdren, búvrán.
Bowe, ó buavaiʒ
Bowen, ve botún, bóinn, 45,
  72; ó buavácáin 77; ó
  cnáimín 46.

* Bohane, in the neighbourhood of Skibbereen, is generally used as
a nickname for a branch of the O'Sullivans (? na mbotán).

Bowes, Ó buaḋaiġ 11; Ó baocġalaiġ 62.
Bowie, Ó buaḋaiġ.
Bowland, v. Boland.
Bowle, v. Bole.
Bowler, bóiléiṗ, boḃléiṗ.
Bowles, v. Boles.
Bowman, buaman.
Bownes, v. Bones.
Bowsher, v. Busher.
Boyan, v. Boyhan.
Boyce, ve búṗ 10; Ó buaḋaiġ 16.
Boyd, ve búiṫ, a búiṫ, búiṫeaċ.
Boyes, v. Boyce.
Boyhan, (?) Ó buaḋacáin 77.
Boylan, Boyland, Ó baoiġealláin.
Boyle, Ó baoiġill.
Boyne, Ó baoiṫín 2; mac baoiṫín 2.
Boyse, v. Boyce.
Boyton, ve baóṫún, baióṫún.
Brabazon, brabarún 11; Ó brolċáin 67.
Bracken, Ó breacáin.
Bradagan, Ó branaġáin, Ó braḋaċáin.
Bradan, Ó braḋáin.
Braddell, Ó braḋġail, Ó braḋġaile.
Bradden, Ó braḋáin.
Braddigan, Ó braḋaġáin.
Bradacan, Ó braḋacáin, Ó braḋaġáin.
Bradigan, Ó braḋaġáin.
Bradley, Bradly, Ó brolċáin, Ó broilaċáin,(s.l.) Ó broileaċáin 19.
Brady, mac bráḋaiġ 6, 8; Ó bráḋaiġ 2; Ó braḋacáin, Ó braḋaġáin 19.
Bragan, Ó braġáin.
Brahan, Ó braċáin.
Braidon, v. Breadon.
Bran, bran.
Branagan, Ó branaġáin.
Branagh, breaṫnaċ.

Branan, v. Brannan.
Brand, branṫ.
Brandon, mac breanḋáin 49; ve branḋún, branḋún 37.
Brangan, v. Branagan.
Braniff, Ó branḋuiḃ.
Branigan, Brankin, Ó branaġáin.
Brannagh, breaṫnaċ.
Brannan, Ó branáin 11; mac branáin 34.
Branne, bran.
Brannick, ve breannóc, breannóc, brannóc.
Brannigan, Ó branaġáin.
Brannock, v. Brannick.
Brannon, Branon, v. Brannan.
Bransfield, ve prionnbíol, prionnbíol.
Brant, branṫ.
Brassill, Ó brearail.
Brauders, Ó bruaḋair.
Brawley, Ó brólaiġ.
Brawn, Ó bioráin.
Brawnick, v. Brannick.
Bray, ve brí 1; Ó breaġaiġ, Ó breaġḋa 71; Ó bróiṫ 772.
Brayden, v. Breadon.
Brazel, Brazil, Ó brearail.
Breadon, ve bréaḋún.
Bready, v. Brady.
Breanon, v. Brennan.
Brearton, v. Brereton.
Breckley, v. Brickley.
Bredin, Bredon, ve bréaḋún.
Bree, v. Bray.
Breedeth, mac ġiolla Bríġve.
Breen, Ó braoin 1; mac braoin 24.
Breheny, Brehony, mac an breiṫeaṁan, mac an broiṫeaṁnaiġ 11, mac an breiṫiṁ 19.
Brenan, v. Brennan.
Brendon, v. Brandon.
Brennagh, breaṫnaċ.
Brennan, Ó braonáin 11, (s.l.) Ó brianáin 192; Ó branáin 6, 91; mac branáin 34.

Brennigan, Ó Branagáin.
Brennock, ᴅe Breannóc, Breannóc.
Brennon, Brenon, v. Brennan.
Brereton, Brerton, Breártún
Bresland, Breslane, Breslaun, Breslawn, Breslin, Ó Breaslán, Ó Breirleáin, Ó Breirlein, (s.l.) Ó Brioráin, Ó Brirleáin, &c.
Bresnahan, Bresnane, Bresnehan, Bresnihan, Ó Brosnacáin, Ó Broirneacáin.
Brett, ᴅe Brit, ᴅe Breic, Bric.
Bretton, ᴅe Breacún, ᴅe Briocún.
Brew, Ó Brugaᴅa.
Breydon, ᴅe Bréaᴅún.
Brian, v. Bryan.
Briceson, Ó Brioráin. (o.f.) Ó Muirgearáin.
Brick, Ó Bruic 49; Ó Bric 47.
Brickley, Bruicléig, Bruicléit.
Bride, Bríᴅe, Bríᴅeac 2; na Brígᴅe 77
Bridge, ᴅe Brig, Brigeac.
Bridgeman, Ó Droicíᴅ.
Bridson, Mac Giolla Bríġᴅe.
Brie, ᴅe Brí.
Brien, Briens, v. O'Brien, Mac Brien, & Bryan.
Brigg, Briggs, ᴅe Brig, Brigeac.
Brinan, Brinane, v. Brennan.
Briody, Ó Bruaiᴅeaᴅa.
Brisco, Briscoe, Briorcú.
Brislan, Brislane, Brislaun, Brislawn, Brislin, v. Bresland, Breslane, &c.
Briton, v. Britton.
Britt, ᴅe Brit, Bric.
Brittan, Britten, Britton, ᴅe Briocún.
Brock, Broc.
Brodders, Broder, Broderick, Ó Bruaᴅair.
Brodie, v. Brody.
Brodigan, v. Bradigan.
Brodrick, v. Broderick.

Brody, Mac Bruaiᴅeaᴅa.
Broe, Ó Brugaᴅa.
Brofie, v. Brophy.
Brogan, Ó Brógáin.
Broggy, Ó Brogaiᴅ.
Brohan, Ó Bruacáin.
Brohoon, Mac an Breiteamán.
Brolan, Ó Breólláin.
Brollaghan, Ó Brolcáin, Ó Brolacáin.
Brolly, Broly, Ó Brólaig.
Brooder, Ó Bruaᴅair.
Broone, v. Bruen.
Broothers, v. Brothers.
Brophy, Ó Bróite 11, (s.l.) Ó Bróit 772.
Broslin, v. Breslin.
Brosnahan, Brosnahen, Brosnahin, Brosnan, Brosnihan, Ó Brosnacáin.
Brother, Brothers, Brouder, Ó Bruaᴅair.
Broudin, Mac Bruaiᴅín.
Broughan, Ó Bruacáin.
Broughton, ᴅe Bruocún.
Browder, v. Brouder.
Browe, Ó Brugaᴅa.
Brown, Browne, ᴅe Brún, Brún
Bruce, ᴅe Brúr, ᴅe Brúr.
Bruder, Brudher, v. Brouder.
Bruen, Bruin, Ó Braoin, (s.l.) Ó Brúin.
Brunnock, Brannóc.
Brunty, v. Prunty.
Bruodin, Mac Bruaiᴅín.
Brusnahan, Brusnehan, Brusnihan, v. Brosnahan.
Bruton, v. Britton.
Bryan, Bryans, Bryen, Bryne, Brynes, Brian 24, 28; Ó Briain 2; Mac Briain 2.
Bryson, Ó Brioráin, (o.f.) Ó Muirgearáin.
Buckley, Ó Buacalla 1; Ó Baclaig 19.
Bueg, Beag.
Buggy, Ó Bogaig.
Buhilly, Ó Buacalla.

Buie, Ó buaóaiġ 16 ; mac ġiollabuióe 68.
Bulfin, bulfin.
Bulger, Ó bolġuióir.
Bunfield, Bunfill, ꝺe buinḃfol.
Bunyan, buinneán.
Burbage, búrbać.
Burchell, buirréil.
Burdon, ꝺe burꝺún.
Burges, Burgess, Burgiss, buirġéir, buirġéir 1 ; ꝺe ḃruġa, ḃruġa 2.
Burke, ꝺe búrc, ꝺe búrca.
Burn, v. Byrne.
Burney, v. Birney.
Burns, Ó broin 6, 8, 71 ; Ó ḃeirn, Ó birn 91 ; Ó bioráin 75, 97 ; Ó bioráinn 499 ; Ó boirne 192, mac conboirne 192 ; Ḃran 469.
Burrell, boiréil.
Burris, buirġéir 1 ; ꝺe ḃruġa 2,
Burrowes, Burrows, ꝺe ḃruġa, ḃruġa.
Burton, ꝺe burꝺún.
Bury, ꝺe ḃruġa.
Busher, búiréir.
Buskin, Ó baircinn.
Bussher, v. Busher.
Bustard, burꝺáꝺ.
Butler, ꝺe buiꝺiléir, ꝺe buiꝺiléir, buiꝺiléir, buiꝺiléir, builꝺéir, builꝺéir.
Butt, ꝺe boꝺ.
Butterly, buꝺarlaiġ.
Buttimer, buiꝺiméir.
Bwee, Ó buaóaiġ 16 ; mac ġiollabuióe 68.
Byran, Byrane, Ó bioráin.
Byrne, Byrnes, Ó broin 11 ; Ó ḃeirn, Ó birn 91 ; Ó bioráin 75, 97 ; mac broin 62 ; Ó boirne 192.
Byron, Ó bioráin 75 ; Ó birn 2 ; Ó broin 2.
Byrrane, Ó bioráin.
Bywater, Ó sruꝺáin, Ó sruiꝺeáin.

Cadagan, v. Cadigan.
Cadan, Ó caꝺáin.
Caddell, Caꝺal.
Cadden, Ó caꝺáin 6 ; mac Áꝺuín, (s.l.) Ó Cáꝺuín 9.
Caddle, Cadell, v. Caddell.
Caden, v. Cadden.
Cadigan, Cadogan, Ó céaꝺaġáin 77, Ó céaꝺacáin 49.
Caddow, v. MacCaddo.
Cafferky, Cafferty, mac eaċṁarcaiġ 11, (s.l.) Ó Ceararcaiġ 19.
Caffery, Caffrey, mac ġafraió, mac Cafraió, maġ Cafraió, &c.
Cagney, Ó Cainġne.
Cahalan, Cahalane, Cahalin, Cahallane, Ó Caċaláin.
Cahan, Cahane, Ó caċáin 1 ; mac eaċáin 62.
Caheerin, mac eaċꝺiġeirn.
Cahelan, Cahelin, v. Cahalan.
Caheny, Ó Caiꝺniaó.
Cahill, Ó Caċail.
Cahillane, Ó Caċaláin.
Cahir, Ó Caċaoir 76 ; mac Caċaoir 2.
Cahy, mac eaċaió 1 ; Ó Caċaiġ 25.
Cain, Caine, Ó Caċáin.
Cairn, Cairnes, Cairns, Ó céirín 1, Ó Ciaráin. 2.
Calaghan, Calahan, v. Callaghan.
Caldwell, Ó huaruirce 63 ; mac conluain 93 ; mac Caċṁaoil 62.
Calhoun, Ó Caċluain.
Calinan, v. Callinan.
Callaghan, Ó Ceallacáin 11 ; Ó Céileacáin 64 ; Ó Cloċacáin 469.
Callagy, Ó Calġaiġ.
Callahan, v. Callaghan.
Callaly, mac Áilġile.
Callan, Ó Caċláin, Ó Caċaláin.
Callanan, Callanane, Ó Callanáin 11 ; Ó Cuileannáin 779.

Callaughan, Calleghan, v.
Callaghan.
Callen, v. Callan.
Callender, Cuiteanoap.
Callery, mac ʒiollaɹabaiʒ 5 ;
(?) mac ʒiolla appaic 2.
Calligan, Callighan, v. Callaghan.
Callily, mac aiʒile.
Callin, v. Callan.
Callina, (?) mac an laiʒniʒ.
Callinan, Ó Callanáin 11 ; Ó
Cuileannáin 779.
Calliry, v. Callery.
Callister, mac Alaptaip.
Callnan, v. Callanan.
Callwell, v. Caldwell.
Calnan, v. Callanan.
Calvey, mac an Calbaiʒ, mac
Calbaiʒ.
Cambell, v. Campbell.
Cambridge, mac Ambpóip.
Cameron, Camppón 1 ; Ó
Cumpáin, (s.l.) Ó Cumapán 19.
Campbell, Caimbéal S ; mac
Cailín 66 ; mac Cacṁaoil 19,
61 ; mac Callanáin 132.
Campion, Caimpion.
Canally, mac an pailʒiʒ. V.
MacNally.
Canavan, Ó Ceannoubáin.
Canaway, v. Conway.
Candless, Candlish, v. MacCand-
lish and Quinlish.
Cane, Ó Catáin.
Cangney, Ó Caingne.
Caning, v. Canning.
Cannan, v. Cannon.
Cannavan, v. Canavan.
Canniff, Canniffe, Ó Ceannouib.
Canning, Ó Cainín, 52, Ó Canáin
97; MacCoinín 2; ÓCanann 16.
Cannon, Ó Canann 16; Ó Canáin,
Ó Conáin, Ó Cuineáin, 9.
Canny, Ó Caicniaō 19 ; mac
Annaiō, (s.l.) mac Cannaiō,
Ó Cannaiō 46.
Canon v. Cannon.

Cantillon, Cantlin, Cantlon, oe
Canncalún, Canncalún.
Canton, oe Canncún, Canncún,
Cancún.
Cantwell, oe Canncual, oe
eanncual, Canncual, Cancual.
Canty, Ó an Cáince, Ó Cáince 11,
(s.l.) Ó Canncaōa, Ó Canncaiō
72.
Caorish, mac peópaip, mac
peópuip.
Capeless, Caples, Caplice
Cáplaip.
Cappack, v. Cappock.
Capples, Capplis, eáplaip.
Cappock, Cappuck, oe Ceapóc,
oe Ceapóʒ.
Carabine, v. Coribeen.
Caragher, Caraher, mac peapcaip.
Carberry, Carbery, Carbry, Ó
Caipbpe 8 ; mac Caipbpe 2.
Cardell, mac Apoʒail.
Carden, Cáipoín.
Cardiff, oe Capouib.
Cardin, Cáipoín.
Cardle, mac Apoʒail.
Cardwell, mac Apoʒail 62 ;
mac Ceapbaill 62.
Carellan, Ó Caipealláin.
Caren, Ó Cappaiōín.
Carew, oe Cappún, Cappún.
Carey, Ó Ciapōa 14, 15, 43, 46,
75, 979 ; mac piacpa, mac
piacpac 972 ; Cappún 71 ; Ó
Cappáin, Ó Coppáin 72 ;
Ó Ciapáin, Ó Ceapáin, Ó
Ciopáin, 197, 199, Ó Céipín
2 ; Ó Ciapṁacáin, 779.
Cargill, mac peapʒail.
Carha, mac Cápcaiʒ.
Carigan, v. Carrigan.
Carkill, mac peapʒail.
Carlan, Carland, Ó Caipealláin,
Ó Coipealláin 11 ; Ó Ceap-
balláin 62.
Carleton, oe Caplcún 2 ; Ó
Caipealláin 6.

63

Carley, mac feargaile.
Carlin, v. Carlan.
Carlon, Ó Cearballáin.
Carlos, mac Carluir.
Carlton, v. Carleton.
Carmichael, mac giolla míchíl.
Carmody, Ó Cearmada.
Carnahan, Ó Cearnacáin.
Carney, Ó Cearnaig 11; mac Cearnaig 13, 16, 38, 43; Ó Catarnaig 172, 192; Ó Ceitearnaig 192.
Carnohan, Ó Cearnacáin.
Carns, Ó Céirín.
Carny, v. Carney.
Carolan, Carolin, Carollan, Ó Cearballáin.
Carpenter, mac an tSaoir.
Carr, Ó Carra 68, 72 97; Ó Carraiúin 19, 97; Ó Cearáin, Ó Cioráin 19, 29, 976; mac giolla Ceara 97; mac Ceara (S.L.) 976; mac giolla Catáir 16; mac Catáoи 2; de Catair 17.
Carragher, Carraher, mac fearcair.
Carre, v. Carr.
Carrick, mac Concairrge, mac Concarraige 11; mac Concatpac 93; de Carruaig 2.
Carrigan, Ó Carragáin.
Carrigee, Carrigy, mac Concairrge, mac Concarraige.
Carrolan, Carrolin, Ó Cearballáin.
Carroll, Ó Cearbaill 11; mac Cearbaill 62, 992.
Carrolly, mac feargaile.
Carry, Ó Carraio 2; Ó Cártaig s.
Cartan, Cartayne, Carten, Ó Cartáin, mac Cartáin, mac Artáin 1; Ó Cártain (S.L.) 99.
Carter, Carthur, mac Artúir.
Carthy, Ó Cártaig 11; mac Cártaig 49, 77, &c; Ó Cártain (S.L.) 976.

Cartin, Carton, v. Cartan.
Carty, v. Carthy.
Carvan, Ó Cearbáin.
Carver, geanptóir.
Carvill, Ó Cearbaill 2; mac Cearbaill 2.
Carvin, Ó Cearbáin.
Casaday, v. Cassidy.
Casement, mac Armuint.
Casey, Ó Cataraig 11; mac Cataraig 62.
Cash, Ó Cair.
Casheen, v. Cashen.
Cashel, Cashell, de Caireal 37; Ó Caipil 69; Ó maoilcairil 7.
Cashen, Cashin, Cashion, mac Cairín 11, Ó Cairín 7.
Cashlan, Ó Cairealáin.
Cashman, Ó Cioráin.
Cashon, v. Cashen.
Casidy, v. Cassidy.
Caskey, mac Arcaió.
Casley, Ó Cairile, Ó Caraile.
Caslin, Ó Cairealáin.
Cass, Car.
Cassan, mac Caráin.
Cassedy, v. Cassidy.
Cassell, Cassells, Ó Cairil.
Casserly, mac Caraplaig.
Cassian, v. Cassin.
Cassiday, Cassidy, Ó Cairioe, Ó Caraioe 1; mac Caraplaig 972.
Cassilly, Ó Caraile, Ó Cairile.
Cassin, mac Cairín 11, Ó Cairín 7.
Cassle, Cassles, Castle, Castles, de Caireal 1; Ó Cairil 69.
Cattigan, mac Aitigín, (s.l.) Ua Caitigín.
Caughey, mac eacaió.
Caughran, Ó Cogaráin, (s.s.) mac Cogaráin, 46, 97.
Caughy, mac eacaió.
Caulfield, mac Catmaoil 6,48,92; mac Congamna 19, 55, 77, 97; mac Carrgamna 52, 72; Ó gamna 2; Ó gamnáin 97, 199.

64

Caulin, Ó Caċaláin.
Cavan, Ó Caomáin, Ó Caoimín.
Cavanagh, v. Kavanagh.
Cave, mac Óáibiú.
Cavendish, Ó Caomáin 19.
Cavey, mac Óáibiú.
Cavish, mac Ćámair.
Caviston, mac Aibirtín.
Cawley, mac Amalġaúa, mac Amalġaiú 5; mac Amlaoiú ß.
Cawlin, Ó Caċaláin, Ó Caċláin.
Chaff, Ó Lóċáin.
Chamberlain, Chambers, Seambaр, Seambaрр, Seambраċ.
Charles, Séaplur E. 2; mac Séapluir, mac Séaplaiр 1; mac Caċail 19.
Charleson, mac Séapluir, mac Séaplaiр.
Cheasty, Ó Searta, Ó Siorta.
Cheevers, Chevers, Síbeaр.
Cheyne, Chine, mac Seáin, mac Seaġáin.
Chisholm, Chissell, Sireal.
Chivers, Síbeaр.
Christian, mac Cpirtín.
Christie, mac Cpíorta.
Christopher, Cpíortóiр.
Christopherson, mac Cpíortópa.
Christy, Chrystie, Chrysty, mac Chute, Siúit.   (Cpíorta.
Clabby, Ó Clabaiġ.
Claffey, Claffy, mac Flaitim, mac Laitim, mac Laċaiġ.
Clahane, Ó Claċáin, (o.f.) ó Caċláin, Ó Caċaláin.
Clair, v. Clare.
Clanchy, Clancy, mac Flanncaúa, mac Flanncaiú.
Clandillon, Clannioiúin.
Clare, пе Cláр, Cláр.
Clarey, v. Cleary.
Clark, Clarke, Cléiреаċ E 2; ó Cléipuiġ 11; mac an Cléipuiġ, mac Cléipuiġ 32; ó Cléiрċín 64, Ó Cléiреаċáin 56, 192; mac Ġiolla apраiċ 29.

Clarkins, Ó Cléiреаċáin, Ó Cléipċín.
Clarkson, Clarson, mac Cléipuiġ.
Classon, Clausson, mac niocláiр
Clavan, Ó Clamáin.
Claveen, Clavin, Ó Claimín.
Clay, mac an Leaġa.
Clayton, пе Cléatún.
Clear, пе Cléiр.
Cleary, Ó Cléipuiġ 11; mac an Cléipuiġ, mac Cléipuiġ 67; mac Ġiolla apраiċ 29.
Cleeland, mac Ġiolla Fao' áin.
Cleere, пе Cléiр.
Cleery, v. Cleary.
Clehane, Ó Claċáin (o.f.), Ó Caċláin, Ó Caċaláin.
Cleland, Clelland, Clellond, mac Ġiolla Faoláin.
Clemens, Clement, Clements, Climéiр, Climéiреаċ 2; mac Laġmainn 2.
Clenaghan, mac Leannaċáin.
Clerihan, Ó Cléiреаċáin.
Clerkan, Ó Cléiреаċáin, Ó Cléipċín.
Clerke, v. Clarke.
Clerkin, Ó Cléipċín, Ó Cléiреаċáin.
Clery, Ó Cléipuiġ 11; mac an Cléipuiġ, mac Cléipuiġ 67.
Clifford, пе Cliorort, Cliorort E 2; Ó Clúmáin 79a, 93.
Climents, Climons, v. Clemens.
Clinane, Ó Claonáin.
Clinch, Clinre, Clinreaċ.
Clinchy, mac Loinsriġ.
Cline, mac Ġiollaċlaoin.
Clinton, пе Cliontún, Cliontún 2; Ġleantún 2.
Clisham, mac Clireаm (S.L.) 19.
Clogan, Ó Cloċaċáin.
Clogherty, Ó Cloċaptaiġ.
Cloghery, mac Cloċaiре.
Cloghessy, Ó Cloċapaiġ.
Cloherty, Ó Cloċaptaiġ.

Clohessy, Ó Cloċaraiġ.
Cloney, v. Clooney.
Cloonan, Ó Cluanáin.
Clooney, Cloony, Ó Cluanaiġ 1; mac Cluanaiġ 2.
Cloran, mac Labráin.
Close, Ó Cluaraiġ.
Closkey, mac Bloreaiḋ.
Cloughry, mac Cloċaire.
Clovan, Cloven, Ó Clúmáin.
Clowney, Clowny, v. Clooney.
Clowry, mac Labraḃa.
Cloyen, mac Giollaċłaoin.
Clucas, mac Lúcáir.
Clunan, Ó Cluanáin.
Clune, Ó Cluain 87; mac Glúin 76.
Cluney, v. Clooney.
Clusby, mac Giolla earpuiġ.
Clusker, mac Bloreaire.
Cluskey, mac Bloreaiḋ.
Cluvane, Ó Clúmáin.
Clymens, v. Clemens.
Clymonds, mac Laġmainn.
Clynch, Clinre, Clinreaċ.
Clyne, Clynes, mac Giollaċłaoin.
Coady, mac Óda.
Coakley, mac Caoċlaoiċ, mac Claoċlaoiċ 77.
Coall, v. Cole.
Coalter, Ó Coltair, Ó Coltaráin
Coan, v. Coen.
Coates, Cat.
Cochrane, Cockrane, Ó Cogaráin, mac Cogaráin 46, 97.
Codd, Coda.
Cody, mac Óda 11; Ó Cuiroiġċiġ 782.
Coe, Ó Coḃċaiġ.
Coen, Ó Comḃáin, Ó Comġáin 11; mac Eoġain 2.
Coey, Ó Coḃċaiġ.
Coffee, Coffey, Ó Coḃċaiġ 11; Ó Caṫṁuaḃaiġ 49; Ó Caṫḃaḃa 27; Ó Caṫṁoġa 97.

Cogan, Ó Cuagáin 1; mac Cogáin 43, 58; mac Eoċagáin 62; De Cogán, Gogán 77.
Cogavin, Cogeen, mac Cogaiḃín.
Coggan, Coggins, mac Cogáin.
Coghlan, Coghlen, Coghlin, Ó Coċláin 1; mac Coċláin, mag Coċláin 25.
Coghran, Ó Cogaráin, mac Cogaráin.
Cogley, Ó Coiglig.
Cogran, v. Coghran.
Cohalan, Cohalane, Ó Caṫaláin.
Cohane, Ó Caṫáin 1; Ó Ceoċáin 779.
Cohen, v. Coen.
Coholane, v. Cohalane.
Coid, mac Uaiḋ.
Coiles, v. Coyle.
Cokely, v. Coakley.
Colahan, mac Uallaċáin.
Colavin, mac Conluain.
Colbert, a Colbárd, Colbárd.
Colclogh, Colclough, Colcloċ.
Coldrick, mac Ualġairg.
Coldwell, Ó húaruirce 63; mac Conluain 93.
Cole, Cól E 2; mac Giolla Coṁġaill 16; mac Duḃġaill 2
Coleman, Ó Colmáin 11; mac Colmáin 2; Colmán E 2; Ó Clúmáin 17, 19, 49, 87, &c.
Coles, v. Cole.
Colgan, Ó Colgan 8, 9; mac Colgan 6.
Colhoon, Colhoun, Colċún 1; Ó Caċluain 6; Ó Cuileaṁain 87.
Coligan, v. Colgan.
Colin, Ó Coċláin 2; Ó Caṫaláin 2.
Colins, v. Collins.
Coll, mac Colla 2; Ó Colla 2; Col 17.
Collagan, v. Colligan.
Collatan, Ó Coolatáin, mac Coolatáin.

Collen, v. Cullen.
Collender, Cuıleanoaʀ.
Colleran, Ó Callaʀáın l, mac
Alltṁuʀáın 2.
Collery, mac ᵹıolla oʀʀaıċ.
Colleton, Ó Coolacáın. mac
Coolacáın.
Collier. Ccıléıʀ.
Colligan, Ó Colᵹan 8. 9 : mac
Colᵹan 6.
Collina, Colliney (?), mac aʀ
Laıᵹnıᵹ.
Collins, Ó Coıleáın, Ó Cuıleáın
l : mac Coılín 6.
Collopy, Ó Colʀċa, Ó Colʀa.
Colloton, v. Collatan.
Collum, Collumb, mac Coluım.
Collwell, v Coldwell.
Colman, v Coleman.
Colohan, mac Uallaċáın
Colomb, mac Coluım.
Colovin, mac Conluaın.
Colquhoun, Colquohoun, Colċún.
Colreavy, mac Cúıʀʀıaḃaıᵹ.
Colter, Ó Colcaıʀ, Ó Colcaʀáın.
Colthurst, Collcıʀ.
Colton, Colcún l; Ó Coṁalcáın 2.
Colum, Columb, mac Coluım
Colvan, mac Conluaın
Colville, v. Coldwell.
Colvin, v. Colvan.
Colwell, v. Coldwell.
Coman, Ó Comáın.
Comaskey, mac Cumaʀcaıᵹ.
Comba, v. Conba.
Comber, oe Cómaʀ,Cómaʀ 99 ; Ó
Cıaʀáın 976; Ó Cıaʀaᵹáın 19,94
Combes, mac Cómaıʀ.
Comer, v. Comber.
Comerford, Comaʀcún l ; mac
Cumaʀcaıᵹ 53.
Comerton, Comaʀcún.
Comesky, v. Comaskey.
Comey, mac ᵹıolla Cóımḃeaó.
Comford, Comfort, v. Comerford
Comish, mac Cómaıʀ.
Comiskey, mac Cumaʀcaıᵹ.

Commane, Ó Comáın.
Commaskey, v. Comıskey.
Commerford, Commerfort, v.
Comerford.
Commins, Ó Comáın 11 ; mac
Coımín 62.
Common, Commons, Ó Comáın.
Comyn, Comyns, Coımín,
Cuımín 46, 57, 77, 78 ; mac
Coımín, mac Cuımín 6, 42 :
Ó Coımín, Ó Cuımín 29, 72.
Conaboy, v. Conboy.
Conacher mac Conċoḃaıʀ.
Conaghan, Ó Connaċáın.
Conaghty, Ó Connaċcaıᵹ.
Conallan, Ó Conalláın. V.
Conlon.
Conally, v. Connelly.
Conalty, Ó Conallca.
Conan, Ó Conáın l ; Ó Cuanáın 29.
Conarchy, Ó Conaʀċce.
Conary, Ó Conaıʀe.
Conaty, Ó Connaċcaıᵹ.
Conba, Conbay, Ó Conbáᵹa, Ó
Conbáıó,
Conboy, Ó Conbuıóe 9 ; Ó
Conbáᵹa, Ó Conbáıó 99.
Concannen, Concannon, Ó Con-
ċeannaınn, Ó Conċeanaınn.
Conderick, v. Condrick.
Condon, Connoún, Conoún l ;
Ó Conoubáın 23, 33.
Condrick, mac Annʀaıc, mac
eanʀaıc, mac eannʀaıc.
Condrin, Condron, Ó Conaʀáın.
Coneely, Ó Conᵹaıle 11 : mac
Conᵹaıle 92.
Conefry, mac Conʀʀaoıċ.
Conelly, v. Connelly.
Coner, v. Connor.
Coney, v. Cooney.
Conheeny, mac Conaonaıᵹ.
Conify, mac Óonnċaıó.
Conlan, Conland, v. Conlon.
Conley, mac Connla, mac
Connlaoóa. V. Connelly.
Conliffe, Ó Conouıó.

Conlogue, ṁac Conaill Óiʒ.
Conlon, Ó Conallán 11; Ó
  Caoinḋealḃáin 43; Ó
  Claonáin 19.
Conly, v. Conley.
Conmee, Conmey, Conmy, ṁac
  Conṁeaḋa 5; ṁac Conṁiḋe
  6.
Connaghton, Ó Connaċtáin.
Connaghty, Ó Connaċtaiʒ.
Connally, Connaly, Ó Conʒalaiʒ
Connaughton, Ó Connaċtáin.
Conneally, Connealy, Conneely,
  Ó Conʒaile 11; ṁac Con-
  ʒaile 92; ṁac Conʒaola 972.
Conneff, Conneffe, ṁac Conḋuiḃ
Connell, Ó Conaill.
Connellan, Ó Conallán 11;
  Ó Caoinḋealḃáin 43.
Connelly, Connely, Ó Conʒalaiʒ
  12; Ó Conʒaile 91; ṁac
  Conʒaile 197; Ó Coinʒeall-
  aiʒ, ṁac Coinʒeallaiʒ 77, 78.
Conner, v. Connor.
Connerney, ṁac an Oiṗċinniʒ,
  ṁac an Aiṗċinniʒ.
Connerton, Ó Connaċtáin.
Connery, Ó Conaire.
Conney, Ó Coinne 6; ṁac
  Connaiḋ 2.
Connick, ṁac Conṁaic.
Conniff, Conniffe, ṁac Conḋuiḃ
  9; Ó Conḋuiḃ 46.
Connigan, Ó Connaʒáin.
Connington, Ó Connaċtáin.
Connison, ṁac Coinniʒ.
Connole, Ó Coineóil.
Connollan, v. Connellan.
Connolly, Connoly, Ó Conʒalaiʒ
  12; Ó Conʒaile 91; ṁac
  Conʒaile 197; Ó Coinʒeallaiʒ,
  ṁac Coinʒeallaiʒ 77, 78.
Connor, Connors, Ó Conċoḃair
  11; ṁac Conċoḃair 66.
Connorton, Ó Connaċtáin.
Connoway, v. Conway.
Conole, Ó Coineóil.

Conolly, Conoly, v. Connolly.
Conoo, Ó Connṁaiʒ.
Conor, Conors, v. Connor.
Conotty, Ó Connaċtaiʒ.
Conrahy, Ó Conṗaċa, ṁac
  Conṗaċa.
Conran, Ó Conaráin.
Conree, ṁac Conṗaoi.
Conrick, ṁac Annṗaici
Conron, Ó Conaráin.
Conroy, ṁac Conṗaoi 73, 97;
  Ó Conṗaoi 62, 92; Ó Conaiṗe
  99; Ó Conṗaċa, ṁac Conṗaċa
  25, 45; Ó Maolċonaiṗe 92,
  462.
Conry, ṁac Conṗaoi 97; Ó Con-
  ṗaċ, Ó Conṗa 92; Ó Conaiṗe 7;
  Ó Maolċonaiṗe 29, 34, 46.
Considine, ṁac Conṗaiḋín.
Convery, ṁac Ainṁiṗe.
Convey, v. Conway.
Conway, Ó Connṁaiʒ 7, 8, 34,
  67; ṁac Connṁaiʒ 252, 462;
  Ó Conḃuiḋe 92; Ó Conṁeaḋa
  2; ṁac Conṁeaḋa 2; Ó
  Connṁaċáin 91; ṁac Nuaḋaḋ,
  ṁac Nuaḋat 252.
Conwell, ṁac Conṁaoil.
Conwy, v. Conway.
Conyeen, Ó Coinín 5; ṁac
  Coinín 2.
Conyngham, v. Cunningham.
Cooey, Ó Coḃtaiʒ.
Coogan, Ó Cuaʒáin 1; ṁac
  eoċaʒáin 62.
Cooke, Cúc 1; ṁac Ḋaḃóc,
  ṁac Ḋaḃóg, (s.l.) ṁac Cuaʒ,
  ṁac ʒuaʒ, ʒuaʒ 97.
Cooken, v. Coogan.
Coolahan, Ó Cúlaċáin 17, 19,
  27; ṁac Uallaċáin 97.
Coole, ṁac Ḋuḃʒaill.
Cooley, Ó Cúile 77; ṁac
  ʒiolla Cúile 46, 97.
Coolican, Coolihan, Ó Cúlaċáin
  11; Ó Cioḃlaċáin 92.
Coomey, Ó Camċa.

Coonaghan, Coonahan, Ó Cuanacáin.
Coonan, Ó Cuanáin.
Coonerty, Ó Cuanartaiġ.
Cooney, Ó Cuanać, Ó Cuana 11; Ó Cuanacáin 72.
Coonihan, Ó Cuanacáin.
Cooper, Cúipéir.
Coote, Cúc.
Copinger, Coipinġéir.
Copley, Cóiplióe.
Coppinger, Coipinġéir.
Corbally, ve Coirbaile.
Corban, Corbane, Ó Coirbáin.
Corbett, Coirbaiv 25, 43, 99; Ó Coirbáin 1, Ó Coirbín 2; Ó Conbáġa, Ó Conbáiv, 179.
Corbin, Ó Coirbín.
Corbitt, v. Corbett.
Corboy, Corby, Ó Coirbuiv́e 77; mac Coirbuiv́e 27, 45.
Corcoran, Corcorin, Ó Coircráin 7, 91; mac Coircráin 25; Ó Coircáin 19, 52, 97.
Cordan, Ó Coirraváin.
Corduff, Coirrvub.
Corey, Ó Cómraive.
Coribeen, Ó Coirbín.
Corish, mac Feórair, mac Feóruiᵹ.
Corken, Ó Coircáin 1; mac Coircáin 48.
Corkeran v. Corcoran.
Corkerry, Corkery, Ó Coircra.
Corkhill, mac Corcaill.
Corkin, Ó · Coircáin 1; mac Coircáin 48.
Corkoran, Corkran, v. Corcoran.
Corless, mac Carluir 11; mac Cacail 197.
Corley, mac Coirvealbaiᵹ.
Cormac, Cormack, Ó Coirmaic 1; Ó Coirmacáin 2; mac Coirmaic 2.
Cormican, Ó Coirmacáin.
Cormick, v. Cormack.
Cormocan, v. Cormican.

Corneen, Ó Cuirnín.
Corr, Corra, Ó Coirrra 1; mac Coirra 2.
Corran, Ó Coirráin.
Corree v. Corry.
Corridon, Ó Coirraváin.
Corrie, v. Corry.
Corrigan, Ó Coirraᵹáin.
Corry, Ó Coirra, Ó Coirraiv́ 1; mac Coirra, mac Coirraiv́ 2; Ó Cómraiv́e 15, 46, 77; mac Ᵹoċraiv́ 23, 67.
Coscor, Ó Coircair 4; mac Oircair 3; mac Ᵹiolla ċorcair 32.
Cosgrave, Cosgreave, Cosgreve, Cosgriff, Cosgrive, Cosgrove, Cosgry, Ó Coircraiᵹ 11; mac Coircraiᵹ 35; Ó Coircracáin 62; mac Coircracáin 38; mac Oircair 62; mac Ᵹiolla ċorcair 32; mac Ᵹiolla ċoircle 32; mac Bloircaire 132.
Cosker, v. Coscor.
Coskeran, Coskerin, Ó Coircracáin 1; mac Coircracáin 38.
Coskerry, Coskery, Ó Coircraiᵹ.
Costello, Costelloe, mac Coirtealb, mac Coirtealbaiᵹ, (o.f.) mac Oirvealb 11; mac Ᵹiolla ċoircle 62, (s.l.) ma'l ċuirleać 37.
Costen, mac Oirtín, (s.l.) Ó Coirtín.
Costigan, mac Oirticín, mac Oirtiᵹín, (s.l.) mac Cortaᵹáin, Ó Cortaᵹáin.
Costillo, Costily, v. Costelloe.
Costin, Costine, mac Oirtín, (s.l.) Ó Coirtín.
Costolloe, Costoloe, Costley, v. Costelloe.
Costum, Costune, Cortún.
Cotter, Cottier, Cottiers, mac Oitir, (s.l.) mac Coitir.
Cottle, Ó Coitil.
Cotton, vo Cotún.

Coughlan, Coughlen, Coughlin, Ó Coċláin 1; Mac Coċláin, Mag Coċláin 25.

Coulahan, Coulihan, Ó Cúlaċáin 17, 19, 27; Mac Uallaċáin 97.

Coulter, Ó Colċair, Ó Colċapáin.

Coulton, v. Colton.

Coumey, v. Coomey.

Counihan, Ó Cuanaċáin.

County, v. Canty.

Courcey, ᴅe Cúrra, Cúrraċ.

Courigan, Ó Corragáin.

Courn, Ó Corráin.

Cournane, Ó Cúrnáin, Ó Curnáin.

Courneen, Ó Cúirnín, Ó Cuirnín.

Coursey, ᴅe Cúrra, Cúrraċ.

Courtayne, Mac Cuirċáin.

Courtney, Ó Cúrnáin, Ó Curnáin 17, 25, 46, 49; Ó Cúirnín, Ó Cuirnín, 93, 462; Mac Cuarca, Mac Cuairc 37, 99.

Cousin, Cousine, Cousins, Cúirín.

Covaddy, Mac an Mavaiᴅ.

Coveney, Ó Coibᴅeanaiġ 24, 45; Mac Coibᴅeanaiġ 2.

Cowan, Cowen, Ó Comᴅain, Ó Comġain 11; Mac Giolla Comᴅain, Mac Giolla Comġain 62; Mac Eoġain 2.

Cowey, Cowhey, Cowhig, Cowie, Ó Cobċaiġ.

Cowin, v. Cowen.

Cowley, Mac Amalġaiᴅ, Mac Amalġaᴅa 5, 9; Mac Amlaoib 2; E 2.

Cowman, Ó Comáin.

Cowmey, Ó Camċa.

Cowper, Cúipéir.

Cowran, Ó Cubráin.

Cox, Coxe, Cocr, Cocraċ 34; Mac an Coiliġ, Mac Coiliġ, Mac Coiliᴅ 34; Ó Coiliġ 16, 92; Mac Coiligin 77; Mac Conċoille, Mac Conċoilleaᴅ 17, 63, 79a, 84.

Coy, v. MacCoy.

Coyd, Mac Uaiᴅ.

Coyle, Mac ᵭubġaill.

Coyne, Ó Caᴅáin 91; Ó Cuinn (Ó Cuínn) 81; Ó Cuain 93; Ó Comᴅain, Ó Comġain 92; Mac Giollaċaoin 39, 82; Mac Eoġain 92.

Craan, Ó Corráin.

Craddock, Creavóc. Creavóg.

Craford, v. Crawford.

Crage, v. Craig.

Crahan, Ó Carráin, Ó Corráin.

Craig, ᴅe Carraig, ᴅe Craig, ᴅe Creag, Creag, Creog.

Craigan, v. Cregan.

Crain, Ó Carráin, Ó Corráin.

Crampsey, Crampsie, Crampsy, Cramsie, Ó Cráimhriġe, (o.f.) Ó Cnáimhriġe.

Crane, Ó Carráin, Ó Corráin.

Cranley, Ó Crónġaile.

Crangle, Ó Crónġail.

Cranny, Crany, (?) Mac ᵭranaiġ

Crauford, v. Crawford.

Craughwell, Ó Creaċṁaoil (S.L.)

Cravane, Ó Crábáin.

Craven, Cravin, Ó Crábáin, Ó Cráibín 1; Mac Crábáin 64.

Crawford, ᴅe Cráforc, Cráforc 1; Mac Crábaġáin 64.

Crawley, Mac Ráġallaiġ. V. Crowley.

Crayford, v. Crawford.

Creagh, Craobaċ.

Creaghan, Ó Créaċáin 1; Ó Carráin 2.

Crean, Creane, Ó Croiᴅeáin 16, 19, 29; Ó Créaċáin 72, 97; Ó Carráin, Ó Corráin, Ó Corraᴅín, Ó Cuirín 77, 87.

Creaton, Ó Créaċáin, Ó Críoċáin.

Creaven, Creavin, Ó Cʀábáin,
Ó Cʀáibín 1 ; Ó Cʀaobáin 29 !
mac Cʀábáin 64.
Creed, Creedon, Ó Cʀíováin,
(o.f.) mac Cʀíováin.
Creegan, v. Cregan.
Creehan, v. Crehan.
Creely, mac Raʒailliʒ.
Creen, v. Crean.
Creevey, Creevy, Ó Cʀaoioc.
Crⷧgan, Ó Cʀiaʒáin, (o.f.) mac
Riaʒáin.
Cregg, ve Cʀaiʒ, Cʀeaʒ, Cʀeoʒ.
Creghan, Crehan, Ó Cʀéacáin,
Ó Cʀiocáin, Ó Cʀíocáin 1 ;,
Ó Caʀʀáin, Ó Coʀʀáin 2.
Creigan, v. Cregan.
Creighan, Creighton, Ó Cʀéac-
áin, Ó Cʀíocáin.
Creilly, Crelly, mac Raʒailliʒ.
Cremeen, Cremen, Cremin, Ó
Cʀoimín, Ó Cʀuimín.
Crenegan, Ó Cʀionaʒáin.
Crennan, Ó Cʀíonáin, mac
Cʀíonáin.
Cribbin, Cribbins, Cribbon, Ó
Cʀoibín.
Crickard, mac Riocaiʀv.
Cricket, mac Ricéiv.
Crigley, mac Raiʒilliʒ.
Crilly, mac Raʒailliʒ.
Crimmeen, Crimmins, Ó Cʀuimín.
Crinigan, Ó Cʀionaʒáin.
Crinion, Crinneen, Ó Cʀíonáin,
mac Cʀíonáin.
Cristy, mac Cʀíoʀta.
Croake, Cʀóc.
Croan, v. Crohan.
Crofton, ve Cʀoctún.
Crofts, ve Cʀoctaʀ.
Croghan, Crohan, mac Con-
cʀuacán.
Croke, Cʀóc.
Crolly, Croly, mac Roʒallaiʒ ;
(s.l.), Ó Cʀovlaoic, Ó Cʀuav-
laoic.

Crombie, Cromie, Crommie.
Cʀomca.
Cromwell, Cʀomail.
Cronan, Ó Cʀónáin, Ó Cʀóinín
Crone, Cʀón 2; Ó Cʀóin 2.
Cronekan, Ó Cʀónaʒáin.
Cronelly, Ó Cʀónʒaile 1; mac
Cʀónʒaile 2.
Croniken, Ó Cʀónaʒáin.
Cronin, Ó Cʀóinín.
Cronley, v. Cronelly.
Cronyn, v. Cronin.
Crook, Crooke, Crookes, Crooks,
Cʀóc, Cʀúc.
Crosbie, E 1 ; mac an Cʀoʀáin 2.
Cross, ve Cʀúiʀ, Cʀúiʀ 2 ; mac
an Cʀoʀáin 2.
Crossan, Crossen, Crossin,
Crosson, mac an Cʀoʀáin.
Crotty, Ó Cʀotaiʒ.
Crough, v. Crowe.
Croughan, mac Concʀuacán.
Crowe, mac Concʀava.
Crowley, Ó Cʀuavlaoic 9 ; mac
Roʒallaiʒ, (s.l.) Ó Cʀo-
ʒallaiʒ, Ó Cʀovlaoic, Ó
Cʀuavlaoic 7.
Crozier, Cʀúiʀéiʀ.
Crudden, mac Rováin.
Cruice, Cruise, ve Cʀúiʀ,
Cʀúiʀ.
Crumley, *Ó Cʀomlaoic.
Crumlish, (?) Ó Cʀompuiʀc.
Crummell, Cʀomail.
Crummy, Ó Cʀomca.
Cryan, Ó Cʀaioeáin.
Cudahy, Cuddehy, Cuddihy,
Cuddy, Cudihy, Ó Cuiviʒciʒ.
Cudden, v. Cadden.
Cuffe, mac Ꝺuio 1 ; Ó Cooⷷcaiʒ
469 ; Ꝙ Ꝺoiʀnín, Ó Ꝺuiʀnín
19, 62.
Cuhy, mac Eocaiv.
Cuinane, Ó Cuineáin.
Culgan, Culgin, Ó Colʒan.
Culhane, Ó Cacláin, Ó Cacaláin,
(s.l.) Ó Caltáin.

Culhoun, Colċún 1; Ó Caṫluain, 6; Ó Cuileaṁain 87.
Culkeen, Culkin, mac uilcín.
Cull, v. Coll.
Cullan, Ó Cuileáin.
Cullanan, Ó Cuileannáin.
Cullane, Ó Cuileáin.
Cullen, Ó Cuilinn 81; mac Cuilinn 64; Ó Cuileáin, Ó Cuilín 777; mae Coilín, 16, 39, 68; Ó Caṫluain 62· Ó Cuileaṁain 87.
Culleton, Ó Coolaċáin 11, mac Coolaċáin 87.
Cullian, v. Cullen.
Culligan, Ó Colgan 4; mac Colgan 6.
Cullin, v. Cullen.
Cullinan, Cullinane, Ó Cuileannáin.
Culliney, (?) mac an Laiġniġ.
Cullington, Ó Coolaċáin, mac Coolaċáin.
Cullins, v. Cullen.
Culliton, v. Culleton.
Cullity, Ó Coolaṫa, (s l.) Ó Collaṫa.
Cullivan, mac Conluain.
Culloo, mac Conulaḃ.
Culloon v. Culhoun.
Culloty v. Cullity.
Cully, Ó Colla.
Culnane, v. Cullinane.
Culreavy, mac Cúilriaḃaiġ.
Cumaskey, mac Cumarcaiġ.
Cumbaw, v. Conba.
Cumberford, v. Comerford.
Cumesky, mac Cumarcaiġ.
Cumin, Cuming, Cumings, Cumins, v. Cummings.
Cumisk, Cumiskey, Cumisky, mac Cumarcaiġ.
Cummane, Ó Comáin.
Cummens, v. Cummins.
Cummerford, v. Comerford.

Cummin, Cumming, Cummings, Cummins, Ó Comáin 71, 81, 91, Ó Cuimín 72, 82, 92'; mac Cuimín 6, 72; Cuimín 46, 57' 77, 78.
Cummiskey, v. Cumiskey.
Cunagum, v. Cunningham.
Cundlish, Ó Cuinnoliṙ.
Cuneen, v. Cunneen.
Cunhane, Ó Conáin 976.
Cunif, Cuniff, v. Cunniffe.
Cunihan, v. Cunnahan.
Cunion, v. Cunneen.
Cunlish, Ó Cuinnoliṙ.
Cunlisk, Ó Coinliṙc, Ó Coinleiṙc.
Cunnahan, Ó Cuinneaċáin.
Cunnane, Ó Cuineáin 11, Ó Conáin 92.
Cunnea, Ó Coinne.
Cunnean, v. Cunneen.
Cunneely, v. Conneely.
Cunneen, Ó Coinín 5; mac Coinín 9.
Cunneeny, mac Conaonaiġ.
Cunniam, Cunnien, v. Cunneen.
Cunniffe, mac Conouiḃ 9; Ó Conouiḃ 46, 92.
Cunning, Ó Conaing.
Cunningan, Ó Cuinneagáin, mac Cuinneagáin.
Cunningham, Ó Cuinneagáin 11, Ó Connagáin 2, mac Cuinneagáin 2. Ó Cuinneaċáin 2, Ó Connaċáin 2.
Cunnion, v. Cunneen.
Cunnoo, Ó Connṁaiġ.
Cunny, Ó Coinne.
Cunree, mac Conriaoi.
Cunreen, mac Conriain.
Cunvane, Ó Conḃáin.
Cuolahan, Cuolohan, v. Coulahan.
Curby, v. Corby.
Curland, Ó Coiṙealláin.
Curley, mac Toiṙroealḃaiġ.
Curnane, Ó Cuṙnáin, Ó Cúṙnáin.

Curneen, Curneene, Curnin, Ó
Cuirnín, Ó Cúirnín.
Curoe, (?) mac ʒocṗaḋa.
Curran, Currain, Currane, Ó
Corráin, Ó Curráin 11,
Ó Corraiḋín (Ó Coiṙín,
Ó Cuirín), 19, 77, 87, 97.
Curreen, Curren, Ó Corraiḋín
(Ó Cuirín) 1 ; mac Corraiḋín
(mac Corraoin) 29, 39.
Currid, Ó Corċaiḋ (S.L.).
Currie, v. Curry.
Currigan, Ó Corraʒáin.
Currin, Ó Corraiḋín 1 ; mac
Corraiḋín 29, 39. V. Curreen.
Curry, Ó Corra, Ó Corraiḋ 1 ;
mac Corra, mac Corraiḋ 2 ;
Ó Coṁraiḋe 15, 46, 77 ; mac
ʒocṗaiḋ 23, 67 ; mac
ṁuireaḋaiʒ 62.
Curtain, Curtan, Curtayne, mac
Cuirtáin 1, mac Cairteáin 2.
Curteis, v. Curtis.
Curten, v. Curtin.
Curties, v. Curtis.
Curtin, mac Cuirtín, (o.f.) mac
Cruitín 46, 178 ; mac Cuirtáin
79a, mac Cairteáin 772, Ó
Cuirtáin 49, 179.
Curtis, ḋe Cuirtéir, Cuirtéir
1 ; mac Cruitín 64.
Cusack, ḋe Cíoṁróʒ, ḋe
Ciúṁróʒ, Cíoṁróʒ, Ciúṁróʒ,
Cíoróʒ 1 ; mac Íoróʒ, mac
Íoróʒ 16, 46, 94, mac Íreóʒ
972, (s.l.) Círeóʒ 976.
Cushanan, Ó Cornaċáin.
Cushen, Cushing, Cushion, Cúiṙn.
Cushlane, Ó Cairealáin.
Cushley, mac ʒiolla ċoircle.
Cushnahan, Ó Cornaċáin.
Cusick, v. Cusack.
Cuskelly, v Cuskley.
Cusker, Ó Corcair 4 ; mac
Orcair 3 ; mac ʒiolla
ċorcair 32.
Cuskern, Ó Corcraċáin 1 ; mac
Corcraċáin 38.

Cuskery, Ó Corcraiʒ.
Cuskley, mac ʒiolla ċoircle.
Cuskor, v. Cusker.
Cusnahan, Ó Cornaċáin.
Cussack, v. Cusack.
Cussane, Ó Coráin (o.f.) Ó Car-
áin, (s.s.), mac Ṗáiḋín 197,
976
Cussen, Cúirín.
Cussick, v. Cusack.
Cuthbert, Cuthbertson, mac
Cúicḃreic.

Dade, mac ḋaiḃéiḋ.
Daffy, Ó ḋeaḃċaiʒ.
Dahill, Ó ḋaċail, Ó ḋaiċʒil.
Dahony, Ó ḋuḃċonna.
Daid, mac ḋaiḃéiḋ.
Daily, v. Daly.
Dallaghan, Ó ḋalaċáin.
Dallagher, Ó ḋalaċair.
Dallon, Ó ḋalláin.
Dalton, D'Alton, ḋalatún 11,
ḋaltún 72; ḋátún 24.
Daly, Ó ḋálaiʒ.
Danagher, Danaher, Ó ḋuine-
aċair.
Danahy, Ó ḋuineaċḋa.
Dane, v, Dean.
Danger, ḋáinréir.
Daniel, Daniels, Ó ḋoṁnaill
7 ; mac ḋoṁnaill 2.
Daniher, Ó ḋuineaċair.
Danihy, Ó ḋuineaċḋa.
Dannaher, Ó ḋuineaċair.
Dannahy, Ó ḋuineaċḋa.
Daragh, v. Darragh.
Darby, Ó ḋiarmaḋa, 2 ; mac
ḋiarmaḋa 2.
Darcy, D'Arcy, ḋairriʒ,
ḋairriʒeaċ 15, 83, 97 ; Ó
ḋorċaiḋe 1, 84, 97.
Dardis, ḋairoir.
Dargan, Ó ḋearʒáin.
Darkey, Ó ḋorċaiḋe.
Darmody, Ó ḋiarmaḋa 4, (s.l.)
Ó ḋearmaḋa 979 ; mac
ḋiarmaḋa 2.

Darney, Ó ᴅoiṗinne.
Darra, Darragh, Darrah, mac ᴅaṗa, mac ᴅaṗaċ, (o.f.) mac ᴅuḃᴅaṗaċ 2; Ó ᴅaṗa, Ó ᴅaṗaċ, (o.f.) Ó ᴅuḃᴅaṗaċ 62.
Darrick, Ó ᴅuḃṗaic.
Darrock, v. Darragh.
Daton, ᴅáᴄún.
Daugherty, v. Dogherty.
Daughton, v. Daton.
Davane, Ó ᴅaṁáin.
Davenny, Ó ᴅuiḃeannaiġ.
Davenport, Ó ᴅonnᴅuḃaṗᴄaiġ 46.
Davern, Ó ᴅáḃoiṗeann, (o.f.) Ó ᴅuḃᴅáḃoiṗeann 1; Ó ᴅoḃaṗáin 197.
Daveson, Davey, Davidson, Davies, mac ᴅáiḃiᴅ.
Davin, Davine, Ó ᴅaiṁín.
Davis, ᴅáiḃiṗ 1; mac ᴅáiḃiᴅ 6; mac ᴅáiḃiᴅ móṗ 28; Ó ᴅaiṁín 972.
Davison, Davisson, mac ᴅáiḃiᴅ.
Davitt, Davits, mac ᴅáiḃiᴅ 10, mac ᴅaiḃéiᴅ 19.
Davoran, Davoren, Ó ᴅáḃoiṗeann 1; Ó ᴅoḃaṗáin 197.
Davy, Davys, mac ᴅáiḃiᴅ 1; Ó ᴅaiṁín 972.
Daw, Ó ᴅeaġaiᴅ, Ó ᴅeaᴅaiᴅ.
Dawley, Dawly, Ó ᴅálaiġ.
Dawney, v. Dahony and Downey.
Dawson, mac ᴅáiḃiᴅ, ᴅáṗon ᴅáṗan.
Dawtin, ᴅáᴄún.
Day, Ó ᴅeaġaiᴅ, Ó ᴅeaᴅaiᴅ.
Dayly, v. Daly.
D'Aylmer, v. Aylmer.
Dea, Ó ᴅeaġaiᴅ, Ó ᴅeaᴅaiᴅ 1, (s.l.) Ó ᴅiaġaiᴅ, Ó ᴅiġe 74, 79, 99.
Deacon, Ó ᴅeocáin.

Deady, Ó ᴅéaᴅaiġ 1, Ó ᴅaoᴅa 17, 49.
Deakin, Ó ᴅuiḃcinn.
Dealy, Ó ᴅuiḃġiolla.
Dean, Deane, Ó ᴅéaġáin 42, 16; mac an ᴅeaġánaiġ 31, mac an ᴅeaġáin 16, 19, 28; Ó ᴅuiḃne 49.
Deanie, Ó ᴅuiḃne.
Dearan, Ó ᴅeaṗáin.
Dease, ᴅéiṗe.
Deasey, Deasy, ᴅéiṗeaċ 1; mac an ᴅéiṗiġ 29.
De Burgh, ᴅe búṗc, ᴅe búṗca.
De Courcey, De Courcy, ᴅe cúṗṗa, cúṗṗaċ, cúiṗṗeaċ.
Dee, v. Dea.
Deegan, Deegin, Ó ᴅuiḃġinn, Ó ᴅuiḃcinn.
Deehan, Ó ᴅíoċon.
Deely, Ó ᴅuiḃġiolla.
Deen, v. Dean.
Deeney, Ó ᴅuiḃne.
Deenihan, Ó ᴅuinneaċáin.
Deeny, Ó ᴅuiḃne.
Deere, Ó ᴅuiḃᴅíṗ.
Deering, ᴅíṗinġ.
De Ermott, v. Dermott.
Deery, Ó ᴅaiġṗe, Ó ᴅoiġṗe.
Deevey, Deevy, Ó ᴅuiḃᴅḃe, Ó ᴅuḃuiᴅe.
Deffely, Ó ᴅuiḃġiolla.
Degidan, Ó ᴅuiḃġeaᴅáin.
Dehan, Ó ᴅíoċon.
Deharty, Ó ᴅoiċeaṗᴄaiġ.
Deheny, Ó ᴅuḃċonna.
Deherty, Dehorty, Ó ᴅoiċeaṗᴄaiġ.
Deighan, Ó ᴅíoċon 2; Ó ᴅuiḃġinn 2.
Deignan, Ó ᴅuiḃġeannáin.
Delacour, Ó ᴅuḃluaċṗa.
De Lacy, ᴅe léiṗ, léiṗeaċ. V. Lacy.
Delahan, Ó ᴅuiḃleaċáin.
Delahide, Delahoyde, ᴅalaiᴄíᴅ 8; Ó scinġín 6.

Delahunt, Delahunty, Ó 'Oulċaoinṫiᵹ, Ó 'Oulċonᴄa.
Delamar, Delamere, 'Oaⱡamaᶈa.
Delane, Ó 'Oallain.
Delaney, Delany, Ó 'Ouḃᶄláine, Ó 'Ouḃᶄláinᵹe 1 ; Ó 'Oallain 91 ; Ó 'Ouḃláin 976.
Delap, De Lapp, Ó Ⱡaᶈáin.
Delargey, De Largey, Delargy, Ó 'Ouiḃleaᶈᵹa.
Delaroe, Ó 'Oaⱡaᶈuaiꝺ (S.L.).
Delay, Delea, Ó 'Ouinnᶄléiḃe.
Deleacy, v. De Lacy.
Deleany, v. Delaney.
Delee, v. Delea.
Delemar, 'Oaⱡamaᶈa.
Deleney, v. Delaney.
Delhunty, Dellunty, Ó 'Oulċaoinṫiᵹ, Ó 'Oulċonᴄa.
Delmar, 'Oaⱡamaᶈa.
Delohery, Delooghery, Deloorey, Deloughery, Delouhery, Delury, Ó 'Ouiḃluaċᶈa, Ó 'Ouḃluaċᶈa.
De Moleyns, Ó maoláin.
Dempsey, Ó 'Oíomaᶈaiᵹ.
Denahy, v. Dennehy.
Denanny, Ó 'Ooineannaiᵹ.
Denegan, Ó 'Ouinneaᵹáin.
Denehan, Ó 'Ouinneaċáin.
Deneher, Ó 'Ouineaċaiᶈ.
Denehy, v. Dennehy.
Deney, v. Deeney and Dennehy.
Denigan, Ó 'Ouinneaᵹáin.
Denis, Denison, Ó 'Oonnᵹuᶈa 2 ; mac 'Oonnċaiꝺ 2.
Denn, 'Oenn.
Dennahy, v. Dennehy.
Dennan, Dennany, Ó 'Ooineannaiᵹ.
Dennehy, Ó 'Ouineaċóa.
Denning, Ó 'Ouinnín.
Dennis, Dennison, Ó 'Oonnᵹuᶈa 2 ; mac 'Oonnċaiꝺ 2.
Dennivan, Ó 'Ouinneaḃáin.
Denny, Ó 'Ouiḃne 11 ; Ó 'Ouineaċóa 77.

Denroche, Ó 'Ouiḃinnᶈeaċᴄaiᵹ.
Denson, v. Dennison.
Dergan, Ó 'Ooᶈᵹáin.
Derham, v. Durham.
Derivan, Derivin, Ó 'Ooᶈḃáin.
Dermid, v. Dermott.
Dermody, Ó 'Oiaᶈmaꝺa 4 ; mac 'Oiaᶈmaꝺa 2.
Dermond, v. Dermott.
Dermoody, v. Dermody.
Dermott, D'Ermott, Ó 'Oiaᶈmaꝺa 1 ; mac 'Oiaᶈmaꝺa 2 ; Ó 'Ouiḃꝺíoᶈmaiᵹ 32, (s.l.) Ó 'Oíoᶈma 16.
Dermoty, v. Dermody.
Deroe, Derow, Ó 'Oaiᶈḃᶈe.
Derrane, O 'Oeaᶈáin.
Derrick, Derrig, Ó 'Oeiᶈiᵹ.
Derry, Ó 'Ooiᶈeiꝺ, Ó 'Ooiᶈiꝺ 62 ; Ó 'Oaiᵹᶈe, Ó 'Ooiᵹᶈe 62.
Derwin, Ó 'Ooiᶈḃín.
Desmond, Ó 'Oeaᶈṁuṁnaiᵹ.
de Valera, 'oe Ḃailéaᶈa.
Devane, Ó 'Ouḃáin 7, 9 ; Ó 'Oaṁáin 6.
Devaney, Devanny, Devany, Ó 'Ouiḃeannaiᵹ 16, 68 ; Ó 'Ouiḃeaṁna 65 ; Ó 'Ouḃánaiᵹ 16, 29 ; Ó 'Ouḃáin 19, 97, Ó 'Ouiḃín 192, 972.
Deveen, Ó 'Ouiḃín.
Develin, D'Evelyn, v. Devlin.
Deven, Ó 'Oaiṁín, Ó 'Ooiṁín.
Devenish, 'Oeiḃniᶈ.
Devenny, Deveny, v. Devanny.
Dever, Ó 'Ouiḃíoᶈ.
De Vere, 'oe Ḃéiᶈ.
Devereux, 'Oéaḃᶈúᶈ 2, 28 ; Ó 'Ouiḃᶈic 276 ; Ó 'Oeiᶈḃᶈeó 25.
Devers, Ó 'Ouiḃíꝺiᶈ.
Devery, v. Devereux.
Devett, mac 'Oaiḃéiꝺ.
Devilly, Devily, Ó 'Ouiḃᵹioⱡⱡa.
Devin, Devine, Ó 'Oaiṁín, Ó 'Ooiṁín 6, 37 ; Ó 'Ouiḃín 71, 91, Ó 'Ouḃáin 72, 92.
Devinney, v. Devanny.

Devins, Ó 'ʋaιṁín, Ó 'Ooιṁín.
Devitt, mac 'Oaιḃéιᵈ.
Devlin, Ó 'Ooḃaιleιn, Ó 'Ooιḃιleιn, Ó 'Ooιḃιlín.
Devon, Ó 'Oaιṁín 6 ; Ó 'Ouιḃín 9.
Devoy, Ó 'Oúḃuιᵈc.
Dewane, Ó 'Ouḃáιn.
DeYermond, Deyermott, Ó 'Ouιḃ-víoɼmaιᵹ, Ó 'Ouιḃóίoɼma.
Diaman, Diamon, Diamond, Ó 'Oιamáιn, Ó 'Oíomáιn, Ó 'Oéamáιn 6 ; Ó maoιleaċáιn 97.
Diarmid, Diarmod, Diarmond, v. Dermott.
Dickson, mac Rιocaιɼᵈ.
Diermott, v. Dermott.
Diffely, Diffily, Ó 'Ouιḃᵹιolla.
Diffin, Ó 'Ouιḃɼιnn.
Diffley, Ó 'Ouιḃᵹιolla.
Digan, Ó 'Ouιḃᵹιnn.
Digany, mac an 'Oeaᵹánaιᵹ.
Diggin, Ó 'Ouιḃᵹιnn.
Dignam, Dignan, Ó 'Ouιḃ-ᵹeannáιn.
Dillahan, Ó 'Ouιḃleaċáιn.
Dillane, Ó 'Ouιlleáιn.
Dilleen, Ó 'Ouιllín.
Dillon, 'Oíolún, 'Oíolṁaιn 1 ; Ó 'Ouιlleáιn 73, 97 ; Ó 'Ouιḃleaċáιn 2.
Dilloughery, Dillury, Dillworth, Dilworth, Ó 'Ouḃluaċɼa, Ó 'Ouιḃluaċɼa.
Dimond, v. Diamond.
Dinahan, Ó 'Ouιnneaċáιn.
Dinan, Ó 'Oaᵹnáιn.
Dineen, Ó 'Ouιnnín.
Dingavan, Ó 'Ouιnneaḃáιn.
Dinihan, Ó 'Ouιnneaċáιn.
Dinkin, Ó 'Ouιnnċιnn.
Dinneen, Ó 'Ouιnnín.
Dinnegan, Ó 'Ouιnneaᵹáιn.
Direen, Ó 'Oιɼín.
Dirrane, Ó 'Oιoɼáιn, Ó 'Oeaɼáιn.
Diskin, Ó 'Oíɼcín.
Diurmagh, Ó 'Oíoɼmaιᵹ, Ó 'Oíoɼma.

Divan, Divane, Ó 'Ouḃáιn.
Diveen, Ó 'Ouιḃín.
Divenney, Divenny, Ó 'Ouιḃ-eannaιᵹ. V. Devanny.
Diver, Ó 'Ouιḃíoιɼ.
Diviney, Ó 'Ouιḃeannaιᵹ. V. Devanny.
Divitt, mac 'Oaιḃéιᵈ.
Divver, Ó 'Ouιḃíoιɼ.
Dixon, mac Rιocaιɼᵈ 1 ; Ó 'Ouιḃᵹeaváιn 469.
Doag, Doake, mac 'Oaḃóc, mac 'Oaḃóᵹ.
Doane, Ó 'Ouḃáιn.
Dobbin, Dobbins, 'Ooιḃín 1 ; ḃιḃíne, ḃιḃíneaċ 376.
Dobbs, 'Ooḃ.
Dobbyn, Dobbyns, Dobin, v. Dobbin.
Dockeray, Dockery, Dockrey, Dockry, Ó 'Oocɼaιᵈ, Ó 'Oocɼaιᵹ.
Dodd, 'Ooᵈa.
Dodding, 'Ooιvín.
Dodds, 'Ooᵈa.
Doey, Ó 'Ouḃċaιᵹ.
Dogheny, v. Doheny.
Dogherty, v. Doherty.
Dohenny, Doheny, Ó 'Ouḃċonna.
Doherty, Ó 'Ooċaɼtaιᵹ 11, Ó 'Ooιċeaɼtaιᵹ 72 ; Ó 'Ouḃaɼtaιᵹ 17.
Dohony, v. Doheny.
Dohorty v. Doherty.
Doig v. Doag.
Dolaghan, Ó 'Oalaċáιn 5 ; Ó 'Ouḃlaċáιn 6.
Dolaher, Ó 'Oalaċaιɼ.
Dolan, Ó 'Ouḃláιn.
Dolfin, 'Ooιlɼín.
Dollard, 'Oollaɼᵈ, 'Oollaɼt.
Dollery, Ó 'Oaιlḃɼe, Ó 'Oala-ɼuaιᵈ.
Dolly, Ó 'Oaċlaoιċ.
Dologhan, v. Dolaghan.
Dolohunty v. Delahunty.
Dolphin, 'Ooιlɼín.

Domegan, Ó Domaġáin.
Donagan, v. Donegan.
Donagh, Donaghey, mac Donncaiḋ 1; Ó Donncaiḋ 2.
Donaghoe, Ó Donncaḋa.
Donaghy, mac Donncaiḋ 1; Ó Donncaiḋ 2.
Donaher, Ó Duineacair.
Donahoe, Ó Donncaḋa.
Donahy, v. Donaghy.
Donald, Donaldson, mac Domnaill.
Donarty, Ó Donnḋubartaiġ.
Dondon, Donḋún, Donnḋún.
Donegan, Ó Donnaġáin 11; Ó hOncon 44.
Donelan, Donellan, Ó Domnalláin.
Donely, v. Donnelly.
Doney, v. Downey.
Dongan, Ó Donnaġáin 11; Donġán 14, 18.
Donigan, v. Donegan.
Donlan, Donlon, Ó Domnalláin.
Donly, Donnally, v. Donnelly.
Donnan, Ó Donnáin, Ó Dúnáin.
Donneely, Ó Donnġaile.
Donnegan, v. Donegan.
Donnell, Ó Domnaill 1; mac Domnaill 2.
Donnellan, Ó Domnalláin.
Donnelly, Ó Donnġaile 11; Ó Donnġalaiġ, Ó Dúnġalaiġ 72, 97.
Donney, v. Downey.
Donnolly, v. Donnelly.
Donogh, mac Donncaḋa.
Donogher, Ó Duineacair.
Donoghue, Donohoe, Donohue, Ó Donncaḋa 11; mac Donncaḋa 976.
Donor, Ó Donnabair.
Donoughoo, v. Donoghue.
Donovan, Ó Donnabáin 11; Ó Donnamáin 777.
Donworth, Ó Donnḋubartaiġ.
Dooal, Ó Duḃġaill.
Dooan, Ó Duḃáin.

Doocey, Doocie, Doocy, Ó Duḃġusa, Ó Duḃasa.
Doody, Ó Duḃḋa.
Dooey, Ó Duḃṫaiġ.
Doogan, Ó Duḃaġáin.
Doohan, Ó Duḃcon,
Doohane, Ó Duacáin.
Dooher, Ó Duḃcair.
Dooherty, Ó Duḃartaiġ. V. Doherty.
Dooladdy, Doolady, Ó Duḃlaḋaiġ.
Doolaghan, Ó Duḃlacáin.
Doolaghty, Ó Duḃlacta, Ó Duḃlactna.
Doolan, Ó Duḃlainn, 2; Ó Duḃláin 2; Ó Dúnlainġ 2.
Doole, v. Doyle.
Doolen, v. Doolan.
Dooler, Ó Dalacair.
Dooley, Ó Duḃlaoic, Ó Duḃluiġc.
Doolin, v. Doolan.
Dooling, v. Dowling.
Dooloughty, Ó Duḃlacta, Ó Duḃlactna.
Dooly, v. Dooley.
Doon, Ó Duḃáin.
Doona, A' Dúna.
Doonan, Ó Dúnáin.
Dooner, Ó Donnabair.
Dooney, Ó Dúnaḋaiġ 11, mac Dúnaḃaiġ 97.
Doonican, Ó Donnacáin, Ó Dúnacáin.
Doordan, mac Duḃradáin.
Doorigan, (?) Ó Dorcáin.
Dooris, Ó Duḃrosa.
Doorley, Doorly, Ó Duḃurtuile.
Doorty, Ó Duḃartaiġ.
Dooyearma, Ó Duiḃḋíorma.
Doran, Ó Deóráin.
Dorcey, Ó Dorcaiḋe.
Dordan, mac Duḃradáin.
Dore, Ó Doġair.
Dorgan, Ó Dorcáin 77; Ó Dearġáin 772.

Þrian, Ó ᴅeópáın, Ó ᴅeóᴘ-
aᴅáın, Ó ᴅeóᴘaıᴅín.
Doris, Ó ᴅuᴄᴘoᴘa.
Dornan, Ó ᴅoᴘnáın, l, Ó
ᴅuıᴘnín 2.
Dorney, Ó ᴅoıᴘınne.
Dornin, Ó ᴅoıᴘnín, Ó ᴅuıᴘnín
Dorran, Dorrian, Ó ᴅeóᴘ.ın, Ó
ᴅeóᴘaᴅáın, Ó ᴅeóᴘaıᴅín.
Dorr, (?) Ó ᴅoᴘaıᴅ.
Dorrigan, v. Dorgan.
Doud, v. Dowd.
Doudall, v. Dowdall.
Douey, v. Dowey.
Dougall, ᴍac ᴅuᴄᴊáıll.
Dougan, Ó ᴅuᴄaᴊáın.
Doughan, Ó ᴅuaᴄáın 16; Ó
ᴅuᴄᴄon 42.
Doughar, Ó ᴅuᴄᴄaıᴘ.
Dougheny, Ó ᴅuᴄᴄonna.
Dougher, Ó ᴅuᴄᴄaıᴘ.
Dougherty, Ó ᴅoᴄaᴘᴄaıᴊ.
Doughney, v. Dougheny.
Douglas, ᴅuᴄᴊᴌaᴘ.
Dougle, v. Dougall.
Douie, v. Dowey.
Dowd, Dowda, Ó ᴅuᴄᴅa.
Dowdall, Dowdell, ᴅuᴄᴅaᴌ.
Dowdican, Ó ᴅuᴄᴅacáın, Ó
ᴅuᴄᴅaᴊáın.
Dowdie, Dowds, Ó ᴅuᴄᴅa.
Dowell, ᴍac ᴅuᴄᴊaıll 2; Ó
ᴅuᴄᴊaıll 2.
Dower, Ó ᴅoᴊaıᴘ.
Dowey, Dowie, Ó ᴅuᴄᴄaıᴊ.
Dowlan, v. Doolan.
Dowler, Ó ᴅaᴌaᴄaıᴘ.
Dowley, Ó ᴅuᴄᴌaoıᴄ, Ó ᴅuᴄ-
ᴌuıᴊe.
Dowlin, Dowling, Ó ᴅúnᴌaınᴊ
l : Ó ᴅuᴄᴌaınn 2.
Down, Downes, Ó ᴅuᴄáın.
Downey, Ó ᴅúnaᴅaıᴊ 4, 9, ᴍac
ᴅúnaᴅaıᴊ 97 ; Ó ᴍaoᴌᴅoᴍn-
aıᴊ 62; ᴍacᴊıoᴌᴌaᴅoᴍnaıᴊ 62
Downing, Ó ᴅúınín, Ó ᴅuıᴙnín
77 ; Ó ᴅúnaᴅaıᴊ 499.

Doyle, Ó ᴅuᴄᴊaıll l ; ᴍac
ᴅuᴄᴊaıll 34 ; Ó ᴅuᴄᴊaıᴌe 2.
Doyne, Ó ᴅuınn.
Draddy, Ó ᴅᴘeaᴅa 7 ; Ó
ᴅᴘaoᴅa 9.
Drain, Draine, Ó ᴅᴘeáın.
Drake, ᴅᴘaᴄ.
Draper, ᴅᴘaoᴘaᴘ.
Drea, Ó ᴅᴘae 49, 179, Ó
ᴅᴘaoı 46.
Dreelan (?) Ó ᴅᴘaoıᴌeáın.
Dreinan, Drennan, Ó ᴅᴘaᴊnáın,
Ó ᴅᴘaıᴊneáın.
Drew, Ó ᴅᴘaoı, Ó ᴅᴘae, Ó
ᴅᴘuaıᴅ 73 ; ᴍac an ᴅᴘuaıᴅ
34, 35 ; ᴅᴘoᴊ, ᴅᴘú, ᴅᴘıú,
15, 25.
Drewry, v. Drury.
Drinan, Drinane, Ó ᴅᴘaıᴊneáın,
Ó ᴅᴘaᴊnáın.
Driscall, Driscoll, Driskell, Dris-
kill, Ó ᴅᴘıᴘceóıl, (o.f.) Ó
hᴇıᴅıᴘᴘceóıl.
Drislane, Ó ᴅᴘıᴘᴌeáın.
Drohan, Drohane, Ó ᴅᴘuaᴄáın.
Droman, Ó ᴅᴘomáın.
Dromey, Ó ᴅᴘoma.
Dromgoole, ᴅe ᴅᴘomᴊúᴌ,
ᴅᴘomᴊúᴌ.
Dr ney, Ó ᴅᴘóna.
Droody, Ó ᴅᴘaoᴅa.
Droohan, Ó ᴅᴘuaᴄáın.
Drough, ᴅᴘoᴊ.
Drought, Ó ᴅᴘoᴄᴄaıᴊ.
Drudy, Ó ᴅᴘaoᴅa.
Drum, Ó ᴅᴘoma.
Drumgoold, Drumgoole, ᴅo
ᴅᴘomᴊúᴌ, ᴅᴘomᴊúᴌ.
Drumm, Ó ᴅᴘoma.
Drummin, Ó ᴅᴘuımín.
Drummond, Drummy, Ó ᴅᴘoma
Drury, ᴅᴘúıᴘıᴅe E 2; Ó ᴅᴘuaıᴅ,
Ó ᴅᴘaoı, Ó ᴅᴘae 73 ; ᴍac
an ᴅᴘuaıᴅ 34.
Duan, Duane, Ó ᴅuᴄáın.
Duany, Ó ᴅuᴄánaıᴊ.
Duarty, Ó ᴅuᴄaᴘᴄaıᴊ.

Ducey, Ó Oubġuṛ⸱⸱, Ó Oubⱥ⸱ṛⱥ.
Duck, Ó Lⱥċⱥ⸱n, Ó Leoċⱥ⸱n 43
(O'D.).
Duddie, Duddy, Ó Oubⱦⱥ.
Dudican, Ó Oubvⱥcⱥ⸱n, Ó
Oubvⱥ⸱ⱽⱥ⸱n.
Dudley, Ó Oubvⱥ́le⸱ⱦe, 777.
Duff, Oub 2 ; Ó Ou⸱b 36, 45,
92 ; mⱥc Ⱬ⸱ollⱥⱦu⸱b 62.
Dufferly, Ó Oubu⸱ṫu⸱le.
Duffin, Ó Ou⸱bṛ⸱nn.
Duffiley, Ó Ou⸱bⱫ⸱ollⱥ.
Duffy, Ó Oubⱦⱥ⸱Ⱬ 11, (s.l.) Ó
Oú⸱ⱦⱦe 62, 92 ; Ó Oo⸱ⱦe 99.
Dugald, mⱥc OubⱫⱥ⸱ll.
Dugan, Duggan, Duggen, Ó
Oubⱥ⸱Ⱬⱥ⸱n 11 ; Ó Ou⸱bⱫ⸱nn
2 ; (?) Ó Oubⱦú⸱n 2.
Dugidan, Ó Ou⸱bⱫeⱥⱦⱥ⸱n.
Duhig, Duhy, Ó Oubⱦⱥ⸱Ⱬ.
Duigan, Ó Ou⸱bⱫ⸱nn.
Duigenan, Duignam, Duignan,
Ó Ou⸱bⱫeⱥnnⱥ⸱n.
Dulanty, Dulinty, Ó Oul-
ċⱥo⸱nⱦ⸱Ⱬ, Ó Oulċonⱦⱥ.
Dullaghan, Ó Oⱥlⱥċⱥ⸱n 5 ; Ó
Oublⱥċⱥ⸱n 6.
Dullard, Oollⱥṛv, Oollⱥṛⱦ.
Dullea, Ó Ou⸱nnⱥ̇le⸱be.
Dullenty, Ó Oulċⱥo⸱nⱦ⸱Ⱬ.
Dumegan, Ó OomⱥⱫⱥ⸱n.
Dun, Ó Ou⸱nn.
Duncahy, Ó Oonnċⱥⱦⱥ⸱Ⱬ, Ó
Ou⸱nnċⱥⱦⱥ⸱Ⱬ.
Duncan, mⱥc Oonnċⱥ⸱ⱽ S 6 ;
Ó Oonnⱥċⱥ⸱n, Ó OonnⱥⱫⱥ⸱n
5 ; Ó Ou⸱nnċ⸱nn 29, 82 ;
OonⱫⱥ́n 14, 18.
Dundas, Ó Ⱨⱥ́ṛⱥ (S.L.) 979.
Dundon, Oonnⱦú⸱n, Oonⱦú⸱n.
Dune, Ó Oubⱥ⸱n.
Dunford, Dunfort, Ó Oonnⱦub-
ⱥṛⱦⱥ⸱Ⱬ.
Dunfy, v. Dunphy.
Dungan, OonⱫⱥ́n 14, 18 ; Ó
OonnⱥⱫⱥ⸱n 2.
Dunican, Ó Oúnⱥċⱥ⸱n, Ó Oonn-
ⱥċⱥ⸱n.

Dunigan, v. Donegan.
Dunion, Ó Oú⸱n⸱n, Ó Ou⸱nn⸱n.
Dunkin, Ó Ou⸱nnċ⸱nn.
Dunlavy, Dunlea, Dunleavy, Dun-
leevy, Dunlevy, Ó Ou⸱nnⱥ̇-
le⸱be ; (s.s.) ulⱦⱥċ, ulⱦⱥċⱥ́n.
Dunlief, Dunlop, mⱥc Ou⸱nn-
ṛ̇le⸱be.
Dunn, Dunne, Ó Ou⸱nn 1 ; mⱥc
Ⱬ⸱ollⱥⱦu⸱nn 29.
Dunnegan, Ó OonnⱥⱫⱥ⸱n.
Dunner, Ó Oonnⱥⱦⱥ⸱ṛ.
Dunnigan, v. Dunnegan.
Dunning, Ó Oú⸱n⸱n, Ó Ou⸱nn⸱n.
Dunny, Ó Oúnⱥⱦⱥ⸱Ⱬ.
Dunphy, Ó Oonnċⱥⱦⱥ, Ó
Oonnċⱥⱦ.
Dunroche, Ó Ou⸱b⸱nnṛeⱥċⱦⱥ⸱Ⱬ.
Dunworth, Ó OonnOubⱥṛⱦⱥ⸱Ⱬ.
Durack, Ó Oubṛⱥ⸱c.
Durcan, mⱥc Ouⱥṛcⱥ⸱n.
Durham, ⱦe Ouṛⱥm.
Durick, Ó Oubṛⱥ⸱c.
Durkan, Durkin, mⱥc Ouⱥṛcⱥ⸱n
Durmody, v. Dermody.
Durnan, Ó Ooṛnⱥ⸱n.
Durnian, Durnin, Durnion, Ó
Ou⸱ṛn⸱n.
Durr, (?) Ó Ooṛⱥ⸱ⱦ.
Durrane, Ó O⸱oṛⱥ⸱n.
Durrian, v. Dorrian.
Durrig, Ó Oe⸱ṛ⸱Ⱬ.
Durry, Ó Ooṛⱥ⸱ⱦ.
Dwain, Dwan, Dwane, Ó Oubⱥ⸱n.
Dwire, Dwyer, Ó Oubu⸱ⱦ⸱ṛ, Ó
Ou⸱b⸱ⱦ⸱ṛ.
Dyer, Ó Ou⸱b⸱ⱦ⸱ṛ, 6, 8 ; mⱥc
Ou⸱b⸱ⱦ⸱ṛ 29.
Dyermott, Ó Ou⸱bⱦ⸱oṛmⱥ, Ó
Ou⸱bⱦ⸱oṛmⱥ⸱Ⱬ.
Dygnam, v. Dignam.
Dyle, v. Doyle.
Dynan, Ó OⱥⱫnⱥ⸱n.
Dyne, Ó Ou⸱nn.

Eagan, v. Egan.
Eagar, é⸱Ⱬeⱥṛ.

Eagleton, mac ιoιρacáin, Ó hιoιρacáin.

Eakin, Eakins, Ó hαoòaзáin.

Earl, Earle, Earls, mac an ιaρla 2; ιaρlaιòe 979.

Early, Ó maolmoιceιρże, (s.l.) Ó maolmoćóιρże 1, Ó maolmoćóιρ 192, Ó moćóιρże 95, Ó moćóιρ 192.

Earner, Earnor, Ó Saoρaιòe, Ó Saoċραιòe.

Eason, mac Aoòa.

Eaton, éaċún.

Edmonds, Edmondson, Edmunds, Edmundson, mac éamoinn, mac éamuinn.

Edwards, mac éaòbáιρò.

Egan, mac Aoòaзáin 11; Ó hαoòaзáin 2.

Egar, éιзeaρ.

Eggleton, v. Eagleton.

Egnew, Ó зním.

Eivers, Ó híomaιρ 76, 93; mac íomaιρ 19.

Elfred, Oιleaòáρò.

Ellard, Aιòleaρò, Aláρò, Oláρò.

Ellison, Ó heιlżeaρáin 62, Ellmore, Ó híomna (G. J.).

Ellwood, Oιleaòáρò, Oιleaòaρò

Elmer, v. Aylmar.

Elshander, Elshinder, v. Alexander.

Elward, v. Aylward & Ellard.

Elwood, v. Ellwood.

England, Aιnзleanò, Aιnзleonċ.

English, Aιnзléιρ, ιnзléιρ, ιnзlιρ 1; mac an зallóзlaιż 15, 86.

Englishby, mac an зallóзlaιż.

Englishe, v. English.

Ennes, Ennis, Ó hαonзuιρ 1; mac Aonзuιρ 2.

Enraght,Enright, mac ιonnρaċtaιż 11, mac ιnnρeaċtaιż 2.

Enroe, mac Conρuòa.

Erke, Ó heιρc.

Erksine, Aρaρcain.

Erought, Erraght, Erraught Ó hOιρeaċtaιż.

Errington, Ó háρραċtáin.

Ervine, Erwin, Ó heιρeamóιn 1; Ó Cιαρmacáin 772.

Esbald, Esball, Áιρeaòóιò.

Esmond, Esmonde, eaρmonn.

Etchingham, eιċιnзeam.

Eurell, òe Oιρżιall.

Eustace, Eustice, ιúρtáρ.

Evans, Evens, Aoιbιn, Aoιbιnn 47, 49; Ó héιmín, Ó héamáin 73.

Everard, éιòeaρáρò, éaòραρò. éaòρóιò.

Everett, Everitt, éaòρóιò.

Evers, v. Eivers.

Evins, v. Evans.

Evoy, v. MacEvoy.

Eyre, Eyres, ιαρραċ.

Fadden, Faddin, mac páιòín.

Fade, mac páιò.

Fadian, mac páιòín.

Fagan, ράзán 15, 18, 43; Ó ράзáin 65; Ó ραoòaзáin 37, 38; Ó ριacáin 2; mac páιòín 16.

Faggy, mac páιòín (mac ραιòι)

Faghy, Ó ραċaιż.

Fagin, v. Fagan.

Faheney, Ó ριacna.

Faherty, Ó ραċαρταιż.

Fahey, Fahy, Ó ραċaιż 11, (s.l.) Ó ραιċ 92.

Fair, ριonn.

Falahee, Falahy, Ó ρalċaιò, (o.f.) Ó ραolċaιò.

Falconer, Falkner, ρácnaρ 11; Ó ρaċtna 9.

Fallaher, Ó ρalċaιρ ,(o.f.) Ó ραolċaιρ.

Fallen, Fallin. Fallon, Falloon, Faloon, Faloona, Ó ρallamáin, Ó ρollamáin.

Falsey, Ó ρalċaιò

Falvey, Ó ράιlbe

Fanagan, Ó ριonnaзáin.

Fane, Ó ꝼiacáin, Ó ꝼéicín.
Fannerty, Ó ꝼionnaċtaiġ.
Fannin, Fanning, ꝼainín, (o.f.) ꝼainín 7, 8 ; Ó ꝼionnáin, Ó ꝼionáin 9 ; Ó ꝼinġin 87.
Fannon, Ó ꝼionnáin.
Fant, ꝼannt.
Faragher, Faraher, Ó ꝼeaṟċaiṟ.
Faran, v. Farren.
Farelly, v. Farrelly.
Faren, v. Farren.
Farghur, mac ꝼeaṟċaiṟ.
Farguson, v. Ferguson.
Farin, v. Farren.
Faris, v. Farris.
Farker, mac ꝼeaṟċaiṟ.
Farley, Ó ꝼaiṟċeallaiġ.
Farmer, mac an Scolóiġe, mac Scolóiġe.
Farnan, Farnand, Farnham, Farnon, Ó ꝼaṟannáin, Ó ꝼoṟannáin.
Farquehar, Farquer, Farquharson, Farquher, mac ꝼeaṟċaiṟ·
Farragher, Farraher, Ó ꝼeaṟċaiṟ.
Farrahill, Ó ꝼeaṟġail.
Farrally, v. Farrelly.
Farran, v. Farren.
Farrell, Ó ꝼeaṟġail 11, Ó ꝼeaṟġaile 2.
Farrelly, Farrely, Ó ꝼaiṟċeallaiġ 1 ; Ó ꝼeaṟġaile 2.
Farren, Ó ꝼeaṟáin 26, 33 ; Ó ꝼaṟacáin 16.
Farris, Farrissy, Ó ꝼeaṟġuiṟ, Ó ꝼeaṟġuṟa.
Farron, v. Farren.
Farry, Ó ꝼeaṟaḋaiġ 6 ; Ó ꝼaṟṟaiġ 9.
Farshin, ꝼaiṟṟinġ.
Faughnan, Ó ꝼaċtnáin.
Faughy, Ó ꝼaċaiġ.
Faulkner, v. Falconer.
Faulkney, Ó ꝼaċtna.
Fausset, Faussette, Fawcett, ꝼóiꝼéiṫ.

Fay, Ó ꝼéiċ, Ó ꝼiaiċ 1, 91 ; Ó ꝼaiṫ 97 ; ᵼe ꝼae, a ꝼae, ꝼaeḋeaċ 15.
Feagan, Ó ꝼaoḋaġáin.   V.
Fagan.
Fealan, Ó ꝼaoláin.
Fealey, Fealy, Ó ꝼióġeallaiġ 1 ; Ó ꝼáile (Ó ꝼáilḃe) 496.
Feane, Ó ꝼiacáin, Ó ꝼéicín.
Fearen, Fearn, Fearon, Ó ꝼeaṟáin.
Feary, Ó ꝼiaċṟa, Ó ꝼiaċṟac.
Fedigan, Ó ꝼéaḋaġáin.
Fee, Ó ꝼiaiċ 11 ; Ó ꝼiaċa 35.
Feehan, Ó ꝼiacáin.
Feeharry, mac annṟaoi, mac hannṟaoi.
Feehely, Ó ꝼiċċeallaiġ.
Feeheny, Ó ꝼiaċna.
Feehery, Ó ꝼiaċṟa.
Feehily, Ó ꝼiċċeallaiġ.
Feehin, Ó ꝼéicín.
Feeley, Feely, Ó ꝼiċċeallaiġ, Ó ꝼióġeallaiġ, (s.l.) Ó ꝼiċille 976.
Feen, Ó ꝼéicín.
Feenaghty, Feenaghy, Ó ꝼiannaċta, Ó ꝼionnaċtaiġ.
Feeney, Feeny, Ó ꝼéinneaḋa, (s.l.) Ó ꝼiannaiḋe, Ó ꝼianna 93 ; Ó ꝼiḋne, (s.l.) Ó ꝼinne, Ó ꝼine 94.
Feerey, Ó ꝼiaċṟa.
Feerick, mac ꝼiaṟuic, mac ꝼiaṟaic, (s.l.) Ó ꝼiaṟaic, ꝼiaṟac.
Fegan, Ó ꝼaoḋaġáin 1 ; Ó ꝼiacáin 2.   V. Fagan.
Feghany, Ó ꝼiaċna.
Fehan, Fehane, Ó ꝼiacáin.
Fehely, v. Fehily.
Fehen, Ó ꝼéicín.
Fehill, Ó ꝼiċċill.
Fehilly, Fehily, Ó ꝼiċċeallaiġ.
Feighan, Ó ꝼiacáin.
Feighery, Ó ꝼiaċṟa.
Feighney, Ó ꝼiaċna.

Feighry, Ó Ḟiaċra.
Felan, Ó Ḟaoláin 7. V. Phelan.
Feley, mac Seanṁaiġ.
Fenaghty, Fenaughty, Ó Ḟionn-
aċta, Ó Ḟionnaċtaiġ, Ó
Ḟinneaċta, &c.
Fendlon, v. Fenlon.
Fenelly, v. Fennelly.
Fenelon, Ó Ḟionnalláin.
Fenihan, Ó Ḟionnaċáin.
Fenley, v. Fennelly.
Fenlon, Ó Ḟionnalláin.
Fennell, Ó Ḟionnġail, Ó Ḟionn-
ġaile.
Fennelly, Ó Ḟionnġalaiġ.
Fennerty, Ó Ḟionnaċta, Ó
Ḟinneaċtaiġ, &c.
Fennessy, Ó Ḟionnġura.
Fennors, Ḟionúiṙ, Ḟionnúiṙ.
Fenton, Ó Ḟiannaċta 71 ; Ó
Ḟiaċna 72.
Feoghney, Ó Ḟiaċna.
Feore, Ó Ḟioṁaḃaiṙ.
Feran, Ó Ḟearáin.
Fergison, Ferguison, v. Fergu-
son.
Fergus, Ó Ḟearġuiṙ, Ó Ḟear
ġura 9 ; mac Ḟearġuiṙ 6.
Ferguson, Fergusson, mac Ḟear
ġura, mac Ḟearġuiṙ.
Feris, v. Ferris.
Ferley, Ferly, v. Farrelly.
Fern, Ó Ḟearáin. V. Ferns.
Fernan, Fernane, Ó Ḟearnáin.
Ferns, Ó Reannaċáin.
Feron, v. Fern.
Ferrall, Ó Ḟearġail.
Ferran, Ó Ḟearáin.
Ferreter, v. Ferriter.
Ferris, Ó Ḟearġuiṙ, Ó Ḟearġura
7, 9.
Ferriter, Ḟeiriteiṙ, Ḟeirteiṙ,
Ḟiriteiṙ, Ḟirteiṙ.
Ferrons, Ó Reannaċáin.
Ferry, Ó Ḟearaḃaiġ 6 ; (?) Ó
Ḟoiṙṙeiḋ 62.
Fetton, Ḟiotún, Ṗiotán.

Fettridge, mac Ṗeaḋruiṙ.
Fey, Ó Ḟéiċ, Ó Ḟiaiċ.
Fidgeon, v. Pidgeon.
Fie, v. Fye.
Field, ve Ḟílve 18 ; Ó Ḟiċ-
ċeallaiġ 4, Ó Ḟróġeallaiġ 2, Ó
Ḟiċċill 2.
Fielding, Fihelly, Fihily, Ó
Ḟiċċeallaiġ.
Filan, v. Phelan.
Filbin, mac Ṗilibín, mac
Ṗilbín, mac Ḟilibín, (s.l.) Ó
Ḟilibín.
Finaghty, Ó Ḟionnaċta.
Finalay, v. Finlay.
Finamore, Ḟionaṁúiṙ.
Finan, Ó Ḟionáin, Ó Ḟionnáin
Finch, Ḟúinṙe.
Findlay, Findley, v. Finlay.
Finegan, Ó Ḟionnaġáin.
Finelly, v. Finnelly.
Finerty, Ó Ḟinneaċta, Ó Ḟionn-
aċta, &c.
Finglas, ve Ḟionnġlaṙ, Ḟionġlaṙ.
Finigan, v. Finegan.
Finlay, Finley, Ó Ḟionnġalaiġ
1, Ó Ḟianġalaiġ 2.
Finn, Ó Ḟinn.
Finnaghty, Ó Ḟinneaċta, Ó
Ḟinneaċtaiġ, &c.
Finnally, v. Finnelly.
Finnamore, Finnamure, Ḟiona-
ṁúiṙ.
Finnan, Ó Ḟionnáin.
Finne, Ó Ḟinn.
Finnegan, Ó Ḟionnaġáin.
Finnell, Ó Ḟionnġail, Ó Ḟionn-
ġaile.
Finnelly, Ó Ḟionnġalaiġ, Ó
Ḟianġalaiġ.
Finnemor, Ḟionaṁúiṙ.
Finneran, Ó Ḟinnċiġearn.
Finnerell (?) Ó Ḟiongarvail,
Finnerty, Ó Ḟionnaċta, Ó
Ḟionnaċtaiġ, Ó Ḟinneaċta,
Ó Ḟinneaċtaiġ, Ó Ḟiannaċt-
aiġ, Ó Ḟiannaċta, &c.

82

Finnessy, Ó Fionnġuṡa.
Finney, v. Feeney.
Finnigan, Ó Fionnaġáin.
Finning, Ó Finġin.
Finnucane, Ó Fionnṁacáin.
Finny, v. Feeny.
Finucane, Ó Fionnṁacáin.
Fisher, mac an Iarcaire 1; Ó Ḃraḋáin 16.
Fitton, Piotún, Piotún.
Fitsimmons, Fitsimons, v. Fitzsimons.
Fitzgerald, FitzGerald, mac Ġearailt.
Fitzgibbon, mac Ġiobúin.
Fitzharris, Fitzhenry, mac Annraoi, mac hanraoi, mac Éinrí.
Fitzherbert, mac hoipeabairo.
Fitzmartin, mac Máirtín.
Fitzmaurice, Fitzmorice, Fitzmorris, mac muiṗir, mac ṁuiṗir.
Fitzpatrick, mac Ġiolla ṗáoraiġ 11; (s.s.) mac Séarṫa, mac Séarṫaiṁ 75, 78; mac ṗáoraiġín 2.
Fitzsimmons, Fitzsimon, Fitzsimons, Fitzsummons, mac Síomóin, mac Síomoinn 11; (s.s.) mac an Rioire 15.
Fitzstephen, Fitzstephens, mac Steaṗáin, mac Stioṗáin, &c V. Stephens.
Flagherty, v. Flaherty.
Flahavan, Ó Flaiṫeaṁáin, Ó Flaṫaṁáin.
Flahavin, Ó Flaiṫiṁín, Ó Flaiṫeaṁáin, Ó Flaṫaṁáin.
Flaherty, Ó Flaiṫḃeartaiġ 11; Ó Faṫartaiġ 972.
Flahevan, v. Flahavan.
Flahive, Flahy, Ó Flaiṫiṁ, (s.l.) Ó Flaṫaiġ.
Flanagan, Ó Flannaġáin.
Flanaghan, Ó Flannacáin.
Flanahy, Ó Flannċaḋa, Ó Flannċaiḋ.

Flang, Ó Flainn.
Flanigan, Flannagan, Ó Flannaġáin.
Flannelly, Ó Flannġaile.
Flannery, Ó Flannaḃra 11; Ó Flannġaile 19, 29.
Flannigan, Ó Flannaġáin.
Flatley, v. Flattley.
Flattery, Ó Flaitire, (o.f.) Ó Flaitile, (o.f.) Ó Flaitṗileaḋ.
Flattley, Ó Flaitile, (o.f.) Ó Flaitṗileaḋ.
Flavahan, Ó Flaiteaṁáin.
Flavell, Ó Flannġail.
Flaverty, Ó Flaitḃeartaiġ.
Flavin, Ó Flaitiṁín, Ó Flaiteaṁáin.
Fleming, Flemming, Flemon, Flemyng, pléamonn, pléimeann.
Fletcher, mac an Fleaṗtaiṗ.
Fleury, v. Fury.
Flinn, Ó Floinn.
Flint, Flint.
Flood, Flóiḋ 62, 82; Ó maoltuile 11, mac maoltuile, mac ṁaoltuile 9, (s.l.) mac an tuile, mac tuile, ó tuile, Ó tuine 192, 972.
Floyd, Flóiḋ. V. Flood.
Flyng, Flynn, Ó Floinn, Ó Flainn.
Fodaghan, Ó Fuaḋacáin.
Foddy, Ó Fuaḋa.
Fodha, Faḋa.
Fogarty, Fogerty, Ó Fógartaiġ 1, (s.l.) Ó Fógarta 499.
Folan, mac Fualáin, (o.f.) mac Faoláin, (s.l.) Ó Cualáin 99.
Foley, Ó Foġlaḋa, Ó Foḋlaḋa 7, 8; mac Searraiġ, 6, 9; Ó Searraiġ 64.
Foody, Ó Fuaḋa.
Foohy, Ó Fuaṫaiġ.
Fooley, Ó Fuallaiġ.
Foorde, Furd, Fúroaċ.

Foote, Ó Cρoiξċiξ 2 (O'D); mac Coiρe 2 (O'D.).

Foran, Ó fuaρτáin, Ó fuaρράin, Ó fuaράin.

Forbes, Forbis, Forbish, mac fiṁbiριξ ,(s.l.) mac foiρbiρ, Coiρbiρ 19, 29; foiρbiρ, foiρbiρeaċ S. 2.

Ford, Forde, fóρc, fóρ'o, fúρ'o 86; mac an áċa, (o.f.) mac Confnáṁa 96, 976; mac ξiolla na ṅaoṁ, (s.l.) mac ξiollaρnáċ, Ó ξiollaρnáċ 97, 197; Ó fuaρċáin, Ó fuaράin 7.

Forehan, Forehane, Ó fuaρċáin, Ó fuaρράin, Ó fuaράin.

Forestall, fuiρeaρcal 11; mac an Coill (S.L.) 197.

Forhan, Ó fuaρċáin.

Forkan, Ó ξabláin.

Forke, Ó ξabalaiξ.

Forker, mac feaρċaiρ.

Forkin, Ó ξabláin.

Forran, Ó faρaċáin 16.

Forrest, foiρéiρ, fuiρéaρc.

Forrestal, Forrester, fuiρeaρcal

Forry, Ó faρρai'o 19.

Forstall, Forster, Foster, fuiρeaρcal.

Fortin, Ó foiρcċeiρn.

Fortune, Ó foiρcċeiρn 1; faiρ- ριṅξ 779.

Fottrell, fucρail.

Foudy, Ó fua'oa.

Fouhy, Ó fuaċaiξ.

Fourhane, Ó fuaρċáin.

Fourker, v. Forker.

Fowcett, fóiféi'o.

Fowhey, Ó fuaċaiξ.

Fox, Foxe, 'oe boρc, boρcaċ 17; Sionnaċ, (o.s.) Ó Caċaρnaiξ 25, 55; Ó Sion- naiξ, Ó Sionaiξ 19, 29, 37, 77; mac an cSionnaiξ 2; Ó Sionaċáin 58; mac Seanċa, mac Seanċai'oe 39.

Foy, Ó fiaiċ 11; Ó faiċ 976.

Foynes, faξan, paξan.

Fraher, Ó fpeaċaiρ, Ó feaρċaiρ.

Frahill, Ó fpeaċail, (o.f.) Ó feaρξail.

Frain, Frainey, Frainy, 'oe fρéin, 'oe fρéine, a fρéin 8, 78; mac an fρanncaiξ 9.

Francey, Francis, ppéinféiρ.

Frane, Franey, v. Frain.

Franklin, fpainclín.

Fraser, fuiρeal; (G.p.) mac Simi'o.

Fraul, Ó fpeaċail, (o.f.) Ó feaρξail.

Frawley, Ó fpeaξaile, Ó feaρ- ξaile.

Frayne, v. Frain.

Frazer, fuiρeal, fuiρealaċ.

Freal, v. Freel.

Free, Ó Saopai'oe.

Freehill, Ó fpiċil, (o.f.) Ó fiṅξil.

Freehily, Ó fpiċile.

Freel, Ó fiṅξil, Ó fipiξil.

Freely, Ó fpiξile, Ó fipξile.

Freeman, Ó Saopai'oe 9; mac an cSaoiρ 67.

Freeney, Freeny, 'oe fρéine 8; mac an fρanncaiξ 9.

Frehen, Ó fpaoiċín.

Frehill, Ó fpiċil.

Frehilly, Ó fpiċile.

Frein, 'oe fρéin, a fρéin. V. Frain.

French, 'oe fρéinρ 28, 97; fpinρe, fpinρeaċ 19; ppionn- ρa, ppionnρaċ 34; Ó fρaoċ- áin 92.

Freney, Freny, 'oe fρéine, a fρéine 8; mac an fρannc- aiξ 9.

Frewen, Frewin, fpiúin.

Freyne, 'oe fρéin, a fρéin 8, 78; mac an fρanncaiξ 9.

Friar, Friary, mac an ppíρ, mac an píopa.

Friel, Ó fpiṅξil, Ó fipξil.

Frier, v. Friar.
Frisell, Frizell, Frizzle, ꝼꝛipeⱥl.
Frost, ⱥn ⱦeⱥcⱥ 76; ꝼuiꝛéⱥꝛⱦ 77.
Frvar, Frver, mⱥc ⱥn ꝑꝛíꝛ, mⱥc ⱥn ꝑꝛioꝛⱥ.
Fullen, v. Fallon.
Fullarton, ꝼulⱥꝛⱦún.
Fuller, mⱥc ⱥn úcⱥiꝛe.
Fullerton, ꝼulⱥꝛⱦún.
Fuohy, Ó ꝼuⱥcⱥiⱅ.
Furey, Fury, Ó ꝼíoⱴⱥⱴꝛⱥ.
Furlong, ꝼuꝛlonⱅ.
Fyans, ꝼⱥⱅⱥn, ꝑⱥⱅⱥn.
Fye, Ó ꝼiⱥic 11; Ó ꝼiⱥcⱥ 35.
Fyfee, Ó ꝼiⱥcⱥ.
Fylan, Fyland, v. Phelan.
Fynn, Ó ꝼinn.

Gabbett, Gabbott, ⱅⱥbóiⱴ.
Gaff, mⱥⱅ eⱥcⱥc.
Gaffeney, v. Gaffney.
Gaffey, mⱥⱅ eⱥcⱥiⱴ.
Gaffikan, Gaffikin, mⱥⱅ eⱥcⱥⱅⱥin.
Gaffiney, Gaffney, Gafiney, Gafney, Ó ⱅⱥṁnⱥ 78, 87, 96; mⱥc ⱅⱥṁnⱥ 18, 55, 67; mⱥc coṁⱅⱥṁnⱥ 19, 55, 77, 97; mⱥⱅ ꝼⱥcⱦnⱥ 52; mⱥc cⱥꝛꝛⱅⱥṁnⱥ 152.
Gagan, Gahagan, mⱥⱅ eⱥcⱥⱅⱥin.
Gahan, Ó ⱅⱥoiⱦín 84; mⱥc ⱅⱥoiⱦín, (s.l.) mⱥⱅ ⱅⱥⱦⱥn 64; Ó ⱅⱥcⱥin (o.f) Ó ⱅⱥiⱴⱦeⱥcⱥin 19.
Gahey, mⱥⱅ eⱥcⱥiⱴ.
Gaine, Ó ⱅéiⱴinn.
Gainer, Gainor, mⱥⱅ ꝼionnⱴⱥiꝛꝛ.
Gairlan, v. Garlan.
Galagher, v. Gallagher.
Galavan, Galavin, v. Gallivan.
Galbally, ⱴe ⱅⱥllⱴⱥile.
Galbraith, Galbreath, ⱅⱥllⱴꝛeⱥcnⱥc.
Galespy, mⱥc ⱅiollⱥ eⱥꝛꝛuiⱅ.

Gall, ⱅⱥll.
Gallagher, Gallaher, Gallaugher, Ó ⱅⱥllcoⱴⱥiꝛ, Ó ⱅⱥllcuⱴⱥiꝛ.
Gallahue, Ó ⱅⱥllcuⱴⱥ, (o.f.) Ó ⱅⱥllcuⱴⱥiꝛ.
Gallen, Ó ⱅⱥlⱥin, Ó ⱅⱥllⱥin 1; Ó ⱅⱥillín 62.
Gallery, mⱥc ⱅiollⱥꝛⱥⱴⱥiⱅ.
Galligan, Ó ⱅeⱥlⱥⱅⱥin.
Galliher, Gallihur, v. Gallaher.
Gallin, v. Gallen.
Gallinagh, Ó ⱅⱥilineⱥc (S.L.) 16.
Gallivan, Ó ⱅeⱥlⱴⱥin.
Gallogher, Ó ⱅⱥllcoⱴⱥiꝛ.
Gallogly, mⱥc ⱥn ⱅⱥllóⱅlⱥiⱅ.
Gallon, Ó ⱅⱥlⱥin, Ó ⱅⱥllⱥin.
Galloway, Gallway, ⱴe ⱅⱥilliⱴe, ⱅⱥilliⱴe.
Galt, ⱅⱥllⱴⱥ.
Galvan, Galven, Galvin, Ó ⱅeⱥlⱴⱥin.
Galway, Galwey, ⱴe ⱅⱥilliⱴe, ⱅⱥilliⱴe.
Gambell, Gamble, ⱅⱥmⱥl.
Gambling, ⱅⱥimlín.
Gambon, ⱅⱥmbún.
Gamel, ⱅⱥmⱥl.
Gamlin, ⱅⱥimlín.
Gammel, ⱅⱥmⱥl.
Gammon, ⱅⱥmbún.
Ganagher, mⱥⱅ ⱴuineⱥcⱥiꝛ.
Ganley, Ganly, mⱥⱅ Seⱥnlⱥoic.
Gannissy, mⱥⱅ ⱥonⱅuꝛⱥ.
Gannon, mⱥⱅ ꝼionnⱥin, (s.l.) Ó ⱅionnⱥin, Ó ⱅeⱥnnⱥin 19, 97.
Gantly, mⱥⱅ Seⱥnlⱥoic.
Gara, Ó ⱅⱥⱴꝛⱥ.
Garagan, v. Gargan.
Garahan, mⱥⱅ ⱅⱥꝛⱥcⱥin, mⱥⱅ ⱥꝛⱥcⱥin.
Garahy, mⱥⱅ ꝼeⱥꝛⱥⱴⱥiⱅ, (s.l.) mⱥⱅ ⱅeⱥꝛⱥcⱥiⱅ.
Garavin, v. Garvin.
Garde, ⱴe ⱅeⱥꝛⱴ, ⱅeⱥꝛⱴ.
Garden, Gardin, ⱅⱥiꝛⱴín.
Gardiner, Gardner, ⱅⱥiꝛⱛéiꝛ.

Gargan, Ó Geargáin, (s.s.) Mac Geargáin.
Garity, Mag Aireaċtaiġ.
Garlan, Garland, Garlin, Gearlann (o.f.) Gearlún, (o.f.) Gearnún
Garner, v Gardner
Garraghan, Mag Garaċáin, Mag Araċáin.
Garratt, Garrett, Gearóid, Gioróid.
Garrigan, v Gargan.
Garrihy, v Garahy.
Garrity, v Garity.
Garron, Mag Garaċáin.
Garry, Mag Fearaḋaiġ 1 ; Ó Gaḋra 2
Gartlan, Gartland, Gartlin, Geartlan, Gearlann. V. Garlan
Garvan, Ó Garbáin.
Garveagh, Ó Gairbḟéiċ, Ó Gairbḟiaiċ.
Garven, v Garvin.
Garvey, Ó Gairbiṫ, Ó Gairbeiṫ 1 ; Mac Gairbiṫ, Mac Gairbeiṫ 16, 64, 67, 192 ; Ó Gairbḟéiċ, Ó Gairbḟiaiċ 49 ; Ó Gairbín 94, 191.
Garvin, Garwin, Ó Gairbín 1, Ó Garbáin 2.
Gascoigne, Gascoyne, Gaskin, de Gascún.
Gasson, Ó Gusáin.
Gaston, Gastún.
Gately, Ó Gatlaoiċ.
Gaughan, Ó Gáibṫeaċáin, (s l) Ó Gáċáin 19 ; Mag Eaċáin 2.
Gaughney, Mag Faċtna.
Gaughran, Mag Eaċráin.
Gaughy, Gaugy, Mag Eaċaiḋ.
Gaul, Gaule, Gall.
Gault, Gallda.
Gaussen, Ó Gusáin.
Gausslin, Géislín.
Gavacan, Gavagan, Gavaghan, Gavahan, Ó Gáibṫeaċáin 9 ; Mag Eaċagáin 6.

Gavan, Gaven, Ó Gábáin.
Gavigan, v Gavagan.
Gavin, Ó Gáibín, Ó Gábáin.
Gaw, Mag Áḋaiṁ.
Gawley, Mag Aṁalġaḋa, Mag Aṁalġaiḋ.
Gay, Mac Giolla Dé.
Gayer, Géar 1 ; Mac an Géairr 2.
Gaynard, Ó Gánaird (S L) 976.
Gaynor, Mag Fionnbairr 1, Mag Fionnbarra 2 ; Ó Gánaird (S L) 976.
Geagan, Mag Eoċagáin.
Gealon, Ó Gialláin.
Geane, Ó Géibinn.
Geaney, Ó Géibeannaiġ.
Geanor, v Gaynor.
Geany, v Geaney.
Gearn, Gearns, Gearon, Ó Géaráin.
Gearty, Mag Oireaċtaiġ.
Geary, Ó Gaḋra 11 ; Mac Gaḋra, (s.l.) Mag Gaora 97 ; Mag Fearaḋaiġ 2.
Geaveney, Geaveny, Mac Géibeannaiġ 6 ; Ó Géibeannaiġ 9.
Gee, Mag Aoiḋ.
Geehan, Ó Gaoiṫín
Geelan, Ó Gialláin.
Geffeken, v Gaffikin.
Gegan, Mag Eoċagáin.
Geghan, Mag Eaċáin, Mag Eoċagáin.
Gehagan, Gehegan, Mag Eoċagáin.
Gelaspy, Mac Giolla Easpuig.
Gellan, Gelland, Ó Gealáin 9 ; Mac Giolla Faoláin 6.
Gellen, Ó Gealáin, Ó Gilín.
Gellespey, v. Gelaspy.
Gelshinan, v. Gilshenan.
Gelvarry, Mac Giolla Bearaiġ.
Gennagh, Mag Cineáiṫ.
Gennell, Mag Fionnġail.
Geogan, Geoghegan, Mag Eoċagáin.

86

Geoghery, Ó ᵹoċꝛⱥıṫ. 4.
Geon, mⱥᵹ eoᵹⱥın.
George, ѕeóıꝛꝛe.
Geraghty, mⱥᵹ Oıꝛeⱥċtⱥıᵹ 11;
Ó hOıꝛeⱥċtⱥıᵹ 16, 29, 99.
Geran, Ó ᵹéⱥꝛáın.
Gerard, ᵹeⱥꝛáꝛo 1, ᵹeⱥꝛóıo 2.
Gerarty, Geraty, Geraughty,
Gerity, v. Gerraghty.
German, ᵹeⱥꝛmán.
Germon, ᵹeⱥꝛmonn.
Gernon, ᵹeⱥꝛnún.
Gerraghty, mⱥᵹ Oıꝛeⱥċtⱥıᵹ 11,
(s.l.) Ó ᵹoıꝛeⱥċtⱥ 92; Ó
hOıꝛeⱥċtⱥıᵹ 16, 29, 99.
Gerrard, v. Gerard.
Gerret, v. Garrett.
Gertey, Gerty, mⱥᵹ Oıꝛeⱥċtⱥıᵹ.
Gervase, Gervis, ᵹeⱥꝛḃáꝛ.
Gery, mⱥᵹ ꝼeⱥꝛⱥṫⱥıᵹ.
Getty, mⱥᵹ eıtıᵹ.
Ghagan, mⱥᵹ eⱥċⱥᵹáın.
Ghee, mⱥᵹ ⱥoıṫ.
Ghegan, mⱥᵹ eoċⱥᵹáın.
Gheraty, v. Gerraghty.
Gibb, ᵹıb.
Gibben, Gibbin, mⱥᵹ ꝼıbín.
Gibbings, Gibbins, mⱥc ᵹıob-
úın 2; mⱥᵹ ꝼıbín 2.
Gibbon, Gibbons, Gibbonson,
mⱥc ᵹıobúın.
Giblin, Ó ᵹıbeⱥⱡⱡáın, Ó ᵹıob-
ⱥⱡⱡáın.
Gibney, Giboney, Ó ᵹıbne.
Gibsey, Ó ᵹıbeⱥⱡⱡáın, Ó ᵹıob-
ⱥⱡⱡáın.
Gibson, mⱥc ᵹıb, ᵹıobꝛon,
ᵹıobꝛⱥn 1; Ó ᵹıbeⱥⱡⱡáın, Ó
ᵹıobⱥⱡⱡáın 197, 976.
Gibulawn, Ó ᵹıbeⱥⱡⱡáın, Ó
ᵹıobⱥⱡⱡáın.
Giffen, mⱥᵹ Ṫuıbꝛınn.
Gihon, Ó ᵹⱥoıċín.
Gilberson, v. Gilbertson.
Gilbert, ᵹıⱡbeⱥꝛt.
Gilbertson, mⱥc ᵹıⱡbeıꝛt, mⱥc
ᵹıⱡⱡıbeıꝛt.

Gilbey, Gilboy, mⱥc ᵹıoⱡⱡⱥ-
ḃuıṫe 16, 93, Ó ᵹıoⱡⱡⱥḃuıṫe
16.
Gilbride, mⱥc ᵹıoⱡⱡⱥ Ḃꝛíᵹṫe.
Gilchreest, Gilchriest, Gilchrist,
Gilcrest, Gilcriest, Gilcrist,
mⱥc ᵹıoⱡⱡⱥ Ċꝛíoꝛt.
Gildea, mⱥc ᵹıoⱡⱡⱥ Ṫé.
Gildowney, mⱥc ᵹıoⱡⱡⱥ Ṫoṁ-
nⱥıᵹ.
Gilduff, mⱥc ᵹıoⱡⱡⱥṫuıḃ.
Giles, Ó ᵹⱡⱥıꝛne 376.
Gilfeather, Gilfedder, mⱥc
ᵹıoⱡⱡⱥ Ꝑeⱥṫⱥıꝛ.
Gilfillan, Gilfilland, mⱥc ᵹıoⱡⱡⱥ
ꝼⱥoⱡáın.
Gilfoyle, mⱥc ᵹıoⱡⱡⱥ Ꝑóıⱡ.
Gilgan, v. Gilligan.
Gilgar, mⱥc ᵹıoⱡⱡⱥᵹeáꝛꝛ.
Gilgrinn, mⱥc ᵹıoⱡⱡⱥᵹꝛınn.
Gilgunn, mⱥc ᵹıoⱡⱡⱥṫuınn.
Gilheany, mⱥc ᵹıoⱡⱡⱥ Cⱥınnıᵹ.
Gilhool, mⱥc ᵹıoⱡⱡⱥ Coṁᵹⱥıⱡⱡ.
Gilhooly, mⱥc ᵹıoⱡⱡⱥᵹuⱥⱡⱥ,
mⱥc ᵹıoⱡⱡⱥꝛúıⱡıᵹ.
Gilkelly, mⱥc ᵹıoⱡⱡⱥ Ceⱥⱡⱡⱥıᵹ.
Gilkeson, Gilkinson. Gilkison
mⱥc Uıⱡcín.
Gill, mⱥc ⱥn ᵹoıⱡⱡ 11; mⱥᵹ
ᵹıoⱡⱡⱥ 64.
Gillan, Gilland, Gillane, Ó
ᵹıoⱡⱡáın.
Gillanders, mⱥc ᵹıoⱡⱡⱥ ⱥın-
oꝛéıꝛ.
Gillaspy, mⱥc ᵹıoⱡⱡⱥ eⱥꝛpuıᵹ.
Gillbee, v. Gilbey.
Gilleece, mⱥc ᵹıoⱡⱡⱥ Íoꝛⱥ.
Gilleen, Ó ᵹıⱡín.
Gilleland, mⱥc ᵹıoⱡⱡⱥ ꝼⱥoⱡáın.
Gillen, Ó ᵹıⱡín 9; Ó ᵹıoⱡⱡáın 6.
Gilleran, mⱥc ᵹıoⱡⱡⱥꝛáın, (o.f.)
mⱥc ᵹıoⱡⱡⱥ éⱥnáın, (s.l.) Ó
ᵹıoⱡⱡⱥꝛáın 92.
Gillesby, Gillespie, mⱥc ᵹıoⱡⱡⱥ
eⱥꝛpuıᵹ.
Gillick, mⱥᵹ Uıⱡıc, mⱥᵹ Uıⱡⱡıc.

Gilligan, Ó Giollagáin 1; Mac Giollagáin 66.
Gillilan, Gilliland, Mac Giolla Faoláin.
Gillinan, Mac Giolla Fionnáin.
Gillinnion, Mac Giolla Finnéin
Gillis, Mac Giolla Íosa.
Gillispie, Mac Giolla Easpuig.
Gillivan, Mac Giollabáin.
Gillon, Ó Gilín 9; Ó Giolláin 6.
Gillooly, Mac Giollaguala.
Gilloon, Mac Giolla Eóin.
Gilloway, Mac Giollabuíde.
Gillowly, Mac Giollaguala.
Gilmartin, Mac Giolla Mhártain
Gilmary, Mac Giolla Mhuire.
Gilmer, Gilmor, Mac Giollamír 29; Mac Giolla Mhuire 68, 92.
Gilmore, Gilmour, Mac Giolla Mhuire.
Gilpatrick, Mac Giolla Pádraig.
Gilpin, Mac Giollapinn.
Gilrain, Gilrane, Mac Giollaráin.
Gilroy, Mac Giollaruaid.
Gilsenan, Gilshenan, Gilshenon, Gilson, Mac Giolla Seanáin, Mac Giolla Sionáin 11, (s.l.) Mag Uinnseannáin, Mag Uinnrionnáin, Ó Cuinriogán, 67, 86.
Giltenan, Giltenane, Giltinane, Mac Giolla tSeanáin.
Gilvanny, Gilvany, Mac Giolla Mheana.
Gilvarry, Mac Giolla Bhearaigh.
Gilvoy, Gilwee, Mac Giollabuíde.
Ginaty, Ginity, Mag Finneachtaigh, Mag Fionnachtaigh, &c;
Ginivan, Mag Duinneabhain.
Ginley, Mag Fionngaile.
Ginn, Mag Finn.
Ginna, Mag Cineáit.
Ginnane, Ó Cuineáin, Ó Cuinneáin 76; Mag Cineáit 762.
Ginnaw, Mag Cineáit.

Ginnell, Mag Fionnghail.
Ginnelly, Mag Fionnghaile.
Ginnity, Ginty, Mag Finneachtaigh, Mag Fionnachtaigh, &c.
Gipsey, Ó Gioballáin, Ó Gibealláin.
Girvan, Girvin, (?) Ó Garbháin, Ó Garbín.
Givan, Giveen, Given, Givin, Mag Duibhín.
Glackan, Ó Glacáin.
Gladdery, Gladdry, Ó Gleadhra 9; Mac Gleadhra 6.
Glaffey, Mag Flaitim, Mag Laitim, Mag Lathaigh.
Glakan, Ó Glacáin.
Glancy, Mag Flanncadha, Mag Flanncaidh.
Glanders, Mac Giolla Aindréis.
Glanfield, de Glainbhíol.
Glanny, a' Gleanna.
Glanton, a' Gleanntáin.
Glanville, de Glainbhíol.
Glashby, Glaspy, Mac Giolla Easpuig.
Glasheen, Ó Glaisín.
Glass, Glas.
Glassett. Glaiséid.
Glavey, Mag Flaitim, Mag Laitim, Mag Lathaigh.
Glavin, Ó Gláimín.
Gleasure, Gléasúr.
Gleeson, Ó Gliasáin, (o.f.) Ó Glasáin.
Glenane, Mag Leannáin.
Glenn, de Glin 2; a' Gleanna 2
Glennon, Mag Leannáin.
Glenny, a' Gleanna.
Glessane, Ó Glasáin.
Glinn, de Glin. V. Glynn, Glenn.
Glissane, Glissawn, Ó Glasáin, Ó Gliasáin.
Gloon, Mac Giolla Eóin.
Glorney, (?) Ó Glóiairn.
Glynn, Mag Floinn 11; de Glinn 2.
Gna, Mag Cineáit.

Goan, v. Gowan.
Gobin, Ó ʒobáin, Ó ʒuibín.
Goddan, Ó ʒováin.
Godfrey, mac ʒoʈpaiʋ 1; Ó
ʒoʈpaiʋ 17, 27; ʒoʈpaiʋ 2.
Godrick, maʒ ualʒairʒ.
Godwin, ʒoiʋín E 1; Ó ʒoiʋín
192, Ó ʒováin 2 (O'D.); Ó
Veaʒaiʋ, Ó Viaʒaiʋ 91.
Goff, ʒoʈ 7, 8; maʒ eoʈaʈ,
maʒ eoʈava 6, 9.
Gogan mac eoʈaʒáin 1; ʒoʒán,
ʒóʒan, ʒaʒain, 2.
Gogarty, Gogerty, maʒ ʈóʒaʈt-
aiʒ.
Goggan, Goggin, Goggins, ve
coʒán, ʒoʒán.
Gogin, v. Gogan, Goggin.
Gohary, v. Godfrey.
Going, mac an ʒovann.
Golagley, Golagly, mac an
ʒallóʒlaiʒ.
Golden, ʒúilín 8, 72; Ó ʒoill-
iʋe, (o.f.) Ó ʒoillín 49, 77;
mac cuallaʈta, (s.l.) Ó
ʒuallaʈta 19, 29; maʒ ual-
ʒairʒ 91; Ó ʒavláin 976.
Goldie, ʒúiliʋe.
Golding, v. Golden.
Goldrick, maʒ ualʒairʒ, (s.l.)
mac ʒualpaiʒ, mac ʒual-
paic.
Goligher, Gollagher, Golligher,
Golliher, Gollogher, Golloher.
Ó ʒallʈovaip, Ó ʒallʈuvaip,
Gollan, Ó ʒaláin, Ó ʒalláin,
Gologly, mac an ʒallóʒlaiʒ.
Golrick, maʒ ualʒairʒ.
Gomory, mac iomaipe.
Gonn, ʒunna.
Gonoude, maʒ nuavav, maʒ
nuavat.
Good, ʒuv.
Goodman, ʒoʈmonn E 1; mac
ʒiollamait 64.
Goodwin, v. Godwin.
Googan, maʒ eoʈaʒáin.

Googarty, maʒ ʈuaʒaptaiʒ,
maʒ ʈóʒaptaiʒ.
Goold, Goolde, ʒúl.
Goolden, v. Golden.
Gooley, ʒúiliʋe 1; Ó ʒavalaiʒ
15.
Goonan, Goonane, Ó ʒamnáin.
Goonery, Goonry, Ó ʒamnaipe.
Gooney, Ó ʒamna.
Gooravan, maʒ Sampaváin,
Goorey, Ó ʒuaipe.
Gordon, ve ʒópvún, ʒópvún,
ʒópvan 1; maʒ muipneaʈ-
áin 19, 38, (s.l.) maʒ ʒuap-
naʈáin 19; mópvoipneaʈ
19.
Gore, ve ʒaop.
Gorevan, maʒ Sampaváin.
Gorey, Ó ʒuaipe.
Gorham, ve ʒupam, (s.l.) Ó
ʒuaipim 97.
Gorish, maʒ ʈeópaip.
Gormagan, Ó ʒopmaʒáin.
Gormally, Gormaly, v. Gormley.
Gorman, Ó ʒopmáin 11; mac
ʒopmáin 35, 76; Ó ʒopmóʒ
192 (O'D.); Ó ʒopmʒail,
(s.l.) Ó ʒopmʈúil 19, 97, Ó
ʒopmʒaile, (s.l.) Ó ʒopm-
ʈúiliʒ 192.
Gormican, Ó copmaʈáin.
Gormilly, Gormley, Ó ʒoipm-
ʈleaʒaiʒ, Ó ʒoipmleaʒaiʒ 6;
Ó ʒopmʒaile, (s.l.) Ó ʒopm-
ʈúiliʒ 91, Ó ʒopmʒail, (s.l.)
Ó ʒopmʈúil 192; mac
ʒopmʒaile 2.
Gorry, mac ʒoʈpaiʋ.
Goslin, Gosling, ʒóiplín.
Gosnall, Gosnell, ʒóiʈéip.
Gossan, Ó ʒuráin.
Gosselin, ʒóiplín.
Gosson, Ó ʒuráin.
Gostlin, ʒóiplín.
Gough, ʒoʈ 7, 8; maʒ eoʈaʈ
6, 9; Ó cuaʈáin 192 (O'D.)
Gould, ʒúl.

Goulding, Ṡúilín 8, 72; Ó
Ṡoilliḋe, (o.f.) Ó Ṡoillín 49
77; Ó Ṡaḃláin 976; Mag
Ualġairiġ 91; Mac Cuallaċta,
(s.l.) Ó Ṡuallaċta, 19, 29

Gouldrick, Goulrick, Mag Ualġairiġ.

Gouldy, Ṡúiliḋe.

Gourley, Mag Ṫoirḋealḃaiġ.

Governey, (?) Mac Coiḃḃeanaiġ.

Gow, Ṡoḃa 2; Mac an Ṡoḃa 2.

Gowan, Gowen, Gowing, Mac
an Ṡoḃann, Mac an Ṡaḃann
1; Ó Ṡoḃann, Ó Ṡaḃann 67.

Gowran, Ó Ṡaḃráin.

Grace, Ṡráp.

Graddy, Ó Ṡreaḋa.

Graden, Mag Ḃraḋáin.

Grady, Ó Ṡráḋa 11; Ó Ṡreaḋa
72; Mag Riaḋa, (s.l.) Ó
Ṡraḋa 19, 97.

Graeme, Graham, Ó Ṡréaċáin
11, (s.l.) Ó Ṡreióm 72.

Grainger, Ṡráinréir.

Grame, v. Graham.

Grandan, Grandon, ḋe Ṡranḋún, Ṡranḋún.

Grange, Ṡráinreaċ.

Granger, Ṡráinréir.

Grannell, Mag Raṡnaill.

Grannon, Ó Ṡranáin.

Granny, Mag Ráiċne, Mag
Ṡráinne, Mag Ṡránna 2;
Ṡránna, Ṡránḋa 2.

Grant, ḋe Ṡrannt, Ṡrannt 11;
Mag Ṡránna 64; Ṡránḋa 2.

Grattan, (?) Mag Reaċtain,
(o.f.) Mag Neaċtain. Cf.
Natton.

Graves, v. Greaves.

Gray, ḋe Ṡrae, Ṡrae E 1; Liaċ
976; Mac Ṡiollaṁraḃaiġ ḃ.

Grayhan, Ó Ṡréaċáin.

Gready, v. Grady.

Greaghan, Greaham, Greahan,
Ó Ṡréaċáin.

Grealish, Ó Ṡriall. uir, Mag
Riallġuir, (o.f.) Mag Niallġuir.

Greally, Grealy, Mag Raṡall
aiġ, (s.l.) Ó Ṡrálaiġ, Ó
Ṡraolaiġ 19; Ó Ṡriall.uir,
Mag Rialluir, (o.f.) Mag
Niallġuir 972.

Greame, Greames, Ó Ṡréaċáin.

Greaney, Greany, Ó Ṡráinne.

Grear, v. Greer.

Greaven, Ó Ṡríoḃċáin, (s.l.) Ó
Ṡraḃáin.

Greaves, ḋe Ṡréiḃ E 1; Ó
Ṡríoḃċáin, (s.l.) Ó Ṡraḃáin
976.

Greehy, Ó Ṡríoċa, (o.f.) Ó
Ṡríoḃċa.

Greely, v. Grealy.

Green, ḋe Ṡraoin 17, 18, 47;
Ó huaiċne, Ó huainiḋe 779,
Ó huaiċnín 19, 27, 46; Mac
Ṡlaráin, Mac Ṡlairín 26, 64;
Mac Ṡiollaṡlair 16; uaiċne,
2; Ṡlar 2; Ó huiḋrín 992;
Ó faċaiġ 972 (O'D.)

Greenan, Ó Ṡranáin, (o.f.) Mag
Ḃraonáin 29.

Greene, v. Green.

Greer, Mac Ṡrioġair 1 (s.i.)
Ṡraḃar. 19.

Gregan, Ó Ṡréaċáin.

Gregory, Ṡréaṡóir 1; Mac
Ṡréaṡair, Mac Ṡrioṡair 2.

Greham, Grehan, Ó Ṡréaċáin.

Greir, v. Greer.

Grene, v. Green.

Grennan, Ó Ṡranáin.

Grevin, v. Greaven.

Grey, v. Gray.

Greyhan, Ó Ṡréaċáin.

Gribben, Gribbin, Gribbon, Mag
Roiḃín 1; Ó Ṡriḃín 16.

Grier, v. Greer.

Grieves, v. Greaves.

Griffey, Ó Ṡríoḃċa.

Griffin, Ᵹᴘᴉᴘᴉn 47 ; Ó Ᵹᴘᴉᴘᴉn, Ó
Ᵹᴘᴉ́ᴠᴄᴉn 79 ; Ó Ᵹᴘᴉoᴠᴄᴀ 71,
91 ; Ó Ᵹᴘᴉoᴠᴄᴀᴉn 27, 972 ;
ᴍᴀᵹ nᴉᴀᴌᴌᵹᴜᴉᴘ, (s.l.) ᴍᴀᵹ
Rᴉᴀᴌᴌᵹᴜᴉᴘ, Ó Ᵹᴘᴉᴀᴌᴌᴜᴉᴘ 192,
972.
Griffith, Griffiths, Ó Ᵹᴘᴉoᴠᴄᴀ
91, Ó Ᵹᴘᴉoᴠᴄᴀᴉn 976.
Griffy, Ó Ᵹᴘᴉoᴠᴄᴀ.
Grimes, Ó Ᵹᴘᴇᴉ́oᴍ (S.L.) 7 ;
Ó Ᵹᴘᴇ́ᴀᴄᴀᴉn 62, 91 ; Ó Ᵹoᴘᴍ-
ᵹᴀᴉᴌᴇ 192 ; Ó Coᴉnᴌᴇᴉᴘc, Ó
Coᴉnᴌᴉᴘc 199.
Grimley, v. Gormley, Grumley.
Groarke, ᴍᴀᵹ Rᴜᴀᴉᴘc.
Groden, ᴍᴀᵹ Roᴠᴀᴉn 29 ; ᴍᴀᵹ
Ꝺᴘᴀᴠᴀᴉn 38.
Grogan, Groggan, Ó Ᵹᴘᴜᴀᵹᴀᴉn,
Ó Ᵹᴘᴜ́ᵹᴀᴉn.
Gronel, ᴍᴀᵹ Rᴀᵹnᴀᴉᴌᴌ.
Groogan, v. Grogan.
Grosby, ᴍᴀc ᴀn Cᴘoᴘᴀᴉn.
Grourke, ᴍᴀᵹ Rᴜᴀᴉᴘc.
Grubb, ᴍᴀᵹ Roᴠ.
Grumley, Ó Ᵹoᴉᴘᴍᴌᴇᴀᵹᴀᴉᵹ.
Grummell, Ᵹᴘoᴍᴀᴉᴌ.
Gubbins, Ó Ᵹᴜᴉᴠᴉn, Ó Ᵹoᴉᴠᴉn.
Guckeane, Gucken, Guckian,
ᴍᴀᵹ ᴇoᴄᴀᴉᴠᴉn.
Guerin, Ó Ᵹᴇ́ᴀᴘᴀᴉn 7 ; ᴍᴀᵹ
ᴜᴉᴠᴘᴉn 38.
Guigan, ᴍᴀᵹ ᴇoᴄᴀᴉᴠᴉn, ᴍᴀᵹ
ᴇoᴄᴀᴉn.
Guighan, Guihan, Guiheen,
Guihen, Ó Ᵹᴀoᴉᴄᴉn 2 ; ᴍᴀc
Ᵹᴀoᴉᴄᴉn 2.
Guiken, ᴍᴀᵹ ᴇoᴄᴀᴉᴠᴉn.
Guilchrist, ᴍᴀc Ᵹᴉoᴌᴌᴀ Cᴘᴉoᴘc.
Guilfoyle, ᴍᴀc Ᵹᴉoᴌᴌᴀ ᴘóᴉᴌ.
Guilliland, ᴍᴀc Ᵹᴉoᴌᴌᴀ ꝼᴀoᴌᴀᴉn.
Guilmartin, ᴍᴀc Ᵹᴉoᴌᴌᴀ ᴍᴀᴘ-
ᴄᴀᴉn.
Guina, ᴍᴀᵹ Cᴉnᴇᴀᴉᴄ.
Guinan, Guinane, Ó Cᴜᴉnᴇᴀᴉn, Ó
Cᴜᴉnnᴇᴀᴉn l ; Ó Ᵹᴀᴉᴠnᴇᴀᴉn 778.
Guinea, Guinee,Ó Ᵹᴜᴉnᴉᴠᴇ(S.L.).
Guinevan, ᴍᴀᵹ Ꝺᴜᴉnnᴇᴀᴠᴀᴉn.

Guiney, Ó Ᵹᴇᴉᴠᴇᴀnnᴀᴉᵹ 7 ; Ó
Ᵹᴜᴉnᴉᴠᴇ. Ó Ᵹᴉnᴉᴠᴇ 49, 776.
Guinna, ᴍᴀᵹ Cᴉnᴇᴀᴉᴄ.
Guinnane, Ó Cᴜᴉnnᴇᴀᴉn.
Guinnaty, ᴍᴀᵹ ꝼᴉonnᴀᴄᴄᴀ, ᴍᴀᵹ
ꝼᴉonnᴀᴄᴄᴀᴉᵹ, &c.
Guinness, ᴍᴀᵹ ᴀonᵹᴜᴉᴘ, ᴍᴀᵹ
ᴀonᵹᴜᴘᴀ.
Guiny, v. Guiney.
Guiry, Ó Ᵹᴀᴠᴘᴀ.
Gulan, Gullan, Ó Ᵹoᴌᴌᴀᴉn.
Gullion, Ᵹᴉᴌᴌᴇᴀn.
Gully, v. Gooley.
Gumbleton, Ᵹᴜᴍᴀᴘᴄᴜn.
Gunn, Ᵹᴜnnᴀ l ; ᴍᴀc Ᵹᴉoᴌᴌᴀ-
ᴠᴜᴉnn 29.
Gunnell, ᴍᴀᵹ Conᵹᴀᴉᴌ.
Gunner, Ᵹᴜnnᴀᴘ.
Gunnigan, ᴍᴀᵹ Ꝺonnᴀᵹᴀᴉn.
Gunnigle, ᴍᴀᵹ Conᵹᴀᴉᴌ.
Gunning, Ó Conᴀᴉnᵹ 76 (O'D.) ;
Ó Ᵹᴀᴍnᴀᴉn 46, 87.
Gunshinan, ᴍᴀᵹ ᴜᴉnnᴘᴇᴀnnᴀᴉn,
ᴍᴀᵹ ᴜᴉnnᴘᴉonnᴀᴉn, Ó Cᴜᴉn-
ᴘᴉoᵹᴀn, (o.f.) ᴍᴀc Ᵹᴉoᴌᴌᴀ
Sᴇᴀnᴀᴉn.
Gurrin, ᴍᴀᵹ Coᴘᴘᴀᴉn, ᴍᴀᵹ
Coᴘᴘᴀᴉᴠᴉn.
Gurdan, v. Jordan.
Gurry, ᴍᴀc Ᵹoᴄᴘᴀᴠ.
Gutherie, Guthrie, Guttery, Ó
ᴌᴀᴉᴄᴉᴍ, Ó ᴌᴀᴄᴀᴉᵹ.
Guy, Ᵹᴜᴉᴠ.
Gware, ᴠᴇ Ᵹᴀoᴘ.
Gweehin, Ó Ᵹᴀoᴉᴄᴉn.
Gwyn, Gwynn, Gwynne, Ᵹᴜᴉn.
Gyles, Ó Ᵹᴌᴀᴉᴘnᴇ 64.

Habbagan, ᴎoᴠᴀᴄᴀn.
Habbert, ᴎoᴉᴠᴇᴀᴘᴠ.
Hackett, ᴎᴀᴉcᴇᴉᴠ l : ᴎᴀᴄᴀᴇᴠ,
ᴀᴉcᴇᴉᴠ, ᴀᴄᴀᴠᴠ 2 ; ᴍᴀc ᴎᴀᴉc-
ᴇᴉᴠ 972 ; ᴍᴀc ᴇᴀᴄᴀᴉᴠ, ᴍᴀᵹ
ᴇᴀᴄᴀᴉᴠ 23, 35.
Hadden, v. Haddon.
Haddigan, Ó ᴎᴇᴉᴠᴇᴀᵹᴀᴉn.
Haddon, Haden, Hadian, Ó ᴎᴀᴉᴠ-
ᴉn, Ó ᴎᴇᴉᴠᴉn, Ó ᴎᴇᴉᴠᴇᴀᴉn.

Hadnet, v. Hodnett.
Hafferon, Haffron, Ó hAṁṗáɲ.
Haffy, Ó heAċAıṁ.
Hagan, Hagans, Ó háɠáın
(o.f.) Ó hÓɠáın 61 ; Ó hAoṁ-
Aɠáın 8, 62 ; mAc AoṁAɠáın
2.
Hagarty, Hagerty, Ó héıɠceAɲc-
Aıɡ, Ó héıɠeAɲcAıɡ 19, 46,
63, 77 ; Ó háɠAɲcAıɡ, Ó
háɠAɲcAıɡ 64, 82.
Haggan, Haggans, v. Hagan.
Haggarty, v. Hagarty.
Haggens, v. Hagans.
Haggerty, v. Hagerty.
Haghan, Haghen, Ó heAċáın.
Haghey, Ó heAċAıṁ.
Hagin, v. Hagan.
Hahasy, Hahessy, Ó hAıċeAɲA.
Hahee, Ó heAċAıṁ.
Haidee, Haidy, Ó háıoıċ, Ó
háıoıṁe, Ó háıoeıċ, Ó
héıoıṁ, Ó héıoeAṁA.
Haier, Ó hOıċıɲ.
Haigney, v. Heagney.
Hainen, v. Heanen.
Haines, Ó héıṁın.
Hainey, v. Heaney.
Hair, Haire, Ó híɲ 3 ; Ó hAıċıɲ,
Ó hOıċıɲ 4 ; Ó ɠıoɲɲAıṁe,
(o.f.) mAɠ ḟeAɲAṁAıɡ 976.
Hale, Hales, mAc hAol.
Halferty, Ó hAılḃeAɲcAıɡ.
Halfpenny, Ó hAılpín, (o.f.) Ó
hAılpene, (s.l.) Ó hAlpAn
376.
Hall, ṽe hál.
Hallaghan, Hallahan, Ó hAllAċ-
áın, Ó hAılleAċáın.
Hallan, Ó hAllAṁAın, (o.f.) Ó
ḟAllAṁAın.
Hallanan, Ó hAılɠeAnáın.
Halleran, Ó hAllṁuɲáın.
Hallessy, Ó háılɠeAɲA.
Halley, v. Hally.
Halligan, Ó hAllAɠáın, Ó
hAılleAɠáın.

Hallihan, Hallihane, Ó hAılleAċ-
áın.
Hallin, Ó hAılín, Ó hAıllín.
Hallinan, Ó hAılɠeAnáın.
Hallion, Ó hAılín, Ó hAıllín.
Hallissey, Hallissy, Ó háıl-
ɠeAɲA.
Halloran, Ó hAllṁuɲáın.
Hally, Ó hAılċe 17, 27 ; Ó
hAılle 46 ; Ó hAllAıṁe 47.
Halpeny, Halpin, Ó hAılpín.
Haltigan, Ó hulcAċáın.
Halton, ṽe hálcún.
Halvey, ṽe hAlḃuıṁe, hAl-
ḃuıṁe, hAluıṁe 1 ; Ó hAıl-
ṁıc 19, 97.
Hamell, Hamill, Ó háṁmAıll,
Hamilton, ṽe hAmAlcún,
hAmAlcún 1, (s.l.) Ó hAm-
Aıllcín 469 ; Ó huɲmolcAıɡ
7779.
Hamlen, Hamlin, Hamlyn,
hAımlín.
Hammell, Hammill, Ó háṁ-
mAıll, Ó háɡmAıll.
Hammon, Hammond, hámonn
1 ; hAmon 2 ; mAc Amoınn
2.
Hamondson, mAc Amoınn.
Hampton, ṽe hAmcún.
Hamrock, Hamrogue, hAmɲóc,
hAmɲóɡ 1 ; SeAmɲóɡ 976.
Hanafey, v. Hanify.
Hanafin, Ó hAınɲeáın, Ó hAın-
ɲín, Ó hAınıɲeáın, Ó hAını-
ɲín, (o.f.) Ó hAınḃċeáın, Ó
hAınḃċín.
Hanafy, v. Hanify.
Hanan, Ó hAnnáın.
Hanaty, Ó hıonnAċcAıɡ, (o.f.)
Ó ḟıonnAċcAıɡ.
Hanberry, Hanbery Hanbury
ṽe hAnḃɲuɠA 2, Ó hAın-
ṁıɲe, Ó hAınṁıɲeAċ, (s.l.) Ó
hAınmneAċ, Ó AınmneAċ 97.
Hancock, hAncóc.

Hand, Mᴀꞅ Lᴀɪᴄɪṁ (s.l.) Mᴀꞅ
Lᴀɪṁ 29, 39, 55 ; Mᴀꞅ Lᴀɪᴄ-
ɪṁín, (o.f.) Mᴀꞅ Flᴀɪᴄɪṁín,
(s.l.) Mᴀꞅ Lᴀɪṁín 19, 34.
Handbury, v. Hanbury.
Handcock, hᴀncóc.
Handlon, v. Hanlon.
Handly, v. Hanly.
Handrahan, v. Hanrahan.
Handrick, v. Hanrick.
Hands, v. Hand.
Haneen, v. Hanneen.
Hanefan, v. Hanifan.
Hanephy, v. Hanify.
Hanheen, v. Hanneen.
Hanick v. Hanwick.
Hanifan, Hanifin, Ó hᴀɪnꝼeᴀɪn,
Ó hᴀɪnꝼín, Ó hᴀɪnɪꝼeᴀɪn, Ó
hᴀɪnɪꝼín, (o.f.) Ó hᴀɪnḃ-
ᴄeᴀn, Ó hᴀɪnḃᴄín.
Hanify, Ó hᴀɪnꝼɪᴄ, Ó hᴀɪnꝼɪṁ,
(o.f.) Ó hᴀɪnḃeɪᴄ, Ó hᴀɪnḃɪᴄ,
(s.l.) Ó hᴀɪnᴄe, Ó hᴀnᴀɪᴄe
972.
Hanihan, Ó hᴀnnᴀcᴀɪn.
Hankard, hᴀncᴀꞃᴅ.
Hanlan, v. Hanlon.
Hanley, Ó hᴀɪnlɪꝛe, Ó hᴀɪn-
lɪꝛe, Ó hᴀɪnle, Ó hᴀɪnle.
Hanlin, Hanlon, Ó hᴀnnlᴜᴀɪn,
Ó hᴀnlᴜᴀɪn 1, (s.l.) Ó hᴀnn-
lᴀɪn 2.
Hanly, v. Hanley.
Hanna, *Ó hᴀnnᴀɪṁ.
Hannafy, v. Hanify.
Hannahan, Ó hᴀnnᴀcᴀɪn.
Hannan, Ó hᴀɪnnín, Ó hᴀɪncín
11 ; Ó hᴀnnᴀɪn 17, 75 ; Ó
hᴀnnᴀcᴀɪn 2 ;.
Hannaway, v. Hanway.
Hanneen, Ó hᴀɪnnín, Ó hᴀɪn-
cín.
Hannell, Ó hɪonnꝶᴀɪl, (o.f.) Ó
Fɪonnꝶᴀɪl.
Hannen, v. Hannan.
Hannerty, Ó hɪonnᴀcᴛᴀɪꝶ.
Hannify v. Hanify

Hannigan, Ó hᴀnnᴀꝶᴀɪn.
Hannin, Hannon Hanon.
Hannan.
Hanrahan, Ó hᴀnꞃᴀcᴀɪn.
Hanratty, Ó hᴀnꞃᴀᴄᴛᴀɪꝶ.
Hanrick, Ó hᴀnnꞃᴀɪc, Ó heᴀn
ꞃᴀɪc.
Hanvey, Hanvy, Hanway, Ó
hᴀɪnḃɪᴄ, Ó hᴀɪnḃeɪᴄ.
Hanwick, (?) Ó hᴀɪlṁɪc.
Hara, Ó heᴀꝶꞃᴀ, Ó heᴀóꞃᴀ.
Haraghy, Ó heᴀꞃᴄᴀṁᴀ, Ó heᴀꞃ-
ᴄᴀɪṁ.
Harald, v. Harold.
Haran, Ó heᴀꞃᴀɪn 6 ; Ó heᴀꝶ-
ꞃᴀɪn 97, Ó heᴀᴄꞃᴀɪn 2 ; Ó
hᴀꞃꞃᴀᴄᴀɪn 27, 45 ; Ó hᴀnn-
ꞃᴀɪn 732.
Harberd, Harbert, hoɪꞃeᴀḃᴀꞃᴅ,
hoɪꞃeᴀḃᴀꞃᴅ.
Harbin, hoɪꞃḃín.
Harbinson, Harbison, Mᴀc
hoɪꞃḃín.
Harden, Mᴀc ꝶɪollᴀ ᴅeᴀcᴀɪꞃ.
Hardford, ᴅe heᴀꞃꝼoꞃᴛ.
Hardiman, Ó hᴀꞃꝶᴀṁᴀɪn, Ó
hᴀɪꞃꝶeᴀṁᴀɪn.
Harding, Hardinge, hᴀɪꞃṁín.
Hardman, heᴀꞃmᴀn.
Hardwood, hᴀꞃóᴅ.
Hardy, Mᴀc ꝶɪollᴀ ᴅeᴀcᴀɪꞃ.
Hare, Ó híꞃ 3 ; Ó hᴀɪcɪꞃ, Ó
hoɪcɪꞃ 4 ; Ó ꝶɪoꞃꞃᴀɪᴅe, (o.ᴄ.)
Mᴀꞅ Feᴀꞃᴀṁᴀɪꝶ 976.
Harel, v. Harrell.
Haren, v. Haran.
Harford, ᴅe heᴀꞃꝼoꞃᴛ.
Hargadan, Hargaden, Harga-
don, Ó hᴀꞃꝶᴀṁᴀɪn, Ó hᴀɪꞃ-
ꝶeᴀṁᴀɪn.
Hargan, v. Horgan.
Harhan, Harhen, v. Haran.
Harkan, Ó heᴀꞃcᴀɪn 6 ; Ó
hoꞃcᴀɪn 19, 46.
Harkey, Ó heᴀꞃcᴀɪṁ.
Harkin, Harkins, Harkon, v.
Harkan.

Hartey, Ó heαrgαile.
Harman, Harmon, heαrmαn 1; Ó hαrgαdáin 97; mαcgiollα ʋeαcαir 37.
Harnedy, Harnett, Ó hαirtnéαʋα.
Harney, Ó hαtαirne, (s.l.) Ó háirne.
Harnon, Ó heαrnáin.
Harold, hαróiʋ, αróiʋ, αrαlt 1; Ó hαrαilt 17.
Haroughten, Haroughton, Ó hαrrαctáin.
Harper, Harpur, ʋe hαrpúr, hαrpúr.
Harragher, Harraher, Ó heαrcαir, (o.f.) Ó feαrcαir.
Harren, v. Haran.
Harrel, Harrell, Ó heαrgαil, (o.f.) Ó feαrgαil.
Harren, v. Haran.
Harrett, v. Harrot.
Harricks, Ó heirc.
Harries, v. Harris.
Harrigan, Ó hαrrαgáin.
Harrihy, Ó heαrcαiʋ.
Harrington, Ó hαrrαctáin 73, 95; Ó hαireαctαig 16, 29, 55, 462, 498; Ó hiongαrʋαil, (s.l.) Ó húrʋαil 77, 277, 497.
Harris, hαirir E 1; mαc hαnnrαoi, mαc αnnrαoi 2; mαc eαnnrαic 47; Ó heαrcαʋα, Ó heαrcαiʋ 19.
Harrison, mαc αnnrαoi, mαc hαnnrαoi 1; Ó heαrcαʋα, Ó heαrcαiʋ 19.
Harrity, Ó hαireαctαig.
Harroe, Ó heαrcαʋα.
Harrold, v. Harold.
Horron, v. Haran.
Harroughton, Ó hαrrαctáin.
Harrot, hαróiʋ.
Hart, Harte, Ó háirt 11; mαc áirt 2; hαrt E 62.
Hartan, Harten, Ó hαrtáin.
Hartery, Ó hαirtrí.

Hartford, ʋe heαrrort.
Hartican, Hartigan, Ó hαrtαgáin.
Hartin, Ó hαrtáin.
Hartley, Ó hαrtgαile.
Hartnane, Ó heαrnáin.
Hartnett, Ó hαirtnéαʋα.
Hartney, Ó hαtαirne.
Harton, Ó hαrtáin.
Hartry, Ó hαirtrí.
Harty, Ó hαtαrtαig, (s.l.) Ó hártαig, Ó hártα 4; mαc αrtα 197; Ó hαireαctαig 52.
Harvey, Ó hαirmheαʋαig 1; E 28.
Harwood, hαróiʋ.
Hasken, Haskin, Ó hoircín.
Hassan, Ó horáin.
Hassett, Hassey, Ó hαireαʋα.
Hassin, Hasson, Ó horáin.
Hastie, mαc hoirte, mαc oirte
Hasting, Hastings, Ó hoircín.
Hasty, mαc hoirte, mαc oirte.
Hatton, mαc giollα cαtáin 26, 62.
Haugh, Ó heαcαc.
Haughan, Ó heαcáin.
Haughean, Ó heαcαiʋín.
Haughey, Ó heαcαiʋ, Ó heαcαʋα.
Haughian, Ó heαcαiʋín.
Haughran, Ó heαcráin.
Haughton, ʋe hoctún 11; Ó heαcáin 38.
Haveran, Havern, Haveron, v. Heveran.
Haverty, Ó hábαrtαig.
Havey, v. Heavey.
Havron, v. Heveran.
Havy, v. Heavey.
Hawe, Hawes, Hawey, Ó heαcαc, Ó heαcαʋα, Ó heαcαiʋ.
Hawkins, háicín E 1; Ó heαcáin, Ó heαcαiʋín 38.
Hay, ʋe hαe 28; Ó hαoʋα 2.

Hayden, Haydin, Haydon, Ó heroeáin, Ó héroeáin, Ó heroín, Ó héroín 11 ; ve héavún 18.

Hayes, Ó haová 11 ; mac aová 197 ; ve hae 28.

Haytron, v. Haffron and Heveran.

Hayles, mac haol 2 ; Ó healaíve 37.

Haynan, v. Heenan.

Haynes, Ó héroín.

Hays, v. Hayes.

Hayward, héibeapt.

Hazel, Hazelton, Hazleton. Hazelwood mac Concollcoille.

Headen, Headon, v. Hayden.

Heafy, v. Heaphy.

Heagan, Ó haováşáin.V.Hagan.

Heagney, Ó heişniş, Ó héişniş.

Healion, Ó haoláin.

Heally, Healy, Ó héilíve, Ó héilişe 11, Ó healaíve 2, Ó hcaluişte 77, Ó healuişte 2, (o.f.) Ó healavaiş ; Ó haille 762 ; Ó ceipipe 498.

Heanaghan, Heanahan, Ó héineacáin, Ó héanacáin.

Heanen, v. Heenan.

Heaney, Ó héanna 7, 91, (s.l.) Ó héanaiş 2, Ó héinne 2 ; Ó héiniş 6, 92 ; Ó héanaóa 972 ; mac şiolla Coinniş (s.l.) ma'l ceanac 376.

Heanue, Ó héanaóa, Ó héineaóa.

Heany, v. Heaney.

Heaphy, Ó héaṁtaiş, (s.l.) Ó héapa, (o.f.) Ó héaṁaiş.

Hear, Ó híp.

Hearaghty, Ó hoipeactaiş.

Heare, Ó hípi.

Hearn, Hearne, Ó heactişeipn 7 ; Ó heapáin 6 ; Ó huipóipín 85 ; héapún 87.

Hearnon, Ó hiapnáin.

Hearon, v. Hearn.

Hearty, Ó haşaptaiş, (s.l.) Ó haoptaiş 1 ; mac apta 197.

Heary, Ó hiopuaió.

Heavern, v. Heveran.

Heavey, Heavy, Ó héaṁaiş, Ó héiṁiş.

Hedderman, Ó héavopomáin.

Hedegan, Ó heroeaşáin.

Heden, Ó heroín, Ó héroín. V. Hayden.

Hedigan, Ó heroeaşáin 1 ; Ó haoilleacáin 469.

Hedivan, Heduvan, Ó hcavaṁáin.

Heelan, Ó haoláin, (o.f.) Ó paoláin.

Heenan, Ó héanáin 11 ; Ó héineacáin, Ó héanacáin 192.

Heeney, Heeny, v. Heaney.

Heery, Ó hiopuaió.

Heever, Ó hioṁaip.

Hefferan, Hefferin, v. Heffron.

Heffernan, Heffernin, Heffernon, Ó hipeapnáin 11, Ó heapnáin 72, 82.

Heffron, Ó héiṁpín 19 ; Ó haṁpáin 68 ; Ó huipóipín 85 ; Ó hipeapnáin 7, 78.

Hegan, Hegans, Ó haováşáin. V. Hagan.

Hegarty, Hegerty, Heggarty, Ó héişceaptaiş, Ó héişeaptaiş 19, 46, 63, 77 ; Ó haşaptaiş, Ó haşaptaiş 64, 82.

Heggert, Ó haşaipt.

Heggerty, v. Hegarty.

Hegher, Ó hoicip, Ó haicip.

Hegney, Ó heişniş, Ó héişniş.

Hehir, Ó haicip, Ó hoicip.

Heify, v. Heaphy.

Heins, Ó heroín.

Helbert, Helbet, hoileabaro.

Helehan, Ó haoilleacáin.

Helen, v. Heelan.

Helihan, Hellican, Ó haoilleacáin.

Hely, v. Healy.

Henaghan,Henahan, Ó hĊineaċáin, Ó héanaċáin.

Henan, v. Heenan.

Henchy, Ó háonġuṗa 2 ; mac áonġuṗa 2.

Henderson, mac áinopéiṗ, mac áinoṗiaṗa, mac áinopiú.

Hendrick, Ó heanṗaic.

Hendry v. Henry.

Heneberry, Henebery, Henebry, oe hionbuṗġa, (oe hinoebeṗġ).

Heneghan,Henehan, Ó héineaċáin, Ó héanaċáin.

Henekan, Ó héanaġáin, Ó héanaċáin.

Henery, Ó hinneiṗġe. V. Henry.

Henesy, v. Hennessy.

Heney, v. Heaney.

Henihan, v. Henehan.

Henissy, v. Hennessy.

Henley, v. Hanley.

Hennan, v. Heenan.

Henneberry, Hennebry, oe hionbuṗġa.

Hennelly, Ó hionnġaile.

Hennerty, Ó hionnaċtaiġ, Ó hinneaċtaiġ.

Hennessy, Ó háonġuṗa.

Hennigan, Ó héanaġáin.

Henrick, Ó heanṗaic, Ó heanṗaic.

Henright, v. Enright.

Henrion, Ó hionṗáin, Ó hionnṗáin, (o.f.) Ó hionṗaoáin, Ó hánṗaoáin.

Henry, mac éinṗí, mac ánnṗaoi, mac hannṗaoi 11 ; Ó hinneiṗġe 6.

Hensy, Ó háonġuṗa.

Heraghty, Ó hOiṗeaċtaiġ.

Herald, Ó heaṗġail, (o.f.) Ó ṗeaṗġail.

Heran, v. Hearn.

Heraty, Ó hOiṗeaċtaiġ.

Herbert, hoiṗeabáṗo, hoiṗeabáṗo 11, hoibeáṗo 17, 77.

Herbertson, Herbison, mac hoiṗeabáiṗo, mac hoiṗeabáiṗo.

Herdman, heaṗman.

Hereward, hoiṗeabáṗo.

Herford, oe heaṗṗoṗt.

Herguson, mac ṗeaṗġuṗa.

Herley, Herly, Ó heaṗġaile, Ó hiṗġile 10 ; Ó hiaṗṗlaċa 79.

Herlihy,Ó hiaṗlaċa,Ó hiaṗṗlaċa

Herne, v. Hearne.

Hernon, Ó hiaṗnáin 9, Ó heaṗnáin 2.

Heron, v. Hearn.

Herr, Ó hOiċiṗ.

Herran, Ó heaṗáin. V. Hearn.

Herreran, Herrerin, Ó heaṗaṗáin, Ó heaṗoiṗín.

Herrick, Herricks, Ó heiṗc.

Herrigan, Ó háṗṗaġáin.

Herron, v. Hearn.

Hertnan, Hertnon, Ó heaṗnáin.

Hervy, v. Harvey.

Herward, hoiṗeabáṗo.

Heskin, Ó hOiṗcín, Ó huiṗcín.

Heslin, Ó heiṗlin, Ó heiṗleanáin.

Hessian, Hession, Ó hOiṗín.

Hester, Ó hOiṗtiṗ.

Hestin, Hestings, Hestion, Ó hOiṗtín.

Heuson, mac áoóa.

Hevaghan, Ó héamaċáin, Ó héimeaċáin.

Hever, Ó hiomaiṗ.

Heveran, Heverine, Heveron, Ó héimṗín 9 ; Ó huioṗín 8. Cf. Heffron.

Hevey, Ó héimiġ, Ó héamaiġ.

Hewett, Hewitt, húiġéio.

Hewlett, Hewlitt, húiléio.

Hews, v. Hughes.

Hewson, mac áoóa.

Heydon, v. Hayden.

Heyfron, v. Heffron.

Heyland Ó hAoláin.
Hibbard, hibeáṗ, hiobáṗ.
Hickey Hickie, Ó hiceavá, Ó hicíve.
Hiffernan, Ó hiṗeaṗnáin.
Higerty, Ó héiġeaṗcaiġ.
Higgans, Ó hAováġáin.
Higgens v. Higgans and Higgins
Higgins, Ó huiġinn, Ó huiġín. 1; Ó huiġe 778.
Higginson, mac huiġín.
Highland, Hiland, Ó hAoláin. V. Hyland.
Hilbert, hoileabaṗ.
Hilferty, Ó háilḃeaṗcaiġ.
Hill, a' Cnuic.
Hillan, Hilland, Hillane, Ó hioláin, Ó hAoláin. V. Hyland.
Hillee, Ó hicceallaiġ, (o.f.) Ó ṗicceallaiġ.
Hillen, v. Hillan.
Hilligan, Ó háilleaġáin.
Hillind, v. Hilland.
Hilly, v. Hillee.
Hinan, Ó heivneáin.
Hinchey, Hinchy, Ó hAonġuṗa, (s.l.) Ó hínṗe 2; mac Aonġuṗa 2.
Hinds, Hines, v. Hynes.
Hiney,Ó hAvnaiv,Ó hAivne &c
Hingerty, Hinnerty,Ó hinneáċaiġ, Ó hionnáċaiġ, &c., (o.f.) Ó ṗinneáċaiġ, Ó ṗionnáċaiġ, &c.
Hinsy, v. Hennessy.
Hiraghy, Ó heaṗcaiv.
Hirl, Ó hinġil.
Hishon, Ó huiṗeáin, Ó hoiṗeáin, Ó hoiṗín.
Hiskey, Ó huiṗce.
Histion, Histon, Ó hoiṗcín.
Hoad, Hoade, hóv, hóvaċ.
Hoar, Hoare, ve hóṗ, ve hóṗa, a hóṗa, 17, 18, 74, 84; Ó huiviṗ 772; Ó heaṗcavá 29; Ó hiomaiṗ 762.

Hoban, Ó húbáin.
Hobart, Hobard, hoibeáṗ, hiobáṗ.
Hobbagan, hobacán.
Hobbard, Hobbart, v. Hobart.
Hobbikin, mac hoibicín, mac Oibicín. V. Hopkins.
Hobbs, hob.
Hobert, v. Hobart.
Hobson, mac hob.
Hoctor, Ó heáċaiṗ.
Hodge, hoiṗce.
Hodgkin, hoiṗcicín.
Hodgkins, Hodgkinson, mac hoiṗcicín.
Hodnett, hovnae; (G.p.) mac séaṗca.
Hoey, Ó heocaiv, Ó heácaiv.
Hogan, Ó hóġáin 11; Ó heocaġáin 977; Ó hAováġáin 2.
Hogart, Ó hóġaiṗc.
Hogarty, Hogerty, Ó hóġaṗcaiġ (o.f.) Ó póġaṗcaiġ.
Hogg, Hogge, hoiṗce.
Hoins, Ó heoġáin.
Holahan, Ó huallaċáin.
Holey, Ó hoġlavá, (o.f.) Ó poġlavá.
Holian, Ó hóileáin, (o.f.) Ó paoláin.
Holland, Ó hAoláin 8, 9, 61, (o.f.) Ó paoláin, (s.l.) Ó hualáin 6, 82, Ó holáin 19, Ó hioláin 97; Ó huallaċáin 77; Ó maol Callann 63.
Holleran, Holloran, Ó hallmupáin.
Holloway, Hollway, ve halbuive.
Holly, Ó Cuilinn 2; mac Cuilinn 2.
Hollywood, ve halabóiv, halabóiv 86; Ó Cuileannáin 2.
Holmes, mac Cómaiṗ, mac Támaiṗ, mac Comáiṗ.

Holohan, Holoughan, Ó huaʟʟać-
áın.
Holoway, ᴠe haʟḃuıᴠe.
Holt, Holte, hóʟᴄ.
Holywood, haʟaḃóıᴠ.
Homes, v. Holmes.
Honahan, Ó huaṁnaćáın.
Honan, Ó heoġanáın.
Hone, Ó heoġaın.
Honeen, Ó huaıᴄnín.
Hooban, Ó húḃáın.
Hood, Ó huıᴠ.
Hoolaghan, Hoolahan, Hooli-
han, Hoologhan, Ó huaʟʟać-
áın.
Hooney, Ó huaıᴄne, Ó huaınıᴠe
Ó huaıᴄnıż.
Hop, Hope, hoḃ.
Hopkin, Hopkins, Hopkinson,
mac hoıbıcín, mac Oıbıcín,
(s.l.) Ó hoıbıcín, Ó Coıbıcín,
&c., 19.
Hopps, Hopson, mac hoḃ.
Horogan, v. Horrigan.
Horahan, Ó happaćáın.
Horaho, Horahoe, Ó heapćaᴠa.
Horan, Ó hoᴠpáın 1 ; Ó hoż-
páın, (o.f.) Ó hużpóın 19, 97 ;
Ó hannpáın 73, 85, Ó happ-
aćáın 27, 45.
Hore, v. Hoare.
Horgan, Ó hapżáın, Ó happ-
żáın.
Horish, Ó huapżuıp.
Horisky, Ó huapuıpce.
Horkan, Horkin, Ó hOpcáın.
Horoho, Horohoe, Ó heapćaᴠa.
Horrigan, Ó happażáın, (o.f.)
Ó hanpaᴠáın.
Horsey, ᴠe hóppaıż.
Hosey, Hosie, Ó heoᴠapa, Ó
heoᴠupa, Ó heożapa.
Hoskins, Ó huıpcín, Ó hOıpcín.
Hosty, mac hoıpce, mac
Oıpce.
Hotchkin, hoıpᴄıcín.
Hough, Ó heoćać.

Houghegan, Ó heoćażáın.
Houghney, v. Hooney.
Houghton, ᴠe hoćᴄún.
Houghy, Ó heoćaıᴠ.
Houlaghan, Houlehan, Houli-
han, Ó huaʟʟaćáın.
Houneen, Ó huaıᴄnín.
Hourahan, Hourican, Ó hann-
paćáın.
Hourigan, Ó hannpażáın 17,
27 ; Ó hoᴠpażáın 779.
Hourihan, Hourihane, Ó hann-
paćáın.
Hourisky, Ó huapuıpce.
Houstin, Houston, mac úıpᴄın.
Hoverty, Ó hóżapᴄaıż 1 ; Ó
héıżeapᴄaıż 198.
Howard, hıobápᴠ 48, 49 ; héı-
ḃeapᴄ 19 ; Ó hıoṁaıp 76 ;
Ó hożaıpᴄ 2.
Howay, Ó heoćaıᴠ.
Howe, Ó heoćaᴠa.
Howel, Howell, Howells, haoʟ,
mac haoʟ.
Howen, Ó heoġaın.
Howes, Ó heoćaᴠa.
Howett, húıżéıᴠ.
Howey, Howie, Ó heoćaıᴠ.
Howitt, húıżéıᴠ.
Howlen, v. Howlin.
Howlet, Howlett, húıżléıᴠ,
húıléıᴠ.
Howley, Ó huaʟʟaıż.
Howlin, Howling, huıżlín,
húılín.
Hoy, Hoye, Ó heoćaıᴠ, Ó
heoćaᴠa.
Hoyle, Hoyles, (?) mac żıoʟʟa-
ćoıʟʟe.
Hoyne, Hoynes, Ó heoġaın.
Huban, Ó húḃáın.
Hubbard, Hubbart, Hubbert,
hoḃápᴠ, hoıḃeápᴠ, hıobápᴠ,
híḃeápᴠ.
Hubbock, húḃuc, hoḃac.
Huddy, Ó huaᴠa, (s.l.) Ó
huᴠaıż 976.

Hue, Hueson, mᴀc ᴀoóᴀ.
Huett, húiséiᴅ.
Huey, Ó heoċᴀiᴅ.
Huggins, Ó hᴀoóᴀsáin.
Hugginson, mᴀc huisín.
Hughes, Ó hᴀoóᴀ 11 ; mᴀc ᴀoóᴀ 192.
Hughey, mᴀc eoċᴀiᴅ.
Hughs, v. Hughes.
Hughston, mᴀc úirᴄin.
Huleat, huisléiᴅ, húiléiᴅ.
Hulihan, Ó huᴀllᴀċáin.
Hultaghan, Hultahan, Ó hulᴄᴀċáin.
Humfrey, Humphrey, unᵽᵽᴀiᴅ.
Humphreys, Humphries, mᴀc unᵽᵽᴀiᴅ, mᴀc hunᵽᵽᴀiᴅ.
Huneen, Ó huᴀiᴄnín.
Hunt, Ó ᵽiᴀiċ 11, Ó ᵽéiċ 2 ; Ó ᵽiᴀċᴀ, Ó ᵽiᴀċᴀċ 47, 72 ; Ó ᵽiᴀċnᴀ, Ó ᵽiᴀċnᴀċ 29, 34, 172, 192, 272, 772 ; Ó ᵽiᴀċᵽᴀ, Ó ᵽiᴀċᵽᴀċ 25, 33, 48 ; hunᴄ E 2.
Hunter, (?) Ó ᵽiᴀċᴀ, Ó ᵽiᴀċᴀċ 7.
Hurley, Ó húrᴄuile, Ó huirᴄuile 11 ; Ó Coṁáin 197, 462 772 ; Ó hiᴀᵽᵽlᴀċᴀ 7792 ; Ó murᴄuile 7792.
Hurney, Ó húrnᴀiᴅe.
Hurroe, Ó heᴀᵽċᴀóᴀ.
Hurst, ᴅe hóᵽᵽᴀis, (s.l.) Ó hóᵽᵽᴀis 47.
Hussey, ᴅe horᴀe, ᴅe húrᴀe, húrᴀe, hiorᴀe 17, 18, 43, 49 ; Ó heoóurᴀ 6, 9. 72, 82.
Hussian, Ó hoirín.
Huston, mᴀc úirᴄin.
Hutch, huirᴄe
Hutchinson, huiᴄeᴀċáin 979.
Hyde, ᴅe híᴅe 1 ; Ó Seiᴄeᴀċáin 779.
Hylan, Hyland, Ó hᴀoláin, 1, (o.f.) Ó ᵽaoláin, (s.l.) Ó hᴀoileáin 72, Ó hoileáin 82, 191, Ó holáin 192, Ó hioláin 97.

Hyle, Hyles, v. Hoyle, Hoyles'
Hynan, Ó heiónᴀáin.
Hyndes, Hynds, v. Hynes.
Hynes, Ó heióin 11, Ó héióin 2 ; Ó heosᴀin 6, 24, 44.
Hyney, Ó hᴀónᴀiᴅ, Ó hᴀónᴀis, Ó hᴀióne, Ó heiónis.

Iago, iᴀsó 1 ; mᴀc iᴀsó 9.
Igo, Igoe, mᴀc iᴀsó 11, mᴀc iᴀsós 92.
Ildowney, mᴀc siollᴀ ᴅoṁnᴀis.
Ilhinney, mᴀc siollᴀ Coinnis.
Ilroy, mᴀc siollᴀᵽuᴀiᴅ.
Ilwee, mᴀc siollᴀóuiᴅe.
Inglesby, v. Ingoldsby.
Inglis, insléiᵽ, insliᵽ. V. English.
Ingoldsby, mᴀc ᴀn sᴀllósᴌᴀis.
Ingram, ionsᵽᴀm.
Innes, Innis, mᴀc ᴀonsuiᵽ.
Inright, v. Enright.
Insgelby v. Ingoldsby.
Ireland, ᴅe íᵽleonᴄ, íᵽleonᴄ.
Irish, ᴅe íᵽéiᵽ, íᵽéiᵽ.
Irrington, Ó hᴀᵽᵽᴀċᴄáin.
Irvine, Irving, Irwin, Ó heiᵽeaṁóin 1 ; Ó Ciᴀᵽṁᴀcáin 772
Ivers, Ivor, Ivors, Ó hioṁᴀiᵽ 76, 93 ; mᴀc ioṁᴀiᵽ 19.

Jack, Jacke, Jackman, Seᴀc.
Jackson, mᴀc siᴀcᴀiᵽ, mᴀc siᴀcuiᵽ.
Jacob, iᴀcob.
Jacques, siᴀcuᵽ.
Jaffery, Jaffrey, Seᴀᵽᵽᴀiᴅ.
Jago, Jagoe, iᴀsó.
James, Séᴀmuᵽ.
Jameson, Jamieson, Jamison, mᴀc Séᴀmuiᵽ.
Jarman, Jarmyn, Seᴀᵽmán.
Jarrett, Seᴀᵽóiᴅ.
Jarvis, Seᴀᵽbáᵽ
Jeffers. Jefferson, Jeffreson, mᴀc Seᴀᵽᵽᴀiᴅ.
Jeffery, Jeffrey, Seᴀᵽᵽᴀiᴅ.

99

Jeffries, mac Seaffraið.
Jemison, mac Séamuir.
Jenkin, Seinicín.
Jenkins, Jenkinson, Jenkison, mac Seinicín.
Jennens, Jennings, mac Seinín 10; mac Séoinín 9, (s.l.) Ó Ceóinín 19.
Jerety, mas Oireactais.
Jerman, Jermyn, Seanmán.
Jerrett, Seanóið.
Jervaise, Jervis, Seanbár.
Jimison, mac Séamuir.
Jinkins, mac Seinicín.
Johnson, Johnston, Johnstone, mac Seáin, mac Seagáin 1, mac Seóin 2, mac Eóin 2.
Joie, Seóig.
Jones, mac Seóin, Seónr.
Jordan, Jorden, Jordon, Jourdan, Siúrðán, Siúrtán 10; mac Siúrtáin 9.
Joy, Seog, Seóig, Seogac, Seoigeac.
Joyce, Seogar, Seórac 24, 77; Seog, Seóig, Seogac, Seoigeac 1, Seoigeac 2.
Joyner, Siúinéir.
Joynt, ðe Siúnta.
Judge, mac an Óreiteaman, mac an Óreiteamnais, mac an Óreitim.
Julian, Julien, Silleán.
Jurdan, v. Jordan.

Kadell, Kadle, Caðal.
Kain, Kaine, v. Kane.
Kairns, v. Kearns.
Kanavaghan, Ó Connmacáin.
Kane, Ó Catáin 11; mac Aoðáin, (s.l.) Ó Caoðáin 92.
Kangley, Ó Coingeallais, mac Coingeallais 78, 779; mac Ceanglais 53, 67.
Kappock, ðe Cearóc, ðe Cearóg.
Karey, v. Carey.

Karr, v. Carr.
Kavanagh, Kavenagh, Caománac, (o.s) mac Murcaða Caománac 81; Ó Caománn, Ó Caománais 7, 9, 15, 24, 25.
Keady, Ó Céaðais, mac Céaðais 9; mac Céiðis, (o.f.) Ó Meicéiðis 77.
Keag, mac Taiðg.
Keaghery, mac Fiacra, mac Fiacrac.
Keague, mac Taiðg.
Keahan, Ó Caocáin, mac Caocáin.
Keahery, mac Fiacra, mac Fiacrac.
Kealahan, Ó Céileacáin.
Kealy, Ó Caollaiðe, Ó Caollaige 45, 78, 87; Ó Caðlá 9; Ó Céile 86.
Kean, Keane, Ó Catáin 11; Ó Céin 47; mac Aoðáin, (s.l.) Ó Caoðáin 92.
Keaney, Keany, Ó Cianais (S.L.) 97.
Keappock, ðe Cearóc, ðe Cearóg.
Kearin, Kearn, Kearnes, v. Kearns.
Kearney, Ó Cearnais 11; mac Cearnais 13, 16, 38, 43; Ó Catarnais 172, 192; Ó Ceitearnais 192.
Kearns, Kearon, Kearons, Ó Céirín, Ó Ciaráin 11, (s.l.) Ó Cearáin, Ó Cioráin 19; Ó Ceitearnais 2.
Kearsey, ðe Céarrais, (s.l.) Ciararac.
Kearson, mac Fiararir.
Keary, Ó Ciarða 8; mac Fiacra, mac Fiacrac 9; (?) mac Siolla Céire 2.
Kearse, mac Fiarair.
Keating, Keatinge, Céitinn 11; Ó Céatraða 462.
Keatley, Ó Satlaoic.

Keaty, Ó Céatfaḋa.
Keaveney, Keaveny, Ó ჳéiḃeannaiჳ 94 ; mac ჳéiḃeannaiჳ 6, 93 ; Ó Coiḃḋeannaiჳ 8 ; Ó Caománaiჳ 2.
Keavy, Ó Ciaḃaiჳ.
Keawell, mac Caṫṁaoil
Kedney, v Kidney.
Kee, mac Aoiḋ
Keefe, Keeffe, Ó Caoiṁ.
Keegan, mac Aoḋaჳáin, 1 (s.l.) Ó Caoჳáin 9.
Keehan, Ó Caocáin, mac Caocáin.
Keelaghan, Ó Céileacáin.
Keelan, Ó Caoláin.
Keeley, v. Kealy.
Keelighan, Ó Céileacáin.
Keelin, Keeling, v. Keelan.
Keelty, Ó Caoilte, Ó Caoiltiჳ.
Keely, v. Kealy.
Keena, v. Keeny.
Keenaghan, Ó Coinneacáin, Ó Cuinnéacáin.
Keenan, Ó Cianáin 1 ; mac finჳin, (s.l.) mac Cinín 34 ; Ó Cuinneacáin 2.
Keene, v. Keane.
Keeney, Keeny, Ó Cianaiჳ.
Keerawin, Ó Ciarḋuḃáin, Ó Cíorḋuḃáin.
Keerivick, Ó Ciarṁaic, Ó Círṁic.
Keern, v. Kieran.
Keesack, v. Cusack.
Keeshan, Ó Cireáin.
Keevan, Keevane, O Caomáin 11 ; Ó Ciaḃáin 779.
Keevers, mac íomair.
Keevey, Ó Ciaḃaiჳ.
Keevlin, Ó Ciḃlín 1, Ó Ciḃleacáin 976.
Kegley, Ó Coiჳealaiჳ, Ó Coiჳliჳ.
Keheerin, mac eicciჳeirn.

Kehelly, mac Caoclaoiċ, (o.f.) (?) mac Caoċfile, (s.l.) mac Claoclaoiċ.
Kehering, v. Ke ꝓeerin.
Keherny, Ó Ceitearnaiჳ, mac Ceitearnaiჳ.
Kehigan, mac eoċaჳáin.
Kehilly, v. Kehelly.
Kehoe, mac eoċaḋa
Keighron, Ó Cíocaráin.
Keighry, mac fiacra, mac fiacraċ.
Keightley, Ó ჳaclaoiċ.
Keilly, v. Keily.
Keiltagh, Ó Caoilte, Ó Caoiltiჳ.
Keily, Ó Caḃla 11 ; mac Caoclaoiċ 779.
Keiran, Keirans, Ó Ciaráin.
Keitley, Ó ჳaclaoiċ.
Kelaghan, Keleghan, Kelihan, Kellaghan, Ó Céileacáin.
Kellard, v. Keller.
Kelledy, Ó Callaḋa.
Kellegher, Ó Céileacáir.
Kellegy, Ó Calჳaiჳ.
Kelleher, Keller, Ó Céileacáir
Kelley v. Kelly.
Kelliher, Ó Céileacáir.
Kellops, mac filiḃ.
Kelrick, (?) mac ჳiollaḃ ꝑic.
Kelly, Ó Ceallaiჳ (s.l.) Ó Cealla 11 ; mac Ceallaiჳ 2 ; Ó Caollaiḋe, Ó Caollaiჳe 17, 24, 49 ; mac ჳiolla Ceallaiჳ 972 ; Ó Caḃla 492 ; mac Caoclaoiċ 7792.
Kenah, v. Kenna.
Kenchyla, v. Kinsella.
Kendellan, Ó Caoinḋealḃáin.
Kendrick, mac eanraic, mac eanrpaic.
Kenealy, Kenelly, v. Kenneally.
Kenerney, mac an Oirċinniჳ.
Kenlan, v. Kennellan.
Kenna, Kennah, Ó Cionaoiċ 4, (s.l.) Ó Cionáiċ, Ó Cineáiċ, Ó Cnáċ.

Kennane, Ócoıneáın, Ó Cuıneáın.
Kenneally, Kennealy, Ó Cınnfaolaıᵭ 11 ; Ó Coınᵹeallaıᵹ, mac Coınᵹeallaıᵹ 24, 779.
V. Kennelly.
Kennedy, Ó Cınnéıᵭe, Ó Cınnéıᵭıᵭ, Ó Cınnéıᵭıᵹ.
Kennefeck, ᵭe Cınıféıc, Cınıféıc.
Kennellan, Ó Caoınᵭealᵬáın.
Kennelly, Ó Eınnfaolaıᵭ 71 ; Ó Coınᵹeallaıᵹ, mac Coınᵹeallaıᵹ 24, 779 ; Ó Conᵹaıle, mac Conᵹaıle 19, 97.
Kennifeck, ᵭe Cınıféıc, Cınıféıc.
Kenning, Kennon, mac Coınín 2 ; mac fınᵹın 2.
Kenny, Ó Cıonaoᵭa, Ó Cıonaoıᵭ 11 ; mac Cıonaoᵭa, mac Cıonaoıᵭ 2 ; Ó Coınne 38, Ó Coınnıᵹ 32 ; mac ᵹıolla Coınnıᵹ 2.
Kennyon, Kenyon mac Coınín 2 ; mac fınᵹın 2.
Kenrick, mac eanpaıc, mac eannpaıc.
Kent, ᵭe Ceannᵭ, Ceannᵭ, Cınᵭ.
Kenure, mac fıonnᵬaıpp.
Keogan, mac eoᵭaᵹáın, (s.l.) Ó Ceoᵹáın.
Keogh, mac eoᵭaᵭa, mac eoᵭaᵭ, (s.l.) mac Ceoᵭ, mac Ceoᵭaᵭ.
Keoghane, mac eoᵭáın, (s.l.) Ó Ceoᵭáın.
Keoghoe, Keoghy, mac eoᵭaᵭa, mac eoᵭaıᵭ.
Keohane, mac eoᵭáın, (s.l.) Ó Ceoᵭáın.
Keon, mac eóın 2 ; mac eoᵹaın 2.
Keoneen, mac Seóınín, (s.l.) Ó Ceóınín.
Keough, v. Keogh.
Keown, mac eoᵹaın 2 ; mac eóın 2.

Keppock, ᵭe Ceapóc, ᵭo Ceapóᵹ.
Kerans, Ó Cıapáın.
Kerbin, Ó Coıpbín.
Kerby, v. Kirby.
Kerdiffe, ᵭe Capᵭuıᵬ.
Kereen, Ó Céıpín.
Kerevan, Ó Cıapᵭuᵬáın.
Kergan, Kerigan, Ó Cıapaᵹáın.
Kerin, Kerins, Ó Céıpín.
Kerisey, v. Kearsey.
Kerivan, Kerivin, Ó Cıapᵭuᵬáın, Ó Cíopᵭuᵬáın.
Kerley, mac feapᵹaıle 2 ; mac ᵭoıpᵭealᵬaıᵹ 2.
Kerlin, Ó Coıpealláın.
Kerly, v. Kerley.
Kermode, mac ᵭıapmaᵭa.
Kermody, Ó Ceapmaᵭa.
Kernaghan, Kernahan, Ó Ceapnaᵭáın.
Kernan, Ó Ceapnaᵭáın 16, 29 ; mac ᵭıᵹeapnáın 67.
Kerney, Ó Ceıᵭeapnaıᵹ, mac Ceıᵭeapnaıᵹ.
Kernohan, v. Kernahan.
Kernon, v. Kernan.
Kerns, Kerons, v. Kearns.
Kerr, v. Carr.
Kerragher, mac feapᵭaıp.
Kerragy, v. Carrigy.
Kerraher, mac feapᵭaıp.
Kerrane, Ó Ceapáın, Ó Cıopáın.
Kerrigan, Ó Cıapaᵹáın 11 ; Ó Cíocapáın 972.
Kerrin, Kerrins, Ó Céıpín 1, Ó Cıapáın 2.
Kerris, Kerrish, Kerrisk, Kerrison, mac fıapaıp 1, (s.l.) Ó Ceıpıᵭc 498.
Kervan, Ó Ceapᵬáın.
Kerwick, Ó Cıapmaıc, Ó Cfrᵮıᵭc.
Kerwin, Ó Cıapᵭuᵬáın.
Keshin, v. Cashin.
Kessidy, v. Cassidy.
Kett, Ó Ceıᵭ, Ceaᵭaᵭ.
Kettle, Kettyle, mac Coıᵭıl.

Kevane, Kevans, Ó Caomáin.
Kevany, Kevanny, Keveney, Keveny, Kevney, Ó ᵹéıḃeannaıᵹ 94 ; mac ᵹéıḃeannaıᵹ 6, 93 ; Ó coıḃḋeanaıᵹ 8 ; Ó caománaıᵹ 2.
Keverney, (?) Ó coıḃḋeanaıᵹ.
Keville, Ó cıḃıl 1, Ó cıḃlín 192.
Kevin, Ó caoımín.
Kevlean, Ó cıḃlín 1, Ó cıḃleacáın 92.
Kevlihan, Ó cıḃleacáın.
Keyes, Keys, mac aoıḋ, mac aoḋa 979 ; (?) mac an Caoıc 58, 73.
Kickham, cıceam.
Kidney, Ó ᵒuḃáın 77.
Kielly, Ó caḋla.
Kielt, Kielty, Ó caoılte, Ó caoıltıᵹ.
Kiely, Ó caḋla.
Kieran, Ó cıapáın.
Kiernan, mac tıᵹeapnáın 11 ; Ó ceapnacáın 62.
Kiervan, Ó cıapᵒuḃáın, Ó cíopᵒuḃáın.
Kierce, mac ᵱıapaıp.
Kilahy, mac ᵹıolla acaıḋ (O'G.).
Kilamartin, mac ᵹıolla máptaın.
Kilbane, mac ᵹıollaḃáın.
Kilbeg, mac ᵹıollaḃıᵹ.
Kilboy, mac ᵹıollaḃuıḋe.
Kilbride, mac ᵹıolla ḃríᵹᵒe.
Kilby, mac ᵹıollaḃuıḋe.
Kilcar, Kilcarr, mac ᵹıolla Cacaıp.
Kilcash, mac ᵹıollacaıᵱ.
Kilchreest, Kilchriest, Kilchrist, mac ᵹıolla Críoᵱt.
Kilcline, mac ᵹıollaclaoın.
Kilcommons, mac ᵹıolla Comáın.
Kilcooley, mac ᵹıolla Cúılle.
Kilcourse, (?) mac ᵹıollaᵹaıpḃ.

Kilcoyne, mac ᵹıollacaoın, mac ᵹıolla Caoıne.
Kilcrow, mac ᵹıollaᵹaıpḃ.
Kilcullen, mac ᵹıolla Coıllın, mac ᵹıolla Caıllın.
Kilday, Kildea, mac ᵹıolla ᵒé.
Kilduff, mac ᵹıollaḋuıḃ.
Kildunn, mac ᵹıollaḋuınn.
Kilfedder, Kilfeder, mac ᵹıolla ᵱeaᵒaıp.
Kilfillan, mac ᵹıolla ᵱaoláın.
Kilfoyle, mac ᵹıolla ᵱóıl.
Kilgallen, Kilgallon, mac ᵹıolla Caıllın.
Kilgannon, mac ᵹıolla ᵹannáın.
Kilgar, mac ᵹıollaᵹeáıpp.
Kilgarriff, mac ᵹıollaᵹaıpḃ.
Kilgray, mac ᵹıollapıaḃaıᵹ.
Kilgrew, mac ᵹıollaᵹaıpḃ.
Kilgrist, mac ᵹıolla Críoᵱt.
Kilgunn, mac ᵹıollaḋuınn.
Kilkeary, mac ᵹıolla Céıpe.
Kilkelly, mac ᵹıolla Ceallaıᵹ.
Kilken, mac uılcín.
Kilkenny, mac ᵹıolla Coınnıᵹ.
Kilker, mac ᵹıollaᵹéıp.
Kilkey, mac ᵹıollacaoıc.
Kilkison, Kilkisson, mac uılcín.
Killackey, mac ᵹıolla acaıḋ (O'G.).
Killan, Killane, Ó cılleáın.
Killby, mac ᵹıollaḃuıḋe 11 ; Ó ᵹıollaḃuıḋe 62.
Killeavy, mac ᵒuınnᵱléıḃe.
Killeen, Ó cıllín.
Killelea, mac ᵹıollaléıc.
Killemeade, Killemet, mac uıllıméıᵒ.
Killen, Ó cıllín.
Killeran, mac ᵹıollapáın, (o.f.) mac ᵹıolla Éanáın.
Killerlean, mac an ᵱıpléıᵹınn.
Killery, mac ᵹıollapıaḃaıᵹ.
Killevy, mac ᵒuınnᵱléıḃe.
Killgore (?) mac ᵹıollaᵹaıpḃ.
Killian, Ó cıllín, Ó cılleáın.

Killiger, ᴀ Cliʒeóip (S.L.) 77.
Killimith, mᴀc uilliméiꝺ.
Killin, Killion, Ó Cillín, Ó Cilleáin.
Killips, mᴀc Ƒilib.
Killkelly, mᴀc ʒiollᴀ Ceallᴀiʒ.
Killooley, mᴀc ʒiollᴀʒuᴀlᴀ.
Killops, mᴀc Ƒilib.
Killoran, mᴀc ʒiollᴀ Luᴀiċ-ᴘinn.
Kilmartin, mᴀc ʒiollᴀ ṁáp-ᴛᴀin.
Kilmary, mᴀc ʒiollᴀ ṁuipe.
Kilmet, mᴀc uilliméiꝺ.
Kilmore, Kilmurry, mᴀc ʒiollᴀ ṁuipe.
Kiloughry, Kiloury, mᴀc Con-luᴀċpᴀ.
Kilpatrick, mᴀc ʒiollᴀ ᴘáꝺ-pᴀiʒ.
Kilrain, Kilrane, mᴀc ʒiollᴀ-páin, (o.f.) mᴀc ʒiollᴀ Eánáin.
Kilroe, mᴀc ʒiollᴀpuᴀiꝺ.
Kilronan, mᴀc ʒiollᴀ Rónáin.
Kilroy, mᴀc ʒiollᴀpuᴀiꝺ.
Kilty, Ó Cᴀoilᴛe, Ó Cᴀoilᴛiʒ.
Kilvey, mᴀc ʒiollᴀbuiꝺe.
Kimins, Kimmings, Kimmins, mᴀc Coimín, mᴀc Cuimín.
Kinaghan, Kinahan, Ó Coinneᴀċáin, Ó Cuinneᴀċáin.
Kinane, Ó Cuinneáin.
Kinarney, mᴀc ᴀn ᴀipċinniʒ.
Kinavan, Ó Ceᴀnnꝺubáin.
Kincaid, Cinnicéiꝺ.
Kincart, mᴀc ᴀn Ceᴀipᴛ (S.L.) 19.
Kinchela, Kinchella, Kinchley Cinnpeᴀlᴀċ 1; Ó Cinnpeᴀlᴀiʒ 2.
Kindellan, Ó Cᴀoinꝺeᴀlbáin.
Kindregan, Ó Cinnꝺeᴀpʒáin.
Kine, Ó Cᴀꝺᴀin.
Kinealy, v. Kenneally.
Kineavy, Ó Cinncnáṁᴀ nó mᴀc Conƒnáṁᴀ.

Kinerney, mᴀc ᴀn Oipċinniʒ.
King, Ó Cinʒeᴀꝺ, Ó Cionʒᴀ 88, 89, 97, 199, 462; mᴀc Con-pᴀoi 17, 19, 49, 64, 97; mᴀc Ƒeᴀpᴀꝺᴀiʒ 2; mᴀc Conpuᴀin 2; mᴀc ʒiollᴀpuᴀiꝺ 2.
Kingarty, Kingerty, mᴀc Ƒinn-eᴀċᴛᴀ, mᴀc Ƒinneᴀċᴛᴀiʒ.
Kinghan, Ó Cuinneáin.
Kingsley, Ó Cinnpeᴀlᴀiʒ (O'D.)
Kingston, Kingstone, mᴀc Cloċ-ᴀipe 55; mᴀc Oinpeᴀmáin, (s.l.) Ó Cinnpeᴀmáin, Cinn-peᴀmáin 779.
Kinighan, Kinihan, Ó Coinneᴀċáin, Ó Cuinneᴀċáin.
Kiniry, mᴀc inneipʒe.
Kinlan, Kinlen, Ó Cᴀoinleáin, (o.f.) Ó Cᴀoinꝺeᴀlbáin.
Kinlough, mᴀc Conloċᴀ.
Kinna, v. Kenna.
Kinnan, Ó Ciᴀnáin 62; mᴀc Ƒionnáin 2; Ó Cuinneᴀċáin 2.
Kinnane, Ó Cuinneáin, Ó Cuin-eáin.
Kinnavane, Ó Ceᴀnnꝺubáin.
Kinnavy, v. Kineavy.
Kinneally, Kinnealy, v. Ken-neally.
Kinnear, mᴀc ᴀn Ƒip.
Kinneen, mᴀc Coinín.
Kinneevy, v. Kineavy.
Kinnegan, Ó Cuinneᴀʒáin, mᴀc Cuinneᴀʒáin.
Kinner, mᴀc ᴀn Ƒip.
Kinnerk, mᴀc ᴀn ᴀipċinn, mᴀc ᴀn Oipċinn 1; mᴀc Eᴀnpᴀic 469.
Kinnevane, Ó Ceᴀnnꝺubáin.
Kinney, v. Kenny.
Kinnian, Ó Coinín, Ó Cuinín.
Kinnier, mᴀc ᴀn Ƒip.
Kinnighan, Ó Cuinneᴀċáin, Ó Cuinneᴀʒáin.
Kinnock, Ó Cuineóʒ.
Kinregan, Ó Cinnꝺeᴀpʒáin.
Kinrock, mᴀc Eᴀnpᴀic.

Kinsela, Kinsella, Kinshela, Kinsley, Cınnrealaċ 1, Ó Cınnrealaıġ 2.
Kinucane, mac Fıonnṁacáın.
Kirby, Ó Cıarṁaıc 1, (s.l.) Ó Cıarba 17, 46, 49 ; Ó Coırbín 92 ; mac Ġeırble 192.
Kirivan, Ó Cıarouḃáın, Ó Cíoroubáın.
Kirk, Ó Cuırc.
Kirkpatrick, mac Ġıolla Páoraıġ.
Kirland, Ó Coıreallaın.
Kirley, v. Kerley.
Kirlin, Ó Coıreallaın.
Kiroy, mac Cıocruaıo.
Kirrane, Ó Cıoráın, (o.f.) Ó Cıaráın.
Kirrell, Ó Coırıll.
Kirvan, Kirwan, Kirwen, Kirwin, Ó Cıarouḃáın, Ó Cıoroubáın 11 ; Ó Cearḃáın 82 ; Ó Cıaraġáın 972.
Kissack, v. Cusack.
Kissane, Ó Cıoráın, (o.f.) Ó Caráın.
Kissick, Kissock, v. Cusack.
Kitson, mac Ceıt 469.
Kitterick, Kittrick, mac Śıtrıc.
Kiville, Ó Cıbıl 1. Ó Cıblín 192.
Klyne, v. Cline.
Klisham, mac Clırcam (S.L.) 19.
Kneafsey, Ó Cnáımrıġe.
Knee, Ó nıao.
Kneeland, Ó nıalláın.
Knight, mac an Rıoıre 2 ; mac neáctaın 62.
Kniland, Knilans, Ó nıalláın.
Knowd, Ó nuaoac.
Knowels, Knowles, Ó Cnútaıl, Ó Cnútġaıl.
Knox, oe Cnoc.
Koen, Ó Coṁḃáın, Ó Coṁġaın 11 ; mac Eoġaın 2.
Korish, mac Feóraır, mac Feóruır.

Kough, mac Eocáoa.
Kulkeen, Kulkin, mac Uılcín.
Kyley, Ó Caola.
Kyne, Ó Caoaın.

Lacey, v. Lacy.
Lachlin, Ó Laclaınn.
Lacy, oe Léır, Léıreac 1 ; Ó Laıteara, Ó Laıtġeara, (o.f.) Ó Flaıteara, Ó Flaıtġeara 87.
Ladden, Ó Laıoeáın, Ó Loıoeáın.
Ladrigan, v. Landregan.
Laffan, Laffen, Lapán.
Lafferty, Ó Laıtḃeartaıġ, (o.f.) Ó Flaıtḃeartaıġ.
Laffey, Laffy, Ó Laıtıṁ, (s.l.) Ó Laıtṁe, Ó Lataıġ, (o.f.) Ó Flaıtıṁ.
Lagan, Ó Leoġáın.
Laghlen, Laghlin, Ó Laclaınn.
Lahan, Ó Lacáın 2 ; Ó Leacáın 976.
Laheen, (?) Ó Laıtín, (o.f.) Ó Laıtıṁín, Ó Flaıtıṁín.
Laherty, Ó Laıtḃeartaıġ, (o.f.) Ó Flaıtḃeartaıġ.
Lahey, Lahiff, Lahiffe, Lahive, Lahy, Ó Laıtıṁ, Ó Lataıġ, (o.f.) Ó Flaıtıṁ.
Laine, Ó Leatáın 976.
Laing, Ó Laınn, (o.f.) Ó Flaınn.
Laird, v. Lord.
Lally, Ó maolalaıo, (o.f.) Ó maol Falaıo.
Lalor, Ó Leatloḃaır.
Laman, v. Lammon.
Lamb, v. Lambe.
Lambart, v. Lambert.
Lambe, Ó Luaın 11 ; Ó Luanáın 16 ; Ó nuaoan, Ó nuaoaın 5, 9.
Lambert, Laımbcart 1 ; Lamport 28.
Lambin, Lambyn, Laımbín.

Lammon, Lamon, Lamond,
Lamont, mac Laʒmainn, mac
Laómainn.
Lampart, Lampert, v. Lambert.
Landers, ɒe Lonɒrar, ɒe Lun-
ɒrar, Lomɒrarać, Lunɒrarać
1, ɒe Lonɒra, Lonɒrać 79 ;
Leainɒi (S.L.) 47.
Landon, ɒe Lonɒún.
Landregan, Ó Lonʒarʒáin.
Landrey, ɒe Lonɒra. V.
Landers.
Landy, Leainɒi.
Lane, Ó Laiʒin, Ó Laióin 1,
(s.l.) Ó Liaʒain, Ó Liaóain,
Ó Liʒin, Ó Lióin 47, 79, Ó
Leiʒin, Ó Leióin 772 ; Ó
Leaćáin 976 ; ɒe Léiʒinn, ɒe
Léin, Léiʒinn E 2.
Laney, Ó ɒubṗláine, Ó ɒub-
ṗláinʒe.
Lang, Ó Lainn, (o.f.) Ó ṗlainn.
Langan, Ó Lonʒáin.
Langford, Lanʒṗorc, Lonʒṗorc.
Langin, Ó Lonʒáin.
Langton, ɒe Lanʒcún, Lanʒcún.
Lanigan, Ó Lonaʒáin, Ó Luin-
eaʒáin.
Lannan, Lannen, Ó Leannáin
1 ; Ó Lonáin, (s.l.) Ó Lionáin
779.
Lannigan, v. Lanigan.
Lannin, Lannon, Lanon, v.
Lannan.
Lant, Lannc.
Laphin, Ó Lapáin 3 ; Lapán 4.
Lapin, Lappin, Ó Lapáin.
Laracy, Ó Learʒura.
Lardner, Ó Lorʒnáin, Ó Loirʒ-
neáin.
Larens, Labranc, Labrár.
Largan, Ó Lorʒnáin, Ó Loirʒ-
neáin.
Larken, Larkin, Larkins, Ó
Lorcáin.

Larney, Ó maoil earna 89,
(s.l.) Ó Leárnać 64.
Larrissy, Ó Learʒura.
Latten, Laicín.
Lauder, Láiɒir.
Laugheran, v. Lougheran.
Laughlin, v. Loughlin.
Laughnan, Ó Laćnáin.
Launders, v. Landers.
Laurence, Labranc, Labrár.
Laurison, mac Labrainn, mac
Labráir.
Lavallen, Lavallin, Leabailin.
Lavan, Ó Láiṁín 91, Ó Láṁáin
92, (o.f.) Ó ṗlaicṁín, Ó
ṗlaiceaṁáin.
Lavelle, Ó maolṗábail.
Laven, v. Lavan.
Laverty, Ó Laicbearcaiʒ, (o.f)
Ó ṗlaicbearcaiʒ.
Lavery, Ó Labraóa.
Lavin, v. Lavan.
Lavins, v. Levins.
Lawder, Láiɒir.
Lawell, Ó maolṗábail.
Lawlee, Lálaióe.
Lawler, Ó Leaćlobair.
Lawless, Laiʒléir 11 (s.l.) Laiʒ-
réir 972.
Lawlor, Ó Leaćlobair.
Lawrance, Lawrence, Labranc,
Labrár.
Lawrenson, Lawrinson, Lawri-
son, Lawson, mac Labrainn,
mac Labráir.
Lawton, Ó Laćnáin.
Layne, Ó Laiʒin, Ó Laióin. V.
Lane.
Layng, Ó Lainn, (o.f.) Ó ṗlainn.
Lea, v. Lee.
Leach, Leache, v. Leech.
Leacy, v. Lacy.
Leader, Léaɒar.
League, v. Leeogue.
Leahey, Leahy, Ó Laoćóa 11,
(s.l.) Ó Laoćra 469 ; Ó Laćaiʒ,
(o.f.) Ó Laicíṁ, Ó ṗlaicíṁ 782.

Leamy, Ó Laomḋa, Ó Léime (K.).

Lean, Leane, Ó Liaġáin, Ó Liaḋáin, Ó Liġin, Ó Liḋín, (o.f.) Ó Laiḋín, Ó Laiġin.

Learhinan, Ó Loirgneáin.

Leary, Ó Laoġaire.

Leavy, Mac Ḋuinnṡléiḃe.

Leddan, Ó Loiḋeáin, Ó Luiḋeáin 11 (o.f.) Ó Loḋáin, (s.l.) Ó Lioḋáin 92.

Leddy, Ó Liḋeaḋá.

Ledger, ᴠe Sailiġéir, Sailiġéir Sailinġéir, Sailinéir, Sai-leartar.

Ledwich, Ledwidge, Ledwitch Ledwith, ᴠe Léaḋúr, Léaḋúr.

Lee, Ó Laiḋiġ 9, Ó Laoiḋiġ 7 ; Mac Laiḋiġ, Mac Laoiḋiġ 45 ; Mac an Leaġa 3 ; Liaċ 2 ; ᴠe Léiġ 14, 24, 43, &c.

Leeane, Ó Liaċáin.

Leech, Liaiġ 1 ; Ó Laoġóg, Ó Laoḋóg 94.

Leehan, Leehane, Ó Liaċáin.

Leehy, v. Leahy.

Leeman, Leemon, v. Lemon.

Leen, v. Lean.

Leeney, Ó Laiġniġ.

Leeogue, Ó Laoġóg, Ó Laoḋóg.

Leery, v. Leary.

Lees, v. Lee

Leeson, * Ó Lireáin.

Leetch, v. Leech.

Legge, ᴠe Léiġ ; Mac Coire (O'D.).

Lehane, Ó Liaċáin.

Lehy, v. Leahy.

Leicester, ᴠe Leartar.

Leigh, ᴠe Léiġ 1 ; Mac Laiḋiġ 82 ; Mac an Leaġa 62.

Leland, Mac Giolla Ḟaoláin.

Lemmon, Lemon, Mac Laġmainn 6 ; Ó Lomáin 4.

Lenagan, Ó Luineaġáin.

Lenaghan, Lenahan, Ó Léanaċáin, Ó Líonaċáin 9.

Lenane, Ó Lonáin, (s.l.) Ó Lionáin 779 ; Ó Luinġeáin, (o.f.) Ó Lonġáin 47. V.

Lennon.

Lenard, v. Leonard.

Lenden, Ó Leanᴠáin, Ó Leann-áin.

Leneghan, Lenehan, Ó Léanaċáin, Ó Líonaċáin 9.

Lenigan, Ó Luineaċáin.

Lenihan, Ó Léanaċáin, Ó Líonaċáin 9 ; Ó Luinġeaċáin 71, (s.l.) Ó Luineaċáin, Ó Laoin-eaċáin 72.

Lennard, v. Leonard.

Lennihan, v. Lenihan.

Lennon, Ó Leannáin, Ó Lionnáin 1; Ó Lonáin 77,82, Ó Luinín,23.

Lennox, Lenox, Leaṁnaċ.

Lenord, v. Leonard.

Lenton, v. Linton.

Leo, ᴠe Liaċ.

Leogue, Ó Laoġóg, Ó Laoḋóg.

Leonard, Lionáirᴅ E 2 ; Ó Lionnáin, Ó Leannáin 61, 91 ; Ó Lonáin 77, 78, (s.l.) Ó Lionáin 779 ; Ó Luinġeáin, (o.f.) Ó Lonġáin 79a ; Ó Luinín 23, 34, 35 ; Mac Loineáin 976 ; Mac Giolla Ḟinnéin 23, Mac Giolla Ḟionn-áin 2 ; Mac Giolla Seanáin. Mac Giolla Sionáin, (s l.), Maġ Uinnreannáin, Maġ Uinnrionnáin 33, 43, 67.

Lerhinan, Lerkinan, Ó Loirg-neáin.

Leslie, ᴠe Liorla, Leartaoi.

Lester, ᴠe Leartar, Leartar 2 ; Mac Alartair 62.

L'Estrange, Stráinre 1 ; Mac Conċoigcríċe 15, 25.

Letter, Letters, (?) Mac Con-leitreaċ.

Levenston, v. Levinston.

Leveson, Levey, Mac Ḋuinn-ṡléiḃe.

Levinge, Levins, Levinson, Levinston, Levingston, Levingstone, Leviston, mac ᏧuinnᚱléiᏏín.
Levett, LuiᏏéiꝺ.
Lewis, loᏏaoiꝛ.
Leycester, ꝺe leaꝛcaꝛ.
Leyden, Ó loiꝺeáin, Ó luiꝺeáin 11, (o.f.) Ó loꝺáin, (s.l.) Ó lioꝺáin 92, Ó liaꝺꝛáin 469.
Leyhane, Ó liacáin.
Leyne, Ó laiᵹin, Ó laiᏏin, (s.l.) Ó leiᵹin, Ó leiᏏin.
Liddane, Ó loiꝺeáin, Ó luiꝺeáin. V. Leyden.
Liddy, Ó liꝺeaꝺa.
Lidwich, ꝺe léaꝺúꝛ, léaꝺúꝛ.
Lihane, Ó liacáin.
Lilley, v. Lilly.
Lillis, laiᵹléiꝛ, (s.l.) laoiᵹléiꝛ 462, líleaꝛ 17, 77.
Lilly, mac ailᵹile.
Liman, mac laᵹmainn.
Limerick, Ó luimbꝛic.
Linagh, v. Lynagh.
Linahan, v. Linehan.
Linane, v. Linnane.
Linchey, Linchy, Ó loinᵹꝛiᵹ.
Lincoln, ꝺe lioncól.
Lind, Ó loinn, (o.f.) Ó ꝼloinn.
Linden, Lindin, Lindon, Ó lionꝺáin, Ó leanꝺáin 1; mac ᵹiolla ꝼinꝺéin 62.
Lindsay, Lindsy, Ó loinᵹꝛiᵹ 38; Ó loinn, (o.f.) Ó ꝼloinn 68 (O'D.); mac ᵹiolla ꝼionncóᵹ 62.
Line, v. Lyne.
Lineen, Ó luinín.
Lineham, v. Lynam.
Linehan, Ó líonacáin 9; Ó luinᵹeacáin 7. V. Lenihan.
Lines, v. Lyons.
Lingane, Ó luinᵹeáin.
Lingard, líonᵹáꝺ.
Linham, v. Lynam.

Linighan, v. Linehan.
Linn, Ó loinn, (o.f.) Ó ꝼloinn.
Linnagar, Ó luinín.
Linnahaa, v. Linehan.
Linnane, Ó lionnáin 9, 46; Ó luinᵹeáin 79a.
Linneen, Ó luinín.
Linnegar, Ó luinín.
Linnehan, v. Linehan.
Linnen, Ó luinín.
Linnox, leamnac.
Linskey, Ó loinꝛciᵹ.
Linton, ꝺe lioncún 1; mac ᵹiolla ꝼionncáin 62.
Lion, Lions, v. Lyons.
Lister, ꝺe leaꝛcaꝛ, leaꝛcaꝛ 2; Saileaꝛcaꝛ 2.
Liston, ꝺe lioꝛcún, lioꝛcún.
Little, beaᵹ 2; Ó beiᵹ 2; Ó beaᵹáin 2; ꝛeicío 28.
Littleton, Ó beaᵹáin 1, Ó biᵹeáin 17, 46.
Livingston, Livingstone, mac ᏧuinnᚱléiᏏín.
Livott, lioᏏóiꝺ.
Lloyd, laoiꝺe, lóiꝺ, lúiꝺ.
Loag, Loague, v. Logue.
Loane, Ó luain.
Lochlin, Ó loclainn.
Lochrane, Ó lucaiꝛeáin, Ó lucꝛáin.
Lockard, Lockart, locáꝺ.
Lockery, v. Loughrey.
Lockhart, locáꝺ.
Loftis, Loftus, ꝺe loccúꝛ 20, 23, 28; Ó laccnáin 19, 97, (s.l.) Ó locláin 192; mac loclainn 192.
Logan, Ó lóᵹáin, Ó leoᵹáin.
Loghan, Ó lócáin, (o.f.) Ó loccáin, Ó leocáin.
Loghlin, Ó loclainn.
Logue, Ó laoᵹóᵹ 11; Ó maol aoꝺóᵹ 16, 19.
Lohan, Ó lócáin. V. Loghan.
Loman, Lomand, Ó lomáin 4; mac laᵹmainn 6.

Lombard, Lombáro.
Lomond, v. Lomand.
Lomosney, Ó Lomarna, Ó Lomarnaig.
Lomdergan, v. Londregan.
London, oe Lonoún.
Londregan, Londrigan, Lonergan, Ó Longargáin, (s.l.) Ó Lonnargáin, Ó Lonnragáin.
Loney, Ó Luinig.
Long, oe Long 2; Ó Longaig 79a; Ó Longáin 2; ғаоа 2.
Longan, Ó Longáin.
Lonican, Ó Luingeacáin.
Lonney, Ó Luinig.
Looby, Ó Lúbaig.
Looney, Loony, Ó Luanaig 7; Ó Luinig 6.
Loran, Ó Labráin.
Lord, Ó Tigearnaig 97; mac Tigearnáin 67.
Lordan, Ó Lóroáin.
Lorkan, Lorkin, Ó Lorcáin.
Lorrigan, v. Lonergan.
Lough, (?) mac Conloca.
Loughan, Ó Lócáin. V. Loghan.
Lougheran, Ó Lucaireáin.
Loughlan, Loughlen, Loughlin, Ó Loclainn 41; mac Loclainn 6; Ó Locláin, (o.f.) Ó Lactnáin 19, 24; Ó maoil Seaclainn 2.
Loughnan, Loughnane, Ó Lactnáin.
Loughney, Ó Lactna.
Loughran, Loughraue, Ó Lucaireáin, Ó Lucráin 3; Ó Locráin, (o.f.) Ó Lactnáin 46.
Loughrey, Loughry, Ó Luacra 19; (?) mac Conluacra 46.
Louney, v. Looney.
Lovat, v. Lovett.
Love, mac Ionṁain.
Lovell, Luibéil.
Lovett, Lovitt, Luibéro 1, Libéro 499.

Lowe, mac Lugaóa.
Lowery v. Lowry.
Lowney, Ó Luanaig. V. Looney
Lowroo, Ó Labraóa.
Lowry, Ó Labraóa, Ó Labraró 1; (?) mac Conluacra 462.
V. Loughry, Kiloughry.
Luby, Ó Lúbaig.
Lucas, Lúcár.
Lucet, Lúiréro.
Lucey, Ó Luaraig.
Lucid, Lúiréro.
Lucy, Ó Luaraig.
Ludden, Ó Looáin, Ó Loioeáin, Ó Luioeáin.
Luddy, Ó Loioió.
Ludwig, oe Léaoúr, Léaoúr.
Luke, Lúcár.
Lumbard, Lombáro.
Lundergan, v. Lonergan.
Lundon, oe Lonoún.
Lunican, Ó Luingeacáin.
Lunneen, Ó Luinín.
Lunney, Lunny, Luny, Ó Luinig.
Luogue, v. Logue.
Lupane, Ó Lapáin.
Lutterel, Luttrell, Locairéil, Locrail.
Lydden, Lyden, Lydon, Ó Lioo-áin, Ó Loioeáin, &c. V. Leyden.
Lyhan, Lyhane, Ó Liacáin.
Lyle, Ó Laoigill.
Lynagh, Laigneac.
Lynam, Ó Laioġeanáin 1; Laigneac 25.
Lynan, Ó Laioġeanáin, Ó Laioeanáin, Ó Laigeanáin, Ó Laioġneáin, Ó Laioneáin, Ó Laigneáin.
Lynane, v. Linnane.
Lynch, Ó Loingrig 11, Ó Loingreacáin 16, 93; oe Línre, a Línre 43, 97.

Lynchahan, Lynchahaun,
Lynchehan, Ó Loingreacáin
11, (o.f.) mac Loingreacáin
16.
Lynchy, Ó Loingrig.
Lyne, Ó Laigin, Ó Laidín, 10,
(sl.) Ó Leigin, Ó Leidín 17,
49..
Lynegan, Ó Luineagáin.
Lynegar, Ó Luinín 23.
Lyneham, v. Lynam.
Lynes, v. Lyons.
Lynham, v. Lynam.
Lynn, Ó Loinn, (o.f.) Ó Floinn.
Lynott, Lionóid.
Lynskey, Ó Loinrcig.
Lynton, ve Liontún 1; mac
Giolla Fionntáin 2.
Lyon, ve Líon.
Lyons, ve Líon 86; Ó Laigin,
Ó Laidín 1, (s.l.) Ó Leigin, Ó
Leidín 17, 49; Ó Laignig 19;
Laigneac 19; Ó Liatáin 16,
772.
Lysaght, Lysatt, mac Giolla
Iaracta.
Lyster, ve Leartar, Leartar
2; Saileartar 2.
Lyttle, v. Little.
Lyttleton, v. Littleton.
Lyvott, v. Livott.

Mabe, máb.
Macabe, mac Cába.
MacAbee, mac an Beaca (O'G).
MacAboy, v. MacAvoy.
MacAdam, MacAdams, mac
Ádaim, mac Ádain.
MacAdarra, MacAdarrah, mac
 Dubdara, mac Duibdara,
(o.f.) mac Duibdarac, (s.l.)
mac Dara, mac Darac.
MacAdo, MacAdoo, mac Con-
duib.
MacAdorey, mac an Deóraid.
MacAfee, MacAffee, mac Duib-
fíce.
MacAfferty, mac Eacmarcaig.

MacAffie, mac Duibfíce.
MacAghy, mac Eacaid.
MacAimon, mac Eamoinn, mac
Éamuinn.
MacAlarry, MacAlary, mac
Giolla arraic 2; mac Giolla
carraig 2.
MacAldin, mac Ailín.
MacAlea, mac an leaga 2;
mac Duinnfléibe 2.
MacAlean, mac Aileáin 9
mac Giolla Eáin 6.
MacAlearney, mac Giolla
Eanna.
MacAleavy, mac Duinnfléibe.
MacAlee, mac an leaga 2; mac
Duinnfléibe 2.
MacAleece, mac Giolla Íora.
MacAleenan, mac Giolla
Finnéin.
MacAleer, mac Giolla uidir.
MacAleery, mac Giolla arraic.
MacAleese, mac Giolla Íora.
MacAlen, mac Ailín.
MacAleney, mac Giolla Coin-
nig.
MacAlernon, mac Giolla Ear-
náin.
MacAlery, mac Giolla arraic.
MacAlester, mac Alartair.
MacAlilly, mac Ailgile.
MacAlin, mac Ailín.
MacAlinda, (?) mac Giolla
Fionda.
MacAlinden, mac Giolla Find-
éin, mac Giolla Finnéin.
MacAlindon, mac Giolla
Fionntáin.
MacAlingen, MacAlinion, mac
Giolla Finnéin, mac Giolla
Findéin.
MacAlinney, mac Giolla Coinnig
MacAlinon, mac Giolla Finn-
éin.
MacAlish, mac Giolla Íora.
MacAlister, mac Alartair.
MacAlivery, mac Giolla geim-
rid.

MacAll, v. MacCall.

MacAlleaon, MacAllen, Mac-Allion, ᵯᴀᴄ ᴀɪᴸín.

MacAllester, MacAllister, ᵯᴀᴄ ᴀᴸᴀ⒭ᴛᴀɪ⒭.

MacAllon, Macallon, ᵯᴀᴄ ᴀɪᴸín.

MacAlonan, ᵯᴀᴄ ᵹɪᴏᴸᴸᴀ ᴀⱱᴀ⒥ɴáɪɴ.

MacAloney, ᵯᴀᴄ ᵹɪᴏᴸᴸᴀ ᴄᴏɪɴɴɪᵹ.

MacAloon, MacAloone, ᵯᴀᴄ ᵹɪᴏᴸᴸᴀ éóɪɴ.

MacAlpin, MacAlpine, ᵯᴀᴄ ᴀɪᴸᴘɪɴ.

MacAlroy, ᵯᴀᴄ ᵹɪᴏᴸᴸᴀ⒭ᴜᴀɪⱱ.

MacAlshander, MacAlshender, MacAlshinder, ᵯᴀᴄ ᴀᴸ⒭ᴀɴⱱᴀɪ⒭.

MacAlunney, MacAlunny, ᵯᴀᴄ ᵹɪᴏᴸᴸᴀ ᴄᴏɪɴɴɪᵹ.

MacAmbrose, ᵯᴀᴄ ᴀ⒥ʙ⒭óɪ⒭.

Macan, v. MacCann.

MacAnabb, ᵯᴀᴄ ᴀɴ ᴀʙʙᴀⱱ 11 ; ᵯᴀᴄ ᴀɴᴀʙᴀⱱᴀ 62.

MacAnallan, MacAnallen, ᵯᴀᴄ ᴀɴ ᴀɪᴸín (S.L.).

MacAnally, ᵯᴀᴄ ᴀɴ ᶠᴀɪᴸᵹɪᵹ. V. MacNally.

MacAnalty, ᵯᴀᴄ ᴄᴏɴᴀᴸᴛᴀ.

MacAnanama (?),

MacAnaspie, ᵯᴀᴄ ᴀɴ ᴇᴀ⒭ᴘᴜɪᵹ.

MacAnaul, ᵯᴀᴄ ᴄᴏɴᴜᴸᴀⱱ, ᵯᴀᴄ ᴄᴏɴ ᴜᴸᴀⱱ.

MacAnave, ᵯᴀᴄ ᵹɪᴏᴸᴸᴀ ɴᴀ ɴᴀᴏ⒥.

MacAnawe, ᵯᴀᴄ ᴄᴏɴ⒭ɴá⒥ᴀ, (s.l.) ᵯᴀᴄ ᴀɴ áᴄᴀ.

MacAndless, ᵯᴀᴄ ᴄᴜɪɴⱱᴸɪ⒭.

MacAndrew, ᵯᴀᴄ ᴀɪɴⱱ⒭ɪú 11 ; ᵯᴀᴄ ᴀɪɴⱱ⒭éɪ⒭, ᵯᴀᴄ ᴀɪɴⱱ⒭ɪᴀ⒭ᴀ 2.

MacAneany, ᵯᴀᴄ ᴄᴏɴᴀᴏɴᴀɪᵹ, (s.l.) ᵯᴀᴄ ᴀɴ éᴀɴᴀɪᵹ.

MacAneave, ᵯᴀᴄ ᵹɪᴏᴸᴸᴀ ɴᴀ ɴᴀᴏ⒥.

MacAneeny, MacAneny, ᵯᴀᴄ ᴄᴏɴᴀᴏɴᴀɪᵹ, (s.l.) ᵯᴀᴄ ᴀɴ éᴀɴᴀɪᵹ.

MacAnern, ᵯᴀᴄ ᴀɴ ᴀɪ⒭ᴄɪɴɴ, (o.f.) ᵯᴀᴄ ᴀɴ ᴀɪ⒭ᴄɪɴɴɪᵹ.

MacAnerney, ᵯᴀᴄ ᴀɴ ᴀɪ⒭ᴄɪɴɴɪᵹ, ᵯᴀᴄ ᴀɴ ᴏɪ⒭ᴄɪɴɴɪᵹ.

MacAniff, ᵯᴀᴄ ᴄᴏɴⱱᴜɪʙ.

MacAnilly, ᵯᴀᴄ ᴀɴ ᶠɪᴸᴇᴀⱱ, ᵯᴀᴄ ᴀɴ ᶠɪᴸɪⱱ.

MacAnliss, ᵯᴀᴄ ᴄᴜɪɴⱱᴸɪ⒭.

MacAnn, v. MacCann.

MacAnnally, ᵯᴀᴄ ᴀɴ ᶠᴀɪᴸᵹɪᵹ. V. MacNally.

Mac-an-Ree, ᵯᴀᴄ ᴄᴏɴ⒭ᴀᴏɪ, (s.l.) ᵯᴀᴄ ᴀɴ ⒭ᴀᴏɪ.

MacAnspie, ᵯᴀᴄ ᴀɴ ᴇᴀ⒭ᴘᴜɪᵹ.

MacAntire, MacAntyre, ᵯᴀᴄ ᴀɴ ᴛ⒮ᴀᴏɪ⒭.

MacAnuff, ᵯᴀᴄ ᴄᴏɴⱱᴜɪʙ.

MacAnulla, ᵯᴀᴄ ᴄᴏɴ ᴜᴸᴀⱱ, ᵯᴀᴄ ᴄᴏɴᴜᴸᴀⱱ.

MacAnulty, ᵯᴀᴄ ᴀɴ ᴜᴸᴛᴀɪᵹ.

MacArchey, MacArchy, ᵯᴀᴄ ⱱᴏ⒭ᴄᴀɪⱱ.

MacArdell, MacArdle, ᵯᴀᴄ á⒭ⱱᵹᴀɪᴸ.

MacAready, ᵯᴀᴄ ᴄᴏɴ⒭ᴀⱱᴀ.

MacAreavy, ᵯᴀᴄ ᵹɪᴏᴸᴸᴀ⒭ɪᴀʙᴀɪᵹ.

MacAree, ᵯᴀᴄ ᴄᴏɴ⒭ᴀᴏɪ, (s.l.) ᵯᴀᴄ ᴀ' ⒭ᴀᴏɪ 2 ; ᵯᴀᴄ ᶠᴇᴀ⒭ᴀⱱᴀɪᵹ, (s.l.) ᵯᴀᴄ ᴀ' ⒭íoᵹ 2.

MacArevy, ᵯᴀᴄ ᵹɪᴏᴸᴸᴀ⒭ɪᴀʙᴀɪᵹ.

MacArgle, ᵯᴀᴄ ᶠᴇᴀ⒭ᵹᴀɪᴸ.

Macarha, ᵯᴀᴄ ᴄá⒭ᴛᴀɪᵹ.

MacArory, ᵯᴀᴄ ⒭ᴜᴀɪⱱ⒭í.

MacArt, ᵯᴀᴄ ᴀɪ⒭ᴛ.

Mac Artarsney, ᵯᴀᴄ ᴀɴ ᴛ⒮ᴀ⒭ᴀɴᴀɪᵹ.

MacArthur, ᵯᴀᴄ ᴀ⒭ᴛúɪ⒭.

MacArthy, ᵯᴀᴄ ᴄá⒭ᴛᴀɪᵹ 11 ; ᵯᴀᴄ ᴀɪ⒭ᴛ 192.

MacArtie, ᵯᴀᴄ ᴄá⒭ᴛᴀɪᵹ.

Macartney, v. MacCartney.

MacAsey, Macasey, ᵯᴀᴄ ᴄᴀᴛᴀ⒭ᴀɪᵹ.

MacAshinah, ᵯᴀᴄ ᴀɴ ᴛ⒮ɪᴏɴɴᴀɪᵹ.

MacAskie, ᵯᴀᴄ ᴀ⒭ᴄᴀɪⱱ.

MacAskill, ᵯᴀᴄ ᴀ⒭ᴄᴀɪᴸᴸ.

MacAsparan, ᵯᴀᴄ ᴀɴ ⒮ᴘᴀ⒭áɪɴ.

MacAssie, Macassy, Ó mᴀcᴀrᴀ 4; mᴀc Cᴀtᴀrᴀiᵹ 6.
MacAstocker, mᴀc ᴀn Stocᴀipe
Mac A'Taghlin, mᴀc ᵹiollᴀ tSeᴀclᴀinn, (s.l.) mᴀc 'ᴀ tSeᴀclᴀinn.
MacAtaminey, Mac Atamney, mᴀc ᴀn Tiompánᴀiᵹ.
MacAtasney, mᴀc ᴀn tSᴀrᴀnᴀiᵹ
MacAtear, mᴀc ᴀn tSᴀoip.
MacAtee, mᴀc ᴀn tSᴀoi.
MacAteer, mᴀc ᴀn tSᴀoip.
MacAteggart, mᴀc ᴀn tSᴀᵹᴀipt.
MacAtier, v. MacAteer.
MacAtilla, mᴀc ᴀn Cuile, (o.f.) mᴀc ṁᴀoltuile.
MacAtimeny, MacAtimney, mᴀc ᴀn Tiompánᴀiᵹ.
MacAulay, Macaulay, Mac Auley, MacAuly, mᴀc Aṁᴀlᵹᴀóᴀ 5; mᴀc Aṁlᴀoiḃ 6.
MacAuliffe, mᴀc Aṁlᴀoiḃ.
MacAvaddy, MacAvady, mᴀc ᴀn ṁᴀoᴀió.
MacAveely, mᴀc ᴀn ṁileᴀóᴀ.
MacAveigh, mᴀc ᴀn ḃeᴀcᴀ, mᴀc ᴀn ḃeᴀcᴀó.
MacAvenue, mᴀc Aiḃne.
MacAvey, mᴀc ᴀn• ḃeᴀcᴀ, mᴀc ᴀn ḃeᴀcᴀó 1; mᴀc ᵹiollᴀ-ḃuióe, (s.l.) mᴀc 'ᴀ ḃuióe 38.
MacAvin, mᴀc Óuiḃín.
MacAvinchy, mᴀc Óuiḃinre.
MacAvinue, mᴀc Aiḃne 26; mᴀc Óuiḃne 67.
MacAvish, mᴀc Cáṁᴀip.
MacAvock, mᴀc Óᴀḃuc.
MacAvoy, mᴀc ᵹiollᴀḃuióe, (s.l.) mᴀc 'ᴀ ḃuióe 2; mᴀc Aoóᴀ ḃuióe 2; mᴀc fíoóḃuióe, (o.f.) mᴀc fíoóḃᴀóᴀiᵹ 45; mᴀc ᴀn ḃeᴀcᴀ, mᴀc ᴀn ḃeᴀcᴀó 2.
MacAward, mᴀc ᴀn ḃáipo.
MacAweeny, mᴀc ṁᴀonᴀiᵹ.
MacAwley, MacAwly, mᴀc Aṁᴀlᵹᴀóᴀ 5; mᴀc Aṁlᴀoiḃ 6.

MacBain, mᴀc ḃeᴀcᴀn.
MacBarron, mᴀc ᴀn Ḃᴀpúin.
MacBay, mᴀc ḃeᴀcᴀ, mᴀc ḃeᴀcᴀó.
MacBean, mᴀc ḃeᴀcᴀn.
MacBeath, MacBeith, mᴀc ḃeᴀcᴀ, mᴀc ḃeᴀcᴀó.
MacBennett, mᴀc ḃeinéio, mᴀc ḃinéio.
MacBeth, MacBey, mᴀc ḃeᴀcᴀ, mᴀc ḃeᴀcᴀó.
MacBirne, mᴀc ḃpoin.
MacBirney, mᴀc ḃiopnᴀ.
MacBrairty, mᴀc ḃpiᴀptᴀiᵹ, (o.f.) mᴀc muipceᴀptᴀiᵹ.
MacBratney, mᴀc ḃpeᴀcnᴀiᵹ.
MacBrearty, mᴀc ḃpiᴀptᴀiᵹ, (o.f.) mᴀc muipceᴀptᴀiᵹ.
MacBreatney, mᴀc ḃpeᴀcnᴀiᵹ.
MacBreen, mᴀc ḃpᴀoin.
MacBretney, mᴀc ḃpeᴀcnᴀiᵹ.
MacBride, mᴀc ᵹiollᴀ Ḃpíᵹoe, (s.l.) mᴀc 'ᴀ Ḃpíᵹoe 1, mᴀ'l Ḃpíᵹoe 376.
MacBrien, mᴀc ḃpiᴀin.
MacBrin, MacBrinn, mᴀc ḃpoin.
MacBrody, mᴀc ḃpuᴀioeᴀóᴀ.
MacBroudin, MacBruodin, mᴀc ḃpuᴀioín.
MacBryan, MacBryen, mᴀc ḃpiᴀin.
MacBurney, mᴀc ḃiopnᴀ.
MacByrne, mᴀc ḃpoin.
MacCabe, mᴀc Cáḃᴀ.
MacCadam, MacCaddam, mᴀc Aoᴀim, mᴀc Aoᴀim.
MacCadden, mᴀc Cᴀoáin, mᴀc Aoáin.
MacCaddo, MacCadoo, mᴀc Conouiḃ.
MacCady, mᴀc Aoᴀ, mᴀc Aoᴀió.
MacCaet, mᴀc Óᴀiḃéio.
MacCaffaley, mᴀc eᴀcṁílió, mᴀc eᴀcṁileᴀóᴀ.
MacCaffarky, mᴀc eᴀcṁᴀpcᴀiᵹ.
MacCaffely, mᴀc eᴀcṁílió, mᴀc eᴀcṁileᴀóᴀ.

MacCafferty, mac eᴀċṁᴀpcᴀiṡ.
MacCaffery, MacCaffray, Mac
Caffrey, MacCaffry, Mac
Cafry, mac ṡᴀppᴀiꝺ, mac
Cᴀppᴀiꝺ, mac ṡoppᴀiꝺ, mac
ṡoppᴀꝺᴀ, mᴀṡ Cᴀppᴀiꝺ, mᴀṡ
ṡᴀppᴀiꝺ.
MacCagheron, mac eᴀċpáin.
MacCagherty, mac eᴀċṁᴀpcᴀiṡ.
MacCaghey, MacCaghy, mac
eᴀċᴀiꝺ.
MacCague, mac ċᴀióṡ.
MacCahan, mac Cᴀċáin 21;
mac eᴀċáin 68.
MacCaharty, mac eᴀċṁᴀpcᴀiṡ.
MacCahern, mac eᴀċpáin 2;
mac eᴀċċiṡeipn 2.
MacCaherty, mac eᴀċṁᴀpcᴀiṡ.
MacCahon, v. MacCahan.
MacCahugh, mac eᴀċᴀꝺᴀ, mac
eoċᴀꝺᴀ.
MacCahy, mac eoċᴀiꝺ.
MacCaig, MacCaigue, mac
ċᴀióṡ.
MacCain, mac eáin 1; mac
Cᴀċáin 2.
MacCalden, mac ᴀilín.
MacCall, mac Cᴀċṁᴀoil 1; mac
Cᴀċᴀil 62.
MacCalla, v. MacCauley.
MacCallan, MacCallen, Mac
Callion, mac Cᴀilín.
MacCalliskey, MacCallisky, (?)
mac Conuipce.
MacCallister, mac ᴀlᴀpᴄᴀip.
MacCallnon, mac Cᴀllᴀnáin.
MacCallum, mac Cᴀluim
MacCally, mac eᴀċṁiliꝺ.
MacCalman, MacCalmont, mac
Cᴀlmáin, mac Colmáin.
MacCalpin, mac ᴀilpín.
MacCals ander, MacCalshender,
MacCalshinder, mac ᴀlpᴀn-
ꝺᴀip.
MacCalum, mac Cᴀluim.
MacCalvey, mac ᴀn Cᴀlḃᴀiṡ,
mac Cᴀlḃᴀiṡ.

MacCalvin, mac Conluᴀin.
MacCambridge, mac ᴀmḃpóiṡ.
MacCamley, (?) mac Cᴀmlᴀoiċ.
MacCammon, MacCammond,
mac ᴀmoinn.
MacCance, (?) mac ᴀonṡuip.
MacCandlass, MacCandleish,
MacCandless, MacCandlis,
MacCandliss, MacCanlis, mac
Cuinꝺilip, mac Cuinꝺlip.
MacCann, mac ᴀnnᴀ, mac
Cᴀnnᴀ, mac Cᴀnᴀ 11; mac
Cᴀnᴀnn 192.
MacCanuff, mac Conꝺuiḃ.
MacCardle, mac ᴀpꝺṡᴀil.
MacCarha, mac Cᴀpċᴀiṡ.
MacCarney, mac Ceᴀpnᴀiṡ.
MacCarnon, mac ċiṡeᴀpnáin.
MacCaron, mac Cᴀppṡᴀṁnᴀ.
MacCarragher, mac ᵽeᴀpċᴀip.
MacCarrell, mac ᵽeᴀpṡᴀil.
MacCarrick, mac Conċᴀippṡe,
mac Conċᴀppᴀiṡe 1; mac
Conċᴀċpᴀċ 93.
MacCarrie, v. MacCarry.
MacCarrogher, mac ᵽeᴀᴅċᴀip.
MacCarroll, mac Ceᴀpḃᴀili 2;
mac ᵽeᴀpṡᴀil 2.
MacCarron, mac Ceᴀpáin, (o.f.)
mac Ciᴀpáin.
MacCarroon, mac Cᴀppṡᴀṁnᴀ.
MacCarry, mac ᵽeᴀpᴀꝺᴀiṡ 2;
mac ᴀn Cᴀppᴀiṡ 2.
MacCart, mac ᴀipᴄ.
MacCartan, MacCarten, mac
ᴀpᴄáin, (s.l.) mac Cᴀpᴄáin.
MacCarter, MacCarthur, mac
ᴀpᴄúip.
MacCarthy, mac Cᴀpᴄᴀiṡ 1;
mac eᴀċṁᴀpcᴀiṡ 692.
MacCartie, mac Cᴀpᴄᴀiṡ.
Mac Cartin, mac ᴀpᴄáin, (s.l.)
mac Cᴀpᴄáin.
MacCartiney, MacCartney, mac
Cᴀpᴄᴀine
MacCarton, mac ᴀpᴄáin, (s.l.)
mac Cᴀpᴄáin.
MacCarty, mac Cᴀpᴄᴀiṡ.

MacCarvill, MacCarville, mac Ceapḃaill.
MacCasey, mac Caṫaraiġ.
MacCassarly, mac Casarlaiġ.
MacCashin, mac Caisín.
MacCaskie, mac Arcaiḋ.
MacCaslan, (?) mac Caisealáin,
MacCateer, mac an tSaoir.
MacCaufield, mac Caṫṁaoil.
MacCaughan, mac Eaċáin.
MacCaugherty, mac Eaċṁarcaiġ.
MacCaughey, mac Eaċaiḋ.
MacCaughin, mac Eaċáin.
MacCaughley, mac Eaċṁíliḋ, mac Eaċṁíleaḋa.
MacCaul, mac Caṫṁaoil 1; mac Caṫail 62.
MacCaulay, MacCauley, mac Aṁalġaḋa, mac Aṁalġaiḋ 5; mac Aṁlaoiḃ 6.
MacCaulfield, mac Caṫṁaoil.
MacCauliffe, mac Aṁlaoiḃ.
MacCausland v. Mac Caslan
MacCavanagh, (?) mac Caoṁánaiġ.
MacCave, mac Ḋáiḃiḋ.
MacCaverty, mac Eaċṁarcaiġ.
MacCavey, mac Ḋáiḃiḋ 1. V. MacAvey.
MacCavill, mac Caṫṁaoil.
MacCavish, mac Ṫáṁais.
MacCavitt, mac Ḋaiḃéiḋ.
MacCavock, mac Ḋaḃuc.
MacCaw, mac Áḋaiṁ.
MacCawel, MacCawell, mac Caṫṁaoil.
MacCawl, mac Caṫṁaoil 1; mac Caṫail 62.
MacCawley, MacCawly, mac Aṁalġaḋa, mac Aṁalġaiḋ 5; mac Aṁlaoiḃ 6.
MacCay, mac Aoḋa.
MacCeig, mac Taiḋg.
MacCheyne, mac Seáin, mac Seaġáin.
MacChrystall, mac Criostail.

MacClachlin, mac Laċlainn 6; mac Giolla Seaclainn 86.
MacClafferty, mac Laiṫḃeartaiġ, (o.f.) mac Flaiṫḃeartaiġ.
Mac Clafflin, v. Mac Clachlin.
MacClain, v. MacClean.
MacClamon, mac Laġmainn, mac Laoṁainn.
MacClancy, mac Flannċaḋa, mac Flannċaiḋ.
MacClane, v. MacClean.
MacClarnon, mac Giolla Earnáin.
MacClary, v. MacCleary
MacClatton, mac Giolla Caṫáin
MacClave, mac Laiṫiṁ, (o.f.) mac Flaiṫiṁ, (s.l.) mac Láiṁ.
MacClaverty, mac Laiṫḃeartaiġ.
MacClavish, mac Giolla Ḟáṁair
MacClay, mac an Leaġa 2; mac Ḋuinnḟléiḃe 2.
MacClean, mac Giolla Eáin 1; mac Aileáin 9, 62; mac an Leaġa 192.
MacClearnon, mac Giolla Earnáin.
MacCleary, MacCleery, mac an Cléiriġ, mac Cléiriġ 11; mac Giolla arraiṫ 29, 36.
MacCleish, mac Giolla Íosa.
MacClellan, MacClelland, mac Giolla Faoláin.
MacClement, MacClements, Mac Clemonts, mac Laġmainn,
MacClenaghan, MacClenahan, MacCleneghan, MacClenighan, MacClennon, mac Leannaċáin.
MacCleod, mac Leóiḋ.
MacClernand, MacClernon, mac Giolla Earnáin.
MacClery, v. MacCleary.
MacClester, mac Alastair.
MacCleverty, mac Laiṫḃeartaiġ, (o.f.) mac Flaiṫḃeartaiġ.
MacClew, mac Ḋuinnḟléiḃe.

MacCliment, MacClimond, Mac Climont, mac Laʒmainn, mac Laómainn.
MacClinchy, mac Loinʒriʒ.
MacClintock, mac ʒiolla ꝼionntóʒ.
MacClinton, mac ʒiolla ꝼionntáin
MacCloghery, mac Clocaiɼe.
MacClory, mac Labɼaóa.
MacCloskey, mac bloɼcaió.
MacCloud, mac Leóió.
MacCloughery, MacCloughry mac Clocaiɼe.
MacCloy, mac Ouinnꝼléibe.
MacCluggage, (?) mac Lúcáiɼ.
MacClughan, (?) mac Clúcáin.
MacClune, mac ʒiolla eóin.
MacClung, mac Luinʒe.
MacClure, mac ʒiolla uióiɼ.
MacClurg, mac Luiɼʒ.
MacClusker, mac bloɼcaiɼe.
MacCluskey, mac bloɼcaió.
MacClymon, mac Laʒmainn, mac Laómainn.
MacClyntock, mac ʒiolla ꝼionntóʒ.
MacCobrie, mac Cúicbɼéic.
MacCogan, MacCoggan, mac Coʒáin, (o.f.) mac Coʒaóáin 1; mac eocaʒáin 62.
MacCoghlan, mac Cocláin.
MacCole, mac ʒiolla Comʒaill 16; mac Comʒaill 2; mac Oubʒaill 2.
MacColgan, mac Colʒan.
MacColl, mac Colla.
MacCollom, mac Coluim.
MacCollough, mac Colla, (s.l.) mac Collac.
MacCollum, mac Coluim.
MacCollyams, mac Uilliam.
MacColman, mac Colmáin.
MacColum, mac Coluim.
MacComb, MacCombes, Mac-Combs, mac cóm, mac cómaiɼ.
MacComick, mac cómuic.

MacComish, mac cómaiɼ.
MacComiskey, mac Cumaɼcaiʒ.
MacComley, (?) mac Camlaoic.
MacComming, mac Coimín.
MacComoskey, mac Cumaɼcaiʒ.
MacCona, mac Oonncaóa.
MacConachie, Mac Conaghy, mac Oonncaió.
MacConamy, MacConaway, mac Conmeaóa, mac Conmeaóa 5; mac Conmióe 6.
MacConchie, mac Oonncaió.
MacCone, mac eoʒain 1; mac Comósin, mac Comʒain 62.
MacConell, mac Oomnaill.
MacCongail, MacConigly, mac Conʒail, mac Conʒaile.
MacConkey, mac Oonncaió.
MacConloy, mac Ouinnꝼléibe.
MacConn, mac miolcon.
MacConnachie, MacConnaghy, Mac Connaughey, mac Oonncaió.
MacConnaughty, mac Connac-taiʒ.
MacConnell, mac Oomnaill 1; mac Conaill 2.
MacConnellogue, macConaillóiʒ
MacConnerty, mac Connactaiʒ.
MacConnon, mac Canann.
MacConohy, mac Oonncaió.
MacConol, mac Oomnaill.
MacConomy, mac Conmióe.
MacConready, mac Conɼiaóa.
MacConvery, mac Ainmiɼe.
MacConville, mac Conmaoil.
MacConway, mac Conmeaóa.
MacCoo, mac Aoóa.
MacCooey, mac Cobcaiʒ.
MacCoog, MacCook, mac Oabuc (s.l.) mac Cuaʒ.
MacCool, v. MacCole.
MacCorcadale, mac coɼcaóail.
MacCord, mac Cuaiɼc.
MacCordick, (?)
MacCorkell, MacCorkill, Mac-Corkle, mac coɼcaill, mac cuɼcaill.

MacCorley, mac coipʋealḃaiᵹ.
MacCormac, MacCormack, Mac Cormick, mac copmaic, 11; mac copmacáin 197; Ó copmacáin 462.
MacCormicken, maccopmacáin.
MacCormilla, mac ᵹopmᵹaile.
MacCorquodale, mac copcaʋail.
MacCorrikle, mac copcaill, mac cupcaill.
MacCorry, mac coppaiʋ 2; mac ᵹocpaiʋ 2.
MacCosh, mac coipe.
MacCoskar, MacCosker, mac Opcaip..
MacCosbey, mac Oppaic.
MacCottar, MacCotter, Mac-Cottier, mac Oicip, (s.l.) mac coicip.
MacCoubrey, mac Cúicḃpéic.
MacCoughey, mac eoċaiʋ.
MacCoughlan, MacCoughlin, mac Coċláin.
MacCoughy, mac eoċaiʋ.
MacCoulaghan, mac uallaċáin.
MacCourt, MacCourtney, mac Cuapca, mac Cuaipc.
MacCovera, mac Cúicḃpéic.
MacCovey, mac Coḃcaiᵹ.
MacCowan, mac Comʋain, mac Comᵹain 1; mac eoᵹain 2; mac ᵹiolla Comʋain, mac ᵹiolla Comᵹain 62.
MacCowell, MacCowhill, mac Caċmaoil.
MacCowley, mac Amalᵹaʋa, mac Amalᵹaiʋ 5; mac Amlaoiḃ 6.
MacCownley, mac Annlaoiḃ.
MacCoy, mac Aoʋa.
MacCracken, mac Reaċcain, (o.f.) mac neaċcain.
MacCrail, mac Réill, (o.f.) mac néill.
MacCrainor, mac cpéinpip.
MacCraith, mac Cpaic, (o.f.) mac Raic.

MacCrann, mac Ḃpain.
MacCranor, mac cpéinpip.
MacCray, MacCrea, mac Raic, mac Cpaic.
MacCready, mac Riaʋa 11; mac Conpiaʋa 62.
MacCreanor, mac cpéinpip.
MacCreary, mac Ruiʋpí (mac Ruaiʋpí).
MacCreavy, mac Riaḃaiᵹ.
MacCreech, mac Raoip, (o.f.) mac Aonᵹuip.
MacCreedy, v. MacCready.
MacCreery, v. MacCreary.
MacCreesh, mac Raoip, (o.f.) mac Aonᵹuip.
MacCreevy, MacCrevey, mac Riaḃaiᵹ.
MacCrifferty, mac Ricḃeapcaiᵹ.
MacCrilly, mac Raᵹailliᵹ.
MacCrindle, mac Raᵹnaill.
MacCrink, (?) mac ṗpainnc.
MacCroberts, mac Roibeáipʋ, mac Roibeaipʋ.
MacCroghan, mac Conċpuaċan 9.
MacCrohan, mac Cpiomċainn 49, (s.l.) mac Cpioċan.
MacCrorken (?) mac Ruapcáin.
MacCrory, mac Ruaiʋpí.
MacCrossan, mac an Cpopáin. mac Cpopáin.
MacCrub, mac Rob.
MacCrudden, mac Roʋáin.
MacCrum, MacCrumb, (?) mac Cpuim.
MacCrystall, mac Cpiopcail.
MacCubrae, mac Cúicḃpéic.
MacCudden, mac Caʋáin, (s.l.) ma' Cuʋan.
MacCudy, mac Óʋa.
MacCue, mac Aoʋa.
MacCull, MacCulla, MacCullagh, MacCullah, mac Colla, (s.l) mac Collaċ.
MacCullen, MacCullion, mac Coilín 68, 69; mac Cuilinn 64.

MacCulloch, MacCullogh, ṁac
Colla, (s.l.) ṁac Collaċ.
MacCullough, MacCullow, ṁac
Colla, (s.l.) ṁac Collaċ 1 ;
ṁac Con ulaó 2.
MacCullum, ṁac Coluim.
MacCully, ṁac Colla.
MacCullyam, ṁac Uilliaṁ.
MacCumesky, Mac Cumisky,
ṁac Cuṁarcaiġ.
MacCumming, MacCummings,
ṁac Cuimín.
MacCune, ṁac eoġain.
MacCunneela, ṁac Conġaola.
MacCunnigan, ṁac Cuinne-
aġáin.
MacCunny, ṁac Connaió.
MacCurdy, ṁac Ṁuircearcaiġ,
(s.l.) ṁac Cuirciġ.
MacCure, ṁac Íoṁair.
MacCurry, ṁac Corraió 2 ;
ṁac Ġorraió 2.
Mac Curtain, ṁac Cuircáin.
MacCurtin, ṁac Cuircín, (o.f.)
ṁac Cruicín 76.
Mac Cushen, ṁac Oirín.
MacCusker, ṁac Orcair.
MacCuskern, ṁac Corcraċáin.
MacCuskin, (?) ṁac Uircín.
MacDacker, ṁac Ġiolla oea-
cair.
MacDade, MacDaid, ṁac Oaiḃ-
éió, (s.l.) ṁac Oaéió.
MacDaniall, MacDaniel, ṁac
Oomnaill.
MacDara, ṁac Oara, ṁac
Oarać, (o.f.) ṁac Ouiḃoarać.
MacDarby, ṁac Oiarmaoa.
MacDary, ṁac Oáire.
MacDavid, MacDavitt, ṁac
Oáiḃió, ṁac Oaiḃéió.
MacDermot, ṁac Oiarmaoa 1,
ṁac Oiarmaoa 97; Ó Ouiḃ-
óíorma, Ó Ouiḃóíormaiġ 16,
26.
MacDermott Gall, ṁac Oiar-
maoa Ġall ṁac Oiarmaoa
Ġalloa.

MacDermottroe, ṁac Oiar-
maoa Ruaó.
MacDevitt, ṁac Oaiḃéió.
MacDiarmod, v. MacDermott.
MacDigany, ṁac an Oeaġánaiġ.
MacDire, ṁac Ouiḃióir.
MacDivitt, ṁac Oaiḃéió.
MacDole, ṁac Ouḃġaill.
MacDona, MacDonagh, ṁac
Oonnċaóa 1, ṁac Óonnċaóa,
(s.l.) Ó Connċaóa 192.
MacDonald, ṁac Oomnaill.
MacDonnagh, v. MacDonagh.
MacDonnell, ṁac Oomnaill 1,
ṁac Óomnaill, (s.l.) Ó Coṁ-
naill 19.
MacDonogh, MacDonough, v.
MacDonagh.
MacDool, MacDougal, Mac
Dougald, MacDougall, Mac
Dowall, MacDowell, ṁac
Ouḃġaill.
MacDorcy, ṁac Oorċaió (O'D.)
MacDowney, ṁac Ġiolla Ooṁ-
naiġ 6.
MacDrury, ṁac an Oruaió.
MacDuff, ṁac Ouiḃ.
MacDugal, MacDugald, ṁac
Ouḃġaill.
MacDunn, ṁac Ouinn.
MacDunphy, ṁac Oonnċaió.
MacDwyer, ṁac Ouḃuióir, ṁac
Ouiḃióir.
MacEchern, ṁac eiċciġeirn.
MacEgan, ṁac Aoóaġáin.
MacElany, v. MacElhenny.
MacElcuddy, ṁac Ġiolla Cuoa,
ṁac Ġiolla Ṁocuoa.
MacElderry, (?) ṁac Ġiolla
oorċa.
MacEldowney, ṁac Ġiolla
Oomnaiġ.
MacEldrew, (?) ṁac Ġiolla
oorċa.
MacElduff, ṁac Ġiollaóuiḃ.
MacEleary, ṁac Ġiolla arraiċ.
MacEleavy, ṁac Ouinnṡléiḃe.
MacElerney, ṁac Ġiolla earna.

MacElestrim, mac Alarcpuim.
MacElfatrick, MacElfedrick,
mac ʒiolla Pápraiʒ.
MacElgan, mac ʒiollaʒáin.
MacElgun, MacElgunn, mac
ʒiolla ʋuinn.
MacElhair, MacElhar, mac
ʒiolla Cacaip.
MacElharry, mac ʒiolla
cappaiʒ.
MacElhatton, mac ʒiolla
Cacáin.
MacElhenny, MacElheny, mac
ʒiolla Coinniʒ.
MacElhill, mac ʒiolla coille.
MacElhinney, mac ʒiolla
Coinniʒ.
MacElholm, mac ʒiolla Colm,
mac ʒiolla Coluim.
MacElhone, mac ʒiolla Com-
ʒain, mac ʒiolla Comʋain.
MacElhoney, mac ʒiolla Coin-
niʒ.
MacElhoyle, mac ʒiolla coille.
MacElhuddy, mac ʒiolla Cuʋa,
(o.f.) mac ʒiolla mocuʋa.
MacElistrum, mac Alarcpuim.
MacElkenny, mac ʒiolla Coin-
niʒ.
MacEllen, mac Ailín.
MacElligott, mac Uileaʒóiʋ.
MacElin, mac Ailín.
MacEllister, mac Alarcaip.
MacEllistrim, MacEllistrum,
mac Alarcpuim.
MacElmeel, mac ʒiolla Micil
1 ; mac ʒiolla Maoil 2.
MacElmoyle, mac ʒiolla Maoil
MacElmurray, mac ʒiolla
Muipe.
MacElnea, mac ʒiolla na
naom.
MacElrath, MacElreath, Mac
Elreavy, mac ʒiollapiaʋaiʒ.
MacElroe, mac ʒiollapuaiʋ.
MacElrone, mac ʒiolla Ruaʋ-
áin.
MacElroy, mac ʒiollapuaiʋ.

MacElshander, Mac Elshender,
mac Alpanʋaip.
MacElsinan, mac ʒiolla Sion-
áin.
MacElvaine, mac ʒiollabáin.
MacElvee, mac ʒiollabuiʋe.
MacElveen, mac ʒiollamín.
MacElvenna, MacElvenny, mac
ʒiolla meana.
MacElvie, mac ʒiollabuiʋe.
MacElvogue,mac ʒiolla maoʋ-
óʒ.
MacElwain, MacElwane, Mac-
Elwean, mac ʒiollabáin.
MacElwee, mac ʒiollabuiʋe.
MacElwreath, mac ʒiollapiaʋ-
aiʒ.
MacEnally, mac an pailʒiʒ.
V. MacNally.
MacEnchroe, MacEncroe, mac
Concpaʋa.
MacEndoo, mac Conʋuiʋ.
MacEndry, mac Einpí, mac
Annpaoi.
MacEneaney, MacEneany, mac
Conaonaiʒ, (s.l.) mac an
éanaiʒ.
MacEneilis, mac niallʒuip.
MacEnerney, MacEnerny, mac
an Oipcinniʒ, mac an Aip-
cinniʒ.
MacEnery, mac Einpí, mac
Annpaoi 10 ; mac inneipʒe
7.
MacEniff, mac Conʋuiʋ.
MacEniry, mac inneipʒe.
MacEnnis, mac Aonʒuip.
MacEnright, mac ionnpaccaiʒ,
mac innpeaccaiʒ.
MacEnroe, mac Conpuʋa.
MacEnry, v. MacEnery.
MacEntagart, MacEntaggart,
MacEntaggert, mac an cSaʒ-
aipc.
MacEntee, mac an cSaoi.
MacEnteer, mac an cSaoip.
MacEntegart, mac an cSaʒaipc.
MacEntire, mac an cSaoip.

MacEntosh, mac an τaoıꞃıᵹ.
MacEoin, MacEown, mac eóın
2; mac eoᵹaın 2.
MacErchar, mac ꝼeaꞃċaıꞃ.
MacErlain, MacErlane, Mac-
Erlean, MacErleen, mac ꝼıꞃ-
léıᵹınn.
MacErrigle, mac ꝼeaꞃᵹaıl.
MacErrilly, mac ꝼeaꞃᵹaıle.
MacErvel, mac Ceaꞃbaıll.
MacEtavey, mac an τSámaıᵹ.
MacEvaddy, MacEvady, mac
an maᴅaıᴅ.
MacEvanny, MacEvany, mac
an manaıᵹ.
MacEvely, mac an mílıᴅ, mac
an míleaᴅa.
MacEver, mac éımıꞃ 2; mac
íomaıꞃ 2.
MacEvilly, mac an mílıᴅ, mac
an míleaᴅa.
MacEvin, mac Ɗuıbín.
MacEvinie, MacEvinney, mac
Ɗuıbne 67; mac aıbne 26.
MacEvoy, mac ᵹıollabuıᴅe,
(s.l.) mac 'a Ɗuıᴅe 2; mac
aoᴅa Ɗuıᴅe 2; mac ꝼíoᴅ-
buıᴅe, (o.f.) mac ꝼíoᴅbaᴅaıᵹ,
45; mac an Ɓeaċa, mac an
Ɓeaċaᴅ 2.
MacEwan, MacEwen, mac
eoᵹaın.
MacFaal, ó maolꝼábaıl.
MacFadden, MacFaddin, Mac-
Faddon, MacFaden, Mac-
Fadian, MacFadyen, Mac-
Fadzen, mac ꝼáıᴅín.
Mac Fall, MacFalls, mac ꝼáıl
1; ó maolꝼábaıl 62.
MacFarlaine, MacFarland, Mac-
Farlane, mac ꝼaꞃċaláın,
mac ꝼáꞃċaláın.
MacFarson, mac an ꝼeaꞃꝼúın,
mac an ꝼeaꞃꝼaın.
MacFate, mac ꝼáıᴅ.
MacFatridge, mac ꝼeaᴅoꝼuıꞃ.
MacFattrick, mac ꝼáτꞃaıc.

MacFattridge, mac ꝼeaᴅoꝼuıꞃ.
MacFeat, mac ꝼáıᴅ.
MacFeddan, mac ꝼáıᴅín.
MacFee, mac Ɗuıbꝼíċe.
MacFeeley. MacFeely, (?) mac
ꝼıċċeallaıᵹ.
MacFeerish, mac ꝼıaꞃaıꞃ.
MacFeeters, mac ꝼeaᴅaıꞃ.
MacFerran, mac meaꞃáın.
MacFerson, mac an ꝼeaꞃꝼúın,
mac an ꝼeaꞃꝼaın.
MacFetridge, MacFetrish, mac
ꝼeaᴅoꝼuıꞃ.
MacFettrick, mac ꝼáτꞃaıc.
MacFettridge, mac ꝼeaᴅoꝼuıꞃ.
MacFie, mac Ɗuıbꝼíċe.
MacFirbis, mac ꝼıꞃbıꞃıᵹ.
MacFlinn, MacFlynn, mac
ꝼloınn.
MacGaffigan, maᵹ eaċaᵹáın.
MacGaffin, maᵹ Ɗuıbꝼınn.
MacGaffrey, mac ᵹoꝼꞃaıᴅ, maᵹ
Caꝼꞃaıᴅ, maᵹ ᵹoꝼꞃaıᴅ.
MacGaggy, maᵹ eaċaıᴅ.
MacGagh, maᵹ eaċaċ, maᵹ
eaċaᴅa.
MacGahan, mac ᵹaoıċín 1,
(s.l.) maᵹ ᵹaċan 64; maᵹ
eaċáın 52.
MacGaheran, maᵹ eaċꞃáın.
MacGahey, maᵹ eaċaıᴅ.
MacGahran, maᵹ eaċꞃáın
MacGahy, maᵹ eaċaıᴅ.
MacGale v. Mac Call.
MacGaley, v. Mac Gawley.
MacGall, v. MacCall.
MacGalliogly, mac an ᵹallóᵹ-
laıᵹ.
MacGan, MacGann, maᵹ Canna,
maᵹ Cana 1, maᵹ annaıᴅ 34
maᵹ eaċáın 52; maᵹ Canann
46.
MacGannon, maᵹ ꝼıonnáın 9;
maᵹ Canann 46.
MacGaraghan, MacGarahan,
maᵹ aꞃaċáın, maᵹ ᵹaꞃaċáın
mac ᵹaꞃaċáın.

MacGarahy, mᴀ5 ⱶeᴀpᴀóᴀі5, (s.l.) mᴀ5 5eᴀpᴀċᴀі5.
MacGaraty, MacGarity, mᴀ5 ᴀіpeᴀċᴛᴀі5.
MacGarr, mᴀc ᴀn 5eᴀіpp.
MacGarran, mᴀ5 ᴀpᴀċᴀіn, mᴀ5 5ᴀpᴀċᴀіn, mᴀc 5ᴀpᴀċᴀіn 23 ; (?) mᴀ5 eᴀċpᴀіn 692.
MacGarrell, mᴀ5 ⱶeᴀp5ᴀіl.
MacGarrett, mᴀc 5eᴀpóіⱱ.
MacGarrigal, mᴀ5 ⱶeᴀp5ᴀіl.
MacGarrigan, mᴀc 5eᴀp5ᴀіn.
MacGarrigle, mᴀ5 ⱶeᴀp5ᴀіl.
MacGarrity, mᴀ5 ᴀіpeᴀċᴛᴀі5, mᴀ5 Oіpeᴀċᴛᴀі5.
MacGarroll, mᴀ5 ⱶeᴀp5ᴀіl.
MacGarry, mᴀ5 ⱶeᴀpᴀóᴀі5 1, (s.l.) mᴀ5 5ᴀpᴀіⱱ 34, mᴀc 5éᴀpᴀіⱱ 197.
MacGartlan, mᴀc 5ᴀpᴛlᴀn, uᴀ 5ᴀpᴛlᴀn (S.L.). V. Garlan.
MacGarty, v. MacGaraty.
MacGarvey, mᴀc 5ᴀіpⱱeіⱅ, mᴀc 5ᴀіpⱱіⱅ.
MacGaskell, mᴀ5 ᴀpcᴀіll.
MacGaugh, mᴀ5 eᴀⱅᴀċ, mᴀ5 eᴀⱅᴀóᴀ.
MacGaughey, mᴀ5 eᴀⱅᴀіⱱ.
MacGaughran, mᴀ5 eᴀⱅpᴀіn.
MacGaughy, MacGaugie, mᴀ5 eᴀⱅᴀіⱱ.
MacGaulay, MacGauley, mᴀ5 ᴀmᴀl5ᴀⱱᴀ, mᴀ5 ᴀmᴀl5ᴀіⱱ.
MacGauran, MacGaurn, Mac-Gavern, mᴀ5 Sᴀmpᴀіn, (o.f.) mᴀ5 Sᴀmpᴀⱱᴀіn.
MacGaver, mᴀ5 éіmіp 2 ; mᴀ5 іomᴀіp 2.
MacGavick, MacGavock, mᴀ5 óᴀⱱuіc, mᴀ5 óᴀⱱuc.
MacGaw, mᴀc óᴀⱱᴀіm.
MacGawlay, MacGawley, mᴀ5 ᴀmᴀl5ᴀⱱᴀ, mᴀ5 ᴀmᴀl5ᴀіⱱ.
MacGawran, mᴀ5 Sᴀmpᴀіn 1 ; (?) mᴀ5 eᴀċpᴀіn 62.
MacGeady, (?) mᴀc Céᴀⱱᴀі5.
MacGeagh, mᴀ5 eᴀⱅᴀċ, mᴀ5 eᴀⱅᴀóᴀ.

MacGean, mᴀc 5ᴀoіⱅín.
MacGeany, (?) mᴀ5 éᴀnnᴀ.
MacGeary, mᴀc 5ᴀⱱpᴀ 91, (.l.s) mᴀc 5ᴀopᴀ 97 ; mᴀ5 ⱶeᴀpᴀóᴀі5 6, 92.
MacGee, mᴀ5 ᴀoⱱᴀ, mᴀ5 ᴀoіⱱ 11, (s.l.) Ó 5ᴀoіⱱ 976 ; mᴀc 5ᴀoіⱅe 16 ; Ó mᴀol5ᴀoіⱅe 16, 19.
MacGeehan, mᴀc 5ᴀoіⱅín.
MacGeehee, mᴀc 5ᴀoіⱅe.
MacGeehin, mᴀc 5ᴀoіⱅín.
MacGeever, MacGeevor, mᴀ5 іomᴀіp.
MacGehan, mᴀc 5ᴀoіⱅín.
MacGellan, mᴀc 5eᴀlᴀіn.
MacGellick, mᴀ5 uіlіc.
MacGennis, MacGenniss, mᴀ5 ᴀon5uіp, mᴀ5 ᴀon5upᴀ.
MacGeoghegan, mᴀ5 eoċᴀ5ᴀіn.
MacGeough, mᴀ5 eoⱅᴀċ, mᴀ5 eoċᴀóᴀ.
MacGeown, mᴀ5 eo5ᴀіn 2 ; mᴀ5 éóіn 2.
MacGeraghty, MacGerety, mᴀ5 Oіpeᴀċᴛᴀі5.
MacGerr, mᴀc ᴀn 5іpp.
MacGerraghty, mᴀ5 Oіpeᴀċᴛᴀі5.
MacGerrigan, mᴀc 5eᴀp5ᴀіn.
MacGerrity, mᴀ5 Oіpeᴀċᴛᴀі5.
MacGerry, mᴀ5 ⱶeᴀpᴀóᴀі5.
MacGetrick, MacGetterick, mᴀ5 Sіⱅpіc.
MacGettigan, mᴀ5 eіⱅeᴀ5ᴀіn, mᴀ5 eіⱅі5eіn.
MacGhee, v. MacGee.
MacGherry, mᴀ5 ⱶeᴀpᴀóᴀі5.
MacGhie, v. MacGee.
MacGhoon, v. MacGowan.
MacGibben, MacGibbin, mᴀ5 ⱶіⱱín 2 ; mᴀc 5іoⱱúіn 2.
MacGibbon, mᴀc 5іoⱱúіn.
MacGibney, mᴀc 5іⱱne.
MacGiff, mᴀ5 óuіⱱ.
MacGiffen, mᴀ5 óuіⱱⱶínn.
MacGihan, MacGihen, mᴀc 5ᴀoіⱅín.

MacGilduff, mac ʒiollaóuiḃ.
MacGilfoyle, mac ʒiolla póil.
MacGilharry, mac ʒiollacáṙpaiʒ.
MacGill, mac an ʒoill 11 ; mac ʒiolla 62.
MacGillacowan, mac ʒiolla comṡain, mac ʒiolla comḋáin.
MacGillacuddy, mac ʒiolla cuóa, mac ʒiolla moċuóa.
MacGillan, mac ʒileáin.
MacGillbride, mac ʒiolla ḃríʒóe.
MacGilldowie, mac ʒiolla óuḃċaiʒ.
MacGilldowney, mac ʒiolla óoṁnaiʒ.
MacGillecuddy, mac ʒiolla cuóa.
MacGillen, mac ʒileáin.
MacGillerov, mac ʒiollaṙuaió.
MacGillespie, mac ʒiolla eaṙpuiʒ.
MacGillick, maʒ uillic, maʒ uilic.
MacGillicuddy, mac ʒiolla cuóa, mac ʒiolla moċuóa.
MacGilligan, mac ʒiollaʒáin.
MacGillivray, mac ʒiolla ḃráċa.
MacGilloway, MacGillowy, mac ʒiollaḃuióe.
MacGill Patrick, MacGillpatrick, mac ʒiolla páóraiʒ.
MacGillreavy, mac ʒiollaṙiaḃaiʒ.
MacGillroy, mac ʒiollaṙuaió.
MacGillshenan, mac ʒiolla seanáin.
MacGilly, maʒ coilió.
MacGillycuddy, mac ʒiolla cuóa, mac ʒiolla moċuóa.
MacGilpatrick, mac ʒiolla páóraiʒ.
MacGilpin, mac ʒiollaṙinn.
MacGilrea, mac ʒiollaṙiaḃaiʒ.
MacGilroy, mac ʒiollaṙuaió.

MacGilvane, macʒiollaḃáin.
MacGilvie, MacGilway, Mac Gilwee, mac ʒiollaḃuióe.
MacGimpsey, mac óíomaṙaiʒ.
MacGin, maʒ finn.
MacGindle, maʒ fionnʒail.
MacGinety, maʒ fionnaċtaiʒ, maʒ finneaċtaiʒ, &c.
MacGing, maʒ finn.
MacGiniss, maʒ aonʒuiṙ.
MacGinity, maʒ fionnaċtaiʒ, maʒ finneaċtaiʒ, &c.
MacGinley, MacGinly, mac fionnʒaile.
MacGinn, maʒ finn.
MacGinness, maʒ aonʒuiṙ, mac aonʒuṙa.
MacGinnety, v. MacGinety.
MacGinnis, maʒ aonʒuiṙ, maʒ aonʒuṙa.
MacGinnitty, MacGinty, maʒ fionnaċtaiʒ, maʒ finneaċtaiʒ 11 ; mac an tSaoi 352,
MacGirl, maʒ feaṙʒail.
MacGirr, mac an ʒiṙṙ.
MacGivena, maʒ óuiḃne.
MacGiver, maʒ uióiṙ.
MacGiveran, MacGiverin, Mac Givern, maʒ uióṙín.
MacGivney, maʒ óuiḃne.
MacGladdery, mac ʒleaóṙa.
MacGlade, maʒ léió.
MacGladery, mac ʒleaóṙa.
MacGlan, (?) maʒ flainn.
MacGlancy, maʒ flannċaóa, maʒ flannċaió.
MacGlare (?) mac ʒiolla ċaċaiṙ
MacGlashan, MacGlashin, mac ʒlaṙáin, mac ʒlaiṙín.
MacGlathery, mac ʒleaóṙa.
MacGlaughlin, maʒ loċlainn 11 ; mac ʒiolla seaċlainn 25, 37, 97.
MacGlave, maʒ laiċiṁ, (o.f.) maʒ flaiċiṁ, (s.l.) maʒ láiṁ.
MacGleish, mac ʒiolla íoṙa.
MacGlew, (?) mac óuinnṗléiḃe.

MacGlin, mᴀᴈ ꝼloınn.
MacGlinchey, MacGlinchy, mᴀᴈ loınᴈꞃıᴈ.
MacGloin, MacGlone, mᴀc ᴈıollᴀ eóın.
MacGlory, mᴀᴈ lᴀbꞃᴀóᴀ.
MacGloughlin, mᴀᴈ loċlᴀınn.
MacGlue (?) mᴀc Úuınnꝼléıbe.
MacGlynn, mᴀᴈ ꝼloınn.
MacGoey, mᴀᴈ eóċᴀıó.
MacGoff, mᴀᴈ eoċᴀċ, mᴀᴈ eoċᴀóᴀ.
MacGoggy, mᴀᴈ eoċᴀıó.
MacGoldrick, MacGolrick, mᴀᴈ uᴀlᴈᴀıꞃᴈ (s.l.) mᴀᴈ ᴈuᴀlꞃᴀıc.
MacGonagle, MacGonegal, Mac Gonegle, MacGonigal, Mac Gonigle, mᴀc conᴈᴀıl.
MacGonnell, v. MacConnell.
MacGonnigle, mᴀc conᴈᴀıl.
MacGoogan, mᴀᴈ ᴈuᴀᴈáın, (o.f.) mᴀᴈ eoċᴀᴈáın.
MacGoohan, mᴀc cuᴀċáın 39 ; mᴀᴈ eoċáın 2.
MacGookin, mᴀc ᴈuᴀıcín, (o.f.) mᴀᴈ eoċᴀıóín.
MacGoorty, mᴀᴈ Úoꞃċᴀıó, mᴀᴈ Úoꞃċᴀıóe.
MacGorish, MacGorisk, mᴀᴈ ꝼeóꞃᴀıꞃ, mᴀᴈ ꝼeóꞃuıꞃ.
MacGorl, mᴀᴈ ꝼeᴀꞃᴈᴀıl.
MacGorley, mᴀᴈ coıꞃóeᴀlbᴀıᴈ.
MacGorlic, MacGorlick, mᴀᴈ uᴀlᴈᴀıꞃᴈ.
MacGorman, mᴀc ᴈoꞃmáın.
MacGorrian, MacGorrin, mᴀᴈ coꞃꞃᴀıóín.
MacGorry, mᴀc ᴈoċꞃᴀıó.
MacGorty, mᴀᴈ Úoꞃċᴀıó, mᴀᴈ Úoꞃċᴀıóe.
MacGough, mᴀᴈ eoċᴀċ, mᴀᴈ eoċᴀóᴀ.
MacGouldrick, mᴀᴈ uᴀlᴈᴀıꞃᴈ, (s.l.) mᴀᴈ ᴈuᴀlꞃᴀıc.
MacGouran, mᴀᴈ sᴀṁꞃáın.
MacGourkey, MacGourty, mᴀᴈ Úoꞃċᴀıó, mᴀᴈ Úoꞃċᴀıóe.

MacGovern, MacGovran, mᴀᴈ sᴀṁꞃáın, (o.f.) mᴀᴈ sᴀṁꞃᴀóáın.
MacGoverney, (?) mᴀc coıbóeᴀnᴀıᴈ.
MacGowan, MacGowen, MacGown, mᴀc ᴀn ᴈobᴀnn, mᴀc ᴀn ᴈᴀbᴀnn, mᴀc ᴈobᴀnn, mᴀc ᴈᴀbᴀnn 1 ; mᴀc ᴈᴀṁnᴀ, 2 ; mᴀᴈ Úubáın 19.
MacGowran, mᴀᴈ sᴀṁꞃáın.
MacGra, mᴀᴈ Rᴀıċ, mᴀᴈ cꞃᴀıċ.
MacGrade, MacGrady, mᴀᴈ Úꞃáoᴀıᴈ.
MacGragh, mᴀᴈ Rᴀıċ, mᴀᴈ cꞃᴀıċ.
MacGranahan, mᴀᴈ Reᴀnnᴀċáın.
MacGrane, mᴀᴈ Ráıᴈne, (s.l.) mᴀ ᴈꞃáıne, mᴀ ᴈꞃánᴀ 64.
MacGranell, mᴀᴈ Rᴀᴈnᴀıll.
MacGrann, mᴀᴈ Úꞃᴀın.
MacGrath, mᴀᴈ Rᴀıċ, mᴀc cꞃᴀıċ, mᴀᴈ cꞃᴀıċ.
MacGrattan, (?) mᴀᴈ Reᴀċċᴀın, (o.f.) mᴀᴈ neᴀċċᴀın. Cf. MacCracken.
MacGraun, v. MacGrann.
MacGraw, v. MacGrath.
MacGreal, mᴀᴈ Réıll, (o.f.) mᴀᴈ néıll.
MacGrean, mᴀᴈ Rᴀıᴈne.
MacGreen, mᴀᴈ Rᴀıᴈne 2 ; mᴀc ᴈlᴀꞃáın 2.
MacGreer, mᴀc ᴈꞃıoᴈᴀıꞃ.
MacGreevy, mᴀᴈ Rıᴀbᴀıᴈ.
MacGregan, mᴀᴈ Rıᴀᴈáın.
MacGregar, MacGregor, MacGregory, mᴀc ᴈꞃéᴀᴈóıꞃ, mᴀc ᴈꞃeᴀᴈᴀıꞃ, mᴀc ᴈꞃıoᴈᴀıꞃ.
MacGrenahan, MacGrenehan, mᴀᴈ Reᴀnnᴀċáın.
MacGrenor, mᴀᴈ Cꞃéınꝼıꞃ.
MacGrievy, mᴀᴈ Rıᴀbᴀıᴈ.
MacGriffin, mᴀc ᴈꞃıꝼín.
MacGrillan, (?) mᴀᴈ Rıᴀlláın, (o.f.) mᴀᴈ nıᴀlláın.

MacGrillish, ᴍᴀʒ Ríᴀʅʅʒuıꝛ, (o.f.) ᴍᴀʒ nıᴀʅʅʒuıꝛ, (s.l.) ᴍᴀʒ Ꞡꝛıᴀʅʅuıꝛ.
MacGriskin, ᴍᴀc Cꝛıꝛcín.
MacGroany, ᴍᴀʒ Cᴀꝛꝛʒᴀṁnᴀ,
MacGronan, ᴍᴀʒ Rᴀʒnᴀınn, (o.f.) ᴍᴀʒ Rᴀʒnᴀıʅʅ.
MacGrory, ᴍᴀʒ Ruᴀıᴅꝛí.
MacGrotty, (?) ᴍᴀʒ Rᴀcᴀ.
MacGrudder, ᴍᴀʒ Ḃꝛuᴀᴅᴀıꝛ.
MacGuane, ᴍᴀʒ Ḋuḃáın.
MacGuckian, MacGuckin, ᴍᴀʒ eoċᴀıᴅín, (s.l.) ᴍᴀc ʒuᴀıcín.
MacGueran, (?) ᴍᴀc ʒéᴀꝛáın 46.
MacGuff, ᴍᴀʒ Ḋuıḃ.
MacGuffin, ᴍᴀʒ Ḋuıḃꝼınn.
MacGughian, MacGuickian, ᴍᴀʒ eoċᴀıᴅín.
MacGuiehan, ᴍᴀc ʒᴀoıċín.
MacGuigan, MacGuiggan, ᴍᴀʒ eoċᴀʒáın, (s.l.) ᴍᴀc ʒuᴀʒáın, ᴍᴀc ʒúıʒeᴀn.
MacGuighan, ᴍᴀʒ eoċáın.
MacGuill, ᴍᴀc Cuıʅʅ.
MacGuillan, ᴍᴀc Coıʅín.
MacGuinn, ᴍᴀc Cuınn.
MacGuinness, MacGuinnessy, ᴍᴀʒ ᴀonʒuıꝛ, ᴍᴀʒ ᴀonʒuꝛᴀ.
MacGuire, ᴍᴀʒ Uıᴅıꝛ.
MacGuirk, ᴍᴀʒ Cuıꝛc, ᴍᴀc Cuıꝛc.
MacGullian, MacGullion, ᴍᴀc Coıʅín.
MacGuone, MacGuown, v. MacGowan.
MacGurgan, (?) ᴍᴀc Ḋuᴀꝛcáın.
MacGurk, MacGurke, ᴍᴀc Cuıꝛc, ᴍᴀʒ Cuıꝛc.
MacGurkin, (?) ᴍᴀc Ḋuᴀꝛcáın.
MacGurl, v. MacGorl.
MacGurn, MacGurran, MacGurrin ᴍᴀʒ Coꝛꝛáın, ᴍᴀʒ Coꝛꝛᴀıᴅín.
MacGurrell, v. MacGarrell.
MacGurry, ᴍᴀc ʒoċꝛᴀıᴅ.
MacGushion, ᴍᴀʒ Oıꝛín.
MacGuskin, ᴍᴀʒ Uıꝛcín.

MacGusty, ᴍᴀc Oıꝛce, ᴍᴀʒ Oıꝛce.
MacHaffie, MacHaffy, ᴍᴀc Ḋuıḃꝼíce.
MacHaig, ᴍᴀc Cᴀıᴅʒ.
MacHale, ᴍᴀc hᴀoʅ, ᴍᴀc hᴀeʅ, ᴍᴀc héıʅ.
MacHall, ᴍᴀc Cᴀċᴀıʅ 2; ᴍᴀc Cᴀċṁᴀoıʅ 62.
MacHanfry, Machanfry, ᴍᴀc hunꝛꝛᴀıᴅ.
MacHarnon, ᴍᴀc Cıʒeᴀꝛnáın.
MacHarroll, ᴍᴀc Ꝼeᴀꝛʒᴀıʅ 2; ᴍᴀc Ceᴀꝛḃᴀıʅʅ 2.
MacHarry, ᴍᴀc Aᴍꝛᴀoı 2; ᴍᴀc Ꝼeᴀꝛᴀᴅᴀıʒ 2; ᴍᴀc ʒıoʅʅᴀċᴀꝛꝛᴀıʒ 29.
MacHay, ᴍᴀc Aoᴅᴀ.
MacHeath, ᴍᴀc Síċıʒ.
MacHeffey, ᴍᴀc eᴀċᴀıᴅ.
MacHendrie, MacHendry, v. MacHenry.
MacHenery, v. MacEnery.
MacHenry, ᴍᴀc éınꝛí, ᴍᴀc Anꝛᴀoı, ᴍᴀc hᴀnnꝛᴀoı.
MacHinch, ᴍᴀc Aonʒuıꝛ.
MacHinny, v. MacKinny.
MacHue, MacHugh, ᴍᴀc Aoᴅᴀ 1, ᴍᴀc Aoıᴅ 2.
MacIlboy, ᴍᴀcIlbwee, ᴍᴀc ʒıoʅʅᴀḃuıᴅe.
MacIlchon, ᴍᴀc ṁıoʅċon.
MacIlderry, (?) ᴍᴀc ʒıoʅʅᴀ ᴅoꝛċᴀ.
MacIldoon, ᴍᴀc ṁᴀoıʅᴅúın.
MacIldowie, ᴍᴀc ʒıoʅʅᴀ Ḋuḃꝛᴀıʒ.
MacIldowney, ᴍᴀc ʒıoʅʅᴀ Ḋoṁnᴀıʒ.
MacIlduff, ᴍᴀc ʒıoʅʅᴀᴅuıḃ.
MacIleboy, ᴍᴀc ʒıoʅʅᴀḃuıᴅe.
MacIleese, ᴍᴀc ʒıoʅʅᴀ íoꝛᴀ.
MacIlfatrick, MacIlfederick, ᴍᴀc ʒıoʅʅᴀ Ꝑáᴅꝛᴀıʒ.
MacIlgorm, ᴍᴀc ʒıoʅʅᴀʒuıꝛm.
MacIlhair, ᴍᴀc ʒıoʅʅᴀ Cᴀċᴀıꝛ.
MacIlhaney, ᴍᴀc ʒıoʅʅᴀ Cᴀınnıʒ.

MacIlhar, mac Ġiolla Ċaṫair.
MacIlhargy, mac Ġiolla Ḟearġ.
MacIlharry, mac Ġiollaċarraiġ
MacIlhatton, mac Ġiolla Ċaṫáin.
MacIlhenny, mac Ġiolla Ċoinniġ.
MacIlherron, mac Ġiolla Ciaráin.
MacIlhone, mac Ġiolla Ċomġáin, mac Ġiolla Ċoṁáin.
MacIlhoney, mac Ġiolla Ċoinniġ.
MacIlhoyle, mac Ġiolla ċoille.
MacIlhun, mac ṁíolċon.
MacIllhatton, mac Ġiolla Ċaṫáin.
MacIllicuddy, mac Ġiolla Ċuda
MacIllwain, mac Ġiollabáin.
MacIlmoil, MacIlmoyle, mac Ġiollaṁaoil.
MacIlmurray, mac Ġiolla ṁuire.
MacIlpatrick, mac Ġiolla Pádraig.
MacIlravy, MacIlrea, mac Ġiollaṙiaḃaiġ.
MacIlroy, mac Ġiollaruaiḋ.
MacIlvany, mac Ġiolla ṁeana.
MacIlveen, mac Ġiollaṁín.
MacIlwaine, mac Ġiollabáin.
MacIlwee, mac Ġiollabuiḋe.
MacIlwraith, MacIlwrath, mac Ġiollaṙiaḃaiġ.
MacInally, mac an Ḟailġiġ. V. MacNally.
MacInch, mac Aonġuir.
MacIndoo, mac Conduiḃ.
MacIneely, mac Congaile.
MacInerney, MacInerny, Mac Innerney, mac an Airċinniġ, mac an Oirċinniġ.
MacInnes, mac Aonġuir.
MacIntagert, MacIntaggart, mac an tSagairt.
MacIntee, mac an tSaoi.
MacInteer, mac an tSaoir.

MacInteggart, mac an tSagairt
MacIntire, mac an tSaoir.
MacIntosh, mac an taoiriġ.
MacIntyre, mac an tSaoir.
MacIveagh, mac an Ḃeaṫa, mac an Ḃeaṫaḃ.
MacIver, MacIvers, MacIvor, mac íoṁair.
MacJimpsey, mac Díomasaiġ.
MacKage, MacKague, Mac Kaige, mac Caiḋg.
MacKain, mac eáin 1; mac Caṫáin 2.
MacKalshander, mac Alṙanḋair.
MacKane, mac eáin 1; mac Caṫáin 2.
MacKann, v. MacCann.
MacKaree, mac Ḟearaḋáiġ.
MacKarel, mac Ḟearġail.
MacKay, Mackay, mac Aoḋa.
MacKeady, mac Céaḋaiġ 5; mac Céiḋiġ, mac éiḋiġ 779.
MacKeag, MacKeague, mac Caiḋg.
MacKean, mac eáin, mac Iain 1; Ó Mocáiḋein 64.
MacKeane, mac Aoḋáin, 19, 97.
MacKeany, mac éanna 4; mac Cionaoiḋ 6.
MacKearney, mac Cearnaiġ.
MacKeary, mac Ḟiacra, mac Ḟiacraċ 1; mac Ḟeraḋáiġ 2.
MacKeating, (?) mac Céitín.
MacKeaveney, MacKeaveny, mac Ġéiḃeannaiġ.
MacKeaver, mac íoṁair.
MacKee, mac Aoiḋ 11; mac an Ċaoiċ 67, 82.
MacKeefrey, mac Ḟiacra, mac Ḟiacraċ.
MacKeegan, mac Aoḋaġáin.
MacKeeman, MacKeemon, mac Síomóin, mac Síomoinn.
MacKeen. mac Caṫáin 46.
MacKeeney, MacKeeny, v. MacKeany.

MacKeever, MacKeevor, ᵯac ᵼoṁaıᵽ.

MacKeighry, ᵯac ᵼıaċᵽa, ᵯac ᵼıaċᵽaċ.

MacKeigue, ᵯac ᴛaıóʒ.

MacKeith, ᵯac Síᴛıʒ.

MacKeiver, ᵯac ᵼoṁaıᵽ.

Mackel, v. Magill.

MacKeleghan, ᵯac Ceallacáın

MacKellan, MacKellen, ᵯac Aıleáın, ᵯac Coılín.

MacKellop, ᵯac ᵼılıb.

MacKelly, ᵯac Ceallaıʒ.

MacKelshenter, ᵯac Alᵽan-ᴅaıᵽ.

MacKeivey, ᵯac ʒıollaƀuıᴅe.

MacKemmin, ᵯac Ámoınn.

Mackelwaine, ᵯac ʒıollabáın.

Macken, Ó ᵯaıcín 1, Ó ᵯacáın, 2 ; ᵯac ᵯaıcín 16.

MacKendrick, ᵯac Annᵽaıc, ᵯac eanᵽaıc.

MacKendry, v. MacHenry.

MacKenery, v. MacEnery.

MacKeniry, ᵯac ınneıᵽʒe.

MacKenna, ᵯac Cıonaoᴅa, ᵯac Cıonaoıᴛ 1, (s.l.) ᵯaʒ Cıneáıᴛ 7 ; ᵯac eanna 2.

MacKennery, v. MacEnery.

MacKenny, ᵯac Cıonaoıᴛ.

MacKensie, v. MacKenzie.

MacKenty, ᵯac an ᴛSaoı.

MacKenzie, Mackenzie, ᵯac Coınnıʒ.

MacKeo, ᵯac eocaᴅa.

MacKeoan, ᵯac eoʒaın.

MacKeogh, ᵯac eocaᴅa, ᵯac eoᴛaċ, (s.l) ᵯac Ceoᴛaċ, ᵯac Ceóċ.

MacKeon, MacKeone, ᵯac eóın 2 ; ᵯac eoʒaın 2.

MacKeough, ᵯac eocaᴅa.

MacKeowen, MacKeown, ᵯac eóın 2 ; ᵯac eoʒaın 2.

MacKerel, ᵯac ᵼeaᵽʒaıl.

MacKerley, MacKerlie, ᵯac ᵼeaᵽʒaıle 2 ; ᵯac ᴛoıᵽᴅealb-aıʒ 2.

MacKernan, ᵯac ᴛıʒeaᵽnáın.

MacKerr, (?) ᵯac Coᵽᵽa, ᵯac Caᵽᵽa.

MacKerrall, MacKerrell, ᵯac ᵼeaᵽʒaıl.

MacKerrigan, ᵯac Cıaᵽaʒáın.

MacKerrow, ᵯac Cıoċᵽuaᴅa.

MacKervel, ᵯac Ceaᵽƀaıll.

Mackessy, Ó ᵯacaᵽa.

MacKetian, (?) ᵯac Céıᴛín.

MacKetterick, MacKettrick, ᵯac Síᴛᵽıc.

MacKevin, ᵯac Ꝺuıbín.

MacKevitt, ᵯac Ꝺaıƀéıᴅ.

MacKevor, ᵯac ᵼoṁaıᵽ.

MacKew, ᵯac Aoᴅa.

MacKewen, ᵯac eoʒaın 2 ; ᵯac eóın 2.

MacKey, ᵯac Aoᴅa, ᵯac Aoıᴅ.

Mackey, ᵯac Aoᴅa, ᵯac Aoıᴅ 1 ; Ó ᵯacᴅa 17, 27, 77.

MacKibben, MacKibbin, ᵯac ᵼıbín.

MacKibbon, ᵯac ʒıobúın.

MacKie, ᵯac Aoıᴅ.

MacKiernan, ᵯac ᴛıʒeaᵽnáın.

MacKiever, ᵯac ᵼoṁaıᵽ.

MacKilbouy, ᵯac ʒıollaƀuıᴅe.

MacKilbride, ᵯac ʒıolla Ꝺᵽíʒᴅe.

MacKilkelly, ᵯac ʒıolla Ceall-aıʒ.

MacKillen, MacKillian, Mac Killion, ᵯac Coılín, ᵯac Aıleáın.

MacKillip, MacKillop, **Mac** Killops, ᵯac ᵼılıb.

MacKilmurray, ᵯac ʒıolla ṁuıᵽe.

MacKilveen, ᵯac ʒıollaṁín.

MacKilvie, ᵯac ʒıollaƀuıᴅe.

MacKilwane, ᵯac ʒıollabáın.

MacKim, ᵯac Sím.

MacKimmie, ᵯac Símıᴅ.

MacKimmon, Mackimmon, ᵯac Síomóın, ᵯac Síomoınn.

Mackin, Ó ᵯaıcín 1, Ó ᵯacáın 2 ; ᵯac ᵯaıcín 16.

MacKinaul, Mackinaul, mac Con ulaṫ.
MacKinch, mac ᴀonᵹuıṗ.
MacKinerkin, MacKinerking, mac ᴀn ᴀıṗċınn, mac ᴀn Oıṗċınn.
MacKinestry, mac ᴀn ᴀıṗᴄṗıᵹ.
MacKing, mac ṗınn.
MacKiniff, mac Conᴏuıḃ.
MacKinirking,v. Mac Kinerking.
MacKinlay, MacKinley, mac ṗıonnlᴀoıċ S 2, (o.f.) mac ṗıonnloᵹᴀ, (s.l.) mac Cıúllᴀ ; mac Conleᴀᵹᴀ, (o.f.) mac ᴀn leᴀᵹᴀ 2.
MacKinn, mac ṗınn.
MacKinnawe, mac Conṗnáṁᴀ.
MacKinney, MacKinnie, mac Cıonᴀoıċ 2 ; mac Coınnıᵹ 2.
MacKinnon, mac ṗıonᵹuıne. (s.l.) mac ṗıonúın.
MacKinny, v. MacKinney.
MacKinstry, mac ᴀn ᴀıṗᴄṗıᵹ.
MacKintosh, Mackintosh, mac ᴀn ᴄᴀoıṗıᵹ.
MacKinty, mac ᴀn ᴄSᴀoı.
MacKinzie, v. MacKenzie.
MacKirdy, mac ṁuıṗċeᴀṗᴄᴀıᵹ.
MacKirtrick, mac Sıᴄṗıc.
MacKissock, mac íoṗóc, mac íoṗóᵹ.
MacKitterick, MacKittrick, mac Sıᴄṗıc 1 ; mac Cıoᴄṗᴀṫᴀ 376.
MacKiver, Mackiver, mac íoṁᴀıṗ.
Mackle, v. Magill.
Macklebreed, mac ᵹıollᴀ Ḃṗíᵹᴅe.
Macklehattan, mac ᵹıollᴀ Ċᴀᴄáın.
Macklemoyle, mac ᵹıollᴀṁᴀoıl.
MacKlern, mac ᵹıollᴀ Cıᴀṗáın.
Macklewaine, mac ᵹıollᴀḃáın.
Macklewraith, mac ᵹıollᴀṗıᴀḃᴀıᵹ.
MacKneight, v. MacKnight.

MacKniff, mac Conᴏuıḃ.
MacKnight, mac ᴀn Rıᴏıṗe 2 ; mac eᴀċᴀıṫ 35 ; mac neᴀċᴄᴀın 62.
MacKnulty, mac ᴀn ultᴀıᵹ.
MacKoen, MacKone, mac eoᵹᴀın 2 ; mac Coṁᵹᴀın, mac Coṁṫᴀın 2.
MacKonkey, mac Ḃonnċᴀıṫ.
MacKonnigham, mac Coınneᴀᵹáın.
MacKough, mac eoċᴀṫᴀ, mac eoᴄᴀċ.
MacKoy, mac ᴀoṫᴀ.
MacKrann, mac Ḃṗᴀın.
MacKrell, mac ṗeᴀṗᵹᴀıl.
MacKurdy, mac ṁuıṗċeᴀṗᴄᴀıᵹ.
MacKuscar, MacKusker, mac Oṗᴄᴀıṗ.
MacKussack, mac íoṗóc, mac íoṗóᵹ, mac íṗeóc.
MacLachlan, MacLachlin, mac lᴀċlᴀınn.
MacLagan, mac ᵹıollᴀ ᴀṫᴀṁᴀᵹáın.
MacLaghlan, mac lᴀċlᴀınn.
MacLain, MacLaine, v. Mac Lean.
MacLamond, mac lᴀᵹmᴀınn, mac lᴀṫmᴀınn.
MacLandrish, mac ᵹıollᴀ ᴀınᴏṗéıṗ.
MacLane, v. MacLean.
MacLaren, mac lᴀḃṗᴀınn.
MacLarenon, MacLarinon, mac ᵹıollᴀ eᴀṗnáın.
MacLarney, ó mᴀoıl eᴀṗnᴀ 89. V. MacLerney.
MacLarnon, mac ᵹıollᴀ eᴀṗnáın
MacLary, mac ᵹıollᴀ ᴀṗṗᴀıᴄ.
MacLauchlin, mac lᴀċlᴀınn, mac loċlᴀınn.
MacLaughlin, mac lᴀċlᴀınn, mac loċlᴀınn 11 ; ó mᴀoıleᴀċlᴀınn, ó mᴀoıl Seᴀċlᴀınn 8, 9 ; ó lᴀċᴄnáın 99.
MacLauren, MacLaurin, mac lᴀḃṗᴀınn.

MacMagh, mac maca.
MacMaghen, MacMaghon, Mac Maghone, MacMahan, Mac Mahon, mac macgamna 11; ó macgamna 37, 38.
MacManaman, MacManamon, mac meanman.
MacManamy, mac meanma.
MacManis, v. MacManus.
MacMann, v. MacMahon.
MacMannion, MacMannon, mac manainn.
MacMannus, MacManus, mac magnuir, mac magnura.
MacMaster, mac an maigirtir.
MacMath, mac maca.
MacMay, mac maige, (s.) mac maigeóc, mac maigeóg.
MacMearty, mac muirceartaig
MacMechan, MacMeckan, Mac Meckin, MacMeechan, Mac Meekan, MacMeeken, Mac Meekin, (?) mac miavacáin.
MacMeel, mac giolla mícil 1, mac mícil 2; mac giolla-maoil 2.
MacMeenamon, v. MacMenamin.
MacMeichan, v. MacMechan.
MacMenamen, MacMenamin, MacMenamon, mac meanman.
MacMenamy, mac meanma.
MacMenemen, mac meanman
MacMenemy, mac meanma.
MacMenim, mac meanman.
MacMenimey, mac meanma.
MacMenimin, mac meanman.
MacMerty, mac muirceartaig.
MacMey, v. MacMay.
MacMichael, mac giolla mícil, mac mícil.
MacMichalin, mac mícilín.
MacMichall, v. MacMichael.
MacMichan, v. MacMechan.
MacMighall, v. MacMichael.
MacMillan, mac maolmáin.
MacMillen, MacMillin, mac maolmáin, mac maoilín.

MacMinamy, mac meanma.
MacMinimin, mac meanman.
MacMinn, (?)
MacMonagle, MacMonegal, Mac Monigal, MacMonigle, mac maongail.
MacMoran, mac mugróin, (s.l.) mac mogmáin 39, 97; mac muircáin 2.
MacMordie, mac muirceartaig.
MacMorin, MacMorns, Mac Morran, v. MacMoran.
MacMorray, v. MacMurray.
MacMorris, mac muirir, mac muirir 2; mac muirguir, mac muirgeara 2.
MacMorrow, mac muircava 1; mac muireavaig 67.
MacMorry, mac muireavaig.
MacMouran, v. MacMoran
MacMoyler, mac maoilir.
MacMrearty, mac muirceart-aig.
MacMullan, MacMullen, Mac Mullin, MacMullon, mac maolmáin.
MacMunaway, (?)
MacMunigal, mac maongail.
MacMurdy, mac muirceartaig.
MacMurlan, MacMurland, mac muirgaláin.
MacMurran v MacMoran.
MacMurray mac muireavaig 1; mac muircava 33 (O'D); mac giolla muire 2.
MacMuren, MacMurrin, v. Mac Moran.
MacMurrough, mac muircava.
MacMurrough Kavanagh, mac muircava caománac.
MacMurry, mac muireavaig.
MacMurtery, MacMurthry, Mac Murtie, MacMurtry, mac muirceartaig.
MacNabb, mac an abbav 11 mac anabava 62.
MacNabo, MacNaboe, Mac Nabow, mac anabava.

MacNaboola, mac Con na buaile
MacNaghten, MacNaghton, mac neaċtain.
MacNail, mac néill.
MacNair, mac an maoir.
MacNairn, mac an aircinn.
MacNale, mac néill.
MacNally, mac an failġiġ 11 ; mac Con ulaḃ 62.
MacNalty, mac Conallta.
MacNama, mac Conmeaḋa.
MacNamanamee, (?)
MacNamara, MacNamarra, Mac Namarrow, mac Conmara.
MacNamee, mac Conmíḋe.
MacNarry, mac náraḋaiġ.
MacNaugher, mac Conċoḃair.
MacNaught, MacNaughten, Mac Naughton, mac neaċtain.
MacNay, MacNea, MacNeagh, mac niaḃ, mac néiḋe.
MacNeal, mac néill.
MacNealey, MacNeally, Mac Nealy, mac Conġaile 91 ; mac Conġaola 92 ; mac an fileaḃ, mac an filiḃ 6.
MacNearney, mac an Oirċinniġ.
MacNeary, mac náraḋaiġ.
MacNee, mac niaḃ, mac néiḋe.
MacNeece, mac naoir, mac naora, (o.f.) mac Aonġuir, mac Aonġura.
MacNeel, mac néill.
MacNeela, v. MacNealy.
MacNeeld, MacNeele, mac néill.
MacNeely, v. MacNealy.
MacNeeny, mac Conaonaiġ.
MacNeese, mac naoir, mac naora (o.f.) mac Aonġuir, mac Aonġura.
MacNeffe, mac Conḋuiḃ.
MacNeice, mac naoir, mac naora (o.f.) mac Aonġuir, mac Aonġura.
MacNeigh, mac néiḋe, mac niaḃ.

MacNeight, mac neaċtain.
MacNeilage, mac niallġuir.
MacNeile, MacNeill, mac néill.
MacNeilly, v. MacNealy.
MacNeiry, mac inneirġe.
MacNelis, mac niallġuir.
MacNella, MacNello, v. Mac Nealy.
MacNeney, mac Conaonaiġ, (s.l.) mac an éanaiġ.
MacNerhenny, mac an aircinniġ, mac an Oirċinniġ.
MacNerland, MacNerlin, mac an firléiġinn.
MacNern, mac an Oirċinn.
MacNerney, MacNertney, mac an aircinniġ, mac an Oirċinniġ.
MacNestry, mac an airtriġ.
MacNevin, mac Cnáiṁín.
MacNicholas, mac niocláir.
MacNickle, MacNicol, mac niocoil, mac niocóil.
MacNiece, mac naoir, mac naora, (o.f.) mac Aonġuir, mac Aonġura.
MacNielly, v. MacNealy.
MacNiff, mac Conḋuiḃ.
MacNight, mac neaċtain.
MacNilly, mac an fileaḃ, mac an filiḃ.
MacNinch, mac Aonġuir.
MacNirny, MacNirney, mac an Oirċinniġ, mac an aircinniġ.
MacNish, mac naoir, (o.f.) mac Aonġuir.
MacNite, v. MacNight.
MacNiven, mac naoiṁín.
MacNoger, MacNogher, Mac Noher, mac Conċoḃair.
MacNuff, mac Conḋuiḃ.
MacNulty, mac an ultaiġ.
MacNutt, mac nuaḋaḋ, mac nuaḋat.
MacOscar, mac Orcair.
MacOstrich, (?) mac Orraic.
MacOubery, MacOubery, mac Cúiṫḃréiċ.

MacOwen, mac eoġain 1 ; mac
eóin 2.

MacPadden, MacPadden, Mac
Paden, MacPadgen, Mac
Padian, mac pároín.

MacPake, mac péice.

MacParland, MacParlin, Mac
Partlan, MacPartland, Mac
Partlin, mac paptaláin, mac
páptaláin, mac páptláin,
mac paplám.

MacPaul, mac póil 62 ; ó
maolpábail 66.

MacPeake, mac péice.

MacPhadden, mac pároín.

MacPhail, mac póil, mac póil,
mac páil.

MacPharland, mac paptaláin,
mac páptaláin.

MacPhatrick, mac pátraic.

MacPhee, mac óuibríte.

MacPhelan, mac paoláin.

MacPhelimy, Mac Phellimy,
mac peiólimió.

MacPherson, mac an peappúin.

MacPhettridge, mac peaopuir.

MacPhilbin, mac pilibín.

MacPhillemy mac peiólimió..

MacPhillips, mac pilib.

MacPhilpin, mac pilibín, mac
pilbín, mac pilibín.

MacPhun, mac munna.

MacPolin, mac póilín.

MacQuade, MacQuaid, Mac
Quaide, mac uaió.

MacQualter, mac ualtaip.

MacQuarrie, mac suaipe.

MacQuatters, mac uaitéip.

MacQuay, mac aoóa.

MacQueen, Macqueen, mac
Suibne.

MacQuestion, MacQueston, mac
úirtin.

MacQuey, mac aoóa.

Macquien, v. MacQueen.

MacQuiggan, mac suaiġín, mac
súiġean, (o.f.) mac eocaióín.

MacQuilin, v. MacQuillin.

MacQuilkan, MacQuilkin, mac
uilcín.

MacQuill, mac cuill.

MacQuillan, MacQuillen, mac
coilín 69 ; mac cuilinn 64 ;
mac uióilín, mac uiólín,
mac uiġilín 36.

MacQuilliams, mac uilliam.

MacQuillian, MacQuillin, Mac
Quillion, MacQuillon, v. Mac
Quillan.

MacQuilly, mac an coiliġ, mac
coiliġ, mac coilió 2 ; mac
uiólió 36.

MacQuilquane, mac uilcín.

MacQuin, mac cuinn.

MacQuiney, (?) mac Suibne.

MacQuinn, mac cuinn.

MacQuinney, (?) mac Suibne.

MacQuirk, MacQuirke, mac
cuirc.

MacQuish, mac coire.

MacQuiston, mac úirtin.

MacQuoid, mac uaió.

MacQuorcodale, mac corcao-
ail, mac curcaóail.

MacRae, mac Rait.

MacRanald, MacRandell, mac
Raġnaill.

MacRann, mac Upain.

MacRannal, MacRannall, mac
Raġnaill.

MacRay, MacRea, mac Rait.

MacReady, mac Riaóa.

MacReavy, mac Riabaiġ.

MacRedmond, mac Réamoinn.

MacReedy, mac Riaóa.

MacReery, mac Ruióří.

MacRenn, mac Upoin.

MacReynold, MacReynolds,
mac Raġnaill.

MacRichard, mac Riocáiro,
mac Riocairo, mac Rir-
teáiro, mac Rirteairo.

MacRoarty, mac Robaptaiġ.

MacRoary, mac Ruaióří.

MacRoberts, mac Roibeáiro,
mac Roibeairo.

MacRobin, mac Roibín.
MacRory, mac Ruaiḋrí.
MacRub, MacRubs, mac Rob.
MacRuddery, mac an Rioire.
MacRum, mac Cruim.
MacRynn, mac Ḃroin.
MacScollog, mac an Scolóige, mac Scolóige.
MacSeveney, mac Suiḃne.
MacShaffrey, MacShafrey, mac Seaffraiḋ.
MacShan, mac Seáin, mac Seaġáin.
MacShanaghy, mac Seancá, mac Seancaiḋe.
MacShane, mac Seáin, mac Seaġáin.
MacShanley, mac Seanlaoiċ.
MacShannon, mac Seanáin 2; mac Seanacáin 2.
MacSharry, mac Searraiġ.
MacSheehy, mac Síṫiġ.
Mac Sheffrey, mac Seaffraiḋ.
MacSherry, mac Searraiġ.
MacShufrey, mac Sioffraiḋ, mac Seaffraiḋ.
MacSkeaghan, MacSkean, mac Sceacáin.
MacSkimmins, (?), mac Cuimín
MacSliney, MacSliny, mac Sleimne.
MacSlowey, MacSloy, mac Sluaġaḋaiġ.
MacSoley, MacSolly, mac Soilliġ.
MacSoreley, MacSorely, Mac Sorley, mac Somairle.
MacSpaddin, mac Spáidín.
MacSparran, mac an Spartáin.
MacSpeddin, mac Spáidín.
MacStay, M'Stay, ó maoilṡréiġe.
MacSteen, mac Stiḃín, mac Stín.
Mac Stocker, mac an Stocaire.
MacStravick, (?)
MacSurley, mac Somairle.

MacSwan, mac Suain.
MacSween, MacSweeney, Mac Sweeny, MacSweney, mac Suiḃne.
MacSwiggan, MacSwiggin, Mac Swigin, (?) mac Suigin.
MacSwine, MacSwiney, mac Suiḃne.
MacTaggart, mac an tSagairt.
MacTaghlan, MacTaghlin, mac Giolla tSeaclainn.
MacTague, mac Taiḋg.
MacTamney, mac an Tiompánaiġ.
MacTavish, mac Táṁair.
MacTeague, mac Taiḋg.
MacTeer, mac an tSaoir.
MacTeggart, mac an tSagairt.
MacTegue, MacTeigue, mac Taiḋg.
MacTernan, mac Tiġearnáin.
MacTier, mac an tSaoir.
MacTiernan, mac Tiġearnáin,
MacTierney, mac Tiġearnaiġ.
MacTigue, mac Taiḋg.
MacTimney, mac an Tiompánaiġ.
MacToole, mac Tuaṫail.
MacTucker, mac Tuatcaire.
MacTurk, mac Tuirc,
MacUsker, mac Oscair.
MacVady, mac an Ṁaḋaiḋ.
MacVail, mac Páil, mac Póil.
MacVanamy, mac Ṁeanma.
MacVann, mac Ḃeaṫan.
MacVany, mac an Ṁanaiġ.
MacVarry, mac Fearaḋaiġ.
MacVay, MacVea, MacVeagh, mac an Ḃeaṫa, mac an Ḃeaṫaḋ.
MacVean, mac Ḃeaṫan.
MacVeigh, mac an Ḃeaṫa, mac an Ḃeaṫaḋ.
MacVeety, MacVeity, mac an Ḃiaḋṫaiġ.
MacVerran, mac Ṁearáin.
MacVerry, mac Fearaḋaiġ.

MacVey, mac an beaċa, mac
an beaċaḃ.
MacVicar, MacVickar, Mac
Vicker, mac an ḃiocáire,
mac an ḃiocapa.
MacVitty, MacVity, mac an
ḃiaóċaiġ.
MacVoy, v. MacAvoy.
MacWade, mac uaiṿ.
MacWalter, mac ualcair.
MacWard, mac an ḃáirṿ.
MacWatters, mac uaiċéip.
MacWeeney, MacWeeny, mac
maonaiġ 9; mac Suiḃne 6.
MacWherter, mac apcair.
MacWhinney, MacWhinny, (?)
mac Suiḃne.
MacWhirter, mac apcair.
MacWhiston, mac úircin.
MacWhite, MacWhitty, mac
faoiciġ.
MacWhorter, mac apcair.
MacWiggan, MacWiggin, mac
Suaiġín, mac Suiġean, (o.f.)
mac eoċaiḃín.
MacWilkin, mac uilcín.
MacWilliam, MacWilliams, mac
uilliam.
MacWillie, mac uiṿliṿ.
MacWiney, MacWinney, Mac
Winny, (?) mac Suiḃne.
MacWray, mac Raiċ.
Madden, ó maṿáin 1, ó maṿaiṿ-
ín, ó maiṿín, 19, 97, (s.)
mac an ṁaṿaiṿ 192.
Maddigan, ó maṿaġáin.
Maddock, Maddocks, Maddox,
Maddux, maṿóc, maṿóġ.
Maddy, ó maṿaiṿ.
Madigan, ó maṿaġáin.
Madole, Madowell, mac ṿuḃ-
ġaill.
Madox, maṿóc.
Magahan, mac ġaoicín 1, (s.l.)
maġ ġaċan 64; maġ eaċáin 52
Magaharan, Magaheran, Mag-
ahern, maġ eaċpáin.
Magall, v. MacCall.

Magan, Magann, maġ Canna,
maġ Cana 1, maġ annaiṿ
34; maġ Canann 46. ; maġ
eaċáin 52.
Magarry, maġ fearaṿaiġ.
Magauran, Magaurn, maġ Saṁ-
páin, (o.f.) maġ Saṁpaṿáin.
Magaw, maġ áṿaiṁ.
Magawley, maġ aṁalġaṿa,
maġ aṁalġaiṿ.
Magawran, maġ Saṁpáin, (o.f.)
maġ Saṁpaṿáin.
Magee, maġ aoṿa, maġ aoiṿ
11 ; mac ġaoiċe 16 ; ó maol-
ġaoiċe 16, 19.
Mageehan, Magean, Mageen,
mac ġaoiċín.
Magenis, Magennis, maġ aon-
ġuir, maġ aonġupa.
Mageogh, maġ eoċaṿa, maġ
eoċaċ.
Mageoghegan, maġ eoċaġáin.
Mageown, maġ eoġáin 2 ; maġ
eóin 2.
Mageraghty, maġ oireaċcaiġ.
Magettigan, maġ eiceaġáin,
maġ eiciġein.
Magetty, maġ eiciġ.
Maghan, ó maċáin.
Magher, ó meaċaip.
Maghery, an ṁaċaipe.
Magill, mac an ġoill 11 ; mac
ġiolla 62.
Magillowy, mac ġiollaḃuiṿe.
Magilly, maġ Coiliṿ.
Maginess, maġ aonġuir.
Maginley, maġ fionnġaile.
Maginn, maġ finn.
Maginness, maġ aonġuir.
Maginnetty, maġ fionnaċcaiġ,
maġ finneaċcaiġ, &c.
Maginnis, maġ aonġuir.
Maginty, maġ fionnaċcaiġ,
maġ finneaċcaiġ, &c.
Magiveran, Magiverin, Magivern
maġ uiṿpín.
Maglade, maġ Léiṿ.
Maglamery, (?) maġ laḃpaiṿ.

Maglanchy, mag flannċaḋa, mag flannċaiḋ.
Maglennon, mag leannáin.
Magloin, Maglone, mac giolla eóin.
Magner, Magnier, Magnir, Magnor, maingnéiṗ.
Magolrick, mag ualġaiṗg, (s.l.) mag gualṗaic.
Magone, mag eoġain.
Magonigle, mag congail.
Magorish, Magorisk, mag feóṗaiṗ, mag feóṗuiṗ.
Magorlick, mag ualġaiṗg, (s.l.) mag guarlaic.
Magough, mag eoċaċ, mag eoċaḋa.
Magournahan, mag guaṗnaċáin.
Magoveran, Magoverin, Magovern, mag Samṗáin, (o.f.) mag Samṗaḋáin 11 ; mag uiḋṗín 62.
Magowan, Magowen, mac an ġobann, mac an ġabann mac gobann, mac gabann 1 ; mac gaṁna 2 ; mag ḋuḃáin 19.
Magra, Magragh, mag Raiċ, mag craiċ.
Magrane, mag Ráiġne, (s.l.) ma gráine, ma gṗána 64.
Magrannell, mag Raġnaill.
Magrath, Magraw, mag Raiċ, mag craiċ.
Magrean, mag Raiġne.
Magreavy, mag Riaḃaiġ.
Magreece, mag Raoiṗ, mag Raoṗa. (o.f.) mag aonġuiṗ, mag aonġuṗa.
Magreely, mag Raġallaiġ, (s.l.) mag Raoġallaiġ.
Magreevy, mag Riaḃaiġ.
Magrery, mag Ruiḋṗí.
Magrillan, (?) mag Rialláin, (o.f.) mag nialláin.
Magroarty, mag Roḃaṗtaiġ.
Magroder, mag Ḃṗuaḋaiṗ.

Magrory, mag Ruaiḋṗí.
Magrudden, mag Roḋáin.
Maguane, mag Ḋuḃáin.
Maguigan, mag eoċaġáin, (s.l.) mag guaġáin, mag ġuiġean.
Maguil, mac an ġoill.
Maguiness, Maguinis, Maguinness, mag aonġuiṗ, mag aonġuṗa.
Maguire, mag uiḋṗ.
Maguirke, mag cuirc.
Magullion, mac coilín.
Maguran, Magurn, mag coṗṗáin 9 ; mag Samṗáin 6.
Mahady, Ó moiċiḋe.
Mahaffy, mac Ḋuiḃṗíċe.
Maharry, mac feaṗaḋaiġ.
Mahedy, Ó moiċiḋe.
Maher, Ó meaċaiṗ.
Mahew, máiġiú 1 ; mac máiġiú 19.
Maholland, Ó maolċallann.
Mahollum, Maholm, Ó maol Coluim, Ó maol Colm.
Mahon, Ó maċáin 61, Ó moċáin 91 ; Ó matġaṁna 68 ; mac matġaṁna 92.
Mahoney, Mahony, Ó matġaṁna.
Mailey, v. Malley.
Main, v. Mayne.
Mainey, v. Meany.
Maires, v. Mears.
Makenry, v. MacEnery.
Makeon, v. MacKeon.
Malady, Ó maoiléiḋiġ.
Malarky, Ó maol eaṗca.
Malcolm, Ó maol Colm 2 ; mac maol Coluim 2.
Malcolmson, Malcomson, mac maol Colm, mac maol Coluim.
Maley, v. Malley.
Malia, v. Melia.
Malick, v. Mallick.
Malie, v. Malley.
Maliffe, Ó maolḋuiḃ.
Malise, mac maoil íoṗa.

Mallagh, Ó máille, máilleaċ.
Mallaghan, Ó maolaċáin.
Mallan, Ó mealláin.
Mallavin, Ó maoiléimín.
Mallen, Ó mealláin.
Mallew, Ó maol aoḃa.
Malley, Ó máille 76, 91 ; Ó
  meallaiġ 99 ; Ó maol aoḃa
  6, 78, Ó maoil aoḃa 47.
Mallia, v. Malley.
Mallick, mac míoluic.
Mallin, Mallon, Ó mealláin.
Malloney, Mallowny, Ó maol
  ḃoṁnaiġ.
Mallyn, v. Mallin.
Malmona, Ó maolmóna.
Malone, Ó maoil eóin 11 ; mac
  ġiolla eóin 64 ; Ó maol-
  ḃloġain 73.
Malony, Malowny, Ó maol
  ḃoṁnaiġ.
Maloy, v. Molloy.
Manachan, Manahan, Ó manaċ-
  áin, Ó manċáin 1, Ó mainċín
  7.
Manally, mac an ḟailġiġ.
Manary, mac náraḃaiġ.
Manasses, mac maġnura.
Mandevile, ḃe móinḃíol, móin-
  ḃíol, múinḃíol.
Maneely, Maneilly, mac an
  ḟileaḃ, maac an ḟiliḃ.
Manelis, mac niallġuir.
Mangan, Manghan, Manghen,
  Mangin, Ó monġáin 1, Ó
  muinġeáin 2 ; Ó manċáin 2,
  Ó manaġáin 49 ; Ó mainnín
  972.
Mangner, maingnéir.
Manice, mac naoir. (o.f.) mac
  aonġuir.
Manihan, Manihin, Ó mainċín.
Manion, Ó mainnín.
Manley, Ó maonġaile.
Mann, Ó macáin.
Mannering, Ó manaráin.
Mannice, mac naoir, (o.f.) mac
  aonġuir.

Mannight, mac neaċtain.
Mannin, Ó mainnín.
Manning, Ó mainnín 11 ; Ó
  monġáin 779.
Mannion, Ó mainnín 11 ; Ó
  monġáin 192.
Mannix, Ó mainċín 79a, Ó
  manóġ, Ó muineóġ 25, 46,
  97 ; mac naoir, (o.f.) mac
  aonġuir 6.
Manogue, Ó manóġ, Ó muin-
  eóġ.
Manron, Ó manaráin.
Mansell, móinréil.
Mansfield, móinréil 1 ; ḃe
  móinḃíol, móinḃíol 47, 772.
Mansill, móinréil.
Manus, mac maġnuir.
Many, Ó maine.
Mape, máp.
Maqueen, mac Suiḃne.
Mara, Ó meaḃra, Ó meára.
Maragan, Ó muireaġáin.
Marchal, v. Marshall.
Marcom, Marcum, v. Markham.
Maree, Mariga, Ó mearaḃaiġ,
  Ó mearḃa.
Marinane, Ó marannáin, Ó
  marnáin.
Mark, mac marcuir.
Markahan, Markan, Ó marcaċ-
  áin.
Markey, Ó marcaiġ.
Markham, Ó marcaċáin.
Marks, mac marcuir.
Marley, Ó murġaile 16, Ó
  mearlaiġ 19.
Marmion, (?) mac meanman.
Marnan, Marnane, Ó marnáin.
Marren, Ó mearáin.
Marrilly, Ó murġaile.
Marrinan, Ó marannáin, Ó
  marnáin, (o.f.) Ó manann-
  áin.
Marron, Ó mearáin.
Marsh, ḃe moiréir.
Marshall, maparcal.

134

Marten, Martin, ó má|ctáin, 15, 24, 97, ó máiptín 77, 97 ; mac máiptín 33 ; ó maol máptaim 67 ; mac giolla máptain 34, 35 ; máiptín 17, 77, 97, &c.
Martinson, mac máiptín.
Martyn, v. Martin.
Mason, mapún.
Massey, meapaig.
Master, Masterson, mac an máigiptip.
Mateer, mac an tsaoip.
Matheson, mac íhata ; mac matain.
Mathew, maitiú.
Mathews, maitiú 11 ; mac matgamna 64.
Mathewson, mac mata.
Mathias, mac maicíp.
Matthew, maitiú.
Matthews, maitiú 11 ; mac matgamna 64.
Maughan, ó mocáin 9, ó macáin 64 ; ó matgamna 68.
Maune, mágún,
Maunsell, móinpéil.
Maurice, mac muipip, mac muipip.
Mavity, mac an biaótaig.
Mawe, mac máige, (s.) mac máigeóc, mac máigeóg,(o.s.) Connoún.
Mawhiney, Mawhinney, Mawhinny, (?) mac Suibne.
Mawhirter, mac Aptaip.
Mawme, (?) mágún.
Mawne, mágún.
Maxel, v. Maxwell.
Maxey, ó macapa.
Maxwell, S 10 ; ó meipcill 46.
May, ó miaóaig 5, 34, 197 ; máigiú 2 ; mac máige, mac máigeóc, mac máigeóg 47' 778 ; mac Conmeaóa 92.
Maybin, máibín.
Maydole, mac oubgaill.
Mayduck, maoóc.

Mayers, v. Meares.
Mayhew, Mayhow, máigiú.
Mayne, Maynes, (?) mac maine.
Mayo, máigiú.
Mayrick, v. Merrick.
Mea, v. May.
Meade, mioeaó.
Meagher, ó meaóaip.
Mealia, Mealley, Meally, Mealy, v. Malley.
Meany, ó maonaig 11 ; ó maine 73.
Meara, ó meaópa, ó meápa.
Meares, ó mióip, ó míp.
Mearn, ó meapáin.
Mears, ó mióip, ó míp.
Meath, mac Con mioe 6 (O'D).
Mecmeckin, (?) mac miaóacáin.
Mecowan, v. MacGowan.
Mecredy, v. MacReady.
Medole, mac oubgaill.
Mee, ó miaóaig 1 ; mac Con mioe 62.
Meegan, Meeghan, ó miaóacáin, ó miaóagáin.
Meehagan, ó maotagáin.
Meehan, ó miaóacáin 11 ; ó micióín 39 ; ó maocáin 99.
Meehegan, ó maotagáin.
Meehen, Meehin, ó miaóacáin 11 ; ó micióín 39.
Meekin, v. Meegan.
Meelderry, ó maoloopaió.
Meenagh, muimneaó, (s.l.) muineaó 19.
Meenan, ó mianáin.
Meenchan, ó muineacáin.
Meenhan, Meenin, ó muingeáin.
Meeny, ó maonaig.
Meere, ó mióip, ó míp.
Megahan, v. Magahan.
Megall, v. MacCall.
Megan, v. Magan.
Megarrity, v. MacGarrity.
Megarry, v. Magarry.
Megarty, v. MacGaraty.
Megaw, v. Magaw.
Megginn, v. Maginn.

Meghan, Ó ꞃꞁꞁꞁᴀᴠᴀᴄᴀꞁn.
Meginniss, v. Maginness.
Meglamry, v. Maglamery.
Meglaughlin, v. MacGlaughlin.
Megowan, v. Magowan.
Megrath, Megraw, v. MacGrath.
Meguiggan, v. Maguigan.
Mehaffy, v. Mahaffy.
Mehan, v. Meehan.
Mehigan, Ó ᴍᴀoċᴀᴣᴀꞁn.
Meighan, Ó ꞁꞁꞁᴀᴠᴀᴄᴀꞁn.
Mekerrell, v. MacKerrell.
Mekill, v. Magill.
Melane, Ó ᴍᴀoʟᴀꞁn.
Melanphy, Ó ᴍᴀoʟᴀnꞃᴀꞁᴠ.
Melarkey, Ó ᴍᴀoꞁʟ eᴀꞃcᴀ.
Melay, Ó ᴍᴀoʟ ᴀoᴠᴀ, Ó ᴍᴀoꞁʟ
    ᴀoᴠᴀ.
Meldon, Ó ᴍᴀoʟᴠúꞁn.
Meleady, Meledy, Ó ᴍᴀoꞁʟéꞁᴠꞁᴣ.
Melia, Ó ᴍᴀꞁʟʟe.
Melican, Ó ᴍᴀoꞁʟeᴀᴄᴀꞁn, Ó
    ᴍᴀoꞁʟeᴀᴣᴀꞁn.
Mellan, Ó ᴍeᴀʟʟᴀꞁn.
Melledy, Ó ᴍᴀoꞁʟéꞁᴠꞁᴣ.
Mellet, Mellett, Mellette, ᴍꞁoʟ-
    óꞁᴠ 11, ᴍéᴀʟóꞁᴠ 92.
Mellis, ᴍᴀc ᴍᴀoꞁʟ íoꞃᴀ.
Mellit, v. Mellet.
Mellon, Ó ᴍeᴀʟʟᴀꞁn.
Mellot, Mellott, ᴍꞁoʟóꞁᴠ 11,
    ᴍéᴀʟóꞁᴠ 92, ᴍᴀʟóꞁᴠ 192.
Mellowes, Ó ᴍᴀoꞁʟ íoꞃᴀ.
Melly, Ó ᴍeᴀʟʟᴀꞁᴣ, 1 ; Ó ᴍᴀꞁʟʟe 2
Melody, Ó ᴍᴀoꞁʟéꞁᴠꞁᴣ.
Meloy, v. Molloy.
Melroy, Ó ᴍᴀoʟꞃᴜᴀꞁᴠ.
Melvenny, Ó ᴍᴀoꞁʟ ꞁꞁꞁeᴀnᴀ.
Melville, Ó ᴍᴀoꞁʟ ꞁꞁꞁċꞁʟ 46; Ó
    ᴍᴀoʟꞃᴀᴠᴀꞁʟ 97.
Melvin, Ó ᴍᴀoꞁʟꞁꞁꞁín.
Menaght, ᴍᴀc neᴀċᴛᴀꞁn.
Menahan, Ó ᴍᴜꞁneᴀᴄᴀꞁn.
Menary, Menarry, ᴍᴀc náꞃᴀᴠ-
    ᴀꞁᴣ.
Menautt, v. Menaght.
Meneely, v. Maneely.
Meneese, v. Manice.

Menemin, ᴍᴀc ᴍeᴀnᴍᴀn.
Menocher, v. MacNogher.
Menton, Ó ᴍᴀnnᴛᴀꞁn.
Meran, Ó ᴍeᴀꞃᴀꞁn.
Mergin, Ó ᴍeꞁꞃᴣín, (o.f.) Ó
    hᴀꞁꞁꞁeꞁꞃᴣín.
Merleban, Ó ᴍéꞁꞃʟeᴀᴄᴀꞁn.
Mernin, (Ó) ᴍéꞁꞃnín.
Merrick, ᴍeꞁᴠꞃꞁc, ᴍeꞁꞃꞁc 1,
    ᴍᴀc ᴍeꞁᴠꞃꞁc, ᴍᴀc ᴍeꞁꞃꞁc,
    ᴍᴀc ᴍíᴠꞃꞁc 2.
Merrigan, Ó ᴍᴜꞁꞃeᴀᴣᴀꞁn 1 ; Ó
    ᴍeꞁꞃᴣín 7.
Merriman, Merryman, ᴍᴀc
    ᴍeᴀnᴍᴀn.
Merry, Ó ᴍeᴀꞃᴀᴠᴀꞁᴣ, Ó
    ᴍeᴀꞃᴠᴀ.
Merwick, v. Merrick,
Mescall, Mescel, Meskell, Ó
    ᴍeꞁꞃcꞁʟʟ.
Meyers, Ó ᴍeꞁᴠꞁꞃ.
Meyler, ᴍᴀc ᴍᴀoꞁʟꞁꞃ 1,
    ᴍᴀoꞁʟꞁꞃ 28, ᴍꞁʟéꞁꞃ 47.
Meyrick, v. Merrick.
Miall, v. Michael.
Michael, ᴍꞁċeᴀʟ E 2 ; Ó ᴍᴀoꞁʟ
    ꞁꞁꞁċꞁʟ 9 ; ᴍᴀc ᴣꞁoʟʟᴀ ꞁꞁꞁċꞁʟ 6.
Michell, v. Michael and Mitchell.
Miell, v. Michael.
Miers, Ó ᴍꞁᴠꞁꞃ, Ó ᴍꞁꞃ.
Mighil, Mihell, v. Michael.
Migrillan, v. Magrillan.
Miland, Ó ᴍᴀoꞁʟeᴀín.
Miles, ᴍꞁʟꞁꞃ, ᴍꞁʟꞁᴠ 2 ; ᴍᴀc
    ᴍꞁʟꞁꞃ, ᴍᴀc ᴍꞁʟꞁᴠ 2 ; Ó ᴍᴀoʟ
    ꞁꞁꞁᴜꞁꞃe 19.
Miley, Ó ᴍᴀoꞁʟ ᴀoᴠᴀ, Ó ᴍᴀoʟ
    ᴀoᴠᴀ, Ó ᴍᴀoꞁʟ ᴀoꞁᴠ.
Milford, Ó ᴍᴀoʟꞃoᴣꞁꞁꞁᴀꞁꞃ, Ó
    ᴍᴀoʟꞃoᴣꞁꞁꞁᴀꞁꞃ.
Miligan, Ó ᴍᴀoꞁʟeᴀᴣᴀꞁn.
Millan, Millane, Ó ᴍᴀoʟᴀín, Ó
    ᴍᴀoꞁʟeᴀín.
Millar, ᴍᴜꞁʟʟeóꞁꞃ.
Millbride, Ó ᴍᴀoꞁʟ ᴠꞃíᴣᴠe.
Millea, Ó ᴍᴀoꞁʟ ᴀoᴠᴀ, Ó ᴍᴀoʟ
    ᴀoᴠᴀ.
Millen, Ó ᴍᴀoꞁʟín.

Miller, muilleóir.
Millerick, ó maoil ɡeiric, ó maoil ɡiric.
Millet, Millett, míolóiv.
Millican, Milligan, Milligen, Millikan, Milliken, Millikin, ó maoileacáin, ó maoileaɡáin.
Mills, an ṁuilinn.
Millin, ó maoilín.
Milmo, Milmoe, ó maolmuaiv.
Milreavy, ó maoilriabaiɡ.
Milroy, ó maolruaiv.
Minagh, muimneac.
Minahan, Minahane, ó mionacáin, (o.f.) ó manacáin 11; ó muimneacáin 19.
Mineely, v. Maneely.
Minett, v. Mannight.
Mingane, ó muingeáin.
Miniece, Miniese, v. Mannice.
Minihane, v. Minahane.
Miniter, minicéir, mincéir.
Minnagh, Minnaugh, muimneac.
Minnis, Minnish, v. Mannice.
Minnitt, v. Mannight.
Minochor, v. MacNogher.
Minnock, ó muineóɡ.
Minogher, v. MacNogher.
Minogue, ó muineóɡ.
Minoher, v. MacNogher.
Minteer, mac an tSaoir.
Mintin, ó manntáin.
Mirreen, ó mirín.
Miscella, mac Scalaiɡe.
Miskell, ó meircill.
Miskella, Miskelly, mac Scalaiɡe.
Missett, ve miréiv, miréiv.
Mitchell, mircéil 1; ó maoil ṁicil 92; mac ɡiolla ṁicil 62.
Moakley, ó motla, ó motlaiɡ.
Moan, ó mocáin.
Moany, ó maonaiɡ.
Mockler, móicléir.
Moen, ó mocáin.
Moeran, v. Moran.
Moghan, Mohan, ó mocáin.

Moher, ó mocáin, ó muicir.
Mohilly, ó motla, ó motlaiɡ.
Molamphy, ó maolanfaiv.
Mollan, ó maoláin.
Mollony, Mollowney, ó maoluoṁnaiɡ 11; ó maol factna 27.
Molloy, ó maolṁuaiv 11; ó maol aova, ó maoil aova, ó maoil aoiv 91, (s.) ó maol aovóɡ 19, (s.) ó maol ṁaovóɡ 16; ó laoɡóɡ, ó laovóɡ 16, 19; ó maolait (o.f.) ó maolaitce, ó maolaitɡein 192; ó Sluaɡavaiɡ 62.
Mologhney, ó maol factna.
Molohan, ó maolacáin.
Moloney, Molony, Molowny, ó maoluoṁnaiɡ 11; ó ṁaol factna 27.
Molphy, v. Murphy.
Moloy, v. Molloy.
Molumby, ó maolcomav.
Molvin, ó maoiliṁín.
Molyneux, ó maol an ṁuaiv 49; ó maolaɡáin 16.
Monaboe, mac anabava.
Monachan, Monaghan, v. Monahan.
Monagle, mac maonɡail.
Monahan, ó manacáin, ó mancáin 11, ó muineacáin 192, 462, ó mionacáin 497, 779, ó maincín 2, ó muineóɡ 342, 462.
Monaher, ó manacair.
Monan, ó maonáin.
Monday, mac ɡiolla eóin.
Monegan, ó managáin.
Monehan, v. Monahan.
Money, ó maonaiɡ.
Mongan, ó monɡáin.
Mongavan, ó monɡabáin.
Mongey, ó monɡaiɡ.
Mongon, v. Mongan.
Monk, Monks, mac an ṁanaiɡ 1; ó manacáin, ó mancáin 2.

Monley, Monnelly, Ó ᵯᴀonᵹᴀιle.
Monohan, v. Monahan.
Monroe, ᵯᴀc ᴀn ᴚócᴀιc, S ; Ó ᵯᴀolᵱᴜᴀιȯ 19.
Monsell, ᵯóιnᵱéιl.
Montague, ᵯᴀc cᴀιȯᵹ.
Montane, Montang, Montangue, Ó ᵯᴀnncᴀιn 11; ᴅe ᵯoncᴀιn, ᵯoncᴀιn 77.
Montgomery, ᵯᴀc ιoᵯᴀιᵱe 97, ᵯᴀᵹoᵯᵱᴀc 469.
Moody, Ó ᵯᴜᴀᴅᴀιᵹ (S.L.).
Moohan, Ó ᵯocᴀιn.
Moon, Ó ᵯocᴀιn 1 ; ᴅe ᵯocún 2.
Moonan, Ó ᵯᴀonᴀιn, (s.l.) Ó ᵯᴜᴀnᴀιn.
Moone, v. Moon.
Mooney, Ó ᵯᴀonᴀιᵹ 11 ; Ó ᵯᴜιᵯᵯιᵹ 2.
Moore, Ó ᵯóᵱȯᴀ 11 ; ᴅe ᵯóᵱᴀ, ᴅe ᵯúᵱᴀ 72, 92 ; Ó ᵯocᴀιᵱ, Ó ᵯᴜιᴄιᵱ 772.
Morahan, Ó ᵯᴜᵱcᴀιn.
Moran, Ó ᵯóᵱᴀιn 11 ; Ó ᵯoᵹᵱᴀιn, (o.f.) Ó ᵯᴜᵹᵱóιn 94 ; ᵯᴀc ᵯoᵹᵱᴀιn, (o.f.) ᵯᴀc ᵯᴜᵹᵱóιn 92 ; Ó ᵯᴜιᵱeᴀιn, Ó ᵯᴜιᵱιn 2 ; Ó ᵯᴜᵱcᴀιn 14.
More, Ó ᵯóᵱȯᴀ 11 ; ᴅe ᵯóᵱᴀ, ᴅe ᵯúᵱᴀ 72, 92.
Moreen, Ó ᵯóιᵱιn.
Moreland, ᵯᴀc ᵯᴜᵱᵹᴀlᴀιn.
Morell, Ó ᵯᴜᵱᵹᴀιl.
Moren, Ó ᵯóιᵱιn.
Moreton, ᴅe ᵯóᵱcún, ᵯóᵱcún.
Morey, Ó ᵯóᵱȯᴀ.
Morgan, Ó ᵯᴜιᵱeᴀᵹᴀιn 1 ; Ó ᵯᴜᵱcᴀιn 2 ; ᵯoᵱᵹᴀn 2, 28.
Moriarty, Ó ᵯᴜιᵱceᴀᵱcᴀιᵹ.
Morice, v. Morris.
Morin, Ó ᵯóιᵱιn.
Morisey, v. Morrissey.
Morison, v. Morrison
Moriss, v. Morris.
Morisson, v. Morrison.
Morissy, v. Morrissey.

Morkan, Morkin, Ó ᵯᴜᵱcᴀιn 1 ; ᵯᴀc ᵯᴜᵱcᴀιn 2.
Morland, ᵯᴀc ᵯᴜᵱᵹᴀlᴀιn.
Morley, Ó ᵯᴜᵱᵹᴀιle, Ó ᵯᴜᵱᴄᴜιle.
Mornan, Ó ᵯᴀᵱnᴀιn, Ó ᵯᴜᵱnᴀιn.
Morohan, Ó ᵯᴜᵱcᴀιn.
Moroney, Moorooney, Ó ᵯᴀolᵱᴜᴀnᴀιȯ, (s.l.) Ó ᵯᴜᵱᵱᴜᴀnᴀιȯ.
Morphy, v. Murphy.
Morran, v. Moran.
Morresh, ᴅe ᵯoιᵱéιᵱ, ᵯoιᵱéιᵱ, ᵯᴜιᵱéιᵱ.
Morriessey, v. Morrissey.
Morrin, Ó ᵯᴜιᵱιn, Ó ᵯᴜιᵱeᴀιn 1 ; Ó ᵯᴜᵱcᴀιn 2.
Morris, Ó ᵯᴜιᵱᵹιᵱ, Ó ᵯᴜιᵱᵹeᴀᵱᴀ 1 ; ᵯᴀc ᵯᴜιᵱᵹιᵱ, ᵯᴀc ᵯᴜιᵱᵹeᴀᵱᴀ 2 ; ᵯᴀc ᵯᴜιᵱιᵱ, ᵯᴀc ᵯᴜιᵱιᵱ 19 ; ᴅe ᵯoιᵱéιᵱ, ᵯoιᵱéιᵱ, ᵯᴜιᵱéιᵱ 17, 77, 78, 85.
Morrison, Ó ᵯᴜιᵱᵹeᴀᵱᴀιn 11 ; Ó ᵯᴜιᵱᵹeᴀᵱᴀ 2 ; ᴅe ᵯoιᵱéιᵱ, ᵯᴜιᵱéιᵱ 178.
Morrisroe, ᵯᴀc ᵯᴜιᵱιᵱ ᴚᴜᴀιȯ, ᵯᴀc ᵯᴜιᵱιᵱ ᴚᴜᴀιȯ.
Morrissey, Ó ᵯᴜιᵱᵹeᴀᵱᴀ 11 ; ᵯᴀc ᵯᴜιᵱᵹeᴀᵱᴀ 2 ; ᵯoιᵱéιᵱ 47.
Morrisson, v. Morrison.
Morrogh, v. Morrough.
Morrolly, Ó ᵯᴜιᵱᵹᴀιle, Ó ᵯᴜᵱᴄᴜιle.
Morrough, ᵯᴀc ᵯᴜιᵱcᴀȯᴀ.
Morrow, ᵯᴀc ᵯᴜιᵱcᴀȯᴀ 1 ; ᵯᴀc ᵯᴜιᵱeᴀȯᴀιᵹ 67.
Morrowson, ᵯᴀc ᵯᴜιᵱcᴀȯᴀ.
Mortagh, ᵯᴀc ᵯᴜιᵱceᴀᵱcᴀιᵹ.
Mortell, ᵯoιᵱcéιl.
Mortimer, Mortimor, ᴅe ᵯoιᵱcιᵯéιᵱ, ᵯoιᵱcιᵯéιᵱ 43 ; ᵯᴀc ᵯᴜιᵱceᴀᵱcᴀιᵹ 192.
Mortland, ᵯᴀc ᵯᴜᵱᵹᴀlᴀιn.
Morton, ᴅe ᵯóᵱcún, ᵯóᵱcún.
Mortymer, v. Mortimer.
Moss, Ó ᵯᴀolᵯónᴀ.

Moughan, Ó moċáin.
Moughty, Ó moċᴛᴀ.
Mountain, Ó mᴀnnᴛáin 11 ; ᴅe moncáin, moncáin 77.
Mountcashel, Ó mᴀolċᴀiṙil.
Mowen, Ó moċáin.
Moy, Ó muiᵹe 16 (G.J.).
Moyers, mᴀc ᴀn ṁᴀoiṙ. V. Myers.
Moylan, Ó mᴀoileáin, Ó mᴀol- áin.
Moyles, v. Miles.
Moylin, Ó mᴀoilín, Ó mᴀoil- eáin.
Mylott, Mylotte, míolóiᴅ 11, méᴀlóiᴅ 99, máↄóiᴅ 192.
Moynagh, muiṁneᴀċ.
Moynahan, Moynan, v. Moyni- han.
Moyney, Ó muiṁniᵹ.
Moynihan, Ó muiṁneᴀċáin 1 ; Ó mionᴀċáin 2.
Mucbrin, mᴀc ᴠṙoin.
Muckady, mᴀc áᴅᴀ, mᴀc áᴅᴀiᴅ.
Muckaran, mᴀc eᴀċṙáin.
Muckedan, mᴀc cᴀᴅáin.
Muckeen, Muckian, v. MacKean.
Muckilbouy, mᴀc ᵹiollᴀᴠuiᴅe.
Mucklebreed, mᴀc ᵹiollᴀ ᴠṙíᵹᴅe.
Muckler, móicléiṙ.
Muckley, Ó mᴀolċluiċe.
Mugan, v. Magan.
Muir, ᴅe múṙᴀ, ᴅe móṙᴀ.
Muirland, mᴀc muṙᵹᴀláin.
Mulally, Ó mᴀolᴀlᴀiᴅ, (o.f.) Ó mᴀol ṗᴀlᴀiᴅ.
Mulavil, Mulavill, Ó mᴀolṗáb- ᴀil.
Mulbrandon, Ó mᴀoil ᴠṙeᴀnn- ᴅáin.
Mulberry, Ó mᴀoil ᴠeᴀṙᴀiᵹ.
Mulbreedy, Mulbride, Ó mᴀoil ᴠṙíᵹᴅe.
Mulcahy, Ó mᴀol ċᴀċᴀiᵹ 11 ; Ó mᴀolċluiċe 1782.
Mulcair, Ó mᴀoil céiṙe.

Mulcashel, Mulcashell, Ó mᴀoil- ċᴀiṙil.
Mulcessor, (?)
Mulchrone, Ó mᴀolċṙóin.
Mulconry, Ó mᴀol ċonᴀiṙe.
Mulcreevy, Ó mᴀolċṙᴀoiᴠe.
Mulcroan, Mulcrone, Mulcroon, Ó mᴀolċṙóin.
Mulcrowney, Ó mᴀol ċṙóine.
Muldarry, Ó mᴀolᴅoṙᴀiᴅ.
Mulderg, Mulderrig, Ó mᴀoil- ᴅeiṙᵹ.
Mulderry, Ó mᴀolᴅoṙᴀiᴅ.
Muldon, Muldoon, Ó mᴀol- ᴅúin.
Muldooney, Muldowney, Ó mᴀolᴅoṁnᴀiᵹ.
Mulfaal, Ó mᴀolṗáḃᴀil.
Mulgan, Ó mᴀolᴀᵹáin.
Mulgeehy, Ó mᴀolᵹᴀoiċe.
Mulgrave, Mulgrew, Mulgrievy, Mulgroo, Ó mᴀolċṙᴀoiᴠe.
Mulhall, Ó mᴀol ċᴀċᴀil.
Mulhallen, Ó mᴀolċᴀllᴀnn.
Mulhane, Ó mᴀoláin.
Mulhare, Ó mᴀoil céiṙe.
Mulhartagh, Ó mᴀolᴀċᴀṙᴛᴀiᵹ, (o.f.) Ó mᴀol ṗᴀᴛᴀṙᴛᴀiᵹ.
Mulhatton, Ó mᴀol ċᴀċáin.
Mulhearn, Mulheeran, Mulheran, Mulherin, Mulhern, Mulherrin, Mulherron, Ó mᴀoil ċiᴀṙáin.
Mulhollan, Mulholland, Ó mᴀol- ċᴀllᴀnn.
Mulhollum, Mulholm, Ó mᴀol ċoluim, Ó mᴀol ċolm.
Mulholn, Ó mᴀolċᴀllᴀnn.
Mulhooly, Ó mᴀolᵹuᴀlᴀ.
Mulick, v. Mulleague.
Mulkearn, Mulkearns, Ó mᴀoil ċiᴀṙáin.
Mulkeen, Ó mᴀolċᴀoin.
Mulkern, Mulkerns, Mulkerrin, Ó mᴀoil ċiᴀṙáin.
Mulkerry, Ó mᴀoil céiṙe.
Mulkhearn, Mulkieran, Ó mᴀoil ċiᴀṙáin.
Mullagan, Ó mᴀolᴀᵹáin.

Mullahy, Ó mᴀolᴀɩċċe, Ó mᴀol-ᴀɩċ, (o.f.) Ó mᴀolᴀɩċ̇ᵹeɩn.
Mullally, Mullaly, Ó mᴀolᴀlᴀɩ̇ᴅ, (o.f.) Ó mᴀol fᴀlᴀɩ̇ᴅ.
Mullan, Mullane, Ó mᴀolᴀ́ɩn.
Mullaney, Ó mᴀoɩleᴀnᴀɩ̇ᵹ.
Mullanphy, Ó mᴀolᴀnꝑᴀɩ̇ᴅ.
Mullany, Ó mᴀoɩleᴀnᴀɩ̇ᵹ.
Mullarkey, Ó mᴀoɩl eᴀꝃcᴀ.
Mullavin, Ó mᴀoɩl éɩṁín.
Mullavogue, Ó mᴀol ṁᴀoḃóᵹ.
Mullbride, Ó mᴀoɩl Ḃꝛíᵹ̇ᴅe.
Mulleady, Ó mᴀoɩléɩ̇ᴅɩᵹ.
Mulleague, mᴀc míolᴜɩc.
Mullee, Ó mᴀol ᴀoḃᴀ, Ó mᴀol ᴀoɩ̇ᴅ, Ó mᴀoɩl ᴀoḃᴀ, Ó mᴀoɩl ᴀoɩ̇ᴅ.
Mulleen, Ó mᴀoɩlín.
Mullen, Ó mᴀolᴀ́ɩn 11, Ó mᴀoɩleᴀ́ɩn 972 ; mᴀc mᴀolᴀ́ɩn 2 ; Ó meᴀllᴀ́ɩn 62.
Mullerick, Ó mᴀoɩl ᵹeɩꝛɩc, Ó mᴀoɩl ᵹɩꝛɩc.
Mullery, Ó mᴀol ṁᴜɩꝛe.
Mullet, Mullett, míolóɩ̇ᴅ.
Mulligan, Ó mᴀolᴀᵹᴀ́ɩn 11, Ó mᴀoɩleᴀᵹᴀ́ɩn 2 ; Ó mᴀolᴀċ̇-ᴀ́ɩn, Ó mᴀoɩleᴀċᴀ́ɩn 19, 97.
Mullin, Mullins, Ó mᴀolᴀ́ɩn 1, Ó mᴀoɩlín 2 ; Ó mᴀoɩlꝑɩnn 87 ; mᴀc mᴀolᴀ́ɩn 2.
Mullock, mᴀc míolᴜɩc, mᴀc míolᴜc.
Mullogan, Ó mᴀolᴀᵹᴀ́ɩn.
Mullon, Ó mᴀolᴀ́ɩn.
Mulloney, v. Moloney.
Mulloughney, Ó mᴀol fᴀċᴛnᴀ.
Mullowne, v. Malone.
Mullowney, v. Moloney.
Mulloy, v. Molloy.
Mullpeters, Ó mᴀoɩl ꝑeᴀ̇ᴅᴀɩꝛ.
Mullreavy, Ó mᴀoɩlꝛɩᴀḃᴀɩ̇ᵹ.
Mullveen, Ó mᴀoɩlṁín.
Mullvihill, Ó mᴀoɩl ṁɩċɩl, Ó mᴀoɩl ṁɩċíl.
Mulmona, Ó mᴀolmónᴀ.
Muloney, v. Moloney.
Mulooly, Ó mᴀolᵹᴜᴀlᴀ.

Muloy, v. Molloy.
Mulqueen, Ó mᴀolċᴀoɩn 11, Ó mᴀol Ċᴀoɩne 462.
Mulqueeny, Ó mᴀol Ċᴀoɩne.
Mulquin, Ó mᴀolċᴀoɩn.
Mulrain, Ó mᴀoɩl Rɩᴀᵹᴀɩn, Ó mᴀoɩl Rɩᴀɩn.
Mulready, Ó mᴀoɩl Ḃꝛíᵹ̇ᴅe.
Mulreany, Ó mᴀoɩlꝛéᴀnᴀ, (o.f.) Ó mᴀoɩl Ḃꝛéᴀnᴀɩnn.
Mulreavy, Ó mᴀoɩlꝛɩᴀḃᴀɩ̇ᵹ.
Mulrenan, Mulrenin, Mulrennan, Mulrennin, Ó mᴀoɩl Ḃꝛéᴀn-ᴀɩnn, Ó mᴀoɩl Ḃꝛeᴀnᴀɩnn.
Mulrine, Ó mᴀoɩl Rɩᴀɩn.
Mulroe, Ó mᴀolꝛᴜᴀɩ̇ᴅ.
Mulrony, Ó mᴀolꝛᴜᴀnᴀɩ̇ᴅ.
Mulroon, Ó mᴀolꝛᴜᴀɩn, Ó mᴀolꝛᴜᴀnᴀɩ̇ᴅ.
Mulrooney, Ó mᴀolꝛᴜᴀnᴀɩ̇ᴅ.
Mulrow, Mulroy, Ó mᴀolꝛᴜᴀɩ̇ᴅ.
Mulry, Ó mᴀolꝛᴜᴀɩ̇ᴅ 2 ; Ó mᴀol ṁᴜɩꝛe 2.
Mulryan, Mulryne, Ó mᴀoɩl Rɩᴀᵹᴀɩn, Ó mᴀoɩl Rɩᴀɩn.
Mulshinogue, Ó mᴀoɩl Sɩonóᵹ.
Mulumy, Ó mᴀolċomᴀ̇ᴅ.
Mulvagh, Ó mᴀoɩlṁeᴀ̇ᴅᴀ.
Mulvane, Ó mᴀolḃᴀ́ɩn.
Mulvanerty, Ó mᴀoɩlḃeᴀn-nᴀċᴛᴀ.
Mulvanny, Mulvany, Ó mᴀoɩl ṁeᴀnᴀ.
Mulveen, Ó mᴀoɩlṁín.
Mulvenna, Ó mᴀoɩl ṁeᴀnᴀ.
Mulvennon, Ó mᴀoɩl Ḃeᴀnóɩn.
Mulvenny, Ó mᴀoɩl ṁeᴀnᴀ.
Mulverhill, Ó mᴀoɩl ṁɩċɩl.
Mulvey, Ó mᴀoɩlṁᴀ̇ᴅᴀɩ̇ᵹ 39 ; Ó mᴀoɩlṁeᴀ̇ᴅᴀ 76.
Mulvihil, Mulvihill, Ó mᴀoɩl ṁɩċɩl, Ó mᴀoɩl ṁɩċíl.
Mulvin, Ó mᴀoɩlṁín.
Mulvy, v. Mulvey.
Munday, mᴀc ᵹɩollᴀ eóɩn.
Mungavan, Mungavin, Ó monᵹᴀḃᴀ́ɩn.
Mungay, Mungey, Ó monᵹᴀɩ̇ᵹ.

Munkettrick, Munkittrick, mac Sicric.
Munnelly, Ó maongaile.
Munroe, Munrow, v. Monroe.
Munster, Ó muimneacáin.
Muran, v. Murran.
Murchan, Ó murcáin 1 ; mac murcáin 2.
Murchison, mac murcaiö, mac murcaöa.
Murchoe, Ó murcaöa.
Murdoch, Murdock, Murdough, Murdow, Murdy, mac muirceartaig.
Murhilla, Ó murcuile.
Murkin, Ó murcáin 2 ; mac murcáin 2.
Murland, mac murgaláin.
Murley, Ó murcuile.
Murnaghan, Ó muirneacáin.
Murnain, Murnan, Murnane, Ó murnáin, (o.f.) Ó manannáin.
Murney, mac muirnig.
Murphy, Ó murcaöa 11 ; mac murcaöa, mac murcaiö 62.
Murran, Murrane, Ó muireáin.
Murray, Ó muireaöaig 1, (s.l.) Ó muirigte 7, 972 ; mac muireaöaig 62 ; mac giolla muire 232, 332.
Murready, Ó maoil Ürigöe.
Murren, Ó muireáin, Ó muirín.
Murricane, v. Murrigan.
Murricohu, Ó murcaöa.
Murrigan, Ó muireagáin.
Murrihy, Ó muirigte, (o.f.) Ó muireaöaig.
Murrin, Ó muirín, Ó muireáin.
Murroney, Ó maolruanaiö,(s.l.) Ó murruanaiö.
Murrough, mac murcaöa.
Murrow, mac murcaöa 1 ; mac muireaöaig 67.
Murry, v. Murray.
Murt, Murta, mac muirceartaig.
Murtagh, Murtaugh, Ó muirceartaig 1 ; mac muirceartaig 62.

Murtha, v. Murta.
Murtland, mac murgaláin.
Mustay, Ó maoilrtéige.
Myall, v. Michael,
Myers, Ó meiöir 1, Ó miöir, Ó mír 46, 97.
Myhan, Myhane, Ó miaöacáin.
Myhill v. Michael.
Myler v. Meyler.
Myles v. Miles
Mylett, Mylott, Mylotte, míolóir 11, méalóir 99, málóir 192.
Mynahan, v. Moynihan.
Myniter, v. Miniter.
Myres, v. Myers.

Nagel, v. Nagle.
Naghten, Naghton, Ó neactain.
Nagle, Nagill, ve nógla.
Nail, v. Neill.
Naish, v. Nash.
Nale, v. Neill.
Nallen, mac nailín (S.L.).
Nally, mac an failgig. v. MacNally.
Nalty, mac Conallta.
Nanany, mac Conanaonaig.
Nangle, ve nógla ; (G.p.) mac Oirvealb, mac Oirvealöaig.
Nary, Ó náraöaig.
Nash, ve nair 1 ; ve nár 2.
Natton, Ó neactain.
Naugher, mac Concoöair.
Naughtan, Naighten, Ó neactain.
Naughter, mac Concoöair.
Naughton, Ó neactain.
Naulty, v. Nalty and Nulty.
Navan, Navin, mac Cnáimín 46, 99 ; Ó Cnáimín 93.
Nawn, Ó nátan, Ó náan.
Neagle, ve nógla.
Neal, Neale, v. Neill.
Nealis, mac niallguir, mac niallgura.
Nealon, Ó niallláin.
Neaphsey, Ó Cnáimrige.

Neary, Ó nápaóaıʒ.
Neavin, mac Cnáıṁín 1 ; mac naoıṁín 87.
Nee, Ó nıaó.
Neecy, Ó Cnáıṁpıʒe.
Needham, E 6 ; Ó nıaó 7, 9.
Neehan, Ó nıaċáın.
Neelan, Neelands, Ó nıalláın.
Neely, v. MacNealy.
Neenan, Neenin, Ó naoıóeanáın.
Neeson, (?) mac nıaó.
Nehill, Ó neıʒıll.
Neight, mac neaċtaın.
Neilan, Neiland, Neilands, Ó nıalláın.
Neill, Ó néıll 1 ; mac néıll 2.
Neilson, mac neıʒıll.
Nelan, Neland, Nelands, Ó nıalláın.
Neligan, Ó nıallaʒáın.
Nelis, mac nıallʒuıp, mac nıallʒupa.
Nelson, mac neıʒıll.
Nerhenny, Nerney, Nertney, mac an Aıpċınnıʒ, mac an Oıpċınnıʒ.
Nery, Ó nápaóaıʒ.
Nestor, mac an Aʒaptaıʒ, mac an Aóaptaıp, (o.f.) mac ʒıpp an Aʒaptaıp.
Netterfield, Netterville, óe neaópaıbíol.
Neven, v. Nevin.
Neville, óe nuıbíol 87 ; óe neaó 77 ; Ó nıaó 17, 46, 49 ; Ó Cnáıṁín 469.
Nevin, Nevins, Ó Cnáıṁín 7 ; mac Cnáıṁín 9 ; mac naoıṁín 8.
Newcombe, E 11 ; Ó nıaóóʒ 19.
Newell, Newells, Newill, Ó Cnúċʒaıl, Ó Cnúċaıl.
Newman, nuaman.
Newnan, Ó nuanáın. V. Noonan.
Newton; Ó núċáın (S.L.).

Neylan, Neyland, Neylon, Ó nıalláın.
Nichol, Nichold, Nicholds, Nicholl, Nicholls, Nicholson, Nickle, Nickles, Nickleson, Nicol, Nicoll, Nicolls, Nicols, Nicolson, mac nıocoıl, mac nıocóıl.
Niell, v. Neill.
Nielson, mac neıʒıll.
Night, v. Knight.
Nihill, Ó neıʒıll.
Nilan, Niland, Nilon, Ó nıalláın.
Nirney, mac an Aıpċınnıʒ, mac an Oıpċınnıʒ.
Nivin, v. Nevin.
Nix, mac nıocaıp.
Nixon, mac nıc, mac nıocláıp.
Noakley, Ó neoċallaıʒ (S.L.).
Nocher, mac Conċoóaıp.
Nochtin, Nochton, Ó neaċtaın.
Nocker, Nocter, mac Conċoóaıp.
Nocton, Ó neaċtaın.
Noghar, Nogher, mac Conċoóaıp.
Nohally, Ó neoċallaıʒ (S.L.).
Noher, mac Conċoóaıp.
Nohilly, Ó neoċallaıʒ (S.L.).
Nolan, Ó nualláın 11 ; mac nualláın 19 ; Ó huallaċáın 98, Ó nuallaċáın 19 ; Ó hultaċáın 23, 67.
Noland, Nolans, v. Nolan
Nolty, v. Nulty.
Noonan, Noonane, Ó nuanáın 11, (o.f.) Ó hıonṁaıneáın 7 ; Ó nuaóan 19 ; Ó naoıóeanáın 172, 492.
Noone, Ó nuaóan 11, Ó nuanáın 97.
Nooney, Ó hıonṁaıne.
Normile, Normoyle, mac Con popmaoıle, (s.l.) mac Conoıpṁaoıle,
Norris, Norrish, Norries, óe noıpéıp, noıpéıp, nopaıp 1 ; óe nopaó, óe nopaıó 74.

North, Northridge, v. Norris.
Norton, Ó neaċtain 1 ; ᴅe noptún 2.
Norway, ᴅe nopaᴅ, ᴅe nopaıᴅ.
Noud, Ó nuaᴅat 16 ; mac nuaᴅat, mac nuaᴅaᴅ 2.
Noughton, Ó neaċtaın.
Noury, ᴅe nopaᴅ, ᴅe nopaıᴅ.
Nowd, v. Noud.
Nowlan, Ó nuallaın. V. Nolan.
Nowry, ᴅe nopaᴅ, ᴅe nopaıᴅ.
Nugent, ᴅe núınnpean, núınnpean 11 ; uınnpeaᴅún, ínnpeaᴅún 77 ; maʒ uınnpeannaın, maʒ uınnpıonnaın, ua Cuınpıoʒán 43, 64, 67, (o.f.) mac ʒıolla Seanaın, mac ʒıolla Sıonaın.
Nulty, mac an ultaıʒ.
Nunan, Nunun, v. Noonan.
Nyhane, Ó nıaċaın.
Nyhill, Ó neıʒıll.
Nynane, Ó naoıᴅeanaın.

Oak, Oakes, Oaks, mac ᴅapaċ, (o.f.) mac ᴅuıᴅᴅapaċ 1 ; Ó ᴅapaċ, (o.f.) Ó ᴅuıᴅᴅapaċ 2.
Oates, mac Cuıpc, (s.l.) mac Coıpce.
O'Begley, Ó beaʒlaoıċ.
O'Beirne, O'Bierne, Ó beıpn, Ó bıpn.
O'Boyce, Ó buaᴅaıʒ.
O'Boyle, Ó baoıʒıll.
O'Brady, Ó bpáᴅaıʒ 97.
O'Brallaghan, Ó bpolċaın, Ó bpolaċaın, Ó bpoıleaċaın.
O'Brazil, Ó bpeapaıl.
O'Brennan, Ó bpaonaın. V. Brennan.
O'Brian, Ó bpıaın.
O'Brick, Ó bpuıc 49 ; Ó bpıc 47.
O'Brien, Ó bpıaın 12 ; Ó bpaoın 15.
O'Brollaghan, v. O'Brallaghan.
O'Bryan, O'Bryen, Ó bpıaın.
O'Byrne, Ó bpoın 11 ; Ó beıpn, Ó bıpn 9.

O'Cahan, Ó Caċáın.
O'Caharney, O'Caherney, Ó Caċapnaıʒ.
O'Callaghan, O'Callahan, Ó Ceallaċáın 10 ; Ó Céıleaċáın 64.
O'Carrigan, Ó Cappaʒáın.
O'Carroll, Ó Ceapᴅaıll.
O'Carthy, Ó Cápċaıʒ
O'Casey, Ó Caċapaıʒ.
O'Caughan, Ó Caċáın.
O'Clery, Ó Cléıpıʒ.
O'Cloghessy, O'Clohessy, Ó Cloċapaıʒ.
O'Coigley, Ó Coıʒlıʒ.
O'Colohan, Ó Cúlaċáın.
O'Colter, Ó Coltaıp, Ó Coltapaın.
O'Concannon, Ó Conċeanaınn, Ó Conċeannaınn.
O'Connell, Ó Conaıll.
O'Conner, O'Connor, O'Conor, Ó Conċoᴅaıp.
O'Conor Don, Ó Conċoᴅaıp ᴅonn.
O'Corry, Ó Coppa.
O'Crowley, Ó Cpuaᴅlaoıċ 9 ; Ó Cpoᴅlaoıċ 7. V. Crowley.
O'Cuill, Ó Cuıll.
O'Cullane, Ó Cuıleáın, Ó Coıleáın.
O'Curran, Ó Coppáın, Ó Cuppáın
O'Currobeen, Ó Coıpbín.
O'Curry, Ó Compaıᴅe 46.
O'Daly, Ó ᴅálaıʒ.
O'Dea, Ó ᴅeaʒaıᴅ, Ó ᴅeaᴅaıᴅ, (s.l.) Ó ᴅıaʒaıᴅ 72, 92.
O'Deere, Ó ᴅuıbıᴅıp, (s.l.) Ó ᴅuıᴅıp.
O'Dempsey, Ó ᴅíomapaıʒ.
O'Dermott, Ó ᴅıapmaᴅa 1 ; Ó ᴅíopma, (o.f.) Ó ᴅuıbᴅíopma 16, 26.
O'Devine, Ó ᴅaıṁín 6 ; Ó ᴅuıbín 7, 9.
O'Diff, Ó ᴅuıb 8 ; Ó ᴅoıċe 19.
O'Dogherty, O'Doherty, Ó ᴅoċaptaıʒ.

O'Donnell, Ó Domnaill.
O'Donnelly, Ó Donngaile.
O'Donoghue, O'Donohoe,
O'Donohue, Ó Donncadha.
O'Donovan, Ó Donnabáin.
O'Doogan, Ó Dubagáin.
O'Dooghany, Ó Dubconna.
O'Dolan, Ó Dubláin.
O'Doolan, Ó Dublainn 2 ; Ó
Dubláin 2.
O'Doran, O'Dorian, Ó Deóráin,
(o.f.) Ó Deórabáin.
O'Dornan, Ó Dornáin.
O'Doud, Ó Dubda.
O'Dougherty, Ó Docartaig.
O'Dowd, O'Dowda, Ó Dubda.
O'Driscoll, Ó Oirirceóil, (o.f.)
Ó heidirirceóil.
O'Duffy, Ó Dubtaig. V. Duffy.
O'Durnin, Ó Duirnín.
O'Dwane, Ó Dubáin.
O'Dwyer, Ó Dubuidir, Ó Duib-
idir.
O'Falvy, Ó Fáilbe.
O'Farrell, Ó Feargail.
O'Farrelly, Ó Fairceallaig.
O'Fegan, v. Fegan.
O'Ferrall, Ó Feargail.
O'Ferry, Ó Fearabaig.
O'Filbin, Ó Filibín, (o.f.) mac
Filibín.
O'Finan, Ó Fionnáin.
O'Flaherty, Ó Flaitbeartaig.
O'Flanagan, Ó Flannagáin.
O'Flannelly, Ó Flanngaile.
O'Flynn, Ó Floinn, Ó Flainn.
O'Foody, Ó Fuada.
O'Friel, Ó Firgil.
Ogan, Úgán.
O'Gallagher, Ó Gallcobair, Ó
Gallcubair.
O'Gara, Ó Gaóra.
O'Garriga, Ó Gearaga, (o.f.)
mac Fearabaig.
O'Gilbie, O'Gilvie, Ó Giolla-
buide.
O'Gorman, Ó Gormáin 1 ; mac
Gormáin 46.

O'Gormley, Ó Goirmleagaig 6 ;
Ó Gormgaile 9. V. Gorm-
ley.
O'Gowan, Ó Gobann, Ó Gabann.
O'Grady, Ó Gráda 11 ; Ó
Greada 74.
O'Gready, Ó Greada.
O'Growney, Ó Gramna, (o.f.)
mac Carrgamna.
O'Hagan, Ó hágáin, (o.f.) Ó
Ó hógáin 6 ; Ó haobagáin 8.
O'Hahasy, Ó haiteara.
O'Haire, v. O'Hare.
O'Hallaran, O'Halleran, O'Hal-
leron, Ó hallmuráin.
O'Hallinan, Ó hailgeanáin.
O'Halloran, Ó hallmuráin.
O'Hamill, Ó haómaill, Ó
hágmaill.
O'Hanlon, Ó hannluain, Ó
hanluain.
O'Hanrahan, Ó hanracáin.
O'Hara, Ó heagra, Ó heabra.
O'Hare, Ó hír 3 ; Ó haicir, Ó
hoicir, Ó haitcir 4 ; Ó
Giorraide, (o.f.) mag Fearabb-
aig 976.
O'Harra, v. O'Hara.
O'Harran, Ó hearáin 6 ; Ó
heagráin 97.
O'Harrigan, Ó harragáin.
O'Hart, O'Harte, Ó hairt.
O'Hartigan, Ó hartagáin.
O'Hea, Ó haoda.
O'Hear, Ó hír.
O'Hegan, Ó haobagáin 8 ; Ó
hágáin 6.
O'Hehir, Ó hoicir, Ó haicir.
O'Herlihy, Ó hiarflata, Ó
hiarlata, Ó hiarlaite.
O'Hern, v. Hearn.
O'Heyne, Ó heidin.
O'Hickey, Ó hiceada, Ó hicide.
O'Higgin, O'Higgins, Ó huigín,
Ó huiginn 1 ; Ó haoilleac-
áin 472.
O'Hood, Ó huid.
O'Hora, Ó hóra, Ó hoóra.

O'Houlihan, Ó huallacáin.
O'Hourihane, Ó hannpacáin.
O'Huadhaigh, Ó huaóaiġ.
O'Hure, Ó hioṁaiṗ.
O'Hurley, Ó huṗċuile.
O'Kane, O'Keane, Ó Catáin.
O'Kearney, Ó Ceapnaiġ.
O'Keeffe, Ó Caoiṁ.
O'Keenan, Ó Cianáin.
O'Keeney, Ó Cianaiġ.
O'Kelleher, O'Kelliher, Ó Céileaċaiṗ.
O'Keily, Ó Caóla.
O'Kelly, Ó Ceallaiġ 1 ; Ó Caollaióe, Ó Caollaiġe 2. V. Kelly.
O'Kennedy, Ó Cinnéioiġ, Ó Cinnéioió.
O'Keoneen, Ó Ceóinín, (o.f.) mac Seóinín.
O'Kerane, Ó Ciapáin.
O'Kermody, Ó Ceapmaoa.
O'Kibbon, Ó Ciobúin, (o.f.) mac Ġiobúin.
O'Kielt, O'Kielty, Ó Caoilte, Ó Caoiltiġ.
O'Kieran, Ó Ciapáin.
O'Kissane, Ó Ciopáin.
O'Knee, Ó niaó.
O'Kirwan, Ó Ciapoubáin.
O'Lafferty, Ó Laitbeaptaiġ, (o.f.) Ó ḟlaitbeaptaiġ.
O'Lalor, Ó Leatloḃaiṗ.
O'Lane, Ó Laiġin, Ó Leiġin. V. Lane.
O'Laverty, Ó Laitbeaptaiġ, Ó ḟlaitbeaptaiġ.
O'Leary, Ó Laoġaiṗe.
O'Lee, Ó Laióiġ, Ó Laoióiġ.
O'Leery, Ó Laoġaiṗe.
O'Lehane, Ó Liatáin.
O'Leyne, Ó Laiġin, Ó Leiġin, Ó Leióin.
Oliver, Oiliḃéaṗ.
O'Loan, O'Loane, Ó Luain.
O'Loghlen, Ó Loċlainn.
O'Lomasney, Ó Lomapna.

O'Lone, Ó Luain.
O'Looney, Ó Luanaiġ 7 ; Ó Luiniġ 6.
O'Loughlan, O'Loughlin, Ó Loċlainn 11 ; Ó Loċláin, (o.f.) Ó Laċtnáin, 19, 24 ; Ó maoileaċlainn, Ó maoil Seaċlainn 82, 92.
O'Loughran, Ó Luċaiṗeáin, Ó Luċṗáin 6 ; Ó Laċṗáin, (o.f.) Ó Laċtnáin 46.
Olus, Ó heólupa, Ó heóluiṗ.
O'Lynn, Ó Loinn, Ó ḟloinn.
O'Lyons, Ó Laiġin, Ó Laióin 11 ; Ó Liatáin 16, 77 ; Ó hóileáin 19.
O'Madden, Ó maoaióín, Ó maioín.
O'Mahony, Ó matġaṁna.
O'Malley, Ó máille. V. Malley
O'Malone, Ó maoil eóin.
O'Mara, Ó meaópa.
O'Meagher, Ó meaċaiṗ.
O'Meally, Ó máille.
O'Mealue, Ó maol aoóa.
O'Mealy, Ó máille.
O'Meara, Ó meaópa.
O'Mcehan, O'Meehon, Ó miaóaċáin.
O'Mellon, Ó mealláin.
O'Molloy, Ó maolṁuaió. V. Molloy.
O'Moore, O'More, Ó móṗóa.
O'Moran, Ó móṗáin, Ó moġṗáin. V. Moran.
O'Moynan, Ó muiṁneaċáin ; Ó muineaċáin.
O'Mullane, Ó maoláin.
O'Mulrennin, Ó maoil Ḃṗéanainn
O'Muracha, O'Murphy, Ó muṗċaóa.
O'Naughton, Ó neaċtain.
O'Neal, O'Neill, Ó néill.
O'Nial, Ó neiġill.
O'Nolan, O'Nowlan, Ó nualláin.
Oogan, úġán.
Oonin, Ó huaitnín.
O'Phelan, Ó ḟaoláin.

O'Pray, ⱥn ⱣⱤéⱦ, (s.l.) Ó ⱣⱤéⱦ
O'Quigley, Ó CoⱤⱱⱢⱤⱥ.
O'Quin, Ó CuⱤnn.
O'Rafferty, Ó ⱤⱥⱚⱥⱤⱦⱥⱤⱥ, (s.l.)
Ó ⱤⱥⱦⱚeⱥⱤⱦⱥⱤⱥ.
O'Rahill, Ó ⱤⱥⱥⱥⱤⱢⱢ.
O'Rahilly, Ó ⱤⱥⱦⱦⱢe.
O'Rawe, (?)
Orchard, ⱥⱤⱤéⱤⱤ.
O'Realley, Ó ⱤⱥⱥⱥⱢⱢⱥⱤⱥ, Ó
ⱤⱥⱥⱥⱤⱢⱢⱤⱥ, (s.l.) Ó ⱤⱥoⱥⱥⱢⱢ-
ⱥⱤⱥ.
O'Regan, Ó ⱤⱤⱥⱥⱥⱤn 1, (s.l.) Ó
ⱤéⱥⱥⱥⱤn 2.
O'Reiley, O'Reilly, Ó ⱤⱥⱥⱥⱢⱢ-
ⱥⱤⱥ, Ó ⱤⱥⱥⱥⱤⱢⱢⱤⱥ. V.
Reilly.
O'Renehan, Ó ⱤeⱥnnⱥⱦⱥⱤn.
Organ, Ó hⱥⱤⱥⱥⱤn.
O'Rielly, v. O'Reilly.
O'Riordan, Ó ⱤⱤoⱥⱚⱥⱤⱥⱥⱤn,
(s.l.) Ó ⱤⱤoⱤⱥⱥⱤn.
Ormond, Ó ⱤⱥⱥⱤⱥ.
Ormsby, ⱥⱤⱤⱥⱤ, ⱥⱤⱤⱥeⱥⱤ.
O'Roarke, O'Rorke, O'Rourke,
Ó ⱤⱥⱥⱤⱤc.
O'Ryan, Ó ⱤⱤⱥⱤn 8; Ó ⱥⱥoⱤⱢ
ⱤⱤⱥⱤn 7; Ó ⱤⱥⱥⱤⱥⱤn 9. V.
Ryan.
Osborne, ÓⱤⱚⱥⱤ.
O'Scannell, Ó ScⱥnnⱥⱤⱢ.
O'Sevnagh, Ó SⱥⱤⱚne.
O'Shannessy, O Shaughnessy,
Ó SeⱥⱦnⱥⱤⱥⱤⱥ.
O'Shea, O'Shee, Ó Séⱥⱥⱥⱥ.
O'Shiel, Ó SⱥⱥⱥⱥⱤⱢ, Ó SⱤⱥⱥⱥⱤⱢ.
O'Sullivan, Ó SⱥⱤⱢeⱥⱚⱥⱤn, Ó
SⱥⱤⱢⱢeⱥⱚⱥⱤn.
O'Summachan, O'Summahan,
Ó SomⱥⱦⱥⱤn.
Oswald, Oswell, Ó heoⱥoⱤⱥ
23 (O'D.).
O'Thina, Ó ⱦⱥⱤne.
O'Tierney, Ó ⱦⱤⱥeⱥⱤnⱥⱤⱥ. V.
Tierney.
O'Toole, Ó ⱦⱥⱥⱦⱥⱤⱢ, Ó ⱦⱥⱥⱦⱥⱥⱤⱢ.
O'Toomey, Ó ⱦⱥⱥⱥⱥ.
Otterson, ⱥⱥⱦⱥ OⱤⱦⱤⱤ.

O'Twomey, Ó ⱦⱥⱥⱥⱥ.
Ougan, úⱥⱥn.
Ounihan, Ó hOnⱦon.
Owen, Owens, Ó heoⱥⱥⱤn 11;
ⱥⱥⱦⱥ eoⱥⱥⱤn 642.
Padden, Paden, Padian, Padin,
ⱥⱥⱦⱥ ⱣⱥⱤⱥⱤn 2; ⱣⱥⱤⱥⱤn 2.
Paine, Ᵽⱥⱥⱥn.
Pallas, Palles, ⱣⱥⱤⱢⱤⱤ.
Palmer, ⱣⱥⱥⱥⱤ 1; Ó ⱥⱥoⱢⱣoⱥ-
ⱥⱥⱤⱤ, Ó ⱥⱥoⱢⱣoⱥⱥⱥⱤⱤ 19
(O'D.).
Panneen, ⱣⱥⱤnⱤn.
Paragon, v. Parrican.
Paill, ⱣeⱥⱤⱥⱤⱢ.
Parish, ⱥe ⱣⱥⱤⱤⱤ.
Parker, ⱣⱥⱤⱤⱦéⱤⱤ, ⱣⱥⱤⱦⱥⱤ.
Parkins, Parkinson, ⱥⱥⱦⱥ ⱣeⱥⱤⱤ-
ⱦⱤn.
Parle, ⱣeⱥⱤⱥⱤⱢ.
Parlon, ⱥⱥⱦⱥ ⱣⱥⱤⱦⱥⱥⱤn. V.
MacParlan.
Parnell, ⱣeⱥⱤⱤnéⱤⱢ, ⱣⱥⱤⱤnⱥⱤⱢ.
Parrican, ⱥⱥⱦⱥ ⱣⱥⱥⱣⱥⱤⱦⱤn, ⱥⱥⱦⱥ
ⱣⱥⱥⱣⱥⱤⱦⱤn.
Parrott, ⱣeⱥⱤⱥⱥ.
Parsons, ⱥⱥⱦⱥ ⱥn ⱣeⱥⱤⱤⱥⱤn.
Partland, ⱥⱥⱦⱥ ⱣⱥⱤⱦⱥⱥⱤn, ⱥⱥⱦⱥ
ⱣⱥⱤⱦⱢⱥⱤn, ⱥⱥⱦⱥ ⱣⱥⱤⱦⱢⱥⱤn.
Paton, v. Patten.
Patrician, ⱥⱥⱦⱥ ⱣⱥⱥⱣⱥⱤⱦⱤn, ⱥⱥⱦⱥ
ⱣⱥⱥⱣⱥⱤⱥⱤn.
Patrick, ⱣⱥⱥⱣⱥⱤⱥ.
Patten, Ó ⱣeⱥⱦⱥⱤn, Ó ⱣⱤoⱦⱥⱤn
16, 91, Ó ⱣⱤⱦeⱥⱤn 192;
ⱣⱥⱤⱥⱤn E. 2; ⱥⱥⱦⱥ ⱣⱥⱤⱥⱤn
992; Ᵽⱥⱦún 2.
Patterson, ⱥⱥⱦⱥ ⱣⱥⱤⱥⱤn, ⱥⱥⱦⱥ
ⱣⱥⱤⱥⱤn 9; (s.s.) Ó CⱥⱤⱥⱤn, Ó
CoⱤⱥⱤn 197, 976.
Pattin, v. Patten.
Pattinson, Pattisson, ⱥⱥⱦⱥ
ⱣⱥⱤⱥⱤn, ⱥⱥⱦⱥ ⱣⱥⱤⱥⱤn.
Patton, v. Patten.
Paul, Ó ⱥⱥoⱢⱣⱥⱚⱥⱤⱢ 66.
Paulett, ⱣóⱤⱢéⱤⱥ.
Paulson, ⱥⱥⱦⱥ ⱣóⱤⱢ, ⱥⱥⱦⱥ ⱣóⱤⱢ.

Payne, pᵹᵹᵹan.
Payton, ó peᴀᴄáin 16, 92 ; ᴅe
péᴀᴄún 2 ; mᴀc páιᴅín 92,
(s.l.) ó páιᴅín 34.
Peacock, Peacocke, péᴀᴄóc,
péᴀᴄóᵹ.
Peake, mᴀc péιce.
Pearse, pιᴀpᴀɼ 1 ; mᴀc pιᴀpᴀιɼ
2.
Pearson, mᴀc pιᴀpᴀιɼ.
Peck, ó béιce (O'D.).
Peden, Pedian, v. Padden.
Peelan, v. Phelan.
Pegum, péᴀᵹum.
Peirson, mᴀc pιᴀpᴀιɼ.
Pelan, v. Phelan.
Pembroke, ᴅe pιonbɼóc, ᴅe
pιombɼóᵹ, pιombɼóᵹ.
Pender, pιonᴅᴀp 1 ; pιonᴅᴀp-
ᵹáp 2.
Pendergast, Pendergrass, pιon-
ᴅᴀpᵹáp, pιonᴅᴀpᵹɼáp, &c.
V. Prendergast.
Penders, v. Pender.
Pendeville, ᴅe pɼιonnᴅíol.
Peppard, Pepper, pιobᴀp, pιob-
ᴀpc, pιobᴀιpe.
Perkins, mᴀc peáιɼcín.
Perrott, peᴀpóιᴅ, pιopóιᴅ
Perry, ᴅe poιpe.
Peters, Peterson, mᴀc peᴀᴅᴀιɼ.
Petit, Petite, peιcíᴅ, peιcíᴅ.
Peton, v. Payton.
Petters, Petterson, v. Peters.
Pettitt, Petty, peιcíᴅ, peιcíᴅ.
Peyton, v. Payton.
Phair, fιonn.
Pharis, v. Farris.
Phelan, Phelon, ó fᴀoláin 1 ;
ó fιᴀláin 6 ; ó fᴀoιlleᴀᴄáin.
5. V. Whelan.
Phelim, mᴀc feιᴅlιm, mᴀc
feιᴅlιmιᴅ.
Pherson, mᴀc ᴀn peᴀppúιn,
mᴀc ᴀn peᴀppᴀιn.
Phibbs, mᴀc pιb.
Philan, ó fιᴀláin 3; ó fᴀoláin 4.

Philban, Philbin, mᴀc pιlιbín,
mᴀc pιlbín, mᴀc fιlιbín.
Philmey, mᴀc feιᴅlιmιᴅ.
Philpin, mᴀc pιlιbín, mᴀc
fιlιbín.
Philips, v. Phillips.
Philipson, mᴀc pιlιb, mᴀc
fιlιb.
Phillipin, mᴀc pιlιbín, mᴀc
fιlιbín.
Phillips, mᴀc pιlιb 1, mᴀc
fιlιb 19, 97 ; mᴀc fιlιbín,
mᴀc fιlιbín 992.
Philomy, mᴀc feιᴅlιmιᴅ.
Philson, mᴀc pιlιb, mᴀc fιlιb,
mᴀc fιlιb.
Phippen, Phippin, mᴀc pιbín.
Phipps, Phipson, mᴀc pιb.
Phylan, v. Philan.
Pike, píc.
Pickett, pιocóιᴅ.
Pidgeon, v. Pigeon.
Pierce, Pierse, pιᴀpᴀɼ 1 ; mᴀc
pιᴀpᴀιɼ 2.
Pierson, mᴀc pιᴀpᴀιɼ.
Pigeon, mᴀc ᵹuᴀιᵹín 62 ; mᴀc
Cuιlιnn 64 ; mᴀc Coluιm
2 (O'G.).
Piggott, Pigott, pιoᵹóιᴅ,
pιocóιᴅ.
Pilliu, Pillon, pιlιn.
Pindar, Pinder, pιonᴅᴀp 1 ;
pιonᴅᴀpᵹáp, pιonᴅᴀpᵹɼáp 2.
Pindergast, pιonᴅᴀpᵹáp. V.
Prendergast.
Pinders, v. Pinder.
Piper, Pipper, v. Pepper.
Pirrie, ᴅe poιpe.
Plover, mᴀc pιlιbín, mᴀc
fιlιbín, mᴀc fιlιbín 19.
Plunket, Plunkett, pluιncéιᴅ,
pluιnᵹcéιᴅ, ploιnᵹcéιᴅ.
Poer, ᴅe pᴀop, pᴀop.
Poland, Polin, póιlín, mᴀc
póιl n.
Pollard, polᴀɼᴅ.
Pollen, póιlín.
Pollett, póιléιᴅ.

Pollick, Pollock, polóc.
Poison, mac póil.
Pomeroy, Pomroy, ᴅe pompae.
Poor, ᴅe paop, paop.
Portabello, ᴅe poiptingéil, poiptingéil.
Porter, póiptéip 18, 28, 43, 47 ; póptúp 2.
Potter, potap.
Powderly, púᴅaplaiᵹ.
Powel, Powell, a paol, paol 2 ; póil 979 ; mac ᵹiolla póil 25, 27.
Power, ᴅe paop, paop.
Powlett, póiléiᴅ.
Powlson, mac póil, mac póil.
Poyne, paᵹan.
Prat, Pratt, ᴅe ppáṫ.
Pray, a'ppéiṫ, (s.l.) ó ppéiṫ.
Prendergast, ᴅe ppionᴅapᵹáp, ᴅe ppionᴅpaᵹáp, ppionᴅap-ᵹáp, pionᴅapᵹáp, pionᴅap-ᵹpáp, &c. ; (G.p.) mac Seap-ṫúin.
Prenderville, Prendeville, Pren-dible, ᴅe ppionnbíol, ppoinn-bíol.
Preston, ᴅe ppeaptún, ppeap-tún, ppioptún.
Prey, v. Pray.
Priall, ppíoḃáil.
Price, a ppíp, ppíp, ppaiᵹeap 1 ; ó ppíopáin, (o.f.) ó muipᵹeapáin 19.
Prichard,Prickard,a ppipteaipᴅ, a ppiocaipᴅ.
Piiel, ppíoḃáil.
Prindergast, v. Prendergast.
Prinderville, Prindeville, Prindi-ville, v. Prenderville.
Prior, mac an ppíopa, mac an ppíp.
Pritchard, a ppipteaipᴅ.
Prout, ppúṫ.
Prunty, ó ppoinnṫiᵹe.
Pryall, ppíoḃáil.
Pryce, Pryse, a ppíp, ppíp, ppaiᵹeap.

Pryle, ppíoḃáil.
Punch, ponnp, púinpe.
Purcell, Purcill, Pursell, puip-péil 1, ppuipéil 2.
Purtell, Purṫill, Purtle, ᴅe poptuil, poptuil.
Pyke, píc.
Pyne, paᵹan.
Pyper, v. Pepper.

Quade, Quaid, Quaide, mac uaiᴅ 1 ; ó cuain 17.
Quaine, ó cuain.
Qualey, v. Queally.
Qualter, Qualters, mac ualtaip.
Quan, Quane, Quann, ó cuain.
Queally, Queally, ó caollaiᵹe, ó caollaiᴅe 1 ; ó caóla 9.
Queelty, ó caoilte, ó caoil-tiᵹ.
Queen, ó cuinn.
Queenan, Queenane, ó cuine-áin, ó cuinneáin.
Queeney, (?) mac maonaiᵹ 34.
Quenan, v. Queenan.
Querk, Quick, ó cuipc.
Quiddihy, ó cuiᴅiᵹṫiᵹ.
Quigley, ó coiᵹliᵹ.
Quiligan, v. Quilligan.
Quilkin, mac uilcin.
Quill, ó cuill.
Quillan, Quillen, ó cuileáin, ó cuilín 1 ; mac coilín 68, 69 ; mac cuilinn 64 ; mac uiᴅlín 36.
Quillenan, ó cuileannáin.
Quilligan, ó cuileaᵹain, ó coiliᵹin, (o.f.) ó colᵹan.
Quillinan, Quilnan, ó cuileann-áin.
Quilter, ᴅe cuiᴅléip, (s.l.) cuill-téip.
Quilty, ó caoilte, ó caoil-tiᵹ.
Quin, ó cuinn 11 ; ó coinne 62.

148

Quinane, Ó Cuineáin Ó Cuinn-
eáin.
Quinlan, Ó Caoinleáin, (o.f.)
Ó Caoinvealbáin.
Quinlish, Quinlisk, Ó Cuinvlir,
(s.l.) Ó Coinlirc, Ó Coinleirc.
Quinlivan, Ó Caoinvealbáin,
(s.l.) Ó Caoinliobáin.
Quinn, Ó Cuinn 11 ; mac Cuinn
2 ; Ó Coinne 62.
Quinnell, Ó Coingill.
Quinnelly, Ó Coingeallaig, (s.)
mac Coingeallaig.
Quinniff, Ó Convuib 2 ; mac
Convuib 2.
Quinny, Ó Coinne.
Quirk, Quirke, Ó Cuirc.
Quish, Ó Coire.
Quoid, mac Uaiv.

Rabbett, Rabbit, Rabbitt, Ó
Coinín, Ó Cuinín 11, Ó
Cuineáin 192, 972; mac
Coinín 92 ; mac Conaonaig
972.
Ractigan, Ó Reactagáin
Rae, v. Rea
Rafe v. Ralph.
Raferty, Rafferty, Ó Rabartaig
(s.l.) Ó Raitbeartaig.
Rafter, Ó Reactabair.
Raftery, Ó Reactabra, Ó React-
aire.
Raftiss, Ó Reactabair, (s.l.) Ó
Reactabair.
Raggett, Ragav, Ragat.
Raghneen, Ó Reactnín.
Raghtigan, Ó Reactagáin.
Raheny, (?) Ó Raitne.
Raher, Ó Reacair, (o.f.) Ó
Freacair, Ó Fearcair.
Rahill, Ó Rágaill.
Rahilly, Ó Raitile.
Rail, Rails, Ó Rágaill, Ó
Ráigill.
Rainey, Ó Raigne, Ó Ráigne
9 ; mac Raigne 2.

Raleigh, ve Ráiléig, Ráiléig,
Rálaig 14, 17, 27 ; Ó Ragall-
aig, Ó Rogallaig 2.
Rall, Ó Rágaill.
Rally, Ó Rágallaig.
Ralph, Rávulb 11, Riap 192.
Ramsay, Ramsey, ve Rampaig,
Rampaig.
Ranaghan, Ranahan, Ó Reann-
acáin.
Ranaldson, mac Ragnaill.
Randall, Randell, Ranval 1 ;
Ragnall 2 ; mac Ragnaill 2.
Randals, Randalson, Randles,
mac Ragnaill.
Raney, Ó Ráigne 9 ; mac
Raigne 2.
Rankin, Raincín.
Rannals, mac Ragnaill 2 ;
Ragnall 2.
Ranny, v. Raheny.
Ranolds, v. Rannals.
Rashford, Ratchford, v. Roch-
ford.
Ratecan, Ó Reactagáin.
Rath, ve Rát.
Ratican, Ratigan, Rattigan, Ó
Reactagáin.
Raverty, Ó Rabartaig, Ó Rait-
beartaig.
Ravery, Ó Rabartaig, Ó Rait-
beartaig, (s.l.) Ó Raitbeartaig.
Ravy, Ó Riabaig.
Rawleigh, Rawley, v. Raleigh.
Ray, Ó Riabaig.
Raymond, Réamonn.
Raynard, Ragnarv.
Rea, Ó Riabaig 1 ; Riabac 2 ;
mac Rait 62.
Read, Reade, v. Reid.
Readdy, Ready, Ó Riava, Ó
Réava.
Reagh, Riabac.
Real, Ó Ragaill, (s.l.) Ó Raogaill.
Realy, Ó Ragaillig, (s.l.) Ó
Raogallaig.
Reaney, Reany, Ó Raigne, Ó
Ráigne 1 ; mac Raigne 2.

Reardan, Reardon, Ó Ríoρⴆáin, (o.f.) Ó Ríoᵹⴆaρⴆáin.
Reaveny,
Reavey, Reay, Ó Rⴈⴆⴈⴈᵹ.
Reckle, Ó Rⴈⴈᵹⴈll.
Redahan, Ó Roⴆⴈcáin, Ó Roⴈⴆ-eⴈcáin.
Reddan, Reddin, Redding, Ó Roⴆáin.
Reddington, Ó Roⴆⴈcáin, Ó Roⴈⴆeⴈcáin 11; Ó mⴈoⴈl-ⴆeⴈⴈᵹ 196.
Reddy, Ó Roⴆⴈᵹ, Ó Roⴈⴆⴈᵹ.
Redehan, Ó Roⴆⴈcáin, Ó Roⴈⴆe'ⴈcáin.
Redington, v. Reddington.
Redmon, Redmond, Redmont, Redmun, Réⴈmonn 1; mⴈc Réⴈmoⴈnn 9; Roⴆmonn 2.
Reed, Reede, v. Reid.
Reel, Ó Rⴈᵹⴈⴈll, (s.l.) Ó Rⴈoᵹⴈⴈll.
Reely, Ó Rⴈᵹⴈⴈllⴈᵹ, (s.l.) Ó Rⴈoᵹⴈⴈllⴈᵹ.
Reen, O Rⴈnn.
Reeves, Ó Rímeⴈⴆⴈ.
Regan, Ó Rⴈⴈᵹáin 1, (s.l.) Ó Réⴈᵹáin 2.
Reid, Réⴈⴆ E 1; ᵹⴈoⴈcⴈc 19; Ó mⴈoⴈlⴆeⴈⴈᵹ 16; Ó mⴈoⴈl Ⴆⴈᵹ́ⴆe 92.
Reidy, Ó Rⴈⴈⴆⴈ.
Reigh, Rⴈⴈⴆⴈc 1; Ó Rⴈⴈⴆⴈⴈᵹ 2.
Reighill, Reihill, Ó Rⴈᵹⴈⴈll, Ó Rⴈⴈᵹⴈll.
Reilly, Reily, Ó Rⴈᵹⴈⴈllⴈᵹ, Ó Rⴈᵹⴈⴈllⴈᵹ, Ó Rⴈⴈᵹⴈⴈllⴈᵹ, (s.l.) Ó Rⴈᵹⴈⴈllⴈᵹ, Ó Rⴈoᵹⴈⴈllⴈᵹ, &c.
Reiny, Ó Rⴈⴈᵹne 2; mⴈc Rⴈⴈᵹne 2.
Reirdan, v. Riordan.
Relehan, Relihan, Ó Roⴈⴈleⴈcáin.
Renaghan, Ranahan, Ó Reⴈnnⴈcáin.
Renan, Ó mⴈoⴈl Ⴆρeⴈnⴈⴈnn, Ó mⴈoⴈl Ⴆρéⴈnⴈⴈnn.
Renard, Rⴈᵹnⴈρⴆ.

Reneghan, Renehan, Renihan, Ó Reⴈnnⴈcáin.
Renken, Renkin, Rⴈⴈncín.
Rennaghan, Ó Reⴈnnⴈcáⴈⴈ.
Rennie, Renny, v. Reiny.
Renolds, v. Reynolds.
Reordan, v. Riordan.
Restrick, Rⴈⴈρⴆρⴈc.
Reville, Roⴈⴆeⴈl.
Rewan, Ó Ruⴈⴆáin.
Reynalds, v. Reynolds.
Reynard, Rⴈᵹnⴈρⴆ.
Reyney, mⴈc Rⴈⴈᵹne 1; Ó Rⴈⴈᵹne 9.
Reynolds, mⴈc Rⴈᵹnⴈⴈll, mⴈᵹ Rⴈᵹnⴈⴈll 11; Rⴈᵹnⴈll 18, Rⴈᵹnóⴈⴆ 2.
Reynoldson, mⴈc Rⴈᵹnⴈⴈll.
Rhategan, Rhatigan, Ó Reⴈcⴆ-ⴈᵹáin.
Riall, Ó Rⴈᵹⴈⴈll, (s.l.) Ó Rⴈoᵹⴈⴈll.
Ribbon, Ó Ruⴈⴆín.
Ricards, v. Rickards.
Rice, Ríρ, Ríρeⴈc 1; Ó mⴈoⴈl-cρⴈoⴈⴆe 38.
Richards, Richardson, mⴈc Rⴈρⴆeⴈⴈρⴆ, mⴈc Rⴈρⴆeⴈⴈρⴆ.
Richmond, ⴆe Rⴈρeⴈmonn.
Rickard, Rⴈocáρⴆ, Rⴈocⴈρⴆ.
Rickards, mⴈc Rⴈocáⴈρⴆ, mⴈc Rⴈocⴈⴈρⴆ.
Rickets, Ricketson, mⴈc Rⴈcéⴈⴆ.
Riddell, Riddle, ⴆe Rⴈoⴆⴈl, Rⴈoⴆeⴈl.
Ridge, mⴈc ⴈomⴈⴈρe 97.
Rieley, Rielly, Ó Rⴈᵹⴈⴈllⴈᵹ, Ó Rⴈᵹⴈⴈllⴈᵹ.
Rierdan, Rierdon, v. Riordan.
Rigley, Ó Rⴈⴈᵹⴈⴈllⴈᵹ.
Rigney, Ó Rⴈⴈᵹne.
Rile, v. Ryle.
Riley, Rilly, v. Reilly.
Rinaghan, Rinahan, Ó Reⴈnnⴈcáin.
Ring, Ó Rⴈnn.
Rinihan, Ó Reⴈnnⴈcáin.
Rinn, Ó Rⴈnn.

Riordan, Riorden, Ó Ríogḃaṟu-áin, (s.l.) Ó Ríoṟuáin.
Roache, ṽe Róiṟce, Róiṟceaċ.
Roan, Roane, Ó Ruaṽáin.
Roantree, Ó Caoṟċannáin.
Roarke, Ó Ruaiṟc.
Roarty, Ó Roḃaṟcaiġ.
Robbins, Robbinson, mac Roibín.
Robb, Robbs, mac Rob.
Robert, Riobáṟu, Roibeaṟu.
Roberts, Riobáṟu, Roibeaṟu 2 ; mac Roibeáiṟu, mac Roibeaiṟu 2, mac Roibiṟu 2.
Robertson, mac Roibeáiṟu, mac Roibeaiṟu 2 ; Roburcún, Roburún 2 ; mac ṽonnċaiṽ S. 2.
Robinson, mac Roibín 1 ; Roburcún, Roburún 2.
Robson, mac Rob.
Roche, ṽe Róiṟce, Róiṟceaċ.
Rochefort, Rochford, Rochfort, *ṽe Roṟṟoṟc, Roṟcaṟu 1, Roṟcún 17 ; Ó Reaċcnín 19.
Rochneen, Ó Reaċcnín.
Rock, ṽe Caṟṟaiġ 1 ; mac Conċaiṟṟġe, mac Conċaṟṟaiġe 9.
Rodan, v. Rodden.
Rodaughan, Ó Roṽaċáin.
Rodden, Roddon, Ó Roṽáin 10 ; mac Roṽáin 13, 16.
Roddy, Ó Roṽaiġ.
Roden, v. Rodden.
Rodger, Rodgers, mac Ruaiṽṟí; maġ Ruaiṽṟí 1 ; Ó Ruaiṽṟí 38, 43, 77, 992, (s.l.) Ó Reiṽṟí 779.
Rodin, v. Rodden.
Rodmont, Rodmund, Roṽmonn
Rody, v. Roddy.
Roe, Ruaṽ, 1 ; Ó Ruaiṽ, 47 ; mac Ruaiṽ 2 ; mac Conṟuḃa 56.
Roe-Lavery, Ó Laḃraṽa Ruaṽ.
Rogan, Ó Ruaṽaġáin, Ó Ruaṽaċáin.
Roger, Rogers, v. Rodgers.

Rogerson, mac Ruaiṽṟí.
Rohan, Ó Roḃaċáin, Ó Reaḃaċáin 4 ; Ó Ruaṽaċáin 6.
Roland, Ó Roċláin, Ó Roiċleáin 9.
Rolfe, Rolph, Roṽulḃ.
Ronaghan, Ó Reannaċáin.
Ronaldson, mac Raġnaill.
Ronan, Ronane, Ronayne, Ó Ronáin 11 ; Ó Ruanáin, Ó Ruanaṽáin 29, 92.
Rone, Ó Ruaṽáin.
Roney, v. Rooney.
Roohan, v. Rohan.
Roon, Ó Ruaṽáin.
Roonan, Roonane, Ó Ruanáin, (o.f.) Ó Ruanaṽáin.
Rooneen, Ó Ruanaiṽín.
Rooney, Ó Ruanaṽa, Ó Ruanaiṽ 1 ; Ó Ruanaiṽín 93 ; Ó maolṟuanaiṽ 23, 29, 97, &c.
Roonoo, Ó Ruanaṽa.
Roorke, Ó Ruaiṟc.
Roragh, Ó Ruaṽṟaic.
Rorison, mac Ruaiṽṟí.
Rorke, Ó Ruaiṟc.
Rory, Ó Ruaiṽṟí.
Rose, ṽe Rúṟ, Róṟ.
Ross, ṽe Roṟ, Roṟaċ ; (G.p.) mac Ainṽṟéiṟ, mac Ainṽṟiaṟa.
Rosseter, Rossiter, Rossitor, Roṟaiceaṟ.
Rossney, Ó Roṟna.
Rostig, Róiṟceaċ.
Roth, Rothe, Rúc.
Rouane, Ó Ruaṽáin.
Roughan, Ó Roḃaċáin, Ó Reaḃaċáin 4 ; Ó Ruaṽaċáin 6.
Roughasy, (?) Ó Ruṽġuṟa.
Roughneen, Ó Reaċcnín.
Rountree, Ó Caoṟċannáin.
Rourke, Ó Ruaiṟc 11, (o.f.) Ó Ruaṽṟaic 2.
Routh, Rúc.
Rowan, Ó Roḃaċáin 76 ; Ó Ruaṽáin 9.

Rowe, Ruaṫ 1; Ó Ruaiṫ 17; mac Ruaiṫ 2; mac Conṗuḃa 56.

Rowen, Ó Ruaiṫín.

Rowland, Roṫlann 1; Ó Roiċláin, Ó Roiċleáin 9

Rowley, Ó Roġallaiġ 1; Ó Roċláin, Ó Roiċleáin 9.

Rowney, Ó Ruanaṫa, Ó Ruanaiṫ.

Roy, mac Ruaiṫ 2; mac Ġiollaṗuaiṫ 62.

Royan, Ó Ruaṫáin, Ó Ruaiṫín.

Royce, v. Rice.

Roynane, Ó Ruanáin, (o.f.) Ó Ruanaṫáin.

Royse, v. Rice.

Ruan, Ruane, Ó Ruaṫáin 11, Ó Ruaiṫín 192.

Ruarke, Ó Ruairc.

Ruckston, Rucrton.

Ruddan, v. Rudden.

Ruddell, v. Ruddle.

Rudden, Ruddin, Ó Roṫáin 1 0; mac Roṫáin 13, 16.

Ruddle, ṿe Rioṫal, Rioṫal.

Ruddy, Ó Roṫaiġ 1; mac Roṫaiġ 16.

Rudican, Rudihan, Ó Roṫacáin, Ó Roiṿeacáin.

Ruhan, v. Rohan.

Ruineen, Ó Ruanaiṫín.

Ruirk, Ó Ruairc.

Runey, v. Rooney.

Runian, Ó Ruanaiṫín.

Ruorke, Rurke, Ó Ruairc.

Rush, Ó Ruir 43, 88; Ó Luacáir, Ó Luacra 9; Ó ruaṫa 62; ṿe Ruir 2.

Rushford, v. Rochford.

Russell, Ruiréil.

Ruth, Rúc.

Ruthledge, Rutledge, Rutlege, Ruicléir, Ruiclir 11; Ó maoilṿeirġ 19.

Ruttle, v. Ruddle.

Ryall, Ó Raġaill.

Ryan, Ó Riain 8; Ó maoil Riain 7; Ó Ruaiṫín 91, Ó Ruaṫáin 92; Ó Spuiċeáin 192.

Ryder, Ó marcaiġ 3; Ó marcáin 4, 9.

Ryely, v. Reilly.

Ryle, Ó Raġaill, (s.l.) Ó Reiġill.

Ryley, v. Reilly.

Reynard, Raġnarṿ.

Ryney, Ó Raiġne 2; mac Raiġne 2.

Rynn, Ó Rinn 7; mac Ḃroin 39.

Sall, ṿe Sál, Sál.

Sallanger, Sallenger, Sallinger, Sailinġéir, Sailiġéir, Sailinéir.

Salmon, Sammon, Ó Ḃraṫáin.

Sampson, Samson, Samrún.

Samuels, Samuelson, mac Samuel.

Sandall, Sandell, ṿe Sanṿál, Sanṿál.

Sanders, Sanṿar, Sanṿair.

Sanderson, mac Sanṿair.

Sanford, ṿe Sanforc.

Santry, ṿe Sainċreaḃ, ṿe Seanċreaḃ 1; Sicric 779.

Sargeant, Sargent, Sargint, Sáirġeanc.

Sarseil, Sáirréil.

Sarsfield, Sáirréil 11, Sáiréil 19, Sainréil 192.

Saul, ṿe Sál, Sál.

Saunders, Sanṿar, Sanṿair.

Saunderson, mac Sanṿair.

Saurin, ṿe Saḃrainn.

Sausheil, Sáiréil.

Savage, Sáḃaoir, Saḃaoir 1, Saḃáirce 24, 47; Ó Saḃáin 27, 49, 77.

Savin, Ó Saḃáin.

Sayer, Sayers Saoġar.

Scahill, Ó Scaċġail, (o.f.) mac Scaiċġil.

Scales, ṿe Scéalar.

Scallan, Ó Sceallái n.
Scally, Ó Scalaiġe, Mac Scalaiġe 11 ; Ó Scollán 92.
Scamaton, Scampton, Scamtún, Sceaimicín.
Scandlon, Scanlan, Scanlon, Ó Scannláin.
Scannell, Ó Scannail.
Schail, Schaill, Ó Scatġail.
Schofield, Scholefield, Scofield, ve Scoful, Scoful.
Scolard, Scollard, Scoláro.
Scott, Scot 1 ; Albanac 2.
Scriven, ve Scribin.
Scuffil, ve Scoful, Scofub.
Scullane, Scullion, Ó Scolláin, (o.f.) Ó Scealláin.
Scully, Ó Scolaiġe, Ó Scolaive 11 ; Ó Scolláin 92.
Scurlock, Scoplóg.
Scurry, Ó Scurra, Ó Scuipe, Ó Scuiprò.
Sdundon, ve Sconnrún, Sconnrún, Sconrún, Scúnrún.
Seagrave, Seagrove, v. Segrave.
Sear, Seares, Sears, Saoġar, Mac Saoġaip, (s.l.) Mac Séarpac 19.
Searson, Mac Saoġaip.
Seaver, Saoṁap.
Seaward, Saobapo.
Seerey, Seery, Ó Saopaive, (o.f.) Ó Síoġpava, Ó Síoġpaiv.
Segrave, Segre, ve Saoġráb.
Segrue, Ó Siocfrava, Ó Siocrava.
Seix, Saġap.
Selenger, Sellinger, Sailinġéip, Sailiġéip, Sailinéip.
Semore, Semour, Saomap.
Sergeant, Sergent, Saipġeanc.
Setright, Mac Sicpic.
Seward, Saobapo 1 ; Ó Suaipo, Ó Suaipc 14 ; Ó Claiṁín 19.
Sewell, Ó Súiliġ 2 ; Saobal 2.
Sexton, Ó Searnáin, Ó Siornáin.

Seymore, Seymour, Saomap.
Shaftery, Mac Searpaiv.
Shahan, Ó Séavacáin.
Shails, Shales, v. Sheils.
Shairp, v. Sharpe.
Shalloe, Shallow, Shally, Shalvey, Ó Sealbaiġ.
Shamrock, Seampóg.
Shanaghan, Ó Seanacáin.
Shanagher (?), Ó Seanacaip.
Shanaghy, Mac Seanca, Mac Seancaive.
Shanahan, Shanahen, Ó Seanacáin, Ó Seancáin.
Shanahy, v. Shanaghy.
Shanan, v. Shannon.
Shane, Mac Seaġáin, Mac Seáin 1 ; Ó Séavacáin 2.
Shanessy, v. Shaughnessy.
Shanihan, v. Shanahan.
Shanley, Mac Seanlaoic.
Shannagh, Ó Seanaiġ.
Shannahan, v. Shanahan.
Shannessy, v. Shaughnessy.
Shannihan, v. Shanahan.
Shannon, Ó Seanáin 10, 87 ; Ó Seancáin, Ó Seanacáin 15, 46, 87 ; Mac Giolla tSeanáin 46, (s.l.) Ó Cillcpeáin 462.
Shanny, Ó Seanaiġ.
Shanon, v. Shannon.
Sharket, Sharkett, Ó Searcóiv.
Sharkey, Ó Searcaiġ.
Sharman, Seapman.
Sharpe, Géap 1 ; Ó Géapáin 16.
Sharry, Mac Searpaiġ 13, 16, 29 56 ; Ó Searpaiġ 16, 36, 64, 77.
Sharvin, Ó Searbáin.
Shasnan, Ó Searnáin.
Shaughness, Ó Seacnair.
Shaughnessy, Ó Seacnarpaiġ 11, (s.l.) Ó Seacnair 2.
Shaw, Seavac, Seaġac.
Shea, Ó Séaġva.
Sheahan, Ó Séavacáin, Ó Síovacáin.
Sheales, Sheals, v. Sheils.
Shealy, Ó Sealbaiġ.

153

Shean, Ó séaóacáin, Ó síoóacáin.
Shearhoon, mac séaptúin.
Shearlock, v. Sherlock.
Shearman, seapman.
Shee, Ó séaġóa.
Sheean, Ó síoóacáin, Ó séaó-acáin.
Sheedy, Ó síoóa 1 ; mac síoóa 76.
Sheehan, Ó síoóacáin, Ó síóeacáin. Ó síotcáin.
Sheehy, mac sítiġ 11, Ó sítiġ 72.
Sheen, Ó síoóacáin, Ó síóeacáin.
Sheenan, Ó sionáin.
Sheera, mac séaptáin.
Sheeran, Sheeren, Ó síopáin, Ó sípín.
Shegrue, Ó siocppaóa, Ó siocpaóa.
Shehan, v. Sheehan.
Sheil, Sheilds, Sheils, Ó siaóail, Ó siaġail.
Sheily, Ó sealbaiġ.
Sheirdan, v. Sheridan.
Sheles, v. Sheils.
Shellew, Shelloe, Shelly, Ó sealbaiġ.
Shera, mac séaptáin.
Sherden, Sherdon, Sheredan, Sheridan, Sheriden, Ó sipióeáin, Ó siopaóáin, Ó seipeaóáin.
Sherin, Ó sípín.
Sherlock, scoplóġ 1, seaplóġ 47.
Sherman, seapman.
Sherodan, v. Sheridan.
Sherra, mac séaptáin.
Sherridan, v. Sheridan.
Sherry, mac seappaiġ 13, 16, 29, 56 ; Ó seappaiġ 16, 36, 64, 77.
Sherwin, Ó seapbáin.
Shevlin, Ó sióbleáin, Ó sióbliain, Ó seibleáin, Ó seiblín.
Shiel, Shields, Shiells, Shiels, Shiles, Ó siaóail, Ó siaġail.
Shinagh, v. Shinnagh.

Shine, Ó seiġin.
Shinkwin, simicín.
Shinnagh, sionnac 2 ; Ó sionnaiġ 2.
Shinnahan, Ó sionacáin.
Shinnan, Ó sionáin.
Shinnick, Ó sionnaiġ, Ó sionaiġ.
Shinnock, sionnac 2 ; Ó sionnaiġ 2.
Shinnor, Shinnors, óe sionúip, sionúip 11, soiniúip 92.
Shinny, Shinwick, Ó sionaiġ, Ó sionnaiġ.
Shirdan, v. Sheridan.
Shirlock, v. Sherlock.
Shirra, mac séaptáin.
Shonagh, Shonogh, sionnac.
Short, ġeapp 1 ; mac an ġeáipp, mac an ġipp 6.
Shortall, Shortell, soiptéil, seaptal.
Shorten, seaptáin.
Shorthall, Shortle, v. Shortall.
Shortice, Shortis, seoptúp.
Shortt, v. Short.
Shoughnessy, v. Shaughnessy.
Shovelin, Shovlin, v. Shevlin.
Shoye, seóiġ.
Shryhane, Ó spuiteáin.
Shughrue, Ó siocppaóa, Ó siocpaóa.
Shunagh, sionnac.
Shunny, Ó sionaiġ, Ó sionnaiġ.
Shurdan, Ó siopaóáin.
Sigerson, mac síoġaip.
Siggins, siġín.
Silk, Ó síoóa.
Silver (?) Ó háipġeaóáin
Simcox, siomcóc, siomcóġ.
Simkin, Simkins, simicín.
Simmonds, Simmons, Simonds, Simons, Simonson, mac síomóin, mac síomoinn.
Simpkin, Simpkins, simicín.
Simpson, S. ms, Simson, mac sim.

Sinclair, Sinclare, Sincler, ᴅe Sincléip, Sincléip ; (G.p.) mac Riocaipᴅ.

Singen, Singin, ᴅe Suingean, Suingean.

Singleton, ᴅe Singealcún, (s.l.) Ó Sinᴅile, Ó Sionᴅuile 46, 77.

Sinjohn, Sinjun, v. Singen.

Sinnott, Sinott, Sionóiᴅ 1 ; Sionúip, Soiniúip 19, 97.

Size, Saᵹap.

Skahill, Ó Scacᵹail, (o.f.) mac Scaiéᵹil.

Skally, Ó Scalaiᵹe, (s.) mac Scalaiᵹe 11 ; Ó Scolláin 92.

Skeahan, Skeane, Ó Scéacáin 4 ; mac Sceacáin 6.

Skeffington, Sceimealcún.

Skehan, v. Skeahan.

Skelly, Ó Scalaiᵹe, (s.) mac Scalaiᵹe.

Skelton, ᴅe Scealcún.

Skerrett, Sceapac, Scipéiᴅ.

Skiddy, Sciᴅiᵹ, Sciᴅiᵹeac.

Skiffington, v. Skeffington.

Skillen, Scilling, Scillinn.

Skinner, Scinéip.

Skinnion, Ó Scinᵹín.

Skivington, Sceimealcún.

Skoolin, Ó Scolláin.

Skryne, ᴅe Scpín.

Slamon, (?) Ó Sléibín.

Slane, ᴅe Sláine.

Slattery, Ó Slacappa, Ó Slacpa.

Slavin, Sleavin, Sleevin, Slevan, Slevin, Ó Sléibín.

Sleyne, Sliney, Sliny, mac Sleimne.

Sloan, Sloane, Ó Sluaᵹáin, (o.f.) Ó Sluaᵹaᴅáin.

Slocombe, Slócúm, Slócum.

Sloey, v. Slowey.

Slone, v. Sloan.

Slowey, Ó Sluaᵹaᴅaiᵹ.

Slown, v. Sloan.

Sloy, v. Slowey.

Sloyan, Sloyne, Ó Sluaᵹáin, Ó Sluaiᵹín, (o.f.) Ó Sluaᵹaᴅáin, Ó Sluaᵹaiᴅín.

Small, beaᵹ 1 ; Ó Caoilce, Ó Caoilciᵹ 64.

Smallen, Ó Smealáin, (o.f.) Ó Spealáin.

Smallwoods, mac Concoillín.

Smart, Smeapc.

Smeeth, Smípc.

Smiddy, Smiᴅiᵹ, Smiᴅiᵹe 1 ; Smípc 2.

Smith, mac an ᵹobann, mac an ᵹabann 11, mac an ᵹoba 2, mac ᵹobann, mac ᵹabann 2 ; Ó ᵹobann, Ó ᵹabann 35, 38, 58, 67, 86 ; ᵹoba 2.

Smithwick, Smiᴅic 1 ; Smiᴅiᵹ, Smiᴅiᵹe 2 ; Smípc, Smípceac 778.

Smollan, Smollen, Smullen, Ó Smoláin, (o.f.) Ó Smealáin, (o.f.) Ó Spealáin.

Smyth, Smythe, v. Smith.

Smythwick, v. Smithwick.

Snee, Ó Sniaᴅaiᵹ.

Snow, an cSneacca.

Soghlahan, Ó Soclacáin.

Solly, mac Soilliᵹ.

Soloman, Solomon, Solomons, mac Solaim.

Somahan, Somahaun, Ó Somacáin.

Somers, Ó Sampaiᴅ 7, 87 ; Ó Somacáin 9 ; maᵹ Sampáin 2.

Somerville, Ó Somacáin.

Sommers, v. Somers.

Sommerville, v. Somerville.

Soolivan, Ó Súileabáin.

Soraghan, Sorahan, Soran, Soroghan, Ó Sopacáin.

Soughly, Ó Soclaiᵹ.

Soutar, Souter, Súcap.

Spain, ᴅe Spáine, Spáineac.

Spalane, Ó Spealáin.

Spearin, Speariug, Spéipinᵹ.

Speed, Speedy, Ó puaᴅa 9, Ó puaᴅacáin 6.

Spelessy, v. Spellessy.
Spellane, Ó Spealáin.
Spellissy, Ó Spealġusa, Ó Spilġeasa.
Spellman, Spelman, Ó Spealáin.
Spencer, Spenser, Mac Spealáin, Mac Spealláin.
Spilacy, v. Spillessy.
Spilane, Spillane, Ó Spealáin, Ó Spioláin.
Spillessy, Ó Spilġeasa, Ó Spealġusa.
Splaine, v. Spilane.
Spollan, Spollane, Ó Spealáin, (s.l.) Ó Spoláin.
Spratt, Sprat.
Sreenan * Ó Srianáin.
Sruffaun, Ó Sruṫáin, Ó Sruiṫeáin.
Stack, Stac.
Stackpole, Stackpoole, Stacpole, de Stacabúl, de Stacapúl; (s.s.) Gallduḃ.
Stafford, de Stafort, Stafort 1; Mac an Stocaire 26.
Staines, de Stáineas.
Stancard, Stanfard, Stancard.
Stanford, de Stanfort.
Stanley, de Stainléiġ.
Stanton, de Stonndún, Stonndún, Stondún; (G.p.) Mac an Ṁíleaḋa, Mac an Ṁíliḋ.
Stapleton, Stapleton, de Stáblatún; (s.s.) Gallduḃ; (G.p.) Mac an Ġaill.
Starkey, Starkie, Starcaiḋ.
Staunton, v. Stanton.
St. Clair, St. Clare, de Sincléir, Sincléir; (G.p.) Mac Riocaird.
Stead, Steadman, Steed, Mac Eaċaiḋ 35.
Steen, Stiḃin.
Steenson, Steinson, Stenson, Mac Stiḃin, Mac Stín.
Stephens, Stiḃin 1; Mac Stiḃin 81, 91, Mac Steafáin. Mac Stiofáin, Mac Stioṗáin, 92; Mac Giolla Steafáin 2; Ó Steafáin 45.
Stephenson, Stevens, Stevenson Stevinson, Mac Stiḃin, Mac Steafáin, Mac Steiṁin, Mac Stiaḃna, &c.
Steward, Stewart, Stíoḃard Stíoḃart, Stiuḃard.
Stinson, Mac Stiḃin, Mac Stín
St. John, de Siúngean, Siúngean.
St. Ledger, St. Leger, Sailingéir, Sailigéir, Sailinéir 11, Saileastar 78.
Stoakes, Stokes, de Stóc. Stóc.
Stone, Ó Maolċluiċe 1; Ó Cloċartaiġ 99.
Storan, Ó Stóirín.
Strachan, Straghan, Strahan, Strain, Ó Sraiṫeáin, Ó Sruiṫeáin, Ó Sruṫáin.
Strange, Stráinse 1; Stronng, Strong 78; Mac Conċoigcríċe 52.
Stritch, Straoit, Straoits, Straoitseaċ.
Strohane, Ó Sruiṫeáin, Ó Sruṫáin.
Strong, Stronge, Stronng, Strong.
Stuart, v. Stewart.
Stubbin, Stubbins, Stóibín.
Studdert, Studart.
Stundon, de Stonndún, Stonndún, Stúndún.
Suche, Súirte.
Suckley, Ó Soċlaiġ.
Suel, Ó Súiliġ 2; Saoḃal 2.
Sugrew, Sugrue, Ó Siocḟraḋa, Ó Sioċraḋa.
Sullahan, Sullehan, Ó Súileaċáin.

Sullevan, Sullivan, Ó Súileaḃáin, Ó Súilleaḃáin 1 ; Ó Súileacáin 37, 55, 67.
Sumahean, Ó Somacáin.
Summerly, Ó Somacáin 19.
Summers, v. Somers.
Summerville, Ó Somacáin 19, 97.
Suppell, Supple, Suipéil.
Surtill, Soirtéil.
Suter, Sutor, Sutter, Sútar.
Sutton, ᵒe Sucún.
Swaine, Suan.
Swainson, mac Suain.
Swan, Suan.
Swanson, mac Suain.
Swanton, ᵒe Suantún.
Swayne, Suan.
Sweeney, Sweeny, mac Suiḃne 11, Ó Suiḃne 772.
Sweetman, Suatman.
Sweney, Sweny, v. Sweeney.
Swift, Ó ꝼuaᵒa 9; Ó ꝼuaᵒacáin 6.
Swine, Swiney, mac Suiḃne.
Switzer, Suiꞇréir.
Sword, Swords, Ó Suairᵒ, Ó Suairꞇ 8 ; Ó Claiṁín 9.
Swyne, mac Suiḃne.
Sylver, v. Silver.
Symmonds, Symmons, Symonds Symondson, Symons, mac Síomóin, mac Síomoinn.
Synan, Ó Sionáin.
Synnott, Synott, Sionóiᵒ 1 ; Sionúiꞇ, Soiniúiꞇ 19, 97.
Syron, (?) mac Séarꞇúin.

Taaffe, Taff, Ꞇáꞇ.
Tagan, Ó Ꞇaᵒɕáin.
Tagart, Tagert, Taggart, Taggert, mac an ꞇSaɕairꞇ.
Tagney, Ó Ꞇeanɕana.
Tague, Ó Ꞇaióɕ 2 ; mac Ꞇaióɕ 2.
Talbot, Ꞇalbóiᵒ.
Tallant, Tallent, Ꞇalanꞇ.
Tallon, Ꞇalún.

Tally, Ó Ꞇaiꞇlιɕ, Ó Ꞇaiꞇliɕ.
Talty, Ó Ꞇailꞇιɕ.
Tamney, mac an Ꞇiompánaιɕ.
Tangney, Ó Ꞇeanɕana.
Tankard. Ꞇanncáꞃᵒ.
Tannan, v. Tannian.
Tanner, Ꞇanúiꞃ.
Tannian, Tannion, Ó Ꞇanaiᵒeáin.
Tansey, Ó ḃliorcáin (S.L.) 9.
Tarmey, Ó Ꞇormaᵒa, Ó Ꞇormaιɕ.
Tarpey, Ó Ꞇarra, Ó Ꞇarraiᵒ, Ó Ꞇarraιɕ.
Tarrant, Ꞇaranꞇ. Ꞇoranꞇa 77; Ó Ꞇaráin, Ó Ꞇoráin 2.
Tarsnane, Ó Ꞇarrnáin.
Taugher, Ó Ꞇuaꞇcaiꞃ.
Taulty, Ó Ꞇailꞇιɕ.
Tavey, mac an ꞇSáṁaιɕ.
Tayler, Taylor, Taylour, Ꞇáilliúiꞃ.
Teaghan, Ó Ꞇéacáin.
Teague, Ó Ꞇaióɕ 2 ; mac Ꞇaióɕ 2.
Teahan, Ó Ꞇéacáin, (o.f.) Ó Ꞇeiꞇeacáin.
Tee, Ó Ꞇaióɕ.
Teegan, Ó Ꞇaᵒɕáin.
Teehan, Ó Ꞇéacáin.
Teeling, Ꞇaoilinɕ.
Teevan, (?) Ó Ꞇeiṁneáin.
Tegan, Ó Ꞇaᵒɕáin.
Tegart, Teggart, Teggarty, mac an ꞇSaɕairꞇ.
Tehan, Tehane, Ó Ꞇéacáin.
Teigan, Ó Ꞇaᵒɕáin.
Teige, Teigue, mac Ꞇaióɕ 1 ; Ó Ꞇaióɕ 4, 9.
Tempany, Tempeny, Tenpeny, mac an Ꞇiompánaιɕ.
Tempest, mac Anꞃaιᵒ.
Ternan, v. Tiernan.
Terney, Terny, v. Tierney.
Terry, Ꞇuiriᵒ, Ꞇoiriᵒ 1 ; Ꞇuraoin 47 ; mac Ꞇoirᵒealḃaιɕ 2.

Tevnan, Tevnane, Ó Ceiṁneáin.
Tew, ᴅe Ciú, Ciú.
Thirkell, mac Coᴘcaill.
Thom, Cóm.
Thomas, Comáᴘ 1; mac Comáᴘ 2, mac Cómaiᴘ, (s.l.) Ó Cómaiᴘ 19, 97.
Thompson, Thomson, mac Comáiᴘ 1, mac Cómaiᴘ, (s.l.) Ó Cómaiᴘ 19, 97, mac Cáṁaiᴘ 6.
Thoran, Thorn, Ó Coᴘáin.
Thornhill, Coᴘnuil
Thornton, Coᴘanca, 47, 77; Ó Coᴘáin, Ó Caᴘáin 2; Ó Oᴘaᴣnáin, Ó Oᴘaiᴣneáin 19, 97; muineaċ 192; Ó muineaċáin 92; mac Sceaċáin 64.
Thulis, Ó Cuaċaláin.
Thunder, Cunᴅaᴘ.
Thurkell, Thurkill, Thurkle, mac Coᴘcaill.
Thynne, Ó Ceiṁin.
Tidins, (?) Ó Cuaᴘuiᴘc.
Tiernan, mac Ciᴣeaᴘnáin 11, mac Ciᴣeaᴘnáin 97; Ó Ciᴣeaᴘnáin 16, 91; Ó Ciᴣeaᴘnaiᴣ 15, 19,
Tierney, Ó Ciᴣeaᴘnaiᴣ 11; Ó Ciᴣeaᴘnáin 91; mac Ciᴣeaᴘnáin 976.
Tighe, Ó Caiᴅᴣ 4, 91; mac Caiᴅᴣ 22, 56; mac Ceanᴣalaiᴣ 43, 67 Ó Ceanᴣlaċáin 19.
Tigue, mac Caiᴅᴣ 19. V. Teigue.
Tilly, Ó Caiċliᴣ, Ó Caiċliᴣ.
Timblin, Timlin, mac Coimilín, mac Coimilín, (s.l.) Ó Cuimlin, Ó Cuimlín 19.
Timmin, Timmins, Timmons, Coimín 14, 87; mac Coimín 19, Ó Coimín 2; Ó Ciomáin 692, 872.

Timony, Ó Ciománaiᴣ 69; mac an Ciompánaiᴣ 62.
Timothy, mac Comalcaiᴣ 97
Timpany, mac an Ciompánaiᴣ
Tinan, Ó Ceiṁneáin, Ó Ceiṁnín
Tinckler, Cincléiᴘ.
Tinin, Ó Ceiṁnin.
Tinkler, Cincléiᴘ.
Tinsley, Ó Ceinnᴘealaiᴣ (O'D.).
Tivane, (?) Ó Ceiṁneáin.
Tivnane, Ó Ceiṁneáin.
Toal, Toale, Ó Cuaċail, Ó Cuaċᴣail.
Tobin, Tobyn, Cóibín.
Togher, Ó Cuaċċaiᴘ.
Toghill, Tohall, Ó Cuaċail, Ó Cuaċᴣail.
Toher, Ó Cuaċċaiᴘ.
Tohill, Ó Cuaċail, Ó Cuaċᴣail.
Toke, Cóc.
Tolan, Toland, Ó Cuaċaláin.
Toler, Ó Calċaiᴘ.
Tolin, Ó Cuaċaláin, (s.l.) Ó Coláin 19.
Tolleran, Ó Calċaᴘáin.
Toman, Ó Cuamáin, Ó Comáin.
Tomblin, Tomblinson, mac Coimilín.
Tomilty, mac Comalcaiᴣ 1; Ó Comalcaiᴣ 87, 88.
Tomkin, Tomkins, Cóimicín.
Tomkins, Tomkinson, mac Cóimicín.
Tomlin, Tomlins, Tomlinson, Tomlyn, mac Coimilín.
Tompkins, mac Cóimicín.
Toner, Ó Coṁnaiᴘ, (o.f.) Ó Coṁᴘaiᴘ.
Tonra, Tonry, Ó Coṁnᴘa (o.f.) Ó Coṁᴘaiᴘ.
Tooey Ó Cuaċaiᴣ.
Tooher Ó Cuaċċaiᴘ.
Toohig, Ó Cuaċaiᴣ.
Toohill, Ó Cuaċail, Ó Cuaċᴣail.
Toohy, Ó Cuaċaiᴣ.
Took, Tooke, Cóc.
Tooker, Ó Cuaċċaiᴘ.
Toolan, Ó Cuaċaláin.

Toole Ó Tuathail 11 Ó Tuathghail 2 ; Mac Tuathail 92.
Tooley (?) Ó Tuathghaile.
Toolis, Ó Tuathaláin.
Tooman, Ó Tuamáin.
Toomey, Ó Tuama.
Toompane, (?) Ó Tuamáin, nó Mac an Tiompánaigh.
Toorish, Ó Tuaruir.
Toran Ó Toráin Ó Taráin.
Torley, Mac Toirdhealbhaigh.
Tormey, Ó Tormadha, Ó Tormaigh.
Torney, Ó Tórna.
Torpy, Ó Tórpa, Ó Tórpaigh.
Torran, Ó Toráin, Ó Taráin 2; Turaoin 2.
Torrance, Torrans, Torrence, Torrens, Torrins, Ó Toráin, Ó Taráin 1 ; Turaoin 47; Mac Toirdhealbhaigh 2
Torry, v. Terry.
Tothill, Ó Tuathail (O'M).
Toughall, v. Toughill.
Tougher, Ó Tuathchair.
Toughill, Ó Tuathail, Ó Tuathghail.
Touhig, Ó Tuathaigh.
Touhill v. Toughill.
Touhy Ó Tuathaigh.
Toulhan, Ó Tuathaláin, (s.l.) Ó Tualcháin.
Tourisk Ó Tuaruirc.
Towell Ó Tuathail.
Towey Ó Toghdha 19 34 ; Ó Tuathaigh 20.
Towhig, Ó Tuathaigh.
Towill. Ó Tuathail.
Towmey, Ó Tuama.
Townley, de Túinléigh, Túinléigh, Túnluidh.
Toy, Toye, Ó Tuaith (S.L.) 19.
Tracey, Tracy, Ó Treasaigh.
Trahey, Ó Traighthigh.
Trainor, Tranor, Mac Tréinfir.
Trant, de Treant, Treant, Treannt.

Trassy, Ó Treasaigh.
Travers, Travors, de Tráibhearr, Tráibhearr 1 ; Ó Treabhair 35, 39, 55.
Trayner, Traynor, Mac Tréinfir.
Treacy, Ó Treasaigh.
Treanor, Mac Tréinfir.
Trehy, Ó Traighthigh, Ó Troighthigh.
Trench, Trinre, Trinnre.
Trenor, Mac Tréinfir.
Tressy, Ó Treasaigh.
Trevor, Ó Treabhair.
Trevors, v. Travers.
Trew, Triú.
Trim, de Truim.
Trim-Lavery, Trin-Lavery Ó Labhradha Tréan.
Tristan, Tristram, Trortan.
Trodden, Troddyn, Ó Treodháin.
Trower, Ó Treabhair.
Troy, de Treó, Treó 24, 47 ; Ó Traighthigh, Ó Troighthigh 2 ; Ó Tréamhain 469.
Trueman. Triúman.
Tryn-Lavery, v. Trin-Lavery.
Tubridy, Tubrit Ó Tiobraide.
Tucker, Ó Tuathchair.
Tuffy, Ó Toghdha.
Tuhill, Ó Tuathail.
Tuhy, Ó Tuathaigh.
Tuite, de Tiúit, Tiúit, (o.f.) de Diúid, Diúid.
Tuke, Tóc
Tully, Ó Taichligh, Ó Taichligh 65 ; Ó Maoltuile 8, 67, 97, (s) Mac Mhaoltuile. (s l.) Mac an Tuile, Mac Tuile 16, 95, Ó Tuile 99.
Tumalty, Tumblety, Tumelty, Tumilty, Mac Tomaltaigh 1 ; Ó Tomaltaigh 87, 88.
Tumman, Tummon, Ó Tuamáin, Ó Tomáin.
Tumpane, v. Toompane.
Tumulty, v. Tumalty.
Tunney, Tunny, Ó Tonnaigh 11 ; Ó Tuine 192.

Tuohig, Ó Cuaċaıᵹ.
Tuohill, Ó Cuaċaıl.
Tuohy, Ó Cuaċaıᵹ.
Tuomy, Ó Cuama.
Turbett, Turbit, Coɾbóıᴅ.
Turish, Ó Cuaɾuıɾ.
Turley, mac Coıɾᴅealbaıᵹ.
Turner, Coɾnóıɾ.
Turney, Ó Cóɾna.
Turnor, Turnour, Coɾnóıɾ.
Tuthill, Tuttell, Tuttill, Tuttle Ó Cuaċaıl (O'M.).
Tutty, Ó Cuaċaıᵹ.
Twigley, Ó Coıᵹlıᵹ.
Twohig, Ó Cuaċaıᵹ.
Twohill, Ó Cuaċaıl.
Twohy, Ó Cuaċaıᵹ.
Twomey, Ó Cuama.
Twoohy, v. Twohy.
Twoomy, Ó Cuama.
Tye, Tyghe, v. Tighe.
Tymmany, v. Timony.
Tymmins,   Tymmons,   v. Timmins, Timmons.
Tynan, Ó Ceıṁneáın.
Tyne, Ó Ceıṁın.
Tynnan, v. Tynan.
Tynne, v. Tyne.
Tyrrell, Cıɾıal, Cɾıal.

Uiske, mac Conuıɾce.
Ultagh, ulcaċ.   V. Dunleavy.
Umphrey, unɸɾaıᴅ.
Unehan, Ó hOnċon.
Uniack, Uniacke, Uniake, ᴅoın-ᵹeáɾᴅ, ᴅoınneáɾᴅ, ᴅuın-ᵹeáɾᴅ, ᴅuınneáɾᴅ.
Upton, uɾcún.
Urrell, ᴅe Oıɾᵹıall.
Usher, Ussher, uıɾéıɾ.
Ustace, Iúɾcáɾ.

Vaddock, mac ṁaᴅóc, mac ṁaᴅóᵹ.
Vadin, mac ɸáıᴅın.
Vahey, Vahy, mac an beaċa, mac an beaċaᴅ.
Vail, mac ɸáıl, mac ɸóıl.

Valentine, baılıncín.
Vallely, Vallily, (?) mac ᵹıolla ṁuıɾe
Vally, mac an ballaıᵹ.
Varden, ᴅe beaɾᴅún 1 ; mac ɸáıᴅın 99.
Vargis, Vargus, mac ɸeaɾᵹuɾa.
Varily, Varley, Varrelly, Varrilly, mac an beaɾɸúılıᵹ.
Vaughan, Ó maċáın, Ó moċáın 1 ; uaċan 18, 28, 82.
Veale, ᴅe béal, ᴅe bıal.
Veasy, mac an beaċa, mac an beaċaᴅ 19.
Veigh, mac an beaċa, mac an beaċaᴅ.
Veldon, ᴅe béalacún, béala-cún.
Verdin, Verdon, ᴅe beaɾᴅún.
Verlin, Verling, ɾeóıɾlınᵹ.
Vesey, v. Veasy.
Vicars, Vickers, Vickery, mac an bıocáıɾe, mac an bıocaɾa.
Victory, mac ⱥnabaᴅa.
Vikers, v. Vickers.
Vincent, uınɾeann.
Vingin, Ó ɸıaċa, Ó ɸıaċaċ 47.
Vogan, úᵹán.

Wadden, uaıᴅín.
Waddick, mac ṁaᴅóc.
Wadding, uaıᴅín.
Waddock, mac ṁaᴅóc, mac ṁaᴅóᵹ.
Wade, uaᴅa 1 ; mac uaıᴅ 6 mac meaᴅ́aċaın (S.L.) 19.
Wadick, Wadock, mac ṁaᴅóc, mac ṁaᴅóᵹ.
Waid, Waide, v. Wade.
Waldron, ualᴅɾán 19 ; mac ualᴅáın, mac balᴅáın 92, mac ualɾonca, mac balɾonca 8 ; mac uaılᴅín, mac uaılcɾín, mac baılᴅín, mac baılcɾín 192.
Walker, an cSıubaıl.
Wall, ᴅe bál, ɾálcaċ.

Wallace, Wallice, Wallis, ᴠe
ⱱⱥⷱléⷠⱃ, ᴠe ⱱⱥⷱⳑⷠⱃ, ᴠe ⱱⱥⷱⳑⷠⱃ,
ⱱⱥⷱⳑⷠⱃ.

Walsh, Walshe, ⱱⱃeⱥⱦⱀⱥⱦ 11 ;
ᴠe ⱱⱥⷱléⷠⱃ, ᴠe ⱱⱥⷱⳑⷠⱃ, ᴠe
ⱱⱥⷱⳑⷠⱃ, ⱱⱥⷱⳑⷠⱃ 2 ; ⱱⱥⱃⱥⷱⱀ,
ⱱⱥⱃⱥⱀⱦⱥⱦ 493.

Walter, Walters, ⰿⱥⱄ ⱂⱥⳑⱦⱥⷠⱃ.

Walton, ᴠe ⱱⱥⳑⱦún.

Ward, ⰿⱥⱄ ⱥⱀ ⱱⱥⷠⱃᴠ.

Warnock, ⰿⱥⱄ ⰿeⱥⱃⱀóⳢ, (o.f.)
ⰿⱥⱄ Ⳣⷠoⳑⳑⱥ ⰿeⱥⱃⱀóⳢ.

Warren, Warrin, ⱱⱥⱃⱥⷠⱀ 11 ; ó
ⰿⱃⱐⱀⱥⷠⱀ 497.

Waters, ⰿⱥⱄ ⱂⱥⷠⱦéⷠⱃ 1 ; ⰿⱥⱄ
Conⱐⷠⱃⱄe, (s.l.) ⰿⱥⱄ ⱥⱀ ⱐⷠⱃⱄe
19, 35 ; ó ⱨⱐⷠⱃⱄe, ó ⱨoⷠⱃⱄe
92 ; ó ⱨⱐⷠⱃⱄín, ó ⱨoⷠⱃⱄín
972; ó ⱃⱐⱥⱃⱐⷠⱃⱄe, ó ⱨⱐⱥⱃⱐ-
ⱐⷠⱃⱄe 16, 29 ; ó ⱦⱐⱥⱃⱐⷠⱃⱄ 16,
92.

Waterson ⰿⱥⱄ ⱂⱥⷠⱦéⷠⱃ.

Watson ⰿⱥⱄ ⱂⱥⷠⱦ.

Watters, v. Waters.

Watterson, ⰿⱥⱄ ⱂⱥⷠⱦéⷠⱃ.

Watts, ⰿⱥⱄ ⱂⱥⷠⱦ.

Wayland, (?) ó ⱃⱥoⳑⱥⷠⱀ.

Weadock, ⰿⱥⱄ ⰿⱥᴠóⱄ, ⰿⱥⱄ
ⰿⱥᴠóⳢ.

Wear, Weere, Weir, ⰿⱥⱄ ⱥⱀ
ⰿⱥoⷠⱃ 1 ; ó Coⱃⱃⱥ 62.

Welch, v. Walsh.

Weldon, ᴠe ⱱéⱥⳑⱥⱦún, ⱱéⱥⳑⱥⱦún.

Wellesley, ⱂⱥⷠⱃléⷠⳢ ; (G.p.) ⰿⱥⱄ
ⱂⱥⷠⱃⱂoⱀⱦⱥ, ⰿⱥⱄ ⱱⱥⷠⱃⱂoⱀⱦⱥ.

Welsh, v. Walsh.

Were, v. Wear.

Welsey, v. Wellesley.

Weston, ⱂⱥⱃᴠún, ⱂⱥⱃⱦún.

Whalan Whealan Whealon, v.
Whelan.

Whearty, ó ⱃⱥⳢⱥⱃⱦⱥⷠⳢ.

Wheelahan, ó ⱃⱥoⷠⳑⳑeⱥⱄⱥⷠⱀ.

Wheelan, v. Whelan.

Whelahan ó ⱃⱥoⷠⳑⳑeⱥⱄⱥⷠⱀ.

Whelan ó ⱃⱥoⳑⱥⷠⱀ 11 (s.l.) ó
ⱃⱥoⷠⳑeⱥⷠⱀ, ó ⱃⱐⱥⳑⱥⷠⱀ 2, ó
ⱃoⷠⳑeⱥⷠⱀ 92, ó ⱨⱐⱥoⳑⱥⷠⱀ 2,
ó ⱨoⷠⳑeⱥⷠⱀ, ó ⱨóⷠⳑeⱥⷠⱀ, ó
ⱨoⳑⱥⷠⱀ 91, ó ⱨⱐⷠⳑeⱥⷠⱀ, ó
ⱨⷠoⳑⱥⷠⱀ 99 ; ó ⱃⱥoⷠⳑⳑeⱥⱄⱥⷠⱀ
52.

Wheleghan, Whelehen ó ⱃⱥoⷠⳑ-
ⳑeⱥⱄⱥⷠⱀ.

Whelen, Whelon, v Whelan.

White, ᴠe ⱃⱥoⷠⱦ 1, ᴠe ⱃⱥoⷠⱦe
72 ; ⱱⱥⱀ 2 ; ó ⱱⱥⱀⱥⷠⱀ 23,
29 ; ó ⳢeⱥⳑⱥⳢⱥⷠⱀ 2.

Whitehead, ó Ceⱥⱀⱀᴠⱐⱱⱥⷠⱀ.

Whiteley, ᴠe ⱃⱐⷠⱦléⷠⳢ.

Whitesteed, ó ⱨeⱥⱄᴠⱐⱱⱥⷠⱀ.

Whitley, ᴠe ⱃⱐⷠⱦléⷠⳢ.

Whitney, ᴠe ⱃⱐⷠⱦⱀⷠⳢ.

Whitty, ᴠe ⱃⱐⷠⱦe.

Wholey, ó ⱨⱐⱥⳑⳑⱥⷠⳢ, (s.l.) ó
ⱃⱐⱥⳑⳑⱥⷠⳢ.

Wholihan, Wholihane, ó ⱨⱐⱥⳑⳑ-
ⱥⱄⱥⷠⱀ (s l) ó ⱃⱐⱥⳑⳑⱥⱄⱥⷠⱀ.

Wholy v. Wholey.

Whoolahan, Whoolehan, v.
Wholihan.

Whooley, Whooly, v. Wholey.

Whoriskey, Whorriskey, ó ⱃⱐⱥⱃ-
ⱐⷠⱃⱄe.

Whyte v. White.

Wier ⰿⱥⱄ ⱥⱀ ⰿⱥoⷠⱃ.

Wigin, ⰿⱥⱄ ⳢúⷠⳢín, ⰿⱥⱄ ⳢúⷠⳢ-
eⱥⱀ.

Wigmore ᴠe ⱂⷠⳢeⱥⰿóⱃ.

Wilhair, Wilhere, ó ⰿⱥoⷠⳑ Céⷠⱃe.

Wilkins, Wilkinson, Wilkisson,
ⰿⱥⱄ ⱂⷠⳑⱄín.

Williams, Williamson, ⰿⱥⱄ
ⱂⷠⳑⳑⷠⱥⰿ.

Willis, ⱂⷠⳑⷠⱃ.

Willmit, Willmott, v. Wilmot.

Wills ⱂⷠⳑⷠⱃ.

Wilmot, ⱂⷠⳑeⱥⰿóⷠᴠ, ⱂⷠⳑⰿⷠⱦ.

Wilson, ⰿⱥⱄ ⳑⷠⱥⰿ.

Windham, ó Ⳣⱥoⷠⱦín 97.

Windle, ⱂⷠⱀⳢⷠⳑ.

Wingfield, ⱂⷠⱀⳢⱃéⷠⳑ, ⱂⷠⱀⳢⷠⳑ.

Wingle, Winkle, ⱂⷠⱀⳢⷠⳑ.

Winn, v. Wynne
Winters, ᴀn ᵹeimpᴒ 1 ; mᴀc
ᵹiollᴀ ᵹeiṁpᴒ 62.
Wire, mᴀc ᴀn ṁᴀoip.
Wisdom, Ó Céile.
Wise, ᴏe UiᴒeᴀⱤ, UiᴒeᴀⱤ.
Wixted, UicⱤτéiᴒ.
Wogan, Úᵹán.
Wofe, UlⱤ 2; Ó mᴀcτípe, Ó mic-
τípe 778; ᴏe Ƀulƀ, ᴏe Ƀul 73.
Woodlock, Uᴀᴏlóc, Uᴀᴏlóᵹ.
Woods, ᴏe Ƀóiᴒ E 2 ; mᴀc
Conċoille, mᴀc Conċoilleᴀᴒ
26, 33, 72, 82 ; mᴀc Con-
ċoillín 2 ; mᴀc ᵹiollᴀ ċoille
62, 92 (O'D.) ; Ó Ċoilliᵹ 9
(O'D.) ; Ó Cᴀoilτe 92 ; Ó
Cuill 792.
Wooley, ᴏe Ƀulƀ, (s.l.) ᴀ Ƀulᴀ
197.
Wooloughan, Ó hUᴀllᴀċáin,
(s.l.) Ó Ⱡuᴀllᴀċáin.
Woulfe, ᴏe Ƀulƀ, ᴏe Ƀul.

Wrafter, Ó ReᴀċτᴀƀᴀiⱤ.
Wray, v. Rea.
Wren, Wrenn, Ó Rinn 10 ; mᴀc
ɃⱤoin 9.
Wright, Rᴀᵹᴀiτ 1 ; mᴀċ ᴀn
ĊeᴀiⱤτ (S.L.) 19 ; Ó ᴏeiⱤeᴀl
97.
Wrynn, Ó Rinn 7 ; mᴀc ɃⱤoin 9.
Wyer, mᴀc ᴀn ṁᴀoiⱤ.
Wynne, ᵹuin 1 ; ᴏe Ƀuinn 47 ;
Ó ᵹᴀoiτín 19, 97; mᴀc
ᵹᴀoiτín 39 ; Ó mᴀolᵹᴀoiτe
2 ; mᴀc ᵹᴀoiτe 2.
Wyse, v. Wise.

York, Yorke, mᴀc Con ĊeᴀⱤcᴀ,
mᴀc ConċeᴀⱤcᴀ.
Young, Younge, ᴏe Siún.
Yourell, ᴏé OiⱤᵹiᴀll.

Zorkin, mᴀc ɃuᴀⱤcáin.
Zouche, SúiⱤτe.

SUPPLEMENT

Ashlin, airlinn.
Auterson, v. Otterson.
Barnidge, beapnair.
Beades, na bpaioip.
Beazley, v. Beasley.
Begaddon, ó beaʒacáin.
Biesty, v., Beasty.
Blackwell, oe blácual.
Blood, a blóio, blóio.
Branley, Brannelly, ó bpan-
ʒaile.
Bratton, oe bpácún.
Brinn, mac bpoin.
Brooke, Brookes, Brooks, oe
bpóc, oe bpúc.
Brunton, oe bpúncún.
Butcher, búircéip.
Cady, mac áoaio.
Candon, v. Canton.
Cargin, ó Cappaʒáin.
Carron, mac Ceapáin.
Clafflin, v. MacClachlin.
Condra, mac annpaic.
Connon, mac Canann.
Corket, Copcaic.
Cott, Cac.
Cranitch, Cpanuic.
Croarkien, (?) mac Ruaipcín.
Cush, mac Coipe.
Dagney, mac an Oeaʒánaiʒ.
Dergan, ó Oeapʒán.
Digney, mac an Oeaʒánaiʒ.
Divilly, ó Ouibʒiolla.
Domigan, ó Oomaʒáin.
Doorish, ó Oubpuip.
Emmet, eiméio.
Fagarthy, ó faʒapcaiʒ.
Fawsitt, fóiréio.
Feenan, ó fionnáin.
Funge, fúinpe.
Gaan, mac an ʒobann.
Garrahan, Garrahen, v. Gar-
raghan.
Gatchell, ʒairceal.
Giles, mac ʒoill 97.
Gilloran, v. Killoran.
Glendon, mac ʒiolla finoéin
Goodbody, mac ʒiolla maic.
Goodfellow, macʒiolla maic.

Gonagle, mac Conʒail.
Green, ó ʒpiana (S.L.) 16.
Grierson, mac ʒpioʒaip.
Herky, ó heapca.
Horton, ó hapcáin.
Houston, mac ʒiolla cseac-
lainn (s.l.) mac 'a cseac-
lainn 162
Huggins, huʒúin.
Kennish, mac naoip.
Killyleigh, v. Killelea.
Kinnish, mac naoip.
Law, oe lá.
Leahane, ó liacáin.
Loran, Loughran, ó lucaipeáin,
ó lucpáin.
MacAnespic, mac an earpuiʒ.
MacBarklie, mac papclóin.
MacBlain, mac maoláin.
MacCaughern, mac eacpáin.
MacCooe, mac Cobcaiʒ.
MacEdmond, mac éamoinn.
MacGeaveny, mac ʒéibeannaiʒ.
MacLysaght, mac ʒiolla
iapacca.
MacMunn, mac munna.
MacNamanamee, mac Conan-
aonaiʒ.
MacNully, mac Conulao.
MacPoland, mac póilín.
MacQuatt, MacWatt, mac uaic.
Marry, ó meapaoaiʒ.
Meldron, ó maolpuain.
Mucleen, Mulkeen, ó maol-
claoin 19.
Mulroyan, ó maoilpiain.
O'Loran, ó lucaipeáin, ó luc-
páin.
O'Mullan, ó maoláin.
O'Prey, ó ppéic, (o.f.) a'ppéic.
O'Shannon, ó Seanáin.
Proud, ppúc.
Rouine, ó Ruaioín.
Temple, ciompail.
Tinney, mac an csionnaiʒ.
Tone, cón.
Weddick, v. Waddick.
Yanahan, ó hannacáin.
Yeats, oe ʒeaca.

II

EXPLANATORY NOTE

Names of Men and Women.—These are given in both the nom. and gen. case (cf. § 6, p. 14). English or angl. forms not derived from the Irish name either phonetically or by translation, but substituted by attraction or assimilation (see p. 38), are enclosed in brackets. Our names are drawn from several different languages. The original form of each name is given, together with its signification, as far as it is possible to ascertain it. The manner in which foreign names found their way into Ireland is indicated. Finally, a Latin form is added which it is hoped will prove useful for purposes of registration.

Surnames.—Each surname is given in the nom. case masculine, but in several classes of surnames the same form is common to males and females. The declension of surnames is explained in § 6, pp. 24-7. The form of the surname to be used with names of females is shown in § 7, pp. 27-9. The class to which a surname belongs is indicated by a Roman numeral immediately following the surname. These numerals (I-XIV) refer to § 5, p. 23, but for the convenience of the reader an amplified table of the different classes of surnames is given below, The older English or angl. forms, now obsolete, are printed in italics. These, which are nearly all taken from the Fiants of Elizabeth and the Patent Rolls of James I, show the different steps in the process of anglicising our surnames and generally supply the links between the Irish surname and its present-day angl. equivalents. The modern angl. forms are printed in Roman characters. These have not always been derived from the Iiish surname either phonetically or by translation (see pp. 35-7), but substituted by attraction or assimilation (see pp. 37-9). These substituted forms are generally enclosed in round brackets. In consequence of the interchange of surnames (see § 9, pp. 33-5), there is often apparently no connection between the Irish surname and its present English or angl. equivalents. In this case the English or angl. form is enclosed in square brackets. English surnames which are merely equivalents of Irish surnames are similarly enclosed. The original form of the surname, with its meaning, is given whenever possible. The former and present location of the surname is generally noted, and a short sketch added of the family or families who bore it. I have aimed at giving all the genuine variants of each Irish surname, but in the case of certain classes of variants, where to insert all would greatly increase the size of the book, the uniform use of one of the variants was considered sufficient. Thus, Ó is used instead of

ᥙᴀ throughout. The combinations ʀc, ʀp, ʀᴄ are, with a few
exceptions which explain themselves, used instead of ʀꞡ, ʀb, ʀᴅ
respectively. The uninflected form ᴍᴀoʟ- is used instead of
ᴍᴀoiʟ- when followed by a broad vowel in the next syllable.
ᴅuʙ- in similar circumstances is used instead of ᴅuiʙ-. -éiʟ and
-éiʀ are used instead of -éᴀʟ and -éᴀʀ respectively in the final
syllable of Norman surnames. The alternative forms treated of
above (pp. 21, 22) are not included, except in a few instances and
for some special reason. See also remarks p. 9, note.

CLASSES OF SURNAMES

I.—Surnames of this class are formed by prefixing ó or ᥙᴀ, grandson, descendant, to the gen. case of a native Irish personal
name, as ó ʙʀiᴀin, des. of ʙʀiᴀn ; ó hᴀoᴠᴀ, des. of ᴀoᴠ ;
ó néiʟʟ, des. of niᴀʟʟ (see p. 15). This is our oldest and most
numerous class of surnames. For declension, see p. 25.

II.—Surnames of this class are formed by prefixing ó or ᥙᴀ, grandson, descendant, to the gen. case of a name of foreign origin,
as ó ʙʀuᴀᴅᴀiʀ, des. of ʙʀuᴀᴅᴀʀ ; ó ᴅuʙꞡᴀiʟʟ, des. of ᴅuʙ-
ꞡᴀʟʟ ; ó hᴀʀᴀiʟᴄ, des. of Harald. Surnames of this class are
mostly of Norse and Danish origin. See p. 16, and for declension, p. 25.

III.—Surnames of this class are formed by prefixing ó or ᥙᴀ,
grandson, descendant, not to the personal name of the ancestor,
but to the gen. case of a word indicative of his trade, profession,
rank, or occupation, as ó ꞡoʙᴀnn, des. of the smith ; ó
hiceᴀᴠᴀ, des. of the healer (see p. 15). Only a comparatively
small number of surnames belongs to this class. For declension, see p. 25.

Note.—The above three classes comprise all genuine surnames in ó or ᥙᴀ. Many apparently ó-surnames are merely
corruptions of surnames in ᴍᴀc- or ᴍᴀꞡ- (see p. 32).

IV.—Surnames of this class are formed by prefixing ᴍᴀc or ᴍᴀꞡ,
son, to the gen. case of a native Irish personal name, as ᴍᴀc
ᴀoᴠᴀꞡᴀin, son of ᴀoᴠᴀꞡᴀn ; ᴍᴀc cᴀʀᴄᴀiꞡ, son of cᴀʀᴄᴀc ;
ᴍᴀꞡ uiᴅiʀ, son of oᴅᴀʀ (see p. 15). This is an old and
numerous class of surnames. For declension, see p. 25.

V.—Surnames of this class are formed by prefixing ᴍᴀc or ᴍᴀꞡ,
son, to the gen. case of a name of foreign origin, as ᴍᴀc
íoᴍᴀiʀ, son of Ivor ; ᴍᴀc ᴍᴀꞡnuiʀ, son of Magnus ; ᴍᴀc
ᴘéoʀᴀiʀ, son of Piers ; ᴍᴀc Seóinín, son of little John. Surnames of this class are mostly of Norse and Norman origin.
See pp. 16, 19.

VI.—This class comprises surnames of Welsh origin, formed by
prefixing ' ab ' or ' ap ', son, to a Welsh personal name (see
p. 17). Only a few surnames belong to this class. For declension, see p. 26.

VII.—Surnames of this class are formed by prefixing mac, son, not to the personal name of the ancestor, but to the gen. case of a word indicative of his trade, profession, rank, or occupation, as mac an báiñt, son of the bard ; mac an tSaoiñ, son of the craftsman ; mac an Rioiñe, son of the knight (see p. 15). Families bearing surnames of this class may be of either Irish or foreign origin.

VIII.—This class comprises all patronymic surnames of foreign origin in which the father's name appears in its simple and un-altered form, without prefix or desinence (see pp. 17, 19). The great bulk of Anglo-Norman patronymic surnames belong to this class. For declension, see p. 26.

IX.—This class comprises Irish descriptive adjectives which have supplanted the real surnames (see p. 21). For declension, see p. 26.

X.—This class comprises surnames in -aċ, -eaċ, indicative of nationality, place of origin, fosterage, &c. (see p. 21). They may be either substantives or adjectives. For declension, see p. 26.

XI.—This class comprises foreign surnames of local origin (see pp. 18, 19, 20). This class is very numerous. For declension, see p. 26.

XII.—This class comprises occupative and descriptive surnames of foreign origin (see pp. 18, 19, 20). This class is very numerous. For declension, see p. 26.

XIII.—This class comprises Irish surnames formed from the gen. case of place of residence, or some peculiarity (see p. 21). They were not originally surnames in the strict sense, but took the place of real surnames which are now lost. For declension, see p. 26.

XIV.—This class comprises alternative forms of surnames (see p. 21). For declension, see p. 26.

NAMES OF MEN

IRISH—ENGLISH

ⱭⱵⱵⱭⁿ, *g.* -Ɑⁱⁿ, Abban; dim. of ⱭⱵⱵ, an abbot; the name, of a famous Leinster saint of the 6th century; associated chiefly with Wexford. Lat. Abbanus.

ⱭⱵRⱭⱧⱭⱩ, *g.* -ⱭⁱⱩ, Abraham; Heb. Abbrahám, father of a multitude (cf. Gen. XVII, 5); the name of the progenitor of the Jewish nation; propagated in France and the Netherlands through St. Abraham of Auvergne; introduced into Ireland by the Anglo-Normans, but never became common. Lat. Abraham, -ae.

ⱭⱵⱵⱽⱭⱵⱱⱩ, *v.* ⱵⱶⱽⱽⱵⱱⱩ.

ⱭⱵⱭⱩ, *g.* -ⱭⁱⱩ, ⱭⱵⱭⱩ, *g.* -ⱭⁱⱩ, Adam; Heb. Adám, one made or produced, hence creature; the name of the first man; apparently in use in Ireland and Scotland from early Christian times; one of the most popular names among the Anglo-Normans. Lat. Adam, -ae, Adamus.

ⱭⱵⱭⱩⱱⱭⱱ, *g.* -ⱭⁱⱩ, Adamnan, Eunan; dim. of ⱭⱵⱭⱩ (q.v.); the name of a celebrated Abbot of Iona in the 7th century, author of the Life of St. Columba and patron of the Diocese of Raphoe. Lat. Adamnanus, Eunanus.

ⱵⱶⱽⱵⱱⱩ, ⱵⱶⱽⱵⱱⱩ, *g.* id., Augustine, Augustin, Austin, &c.; Lat. Augustinus, dim. of Augustus, venerable; the name of the renowned Bishop of Hippo and Doctor of the Church; also of the Apostle of England. To the latter it was that it owed its popularity in England, where it was formerly common as Austin. It is only in comparatively recent times that it has come much into use in Ireland. Also ⱭⱵⱵⱽⱵⱱⱩ, ⱭⱵⱵⱽⱵⱱⱩ and ⱣⱵⱵⱱⱩ.

Aıbısⲧín, g. id., Augustine, Augustin, Austin, Avvy, Affy; a var. in Connacht of Áᵹuıⲣⲧín, q.v. Also Abuıⲣⲧín.

Aıbne, g. id., Eveny; a Derry name, peculiar to the O'Kanes, MacCloskeys and O'Brallaghans.

Aılbe, g. id., Alby, Alvy, (Albert, Bertie); the name of the patron of the Diocese of Emly; revived in recent times, but the angl. form is generally Albert (Bertie), which is incorrect. St. Ailbe died in 541. His feast is kept on 12 September. Lat. Albeus.

Aılⲝⲣıꝺ, g. id., Alfred; Ang.-Sax. Ælfred, elf-counsel; the name of a king of the West Saxons, known as Alfred the Great; came into Ireland at the time of the Anglo-Norman invasion, but did not long survive. Aılⲝⲣıꝺ is a recent revival. Lat. Alfredus, Aluredus.

Aılín, g. id., Allen; an ancient Irish personal name, probably dim. of some name commencing with Aıl-, noble. Lat. Ailenus.

Aınꝺⲣéas, Aınꝺⲣıas, g. -ⲣéıⲣ, -ⲣıaⲣa, Andrew; Gr. Ἀνδρέας (Andréas), from ἀνήρ (anér), g. ἀνδρός (andrós), man; the name of one of the Twelve Apostles, the brother of St. Peter. The adoption of St. Andrew as the patron of Scotland made Andrew a national name. It was also one of the commonest names among the Anglo-Norman settlers in Ireland (v. Aınꝺⲣıú). Lat. Andreas, -ae.

Aınꝺⲣıú, g. id, Andrew; a var. of Aınꝺⲣéaⲣ (q.v.), through the Norman-French Andreu; very common among the Anglo-Norman settlers in Ireland.

Aıneıslıs, g. id., Aneslis, (Standish; Stanislaus); comp. of aın-, negative, and éıⲣlıⲣ, neglect, forgetfulness, hence careful, thoughtful; an Irish name formerly in use among the O'Gradys, O'Donovans, O'Heynes, etc.

Alabaoıs, g. id., Aloys, Aloysius; Teut. Hlúdwig, famous battle, Frank. Hluodowig, Cluodowic, Cludowich (Lat. Chlodovisus and Ludovicus), Clovis, Clouis, Fr. Louis, Provençal Aloys (Lat. Aloysius); adopted in Ireland in honour of St. Aloysius Gonzaga.

Alas𝚌Aʀ, g. -aıp, Allister, Alexander, &c.; an Irish form of Alexander. V. Alpan𝚘ap.

Alas𝚌ʀann, g. -aınn, Alestren, Alexander, &c.; an Irish form of Alexander. V. Alpan𝚘ap.

Alas𝚌ʀom, g. -𝚌puım, Alexander, &c.; an Irish form of Alexander. V. Alpan𝚘ap.

Alɓán, g. -áın, Alban; Lat. Albanus, from 'albus,' white; the name of the proto-martyr of England.

Alponsus, Alᵽonsus, g. -uıp, Alphonsus, Alfons; Teut. Adalfuns, noble eagerness; a name adopted in Ireland in honour of St. Alphonsus Liguori, founder of the Congregation of the Most Holy Redeemer and Doctor of the Church. Lat. Alphonsus.

Alsan𝚘Aʀ, g. -aıp, Alexander, Alex, Alick; Gr. Αλέξανδρος (Aléxandros), defending men; perhaps the most widespread as well as the most famous of all personal names. The conquests of Alexander the Great caused it to become widely diffused among eastern nations, while the large number of saints and martyrs of the name in the early Church—the Roman Martyrology mentions no fewer than thirty-nine—popularised it all over Europe. It was introduced into Scotland by Queen Margaret, where it was borne by three of the Scottish kings and became a national name. It was also very common among the early Anglo-Norman settlers in Ireland. The ordinary Gaelic form of the name in Ireland and Scotland was Alapᴄap or Alapᴄpom, q.v. Lat. Alexander, -dri.

Amɓʀós, g. -óıp, Ambrose; Gr. Aυβρόσιος (Ambrósios), immortal, divine; the name of the great Bishop of Milan and Doctor of the Church; never, however, very common in Ireland. Lat. Ambrosius.

Amɓʀus, g. -uıp, Ambrose; an Ulster var. of Amɓpóp, q.v.

Amᵽlaoıɓ, g. id., Auliffe, Olave, (Humphrey); Norse, Ólafr, ancestral relic; also written Onlaf and Anlaf; a name introduced by the Norsemen and adopted by the Irish; it first occurs in the Annals at the year 851; still common in West Munster, but absurdly angl. Humphrey. St. Olave, King of Norway, who was slain in battle, July 29, 1030, has made it one of the most popular of Scandinavian names. Lat. Olavus.

ᴀɴ Cᴀʟbᴀċ g. ᴀn Cᴀʟbᴀɪ꜔, Callough, (Charles). V. Cᴀʟbᴀċ.

ᴀnʟuᴀn, g. -ᴀɪn, Anlon, (Alphonsus) ; comp. of ᴀn, great, and ʟuᴀn, a hero, champion, or warrior ; a rare name, found only among the O'Briens and a few other families ; angl. Alphonsus among the MacEgans of Kerry ; also, but less correctly, written ᴀnnʟuᴀn. Lat. Anluanus.

ᴀnmċᴀb, g. -ᴀɪb and -ᴀbᴀ, (Ambrose) ; a rare name, peculiar to the O'Maddens, among whom it was angl. Ambrose. Lat. Anmchadus and Animosus.

ᴀnnʟuᴀn, v. ᴀnʟuᴀn.

ᴀnnʀᴀoɪ, g. id., Henry, Harry. V. Єɪnʀɪ.

ᴀnnʈoɪn, ᴀnʈoɪn, ᴀnʈoɪne, g. id., Antony, Anthony, Anthin ; Lat. Antonius, an ancient Roman name, popularised by St. Antony of Egypt and St. Antony of Padua. It was introduced into Ireland by the Anglo-Normans, but never became very common.

ᴀob, g. ᴀobᴀ and ᴀoɪb, Ea, (Hugh) ; Celt. *Aidu-s, fire, Old Ir. Aed ; an ancient and very common Irish name ; a favourite name among the O'Connors of Connacht and the ONeills and O'Donnells of Ulster ; now always angl. Hugh. Lat. Aidus, Ædus.

ᴀobᴀ꜔ᴀn, g. -ᴀɪn, Egan ; dim. of ᴀob, q.v. ; Old Ir. Aidacan. Lat. *Aidacanus.

ᴀobᴀɪ꜔, g. id., Hughey ; a pet form of ᴀob, q.v.

ᴀobᴀn, g. -ᴀɪn, Aidan, Aedan, Edan ; dim. of ᴀob, q.v. ; fairly common in the 8th and 9th centuries. Twenty-three saints of the name are mentioned in the Martyrology of Donegal. Lat. Aidanus, Edanus.

ᴀon꜔us, g. -꜔uʀᴀ and -꜔uɪʀ, Angus, Aeneas, Eneas, Neese, Neece, Niece ; Celt. *Oino-gustu-s (from oinos, one, and gustus, choice), Old Ir. Oingus, g. Oingusso, Mid. Ir. Oengus, Aengus, g. -gusa ; an ancient and once common Irish name, frequent among the MacDonnells, O'Dalys, O'Leynes, &c.; sometimes shortened to ⁿⱥoꞃ, q.v. Five saints of the name are mentioned in the Martyrology of Donegal. Lat. Ængussius, Æneas.

ⱥʀⱥlⱦ, *g.* -ⱥilⱦ, Harold; Norse, Haraldr, army-might; a name brought into Ireland by the Norsemen. Lat. Haraldus.

ⱥʀꝺᵹⱥl, *g.* -ᵹⱥil. Ardal, (Arnold); comp. of ⱥꞃꝺ, high, and ᵹⱥl, valour; a favourite name among the Mac Kennas and MacMahons of Ulster by whom it was angl. Arnold; still in use. Lat. Ardgalus.

ⱥʀⱦ, *g.* ⱥiꞃⱦ, Art, (Arthur); Celt. *Arto-s, a stone, or bear; an ancient Irish personal name; common among the MacMurrough Kavanaghs, O'Connors and O'Molloys in Leinster, the O'Keeffes and O'Learys in Munster, the O'Haras and O'Rourkes in Connacht, and the O'Neills in Ulster; now generally angl. Arthur. Lat. Artus.

ⱥʀⱦûʀ, *g.* -ûiꞃ, Arthur; a name of uncertain origin; in use in Ireland in the 9th century and among the Scoto-Irish in the time of St. Columcille, in the form of Artuir, Lat. Arturius by Adamnan. Lat. Arturus, Arthurus.

ⴱⱥil, Val; a pet form of ⴱⱥilinⱦín, q.v.

ⴱⱥilinⱦín, *g.* id., Valentine; Lat. Valentinus, dim. of valens, strong, healthy; the name of several martyrs in the early Church; never common in Ireland.

ⴱⱥoⱦᵹⱥlⱥċ, *g.* -ⱥiᵹ, *Behellagh, Beolagh,* (Boetius, Bowes); comp. of ⴱⱥoⱦ, vain, foolish, and ᵹⱥlⱥċ, valorous; a name peculiar to the MacEgans, O'Dalys, and a few other families. Lat. Boetgalachus, Boetius.

ⴱⱥʀʀⱥ, *g.* id., Barry; a pet form of ⴱⱥiꞃꝝꞽonn or ꝝionn-ⴱⱥꞃꝝ, q.v.; the name of the patron of the Diocese of Cork. Lat. Barreus.

ⴱeⱥcⱥn, *g.* -ⱥin, Becan; dim. of ⴱeⱥᵹ, small; the name of a celebrated Munster saint of the 6th century. His feast was kept on 26th May. Lat. Becanus.

ⴱeⱥnón, *g.* -óin, Benen, Benignus. V. ⴱeineón.

 beⱭRⱭⱦ, *g.* -Ⱥⱶ, Barry ; deriv. of beⱭⱦ, a spear, javelin, or anything pointed ; the name of a celebrated Connacht saint of the 6th century, Abbot of Cluain Coirpthe, in the present Co. Roscommon, and patron of the O'Hanlys ; explained in the Life of the saint as signifying "one who takes a direct aim at an object, or reaches it, as it were, with the point of the sword." "Rightly has this name been given to him," said the priest, Froech, by whom he was baptised, "for he shall be a saint and his place shall be in heaven." beⱭⱦⱭⱦ, angl. Barry, continued in use as a Christian name among the O'Hanlys down to recent times. Lat. Berachius.

beⱭRⱦⱭn, *g.* -Ⱥⱶⱶ, Bercan ; dim. of beⱭⱦⱭⱦ, q.v. ; the name of five Irish saints. Lat. Berchanus.

beⱭRnⱭRⱃ, *g.* -Ⱥⱶⱃⱃ, Bernard ; Frank. Bernhard, strong bear, brave warrior ; the name of the celebrated Abbot of Clairvaux, whose fame made it universal in Europe ; introduced into Ireland by the Anglo-Normans, among whom it was rather common, and later adopted as a synonym for the native name bⱤⱭⱶ, q.v. Lat. Bernardus.

beⱭRⱦLⱭⱃ, *g.* id., Bartley ; a modern rendering of the English name Bartley. V. pⱭⱤⱦⱭLⱭn.

beⱶⱶeⱭn, *g.* -Ⱥⱶⱶ, Benignus, Benen ; a var. of beⱶⱶeⱶn, q.v.

beⱶⱶeⱶn, *g.* -ⱶⱶⱶ, Benignus, Benen ; Lat. Benignus, good, kind, mild ; the name given by St. Patrick to his favourite disciple and successor in the See of Armagh.

beⱶRⱦeⱭRⱦ, *g.* -ⱦeⱶⱤⱦ, (Benjamin, Ben ; Bernard ; Bertie) ; Ang.-Sax. Beorhthere, bright-army ; the name of an Anglo-Saxon saint who settled at Tullylease, Co. Cork, where he died on 6th December, 839 ; common in many parts of Cork, Kerry and Limerick under the angl. form of Benjamin ; in parts of Tipperary, it is made Bernard. Lat. Berichertus.

bⱶⱶeⱭn, *g.* -Ⱥⱶⱶ, Benignus, Benen ; a var. of beⱶⱶeⱶn, q.v. Lat. Bineanus.

bRⱭn *g.* bⱤⱭⱶⱶ and bⱤⱶⱶⱶ Bran ; and old and once

common Irish name meaning ' raven ' ; in use in the family of O'Byrne down to the middle of the 17th century or later. Lat. Branius.

 bⱤéⱭnⱭınn, g. id., Brendan ; the name of several Irish saints, of whom the most celebrated were St. Brendan, Abbot of Clonfert, and St. Brendan of Birr. The name in modern Irish is bⱤeⱭnⱱⱭn or bⱤeⱭnnⱱⱭn. Lat. Brendanus.

bⱤeⱭnⱱⱭn, bⱤeⱭnnⱱⱭn, g. -Ɑın, Brendan. V. bⱤéⱭnⱭınn.

bⱤeⱭsⱭl, g. -Ɑıl, Brasil, (Basil) ; Old Ir. Bressal, from Celt *brestelo-s, strife, war ; the name of an Irish saint whose feast-day was 18th May ; common among the O'Kellys and O'Maddens of Connacht. Lat. Bressalius.

bⱤıⱭn, g. -Ɑın, Brian, Bryan, (Bernard ; Barnaby, Barney); a name made famous by King Brian Boru, victor of Clontarf, and ever since common in most Irish families. Lat. Brianus.

bⱤoċⱭⱱ, Morgan ; a corruption in West Connacht of mⱯⱭⱤċⱭⱱ, q.v.

buⱭⱱⱭċ, g. -Ɑıꞡ, Buagh, (Boetius), Victor ; deriv. of buⱭıⱱ, victory ; formerly a favourite name among the O'Sullivans.

CⱭıleⱭn, g. -eın, Colin ; a Scottish-Gaelic form of the Irish CoıleⱭn, q.v. ; more of less peculiar to the Campbell family. Lat. Colinus.

CⱭınneⱭċ, g. Ɑıꞡ, Canice ; an older form of CoınneⱭċ, q.v. ; Lat. Cainnechus in the Book of Armagh.

CⱭıⱤbⱤe, g. id., Carbry ; Old Ir. Coirbre, charioteer ; formerly a common name among the O'Farrells, O'Beirnes, &c. ; in use in a few families down to recent times. Four saintly bishops of the name are mentioned in the Martyrology of Donegal. Lat. Corbreus.

CⱭlⱱⱭċ, g. -Ɑıꞡ, Calvagh, Callough, (Charles) ; an Irish name, meaning ' bald ' ; once common among the O'Connors of Offaly, O'Carrolls of Ely, O'Molloys,

O'Donnells, O'Reillys, &c.; now generally angl. Charles. Also ᴀn Cᴀʟbᴀċ. Lat. Calvachus.

Cᴀoιṁᵹιn, g. id., Kevin; Old Ir. Coemgen, comely birth; the name of the celebrated Abbot of Glendalough; fast becoming a popular mane. Lat. Coemgenus.

Cᴀoʟᴀn, g. -ᴀιn, Kealan, Kelan; dim. of cᴀoʟ, slender; the name of seven Irish saints. Lat. Coelanus.

Cᴀoṁᴀn, g. -ᴀιn, Kevan; dim. of cᴀoṁ, comely, mild, &c.; sometimes Latinised Pulcherius by translation; the name of no fewer than fifteen Irish saints. Lat. Coemanus.

Cᴀꞃʟus, g. -uιꞃ, Charles; the Latin name Carolus which was adopted by the Norsemen in honour of Charlemagne (Carolus Magnus) and by them introduced into Ireland.

Cᴀꞃᴛᴀċ, g. -ᴀιᵹ, Cartagh, Carthage; Old Ir. Carthach, from Celt. *karatako-s, loving; an ancient Irish name borne by the celebrated Abbot and Bishop of Lismore and patron of that diocese. Lat. Carthachus, Carthagus.

Cᴀᴛᴀιꞃ, g. id., Cahir; a Donegal var. of Cᴀᴛᴀoιꞃ, q.v.; found chiefly in the families of O'Doherty and O'Gallagher. Lat. Cathirius.

Cᴀᴛᴀʟ, g. -ᴀιʟ, Cahal, (Charles); Celt. *Katu-valo-s, battle-mighty; an ancient and very common Irish name, especially among the O'Connors of Connacht, O'Farrells, O'Reillys, O'Rourkes and Maguires; now generally angl. Charles. Lat. Cathalus, Cathaldus.

Cᴀᴛᴀoιꞃ, g. id., Cahir, (Charles); Celt. *Katu-viro-s, Old Ir. Cathfer, Cather, battle-man, warrior; an ancient Irish name, most frequent amongst Leinster families, especially the O'Connors of Offaly, the Mac Coghlans, O'Molloys and O'Byrnes; now always angl. Charles. In Donegal, Cᴀᴛᴀιꞃ (q.v.) is a variant. Lat. Cathirius.

Cᴀᴛbᴀꞃꞃ, g. -ᴀιꞃꞃ, Caffar; comp. of cᴀᴛ, battle, and bᴀꞃꞃ, head, hence a helmet; a name peculiar to the O'Donnells of Tirconnell. Lat. Caffarrus.

ceaᴌᴌaċ, *g.* -aⁱᵹ, Kellagh, (Celsus) ; an ancient and once very common Irish name, meaning ' war ' or ' strife ' ; borne by at least three saints, of whom one was the celebrated Archbishop of Armagh, better known as St. Celsus, who died at Ardpatrick in Munster, on 1st April, 1129. Lat. Cellachus, Kellachus.

ceaᴌᴌaċán, *g.* -áⁱn, Callaghan ; the name of two Irish saints in the Martyrology of Donegal ; also that of a celebrated King of Munster in the tenth century, still borne by his descendants, the MacCarthys and O'Callaghans. Lat. Cellachanus, Kellachanus.

ceaᴚᴅaᴌᴌ, *g.* -aⁱᴌᴌ, Carroll, (Charles) ; a once common Irish name, especially among the O'Dalys, now angl. Charles. Lat. Kervallus.

Cⁱan, *g.* Céⁱn, Kian, Kean, Cain ; an old Irish name, meaning ' ancient ' ; common among the O'Haras and O'Garas of Connacht and the O'Carrolls of Ely, who, no doubt, took it from their great ancestor, Cⁱan, the son of Olioll Olum, King of Munster, and among the O'Mahonys of South Munster, after their great ancestor, Cⁱan, the son-in-law of Brian Boru, who led the forces of Desmond at the battle of Clontarf ; still in use, but sometimes ridiculously angl. Cain. Lat. Cianus, Kianus.

Cⁱanán, *g.* -áⁱn, Kienan, Kenan ; dim. of Cⁱan, q.v. ; the name of three Irish saints, of whom one was the celebrated Bishop of Duleek. Lat. Ciananus, Kenanus.

Cⁱaᴚán, *g.* -áⁱn, Kieran ; dim. of cⁱaᴚ, black ; the name of no fewer than fifteen Irish saints mentioned in the Martyrology of Donegal, of whom the best known are St. Kieran of Saighir, patron of the Diocese of Ossory, and St. Kieran, Abbot of Clonmacnoise and patron of that diocese. Their feasts occur respectively on 5th March and 9th September. Cⁱaᴚán is still a common Christian name in Cape Clear and is also in use in parts of Connacht. Lat. Ceranus, Kiranus, Kieranus.

Cⁱᴌᴌⁱan, *g.* -ᴌéⁱn, Killian ; ' pet ' dim. of Ceaᴌᴌaċ, q.v. ;

the name of a celebrated Irish missionary who was martyred at Wurtzburg in Germany, on 8th July, about the year 689. Lat. Chilianus, Kilianus, Killianus.

Cıllín, g. id., Killian; a var. of Cıllıan, q.v. Lat. Cillenus, Killinus.

Cınnéıoıo, cınnéıoıʒ, g. id., Kennedy; comp. of ceann, a head, and éıoe, armour, hence 'helmeted-head'; the name of the father of Brian Boru; still in use among the O'Briens. Lat. Kinnedius.

Coıleán, g. -áın, Colin; also written Cuıleán; an old Irish personal name meaning 'whelp,' the same as the Scottish Cailean or Colin among the Campbells; rather rare and in later times almost peculiar to the family of O'Dempsey. Lat. Culanus, Culenus.

Coılín, g. id., Colin; a var. ot Coıleán, q.v. Coılín was also in use among Anglo-Irish families as a 'pet' form of Nicol or Nicholas. Lat. Colinus.

Cóılín, g. id., Colman; dim. of Colmán, q.v.; in use in Connemara.

Coınneaċ, g. -nıʒ, Canice, Kenny; older Caınneaċ, fair one; the name of the patron of Kilkenny. Lat. Cainnechus, Canicius.

Coıreall, g. -ŋıll, Kerill, (Cyril); the name of a saintly Irish Bishop whose feast was kept on 13th June. Lat. Carellus, Cyrillus.

Colla, g. id, Colla; an ancient Irish name, formerly common among the MacDonalds, MacSweenys and MacMahons of Ulster. Lat. Colla.

Colm, g. id., Colm, Colum, Columba; also written Colum; an old Irish name, signifying 'dove'; made famous by St. Columcille, Apostle of Scotland, whose name signifies 'dove of the church.' Lat. Columba.

Colmán, g. -áın, Colman, Columban; dim. of colm, a dove; formerly one of the commonest of Irish names; borne by nearly one hundred Irish saints, of whom three are patrons of Irish dioceses, namely, Cloyne, Dromore and Kilmacduagh. Lat. Colmanus.

Colum, g. -uım, Colum, Columba; a var. of Colm, q.v.

comán, *g.* -áin, Coman; dim. of cam, bent; the name of twelve Irish saints, from one of whom Roscommon was so called. Lat. Comanus.

comḃan, v. Comġan.

comġall, *g.* -aill, Cole; Old Ir. Comgell, co-pledge, fellow-hostage; the name of the celebrated Abbot of Bangor and six other saints mentioned in the Martyrology of Donegal. Lat. Comgallus.

comġan, *g.* -ain, Cowan; also written Comḃan; Old Ir. Comgan, co-birth, perhaps meaning 'twin' (cf. Tomár); the name of three Irish saints. Lat. Comganus.

conaire, *g.* id., Conary; an ancient Irish name. Lat. Conarius.

conall, *g.* -aill, Conall, Connell; Celt. *Kuno-valo-s, high-mighty; an ancient and once common Irish personal name; still in use among a few families. Eight saints of the name are mentioned in the Martyrology of Donegal. Lat. Conallus.

conán, *g.* -áin, Conan; the name of at least six Irish saints, of whom one was St. Conan of Assaroei, Co. Donegal, a relative of St. Columcille, who flourished in the 6th century and was venerated on 8th March. Lat. Conanus.

concoḃar, *g.* -air, Conor, Connor, Naugher, Noghor, Nohor, Conny, Con, (Cornelius, Corney, Neil); an ancient and very common Irish name, meaning 'high will' or 'desire'; found in most Irish families; still very much in use, but generally angl. Cornelius. Lat. Conchovarius, Conquovarus.

conn, *g.* Cuinn, Conn, Con, (Constantine); Old Ir. Cond, from Celt. *kondo-s, sense, reason, intelligence; also a freeman; an ancient Irish name, common among the O'Neills, O'Donnells and O'Rourkes. In the 17th century, it was angl. Constantine by the O'Neills. Lat. Connus.

connlaoḋ, *g.* -aoḋa, connlaoť, *g.* -aoťa, Conleth, Conley; comp. of connla, prudent, chaste, and aoḋ, fire; written Conlaid in the Book of Armagh; the name

of the patron of the Diocese of Kildare. Lat. Con-
laethus, Conlethus.

Consaroín, *g.* id., Constantine ; Lat. Constantinus, a
name which seems to have been adopted by the
O'Briens in the 12th century, but never became
common.

Cormac, *g.* -aic, Cormac, (Charles) ; Old Ir. Corbmac,
chariot-son, charioteer, or son of Corb ; an ancient
Irish name, very common among the MacCarthys,
MacDermotts, MacDonoughs, Maguires, O'Clerys,
O'Connors of Connacht, O'Donnells and O'Farrells ;
now generally angl. Charles. Eight saints of the name
are mentioned in the Martyrology of Donegal. Lat.
Cormacus.

Criomtann, *g.* -ainn, Crevan ; an old, but rare, name,
meaning 'fox' ; common among the Kavanaghs of
Leinster. It was the first name of St. Columcille.
St. Criomhthann was venerated on 23rd May. Lat.
Crimthanus.

Criostal, *g.* -ail, Christopher, Christy ; a Scottish and
North of Ireland form of Críortóir, q.v.

Críostóir, *g.* -óra, Christopher, Christy ; Gr.Χριστοφόρος,
(Christophóros), Christ-bearing ; a name in use
from early Christian times and popularised through
Europe by the legend of St. Christopher. It does not
appear to have been frequent among the first Anglo-
Norman settlers in Ireland, but by the end of the 16th
century it had become rather common. Lat. Christo-
phorus.

Crócán, *g.* -áin, Crohan ; the name of a Kerry saint, still
much venerated in Cahirdaniel and neighbourhood,
where Crohan is rather common as a Christian name.
Lat. Crocanus.

Crónán, *g.* -áin, Cronan ; dim. of crón, dark-brown ; the
name of the celebrated Abbot of Roscrea and more
than twenty other Irish saints. Lat. Cronanus.

Cuan, *g.* -ain, Cuan, the name of four Irish saints. Lat.
Cuanus.

Cúcoigcríce, *g.* Concoigcríce, Peregrine ; an Irish

name meaning 'hound of the border'; peculiar to the Mageoghegans, O'Molloys, and a few other families in Westmeath and Offaly; probably now obsolete. Peregrine was supposed to be a translation. Lat. Peregrinus.

Cúconnaċt, *g.* Conċonnaċt, (Constantine); a favourite name among the Maguires, meaning 'hound of Connacht.' Lat. Cuconnactus.

Cúcríċe, *g.* Conċríċe, Peregrine; the same as Cúcoiġcríċe, q.v.

Cuimín, *g.* id., Cumin, Comyn; dim. of cam, bent; the name of several Irish saints; still in use. Lat. Cominus, Cuminus.

Cúmaiġe, *g.* Conṁaiġe, Cooey, Hughey, (Quintin, Quinton); a rare Derry name, meaning 'hound of the plain'; peculiar to the family of O'Kane and MacCloskey, by whom it is angl. Quintin.

Cúmeaḋa, *g.* Conṁeaḋa, Covey; an Irish name signifying 'hound of Meaḋ' (a place-name); peculiar to the MacNamaras.

Cú ulaḋ, *g.* Conulaḋ, Cullo, Cooley; an Irish name, meaning 'hound of Ulidia'; formerly in use among the MacMahons, MacCawels, MacCanns, &c., but now very rare, if not obsolete.

Daibéid, *g.* id., David; Nor. Davet, dim. of David (v. Dáibid).

Dáibid, Dáibíd, *g.* id., David; Heb. Dávídh, beloved, probably a shortened form of Dōdavahu, beloved of Jehovah; the name of the great King of Israel, psalmist and prophet; the national name in Wales, out of reverence for St. David of Menevia; rather common among the Anglo-Normans, who brought it into Ireland, where it has ever since enjoyed a steady popularity. In the spoken language it is often shortened to Dáit and Dát, with dim. Dáitín. Lat. David, -is.

Dáire, *g.* id., Dary; an old Irish name. Lat. Darius.

Dáit, *g.* id., Davy; a pet form of Dáibid, q.v.

ⱱⱭⁱɔⁱ, g. id., Dahy, Davy, David ; (1) an old Irish name, meaning 'swiftness,' 'nimbleness'; borne by the celebrated King Dahy and retained by his descendants, the O'Dowds, down to recent times ; and (2) a form of ⱱⱭⁱⱱ⹐ⱱ, q.v.

ⱱⱭⁱɔín, g. id., Davy ; dim. of ⱱⱭⁱɔ or ⱱⱭⁱⱱ⹐ⱱ, q.v.

ⱱⱭⱂⱢⱭⁱc, g. id., Dominic, Dominick ; very common in Derry for ⱱoⁱⱱⁱⱂⱢc, q.v.

ⱱⱭⱂⱢⱂⱭⁱc, g. id., Dominic, Dominick.; an Irish form of Dominic ; in use in Co. Derry.

ⱱⱭɔ, g. ⱱⱭⁱɔ, Davy ; a pet form of ⱱⱭⁱⱱ⹐ⱱ, q.v.

ⱱÉⱭⱢⱢⱭⁱⱂ, g. -Ɑⁱⱂ, Declan ; the name of the patron of Ardmore, where his feast is kept on 24 July ; a rather common name in Co. Waterford. Lat. Declanus.

ⱱeⱭⱢⱂⱢuⱂⱢⱂⱭɔ, g. -ⱭⁱⱢ, Desmond ; an old Irish name or designation, meaning native of, or belonging to, Desmond or South Munster. Lat. Desmundus.

ⱱⁱⱭRⱂⱢⱭⁱⱱ, g. -ⱭⱱⱭ, Dermod, Dermot, (Darby ; Jeremiah, Jarmy, Jerry ; Jerome) ; Old Ir. Diarmait, comp. of di, without, and airmit, injunction, hence a freeman ; an ancient and very common name, especially among the MacCarthys, MacDermotts, O'Briens, and O'Connors ; still found in every part of Ireland, but generally angl. Jeremiah. Eleven saints of the name are mentioned in the Martyrology of Donegal. Lat. Diermitius, Dermitius.

ⱱoⁱⱱⁱⱂⱢc, g. id., Dominic, Dominick ; Lat. Dominicus, belonging to the Lord, or born on Sunday ; the name of the founder of the Order of Preachers, in whose honour it was adopted in Ireland.

ⱱoⱂⱢⱂⱭⱢⱢ, g. -ⱭⁱⱢⱢ, Donall, Donald, (Daniel) ; Old Ir. Domnall, from Celtic *Dumno-valo-s, world-mighty, *Dubno-valo-s, mighty in the ' deep '; one of the most ancient and popular of Irish names, still in use in every part of the country, but generally angl. Daniel ; also one of the most popular names in Scotland, where it is angl. Donald. Only one saint of the name is mentioned in the Irish martyrologies ; his feast was kept on 26th April. Lat. Domnaldus, Donaldus.

ᴅᴏɴɴ, *g.* ᴅuɪɴɴ, Donn ; a rare name, almost peculiar to the family of Maguire. Lat. Donnus.

ᴅᴏɴɴáɴ, *g.* -áɪɴ, Donnan ; dim. of ᴅᴏɴɴ, brown ; the name of four Irish saints. Lat. Donnanus.

ᴅᴏɴɴċᴀᴅ, *g.* -ᴀᴅᴀ, -ᴀɪᴅ, Donogh, Donough, Donaghy, (Donat, Denis, Duncan) ; Old Irish Donnchad, Dunchad, from Celt *Donno-catu-s, *Duno-catu-s, brown warrior, or strong warrior ; an ancient and very common Irish name, still found in every part of the country, but generally angl. Denis. The Scots make it Duncan. St. Dunchadh was Abbot of Iona ; his feast was kept on 25th May. Lat. Donnchadus, Donatus.

ᴅuᴃᴀʟᴛᴀċ, *g.* -ᴀɪʒ, Dualtagh, Duald, (Dudley) ; a rare Irish name, meaning ' black-jointed ' ; borne by the celebrated antiquary ᴅuᴃᴀʟᴛᴀċ ṁᴀc ꝼɪ̇ᴃɪ̇ʀɪ̇ʒ, called in English Duald or Dudley MacFirbis. Lat. Dubaltachus.

ᴅuᴃáɴ, *g.* -áɪɴ, Dowan ; dim. of ᴅuᴃ, black ; the name of two Irish saints, whose feasts were kept on 11th February and 11th November respectively. Lat. Dubanus.

ᴅuᴃᴅáʟeɪᴛe, *g.* ᴅuɪᴃᴅáʟeɪᴛe, (Dudley) ; an ancient Irish personal name, meaning ' the black-man of the two sides, or halves ' ; now very rare, if not actually obsolete.

ᴅuᴃᴅᴀʀᴀ, ᴅuᴃᴅᴀʀᴀċ, *g.* ᴅuɪᴃᴅᴀʀᴀċ, (Dudley) ; an old Irish name, meaning ' the black-man of the oak ' ; still in use in West Connacht, angl. Dudley. Lat. Dubdarus.

ᴅuᴃʒᴀʟʟ, *g.* -ᴀɪʟʟ, Dugald ; comp. of ᴅuᴃ, black, and ʒᴀʟʟ, a foreigner ; a name given by the Irish to the Danes ; still in use among the Scots, angl. Dugald. Lat. Dugaldus.

ᴅuᴃʒʟᴀs, *g.* -ᴀɪʀ, Douglas.

eᴀċᴀɪᴅ, *g.* id. and -ᴀᴅᴀ, Aghy ; a var. of eoċᴀɪᴅ, q.v.

eᴀċᴀɪɴɴ, *g.* -ᴀɪɴɴ, Hector ; older eᴀċᴅonn, horse-lord ;

an old Irish name, still in use among the Scots, angl. Hector.

Ɛᴀᴅᴛᴀᴚᴅ, g. -ᴀɪᴘᴅ, Edward; Ang.-Sax. Eadweard, blessed-guard; the name of two saintly kings of England, known respectively as Edward the Martyr and Edward the Confessor; introduced into Ireland by the Anglo-Normans, but has been almost completely absorbed by Ɛᴀmonn, q.v. Lat. Eduardus.

Ɛᴀmonn, g. -oɪnn, -uɪnn, Eamon, Edmund, Edmond, (Edward); Ang.-Sax. Eadmund, blessed-protection; the name of a saintly King of England, who was martyred on 20th November, 870; introduced into Ireland by the Anglo-Normans, where it has become very popular and has almost completely absorbed the other great Anglo-Saxon name Edward, the Irish Ɛᴀmonn generally standing for both names. Lat. Eadmundus, Edmundus.

Ɛᴀnᴀn, g. -ᴀɪn, Enan; the name of several Irish saints. Lat. Enanus.

Ɛᴀnnᴀ, g. id., Enda; an old Irish name, made famous by St. Enda, Abbot of Aran, whose feast is on 21st March. Lat. Endeus.

Ɛᴀᴚᴄᴀn, g. -ᴀɪn, Ercan, Erkan; dim. of eᴀᴘᴄ, red, or speckled; the name of several saintly Irish bishops and priests. Lat. Ercanus.

Ɛᴀᴚnᴀn, g. -ᴀɪn, Ernan, (Ernest); dim. of eᴀᴘnᴀ, knowing, experienced; the name of eight Irish saints. Lat. Ernanus.

Ɛɪᴃeᴀᴚ, g. -ᴃɪᴘ, Ever, Heber, (Ivor); a common name among the MacMahons and a few other families in Ulster; also common in Cape Clear Island, angl. Heber; in the North, sometimes angl. Ivor. Also written Ɛɪ́meᴀᴘ. Lat. Heberus, Eberus, Iberus.

Ɛɪꝣneᴀᴄᴀn, eɪꝣneᴀᴄᴀn, g. -ᴀɪn, (Æneas, Eneas; Ignatius); dim. of Ɛɪꝣnᴀᴄ or eɪꝣnᴀᴄ; an old Irish name, peculiar to the O'Donnells, O'Dohertys, and a few other families of Tirconnell, pronounced locally eɪꝣneᴀᴄᴀn or ɪꝣneᴀᴄᴀn. Lat. *Egnechanus.

éiṁeaR, g. -ṁiṗ, Ever, Heber, (Ivor) ; a var. of éiḃeaṗ, q.v. Lat. Emerus.

éiṁín, g. id., Evin ; dim. of eiṁ, swift, active ; the name of three Irish saints, one of whom was the founder of Monasterevan and patron of the O'Dempseys. Lat. Eminus.

éinRí, g. id., Henry ; Teut. Heimrich or Heinrich, home-ruler ; one of the commonest names among the early Anglo-Norman settlers in Ireland ; largely adopted by Irish families, especially the O'Neills. Lat. Henricus.

eiReaṁón, g. -óin, Erevan, Heremon, Hermon, (Irving) ; an ancient Irish name, still in use in Cape Clear Island ; now pronounced eiṗeaṁán. Lat. Heremon, Eremon, -onis.

eiRnín, g. id., Ernin ; dim. of eaṗna, knowing, experienced; the name of no fewer than seventeen Irish saints. Lat. Erninus.

eoċaiḋ, g. id., and -aḋa, Oghie ; formerly a very common name, but now almost obsolete. It was a favourite name among the O'Hanlons. Lat. Eochodius

eóin, g. id., Eoin, John, (Owen) ; Heb. Jochanan, grace, or gracious gift of Jehovah ; the name of the precursor of Our Lord, and of the beloved disciple ; common in all Christian countries ; in use in Ireland from early Christian times ; one of the most frequent names among the Anglo-Norman settlers, and now by far the most popular name in Ireland. V. Seaġán, Seán and Seón. Lat. Joannes, -is.

eóin baiste, John Baptist.

eoġan, g. -ain, Eoghan, Owen, (Eugene) ; an ancient and rather common Irish name, explained as meaning ' well-born ' ; still in use, but generally angl. Eugene. Lat, Eoganus, Eugenius.

eoġainín, g. id., Oynie ; a dim. of eoġan, q.v.

ᵹaċtna, g. id. and -nan, Fachnan, (Festus) ; the name of four Irish saints, one of whom is patron of the Dioceses of Ross and Kilfenora ; formerly in use among the O'Kellys of Connacht by whom it was angl. Festus. Lat. Fachtnanus.

ꝼáιℓbe, g. id., Falvy; an ancient Irish name, borne by fourteen Irish saints. Lat. Falbeus.

ꝼaoℓán, g. -áιn, Felan; dim. of ꝼaoℓ, a wolf; the name of fourteen Irish saints, one of whom was a brother of St. Fursey and a famous missionary in Flanders, where he was killed about the year 656. Lat. Foelanus.

ꝼeaꞃaὁaċ, g. -aιꞅ, Farry, (Ferdinand); an ancient Irish name, meaning 'manly'; rather common in early times; retained until recently among the O'Maddens and O'Naughtons of Connacht, by whom it was angl. Farry. Finally it was turned into Ferdinand. Lat. Ferdachus.

ꝼeaꞃὁoꞃċa, g. ꝼιꞃὁoꞃċa, Fardoragh, (Frederick; Ferdinand); also an ꝼeaꞃὁoꞃċa; comp. of ꝼeaꞃ, a man, and ὁoꞃċa, dark, hence ' the dark-complexioned man '; a rather common name in the 16th century and in use down to comparatively recent times, but probably now obsolete. Lat. Fardorchus.

ꝼeaꞃꞅaℓ, g. -ꞅaιℓ and -ꞅaιℓe, Fergal, Farrell; an ancient and once very common name, especially among the MacDonnells, MacDonoughs, Mageoghegans, O'Farrells, O'Neills and O'Rourkes; still in use, but rare. It is supposed to have been the Irish name of the celebrated St. Virgilius, the Irish ꝼeaꞃ- having been equated with the Latin Vir-(man). Lat. Fergalius.

ꝼeaꞃꞅanaιnm, g. ꝼιꞃꞅanaιnm, Fergananym, (Ferdinand); comp. of ꝼeaꞃ, a man, ꞅan, without, and aιnn, a name, hence ' anonymous, nameless.' This peculiar name was formerly rather common in Ireland. It is supposed to have been first given to persons who had not been baptised in their childhood.

ꝼeaꞃꞅuꞅ, g. -ꞅuꞃa, -ꞅuιꞃ, Fergus, (Ferdinand); Celt. *Ver-gustu-s, super-choice, super-selection, Old Ir. Fergus, g. -gosso; formerly a rather common name in Ireland and Scotland. Ten saints of the name are mentioned in the Martyrology of Donegal. Lat. Fergusius.

ꝼeıcín, g. id., Fehin, (Festus) ; dim. of ꝼıaċ, a raven ; the name of five Irish saints, one of whom was Abbot of Fore and patron of West Connacht, where the name is now angl. Festus. St. Feichin's Day is 20 January. Lat. Fechinus.

ꝼeıꝺlım, g. id., Phelim, (Felix ; Philip) ; a shortened form of ꝼeıꝺlımıꝺ, q.v. Lat. Fedelmius, Fedlimius.

ꝼeıꝺlımıꝺ, g. id., Felimy, Phelimy, Phelim, (Felix ; Philip) ; an ancient Irish name, explained as meaning 'the ever good' ; common among the Maguires, O'Connors, O'Donnells, O'Neills and O'Reillys ; and borne by six Irish saints, one of whom is patron of the Diocese of Kilmore. Lat. Fedelmidius, Fedlimidius.

ꝼeóRas, g. -aır, Pierce ; an Irish form of the Norman Piers (Fr. Pierre, Lat. Petrus, Peter).

ꝼıaċa, g. -aċ, Feagh ; a name among the O'Byrnes, borne by the famous Feagh MacHugh. St. Fiacha's Day was 27 December. Lat. Fiachus.

ꝼıaċRa, g. -aċ, Fiachra, Feary ; the name of eight Irish saints, of whom the most celebrated was St. Fiachra the Solitary, founder of the monastery of Breuil, in France, whose shrine is a constant place of pilgrimage, where innumerable miracles are said to have been performed. The French form of the name is Fiacre. Lat. Fiachrius.

ꝼılıb, g. id., Philip ; usually pılıb, q.v.

ꝼınᵹın, g. id., Fineen, Finneen, Finnin, (Florence, Florry); an ancient Irish name, explained as meaning 'fair birth' or 'fair offspring' ; common among the Mac Carthys, O'Sullivans, O'Mahonys, O'Driscolls, and other families in West Munster, by whom it is absurdly angl. Florence. St. Finghin's Day was 5 February. Lat. Fingenus, Finginus.

ꝼınnıan, g. -eın, Finnian, Finian ; dim. of ꝼıonn, fair ; the name of several Irish saints, of whom the most celebrated were St. Finnian, Abbot of Moville, and St. Finnian, Abbot of Clonard and founder of the famous school of that place. Lat. Finnianus.

ꝼ1on&n, g. -&ın, Fionan, Finan ; also written ꝼıonn&n ;
dim. of ꝼıonn, fair ; the name of at least nine Irish
saints, some of whom were very celebrated, as St.
Fionan Cam and St. Fionan, the Leper. Lat.
Fionanus.

ꝼ1onn, g. ꝼınn, Finn ; an ancient and once common
name ; made famous by Fionn MacCumhal. It was
borrowed by the Norsemen and is still in use as a
Christian name in Scandinavia and Iceland. Lat.
Finnius.

ꝼ1onn&n, v. ꝼıon&n.

ꝼ1onnᵬ&RR, g. -&ıꝶꝶ, Finbar ; comp. of ꝼıonn, fair, and
ᵬ&ꝶꝶ, a head ; the name of several Irish saints, of
whom one is patron of the Diocese of Cork ; also
called ᵬ&ıꝶꝶꝼıonn, shortened to ᵬ&ꝶꝶ&, q.v. Lat.
Finnbarrus.

ꝼ1onnc&n, g. -&ın, Fintan ; dim. of ꝼıonn, fair ; the
name of upwards of twenty Irish saints, of whom one
of the most celebrated was St. Fintan of Clonenagh.
Lat. Fintanus.

ꝼ1ce&l, g. -cıl, (Florence, Florry) ; a corruption of
ꝼıcce&ll&c (whence the surname Ó ꝼıcce&ll&ıꝅ) ;
in use among the O'Mulconrys, by whom it was angl.
Florence.

ꝼl&nn, g. ꝼl&ınn and ꝼloınn, Flann, Flan, (Florence,
Florry) ; an ancient and once common Irish name,
meaning ' ruddy.' It survived among the MacEgans
and O'Mulconrys down to comparatively recent
times. Several saints of the name are mentioned in
the Martyrology of Donegal. Lat. Flannus.

ꝼl&nn&n, g. -&ın, Flannan ; dim. of ꝼl&nn, ruddy ; the
name of the patron of the Diocese of Killaloe, whose
feast is kept on 18th December. Lat. Flannanus.

ꝼolc, Foulk ; a Frankish name introduced by the Normans
and still found among a few families. It was generally
pronounced ꝼúc. Lat. Fulcus.

ꝼR&ınc, g. id., Frank ; a pet form of Francis. V.
ꝑꝶoınnꝶı&ꝶ.

ᵹᴀᴿƀᴀɴ, g. -ᴀin, Garvan ; dim. of ᵹᴀᴿƀ, rough ; the name of five Irish saints. Lat. Garvanus.

ᵹeᴀᴿᴀLᴄ, g. -ᴀiLᴄ, Gerald ; Teut. Gerwald, spear-might ; a name introduced into Ireland by the Anglo-Normans. It was rare at first, but by the end of the 16th century had become very common. Its popularity has again declined. V. ᵹeᴀᴿᴀᴿƀ and ᵹeᴀᴿóiƀ. Lat. Giraldus, Geraldus.

ᵹeᴀᴿᴀᴿƀ, g. -ᴀiᴿƀ, Gerard ; Frank. Gerhard, spear-brave ; a name borne by two saints, one Bishop of Toul and the other Abbot of Namur, after whom it became popular among the Normans, who introduced it into Ireland. It appears, however, to have soon died out, having been apparently absorbed by Gerald (v. ᵹeᴀᴿᴀLᴄ). The present popularity of the name in Ireland is due to St. Gerard Majella. Lat. Gerardus.

ᵹeᴀᴿóiƀ, g. id., Garrett, Gerald, Gerard ; apparently not a dim. of Gerald (v. ᵹeᴀᴿᴀLᴄ), but merely the Norman pronunciation of that name. Lat. Giraldus, Geraldus.

ᵹeᴀꞅpᴀᴿ, g. -ᴀiᴿ, Jasper ; a fancy name given to one of the Magi who came from the East to adore the Infant Saviour. The Magi, according to tradition, were three kings named Gaspar, Melchior and Balthasar, who afterwards suffered martyrdom. The translation of their supposed relics from Constantinople to Milan, and thence to Cologne in the 12th century, made their names known in Europe. Gaspar became very common in Germany, and was in use in France as Gaspard and in England as Jasper. All three names were at one time in use in Ireland, but none of them ever became common. Gaspar was represented in the Fiants of Elizabeth by ' Gaspar Synnott,' ' Jasper Browne,' and ' Jasper Butler,' and is still in use. Melchior was current in the neighbourhood of Youghal, while Balthasar was a name among the Nugents. Lat. Caspar.

ᵹiLibeiᴿᴄ, g. id., Gilbert ; Frank. Giselbert, hostage-bright ; very common as Gilbert among the Normans, who introduced it into Ireland. Lat. Gilbertus.

ᵹᴉobún, g. -úᴉn, Gibbon ; a dim. of Gilbert (v. ᵹᴉᴜᴉbeᴉ\p̃c).

ᵹᴉoᴜᴌᴀ beᴀ\pᴀᴉᵹ, g. id., Gilvarry ; an Irish name, meaning ' servant of St. Barry ' (v. beᴀ\pᴀᴄ). Lat. Berachianus.

ᵹᴉoᴜᴌᴀ b\pᴉᵹ'oe, g. id., Gilbride ; an Irish name, meaning ' servant of St. Brigid ' (v. b\pᴉᵹᴉ'o). Lat. Brigidianus.

ᵹᴉoᴜᴌᴀ ᴄ\pᴉoꞅc, g. id., Christian ; an Irish name, meaning ' servant of Christ.' Lat. Christianus.

ᵹᴉoᴜᴌᴀ 'oé, g. id., Gildea ; an Irish name, meaning ' servant of God.' Lat. *Gildeus.

ᵹᴉoᴜᴌᴀ eᴀꞅpuᴉᵹ, g. id., Archibald ; an Irish name, meaning ' bishop's servant ' ; strangely angl. Archibald in the North of Ireland and in Scotland.

ᵹᴉoᴜᴌᴀ ᴉoꞅᴀ, g. id., Gillisa, Gillesa, Gill ; an Irish name, meaning ' servant of Jesus.' Lat. *Gilisius.

ᵹᴉoᴜᴌᴀ nᴀ nᴀoᴍ̃, g. id., (Nehemiah) ; an Irish name, meaning ' servant of the saints.' Lat. *Sanctianus.

ᵹᴉo\pá\p'o, g. -áᴉ\p'o, Gerard ; a var. of ᵹeᴀ\pá\p'o, q.v.

ᵹᴉo\póᴉ'o, g. id., Garrett, Gerald, (Gerard) ; a var. of ᵹeᴀ\póᴉ'o, q.v.

ᵹᴌᴀᴉꞅne, g. id., Glasny ; formerly a favourite name in several Ulster families ; survived down to recent times. Lat. Glasnaeus.

ᵹo\p'oᴀn, g. -ᴀᴉn, Gordan ; a name among the O'Neills of Ulster, first borne by a son of Sir Phelim O'Neill, who was so called from his grandfather, the Marquis of Huntly in Scotland, whose family name was Gordon. Lat. * Gordanus.

ᵹoc\pᴀᴉ'o, ᵹoc\pᴀᴉ'o, g. id. and -ᴀ'oᴀ, Godfrey, Gorry ; Norse Gothfrithr, God-peace ; a Norse name early adopted by the Irish, among whom it was at one time rather common. Lat. Godefridus.

ᵹ\péᴀᵹóᴉ\p, g. -óᴘᴀ, Gregory ; Gr. Γρηγόριος (Gregórios), watchman ; a frequent episcopal name in the Eastern Church from early times, and borne by no fewer than sixteen Popes. Although rather common among the early Anglo-Norman settlers, it never became popular in Ireland. Lat. Gregorius.

GRIOĠAR, g. -air, Gregory; a var. of Gréagóir, q.v.

HANNRAOI, HANRAOI, g. id., Henry, Harry; common var. of Éinrí, q.v.

HOIBEARD, g. -aird, Hubert, (Hugh); Teut. Hugibert, mind-bright; a common name in France; introduced into Ireland by the Anglo-Normans, but never became popular. St. Hubert was the patron of hunters. Lat. Hubertus.

HOIREABARD, g. -aird, Herbert; Frank. Haribert, Heribert, army-bright; common as Herbert among the Anglo-Norman settlers in Ireland, but it quickly declined in popularity and for centuries has been very rare. Lat. Heribertus.

IARḞLAIṪ, g. -aṫa, Jarlath; the name of the patron of the Diocese of Tuam. Lat. Iarlathus.

ÍOṀAR, g. -air, Ivor; Norse Ivarr; a name borrowed by the Irish from the Norsemen.

ÍOSAC, g. -aic, Isaac; Heb. Yitschaq, laughter; the name of the Jewish patriarch, son of Abraham and father of Esau and Jacob; probably so called on account of the joy occasioned by his birth (cf. Gen. XVII, 17); always exceedingly rare in Ireland. Lat. Isaac.

IÓSEP, IÓSEḂ, g. id., Joseph; Heb. Yoseph, May God add (cf. Gen. XXX, 23-24); the name of one of the sons of Jacob and Rachel, afterwards prime minister of Pharaoh in Egypt, and also of the spouse of the B. V. Mary and foster-father of Jesus Christ; in use in Ireland from early Christian times and re-introduced by the Anglo-Normans, but it is only within comparatively recent times that it has become really popular. Lat. Josephus.

ÍOSÓC, ÍOSÓG, g. id., Isaac; var. of Íosac, q.v.

IRIAL, g. -ail, Irial; an ancient Irish name; formerly in use among the O'Farrells, O'Kennedys and O'Loghlens. Lat. Irialus.

1ÚSⅭÁS, g. -áıp, Eustace ; **Gr.** Εὐστάκυς (Eustachus), fruitful ; the name of a Roman martyr whose relics were translated to the Church of St. Denis at Paris in the 12th century, making the name common in France. It was brought into Ireland by the Anglo-Normans, but has always been very rare. Lat. Eustachius, Eustasius.

LAⒷⒸÁS, g. -áıp, Luke ; a var. in parts of Connacht of Lúcáp, q.v.

LAⓊRÁS, g. -áıp, Laurence ; Lat. Laurentius, i.e., belonging to Laurentum, a town in Latium ; the name of a celebrated Roman deacon who suffered martyrdom under Valerian, in the 3rd century ; popular among the Anglo-Normans, who introduced it into Ireland. Sometimes Laбpap and Luбpáp.

LAⒸTNA, g. id., (Lucius) ; the name of the great-grandfather of Brian Boru ; hence the name Lucius among the O'Briens.

LAISRIAN, v. Lapaıpıan.

LAOıżseAⒸ, LAOıseAⒸ, g. -ıż, Lysagh, (Lucius, Lewis, Louis) ; deriv. of Laoıżıp, i.e., belonging to Leix ; a name in use among the O'Mores and a few other families.

LASAIRIAN, g. -éın, Laserian ; dim. of Lapaıp, a flame ; the name of four Irish saints, one of whom is patron of the Diocese of Leighlin. Lat. Lassarenus, Laserianus.

LeAⒸLAınn, g. id., Laughlin, Lanty ; a shortened form of mAeLeAⒸLAınn, q.v.

León, g. -óın, Leo ; Lat. Leo, g. -onis, lion ; a common Latin name, borne by thirteen Popes in honour of the last of whom—the great Pope Leo XIII—it was adopted in Ireland.

LıAm, g. id., William ; a pet form of UıLLıAm, q.v.

LoⒸLAınn, g. id., Loughlin, Laughlin ; a name borrowed from the Northmen. The native home of the northern invaders was known to the Irish as LoⒸLAınn, a name which is supposed to signify ' Lakeland ' or ' Fiordland.' This was quickly adopted by the Irish as a personal name and became very popular. Dr. MacBain suggests that it was originally ᵐᵃᶜloᴄᴌᴀⁱⁿne ' son of Scandinavia,' hence a Scandinavian. It still survives, angl. Loughlin and Laughlin. Lat. Lochlunius.

loᴄᴌᴀⁿⁿ, g. -ᴀⁱⁿⁿ, Loughlin, Laughlin ; a var. of loᴄ-ᴌᴀⁱⁿⁿ, q.v.

lomáⁿ, g. -áⁱⁿ, Loman ; dim. of lom, bare ; the name of four Irish saints, one of whom was a disciple of St. Patrick. Lat. Lomanus.

lonáⁿ, g. -áⁱⁿ, Lonan ; dim. of lon, a blackbird ; the name of eight Irish saints. Lat. Lonanus.

loRcáⁿ, g. -áⁱⁿ, Lorcan, (Laurence) ; dim. of loᴨc, fierce ; the Irish name of St. Laurence O'Toole, patron of the Diocese of Dublin. Lat. Lorcanus.

lúcáⁿ, g. -áⁱⁿ, Lucan ; the name of four Irish saints. Lat. Lucanus.

lúcáS, g. -áⁱᴨ, *Lucas*, Luke ; Gr. Λουκᾶς (Loukas), traced by St. Jerome to the Hebrew and explained by him as meaning ' resurrection,' but generally considered to be a contraction of the Greek form, Λουκανοs (Loukanos), of the Latin Lucanus, a Roman forename probably derived from Lucania, a district in Southern Italy ; the name of one of the Four Evangelists, native of Antioch and physician by profession. ' Lucas ' was the old English form of the name, as it is still in Spanish and Portuguese. Lat. Lucas, -ae.

luᵹᴀⁱᴅ, g. -ᴀᴅᴀ, Lewy, (Lewis, Louis, Aloysius) ; an ancient Irish name, borne by ten saints ; a favourite name among the O'Clerys. Lat. Lugadius.

ᵐᴀeleᴀᴄᴌᴀⁱⁿⁿ, ᵐᴀelSeᴀᴄᴌᴀⁱⁿⁿ, g. ᵐᴀoⁱleᴀᴄ-ᴌᴀⁱⁿⁿ, Melaghlin, Laughlin, Lanty, (Malachy ; Milo ; Miles, Myles) ; an Irish name, meaning ' servant of St. Secundinus,' disciple of St. Patrick and patron of the family of Ó ᵐᴀoⁱlᴦeᴀᴄᴌᴀⁱⁿⁿ, or O'Melaghlen ; rather common in the tenth and succeeding centuries, especially among the O'Melaghlens, O'Farrells, O'Kellys and O'Connors ; still in use, but generally disguised as Malachy. Lat. Malachias.

ⅿᴀeⱡíosᴀ, g. ⅿᴀoⱡ íorᴀ, Maelisa ; formerly a not uncommon Irish name signifying 'servant of Jesus.'
Lat. Moelisa.

ⅿᴀᵹnus, g. -urᴀ and -uir, Manus, (Manasses) ; Lat.
Magnus, great ; a name adopted by the Northmen in
honour of Charlemagne (Carolus Magnus), and by
them introduced into Ireland. It became very
common among some Irish families, especially the
O'Donnells of Tirconnell. Often pronounced ⅿᴀᵹnur
or ⅿᴀonur. Eight saints of the name are mentioned
in the Roman Martyrology.

ⅿᴀincín, g. id., Munchin ; dim. of ⅿᴀnᴀċ, a monk ; the
name of several Irish saints, one of whom is patron
of the Diocese of Limerick. Lat. Manchinus,
Munchinus.

ⅿᴀiⱃⱦín, g. id., Martin ; Lat. Martinus, dim. of Martius
(deriv. of Mars, the Roman god of war) ; the name of
the celebrated St. Martin of Tours, said to have been
a relative of St. Patrick, in whose honour it was
popular in France, whence the Normans brought it
into England and Ireland. Under the form of ⅿᴀrⱦᴀn,
however, it had been already in use in Ireland from
early Christian times.

ⅿᴀiⱦ, g. id., Mat ; a pet form of ⅿᴀiⱦiú, q.v.

ⅿᴀiⱦín, g. id., Mat ; a dim. of ⅿᴀiⱦiú, q.v.

ⅿᴀiⱦiᴀs, g. -ⱦír, ⅿᴀiⱦiᴀs, g. -ⱦír, Matthias ; probably
of same origin as ⅿᴀiⱦiú, q.v. ; the name of the Apostle
who supplied the place of Judas ; always rare in
Ireland. Lat. Mathias, -ae.

ⅿᴀiⱦiú, g. id., Matthew ; Heb. Mattattjah, gift of
Jehovah ; the name of one of the Twelve Apostles
and the first of the Four Evangelists ; a rare name
among the early Anglo-Norman settlers in Ireland.
Lat. Mattheus.

ⅿᴀoⱱóᵹ, g. id., Mogue, (Aidan, Moses) ; a var. of ᴀoⱱᴀn,
q.v. The initial ⅿ represents the possessive pronoun
ⅿo, my, prefixed as a term of endearment to the
names of saints, while -óᵹ is merely another dim.
termination. Lat. Maidocus.

Mᴀoilir, g. id. Meyler; Welsh Meilir or Meilyr; very
rare. Lat. Milerus, Mylerus.

Mᴀolbeᴀnnᴀċᴛᴀ, g. Mᴀoilbeᴀnnᴀċᴛᴀ, Benedict; an
ancient Irish name, signifying 'one desirous of the
blessing.'

Mᴀolċolm, Mᴀolċoluim, g. Mᴀoilċolm, Malcolm;
an Irish name signifying 'servant of St. Columcille';
a royal name in Scotland, where it is still in use. It
does not appear to have been at any time a very
common name in Ireland. Lat. Malcolmus.

Mᴀolmórᴅᴀ, g. Mᴀoilmórᴅᴀ, (Miles, Myles); an
ancient Irish name signifying 'majestic chief'; a
favourite name among the O'Reillys, by whom it
was angl. Miles or Myles. Lat. Maelmorus.

Mᴀolṁuire, g. Mᴀoilṁuire, (Meyler, Milo, Miles,
Myles); an Irish name, signifying 'servant of the
B. V. Mary'; a favourite name among the Mac
Sweenys, by whom it was angl. Miles or Myles. Lat.
Maelmarius.

Mᴀolruᴅᴀin, g. Mᴀoilruᴀᴅáin, Melrone an Irish
name, meaning 'servant of St. Ruadhan.' Lat.
Maelruadanus.

Mᴀrcus, g. -uiʀ, Marcus, Mark; Lat. Marcus, a common
name in ancient Rome and its provinces; of uncertain
origin, but supposed to be a deriv. of Mars, the Roman
god of war; the name of the second of the Four Evangelists. The Anglo-Normans brought it into Ireland,
but it never became common.

Máʀᴛᴀin, g. id., Martin; a var. of Máiʀᴛín, q.v.

Máʀᴛᴀn, g. -ᴀin, Martin; a var. of Máiʀᴛín, q.v.

Mᴀᴛᴀ, g. id., Matthew; a var. of Mᴀiᴛiú, q.v.

Mᴀᴛṡᴀṁᴀin, g. -ᴀṁnᴀ, Mahon, (Matthew); a well-
known Irish name, signifying 'a bear'; borne by the
brother of Brian Boru, and common among the
O'Briens, O'Connors, O'Farrells, &c., but now disguised under the angl. form of Matthew. Lat. Math-
gamanius.

Meᴀllán, g. -áin, Mellan, Meldan; dim. of meᴀll,
pleasant; the name of four Irish saints. Lat. Mellanus.

meilseóir, g. -óra, Melchor ; a fancy name given to one of the Magi (v. Seaspar) ; still in use in the neighbourhood of Youghal. Lat. Melchior, -oris.

míceál, míceál, g. -cíl, Michael ; Heb. Mikael, Who like God ? ; the name of one of the archangels, chief of the heavenly hosts and conqueror of Satan ; rare until comparatively recent times, but now one of the most popular names in Ireland. Lat. Michael, -is.

muirceartac, g. -aig, Murtaugh, Murty, (Mortimer) ; comp. of muir, sea, and ceart, right, meaning ' sea-director,' ' expert at sea,' ' able navigator ' ; an ancient Irish name, common among the O'Briens, O'Connors, &c. ; still in use, but generally angl. Mortimer, with which it has no connection. Lat. Murchertachus.

muireaḋac, g. -aig, Murry ; deriv. of muir, sea, meaning ' seaman ' ; also ' lord ' ; formerly a very common Irish name ; borne by two saints, one of whom is patron of the Diocese of Killala. Lat. Muredachus.

muirgeas, g. -geara and -gir, (Maurice) ; comp. of muir, sea, and -gur, choice ; formerly a common Irish name ; now merged in muirir, q.v. Lat. Murgessius.

muiris, g. id., Maurice ; Lat. Mauritius, Moorish, a Roman name for a man of Moorish lineage ; borne by the captain of the Thebean legion who was martyred, together with his companions, in Switzerland, by order of Maximian, in the 3rd century ; common among the Anglo-Norman settlers in Ireland.

murcaḋ, g. -aḋa and -aiḋ, Murrough, (Morgan) ; Celt. *Mori-catu-s, sea-warrior ; an ancient Irish name, formerly common in most Irish families, especially among the O'Briens, O'Flahertys, &c. ; still in use, but generally angl. Morgan. Lat. Murchadus.

naoṁán, g. -áin, Nevan ; dim. of naoṁ, holy ; the name of an Irish saint whose feast was kept on 13 September. Lat. Sanctanus.

naos, g. -ra, Neece, Neese, Niece, (Nicholas) ; a pet

form of ᴀóngup, q.v. ; formerly common in Ulster and still extant in that province.

neᴀsᴀ́n, g. -ᴀ́in, Nessan ; the name of five Irish saints, of whom the best known is St. Nessan, the deacon of Mungret. Lat. Nessanus.

néill, v. niᴀll.

niᴀll, g. néill, Niall, Neal, Neale, Neil ; an ancient Irish name, specially common in Ulster among the O'Neills, O'Donnells, O'Dohertys, O'Boyles, &c. ; still in use, but the gen. néill is sometimes used instead of the nominative. Lat. Niallus, Niellus, Nellus.

niᴀllᴀ́n, g. -ᴀ́in, Niallan ; dim. of niᴀll, q.v. Lat. Niallanus.

nioclᴀ́s, g. -ᴀ́ip, Nicholas ; Gr. Νικόλαος (Nikólaos), victory of the people ; the name of one of the seven first deacons. The legend of St. Nicholas, Bishop of Myra, made it universal. It was one of the commonest names among the early Anglo-Norman settlers in Ireland, and still retains its popularity. Lat. Nicolaus.

niocol, g. -oil, Nicol ; a short form of nioclᴀ́p, q.v.

oóRᴀ́n, g. -ᴀ́in, Oran ; dim. of oóᴀp, pale-green ; the name of nine Irish saints, one of whom is patron of Waterford. Lat. Odranus, Otteranus.

oilibéᴀR, g. -éip, Oliver ; almost certainly a Gallicised form of the Norse Ōlafr or Ōleifr, ancestor's relic (v. ᴀṁlᴀoib) ; a name introduced into Ireland by the Anglo-Normans and once fairly common, until its association with Cromwell made it unpopular. With the beatification of Blessed Oliver Plunket it is likely to be revived. Lat. Oliverus, Oliverius.

oisín, g. id., Ossin, Ossian ; dim. of op, a deer ; the name of the Fenian poet, son of Fionn MacCumhail ; also borne by four Irish saints. Lat. Ossenus.

oiscín, g. id., Austin ; a Norse form of Augustine. It occurs in the Annals of Ulster, at the year 874, as the

name of a son of Aṁlaoiḃ, king of the Norsemen. V.
Áṡuirtín.

OSCAR, g. -air, Oscar; Norse Asgeirr, a common Norse
name, meaning 'divine spear' or 'spear of the Anses
or gods,' the same as the Ang.-Sax. Osgar (occurring
in Domesday Book); but 'oscar' is also an Irish
word, meaning 'champion' or 'combatant'; the
name of the son of Oisin and grandson of Fionn Mac
Cumhail; also a name among the Maguires in the
14th century. Lat. Osgerus.

Paḋra, g. id., Paddy; a pet form of Páoraiṡ, q.v.

Páoraic, Páoraic, Páoraiṡ, Páoraiṡ, g. id.,
Patrick; Lat. Patricius, Patritius, patrician, noble;
the name of the National Apostle of Ireland.

Páio, g. id., Pat; a pet form of Páoraiṡ, q.v.

Páioi, g. id., Paddy; a pet form of Páoraiṡ, q.v.

Páioín, g. id., Padden, Paddy, Pat; a pet dim. of Páoraiṡ, q.v.

Parra, g. id., Paddy; a pet form of Páoraiṡ, q.v.

Parṫalán, párṫalán, párṫlán, párṫlán,
pártnán, g. -áin, parṫlón, g. -óin, Bartholomew,
Bartlemy, Bartley, Barkley, Berkley, Barclay, Bartel,
Parlan, Bat, Batt; Heb. Bār Talmai, son of Talmai;
the name of one of the Twelve Apostles; fairly common
in Ireland. Lat. Bartholomaeus.

Peaoar, g. -air, Peter; Lat. Petrus, rock; the name
given by Christ to Simon, son of Jonas, whom He made
Chief of the Apostles and the foundation-stone of
His Church. This form of the name is comparatively
recent, Piaṙar (q.v.) being the form previously in
general use.

Peaoair, g. id., Peter; a var. of Peaoar, q.v.

Piaras, g. -air, *Piers*, Pierce; the Norman form of
Peter (v. Peaoar), from French Pierre; a common
name among the early Anglo-Norman settlers in
Ireland. Lat. Petrus, Piercius, Percius.

Pilib, g. id., Philip; Greek Φίλιππος (Philippos), horse-
lover; the name of one of the Twelve Apostles; in

use in Ireland in early Christian times ; a very common name among the Anglo-Norman settlers. Lat. Philippus.

pius, g. id., Pius ; Lat. Pius, pious ; the name of eleven Popes.

pól, g. póil, Paul ; Lat. Paulus, small ; the name of the Apostle of the Gentiles ; never a common name in Ireland.

pReannoaiġ, g. id., Frank ; a pet form of pRoinnriar ; in use in Omeath.

pRoinnsias, pRoinnséas, pRóinsias, g. -réir, Francis ; Lat. Franciscus, Frenchman, a name given in his youth to St. Francis of Assisi (whose original name was John), from the readiness with which he acquired and spoke the French language, and which from him became a name of world-wide popularity.

Raðulb, g. -uilb, Ralph ; Teut. Raedwulf, swift-wolf, or counsel-wolf, Frank. Radulf ; one of the most frequent names among the Anglo-Norman settlers in Ireland, but it rapidly declined in popularity, and even in the 16th century was very rare. Lat. Radulfus.

Raġnall, g. -aill, Reginald, *Reynald*, Ronald, (Randal, Randulph) ; Teut. Raginwald, Reginwald, mighty-power, Norse Rognvaldr, Nor. Ragenald, Regnault, Reynald, Eng. Reynold ; a Teutonic name which reached us by two channels, first through the Norsemen when it was largely borrowed by the Irish and Scottish Gaels, especially the MacDonnells, by whom it was incorrectly angl. Randal, and again through the Anglo-Normans, among whom it was very common. The pronunciation is often Raġnall or Raonall. Lat. Raganaldus, Reginaldus.

Raibilin, Revelin. V. Roibilin.

RaiðRí, v. Ruaiðrí.

Rannulb, g. -uilb, Randulph ; Frank. Randulf, shield-wolf ; a name introduced by the Anglo-Normans, but always very rare. Its angl. form, Randal, has been absorbed by Raġnaḷḷ, q.v. Lat. Randulfus, Randulphus.

Réamonn, g. -oinn, Raymond, Redmond, Mundy; Teut. Raginmund, Reginmund, mighty-protection, Fr. Raimond, or Ang.-Sax. Raedmund, counsel-protection ; a name introduced by the Anglo-Normans and formerly not uncommon in many Irish families. Lat. Raymundus, Reymundus, Remundus.

Reiórí, v. Ruaióṗí.

Ribeaṙo, g. -aiṗo, Ribeaṙt, g. -biṗt, Ribiṙt, g. id., Rioḃáṙo, g. -áiṗo, Rioḃáṙt, g. -aiṗt, Robert. V. Roiḃeáṗo.

Riocáṙo, g. -áiṗo, Riocáṙo, g. -aiṗo, Rickard, Richard; Teut. Rikhard, Richard, powerful-brave, Fr. Ricard, Ricart, Richard ; one of the most frequent names among the Anglo-Norman settlers in Ireland. It owed its popularity to an Anglo-Saxon king of Kent, who in the 7th century left his throne to become a monk at Lucca, where he was reputed to have wrought many miracles. Lat. Richardus.

Risteáṙo, g. -áiṗo, Richard ; a var. of Riocáṗo, due to French influence. This is the common form of the name. Cf. Italian Ricciardo for Riccardo.

Roóḷaióe, g. id., Roland, Rowland ; a pet form of Roóḷann, q.v.

Roóḷann, g. -ainn, Roland, Rowland ; Teut. Hruodlant, Hrothland, famous-land, Nor. Rollant, Roland ; a name introduced by the Anglo-Normans, among whom, however, it was not of frequent occurrence. Lat. Rotlandus, Rolandus.

Roóuḷḃ, g. -uiḷḃ, (Ralph) ; Teut. Hruodwulf, Hrothwulf, famous-wolf, Nor. Rodulf (Rolf in Domesday Book) ; a rare Anglo-Norman name ; absorbed by Ráóuḷḃ, q.v. Lat. Rodulfus, Rodulphus.

Roiḃeán, v. Roiḃín.

Roiḃeáṙo, g. -áiṗo, Roiḃeáṙo, g. -aiṗo, Robert ; Teut. Hruodberht, Hrothberht, fame-bright, Nor. Rodbert, Fr. Robert ; one of the commonest names among the early Anglo-Norman settlers in Ireland, but it has greatly declined in popularity and is now a rather rare name. Roibín (q.v.) is a diminutive. Lat. Robertus.

Roibilín, g. id., Revelin, (Roland, Rowland) ; a rare name, peculiar to the MacDonnells and the Savages of the Ards, Co. Down ; perhaps the same as Ravelin of Domesday Book ; also written Raibilín and Ruibilín.

Roibín, g. id., Robin ; dim. of Roibeáro, q.v. Roibean is sometimes a variant.

Rónán, g. -áin, Ronan ; dim. of rón, a seal ; an ancient Irish personal name, borne by twelve saints. Lat. Ronanus.

Ros, g. -ra, Ross ; a rare name, formerly in use among the Mageoghegans, MacMahons, Maguires, O'Loghlens, &c. Lat. Rossius.

Ruaóán, g. -áin, Rowan ; dim. of ruaó, red ; the name of the celebrated Abbot of Lorrha, whose feast was kept on 15 April. Lat. Ruadanus.

Ruaiórí, g. id., Rory, Roderick, (Roger, Roddy) ; Teut. Hruodric, Norse Rothrekr, fame-ruler ; a name introduced by the Norsemen and which became very common in many Irish families ; now often incorrectly angl. Roger. Raiórí and Reiórí are dialectical variants. Lat. Rodericus, Rudericus.

Ruibilín, v. Roibilín.

Saerbreatac, g. -aig, Justin ; comp. of raor and breatac, meaning 'noble judge' ; a common name among the MacCarthys, borne by the father of Cártac, from whom the family name. Lat. Justinus.

Sailbeastar, g. -air, Sylvester ; Lat. Silvester, -tri, living in a wood ; the name of two Popes ; brought into Ireland by the Anglo-Normans, but always very rare.

Samairle, g. id., (Charles) ; a dialectical var. of Somairle, q.v.

Séaona, g. id., (Sidney) ; an ancient Irish name, borne by four saints. Lat. Sednaeus, Sedonius, Sidonius.

Séafra, Seafraid, g. id., Geoffrey; a var. of Gotfraid (q.v.) owing to French influence; a common name among the early Anglo-Norman settlers in Ireland; now rare. Lat. Galfridus.

Seagán, g. -áin, Shane, John. V. Seán.

Séamus, g. -uis, Shemus, James; Heb. Yākōb, literally one who takes by the heel (Gen. XXV. 25, XXVII, 36), from yekeb, a heel, hence to trip up, defraud, supplant by subtlety; the name of the Jewish patriarch (Jacob) and of two of the Twelve Apostles; common among the Anglo-Norman settlers, and ever growing in popularity. It is in honour of St. James the Greater that the name is used in Ireland, as in Europe generally. The angl. form James is derived from the Spanish Jayme. Lat. Jacobus.

Seán, g. -áin, Sean, Shane, John; Old Fr. Jehan, Fr. Jean; a var. of Eóin, q.v.; one of the commonest names among the early Anglo-Norman settlers in Ireland and now by far our most popular man's name; also written Seagán and Seón. Lat. Joannes, -is.

Seanán, g. -áin, Senan, Sinan, Synan, Sinon; dim. of sean, old, wise; the name of upwards of twenty Irish saints, of whom the most celebrated is St. Senan of Iniscathy; his feast is kept on 8th March. Lat. Senanus.

Séarlas, g. -ais, **Séarlus**, g. -uis, Charles; Teut. Carl, Karl, man, Fr. Charles; a rare name in Ireland until James I called his son and heir Charles as a lucky royal name. Lat. Carolus.

Séarta, g. id., Sheary, Geoffrey, Jeffrey; a var. of Seafra, q.v.

Seartún, v. Séatrún.

Séatra, v. Séarta.

Séatrún, Seatrún, g. -úin, Sheron, Geoffrey, Jeffrey; probably from Fr. dim. of Geoffrey.

Seóirse, g. id., George; Greek Γεωργος (Georgos), husbandman, rustic; the name of the patron saint of

England; rare in Ireland before the advent of the Hanoverian dynasty. Seórsa is sometimes a variant. Lat. Georgius.

Seón, g. -óin, John; a var. of Seán, q.v.; a late form from the English John.

Seórsa, v. Seóirse.

Seosaṁ, g. -aiṁ, **Seosap**, **Seosaḃ**, Joseph; var. of Iósep, q.v.

Siaḋal, **Siaġal**, g. -ail, Shiel; an old Irish name, borne by two saints, one of whom is said to have been Bishop of Dublin. Lat. Sedulius.

Simiḋ, g. id., Jimmy; a pet form of Séamus, q.v.

Sioḟraiḋ, g. id., Geoffrey; a var. of Seaffraiḋ, q.v.

Siomaiḋ, g. id., Jimmy; a pet form of Séamus, q.v.

Síomón, g. -óin, **Síomonn**, g. -oinn, **Síomún**, g. -úin, Simon; Heb. Shim'ón (Simeon), from the root sháma', to hear (cf. Gen. XXIX 33); Greek form Σιμόν (Simon), confused with Ang.-Sax. Sigemund, 'victory-protection'; the first name of St. Peter and the name of another of the Apostles; rather common among the early Anglo-Norman settlers in Ireland. Lat. Simon, -onis.

Sionán, g. -áin, Sinan, Synan, Sinon; a var. of Seanán, q.v.

Siseal, g. -sil, Cecil; Lat. Caecilius, dim. of caecus, blind.

Solaṁ, g. -aiṁ, Solomon; doubtless the Scriptural name; formerly in use among the MacNamees and O'Mellans of Ulster.

Soṁairle, g. id., Sorley, (Samuel, Charles); Norse Sumerlide, summer-sailor; a name of Norse origin; specially common among the MacDonnells, by whom it was angl. Sorley; now disguised as Samuel and Charles. Lat. Somerledus.

Steafán, g. -áin, **Steiṁin**, g. id., **Stiaḃán**, g. -áin, **Stiaḃna**, **Stiana**, **Stiḃin**, g. id., **Stiofán**, g. -áin, Stephen; Greek Στέφανος (Stephanos), crown, or wreath; the name of the proto-martyr of the Christian faith; a rather common name among the early Anglo-Norman settlers in Ireland. Lat. Stephanus.

suibne, g. id., Sivney, (Simon); an old Irish name meaning 'well-going'; borne by seven Irish saints. Lat. Suibneus.

Caȯʒ, g. Caiȯʒ, Teige, Teague, (Thaddeaus, Thaddeus, Thady, Thade, Timothy, Tim); an ancient and very common Irish name, meaning 'poet' or 'philosopher'; still found in every part of Ireland, but now generally angl. Timothy. St. Caȯʒ was martyred at Wurtzburg; his feast was kept on 8 July. Lat. Thaddaeus.

Caiȯʒín, g. id., Tim; a dim. of Caȯʒ, q.v.

Carla, v. Coirȯealȯać.

Ceaȯóiȯ, g. id., Tibbot, Theobald, (Tobias, Toby); Teut. Theodbald, people-bold, Nor. Thebault, Thebaut, Thibault, Thibaut; a rare name, introduced by the Anglo-Normans. Lat. Theobaldus.

Céaȯóir, g. -óra, Theodore; Greek Θεόδωρος (Theodoros), God-gift. Lat. Theodorus.

Tiʒearnać, g. -aiʒ, Tierney; deriv. of tiʒearna, a lord, and meaning 'lordly'; an old Irish name, borne by four saints, of whom the best known is St. Tierney of Clones. Lat. Tigernachus.

Tiʒearnán, g. -áin, Tiernan; dim. of tiʒearna, a lord; a common name among the O'Rourkes. St. Tiernan's Day was 8 April. Lat. Tigernanus.

Cioȯóiȯ, a var. of Ceaȯóiȯ, q.v.

Ciomóiȯ, g. id., Timothy; Greek Τιμόθεος (Timotheos), honouring God; an ancient name, in use even in pagan times; borne by the disciple of St. Paul. In Ireland, it appears to be of comparatively recent introduction and is very rare. Timothy as an angl. form of Caȯʒ (q.v.) is, however, very common, but does not appear to have been in use before the Cromwellian period. Lat. Timotheus.

Coirȯealȯać, g. -aiʒ, Turlough, (Terence, Terry, Charles); an Irish name, meaning 'shaped like Thor,' the Norse Jupiter; a common name among the O'Briens, O'Neills, O'Donnells, O'Connors of Connacht, MacSweenys, &c. ; now generally angl. Terence. Lat. Tordelvachus.

τοmᴀisín, g. id., Tommy ; a dim. of τomᴀ́ρ, q.v.

τomᴀlτᴀċ, -ᴀiȝ, Tomaltagh, Tumelty, (Timothy) ; an old Irish name, formerly rather frequent, especially among the O'Connors of Connacht ; still in use, but disguised under the angl. form of Timothy. Lat. Tomaltachus, Tumultachus.

τomᴀ́s, g. -ᴀiρ, Thomas ; Heb. Tōmā, from tōm, a twin, the same as the Greek δι8υμος (Didymus) ; the name of one of the Twelve Apostles ; very common among the early Anglo-Normans out of devotion to St. Thomas a Becket. Lat. Thomas, -ae.

τRᴀelᴀċ, a dialectical var. of τoiρoeᴀlbᴀċ, q.v.

τuᴀτᴀl, g. -ᴀil, Toal, Tully ; Celt. *Touto-valo-s, people-mighty ; an ancient and once rather common name in Ireland ; still in use, but now very rare. Lat. Tuat-halius, Tulius.

uᴀiτéiR, g. id., Walter ; a var. of uᴀlτᴀρ, q.v.

uᴀiτne (recte. uᴀiτne), g. id., Hewney, Oney, Owney, Oynie, (Antony, Anthony) ; an old Irish name, found among the O'Mores, O'Loghlens, &c., by whom it was angl. Antony.

uᴀlτᴀR, g. -ᴀiρ, Walter ; Teut. Waldhar, Walthar, Walther, power-army, Nor. Walter ; one of the commonest names among the early Anglo-Normans in Ireland, but now rather rare. Lat. Valterius.

uileóȝ, g. id., Ulick, (Ulysses) ; a dim. of uilliᴀm, q.v. Lat. Ulligus.

uilfRio, g. id., Wilfrid ; Ang.-Sax. Wilfrith, will-peace.

uilleᴀc, g. -lic, Ulick, (Ulysses) ; a var. of uileóȝ, q.v.

uilliᴀm, g. id., William ; Teut. Willehelm, Wilhelm, will-protection, Nor. Willaume ; the most common name among the early Anglo-Norman settlers in Ireland. It owed its popularity to William the Conqueror. Lat. Gulielmus.

uillioc, v. uilleᴀc and uileóȝ.

uinseᴀnn, uinsionn, g. -ρinn, Vincent ; Lat. Vincentius, conquering; a name introduced by the Anglo-Normans; always rare.

 úısⅽeⅾn, g. -ⅽın, Euston; Nor. Hutchen, dim. of Hugh; a name among the MacDonnells.

ulⅽⅾn, g. -ⅾın, Ultan; the name of eighteen Irish saints mentioned in the Martyrology of Donegal. Lat. Ultanus.

unⱷⱤⅾıⅾ, g. id., Humphrey; Teut. Hunfrid, Hunfrith, Hun-peace; a rare name among the Anglo-Normans. It appears to have gone entirely out of use, except as an angl. form of ⅾṁlⅾoıⅾ, q.v. Lat. Hunfridus, Onuphrius.

NAMES OF WOMEN
IRISH—ENGLISH

ⱯⱠⱯ1ȝeⱯⱡ, g., id., Abigail; Heb. Abigail father of joy, joyfulness; the name of the wife of King David, noted for her prudence and beauty; in use in Derry and Omeath. Lat. Abigail.

ⱯⱠⱯ1ȝ, g. id., Abbey, Abbie; a pet form of ⱯⱠⱯ1ȝeⱯⱡ, q.v.

ⱯȝⱯⱺⱯ, g. id., Agatha; Gr. Ἀγαθη (Agathé), good; the name of a celebrated Sicilian virgin and martyr of the 3rd century. O'Connell's heart rests in her church at Rome. Lat. Agatha.

ⱯȝnⱯ, g. id., Ina; the name of two Irish saints; probably an Irish form of Agnes (v. Ɐ1ȝné1r).

Ɐ1Ⱡ1ⱡín, g. id., Aileen, Eveleen, Evelyn; a var. of e1Ⱡín, q.v.

Ɐ1ⱤⱤ1ⱺ, g. -1ce, Afric, Africa, Aphria; the name of two abbesses of Kildare, one of whom died in 738 and the other in 833; also in use in Scotland and the Isle of Man. It was a lady of this name, Africa, daughter of Godred, King of Man, and wife of John de Courcy, that founded the Cistercian Abbey, known as the Grey Abbey, in the Ards of Co. Down. Now very rare. Lat. Affrica, Africa.

Ɐ1ȝné1s, g. id., Agnes; Gr. Ἀγνη (Agné), sacred, pure; the name of a Roman virgin, martyred in 304; introduced into Ireland by the Anglo-Normans. Lat. Agnes, -etis.

Ɐ1ⱡⱠe, g. id., Alvy, Elva; also written O1ⱡⱠe; formerly common as a woman's name in Ireland. Lat. Albea.

Ɐ1ⱡ1ⱺ, g. id., Alley; a pet form of Ɐ1ⱡír, q.v.

Ailis, Ailís, Ailíse, Ailse, g. id., Alicia, Alice, Aylice, Elsha; a pet form of Adelaide (Teut. Adalheid, noble rank); a name introduced by the Anglo-Normans. Lat. Alicia.

Aimilíona, g. id., Amelina; a Nor. dim. of Æmilia (v. eimile); a name introduced by the Anglo-Normans. Lat. Æmiliana.

Áine, g. id., Anne, Anna; an ancient Irish name; still common, but now merged in the Hebrew Anna, q.v.

Aingeal, g. id., Angela; Lat. Angela, angel.

Aisling, Aislinn, g. -e, (Esther); an Irish name, meaning 'a dreamh'; in use in Derry and Omeath.

Aitce, g. id., Atty; the name of a holy virgin, patroness cf Cill Aitce in the barony of Kenry, Co. Limerick, where her feast-day (Jan. 15) was formerly kept as a holiday and a station held.

Alaid, g. id., Alley; a pet form of Ailír, q.v.

Alastríona, g. id., Alastrina, Alexandra; the fem. form of Alartar, q.v. Lat. Alexandra.

Allsún, g. id., Allison; dim. of Ailír, q.v.; in use down to recent times.

Anna, Anna, g. id., Anna, Anne; Heb. Hannáh, grace; a Biblical name, borne by the mother of Samuel, the wife of Tobias, and the mother of the Blessed Virgin Mary. It is to the last of these that the name owes its popularity. Very common in Ireland; confused with the native name Áine, q.v. Lat. Anna.

Annábla, g. id., Annabel, Annabella, Arabella, Bella; a name of uncertain origin; introduced into Ireland by the Anglo-Normans, but never became popular. Lat. Annabella.

Annstás, g. id., Anastasia; Gr. Ἀναστάσια (Anastasia), from ἀνάστασις (anástasis), resurrection; a name given by the early Christians to newly baptised, to signify that they had arisen to a new life; introduced into Ireland by the Anglo-Normans. Lat. Anastasia.

Aodnait, g. id. -ata and -atan, Enat, Ena, Eny; fem. dim. of Aod (q.v.), corresponding to the masc. Aodán (q.v.);

the name of an Irish saint whose feast was kept on 9 November. Lat. Aidnata.

ᴀᴏɪʙᴇᴀɴɴ, g. -ʙne, Eavan ; Old Ir. Aibfinn, Aebfind, fair form ; an ancient Irish name, borne by the mother of St. Enda. Lat. Aibfinnia.

ᴀᴏɪꝼᴇ, g. id., Eva ; an ancient Irish name. Lat. Eva.

ᴀᴄʀᴀᴄᴛ, g. id. and -ᴀ, Attracta ; the name of an Irish virgin saint, of Ulster origin, who flourished in the 6th century and founded the nunnery of Killaraght, near Lough Gara, Co. Sligo, where her memory is revered on 11 August. Lat. Attracta.

ʙᴀʙ, Babe ; a pet name.

ʙᴀɪʙín, g. id., Barbara, Barbary, Bab ; a pet dim. of ʙᴀɪʀʙʀe, q.v. ; common in West Galway.

ʙáɪʀʙʀᴇ, ʙᴀɪʀʙʀᴇ, g. id., Barbara, Barbary ; Gr. βάρβαρή (Bárbaré), stranger ; a name in use among the ancient Romans ; borne by a holy virgin and martyr of Nicodemia in the 3rd century, who became the patroness of architects and engineers ; common in Connacht. Lat. Barbara.

ʙᴇᴀɴ ṁuṁᴀɴ, Benvon ; an Irish name, meaning 'Lady of Munster' ; in use down to the beginning of the 17th century.

ʙᴇᴀɴ ṁɪʙᴇ, Benvy ; an Irish name, meaning 'Lady of Meath' ; in use down to the beginning of the 17th century.

ʙéʙɪɴɴ, g. -ʙɪnne, Bevin, (Vivian) ; an ancient Irish name, meaning 'melodious lady' ; borne by, among others, the mother and a daughter of Brian Boru.

ʙlᴀᴄ, g. -áɪᴄe, Flora ; an ancient Irish name, meaning 'blossom,' or 'flower-bud' ; borne by two virgin saints. Lat. Flora.

ʙlᴀᴄnᴀɪᴅ, g. id., Florence ; dim. of ʙlᴀᴄ, q.v. ; an ancient Irish personal name. Lat. Florentia.

ʙlɪnne, g. id., Blanche ; a corruption of ṁonɪnne ; the name of an Irish virgin, patroness of Killevy, Co. Armagh, whose feast-day is 6 July ; still in use, angl. Blanche. Lat. Moninna.

bluinse, g. id., Blanche; perhaps a corruption of blinne, q.v.

bRigoe, v. bṟíġıo.

bRigoín, g. id., Bridie, Breeda, Bidina, Bidelia, Dina, Delia, Dillie, Beesy, &c.; dim. of bṟíġıo, q.v.

bRigio, g. -goe, Brigid, Bride, Breeda (Bridget); an ancient Irish name, probably derived from bṟíġ, strength; the name of the goddess of poetry in pagan Ireland; sanctified and made for ever illustrious by St. Brigid of Kildare, patroness of Ireland. It does not appear to have come into common use as a woman's name until the 17th or 18th century. In the spoken language, the gen. case, bṟíġoe, is sometimes used for the nominative. The frequent angl. form Bridget is due to the resemblance of the Irish name to that of the celebrated Swedish widow, St. Bridget. Lat. Brigida.

Cáıṫ, g. id., Kate; a pet form of Catherine (v. Caıṫṟín); very common.

Cáıṫı, g. id., Katty; a pet form of Caıṫṟín, q.v.

Cáꞏṫılín, g. id., Kathleen, Catherine; a var. of Caıṫṟín, q.v. Cf. Spanish Catalina and Hungarian Katalin.

Cáıṫín, g. id., Katie, Katty; dim. of Cáıṫ, q.v.

Cáıṫlín, g. id., Kathleen, Catherine; a var. of Caıṫılín, q.v.

Cáıṫṟín, Cáıṫṟíona, g. id., Catherine; Gr. Καθαρινή (Kathariné), from καθαρός (katharos), pure; the name of a celebrated virgin and martyr of Alexandria, brought into Europe by the crusaders; but the popularity of the name is mainly due to St. Catherine of Sienna. Lat. Catharina.

Caoılṟıonn, g. -ṟınne, Keelin; comp. of caol, slender, and ṟıonn, fair; the name of an Irish virgin saint who was venerated on 3rd February. Lat. Coelfinnia.

Caoıṁe, g. id., Keavy; an Irish name, signifying 'gentleness,' 'beauty,' 'grace,' 'courtesy'; borne by a Scoto-Irish saint whose feast-day is 2 November. Lat. Pulcheria.

Cazraoine, g. id., Catherine ; a var. of Caizpín, q.v.

Ciannaiz, g. id. -aza and -azan, Kinnat, Keenat ; fem. dim.
of Cian (ancient), corresponding to the masc. Cianán,
q.v. ; the name of an Irish virgin saint, commemorated
on 23 March. Lat. Ciannata.

Criszín, Crisziona, g. id., Christina ; Lat. Christina,
deriv. of Christus, a Christian ; the name of a Roman
virgin who was martyred at Bolsena in 295 ; brought
into Scotland by Queen Margaret, and into Ireland
by the Anglo-Normans.

Damnaiz, g. id., -aza, -azan, Devnet, Downet, Dymphna ;
fem. dim. of Dam, a poet, corresponding to the masc.
Damán ; the name of a celebrated Irish virgin who
was martyred at Gheel in Belgium. She is patroness
of Gheel where her feast is kept on 15th May. Lat.
Dymphna.

Dearbáil g. *-áile, Derval, Dervilia ; comp. of deapb,
true, and áil, desire ; an ancient Irish name. Lat.
Dervilia.

Doireann, g. -pinne, Dorren, (Dorothy, Dolly) ; an
ancient Irish name, meaning 'the sullen.' Lat.
Dorinnia.

Eadaoin, g. -ine, Edwina ; the name of a holy virgin
of Moylurg (Boyle), Co. Roscommon, whose festival-
day was 5 July. Lat. Edwina.

Earnaiz, g. id. -aza and -azan, Ernet, fem. dim. of eapna,
knowing, corresponding to the masc. eapnán, q.v.
Lat. Ernata.

Eibilín, Eiblín, g. id., Eileen, Eveleen, Evelyn, Aileen,
Ellen, Helen, Ellie, Eily, Nellie, Nell, Lena ; Gr.
Ἑλένη (Elené), from ἐλη (elé), sunlight ; the name
of the mother of Constantine ; introduced into Ireland
by the Anglo-Normans. Lat. Helena.

Eileanóir, Eileanóir, Eilíonóra, g. id., Eleanor,
Eleanora ; supposed by some to be a distinct name,
but really only a Provençal form of Helena (v. Eiblín) ;
introduced into Ireland by the Anglo-Normans.

eıƚís, eıƚíse, g. id. Elizabeth, Eliza, Elsie, Lizzie,
Bessie, Betsey, Betty, (Alicia, Alice, Aylice) ; Heb.
Eliscéba', from 'el, God, and scéba', an oath, meaning
' God hath sworn,' or ' God is an oath ' ; the name of
the wife of Zachary and mother of John the Baptist,
and of many other holy women ; Isabella was the
form under which it first came into Ireland, where
it is very common. Lat. Elisabetha.

eımíƚe, g. id., Emily ; Lat. Æmilia, the fem. form of
Æmilius, the cognomen of one of the most ancient of
the patrician gentes of Rome, and the name of several
early martyrs.

eıs⁀cır, g. id., Esther ; Heb. 'Estér, of Persian origin ;
the name of the Hebrew lady who was wife of Assuerus,
King of Persia ; popularised in France by Racine ;
in Ireland, given to children born about Easter. Lat.
Esther.

eı⁀cne, g. id., Eithne, Ethna, Etney, (Annie) ; an Irish
personal name, meaning ' a kernel ' ; borne by three
virgin saints. Lat. Ethnea.

ꝼaınċe, g. id., Fanny ; the name of two saintly Irish
virgins, one the sister of St. Enda of Aran and
patroness of Rossory, on Lough Erne, whose feast
was kept on 1 January ; and the other patroness of
Cluain-caoi, in the neighbourhood of Cashel, who was
venerated on 21 of same month. Lat. Fanchea.

ꝼaoıƚ⁀cıᵹearna, g. id., Whiltierna ; comp. of ꝼaoƚ,
wolf, and ⁀cıᵹeaꝛna, lady ; the name of an Irish virgin
saint whose feast-day was 17 March. Lat. Fail-
tigerna.

ꝼıaᵭnaı⁀c, g. id. -a⁀ca, and -a⁀can, Feenat, Feena ; fem. dim.
of ꝼıaᵭ, a deer ; the name of a saintly Irish virgin
whose festival was celebrated on 4 January. Lat.
Fiadnata.

ꝼıonnᵹuaƚa, g. id., Finola, Nuala, (Flora, Penelope,
Penny, Nappy) ; comp. of ꝼıonn, fair, and ᵹuaƚa, a
shoulder ; an ancient Irish name, common down to
the end of the 17th century and still in use, but often

shortened to ⁊uaⱡa (q.v.) and generally disguised under the angl. form of Penelope. Lat. **Finguala**, Finola.

ᵹobnaiⱅ, g. id., -aⱅa and -aⱅan, Gobinet, Gobnet, Gubby, (Abigail, Abbey, Abbie, Abina, Deborah, Debby, Webbie) ; fem. dim. of ᵹob, a mouth, corresponding to the masc. ᵹobán ; the name of a celebrated Munster virgin, the patroness of Ballyvourney, whose feast is kept on 11 February ; still common in Cork, Kerry and Limerick, but generally angl. Abbey and Debby. Lat. Gobnata.

ᵹoRmⱉlaiⱅ, g. -aⱅa, Gormlaith, Gormley, (Barbara, Barbary) ; comp. of ᵹoⱃm, blue, and ⱉlaiⱅ, lady ; still in use, but rare. Lat. Gormlata.

ᵹRáinne, g. id., (Grace, Gertrude, Gertie) : an ancient Irish name, still in use. Lat. Grania.

ⱨilⱅe, g. id., Hilda, Hildy ; the name of a saintly Irish abbess, who was venerated on 18 November. Lat. Hilda.

íⱅe, g. id., Ida, Ita ; Old Ir. Itu, thirst ; the name of the celebrated Abbess of Kileedy, in West Limerick, whose feast is kept with great solemnity on 15 January. Lat. Ita.

iseabaⱡ, v. iⱃibéaⱡ.

isibéaⱡ, g. id., Isabella, Sybil, Sibby, Elizabeth, Eliza, Bessie, (Annabel, Annabella, Bella) ; the French form of Elizabeth (v. aiⱡíⱃ) ; apparently the form in which the name first came into Ireland ; still in use, but rare ; also Sibéaⱡ.

labaoise, g. id., Louisa ; the fem. form of alabaoiⱃ, q.v. Lat. Aloysia, Ludovica.

lasaiRⱉíona, g. id., Lassarina ; comp. of laⱃaiⱃ, a flame, and ⱉíona, of wine ; an ancient Irish name, still in use in parts of Connacht. Lat. Lassarina.

léan, g. id., Eleanor, Eleanora ; a pet form of eiléanóiⱃ, q.v.

Lıl, Lᵢle, g. id., Lily, Lelia.   Lat. Lelia.

Luıᵹseᴀċ, g. -ᵱıᵹe, Lucy ; the fem. form of Luᵹᴀıᴅ, q.v. ; the name of an Irish virgin saint who was venerated on 22 May.   Lat. Lugsecha.

Mᴀᴅᴀ, g. id., Maud ; a contraction of Matilda (v. Mᴀıᴄılᴅe).

Mᴀᴅᴀıléın, g. id., Madeline ; a name assumed in honour of St. Mary Magdalen.   Lat. Magdalena.

Mᴀıble, g. id., Mabel ; a shortened form of Amabel, from Lat. Amabilis, loveable.

Mᴀıᵹᴅlín, g. id., Madeline.   V. Mᴀᴅᴀıléın.

Mᴀıᵹᵣéᴀᴅ, g. id., Margaret, Maggie, Madge.   V. Mᴀıᵱᵹᵱéᴀᴅ.

Mᴀılle, Mᴀılse, Mᴀılᴄı, g. id., Molly, (Margery, Marjory) ; pet form of Mᴀıᵱe, q.v.

Mᴀıᵣe, g. id., Mary, Moira, Maria.   V. Muıᵱe.

Mᴀıᵣéᴀᴅ, Mᴀıᵣéᴀᴅ, v. Mᴀıᵱᵹᵱéᴀᴅ.

Mᴀıᵣᵹᵣéᴀᴅ, Mᴀıᵣᵹᵣéᴀᴅ, g. id., Margaret, Maggie, Madge ; Gr. Μαργαρίτης (Margarítés), a pearl ; the name of a Christian virgin who was martyred at Antioch in the last general persecution ; brought to Europe by the crusaders, when it became very common in France and England ; introduced by the Anglo-Normans into Ireland, where it has ever since been very popular, and is now found under a great variety of forms.   Lat. Margarita.

Mᴀıᵣín, g. id., Maureen, May, Molly ; a dim. of Mᴀıᵱe, q.v.

Mᴀıᵣsıl, Mᴀıᵣsıle, g. id., Marcella ; Lat. Marcella, a fem. dim. of Marcus (v. Mᴀᵱcuᵱ) ; the name of a saintly Roman widow ; common in France, whence apparently it came into Ireland.

Mᴀıᴄı, g. id., Matty ; a pet form of Mᴀıᴄılᴅe, q.v.

Mᴀıᴄılᴅe, g. id., Matilda ; Ger. Mahthild, might-heroine ; the name of a royal German saint, the mother of the Emperor Otho I, a lady remarkable for her humility and patience ; formerly very common in France ; brought to England by the wife of William the Conqueror and into Ireland by the Anglo-Normans. The Flemings called the name Mahault, whence the Norman forms, Molde and Maud. Both Matilda and Maud were in use in England, but neither ever became common in Ireland. Lat. Mathildes, -is.

mᴀʟʟᴀɪ𐭃, g. id., Molly ; a pet form of **mᴀɪᴘe**, q.v.

muʀᴀoᴅ, v. **mᴀɪᴘᵹᴘéᴀᴅ**.

mᴀʀᴛᴀ, g. id., Martha ; a Biblical name of uncertain origin ; borne by the sister of Lazarus and Mary, and by an Abbess of Kildare, in the 8th century. Lat. Martha.

meᴀᴅᴅ, g. **meɪᴅᴅe**, **meᴀᴅᴅᴀ**, Meave, (Maud, Mabbina, Mabel, Margery, Marjory, Madge) ; the name of the celebrated Queen of Connacht in the first century ; also borne by an Irish saint who was venerated on 22 November. Lat. Meba.

meᴀʟʟᴀ, g. id., Mella ; the name of several holy women in ancient Ireland. Lat. Mella.

meᴀʀs, g. id., Mary ; a form of **mᴀɪᴘe**, q.v. ; in use in Kerry until recent times.

meɪᴅᴅín, g. id., Meaveen, (Mabbina) ; a dim. of **meᴀᴅᴅ**, q.v.

míᴅe, g. id., Meeda ; a var. of **íᴅe** (q.v.) by the prefixing of **mo**, my, as a term of endearment. Lat. Mita.

móɪʀín, g. id., Moreen ; dim. of **móᴘ**, q.v.

monᴄᴀ, g. id., Monica ; a name of unknown origin, borne by the mother of St. Augustine. Lat. Monica.

móʀ, g. **móɪᴘe**, More, (Martha, Mary, Agnes) ; an ancient and, until comparatively recent times, very common Irish name, signifying ' great ' ; still in use, but disguised under the angl. forms of Martha, Mary, or Agnes. Lat. *Mora.

muᴀᴅnᴀɪᴛ, g. id., -ᴀᴛᴀ and -ᴀᴛᴀn, Monat, Mona ; dim. of **muᴀᴅ**, noble ; the name of an Irish virgin saint, whose festival-day was 6 January. Lat. Muadnata.

muɪʀe, g. id., Mary ; Heb. Mrjám, which can be read Mirjám, or better Mariám, a name of difficult interpretation, as are all names which appear in a very contracted form and in which it is difficult to discover

the root-word from which they are derived. About
seventy different meanings are given to Mary, in great
part suggested by devotion to the Mother of God
rather than by solid critical sense. Historically and
grammatically examined, it seems very likely that it
is a Hebrew name signifying ' bitterness,' in the sense
of grief, sorrow, affliction, either in reference to the
pains of childbirth, or to the moral condition of the
mother and family, oppressed by some great mis-
fortune, or perhaps to the sad period of the Egyptian
bondage, to which the Israelites were subject at the
time of the birth of the first Mary, the sister of Moses.
It was afterwards the name of several Jewish women,
including the Blessed Virgin Mary, Mother of Jesus
Christ, but was very slow in creeping in to the Western
Church. It is only about the middle of the 12th
century that we find the first instances of its use in
Europe, whither apparently it had been brought by
the devotion of the crusaders. Even in Ireland,
there were few Marys until comparatively recent
times. I find only a few instances of the use of the
name before the 17th century. At present one-
fourth of the women of Ireland are named Mary.
The ordinary form of the name, however, is Máiꞃe,
muiꞃe being used exclusively for the Blessed Virgin
Mary, and, therefore, the most honoured of all names
of women. Lat. Maria.

muiꞃéaꝺ, muiꞃ᷾éaꝺ, v. Máiꞃᵹꞃéaꝺ.

muiꞃeann, muiꞃinn, g. -ꞃinne, Morrin, (Marion,
Madge) ; an ancient Irish name, meaning ' of the long
hair.' Lat. Murinnia.

muiꞃᵹeal, g. -ᵹile, Murel, Muriel ; comp. of muiꞃ,
sea, and ᵹeal, bright, meaning ' sea-bright,' or ' fair
one of the sea.' Lat. Murgela.

muꞃáiꝺ, v. Máiꞃᵹꞃéaꝺ.

muꞃainn, v. muiꞃeann, of which it is a variant.

nábla, náible, g. id., Annabel, Annabella, Nabla,
(Mabel), Bella ; a shortened form of annábla, q.v.

Ⅾáinseáⱷ, neáⱱs, g. id., Nancy, Nance, Nan, Anne;
popular variants of Ánná, q.v.

neiⱢⱢ, neiⱢⱢi, g. id., Nell, Nellie; pet forms of eiⱱⱢín, q.v.

nóinín, nóirín, Nonie, Daisey; pet form of nórá, q.v.

nórá, g. id., Nora, Norah, Honor, Honora, Honoria
Nonie, Nanno, (Hannah); a shortened form of Onórá.
q.v.

nuáⱢá, g. id., Nuala, (Nappy, Penelope, Penny); a shortened form of ſionnξuáⱢá, q.v.

oⱷárnáiⱬ, g. id., -áⱬá, and -áⱬán, Ornat, Orna; fem. dim.
of oⱷár, pale, olive-colour, corresponding to the masc.
oⱷrán, q.v.; the name of an Irish saint, venerated
on 13 November. Lat. Odarnata.

oiⱢⱷe g. id. Elva; (Olive); a var. of ÁiⱢⱷe q.v.

onórá g. id., Honor, Honora, Honoria, Nora, Norah,
(Hannah); Lat. Honoria, fem. dim. of Honorius,
honourable; a name introduced into Ireland by the
Anglo-Normans and still very popular under the
shortened form of nórá, q.v.

órſⱢáiⱬ, g. -áⱬá, Orlaith; an old Irish name, meaning
'the golden lady.' Lat. Orlata.

páiⱢi, páiⱢs, páⱢ, Poll, Polly; var. of máⱢⱢáiⱷ, q.v.

peiξ, peiξi, g. id., Peg, Peggy; rhymed var. of Meg
and Meggy, for Margaret (v. máirξréáⱷ).

proinnséás, próinséás, g. id., Frances, Fanny;
Lat. Francisca, fem. form of Franciscus, or Francis;
a name adopted in honour of St. Francis of Assisi
and borne by a saintly Roman widow, whose feast-
day is 9 March.

ráⱬnáiⱬ, g. id., -áⱬá and -áⱬán, Renny; fem. dim. of ráⱬ,
grace, or prosperity; the name of an Irish saint who is
patroness of Kilrenny, Co. Kildare. Lat. Ratnata.

riceáⱢ, g. -ciⱢe, Richella; the name of a virgin saint
whose feast-day was 19 May. Lat. Richella.

ríoξnác, g. -áiξe, Regina; the name of a saintly Irish
virgin, whose feast was kept on 18 December; she was
the sister of St. Finnian of Clonard. Lat. Regnacia.

róis, róise, g. id., Rose; Teut. Hros, a horse, Nor.

Rohais, Roese, Roesia ; a name introduced, no doubt, by the Anglo-Normans and borne by a lady of the Maguires in the early part of the 16th century. The name of St. Rose of Lima is derived from the Latin rosa, a rose. She was first named Isabella, but was afterwards called Rose from the rose-like appearance of her face in childhood. Róiṗ was, however, a woman's name in Ireland long before the birth of St. Rose. Lat. Rosa.

Róisín, g. id., Rose, Rosie ; a dim. of Róiṗ, q.v.

Saḃa, g. id., Sive, (Sally) ; a var. in West Connacht of Saḋḃ, q.v.

Saḋḃ, g. id., and Saiḋḃe, Sive, (Sabia, Sophia, Sophy, Sarah, Sally) ; an ancient Irish name, meaning ' goodness ' ; still in use, but generally angl. Sally. Lat. Sabia.

Saḋḃa, g. id., Sive, (Sophia, Sophy) ; a var. of Saḋḃ, q.v. ; in use in Donegal and Derry.

Saiḋḃín, g. id., Sabina ; dim. of Saḋḃ, q.v. Lat. Sabina.

Séarlait, g. id., Charlotte ; fem. dim. of Charles ; a name of comparatively recent formation. Lat. Carlotta.

Seósaiṁtín, g. id., Josephine ; fem. dim. of Joseph (v. Ióṗep) ; a name of comparatively recent formation ; borrowed from the French. Lat. Josephina.

Siḃéal, v. Iṗiḃéal.

Siḃi, Sioḃaiġ, g. id., Sibby ; pet forms of Siḃéal or Iṗiḃéal, q.v.

Síle, g. id., Cecelia, Cecily, Celia, Selia, Sheila, Sheela, (Sabina, Sibby, Sally, Julia, July, Judith, Judy, Jude) ; Lat. Caecilia, dim. of caeca, blind ; the name of a celebrated Roman virgin and martyr, the patroness of musicians ; introduced by the Anglo-Normans and ever since common in Ireland, but generally wrongly angl. Julia, &c.

Sine, g. id., Jane, Jannet, Jenny ; a var. of Sinéaḋ, q. v.; in use in Co. Derry.

ѕıпéᴀ'ᴏ, g. id., Jane, Jannet, Jenny; a dim. of Fr.
Jeanne, from Johanna (v. Sıoḃán).
ѕıпeᴀıᴏ, g. id., Jane, Jannet, Jenny; a var. of Sınéᴀᴏ,
q.v.; in use in Co. Derry.
ѕıoḃáınín, g. id., Hannah, (Josephine); a dim of
Sıoḃán, q.v.
ѕıoḃán, g. id., Joan, Johanna, Hannah, (Julia, July,
Judith, Judy, Jude, Susanna, Susan, Nonie); the
fem. form of Joannes, or John (v. eóın and Seán), which
became common in France in the 12th century
as Jehanne and Jeanne, and in England as Joan;
brought into Ireland by the Anglo-Normans, where
it has ever since been one of the most popular of
women's names. Lat. Joanna.
ѕıѕıĺe, g. id., Cecilia, Cecily; a late form of Sıĺe, q.v.
ѕıuḃáınín, a var. of Sıoḃáınín, q.v.
ѕıuḃán, a var. of Sıoḃán, q.v.
ѕıúı, a pet form of Súrᴀnnᴀ, q.v.
ѕĺáıne, g. id., Slany; an old Irish name, meaning
'health'; common among the O'Briens. Lat. Slania.
ѕorċᴀ, g. id., Sorcha, (Sarah, Sally); an old Irish name,
signifying 'clear' or 'bright'; still in use, but now
always angl. Sarah or Sally. Lat. Sorcha.
ѕóѕᴀıᴏ, g. id., Susie; a pet form of Sórᴀnnᴀ or Súrᴀnnᴀ,
q.v.
ѕóѕᴀnnᴀ, g. id., Susanna, Susan; a var. of Súrᴀnnᴀ, q.v.
ѕcéıѕe, a pet form of ᴀnnrcár, q.v.
ѕúѕᴀnnᴀ, g. id., Susanna, Susan; Gr. Σ ουσανα
(Sousana); the name of a Hebrew maiden who, on
being falsely accused of adultery, was condemned to
death, but saved by Daniel who showed that her
accusers were calumniators; introduced into Ireland
by the Anglo-Normans. Lat. Susanna.

cıĺᴏe, g. id., Tilda; a shortened form of mᴀıcıĺᴏe, q.v.
coıréᴀѕᴀ, g. id., Teresa, Tessie; a name of uncertain
origin; peculiar to Spain until the 16th century,
when the fame of St. Teresa made it world-wide. Lat.
Teresia.

ᴄᴿᴀoɪne, ᴄᴿíoᴎᴀ, g. id., Trina, Katie, Katty; pet
forms of Cᴀᴄᴘᴀoɪne or Cᴀɪᴄᴘíoᴎᴀ, q.v.

ᴄᴿeᴀsᴀ, ᴄᴿeɪse, g. id.,; an old Irish name, meaning
'strength'; adopted as the Irish equivalent of Teresa
(v. ᴄoɪᴘéᴀᴘᴀ).

úᴎᴀ, g. id., Una, Uny, (Unity, Winifred, Winefred,
Winnie, Winny, Agnes); an ancient and once common
Irish name; still in use, but generally angl. Winifred.
Lat. Una.

uᴿsuʟᴀ, g. id., Ursula; Lat. Ursula, little bear; the
name of a Breton maiden who was martyred by the
Huns at Cologne in the 5th century.

SURNAMES

IRISH—ENGLISH

---

a Barra, Barry. V. de Barra.

Abbóid—VIII—*Abbod*, Abbott; 'son of Abbot' (dim. of Abraham); an old Anglo-Irish surname, found at least as early as the beginning of the 14th century.

a Blác, Blake. V. de Blaca.

a Blóid—VI—Blood; Welsh 'ab-Lloyd,' i.e., 'son of Lloyd'; a Clare surname. Cf. Flóid and Lóid.

Ábraham—VIII—Abraham; 'son of Abraham.' This surname in Ireland dates back to the early part of the 13th century.

a Briús, Bruce. V. de Briús.

a Ḃula, Wooley. V. de Ḃulḃ.

a Búrc, Burke, Bourke. V. de Búrca.

Acaod, Hackett. V. Hacaed, Haicéid.

a Cligeóir, Killiger.

a' Ċnuic—XIII—Hill; Ir. 'an Ċnuic,' i.e., of the hill, from residence thereon.

a Colbard, *Acollobert*, Colbert. V. Colbárd.

a' Dúna—XIII—Doona; Ir. 'an Dúna,' i.e., of the dun or fort, from residence in or thereby; a rare surname, found in parts of Kerry.

a Fae, *Aphaye, Affay, Faie*, Fay. V. de Fae.

a Fréin, Freyne, Frein, etc. V. de Fréin.

Ágas—XI—*Aase, Asshe*, Ashe; Mid. Eng. 'atte Asse,' 'atte Ashe,' corrupted to 'de Ass,' 'de Asse,' i.e., at the ash, from residence beside an ash-tree. This form of the surname is common in Kerry and parts of Limerick. V. Ais, de Nais, and de Nás.

ᴀ' ᵹⅼeᴀɴɴᴀ—XIII—Glanny, Glenny, Glenn; Ir. 'ᴀɴ
ᵹⅼeᴀɴɴᴀ,' i.e., of the glen, from residence therein.

ᴀ' ᵹⅼeᴀɴɴᴄᴀ́ɪɴ—XIII—Glanton; Ir. 'ᴀɴ ᵹⅼeᴀɴɴᴄᴀ́ɪɴ,'
i.e., of the little glen, from residence therein.

ᴀ ɴóʀᴀ, Hore, Hoare. V. ᴅe ɴóʀᴀ.

ᴀɪᴄéɪᴅ, Hackett. V. ɴᴀɪᴄéɪᴅ.

ᴀɪᴅⅼeᴀʀᴄ—VIII—*Athelard, Adelard, Ayllard, Eylard,*
Ellard; 'son of Adelard' (a Frankish personal name,
also written Adelhard and Athelard, the same as the
Anglo-Saxon Æthelheard); an old Anglo-Irish surname,
dating back at least to the middle of the 13th century.
In the time of Edward I, Robert Athelard of Athel-
ardestoun, Co. Louth, was tenant-in-capite of the king.

ᴀɪᵹⅼeᴀʀᴄ—VIII—*Aylwert, Eylward, Ayleward,* Ailward,
Aylward, Alyward, etc.; 'son of Ailward' (Anglo-
Saxon Æthelweard); the name of an Anglo-Norman
family who came into Ireland at the time of the
invasion and settled at Aylwardstown, Co. Kilkenny,
and at Faithleg, near Waterford. The Aylwards
were frequently mayors of Waterford. Their castle
at Faithleg was besieged and taken by Cromwell in
1649.

ᴀɪᵹⅼmeᴀʀ—VIII—*Ailmar, Eilmer,* Aylmer, Elmer, etc.;
'son of Ailmar' (Anglo-Saxon Æthelmaer); the name
of a distinguished Anglo-Irish family who settled in
the 13th century in Dublin, Meath and Kildare. In
the wars of the 16th century, the Aylmers adhered to
the Stuart cause, and many of them were in consequence attainted and lost their property.

ᴀɪⅼéɪɴ—VIII—*Aleyne, Alleyne, Allaine,* Allan, Allen,
etc.; 'son of Alan' (a Breton personal name introduced by the Normans). Families of this name came
into Ireland at the time of the invasion and settled
in Dublin, Kildare, and other parts of Leinster.

ᴀɪⅼíɴ—VIII—*Alwine, Allyne,* Allin, Allen, etc.; 'son of
Ailwin' (Anglo-Saxon Æthelwine); the name of an
English family who settled in Ireland at or soon after
the invasion. It can hardly be now distinguished
from ᴀɪⅼéɪɴ, q.v.

ᴀɪɴ'ᴅʀɪú—VIII—*Andreu, Andrewe*, Andrew, Andrews ; ' son of Andrew.'

ᴀɪɴᵹʟᴇᴀɴ'ᴅ, Angland, Ankland, England. V. ᴀɪɴᵹʟᴇᴏɴᴄ.

ᴀɪɴᵹʟᴇɪꜱ—XII—*Ainglishe*, English, Englishe ; Nor. ' l'Engleys,' i.e., the Englishman ; a descriptive surname evidently applied by Norman-French settlers to their English comrades ; common in many parts of Ireland, but especially in Tipperary where there are still some old and respectable families of the name. Also ɪɴᵹʟᴇɪꜱ, q.v.

ᴀɪɴᵹʟᴇᴏɴᴄ—XI—*Angylont, Anglant, Englant, Anglound*, Angland, Ankland, England ; Nor. ' de Englond,' Lat. ' de Anglia,' i.e. from England. This surname, strange to say, is very rare. The few families who bear it are located chiefly in Limerick and Cork. Cf. ᴀɪɴᵹʟᴇɪꜱ above.

ᴀɪʀɪᵹ—XI—Airey ; i.e., ' of Airey ' in Cumberland.

ᴀɪʀᴍᴇᴀꜱ—XI—Ormsby ; i.e., ' of Ormsby ' in England ; a late English surname.

ᴀɪʀꜱᴇᴀᴃᴏɪ'ᴅ—VIII—*Archebaud, Archibaud*, Archabold, Archibold, Archbold, etc. ; ' son of Arcenbald' or ' Eorconbeald ' (a Teutonic personal name). This family settled in Ireland at an early period and obtained extensive possessions in Dublin, Wicklow and Kildare. Even as early as 1315, they were in alliance with the O'Byrnes and O'Tooles. They were prominent in the wars of the 17th century, and in 1641 and 1691, several of the name in Dublin, Kildare and Wicklow were indicted of treason and attainted. The name was early corrupted to Ashpole, Ashpool, etc.

ᴀɪʀꜱᴇɪʟ, Archfield.

ᴀɪʀꜱᴇɪʀ—XII—Archer, Orchard ; Nor. ' le Archer,' i.e., the archer or professional bowman ; the name of an Anglo-Norman family who came into Ireland at the time of the invasion and settled in Kilkenny, where they became wealthy and influential. To this family belonged the celebrated Irish Jesuit, Father James Archer.

ᏗꞮꞂꙄꞮꝹᎬᏗᏞ—VIII—Archibald; the same origin as ᏗꞯꞁᏒᎬᏗꝹᏅꝹ, q.v.; the name of a Scottish family who settled in the north of Ireland.

ᏗꞮꞂꙄꝹᎬꞮᏟꞮꞃ—XII—*Arstekin, Archedekyn,* Archdeacon; Nor. ' le Erchedekine,' ' le Ercedekne,' ' le Ercedecne,' i.e., the archdeacon; the name of an Anglo-Norman family who settled soon after the invasion in Co. Kilkenny. They were descended from Odo le Ercedekne, from whom, when they became Irish, they took the surname of ᏔᏗᏟᎤꝹᏗ (q.v.), now angl. Cody and Coady. At the beginning of the 17th century, the name was also found in Wexford, Waterford and Cork.

ᏗꞮꙄ—XI—*Aysh, Ayshe, Asshe,* Ashe; Mid. Eng., ' atte Ashe,' i.e., at the ash, from residence beside an ash-tree. Families of this name settled soon after the invasion in Meath and Kildare. The following were indicted of treason in the King's Bench and outlawed in 1641 : Thomas Aysh, of Naas, gentleman ; Henry Aysh, of same, gentleman ; and Walter Aysh, of same, merchant. V. ᏗᵹᏗꞃ and ꝹᎬ ꞃᏗꞮꞃ.

ᏗꞮꙄᎬᏗꝹᏅꝹ, *Ashbould, Ayshpool, Asbold, Aspoll,* Aspel, Esbald, etc. ; a corruption of ᏗꞯꞁᏒᎬᏗꝹꝹ, q.v.

ᏗꞮꙄᎬꞮꞂ, Archer ; a corruption of ᏗꞯꞁᏒᎬꞮꞁ, q.v.

ᏗꞮꙄᏞꞮꞃꞃ, Ashlin.

ᏗꞮꙄᏟᎬꞮᏟꞮꞃ, *Astekine, Asteken,* Archdeacon ; a corruption of ᏗꞯꞁꞃꝹᎬꞮᏟꞮꞃ, q.v.

ᏗᏞᏗᏔᎧꞃ—XI—*Aleman,* Allman ; Nor. ' de Alemayne,' i.e., from Alemaigne, or Germany ; an old but rare surname in Ireland. It still survives in Kerry.

ᏗᏞᎧꞂꝹ, Ellard. V. ᏗꞮꝹᏞᎬᏗꞃꞇ.

ᏗᏞᏰᏗꞃᏗᏟ—X—*Albanagh,* Scott; Ir. ' ᏗᏞᏰᏗꞃᏗᏟ,' i.e.' the Scot, native of Scotland ; a generic name for the Scottish galloglasses, especially the MacDonnells, who came over to Ireland in the 14th, 15th and 16th centuries.

ᏗᏞᏟᎧᏟ—VIII—*Alekoc, Alcoc,* Alcock ; ' son of Alcoke ' (a dim. of Alan).

Ꮧ ᏞꞮꞃꙄᎬ, Lynch. V. ꝹᎬ ᏞꞮꞃꞃᎬ.

ᴀʟsᴀnᴅᴀıʀ—VIII—*Alesaundre, Alisander, Elysandyr,* Elshander, Alexander, etc. ; ' son of Alexander.' This surname is of early record in Ireland, but like many others of the same class, it doubtless came in at different periods. It is now found chiefly in Ulster.

ᴀʟᴛún—XI—*Altoun,* Alton ; Nor. ' de Alleton,' 'de Alton,' i.e., of Alton, the name of more than one place in England ; an old Anglo-Irish surname.

ᴀmᴅᴙós, ᴀmᴙós, ᴀmᴙus—VIII—*Ameros,* Ambrose ; ' son of Ambrose ' ; a not uncommon surname in Limerick and Cork. In Ireland it dates back at least to the end of the 13th century. In 1601, William Ambrose of Annagh obtained a grant of pardon from Queen Elizabeth.

ᴀnᴄoıᴄıʟ—VIII—*Ankettill,* Anketell, Ankethill, etc. ; ' son of Ancytel,' a Teutonic personal name found in Domesday Book and early Dublin rolls.

ᴀnᴅᴙᴀosán—VIII—Anderson ; a phonetic rendering of the English surname Anderson.

ᴀn ᴅúnᴀ—XIII—Doona. V. ᴀ'ᴅúnᴀ.

ᴀn ᵹeımᴙıᴅ—XIII—Winters ; probably a translation of the English surname Winters.

ᴀn ᵹʟeᴀnnᴀ—XIII—Glanny, Glenny, Glenn. V. ᴀ'ᵹʟeᴀnnᴀ.

ᴀn ᵹʟeᴀnnᴄáın—XIII—Glanton. V. ᴀ'ᵹʟeᴀnnᴄáın.

ᴀn mᴀᴄᴀıᴙe—XIII—Maghery ; Ir. ' ᴀn mᴀᴄᴀıᴘe,' i.e., of the field, from residence in or thereby.

ᴀn muıʟınn—XIII—Mills ; Ir. " ᴀn mᴜıʟınn,' i.e., of the mill,' from residence in or thereby.

ᴀn ᴘᴙéıᴄ—XIII—'O'Pray, O'Prey, Pray, Prey. V. ᴀ' ᴘᴘéıᴄ.

ᴀnᴄóın, ᴀnᴄoıne—VIII—*Anton,* Antony, Anthony ; ' son of Antony.'

ᴀn ᴄseᴀᴄᴀ—XIII—Frost ; a translation of the English surname Frost. The Frosts are a well known family about Limerick.

ᴀn ᴄsıuᴅᴀıʟ—XIII—Walker ; Ir. ' ᴀn ᴄᴘıuᴅᴀıʟ,' i.e., the pedestrian, one given to walking ; but perhaps a translation of the English surname Walker, which however has a different meaning.

ᴀn ᴄsneᴀᴄᴛᴀ—XIII—Snow; Ir. 'ᴀn ᴄsneᴀᴄᴛᴀ,' i.e., of the snow, perhaps born in time of snow.

ᴀ pᴀol—VI—*Apowell*, Powell; 'son of Howel'; the name of a family of Welsh origin who settled in Ireland some time prior to the beginning of the 17th century.

ᴀ' pᴚéιᴛ—XIII—*A praye*, O'Pray, O'Prey, Pray, Prey; Ir. 'ᴀn pᴚéιᴛ,' i.e., of the cattle-spoil; a Co. Down surname.

ᴀ pᴚιoᴄᴀιᴚᴅ—VI—Prickard, Prichard; 'son of Richard'; a Welsh surname, long established in Ireland.

ᴀ pᴚís—VI—*Apprise, Apprice*, Pryse, Price, etc.; 'son of Rhys' (a well-known Welsh personal name). This surname, which is the same as the Welsh Ap-Rice or Ap-Rees, is long established in Ireland.

ᴀ pᴚιsᴄeᴀιᴚᴅ—VI—Pritchard; a variant of ᴀ pᴚιo-ᴄᴀιᴚᴅ, q.v.

ᴀᴚᴀlᴛ—VIII—Harald, Harold, Harrold; 'son of Harald'; the name of a family of Danish origin who settled early in Dublin and Wicklow. In 1315, they were in alliance with the O'Byrnes and O'Tooles, when they plundered the English of Wicklow. V. ᴀᴚóιᴅ and Ó hᴀᴚᴀιlᴛ.

ᴀᴚᴀsᴄᴀιn—XI—Erskine, Erksine; a well-known Scottish surname.

ᴀᴚᴅᴀᴄᴀ—XI—Ardagh; Nor. 'de Ardagh,' i.e., of Ardagh in Co. Longford; the name of an early Anglo-Norman family who settled at, and took its name from, Ardagh. It has always been very rare.

ᴀᴚmᴀs, Ormsby. V. ᴀιᴚmeᴀᴚ.

ᴀᴚnóιᴅ—VIII—*Arnolle, Arnoud*, Arnold, Arnott; 'son of Arnald,' a common Teutonic personal name.

ᴀᴚóιᴅ—VIII—*Arot, Arrot, Harrod*, Harrot, Harold, etc.; a var. of ᴀᴚᴀlᴛ, (q.v.), of which it is merely the Norman pronunciation.

ᴀᴚᴄûᴚ—VIII—*Arthour, Arthure*, Arthur, Arthurs; 'son

of Arthur.' The Arthurs settled in Ireland soon after the invasion, and were located in Dublin, Meath, Cork and Limerick. They were at one time an influential family in the City of Limerick.

Ⰰⱅⰰⱁⰻ—XI—Athy ; Nor. ' de Athi," de Athy,' i.e., of Athy in Co. Kildare : the name of an Anglo-Norman family who first settled at Athy. They removed at an early period to Galway, where tradition relates that one of them erected the first stone house or castle. The surname is now very rare.

Ⰰⱅⰰⱄⰰⱍ—XIV—Ashe. V. Ⰰⰷⰰⱃ.

ⰁⰰⰀ—XII—Babe ; Eng. ' the babe,' i.e., one of guileless disposition, corresponding to the Norman l'Enfant ; the name of an old Anglo-Norman family who settled at Ardee and other places in Co. Louth.

Ⰱⰰⱄⰰⰵⰻⱃ, Baker. V. Ⰱⰰⰻⱍⰵⰻⱃ.

Ⰱⰰⱍⱏⱀ—XII—*Bakun, Bacoun*, Bacon. V. ⰺⰵ Ⰱⰰⱍⱏⱀ.

Ⰱⰰⱁⱅⱏⱀ, Boyton. V. ⰺⰵ Ⰱⰰⱁⱅⱏⱀ.

Ⰱⰰⰷⱀⰰⰾ—XI—Bagnall, Bagnell, etc. ; i.e., ' of Bagnall,' in Staffordshire.

Ⰱⰰⰷⱁⰺⱁ—VIII—*Bagod, Bagote*, Bagot, Bagott, Baggot, Baggott ; ' son of Bagot ' (dim. of a common Anglo-Saxon personal name Baga, Bago, etc.). This family came into Ireland soon after the Anglo-Norman invasion and settled in Dublin, Meath, Kildare, Carlow and Limerick. In 1280, Robert Bagod, chief justiciary of Ireland, obtained a grant of the manor of Rath, near Dublin, since known as Bagot-rath, and of Bonevilstøne and Brownstown, in Co. Limerick, since known as Bagottstown. Maurice Baggot of Baggotstown was one of the twenty exempted from pardon by Ireton when he obtained possession of Limerick in 1651.

Ⰱⰰⰻⱍⰵⰻⱃ—XII—Baker ; Nor. ' le Bakere,' ' de Bakere,' i.e., the baker.

Ⰱⰰⱃⱁⱅⰻⱏⱀ. V. ⰺⰵ Ⰱⰰⱁⱅⱏⱀ.

Ⰱⰰⰻⰾⰻⱀⱄⰵⰻⱃ—XI or XII—*de Belynger*, Ballinger ; Nor. ' de Belynger,' i.e., of Bellinger, probably an English place-name ; or possibly Nor. ' le Bulenger,' i.e., the baker (Fr. boulanger).

ḃⱭıłınⱱⓘⓝ—XI—Ballentine ; a surname of Scottish origin.

ḃⱭıłınⱱⓘⓝ—VIII—Valentine ; ' son of Valentine.'

ḃⱭıłıſ, Wallace, Wallis, Walsh. V. ꝺe ḃⱭıłıꝛ.

ḃⱭıłıſⱱe—XII—*Baliste*, Ballesty ; Nor. ' balestier,' Lat. ' balistarius ' i.e., the cross-bowman ; an old, but rare, surname in Ireland. It occurs as ' Baliste ' in Gilbert's Municipal Documents.

ḃⱭıłłe—XII—Bailie, Bailey, Bayly ; Nor. ' le Baillif,' Eng. ' the Bailie,' i.e., the bailiff ; an old surname in Ireland.

ḃⱭıꞃéıꝺ—VIII—*Bared, Baret*, Barrett ; ' son of Baret.' Bared, Baret, Boret, Borret, and Borred occur in Domesday Book as names of persons holding land in the time of Edward the Confessor. The name is, therefore, most probably Anglo-Saxon and distinct from ḃⱭꝺóıꝺ, q.v. The Barretts settled in the 13th century in Tirawley, where they became numerous and powerful. In later times they formed a clan after the Irish fashion, the head of which was known as ⱮⱭc ḃⱭıⱱín ḃⱭıꝺéıꝺ ; and there were sub-clans known as CłⱭnn ⱱóıⱮín and CłⱭnn Ɐınꝺꞃıú.

ḃⱭıſéıꝺ—XII—*Basset*, Bassett ; O. Fr. ' basset,' i.e., the dwarf. In Ireland, this surname is as old at least as the beginning of the 13th century.

ḃⱭıſnéıꝺ—XII—*Basnede*, Basnet ; O. Fr. ' Bassinet,' a double dim. of Bass, low-sized. V. ḃⱭıꝺéıꝺ above. This family was located in Dublin and Wicklow. There is a Bosnetstown near Kilfinane, Co. Limerick.

ḃⱭł—VIII—Ball ; ' son of Ball,' (very probably a short form of Baldwin) ; the name of an old Anglo-Norman family in Dublin and Meath.

ḃⱭłḃ—IX—Balfe ; Ir. ' ḃⱭłḃ,' Lat. ' balbus,' i.e., the stammerer. Though the name is Irish, the family is of foreign origin. The Balfes came to Ireland at, or soon after, the Anglo-Norman invasion and settled in Dublin and Meath.

ḃáloᴜⁱⁿᵹ—VIII—Baldwin; 'son of Baldwin.' This form of the surname, which is found in Co. Cork, is apparently modern. V. ḃáloún.

ḃáloún—VIII—*Baldone*, Baldoon, Ballon, Baldin, Baldwin; 'son of Baldon' (a dim. of Baldwin). Families of this name settled soon after the Anglo-Norman invasion in Dublin, Wexford, Kilkenny, Waterford and Cork. The pronunciation is sometimes ḃállún or ḃallún. The town of Cobh stands in the townlond of Ballyvaloon, so called from Baldwin Hodnett, a member of the family who once owned the Great Island.

ḃalláṘo—XII—Ballard, Bollard; Mid. Eng. 'the ballard,' i.e., baldheaded; the name of an Anglo-Norman family who settled in Dublin and Meath soon after the invasion.

ḃán—IX—Baun, Bawn, Bane, Bayne, Baynes, and sometimes, by translation, White; Ir. 'bán,' i.e., fair, white; a descriptive epithet which supplanted the real surname.

ḃáꞃⱥⁱⁿ—XI—Warren, Warrin, and, in parts of Kerry, Walsh; Nor. 'de Warenne,' i.e., at the warren, or game-preserve, from residence thereby. This surname came into Ireland at the time of the Anglo-Norman invasion, and was not uncommon in Dublin, Meath, and other parts of Ireland. In East Kerry it has been strangely re-anglicised Walsh. Possibly the Warrens of that locality had two surnames; but at present they are called only by the one in Irish and the other in English. The adj. form is ḃaꞃⱥⁿⱦⱥċ (ḃ not aspirated).

ḃaꞃċaꞃ—XII—Barker; Nor. 'le Barker,' Eng. 'the barker,' i.e., one who stripped trees of bark for the tanner. This surname does not appear to be old in Ireland. The Barkers of Waterford were a Cromwellian family.

ḃáꞃóⁱo—VIII—Barrett; 'son of Baraud' (a Norman form of the Teutonic Berwald). Families of this name settled in Ireland at the time of the Anglo-Norman invasion. The Barretts were an influential family in Cork, and the name is still well known throughout Munster. Cf. ḃáiṗéiṫ.

ḃᴀᴚᴄún, Barton. V. ᴅe ḃᴀᴘᴄún.

ḃᴀᴚún—XII—*Baroun*, Baron, Barron ; Mid. Eng. ' barun,' i.e., the baron, either a real baron, or one who put on the airs of a baron. Robert Barun was a member of the Dublin Guild-Merchant in 1226. A branch of the Fitzgeralds who were barons of Burn-church, Co. Kilkenny, assumed the surname of Barron, and were a highly respectable family in Kilkenny, Tipperary and Waterford.

ḃáċ—XI—Bath, Baith, Bates, etc. V. ᴅe ḃáċ.

ḃeᴀᴣ—IX—Bueg, Begg, Begge, and sometimes, by translation, Little and Small ; Ir. ' ḃeᴀᴣ,' i.e., little, small ; a descriptive epithet which supplanted the real surname. Cf. ḃán. Note, however, that Bagge, Bege, and Beg occur frequently as English surnames in our early Anglo-Irish records.

ḃeᴀᴌᴀᴄún, Belton, Weldon, Veldon. V. ᴅe ḃeᴀᴌᴀᴄún.

ḃeᴀᴚnᴀḃáᴌ, Barnwell, etc. V. ᴅe ḃeᴀᴘnᴀḃáᴌ.

ḃeᴀᴚnᴀis, *Barnise*, *Barneis*, *Barnyshe*, Barnidge, Bearnes, Barnes.

ḃeᴀᴚnáᴚᴅ—VIII—Barnard, Bernard ; ' son of Bernard'; an old surname in Ireland, but always very rare.

ḃeᴀᴚᴄᴚᴀm—VIII—Bertram ; ' son of Bertram,' a Teutonic personal name.

ḃeᴀsᴌᴀiᴣ, ḃeᴀsᴌᴀoi—XI—Beazley, Beasley ; i.e., ' of Beazley,' or ' Beasley,' in England.

ḃeᴀsᴄún—XI—Baston, Beston ; probably ' of Beston,' or ' Baston,' in England, but I can find no instance earlier than the 16th century. The name was peculiar to Tipperary and Waterford where it still survives.

ḃeiᴌᴌe, ḃeiᴌᴌiú—XI—*Belewe*, Bellew ; Nor. *' de Belleau,' Lat. ' de Bella Aqua,' i.e., of Belleau (the fair water), in France ; the name of a family of Norman origin who came into Ireland about the time of the invasion and settled in Meath and Louth. For much

information about this ancient family, see D'Alton's
'King James' Irish Army List, 1689.'

beilleaʒam—XI—Bellingham; i.e., 'of Bellingham,'
in England. The founder of this family came to
Ireland in the 17th century and obtained a grant of
the estate now called Castle Bellingham, in Co. Louth.

beinéiꝺ—VIII—*Benet*, Bennett; 'son of Benet' (dim.
of Benedict), formerly one of the most popular names
in England. As a surname, Bennett came into
Ireland at different periods since the invasion, and
is now common in many parts of the country. Also
bionóiꝺ, q.v.

beiRʈ, Berth; a var. of ꝺe bꞃeiʈ, q.v.; cf. 'le Birt,' for
'le Brit'; in use in West Clare.

biaꝺʈaċ—XII—Betagh, Beatagh, Beatty, etc.; Ir.
'biaꝺʈaċ,' i.e., the hospitaller, public victualler.
This family is said to be of Danish descent, but in the
early Anglo-Irish records the Christian names are
Norman. They were seated in Moynalty, in Co.
Meath, from an early period, and possessed considerable property down to Cromwellian times when, by
fraud and perjury, Francis Betagh was stripped of
his estates. Branches of the family appear to have
settled in Mayo, Galway and Clare.

bibíne, Dobbin, Dobbins

biʒeaR, Biggar, Bigger; a surname of doubtful origin,
but probably 'of Biggar' in Scotland.

binéiꝺ, Bennett. V. beinéiꝺ.

binnse, Binchy.

bionʒam—XI—Bingham, Bigham; i.e., 'of Bingham,'
in Nottinghamshire.

bionóiꝺ, Bennett. V. beinéiꝺ, and cf. Fr. Benoit.

biséiꝺ—VIII—*Biset*, Bissett; 'son of Biset' (dim. of
an old Teutonic personal name Bis). The Bissetts
were an English family who settled at an early period
in Scotland. In 1242, John Bisset and Walter, his
uncle, were outlawed and fled to Ireland, where they
took refuge in the Glynns of Antrim and effected a
settlement under de Burgo, Earl of Ulster. From

this John the family in after times assumed the Irish patronymic surname of mac eóin. By marriage with an heiress of the Bissetts, the Glynns at a later period came into the possession of the MacDonnells.

blácac—XIV.—Blacagh, Blake. V. oe bláca.

blaoo—XII—*Bluet, Bloet, Blowet*, Bluett, Blewett, etc.; Nor. ' Bluet,' i.e., of blue complexion or dress. This family came into Ireland at the time of the Anglo-Norman invasion. Walter Bloet (circa 1174) was witness to a grant of land to Holy Trinity Church, Dublin. In the 16th century, the name was peculiar to Cork and Limerick, where it still survives. Also bliúit, q.v.

bléine, *Bleyne*, Bleney, Bleaney, Blaney, Blainey, Blayney.

bliúit, Bluett, Blewett. V. blaoo.

blóro, Blood. V. a blóro.

bluinnsín, Blanchville, Blanchfield. V. oe bluinnriol.

booléir, Bowler. V. bóiléir.

booún—VIII—*Boudun, Boudoun, Boudon*, Bowden, Boden, etc.; ' son of Baldon ' (dim. of Baldwin, sometimes written Bawdewyn in old Anglo-Irish records); a var. of báloún, q.v. The family so called came into Ireland about the time of the Anglo-Norman invasion and settled at Bodenstown, in Co. Kildare.

bóroicín—VIII—*Bawdekyn, Baudekin, Boudekyn, Bodekine*, Bodkin; ' son of Baldkin ' (dim. of Baldwin). The Bodkins, who are said to be a branch of the Fitzgeralds, appear to have first settled at Athenry and taken an active part in the affairs of that town. Later on, apparently towards the end of the 14th century, they removed to Galway, where they acquired a considerable amount of property and became one of the ' tribes ' of that city, of which many of them were mayors and sheriffs down to the time when it surrendered to Sir Charles Coote in 1652.

bóroín—VIII—*Boydyn, Boydin*, Boden, etc.; ' son of Baldin ' (dim. of Baldwin). Cf. bóroicín and booún.

ḃóıléır—XII—Bowler; Nor. 'le Boller,' i.e., the bowler, maker of wooden bowls; an old Kerry surname.

ḃóınn, Bowen, V. ꝺe ḃoṫún.

ḃoıréıl—XII—*Borel, Burell, Berle,* Burrell, Berrell, Berrall, Berrill, Birrell, etc.; Nor. 'borel,' 'burel,' i.e., one of reddish-brown complexion. The family so called came into Ireland soon after the Anglo-Norman invasion and settled in Co. Louth.

ḃólṫún, Bolton. V. ꝺe ḃoıltún.

ḃórṫuıc—XI—Borthwick; i.e., 'of Borthwick,' in Scotland.

ḃoscaċ—XIV.—*Boskagh,* Fox. V. ꝺe ḃorc.

ḃraḃasún—XII—*Brabasun,* Brabazon; Nor. 'le Brabansun,' 'le Brabazoun,' i.e., native of Brabant in Flanders. This surname was not unknown in Ireland as early as the 13th century, but the family to which belongs the Earl of Meath came hither only in the 16th century.

ḃran, Bran, Branne; Burns; a West Clare surname.

ḃranꝺún—XI—Brandon, etc.; Nor. 'de Brandon,' i.e., of Brandon (a frequent place-name in England); the name of an old Anglo-Norman family who settled in Co. Louth.

ḃrannóc, *Brayhenoc, Braynoc, Bronoke, Bronicke,* Brannock, Brannick, etc. V. ꝺe ḃreannóc.

ḃranṫ—VIII—Brant, Brand; 'son of Brand' (the Norse personal name Brandr); an old surname in Ireland.

ḃreannóc, *Brayhnock, Breynoc, Brenoke,* Brennock, etc. V. ꝺe ḃreannóc.

ḃréarṫún—XI—Brearton, Brerton, Brereton; i.e., 'of Brereton,' in England.

ḃreaṫnaċ—X—*Brathnagh, Brethnagh, Brehnagh,* Brennagh, Brannagh, and by translation Walsh, Walshe, etc.; Ir. 'ḃreaṫnac' (more correctly ḃreaṫnaċ), i.e., the Welshman; a descriptive surname applied generically to the early Anglo-Norman invaders who came hither from Wales; now one of our most numerous surnames. There are naturally many distinct families so called. See also ᵒe Ɗᴀɪᴌᴇɪᵱ, ᵒe Ɗᴀɪᴌɪᵱ, which is the Norman equivalent.

Ɗᴙɪᴀn—VIII—Brian, Bryan, Brien, etc. ; ' son of Brian ' (a common Breton personal name introduced into England at the Conquest). The family so called settled in Kilkenny and Wexford.

Ɗᴙɪᴅe—XI—*Bryde*, Bride ; Lat. ' de Sancta Brida,' i.e., of St. Bride's ; an early Anglo-Norman surname in Ireland. ' Henricus de Sancta Brida ' occurs in the Dublin Roll of Names soon after the invasion. But see nᴀ Ɗᴙɪᵹᵒe.

Ɗᴙɪᴅeᴀċ—XIV.—*Bridagh*, Bride. V. Ɗᴙɪᴅe.

Ɗᴙɪᵹeᴀċ—XIV—*Brigaghe*, Brigg, Bridge. V. ᵒe Ɗᴙɪᵹ.

Ɗᴙɪoꞅᴄū—XI—*Briskoo*, Briscoe, Brisco ; Eng. ' of Briscoe,' in Cumberland. The family of this name has long been settled in Ireland.

Ɗᴙɪꞇ, Britt, Brett. V. ᵒe Ɗᴙɪꞇ.

Ɗᴙɪꞇeᴀċ—XIV—*Brittagh*, Britt, Brett. V. ᵒe Ɗᴙɪꞇ.

Ɗᴙoꞓ—XII—Brock ; Nor. ' le Broc,' i.e., the badger ; an English surname.

Ɗᴙuᵹᴀ, Burrowes, Burrows ; Burgess. V. ᵒe Ɗᴙuᵹᴀ.

Ɗᴙuɪꞓᴌᴇɪᵹ, Ɗᴙuɪꞓᴌᴇɪꞇ—XI—*Bricklea*, Brickley ; ' of Brockley ' in Suffolk ; the name of an English family who were seated at Ballycahan in Co. Limerick. About the middle of the 17th century they removed to South Cork, where they still survive.

Ɗᴙūn, Brown, Browne. V. ᵒe Ɗᴙūn.

Ɗuᴀmᴀn—XII—Bowman.

Ɗuᴀmonn, Beaumont. V. ᵒe Ɗuᴀmonn.

Ɗuᴅᴀᴙᴌᴀɪᵹ—XI—Butterly ; i.e., of Butterley ; an English place-name.

Ɗūᴅᴙᴀn, *Budran, Boudran, Bowdran*, Bowdren ; the name of an old Anglo-Irish family in East Cork. I cannot trace its origin.

Ɗuɪᴌꞇᴇɪᴙ, Ɗuɪᴌꞇᴇɪᴙ, Butler. V. ᵒe Ɗuɪꞇᴌᴇɪᵱ.

Ɗuɪnneᴀn, *Bonane, Bonan*, Banane, Binane, Bunyan, and incorrectly Bennett ; the name of an old Kerry family who were seated at, and gave its name to,

Ballybunion in North Kerry. Latterly it is being turned into Bennett, which is altogether wrong and equivalent to the assumption of a new name.

ḃuıRʒéıs, ḃuıRʒéıs—XII—*Burgeis, Burys*, Burgess, Burges, etc. ; Mid. Eng. ' Burgeys,' the burgess, the citizen.

ḃuıRséıl, Burchell.

ḃúıséıR—XII—*Boucher, Bossher*, Bowcher, Busher, Bussher, etc. ; Nor. ' le boucher,' i.e., the butcher. Families of this name settled soon after the Anglo-Norman invasion in the counties of Kilkenny, Carlow and Wexford. The name came in again in the 16th century. The older families spell the name with *sh* instead of *ch*. The corresponding English surname is Butcher.

ḃúısᴄéıR, Butcher. V. ḃúıréıṗ.

ḃúıᴄeaċ—XIV—*Bowet, Boyt, Boyde*, Boyd. V. ṽe ḃúıᴄ.

ḃuıᴄıléıR, Butler. V. ṽe ḃuıᴄléıṗ.

ḃuıᴄıméıR, *Bottymer*, Buttimer ; an old but rare Anglo-Irish surname in Co. Cork, the origin of which I have failed to trace.

ḃuıᴄléıR, Butler. V. ṽe ḃuıᴄléıṗ.

ḃulᵱın, Bulfin.

ḃúRḃaċ—XI—Burbage ; i.e., ' of Burbach ' or ' Burbage,' an English place-name.

ḃuRṽún, *Burdun*, Burdon. V. ṽe ḃuṗṽún.

ḃusᴄáRṽ—XII—*Bostard*, Bustard ; Eng. ' the bustard,' a large bird once common in England. This old surname has long been peculiar to Donegal.

caṽal—VIII—Cadell, Caddell, etc. ; ' son of Cadell ' (a Welsh personal name corresponding to the Irish Cathal) ; the name of a family of Welsh origin who came to Ireland in the 13th century and settled in Dublin, Meath and Galway. The Caddells of Galway have long since assumed the surname of Blake. V. ṽe ḃláca.

caımḃéal—XII—Cambell, Campbell, etc. ; Ir. ' cam ' and ' ḃéal,' i.e., wry-mouthed, originally an epithet

or nickname which in course of time supplanted the
real surname ; not from Norman ' de Campobello,'
as some have imagined. The original surname is
said to have been Ó Ɗuıɓne. Sir Colin Mór Caimbéal, lord of Lochawe, who was knighted by Alexander III, and from whom the Duke of Argyll derives
the title of Mac Cailean Mór by which he is known
in the Highlands to the present day, was the seventh in
descent from Ɗuıɓne, the ancestor from whom the
family took their original surname of Ó Ɗuıɓne.
The Campbells were long the most formidable of the
Scottish clans, and the name is now one of the most
numerous in Scotland.

Cαιmpıon—XII—Campion ; Nor. ' le Campion,' i.e.,
the champion, victor in the village sports.

Cáıroín—XI—Cardin, Carden ; i.e., ' of Carden,' a
parish in Cheshire.

Camŝron—XII—Cameron ; Ir. ' cαm ' and ' ʃ̧ʃ̧ón,' i.e.,
wry-nosed, an epithet like Cαımbéαl, q.v. ; the name of a
distinguished Scottish clan. The Camerons were
seated in Inverness and were divided into four septs,
of which the best known are the Camerons of Lochiel.
In the civil wars of the 17th century, the Camerons
were loyal to the Stuart cause, and in 1745 the whole
clan was out for Prince Charlie.

Cαnnꞇαlún, Cantillon, Cantlon, etc. V. ɗe Cαnnꞇαlún.

Cαnnꞇuαl, Cαnꞇuαl, Cantoell, Cantowle, Cantwell.
V. ɗe Cαnnꞇuαl.

Cαnnꞇún, Cαnꞇún, Canton, Candon. V. ɗe Cαnnꞇún.

Cαománαċ—X—Cavanagh, Kavanagh, etc. ; Ir.
' Cαománαċ,' i.e., belonging to Cαomán. This
family derives its name and descent from Domhnall
Caomhanach, son of Diarmaid Mac Murchadha
who was King of Leinster at the time of the Anglo-
Norman invasion. He was so called from having been
fostered by the comharb or successor of St. Cαomán
at Kilcavan, near Gorey ; and the agnomen, contrary
to the usual Irish practice, has for many centuries
been adopted as a surname by his descendants. Modern

writers sometimes wrongly prefix an Ó to this surname, making it Ó Caoṁánaiġ. The patrimony of the family lay in the present counties of Carlow and Wexford, where the name is now very common.

Cáplais, Capples, Caplis, Caplice ; an hibernicised form of the English surname Caples.

Carrún, *Carrune, Carun,* Carew, Carey. V. ꝺe Carrún.

Cas—VIII—*Casse,* Cass, Cash ; ' son of Casse ' (a common French name, the same as the Latin Cassius) ; an old surname in Co. Cork, and other parts of the South of Ireland.

Cat—XI—*Kot, Cote,* Cott, Coates ; Mid. Eng. ' atte cote,' i.e., at the cot, or cottage, from residence.

Ceannt, Kent. V. ꝺe Ceannt.

Ceárꝺ—XII—Caird ; Gaelic ' ceárꝺ,' a craftsman ; a Scottish-Gaelic surname.

Ceatac—XIV—Kett. V. Ó Ceit.

Céitinn—XI—Keating, Keatinge ; Nor. ' de Ketyng,' i.e., of Ketyng, a place-name, possibly in England. I cannot find the spot. The Keatings were among the earliest of the Anglo-Norman invaders. They settled first in Wexford, where they obtained large grants of land, and afterwards spread into Carlow, Kildare, Tipperary, Waterford and Cork. Dr. Geoffrey Keating has made the name famous in Irish literary history

Ciarasac—XIV—Kearsey. V. ꝺe Céarraiġ.

Ciceam—XI—Kickham ; i.e., ' of Kickham,' an English place-name ; a late English surname, made famous by Charles J. Kickham.

Cinipéic—XI—Kennifeck, Kennefick. V. ꝺe Cinipéic.

Cinnicéiꝺ, Kincaid, Kinkead.

Cinnsealac—X—*Kinshellagh, Kinselagh,* Kinshela, Kinsella, etc. ; Ir. ' Cinnrealac ', i.e., belonging to Ui Cinnsealaigh, in Wexford ; the name of a Wexford family who are descended from Enna Cinnsealach, son of Diarmaid Mac Murchadha, King of Leinster at the time of the Anglo-Norman invasion. Cinnrealac was, like Caoṁánac (q.v.), an agnomen which supplanted the real surname. Ó Cinnreataíg is also, though rarely, used.

cinnseamán, Kingston. V. Ó Cinnreamáin.

cinc, Kent. V. de Ceannc.

cíomsóg, cíosóg, ciúmsóg, Cusack, Cussack, etc. V. de Ciúmróg.

clanndiolúin, Clandillon; probably from an Irish place-name.

clár, Clare, Clair. V. de Clár.

cléireac—XII—Clarke; Ir. ' Cléireac,' i.e., the clerk; a very common surname in early Anglo-Irish records. Most of our Irish Clarkes are, however, O'Clerys or MacClerys.

climéis—VIII—climéiseac—XIV—Clement; ' son of Clement ' (Lat. Clemens, Fr. Clemence).

clinse, Clinshe, Clenche, Clinch, Clynch. I can discover nothing to throw light on the origin of this surname which was borne by an old Anglo-Irish family of the Pale. The Clinches ranked among the gentry of Dublin and Meath at the end of the 16th century.

cliororc, Clifford. V. de Cliororc.

clioncún, Clinton. V. de Clioncún.

cocs, Cox; an hibernicised form of the English surname Cox.

coda—VIII—Cod, Codde, Codd; ' son of Cod,' (an old Anglo-Saxon personal name; a short form of Cuthbert, Cuthwine, or some other name commencing with Cuth; variously written in Searle's Onomasticon, Coda, Cuda, Cudda, Cudd, Cuta, Cutta, etc. Code appears in Domesday Book as a holder of land in the time of Edward the Confessor). The Codds are an old and respectable family of Co. Wexford, to which county the name is peculiar.

coiléir—XII—Collier; ' the Coller,' i.e., the collier, or charcoal-burner, a term still used in the north of England.

coilldub, Blackwood; a translation of the English surname Blackwood.

coimín—XI or VIII—Comin, Comyn, Comyns, Cummins, etc. ; possibly from Fr. ' de Comminges,' i.e., of Commimges in Gascony, or ' de Comines,' i.e., of Comines in the north of France bordering on Belgium, but in old records the prefix ' de ' is never found. Harrison suggests that it is from a Frankish personal name, Comin or Cumin. The family in any case came over to Ireland at the time of the Anglo-Norman invasion. John Comyn was the first Anglo-Norman Archbishop of Dublin. The name became very common throughout the southern half of Ireland, and also in Westmeath and Roscommon, but is now difficult to distinguish from Mac Cuimín and Ó Cuimín (q.v.), which are similarly anglicised.

coipinséir—XII—Copinger, Coppinger ; Norse ' Kaupungr,' (a nickname) ; the name of a family of Norse extraction long settled in Cork, where in 1319 Stephen Coppinger was mayor of the city, as was William Coppinger in 1535. The Coppingers formed a kind of clan after the Irish fashion. Many of them were attained in 1642 and again in 1691. The name is generally pronounced Coipinéiɼ.

cóipliɖe—XI—Copley ; Eng. ' of Copley,' a parish in the West Riding of Yorkshire ; not an old surname in Ireland.

cól—VIII—Cole ; ' son of Cole ' (Norse Colr or Kolr, also in use among the Anglo-Saxons ; Cole, Cola, Colo, etc. appear in Domesday Book as names of persons holding land in the time of Edward the Confessor). A family of this name settled in Fermanagh at the time of the plantation of Ulster, but most of our Coles are of Irish origin.

col—VIII—Col, Coll ; ' son of Colle ' (Norse Kollr ; Colle, Col, etc. among the Anglo-Saxons, but not easily distinguishable from Cole, Cola, etc.) Colle was the name of a landholder in the time of Edward the Confessor, and Collo that of an undertenant at the time of the Domesday survey. The name is of record in Ireland since the end of the 14th century, and is chiefly associated with the district around Kilmallock in Co. Limerick, where the family is of long standing respectability.

colbáꞃ𝓭—VIII—Colbert; 'son of Colbert' (the Anglo-Saxon Colobert or Colbeorht); Colbert and Colibert appear in Domesday Book as the names of landholders in the time of Edward the Confessor and of undertenants at the time of the survey, an indication that the name is derived from the Anglo-Saxon and not from its Frankish cognate. In Ireland, the Colberts are found chiefly in Cork and Limerick. The Irish form of the name as I have heard it is ᴀ Colbáꞃ𝓭.

colcloċ—XI—Colclogh, Colclough; i.e., 'of Colclough' in Staffordshire. A family of this name settled in Wexford in the 16th century.

colċún—XI—*Colchoun*, Colhoun, Colquhoun, etc.; i.e., 'of Culchone' or Colquhoun, in Dumbartonshire; the name of a Scottish clan, some of whom settled in Ireland.

colmán—VIII—*Colman*, Coleman; 'son of Colman' (a name in use in England in Anglo-Saxon times, but doubtless borrowed from the Irish. Searle gives it in three forms: Colman, Coloman, and Coleman, under the last of which it appears as the name of a landholder in the time of Edward the Confessor). A family of the name came to Ireland about the period of the Anglo-Norman invasion and settled in Dublin and other places in Leinster.

colcún—XI—Colton; 'of Colton,' a common place-name in England.

cómᴀꞃ, Comber. V. 𝓭e Cómᴀꞃ.

comᴀꞃcún—XI—Comerton, Comerford, etc.; i.e., 'of Comberton,' a parish in Cambridgeshire, if not 'of Comberford,' a village in Staffordshire. The Irish form would seem to point to the former as the origin, but cf. Ꞃoꞃcún for Rochford. The Comerfords, as they are usually called, are an old and respectable family in Kilkenny and Waterford. The head of the family was Baron of Danganmore.

con𝓭ún, conn𝓭ún, Condon. V. 𝓭e Cᴀnncún.

COᴎbᴀɪᴅ—VIII—Corbett ; 'son of Corbet' (dim. of French corbeau, a raven, a personal name in Domesday Book). The Corbetts, who are a family of Norman origin, settled in Meath and Offaly, but the name has always been very rare. Nearly all our Corbetts are of Irish origin. V. Ó Coꞃbáın, Ó Coıꞃbín and Ó Conbáᵹa.

COᴎcᴀɪᴄ, Corket ; a rare Galway surname.

COᴎᴎᴅub, Corduff ; more correctly Ó Coꞃꞃouıb, q.v.

COꞅᴄûn, Costune, Costume.

CᴎáꝼOᴎᴄ—XI—Craforte, Crawford, etc. V. ᴅe Cꞃáꝼoꞃᴄ.

Cᴎᴀnuıᴄ, Cranwich, Cranitch ; i.e., probably 'of Cranwich' in England.

CᴎᴀObᴀᴄ—IX—*Creavagh*, Creagh ; Ir. 'cꞃaobaᴄ,' branching, or possibly belonging to Cꞃaob, a common Irish place-name. The Creaghs are, according to tradition, a branch of the O'Neills of Clare and obtained the cognomen of Cꞃaobaᴄ from one of their ancestors who carried a green branch in a battle fought at Limerick with the Danes. They were an ancient and respectable merchant family in Limerick where the name frequently appears in the list of mayors and bailiffs. Many of them, too, attained to high ecclesiastical distinctions. In 1459, William Creagh was Bishop of Limerick ; in 1483 David Creagh was Archbishop of Cashel ; a century later Richard Creagh was appointed by the Pope to the primacy of Armagh ; and at the beginning of the 18th century, Pierce Creagh was Archbishop of Dublin. All these were natives of Limerick. The Creaghs were also an old and wealthy merchant family in Cork.

CᴎeᴀᴅóC, Cᴎeᴀᴅóꜱ—VIII—*Cradok*, *Craddok*, Craddock ; 'son of Caradoc,' (a Welsh personal name, famous in British history as Caractacus) ; not from the place-name Cradoc in Brecnockshire, or Craddock in Devonshire, as in old records it never takes the prefix 'de.' The Craddocks, who are a family of Welsh origin, settled at an early period at Crad-

dockstown in Co. Kildare, whence the name has
spread to other parts of Ireland. The Irish form is
possibly more correctly Cɾaʋóc.

creaᵹ, creoᵹ, Cregg, Craig. V. ʋe Cɾaiᵹ.

críoscóir—VIII—*Cristor*, Christopher; 'son of Christopher.'

cróc—VIII—*Croc, Crok*, Croke, Croake; Crooke, Crooks,
etc.; 'son of Croc' (old Norse Krokr, a personal
name which appears more than once in Domesday
Book and was borne by holders of land in the time
of Edward the Confessor and by tenants-in-chief and
undertenants at the time of the survey). The
Crokes settled at an early period in Kilkenny, Tipperary and Cork. Crooke represents a later immigration, and is more widespread.

cromaıl—XI—*Cromall*, Crummell, Grummell, Cromwell; i.e., 'of Cromwell,' a parish in Nottinghamshire;
the name, strangely enough, of an old Anglo-Irish
family in Limerick, where James Cromwell was
mayor in 1598. It has now disappeared from
Limerick, but is still found in other parts of the
country.

cromċa—IX—Crombie, Cromie, Crommie; Ir. 'cɾomċa,'
i.e., bent, crooked.

crón—IX—Crone; Ir. 'cɾón,' i.e., brown; an epithet
which supplanted the real surname which is now lost.
Cf. ʋán.

crúc, Crooke, Crooks, etc. V. Cɾóc.

crúıs, Cruice, Cruise, Cross. V. ʋe Cɾúıɾ.

crúıséır—XII—Crozier.

cúc—XII—Cooke; i.e., 'the cook,' a common name in
early Anglo-Irish records.

cuıleanʋar—XII—Collendar, Callender; i.e., 'the
calender,' one who calenders cloth; in use in Co.
Waterford.

cuılcéır, Quilter. V. ʋe Cuıcléıɾ.

cuımín, Comyn, Cumming, Cummins, etc. V. Coımín.

cúıpéır—XII—Cooper, Cowper; i.e., 'the cooper.'

cuırcéıs, Curtis, etc. V. ʋe Cuıɾcéıɾ.

Cuisín—XII—*Coushine, Cushine,* Cousin, Cushen, Cussen Cousins, etc. ; Nor. ' le cosyn,' i.e., the cousin, kinsman ; the name of an Anglo-Norman family who settled in Ireland soon after the invasion ; found in nearly all the counties of Munster, and also in Connacht and Westmeath.

Cúrsac—XIV—De Courcy, Courcey, Coursey. V. oe Cúppa.

Cúc—XII—Coote ; i.e., ' the coot,' the waterfowl so called.

Dáibís, Davis ; an hibernicised form of the English or Welsh surname Davis.

Dáinséir—XI—*de Aungers,* Aungier, Danger ; Nor. ' de Aungers,' i.e., of Angers, a city of Anjou ; an old surname of Norman origin.

Dáiroís—XI—*de Ardis,* Dardis ; Nor. ' de Ardis,' probably, ' of the Ards ' in Co. Down ; the name of an Anglo-Norman family who settled soon after the invasion in Meath and Westmeath.

Dáirsig—XI—*de Arcy,* D'Arcy, Darcy ; Nor. ' de Arcy,' i.e. from Arci in Normandy. The D'Arcys were one of the most distinguished of the Norman families who settled in England after the Conquest. The founder of the Irish family of the name was Sir John D'Arcy, chief justiciary of Ireland, in the second quarter of the 14th century. He received large grants of land in Meath, which remained in the possession of his descendants down to the Cromwellian and Williamite confiscations. The first home of the D'Arcys in Ireland, and their chief seat for many centuries, was at Platten, in Co. Meath, from which branched out all the other houses of the name in Ireland. But see Ó Dopcaroe, which is also angl. Darcy.

Dalaitío—XI—*de la Hide,* Delahide, Delahoyde ; i.e., of the hide,' a measure of land sufficient to support a family (about 120 acres), from residence on or thereby ; an early Anglo-Norman surname. ' Roger de la Hide' was a member of the Dublin Guild-Merchant in 1226. The family settled in Dublin, Meath and Kildare.

ⅮⱰⱢⱰⱮⱰⱤⱰ—XI—Delamar, Delamere, etc.; Nor. 'de la Mare,' i.e. of la Mare in Normandy. This family settled in England at the time of the Norman Conquest, and came to Ireland soon after the Anglo-Norman invasion. The Delameres had extensive estates in Co. Westmeath down to the Cromwellian confiscations. They assumed the Irish patronymic surname of MacHerbert.

Ⰴⰰⰾⰰⱅⱗⱀ, Ⰴⰰⰾⱅⱗⱀ—XI—*de Daltune*, Dalton, D'Alton; i.e., 'of Dalton,' a common place-name in the north of England; or it might be from ' de Aletone,' i.e. of Alton. Both forms occur in early Anglo-Irish records. Robert de Daltune and William de Daltune were members of the Dublin Guild-Merchant in 1226. In later times the Daltons were lords of Rathconrath, in Co. Westmeath, but they lost their estates in the Cromwellian and Williamite confiscations.

Ⰴⰰⱄⰰⱀ, Ⰴⰰⱄⱁⱀ, Dawson; hibernicised forms of the English surname Dawson.

Ⰴⰰⱅⱗⱀ—XI—*de Autun, Dawtone*, Daton, Daughton, Dawtin; Nor. ' de Autun,' i.e. of Autun in Normandy; the name of an old Kilkenny family, sometimes incorrectly re-anglicised Dalton.

Ⰴⰵⰰⰱⱃⱗⱄ—XI—*de Evereux*, Devereux; i.e. ' of Evereux' in Normandy. This family came into England at the time of the Norman Conquest, and into Ireland at the time of the Anglo-Norman invasion, when they settled in Co. Wexford. "The Devereuxes," writes Dr. E. Hogan, "were the wealthiest and most powerful of all the Strongbowian race in Wexford."

Ⰵⰵ ⰱⰰⰽⱗⱀ—XII—*de Bacoun*, Bacon; Nor. ' le Bacoun,' i.e. the bacon, the pig, reminiscent of a time when ' the bacon ' meant the live pig; the name of an English family who came into Ireland soon after the Anglo-Norman invasion and settled in Co. Meath. Cf. ⱂⱆⰺⱃⰵⰺⰾ.

ᴠe ⰁⰀⰅⰕⰆⱀ—XI—*de Boytoun,* Boyton ; ' of Boyton,' somewhere in England. The name is in Ireland at least since the 13th century, and was chiefly associated with Cashel.

ᴠe ⰁⰀⰉⰎⰅⰀⰓⰀ—XI—De Valera, de Valera ; i.e., ' of Valera,' an ancient city in Spain.

" VALERA, Valeria. C'étoit anciennement une Ville considerable des Celtiberiens, en Espagne. Elle fut ensuite épiscopale, et enfin ruinée. On a bâte de ses rûines trois villages nommez Valera-Quemada, Valera-de-Suso, et Valera-la-Veja, dans la nouvelle Castille, sur le Xucar, à six lieues de Cuença, qui a succedé à l'Episcopat."—*Baudrand, Dictionnaire Geographique et Historique.*

ᴠe ⰁⰀⰉⰎⰅⰉⰏ, ᴠe ⰁⰀⰉⰎⰉⰎ, ᴠe ⰁⰀⰉⰎⰉⰎ—XII—*le Waleys, le Waleis, the Walish,* Wallis, Wallace, Walsh, etc. ; i.e. ' the Welshman'; the Norman equivalent of the Irish ⰁⱃⰅⰀⱍⱀⰀⱍ, q.v.

ᴠe ⰁⰀⰎ—XI—*de Val, de Vale, de Vaal, de Wale,* Wall ; Nor. ' du Val,' i.e. of the vale, or valley, from residence therein. This surname dates back at least to the 13th century, and is found in many parts of Ireland. In 1335, John de Vale and Walter de Vale were among those summoned to attend Sir John D'Arcy on his expedition to Scotland. In the same century three bishops of the name filled Irish Sees, among whom was Stephen de Wale who became Bishop of Limerick in 1360, and was afterwards translated to Meath and made Lord High Treasurer of Ireland. The Walls were numerous and respectable in the 16th century in Kildare, Carlow, Kilkenny, Tipperary, Cork, Limerick and Galway, and in the last-named county appear to have formed a distinct clan after the Irish fashion, with a chief of the name. In Limerick, the Walls held the manor of Dunmoylan from the 13th century down to 1580 when Ulick de Wale, although blind from his birth, was shamefully put to death by Pelham, and his lands confiscated.

ᴠe ⰁⰀⰎⰕⱀ—XI—*de Waletone, de Walton,* Walton ;

i.e., ' of Walton,' a common place-name in England ; the name of a family who settled in Dublin in the 13th century.

ᴅe ᴅᴀʀʀᴀ—XI—*de Barry*, Barry ; Nor. ' de Barri,' i.e., of Barri, probably in Normandy ; one of the oldest and most illustrious of the Anglo-Norman families in Ireland. The name occurs in the earliest Anglo-Irish records, and has always been specially associated with the County of Cork. In the year 1179, Robert FitzStephen granted to his nephew, Philip de Barry, the three cantreds of Ui Liatháin, Mus-craighe-trí-máighe, and Cinel Aodha, now repre-sented respectively by the baronies of Barrymore, Orrery, and Kinelea ; and this grant was con-firmed by King John in 1207 to William de Barry, son and heir of Philip. In the course of time the Barrys became one of the most numerous and power-ful families in Munster. They divided into several branches, the heads of which were known respectively as ᴀn ᴅᴀᴘᴘᴀᴄ ᴍóᴘ (the Great Barry), ᴅᴀᴘᴘᴀᴄ ʀuᴀᴅ (Red Barry), ᴅᴀᴘᴘᴀᴄ óɢ (Young Barry), ᴅᴀᴘᴘᴀᴄ ᴍᴀoᴌ (Bald Barry), ᴅᴀᴘᴘᴀᴄ ᴌáᴘoᴘ (Strong Barry) ; and one branch adopted the Irish patronymic sur-name of ᴍᴀᴄ ᴀᴅᴀᴍ, q.v. The Barrys suffered considerably in the wars of the 17th century, but are still numerous and respectable throughout Munster. There was also a family of the name in Co. Wexford. The Barrys of Co. Limerick, in many instances, be-long to the old Irish family of ó ᴅeᴀᴘɢᴀ (q.v.), and not to the Anglo-Norman Barrys.

ᴅe ᴅᴀʀᴛún—XI—*de Bartoun, de Barton*, Barton ; i.e., ' of Barton ' in England. This surname in Ireland dates back to the early part of the 13th century, but in many instances represents more recent immigra-tion.

ᴅe ᴅᴀs—XII—Bass ; Nor. ' le Bas,' i.e. of low stature ; an old but rare surname in Ireland.

ᴅe ᴅᴀsᴛᴀᴅᴌᴀ—XI—Bastable, Bastible ; Nor. ' de Bardastabla,' i.e., of Barnstable, in Devonshire. This

surname occurs in old Anglo-Irish records. It appears
to be now peculiar to Cork.

ꝺe bᴀṫ—XI—*de Baa, de Bathe*, Bath, Baith, Bates ;
i.e., ' of Bath,' in Somerset. This family came into
Ireland about the time of the Anglo-Norman invasion
and settled in Dublin, Meath and Louth. Many of
the name held high offices under the English crown in
the 14th and following centuries, until they lost their
lands in the Cromwellian and Williamite confiscations.

ꝺe béᴀl—XII—*de Veel*, Veale ; Nor. ' le Veel,' i.e., the
veal, the calf. Cf. ꝺe bᴀcún. This surname, which
came into Ireland at the period of the Anglo-Norman
invasion, is still well known in Co. Waterford, where
it is pronounced ꝺe bíᴀl.

ꝺe béᴀlᴀtún—XI—*de Beletune, de Weleton*, Belton,
Veldon, Weldon ; i.e., ' of Belton ' or ' of Welton,' in
England ; the name of a family who settled in Dublin
in the 13th century.

ꝺe beᴀꝛꝺún—XI—*de Verdoun, de Fardun*, Verdon,
Varden, etc. ; Nor. ' de Verdun.' i.e., of Verdun, the
historic town in the east of France. The de Verduns
came to England with William the Conqueror and
settled in Leicestershire. Bertram de Verdun, the
founder of the Irish branch of the family, came hither
at the period of the Anglo-Norman invasion, was
made seneschal of Ireland by Henry II and granted
the manors of Dundalk and Clonmore, and other
estates in Co. Louth. His great-grandson, John de
Verdon, by marriage with an heiress of the de Lacys,
added to his already extensive patrimony a moiety of
Meath, and succeeded to the office of constable of
Ireland, which had been originally granted to Hugh
de Lacy. He also possessed the castle and manors of
Croom and Castle Robert in Co. Limerick. In 1314,
Theobald de Verdon became justiciary, but dying in
1317 without heirs male, his estates were divided
between four daughters who all married English
noblemen. The name however continued to be
represented in Louth down to the end of the 17th

century, as we find among those attainted in 1642 a John Verdon, and in 1691 another John Verdon, a descendant of the former. Of the Limerick Verdons, William was mayor of the city in 1553 ; and John Verdon, in 1579, was sovereign of Kilmallock, and in 1585 represented that town in parliament. Several of the Verdons of Kilmallock were transplanted to Connacht in 1653.

ᴅe Ɓeᴀʀnᴀƀᴀᴌ—XI—*de Bernevale*, Barnewall, Barna-vill, Barnwell ; i.e., ' of Bernevale,' probably in Normandy. This family came into Ireland about the time of the Anglo-Norman invasion and settled in Dublin and Meath. They were long one of the most influential families of the Pale, and played an important part in the history of the country.

ᴅe Ƀeɩc—XI—*de Bec*, Beck, Bex ; i.e., ' of Bec,' in Normandy ; the name of a family of Norman origin who came to Ireland about the time of the invasion.

ᴅe Ƀeɩᴌ—XII—*de Bel*, Bell ; Nor. ' le bel,' i.e., the beauti-ful. This family, which is of Norman origin, first came to Ireland about the time of the invasion.

ᴅe Ƀéɩʀ—XI—*de Ver*, De Vere ; i.e., ' of Ver,' in Nor-mandy.

ᴅe Ƀɩᴀᴌ, Veale. V. ᴅe Ƀéᴀᴌ.

ᴅe Ƀᴌᴀcᴀ—XII—*le Blak*, *le Blake*, Blake ; i.e., ' the black,' from the complexion ; a descriptive epithet which in course of time supplanted the original sur-name, which was Caddell. Caddel was used as an alias for Blake as late as the 17th century, when it fell into disuse. The Blakes were one of the ' tribes' of Galway. The first of the family to come into prominence was Richard Caddel, or Blake, who was sheriff of Connacht in the early years of the 14th century, and from him are descended the many dis-dinguished families of Blake in Ireland.

ᴅe Ƀᴌᴀcᴀᴌ—XI—Blackhall ; i.e., ' of the black hall,' or ' of Blackhall ' ; a late English surname.

ᴅe Ƀᴌᴀcᴀm—XI—*de Blakeham*, Blackham ; i.e., ' of Blackham ' in England.

ᴅe ᴃláᴄuaᴌ—XI—Blackwell ; i.e., ' of Blackwell,' in England.

ᴅe ᴃᴌaᵹᴅ—XI—*de Blythe,* Blythe ; i.e., ' of Blyth,' in England.

ᴅe ᴃᴌuɪnnsíoᴌ—XI—*de Blauncheuill, de Blancheville,* Blanchville, Blanchfield ; i.e. ' of Blanchville,' probably somewhere in Normandy. This family, which is of Norman origin, came into Ireland soon after the invasion and settled in Co. Kilkenny, where they held a prominent position down to the Cromwellian confiscations. Sir Edmund Blanchville forfeited his estates by attainder in 1641. The name, in the spoken language, is corrupted to ᴃᴌuɪnnᴘín, and is even so written by Keating.

ᴅe ᴃóɪᴅ—XI—*de Wode, Void, Voide, Woayde,* Wood, Woods ; Mid. Eng. ' atte Wode,' i.e., at the wood, from residence thereby ; a rather common surname in early Anglo-Irish records, but it is now impossible to distinguish it from the many Irish surnames that have been anglicised Wood or Woods.

ᴅe ᴃoᴌᴌᴄun—XI—*de Boulton, de Bolton,* Bolton ; i.e., ' of Bolton,' in England.

ᴅe ᴃonᴅ—XII—Bonde, Bond ; Nor. ' le Bonde,' i.e., the bond, householder, husbandman, one who held under the tenure styled bondage. The surname is old in Ireland.

ᴅe ᴃosᴄ—XII—Fox ; i.e., ' the fox,' one of somewhat sly and cunning disposition ; the name of a once respectable old English family in Co. Limerick. Mountfox, near Kilmallock, is called in Irish móɪn an ᴃoᴘᴄaɪᵹ, Fox's bog, from a member of this family.

ᴅe ᴃosᴄóᴄ—XI—*de Bostock, Bostoke,* Bostock ; i.e., ' of Bostock,' in Cheshire ; the name of an old family in Cork and Waterford ; now very rare.

ᴅe ᴃoᴄ—XII—*le Bot, le But, But,* Butt ; Nor. ' le bot,' i.e., the short, stumpy person.

ᴅe ᴃoᴄûn—XI—*de Bohun, de Bohoun,* Boone, Bone, Bowen ; i.e., of Bohun. It occurs as a surname in Domesday Book.

ᴅe ⒷⓇⒶⓃⓄⓊⓃ—XI—*de Brandon*, Brandon; i.e., 'of Brandon,' a frequent place-name in England; the name of an old English family who settled in Co. Louth.

ᴅe ⒷⓇⒶⓉⓊⓃ—XI—Bratton; i.e., 'of Bratton' in England.

ᴅe ⒷⓇⒺⒶⓄⓊⓃ—XI—*de Bredun*, *de Bredone*, Bredon, Breadon, Breydon, etc.; i.e., 'of Bredon' in England.

ᴅe ⒷⓇⒺⒶⓃⓃⓄⒸ—XI—*de Brechnok*, *de Braynok*, Brennock, Brannock, Brannick, etc.; i.e., 'of Brechnock' in Wales. Families of this name settled in Ireland at the time of the Anglo-Norman invasion, and in the 16th century were most numerous in Tipperary, Kilkenny and Waterford. Not to be confounded with Ⓑⓡⓔⓐⓒⓝⓐⓒ, q.v.

ᴅe ⒷⓇⒺⒶⓉⓊⓃ, v. ᴅe ⒷⓡⓘⓄⓉúⓝ.

ᴅe ⒷⓇⒺⒾⓉ, Brett. V. ᴅe ⒷⓡⓘⓉ.

ᴅe ⒷⓇⒾ—XI—*de Bree, de Bre, de Bray*, Bree, Bray; i.e., 'of Bree,' in England, or 'of Brie,' in Normandy, or possibly 'of Bray' in Co. Wicklow (Irish Ⓑⓡⓘ).

ᴅe ⒷⓇⒾⒼ—XI—*de Brugge*, Brigg, Briggs, Bridge; Mid. Eng. 'atte Brigge,' i.e., at the bridge, from residence thereby. Brugge and Brigge were Mid. Eng. forms of Bridge. 'Sibrecht of Brigg' occurs in the Dublin Roll of Names (A.D. 1216).

ᴅe ⒷⓇⒾⓄⓉⓊⓃ—XII—*de Breton, Britun*, Bretton, Britton, etc.; Nor. 'le Breton,' i.e., the Breton, an immigrant from Brittany. Also ᴅe ⒷⓡⓔⓐⓉúⓝ.

ᴅe ⒷⓇⒾⓉ—XII—Britt, Brett; Nor. 'le Brit,' 'le Bret,' i.e., the Breton, native Brittany, the same as ᴅe ⒷⓡⓘⓄⓉúⓝ, q.v. Families of this name came to Ireland at the time of the Anglo-Norman invasion, or soon after, and settled in different parts of the country. ᴅe ⒷⓡⓔⓘⓉ (q.v.) is a variant.

ᴅe ⒷⓇⒾⓊⓈ, Bruce. V. ᴅe Ⓑⓡúⓢ.

ᴅe ⒷⓇⓄⒸ—XI—Brooke, Brookes, Brooks; Mid. Eng., 'atte Brok,' i.e., at the brook, from residence thereby.

ᴅe ⒷⓇⓄⒸⓉⓊⓃ—XI—*de Broghton, de Broughton*, Broughton; i.e., 'of Broughton,' in England.

ᴅe ⒷⓇⓊⒸ, Brookes, etc. V. ᴅe Ⓑⓡóⓒ.

ᵭe bꞦuᵹᴀ—XI—*de Bury, Burewe, Bru,* Bury, Burrows, Burrowes, etc., and indirectly Burgess; i.e., ' at the borough,' from residence therein; the English equivalent of the Norman de Burgo or Burke, being derived from the dative form of the Old English ' burg.'

ᵭe bꞦúп—XII—*de Brune,* Brown, Browne; Nor. ' le Brun,' i.e., the brown, from the complexion; an old Norman surname, extremely common in England. It came into Ireland at the time of the Anglo-Norman invasion, and is now also very common in this country. The most important families of the name in Ireland in the 16th century were those (1) of Galway, of which the Brownes were one of the ' tribes '; (2) of the Neale, Co. Mayo; (3) of Malrancan, Co. Wexford; (4) of Hariston, Co. Waterford; (5) of Aney, Co. Limerick; (6) of Kilpatrick, Co. Westmeath; and (7) of Dunbrowne, Co. Kerry. The Brownes of Kenmare came to Ireland only in the reign of Elizabeth, but by purchase and intermarriage succeeded to the vast estates of MacCarthy More, O'Sullivan More, and O'Donoghue of Ross, and as Earls of Kenmare have held an important place in the social and public life of the country.

ᵭe bꞦúпᴄúп—XI—Brunton; i.e., ' of Brunton,' in England.

ᵭe bꞦús—XI—*de Brus, de Bruis, de Bruce,* Bruce, etc.; i.e., ' of Brus ' or ' Brousse,' in France. This family came into England with William the Conqueror, and obtained large grants of land in Yorkshire and other places in the north of England. Robert de Bruce, whose father had obtained from David I of Scotland the Lordship of Annandale and other great possessions, was the founder of the royal house of Bruce in Scotland. The name is also old in Ireland, but has always been very rare.

ᵭe buᴀmoпп—XI—Beaumont; Nor. ' de Beaumont,' Lat. ' de Bello Monte.' i.e., of Beaumont (the fair mount), a frequent place-name in France.

de Ḃuinn—XII—Wynne, Winn; Welsh 'gwyn'; i.e., white, fair.

de Ḃuinḃíol—XI—*de Boneville,* Banville, Bonfield, Bunfield, etc.; i.e., 'of Bonville' in Normandy; the name of a Norman family who settled in Ireland soon after the invasion. In the early part of the 14th century, John de Boneville was seneschal of the counties of Kildare and Carlow, and the de Bonevilles were among the earliest Anglo-Norman settlers in Co. Limerick. For more than three centuries, the name has been associated chiefly with the district around Killaloe.

de Ḃúit—XI—*Bowet, Boyt, Boyde,* Boyd; perhaps 'of Bute' in Scotland; an old surname in Ireland, still found in Co. Mayo.

de Buitiléir, de Buitléir—XII—Butler; Nor. 'le Botiller,' 'le Buitiler,' i.e., the butler. This surname originated in the appointment by Henry II of Theobald Walter, the first of the family who settled in this country, to the office of chief butler of Ireland. Theobald, besides being made chief butler, was granted the baronies of Upper and Lower Ormond and other great possessions, and became the founder of one of the most illustrious of the Anglo-Norman families in Ireland.

de Ḃul, de Ḃulḃ—XII—Woulfe, Wolfe; Nor. 'le Wulf,' 'le Wolf,' i.e., the wolf, one of a rapacious disposition. This family came into Ireland at the time of the Anglo-Norman invasion and settled in Kildare and Limerick. In the former county, they were seated at Baile nuadh, now Newtown, near Athy, and possessed a district, called Críoċ Ḃulḃaċ, or Woulfe's country, on the east side of the Barrow, extending towards Monasterevan. Baile nuadh continued to be the home of the family until forfeited on the attainder of Nicholas Wolfe in 1641. The Woulfes of Limerick, from the 14th to the middle of the 17th century, took an active part in the affairs of the city. Among those exempted from pardon by Ireton, when he took possession of Limerick in 1651, were Father Francis Woulfe and Captain George Woulfe. In the county, Ballywilliam and Inniscouche, the lands of Patrick Woulfe, and Ballywinterrourke, the property of John Woulfe, were confiscated after the Geraldine war in the last quarter of the 16th century; and in 1653, David Wolfe was transplanted to Connacht. Some of the name about the same time settled in Clare.

ꝺe bÚRC, ꝺe bÚRCA—XI—*de Burgo*, De Burgh, Burke, Bourke; i.e., 'of the burgh' or 'borough.' This family ranks with the Fitzgeralds and Butlers as among the most illustrious of the Anglo-Norman settlers in Ireland. They derive their descent from William Fitz Adelm de Burgo who, in 1171, accompanied Henry II to Ireland, was made governor of Wexford, and in 1178 succeeded Strongbow as chief governor of Ireland. In 1179, Fitz Adelm obtained a grant of a great portion of Connacht. By marriage with an heiress of the de Lacys, Walter de Burgo acquired, in addition to his other possessions, the earldom of Ulster; and the Burkes became the greatest Anglo-Norman family in Ireland. On the murder, in 1333, of William, the Brown Earl of Ulster, leaving only an infant daughter, the leading male representatives of the name adopted the Brehon law, which provided for a male succession, and dividing the lordship of Connacht between them, proclaimed themselves Irish chiefs under the style of MacWilliam Uachtar and Mac William Iochtar, that is, the Upper and Lower MacWilliam, the former seated in Co. Galway and the latter in Co. Mayo. And so Irish did the Burkes of Connacht become, that they were at one time regarded as 'mere Irish.' Minor branches assumed the surnames of MacDavid, MacPhilpin, Mac Seoinin, MacGibbon, MacRedmond, etc., from their respective ancestors. The Burkes were also lords of the barony of Clanwilliam in Co. Limerick. The name is now very common all over Ireland.

ᵈe **ᵇⁱuⱤᵒᵘⁿ**—XI—*de Burdune, Burdoun,* Burdon ; i.e., ' of Burdon,' in England. This surname, which is of record in Ireland since the 14th century, has long been peculiar to Co. Cork, but even there is very rare.

ᵈe **ᵇⁱuⱤᴄᵘⁿ**—XI—*de Burtoun, de Burton,* Burton ; i.e., ' of Burton ' in England. This surname came into Ireland at different times since the middle of the 13th century.

ᵈe **ᵇⁱuꞩ**—XI—*de Bois, de Boys,* Boyse, Boyes, Boice, Boyce ; Nor. ' del Bois,' ' de Bois,' i.e., of the wood, from residence by or near a wood ; a surname of Norman origin which has been known in Ireland at least since the early 13th century. Cf. the English ᵈe **ᵇⁱᴏⁱᵒ** above.

ᵈe **ᴄᴀⁱꞩeᴀᴌ**—XI—*de Cassell,* Cassell, Cashel, etc. ; Nor. ' de Cassell,' Lat. ' de Castello,' i.e., of Cashel, or at the castle, from residence thereby or therein ; the name of an Anglo-Norman family who settled at Dundalk soon after the invasion.

ᵈe **ᴄᴀⁿⁿᴄᴀᴌᵘⁿ**—XI—*de Cantelon,* Cantillon, Cantlon, etc.; Nor. ' de Cauntelowe,' Lat. ' de Cantulupo,' i.e., of Chanteloup in France (Seine-et-Oise) ; the name of an early Anglo-Norman family in Ireland. They were among the first of the invaders, and settled in Limerick and Kerry. In the reign of Edward I, Richard de Cantelupo was sheriff of Kerry, and at the same period Master Thomas de Cantulupo was official of the church of St. Mary at Limerick. The Cantillons were lords of Ballyheigue in Co. Kerry until after the Jacobite wars in the latter part of the 17th century. Many of the name afterwards gained distinction in France where in the last century Antoine Sylvaine de Cantillon was created Baron de Ballyheigue. The name, though never very numerous, still survives in Kerry and Limerick.

ᵈe **ᴄᴀⁿⁿᴄuᴀᴌ**, ᵈe **ᴄᴀⁿᴄuᴀᴌ**—XI—de *Cantewell, de Cantwell,* Cantwell ; i.e., ' of Cantwell,' or ' Kentwell,' a spot somewhere in England. This family came to

Ireland at the time of the Anglo-Norman invasion and settled in Kilkenny and Tipperary, where they obtained large grants of land from the Butlers. The original seat of the family was at Cantwell's Court, about four miles to the north-east of Kilkenny. The Cantwells are still a well-known and respectable family in Kilkenny and Tipperary.

ᴅe Cᴀnnᴄūn—XI—*de Cauntoun, de Caunton, de Canton,* Canton, Candon and Condon ; Nor. ' de Countyntoun,' ' de Cauntyton,' ' de Caunteton,' i.e., of C————, probably the present parish of Canton in Glamorganshire ; an old Norman surname, sometimes angl. Canton and Candon, but generally corrupted to Connᴅún (pronounced locally Cúnún) and anglicised Condon. The Condons are a well-known family in Cork, Waterford and Limerick who formerly possessed considerable property in the neighbourhood of Mitchelstown, from one of whom that town got its name.

ᴅe CᴀRᴅuiᴅ—XI—*de Cardif, de Kerdyff,* Cardiff, Kerdiffe ; Nor. ' de Cardif,' i.e., of Cardiff in Wales. Families of this name settled at an early period in Dublin, Meath, Kildare and Wexford. The name, though never very common, still survives in Leinster.

ᴅe CᴀRlᴄūn—XI—*de Carletoun, de Carltoun,* Carleton, Carlton ; Nor. ' de Carletoun,' i.e., of Carleton or Carlton, a frequent place-name in England. This surname is old in Ireland. But see Ó Cᴀiᴘeᴀllᴀ́in, which has been anglicised Carleton.

ᴅe CᴀRRᴀiᴢ—XI—*de Carricke, de Carrig,* Carrick, Craig, etc., and by translation Rock ; Nor. ' de Carraig,' i.e., of Carrick, a common place-name in Ireland and Scotland, meaning ' the rock ' ; a not uncommon surname in Ireland in the 13th century. But see Mᴀc Conᴄᴀiᴘᴘᴢe and Mᴀc Conᴄᴀᴄᴘᴀᴄ, which are similarly anglicised.

ᴅe CᴀRRūn—XI—*de Carron, de Carrew,* Carew, Carey, etc. ; Nor. ' de Carreu,' i.e., of Carew, a parish in Pembrokeshire ; an Anglo-Norman surname which came into Ireland soon after the invasion and is still common in Munster. V. Cappún.

ᴅe Catain—XI—*de Cathyr, de Cather, de Caher,* Carr; Nor. 'de Cathyr,' i.e., of Cahir, an Irish place-name, found very frequently all over the country; the name of an old Co. Limerick family of which we have record since the last quarter of the 13th century and which, though never numerous, is still extant in the county.

ᴅe Ceannt—XI—*de Kent,* Kent; Nor. 'de Kent,' i.e., of Kent in England; a not uncommon surname in early Anglo-Irish records; still well known in Co. Cork.

ᴅe Ceapóc—XI—*de Keppoc, de Keppok,* Keappock, Keppock, Cappock, etc.; Nor. 'de Keppoc,' i.e., of Ceapóg, an Irish place-name signifying a green plot before a house (Dinneen). The ceapóg from which the family took its name was in Co. Louth, where they settled early in the 13th century.

ᴅe Céarsaig—XI—*de Kersey,* Kearsey; Nor. 'de Kersey,' i.e., of Kersey, a parish in Suffolk. This family settled in Ireland in the 13th century. The name still survives in Co. Waterford.

ᴅe Céitinn—XI—*de Ketyng,* Keating. V. Céitinn.

ᴅe Cinipéic—XI—*de Kenefec, de Kenefeg, Kynnepeke,* Kennifeck, Kennefick, etc.; Nor. 'de Kenefeg,' i.e., of Kenfig, a parish and ancient town in Glamorganshire. This surname occurs very frequently in the Dublin Roll of Names (A.D. 1216). The family finally settled in Co. Cork where the name, though rare, is still well known.

ᴅe Ciomsóg, ᴅe Ciúmsóg—XI—*de Kisshok, de Keusaac, de Cusaak, de Cusack,* Cusack, etc.; Nor. 'de Cusak,' i.e., of Cussac in France. This family came to Ireland at the time of the Anglo-Norman invasion and settled in Meath and other parts of Leinster. They were one of the most distinguished families of the Pale and many of them filled high judicial posts under the Anglo-Irish government. In the wars and confiscations of the 17th century they lost their property and were dispersed. The name is now more common in Munster than in Leinster.

ᴅe Clᴀʀ—XI—*de Clare*, Clare ; Nor. ' de Clar,' i.e., of Clare, a parish in Suffolk.

ᴅe Cléᴀᴛún—XI—*de Clayton*, Clayton ; Nor. ' de Clayton,' a parish in Essex, Yorkshire or Lancashire.

ᴅe Cléiʀ—XI—*de Clere*, Cleere, Clear ; Nor. ' de Clere,' from some spot perhaps in Normandy ; the name of an old Anglo-Norman family in Co. Wexford and other parts of the south-east of Ireland.

ᴅe Cliofoʀᴛ—XI—*de Clifford*, Clifford ; Nor. ' de Clifford,' i.e., of Clifford, a parish in Herefordshire. The name is old in Ireland, but the vast majority of our Cliffords are of Irish origin. V. Ó Clúmáin and Ó Colmáin.

ᴅe Clionᴛún—XI—*de Clyntoun, de Clynton*, Clinton ; Nor. ' de Clinton.' i.e. of Clinton, some spot in England, if not ' of Glinton,' a parish of Northamptonshire. V. Ɉleᴀnᴛún. The Clintons were an old family in Co. Louth.

ᴅe Cnoc—XI—*de Cnocke, Cnok*, Knox ; Nor. ' de Cnocke,' i.e., of the cnoc (or hill), from residence thereon, a Norman-Irish surname, corresponding to the Irish ᴀ' Cnuic, the English Hill. Cf. ᴅe Cappaiɉ above.

ᴅe Coɉán—XI—*de Cogan, Cogane*, Cogan, Goggin ; Nor. ' de Cogan,' i.e., of Cogan, a parish in Glamorganshire. This surname came into Ireland at the time of the Anglo-Norman invasion. Milo de Cogan was the first constable of Dublin. He received, jointly with Robert FitzStephen, a grant of the whole of Co. Cork from Henry II. The name is now pronounced Ɉoɉán, sometimes Ɉóɉán, and is generally anglicised Goggin in Munster.

ᴅe Cómᴀʀ—XII—Comber ; Nor. ' le Comber,' i.e., the (wool-) comber ; an old surname in Ireland. I find it still in this form in Connemara.

ᴅe Coʀbᴀile—XI—*de Corbaly*, Corbally ; Nor. ' de Corbaly,' i.e., of Corbally ; a surname formed after the Norman fashion from an Irish place-name.

ᴅᴇ COCÚn—XI—*de Cotun, de Cottoune,* Cotton ; Nor. ' de Cotun,' i.e., of Cotton, the name of several places in England. Cotton is a Wicklow surname.

ᴅᴇ CRÁ̇FORC—XI—*de Crauford,* Crawford, etc. ; Nor. ' de Crauford,' i.e., of Crawford, a parish in Lanarkshire. The name is found in Anglo-Irish records as early as 1218, but, except in Donegal, there is no old family of Crawfords in Ireland. The Crawfords are for the most part descendants of Scottish settlers who came over at the time of the plantation of Ulster.

ᴅᴇ CRᴀ1ᵹ, ᴅᴇ CRᴇᴀᵹ—XI—*de Creck,* Cregg, Craig, etc. ; Nor. ' de Creck,' i.e., of the craig or rock, the same as ᴅᴇ Cᴀ̇ᵽᵽᴀ1ᵹ, q.v. The craig in question must have been in Scotland or in Wales.

ᴅᴇ CROĊCᴀS—XI—*de Croftus,* Crofts ; i.e., ' of the crofts,' or small farms.

ᴅᴇ CROĊCÚn—XI—*de Croftune,* Crofton ; Nor. ' de Croftune,' i.e., of Crofton in Yorkshire or Hampshire.

ᴅᴇ CRÚ1S—XI—*de Cruce, de Crosse,* Cruice, Cruise, Cross ; Nor. ' de Cruys,' Lat. ' de Cruce,' i.e., of the cross, from residence by the roadside or market cross (Mid. Eng. crouche, cruche) ; the name of an Anglo-Norman family who came to Ireland at the time of the invasion and obtained lands in Dublin and Meath. The chief seat of the family was at the Naul, where the ruins of their castle are still to be seen. In 1653, Peter Cruise of the Naul was transplanted to Connacht, and in 1691 many of the name were attainted. There was also an old family of Cruises in Co. Clare.

ᴅᴇ CU1RĊÉ1S—XII—Curteis, Curties, Curtis ; Nor. ' le Curteis,' i.e., the courteous, one of courtly manners (Old Fr. curteis). The name is of record in Ireland since the 13th century.

ᴅᴇ CU1CLÉ1R—XII—Quilter ; Nor. ' le Cutiler,' i.e., the cutler, maker of knives. This surname had come into Ireland before the end of the 13th century. Though always very rare, it still survives, but is now found chiefly in the neighbourhood of Listowel in Co.

Kerry, where it is pronounced corruptly Cuıllτéıṗ in Irish and made Quilter in English.

ᴅe Cúrsᴀ—XI—De Courcy, Courcey, Coursey; Nor., ' de Courcy,' i.e., of Courcy in Normandy; the name of a distinguished Norman family whose ancestors came to England with William the Conqueror. In 1177, Sir John de Courcy came to Ireland and having obtained from Henry II a grant of Ulster, invaded that province, committing dreadful slaughter of the inhabitants. His son, Milo de Courcy, was created Baron of Kinsale by Henry III, since which time the name has been associated chiefly with Co. Cork.

ᴅe ᴅıúıᴅ, Tuite. V. ᴅe Cıúıτ.

ᴅe ᴅromᵹúl—XI—de Dromgol, Dromgoull, Dromgole. Drumgole, Dromgoole, Drumgoole, Drumgoold; Nor. ' de Dromgole,' i.e., of ᴅruımᵹᴀᴅᴀıl, a frequent Irish place-name; the name of an old Co. Louth family. Dromgold of Dromgoldstown was one of the gentlemen of Co. Louth in 1598.

ᴅe ᴅurᴀm—XI—de Durame, Durham, Derham; i.e., ' of Durham.'

ᴅe fᴀe--XI--de Faie, Faie, Fay; Nor. 'de Faie,' i.e.,of Faie, in Normandy; the name of an Anglo-Norman family who settled in Co. Westmeath. They were seated at Tromroe and Derrynegarragh, and seem to have been a family of considerable local importance in the 16th and 17th centuries. The name is to be distinguished from the Irish Ó féıc which is also angl. Fay.

ᴅe fᴀoıc, ᴅe fᴀoıce—XII—White, Whyte; Nor. ' le White,' ' le Whyte,' i.e., the white, of fair complexion; the name of an Anglo-Norman family who came to Ireland at the time of the invasion. There are several respectable families of the name, which is common in all parts of Ireland.

ᴅe fılᴅe—XI—de Felda, Field; Nor. ' de la Felde,' de Felda,' i.e., at the field, from residence therein or thereby; the name of an Anglo-Norman family who settled in Co. Dublin soon after the invasion.

ᴅe fıonnᵹlᴀs—XI—de Fyneglas, Finglas; Nor. ' de

Fyneglas,' i.e., of Finglas; the name of an Anglo-Norman family who settled at, and took its name from, the village of Finglas in Co. Dublin.

ᴅe ꝼʀéın, ᴅe ꝼʀéıne—XI—*de Freyne*, Freyne, Frein, Frayne, Freyne, Freney, Freeney, etc; Nor. ' de la Freyne,' Lat. ' de Fraxineto,' i.e., ef the ash-tree (French frêne), from residence thereby; the name of an Anglo-Norman family who settled at an early period in Co. Kilkenny. The head of the family lived at Ballyreddy and was usually seneschal of Ormond.

ᴅe ꝼʀéıns—XI—*de Freynes, de Freyns, Freins, Frensh, Freynshe, Frensche*, French; Nor. ' de Freynes,' Lat. ' de Fraxinis,' i.e., of the ash-trees (cf. ᴅe ꝼʀéıne above), from residence thereby; the name of an Anglo-Norman family in Co. Wexford. A branch of this family settled in Galway in the 15th century and became one of the ' tribes '; now represented by Lord ffrench and Lord De Freyne.

ᴅe ꝼuıꞇe—XI—*Whittay*, Whitty; Mid. Eng. ' atte Wytheg,' i.e., at the white hey or enclosure, from residence thereby; the name of an old Anglo-Norman family in Co. Wexford.

ᴅe ꝼuıꞇléıᵹ—XI—Whiteley, Whitley; Nor. ' de Whit-leghe,' i.e., of Whiteley (white meadow), in Northumberland.

ᴅe ꝼuıꞇnıᵹ—XI—Whitney; Nor., ' de Whytene,' i.e., of Whitney in Hereford.

ᴅe ᵹaıllıᴅe—XI—*de Gallweia, de Galloway*, Galloway, Gallway, Galway, etc.; Nor. ' de Gallweia,' i.e., of Galloway in the S.W. of Scotland; the name of an Anglo-Norman family who settled in Ireland in the early part of the 13th century. The Galways were wealthy merchant families in Limerick, Cork, Kinsale and Youghal.

ᴅe ᵹallᴅaıle—XI—*de Galbally*, Galbally; i.e., ' of Galbally,' one of the small group of surnames formed after the Norman fashion from Irish place-names.

ᴅe ᵹaoʀ—XI—*de Guher, de Guer, de Goer, Goer, Gower, Gwerre, Goore*, Gware, Gore; Nor. ' de Guher,' ' de

Guer,' ' de Goer,' i.e., of Gwyr or Gower, a peninsula in South Wales, projecting into the Bristol Channel, where, since the time of Henry I, there had been a colony of Flemings. This family, which is probably of Flemish origin, came into Ireland about the time of the Anglo-Norman invasion, but has never been very numerous. The name is now found chiefly in Limerick, Kerry and Waterford.

ᴅe Ʒᴀ걽cúɴ—XI—*de Gascoyn*, Gascoigne, Gaskin ; Nor. ' de Gascoyne,' i.e., of Gascony, Fr. Gascogne, an old province in the S.W. of France ; the name of an old Norman family in Dublin. The form ' Gascoigne ' represents a later immigration.

ᴅe Ʒeᴀꞃᴅ—XI—*de Gard*, Garde ; probably of same origin as Ꝺoɩɴʒeᴀꞃᴅ, q.v. ; an old surname, still surviving in East Cork.

ᴅe Ʒeᴀꞇᴀ—XI—Yeates ; Mid. Eng. ' atte Yate,' ' atte Yeate,' i.e., at the gate (Old Eng. ' geat '), from residence thereby.

ᴅe Ʒᴌᴀɩɴbíoᴌ—XI—*de Glanvilla*, Glanville, Glanfield ; Nor. ' de Glanville,' i.e., of Glanville in Normandy ; an early Norman surname, but always very rare.

ᴅe Ʒᴌɩɴ—XI—*de Glyne, de Glen*, Glynn, Glinn, Glenn ; Nor. ' de Glyn,' ' del Glyn,' i.e., of Glyn, a parish in Brecknockshire, or of the glyn, or glen. Glyn enters largely into the formation of Welsh place-names. The surname came into Ireland at an early period, but has always been very rare.

ᴅe Ʒóꞃᴅúɴ—XI—*de Gordon*, Gordon ; Nor. ' de Gordon,' i.e., of Gordon, a parish in Berwickshire ; the name of a celebrated Scottish clan whose history goes back to Richard, lord of Gordon, about the middle of the 12th century. There were Gordons in Ireland as early as the middle of the 14th century, but the name was rare until after the plantation of Ulster. The modern Scottish form of the name is Ʒóꞃꝺoɴ or Ʒóꞃꝺᴀɴ.

ᴅe Ʒꞃᴀe—XI and XII—*de Grey, de Graye*, Grey, Gray ; (1) Nor. ' de Grey,' i.e., of Grey, some spot in England, probably; (2) Nor. 'le Grey,' i.e., the grey, from the colour of the hair. Both forms occur in early Irish records, but ' de Grey ' was by far the more common.

ᴅe ᵹᴙᴀɴᴐúɴ—XI—*de Grendun*, Grandon, Grandan; Nor. ' de Grendun,' i.e., of Grendon, a parish in Warwickshire, also a parish in Northamptonshire; an old but extremely rare surname in Ireland.

ᴅe ᵹᴙᴀɴɴᴄ—XII—*de Graunt*, Grant; Nor. ' le Graunt,' ' le Grant,' i.e., the great, gigantic in size; the name of a Norman family who came to Ireland some time before the end of the 13th century and settled in Kilkenny, Tipperary, Waterford and Cork. The Grants were also a Scottish clan, some of whom settled in Ulster at the time of the plantation, and are still represented in that province.

ᴅe ᵹᴙᴀᴏɪɴ—XI—*de Grene, Grene*, Greene, Green; Nor. ' de Grene,' i.e., at the green, or village common, from residence thereby; the name of an English family who settled in Dublin, Waterford, Limerick, etc. It can hardly now be distinguished from the many Irish surnames that have been anglicised Green.

ᴅe ᵹᴙéɪᴃ—XI—*de Greve, Grave*, Graves, Greaves; Nor. ' de Greve,' i.e., at the grove (Ang.-Sax. graef), from residence thereat.

ᴅe ᵹúᴙᴀm—XI—*de Gorham*, Gorham; Nor. ' de Gorham,' i.e., of Gorham in England. This surname has been in Ireland since the reign of Edward I. It is, no doubt, the origin of the surname which is pronounced Ó ᵹuᴀɪꝓm in Co. Galway and anglicised Gorham.

ᴅe ɦᴀe—XI—*de Haia, de Haya, de Hay*, Hay, Hays, Hayes; Nor. ' de la Haye,' Eng. ' atte Haye,' i.e., at the hay, or hedged field, from residence therein; the name of an Anglo-Norman family who settled about the time of the invasion in Co. Wexford.

ᴅe ɦᴀl—XI—Hall; Mid. Eng. ' atte Hall,' i.e., at the hall, from residence therein; an old surname in Cork and Tipperary. It is only in modern times that it has become common in Ireland.

ᴅe ɦᴀlᴀᴃᴏɪᴅ—XI—*de Halywode, Holywode, Holywood,*

Hollywood ; Nor. ' de Halywode,' and frequently in early Anglo-Irish records Lat. ' de Sancto Bosco ' and ' de Sacro Bosco,' i.e., of Hollywood (the holy wood), a parish in Co. Dublin. The family so named, which was one of the most distinguished of the Pale, settled about the time of the Anglo-Norman invasion in Dublin and Meath, where they possessed the manors of Artane, Great Holywood, and other estates.

ꝺe ɦᴀᴸᴜᴜⱱꝺe—XI—*de Holeweye, de Halee, Halvie,* Halvey, Holloway, Holoway, etc. ; Nor. ' in le Halwye,' ' de Holeweye,' perhaps in the holy, or hollow, way (Mid. Eng. ' halowe,' ' halwe,' ' halghe,' holy) ; apparently an old surname in Ireland ; there is a Bally-hallway in Co. Kildare. The Irish pronunciation is ꝺe ɦᴀᴸᴜᴜꝺe.

ꝺe ɦᴀᴸᴄᴜn—XI—*de Halton,* Halton ; Nor. ' de Halton,' i.e., of Halton, a parish in Buckinghamshire, a frequent place-name in England. Ballyhalton in Wicklow may have been the original home of the family in Ireland.

ꝺe ɦᴀᴍᴀᴸᴄᴜn—XI—*de Hameldon, Hamleton,* Hamil-ton ; Nor. ' de Hambledon,' ' de Hambleton,' i.e., of Hambledon or Hambleton, the name of several parishes in England, or of Hamilton in Scotland. The Hamiltons came over in large numbers from Scotland at the time of the plantation of Ulster.

ꝺe ɦᴀᴍᴄᴜn—XI—*de Hamptun, de Hampton,* Hampton ; Nor. ' de Hamptoun,' i.e., of Hampton in England. V. Ꝺonnꝺún. This name is of record in Ireland since the reign of Edward I, but has always been extremely rare.

ꝺe ɦᴀnᴃᴜRᵹᴀ—XI—*de Haneberge, de Hanburgo, de Haneberwe, de Handbury,* Hanbury, Handbury, Han-bery, Hanberry, Anborough, Anboro, etc ; Nor. ' de Hanburgo,' ' de Haneberge,' etc., i.e., of Hanbury, the name of several places in England. The English -burg and -berg, -bury and -berry, though distinct by origin, have long been confused. The Hanburys in the 14th century were a Co. Louth family.

ɒe ħᴀRpúR—XII—Harpur, Harper; Nor. 'le Harpour,' 'le Harpur,' i.e., the harper; the name of an old Anglo-Norman family who settled, probably in the 13th century, in Co. Wexford, where they are still numerous. The 'Harpers,' as distinct from the 'Harpurs,' are later settlers.

ɒe ħéᴀɒún—XI—*de Hedune,* Heden, Headon, Heydon, Haydon, etc.; Nor. 'de Hedune,' i.e., of Headon or Haydon, the name of several places in England. This surname came into Ireland soon after the Anglo-Norman invasion, but scarcely spread outside Dublin. 'Stephanus de Hedune' occurs in the Dublin Roll of Names, A.D. 1216.

ɒe ħeᴀRɼoRᴄ—XI—*de Herford, Herford,* Harford, Hartford, etc.; Nor. 'de Herford,' i.e., of Hereford; an old surname in Kilkenny.

ɒe ħenebRe, v. ɒe ħᴑonbuꞃᴣᴀ.

ɒe ħíɒe—XI—*de Hyda,* Hyde; Nor. 'de Hyda,' i.e., of Hyde, a market town in Cheshire (other places of the name in Gloucestershire and Hampshire); or it may be Eng. 'atte Hide,' i.e., at the hide, a measure of land, from residence therein. The surname is of record in Ireland since the 13th century. Cf. ᴑᴀʟᴀıᴄíɒ.

ɒe ħᴑonbuꞃᴣᴀ—XI—*de Hynteberge, de Hindeberg, de Hyntebrygh, Hynebrye, Henbury,* Henebery, Heneberry, Hennebry, Henebry, etc.; Nor. 'de Hynteberge, etc.,' i.e., of Hindeberg, the modern Henbury, a parish in Gloucestershire, also a place in Cheshire. The English terminations -burg and -berg, modern -bury and -berry, have been confused. Cf. ɒe ħᴀnbuꞃᴣᴀ above. The first of this family of whom we have record was Philip de Hynteberge who, about the middle of the 13th century, was lord of the manor of Rath, near Dublin, and one of the itinerant justices. His grandson, Nicholas de Hynteberge, in 1280, granted this manor to Robert Bagod, and it has since been known as Bagotrath. The family seems to have then settled in Co. Kilkenny, whence they spread into Waterford and Tipperary.

ⱱe ɦoċⱱun—XI—*de Hochton, de Hoghton, de Houghton,* Houghton, Haughton, etc. ; Nor. ' de Hoghton,' i.e., of Houghton, a common place-name in England. This surname came into Ireland in the 13th century, but has always been very rare.

ⱱe ɦóꞃ, ⱱe ɦóꞃᴀ—XII—*Horie,* Hore, Hoar, Hoare ; Nor. ' le hore,' i.e., the hoary, greyish-white, no doubt from the colour of the hair ; the name of an Anglo-Norman family who came to Ireland at the time of the invasion and settled in Dublin, Wicklow, Wexford, Carlow, Waterford, Cork, Kerry, etc. The Hores of Wexford were a distinguished and influential family.

ⱱe ɦóꞃsᴀıᵹ—*de Horseye,* Horsey, and incorrectly Hurst; Nor. ' de Horseye,' i.e., of Horsey, a parish in Norfolk. The surname is of record in Ireland since the 13th century, In the reign of Elizabeth, Jasper Horsey was seneschal of Imokilly. It still survives in Co. Waterford, but is corrupted to Ó ɦóꞃꞃᴀıᵹ and incorrectly re-anglicised Hurst.

ⱱe ɦosᴀe, ⱱe ɦúsᴀe—XI—*de Hosey, de Husee,* Hussey ; Nor. ' de Hosse,' ' de Heose,' etc., i.e. of Houssaye in Normandy. This family came into Ireland at the time of the Anglo-Norman invasion and settled in Dublin, Louth and Meath. In the last-named county the Husseys obtained large possessions, including Galtrim from which they took the title of baron. A branch of the family settled in the 16th century at Dingle, Co. Kerry. The Husseys suffered much in the wars of the 17th century.

ⱱeıⱱnıs—XII—Devenish, and incorrectly Devereux ; Nor. ' le Deveneis,' i.e., the Devonian, native of Devon ; an old surname in Ireland ; now wrongly re-anglicised Devereux in Co. Waterford.

ⱱe ıꞃéıs—XII—*de Ires,* Irish ; Nor. ' le Ireis,' i.e., the Irishman, a descriptive name given in England to an early emigrant from Ireland ; the Christian names in the Hundred Rolls show, however, that the emigrant was of Norman extraction. The exile, or one of his descendants, brought back the surname to Kilkenny, where, however, it has always been rare.

ᴅe ᴉʀᴌeoⁿᴄ—XI—*de Yrlond, de Yrlonde, Dirland, de Irland*, Ireland ; Nor. ' de Irland,' i.e., from Ireland, a local descriptive surname given in England to an early emigrant from Ireland. Cf. ᴅe Íʀéıʀ above The returned exile in this case also settled in Co. Kilkenny. The late Most Rev. John Ireland, D.D., Archbishop of St. Paul's, Min., was the best-known bearer of the name and an illustrious representative of this family.

ᴅéıꞅe—XI—*Deise, Dece*, Dease ; doubtless ' of Deise,' the barony of Deece in Co. Meath ; a Norman surname formed from an Irish place-name. The Annals at the year 1494 record the death of Gerald Deise, ' a good foreign youth of the Baron of Delvin's people.' The Deases resided at Turbotstown, and are one of the few old families who still retain their ancient patrimony.

ᴅéıꞅeᴀċ—X—*Deasaghe*, Deasy, Deasey ; Ir. ' ᴅéıʀeᴀċ,' i.e., native of the Decies of Waterford ; a descriptive epithet which supplanted the original surname which is now lost. The Deasys are numerous in Co. Cork.

ᴅe ᴌᴀ́—XI—Law ; Mid. Eng. ' atte Lawe,' i.e., at the *law*, or hill, from residence.

ᴅe ᴌᴀⁿᵹᴄúⁿ—XI—*de Langetoun, de Langetone*, Langton ; Nor. ' de Langetoun,' i.e., of Langton, a common place-name in England ; the name of an old Kilkenny family.

ᴅe ᴌéᴀᴅúꞅ—XI—*de Ledwich*, Ledwich, Ledwidge, Ledwitch, Ledwith, Lidwich, Ludwig ; Nor. ' de Ledwich,' i.e., of Ledwich, somewhere in England, but I cannot find the spot. This family settled soon after the Anglo-Norman invasion at Ledwichtown in Co. Westmeath.

ᴅe ᴌeᴀꞅᴄᴀʀ—XI—*de Leycester, de Lestre*, Leicester, Leycester, Lester, Lister, Lyster ; Nor. ' de Leycester,' i.e., of Leicester, in England.

ᴅe ᴌéıᵹ—XI—*de Lega, de Leye*, Leigh, Legge, Lea, Lee,

etc.; Lat. 'de Lega,' Nor. 'de Leye,' Mid. Eng.
'atte Lea,' i.e., at the legh (ley, lye, lea) or meadow,
from residence therein or thereby. The family so
called came to Ireland about the time of the Anglo-
Norman invasion and settled in Meath, Kildare,
Kilkenny, etc.

ꝺe Leiȝinn, ꝺe Lein—XI—*de Lane*, Lane; Nor. 'de
Lane,' Mid. Eng. 'atte Lane,' i.e., at the Lane, from
residence thereby; a very rare surname in Ireland,
nearly all our Lanes being of Irish origin.

ꝺe Leis—XI—*de Lesse, de Lease*, De Lacy, Lacy, Lacey;
Nor. 'de Laci,' i.e., of Lacy or Lassy in France. The
de Lacys came over to England with William the
Conqueror, and some of them appear in Domesday
Book as tenants-in-chief. At the time of the Anglo-
Norman invasion, Hugh de Lacy was granted the
whole of the province of Meath, but owing to failure
of male issue this vast territory soon passed away
into other families. A highly distinguished branch
of the de Lacys settled in Co. Limerick where they
had castles at Ballingarry, Bruree, Bruff, etc. Pierce
Lacy of Bruff was a celebrated captain in the wars
against Elizabeth. Several of the de Lacys became
famous in the service of Continental powers, notably
Count Peter de Lacy, born in Co. Limerick in 1678,
who was a celebrated military commander in Russia,
and his son, Maurice, Marshal de Lacy, who was no
less famous in the Austrian service; while another
Maurice de Lacy, also born in Co. Limerick, in 1740,
became a General in the Russian army. The de Lacys
were also distinguished in Spain, where Count de Lacy
was a famous general and diplomat in the 18th century.

ꝺe Liat—XI—*de Lee, Doleo, Lea*, Leo; of same origin
as ꝺe Leiȝ above; the name of an old Anglo-Irish
family in East Limerick. In 1600, the castle and
lands of Rathmore were held by James oge Leo, and
about the same time Leo of Tullavin was one of the
chief gentlemen of the county. The name is still
well-known in the neighbourhood of Kilmallock.

ꝺe **ꞁinꞅe**—XI—*de Lench, Lenche,* Lynch ; Nor. ' de Lench,' i.e., at the linch, or hill, from residence ; the name of a family who soon after the Anglo-Norman invasion settled at Knock in Co. Meath. A branch of this family, about the beginning of the 14th century, removed to Galway where they became one of the leading ' tribes ' and occupied a distinguished position down to the end of the Jacobite wars when several of the name were attainted and their property confiscated. There are, however, several respectable families of Lynches still in Connacht. This surname is to be distinguished from the Irish Ó ꞁoinꞅꞃiꞅ, q.v.

ꝺe **ꞁion**—XI—*de Leon, de Lyons,* Lyon, Lyons, etc. ; Nor. ' de Leon,' ' de Lyons,' i.e., of Lyons, the city in France, or possibly of Lyons, a parish in Durham ; the name of an Anglo-Norman family who came to Ireland about the time of the invasion and settled in Meath and other parts of the Pale.

ꝺe **ꞁioncóꞁ**—XI—*de Lincole, de Lincoll, Lincole,* Lincoln ; Nor. ' de Lincoll,' i.e., of Lincoln, a city in England ; an old but always extremely rare surname in Ireland.

ꝺe **ꞁionꞇún**—XI—*de Linton, Lyntoun,* Linton, Lynton, Lenton ; Nor, ' de Linton,' i.e., of Linton, a frequent place-name in England ; an old but always rare surname in Ireland.

ꝺe **ꞁioꞅꞁᴀ**—XI—*de l'isula, del Isle, Lisle, Lislie,* Leslie, Lesley ; Nor. ' del Isle,' Lat. ' de Insula,' i.e., of the island, from residence therein. A family of this name came to Ireland about the time of the Anglo-Norman invasion and seem to have settled in Dublin and Meath. Some Scottish Leslies settled in Derry at the time of the plantation of Ulster.

ꝺe **ꞁioꞅꞇún**—XI—*de Lextoun, de Lectone, de Lyston, Lystowne,* Liston ; Nor. ' de Lexington,' ' de Lexintoun,' 'de Lessinton,' ' de Lextoun,' ' de Lyston,' i.e., of Lexington, or Laxton, in Nottinghamshire. This family settled in the 13th century at Kilscannell, in Co. Limerick, which they held down to the year

1595, when it was confiscated and granted to Captain Robert Collum. The Listons are still numerous in Co. Limerick.

ᴅe ʟoᴄᴛús—XI—*de Lofthouse*, Loftus, Loftis ; Nor. 'de Lofthouse,' i.e., of Loftus in Yorkshire, or of the lofthouse (house with an upper story) ; a rare surname in Ireland, found chiefly in Wexford. Nearly all our Loftuses are of Irish origin.

ᴅe ʟonᴅᴙᴀ, ᴅe ʟonᴅᴙᴀs—XI—*de Loundres, Londres, Londra, Londry*, Landrey, Landers, Launders ; Nor. 'de Loundres,' i.e., of London. Families of this name came into Ireland soon after the Anglo-Norman invasion and settled in Dublin, Meath, Wexford, Ormond, etc. The form ᴅe ʟonᴅᴙᴀ is peculiar to West Munster. See also ᴅe ʟonᴅún.

ᴅe ʟonᴅún—XI—*de Lundun, de Lundon, de London*, Lundon, London, Landon ; a var. of ᴅe ʟonᴅᴙᴀᴙ, ᴅe ʟonᴅᴙᴀ, q.v. John de Lundon and Richard de Lundun are mentioned in the Dublin Roll of Names, A.D. 1216. William de London was witness to a grant of land by the dean and chapter of Limerick early in the 13th century, from which period onward the name appears to have been peculiar to the counties of Limerick and Waterford.

ᴅe ʟonᴈ—XII—Long ; Nor. 'le Lung,' 'le Loung,' i.e., the long, one of remarkably tall stature. This surname came into Ireland about the time of the Anglo-Norman invasion, and was not uncommon in many parts of the country. It cannot now be easily distinguished from the many Irish surnames that have been anglicised Long.

ᴅe ʟunᴅᴙᴀs, Landers, Launders. V. ᴅe ʟonᴅᴙᴀᴙ.

ᴅe mɪséɪᴅ—XI—*de Miset*, Misset ; Nor. 'de Miset,' i.e., of Miset, some spot probably in Normandy ; the name of a Norman family who settled with de Lacy in Meath ; now very rare, if not obsolete.

ᴅe móɪnᴠɪoʟ—XI—*de Manneville, de Maundeville*, Mandeville, and incorrectly Mansfield in Waterford and parts of Cork ; Nor. 'de Magneville,' 'de Mandeville,' Lat. 'de Magnavilla,' i.e., of Magneville, corruptly Mandeville, a place-name in Normandy. Among those who attended William the Conqueror to England was Sire de Magneville; and 'de Manneville,' or 'de Monneville' occurs in Domesday Book. The name is of record in Ireland since the early part of the 13th century, but is now very rare, especially as Mandeville, the form Mansfield having been substituted for it in English. The family settled in Tipperary and Waterford.

ꝺe moıꞃéıs—XI—*de Mareys, de Marries, Morreis,* Morris, and incorrectly Morrison; Nor. 'de Mareys,' 'de Marreis,' Lat. 'de Marisco,' i.e., of the marsh (Fr. marais), from residence thereby; a common surname in many parts of the south of Ireland, especially in Kilkenny, Tipperary, Offaly, Leix, Cork and Limerick, where it is now generally anglicised Morris. In the neighbourhood of Kilmallock, the angl. form is popularly Morresh, but officially it is incorrectly turned into Morrison. A family of the name settled, in 1485, at Galway and became one of the 'tribes' of that city.

ꝺe moıꞃꞇıméıꞃ—XI—*de Mortimer,* Mortimer, etc. Nor. 'de Mortemer,' i.e., of Mortemer in Normandy; incorrectly Latinised 'de Mortuo Mari' (of the Dead Sea), for which reason it was supposed to have arisen in crusading times. One of the de Mortimers accompanied William the Conqueror to England, and the name appears in Domesday Book. It came into Ireland about the time of the Anglo-Norman invasion. In 1185 Robert de Mortemer was witness to King John's Dublin Charter. The family settled in Meath, but was never very numerous.

ꝺe monꞇáın—XI—*Montaine, Montayn,* Montane, Mountain, etc.; Nor. 'de la Montayne,' i.e., of the mountain (Old Fr. montaine, mod. Fr. montagne), from residence thereby; a rare Norman surname, found chiefly in Co. Cork. To be distinguished from Ó mannꞇáın q.v.

ᴠe **mÓRᴀ**—XI—*de Mora*, More, Moore, etc. ; Nor. ' de
la More,' Mid. Eng. ' atte Mor,' Lat. ' de Mora,' i.e.,
at the moor or heath, from residence thereby ; an old
Anglo-Norman surname in Ireland ; still found in
parts of Munster and Connacht. Its angl. forms
cannot be distinguished from those of the Irish Ó
mÓrᴅᴀ, q.v.

ᴠe **mÓRᴄûn**—XI—*de Mortun*, *de Mortoun*, *de Morton*,
Moreton, Morton ; Nor. ' de Mortun,' i.e., of Morton,
a common place-name in England.

ᴠe **moᴄûn**—XI—*de Mohun*, *de Moun*, Moon, Moone ;
Nor. ' de Mohun,' i.e., of Mohon or Moon in France.

ᴠe **mûRᴀ**, More, Moore ; a var. of ᴠe mÓrᴀ, q.v.

ᴠe **nᴀ1s**—XI—*de Nasshe*, Nash, Naish ; Mid. Eng.
' atten Ash,' ' atte Nash,' i.e., at the ash, from residence beside an ash-tree ; the *n* of the article, having
been attracted over, became the initial of the surname. Etymologically, therefore, Nash is precisely
the same as Ashe (v. ᴀ1r). This surname appears
in Ireland soon after the Anglo-Norman invasion, and
is now fairly common in Limerick and Kerry. In the
latter county it is sometimes corrupted to ᴠe Rᴀ1r.
Cf. ᴠe nᴀr below.

ᴠe **nᴀs**—XI—*de Naas*, Nash, Naish ; Nor. ' de Naas,'
i.e., of Naas in Co. Kildare ; a surname taken by an
early Anglo-Norman family from their place of settlement ; now confused with, and absorbed by, ᴠe nᴀ1r,
q.v. It is possible also that, owing to false analogy,
it has, by a process the reverse of that which took
place in the case of ᴠe nᴀ1r (see above), been corrupted to ' de As,' ' de Asse,' and so may now be
sometimes represented by Ashe. (v. ᴀ̄ᴣᴀr).

ᴠe **néᴀᴠ**—XI—*de Nethe*, now incorrectly Neville ; Nor.
' de Nethe,' i.e., of Neath, in Wales. This surname
is in use in Co. Cork, where it is strangely anglicised
Neville.

ᴠe **neᴀᴠRᴀ1ᴠ1oᴌ**—XI—*de Netterville*, *Nettervilde*,
Netterfield, Netterville ; Nor. ' de Netterville,' i.e.,
of Netherfield (lower field), name of a parish in

Sussex, and of another in Nottinghamshire. This family came to Ireland about the time of the Anglo-Norman invasion and settled in the counties of Dublin and Meath. Luke Netterville was Archbishop of Armagh in the early part of the 13th century. The Nettervilles were a very distinguished family. They took an active part in public affairs and were prominent in the Confederate and Jacobite wars.

ⴅenn—XI—*de Dene*, Denn ; Mid. Eng. ' atte Dene,' i.e., at the deane, or wooded valley, from residence therein ; an old, but rare, Kilkenny surname.

ⴅe nóꝲlⴀ—XI—*de Nangle, de Nongle, de Nougle, Nogle*, Nangle, Nagle, Neagle, etc. ; Mid. Eng. ' atten Angle,' ' atte Nangle,' Lat. ' de Angulo,' i.e., at the angle or corner, from residence thereat ; the *n* of the article was attracted over, as in the case of ⴅe nⴀⵑ (q.v.), and thus became the initial of the surname proper. The Nangles or Nagles derive their descent from Gilbert de Angulo, one of the earliest of the Anglo-Norman invaders. They obtained large grants of land in Meath, and were barons of Navan. Branches of the family settled in Westmeath, Kildare, Waterford and Cork. In Munster the name is now always Englished Nagle or Neagle.

ⴅe noⵑꝴⵑeⵑⵑ—XII—*Norreys*, Norrish, Norris, etc. ; Nor. ' le Norreys,' ' le Noreis,' i.e., the Northman, the Northerner. Families of this name settled in Ireland about the time of the Anglo-Norman invasion.

ⴅe noⵑⴀⴅ, ⴅe noⵑⴀⵑⴅ—XI—*de Norragh, de Norroy, de Norwey*, Noury, Nowry, and incorrectly Norris in Waterford, Kerry, etc. ; Nor. ' de Norwey,' i.e., from Norway, Norwegian settler ; synonymous with ⴅe noⵑⵑéⵑⵑ, (q.v.) and often similarly anglicised.

ⴅe noⵑⵞún—XI—*de Nortune*, Norton ; Nor. ' de Nortune,' i.e., of Norton, a common place-name in England. This surname came into Ireland soon after the Anglo-Norman invasion, but has always been very rare. Most of our Nortons are really O'Naughtons.

de Nuiḃíol—XI—*de Neuville, de Neville,* Neville; Nor. 'de Neuville,' 'de Neville,' i.e., of Neville or Neuville, a common place-name in France. This family came into Ireland about the time of the Anglo-Norman invasion and settled in Wexford, Carlow and Kilkenny. The Nevilles of Limerick and Cork are of a different origin. See Ó Niaḋ and de Néaḋ. In Co. Clare, Ó Cnáiṁín (q.v.) is sometimes anglicised Neville.

de Núinnseann—XI—*de Nungent, de Nugent,* Nugent; Nor. 'de Nugent,' i.e., of Nogent, a common place-name in France. The Nugents came to England with William the Conqueror, and settled in Ireland at the time of the Anglo-Norman invasion. Gilbert de Nugent was made baron of Delvin by Hugh de Lacy, and the title continued in the family down to the year 1621 when Richard Nugent, Baron of Delvin, was created Earl of Westmeath. The Nugents were one of the most illustrious of the Norman families in Ireland. For special reference to the Nugents of Cork, see under Uinnseaḋún.

de Oirġiall—XI—*de Uriel,* Urrell, Eurell, Yourell; Nor. 'de Uriel,' i.e., of Oriel; the name of an old Anglo-Norman family who settled in Co. Louth and afterwards in Westmeath; now very rare.

de Páiris—XI—*de Paris, de Parys,* Parish; Nor. 'de Paris,' i.e., of Paris. In 1295, Peter de Paris was burgess and merchant of Youghal, and Parish is, or was at the beginning of the 17th century, a Co. Cork surname.

de Paor—XII—Poer, Poor, Power; Nor. 'le Pover,' 'le Pouer,' 'le Power,' 'le Poer,' 'le Poor,' i.e., the poor (Old Fr. 'povre, paure,' Lat. pauper), a sobriquet hardly bestowed because of ordinary poverty, which must always have been too common to be a mark of distinction, but probably, as Bardsley suggests, of poverty consequent on a vow. The ancestor of this family came to Ireland with Strongbow, from whom he obtained a grant of the territory of Waterford. In 1535, Sir Richard le Poer was created Baron of Curraghmore, but through failure of the male line, at the beginning of the 18th century, the estates of Curraghmore passed by marriage into the family of Beresford. The name is now very common and widespread, especially in Munster and Leinster.

ᵹe peᵹᴄún—XI—*de Peton, de Peyton,* Peyton, Payton; Nor. ' de Peton,' i.e., of Peton, Peyton, or Payton in England.

ᵹe pioṁbróᵹ, ᵹe pionbróc—XI—*de Pembrog, de Penbroc,* Pembroke; Nor. ' de Penbroc,' i.e., of Pembroke in Wales; an old, but rare, surname in Ireland. Many of the early Norman invaders came from Pembrokeshire.

ᵹe poiṙe—XI—*de Pirye, Pyrry,* Pirrie, Perry; Nor. ' de la Pirie,' Mid. Eng. ' atte Perye,' i.e., at the perry, or pear-tree (Fr. poire), from residence thereby.

ᵹe poiṙᴄinᵹéiᴌ—XI—*de Portyngale, Portingale, Portingall,* Portabello; i.e., from Portugal; a rare surname, peculiar to Youghal and district. In 1569, John Portingale was one of the townsmen of Youghal, as was Arthur Portingall thirty years later. The name is now strangely anglicised Portabello.

ᵹe pomṙᵹe—XI—*de Pomeray,* Pomeroy, Pomroy; Nor. ' de Pomeray,' i.e., of the apple-orchard (Fr. pommeraie), from residence thereby; a Co. Cork surname.

ᵹe pṙᵹᴄ—XI—*Prat,* Pratt; Lat. ' de Prato,' same as the Fr. Duprat, Dupray, i.e., at the meadow (Old Fr. ' prat,' Fr. ' pré,' Lat. pratum), from residence thereby or therein. In early Anglo-Irish records, it generally appears in the Lat. form of ' de Prato.' ' Martinus de Prato ' occurs in the Dublin Roll of Names, A.D. 1216; and Richard Prat was a witness to a document in the Black Book of Limerick.

ᵹe pṙeᵹsᴄún—XI—*de Preston,* Preston; Nor. ' de Preston,' i.e., of Preston, a common place-name in England. This surname is of record in Ireland since the middle of the 13th century. In 1361, Robert de Preston was knighted by Lionel, Duke of Clarence,

and obtained a grant of the manor of Gormanstown ;
and his great-grandson, another Sir Robert Preston,
was, in the year 1478, elevated to the peerage by the
title of Viscount Gormanston. It was on the in-
vitation of Nicholas, the sixth Viscount Gormanston,
that the noblemen and gentry of the Pale assembled
at the historic meeting on the Hill of Crofty in 1641.
The Prestons took a prominent part in the Confederate wars, and Viscount Gormanston was exempted by Cromwell from pardon for life and estate.
His son and successor, Jenico Preston, was likewise
attainted in 1691. It was only in the year 1800
that these outlawries were removed and the family
honours restored.

ᵒe ρ̱ꞃⁱoⁿᴅᴀꞃᵹᴀ́s, ᴅe ρ̱ꞃⁱoⁿᴅꞃᴀᵹᴀ́s—XI—*de
Prendergast*, Prendergast, Prindergast, Pendergast,
Pendergrass, Pender, Pinder, etc. ; Nor. ' de Prendergast,' i.e., of Prendergast, a parish in Pembrokeshire.
Maurice de Prendergast was one of the knights who
accompanied Strongbow to Ireland. He and his
descendants obtained large grants of land in different
parts of the south and west of Ireland. The principal branches of the family were seated in the present
counties of Wexford, Kilkenny, Tipperary, Limerick,
Mayo and Galway. The surname is variously corrupted in Irish as well as in English.

ᴅe ρ̱ꞃⁱoⁿⁿᵬⁱoꞁ—XI—*de Prendeville*, Prendeville, Prindeville, Prendible, Prenderville, Pendiville, etc., and
incorrectly Bransfield ; Nor. ' de Frendeville,' i.e.,
of Frendeville, some spot, no doubt, in **Normandy;**
the name of an old Kerry family. Thomas de Frendeville was sheriff of Kerry in 1235. In Co. Cork
the name has been strangely changed to Bransfield.

ᴅe ꞃᴀⁱꞁéⁱᵹ—XI—*de Rayleg, de Raleigh, de Raley*,
Rally, Rawley, Rawleigh, Raleigh ; Nor. ' de Ralegh,'
i.e., of Raleigh in England ; the name (1) of an old
Anglo-Norman family who settled at Rawleystown
and other places in Co. Limerick and the adjoining
parts of Tipperary, where it is still common ; and

(2) of an old Anglo-Norman family in Co. Kildare. This surname appears in old Anglo-Irish records under a great variety of spellings, and the same is true of English records; Bardsley gives seventeen different forms from the Index to the Register of Oxford University alone. In Co. Limerick 'de Raley' and 'de Roley,' 'Rawlie' and 'Rowlie,' 'Rawley' and 'Rowley,' occur side by side down to the end of the 16th century, when Richard Rowlie, alias Raleigh, of Raleighston (also called Rawleystown, Rolleston, and Ballynrowley), Co. Limerick, gentleman, was the recipient of a pardon from Queen Elizabeth; and Raleigh, Rowley, Roley, etc., as English place-names, are, or were, similarly interchangeable.

ᴅe ꞃᴀmꞄᴀιᵹ—XI—*de Ramsey, Ramesey*, Ramsey, Ramsay; Nor. 'de Ramsey,' i.e., of Ramsey, the name of more than one place in England. Though this surname is an old one in Ireland, most of those who now bear it are the descendants of late immigrants, who came hither from Scotland.

ᴅe ꞃᴀᴛ—XI—*de Rath*, Rath; Nor. 'du Rath,' i.e., of the rath, some spot near Dublin. The surname survives in Co. Louth.

ᴅe ꞃιoᴅᴀⳑ—XI—*de Ridal, de Rydale*, Riddell, Riddle, Ruddell, Ruddle; Nor. 'de Ridal,' i.e., of Ridal (?), some spot in England. 'de Rydale' and 'Rydalagh' occur in old documents relating to Co. Limerick, where Ruddle is a well-known surname. V. ꞃιoᴅᴀⳑ.

ᴅe ꞃιꞄeᴀmonn—XI—*de Richemond*, Richmond; Nor. 'de Richemond,' i.e., of Richmond, the well-known town in Surrey.

ᴅe ꞃóιꞄᴛe—XI—Roche, Roache; Nor. 'de la Roche,' Lat. 'de Rupe,' i.e., of the rock, from residence beside some prominent rock; an old Norman surname. Families of this name settled in different parts of Ireland, but the best known were those of Cork, Limerick and Wexford. In the first-named county, the Roches obtained by marriage the district about Fermoy known as Cꞃιoc ꞃóιꞃᴛeᴀc, or Roche's

Country ; the head of this family was Viscount Fermoy.
The Roches of Limerick were a wealthy and respectable merchant family. Among the twenty exempted
from pardon by Ireton when he obtained possession
of the city in 1651, were Alderman Jordan Roche and
Edmund Roche. Roche of Rochesland was one of
the principal gentlemen of Wexford in 1598.

ⴁe ROS—XI—*de Ros*, Ross ; Nor. ' de Ros,' i.e., of Ross,
a Gaelic place-name, probably in Scotland.

*ⴁe ROSⱵORⱦ—XI—*de Rochefort, de Rocheford, de Rochford*, Rochefort, Rochfort, Rochford, Rushford, etc. ;
Nor. ' de Rochefort,' Lat. ' de Rupe forti,' i.e., of
Rochefort (strong or fortified rock) in France. This
surname came into Ireland at the time of the Anglo-
Norman invasion and soon became very widespread.
In the 16th century, it was found chiefly in Meath,
Westmeath, Kildare, Carlow, Wexford, Waterford
and Limerick. It is now, strange to say, comparatively rare. In Limerick, the Irish forms Roⱃⱦⱥⱃⱁ
and Roⱃⱦún (q.v.) are found.

ⴁe RUIS—XI—*de Rush*, Rush ; Nor. ' de Rush,' i.e.,
probably of Rush, Co. Dublin ; a very rare surname.

ⴁe RÚS—XII—*de Rus*, Rose ; Nor. ' le Rus,' ' le Rous,'
Lat. ' Rufus,' i.e., red-haired ; a descriptive surname.
Cf. Ruiⱃéiⱡ.

ⴁe SⱭⴁRⱭinn—XI—*de Sauverne, Severne, Severn, Saryn*,
Saurin ; Nor. ' de Sauverne,' i.e., of the Severn, from
residence beside the River Severn in England. The
surname is old in Ireland, but has always been very
rare.

ⴁe SⱭiliⵘéiR—XI—*de Seyntlegger, de St. Ledger*, Sallinger, Sellinger, St. Ledger, etc. ; Nor. ' de St. Ledger,'
Lat. ' de Sancto Leodegario,' i.e., of St. Leger's, a
common place-name in France. This family came
to Ireland probably about the beginning of the 14th
century and settled in different parts of the Pale,
especially in Co. Kilkenny. By the 16th century
they had become so Irish that Stanihurst describes
them as ' mere Irish.' Their chief seat was at Tullagh-

anbroge; a branch of the family resided at Bally-
fennon. The head of the family was called Baron of
Slieve Margie. V. Sᴀɪʟeᴀɼcᴀɼ, Sᴀɪʟɪʒéɼ, and Sᴜɪʟ-
ɪɳʒéɼ.

ᴅe SᴀɪɳcReᴀᴅ—XI—*de Santry*, Santry; Nor. 'de
Santry,' i.e., of Santry, Ir. Seᴀɳcɼeᴀᴅ, a village in
Co. Dublin; the name of an early Anglo-Norman
family. It was never very common, and is now
found chiefly in Co. Cork.

ᴅe SᴀɪRSéɪʟ—XI—*de Sarsefield*, Sarsfield, etc.; Nor.
'de Sarnesfeld,' 'de Sarnefield,' 'de Chernesfend,'
i.e., of Sarnesfelde (as the name is written in Domesday Book, where it is mentioned as one of the King's
manors) in Herefordshire, the modern name of which
I have failed to discover. This surname came into
Ireland about the time of the Anglo-Norman invasion,
when the family settled in Dublin, Kildare, Cork and
Limerick. There were many distinguished men of
the name, but it is to Patrick Sarsfield, Earl of Lucan,
the celebrated commander in the wars of the Revolution, that it owes its fame in Irish history.

ᴅe Sᴀʟ—XI—*de Salle, Sale, Sawle*, Sall, Saul; Nor. 'de
la Sale,' i.e., of the hall, from residence therein; the
name of an Anglo-Norman family who settled early
at Cashel, Co. Tipperary, and at Salestown, Co. Meath.
In 1598, Sale of Saleston was one of the chief gentlemen of Co. Meath. The name is now very rare.

ᴅe Sᴀɳᴅᴀʟ—XI—*de Sandale, de Sandall*, Sandall, Sandell; Nor. 'de Sandale,' i.e., of Sandale or Sandal, a
frequent place-name in the north of England; the
name of an Anglo-Norman family who settled early
in the neighbourhood of Carrickfergus.

ᴅe SᴀɳɼoRc—XI—*de Saunford, de Sanford*, Sanford;
Nor. 'de Sanford,' i.e., of Sandford, some spot in
England.

ᴅe SᴀoʒRᴀᴅ—XI—*de Segrave*, Seagrave, Segrave, Seagrove, Segre; Nor. 'de Segrave,' i.e., of Seagrave
(Ang.-Sax. Saegraf), a parish in Leicestershire. This
family came to Ireland probably in the early part

of the 14th century and settled in Meath and Dublin.
Their chief seat was at Killeglan in Co. Meath, with
branches at Cabragh and Ballyboghill, in Co. Dublin.
In 1322 Stephen Segrave was made Primate of Armagh.

ᴅe SCÉᴀLᴀS—XI—*de Scales*, Scales; Nor. ' de Scales,'
i.e., of Scales, a common place-name in the north of
England; an old, but extremely rare, surname in
Ireland. There are a few families of the name in
Limerick.

ᴅe SCEᴀLCÚn—XI—*de Skelton*, Skelton; Nor. ' de
Skelton,' i.e., of Skelton, the name of a parish in Yorkshire and of another in Cumberland.

ᴅe SCOꝶUL—XI—*de Scoville*, Scuffil, Scofield, Schofield,
Scholefield; Nor, ' de Scoville,' i.e., of Scoville or
Escoville in Normandy. This surname is in use in
Co. Mayo, but the present angl. forms are incorrect.
Scovell or Scovill, as in England, would be better.

ᴅe SCRᵻᵬᵻn—XI—*de Screvine, de Skrevyn*, Scriven; Nor.
' de Screvine,' i.e., of Scriven in Yorkshire; a rare
Cork surname.

ᴅe SCRᵻn—XI—*de Scryne, Screne*, Skryne; Nor. ' de
Scryne,' i.e., of Screen, probably in Meath; an extremely rare surname.

ᴅe SEᴀnCREᴀᵬ, Santry. V. ᴅe Sᴀᵻnᴛꞃeᴀᵬ.

ᴅe SᵻnCLÉᵻR—XI—*de Seynclere, de Sencler*, Sinclare,
Sinclair, St. Clair, St. Clare, etc.; Nor. ' de St. Clair,'
Lat. ' de Sancto Claro,' ' de Sancto Clero,' i.e., of St.
Clair, a frequent place-name in Normandy. This
surname came into England with William the Con-
queror, and was borne by an important Scottish clan.
In Ireland also it occurs early, but the family was
never either numerous or important.

ᴅe SᵻnᴣeᴀLCÚn—XI—*de Singleton*, Singleton; Nor.
' de Singleton,' i.e., of Singleton, the name of a parish
in Sussex and of another in Lancashire. This surname in Clare and Cork has been corrupted to Ó
Sᵻnᴅᵻᴛe and Ó SᵻonᴅᵻᵻLe.

ᴅe SᵻOnÚᵻR—XI—*de Synors, de Sinors, de Sunors*,
Shinnor, Shinnors; Nor. ' de Sinors,' etc., i.e., of

Sinors or Sunors, apparently some spot in England ; an old, but rare, Anglo-Norman surname found chiefly in East Limerick and in parts of Connacht. V. Sionúiɼ.

ᴅe Sιūn—XII—*Yonge*, Younge, Young ; Nor. ' le Jeune,' ' le Jouen,' i.e., the young, in the sense of the younger, junior, as opposed to senior. Families of this name settled about the time of the Anglo-Norman invasion in Dublin, Kildare, and other parts of Ireland. Young of Youngstown was one of the principal gentlemen of Co. Kildare in 1598, while at the same time ' Young of Gareston was one of the ' men of name ' in Co. Dublin.

ᴅe Sιūnᴄᴀ, Joynt.

ᴅe Sᴌᴀιne—XI—*de Slane*, *Slaan*, Slane ; Nor. ' de Slane,' i.e., of Slane, in Co. Meath ; an early, but always very rare, Norman surname.

ᴅe Spᴀιne—XI—*de Spainne*, Spain ; Nor. ' de Spainne,' i.e., from Spain, an immigrant from Spain.

ᴅe Sᴄᴀbᴀᴌᴄūn—XI—*de Stapeltoun*, *de Stapulton*, Stapelton, Stapleton ; Nor. ' de Stapeltoun,' i.e., of Stapleton, a common English place-name ; the name of an old and distinguished Anglo-Norman family who settled, soon after the invasion, in Kilkenny and Tipperary. They assumed the Irish surname of mᴀc ᴀn Ӡᴀιᴌᴌ (q.v.), but were also called Ӡᴀᴌᴌᴅᴜᴃ, q.v.

ᴅe Sᴄᴀcᴀbūᴌ, ᴅe Sᴄᴀcᴀpūᴌ—XI—*de Stacepole*, *Stacaboll*, *Stacapoll*, Stackpole, Stackpoole ; Nor. ' de Stacepole,' of Stackpool or Stackpole, a parish in Pembrokeshire ; also called Ӡᴀᴌᴌᴅᴜᴃ, q.v. ; the name of an early Norman family who settled in Tipperary and other parts of the south of Ireland. The name is now very rare.

ᴅe Sᴄᴀɼᴏᴚᴄ—XI—*de Stafford*, Stafford ; Nor. ' de Stafford,' i.e., of Stafford in England ; the name of an old and distinguished Wexford family ; also found in Dublin, Louth and Kilkenny.

ᴅe Sᴄᴀιneᴀs—XI—*de Stanes*, Staines ; Nor. ' de Stanes,' i.e., of Staines in Middlesex, or Stanes in Lincolnshire.

ᴅe Sᴛᴀɪɴᴌéɪᴈ—XI—*de Stanleye, de Stanley*, Stanley"; Nor. ' de Stanley,' i.e., of Stanley, a common English place-name.

ᴅe Sᴛᴀɴꝼoᴚᴛ—XI—*de Stanford*, Stanford, Stancard; Nor. ' de Stanford,' i.e., of Stanford, in England. V. Sᴛᴀɴcᴀᴩᴅ.

ᴅe Sᴛóc—XI—*de Stoke, de Stokes*, Stokes, Stoakes ; Nor. ' de Stoke,' i.e., of Stoke, a common English place-name, from Old Eng. ' stoc,' a village. Mono-syllabic surnames of local origin often add on the genitive *s* after the manner of patronymics. This surname came into Ireland about the time of the Anglo-Norman invasion, and was common in many parts of the country.

ᴅe Sᴛoɴɴᴅúɴ—XI—*de Stauntoun, de Stanton*, Staunton, Stanton, Stundon, Sdundon ; Nor. ' de Stanton,' i.e., of Stanton, a frequent place-name in England. The Stantons were amongst the earliest of the Anglo-Norman invaders. They settled in Dublin, Kildare, Kilkenny, Cork and Mayo. The Stantons of the last-named county, who were followers of the Burkes, obtained extensive possessions in the barony of Carra, and formed a clan after the Irish fashion. They took the Irish surname of ᴍᴀc ᴀɴ ṁíᴌeᴀᴅᴀ, i.e., son of the knight, probably from their ancestor, Milo de Stanton, as did also the Stauntons of Cork.

ᴅe Sᴜᴀɴᴛúɴ—XI—*de Swantun*, Swanton ; Nor. ' de Swanton,' i.e., of Swanton, in Norfolkshire or Kent.

ᴅe Sᴜɪɴᴈeᴀɴ—XI—*de St. John*, St. John, Singen, Singin, etc., Nor. ' de St. Jean' ; Lat. ' de Sancto Johanne,' i.e., of St. Jean, a common French place-name. This family settled early in Wexford, Kil-kenny and Tipperary. Thomas de St. John was sheriff in Tipperary in 1296.

ᴅe Sᴜᴛúɴ—XI—*de Suttoun*, Sutton ; Nor. ' de Suttoun,' i.e., of Sutton, a common place-name in England. The Suttons are an old and respectable Anglo-Norman family who settled soon after the invasion in Kildare and Wexford.

ᴅe ᴄıû—XI—*de Tiwe, de Tywe, Tue,* Tew ; Nor. ' de Tiwe,' i.e., of Tew, in Oxfordshire, more anciently Tiwe ; an old, but rare, surname in Kildare, Kilkenny and Waterford.

ᴅe ᴄıûıᴄ—XI—*de Tuite,* Tuite ; Nor. ' de Tuite,' ' del Tuit,' i.e., of Tuit or Thuit, a frequent place-name in Normandy, of same meaning as the English thwaite, i.e., a woodland clearing. The presence of the article in the old form ' del Tuit ' would seem to show that the surname was taken from the common noun rather than from the place-name. The Tuites were a distinguished Norman family, descended from Richard de Tuite who came over with Strongbow ; and they enjoyed extensive estates in Longford, Meath and Westmeath down to the confiscations of the 17th century. The head of the family was Baron of Moycashel.

ᴅe ᴄʀáıᴅeáʀꜱ—XI—*de Travers, de Tryveres, de Tryvers, Trevers, Trivers,* Travers, Travors, Trevors, etc. ; Nor. ' de Tryvers,' i.e., of Treviers in Normandy ; a rather old surname in Dublin and many parts of the south of Ireland, especially Kildare, Carlow, Tipperary and Cork.

ᴅe ᴄʀeáɴᴄ—XI—*de Trente,* Trant ; Nor. ' de Trente,' i.e., of Trent, a parish in Somerset, also a place in Dorset ; the name of an old and respectable Kerry family. At the end of the 16th century, the Trants of Dingle were one of the chief families of that county. Sir Patrick Trant was a prominent Jacobite. He was attainted, together with several others of the name, in 1691, and lost extensive estates in Kerry and other parts of Ireland.

ᴅe ᴄʀeó—XI—*de Troya, de Troie, de Troye,* Troy ; Nor. ' de Troye,' i.e., of Troyes, a city in France, formerly the capital of Champagne ; an old but rare surname in Kilkenny and Waterford. V. ᴄʀeó.

ᴅe ᴄʀuım—XI—*de Trim,* Trim ; Nor., ' de Trim,' i.e., of Trim in Co. Meath ; very rare.

ᴅe ᴄúıɴꞁéıᵹ—XI—*de Townley,* Townley ; Nor. ' de

Townley,' i.e., of Townley, in Lancashire ; a rather old, but extremely rare, surname in Ireland. Richard Townly is mentioned in the Fiants of Elizabeth.

ᴅe ᴜıᴅeᴀꞅ—XII—*de Wees, de Wyz*, Wise, Wyse ; Nor. ' le Wys,' ' le Wise,' i.e., the wise ; hardly from a place-name, the old ' de ' being for the article ' the,' ' le.' The Wyses were an old family in Waterford.

ᴅe ᴜıᴈeᴀmōʀ—XI—*de Wiggemore, de Wigmore*, Wigmore ; Nor. ' de Wigmore,' i.e., of Wigmore in Herefordshire, more anciently Wiggemore, Wigganmor.

ᴅíoᴌ́mᴀın, ᴅíoᴌ́ún—VIII—*Dylun, Dilloun*, Dillon ; ' son of Dillon ' (a Norman-French personal name formed from an old Teutonic personal name Dill, Dillo, Dilli, by the addition of the French dim. termination '-on.' Dille appears as a surname in older English records, now written Dill ; and Dilkok, another dim. of the same name, now represented by the surname Dilcock in England, is found in the Patent and Close Rolls of Ireland, Henry II-Henry VII. ᴅíoᴌ́mᴀın, the older Irish spelling of the name, may be due to an attempt to assimilate it to the Irish word ᴅíoᴌ́mᴀın). The Dillons came to Ireland at the time of the Anglo-Norman invasion. Sir Henry Dillon received from King John large grants of land in Westmeath and Annaly, known in later times as Dillon's Country, and his descendants were barons of Kilkenny West. A branch of the family also settled in Co. Mayo. In the 17th and 18th centuries, the Dillons were distinguished in the service of continental powers.

ᴅíʀınᴈ—VIII—Deering ; ' son of Deoring,' an Anglo-Saxon personal name, given also as Diring and Dyring by Searle.

ᴅoᴃ—VIII—*Dobbe*, Dobbs ; ' son of Dob,' a pet form of the Norman Robert.

ᴅoᴅᴀ—VIII—*Dode,* Dodd, Dodds ; ' son of Doda ' (a common Anglo-Saxon personal name, probably a shortened form of Dodwine ; given by Searle under a great variety of forms, as Dodda, Doddo, Dodd,

Dodo, Duda, Dudda, etc.). It is an old surname in Tipperary.

ᴅoibín—VIII—*Dobin, Dobyn*, Dobbin, Dobbyn, Dobbins, Dobbyns; 'son of Dobin' (dim. of Dob, a pet form of Robert); the name of an old family in Waterford. Laurence Dobbyn was mayor in 1460, as was Patrick Dobbyn in 1589.

ᴅoidín—VIII—*Dodin*, Dodding; 'son of Dodwine' (an Anglo-Saxon personal name); formerly a surname in Leix, but probably now obsolete in Ireland.

ᴅoilfín—VIII—*Dolfine*, Dolfin, Dolphin; 'son of Dolfin,' a common personal name in England even before the Norman conquest. It occurs in Domesday Book as the name of a landholder in the time of Edward the Confessor, and about 1085 was borne by an Earl of Cumberland. In Ireland, the Dolphins settled in Clanrikard, where in the 16th century they formed a distinct clan after the Irish fashion with a chief of the name.

ᴅoingeárᴅ, ᴅoinneárᴅ—XI—*Donnarde*, Uniacke, Uniake, etc.; Mid. Eng. 'atten yeard,' i.e., at the yard, or enclosure, from residence therein; the old *n* of the article was attracted over as in the case of ᴅe nósla (q.v.), and with the dropping of the preposition 'at', the form became 'the nyeard.' It was evidently a second surname given to the family of Uniacke from their place of residence. It has now no direct equivalent in English, the family being always called Uniacke in that language. The Uniackes are an old Co. Cork family.

ᴅollárᴅ, ᴅollárᴄ—XII—*Dullart*, Dullard, Dollard; i.e., 'the dullard'; an old surname in Dublin and Meath.

ᴅonᴅún, ᴅonnᴅún—XI—*de Aundon, Daundon, Doundowne*, Dondon, Dundon; Nor. 'de Anton,' i.e., of Hampton in Middlesex, near which is the old royal palace of Hampton Court. Hampton is sometimes found in Anglo-Saxon charters as 'Heantune,' and was latinised 'Antona'; Antonae Curia was Hampton Court. The Dundons are an old and respectable family in Co. Limerick. At the end of the 16th century, they held the castle of Ballystine, near Askeaton.

ⲆⲞⲚⳔⳘⲚ—VIII—*Dongane*, Dongan, Dungan, Duncan ; 'son of Duncan,' (the Irish ⲆⲟⲛⲛⲁⳔⳘⲛ which was adopted by the Anglo-Saxons. Searle gives it in three forms : Duncan, Dunecan, and Dunechan ; found along with a few other Irish names in Domesday Book. Cf. ⲤⲟⳑⲙⳘⲛ above). The Dongans settled in Dublin and Kildare. Walter Dongan was created a baronet by James I, and after the Restoration his descendant, Sir William Dongan, was advanced to the Earldom of Limerick. His estates, comprising 30,000 acres, were confiscated by the Williamites.

ⲆⲢⲀⲄ—VIII or XII—*Drak*, Drake ; ' son of Drake ' (old English draca, Lat. draco, meaning ' the dragon,' probably of heraldic origin ; or it may be from ' le drake,' i.e., the dragon, though it never takes the French article in Irish, as it does in English, records). The Drakes came to Ireland about the time of the Anglo-Norman invasion and settled in Louth and Meath. ' Herbertus Draco ' occurs in the Dublin Roll of Names A.D. 1216, and ' Jordanus Drake ' in the list of Free Citizens of Dublin, A.D. 1225-1250. Drake of Drakeston was one of the gentlemen of Co. Louth at the end of the 16th century, as was Drake of Drakerath at the same period in Co. Meath. The name is now very rare.

ⲆⲢⲀⲞⲠⲀⲢ—XII—Draper ; Nor. ' le Draper,' i.e., the draper ; an old surname in Ireland, but now very rare.

ⲆⲢⲓⲨ, Drew ; a late form of Ⲇⲣⲩ, q.v.

ⲆⲢⲞⳔ, ⲆⲢⲞⳔⲀ—VIII—*Drogh*, *Drou*, Drough, Drew ; ' son of Drogo,' (a personal name of Frankish origin borne, among others, by a son of Charlemagne and brought into England by the Normans, where Drogo of Bevrere, a follower of the Conqueror, obtained a grant of Holderness in Yorkshire) ; an old surname in Westmeath and Offaly. Later forms are Ⲇⲣⲩ and Ⲇⲣⲩⲩ, q.v.

DROMGÚL, Dromgoole, Drumgoole, Drumgoold. V. de Dromgúl.

DRÚ—VIII—*Drue*, Drew; 'son of Dru,' a Norman form of Drogo. V. Droġ.

DRÚIRIḊE—XII—*Druerye*, *Drurie*, Drury, Drewry; Old Fr. 'druerie,' i.e., the lover; not an old surname in Ireland. Drury is often merely an incorrect anglicisation of the Irish Mac an Druaiḋ and Ó Druaiḋ, q.v.

DUḂ—IX—Duff; Ir. 'duḃ,' i.e., black; a description epithet which supplanted the real surname which is now lost. Cf. Bán, Beag, etc.

DUḂDAL—XI—*de Duvedale*, *Dovedale*, *Dovedall*, *Dowedale*, Dowdall, Doudall, Dowdell; Nor. 'de Duvedal,' i.e., of Dove Dale, the upper part of the valley of the Dove in Derbyshire and Staffordshire; an old and distinguished family in Dublin, Louth and Meath.

DUḂGLAS—XI—*de Douglas*, Douglas; Nor. 'de Douglas,' i.e., of Douglas, a parish in Lanarkshire; a surname of Scottish origin.

DUINGEÁRD, DUINNEÁRD, Uniacke. V. Doingeárd.

DÚINSMEÁRAĊ, Beresford; a 'translation' of the English surname Beresford, as if Berryfort.

EAḂRÁRD, *Evrard*, Everard. V. Éiḃearárd.

ÉAḂRÓID—VIII—*Everod*, *Evrett*, Everett, Everitt, Everard; 'son of Everhault'; a var. of Éiḃearárd, q.v. Everard and Everhault were probably distinct names, but they were supposed by the Normans to be the same. Cf. Gerard and Gerald.

EASMONN—VIII—*Estmund*, *Eetmond*, Esmond, Esmonde; 'son of Eastmund' (an Anglo-Saxon personal name, written Estmunt in Domesday Book; 'Willielmus filius Estmundi' occurs in the Dublin Roll of Names A.D. 1216). The Esmonds settled at an early period in Co. Wexford. In 1303, Henry Estmund was commissioned by Edward I to provide ships at Wexford and elsewhere for the transporting of his army to Scotland, and in 1371 Thomas Estmunde was constable of Wexford castle. The family is at present represented by Sir Thomas H. G. Esmond.

eᴀꞅpoᵹ—XII—Aspig; Bishop; a translation, probably, of the English surname Bishop.

eᴀᴄún—XI—Eaton; i.e., 'of Eaton,' a common place-name in England.

eiꝺeᴀʀᴀʀꝺ—VIII—Everard; 'son of Everard' (a Norman personal name, from the Frankish ' Eberhard,' ' Ebrard,' the same as the Anglo-Saxon ' Eoforheard ' or ' Eoferard '). The Everards came to Ireland about the time of the Anglo-Norman invasion and settled in Meath and Tipperary. Both families were highly distinguished.

eiᴄinᵹeᴀm—XI—*Echingham*, Etchingham; i.e., ' of Etchingham ' in England.

eiᵹeᴀʀ—VIII—Agar, Eagar, Egar.

eiméʀꝺ—VIII—Emmet; 'son of Emmet' (dim. of Teutonic personal name Emmo); made famous for ever in Ireland by the patriot Robert Emmet.

ꝼᴀᴄnᴀʀ—XII—*Fauconer*, Falconer, Faulkner, etc.; Nor. ' le falconer,' ' le Faukener,' i.e., the falconer, keeper of falcons; a rather common surname in early Anglo-Irish records.

ꝼᴀꝺᴀ—IX—Fodha, Long; Ir. ' ꝼᴀꝺᴀ,' i.e., tall, long; a descriptive epithet which supplanted the real surname; very rare. Cf. ꝺán, ꝺeᴀᵹ.

ꝼᴀeꝺeᴀᴄ—XIV—Fay. V. ꝺe ꝼᴀe.

ꝼᴀᵹán—VIII—*Fagane*, Fagan, Fagin; 'son of Pagan' (Lat. ' Paganus,' the rustic, the pagan, a personal name introduced into England by the Normans); the name of an old and respectable Anglo-Norman family who settled about the time of the invasion in Meath and Westmeath. To be distinguished from Ó ꝼáᵹáin and Ó ꝼᴀoꝺᴀᵹáin, q.v.

ꝼᴀᵹᴀn, *Fyan*, Fyans, Foynes. V. pᴀᵹᴀn and ꝼáᵹán, of which it is a variant.

ꝼᴀinín—VIII—*Fanyne*, Fannin, Fanning; a variant of pᴀinín (q.v.) by the not uncommon change of p to ꝼ ; the name of an old Anglo-Norman family who settled at an early period in many parts of the south of Ireland. There were influential families of the name in Limerick, Tipperary and Kilkenny.

ꝼᴀɪrꞅɪⁿᵹ—IX—*Farshinge*, Farshin, Fortune ; Ir. ' ꝼᴀɪꝑ-ꝑɪⁿᵹ,' i.e., generous ; an epithet applied apparently to members of the family of MacCarthy in West Cork ; very rare. Not the name of the Fortunes of Leinster.

ꝼᴀꞁᴄᴀċ—XIV—*Faltagh*, Wall ; the adjectival form of ꝺe ḃᴀꞁ, q.v.

A.D. 1379—The Bishop of Meath, i.e., ᴀn ꝼᴀꞁᴄᴀċ, died in England—Four Masters.

A.D. 1588—Grant to Oliver Stephenson, of Don Milline, of the manor of Donmilline, Co. Limerick, parcel of the possession of Ulick de Wale alias the Faltagh, of Donmillen, etc.—Fiants Eliz. 5242.

ꝼᴀnnᴄ—XII—*Faunte*, Fant ; Nor. ' le Faunt,' a shortened form of ' l'Enfant,' i.e., the child ; a very common surname in early Anglo-Irish records, but now rare. A family of the name settled at Fantstown near Kilmallock.

ꝼᴀoɪᴄeᴀċ—XIV—White. V. ꝺe ꝼᴀoɪᴄ.

ꝼeɪrɪᴄéɪr, ꝼeɪrᴄéɪr—XII—*Firiter*, Ferriter ; Nor. ' le Fureter,' i.e., the ferreter, probably a dealer in, or manufacturer of, ferret or silk tape, if not one who ferrets, or searches out like a ferret. (Cf. Fr. furet, a ferret). The Ferreters settled in the 13th or 14th century at Ballyferriter in Co. Kerry, where the name still survives. Pierce Ferriter was a well-known Irish poet.

ꝼeóɪrꞁɪⁿᵹ—VIII—*Veerlin*, Verlin, Verling ; ' son of Feorthling ' (an Anglo-Saxon personal name, made Farthing by the Normans. ꝼeóɪꝑꞁɪⁿᵹ is at the present day the Irish for a farthing). ' Elias filius Rogeri fili Farthini ' occurs in the Dublin Roll of Names, A.D. 1216 ; and Warinus Ferthing de Karlel was a member of the Dublin Guild-Merchant A.D. 1226. The family must have settled early in Co. Westmeath, where Farthingstown marks their place of abode ; but for centuries back the name, under the form of Verlin and Verling has been peculiar to Co. Cork.

Ꝼ1ᴀRᴀᴄ, Feerick. V. mᴀᴄ ꝓ1ᴀꝓᴀ1ᴄ.

Ꝼ10nᴀmūR—VIII—*Finamur*, Finamore, Finnamore, etc. ; 'son of Finamour' (Fr. fin amour, fair love, perhaps a nickname). Finamur appears as a surname in the Dublin Roll of Names, A.D. 1212.

Ꝼ10nᴣLᴀS, Finglas. V. ᴅe Ꝼ1onnᴣLᴀꝛ.

Ꝼ10nn—IX—Fair, Phair ; Ir. ' Ꝼ1onn,' fair ; a descriptive epithet which supplanted the real surname. Cf. bᴀn, beᴀᴣ.

Ꝼ10nnū1R, Ꝼ10nū1R—XI—*Fynnor*, Fennors ; probably Nor. ' de Finnure,' i.e., of Ꝼ1onnᴀbᴀ1ꝛ, a frequent Irish place-name ; one of the small group of Norman surnames formed from Irish place-names. There can hardly be any doubt about this derivation, but I have not discovered any early forms that would prove it. The surname is an old one in Tipperary and Kilkenny.

Ꝼ10ᴄūn—VIII—*Fitun*, Fitton, Fetton ; probably ' son of Fitun ' or ' Phitun ' (a Norman personal name). The surname came into Ireland about the time of the Anglo-Norman invasion. ' Hereuic Fitun' occurs in the Dublin Roll of Names, A.D. 1216. Sir Edward Fyton of Gawsworth in Cheshire was President of Connacht in the time of Elizabeth, and Sir Alexander Fytton was Lord Chancellor of Ireland in the time of James II. There are a few families of the name still in Co. Limerick.

Ꝼ1R1ᴄé1R, Ꝼ1Rᴄé1R, *Firiter*, Ferriter. V. Ꝼe1ꝛ1ᴄé1ꝛ.

ꝼL1nᴄ—VIII—*Flynt*, Flint ; ' son of Flint,' a Teutonic personal name, found as a surname in Domesday Book. It came into Ireland some time before the end of the 13th century, but has not extended beyond the City of Dublin.

ꝼLó1ᴅ—XII—*Flode, Floyde*, Floyd, Flood ; merely the English pronunciation of the Welsh surname Lloyd. The name is old in Ireland, but has never been very common.

ꝼoıꞃbıs—XI—Forbes; i.e., ' of Forbes,' a parish in Aberdeenshire.

ꝼoıꞃéıs, Forrest. V. ꝼuıꞃéaꞃꞇ.

ꝼóıséıꝺ, Faussett, Faussette, Fawcett, Fawcitt, Fawsitt, etc.

ꝼóꞃꝺ, ꝼóꞃꞇ—XII—*Forth*, Ford, Forde, etc.; Nor., ' le fort,' i.e., the strong; the name of an Anglo-Norman family who settled in Meath and Louth.

ꝼꞃaınclín—XII—Franklin; Nor. ' le frankelein,' i.e., small freeholder. Walter le frankelein was one of the Free Citizens of Dublin, A.D. 1225-1250. The name is not uncommon in north-east Limerick and Tipperary.

ꝼꞃanncaċ—XII—Beausang; Ir. ' ꝼꞃanncaċ,' i.e., the Frenchman; a descriptive name given to the family of Beausang in Co. Cork who are of French origin.

ꝼꞃéıne, v. ꝺe ꝼꞃéıne.

ꝼꞃıseal—XII—*Fresell*, Frisell, Frizell, Frizzle, Fraser, Frazer, etc.; Nor. ' Frisel,' i.e., the Frisian, native of, or belonging to, Friesland. Simon Fressell came to England with William the Conqueror, and Richard Fresle was one of the tenants-in-chief at the time of the Domesday survey. The name came into Ireland about the time of the invasion. ' Vdardus Fresel' appears in the Dublin Roll of Names, A.D. 1216. Freiselston in Co. Meath was, no doubt, an early home of the family in Ireland. The Frasers were also a distinguished Scottish clan.

ꝼꞃıűın—VIII—Frewin, Frewen; ' son of Freowine,' an Anglo-Saxon personal name, frequent in Domesday Book.

ꝼűınse—VIII—*Founce, Fonce*, Finch, Funge; a variant of ꝑűınꞃe, by change of initial ꝑ to ꝼ; cf. ꝼaınín, for ꝑaınín, ꝼáᵹán for ꝑáᵹán. There is a possibility that the origin is from the obsolete English word ' fonce,' a knowing, cunning person, but the few instances that we have in Irish records are without the article ' le' or ' the.'

ꝼuıꞃéasꞇ—XI—Forrest, Frost; Eng. ' at the forest,'

from residence thereby. The name is common in Cork. Also ꝼoıꝛéıꝛ.

ꝻuıReᴀꞅᴄᴀl—XII—*Furestal*, Forestall, Forrestal, Forstall, Forrester, Forster ; Lat. 'forestarius,' Eng. 'the forester,' i.e., the forest-keeper, custodian of the forest, very common in early Anglo-Irish records ; the name of an Anglo-Norman family long settled in Kilkenny, the head of which held the manors of Kilferagh and Ballyfrunck ; also of a family in Co. Wexford.

ꝼulᴀRᴄūn—XI—Fullarton, Fullerton ; i.e., ' of Fullarton,' a Scottish place-name, in Lanarkshire or Ayrshire ; the name of an old Scottish family who settled in Ireland in the 16th and 17th centuries.

ꝼūRꝺ, *Foord*, Foorde, Forde, Ford ; a variant of ꝼoꝛꝺ, ꝼóꝛᴄ, q.v.　Foord of Foordston was one of the chief gentlemen of Meath in 1598.

ꝼuRlonᵹ—XI—*Forlong*, Furlong ; Eng. ' at the furlong,' a division of an unenclosed corn-field, from residence therein or thereby ; the name of an old and respectable Anglo-Irish family in Co. Wexford.　Their chief seat was at Horestown, but they owned also the manors of Camross, Carrigmanan and Bridestown.　The name is still common in Wexford.

ꝼuᴄRᴀıl—XI—Fottrell ; i.e., ' of Futterill,' a village in Gloucester ; the name of an Anglo-Irish family seated in Co. Dublin.

ᵹᴀbóıꝺ—VIII—Gabbott, Gabbett ; ' son of Gabbot,' dim. of Gabriel.

ᵹᴀıllıꝺe, Galway, Gallway, etc.　V. ꝺe ᵹᴀıllıꝺe.

ᵹᴀımlín—VIII—Gamlin, Gambling ; ' son of Gamelin,' dim. of Gamel (v. ᵹᴀmᴀl).　Gamelin occurs as a personal name in Domesday Book.

ᵹáıRꝺín—XI—Gardin, Garden ; i.e., ' at the garden,' from residence thereby.

ᵹáıRnéıR—XII—*Gardener*, Gardiner, Gardner, Garner ; Nor. ' le gardiner,' i.e., the gardener ; an old surname in Ireland.　' Galfridus le gardiner ' occurs in the Dublin Roll of Names A.D. 1216.

ᵹᴀısceᴀl, Gatchell.

ᵹᴀll—XII—Gall, Gaul, Gaule; Ir. 'ᵹᴀll,' i.e., the foreigner, the Englishman; the designation, and later the name, of a branch of the Burkes, descended from the Red Earl of Ulster, who settled at Gaulstown in Co. Kilkenny. A branch of the family became famous in Austria.

ᵹᴀllbreᴀcnᴀċ—X—Galbraith, Galbreath; i.e., the British or Welsh stranger; a surname of Scottish origin.

ᵹᴀll'oᴀ—IX—*Galdy, Gald, Galte*, Galt, Gault; Ir. 'ᵹᴀll'oᴀ,' i.e., the anglicised; a descriptive epithet which has supplanted the real name of the family, whatever that might have been; now very rare.

ᵹᴀll'ouḃ—XII—*Galduf*, Stackpoole; Stapleton, Stapelton; Ir. 'ᵹᴀll'ouḃ,' i.e., the black foreigner; an Irish designation of members of the family of Stackpoole, and sometimes of Stapleton.

ᵹᴀmbún—XII—Gambon, Gammon; Old Fr. 'gambon,' a leg (cf. English name Foote); an old, but rare, surname in Cork and Waterford.

ᵹᴀmᴀl—VIII—Gamel, Gammel, Gambell, Gamble; 'son of Gamel,' a personal name of Scandinavian origin, frequent in Domesday Book. Cf. the Irish word ᵹᴀmᴀl.

ᵹᴀscún—VIII—*Gastun, Gastoun*, Gaston; 'son of Gaston,' (a Norman personal name apparently). The surname in Ireland dates back to the 13th century.

ᵹéᴀr—IX—*Geare*, Gayer; Sharpe; Ir. 'ᵹéᴀp,' i.e., sharp, bitter; an epithet which has supplanted the real surname.

ᵹeᴀrᴀr'o—VIII—Gerard, Gerrard; 'son of Gerard' (Teutonic Gerhard, a personal name introduced by the Normans, who regarded it as the same name as Gerald). The Gerrards were a Meath family.

ᵹeᴀrḃᴀs—VIII—*Gervase, Gervaise*, Gervais, Gervis, Jervaise, Jarvis, Jervis; 'son of Gervase' (a Norman personal name of Teutonic origin). As a surname, it dates back in Ireland to the reign of Edward I.

ʒeᴀꞃᴅ, Garde. V. ᴅe ʒeᴀꞃᴅ.

ʒeᴀꞃᴌᴀnn, Gairlan, Gartlan, Garland, Gartland, etc.; a corruption of ʒeᴀꞃnún, q.v.

ʒeᴀꞃᴌún, *Garlowne, Garlone, Garlon*, Garlan, Garland, etc.; a corruption of ʒeᴀꞃnún, q.v.; now further corrupted to ʒeᴀꞃᴌᴀnn, q.v.

ʒeᴀꞃmᴀ́n—VIII—German, Jarman, etc; 'son of German,' a Norman personal name which appears occasionally as Germain in early Anglo-Irish records. V. ʒeᴀꞃmonn.

ʒeᴀꞃmonn—VIII—Germon, Jermyn, etc.; 'son of Germund,' a Norman personal name. It is now difficult to distinguish from ʒeᴀꞃmᴀ́n. Both names appear in early Anglo-Irish records, but Germund was much more frequent.

ʒeᴀꞃnún—XII—*Gernoun, Gernone, Garnon*, Gernon, Garlan, Garland, etc.; Nor. Fr. 'gernon,' 'guernon,' i.e., a moustache, hence the wearer of a moustache; a nickname which became a surname. Robert Gernon was one of the tenants-in-chief in England at the time of the Domesday survey. The name came into Ireland about the time of the invasion, and in the 16th century was common in Louth, Meath and Monaghan; but it has long been corrupted to ʒeᴀꞃᴌún and then to ʒeᴀꞃᴌᴀnn, q.v.

ʒeᴀꞃóꞃᴅ—VIII—*Gerot, Garrott*, Garrett, Jerrett, etc.; 'son of Gerald,' a common personal name among the Normans, representing two or three distinct Teutonic names, as Gerwald, Gerhold, and confused with Gerard. V. ʒeᴀꞃᴀ́ꞃᴅ.

ʒeᴀꞃꞃ—IX—Short; Ir. 'ʒeᴀꞃꞃ,' i.e., short, low-sized; an epithet which took the place of the real surname which is now lost.

ʒeᴀꞃꞃᴄóiꞃ—XII—Cárver; a translation of the English surname Carver.

ʒiᴅ—VIII—Gibb; 'son of Gib,' dim. of Gilbert.

ʒiᴌᴅeᴀꞃᴄ—VIII—Gilbert; 'son of Gilbert,' a Norman personal name of Teutonic origin. It appears in Domesday Book in the Lat. form of 'Gislebertus.'

The dim. Gibbon, in Irish ᵹıoḃún, was the usual form of the name among the Anglo-Normans in Ireland, where, as a surname, Gilbert is not very old.

ᵹıɬɬeáɴ—VIII—*Gillian*, Julian, Julien, and probably Gullion ; 'son of Julian' (the Lat. Julianus, popularly Gillian), a personal name introduced by the Normans. Julianstown, Co. Meath, was probably the first home of the family in Ireland.

ᵹıoḃsáɴ, ᵹıoḃsoɴ, Gibson.

ᵹıoɬcáċ, Reade, Reid, etc. ; a mistranslation of the English surname Reade, or Reid, which means simply ' the red,' from the complexion.

ᵹıoróıṫ, v. ᵹeaṗóıṫ.

ᵹɬaıséıṫ, Glassett.

ᵹɬas—IX—Glass, Green ; Ir. ' ᵹɬaṡ,' i.e., green, grey, from the complexion ; an epithet which supplanted the real surname. Cf. ḃáɴ, ḃeaᵹ.

ᵹɬeaɴċúɴ—XI—*Glanton*, Clinton ; i.e., ' of Glanton,' a parish in Northumberland ; wrongly re-anglicised Clinton.

ᵹɬéasúr—XII—Gleasure ; i.e., ' the glazier.'

ᵹoḃa—XII—*Gowe*, Gow, Smith; Ir. ' ᵹoḃa,' i.e., the smith ; a trade designation which took the place of the real surname. Cf. Ceárṗ.

ᵹoċ—XII—*Goch, Gogh, Gooch*, Gough, Goff ; Welsh ' coch,' i.e., the red, from the complexion ; the name of a Welsh family who settled in Dublin and Waterford.

ᵹoᵹáɴ, ᵹóᵹáɴ, *Gogane, Goggane*, Gogan, Goggan, Goggin, etc. V. ṿe Coᵹáɴ.

ᵹoıṫíɴ—VIII—*Godyn, Goodin*, Goodwin, Godwin ; ' son of Godwine,' a very common personal name among the Anglo-Saxons.

ᵹóıséır—XII—Gosnall, Gosnell ; probably Ir. ' ᵹóıṙéıṙ,' a hosier, a dealer in stockings ; the name of a family of late English origin in West Cork who, perhaps, first became known to the Irish as hosiers. Henry Gosnell was Queen's attorney in Munster in the reign of Elizabeth.

ᵹóısᴌín—VIII—Gosselin, Goslin, Gauslin, Gosling, Gostlin; 'son of Goscelin' (dim. of Goshelm, a Norman personal name, frequent in Domesday Book). Goslingstown in Co. Kilkenny commemorates the place of abode of the family in Ireland.

ᵹóʀᴅún, Gordon. V. ᴅe ᵹóʀᴅún.

ᵹoᴄꝼʀᴀıᴅ—VIII—*Godefraye, Godefrey*, Godfrey; 'son of Godfrey,' a Teutonic personal name, variously written as Gothfrith, Guthfrith, etc.; very common among the Normans, by whom it may be said to have been introduced into England, though as Gothfrith it was sometimes found among the Anglo-Saxons.

ᵹoᴄmonn—VIII—*Godmund, Gudmund*, Godman, Goodman; 'son of Godmund,' a Teutonic personal name, not uncommon among the Anglo-Saxons; also written Guthmund. Godman was also a personal name among the Anglo-Saxons, but in early Anglo-Irish records Godmund is the only form found.

ᵹʀᴀᴅᴀʀ, Grier, Greir, Greer, etc.; a Mayo surname, doubtless a phonetic representation of the English surname Grier, Greir, etc. V. mᴀc ᵹʀıoᵹᴀıʀ.

ᵹʀᴀe, Grey, Gray. V. ᴅe ᵹʀᴀe.

ᵹʀᴀınseᴀċ—XI—Grange; i.e., 'at the grange,' (barn, or farm-house) from residence in or thereby.

ᵹʀᴀınséıʀ—XII—*Graunger*, Grainger, Granger; i.e., 'the granger,' the keeper of a grange or granary.

ᵹʀᴀnᴅᴀ—IX—*Grany*, Granny, Grant; Ir. 'ᵹʀᴀnᴅᴀ,' i.e., ugly; an epithet which took the place of the real surname. It is, as might be expected, extremely rare.

ᵹʀᴀnᴅún, Grandon, Grandan. V. ᴅe ᵹʀᴀnᴅún.

ᵹʀᴀnnᴄ, Grant. V. ᴅe ᵹʀᴀnnᴄ.

ᵹʀᴀs—XII—*Graas, Grase*, Grace; Fr. 'le gras,' i.e., the fat; the name of an ancient and distinguished Kilkenny family, said to be descended from Raymond le Gros, one of the companions of Strongbow. The Graces were certainly among the earliest of the Anglo-Norman settlers in Ireland. The head of the family had the title of Baron of Courtstown.

ᵹⱤᵉᴀᵹóⁱⱤ—VIII—Gregory; 'son of Gregory.'

ᵹⱤíꝼín—VIII—*Griffine*, Griffin; 'son of Gruffin' (a common Welsh personal name, from the Latin 'Rufinus,' dim. of Rufus, i.e., of ruddy complexion. The Welsh equivalent of Rufus is Gruffud, or Gruffydd, whence Griffith, Griffiths. Grifin, son of Mariadoc, evidently a Welshman, was one of the tenants-in-chief in England at the time of the Domesday survey. Griffin is very common in early Anglo-Irish records, but Gruffud hardly occurs). The family settled in Ireland about the time of the Anglo-Norman invasion.

ᵹⱤomᴀıᴌ, *Gromwell*, Grunnell. V. CⱤomᴀıᴌ.

ᵹuᴏ—XII—Good; i.e., 'the good.'

ᵹuıᴏ—VIII—Guy; 'son of Guy' or 'Guido,' a Norman personal name.

ᵹuıᴌıᴏe—VIII—Gooley, Goldie, Gouldy; 'son of Goldie,' a pet form of Goldwine, an Anglo-Saxon personal name, Gola in Domesday Book.

ᵹuıᴌín—VIII—Golding, Goulding, Golden, Goolden; 'son of Goldewine,' or 'Goldwine' (Lat. 'Goldinus') an Anglo-Saxon personal name. Under the form of Golding it came into Ireland soon after the Anglo-Norman invasion when the family settled in Dublin, Meath, Kildare, and parts of Munster.

ᵹuın—XII—Gwyn, Gwynn, Gwynne; Welsh 'gwyn,' i.e., white, fair.

ᵹuᴌ—VIII—*Gule, Goule, Goole, Gole, Gold*, Gould, Goold; 'son of Golde,' an Anglo-Saxon personal name, found as Goldus in Domesday Book. The earliest form of the surname in Ireland was Gule: John Gule was a member of the Dublin Guild-Merchant, A.D. 1226; and about a century later Maurice Gule was one of the townsmen of Kilmallock. The Goulds appear to have settled at an early period in the city of Cork, where they were wealthy merchants and long one of the most influential families. No fewer than thirty of the name appear in the list of mayors of that city.

295

ᵹumᴀʀᴄún, Gumbleton; probably only a variant of
Comᴀʀᴄún, q.v.
ᵹunnᴀ—VIII—*Gunne*, Gunn, Gonne; 'son of Gunna,'
a personal name among the Anglo-Saxons, doubtless
a pet form of Gunnar.
ᵹunnᴀʀ—VIII—Gunner; 'son of Gunnar,' a very
common personal name among the Anglo-Saxons,
perhaps of Norse origin.

ħᴀcᴀeᴅ, ħᴀɪcéɪᴅ—VIII—*Hackede, Haket*, Hackett;
'son of Haket' (a Norman personal name). The
Hacketts came into Ireland at the time of the Anglo-
Norman invasion and settled in Dublin, Wicklow,
Kilkenny, Tipperary, etc. The name occurs frequently
in early Anglo-Irish records.
ħᴀɪcín—VIII—*Haukyn*, Hawkins; 'son of Halkin,'
dim. of Harry.
ħᴀɪmlín—VIII—*Hamelyn*, Hamlin, Hamlyn, etc.; 'son
of Hamelin' (double dim. of Hamo). This family
came to Ireland in the 13th century and settled in
Dublin and Meath. Hamlen of Smythstown was one
of the chief gentlemen of Meath in 1598.
ħᴀɪʀᴅín—VIII—*Hardeyne, Hardyn*, Harding, Hardinge;
'son of Heardwine' (an Anglo-Saxon name; not
from 'Harding,' another Anglo-Saxon name, as the
older forms show); an old surname in Ossory and
Ormond.
ħᴀɪʀɪs—VIII—*Harishe, Harreis*, Harris; a phonetic
rendering of the English surname Harris. There
are, no doubt, many old families of the name in Ireland.
ħᴀlᴀᴃóɪᴅ, *Holywode, Holywood*, Hollywood. V. ᴅe
ħᴀlᴀᴃóɪᴅ.
ħᴀlᴃuɪᴅe, ħᴀluɪᴅe, Halvey, Holoway, Hollway, etc.
V. ᴅe ħᴀlᴃuɪᴅe.
ħᴀmᴀlᴄún, *Hamleton*, Hamilton. V. ᴅe ħᴀmᴀlᴄún.
ħᴀmon—VIII—*Hamon, Hammon*, Hammond; 'son of
Hamo,' Norman 'Hamon,' a common personal name
in early Anglo-Irish records. Soon after the invasion
we find the names of 'Adam filius Hamonis' and

'Teboldus filius Haim' in the Dublin Roll. The surname cannot now be distinguished from hámonn, q.v.

hámonn—VIII—*Hamund, Hammound,* Hammond; 'son of Heahmund' (an Anglo-Saxon personal name, Old Norse Hamundr, a name in use among the Danes of Dublin before the Anglo-Norman invasion). About the year 1174, Hamund, son of Torkill, was granted, on behalf of King Henry II, Censale and adjacent lands, held by him before the arrival of the English in Ireland. Families named Hammond also settled early in Louth, Meath and Limerick. V. hámon which is of a distinct origin, but cannot now be distinguished from hámonn.

hamróc, hamróg, Hamrock, Hamrogue; probably 'of Hambrook,' older Hambroke, a hamlet in Gloucestershire. There was a Hamrockstown in Waterford or Cork. V. Seampóg.

hancárd, Hankard; an old, but rare, surname in Co. Cork, the origin of which I cannot trace. Perhaps connected with Tankard.

hancóc—VIII—*Hancok,* Hancock, Handcock; 'son of Hancok,' i.e., little John, from the short form Han (for Johannes) and the dim. suffix. The Hancocks were a Dublin family.

haol—VIII—Howel, Howell, Howels; 'son of Howel' (a Welsh personal name); the name of a Welsh family which came into Ireland as early as the 13th century. V. mac haol.

haróid—VIII—*Haroud,* Harrot, Harwood, Harold, Harrold; 'son of Harold.' V. Apaic and Apóid.

harpúr, Harpur, Harper. V. de happúp.

harc—XII—Hart, Harte; i.e., 'the hart.'

hearman—VIII—*Herman,* Harman, Harmon, Hardman, Herdman; 'son of Hereman' (a Teutonic personal name). This surname came into Ireland in the 13th or early 14th century.

hearún—XII—*Herun, Heyrun, Heyron,* Heron, Hearon, Herron, Hearn, Hearne, Herne, etc.; Mid. Eng. 'herun,' i.e., the heron, one with long slender legs and neck like a heron. This surname in Ireland dates back to the early 13th century, but does nor appear to have been ever very common, and was confined to S. Leinster.

ⵀⴻⵏⴱⴻⴰⵔⵜ—XII—*Heyward, Haward,* Hayward, Howard; Nor. ' le Hayward,' i.e., keeper of the fences (from ' hay ' a hedge, and ' ward,' a guard) ; an old surname in Ireland, but very rare, and now disguised as Howard.

ⵀⵉⴱⴻⴰⵔⴷ, *Hibbard,* Hubbard ; a var. of ⵀⵓⵉⴱⴻⴰⵔⴷ, q.v.

ⵀⵉⵓⴱⴰⵔⴷ,*Hibbard,* Hubbard, Hubbert, Hubbart, Hobart, Hobert, and sometimes incorrectly Howard ; a var. of ⵀⵓⴱⴰⵔⴷ or ⵀⵓⵉⴱⴻⴰⵔⴷ, q.v.

ⵀⵉⵓⵙⴰⴻ, Hussey. V. ⴷⴻ ⵀⵓⵔⴰⴻ. The correctness of this form of the surname, which I got from an old Irish speaker, is corroborated by the fact that Hissey is still a var. of Hussey in England.

ⵀⵓⴱ—VIII—*Hobbe, Hoppe,* Hop, Hobbs, Hope ; ' son of Hob,' (a short form of Robert). The Hopes were once an influential family about Mullingar.

ⵀⵓⴱⴰⵛ, ⵀⵓⴱⵓⵛ—VIII—*Hobbok, Hobbuge,* Hubbock ; ' son of Hobac ' (dim. of Hob, i.e., Robert). This surname was formerly in use in Co. Cork, but was always extremely rare, and is now probably obsolete.

ⵀⵓⴱⴰⵛⴰⵏ—VIII—*Hobbocane,* Habbagan ; ' son of ⵀⵓⴱⴰⵛⴰⵏ ' (double dim. of Hob, i.e., Robert) ; an old surname in Ireland, but always extremely rare.

ⵀⵓⴱⴰⵔⴷ—VIII—*Hobbard,* Hobart, Hubbard ; a var. of ⵀⵓⵉⴱⴻⴰⵔⴷ, q.v.

ⵀⵓⴷ—VIII—*Hod, Hode,* Hoad, Hoade ; probably ' son of Hod ' or ' Hoda ' (an Anglo-Saxon personal name. ' Hod ' was also an Anglo-Saxon word meaning a hood, cap, or helmet). John Hod was a member of the Dublin Guild-Merchant, A.D. 1226. The name, which was very rare, survives in Co. Mayo.

ⵀⵓⴷⵏⴰⴻ—XI—*Hodney, Hodynet,* Hodnett, Hadnett ; i.e., ' of Hodnet,' a parish in Shropshire. The Hodnets settled at Courtmacsherry, near Timoleague, in Co. Cork. They assumed the Irish patronymic surname of Mac Séaᵱcᴀ (q.v.). Courtmacsherry is still called in Irish Cúiᵱc 'ic Séaᵱcᴀiᵹ.

hoibeáꝶꝺ—VIII—*Hebbard, Habert,* Habbert, Hobart, Hobert, Hubbert, Hubbard, Herbert ; ' son of Herbert,' not ' son of Hubert,' as one would be inclined to make it. It was a var. of hoiᵱeᴀbáᵱꝺ (q.v.), and was formerly common in Limerick and Cork.

hoileᴀbáꝶꝺ—VIII—*Halberd,* Helbert, Hilbert, Helbet; ' son of Halbert,' (perhaps for Anglo-Saxon Haligbeort, if not a corruption of Heldbeorht or Hildebeorht, names found in Searle). The surname is old in Ireland. Robert Halberd was a member of the Dublin Guild-Merchant in 1226.

hoiꝶbín—VIII—Harbin ; ' son of Harbin,' dim. of Herbert.

hoiꝶeᴀbáꝶꝺ, hoiꝶeᴀbáꝶꝺ—VIII—*Herbard,* Herbert, Harbert, Harberd ; ' son of Herbert ' (a Norman personal name, already very common among the Anglo-Saxons as Herebeorht). The Herberts came into Ireland about the time of the Anglo-Norman invasion and settled in Kildare, Meath and Limerick. V. hiobáᵱꝺ, hobáᵱꝺ, and hoibeáᵱꝺ, which are variants.

hoiꝶeᴀbáꝶꝺ—VIII—Hereward, Herward ; ' son of Hereweard ' (an Anglo-Saxon personal name) ; an old surname in Ireland. ' Adam Hereward ' occurs in the Dublin Roll of Names, A.D. 1216, and somewhat later in the same century Simon Hereward was mayor of Limerick.

hoisce—VIII—Hodge, Hogg, Hogge ; ' son of Hodge, i.e., Roger. V. Mac hoiᵱce.

hoiscicín—VIII—*Hosteken,* Hotchkin, Hodgkin ; ' son of Hodgkin,' i.e., little Roger. Cf. Mac Oiᵱcicín.

hólc—VIII—Holt, Holte ; ' son of Holt ' (a personal name, or nickname, apparently of Norse origin, found in Domesday Book) ; an old surname still in use in Kildare and Wicklow. It is to be distinguished from the Anglo-Norman surname ' le Holde,' i.e., the freeholder, which was in use in Ireland in the 13th century when William de Holde was one of the townsmen of Kilmallock.

ħubuc, Hubbock. V. ħobᴀc.

ħuᵹúιn—VIII—Huggins ; 'son of Hugin' or 'Hugon' (dim. of Hugh). Huguin and Hugon are still French surnames.

ħúιᵹéιᴅ—VIII—Hewett, Hewitt, Huet, etc. ; 'son of Hughet,' i.e., little Hugh ; a surname which first came into Ireland in the 13th century.

ħúιᵹléιᴅ, v. ħúιléιᴅ.

ħúιᵹlín, v. ħúιlín.

ħúιléιᴅ—VIII—Hewlett, Hewlitt, Huleat, Howlett, etc. ; 'son of Hughelet' (double dim. of Hugh) ; the name of an Anglo-Norman family who settled in Co. Kildare.

ħúιlín—VIII—Howlen, Howlin, Howling, Holing ; 'son of Hughelin' (double dim. of Hugh) ; the name of an Anglo-Norman family who settled early in Wexford and Kilkenny.

ħuιsce, Hutch ; a var. of ħoιᵹce, q.v.

ħuιceᴀcáιn, Hutchinson ; a phonetic rendering of Hutchinson.

ħunᵹRᴀιᴅ—VIII—Humfrey, Humphrey ; 'son of Hunfrid' (a Teutonic personal name, long corrupted to Humfrid and Humphrey). This surname came into Ireland soon after the Anglo-Norman invasion. There is a Humphreystown in Co. Wicklow. Also Unᵹꞃᴀιᴅ, q.v.

ħunc—XII—Hunt ; Nor. 'le Honte,' 'le Hunte,' i.e., the huntsman ; the name of an Anglo-Norman family who came to Ireland about the time of the invasion and settled in Dublin and Meath. It was never very common. Nearly all our Hunts are of native origin.

ħúsᴀe, *Husee*, Hussey. V. ᴅe ħúꞃᴀe.

ιᴀcob—VIII—Jacob ; 'son of Jacob.'

ιᴀᵹó—VIII—Iago, Jago, Jagoe ; 'son of Jago' (a form of Jacob, in use in Britain from ancient times). The surname is found chiefly in Co. Cork. Cf. mᴀc ιᴀᵹó.

ꞮꞲꞲꞲꞲꞲꞲꞲe, Earls ; a translation of the English ' Earls.'

ꞮꞲꞲꞲꞲꞲꞲꞲ, Eyre, Eyres, Ayres.

ꞲꞲꞲꞲꞲꞲꞲ, ꞲꞲꞲꞲꞲꞲ, Inglis, English. V. ꞲꞲꞲꞲꞲꞲ.

ꞲꞲꞲꞲꞲꞲꞲꞲ, Nugent. V. ꞲꞲꞲꞲꞲꞲꞲ.

ꞲꞲꞲꞲꞲꞲ—VIII—Ingram ; ' son of Ingram.'

ꞲꞲꞲꞲ, Irish. V. ꞲꞲ ꞲꞲꞲꞲ.

ꞲꞲꞲꞲꞲꞲ, *Irlond*, Ireland. V. ꞲꞲ ꞲꞲꞲꞲꞲꞲ.

ꞲꞲꞲꞲꞲꞲ—VIII—Eustace, etc. ; ' son of Eustace ' (a common personal name in France, introduced into England by the Normans). The Eustaces came to Ireland at the time of the Anglo-Norman invasion, and obtained large estates in the counties of Kildare and Carlow. They were one of the leading families of the Pale, and many of them attained to high distinction. In 1580, James Eustace, Viscount Baltinglas, took up arms in defence of the Catholic faith and, together with the O'Byrnes and O'Tooles, inflicted a crushing defeat on Lord Grey at Glenmalure, in the autumn of the same year. On the failure of the rising he, a few years later, fled to Spain. His estates and those of his followers were confiscated, and many of them were put to death. The confiscations and attainders of the 17th century completed the ruin of the family.

ꞲꞲꞲꞲꞲꞲꞲ, ꞲꞲꞲꞲꞲꞲ—VIII—Larens, Lawrence, etc. ; ' son of Laurence ' (Lat. Laurentius), a rather common personal name among the early Anglo-Norman invaders.

ꞲꞲꞲꞲꞲ—XII—*Lanfant, Lenfaunt, Leffaine, Laffane,* Laffan, Laffen, Laphin, etc. ; Nor. ' l'Enfant,' i.e., the child, probably applied to a person of guileless disposition ; the name of old and respectable families in Tipperary and Wexford. James Laffan of Grayston was sheriff of Tipperary in the reign of Elizabeth ; and in 1598, Laffan of the Slade (Slade Castle) was one of the principal gentlemen of Co. Wexford.

ꞲꞲꞲꞲꞲ—IX—*Lader, Laudir,* Lauder, Lawder ; Ir. ' ꞲꞲꞲꞲꞲ,' i.e., strong, powerful ; a descriptive epithet which took the place of the real surname ; very rare.

Lᴀɪ5ʟéɪs—XII—*Lageles*, *Lagheles*, *Laweles*, Lawless, Lillis, etc. ; Mid. Eng. ' Laghles,' i.e., the lawless, the outlaw ; the name of a family who came into Ireland about the time of the Anglo-Norman invasion and ramified through Leinster and Munster. A branch also settled in Tirawley, Co. Mayo. In Connacht it is sometimes corrupted to Lᴀɪ5ṗéɪṛ, and in Munster to Lᴀoɪ5ʟéɪṛ and Lɪʟeᴀṛ, q.v.

Lᴀɪ5neᴀċ—X—*Leynagh*, Lynagh, Linagh, generally, but incorrectly, Lynam in Offaly, and Lyons in Mayo ; Ir. ' Lᴀɪ5neᴀċ,' i.e., the Leinsterman ; a descriptive epithet which has supplanted the real surname.

Lᴀɪmbeᴀṛc—VIII—*Lamberde*, Lambart, Lambert ; ' son of Lambart' or ' Lambert' (a Teutonic personal name ; both forms occur in Domesday Book). The surname is old in Ireland, but apparently confined to Dublin. To be distinguished from Lᴀmpoṗc, q.v.

Lᴀɪmbín—VIII—Lambin, Lambyn ; ' son of Lambin,' a dim. of Lambert.

Lᴀɪcín—VIII—*Latin*, *Lattine*, Latten ; ' son of Latin ' (a personal name in Domesday Book). In Ireland, the surname was very rare and peculiar to Co. Kildare. The Rev. J. Latin was a priest of the diocese of Kildare in 1612.

Lᴀ́Lᴀɪᴅe—XI—Lawlee ; i.e., ' of Lawley,' a parish in Shropshire ; a rare West Limerick surname ; written Lawley in England where it is not uncommon.

Lᴀmpoṛc—XI—*Lamport*, Lampart, Lampert, Lambert ; i.e., ' of Lamport,' a parish in Northamptonshire, but confused with Lᴀɪmbeᴀṛc, q.v. The Lamports were an old Wexford family.

Lᴀn5ṗoṛc—XI—Langford ; Nor. ' de Langeford,' i.e., of Langford, a common place-name in England. I can find no instance of the surname in Ireland earlier than the 16th century.

Lᴀn5cún, Langton. V. ᴅe Lᴀn5cún.

Lᴀnnc—VIII—*Launt*, *Launte*, *Lownt*, Lant ; ' son of Lant ' (an Anglo-Saxon personal name, found in Domesday Book as the name of a landholder in the time of Edward the Confessor). Lant is an old Kilkenny surname.

Laoroe, *Loyde,* Lloyd ; a var. of Lóro, q.v.

Laoigléis, Lawless, Lillis. V. Laigléir.

Leabáilin — VIII — Lavallin, Lavallen; 'son of Llywelyn' (a Welsh personal name). The Lavallins have been settled in Cork for more than three centuries.

Léaoar, Leader ; a late English surname in Co. Cork.

Léaous, Ledwich, Ledwith, etc. V. oe Léaoúr.

Leainoi, Landy.

Leamnac—X—*Levenach,* Leynox, Lennox, Linnox ; Ir. ' Leamnac,' i.e., a native of, or connected with, Lennox in Scotland ; the name of a Scottish family who settled in the north of Ireland, probably at the time of the plantation of Ulster.

Leaslaoi, Leslie, Lesley. V. oe Liorla.

Leastar, Lester, Lister, Lyster. V. oe Leartar.

Léiginn, Lane. V. oe Léiginn.

Léiseac—XIV—Lacy, Lacey. V. oe Léir.

Liaig—XII—*Leche,* Leech, Leach ; Mid. Eng. ' leche,' i.e., physician, the same as the Irish liaig ; an old surname in Ireland.

Liac—IX—*Leagh,* Lea, Lee, Gray, Grey ; Ir. ' liac,' i.e., grey, hoary ; an epithet which supplanted the real surname. Cf. oán, ouo, etc.

Lioéio, Lovett, Lovitt ; a var. of Luioéio, q.v.

Lileas, *Lelasse, Leales, Liales, Lylles,* Lillis ; a var. in Limerick and Cork of Laigléir, q.v.

Lioóoio—VIII—Livott, Lyvott ; probably ' son of Lovot' (dim. of Love, same as Lovet, a common Norman personal name) ; an old Mayo surname.

Lionáro—VIII—*Leonarde,* Leonard ; ' son of Leonard.' This surname is very rare in Ireland, nearly all our Leonards being of native origin.

Lionjáro, Lingard.

Lionóio—VIII—*Lynoid, Lynod,* Lynott ; ' son of Lionot' (possibly a dim. of Leonard, certainly from the same root, and meaning ' little lion.' Cf. Lionel which is another diminutive). The Lynotts settled at an early period in Tirawley, Co. Mayo.

Lioscún, *Listowne*, Liston. V. ve Liortún.

Lobaois—VIII—*Lowyes, Lowes, Lewes,* Lewis; 'son of Lewis' (for Fr. Louis, a common personal name representing the older Clovis, from the latinised form, 'Chlodovisus,' of the old Frankish Hludwig, mod. German Ludwig). This family came into Ireland about the time of the Anglo-Norman invasion and settled in Dublin, Kildare, Wexford, Waterford, Cork, Limerick, etc. 'Lewes of Leweston,' also called 'Lowes of Lowston,' was one of the principal gentlemen of Co. Wexford in 1598.

Locárd—VIII—*Locard, Loccard, Lokard,* Lockard, Lockart, etc.; 'son of Locard' (a French personal name, from Teutonic Lochard). This surname came into Ireland about the time of the Anglo-Norman invasion. About the year 1200, Jordan Loccard was witness to a grant by Philip de Nugent to Holy Trinity Church, Dublin. There is a Ballylockard, or Lockardstown, in Co. Westmeath which was probably the first home of the family in Ireland.

Loro—XII—*Loyde,* Lloyd; Welsh 'lluyd,' i.e., grey; a well-known surname of Welsh origin. Also Lúiro and Laoroe, q.v.

Lombárd—XII—Lombard, Lumbard; Nor. 'le Lombard,' i.e., native of Lombardy, but later 'lombard' came to mean a banker, money-lender, or pawnbroker. There were old and respectable merchant families of the name in Cork, Waterford and Buttevant. At the beginning of the 17th century, Peter Lombard was Archbishop of Armagh and Primate of Ireland.

Lonorac—XIV—*Londragh,* Landers, Launders. V. ve Lonorá.

Lonorasac—XIV—Landers, Launders. V. ve Lonorar.

Longfort, Langford.

Locáiréil, Locráil—VIII—*Loterell, Luterell,* Lutterell, Lutterel, Luttrell; 'son of Lutherel' (dim. of Lothar or Lothaire, a Frankish personal name). This surname appears in England soon after the Norman Conquest. Sir Geoffrey Lutterell received from King John an estate in the valley of the Liffey which from him took the name of Luttrellstown, and was for centuries the home of his descendants. Branches of the family settled in Meath and Kildare. The Luttrells were one of the chief families of the Pale.

Lúcás—VIII—Lucas, Luke; 'son of Luke.' Lucas, not Luke, was the early form of the name.

Luibéiɒ—VIII—Lovett, Lovitt, Lovat, Levett; 'son of Lovet' (dim. of Love, a Norman personal name, which came into England with William the Conqueror). As a surname it came into Ireland about the time of the Anglo-Norman invasion.

Luibéil—VIII—Lovel; 'son of Lovel' (dim. of Love, a Norman personal name. It occurs in Domesday Book. Cf. Lovet which is another diminutive of the same). As a surname it was rare in Ireland, and found chiefly in Kilkenny.

Lúiɒ—XII—Lloyd; Welsh 'lluyd,' i.e., grey; also Lóiɒ and Laoiɒe, q.v.

Lúiséiɒ—VIII—Lucid, Lucet; probably 'son of Lucet (dim. of Lucas); an old, but rare, Kerry surname.

Lunɒʀasac—XIV—Landers, Launders. V. ɒe Lonɒpaʀ.

Máb—VIII—Mabe; 'son of Mab' (short for Mabel) V. máp.

Mac 'a bʀíʒɒe, MacBride; a shortened form in the spoken language of Mac ʒiolla bʀiʒɒe, q.v.

Mac 'a buiɒe, MacAvoy, MacEvoy, etc.; a shortened form of Mac ʒiollabuiɒe, q.v.

Mac áɒa, Mac áɒaiɒ—V—McCada, MacCady, MacCadie, MacKady, Muckady, Cady; [Addy, Addison]; 'son of Addy' (a pet form of Adam); very rare. Addison is the English equivalent.

Mac áɒaim, Mac aɒaim—V—MacAdam, MacCadam, MacCaddam, MacAdams, Adams, [Adamson]; 'son of Adam' (one of the commonest names among the early Anglo-Norman settlers in Ireland); an Irish

patronymic surname assumed by the Barrys of Rath-
cormac and Ballynagloch, Co. Cork, and other early
Anglo-Norman settlers.

Mac Áoαιm—V—MacCaw; 'son of Adam'; the same as
Mac Áoαιm (q.v.), but from an earlier Gaelic form
of the personal name.

Mac Aoáin—V—M'Caddane, M'Coddan, MacCadden,
MacCudden, etc.; 'son of Adan' (a dim. of Adam);
a rare and scattered surname. Cf. Mac Áιoín.

Mac Aoαmóιo—V—Adams; 'son of Adamot' (a dim.
of Adam); a rare Connacht surname.

Mac Aιbιsτín—V—Caviston, [Austin, Austen]; 'son
of Augustine' (a name in use among the Anglo-Norman settlers); a rare surname which was, doubtless,
assumed by an offshoot of some Anglo-Irish family.

Mac Aιbne—IV—M'Aveny, M'Eveny, MacEvinney,
MacAvinue, MacAvenue; 'son of Aιbne' (a personal
name peculiar to the families of O'Kane and O'Brallaghan of Derry); the name of a branch of the
O'Kanes.

Mac Áιoín—V—M'Adin, M'Aden, Caden, Cadden; 'son
of Adin' (dim. of Adam); very rare; corrupted in the
spoken language to Ó Cáιoín, q.v.

Mac Aιoιcín—V—Adkins, Atkins, Adkinson, Atkinson,
etc.; 'son of Adkin' (a dim. of Adam). Cf. Mac
Aιτιξín.

Mac Aιleáin—IV—M'Elean, M'Elane, M'Ilean, M'Ellen,
M'Kilan, MacAlean, MacClean, MacLean, MacKellan,
MacKellen, MacKillen, etc.; 'son of Aιleáin'; a var. of
Mac Aιlín, q.v.; a scattered surname in Ulster and
Connacht. The following entry in the Fiants of Eliza-
beth throws some light on its origin: A.D. 1602—
Pardon to Elin M'Elane, kern, (in Co. Armagh). The
family is probably an offshoot of the MacDonnells
or Campbells. See also Mac Coιleáin and Mac Coιlín.

Mac Aιlξιle—IV—M'Alylly, MacAlilly, Callily, Lilly;
'son of Aιlξιl'; the name of a branch of the Maguires
in Co. Fermanagh.

Mac Aιlín—IV—M'Aline, M'Alline, MacAllion, MacAllen,

MacAllon, MacEllin, MacEllen, etc. ; 'son of Ꝺilín ';
the name of a branch of the Campbells of Scotland,
some of whom were brought over by the O'Donnells
as fighting-men, about the middle of the 16th century,
and settled in Tirconnell. This surname easily got
confused with Ɱac Cꝺilín, q.v.

Ɱꝺc Ꝺilpín—IV—MacAlpine, MacAlpin, MacCalpin ;
'son of Ꝺilpín '; a surname probably of Scottish
origin. The MacAlpins claim to be the most ancient
of the Highland clans.

Ɱꝺc Ꝺinꝺꝶéis, Ɱꝺc Ꝺinꝺꝶiꝺsꝺ—V—MacAndrew,
[Ross] ; 'son of Andrew' (Lat. Andreas) ; a Gaelic
patronymic surname assumed by the Scottish family
of Ross.

Ɱꝺc Ꝺinꝺꝶiú—V—MacAndrew, [Andrewson, Anderson,
Andrews, Anders] ; 'son of Andrew '; an Irish patron-
ymic assumed by a branch of the Barretts of Tirawley,
Co. Mayo, who were seated in the district called the
Two Bacs, lying between Lough Conn and the River
Moy. It is now angl. MacAndrew, and is very com-
mon in the district.

Ɱꝺc Ꝺinṁiꝶe—IV—M'Anavero, MacConvery, Convery ;
'son of Ꝺinṁiꝶe.' Cf. Ó hꝺinṁiꝶe, angl. O'Hanvire.

Ɱꝺc Ꝺiꝶꞇ—IV—M'Art, M'Arte, MacCart, (MacArthy,
Hart, Harte,) ; 'son of Ꝺꝶꞇ '; very rare.

Ɱꝺc Ꝺiꝶꞇeꝺin—IV—M'Keartan, M'Curtaine, M'Curtayne, Curtayne, Curtain, Curtin, etc. ; 'son of Ꝺꝶꞇán '
(dim. of Ꝺꝶꞇ) ; an attenuated form of Ɱꝺc Ꝺꝶꞇáin,
q.v. ; peculiar to Co. Cork. V. also Ɱꝺc Cꝺiꝶꞇeáin.

Ɱꝺc ꝹiꞇiꝒín—V—Cattigan ; 'son of Atkin '; a Mayo
surname ; in the spoken language Uꝺ CꝺiꞇiꝒín. Cf.
Ɱꝺc Ꝺiꝺicín.

Ɱꝺc Ꝺlꝺsꞇꝺiꝶ—V—M'Alaster, MacAlister, MacAllister,
MacCallister, MacEllister, MacAlester, M'Closter, Mac-
Clester, MacLester, Callister, Lester, etc. ; 'son of
Ꝺlꝺꝶꞇꝺꝶ,' (a Gaelic form of Alexander) ; the name of
a branch of the MacDonalds, long settled in Co.
Antrim.

Ɱꝺc Ꝺlꝺsꞇꝶuiɱ—V—M'Alastrom, M'Alastrum, M'El-

listrom, MacElistrum, MacElestrim, MacEllistram, etc.; 'son of Alarᴄꝛom' (a Gaelic form of Alexander); a var. of ⴅac Alarᴄaiꝛ, q.v. This form of the surname is peculiar to Kerry, where the family has been settled for centuries.

ⴅac Allṁuráin—IV—Colleran; 'son of Allṁuꝛán'; found in parts of Connacht; probably the correct original of Ó Callaꝛáin, q.v.

ⴅac Alsanᴅaiꝛ—V—*M'Alexander, M'Alesandre,* MacAlshander, MacAlshender, MacAlshinder, MacCalshander, MacElshander, MacKalshander, Alexander, etc.; 'son of Alexander,' (a not uncommon personal name among the Normans, specially common in Scotland). The surname, which came to us from Scotland, has assumed a great variety of forms. V. ⴅac Alarᴄaiꝛ and ⴅac Alarᴄꝛuim, which are varients.

ⴅac Ámoinn—V—MacCammon, MacCammond, MacKemman, Hammond, [Hammondson]; 'son of Amundr' (a Norse personal name); a surname of Norse origin.

ⴅac Aṁalᵹaᴅa, ⴅac Aṁalᵹaiᴅ—IV—MacAulay, MacAuley, MacCauley, MacCowley, Cawley, etc.; 'son of Aṁalᵹaiᴅ' (an ancient Irish personal name). There are several distinct families of this name, the best known being that of Co. Westmeath, the head of which was formerly lord of Calraighe, comprising the whole of the parish of Ballyloughloe, in the west of that county. It is sometimes impossible to distinguish the angl. forms of this surname from those of ⴅac Aṁlaoiꝺ, q.v. V. also ⴅaᵹ Aṁalᵹaᴅa, which is a variant.

ⴅac Aⴅⴅbꝛóis—V—MacAmbrose, MacCambridge; 'son of Ambrose'; a rare surname of Scottish origin.

ⴅac Aṁlaoiꝺ—V—MacAuliffe, MacAuley, MacCauliffe, MacCauley, MacCawley, MacCowley, Cawley, Cowley, etc.; 'son of Aṁlaoiꝺ' (an Irish form of the Norse Olaf). There are three well-known families of this name: (1) ⴅac Aṁlaoiꝺ, angl. MacAuliffe, of Co. Cork, a branch of the MacCarthys. The head of this family resided at Castle MacAuliffe, near Newmarket, and his territory comprised the district lying between Newmarket and the boundaries of the counties of Limerick and Kerry. (2) Mac Aṁlaoiḃ of Fermanagh, a branch of the Maguires, whose territory comprised the barony of Clanawley. And (3) Mac Aṁlaoiḃ, angl. MacAulay, of Scotland. The chief seat of this family was at Ardincaple, in Dumbartonshire. A branch of the family settled in Co. Antrim, and many of the Mac-Aulays of the north of Ireland are of this stock. To it belonged also the celebrated Lord Macaulay.

Mac Anabaḋa—VII—*M'Anaboy*, *M'Annovoy*, Mac-Naboe, Monaboe, (MacAnabb, MacNabb), and, by ' translation,' Victory ; ' son of the premature ' (Ir. ' anabaiḋ,' unripe) ; a Breifney surname. It appears to have been early corrupted to Mac na buaḋa, on the erroneous supposition that it was derived from ' buaiḋ,' victory, and has been accordingly sometimes ' translated ' Victory. It is also apt to be confused with Mac an Abbaḋ, q.v.

Mac an Abbaḋ—VII—*M'an Abba*, *M'Enabb*, Mac-Anabb, MacNabb ; ' son of the abbot.' The MacNabbs are mostly of Scottish descent, apparently very few of the name being Irish. They were a branch of the MacKinnons, and at one time a clan of considerable importance.

Mac an Aḋastair, Mac an Aġastair, *M'Innester*, Nestor ; a shortened form of Mac Ṡipp an Aḋartair, Mac Ṡipp an Aġartair, q.v.

Mac an Ailín, *M'Enallen*, MacAnallen, Nallen ; ' son of————' ; a rare surname in Ulster and Connacht, the origin of which I cannot trace. The above represents the pronunciation as I heard it.

Mac an Airċinn, *M'Enarhin*, *M'Enerin*, *M'Kinnertin*, *M'Naryn*, MacAnern, MacNern, MacNairn, MacKinerkin, Kinnerk ; a shortened form of Mac an Airċinniġ, q.v.; also Mac an Oirċinn.

Mac an Airċinniġ—VII—MacAnerney, MacEnerney, MacInerney, MacNerhenny, MacNerney, MacNirney, Mac-

Nertney, Connerney, Kenerney, Kinerney, Nerhenny, Nerney, Nertney, Nirney, etc. ; ' son of the erenagh ' (Ir. 'ᴀɪꞃcɪnneᴀċ', steward of church lands) ; the name of several distinct families, each an offshoot of one or other of the great erenagh families. The Roscommon family of the name, who are apparently a branch of the family of Ó bꞃᴀnᴀɪn (q.v.), were erenaghs of St. Patrick's church at Elphin. The Thomond family, who are numerous in Clare and Limerick, formerly held considerable property in the parish of Ballysally, but lost it in the Cromwellian confiscations. The above is the literary form of this surname, but ⅿᴀc ᴀn Oɪꞃcɪnnɪᵹ, often shortened to ⅿᴀc ᴀn Oɪꞃcɪnn, has long been the popular form.

ⅿᴀc ᴀn ᴀsꞇꞃɪᵹ—VII—MacKinestry, MacKinstry, MacNestry, ; ' son of the traveller ' (Ir 'ᴀɪꞃꞇꞃɪᵹꞇeᴀċ') ; an Ulster surname, probably of Scottish origin.

ⅿᴀc ᴀn ᴀꞇᴀ, MacAnawe ; Ford, Forde ; a corruption of ⅿᴀc Conꞃnᴀⅿᴀ, q.v.

ⅿᴀc ᴀn bᴀɪꞃꝺ—VII—MacAward, MacWard, Ward ; ' son of the bard ' (Ir. ' bᴀꞃꝺ ') ; a very common surname ; found in every county in Ireland, but especially in Donegal, Galway and Dublin. Three families of the name are known to history : (1) ⅿᴀc ᴀn bᴀɪꞃꝺ of Tirconnell, who were bards to the O'Donnells ; (2) ⅿᴀc ᴀn bᴀɪꞃꝺ of Ui Maine, who were bards to the O'Kellys, and were seated at Muine Chasain and Ballymacward ; and (3) ⅿᴀc ᴀn bᴀɪꞃꝺ of Oriel.

ⅿᴀc ᴀn bᴀʟʟᴀɪᵹ—VII—M'Evally, Vally ; ' son of the freckled man ' (Ir. ' bᴀʟʟᴀċ ') ; a rare surname.

ⅿᴀc ᴀn bᴀꞃuɪn—VII—M'Baron, MacBarron ; ' son of the baron ' (Ir. ' bᴀꞃún ') ; the name of an offshoot of the O'Neills ; a rather late surname.

ⅿᴀc ᴀn beᴀꞃsuɪʟɪᵹ—VII—M'Ewaerowly, M'Everrolly, Varrilly, Varrelly, Varily, Varley ; ' son of the sharp-eyed man ' (Ir.' beᴀꞃꞃúɪʟeᴀċ ') ; a rare Connacht surname.

ⅿᴀc ᴀn beᴀꞇᴀ, ⅿᴀc ᴀn beᴀꞇᴀꝺ—IV—M'Evaghe, M'Eveighe, M'Ivagh, M'Vaghe, M'Veha, M'Vehy,

MacAbee, MacIveagh, MacAveigh, MacAvey, (Mac-
Avoy, MacEvoy, MacVoy), MacVeagh, MacVeigh,
MacVey, MacVay, MacVea, Vahy, Veigh, (Veasy,
Vesey), etc. ; ' son of ᵭᴀᴄ ᴀn ᴅᴇᴀᴄᴀᴅ,' (an Irish personal name, meaning ' son of life ') ; a common surname in many parts of Ulster, found also in some parts
of Leinster and Connacht. There is a universal
tendency to assimilate its angl. forms to those of ᵭᴀᴄ
ᵱᴉoᴅᴅuᴉᴅe (q.v.), and consequently it is often disguised
as MacAvoy, MacEvoy, etc. In Co. Mayo, it is sometimes strangely anglicised Veasy and Vesey.

ᵭᴀᴄ ᴀn ᴅᴉᴀᴅᴄᴀᴉᵹ—VII—MacVeety, MacVity, Mac-
Veity, etc. ; ' son of the hospitaller' (Ir. ' ᴅᴉᴀᴅᴄᴀċ').
This surname has apparently come to us from Scot-
land ; at least, I can discover no early instances in
Ireland. Cf. ᴅᴉᴀᴅᴄᴀċ.

ᵭᴀᴄ ᴀn ᴅᴉoᴄᴀ́ᴉᴚe, ᵭᴀᴄ ᴀn ᴅᴉoᴄᴀᴚᴀ—VII — M'Evi-
care, M'Ivickaire, M'Vycare, MacVicar, MacVicker,
MacVickar, Vickery, Vicars, Vickers, Vickars, etc. ;
' son of the vicar' (Ir.. ' ᴅᴉoᴄᴀ́ᴉᴘe.') This surname,
in the great majority of instances, is of Scottish origin.
As an Irish surname, it was exceedingly rare.

ᵭᴀᴄ ᴀn ᴅᴚeᴉᴄeᴀᵭᴀn, ᵭᴀᴄ ᴀn ᴅᴚeᴉᴄeᴀᵭᴨᴀᴉᵹ,
ᵭᴀᴄ ᴀn ᴅᴚeᴉᴄᴉᵭ—VII—M'Abreham, M'Ebrehowne,
M'Evrehune, M'Evrehoona, M'Evrehon, M'Brehuna
M'Brehon, M'Vrehoune, Brehony, Breheny,
Brohoon, and, by translation, Judge ; ' son of the
brehon,' or judge, (Ir. ' ᴅᴚeᴉᴄeᴀᵭ ', gen. -ᴄeᴀᵭᴀn
and -ᴄᴉᵭ, ' ᴅᴚeᴉᴄeᴀᵭᴨᴀċ,' gen. -ᴨᴀᴉᵹ) ; a common
surname in many parts of Ireland, especialy in Connacht and West Ulster. There are, doubtless, several
distinct families so called, each an offshoot of one or
other of the great brehon families. The surname is now
generally angl. Judge, by translation. The form ᵭᴀᴄ
ᴀn ᴅᴚeᴉᴄᴉᵭ, though common in the spoken language,
is apparently modern. This surname is also found in
Scotland, where it is angl. Browne.

ᵭᴀᴄ ᴀn ᴄᴀᴌᴅᴀᴉᵹ—IV—M'Ecallough, M'Ecallowy,
M'Icallowe, MacCalvey, Calvey ; ' son of ᴀn ᴄᴀᴌᴅᴀċ '

(an Irish personal name, meaning ' the bald ') ; a rare surname.

Mac an CaoiC—VII—*M'Echey*, *M'Ekey*, *M'Keegh*, Mac-Kee, and probably Keyes ; ' son of the blind man ' (Ir. ' caoċ '). This was a designation of a branch of the O'Reillys in Cavan and the neighbouring counties, but was also found in other parts of Ireland, especially in Limerick and Tipperary ; hence probably Keyes.

Mac an Carraiġ—VII—*M'Encarie*, *M'Incarrie*, Mac-Carrie, MacCarry ; ' son of the bald man ' (Ir. ' carrac,' bald, scabbed) ; a rare and scattered surname.

Mac an Ceairt—VII—Kincart, Wright ; ' son of the right ' (Ir. ceart ') ; a Co. Mayo surname ; evidently an incorrect ' translation ' of the English surname Wright.

Mac an Cléiriġ—VII—*M'Anclery*, *M'Ecleary*, *M'Eclery*, MacClery, MacCleary, Clery, Cleary, Clarke, [Clarkson, Clarson] ; ' son of the clerk ' (Ir. ' cléireac ') ; a common Cavan surname, probably a var. of Ó Cléiriġ, q.v. It is now nearly always translated Clarke. Clarkson is the exact English equivalent.

Mac an Coiliġ—VII—*M'Akolly*, *M'Anchelly*, MacQuilly, and, by translation, Cox, Coxe ; ' son of the cock ' (Ir. ' coileac ') ; the name of a Roscommon family who were coarbs of St. Barry at Kilbarry, in the east of that county, and perhaps of other families in different parts of Ireland. Its angl. forms are difficult to distinguish from those of Mac Conċoille, q.v. See also Mac Coiliġ.

Mac an Coill, Forrestal ; a Co. Mayo surname ; probably an attempted translation of the English surname Forrestal ; or possibly a shortened form of Mac an Coiliġ above.

Mac an Crosáin—VII—*M'Acrossane*, *M'Ecrossan*, Mac-Crossan, Crossan, Crossin, Cross, (Crosbie), etc. ; ' son of the rhymer ' (Ir. ' crosán ') ; the name (1) of a Tirconnell family, one of whom was Bishop of Raphoe in the 14th century, and who are still numerous in Derry and Tyrone ; and (2) of a Leinster family who were bards to the O'Moores and O'Connors, in Leix and Offaly. This family threw in its lot with the English in the 16th century, and assumed the English surname of Crosbie.

Mac an Ɗeaȝáin, Mac an Ɗeaȝánaȝ—VII—
M'Adegain, M'Adegany, M'Idegane, M'Idigany, M'Deane, MacDigany, Dagney, Digany, Digney, Deane, etc. ; ' son of the dean,' (Ir. ' Ɗeaȝán,' ' Ɗeaȝánaċ,' Lat. ' decanus '). This surname was found in the 16th century in many parts of Ireland, but especially in Donegal, where the families so named seem to have been originally O'Donnells and O'Gallaghers. It is now very often translated Deane.

Mac an Ɗéisiȝ—VII—*M'Edesey,* Deasy, Deasey ; ' son of the Decian ' (Ir. ' Ɗéireaċ,' i.e., native of the Decies of Waterford) ; a Co. Sligo surname.

Mac an Ɗeóraiɗ—VII—*M'Edoire,* MacAdorey ; ' son of the stranger ' (Ir. ' Ɗeóραɗ ') ; very rare.

Mac an Ɗruaiɗ—VII—*M'Adrwy, M'Edrwe,* Drew, and incorrectly MacDrury, Drewry and Drury ; ' son of the druid,' or ' magician ' (Ir. ' Ɗρuaɗ') ; a rare surname ; formerly peculiar to Monaghan and Roscommon. In the latter county, it is incorrectly angl. Drury.

Mac an Éanaiȝ, MacAneany, MacAneeny, MacEneany, MacAneny, MacNeney, and, by ' translation,' Bird ; a corruption of Mac Conaonaiȝ, q.v. The ' translated ' form, Bird, is, of course, incorrect, being founded on the erroneous supposition that the surname is derived from 'éan,' a bird.

Mac an Easpuic—VII—*M'Enaspicke,* MacAnespic, MacAnaspie, Easping, Aspig, [Bishop] ' son of the bishop ' (Ir. ' earpoc ') ; very rare.

Mac Anɽaiɗ—IV—Tempest ; ' son of Anɽaɗ ' (storm).

Mac an ɸailȝiȝ—VII—MacAnally, MacEnally, MacInally, MacNally, Manally, Canally, Nally, etc. ; ' son of the poor man ' (Ir. ' ɸailȝeaċ ') ; cf. Ɗe Paoρ ; a Mayo surname borne by a family of Welsh or Norman origin ; also common, in the 16th century, in many parts of Ulster and Leinster. In the North, it is apt to be confused with Mac Conulaɗ, q.v.

mac an ꝼileaꝺ, mac an ꝼiliꝺ—VII—*M'Anelly,*
M'Enelly, M'Enillowe, M'Enilly, M'Inilly, MacAnilly,
MacNilly, MacNeilly, MacNielly, MacNeely, Mac-
Neally, MacNealey, Maneilly, Maneely, Meneely,
Mineely ; ' son of the poet ' (Ir. ' ꝼile ') ; not a very
common surname, and almost peculiar to N.E. Ulster.
To be distinguished from mac Conᵹaile and mac
Conᵹaola which are sometimes similarly anglicised.
mac an ꝼir—IV—*M'Ener, M'Enir, M'Inner, M'Innier,*
Kinner, Kinnier, etc. ; ' son of an ꝼeaꞃ (the man)',
(a short form of ꝼeaꞃᵹanainm, ꝼeaꞃꝺoꞃċa, or some
other Irish personal name beginning with ꝼeaꞃ) ; a
rare and scattered surname. Not the same as the
Scottish Kinnear, Kinneir,
mac an ꝼiꞃléiᵹinn—VII—*M'Enferline, M'Enyreloyne,*
MacNerlin, MacNerland, Killerlean ; ' son of the
lector ' (Ir. ' ꝼeaꞃléiᵹinn ') ; a rare Sligo surname ;
also mac ꝼiꞃléiᵹinn, q.v.
mac an ꝼleascaiꞃ—VII—*MacAnaleister,* Fletcher,
' son of the fletcher,' i.e., the arrow-featherer.
mac an ꝼꞃanncaiᵹ—VII—Frain, Frayne, Freyne,
Frainey, Freney ; ' son of the Frenchman' (Ir. 'ꝼꞃanncaċ') ; a Mayo surname. I suspect this surname
is modern ; at least, I can discover no early instances.
mac an ᵹaꝺann, v. mac an ᵹoꝺann.
mac an ᵹallóᵹlaiᵹ—VII—*M'Agaloglie,* MacGallogly,
Gallogly, by ' translation,' English, Englishby, and by
assimilation, Ingoldsby ; ' son of the gallowglass ' (Ir.
ᵹallóᵹlaċ') ; formerly a Donegal surname ; now
found chiefly in Louth and Meath.
mac an ᵹaill—VII—*M'Agayll, M'Agoyle, M'Egeill,*
MacGill, Gill, [Stapleton] ; ' son of the foreigner '
(Ir. ' ᵹall ') ; a var. of mac an ᵹoill, q.v. This was
the Irish name assumed by the Stapletons of Co.
Tipperary.
mac an ᵹeaiꞃꞃ, mac an ᵹiꞃꞃ—VII—*M'Iyear, M'Eghir,*
M'Gayer, MacGarr, MacGirr, MacGerr, Gayer,
and by translation, Short ; ' son of the short,
or low-sized, man ' (Ir. ' ᵹeaꞃꞃ ' and ' ᵹioꞃꞃ '). mac

an Geairr, which may be regarded as the Connacht form of this surname, was formerly common in Sligo and Leitrim, and is now well known in Mayo. Mac an Girr is the Ulster form, and was common in Armagh and Tyrone. The family is supposed to be of Scottish origin, but is, more probably, an offshoot of some native family. Both variants were in use in Dublin and Wicklow.

Mac an Goḃa—VII—*M'Gowe,* Gow, Smith; a var. of Mac an Goḃann, q.v.

Mac an Goḃann—VII—*M'Agowne, M'Egowne, M'Igoine, M'Igone,* MacGowan, MacGowen, Magowan, Gowen, Gowing, Goan, etc., and, by translation, Smith, Smyth; 'son of the smith' (Ir. 'goḃa,' gen. 'goḃann'); a very common Irish surname. In the South of Ireland, it is now generally translated Smith, but MacGowan and Magowan are common in the North. Clann an Goḃann of Clare and Tipperary were hereditary historians to the O'Loghlins of Burren and to the O'Kennedys of Ormond respectively.

Mac an Goill—VII—*Macingill, M'Agill, M'Egill,* MacGill, Magill, Gill, etc.; 'son of the foreigner' (Ir. 'gall'); an Irish surname given to the descendants of some of the early Anglo-Norman settlers. There were families of the name in every province. V. Mac an Gaill, which is a variant.

Mac an Iarla—VII—*M'Inierligh, M'an Erle,* Earl, Earle, Earls; 'son of the earl' (Ir. 'iarla'); very rare.

Mac an Iascaire—VII—*M'Inesker,* Fisher; 'son of the fisherman' (Ir. 'iascaire'); a late importation from Scotland, if not a translation of the English surname Fisher. The Scottish-Gaelic form, as I heard it, is Mac an Iascair.

Mac an Laignig—VII—(?) Callina, Collina, Colliney; 'son of the Leinsterman,' (Ir. Laigneaċ).

Mac an Leaga—VII—*M'Enlawe, M'Enlay, M'Enley, M'Enlea, M'Kinlea, M'Elea, M'Ellay, M'Lea,* MacKinlay, MacKinley, MacAlea, MacAlee, MacClay,

MacLee, Lee, Leigh, and sometimes incorrectly Mac-
Lean, MacClean; 'son of the physician' (Ir. 'ℓıaıᵹ').
There were several scattered families of this name,
each doubtless an offshoot of one or other of great medical families. It seems to have been sometimes used as
an *alias* by members of the family of mac Oᴜınn-
ṫℓéıⱱe (q.v.), who were famous medical practitioners.
See also mac Conℓeaᵹa.

mac an ṁaoaıO—VII—MacAvady, MacEvady, Mac-
Avaddy, MacEvaddy, MacVady, Covaddy, (Madden);
'son of the dog' (Ir. 'maoaⱱ'); an old Mayo surname; now very often incorrectly angl. Madden,
with which it is partly synonymous.

mac an ṁaıᵹısᴄıⱤ—VII—M'Amaster, M'Evaster,
M'Master, MacMaster, Master, Masterson; 'son of
the master' (Ir. maıᵹıⱤᴄıⱤ,' Lat. 'magister'). This
surname seems to have originated in Co. Cavan, but
by the end of the 16th century it had spread into
Longford and Roscommon. It is now nearly always
angl. Masterson. The Mastersons of Wexford are of
English descent.

mac an ṁanaıᵹ—VII—M'Ivannagh, M'Vany, Mac-
Evany, MacEvanny, MacVany, [Monk, Monks]; 'son
of the monk' (Ir. 'manaċ'); a rare surname. So far
as I know, it survives only in Co. Mayo. The corresponding English surname is Monk or Monks.

mac an ṁaoıⱤ—VII—M'Ewire, M'Eweir, Wire, Wyer,
Wier, Weir, Wear, Weere, Moyers, and in Scotland MacNair; 'son of the steward' (Ir. 'maoⱤ').
There were families of this name in Armagh, Westmeath, Offaly and Roscommon. The head of
the Armagh family was hereditary keeper of the Book
of Armagh. mac an ṁaoıⱤ is also a Scottish surname,
angl. MacNair.

mac an ṁıℓeaOa, mac an ṁıℓıO—VII—M'Aveely,
M'Evilee, M'Evelly, M'Ivile, Stanton, MacEvely, Mac-
Evilly, [Stanton, Staunton]; 'son of the knight' (Ir.
'ṁıℓeaⱱ'); the Irish surname assumed by the Stauntons (v. Oe SᴄonOún) of the barony of Carra, Co.

Mayo. Many of the family have resumed the original surname, Staunton or Stanton.

ᵯᴀᴄ ᴀnnᴀ--IV—*M'Anna*, *M'Canna*, MacAnn, MacCann, etc. ; ' son of ᴀnnᴀᵭ '; usually written ᵯᴀᴄ Cᴀnnᴀ or ᵯᴀᴄ Cᴀnᴀ, q.v.

ᵯᴀᴄ ᴀnnᴀıᵭ—IV—*M'Anna*, *M'Canna*, MacCanny, Canny ; ' son of ᴀnnᴀᵭ '; the fullest and most correct form of the surname which is usually written ᵯᴀᴄ ᴀnnᴀ or ᵯᴀᴄ Cᴀnnᴀ, q.v. This form is still in use in Co. Clare, angl. Canny. In the 16th century, the MacCannys were seated in Co. Limerick, and in 1598 one of them held the castle of Drombanny, near the city.

ᵯᴀᴄ ᴀnnᴌᴀoıᵭ—V—*M'Awnly*, MacCownley ; ' son of Anlaf' (a form of the Norse Olaf) ; a var. of ᵯᴀᴄ ᴀᵯᴌᴀoıᵭ, q.v. ; very rare.

ᵯᴀᴄ ᴀnnRᴀıc—V—*M'Anrack*, *M'Canricke*, *M'Henricke*, MacKendrick, Kenrick, Conrick, Condrick, Conderick ; ' son of ᴀnnᵱᴀᴄ ' (Norse Heimrekr) ; a surname of Norse origin, formerly in Cork, Waterford, Wexford and Carlow. Also ᵯᴀᴄ eᴀnnᵱᴀıc, q.v.

ᵯᴀᴄ ᴀnnRᴀoı—V—*M'Hanry*, *M'Harrye*, MacHarry, [Fitzharris, Feeharry, Harris, Harrison] ; ' son of Henry ' ; a var. of ᵯᴀᴄ ᴴᴀnnᵱᴀoı and ᵯᴀᴄ eınᵱı, q.v.

ᵯᴀᴄ ᴀn ᴕᵹᴌᴀoıc—VII—*M'Nogly*, now probably Nagle ; 'son of the soldier ' (Ir. ' ᴕᵹᴌᴀoᴄ) ' ; the name of a Sligo family who were erenaghs of the church of Killery, near Lough Gill. It is probably still extant under the angl. form of Nagle.

ᵯᴀᴄ ᴀn oıRcınn, a var. of ᵯᴀᴄ ᴀn ᴀıᵱcınn, q.v.

ᵯᴀᴄ ᴀn oıRcınnıᵹ, a var. of ᵯᴀᴄ ᴀn ᴀıᵱcınnıᵹ, q.v.

ᵯᴀᴄ ᴀn ᵱeᴀRsúın, ᵯᴀᴄ ᴀn ᵱeᴀRsᴀın—VII— *M'Efarson*, *M'Eparson*, *M'Parson*, MacPharson, Mac-Pherson, MacFarson, MacFerson, Pherson, Parsons ; ' son of the parson ' (Ir. ' ᵱeᴀᵱᵲún,' Lat. ' persona ') ; a scattered surname. Many of the name in Ireland are, no doubt, descended from the famous Highland clan, ᵯᴀᴄ ᴀn ᵱeᴀᵱᵲᴀın.

Mac an ṗníORa, Mac an ṗnír—VII—*M'Ipriorie,*
M'Eprior, M'Prior, Friary, Prior, Fryer, etc. ; ' son
of the prior ' (Ir. ' pníoṗ ') ; a scattered surname.

Mac an Raoí, Mac-an-Ree ; King ; a corruption of
Mac Conṗaoí, q.v.

Mac an Rí▵íre—VII—*M'Eridery, M'Iruddery, M'Rud-*
dery, MacRuddery, MacKnight, Knight, [Fitzsimons,
FitzSimons] ; ' son of the knight ' (Ir. ' ṗíoíṗe ') ; the
Irish surname assumed by the FitzSimons of Co.
Westmeath, and perhaps also by offshoots of knightly
houses in other parts of Ireland.

Mac an Róċaíċ, Monroe, Munroe ; a Scottish surname.

Mac an Scolóíġe — VII — *M'Yscollog, M'Scolloige,*
M'Scologe, MacScollog, and, by translation, Farmer ;
' son of the farmer ' (Ir. ' ṗcolóġ ') ; a rare and scattered surname. In the 16th century, it was most
common in Galway, Tyrone and Fermanagh.

Mac an Spaṙáíṇ, MacAsparan, MacSparran ; ' son of
the purse ' (Ir. ṗpaṗáṇ).

Mac an Stocaíre—VII—MacAstocker, MacStocker,
(Stafford) ; ' son of the trumpeter ' (Ir. ' ṗcocaíṗe).

Mac an Caoísíġ—VII—MacIntosh, MacEntosh, Mac-
Kintosh ; ' son of the chieftain ' (Ir. ' caoíṗeaċ ') ; the
name of a famous Highland clan in Inverness,
some of whom settled in the north of Ireland. The
Scottish Gaelic form of the name is Mac an Cóíríċ.

Mac an Cíompáṇaíġ—VII—*M'Itempany, M'Tympane,*
M'Tempane, MacAtimney, MacAtimeny, MacAtamney,
MacAtaminey, MacTimney, MacTamney, Timpany,
Tymmany, Timony, Tamney, Tempeny, Tenpeny, (?)
Toompane, (?) Tumpane ; ' son of the tympanist ' (Ir.
' cíompáṇaċ'). This surname was found chiefly in
Down, Tyrone and Sligo, and it still survives, under
a great variety of angl. forms, in the north and west
of Ireland.

Mac aṇcoíṇe—V—*MacAnthony,* Anthony, Antony ;
' son of Antony.'

Mac an cSaṡaíRc—VII—MacEntaggart, MacEntaggert,
MacEntegart, MacIntaggart, MacInteggart, MacTag-

gart, MacTeggart, Taggart, Teggart, Tegart, Tiger, etc. ; 'son of the priest' (Ir. 'ʀᴀᴢᴀʀᴄ', Lat. 'sacerdos') ; an Ulster surname.

Mᴀc ᴀn ᴄSᴀṁᴀ1ᴢ—VII—*M'Etawey*, Tavey ; 'son of the mild, or pleasant, man' (Ir. 'ʀᴀṁᴀᴄ') ; a Co. Monaghan surname.

Mᴀc ᴀn ᴄSᴀᴏ1—VII—*M'Attye, M'Entie, M'Inty,* Mac-Atee, MacEntee, MacIntee, MacKenty, MacKinty ; 'son of the scholar' (Ir. 'ʀᴀᴏ1') ; a well-known North of Ireland surname. In the 16th century, it was most common in Donegal, Monaghan, Louth and Long-ford.

Mᴀc ᴀn ᴄSᴀᴏ1ʀ—VII—MacAntire, MacEntire, MacEnteer, MacInteer, MacIntyre, MacAteer, MacAtear, Mac-Cateer, MacTeer, MacTier, Minteer, Mateer, etc., and, by translation, Carpenter and Freeman ; 'son of the craftsman' (Ir. 'ʀᴀᴏʀ,' a mason, carpenter ; also a freeman). There are, no doubt, several distinct families so called. About Dublin, this surname has been translated Carpenter. In other places, it has been incorrectly made Freeman, on the erroneous supposition that it is derived from ʀᴀᴏʀ, a freeman. This was also the name of a famous Scottish clan, whose country was Glen O, in Lorn ; and many of the MacIntyres of the North of Ireland are, doubtless, of that race.

Mᴀc ᴀn ᴄSᴀSᴀnᴀ1ᴢ—VII—MacAtasney, MacArtarsney, Atasney ; 'son of the Englishman' (Ir. 'Sᴀʀᴀnᴀᴄ') ; very rare.

Mᴀc ᴀn ᴄS1ᴏnnᴀ1ᴢ—VII—*M'Eteny, M'Etanny,* Mac-Ashinah, Tinney, Fox ; 'son of the fox' (Ir. 'ʀ1ᴏn-nᴀᴄ') ; a rare and scattered surname.

Mᴀc ᴀn ᴄu1ʟe, *M'Cantully, M'Etwille,* MacAtilla, Tully, and by 'translation,' Flood ; a corruption of Mᴀc ṁᴀᴏʟᴄu1ʟe, q.v. ; in the spoken language often further corrupted to Ó ᴄu1ʟe, q.v. ; a Connacht surname.

Mᴀc ᴀn úcᴀ1ʀe—VII—*M'Enookery, M'Inowkery,* [Fuller] ; 'son of the fuller' (Ir. úcᴀ1ʀe ').

Mac an Uisce, Uiske; Water, Waters; a corruption of Mac Conuisce, q.v.

Mac an Ultaigh—VII—MacAnulty, MacKnulty, MacNulty, Nulty; 'son of the Ulidian' (or native of East Ulster, Ir. 'Ultach'); the name of a Donegal family, who are probably a branch of the O'Dunlevys. (V. Ó Duinnshléibhe and Mac Duinnshléibhe). It is now common in Mayo and Meath. In the latter county, it is always angl. Nulty.

Mac Aodha—IV—*M'Ea,* MacKay, MacKey, MacKee, MacCoy, MacHugh, Eason, Hughes, Hueson, Hewson, etc; 'son of Aodh' (a common Irish personal name, now angl. Hugh); a very common surname, especially in Ulster and Connacht. There are several distinct families so called. In the barony of Clare, Co. Galway, Mac Aodha, of the same stock as the O'Flahertys, was chief of Clann Choscraigh. The MacKays of Strathnaver were a well-known Scottish clan, some of whom are, doubtless, to be found among the MacKays of the north of Ireland. The angl. form MacCoy is almost peculiar to Co. Limerick, whither the family migrated from Ulster more than three centuries ago. V. Mac Aoidh and Mag Aodha, which are variants.

Mac Aodha Buidhe—IV—*M'Eabuoy,* MacEvoy, MacAvoy; 'son of yellow Aodh'; very rare.

Mac Aodhagáin—IV—*M'Egaine, M'Hegane, M'Keagan, M'Kiegane,* MacEgan, MacKeegan, Egan, Heagan, Keegan, etc.; 'son of Aodhagán' (a dim. of Aodh); the name of a distinguished brehon family. They belonged originally to the district of Ui Maine in Connacht; but in the 14th and 15th centuries, branches of the family settled in Ormond, Desmond, and many other parts of Ireland. where they became brehons to the local chieftains. They also kept schools of law, and many learned men and eminent professors of the same name are mentioned in the Irish annals.

Mac Aodháin—IV—*M'Kiane, M'Kian,* MacKeane, Keane, Kane; 'son of Aodhán' (a dim. of Aodh). This is undoubtedly the correct form of the surname which, in the spoken language of Connacht, is pronounced Ó Caoṽáın and anglicised MacKeane, Keane and Kane.

Mac Aoıṽ—IV—*M'Ee, M'Eye*, MacKee, MacKie, Kee; 'son of Aoṽ'; a var. of Mac Aoṽa, q.v.

Mac Aonʒuıs, Mac Aonʒusa—IV—*M'Enesse, M'Hinchey, M'Nisse*, MacEnnis, MacInnes, MacInch, MacKinch, MacHinch, MacNeese, MacNeece, MacNiece, MacNish, Mannice, Minnish. Mannix, Kinnish, Ennis, Innes, Hinchey, etc.; 'son of Aonʒuſ' (an ancient Irish personal name); a var. of Maʒ Aonʒuıſ, q.v. Also the name of a Scottish clan in Argyleshire.

Mac Arcaıl—V—Archer; 'son of Arkil' (Ang.-Sax. Arcytel).

Mac Áɼoʒaıl—IV—MacArdel, MacArdle, MacCardle, Cardle, Cardell, Cardwell, ; 'son of Áɼoʒaı' (high valour); a well-known South Ulster surname. The family is probably a branch of the MacMahons.

Mac Arcaıʒ—IV—Harty, Hearty; apparently 'son of Aɼcac,' but probably corrupt; a rare Co. Mayo surname.

Mac Arcáın—IV—*M'Artane, M'Artan, M'Cartane*, MacCartan, MacCarten, MacCarton, MacCartin, Cartan, Carton, etc.; 'son of Aɼcáın' (a dim. of Aɼc). The head of this family was lord of Cinel Faghartaigh, now the barony of Kinelarty, in Co. Down. At the beginning of the 17th century, the name was common in many parts of Leinster, and it seems to have penetrated into Cork and Kerry. The spelling is often Mac Caɼcáın (q.v.), the c of Mac having been attracted over, and this is further corrupted to Ó Caɼcáın, q.v. See also Mac Aıɼceáın and Mac Caıɼceáın.

Mac Arcúıɼ—V—MacArthur, MacCarthur, MacCarter, Carthurs, Arthurs, etc.; 'son of Arthur.' This surname is apparently of Scottish origin. The MacArthurs were a branch of the Campbell clan, and at one time a powerful family in Argyleshire; but early in the 15th century their power was broken, when their chief, John MacArthur, was beheaded by James I and most of their estates forfeited. The Scottish-Gaelic form of the name is Mac Aṛċaiṛ.

Mac Ascaiḋ—V—M'Oskie, MacAskie, MacCaskie, Caskey ; ' son of Aṛcaiḋ,' (a pet form of some Norse or Anglo-Saxon name, perhaps Askell ; Searle has ' Asci ') ; a rare North of Ireland surname, probably of Norse origin.

Mac Ascaill—V—MacAskill ; ' son of Aṛcall,' (the Norse personal name Askell, Ascytel among the Anglo-Saxons) ; a surname of Scoto-Norse origin.

Mac Asmuinꞇ—V—MacCasmund, Casmond, Casement, ' son of Aṛmunḋ ' (the Norse personal name Asmundr, corresponding to the Anglo-Saxon Osmund) ; an old Manx surname, made famous in Ireland by Roger Casement.

Mac Ḃailoṛín, Mac Ḃailꞇṛín—V—M'Waldrin, Waldron ; ' son of little Walter ' (Ir. Ḃailꞇṛín ') ; the name of a Mayo family who are probably a branch of the Costelloes. Also written Mac Uailoṛín, Mac Uailꞇṛín.

Mac Ḃaiꞇín—V—M'Watten ; ' son of little Walter ' (Ir. ' Ḃaiꞇín ') ; the name or title of the head of the Barretts of Tirawley, Co. Mayo.

Mac Ḃaloṛáin—V—Waldron ; a var. of Mac Ḃalṛonꞇa; q.v. ; in use in parts of Connacht. Also written Mac Ualoṛáin.

Mac Ḃalṛonꞇa—V—M'Falronte, M'Valronte, Walronde, Waldron, [Wesley, Welsley, Wellesley] ; ' son of Waleran ' (an Anglo-Saxon personal name) ; a patronymic surname assumed by the family of Wesley in Leinster among whom Waleran was a favourite name. Also written Mac Ualṛonꞇa.

Mac Ḃaoiꞇín—IV—M'Boyhin, Boyne ; ' son of Ḃaoiꞇín ' ; formerly a Co. Leitrim surname ; still in use in Connacht, but very rare.

Mac Ḃeaṛꞇaġṛa, Baragrey, Barragry, Berachry, Berocry, Bearkery, Berkerry, Berkery ; a var. of Mac Ḃioṛꞇaġṛa, q.v.

Mac Ḃeaꞇa,. Mac Ḃeaꞇaḋ—IV—M'Beagh, Mac-

Beath, MacBeth, MacBeith, MacBey, MacBay; 'son of Macbeth'; a Scottish form of ᵯᴀc ᴀn ᵬeᴀᴄᴀ, q.v.; the name of a Scottish family who were hereditary physicians in Islay and Mull, and also historians to the Macleans. Some of them settled in Ulster.

ᵯᴀc ᵬeᴀᴄᴀn—IV—MacBean, MacVean; a var. of ᵯᴀc ᵬeᴀᴄᴀᵬ (q.v.), but the name of a different family. The MacBeans formed a distinct clan under their own chief.

ᵯᴀc ᵬıoᴚnᴀ—V—MacBirney, MacBurney, Burney, etc.; 'son of Bjarni' (a Norse personal name); a Scoto-Norse surname.

ᵯᴀc ᵬıoᴚᴄᴀᴣᴚᴀ—VII—M'Birehagree, M'Birryhaggery, M'Birragra, M'Birrekry, M'Berrickerey, Biracree, Biracrea, Berachry, Berocry, Berkerry, Berkery; also ᵯᴀc ᵬeᴀᴘᴄᴀᴣᴘᴀ, q.v.; 'son of the sharp pleader' (Ir. 'ᵬıoᴘ' or 'ᵬeᴀᴘ,' sharp, and 'ᴄᴀᴣᴘᴀᵬ,' pleading); the name of an Ulster family who were brehons to the O'Neills. They disappeared from Ulster about the middle of the 16th century, and the surname has ever since been peculiar to Tipperary and East Limerick, whither, not improbably, the family migrated in the reign of Elizabeth.

ᵯᴀc ᵬᴌoscᴀıᵬ—IV—M'blosgaid, M'blosgaigh, M'Closkie, M'Loskie, MacCloskey, MacCluskey, MacLoskey, MacLuskey, Closkey, Cluskey; 'son of ᵬᴌoᴘcᴀᵬ' (a personal name among the O'Kanes); the name of a Derry family descended from ᵬᴌoᴘcᴀᵬ Ó Cᴀᴄᴀın, who flourished in the 12th century; still common in Derry and other parts of Ulster.

ᵯᴀc ᵬᴌoscᴀıᴚe—VII—M'Gloskir, M'Gluskir, Mac-Clusker, Clusker, (Cosgrave); 'son of the public crier' (Ir. 'ᵬᴌoᴘcᴀıᴘe'); a Co. Armagh surname; perhaps a popular substitution for ᵯᴀc ᵬᴌoᴘcᴀıᵬ, q.v.

ᵯᴀc ᵬᴚᴀᵬᴀıᴣ—IV—M'Bradie, M'Brady, M'Brade, Brady; 'son of ᵬᴘᴀᵬᴀᴄ' (spirited); the name of a great Cavan family. ᵯᴀc ᵬᴘᴀᵬᴀıᴣ was chief of Cúıᴌ ᵬᴘíᴣᵬe, or Cúıᴌ ᵬᴘíᴣᵬeın, comprising the district around Stradone in Co. Cavan. The surname is

now very common in Ulster and also in many parts
of Leinster.

Mac ḂRáḊáiġ, M'Vraddie. V. Maġ Ḃráḋaiġ.

Mac ḂRáin—IV—M'Bran, M'Bren. V. Mac Ḃṗoin.

Mac ḂRáiṅ, MacCrann, MacKrann, MacRann; a var.
of Mac Ḃṗoin, q.v.

*Mac ḂRáṅáiġ—IV—Cranny, Crany; 'son of Ḃṗáṅáċ.'

Mac ḂRáṅáin—IV—M'Branane, M'Branon, M'Brenan,
Branan, Branon, Brannan, Brennan, etc.; 'son of
Ḃṗáṅáin' (a dim. of Ḃṗáṅ); the name of a great Roscommon family, the head of which was chief of Corca
Achlann, a large district in that county. They are said
to be descended from the noble druid, Ona, who granted
the site of the church of Elphin to St. Patrick. They
appear to have been also called Ó Ḃṗáṅáin (q.v.), and
there is every reason to believe that the Uí Ḃṗáṅáin
who were erenaghs of St. Patrick's church at Elphin
are a branch of this family. (V. Mac áṅ Aiṗċinniġ).
Mac Ḃṗáṅáin is now generally, but not quite correctly,
angl. Brennan.

Mac ḂRáoin—IV—M'Brewne, M'Brune, M'Breane,
MacBreen, Breen; 'son of Ḃṗáon'; the name of a
Kilkenny family, formerly seated in the barony of
Knocktopher.

Mac ḂReáṅḋáin—IV—M'Brandone, M'Brandon, Bran-
don; 'son of Ḃṗeáṅḋáin'; a rare Kerry surname.
To be distinguished from the English surname Brandon
(V. De Ḃṗáṅḋún).

Mac ḂReáṫṅáiġ—VII—MacBratney, MacBreatney,
MacBretney; 'son of the Welshman' (Ir. 'Ḃṗeáṫ-
ṅáċ'); an Ulster surname of Scottish origin.

Mac ḂRiáin—IV—M'Brian, MacBrien, MacBryan,
MacBryen, etc.; 'son of Ḃṗiáṅ.'

Mac ḂRiáRṫáiġ, MacBrearty, MacBrairty; a corruption of Mac Muiṗċeáṗṫáiġ, q.v.

Mac ḂRoiṅ—IV—MacBrin, MacBrinn, MacBirne, Mac-
Byrne, Brinn, Byrne, etc.; 'son of Ḃṗáṅ'; a var.
of Mac Ḃṗoiṅ, q.v.; a rare surname.

Mac ḂRoiṅ—IV—Mac Renn, MacRynn, Rynn, Wrynn,

Wrenn, Wren ; a var. of mᴀc bᴘᴀin, mᴀc bᴘᴀin, and mᴀc bᴘoin, q.v. ; a rare surname, found chiefly in Co. Leitrim.

mᴀc bʀuᴀᴅᴀiʀ, *M'Broder.* V. mᴀᴣ bᴘuᴀᴅᴀiᴘ.

mᴀc bʀuᴀiᴅeᴀᴅᴀ—IV—*M'Brouddie,* *M'Broudy,* *M'Brodie,* MacBrody, Brody, Brodie ; 'son of bᴘuᴀiᴅeᴀᴅ.' The MacBrodys were hereditary bards and historians to the O'Briens of Thomond from whom they held, in virtue of their office, considerable property at Ballybrody, Kilkeedy and Littermoylan, in Co. Clare. Several distinguished members of the family figure in Irish literary history. Conor MacBrody was one of the learned men whose approbation is prefixed to the Annals of the Four Masters. The family estates were confiscated in Cromwellian times. Also mᴀc bᴘuᴀiᴅin, q.v.

mᴀc bʀuᴀiᴅin, *M'Bruodyne, M'Brodyne,* Mac Broudin, Mac Bruodin, Broudin, Bruodin ; a frequent alias for mᴀc bᴘuᴀiᴅeᴀᴅᴀ (q.v.), of which it is the diminutive.

mᴀc cᴀbᴀ—IV—*M'Caba,* MacCabe, Macabe ; 'son of Cᴀbᴀ' (probably a nickname ; cf. 'cᴀbᴀ,' a cap or hood) ; the name of a military family of Norse origin who came over from the Hebrides, in the 14th century, and settled in Breifney, where they became captains of gallowglasses to the O'Rourkes and O'Reillys. Their pedigree is given by MacFirbis, from which it appears that they are a branch of the Mac Leods (V. mᴀc Leóiᴅ). The MacCabes are frequently mentioned in the Annals of the Four Masters, the earliest mention being at the year 1358. They are still numerous in Breifney (Leitrim and Cavan), and in the neighbouring counties of Monaghan and Meath.

mᴀc cᴀᴅᴀin—IV—*M'Coddane, M'Coddan,* MacCadden, MacCudden, Muckedan ; 'son of Cᴀᴅᴀn' (an Irish personal name, Lat. Catanus) ; a rare Ulster surname, peculiar, in the 16th century, to Armagh. It is impossible to distinguish its angl. forms from those of mᴀc Aᴅᴀin, q.v.

mᴀc cᴀfʀᴀiᴅ, v. mᴀc ᴣᴀfᴘᴀiᴅ.

Mᴀc Cᴀιlín—IV—*M'Calline*, MacCallion, MacCallan, MacCallen, [Campbell]; 'son of Cᴀιlín' (the Scottish Colin); also Mᴀc Coιlín, q.v. The family of fighting-men brought over from Scotland by the O'Donnells of Tirconnell in the 15th century, were sometimes called Mᴀc Cᴀιlín, sometimes Mᴀc Ѧιlín (q.v.), and it is impossible to say which form is correct.

Mᴀc Cᴀιrbre—IV—*M'Carbry*, *M'Carbery*, Carbry, Carbery, Carberry; 'son of Cᴀιrbre' (an old Irish personal name). The angl. forms of this surname cannot now be distinguished from those of Ó Cᴀιrbre, q.v.

Mᴀc Cᴀιrτeᴀιn—IV—*M'Keartan*, *M'Curtaine*, *M'Curtayne*, MacCurtain, Curtayne, Curtain, Curtin, &c.; an attenuated form of Mᴀc Cᴀrτᴀιn, q.v. This family, which is a branch of that of MacCartan of Co. Down, had settled in Co. of Cork before the end of the 16th century. Father Connor Mac Cairteain (angl. Curtin), P.P. of Glanmire and an Irish poet of no mean order, died in the year 1737.

Mᴀc Cᴀιsín—IV—*M'Cashine*, *M'Kasshine*, *M'Cassin*, MacCashin, Casheen, Cashin, Cashen, Cashion, Cassin, Keshin, &c.; 'son of Cᴀιrín' (dim. of cᴀr, bent, curly); a well-known family in Leinster and parts of Munster, where they were formerly hereditary medical practitioners; also an Antrim family.

Mᴀc Cᴀlbᴀιʒ—IV—*M'Callvagh*, MacCalvey, Calvey, &c; a shortened form of Mᴀc ᴀn Cᴀlbᴀιʒ, q.v.

Mᴀc Cᴀllᴀnᴀιn—IV—*M'Callenan*, MacCallnon, (Campbell); 'son of Cᴀllᴀnᴀn'; very rare.

Mᴀc Cᴀlmᴀιn—IV—MacCalman, MacCalmont; 'son of Colmᴀn'; a var. of Mᴀc Colmᴀιn, q.v.

Mᴀc Cᴀluιm—IV—MacCalum, MacCallam; 'son of Colum'; a var. of Mᴀc Coluιm, q.v.

*Mᴀc Cᴀmlᴀoιc—IV—MacCamley; 'son of Cᴀmlᴀoc' (bent hero). Cf. Mᴀc Cᴀoċlᴀoιċ.

Mᴀc Cᴀnᴀ, v. Mᴀc Cᴀnnᴀ.

Mᴀc Cᴀnᴀnn—IV—*M'Cannan*, MacConnon, Connon, (MacCann); 'son of Cᴀno' or 'Cᴀnᴀ' (whelp, wolf);

a rare and scattered surname; now very often disguised under the angl. form of MacCann.

Mac Canna—IV—*M'Canna*, MacCann, MacKann; 'son of Annaḋ'; also written Mac Cana and, more correctly, Mac Anna, q.v. The MacCanns were lords of Cinel Aonghusa, or Clann Breasail, on the south side of Lough Neagh, in Co. Armagh.

Mac Cannaiḋ—IV—*M'Canny*, MacCanny, Canny; a var. of Mac Annaiḋ, q.v.

Mac Caoċáin—IV—*M'Keaghane, M'Keahan*, Keahan, Keehan; 'son of Caoċán' (the blind man, perhaps a nickname). This surname is found in the neighbourhood of the city of Limerick and in parts of Connacht.

Mac Caoċlaoiċ—VII—*M'Keaghlie, M'Keighely*, Kehelly, Kehilly, (Coakley, Keily, Kelly); 'son of the blind hero' (Ir. Caoċlaoċ), but probably it was originally Mac Caoċḟile, 'son of the blind poet'; an old West Cork surname. V. Mac Claoċlaoiċ.

Mac Caoilte—IV—MacCaoilte; 'son of Caoilte.'

*Mac Caoṁánaiġ—IV—MacCavanagh, 'son of Caoṁánaċ.'

Mac Carluis—V—Corless, Carlos; 'son of Carlus' (a Norse form of the Lat. 'Carolus,' i.e. Charles); a rare surname in Galway and Roscommon. I can find no early angl. form.

Mac Carrġaṁna—IV—*M'Carrhon*, MacCarroon, MacCaron, *Carrowny, Carony, M'Crony*, MacGroaney, Growney, O'Growney, (*M'Gaffney*, Gaffney, Caulfield); also written Mag Carrġaṁna, and now corruptly Ó Graṁna; 'son of Carrġaṁain' (i.e., spear-calf, an old Irish personal name); the name of an ancient family in Co. Westmeath, of the southern Ui Neill race, who derive their descent from Maine, son of Niall of the Nine Hostages. They were at first surnamed Mac Giolla Ultain, from Giolla Ultain, one of their ancestors, but afterwards adopted the present surname from Carrġaṁain, the grandson of Giolla Ultain. Their clan-name was Muintear ϻαοιιοηηα, taken from another of their ancestors called ϻαοιρ‌ιοηηα, i.e., 'chief of the Shannon,' from the position of his territory near the River Shannon. ϻαοιρ‌ιοηηα was the great-grandfather of ζιοιια ‌ulταιη. The clan-lands of ϻuιηητεαρ ϻαοιρ‌ιοηηα embraced the district of Cuircne, now the barony of Kilkenny West, which some time after the Anglo-Norman invasion passed into the possession of the Dillons ; but that they maintained some shadow of independence as a clan until late in the 16th century is clear from the Fiants of Elizabeth which record that, in the year 1578, ' Hobbert M'Caron, of Killenefaghna, Co. Westmeath, gentleman, was granted the office of chief serjeant of his nation in Co. Westmeath, and certain lands in Kilkeren, Knockan, and the Parke, same co., called the ploughland of Kilmacaron, which of old belonged to the chief of the nation of M'Caron.' This ancient surname has now almost entirely disappeared, being generally disguised under the angl. forms of Caulfield and Gaffney and widely dispersed through Ireland.

ϻαc Cάρταιζ—IV—*M'Carhig*, *M'Carhie*, MacCarha, MacCarthy, MacCartie, MacCarty, MacArthy, &c. ; ' son of Cάρ‌ται ' (Old Celtic Caratacos, loving, an ancient Irish personal name). The MacCarthys were the chief family of the Eoghanacht, i.e., the descendants of Eoghan Mor, son of Oilioll Olum, King of Munster in the 3rd century. They took their name from Cάρ‌ται, lord of the Eoghanacht, whose tragic death, in 1045, is recorded in the Annals. Cάρ‌ται was the son of Sαeρ‌ϐρeατα (a name still in use in the family, angl. Justin), who was the grandson of Ceαιιαcάη of Cashel, King of Munster in the Danish period. Prior to the Anglo-Norman invasion, the MacCarthys were Kings of Desmond, or South Munster ; but shortly after that event they were driven from the plains of Tipperary into the present counties of Cork and Kerry, where, however, they became very numerous and retained considerable possessions down to the revolution of 1688. They were divided into three great branches, the heads of which were known respectively as MacCarthy More who resided chiefly in Kerry, MacCarthy Reagh, lord of Carbery in West Cork, and MacCarthy of Muskerry ; and there were numerous minor branches. In 1565, Donal MacCarthy, the then MacCarthy More, was created Earl of Clancar, and other members of the family were at various periods ennobled as Barons of Valentia, Earls of Clancarthy, Viscounts Muskerry, and Lords Mountcashel.

mac Caꞃᴛáⁿ, *M'Cartane,* *M'Cartayne,* *M'Cartyn,* MacCartan, MacCarten, MacCarton, MacCartin, Cartan, Carton, &c. ; a var. of mac Aꞃᴛáⁿ (q.v.) owing to the attraction of the c of mac over to the second part of the surname.

mac Caꞃᴛᴀⁱ€, MacCartney, MacCartiney ; a var. of macAꞃᴛáⁿ, q.v.

mac Casáⁿ—IV—*M'Chassane,* *M'Cassan,* Cassan, Cassian ; 'son of Caꞃáⁿ' (dim. of Caꞃ) ; an alias for mac Caⁱꞃíⁿ, q.v.

mac Casaꞃᴌaⁱᵹ—IV—*M'Cassarlie,* MacCasserly, Casserly, (Cassidy) ; 'son of Caꞃaꞃᴌaċ' (an Irish personal name, in use as late as the beginning of the 17th century) ; an old Roscommon surname. Cumumhan Mac Cassarlaigh was among those who fell at the battle of Athenry in 1249.

mac Caᴛaⁱᴌ—IV—*M'Cahall,* *M'Cahill,* *M'Cale,* MacCall, MacCaul, MacHall, MacGall ; Charles, Corless ; 'son of Caᴛaᴌ' (battle-mighty, a common Irish personal name, angl. Charles). A family of this name were followers of O'Kelly of Ui Maine, and the surname still survives in Co. Galway under the angl. forms of Charles and Corless. mac Caᴛaⁱᴌ was, no doubt, also in use in other parts of Ireland, but its angl. forms, especially in Ulster, cannot always be distinguished from those of mac Caᴛṁaoⁱᴌ, q.v.

mac Caᴛáⁿ—IV—*M'Cahane,* MacCahan, MacKane, MacKeen, Keane ; 'son of Caᴛáⁿ' ; the name of a

Clare family who were formerly coarbs of St. Senan
at Iniscattery ; still well known about Kilrush, angl.
Keane. Also an Ulster surname, but very rare.

Mac Cataoir—IV—*M'Cahire*, *M'Cahir*, *M'Kahir*,
Cahir, Carr, Kerr ; ' son of Cacaoin ' (a common Irish
personal name) ; a rare surname.

Mac Catasaiġ—IV—*M'Casie*, MacCasey, Casey ; ' son
of Catarac ' (vigilant, watchful) ; an old surname in
Monaghan and Armagh. About the middle of the
14th century, Nicholas Mac Cathasaigh was Bishop
of Clogher ; and several gentlemen of the name in Co.
Armagh are mentioned as having received pardon
from Queen Elizabeth. The name is now very rare.

Mac Catṁaoil—IV—*M'Caughwell*, *M'Cawill*, *M'Kavill*,
MacCavill, MacCawell, MacCowell, MacCowhill, Mac-
Cawl, MacCaul, MacCall, MacHall, MacCaulfield,
Keawell, (Howell, Caulfield, Campbell, Callwell), &c. ;
' son of Catṁaol ' (battle-chief) ; the name of a family
who, says O'Donovan, ' are famous in Irish history
for their learning and the many dignitaries they supplied to the church.' They derive their descent from
Eoghan, son of Niall of the Nine Hostages, and were
for many centuries powerful chiefs in Tyrone. Their
patrimony was Kinel Farry, now the barony of Clogher
in Co. Tyrone, and other districts in the same county
and in Fermanagh. There was amother family of
the same name in Co. Down. In the 16th century,
the name had spread into Connacht, Westmeath
and Carlow. A branch of the family of Tyrone who
settled in Co. Wicklow changed the name to Caulfield.
This fine old name is now often sadly disguised.

Mac Céadaiġ—IV—*M'Keady*, MacKeady, (?) Mac-
Geady, Keady ; ' son of Céadac ' (deriv. of céad, a
hundred, hundred-possessing, a common personal
name among the O'Farrells, O'Mores and Mageoghegans) ; an old Galway surname.

Mac Ceallacáin—IV—*M'Keallachayn*, *M'Kelleghane*,
MacKeleghan ; ' son of Ceallacán ' (dim. of Ceallac) ;
a rare Westmeath surname.

Ɱac ceᴀᴌᴌᴀⁱ⅁—IV—*M'Kelly*, Kelly; 'son of Ceᴀᴌᴌᴀ⅀' (war, contention); the name (1) of an Co. Galway family of the same stock as the O'Maddens, and (2) of a Co. Leitrim family. There were, no doubt, several other families of the name in Ireland, but they cannot now be distinguished from the O'Kellys. Ɱac Ceᴀᴌᴌᴀⁱ⅁ is also the name of the Kellys of the Isle of Man.

Ɱac ceᴀⁿ⅁ᴌᴀⁱ⅁—IV—Kangley, Tighe; a rare surname in Meath and Cavan; perhaps a corruption of Ɱac Coⁱⁿ⅁eᴀᴌᴌᴀⁱ⅁, q.v.

Ɱac ceᴀꞄᴀ, Carr; in use in Co. Galway.

Ɱac ceᴀꞄᴀ́ⁿ—IV—*M'Carrane*, *M'Carran*, Mac-Carron, MacCarren, Carron; a var. of Ɱac CⁱᴀꞄᴀ́ⁿ, q.v.; an old surname in Donegal and Derry.

Ɱac ceᴀꞄбᴀⁱᴌᴌ—IV—*M'Carrowle*, *M'Carvell*, *M'Car-well*, *M'Kerwell*, MacCarroll, MacCarvill, MacCarville, MacKervel, MacErvel, Carroll, Carvill, (Cardwell); 'son of CeᴀꞄбᴀᴌᴌ'; a celebrated family of musicians in Ulster. In 1594, Ballym'Carroll, parcel of the lands of Gillekeaghe M'Carroll, of Ballymack-Carroll, was escheated. There was also a family of the name in Leix.

Ɱac ceᴀꞄⁿᴀⁱ⅁—IV—*M'Carny*, *M'Kearnie*, *M'Karney*, MacKearney, MacCarney, Kearney, Carney; 'son of CeᴀꞄⁿᴀ⅀' (victorious). The original home of this family appears to have been Ballymacarney in Co. Meath, but in the 16th century the name was found chiefly in Ulster, in the counties of Down, Armagh and Donegal.

Ɱac ceⁱᴅⁱ⅁—IV—*M'Keady*, Keady; a corruption of Ó Ɱeⁱceⁱᴅⁱ⅁, an old surname in West Cork.

Ɱac ceⁱᴌe—IV—*M'Hely*, *M'Heile*, *M'Heale*, *M'Keale*, MacHale; 'son of Ceⁱᴌe' (companion); the name of a Mayo family who were erenaghs of Killala and coarbs of St. Caillin at Fenagh, Co. Leitrim. The name has evidently been confused with Ɱac Ꞅeⁱᴌ, q.v.

Ɱac ceⁱꞇ—IV—Kitson; 'son of Ceᴀꞇ'; a rare West Clare surname.

mac ceiteaRnaiȝ—IV—*M'Kehernie*, *M'Keherne*, Keherny, Kerney, (Kearney) ; 'son of Ceiteaṗnaċ'; the name of a Roscommon family who were chiefs of Ciaṗṗaiⱱe, or Kerry, a district in the barony of Castlerea ; also Ó Ceiteaṗnaiȝ (q.v.), which seems to be the only form in which the name has survived.

mac céitín—IV—MacKetian, MacKeating ; 'son of *céitín' (perhaps dim. of Céatṗaiⱱ)

mac ceóċ, mac ceóṫaċ, MacKeogh, Keogh ; var. of mac eoċaⱱa and mac eoṫaċ (q.v.) owing to the attraction of the c of mac over to the second part of the surname.

mac ciaRaȝáin—IV—MacKerrigan ; 'son of Ciaṗaȝán' (dim. of ciaṗ, black) ; very rare.

mac ciaRáin—IV—*M'Kirrane*, *M'Kearrane*, *M'Carrane*, MacCarron ; 'son of Ciaṗán' (dim. of ciaṗ, black) ; an old Donegal surname. V. Ó Ceaṗáin.

mac cinín, Keenan ; a rare Roscommon surname ; probably a corruption of mac Ḟinȝin, q.v.

mac cionaoⱱa, mac cionaoiṫ—IV—*M'Kinna*, *M'Kenay*, *M'Kena*, MacKinney, MacKinny, MacKenny, MacKenna, MacKeany, Kenny, etc.; 'son of Cionaoⱱ'; the name of a family who, though belonging to the southern Ui Neill, were chiefs of the barony of Trough in the north of Co. Monaghan ; and also of a family in Co. Roscommon who were followers of the O'Connors. This surname, in Kerry, Cork and Limerick, is corrupted in the spoken language to maȝ Cineáit (q.v.), but the old angl. forms in these counties show the true origin.

mac cioṫRuaⱱa, mac cioṫRuaiⱱ—V—MacKerrow, Kiroy, (MacKitterick, &c.) ; 'son of Cioṫṗuaiⱱ' (a name of Norse origin) ; a rare Midland surname.

mac claoċlaoiċ, Coakley ; evidently for mac Caoċlaoiċ, q.v.; a West Cork surname.

mac cléiRiȝ—VII—*M'Clerie*, MacClery, MacCleary, Clarke ; a shortened form of mac an Cléiṗiȝ, q.v.

mac cliseam, Clisham, Klisham ; a rare Connacht surname, the origin of which I cannot trace.

mac Cloċaiṅe—VII—*M'Cloghor*, MacCloughry, Cloughry, and, by 'translation,' Kingstone, Kingston; 'son of the stone-cutter,' or 'mason' (Ir. 'cloċaiṅe').

mac Cluanaiġ—IV—*M'Clonnye*, MacLoonie, Clowney, Clowny, Clooney, Cloney; 'son of Cluanaċ' (deceitful, perhaps a nickname).

mac Clúcáin—IV—MacClughan, Luccan; 'son of Lúcán' (?)

mac Cnáiṁ—IV—Bones, Bownes; 'son of Cnáṁ' (?) (Ir. 'cnáṁ,' a bone; probably a nickname). This surname is in use in Co. Mayo, but I have failed to find any early instance. mac Cnáṁaiġ (q.v.) is a variant.

mac Cnáiṁín—IV—*M'Cnavin*, *M'Knavin*, MacNevin, Navin, Neavin, Nevin, Neven, Nivin, Nevins; 'son of Cnáiṁín' (dim. of cnáṁ, a bone); the name of an ancient family in Co. Galway, who were chiefs of a district in Ui Maine and seated at Crannag MacNevin, in the parish of Tynagh. The name is first mentioned in the Annals of the Four Masters at the year 1159. The chief in the time of Elizabeth was Hugh Mac-Knavin. He went out in rebellion, was taken and hanged on the 4th June, 1602, and his lands granted to the Earl of Clanrickard. Other members of the family possessed considerable property at the beginning of the 17th century. The celebrated Dr. MacNevin of the United Irishmen was the last supposed head of the family.

mac Cnáṁaiġ—IV—Bones, Bownes; 'son of Cnáṁaċ' (bony); a var. of mac Cnáiṁ, q.v. Cf. mac Cnáiṁín.

mac Coḃtaiġ—IV—*M'Cooe*, MacCovey, MacCooey, MacCooe; 'son of Coḃtaċ' (victorious); a rare Co. Louth surname.

mac Coċláin—IV—*M'Cochlane*, *M'Coghlane*, Mac-Coghlan, MacCoughlan, Coghlan, Coghlen, Coghlin, Coughlan, Coughlen, Coughlin; 'son of Coċlán' (dim. of 'coċal,' a cape, cowl or hood). The Mac-Coghlans derive their name from Coċlán, lord of Dealbhna Eathra, whose death is recorded in the

Annals at the year 1053; and they were for many centuries lords of Dealbhna Eathra, called in later times Delvin MacCoghlane, which comprised almost the entire of the present barony of Garryċastle, in Offaly. They were once a very powerful family, and the name is still common in the midlands. About the middle of the 18th century, a branch of the family settled near Castlebar, Co. Mayo.

mac coꞁꞁaꞇáin—IV—*M'Colletane, M'Collitan,* Colleton, Collotan, Culleton, Culliton, (Cullington); 'son of Coꞁꞁaꞇán' (sleeper); the name of an old family in Carlow and Wexford. Also Ó Coꞁꞁaꞇáin, q.v.

mac coꞡaꞛáin, mac coꞡáin—IV—*M'Cogane,* Mac-Cogan, MacCoggan, Cogan, Coggan; 'son of Coꞡaꞛán' (a 'pet' form of Cúċoꞡaiꞛ, an Irish personal name, meaning 'war-hound,' 'warrior'); the name of a family in Co. Leitrim who were chiefs of Clann Fearnaighe, now angl. Glanfarne, a district to the east and north-east of Loch Allen. A branch of the family settled in Co. Meath.

mac coꞡaiꞛín—IV—Cogavin, Cogeen; a var. of mac Coꞡaꞛáin, q.v.

mac coꞡaꞃáin—IV—*M'Cogerane,* Coghran, Cochrane, Caughran; 'son of Coꞡaꞃán'; the name of an old Thomond family, descendants, no doubt, of Coꞡaꞃán, 'the confidential servant' of Brian Boru. Also Ó Coꞡaꞃáin, q.v.

mac coiꞛꞛeanaiꞡ—IV—*M'Cuffeny,* Coveney, (?) Mac-Governey, Governey; 'son of Coiꞛꞛeanaċ' (trooper); a rare surname. We have also Ó Coiꞛꞛeanaiꞡ, q.v.

mac coiꞁiꞛ, mac coiꞁiꞡ—VII—*M'Killie,* MacQuilly; Cox; a short form of mac an Coiꞁiꞡ, q.v. Also maꞡ Coiꞁiꞡ.

mac coiꞁiꞡin, Cox; a Cork surname; probably an attenuated form of mac Coꞁꞡan, q.v. Cf. Ó Cuiꞁeaꞡan.

mac coiꞁín—IV—*M'Colline, M'Culline, M'Kellyn,* Mac-Cullion, MacCullen, MacKillen, MacKellen, Mac-Quillin, MacQuillian, MacQuillion, MacQuillan, Collen,

Cullin, Cullian, Cullen, Quillen, Quillan, Collins, &c.; 'son of Coitín'; a var. of Ѿac Caitín, q.v. This form of the surname was very common in Tirconnell, and in Down and Antrim, at the end of the 16th century. Its angl. forms cannot always be distinguished from those of Ѿac Uιóιtín, q.v.

Ѿac coιѿín—IV—*M'Comin, M'Comyn,* MacComming, MacKimmon, Comyn, Comyns, Commons, Kimmins, etc.; 'son of Coιѿín' (dim. of cam, bent). This surname was common in parts of Munster, and in Wexford, Monaghan and Cavan. Its angl. forms cannot always be distinguished from those of Ó Coιѿín, Ó Comáin, nor from the Anglo-Norman Comyn.

Ѿac coιɴ̄ѕeallaιɜ—IV—*M'Cangellye, M'Congillye, M'Cynelig, M'Kennella, M'Connella,* Quinnelly, Kennelly, Connelly, Connolly; 'son of Coιɴ̄ѕeallac' (faithful to pledges); now always Ó Coιɴ̄ѕeallaιɜ, q.v.; the name of a family in West Cork who were formerly retainers of O'Donovan and at one time owned seven ploughlands in the parish of Drinagh, near Drimoleague. Also in use in Ormond.

Ѿac coιɴín—IV—*M'Conine, M'Kenyne, M'Canine,* Cuneen, Cunneen, Conyeen, Kinneen, Kenning, Canning, &c., and, by 'translation,' Rabbit; 'son of Coιɴín' (an old Irish personal name); a scattered surname. There are, no doubt, several distinct families so called. The Mac Coinins of Mayo, anciently seated in Erris, were noted patrons of learning.

Ѿac coιɴleaɜa, v. Ѿac an leaɜa.

Ѿac coιɴɴeaɜáιn—IV—*M'Quenegan, M'Konningham,* Cunningham, &c. V. Ѿac Cuιɴɴeaɜáιn.

Ѿac coιɴɴιɜ—IV—*M'Coinny,* MacKinney, MacKenzie, &c.; 'son of Coιɴɴeac' (fair one); the name of a celebrated Scottish clan. It appears to have been also an Irish surname, but its angl. forms cannot now be distinguished from those of Ѿac Cιonaoιt, q.v. The Scottish-Gaelic is Ѿac Coιɴɴιc.

Ѿac coιRce, Oates; a corruption of Ѿac Cuιɾc, q.v.

Ѿac coιѕe—VII—*M'Cashie, M'Cashy,* MacCosh, Mac-

Quish, Cush; Legge, Foote; probably 'son of the courier,' the 'footman.' Erard MacCoise was a celebrated Irish poet and chronicler. The name is found also in Scotland.

mac coiStealb, mac coiStealbaiġ—IV—Costello, Costelloe; 'son of Oirȯealb'; var. of mac Oirȯealb, mac Oirȯealbaiġ, owing to the attraction over of the c of mac to the second part of the surname.

mac coitil—V—M'Ketyll, Kettyle, Kettle; 'son of Ketill' (a Norse personal name, Ang.-Sax. 'Cytel'); a rare, but well-known Irish surname, probably of Norse origin. In the 16th century, it was peculiar to Co. Louth.

mac coitir—V—M'Cottir, MacCotter, MacCottier, Mac-Cottar, Cotter, Cottier, Cottiers; 'son of Oitir' (the Norse Ottar); a var. of mac Oitir (q.v.) by the attraction over of the c of mac to the second part of the surname.

mac colġan—IV—M'Collgan, MacColgan, Colgan, Collagan, Colligan, Culligan; 'son of Colġa'; more anciently Ó Colġan; the name of a sept of the Oirghialla, who were chiefs of Ui MacCarthainn, now the barony of Tirkeevan, Co. Derry, until dispossessed by the Cinel Eoghain, and afterwards erenaghs of Donaghmore, in Inishowen. The celebrated Father John Colgan, the hagiographer, was of this family.

mac colla—IV—M'Colla, M'Collagh, M'Colly, M'Colle, MacCulla, MacCullagh, MacCollough, MacCullough, MacColl, MacCull, &c.; 'son of Colla' (a common personal name among the MacDonnells and Mac Sweeneys); a scattered surname; in the spoken language, sometimes made mac collaċ.

mac colmáin—IV—M'Collman, MacColman, Coleman; 'son of Colmán' (dim. of colm, a dove, a very common Irish personal name).

mac coluim—IV—MacColum, MacCollum, MacCollom, Colum, Collum, &c.; 'son of Colum' (dove); an Ulster surname, found chiefly in Antrim, Tyrone and

Donegal; also a Scottish surname, written Mac
Caluim, q.v.

Mac Comóain, Mac comġain—IV—*M'Cowane*,
M'Cone, MacCowan, MacKone, MacKoen; 'son of
Comóan,' or 'Comġan'; originally a Meath surname,
but long dispersed through Ulster. It is difficult, if
not impossible, to distinguish its angl. forms from
those of Mac Eoġain, q.v.

Mac Comġaill—IV—*M'Cole*, MacCole; 'son of Comġall'; extremely rare.

Mac Conaill—IV—MacConnell; 'son of Conall' (high-
ruler); very rare; to be distinguished from Mac
Ďomnaill, which in most instances is the origin of
MacConnell.

Mac Conaill óig—IV—*M'Connell oge*, MacConnellogue,
Conlogue; 'son of young Conall'; an old Tirconnell
surname.

Mac Conallta—IV—MacAnalty, MacNalty, Nalty;
'son of Cú-allaið' (wild-dog, wolf); a Sligo surname;
to be distinguished from Mac an Ultaiġ, q.v.

Mac Conanaonaiġ—IV—*M'Anonany*, *M'Anenany*,
MacNamanamee, Nanany; 'son of Cú-an-aonaiġ'
(hound of the fair); a var. in Co. Roscommon of Mac
Conaonaiġ, q.v.

Mac Conaonaiġ—IV—*M'Enanny*, *M'Nenny*, Mac-
Aneany, MacAneeny, MacAneny, MacEneany, Mac-
Neney, MacNeeny, Conheeny, Cunneeny, and, by
'translation' Bird in Ulster, and Rabbit in Connacht;
'son of Cú-aonaiġ' (hound of the fair); the name of a
well-known Monaghan family, who were formerly
seated in the neighbourhood of Clones. The surname
has been corrupted in Ulster to Mac an Éanaiġ and
sometimes ridiculously 'translated' Bird. Also the
name of a Roscommon family, sometimes called Mac
Conanaonaiġ (q.v.), who gave its name to the townland of Kilmacenanny, or Kilmacananneny, in the
parish of Lissonuffy, where some of them were still
inhabiting at the end of the 16th century. In Connacht, the surname is now generally angl. Rabbit,

owing to its similarity in pronunciation to the word
' coınín,' a rabbit. There was a third family of the
name, apparently a branch of the MacDonnells, in
Co. Antrim, who are now probably represented by
MacAneny in Co. Tyrone.

mac conboıꞃne—IV—*M'Conborney*, Burns ; ' son of
Cú-boıꞃne ' (hound of Boirean, a place-name) ; the
name of a family of the Ui Fiachrach race, in Co.
Mayo. O'Donovaın found it still extant under the
angl. form of Burns. It was also written Ó
Conboıꞃne.

mac concáıꞃꞃ5e, mac concáꞃꞃáı5e—IV—*M'En
carrigy*, *M'Incargy*, *M'Necargy*, MacCarrick, Carrigy,
Carrigee, Kerragy, Carrick, and, by translation,
Rock ; ' son of Cú-čáꞃꞃáı5e ' (an Irish personal name
meaning ' hound of the rock ') ; the name of a Thomond
family who were stewards to the O'Briens in West
Clare. In 1641, they were proprietors of Lisbulligeen,
in the parish of Kilfenora. This surname is also found
in Sligo and Leitriıı where, however, it is probably a
substitution for the old surname mac Concáčꞃáč, q.v.

mac concáčá—IV—*M'Conchaa*. *M'Encuha*, Battle,
Battles ; ' son oı Cú-čáčá ' (' hound of battle,' ' war-
hound ') ; the name of an old Sligo family who were
living at the end of the 16th century ın Coolaney. It
is now always absurdly ˙ translated ' Battle or Battles.
MacConcahy would be the proper angl. form.

mac concáčꞃáč—IV—MacCarrick ; son of Cúčáčꞃáč '
(' hound of the čáčáıꞃ' or fort) ; the name of a Sligo
family of the Ui Fiachrach race. O'Donovan found
some of the name in the parish of Templeboy in
Tireragh, angl. MacCarrick. V. mac Concáıꞃꞃ5e.

mac concéáꞃcá—IV—*M'Anyerkaye*, *M'Ingarky*,
M'Egarky, *M'Igarky*, *M'Igarke*, Yorke ; ' son of
Cú-čéáꞃcá ' (hound of Céáꞃc, a place-name) ; a rare
and scattered surname ; in the 16th century, found
chiefly in the midlands, and in Sligo and Galway.

mac concoꞃáıꞃ—IV—*M'Connogher*, *M'Connoghor*,
M'Conoher, *M'Connor*, MacNogher, MacNaugher, Mac-

Noher, MacNoger, Minogher, Minoher, Connor, Nogher, Noher, Naugher, Naughter, Nocter, &c. ; 'son of Conċobap' (an ancient and very common Irish personal name, Lat. 'Cornelius,' and angl. 'Cornelius' and 'Connor ').

mac conċoʒaıʊ—IV—*M'Enchogy, M'Anhoggy, M'Nagcogy* ; 'son of Cú-ċoʒaıʊ' (war-hound) ; an old surname in Roscommon and Longford ; now obsolete or, possibly, changed to **mac Coʒáın, mac Coʒaıʊín,** q.v. O'Donovan gives the angl. form as MacConkey which I have failed to verify.

mac conċoıʒċrɪ́ce—IV—*M'Conchogrye, M'Enkegrie, M'Nikegrie,* and now, by 'translation,' L'Estrange ; 'son of Cú-ċoıʒċpíce ' (border-hound) ; the name of a family who were anciently chiefs of Muinntear Searcachain in Westmeath or Offaly. It still survives in the midlands under the Frenchified form of L'Estrange.

mac conċoıɬɬe, mac conċoıɬɬeaʊ—IV—*M'Ancoyllew, M'Inchelly, M'Enkelly,* and now, by 'translation,' Woods and Cox ; 'son of Cú-ċoıɬɬe(aʊ)' (hound of the wood) ; a scattered surname, chiefly in use in Derry and Tyrone, Wicklow and Wexford, Cork and Limerick, but now everywhere disguised under the angl. forms of Woods and Cox, the latter form being due to its similarity to ' coıɬeaċ,' a cock.

mac conċoıɬɬín—IV—*M'Necollen,* and now, by translation, Smallwoods, Woods ; 'son of Cú-ċoıɬɬín ' (hound of the little wood). Cf. **mac Conċoıɬɬe** above.

mac conċoɬɬċoıɬɬe—IV—Hazlewood, Hazlegrove, Hazleton, Hazelton ; 'son of Cú-ċoɬɬċoıɬɬe ' (hound of the hazelwood).

mac conċraʊa—IV—*M'Concroe, M'Encrogh, M'Ecroe,* MacEnchroe, MacEncroe, Crough, Crowe ; 'son of Conċpaıʊ ' (a rare Irish personal name) ; the name of an old Thomond family, still well known in Clare, Tipperary and Limerick.

mac conċruacan—IV—*M'Encroghan, M'Necroghan,*

M'Icrowghan, Croughan, Croghan, Crohan, Croan ; 'son of Cú-Ċρυαċαη' (hound of Croghan, in Roscommon, Ir. 'Cρυαċu,' gen. 'Cρυαċαη'); an old Roscommon surname.

mac conⱺuiⱺ—IV—MacAnuff, MacAniff, MacEniff, MacKniff, MacNuff, MacNeffe, MacNiff, MacKiniff, MacEndoo, MacIndoo, MacAdoo, MacAdo, MacCaddoo, MacCaddo, Conniff, Conniffe, Conneffe, Cunniffe, Quinniff, Caddow, &c. ; 'son of Cú-ⱺuⱺ' (the black hound) ; a Connacht surname.

mac conⱺoⱃmαoιle—IV—*M'Enormoyele,* Normoyle, Normile ; 'son of Cú Ɽoⱃmαoιle' (hound of Formoyle, a place in Co. Clare) ; the name of a Clare family who are probably a branch of the MacNamaras (v. mac Conmαⱃα) ; now common in Co. Limerick ; in the spoken language mac Conoⱃmαoιle.

mac conⱤⱃαoιċ—IV—Conefry ; 'son of Cú-Ⱡⱃαoιċ' (hound of Ⱡⱃαoċ, a place-name).

mac conⱫαιl, mac conⱫαιle—IV—*M'Congall,* MacCongail, MacConigly; 'son of ConⱫαl'; usually written mαⱫ ConⱫαιl, q.v. ; a Tirconnell surname, the same as mac ConⱫαιle below.

mac conⱫαιle—IV—MacIneely, MacNeely, MacNeela, MacNella, MacNealy, Coneely, Conneely, Conneally, Conneely, Conneelly, Connelly, Cunneely, Kennelly, (Connolly), &c. ; 'son of ConⱫαl' (high-valour, an old Irish personal name) ; an old surname in West Connacht ; still common in Galway and Mayo, but it is difficult, if not impossible, to distinguish its angl. forms from those of mac ConⱫαolα, q.v.

mac conⱫαlαιⱫ—IV—*M'Conalaye, M'Connally, M'Connolly,* Connolly ; 'son of ConⱫαlαċ' (deriv. of ConⱫαl, high-valour) ; a rare surname, formerly in use in Sligo and Leitrim. In Co. Monaghan, it appears to have been sometimes used as an alias for Ó ConⱫαlαιⱫ, q.v.

mac conⱫαⱚnα—IV—*M'Kengawny,* *M'Engawney,* *M'Negowny,* (Gaffney, Caulfield) ; 'son of Cú-Ⱬαⱚnα' (calf-hound) ; the name of a branch of the Ui Fiachrach Aidhne, in the south of Co. Galway. It is still common in Longford and all the adjoining counties, also in Cork and Mayo, but now always disguised under the angl. forms of Gaffney and Caulfield.

mac conȝaola—IV—MacCunneela, MacNeela, Mac Nella, &c. ; 'son of Cú-ȝaola' (hound of ȝaola, a place-name in Co. Galway) ; the name of a family of Ui Fiachrach, in the south of Co. Galway. Its angl. forms can hardly be now distinguished from those of mac Conȝaile, q.v.

mac conleaȝa, M'Kenlagh, M'Kinlea, MacKinlay, MacKinley, &c. ; probably only a misspelling of mac an leaȝa, q.v.

mac conleiτρeaċ—IV—(?) Letter, Letters ; 'son of Cú-leiτρeaċ' (hound of leiτιρ, a place-name) ; the name of an old family in Tirawley, Co. Mayo. They were seated at Ballykinletteragh, in the parish of Kilfian, but the name has long since disappeared from that district. It is not improbable, however, that it is the origin of Letters or Letter in other parts of Ireland.

mac conloċa—IV—M'Anloghie, M'Inlocky, Kinlough, (?) Lough ; 'son of Cú-loċa' (hound of the lake). This surname seems to have originated in Co. Westmeath. It was always exceedingly rare.

mac conluaċρa—IV—M'Elvochra, Kiloughry, Kiloury ; 'son of Cú-luaċρa' (hound of luaċaιρ, a place-name).

mac conluaιn—IV—M'Anleone, M'Anloyne, M'Collone, M'Colwan, Colvan, Colvin, Colavin, Cullivan, (Colvil, Colville, Collwell, Coldwell, Caldwell, &c.) ; a corruption of mac Anluaιn ; the name of a family of the Ui Fiachrach race, formerly seated in the parish of Dromard, Co. Sligo, where O'Donovan found the name under the angl. form of MacColwan. Before the end of the 16th century, it had passed into Co. Leitrim, and is still found in that county, and in the neighbouring county of Cavan, under strange angl. forms.

mac conṁaic—IV—*M'Conwicke*, *M'Conick*, Connick; 'son of Conṁac' (an ancient Irish personal name, meaning 'son of the hound'); a branch of the O'Farreils in Co. Longford.

mac conṁaoil—IV—*M'Convale*, *M'Conwaile*, *M'Conwell*, MacConville, Conwell; 'son of Conṁaol' (high-chief); a well-known Ulster surname; found chiefly in Antrim, Down and Armagh.

mac conmara—IV—*M'Conmara*, MacNamara, Mac-Namarra, MacNamarrow; 'son of Cú-mara' (hound of the sea). The MacNamaras who, next to the O'Briens, were the most powerful of the Dalcassian clans, derive their descent from Cairín, son of Car, the common ancestor of all the Dál gCair. Their original territory was Ui Caisin, corresponding to the present deanery of Ogashin and comprising nine parishes in the east of Co. Clare; but in later times they ruled over a greatly enlarged territory which comprised the whole of Upper and Lower Tulla, and which, from their clan-name, was known as Clann Cuileáin. The MacNamaras were hereditary marshals of Thomond, and it was their privilege to inaugurate O'Brien. A branch of the family settled, sometime before the end of the 16th century, in Co. Down.

mac conmeaḋa, mac conmeaḋa—IV—*M'Conmea*, *M'Conmay*, *M'Convea*, *M'Convey*, *M'Convay*, *M'Conwaie*, *M'Nema*, MacConaway, MacConway, MacNama, Conmey, Convey, &c.; 'son of Cú-meaḋa,' (hound of Meaḋ, a place-name); the name of a family who were anciently chiefs of Muinnteap Laoḋacáin, in Westmeath, but long dispersed.

mac conmiḋe—IV—MacConamy, MacConomy, Mac-Namee, Conmee, Mee, Meath, &c.; 'son of Cú-miḋe' (hound of Meath); the name of a family who were hereditary poets to the O'Neills of Tyrone; still common in Ulster

mac con na buaile—IV—MacNaboola; 'son of Cú na buaile' (hound of Boyle); a rare Roscommon surname.

Mᴀc connᴀċᴛᴀɪʒ—VII—MacConnaughty, MacConnerty; 'son of the Connachtman' (Ir. 'Con-
nᴀċcᴀċ ').

Mᴀc connᴀʒᴀɪn—IV—*M'Connigan, M'Konningham*,
Cunningham, &c.; 'son of Connᴀʒᴀn' (a dim. of
Conn); a var. of Mᴀc Cuɪnneᴀʒᴀɪn, q.v.

Mᴀc connᴀɪᴅ—IV—*M'Conna, M'Conney, M'Cunny,
M'Cony*, MacCona, Conney, and, by 'translation,'
Woods; 'son of Connᴀᴅ' (an old Irish personal
name); a scattered surname. Its angl. forms are
difficult to distinguish from those of Mᴀc Coɪnnɪʒ,
q.v.; and MacCona may sometimes stand for Mac-
Dona. Moore, in his 'Manx Names' (p. 25), gives
Quinney as an angl. form of this surname, but the
pronunciation in spoken Manx, as indicated by him,
would rather point to Mᴀc Coɪnnɪʒ as the origin; and,
as he shows (p. 28), Mᴀc Cᴀɪnnɪʒ was an old Manx
surname.

Mᴀc connlᴀ, Mᴀc connlᴀoᴅᴀ—IV—*M'Connley,
M'Conley, M'Conly*, Conley, Conly; 'son of Conn-
lᴀoᴅ '; apparently an Offaly surname.

Mᴀc connṁᴀɪʒ—IV—*M'Conough, M'Conowe*, Conway;
'son of Connṁᴀċ'; a rare surname in Clare and
Offaly; apparently an alias for Ó Connṁᴀɪʒ, q.v.

Mᴀc conoꞧṁᴀoɪle, Normoyle, Normile. V. Mᴀc
Conꞧoꞧmᴀoɪle.

Mᴀc conꞧᴀoɪ—IV—*M'Conrie, M'Conry*, Mac-an-Ree,
Conree, Cunree, Conry, Conroy, and, by 'translation,' King; 'son of Cúꞧᴀoɪ' (hound of the plain, or of
battle); the name of a family, said to be of Dalcassian
origin, who were anciently lords of Dealbna Thire-da-
locha, in the barony of Moycullen, between Loch
Corrib and Galway Bay, where they are still numerous.
The name was also common in Kerry and Limerick;
but both in Munster and Connacht it is now usually
mistranslated King, owing to the erroneous belief
that it is derived from ' ꞧɪʒ,' a king, and that the Irish
form is Mᴀc ᴀn Ríoʒ, 'son of the king.'

Mᴀc conꞧᴀᴛᴀ—IV—*M'Conraghe, M'Conraye*, Conrahy,

(Conroy) ; ' son of Cúṗᴀᴄᴀ ' (hound of prosperity) ; an old Offaly surname ; also Ó Conṗᴀᴄᴀ, q.v.

ⅿᴀc COnRⅼᴀᴅᴀ—IV—*M'Conryde*, MacConready, Mac-Aready, MacCready ; ' son of Cú-Rⅼᴀᴅᴀ ' (Riada's hound).

ⅿᴀc COnRⅼᴀⅼn—IV—Cunreen, King ; ' son of Cú-Rⅼᴀⅼn ' (Rian's hound) ; extremely rare ; sometimes ' translated ' King on the erroneous supposition that it is derived from ' ⱃⅼⱎ,' a king. Cf. ⅿᴀc Conⱃᴀoⅼ.

ⅿᴀc COnRuᴅᴀ—IV—*M'Conrowe*, *M'Enrowe*, *M'Erowe*, *M'ny Rowe*, MacEnroe, Enroe, Rowe, Roe ; ' son of Cú-Ruᴅᴀ ' (hound of Ruᴅᴀ, or Rowe, a place-name) ; a Breifney surname.

ⅿᴀc COnSᴀⅼᴅⅼn—V—*M'Considine*, Considine ; ' son of Constantine ' ; the name of a branch of the O'Briens in Co. Clare, descended from ᴅoṁnᴀʟʟ ⅿóⱃ Ó ᴅⱃⅼᴀⅼn, King of Munster.

ⅿᴀc COnŚnᴀṁᴀ—IV—*M'Conave*, *M'Kinnawe*, *M'En-awe*, MacAnawe, Kinnavy, Kineavy ; (Adams) ; Forde, Ford ; ' son of Cú-ⱱnᴀṁᴀ ' (the swimming-hound, expert swimmer) ; the name of a family in Co. Leitrim who were formerly chiefs of Muinter Kenny, in the present barony of Dromahaire. It was popularly supposed to be ' ⅿᴀc ᴀn ᴀᴄᴀ,' son of the ford, and was accordingly ' translated ' Ford, Forde. I find it also angl. Adams, which shows that it must have been sometimes mistaken for ⅿᴀc ᴀᴅᴀⅼṁ, q.v.

ⅿᴀc COnuⅼSce—IV—*M'Enuske*, Uiske, Waters ; ' son of Cú-uⅼⱃce ' (the water-hound) ; a Monaghan surname ; now also in use in Co. Mayo. It is popularly supposed to be ' ⅿᴀc ᴀn uⅼⱃce,' son of the water, and is in consequence generally ' translated ' Waters.

ⅿᴀc COnuʟᴀᴅ—IV—*M'Anullo*, *M'Enully*, *M'Annoll*, *M'Cowla*, *M'Cowloe*, *M'Cowley*, MacAnulla, MacNully, MacAnaul, MacKinaul, (MacNall), MacCullow, Culloo ; ' son of Cú-uʟᴀᴅ ' (hound of Ulidia, East Ulster) ; an East Ulster surname. The Cú of this surname is sometimes not inflected ; hence the old angl. forms

M'Cowla, M'Cowloe, and the modern MacCullow, Culloo, &c.

mᴀc ᴄoᴦcᴀ́in—IV—*M'Corkane, M'Corkan,* Corken; 'son of ᴄoᴦcᴀ́n' (dim. of ᴄoᴦc); a rare Wicklow surname.

mᴀc ᴄoᴦcᴦᴀ́in—IV—*M'Corcrane, M'Corkrane,* Corcoran, Corkran, Corkeran, &c.; 'son of ᴄoᴦcᴦᴀ́n' (dim. of 'ᴄoᴦcᴀiᴦ,' purple). The head of this family was chief of Clann Ruainne in Ely O'Carroll.

mᴀc ᴄoᴦmᴀcᴀ́in—IV—MacCormiken, (MacCormack, MacCormick); 'son of ᴄoᴦmᴀcᴀ́n' (dim. of ᴄoᴦmᴀc); a rare Connacht surname. The angl. form is shortened in Co. Mayo to MacCormack and MacCormick.

mᴀc ᴄoᴦmᴀic—IV—MacCormac, MacCormack, MacCormick, Cormac, Cormick, Cormack; 'son of ᴄoᴦmᴀc' (an ancient and very common Irish personal name); a common surname in all parts of Ireland.

mᴀc ᴄoᴦᴦᴀ, mᴀc ᴄoᴦᴦᴀiᴅ—IV—*M'Correy, M'Corr,* MacCorry, MacCurry, Corry, Curry, Corra, Corr; 'son of ᴄoᴦᴦᴀᴅ' (spear); a rare surname. In Co. Leitrim, it seems to have been a var. of mᴀc ᴄoᴦᴦᴀiᴅín, q.v.

mᴀc ᴄoᴦᴦᴀiᴅín—IV—*M'Corrine, M'Curine,* Curreen, Currin, Curren; 'son of ᴄoᴦᴦᴀiᴅín' (a dim. of ᴄoᴦᴦᴀᴅ); the name of a family of the Ui Fiachrach race, formerly seated in the parish of Skreen, Co. Sligo, but, at the end of the 16th century, more numerous in Co. Leitrim; written mᴀc ᴄoᴦᴦᴀoin by MacFirbis.

mᴀc ᴄoᴦᴦbuiᴅe—IV—*M'Corboy, M'Corby,* Corboy, Corby; 'son of ᴄoᴦᴦbuiᴅe' (yellow-crane); a rare surname in Leix and Tipperary.

mᴀc ᴄoscᴦᴀcᴀ́in—IV—*M'Cossrichan,* MacCuskern, Coskeran, Cuskern, (Cosgrave, Cosgrove); 'son of ᴄoᴦcᴦᴀcᴀ́n' (dim. of ᴄoᴦcᴦᴀc,' victorious); a Co. Down surname.

mᴀc ᴄoscᴦᴀiᴈ—IV—*M'Cosegrave,* Cosgrave, Cosgrove; 'son of ᴄoᴦcᴦᴀc (victorious); the name of a family who were anciently erenaghs of Clones. V. Ó ᴄoᴦcᴦᴀiᴈ.

mac COSⱦaȝáın, *M'Costegane*, *M'Costegan*, Costigan; a corruption of mac Oırⱦıcín, q.v.

mac CRáḃaȝáın—IV—Crawford; 'son of Cráḃaȝán' (religious); a rare surname in Louth and Monaghan. I can find no early instance, and suspect that it is a substitution for mac Cráḃáın, q.v.

mac CRáḃáın—IV—*M'Craven*, *M'Cravin*, Craven, Cravin, Creaven; 'son of Cráḃán' (religious); an old surname in Louth and Monaghan; probably now replaced in some instances by mac Cráḃaȝáın.

mac CRaıⱦ—IV—MacCraith, MacCrea, MacGrath, &c., 'son of macRaıⱦ' (an Irish personal name); a var. of mac Raıⱦ, owing to the attraction over of the c of mac to the second part of the name. V. mac Raıⱦ and maȝ Raıⱦ.

mac CRıaȝáın—IV—*M'Crigan*, Cregan; 'son of Rıaȝán'; a form of mac Rıaȝáın (q.v.) due to the attraction over of the c of mac to the second part of the surname; now always Ó Crıaȝáın in the spoken language.

mac CRíoḋáın—IV—*M'Cridane*, *M'Credan*, Creedon, Creed; 'son of Críoḋán'; an old surname in Cork, Limerick and Tipperary; now always Ó Críoḋáın in the spoken language.

mac CRıomⱦaınn—IV—*M'Criffon*, *M'Criohin*, *M'Creohan*, MacCrohan; 'son of Crıomⱦann' (fox); in the spoken language, now mac Crıoⱦán; the name of a branch of the O'Sullivans in Kerry. The MacCrohans once owned Letter Castle.

mac CRíonáın—IV—*M'Crenan*, Crennan; 'son of Críonán.'

mac CRíoSⱦa—V—*M'Cristie*, Christy, Christie, &c.; 'son of Christy' (a pet form of Christian or Christopher).

mac CRıoSⱦaıl—V—*M'Christell*, *M'Christall*, MacChrystall; 'son of Christal' (a form of Christopher); a Co. Down surname.

mac CRíoSⱦóRa—V—Christopherson, Christopher; 'son of Christopher.'

Mᴀc ᴄʀɪꜱᴛɪɴ—V—*M'Christeine*, *M'Christyne*, Mac-Criskin, MacGriskin, Christian ; ' son of Christian.'·

Mᴀc ᴄʀóɴɢᴀɪʟᴇ—IV—*M'Crongully*, *M'Cronilla*, Cronelly ; ' son of ᴄʀóɴɢᴀʟ.' V. Ó ᴄʀóɴɢᴀɪʟᴇ.

Mᴀc ᴄʀᴜɪᴍ—IV—MacCrum, MacCrumb, MacRum ; ' son of ᴄʀom ' (bent, crooked).

Mᴀc ᴄʀᴜɪᴛɪɴ—IV—*M'Crutten*, *M'Cruttan*, MacCurtin, Curtin, (Curtis) ; ' son of ᴄʀᴜɪᴛɪɴ'. (hunch-backed) ; the name of a learned family of antiquaries in Thomond, whose patrimony was Carrowduff, in the parish of Killaspuglonane, and Laghvally, in the parish of Kilmacreehy, Co. Clare. A branch of the family settled in East Limerick some time prior to 1600. Andrew MacCurtin, who lived in the early part of the 18th century, was one of the best Irish scholars of his time.

Mᴀc ᴄᴜᴀᴄáɪɴ—IV—MacGoohan ; ' son of ᴄᴜᴀᴄáɴ ' (dim. of ᴄᴜᴀᴄ, a cuckoo) ; a rare Leitrim surname.

Mᴀc ᴄᴜᴀʟʟᴀᴄᴛᴀ — IV — *M'Gwolaghtie*, *M'Gwllaghty*, (Goolden, Goulding, Golden) ; ' son of ᴄᴜᴀʟʟᴀᴄᴛᴀ ' ; a Sligo surname ; now changed to Ó ɢᴜᴀʟʟᴀᴄᴛᴀ and angl. Goolden, &c.

Mᴀc ᴄᴜᴀʀᴛᴀ, Mᴀc ᴄᴜᴀɪʀᴛ—IV—*M'Cowrty*, *M'Cowart*, *M'Cuyrt*, MacCourt, MacCort, MacCourtney, (Courtney) ; a Co. Louth surname ; not improbably a corruption of Mᴀc Mᴜɪʀᴄᴇᴀʀᴛᴀɪɢ, q.v.

Mᴀc ᴄᴜɪʟɪɴɴ—IV—*M'Cwlin*, *M'Cowlin*, MacCullen, MacQuillen, Cullen, Quillen, and, by translation, Holly ; ' son of ᴄᴜɪʟᴇᴀɴɴ ' (holly) ; in use in Monaghan and Louth.

Mᴀc ᴄᴜɪʟʟ—IV—MacQuill, MacGuill ; 'son of ᴄᴏʟʟ' ; very rare.

Mᴀc ᴄúɪʟʀɪᴀᴃᴀɪɢ—IV—*M'Coulray*, Culreavy, Colreavy and, by translation, Gray, Grey ; ' son of ᴄúʟʀɪᴀᴃᴀᴄ ' (grey-poll), or more probably a corruption of Mᴀc ɢɪᴏʟʟᴀʀɪᴀᴃᴀɪɢ, q.v. ; a midland surname.

Mᴀc ᴄᴜɪᴍíɴ—IV—MacCumming, MacCummings, Cummin, Cuming, Cumming, Cummins, Cummings, Kimmins, &c. ; ' son of ᴄᴜɪᴍíɴ.' Also Mᴀc ᴄoɪᴍíɴ, q.v.

Mac Cuinᴏiᴌis, Mac Cuinᴏᴌis—IV—MacCandlis, Mac-Candless, MacCanlis, MacAndless, &c. ; 'son of Cuinᴏᴌeᴀꞃ' (an old Irish personal name). V. Ó Cuinᴏᴌiꞃ.

Mac Cuinn—IV—MacQuinn, MacQuin, MacGuinn, Quinn, 'son of Conn' (sense, reason, also a freeman, an ancient Irish personal name).

Mac Cuinneᴀꞃᴀin—IV—M'Cunnegane, M'Quynegan, MacCunnigan, Cunnigan, Kinnegan, Cunagum, Cunningham ; 'son of Cuinneᴀꞃᴀn' (dim. of Conn) ; a common surname in all parts of Ireland, but Ó Cuinneᴀꞃᴀin (q.v.) was nearly everywhere an alias.

Mac Cuinneᴀin—IV—M'Cunayn, M'Kenane, Cunnane, etc. ; 'son of Cuinneᴀin' (dim. of Conn). V. Ó Cuinneᴀin.

Mac Cuiꞃc—IV—M'Kwirke, MacQuirk, MacQuirke ; 'son of Coꞃc' (heart, an ancient Irish personal name) ; also Maꞃ Cuiꞃc, q.v.

Mac Cuiꞃcín, MacCurtin, Curtin ; a metathesized form of Mac Cꞃuicin, q.v.

Mac Cumᴀscᴀiꞃ—IV—MacCumisky, MacCumesky, MacComiskey, Cumisky, Cumesky, Cumiskey, Comesky, Comiskey, Commiskey, Cumisk, (Comerford, Cummerford), &c. ; 'son of Cumᴀꞃcᴀɓ' (confuser). This surname is almost peculiar to Cavan, Westmeath and Longford.

Mac Cuꞃcᴀin—IV—M'Curtaine, M'Curtayne, MacCurtain, Curtayne, Courtayne, Curtain, Curtin, &c. ; 'son of ᴀꞃcᴀn' (dim. of ᴀꞃc) ; a Munster form of Mac Cᴀꞃcᴀin, q.v. This surname was well established in Cork before the end of the 16th century.

Mac ᴏᴀɓóc, Mac ᴏᴀɓóꞃ, Mac ᴏᴀɓuc, Mac ᴏᴀɓuic — V — M'Davock, M'Davog, M'Dough, Doake, Doag, Doig ; 'son of Davuc' (a dim. of David).

Mac ᴏᴀɓóc, Mac ᴏᴀɓóꞃ, Mac ᴏᴀɓuc, Mac ᴏᴀɓuic—V—M'Cawque, M'Cavoke, M'Cavog, M'Coag, M'Coke, MacAvock, MacCavock, MacCoog, MacCook, Cooke ; a var. of Mac ᴏᴀɓóc, &c. ; the name of a branch of the Burkes in Co. Galway, and perhaps of other families in different parts of Ireland.

Mᴀc Oᴀɪbᴇɪᴅ—V—*M'Daveyd*, *M'Deyt*, MacDavid, Mac-Davitt, MacDaid, MacDevitt, MacDivitt, Davitt, Devitt, Daid, Dade, &c. ; ' son of Davet ' (a dim. of David) ; the name of a branch of the O'Dohertys of Inishowen who derive their name and descent from David O'Doherty who fell in battle in the year 1208 ; numerous in N.W. Ulster where it is generally angl. MacDaid and MacDevitt ; also in use in Co. Mayo, angl. Davitt, but whether, or not, the descent of the family is the same as that of Inishowen, I am unable to say. The local pronunciation is Mᴀc Oᴀᴇɪᴅ.

Mᴀc Oᴀɪbᴇɪᴅ—V—*M'Caveat*, MacCavitt, MacKevitt, MacCaet ; a var. of Mᴀc Oᴀɪbᴇɪᴅ, q.v. ; formerly a Galway surname, now peculiar to S.E. Ulster and Louth.

Mᴀc Oᴀɪbɪᴅ—V—*M'David*, *M'Davie*, *M'Davy*, *M'Dave*, *M'Day*, *M'Da*, MacDavid, MacDavitt, Davy, Davey, Day, Davies, Davis, Davidson, Davison, Dawson, &c. ; ' son of David ' (a common name among the early Anglo-Norman settlers in Ireland). There are several distinct families of this name. Of these, two are native Irish, namely, MacDavid of Thomond and MacDavid of Wexford, the latter of the same stock as the MacMurroughs ; and one Scottish, once numerous and powerful in Badenoch. MacDavid was also the title of the head of a branch of the Burkes who, shortly after the Anglo-Norman invasion obtained possession of the district of Clann Connmhaigh, the ancient patrimony of the O'Finaghtys, in Co. Galway. The head of the MacDavids of Wexford was known as Mᴀc Oᴀɪbɪᴅ Móʀ, q.v.

Mᴀc Oᴀɪbɪᴅ—V—*M'Cavy*, MacCave, Cavey, Ceavey, Cave ; a var. of Mᴀc Oᴀɪbɪᴅ, q.v. ; very rare.

Mᴀc Oᴀɪbɪᴅ Móʀ, Mᴀc Oᴀɪbɪᴅ Móʀ—V—*M'David More*, *M'Davy More*, *M'Damore*, *M'Amore*, Davis ; i.e., the great MacDavid ; the title of the head of the family of Mᴀc Oᴀɪbɪᴅ in Co. Wexford, whose patrimony lay in the north-east of that county. O'Donovan states, on the authority of the Book of Leinster, that this family is descended from Murchadh na nGaedheal, brother of Dermot MacMurrough. The name is now angl. Davis in Wexford.

Ⅿⱥⲥ Ⲅⱥⱦⷮ Ɽⲉ Ⲅⲟⲥⱥⲓɽ—IV—*M'Callredocker, M'Calradocker, M'Gallredocker*; 'son of Ⲅⱥⱦⷮ ɽⲉ ⲅⲟⲥⱥⲓɽ' (an Irish designation); the name, in the 13th and 14th centuries, of followers of O'Donnell; in the 16th, peculiar to Roscommon; now either obsolete or changed into some other form, such as Ó Ⲅⲟⲥɽⱥⲓⱦ, or Ⱦⱥⲥ Ꝣⲓⲟⱡⱡⱥⲅⲉⱥⲥⱥⲓɽ, q.v.

Ⱦⱥⲥ Ⲅⱥⲓɽⲉ—IV—*M'Dary, M'Darey*; 'son of Ⲅⱥⲓɽⲉ'; a famous patronymic in Irish literary history. It does not seem to have ever been a family name.

Ⱦⱥⲥ Ⲅⱥɽⱥ, Ⱦⱥⲥ Ⲅⱥɽⱥⱦⷮ, MacDara, Daragh, Darragh, Darrogh; Oak, Oakes, &c.; a shortened form of Ⱦⱥⲥ Ⲅⱦⲅⲅⱥɽⱥⱦⷮ, q.v.

Ⱦⱥⲥ Ⲅⲓⱥɽⱦⱥⲅⱥ—IV—*M'Dermody, M'Dermot, M'Dermonde, M'Derby*, MacDiarmod, MacDermott, MacDarby, Dermody, Darmody, Diarmid, Dermid, Dermond, Darby, &c.; 'son of Ⲅⲓⱥɽⱦⱥⲓⲅ' (an ancient and very common Irish personal name, angl. Dermot, Darby and Jeremiah). The most important family of this name are the MacDermotts of Moylurg. They were a branch of the Sil-Murray, long the ruling race in Connacht, of which, next to the O'Connors, they were the most powerful family. Their clan-name was Ⲥⱡⱥⲛⲛ Ⱦⱥⲟⲓⱡɽⱦⱥⲛⱥⲓⱦ, so called from Ⱦⱥⲟⱡɽⱦⱥⲛⱥⲓⱦ, who was son of Tadhg O'Connor, King of Connacht, in the 11th century. They are, therefore, of the same stock as the O'Connors. From Ⲅⲓⱥɽⱦⱥⲓⲅ, who was the grandson of Ⱦⱥⲟⱡɽⱦⱥⲛⱥⲓⱦ and died in 1159, they took the surname of Ⱦⱥⲥ Ⲅⲓⱥɽⱦⱥⲅⱥ, angl. MacDermott. About the middle of the 14th century, they divided into three distinct septs, each with a chief of its own, namely: MacDermott of Moylurg, who was overlord of all the MacDermotts, and had his fortress at the Rock of Lough Key, near Boyle;

MacDermottroe, or the Red MacDermott, who was chief of Tir-Thuthail, comprising the parish of Kilronan, and had his residence at Alderford ; and MacDermott Gall (or Gallda), the English or Anglicised MacDermott, who was chief of Artagh, comprising the parish of Tibohine. The two baronies of Boyle and Frenchpark now represent the patrimony of the MacDermotts. The MacDermotts played a conspicuous part in the history of Connacht. They retained their rank as lords of Moylurg down to the end of the 16th century ; and as successors to the O'Garas continued to hold considerable property at Coolavin, in Co. Sligo, down to recent times ; and The MacDermott is still known as Prince of Coolavin. V. ṁac Ḋiaṗmaḋa.

ṁac Ḋiaṙmaḋa — IV — *M'Kiermodie,* *M'Kearmode,* Kermode, &c. ; a var. of ṁac Ḋiaṗmaḋa, q.v. This is the usual form of the surname in the spoken Irish of Connacht, even when the radical Ḋ is retained in the angl. form.

ṁac Ḋiaṙmaḋa ȝall, ṁac Ḋiaṙmaḋa ȝallḋa, MacDermott Gall ; the Anglicised MacDermott. V. ṁac Ḋiaṗmaḋa.

ṁac Ḋiaṙmaḋa Ruaḋ, *M'Dermody Roe,* MacDermottroe ; i.e., the Red MacDermott. V. ṁac Ḋiaṗmaḋa. It was in MacDermottroe's house at Alderford that Torlough O'Carolan, the last of the bards, died in 1737.

ṁac Ḋíomasaiȝ — IV — MacGimpsey, MacJimpsey ; ' son of Ḋíomaṙac ' (proud) ; a rare Ulster surname.

ṁac Ḋoṁnaill—IV—*M'Donaill,* *M'Donall,* MacDonald, MacDonnell, MacDaniel, Donaldson, Donald, &c. ; ' son of Ḋoṁnall ' (world-mighty, an ancient and very common Irish personal name, angl. Donald and Daniel). There are three distinct families of this name : (1) The MacDonalds, or MacDonnells, of Scotland, who derive their name and descent from Ḋoṁnall, or Donald, grandson of Somhairle thane of Argyle about the middle of the 12th century. They

were the most powerful and warlike of all the Highland clans, and as lords of the Isles played an important part in the history of Scotland.   In the 14th
and 15th centuries, the MacDonalds came over in
large numbers to Ireland, where they became famous
as leaders of gallowglasses or heavy armed soldiers.
They formed a military clan under their own chiefs
who were often of high rank, and in reward for their
services obtained grants of land in different parts of
the country.   In this way they seem to have formed
a permanent settlement in Leinster as early as the
middle of the 15th century, and acquired considerable
estates in Leix and the present Co. of Wicklow.
By the marriage John Mor, son of the Lord of the
Isles, with the heiress of MacEoin Bissett, about the
beginning of the 15th century, the Glinns of Antrim
came into their possession, but it was only about the
year 1520 that, in right of this marriage, they effected
a permanent settlement in that county.   The Mac-
Donnells played a conspicuous part in the confederate
and Jacobite wars, and both in Ireland and Scotland,
were true to the last to the Stuart cause.   The great
bulk of our Irish MacDonnells belong to this race.
(2) The MacDonnells of Clan-Kelly.   They were chiefs
of Clan-Kelly in Co. Fermanagh, and even as late as
the end of the 16th century formed a distinct clan,
with a chief of the name.   (3) The MacDonnells of
Thomond.   This family, according to Dr. O'Brien
(Irish Dict. s.v. Ꞩoṁnaʟʟ, Conċoḃaṗ), is a branch of
that of O'Brien, being descended from Ꞩoṁnaʟʟ, who
was son of Murtagh Mor Ó'Brien, King of Ireland.
MacDonnell, or MacDonald, is now one of our most
numerous surnames.   V. ṁac Ꞩoṁnaiʟʟ.
ṁac Ꞩoṁnaiʟʟ—IV—*M'Coenill*, *M'Conill*, *M'Gonell*,
MacConell, MacConnell, MacGonnell, &c. ; a var. of
ṁac Ꞩoṁnaiʟʟ, q.v.   This form of the surname is
common in the spoken language even when the angl.
form is MacDonnell, with the radical Ꞩ retained.
In Co. Mayo it is sometimes pronounced Ó Coṁnaiʟʟ.

Mac ᴅoɴɴċᴀᴅᴀ, Mac ᴅoɴɴċᴀɪᴅ—IV—*M'Donoghue,*
M'Donnoghie, M'Donaghy, M'Donchie, M'Denis, Mac-
Donnagh, MacDonough, MacDonogh, MacDonagh,
MacDona, MacDunphy, Donoghue, Donohoe,
Donaghy, Donogh, Donagh, Dunphy, Duncan, Denni-
son, Denison, Dennis, &c.; ' son of ᴅoɴɴċᴀᴅ '
(brown warrior, or strong warrior, an ancient and
very common Irish personal name, angl. Donough,
Denis.) There are at least three distinct families
bearing this surname : (1) A branch of the
MacCarthys, who were chiefs of Duhallow, in Co.
Cork, and at one time very powerful. Their principal
seat was at Kanturk. (2) A branch of the MacDer-
motts of Moylurg, who were chiefs of Tirerrill and
Corran, in Co. Sligo, and resided at Ballymote. The
Book of Ballymote was compiled under their patronage.
An offshoot of this family settled in Co. Clare, and
thence spread into Co. Limerick. (3) A Scottish clan
in Perthshire, said to be a branch of the MacDonalds.
This family now angl. their name Duncan, and some
of them call themselves Robertson. V. Mac ᴅoɴɴċᴀᴅᴀ.
Mac ᴅoɴɴċᴀᴅᴀ, Mac ᴅoɴɴċᴀɪᴅ—IV—*M'Conogho,*
M'Conough, M'Connagh, M'Conna, MacConachie, Mac-
Connachie, MacConnaghy, MacConaghy, MacCon-
naughey, MacConohy, MacCona, MacConkey, Mac-
Konkey, Conify, (Robertson) ; variants of Mac ᴅoɴɴċᴀᴅᴀ, Mac ᴅoɴɴċᴀɪᴅ, q.v. ; common in the spoken
language even when the radical ᴅ is retained in the
angl. form.
Mac ᴅoᴦċᴀɪᴅ—IV—MacArchy, MacDorcy ; a var. of
Maᵹ ᴅoᴩċᴀɪᴅ, q.v. O'Donovan gives the angl.
form as MacDorcy, Dorcey, which I am unable to
verify.
Mac ᴅuᴀᴦċáɪɴ—IV—MacGurgan, Gurkin, Durcan,
Durkan, Durkin, Zorkin ; ' son of ᴅuᴀᴩcáɴ '; the
name of a well-known North Connacht family who
were anciently lords of Cuil Neiridh, in Co. Sligo, and
are probably a branch of the O'Haras. This surname

is sometimes pronounced Ó Cuaᵽcáin in the spoken language of Mayo.

Mac Oubᴅara, Mac Oubᴅarac—IV—*M'Dwdara,* MacAdarrah, MacAdarra, MacDara, Daragh, Darra, Darragh, Darrock, and, by translation, Oak, Oaks, Oakes ; ' son of Oubᴅaᵽaċ ' (the black-man of the oak) ; also written Mac Ouibᴅaᵽa, Mac Ouibᴅaᵽaċ (q.v.), and shortened to Mac Oaᵽa, Mac Oaᵽaċ, q.v.

Mac Oubᵹaill—IV—*M'Doole, M'Doell, M'Doile,* MacDool, MacDowall, MacDowell, MacDugal, Mac-Dougall, MacDugald, MacDougald, MacDole, Madole, Doole, Dowell, Dougall, Dugald, &c. ; ' son of Oub-ᵹaill ' (the black-stranger, a name given by the Irish to the Danes) ; the name of a Scoto-Irish family of the same stock as the MacDonalds, being descended from Somaiᵽle, thane of Argyle (slain 1165), who was the common ancestor of both families. The Mac-Dugalds were lords of Lorne in Scotland. Some of them, like the MacDonalds, came over to Ireland, in the 14th and 15th centuries, as captains of gallow-glasses, and settled in Co. Roscommon and other parts of the west and north of Ireland. V. Mac Oubᵹaill.

Mac Oubᵹaill—IV—*M'Cowgall, M'Cougald, M'Co-wyle, M'Cooel, M'Cual, M'Coole, M'Cole, M'Coyle,* MacCool, MacCole, Coole, Cole, Coyle, Coiles, &c. ; a var. of Mac Oubᵹaill, q.v. This is the usual form of the surname in the spoken language, even when the radical O is retained in the angl. form. Cf. Mac Oomnaill.

Mac Oubᵲaᴅáin—IV—Doordan, Dordan ; ' son of Oubᵽaᴅán ' (atom, pygmy) ; a rare Connacht surname. Maolṁaoᴅóᵹ, Mac Oubᵽaᴅáin, abbot of Saul, Co. Down, died in the year 1156.

Mac Oubuiᴅiᴚ—IV—MacDwyer ; ' son of Oubóᴅaᵽ ' (black Oᴅaᵽ) ; usually, but less correctly, written Mac Ouibiᴅiᵽ, q.v.

Mac Ouib—IV—*M'Duffe,* MacDuff, Duff, and, by trans-lation, Black ; ' son of Oub ' (an Irish personal name meaning ' black '). Besides the Irish families bearing this surname, there is a Scottish clan mᴀc Ɗuıᴃ, of which the old Earls of Fife were the heads. V. mᴀc Ɗuıᴃ.

mᴀc Ɗuıᴃ—IV—*M'Cuffe*, Cuffe; a var. of mᴀc Ɗuıᴃ, q.v. See also mᴀʒ Ɗuıᴃ.

mᴀc Ɗuıᴃ'ᴅᴀʀᴀ, mᴀc Ɗuıᴃ'ᴅᴀʀᴀċ—IV—Mac-Adarragh, MacAdarra, &c. V. mᴀc Ɗuᴃ'ᴅᴀʀᴀ, mᴀc Ɗuᴃ'ᴅᴀʀᴀċ.

mᴀc Ɗuıᴃeᴀṁnᴀ—IV—*M'Doyaoune*; 'son of Ɗuᴃ-eᴀṁnᴀ' (the black-man of Emania, near Armagh); the name of a family in Co. Down who, according to O'Dugan, were chiefs of Kinelawley. O'Donovan gives the angl. form as Devany, but the surname seems to be obsolete or changed into some other form.

mᴀc Ɗuıᴃꝟınn—IV—*M'Duffin*; 'son of Ɗuᴃꝟıonn' (black ꝟıonn). V. mᴀʒ Ɗuıᴃꝟınn.

mᴀc Ɗuıᴃıᴅıʀ, MacDwyer, MacDire; a var. of mᴀc Ɗuᴃuıᴅıʀ, q.v.

mᴀc Ɗuıᴃın—IV—*M'Kevine, M'Kevyn*, MacKevin, Mac-Evin, MacAvin; 'son of Ɗuıᴃın' (a dim. of ᴅuᴃ, black); a rare surname. In the 16th century, it was almost peculiar to Sligo and Donegal.

mᴀc Ɗuıᴃınse—IV—MacAvinchy; 'son of Ɗuᴃınꞃe' (black-man of the island).

mᴀc Ɗuıᴃne—IV—*M'Duynie*, MacEvinie, MacEvinney, &c.; 'son of Ɗuıᴃne' (ill-going, an ancient Irish personal name, opposed to Suıᴃne); the name of a Breifney fam'y, one of whom was Bishop of Kilmore in the 15th century. Its angl. forms cannot easily be distinguished from those of mᴀc ᴀıᴃne, q.v. See also mᴀʒ Ɗuıᴃne, which is the more common spelling.

mᴀc Ɗuıᴃꞃíᴄe—IV—*M'Duffyhe*, *M'Duffie*, MacAffie, MacAffee, MacAfee, MacHaffie, MacHaffy, MacFie, MacFee, Mahaffy; 'son of Ɗuᴃꞃíᴄe' (the black-man of peace); the name of a Scottish family who for many centuries held the island of Colonsay. They were a brave and warlike clan, and as followers of the Mac-Donalds of Islay and the Camerons of Lochiel, showed their prowess on many a field. They suffered severely at Culloden in 1745, when the whole clan was out for Prince Charlie. A branch of the family settled in Co. Antrim in the 16th century, and others probably came over at a later period.

mac Ꝺuinn—IV—*M'Doyn*, *M'Dun*, MacDunn ; ' son of Ꝺonn ' (lord, strong, brown, dark) ; a rare surname.

mac Ꝺuinnsléibe—IV — *M'Donleiwe*, *M'Donleve*, *M'Donleavy*, Dunlief, Dunlop ; ' son of Ꝺonnṡléibe ' (an Irish personal name, meaning ' Ꝺonn of the mountain') ; now changed to mac Ꝺuinnṡléibe, Ó Ꝺuinnṡléibe, q.v.

mac Ꝺuinnsléibe—IV—*M'Anlevy*, *M'Enlievie*, *M'Enlevie*, *M'Enleve*, *M'Inlewe*, *M'Inlowe*, *M'Colleve*, *M'Colley*, MacConloy, MacEleavy, MacAleavy, MacAlea, MacAlee, Macleavy, MacClew, MacCloy, Killevy, Killeavy, Levy, Leavy, &c. ; a var. of mac Ꝺuinnṡléibe (q.v.), the initial Ꝺ of the second part of the surname being now always aspirated. In Scotland, the final e is dropped, and it would appear from the early angl. forms that this also sometimes happened in Ireland. The MacDunlevys were an ancient and once powerful family in Co. Down. They derive their descent from Ꝺonnṡléibe Ó hEocaḋa, chieftain of Ulidia, who flourished in the 11th century. A remnant of the ancient inhabitants of Ulster, they maintained their independence, though in a greatly circumscribed territory, down to the coming of the English. Their patrimony, which was known as Ulaḋ (Latinised Ulidia), then comprised the present Co. Down and the southern portion of Co. Antrim. The invasion and conquest of Ulidia by John de Courcy, in the year 1177, was the turning point in the history of the clan. Marching his army to Downpatrick, he encountered MacDunlevy, defeated him in battle, though only after a brave resistance, and dispersed his clansmen. From this defeat they never recovered. Though they did not at once cease to exist as a distinct clan, their power was for ever broken, and branches of the family sought new homes in different parts of Ireland, and even in Scotland. In Tirconnell, some of them became famous as physicians to the O'Donnells. The surname has assumed a great variety of forms in Irish; and the corresponding angl. forms are very numerous. V. Ó Ꝺuιnnꝼléιꝺe, ꞁꞁꜰꞁ Ꝺuιnnꝼléιꝺín; also Ultᴀᴄ, Ultᴀᴄᴀ́n, ꞁꞁꜰꞁ ᴀn Ultᴀιꞃ, Ó hUltᴀᴄᴀ́ιn, and ꞁꞁꜰꞁ ᴀn lᴇᴀꞃᴀ.

ꞁꞁꜰꞁ Ꝺuιnnꞁléιꝺín—IV—*M'Inleavin, M'Inlene*, Mac-Lavin, MacLevin, Lavins, Levins, Levinson, Leveson, (Leviston, Levenston, Levinston, Levingston, Livingston, Livingstone, Livingstown); a dim. of ꞁꞁꜰꞁ Ꝺuιnnꝼléιꝺe, q.v. Cf. Ultᴀᴄ and Ultᴀᴄᴀ́n.

ꞁꞁꜰꞁ Ꝺúnᴀꝺᴀιꞃ—IV—*M'Dowany, M'Downey, M'Doney* Dooney, Downey, Doney; 'son of Ꝺúnᴀꝺᴀᴄ' (deriv. of ꝺúnᴀꝺ, of the ꝺún or fort); the name of an old Galway family who are probably a branch of the O'Maddens. Also called Ó Ꝺúnᴀꝺᴀιꞃ, q.v.

ꞁꞁꜰꞁ eᴀᴄᴀꝺᴀ, ꞁꞁꜰꞁ eᴀᴄᴀιꝺ—IV—*M'Kaghoe, M'Caghie*, MacAghy, MacCahugh, MacCaghy, MacCaughey, MacCahy, Caughy, Cahy, (Hackett), and sometimes, by 'translation,' Steed, Steedman; 'son of eᴀᴄᴀιꝺ'; var. of ꞁꞁꜰꞁ eoᴄᴀꝺᴀ, ꞁꞁꜰꞁ eoᴄᴀιꝺ, ꞁꞁ͢ᴀꞃ eoᴄᴀιꝺ, q.v.

ꞁꞁꜰꞁ eᴀᴄᴀ́ιn—IV—*M'Keaghane*, MacCaughan, Mac-Cahan, MacCahon, Cahane; 'son of eᴀᴄᴀ́n' (a dim. of eᴀᴄᴀιꝺ); an Ulster var. of ꞁꞁꜰꞁ eoᴄᴀ́ιn, q.v. See also ꞁꞁ͢ᴀꞃ eᴀᴄᴀ́ιn.

ꞁꞁꜰꞁ eᴀᴄꞁᴀꞃᴄᴀιꞃ — IV—*M'Cafferchie, M'Cafferkie*, MacCaffarky, MacCagherty, MacCaugherty, Mac-Cafferty, MacCaverty, MacCaharty, MacCaherty, (Mac-Carthy, MacCaffry), Cafferky, Cafferty; 'son of eᴀᴄꞁᴀꞃᴄᴀᴄ' (horse-rider); a Donegal surname, now also common in Mayo, but often disguised under the angl. form of MacCaffry. The local pronunciation is sometimes Ó Ceᴀꞃᴀꞃᴄᴀιꞃ. The family is probably a branch of the O'Dohertys, among whom eᴀᴄꞁᴀꞃᴄᴀᴄ was a personal name.

ꞁꞁꜰꞁ eᴀᴄꞁíleᴀꝺᴀ, ꞁꞁꜰꞁ eᴀᴄꞁílιꝺ—IV—*M'Agholy, M'Aughelie, M'Cafely*, MacCaughley, MacCaffaley, MacCaffely; 'son of eᴀᴄꞁíleᴀꝺ' (horse-soldier); a rare East Ulster surname. The family is probably a branch of that of Maguinness, among whom Eaċṁíleaḋ was a favouite name.

Mac Eaċráin—IV—*M'Eacherane, M'Ceagharan,* MacCagheron, MacCaughern, MacCahern, &c.; 'son of Eaċrán'; a var. of Mag Eaċráin, q.v.

Mac Eaċṫiġeirn — IV—*M'Acherin, M'Kagherne,* Caheerin, Keheerin; 'son of Eaċṫiġearna' (horse-lord); a rare and scattered surname. Also Mac Eiċṫiġeirn, q.v.

Mac Éadḃáird—V—*M'Edward,* [Edwards]; 'son of Edward'; an Anglo-Irish patronymic corresponding to the English surname Edwards.

Mac Eáin—V—*M'Eane, M'Keane, M'Cane,* MacKean, MacKane, MacKain, MacCain, &c.; 'son of John'; a var. of Mac Eóin, q.v. The Mac Eains were chiefs of Ardnamurchan in Scotland.

Mac Éamoinn, Mac Éamuinn—V—*M'Eamon, M'Edmond, M'Edmund,* MacAimon, MacEdmund, [Edmond, Edmonds, Edmundson, &c.]; 'son of Edmund'; an Anglo-Irish surname.

Mac Éanna—IV—*M'Enna, M'Eanny, M'Ena,* MacKeany, (MacKenna), 'son of Éanna'; a scattered surname, but found chiefly in Wexford and Carlow. Its angl. forms can hardly be distinguished from those of Mac Cionaoiṫ, q.v.

Mac Eanraic—V—*M'Henricke,* MacKendrick, Kenrick, Kendrick, Kinrock, Condrick, Conderick; 'son of Eanrac' (a Teutonic personal name, the same as the English Henry); a var. of Mac Annraic, q.v.

Mac Éiḃir—IV—MacEver; 'son of Éiḃear'; extremely rare.

Mac Eiċrí—IV—*M'Echrye, M'Keghrie*; 'son of Eiċrí' (horse-king); an Ulster surname; always extremely rare, and probably now obsolete.

Mac Eiċṫiġeirn—IV—MacEchern, Keheerin; a var. of Mac Eaċṫiġeirn, q.v.

Mac Éidiġ—IV—MacKeady, Keady; a corruption of Ó Meicéidiġ, q.v.; a rare West Cork surname.

Mac Éiṁir—IV—MacEver ; a var. of Mac Éibir, q.v.

Mac Éinrí—V—*M'Enree, M'Henrie, M'Henry,* MacEnry, MacEndry, MacHenry, MacHenery, MacHendrie, MacHendry, MacKenery, MacKendry, Fitzhenry, Henry, Hendry, &c. ; 'son of Henry' ; (a very common name among the early Anglo-Norman settlers) ; the name of several distinct families in different parts of Ireland ; common in Ulster and in some parts of Connacht. The Fitzhenrys of Wexford are an Anglo-Norman family. Also Mac Annraoi and Mac Hannraoi, q.v.

Mac Eoċaḋa—IV—*M'Eoghoe, M'Keoghoe,* MacKeogh, MacKeough, MacKeo, MacKough, Keoghoe, Keogh, Keough, &c. ; 'son of Eoċaiḋ' (a very common Irish personal name in ancient times) ; the name (1) of a Leinster family, of the same stock as the O'Byrnes, at one time famous as poets ; (2) of a Co. Roscommon family, a branch of the O'Kellys of Ui Maine, who were chiefs of Moyfinn, in the barony of Athlone ; (3) of a Tipperary family who were anciently chiefs of Owney, but dispossessed many centuries ago by the O'Mulryans ; and (4) of a Roscommon family who were anciently chiefs of Moylurg, now the barony of Boyle, until dispossessed by the MacDermotts. V. Mac Eoċaiḋ, Mag Eoċaiḋ and Mac Eaċaḋa, which are variants.

Mac Eoċagáin — IV — *M'Keoghegane, M'Coghegan, M'Coogan,* Kehigan, MacCogan, Keogan, Coogan, Cooken, Cogan, &c. ; 'son of Eoċagán' (a dim. of Eoċaiḋ) ; a var. of Mag Eoċagáin, q.v. ; rare and found only in Cavan and a few other parts of Ulster.

Mac Eoċaiḋ—IV—*M'Oghie, M'Coghie, M'Cohy,* MacCoughy, Keoghy, Cuhy ; 'son of Eoċaiḋ' ; a var. of Mac Eoċaḋa and Mac Eaċaiḋ, q.v.

Mac Eoċáin—IV—*M'Keoghan,* Keoghane, Keohane, &c. This surname is now almost peculiar to West Cork, where it is pronounced Ó Ceoċáin (with short eo). V. Mac Eaċáin, which is the Ulster form ; also Mag Eoċáin.

mac eoʒᴀ1n—IV—MacOwen, MacEown, MacCone, Mac-Kone, MacKeoan, MacKeown, MacEwan, Keown, Coen, Cowan, Coyne, Owen, Owens, &c. ; 'son of eoʒᴀn' (an old Irish personal name meaning 'well-born') ; a Sligo surname. Its angl. forms and those of mac eó1n (q.v.) are pronounced so nearly alike that it is impossible to distinguish them. V. maʒ eoʒᴀin.

mac eó1n—V—MacEoin, MacKeon, MacKeone, Mac-Keown, Keon, Keown, Johnson, &c. ; 'son of John' an Irish surname assumed by a branch of the Scottish family of Bissett who settled, in the 13th century, in the Glinns of Antrim. Its angl. forms cannot be distinguished from those of mac eoʒᴀin, q.v. See also maʒ eoʒᴀin.

mac eotᴀċ—IV—MacKeogh, Keogh ; 'son of eoċᴀ1ᴅ' ; a var. of mac eoċᴀᴅᴀ, q.v. See also maʒ eotᴀċ.

mac fᴀ́ċtnᴀ—IV—Aughney ; 'son of fᴀċtnᴀ.'

mac fᴀo1t1ʒ—V—MacWhite, MacWhitty.

mac fᴀolᴀ́1n—IV—M'Phillan, MacPhelan ; 'son of fᴀolᴀ́n' (dim. of fᴀol, a wolf) ; extremely rare.

mac feᴀRᴀᴅᴀ1ʒ—IV—M'Farree, M'Farry, M'Ferry, MacVarry, MacVerry ; 'son of feᴀpᴀᴅᴀċ' (an old Irish personal name meaning 'manly') ; an Ulster surname in use in Tyrone, Armagh and Down.

mac feᴀRᴀᴅᴀ1ʒ—IV—M'Karrye, M'Kerry, MacAree, MacKaree, MacCarrie, MacKeary, MacHarry, Maharry, and, by 'translation,' King ; a var. of mac feᴀpᴀᴅᴀ1ʒ, q.v. In the modern spoken language, this surname is sometimes corrupted to mac ᴀ' R1oʒ (son of the king) and accordingly angl. King. V. maʒ feᴀp-ᴀᴅᴀ1ʒ.

mac feᴀRċᴀiR—IV—M'Fearagher, Farquharson, Far-quhar, Farquher, Farquer, Farghur, Farker, Forker, &c. ; 'son of feᴀpċᴀp' (very dear) ; the name of a Scottish clan in Aberdeenshire, some of whom, doubtless, have come over to Ulster. V. mac feᴀpċᴀ1p.

mac feᴀRċᴀiR—IV—M'Eragher, MacErchar, Mac-Carragher, Caragher, Carragher, Caraher, Carraher, Kerragher, Kerraher, &c. ; a var. of mac feᴀpċᴀ1p.

q.v. ; in use in Ulster, but has always been very rare. The initial ꜰ is aspirated, even when pronounced in the angl. form.

mac ꜰeanꞌᵹail—IV—*M'Farrell, M'Freill,* &c. ; 'son of ꜰeanᵹal.' V. mac ꜰeanᵹail.

mac ꜰeanᵹail—IV—*M'Karachill,* MacErrigle, Mac-Argle, Cargill, Carkill ; 'son of ꜰeanᵹal' (super-valour) ; also maᵹ ꜰeanᵹail, q.v. ; a var. of mac ꜰeanᵹail, q.v. ; an Antrim surname. For unaspirated ᵹ, cf. mac Conᵹail.

mac ꜰeanᵹail—IV—*M'Carrell, M'Kerrell,* MacCarrell, MacKerrell, MacKerrall, MacCarroll, MacKarroll, Mackerel, Mackrell, &c. ; a var. of mac ꜰeanᵹail, q.v. Its angl. forms are not always distinguishable from those of mac Ceanbaill, q.v. See also maᵹ ꜰeanᵹail.

mac ꜰeanᵹaile—IV—*M'Carrelly, M'Carley, M'Kearly, M'Errelly, M'Kyrrelly,* MacErrilly, MacKerlie, Car-rolly, Carley, Kerley, Kirley ; a var. of mac ꜰeanᵹail, q.v.

mac ꜰeanᵹusa—IV—*M'Fargus, M'Faryse,* Farguson, Ferguson, Fergus, Vargus, &c. ; 'son of ꜰeanᵹur' (super-choice) ; the name of a Scottish family, some of whom settled in the north of Ireland in the early part of the 17th century.

mac ꜰeanᵹusa—IV—*M'Arrassie,* Hergusson, Fergu-son, &c. ; a var. of mac ꜰeanᵹura, q.v.

mac ꜰeiꝺlim—IV—*M'Phelim, M'Felim,* Phelim, Phelym, &c. ; 'son of ꜰeiꝺlim' (short for ꜰeiꝺlimiꝺ) ; a var. of mac ꜰeiꝺlimiꝺ, q.v.

mac ꜰeiꝺlimiꝺ—IV—*M'Felemy, M'Phelimy,* Mac-Phelimy, MacPhellimy, &c. ; 'son of ꜰeiꝺlimiꝺ' (an ancient Irish personal name, explained as meaning 'the ever good') ; a rare surname.

mac ꜰeónais, mac ꜰeónuis—V—*M'Orish, M'Horishe, M'Keorish, M'Corishe, M'Keoris,* Korish, Corish, [Birmingham, Bermingham, &c.] ; 'son of Piers' (a Norman form of Peter) ; the Irish name assumed by Anglo-Irish family of Bermingham, who are descended from an ancestor called Piers or Peter de Bermingham. V. Ḿac Ṗiaṗaiṗ, ḿac Ṗiaṗaiṗ and ḿaᵹ Ḟeóṗaiṗ, which are variants of the present surname.

Ḿac Ṗiaċṙa, ḿac Ṗiaċṙaċ—IV—*M'Keaghry, M'Keighera*, MacKeighry, MacKeefrey, MacKeary, Keaghery, Keahery, Keary, (Carey) ; ' son of Ṗiaċṙa ' (gen. Ṗiaċṙaċ, but the gen. ending is now generally, if not always, dropped) ; the name (1) of a family of Cinel Eoghain, who were anciently chiefs of Cinel Fearadhaigh, in the barony of Clogher, Co. Tyrone ; (2) of a Galway family who were chiefs of Oga Beathra, in the S.W. of Co. Galway ; and (3) of a family in Co. Meath. The first two families were well represented in the 16th century and are still extant, but the Meath family appears to be long extinct.

Ḿac Ṗiaṙais—V—*M'Keriske*, Kerrison, Kearson, Kerris, Kerrish, Kierce, Kierse, Kearse, Kerisk, Kerrisk, [Healy] ; ' son of Piers ' ; var. of Ḿac Ṗiaṗaiṗ, q.v. ; a rare and scattered surname. In East Kerry, it is corrupted to Ḿac Ceiṗiṙc and Ó Ceiṗiṙc, and very often angl. Healy, the family being probably descended from a person called Ferris O'Helie (Pierce Healy). Cf. Ḿac Ḟeóṗaiṗ above.

Ḿac Ṗibín—V—*M'Fibbin*, MacKibbin, MacKibben, MacKibbon ; ' son of Phipin ' (a dim. of Philip).

Ḿac Ṗilib—V—MacKillip, MacKillop, MacKellop, MacKillops, Killips, Killops, Kellops, Philson, Philipson, Phillips ; ' son of Philip ' ; a var. of Ḿac Ṗilib, q.v.

Ḿac Ṗilibín—V—MacPhilpin, MacPhilbin, Philbin, &c. ; a var. of Ḿac Ṗilibín, q.v. ; common in the spoken language of Co. Mayo.

Ḿac Ṗinᵹin—IV—*M'Kynine*, *M'Kennyne*, Kenning, Kennyon, Kenyon, Kennon, Keenan, &c. ; ' son of Ṗinᵹin ' (fair-offspring), a rare surname. Its angl. forms cannot easily be distinguished from those of Ḿac Coinín, q.v. See also Ḿaᵹ Ṗinᵹin.

Ḿac Ṗinn—IV—*M'Iyn*, MacKinn, MacKing ; ' son of Ṗionn ' (fair) ; a var. of Ḿaᵹ Ṗinn, q.v. ; in use in Derry and Mayo, but rare.

Мac ꝼınneᴀᴄᴛᴀ, мac ꝼınneᴀᴄᴛᴀıᵹ—IV—Kingarty, Kingerty ; ' son of ꝼınneᴀᴄᴛᴀ ' (white-snow) ; var. of Мᴀᵹ ꝼınneᴀᴄᴛᴀ ; extremely rare.

Мac ꝼıoᴅᴠuıᴅe—IV—*M'Eboy, M'Ebwy, M'Ewy,* Mac-Evoy, MacAvoy, MacVoy, Evoy ; a corruption of Мac ꝼıoᴅᴠᴀᴅᴀıᵹ, ' son of ꝼıoᴅᴠᴀᴅᴀᴄ ' (i.e., of the wood, woodman) ; the name of a family in Leix, who were anciently chiefs of Tuath-Fiodhbhuidhe, which appears to have been situated in the barony of Stradbally.

Мac ꝼıonᵹuıne—IV—*M'Kynnoun,* MacKinnon ; ' son of ꝼıonᵹuıne ' (fair-child) ; the name of a celebrated clan in the west of Scotland. The final e is dropped in the spoken language. The pronunciation, as I heard it in Argyleshire, would be represented by Мac Cıonúın.

Мac ꝼıonnáın—IV—*M'Kynnan, M'Kennan,* Kinnan, Kennan ; ' son of ꝼıonnán ' (dim. of ꝼıonn, fair). This surname appears to have been in use in Tyrone, but its present angl. forms cannot be distinguished from those of Ó Cuınneáın and Ó Cıanáın, q.v. See also Мᴀᵹ ꝼıonnáın, which is a variant.

Мac ꝼıonnᴠᴀıRR—IV—*M'Inuyre, M'Kenor,* Kenure ; ' son of ꝼıonnᴠᴀꝛꝛ ' (fair-head) ; a var. of Мᴀᵹ ꝼıonnᴠᴀıꝛꝛ, q.v. ; very rare.

Мac ꝼıonnᵹᴀıl—IV—*M'Kenill* ; ' son of ꝼıonnᵹᴀl ' (fair valour) ; now Мᴀᵹ ꝼıonnᵹᴀıl, q.v.

Мac ꝼıonnlᴀoıᴄ—IV—MacKinley, MacKinlay ; ' son of ꝼıonnlᴀoᴄ ' (fair-hero) ; the name of a Scottish clan ; said to be a substitution for Мac ꝼıonnloᵹᴀ, q.v. The pronunciation in modern Scottish-Gaelic is Мac ꝼıonnlᴀ (Мac Cıúllᴀ). It does not appear to have been at any time an Irish surname, but is now sometimes erroneously substituted for Мᴀᵹ ꝼıonnᵹᴀıle, q.v.

Мac ꝼıonnloᵹᴀ—IV—MacKinley, MacKinlay ; ' son of ꝼıonnluᵹ ' (fair luᵹ) ; now written Мac ꝼıonnlᴀoıᴄ, q.v.

Мac ꝼıonnᵯᴀᴄáın—IV—Kinucane ; ' son of ꝼıonnᵯacán (fair-son). Cf. Ó ꝼıonnᵯacáın.

Mac ꝼiRbisiᵹ—IV—*M'Ferbishy*, *M'Firbisse*, *M'Firbis*, Forbish, Forbis, Forbes; 'son of ꝼeᴀꝶbiꝶiᵹ' (man of prosperity); the name of a celebrated family of historians and antiquaries in Connacht. They belonged to the Ui Fiachrach race, of which for many centuries they were the hereditary poets and chroniclers. Their original patrimony was Magh Broin, in Tirawley, but they afterwards settled at Rosserk, between Ballina and Killala, and finally at Lacken, in the parish of Kilglas, Co. Sligo, which continued to be the home of the family down to the year 1608, when they were dispossessed of their estates by James I. The castle of Lacken, now known as Castle Forbes, was built by Ciothruadh MacFirbis in the year 1560. Duald MacFirbis, the last and greatest scholar of the name, was foully murdered at Dunflin, Co. Sligo, in the year 1670, by an English soldier named Crofton. The MacFirbises were the compilers of the Book of Lecan and other important works on Irish history and antiquities. The surname is now generally angl. Forbes.

Mac ꝼiRléiᵹinn—VII—*Machirleginn*, MacErlean, MacErlane, MacErlain, MacErleen; a var. of Mac ᴀn ꝼiꝶléiᵹinn, q.v. Dermit, Vicar of Drumcliffe, who flourished at the end of the 14th century, is surnamed in the Papal Register, Machinnirlegenn and Machirleginn.

Mac ꝼiᴄᴄeᴀLLᴀiᵹ—IV—MacFeeley, MacFeely; 'son of ꝼiᴄᴄeᴀLLᴀᴄ' (chess-player); very rare.

Mac ꝼLᴀiᴄbeᴀRᴄᴀiᵹ—IV—MacLaverty, MacClaverty, MacClafferty, MacCleverty; 'son of ꝼLᴀiᴄbeᴀꝶᴄᴀb' (bright-lord); a rare Ulster surname.

Mac ꝼLᴀiᴄiᵐ—IV—MacLave, Claffy, Claffey, Hand; 'son of ꝼLᴀiᴄeᴀᵐ' (lord, ruler). V. Maᵹ ꝼLᴀiᴄiᵐ.

Mac ꝼLᴀnnᴄᴀbᴀ, Mac ꝼLᴀnnᴄᴀb—IV—*M'Clanachy*, *M'Clanaghy*, *M'Clanchy*, *M'Clanky*, *M'Clansy*, MacClancy, Clanchy, Clancy; 'son of ꝼLᴀnnᴄᴀb' (ruddy-warrior); the name (1) of an ancient family in Co. Leitrim, who were chiefs of Dartry, now the barony of Rosclogher, and had their seats at Rosclogher and Dungarbry; and (2) of a Thomond family, a branch of the MacNamaras, who were hereditary brehons or judges to the O'Briens, and resided at Knockfin and Cahermaclancy, in the north-west of Co. Clare.

Mac Ḟloinn—IV—*M'Flyn*, MacFlynn; 'son of Ḟlann' (ruddy); a var. of Maᵹ Ḟloinn, q.v.

Mac Ḟloinn—IV—MacLynn; a var. of Mac Ḟloinn and Maᵹ Ḟloinn, q.v.

Mac Ḟualáin—IV—*M'Folaine*, Folan; 'son of Ḟaolán' (dim. of Ḟaol, a wolf); a var. of Mac Ḟaoláin, q.v.; the name of an old family in Co. Galway. The initial Ḟ is aspirated in the present spoken language. Cf. the old angl. form O Folane for Ó Ḟaoláin.

Mac Ᵹabann—VII—MacGowan, Magowan, Gowen, Smith; a var. of Mac an Ᵹobann, q.v.

Mac Ᵹaḋra—IV—*M'Gara*, MacGeary, Geary; 'son of Ᵹaḋra'; an old, but rare, Roscommon surname; pronounced Mac Ᵹaora in Co. Galway where it still survives.

Mac Ᵹaḟraiḋ—V—*M'Gafferie*, MacGaffrey, MacCaffray, MacCaffrey, MacCaffery, Caffrey, Caffery, &c.; 'son of Godfrey'; also written Mac Ᵹoḟraḋa, Mac Caḟraiḋ, &c.; the name of a branch of the Maguires of Fermanagh, now common in Ulster; to be distinguished from Mac Eacṁarcaiᵹ (q.v.), which is sometimes similarly anglicised.

Mac Ᵹairḃeit, Mac Ᵹairḃit—IV—*M'Garvie, M'Garway*, MacGarvey, Garvey; 'son of Ᵹairḃit'; an Ulster surname, very common in Donegal.

Mac Ᵹaṁna—IV—*M'Gawna, M'Gawny, M'Gawne*, (Mac-Gowan, Magowan, Magowen), Gaffney; 'son of Ᵹaṁain' (calf); a rare and scattered surname; now generally assimilated to Mac Ᵹabann, q.v.

Mac Ᵹaoite—IV—*M'Giehie*, MacGeehee, (MacGee, Magee), and, by translation, Wynne; probably a shortened form of Mac Ᵹaoitín, q.v.; now merged in Maᵹ Aoiḋ, q.v. It was a Donegal surname in the 16th century.

Mac ʒᴀoιⳏ1n—IV—MacGeehin, MacGeehan, Mageehan, Mageahan, MacGihen, MacGihan, MacGehan, Mac-Gahan, Magahan, Megahan, MacGean, Magean, Gahan ; 'son of ʒᴀoιⳏ1n' (probably a 'pet' form of mᴀoιʒᴀoιⱅe, chief of the wind) ; an Ulster surname. In the 16th century, it was almost peculiar to the counties of Down and Donegal.

Mac ʒᴀᴩᴀċᴀ́n, v. Mᴀ̄ʒ ʒᴀᴩᴀċᴀ́n.

Mac ʒᴀᴩⱅlᴀn, MacGartlan. V. ʒeᴀᴩlᴀnn.

Mac ʒeᴀlᴀ́n—IV—MacGellan ; 'son of ʒeᴀlᴀ́n' (dim. of ʒeᴀl, bright, white) ; very rare.

Mac ʒeᴀᴩᴀιlⱅ—V—M'Garilt, M'Gerald, FitzGerald, Fitzgerald ; 'son of Gerald' ; the Irish form of the Norman surname FitzGerald. The Fitzgeralds rank with the Burkes and Butlers as one of the most illustrious of the Anglo-Norman families in Ireland. They derive their name and descent from Gerald, Constable of Pembroke, whose wife was Nest, daughter of Rhys Ap Tewdwyr, King of South Wales. Gerald flourished in the early part of the 12th century. His son, Maurice Fitzgerald, was one of the companions of Strongbow, and from him are descended all the families of the name in Ireland. He received large grants of land which continued in the possession of his descendants down to recent times. Members of the family frequently filled the highest offices under the English Crown. The head of the Leinster branch of the family for centuries bore the title of Earl of Kildare, later Duke of Leinster, while the head of the Fitzgeralds of Munster was Earl of Desmond.

Mac ʒeᴀ́ᴩᴀ́1n—IV—(?) MacGueran, Sharpe ; 'son of ʒeᴀᴩᴀ́n' (dim. of ʒeᴀᴩ, sharp).

Mac ʒeᴀᴩʒᴀ́1n—IV—M'Geregan, M'Gergaine, M'Gar-gan, MacGerrigan, MacGarrigan, Garrigan, Gargan ; 'son of ʒeᴀᴩʒᴀ́n' (dim. of ʒeᴀᴩʒ, fierce) ; an old surname in Meath and Cavan ; also Ó ʒeᴀᴩʒᴀ́1n, q.v.

Mac ʒeᴀᴩᴏ́1ᴅ—V—M'Gerode, M'Garrott, MacGarrett ; 'son of Gerald' (a Norman personal name) ; in use in Cork, but very rare.

Mac ʒéıḃeᴀɴɴᴀıʒ—IV—MacGeaveny, MacKeaveny, MacKeaveney, Geaveny, Keaveny, Keaveney, Keveney; 'son of ʒéıḃeᴀɴɴᴀċ' (fettered); originally a Fermanagh surname; found at the end of the 16th century in Sligo and Mayo; now common in Connacht, but very rare in Ulster.

Mac ʒeıʀḃle—IV—M'Keribly, (Kirby); 'son of ʒeıʀḃle'; the name of an old Mayo family from whom the townland of Carrowkeribly, in the parish of Attymas, is so called. It is still extant in Co. Mayo, but always angl. Kirby.

Mac ʒıḃ—V—Gibson; 'son of Gib,' short for Gilbert.

Mac ʒıḃne—IV—M'Gebenay, MacGibney; 'son of ʒıḃne' (grey-hound); an extremely rare surname. It survives in Co. Down.

Mac ʒıleáın—IV—Magillane, MacGillan, MacGillen; 'son of ʒıleáın' (dim. of ʒeᴀl, bright); a var. of Mac ʒeᴀláın, q.v.

Mac ʒılḃeıʀᴄ, Mac ʒıllıḃeıʀᴄ—V—M'Gillebert, M'Gilbert, Gilbertson, Gilberson, Gilbert; 'son of Gilbert.'

Mac ʒıoḃúın—V—M'Gibbone, M'Gibowne, MacGibbon, MacGibben, MacKibbon, O'Kibbon, Gibbonson, Fitz Gibbon, Fitzgibbon, Gibbons, Gibbins, Gibbings, Gibbon; 'son of Gibbon' (a dim. of Gilbert); the name (1) of a branch of the Burkes of Connacht who were seated to the west of Croagh Patrick, in Co. Mayo; and (2) of a Co. Limerick family, usually said to be a branch of the Geraldines, but really descended from Gilbert de Clare who, at the beginning of the 14th century, possessed the manor of Mahoonagh and many other valuable estates in Co. Limerick. The head of this family was known as the White Knight.

Mac ʒıollᴀ—IV—MacGill, Magill, Gill; a shortened form of some surname commencing with Mac ʒıollᴀ.

Mac ʒıollᴀ ᴀċᴀıḋ—IV—Kilahy, Killackey. V. Mac ʒıollᴀ ᴀıᴛċe.

Mac ʒıollᴀ ᴀḋᴀṁɴáın—IV—M'Eleownane, M'Eleownan, MacAlonan, MacLennan, MacLennon; 'son of ᵹ ıoᴸᴸᴀ ᴀ᷈ᴅᴀᵐᴺᴀıᴺ' (servant of Adamnan) ; a Co. Down surname ; also a Scottish surname, said to be the origin of Mac Lennan of Rosshire.

ᵐᴀᴄ ᵹ ıoᴸᴸᴀ ᴀıᴺᴅᴦ́eıs—IV—MacLandrish, Gillanders, [Anderson] ; 'son of ᵹ ıoᴸᴸᴀ ᴀıᴺᴅ᷈ᴩeıᴦ' (servant of St. Andrew) ; a common surname in Rathlin Island, probably of Scottish origin.

ᵐᴀᴄᵹ ıoᴸᴸᴀ ᴀıᴄᴄe—IV—Kilahy, Killackey ; 'son of ᵹ ıoᴸᴸᴀ ᴀıᴄᴄe' (cf. ó ᵐᴀoᴸ ᴀıᴄᴄe).

ᵐᴀᴄ ᵹ ıoᴸᴸᴀ ᴀᴺ ᴄᴸoıᵹ—IV—Bell ; most probably a 'translation' of the English surname Bell.

ᵐᴀᴄ ᵹ ıoᴸᴸᴀ ᴀᴦᴦᴀıᴄ—IV — *M'Elearra, M'Ellearay, M'Elearie, M'Elahray, M'Ellary, M'Calerie, M'Calery,* MacAlarry, MacAlary, MacClary, MacAleery, Mac-Eleary, MacCleary, MacCleery, MacLary, MacLeary, MacLeery, (?) Callery, (?) Calliry, Collery, (Cleary, Clarke) ; 'son of ᵹ ıoᴸᴸᴀ ᴀᴩᴩᴀıᴄ' (probably for ᵹ ıoᴸᴸᴀ ᴀᴺ ᴩᴀıᴄ, the prosperous youth) ; the name of an old Sligo family, the head of which was sometimes chief of the barony of Leyny ; probably of the same stock as the O'Haras. A branch of the family settled with the O'Haras in Co. Antrim, sometime before the end of the 16th century. The name is now often in-correctly angl. Cleary and Clarke.

ᵐᴀᴄ ᵹ ıoᴸᴸᴀ ᴃᴀ́ᴺ—IV—*M'Gilbane, M'Gillevane,* Mac-Gilvane, MacKilwane, MacIlwaine, McElvaine, Mac-Elwain, MacElwane, Macklewaine, Gillivan, Kilbane, and, by translation, White, Whyte ; 'son of ᵹ ıoᴸᴸᴀ ᴃᴀ́ᴺ' (white, or fair youth) ; the name of a family of the Uí Fiachrach, in Co. Sligo, who formerly possessed the townland of Lisnarawer, in the parish of Dromard. O'Donovan found the family still in that neighbour-hood, but the name was always made White in English. It is also a Scottish surname, usually angl. MacIlvaine, but sometimes Whyte.

ᵐᴀᴄ ᵹ ıoᴸᴸᴀ ᴃeᴀᴦᴀıᵹ—IV—*M'Gilleverie,* Gilvarry, Gel-varry ; 'son of ᵹ ıoᴸᴸᴀ ᴃeᴀᴩᴀıᵹ' (servant of ᴃeᴀᴩᴀᴄ, or St. Barry) ; an old, but always very rare, Connacht surname. It still survives.

Mac ʒıollᴀ ᵬıʒ—IV—Kilbeg; 'son of ʒıollᴀ ᵬeᴀʒ' (little fellow); a rare Galway surname.

Mac ʒıollᴀ ᵬRᴀᴄᴀ—IV—MacGillivray; 'son of ʒıollᴀ ᵬRᴀᴄᴀ'; (servant of doom, devotee of the Judgment); a Scottish surname.

Mac ʒıollᴀ ᵬRıʒᴅe—IV—*M'Gillebridy*, *M'Gillvrid*, *M'Killbridy*, *M'Elvride*, MacGillbride, MacKilbride, Macklebreed, MacBride, Gillbride, Kilbride, &c.; 'son of ʒıollᴀ ᵬRıʒᴅe' (servant of St. Brigid). This surname was formerly found in many parts of Ireland, notably in the North, where it is still common under the angl. form of MacBride, having been shortened in the spoken language to Mac 'ᴀ ᵬRıʒᴅe, for which cf. Mac ʒıollᴀ ᵬuıᴅe below.

Mac ʒıollᴀᵬuıᴅe—IV—*M'Gilleboy*, *M'Gilboy*, *M'Gillavoye*, *M'Gillewy*, MacGillowy, Magillowy, MacGilwee, MacGilvie, MacGilloway, MacGilway, MacKilvie, MacKelvey, MacIleboy, MacIlboy, MacIlbwee, MacIlwee, MacElwee, MacElvee, Mackilbouy, MacAboy, MacAvoy, MacEvoy, MacAvey, Gilboy, Gilvoy, Gilloway, Gilwee, Gilbey, Kilboy, Killby, Kilby, Kilvey, Ilwee, &c.; 'son of ʒıollᴀ ᵬuıᴅe' (yellow lad). This surname originated in Co. Mayo, but in the 16th century it was common in Sligo, Leitrim and Donegal. Many of the name at present in Ireland are, no doubt, of Scottish origin. The popular form was often Mac 'ᴀ ᵬuıᴅe; hence the angl. forms MacAvoy, &c.

Mac ʒıollᴀ Cᴀıllín—IV—*M'Gillechallyn*, Kilcullen, Kilgallen, Kilgallon; 'son of ʒıollᴀ Cᴀıllín' (servant of St. Caillin); a rare surname, scarcely found outside the counties of Sligo and Mayo.

Mac ʒıollᴀ Cᴀınnıʒ—IV—MacIlhaney, Gilheany, &c.; a var. of Mac ʒıollᴀ Coınnıʒ, q.v.

Mac ʒıollᴀ Cᴀıs—IV—Kilcash; 'son of ʒıollᴀ cᴀr' (curly youth); the name of an old Sligo family who formerly possessed the townland of Ballykilcash, in the barony of Tireragh. It still survives, but is exceedingly rare.

Mac ʒıollᴀ Cᴀoıᴄ—IV—*M'Kilchy*, *M'Ilky*, Kilkey;

'son of ᵹɪoʟʟᴀ cᴀoċ' (the blind youth) ; a very rare surname.

mᴀc ᵹɪoʟʟᴀ Cᴀoɪn, mᴀc ᵹɪoʟʟᴀ Cᴀoɪne—IV—*M'Gillekyne, M'Gillychyna, M'Gillechyny,* Kilcoyne, Coyne ; 'son of ᵹɪoʟʟᴀ cᴀoɪn' (the gentle youth) or 'son of ᵹɪoʟʟᴀ Cᴀoɪne' (servant of St. Caoine, gentleness) ; apparently only different forms of the same surname which, in the 16th century, was found chiefly in Co. Leitrim and in the neighbourhood of Dublin. mᴀc ᵹɪoʟʟᴀ Cᴀoɪne was probably the original, and mᴀc ᵹɪoʟʟᴀ cᴀoɪn an apocopated form. The same peculiarity, it will be noticed, attaches to Ó mᴀoʟ-cᴀoɪn and Ó mᴀoʟ Cᴀoɪne, q.v.

mᴀc ᵹɪoʟʟᴀ Cᴀʀʀᴀɪᵹ—IV—*M'Gillecharry, M'Gillecarie,* MacGilharry, MacIlharry, MacElharry, MacHarry ; 'son of ᵹɪoʟʟᴀ cᴀʀʀᴀċ' (the scabbed, or bald youth) ; originally a Roscommon surname, but long since removed to Sligo.

mᴀc ᵹɪoʟʟᴀ Cᴀᴛᴀ́ɪn—IV—*M'Gillycattan,* MacIllhatton, MacIlhatton, MacElhatton, Maclehatton, MacClatton, MacHatton, Hatton ; 'son of ᵹɪoʟʟᴀ Cᴀᴛᴀ́ɪn' (servant of St. Catan) ; a well-known Ulster surname.

mᴀc ᵹɪoʟʟᴀ Cᴀᴛᴀɪʀ—IV—*M'Gillacahir, Macgillachair, M'Gillahare,* MacIlhar, MacIlhair, MacElhair, (?) MacGlare, Kilcar, Kilcarr, Carr ; 'son of ᵹɪoʟʟᴀ Cᴀᴛᴀɪʀ' (servant of St. Cathair) ; a Donegal surname.

mᴀc ᵹɪoʟʟᴀ Ceᴀʟʟᴀɪᵹ—IV—*M'Gillakelly, M'Killekelly,* MacKilkelly, Gilkelly, Killkelly, Kilkelly, Kelly ; 'son of ᵹɪoʟʟᴀ Ceᴀʟʟᴀɪᵹ' (servant of St. Ceallach) ; the name of a family of the Ui Fiachrach Aidhne, in Co. Galway, who are of the same stock as the O'Clerys and derive their descent from Guaire the Hospitable, King of Connacht in the 7th century. Their chief resided at the castle of Cloghballymore, in the parish of Killeenavarra. A branch of the family settled in Mayo soon after the Anglo-Norman invasion.

mᴀc ᵹɪoʟʟᴀ Céɪʀe—IV—*M'Gillykeyry, M'Gillicherie, M'Ilkerry,* Kilkeary, Keary ; 'son of ᵹɪoʟʟᴀ Céɪʀe' (servant of St. Ciar) ; once a common surname in many parts of Ireland, especially in Co. Cork. It has now almost disappeared, being probably disguised under the angl. forms of Keary, Carey and Carr. mac ʒ͘ioʟʟᴀ Ceᴀpᴀ, which, according to Father O'Growney, is the Irish for Carr in parts of Co. Galway, is probably a corruption of the present surname.

mac ʒ͘ioʟʟᴀ Ciᴀᴘᴀ́in—IV—*M'Gellecherane*, *M'Gillaghiran*, MacIlherron, MacKlern; 'son of ʒ͘ioʟʟᴀ Ciᴀᴘᴀ́in' (servant of St. Kieran); a rare Midland surname.

mac ʒ͘ioʟʟᴀ Cʟᴀoin—IV—*M'Gillecloyne*, *M'Gillacleyne*, *M'Killeclyne*, Kilcline, Cloyen, Cline, Clyne; 'son of ʒ͘ioʟʟᴀ cʟᴀon' (deceitful youth); an old surname in Roscommon and Longford.

mac ʒ͘ioʟʟᴀ Coiʟʟe—IV—*M'Gillechoile*, *M'Gillechill*, MacIlhoyle, MacElhoyle, MacElhill, (?) Hoyle, (?) Hoyles, (?) Woods; 'son of ʒ͘ioʟʟᴀ Coiʟʟe' (a name given probably to one born on New Year's Day—not from coiʟʟ, a wood); a rare Ulster surname; perhaps sometimes erroneously 'translated' Woods, and sometimes shortened to Hoyle or Hoyles.

mac ʒ͘ioʟʟᴀ Coiʟʟín—IV—Kilcullen; a var. of mac ʒ͘ioʟʟᴀ Cᴀiʟʟín, q.v.

mac ʒ͘ioʟʟᴀ Cóimóeᴀó—IV—*M'Killicomy*, *M'Gilcomy*, Comey; 'son of ʒ͘ioʟʟᴀ Cóimóeᴀó' (servant of the Lord); an old Cavan surmane.

mac ʒ͘ioʟʟᴀ Coinniʒ—IV—*M'Gillekennie*, *M'Gilleconnye*, *M'Gillacunye*, *M'Kilkennie*, MacElkenny, MacIlkenny, MacIlhenny, MacElhenny, MacElhinney, Ilhoney, MacElhoney, MacAloney, MacAlunny, MacAleney, MacAlinney, MacLehenny, Mac Lehinney, MacLhinney, MacLinney, MacLuney, Kilkenny, Ilhinney, Kenny, Heaney, &c.; 'son of ʒ͘ioʟʟᴀ Coinniʒ' (servant of St. Canice, or Kenny). This surname, in the 16th century, was found in Roscommon, Leitrim, Donegal and Down.

mac ʒ͘ioʟʟᴀ Coiscʟe—IV—*M'Gillecosgelie*, *M'Gilkuskley*, *M'Gilkuslie*, Cuskley, Cushley, Cuskelly, (Costello, Cosgrave, Cosgrove); 'son of ʒ͘ioʟʟᴀ coircʟe' (lad of the left leg) ; an old surname in Fermanagh, Monaghan and Offaly ; sometimes, but less correctly, written mᴀc ᵹ101ᴌᴀ ċoıρcuᵹ.

mᴀc ᵹ101ᴌᴀ ċoᴌm, mᴀc ᵹ101ᴌᴀ ċoᴌuım—IV— *M'Gillecolme, M'Gillacollom*, MacElholm ; ' son of ᵹ101ᴌᴀ ċoᴌuım ' (servant of St. Columcille) ; a very rare and scattered surname.

mᴀc ᵹ101ᴌᴀ ċomᴀ́ın—IV—*M'Gillecoman*, Kilcommons; ' son of ᵹ101ᴌᴀ ċomᴀ́ın ' (servant of St. Coman) ; a rare Connacht surname.

mᴀc ᵹ101ᴌᴀ ċomᴅ́ᴀın, v. mᴀc ᵹ101ᴌᴀ ċomᵹᴀın.

mᴀc ᵹ101ᴌᴀ ċomᵹᴀıᴌᴌ—IV—*M'Gillachomhaill, M'Gillacoell, M'Gilleghole, M'Gillecole*, MacCole, MacCool, Glihool, Cole ; ' son of ᵹ101ᴌᴀ ċomᵹᴀıᴌᴌ ' (servant of St. Comgall) ; a Donegal surname.

mᴀc ᵹ101ᴌᴀ ċomᵹᴀın—IV—*M'Gillchoan*, MacIlhone, MacElhone, MacCowan, Cowan ; ' son of ᵹ101ᴌᴀ ċomᵹᴀın ' (servant of St. Comgan) ; also mᴀc ᵹ101ᴌᴀ ċomᴅ́ᴀın ; a rare Ulster surname ; also a Scottish surname.

mᴀc ᵹ101ᴌᴀ ċoscᴀıʀ—IV—*M'Gillcosker, M'Gilcosker*, Cosker, Coscor, Cusker, Cuscor (Cosgrave) ; ' son of ᵹ101ᴌᴀ ċoρcᴀıρ ' (lad of victory, victorious youth).

mᴀc ᵹ101ᴌᴀ ċʀíosᴄ—IV—*M'Gillachrist, M'Gillacrist, M'Gillechreaste*, Gilchrist, Guilchrist, Gilcrist, Gilchrist, Gilchreest, Gilcriest, Gilcrest, Kilchrist, Kilchriest, Kilcreest, Kilgrist ; ' son of ᵹ101ᴌᴀ ċρíosᴄ ' (servant of Christ) ; a scattered surname, found chiefly in Leitrim, Longford, Westmeath and Carlow ; now also common in Ulster, where it is probably of Scottish origin.

mᴀc ᵹ101ᴌᴀ ċuᴅᴀ—IV—MacGillacuddy, MacGillecuddy, MacGillycuddy, MacIllicuddy, MacElcuddy, MacElhuddy ; ' son of ᵹ101ᴌᴀ moċuᴅᴀ ' (servant of St.Mochuda, another name for St. Carthage of Lismore); the name of an old Kerry family, a branch of that of O'Sullivan More. The head of the family is known as MacGillycuddy of the Reeks.

mᴀc ᵹ101ᴌᴀ ċuıᴌᴌe—IV—Kilcooley, Cooley ; ' son of

ʒιοʟʟᴀ ṁoċúιʟʟe' (servant of St. Mochuille) ; a rare
Co. Clare surname.

mᴀc ʒιοʟʟᴀ ꝺé—IV—*M'Gillegea, M'Gillegey, M'Gilgea,*
Gildea, Kildea, Kilday, Gay ; ' son of ʒιοʟʟᴀ ꝺé '
(servant of God) ; an old Donegal surname ; now also
in Mayo.

mᴀc ʒιοʟʟᴀ ꝺeᴀcᴀιn—IV—*M'Gilledogher, M'Gill-
dogher,* MacDacker, Harden, Hardy, Harman, Harmon;
' son of ʒιοʟʟᴀ ꝺeᴀcᴀιn ' (hard youth) ; probably a
var. of mᴀc ꝺáιʟ-ɼe-ꝺoċᴀιn, q.v.   In the 16th century,
it was peculiar to Co. Roscommon.

mᴀc ʒιοʟʟᴀ ꝺoṁnᴀιʒ—IV—MacGilldowney, MacIldowney, MacEldowney, MacDowney, Gildowney, Ildowney, Downey ; ' son of ʒιοʟʟᴀ ꝺoṁnᴀιʒ ' (servant
of the Lord) ; a rare Ulster surname.

mᴀc ʒιοʟʟᴀ ꝺoncᴀ—IV—*M'Gilledoroughe,* (?) Mac-
Ilderry, MacElderry, MacEldrew ; ' son of ʒιοʟʟᴀ
ꝺoɼcᴀ ' (the dark youth, ꝺoɼcᴀ, dark-complexioned).

mᴀc ʒιοʟʟᴀ ꝺuḃcᴀιʒ—IV—MacGilldowie, MacIldowie ; ' son of ʒιοʟʟᴀ ꝺuḃcᴀιʒ ' (servant of ꝺuḃcᴀċ,
the name of two Irish saints) ; an Ulster surname.   I
can find no early instance.

mᴀc ʒιοʟʟᴀ ꝺuιḃ—IV—*M'Gilleduff, M'Gilleguffe,
M'Gilduff, M'Kilduffe,* MacIlduff, MacElduff, Gilduff,
Kilduff, Duff, Black ; ' son of ʒιοʟʟᴀ ꝺuḃ ' (the black
youth) ; the name (1) of a Cavan family, the head of
which was formerly chief of the barony of Tully-
garvey ; (2) of a family in Ui Maine, the head of which
was chief of Caladh, in the barony of Kilconnell, Co.
Galway ; and (3) of a family of the Ui Fiachrach race
in Co. Sligo.   The name was also common in other
parts of Ireland and in Scotland.

mᴀc ʒιοʟʟᴀ ꝺuιnn—IV—*M'Gillydwine, M'Gillyedwn,*
MacElgunn, MacElgun, Gilgunn, Kildunn, Kilgunn,
Dunne, Gunn ; ' son of ʒιοʟʟᴀ ꝺonn ' (the brown
youth) ; an old, but rare, Sligo surname.

mᴀc ʒιοʟʟᴀ eáιn—IV—MacAlean, MacClean, Mac-
Clane, MacLean, MacLaine, MacLane, &c. ; ' son of
ʒιοʟʟᴀ eáιn ' (servant of St. John) ; the name of a

numerous and powerful clan in the western Highlands of Scotland, whose patrimony from a remote period was the island of Mull. Some of this race settled in the 17th century in the North of Ireland.

ℳᴀᴄ ʒɪᴏʟʟᴀ éᴀɴáɪɴ, v. ℳᴀᴄ ʒɪᴏʟʟᴀᴘáɪɴ.

ℳᴀᴄ ʒɪᴏʟʟᴀ éᴀᴚɴᴀ—IV—*M'Elearney*, MacAlearney, MacElerney, MacLerney; 'son of ʒɪᴏʟʟᴀ éᴀᴘɴᴀ' (servant of Earna); an old, but rare Monaghan surname.

ℳᴀᴄ ʒɪᴏʟʟᴀ éᴀᴚɴáɪɴ—IV—*M'Ellerinane*, MacAlernon, MacClearnon, MacClernon, MacClarnon, Mac-Clernand, MacLernon, MacLarnon, MacLorinan, Mac-Larenon, MacLarinon; 'son of ʒɪᴏʟʟᴀ éᴀᴘɴáɪɴ' (servant of St. Ernan); the name of an old Co. Down family who, in the 12th century, were chiefs of Clann Ailebra. At the end of the 16th century, it was still common in that county, but was then also found in parts of Connacht; also a Scottish surname.

ℳᴀᴄ ʒɪᴏʟʟᴀ éᴀꜱᴘᴜɪʒ—IV—*M'Gillaspick*, *M'Gilla-specke*, MacGillespie, Gillespie, Gillaspy, Gillespy, Galesby, Glaspy, Glashby, Clusby, Aspig, Bishop, &c.; 'son of ʒɪᴏʟʟᴀ éᴀᴘᴘᴜɪʒ' (the bishop's servant).

ℳᴀᴄ ʒɪᴏʟʟᴀ éóɪɴ—IV—*M'Ellowen*, *Magloan*, Magloin, Maglone, Malone, MacAloon, MacAloone, MacClune, MacLoone, MacLune, Gilloon, Gloon, and, by 'trans-lation' Monday, Munday; 'son of ʒɪᴏʟʟᴀ éóɪɴ' (servant of St. John); a scattered Ulster surname, found chiefly in Donegal and Tyrone. The popular pronunciation was often ℳᴀᴄ ʒɪᴏʟʟᴀ ʟúɪɴ, which caused the last syllable to be mistaken for ʟᴜᴀɪɴ, Monday; hence the 'translated' forms Monday, Munday. V. ℳᴀᴄ ʒɪᴏʟʟᴀ éáɪɴ.

ℳᴀᴄ ʒɪᴏʟʟᴀ ꜰᴀᴏʟáɪɴ—IV—*M'Gillallen*, MacClellan, MacLellan, MacClelland, MacLeland, Gilfillan, Gil-filland, Kilfillan, Gillilan, Gilliland, Gellan, Gelland, Cleeland, Clelland, Clellond, Leland, &c; 'son of ʒɪᴏʟʟᴀ ꜰᴀᴏʟáɪɴ' (servant of St. Faolan); the name of a family of the Ui Fiachrach race in Co. Sligo; still extant at the beginning of the 17th century, but has apparently since died out. It is, however, at present common in Ulster where it is of late Scottish origin.

Mac ʒɪoʟʟɑ ꝼeɑrʒɑ—IV—MacIlhargy; 'son of ʒɪoʟʟɑ ꝼeɑrʒɑ' (servant of St. Fearga); doubtless a Leitrim surname, but extremely rare.

Mac ʒɪoʟʟɑ ꝼɪnꝺeɪn—IV—*MacGillafyndean*, Mac-Alinden, MacAlingen, MacLinden, Glendon, Linden, Lindon; 'son of ʒɪoʟʟɑ ꝼɪnꝺeɪn' (servant of St. Finnian); a var. of Mac ʒɪoʟʟɑ ꝼɪnneɪn, q.v.

Mac ʒɪoʟʟɑ ꝼɪnn—IV—*M'Gilleffin*, MacGilpin, Gilpin; 'son of ʒɪoʟʟɑ ꝼɪonn' (the fair youth); the name of a family of the Ui Fiachrach who were formerly seated in the townland of Laragh, in the parish of Dromard, Co. Sligo.

Mac ʒɪoʟʟɑ ꝼɪnneɪn—IV—*M'Gillinnion*, *M'Elinnan*, *M'Elynan*, *M'Linnen*, MacAlinion, MacAlinon, Mac-Aleenan, MacLennan, Gillinnion, (Leonard), &c.; 'son of ʒɪoʟʟɑ ꝼɪnneɪn' (servant of St. Finnian); a var. of Mac ʒɪoʟʟɑ ꝼɪnꝺeɪn, q.v. This family, which O'Donovan calls the most royal in Ireland, belongs by race to the Cinel Conaill, and is a branch of the ancient and once powerful family of O'Muldory, being descended from Giolla Finnein O'Muldory who flourished towards the end of the 11th century. Their patrimony was Muinntear Feodachain, on the borders of Fermanagh and Donegal, and their chief was some-times styled 'Lord of Loch Erne.' The family is still numerous in the west of Co. Fermanagh, but the name is often angl. Leonard, which disguises its origin. This is also a Scottish surname, but the Scots write it Mac Gill'innein.

Mac ʒɪoʟʟɑ ꝼɪonnɑɪn—IV—*M'Gullyneane*, Gillinan (Leonard); 'son of ʒɪoʟʟɑ ꝼɪonnɑɪn' (servant of St. Fionnan); very rare.

Mac ʒɪoʟʟɑ ꝼɪonnꞇɑɪn—IV—MacAlindon, MacClin-ton, MacLindon, MacLinton, Linton, Lindon; 'son of ʒɪoʟʟɑ ꝼɪonnꞇɑn' (servant of St. Fintan); a sur-name of Scottish origin, well known in Ulster.

mac ʒιοιιᴀ ϝιοnnᴄóʒ—IV—MacClintock, MacClyntock, MacLintock (Lindsay); 'son of ʒιοιιᴀ ϝιonnᴄóʒ'; the name of a Scottish family who settled in Donegal towards the end of the 16th century.

mac ʒιοιιᴀʒᴀιn—IV—M'Gillegane, M'Gillgan, M'Illegane, MacGilligan, MacElgan, Gilligan, Gilgan; 'son of ʒιοιιᴀʒᴀn' (dim. of ʒιοιιᴀ, youth, lad); an Ulster surname, peculiar to Antrim, Derry and Donegal.

mac ʒιοιιᴀ ʒᴀιᴚᴂ—IV—M'Gilligariffe, Kilgarriff, Kilgrew, Kilcrow, (?) Kilgore, (?) Kilcourse; 'son of ʒιοιιᴀ ʒᴀᴩᴂ' (the rough lad); a rare Connacht surname.

mac ʒιοιιᴀ ʒᴀnnᴀιn—IV—Kilgannon; 'son of ʒιοιιᴀ ʒᴀnnᴀιn' (servant of Gannan); a rare West Connacht surname.

mac ʒιοιιᴀ ʒeᴀιᴚᴚ—IV—M'Gullygar, Gilgar, Kilgar; 'son of ʒιοιιᴀ ʒeᴀᴩᴩ' (short, low-sized youth).

mac ʒιοιιᴀ ʒeιṁᴚιᴂ—IV—M'Gullyghirry, MacAlivery, Winter, Winters; 'son of ʒιοιιᴀ ʒeιṁᴩιᴂ' (winter lad; ʒeιṁᴩeᴀᴂ, winter).

mac ʒιοιιᴀ ʒéιᴚ—IV—M'Kilger, Kilker; 'son of ʒιοιιᴀ ʒéᴀᴩ' (sharp lad); an old, but extremely rare, Mayo surname. Andrew Mac Gillegheir was Abbot of Cong in the 13th century.

mac ʒιοιιᴀ ʒιᴀιs—IV—M'Gilleglas, Green; 'son of ʒιοιιᴀ ʒιᴀᴩ' (grey lad; ʒιᴀᴩ, grey, green); a very rare Donegal surname, angl. Green, according to O'Donovan.

mac ʒιοιιᴀ ʒᴚιnn—IV—Gilgrinn; 'son of ʒιοιιᴀ ʒᴩιnn' (bearded-lad, or humorous-lad); very rare.

mac ʒιοιιᴀ ʒuᴀιᴀ—IV—M'Gillegowly M'Gilgowlye, M'Kellogulie, Gillowly, Gillooly, Gilooly, Gilhooly, Killooley; 'son of ʒιοιιᴀ ʒuᴀιᴀ' (glutton, Ir. ʒuᴀιᴀ, Lat. gula, gluttony); the name of a branch of the family of O'Mulvey in the east of Co. Leitrim, where it is still common. It has been corrupted to mac ʒιοιιᴀ ϝúιιιʒ, q.v.

mac ʒιοιιᴀ ʒuιᴚm—IV—M'Gilgrim, MacIlgorm; 'son

of ʒ1oLLᴀ ʒoꞃm ' (the blue youth) ; a rare North-east Ulster surname.

mᴀc ʒ1oLLᴀ 1ᴀsᴀċtᴀ—IV—*M'Gillesachta*, *M'Gillisachta*, *M'Gillysaghtie*, MacLysaght, Lysaght, Lysat ; 'son of ʒ1oLLᴀ 1ᴀꞃᴀċtᴀ' (strange youth) ; a well-known Clare surname. The family is said to be a branch of the O'Briens, descended from ᴅoṁnᴀLL mᴏ́ꞃ ᴏ́ bꞃ1ᴀ1n, King of Munster (1163-1194).

mᴀc ʒ1oLLᴀ 1osᴀ—IV—*M'Illiosa*, MacIleese, Mac-Aleese, MacAleece, MacAlish, MacLeese, MacLees, Maclise, MacLeesh, MacGleish, MacCleish, Gilleece, Gillis, &c. ; 'son of ʒ1oLLᴀ 1oꞃᴀ' (servant of Jesus) ; an Ulster surname ; also a Scottish surname.

mᴀc ʒ1oLLᴀ Lᴇ́1t—IV—*M'Gillalea*, *M'Gilleley*, Killelea, Killyleigh ; 'son of ʒ1oLLᴀ L1ᴀt' (grey youth ; L1ᴀt, grey) ; a scattered surname, but found chiefly in Co. Galway.

mᴀc ʒ1oLLᴀ Lᴜᴀ1tꞃ1nn—IV—*M'Gillylworin*, *Mc-Gilliworyne*, Gilloran, Killoran ; 'son of ʒ1oLLᴀ Lᴜᴀ1tꞃ1nn' (servant of St. Luaithrenn) ; a rare Sligo surname.

mᴀc ʒ1oLLᴀ mᴀ1t—IV—Goodman [Goodbody, Good-fellow] ; 'son of ʒ1oLLᴀ mᴀ1t' (the good youth) ; a rare Ulster surname. I can find no early instance.

mᴀc ʒ1oLLᴀ mᴀoᴅᴏ́ʒ—IV—MacElvogue ; 'son of ʒ1oLLᴀ mᴀoᴅᴏ́ʒ' (servant of St. Mogue).

mᴀc ʒ1oLLᴀ mᴀo1L—IV—*M'Gullemoyell*, *M'Gilleweele*, MacIlmoyle, MacIlmoil, MacElmoyle, Macklemoyle, MacElmeel, MacMeel ; 'son of ʒ1oLLᴀ mᴀoL' (the bald lad) ; an Ulster surname. It was also in use at one time in Co. Clare.

mᴀc ʒ1oLLᴀ mᴀ́ꞃtᴀ1n—IV—*M'Gillamartin*, *M'Gillavartin*, *M'Gilmartin*, Gilmartin, Guilmartin, Kilmartin, Martin ; 'son of ʒ1oLLᴀ mᴀ́ꞃtᴀ1n' (servant of St. Martin) ; the name of an Ulster family who were anciently chiefs of Cinel Fearadhaigh. In the 16th century, it was common in Monaghan, Sligo and Roscommon, and was also found in many other parts of Ireland. It is, no doubt, in many instances now disguised under the angl. form of Martin.

Mac Ʒiolla Meana—IV—MacElvenna, MacElvenny, MacElvany, MacIlvany, Gilvany; 'son of Ʒiolla Meana' (servant of Meana); an Antrim surname.

Mac Ʒiolla Meaᚱnóʒ—IV—M'Gillavearnoge, Warnock; 'son of Ʒiolla Meaᚱnóʒ' (servant of St. Mearnog); an old Co. Down surname, now shortened to Mac Meaᚱnóʒ, q.v.; also in use in Scotland, where it is Englished Graham.

Mac Ʒiolla Micil—IV—M'Gillemichell, MacMichael, MacMeel, Michael, Mitchell; 'son of Ʒiolla Micil' (servant of St. Michael); the name of a family who were anciently chiefs of Clann Conʒaile, in Co. Fermanagh, but dispossessed by the Maguires in the 15th century. It is said to have been angl. Mitchell. Mac Ʒiolla Micil is also a Scottish surname.

Mac Ʒiolla Mín—IV—M'Gillavyne, M'Gilvine, MacIlveen, MacElveen, MacKilveen; 'son of Ʒiolla Mín' (gentle, tender youth); a Co. Down surname.

Mac Ʒiolla Miᚱ—IV—M'Gilver, M'Gilmer, Gilmer, Gilmor; 'son of Ʒiolla Meaᚱ' (the merry, lively youth); the name of an old family of the Ui Fiachrach race in Co. Sligo, formerly seated in the townland of Finnure, in the barony of Tireragh.

Mac Ʒiolla Mocuda, v. Mac Ʒiolla Cuda.

Mac Ʒiolla Muiᚱe—IV—M'Gilleworry, M'Gilmurry, M'Gilmore, MacIlmurray, MacElmurray, MacKilmurray, MacMurray, Kilmurry, Kilmary, Kilmore, Gilmore, Gilmour, Gilmor, Gilmer, Murry, Murray; 'son of Ʒiolla Muiᚱe' (servant of Mary); the name of a family in Co. Down who were chiefs of Ui Derca Cein, in the barony of Castlereagh. They are a branch of the family of O'Morna, formerly lords of Lecale, being descended from Ʒiolla Muiᚱe Ó Moᚱna, lord of Lecale, whose death is recorded in the Annals of the Four Masters at the year 1276. The name is also in use in Scotland, where it is angl. Morrison (i.e., Muire's son).

Mac Ʒɪoʟʟᴀ ɴᴀ ɴᴀoṁ—IV—*M'Gillinaneave, M'Giller-neve, M'Gillernae*, MacElnea, MacAneave, MacAnave, and, by 'translation' Ford, Forde; 'son of Ʒɪoʟʟᴀ ɴᴀ ɴᴀoṁ' (servant of the saints); a West Connacht surname; corrupted to Mac Ʒɪoʟʟᴀṗɴᴀċ, and erroneously translated Ford, Forde, from the resemblance of the final syllable to ᴀċ, a ford.

Mac Ʒɪoʟʟᴀ ɴᴀ ɴeᴀċ—IV—*M'Gillyneneagh*, Gilnagh; 'son of Ʒɪoʟʟᴀ ɴᴀ ɴ-eᴀċ' (lad of the horses); the name of a family of the Ui Fiachrach in Co. Sligo. It still survives, but is extremely rare.

Mac Ʒɪoʟʟᴀ ṗᴀoʀᴀɪʒ—IV—*M'Gillephadrick, M'Gilla-patrick, M'Kilpatrick*, MacGilpatrick, MacIlpatrick, MacIlfatrick, MacElfatrick, MacIlfederick, MacElfedrick, Gilpatrick, Kilpatrick, Kirkpatrick, Fitzpatrick; 'son of Ʒɪoʟʟᴀ ṗᴀoʀᴀɪʒ' (servant of St. Patrick). The principal family of this name are the MacGillapatricks, or Fitzpatricks, of Ossory, who took their name from Ʒɪoʟʟᴀ ṗᴀoʀᴀɪʒ, son of Donnchadh, lord of Ossory, in the 10th century. In early times they ruled over the entire of Co. Kilkenny and part of the present Leix, but after the Anglo-Norman invasion they were greatly encroached upon by the Butlers and other English settlers in Kilkenny, and their patrimony was limited to the barony of Upper Ossory. Branches of the family settled in Clare, Cavan, Leitrim, and other parts of Ireland. In 1541, Brian Mac Giolla Patrick was created Baron of Upper Ossory. There appears to have been also a Scottish family of this name.

Mac Ʒɪoʟʟᴀ ṗeᴀoᴀɪʀ—IV—*M'Gillepedire*, Gilfedder, Kilfeder, Kilfedder, Gilfeather; 'son of Ʒɪoʟʟᴀ ṗeᴀoᴀɪʀ' (servant of St. Peter); a rare Sligo surname.

Mac Ʒɪoʟʟᴀ ṗóɪʟ—IV—*M'Gillaphoill, M'Gillfoile, M'Killphoill*, MacGilfoyle, Gilfoyle, Guilfoyle, Kilfoyle, (Powell); 'son of Ʒɪoʟʟᴀ ṗóɪʟ' (servant of St. Paul); the name of an ancient family in Ely O'Carroll, who were chiefs of Clann Choinlegan, near Shinrone, in Offaly.

mac 51oLLaRáin—IV—*Magillerane,* Gilleran, Gilrain, Gilrane, Killeran, Kilrain, Kilrane; 'son of 51oLLa Eanáin '(servant of St. Enan) ; a corruption of mac 51oLLa Eanáin.

mac 51oLLa RIaÚa15—IV—*M'Gillereogh, M'Calreogh, M'Calreaghe, M'Callerie,* MacGillreavy, MacGilrea, MacElreavy, MacIlravy, MacElreath, MacElwreath, MacIlwraith, MacIlrea, MacAreavy, MacArevy, Gallery, Callery, Killery, Kilgray, Gray; 'son of 51oLLa puaÚaċ' (the grey youth, from puaÚaċ, grey, brindled) ; the name (1) of a family of the Ui Fiachrach, seated at Creaghaun, in the parish of Skreen, Co. Sligo ; and (2) of a Clare family who were servants of trust to the Earls of Thomond, and held the castle of Craigbrien, in the parish of Clondagad. The family is still in Thomond, but the surname is now always angl. Gallery. In the midlands, it was sometimes made Callery, and sometimes translated Gray. Kilgray is a half translation. mac 51oLLa puaÚai5 is also a Scottish surname. According to Dr. MacBain, it is angl. MacIlwraith, &c.

mac 51oLLa Rónáin—IV—O *Kilronane,* Kilronan ; 'son of 51oLLa Rónáin' (servant of St. Ronan) ; the name of a bishop of Clogher, early in the 13th century. At the beginning of the 17th century, it appears as O Kilronane in Co. Cavan. It has always been very rare.

mac 51oLLa RuaÚáin—IV—*M'Gillaroyn,* MacElrone ; 'son of 51oLLa RuaÚán' (servant of St. Ruadhan).

mac 51oLLa RuaiÚ —IV— *M'Gillarowe, M'Gillaroe, M'Gillaroye, M'Killeroe, M'Killroy,* MacGillroy, Mac-Gilroy, MacIlroy, MacElroy, MacAlroy, MacLeroy, Gilroy, Kilroy, Ilroy, Roy, and, by 'translation,' King; 'son of 51oLLa puaÚ' (red youth) ; the name of a Fermanagh family, the head of which resided at Ballymackilroy, in the parish of Aghalurchur, near Lough Erne. In the 16th century, it was common in Down, Cavan, Roscommon and Offaly. It is sometimes erroneously translated King.

mac ʒιοԼԼᴀ Sᴀ́ṁᴀιS — IV — MacClavish ; 'son of ʒιοԼԼᴀ ƒᴀ́ṁᴀιɼ' (votary of pleasure); a rare Ulster surname, perhaps now obsolete.

mac ʒιοԼԼᴀ SeᴀċԼᴀιnn — IV — M'Gillaghlin, Mac-Glaughlin, MacClachlin, MacClafflin, Clafflin ; 'son of ʒιοԼԼᴀ SeᴀċԼᴀιnn' (servant of St. Secundinus) ; the name of an old Meath family who were lords of Southern Breagh until soon after the Anglo-Norman invasion, when they lost their power and were dispersed. The present angl. forms of mac ʒιοԼԼᴀ SeᴀċԼᴀιnn cannot be distinguished from those of mᴀʒ LοċԼᴀιnn, mᴀʒ LᴀċԼᴀιnn, q.v. ; but that the family is still extant is shown by the variant mᴀc ʒιοԼԼᴀ ᴄSeᴀċԼᴀιnn, q.v.

mac ʒιοԼԼᴀ Seᴀnᴀ́ιn, mac ʒιοԼԼᴀ Sιοnᴀ́ιn — IV — M'Gilsenane, M'Gylsinan, MacGillshenan, Gilshenan, Gilshenon, Gelshinan, Gilsenan, Gunshinan, Gilson, (Nugent, Leonard) ; 'son of ʒιοԼԼᴀ Seᴀnᴀ́ιn' (servant of St. Senan) ; a common surname in Meath, Cavan and Tyrone, but now often disguised under the angl. forms of Nugent and Leonard, especially the former. mᴀʒ Uιnnɼeᴀnᴀ́ιn (q.v.) is a corruption. See also mᴀc ʒιοԼԼᴀ ᴄSeᴀnᴀ́ιn which is a variant.

mac ʒιοԼԼᴀ Sᴄeᴀɼᴀ́ιn — IV — M'Gilsteffan, Stephens ; 'son of ʒιοԼԼᴀ Sᴄeᴀɼᴀ́ιn' (servant of St. Stephen) ; a rare surname in Leix, &c.

mac ʒιοԼԼᴀ Sᴜ́ιԼιʒ — IV — M'Gillehowly, Gilhooly, &c. ; a corruption of mac ʒιοԼԼᴀ ʒᴜᴀԼᴀ, q.v. It is so written in the Annals of Loch Cé and by the Four Masters.

mac ʒιοԼԼᴀ ᴄSeᴀċԼᴀιnn — IV — M'Kintaghlin, M'Taghlin, MacA'Taghlin, MacTaghlin, MacTaghlan, (Houston), &c. ; a var. of mac ʒιοԼԼᴀ SeᴀċԼᴀιnn, q.v. It was still a Meath surname in the 16th century ; now found in Donegal, where it is sometimes angl. Houston.

mac ʒιοԼԼᴀ ᴄSeᴀnᴀ́ιn — IV — Giltenane, Giltinane, Giltenan, Shannon ; a var. of mac ʒιοԼԼᴀ Seᴀnᴀ́ιn, q.v. This form of the name is in use in Co. Clare, where it is corrupted to Ó CιԼԼᴄɼeᴀ́ιn and often angl. Shannon.

mac ᵹΙΟΙ̇Ιᴀ Uι̇Ο̇ιR—IV—*M'Elyre*, MacAleer, MacLear, MacLure, MacClure; 'son of ᵹιΟΙ̇Ιᴀ Ο̇Ο̇ᴀρ' (the pale youth; Ο̇Ο̇ᴀρ, dun, pale); a rare Armagh surname. Eachdonn Mac Giolla uidhir was Primate of Armagh early in the 13th century. It is also a Scottish surname.

mac ᵹιRR ᴀη ᴀΟ̇ᴀᏚᴄᴀιR, mac ᵹιRR ᴀη ᴀᵹᴀᏚᴄᴀιR—VII—*MacGirrenagastyr, MacGirrenastyr, MacGirrnaystar*, Nestor; 'son of the short-(man) of the halter'; now shortened to mac ᴀη ᴀΟ̇ᴀρᴄᴀιρ, q.v.; the name of an old Thomond family who were followers of the O'Loghlens of Burren.

mac ᵹΙᴀιᏚι̇η, mac ᵹΙᴀᏚᴀ́η—IV—MacGlashin, MacGlashan, Green; 'son of ᵹΙᴀιρι̇η,' or 'ᵹΙᴀρᴀ́η' (dim. of ᵹΙᴀρ, grey, green); a West Ulster surname.

mac ᵹΙeᴀΟ̇Rᴀ—IV—MacGladery, MacGladdery, MacGlathery, Gladdry; 'son of ᵹΙeᴀΟρᴀ'; an Ulster surname.

mac ᵹΙᴜ́ιη—IV—*M'Clone, M'Cloane, M'Clowne, MacCloone*, Clune; 'son of ᵹΙᴜ́η' (knee, probably a 'pet' form of ᵹΙᴜ́ηιᴀρᴀιηη, iron-knee, or ᵹΙᴜ́ηᴄρᴀΟ̇ηᴀ, corn-crake knee); the name of an old Thomond family who were seated at Ballymacloon, in the parish of Quin, Co. Clare, where the name is still well known.

mac ᵹΟΟ̇ᴀ, mac ᵹΟΟ̇ᴀηη, v. mac ᴀη ᵹΟΟ̇ᴀηη.

mac ᵹΟᶠRᴀΟ̇ᴀ, mac ᵹΟᶠRᴀιΟ̇—V—*M'Goffrie*, MacCaffrey, &c.; a var. of mac ᵹᴀρρᴀιΟ̇, q.v. See also mac ᵹΟᴄρᴀιΟ̇.

mac ᵹΟιΙΙ—IV—Giles, Gyles; 'son of ᵹΟΙΙ'; a rare Galway surname.

mac ᵹΟιᏚΟeᴀΙΟ̇, mac ᵹΟιᏚΟeᴀΙΟ̇ᴀιᵹ, v. mac ΟιρΟeᴀΙΟ̇, mac Οιρ̇ΟeᴀΙΟ̇ᴀιᵹ.

mac ᵹΟRmᴀ́ιη—IV—*M'Gormane*, , *M'Cormaine*, MacGorman, Gorman, (O'Gorman); 'son of ᵹΟρmᴀ́η' (dim. of ᵹΟρm, blue); the name of a Leinster family who were formerly lords of Ui Bairche, in the barony of Slievemargy, in the south-east of the present Leix. Soon after the Anglo-Norman invasion, they were driven from this territory and settled, some in

Monaghan, others in the barony of Ibrickan, in West Clare, where they became very numerous. The head of the Clare branch of the family was marshal of O'Brien's forces. Even before the end of the 16th century, the name had spread into the neighbouring counties of Galway, Tipperary and Limerick. O'Gorman has been adopted in modern times, but incorrectly, as the angl. form by some of the name in Munster; but MacGorman, the more correct form, is still retained in the North.

mac ʒoꞂmʒail, mac ʒoꞂmʒaile—IV—*M'Gormoyle*, *M'Cormally*, MacCormilla, Gormley; 'son of ʒoꞂmʒal' (blue-valour); a rare surname; perhaps a var. of Ó ʒoꞂmʒail, q.v.

mac ʒoṫꞂaóa, mac ʒoṫꞂaió—V—*M'Gorrie*, *M'Gorhae*, *M'Gorhy*, MacGorry, MacGurry, MacCorry, MacCurry, Godfrey, Gorry, Corry, Curry, (?) Curoe; 'son of Godfrey'; older mac ʒoṫꞂꞂaóa, mac ʒoṫꞂaió; a var. of mac ʒoꞂꞂaóa, mac ʒoꞂꞂaió and mac ʒaꞂꞂaió, q.v.

mac ʒꞂáinne—IV—Granny, Grant; probably for maʒ Ꞃáiʒne, q.v.

mac ʒꞂaiṫ v. maʒ Ꞃaiṫ.

mac ʒꞂeaʒaiꞂ—V—MacGregor, Gregory; 'son of Gregory'; the name of a famous Scottish clan.

mac ʒꞂiꝼin—V—*M'Griffine*, MacGriffin; 'son of Griffin' (a personal name of Welsh origin, the same as the Lat. Rufinus).

mac ʒꞂioʒaiꞂ, v. mac ʒꞂeaʒaiꞂ, of which it is a variant.

mac ʒꞂioʒaiꞂ—V—MacGreer, Greer, Grear, Grier, Grierson; 'son of Gregory'; a var. of mac ʒꞂeaʒaiꞂ, q.v.

mac ʒuaʒáin, mac ʒuaicín, mac ʒuaiʒín—IV—MacGuigan, MacGuiggan, MacGuckian, MacQuiggan, MacGoogan, MacCookin, MacGuckin, MacWiggan, MacWiggin, Pigeon, Pidgeon; a corrupt form of mac eoċaióín, q.v.

mac ʒuaiꞂe—IV—MacQuarrie; 'son of ʒuaiꞂe'; a Scottish surname.

Mac háicéiꝺ—V—*M'Hacket*, *M'Hackett*, Hackett ;
'son of Hacket' (a Norman personal name) ; the
name of a tiny family who were formerly seated at
Island M'Hackett, Co. Galway. V. háicéiꝺ.

Mac hanraoi, Mac hannraoi—V—*M'Hanry*, Mac-
Henry, MacHarry, Fitzhenry, Fitzharris, Feeharry,
Henry, Harris, Harrison, &c. ; 'son of Henry' ; a
var. of Mac Annraoi and Mac Éinri, q.v.

Mac haol—V—*M'Caele*, *M'Keale*, *M'Heale*, *M'Howell*,
MacHale, Hale, Hales, Howell, Howels, &c. ; 'son of
Howel' (a Welsh personal name) ; a surname of Welsh
origin, in use in various parts of Ireland. In Co.
Mayo, it is not infrequently heard, side by side with
Mac héil (q.v.), as the Irish for MacHale. The
diphthong ao has, however, the Munster sound of
ae, the final l being broad. The collective plural is
also peculiar, viz., Clann taol, pronounced Clann
tael (l broad).

Mac héil—V—*M'Keale*, MacHale ; 'son of Howel' ;
a var. of Mac haol, q.v. ; the name of a family,
apparently of Welsh origin, who settled in Tirawley,
in the 12th or 13th century ; now always angl. Mac-
Hale, and probably confused with the native name
Mac Céile, q.v.

Mac hob—V—Hobson, Hopson, Hobbs ; 'son of Hob'
(a 'pet' form of Robert).

Mac hoibicín, v. Mac Oibicín.

Mac hoirbín—V—Harbinson, Harbison, Harbeson,
&c. ; 'son of Harbin' (dim. of Herbert). V. Mac
hoireabáirꝺ.

Mac hoireabáirꝺ, Mac hoireabáirꝺ—V—
M'Harbard, *M'Herbert*, [Fitzherbert, Herbertson, Her-
bison] ; 'son of Herbert' ; an Irish patronymic assumed
by the family of Delamare in Co. Westmeath. V
hoireabáirꝺ.

Mac hoiste—V—*M'Hostie*, *M'Hoste*, Hosty, &c. ;
'son of Hodge' (a 'pet' name for Roger). V. Mac
Oirte.

Mac hoisticín—V—Hodgkins, Hodgkinson, &c. ; 'son

of Hodgkin' (dim. of Hodge, i.e., Roger).   V. mᴀc
Oırᴄıcín.

mᴀc ĥuıᵹín—V—*M'Hugin*,   *M'Hugyn*,   Hugginson,
Higginson; 'son of Hugin' (a dim. of Hugh).

mᴀc ĥunꝼRᴀıᵭ—V—MacHanfry,   Machanfry,   Humphries, Humphreys, &c.; 'son of Hunfrid.' V.
Unꝼꝶᴀıᵭ.

mᴀc ıᴀᵹó—V—*M'Kiego*, *M'Kigo*, *M'Egoe*, Iago, Igo,
Igoe; 'son of ıᴀᵹó' (a Spanish form of James); an
old Roscommon surname; locally supposed, according to O'Donovan, to be of Spanish origin.
V. ıᴀᵹó.

mᴀc ıᴀᵹóᵹ—V—*M'Kigog*, Igo, Igoe; 'son of ıᴀᵹóᵹ'
(a dim. of ıᴀᵹó); a var. of mᴀc ıᴀᵹó (q.v.) in Co. Roscommon.   It is still in use, but has now no distinct
English equivalent.

mᴀc ıᴀın—V—MacKean; 'son of John'; a var. of mᴀc
eᴀın, q.v.

mᴀc ınneıꝶᵹe—VII—*M'Ineirie*, *M'Enerie*, *M'Keneyry*,
MacKeniry, MacEniry, MacNeiry, MacKennery, Mac-
Kenery, MacEnery, MacEnry, Kiniry, &c.; 'son of
ınneıꝶᵹe' (the rising, early riser); the name of an
ancient family in Co. Limerick, who for many centuries were chiefs of Corca Muicheat, now Corcomo-
hide, an extensive district in the south of the county.
The chief resided at Castletown MacEniry, where the
ruins of his castle are still to be seen.   Though greatly
encroached upon by the Anglo-Norman settlers,
the MacEnirys contrived to retain a considerable
portion of their ancient patrimony down to the revolution of 1688.

mᴀc ınnꝶeᴀᴄᴛᴀıᵹ—IV—*M'Inrightighe*,   *M'Enrichty*,
M'Kinraghty, MacEnright, Inright, Enraght, Enright; 'son of ınnꝶeᴀᴄᴛᴀᴄ' (unlawful); a var. of mᴀc
ıonnꝶᴀᴄᴛᴀıᵹ, q.v.

mᴀc ıoʟꝶᴀᴄáın, Eagleton.   I can find no early instance
of this surname, and suspect that it is merely an
attempt to find an Irish equivalent for the English
surname Eagleton.

mac íomair, mac íomair—V—*M'Eiver*, *M'Kewer*, MacIvor, MacIver, MacKiver, MacKiever, MacKiver, MacKever, MacKevor, MacKeever, MacKeevor, Mac-Cure, MacIvers, Ivers, Eivers, Keevers, &c. ; ' son of Ivarr ' (an old Scandinavian personal name) ; a common surname in the North of Ireland, apparently of Scottish origin. See mag íomaiṗ which is the form in use in the West.

mac íomaiṘe, Montgomery, Gomory, Ridge. This seems to be merely an attempt to represent the sound of the English surname Montgomery. Ridge is an attempted translation, on the erroneous supposition that the latter part of the surname is the Irish word ' íomaiṗe,' a ridge. In West Clare it is pronounced maġomṗaċ.

mac íonṁáin—IV—Love ; ' son of íonṁáin ' (beloved).

mac íonnraċtaiġ—IV—*M'Enraghtie*, *M'Kenraghta*, *M'Kenraght*, MacEnright, Enraght, Inright, Enright ; ' son of íonnṗaċtaċ ' (unlawful) ; a well-known Munster surname of Dalcassian origin. In the spoken language, it is pronounced 'a Ciúṗṗaċta.'

mac íosóc, mac íosóġ—V—*M'Isock*, *M'Kysoke*, *M'Kyssock*, *M'Kysog*, MacKissock, MacCussack, Kissack, Cusack ; ' son of Isaac ' ; the name of an old Thomond family ; found also in Galway, Roscommon and Donegal. It was also an old surname in the Isle of Man, where it is still represented by Kissack.

mac íseóġ—V—*M'Ishocke*, Cusack ; a var. of mac íoṗóṡ, q.v. ; still in use in Co. Galway.

mac laḃraḋa—IV—*M'Lawry*, MacLavery, MacClory, Clowry ; ' son of laḃṗaiḋ ' (spokesman, advocate) ; a rare Ulster surname.

mac laḃráin—IV—*M'Loyrane*, *M'Loran*, Cloran ; ' son of laḃṗán ' (a dim. of laḃṗaiḋ) ; an old Cavan surname ; always very rare.

mac laḃrainn—V—MacLaurin, MacLauren, Mac-Laren, [Lawrenson, Lawrinson, Laurison, Lawson], &c. ; ' son of Laurence ' ; a Scottish surname. V. laḃṗanc.

mac Laḃráis—V—*M'Laurence*, [Lawrenson, Lawrinson, Lawson, &c.]; 'son of Laurence.' V. Laḃrár.

mac Laċlainn—V—MacLachlin, MacLachlan, Mac-Laughlin, MacClachlin, MacClaughlin, MacClafflin, Clafflin, &c. 'son of Loċlainn' (a name of Norse origin); the Scottish and Ulster form of mac Loċlainn, q.v. The Scottish clan of this name was seated at Strathlachlan in Argyleshire. V. mac Laóṁainn.

mac Laóṁainn, mac Laȝmainn—V—MacLamond, MacLimont, MacClamon, MacClymon, MacClimond, MacClimont, MacClemonts, MacClement, MacClymonds, Clymonds, Climons, Lammon, Lamond, Lamont, Limond, Limont, &c.; 'son of Laȝmann' (a Norse personal name, meaning 'lawman' or 'lawyer'; found in Domesday Book as Laghemann and Lagman in the time of Edward the Confessor); the name of a Scoto-Irish family in Argyleshire. They are of the same stock as the MacSweenys and MacLachlins, all three families being descended, according to Mac-Firbis (p. 125), from three sons of Donnfléiḃe Ó Néill.

mac Laiḋiȝ, v. mac Laoiḋiȝ.

mac Laitḃeartaiȝ—IV—*M'Lagherlie*, MacLaverty, MacClafferty, MacCleverty; 'son of flaitḃeartaċ'; a var. of mac flaitḃeartaiȝ, q.v. The omission of the initial f when aspirated is not uncommon.

mac Laitiṁ—IV—*M'Glave*, MacLave, MacClave, Claffey, Claffy, and, by 'translation,' Hand; 'son of flaiteaṁ'; a var. of mac flaitiṁ and maȝ Laitiṁ, q.v. The surname was so pronounced as to be mistaken for mac Láiṁ; hence the erroneous translation Hand.

mac Laoiḋiȝ—IV—MacLea, MacLee, Lea, Lee, Leigh; 'son of Laoiḋeaċ' (poetic); the name of an old family in Leix.

mac Lataiȝ, Claffey, Clafry, &c.; a var. in the spoken language of mac Latiiṁ, q.v.

mac Leannaċáin—IV—*M'Clanaghan*, *M'Claneghan*, MacLenaghan, MacLenahan, MacLeneghan, Mac-

Lenighan, MacLennon, MacClenaghan, MacClenahan, MacCleneghan, MacClenighan, MacClennon, Clenaghan, &c.; 'son of Leannaċán' (dim. of Leannaċ, cloaked, mantled); an Ulster surname.

mac Leóiꝺ—V—MacLeod, MacCleod, MacCloud; 'son of Leóꝺ' (the Norse 'Ljotr,' ugly); the name of a well-known Scottish clan, once powerful in Lewis and Harris. Some of them settled in Ireland in the 16th century.

mac Liam—V—Wilson; 'son of Will' (a 'pet' form of William).

mac Loċlainn—V—MacLochlin, MacLoghlin, MacLoughlin, Loughlin, &c., (Loftus); 'son of Loċlainn' (a name of Norse origin); the name of the senior branch of the northern Ui Neill. Before the 13th century, they were the most powerful family in Ulster. They were seated in Inishowen, where the name is still common. A branch of this family settled in Mayo in the 17th century. It would appear that there was also a family of the name in Co. Leitrim, who were followers of the O'Rourkes. This surname is to be distinguished from Ó Maoilṫeaċlainn (q.v.), which is now also angl. MacLoughlin. V. Maᵹ Loċlainn.

mac Loineáin—IV—MacLennan, MacLennon, (Leonard); 'son of Lonán'; a rare Galway surname.

mac Loinᵹseaċáin—IV—M'Linchechane, Lynchehan; 'son of Loinᵹreaċán' (dim. of Loinᵹreaċ); a rare Donegal surname; apparently an alias for mac Loinᵹriᵹ, q.v. See also Ó Loinᵹreaċáin.

mac Loinᵹsiᵹ—IV—M'Kilinsie, MacClinchy, Clinchy; 'son of Loinᵹreaċ' (having, or belonging to, a fleet); a var. of Maᵹ Loinᵹriᵹ, q.v.; a Donegal surname.

mac Lúcáis—V—MacLucas, (?) MacCluggage, Clucas; 'son of Lucas' (an old form of Luke).

mac Luᵹaꝺa—IV—M'Lewe, M'Lowe, Lowe; 'son of Luᵹaiꝺ.'

mac Luinᵹe—IV—MacLung, MacClung; 'son of Lonᵹ' (?); a rare surname of Scottish origin.

Mac Luirg—IV—MacLurg, MacClurg; 'son of Lurg'; a rare surname of Scottish origin.

Mac Mavóc, Mac Mavóg—V—*M'Vadocke, M'Vadog, M'Vadick, M'Vadige,* Vaddock, Wadock, Waddock, Wadick, Waddick, Weadock, Weadick, Weddick, Maddox; 'son of Madoc,' or 'Madog' (a Welsh personal name); the name of an old Wexford family, said to be descended from Murcav na nGaeveal, the brother of Diarmaid Mac Murrough; usually angl. Maddox. V. Mavóc.

Mac Magnuis, Mac Magnusa—V—*M'Manish, M'Moenassa,* MacManus, MacManis, Manus, Manasses; 'son of Magnur' (Lat. 'Magnus,' a name adopted by the Northmen in honour of Charlemagne —Carolus Magnus—and by them introduced into Ireland, angl. Manus); the name (1) of a Roscommon family, descended from Magnur, son of Turlough Mor O'Connor, King of Ireland, who was slain in the year 1181, formerly seated in Tirhoohil; and (2) of a Fermanagh family, descended from Magnur, son of Donn Maguire, chief of Fermanagh, who died in 1302. The head of this family lived at Senadh Mic Maghnusa, now Belle Isle, in Lough Erne. The name is often pronounced Mac Maonuir, or Mac Maonura.

Mac Maicín—IV—*M'Makine, M'Macken,* MacMackin, Mackin, Macken; 'son of Maicín' (youth, dim. of mac, a son); a Donegal surname.

Mac Máige—V—*Mackmawe,* MacMay, Mawe, May, Mea; 'son of May' (short for Maheu, i.e., Matthew); a var. of Mac Máigeóc, Mac Máigeóg, q.v.

Mac Máigeóc, Mac Máigeóg—V—*MacMajoke, M'Maoge, M'Maogh-Condon, M'Mawige, M'Maug, Mackmawe-Condon,* MacMay, Mawe, May, Mea, [Condon]; 'son of Mayoc' or 'Mayog' (dim. of Maheu, the Norman-French form of Matthew); a patronymic surname assumed by a branch of the family of Condon in East Cork and Waterford. The present angl. forms are derived from the shortened form, Mac Máige, q.v.

Mᴀc Mᴀ́ɪᵹɪᴜ́—V—Mahew; 'son of Maheu' (or Matthew); the name of a Mayo family, probably an offshoot of the Barretts, among whom Maheu was a common name; extremely rare.

*Mᴀc Mᴀɪne—IV—M'Many, M'Mane, Mayne, Maynes; 'son of Mᴀɪne.'

Mᴀc Mᴀ́ɪʀᴄɪ́n—V—M'Martin, [Fitzmartin], Martin, Marten, Martyn; 'son of Martin'; the name of a branch of the O'Neills of Tyrone.

Mᴀc Mᴀɪᴄɪ́s—V—M'Mahishe, M'Mahise, Mathias; 'son of Matthias.'

Mᴀc Mᴀnᴀɪnn—IV—M'Mannan, M'Mannian, Mac-Mannon, MacMannion; apparently a shortened form of Mᴀc Mᴀnᴀnnᴀ́ɪn, q.v.; a Donegal surname.

Mᴀc Mᴀnᴀnnᴀ́ɪn—IV—M'Maynanan; 'son of Mᴀnᴀnn-ᴀ́n' (the name of an ancient Irish sea-god); a rare Donegal surname; now obsolete, or shortened to Mᴀc Mᴀnᴀɪnn, q.v.

Mᴀc Mᴀoɪʟᴅᴜ́ɪn—IV—M'Molydon, MacIldoon; 'son of Mᴀoʟᴅᴜ́ɪn' (chief of the fort); a rare Ulster surname. V. Mᴀc Mᴀoʟᴅᴜ́ɪn.

Mᴀc Mᴀoɪʟɪ́n—IV—M'Myline, MacMillin, MacMillen; 'son of Mᴀoɪʟɪ́n' (dim. of Mᴀoʟ, bald); a var. of Mᴀc Mᴀoʟᴀ́ɪn, q.v.

Mᴀc Mᴀoɪʟɪ́osᴀ—IV—(?) M'Myllis, Malise, Mellis; 'son of Mᴀoʟ ɪosᴀ' (servant of Jesus). This surname, which was borne by an Archbishop of Armagh towards the close of the 13th century, is probably now obsolete in Ireland, but survives in Scotland, angl. Malise and Mellis.

Mᴀc Mᴀoɪʟɪʀ—V—M'Miler, M'Meyler, M'Moiler, Mac-Moyler, Meyler; 'son of Meyler' (a Welsh personal name). V. Mᴀoɪʟɪʀ.

Mᴀc Mᴀoʟᴀ́ɪn—IV—M'Mowllane, M'Moylan, Mac-Mullan, MacMullen, MacMullin, MacMullon, Mac-Millan, MacMillen, MacBlain, Mullin, Mullins, &c.; 'son of Mᴀoʟᴀ́n' (dim. of Mᴀoʟ, bald). In the 12th century, Mᴀc Mᴀoʟᴀ́ɪn was lord of Gaileang Breagh, in the north of the present Co. Dublin, but in later ages the name has been confined to North-East Ulster. There is also a Scottish mac maoláin.

mac maolcoluim—IV—Malcolmson, Malcomson, Malcolm ; 'son of maolcoluim' (servant of St. Columcille) ; a surname of Scottish origin.

mac maolcraoibe—IV—M'Elchrive ; 'son of maolcraoibe' (chief of Craob, a place-name) ; a rare Ulster surname, now probably obsolete. V. Ó maolcraoibe.

mac maoldúin—IV—M'Muldowne ; a var. of mac maoildúin, q.v.

mac maoltuile—IV—M'Multully. V. mac maoltuile.

mac maoltuile — IV — M'Cultully, M'Cuntully, M'Cantully, M'Ethwille, MacAtilla, Tully, and, by 'translation,' Flood ; 'son of maoltuile' (devoted to the will, i.e., of God) ; older mac maoltuile, q.v. ; the name of a medical family in Co. Roscommon, who were hereditary physicians to the O'Connors of Connacht. The name has been long corrupted to mac an tuile and mac tuile, erroneously supposed to signify ' son of the flood,' and accordingly angl. Flood. V. Ó maoltuile.

mac maonaiġ — IV — M'Meeney, MacWeeney, (?) Queeney ; 'son of maonac' (wealthy, or dumb) ; the name of an ancient family of Moylurg, in Co. Roscommon.

mac maongail—IV—M'Mounell, M'Monnell, M'Monnyll, MacMonagle, MacMonegal, MacMonigal, MacMonigle, MacMunigal, Monagle ; 'son of maongal' (wealth-valour) ; an old Donegal surname. For unaspirated g, cf. mac Congail.

mac marcuis—V—M'Marcus, M'Markus, M'Markes, Marcus, Marks ; 'son of Mark' (Lat. Marcus) ; the name of an Antrim family who are probably a branch of the MacDonalds.

mac mata—V—M'Mahae, M'Maghie, M'Mah, MacMagh, MacMath, MacMa ; 'son of Matthew' ; a rare Ulster surname. V. mac mata.

ⅯⱰⱭⱭ ⅯⱰⱭⱭ—V—Mathewson, Matheson ; a var. of ⅯⱰⱭⱭ
ⅯⱰⱭⱭ ; a Scottish surname.

ⅯⱰⱭⱭ ⅯⱰⱭⱭⱭⱭ—IV—*Macmaghan*, Matheson ; a Scottish-
Gaelic var. of ⅯⱰⱭⱭ ⅯⱰⱭⱭⱭⱭⱭ, q.v.

ⅯⱰⱭⱭ ⅯⱰⱭⱭⱭⱭⱭⱭ—IV—*M'Mahowna*, *M'Maghowney*,
M'Maghone, *M'Machan*, MacMaghone, MacMaghon,
MacMaghen, MacMachon, MacMahon, MacMahan,
MacMann, Mahony, Mahon, (Matthews, Mathews) ;
' son of ⅯⱰⱭⱭⱭⱭⱭⱭ ' (bear). There are two great
Irish families of this name, viz. : the MacMahons of
Thomond, and the MacMahons of Oriel. The Mac-
Mahons of Thomond are a branch of the O'Briens,
and derive their name and descent from Mahon, son
of Murtagh More O'Brien, King of Ireland (1094-
1119). Their patrimony was Corca Bhaiscinn, which
comprised the baronies of Moyarta and Clonderlaw
in the south-west of Co. Clare. The last chief of the
name was accidentally killed by his own son at Bear-
haven in the year 1602. To this family belonged the
celebrated Marshal MacMahon, Duke of Magenta and
President of the French Republic. The MacMahons
of Oriel were formerly one of the most powerful
families in Ulster. On the decline of the O'Carrolls
in the 13th century, they became lords of Oriel, a
rank which they retained down to the reign of Elizabeth ; and even as late as the Cromwellian wars, they
had considerable possessions and power in Co. Monaghan. The last chief of the family was Hugh Mac-
Mahon who was arrested for complicity in the plot
to seize Dublin Castle in 1641, sent to the Tower of
London, and, in 1644, beheaded at Tyburn. Besides
distinguished chiefs, this family produced many
eminent ecclesiastics, three of whom successively
filled the primatial see of Armagh in the first half of
the 18th century.

ⅯⱰⱭⱭ ⅯⱰⱭⱭⱭⱭⱭⱭ, Wade, Waide ; probably an attempted translation of the English surname Wade ;
in use in Mayo, but rare.

ⅯⱰⱭⱭ ⅯⱰⱭⱭⱭⱭⱭ—IV—*M'Mannamie*, MacManamy, Mac-

Menamy, MacMenemy, MacMinamy ; ' son of ḿeᴀnmᴀ'
(courage, high-spirits) ; a var. of ḿᴀc ḿeᴀnmᴀn, q.v.

ḿᴀc ḿeᴀnmᴀ—IV—MacVanamy ; a var. of ḿᴀc
ḿeᴀnmᴀ, q.v.

ḿᴀc ḿeᴀnmᴀn—IV—MacManaman, MacManamon,
MacMenamon, MacMenamen, MacMenemen, Mac-
Menamin, MacMenimim, MacMeenamon, MacMenim,
Menemin, Merriman, Merryman ; ' son of ḿeᴀnmᴀ '
(courage, high-spirits) ; an old, and still common,
surname in Tirconnell ; also in Thomond.

ḿᴀc ḿeᴀrᴅᴀin—IV—M'Marran, M'Meraine, M'Meran,
MacVerran, MacFerran ; ' son of ḿeᴀpᴀn ' (dim. of
meᴀp, active, lively) ; originally a Westmeath surname,
but long since dispersed and now extremely rare.

ḿᴀc ḿeᴀrnóᵹ—IV—M'Varnocke, Warnock ; apparently short for ḿᴀc ᵹiollᴀ ḿeᴀpnóᵹ, q.v.

ḿᴀc ḿeiᵬric, ḿᴀc ḿeiric, ḿᴀc ḿiᵬric—V—Meyrick, Mayrick, Merrick ; ' son of Merick ' (the common
Welsh personal name Meurug) ; the name of a family
of Welsh origin who settled in the valley of Glenhest,
to the west of Glen Nephin, Co. Mayo ; now more
commonly ḿeiᵬpic, ḿeipic (q.v.) without ḿᴀc.

ḿᴀc mᴀᵬᴀċᴀin—IV—(?) MacMeechan, MacMeekan,
MacMeekin, &c. ; ' son of ḿiᴀᵬᴀċᴀn.'

ḿᴀc miċil—V—MacMichall, MacMichael, MacMighael,
MacMeel ; ' son of Michael ' ; not an old surname in
Ireland, unless short for ḿᴀc ᵹiollᴀ ḿiċil, which is
not improbable.

ḿᴀc miċilín—V—MacMichalin ; ' son of little Michael ' ;
perhaps the same as ḿᴀc miċil, q.v.

ḿᴀc míliᵬ—V—M'Meelye, M'Myle, M'Moylie, Miles,
Myles, Moyles ; ' son of Milo ' (a Norman personal
name). Cf. ḿᴀc ᴀn míliᵬ and miliᵬ.

ḿᴀc mílis—V—M'Myles, M'Myllis, Miles, Myles ; ' son
of Miles ' (a Norman personal name). Cf. miłir.

ḿᴀc ḿiolċon—IV—M'Melchon, MacIlchon, MacConn ;
' son of ḿiolċú ' (grey-hound) ; an old Fermanagh
surname. The ḿ of the second part of the surname
is now aspirated, and sometimes altogether dropped ;

hence the present angl. forms, MacIlchon and Mac-
Conn.

mac miolóit—V—*M'Milode*, *M'Mylod*, *M'Moyloyde* ;
' son of Milot ' (a dim. of Milo) ; probably not a family
name. V. miolóit.

mac mioluic—V—*M'Meleke*, *M'Moylek*, *M'Mulleack*,
Malick, Mulick, Mullock, Mulleague ; ' son of Miluc '
(a dim. of Milo ; cf. miolóit) ; a rare surname ; found
chiefly in Roscommon, Westmeath and Offaly.

mac mogRáin, mac mugRóin—IV—*M'Murrone*, Mac-
Murran, MacMurren, MacMouran, MacMorran, Mac-
Moran, MacMorin, MacMurrin ; ' son of mugrón '
(slave-seal) ; the name of a Co. Leitrim family who
were erenaghs of Killanummery, and apparently also
of a family in Ui Maine, Co. Galway. Like Ó mugróin (q.v.), mac mugróin was early corrupted to
mac mográin.

mac muirceartaig—IV—*M'Murihertie*, *M'Mirirtie*,
M'Moriertagh, *M'Mortagh*, *M'Miertagh*, *M'Murtough*,
M'Murthoe, *M'Morte*, MacMurtrie, MacMurtery, Mac-
Murtry, MacMurdy, MacMordie, MacMutrie, Mac-
Mrearty, MacBrearty, MacBrairty, MacMearty, Mac-
Merty, Murtagh, Mortagh, Murtaugh, Murdough,
Murdoch, Murdock, Murdow, Murtha, Murta, Murdy,
Murt, (Mortimer) ; ' son of muirceartac ' (sea-director,
navigator) ; a very common Irish patronymic which,
in many instances, has undoubtedly become a family
name ; also the name of a Scottish family in Argyle-
shire, some of whom have settled in Ulster. V. mac
muirceartaig.

mac muirceartaig---IV---*M'Urarthie*, MacCurdy, Mac-
Kurdy, MacKirdy ; a var. of mac muirceartaig,
q.v. See also mac cuarta.

mac muireaóaig—IV—*M'Murrey*, *M'Morrye*, Mac-
Murry, MacMorry, MacMorray, MacMurray, (Mac-
Morrow), Murry, Murray, (Morrow) ; ' son of muireaó-
ac ' (belonging to the sea, a mariner ; also a lord) ;
an old Breifney surname, still common in the district,
but generally angl. MacMorrow.

MAC ṀUIREAḊAIĠ—IV—*M'Murrie, M'Murry,* Currie, Curry; a var. in Co. Antrim of Mac Muireaḋaiġ, q.v.; dialectically Mac Ṁuiriċ. It is of Scottish origin.

MAC MUIRĠEASA, MAC MUIRĠIS—IV—*M'Morishey, M'Murrysse,* MacMorris, Morrissey, Morris; 'son of Muirġeas' (sea-choice, an ancient Irish personal name); a rare surname; to be distinguished from Mac Muiris, q.v.

MAC MUIRIS, MAC ṀUIRIS—V—*M'Maurice, M'Morrice, M'Morish,* MacMorris, Morrison, Fitzmaurice, Maurice, Morris, &c.; 'son of Maurice' (a name introduced by the Normans); the name (1) of a branch of the Geraldines in Kerry, who, as lords of Lixnaw, made a great figure in the history of that county; and (2) of a branch of the Prendergasts in Co. Mayo.

MAC MUIRIS RUAIḊ, MAC ṀUIRIS RUAIḊ—V—*M'Morish roe,* Morris-Roe, Morrisroe; 'son of red Maurice'; an old Roscommon surname. V. Mac Muiris.

MAC MUIRNIĠ—IV—*M'Murny, M'Morney, M'Mornie,* Murney; 'son of Muirneaċ' (a loveable person, or member of a troop); extremely rare.

MAC MUNNA, MAC ṀUNNA—IV—MacMunn, MacPhun; 'son of Munna' (i.e., Mo-Ḟionna, a 'pet' form of Fionnán); very rare.

MAC MURĊAḊA—IV—*M'Murroghowe, M'Moroghoe, M'Murphewe,* MacMurrough, MacMurrow, Morrowson, Murrough, Morrough, Morrogh, Murrow, Morrow, Murphy; 'son of Murċaḋ' (sea-warrior, a very common Irish personal name); the name of three distinct families in Ireland, viz.: Mac Murċaḋa of Leinster, Mac Murċaḋa of Muinntear Birn in Ulster, and Mac Murċaḋa of Clann Tomaltaigh in Connacht. The MacMurroughs of Leinster derive their name and descent from Murċaḋ, the grandfather of Dermot MacMurrough, and were long the most powerful family in Leinster, and one of the most powerful in Ireland. From Doṁnall Caoṁánaċ, the son of

Dermot MacMurrough, they took the surname of
Caoṁánac (q.v.), which is that by which they have
been known for centuries. The Ulster family of
Mac Muṙcaḋa was seated in Tyrone, and at the end
of the 16th century was numerous in that county.
Murphy appears to be the angl. form, at least, in many
instances ; O'Donovan gives it as MacMurray, which
I have failed to verify. The Connacht family of this
name was seated in Co. Roscommon.

Mac Muṙcaḋa Caoṁánac—IV—MacMurrough
Kavanagh ; i.e., MacMurrough of St. Cavan's (v.
Caoṁánac) ; the name of the head of the family of
MacMurrough, or Kavanagh, of Leinster. V. Mac
Muṙcaḋa.

Mac Muṙcaiḋ—IV—M'Murchie, M'Murphie, Mac-
Murchy, Murchison, Murphy ; a var. of Mac Muṙcaḋa
of Ulster. V. Mac Muṙcaḋa above.

Mac Muṙcáin—IV—M'Moroghon, M'Morroghin, Mac-
Moran, MacMorin, Murchan, Murkin, Morkin, &c. ;
' son of Muṙcaḋán ' (dim. of Muṙcaḋ).

Mac Muṙġaláin—IV—MacMurlan, Murland, Murtland,
Morland, Mortland, Moreland, &c. ; ' son of Muṙġal-
án ' (dim. of Muṙġal, sea-valour) ; a rare Ulster
surname, apparently of Scottish origin.

Mac Naoiṁín—IV—M'Nyvine, MacNiven, Nivin, Nevin,
Neven, Neavin, Nevins ; ' son of Naoiṁín ' (saintling,
dim. of naoṁ, a saint) ; a South Leinster and also a
Scottish surname. To be distinguished from Mac
Cnáiṁín, q.v.

Mac Náraḋaiġ—IV—MacNarry, MacNeary, Manary ;
' son of Nápaḋac ' (the noble one) ; a rare Ulster
surname.

Mac Naois, Mac Naosa—IV—M'Nyce, M'Nysse, Mac-
Niece, MacNeece, MacNeese, MacNeice, MacNish,
Manice, Mannice, Meneese, Miniece, Minnis, Minnish,
Kinnish, Kennish, Mannix, &c. ; ' son of Aonġus '
(one-choice, an ancient Irish personal name) ; a
dialectical form of Mac Aonġuir, Mac Aonġura,
q.v. ; in use in Ulster and the Isle of Man.

Mac neaċτain—IV—*M'Neaghtane*, MacNaghten, Mac-
Naghton, MacNaughten, MacNaughton, MacCracken,
MacNaught, MacNeight, MacKneight, (MacKnight),
MacNight, MacNite, Mannight, Menaght, Menautt,
Minett, Minnitt, &c. ; 'son of neaċτan' (the
pure one) ; a well-known Scottish surname from the
neighbourhood of Lochow. A branch of the family
settled in Co. Antrim, where it has flourished considerably. This family has produced many distinguished men.

Mac néiʋe—IV—MacNeigh, MacNeagh, MacNay, Mac-
Nea, MacNee ; 'son of nia' (champion) ; a Connacht
family ; probably a branch of the O'Mulconrys.

Mac neiʒill—V—*M'Nigeyll*, *M'Nygel*, Neilson, Nielson,
Nelson ; 'son of Njall' (a Norse form of the Ir. niall,
latinised Nigellus, and angl. Nigel).

Mac néill—IV—MacNeill, MacNeile, MacNeal, &c. ;
'son of niall' (champion) ; the name (1) of a Scottish
clan in Gigha and Barra, two islands off the coast of
Argyle, who were followers of the Lord of the Isles,
and to which belong probably the MacNeills of Antrim
and Derry ; and (2) of a branch of the Ui Fiachrach,
who were seated in Carra, Co. Mayo, where it is still
in use under the form of Maʒ Réill, q.v.

Mac niaʋ—IV—MacNea, MacNee, (?) Neeson ; 'son
of nia' (champion) ; a var. of Mac néiʋe, q.v. ; also
a Scottish surname.

Mac niallʒuis, Mac niallʒusa—IV—*M'Nellus*, Mac-
Nelis, MacEneilis, MacEnealis, MacNeilage, Manelis,
Nealis, Nelis ; 'son of niallʒur' (champion-choice) ;
the name of a West Ulster family, some of whom have
settled in Mayo.

Mac nic—V—Nixon ; 'son of Nick' (short for Nicholas).

Mac niocais—V—Nix, [Woulfe] ; 'son of Nicholas ; a
patronymic surname adopted by a branch of the
Woulfes in Limerick and Clare.

Mac niocláis—V—MacNicholas, Nixon, [Clausson,
Classon] ; 'son of Nicholas' ; a Mayo surname.

Mac niocóil, Mac niocoil—V—*M'Nichoell*, *M'Nicholl*,

MacNicol, MacNickle, Nicolson, Nicholson, Nicholl,
&c. ; ' son of Nicol ' (a form of Nicholas).

Mac nuaⱴaⱴ, mac nuaⱴac—IV—*M'Gnoude*, Mac-
Nutt, Noud, Nowd, (Conway) ; ' son of nuaⱴa ' (an
ancient Irish personal name, the name of a sea-divinity);
extremely rare.

Mac nuallán—IV—Nolan ; 'son of nuallán ' (dim.
of nuall, famous, noble) ; a common surname in Co.
Mayo, but I have failed to discover any early instance.

Mac óⱴa—V—*M'Odo*, *M'Ode*, *M'Codo*, *M'Cody*, Cody,
Coady, [Archdeacon] ; ' son of Odo ' or ' Otho ' (a
Teutonic personal name, introduced by the Normans) ;
a patronymic surname assumed by the family of
Archdeacon, in Co. Kilkenny.

Mac oibicín—V—Hobbikin, Hopkin, Hopkins, Hopkinson ; ' son of Hobkin ' (little Robert) ; a Mayo surname,
often pronounced ó Coibicín.

Mac oinseamáin, Kingston. I find this surname in
use in West Cork, but I have not been able to discover
any early instance, Irish or English.

Mac oisⱴealb, mac oisⱴealbaiᵹ—IV—*M'Cosdal-
lowe*, *M'Costellowe*, *M'Costalighe*, Costelloe, Costello,
Costellow, Costily, Costley, &c. ; ' son of oirⱴealb '
(Os-shaped, shaped like the god Os) ; a patronymic
surname assumed by the family of Nangle. It is
the earliest Anglo-Irish mac-surname recorded in the
Annals (A.D. 1193). It is also written mac ᵹoir-
ⱴealb, mac ᵹoirⱴealbaiᵹ and mac coircealbaiᵹ,
and has numerous variants in the spoken language.

Mac oisín—IV—MacCushen ; ' son of oirín ' (little deer,
dim. of or, a deer) ; an old Meath surname. V. maᵹ
oirín, which is probably the only form under which
it now survives.

Mac oisce—V—*M'Coisht*, *M'Coiste*, *M'Costy*, MacGusty,
Hosty, Hasty, &c. ; ' son of Hodge ' (a ' pet ' form of
Roger) ; the name of a Mayo family of Welsh origin,
so called from an ancestor named Hodge Merrick, who
was killed in 1272 ; also written mac hoirce, q.v.

Mac oisⱴicín, mac oisⱴiᵹín—V—*M'Costikine*, *M'Cos-*

tigine, M'Costegine, Costigan; ' son of Hodgkin ' (dim. of Hodge, i.e., Roger); often corruptly, in the spoken language, mac Corcaʒáin and Ó Corcaʒáin, q.v.; a family of note in Ossory; apparently not of English descent, but a branch of some one of the great Irish families of that district.

mac OISTÍn—V—Costin, Costen; ' son of Hodgin' (a dim. of Hodge), or perhaps 'son of Oirtín' (the Norse form of Augustine; cf. Ó hOirtín); in the spoken language Ó Coirtín.

mac OITIR—V—M'Cottyr, M'Cottir, MacCotter, Mac-Cottier, MacCottar, Cotter, Otterson; ' son of Ottar ' (a Norse personal name); the name of an old and respectable family, doubtless of Norse origin, seated at Carrigtwohil, near the city of Cork; also an Ulster surname; generally written mac Coitir, owing to the attraction of the c of mac over to the second part of the surname.

mac OSCAIR—IV—M'Cosquyr, M'Cowsker, M'Kuesker, MacOscar, MacUsker, MacCosker, MacCusker, Mac-Kusker, MacKuscar, (Cosgrove, Cosgrave); ' son of Oscar ' (a Teutonic personal name, found in Domes-day Book in the time of Edward the Confessor, or it may be from Orcar, a combatant, champion); an Ulster surname.

mac OSPAIC—V—MacCosbey; ' son of Orpac ' (the Norse Ospakr).

*mac OSRAIC—V—MacOstrich; probably ' son of Osric ' (an Anglo-Saxon personal name).

mac PÁTRAIC—V—M'Patrick, MacPhatrick, Mac-Fattrick, MacFettrick; ' son of Patrick '; a surname which came to us from Scotland.

mac PÁORAICÍn, mac PÁORAICÍn, mac PÁO-RAIʒÍn, mac PÁORAIʒÍn—V—M'Pattrickine, M'Padrykine, M'Padrigin, Fitzpatrick, Patrician, Parrican, Paragon; ' son of páoraicín ' (dim. of páoraiʒ or Patrick); very rare.

mac PÁIO—V—MacFate, MacFeat, Fade; ' son of Pate '

(a Scottish and North English form of Pat, or Patrick).
Cf. mac pároin.

mac pároin—V—*M'Paidin*, *M'Padine*, MacPaden, Mac-
Padian, MacPadden, MacPaddan, MacPadgen, Pattinson, Patterson, Pattisson, Paddison, Padian,
Patten, Payton ; ' son of Padin,' or ' Pattin ' (a dim.
of Patrick). V. pároin.

mac pároin—V—*M'Phaddin*, *M'Faddine*, MacPhadden,
MacFaden, MacFaddin, MacFadden, MacFeddan,
Faddin, Vadin, (Fagin, Fagan, Patterson), Padden,
Patten, (Cussane), &c. ; a var. of mac pároin, q.v. ;
a well-known surname in Ulster and in Mayo ; also a
Scottish surname.

mac páil—V—MacFall, MacFalls, MacVail, Vail ; ' son
of Paul ' ; a dialectal var. of mac póil, q.v.

mac partaláin, mac partaláin, mac pártaláin, mac pártaláin mac pártláin, mac
partlóin, mac parláin—V—*M'Parrhelan*,
M'Pharlane, MacParlin, MacParland, MacPartlan,
MacPartland, MacPartlin, MacPharland, MacFarlaine,
MacFarlane, MacFarland, MacBartley, MacBarklie,
Parlon, Partland, Bartley, &c. ; ' son of Bartholomew ' ; found chiefly in Tyrone, Armagh and Leitrim ; also a Scottish surname.

mac peadair—V—MacFeeters, Peterson, Petterson,
Peters, Petters ; ' son of Peter.'

mac peáircín—V—Parkinson, Parkins, Perkins ; ' son
of Peterkin ' (dim. of Peter).

mac peadruis—V—MacFetrish, MacPhettridge, Mac-
Fetridge, MacFettridge, MacFatridge, MacFattridge,
Fettridge ; ' son of Petrus ' (the Latin form of Peter) ;
the name of an Ulster family who are, not improbably,
an offshoot of the O'Breslins.

mac peice—V—*M'Peicke*, MacPeake, MacPake ; ' son of
peic ' (a var. of the Anglo-Saxon Pic) ; a rare
West Ulster surname.

mac piaraic, mac piaruic—V—*M'Feyrick*, *M'Fer-
rick*, Feerick ; ' son of Pieruc ' (dim. of Piers, or Peter) ;
a rare Connacht surname.

Mac Piaras—V—*M'Piers*, *M'Peirs*, *M'Pierce*, Pierson, Peirson, Pearson, Pierce, Pearse, &c. ; ' son of Piers ' (the Norman form of Peter). V. Piapar.

Mac Piaras—V—*M'Fearis*, MacFeerish ; ' son of Piers ' ; a var. of Mac Piapair ; very rare.

Mac Pib—V—*M'Phibbe*, Phipson, Phipps, Phibbs ; ' son of Phib ' (short for Philip).

Mac Pibín—V—*M'Fibbin*, Phippin, Phippen ; ' son of Phipin ' (a dim. of Philip). Cf. Mac Fibín.

Mac Pilib—V—*M'Philip*, *M'Phillip*, MacPhillips, Phillips, Philips, Philipson, Philson, &c.; ' son of Philip ' ; a common surname in Ulster and Connacht. V. Mac Filib, which is a variant.

Mac Pilbín, Mac Pilibín—V—*M'Philibbene*, *M'Phillippine*, MacPhilpin, MacPhilbin, O'Filbin, Philipin, Phillipin, Philbin, Filbin, and, by ' translation,' Plover ; also written Mac Filibín, and often changed in the spoken language to Ó Filibín ; ' son of Philpin ' (dim. of Philip) ; the name of a Mayo family who, according to O'Donovan, are a branch of the Burkes, but more probably are a branch of the Barretts. The head of the family resided at the Castle of Doon, near Westport.

Mac Póil, Mac Póil—V—*M'Poyle*, MacPaul, MacPhail, MacFall, MacFalls, MacVail, Vail, Paulson, Polson, Powlson, &c. ; ' son of Paul.'

Mac Póilín—V—MacPolin, MacPoland, Polin, Poland ; ' son of Paulin ' (dim. of Paul) ; a rare Ulster surname.

Mac Ragailligh—IV—*M'Reily*, *M'Crylly*, MacCrilly, Creilly, Crilly, Crelly, Creely ; ' son of Ragailleach,' or ' Ragallac.' Cf. Mac Rágallaig and Mag Rágallaig.

Mac Rágallaig—IV—*M'Craly*, *M'Crawley*, *M'Crawle*, *M'Crole*, Crawley ; ' son of Ragallac ' ; a var. of Mac Ragailligh and Mag Rágallaig, q.v. See also Mac Rogallaig and Ó Cruadlaoic.

Mac Ragnaill—V—*M'Rainell*, *M'Ranald*, *M'Randal*, MacRannall, MacRanald, MacRandell, MacCrindle, MacReynold, MacReynolds, Randalson, Rondalson,

Reynoldson, Rannals, Randals, Randles, Ranolds, Reynolds, &c. ; 'son of Reginald' (v. Raʒnaɫɫ) ; the name of a family of the same stock as the O'Farrell who were chiefs of Muinntear Eolais, in the south of Co. Leitrim ; also a Scottish surname ; often pronounced mac Ráʒnaiɫɫ and mac Raonaiɫɫ.

mac Raiʒiɫɫiʒ—IV—Crigley ; a var. of mac Raʒaiɫɫiʒ, q.v.

mac Raiʒne—V—*M'Reynie,* *M'Creynie,* *M'Kryny,* Reyney, Ryṅey, Reinny, Rennie, Reany, Rainey, Raney, &c. ; 'son of Rayny' or 'Rennie' (a pet form of Reginald or Reynold ; v. mac Raʒnaiɫɫ and Raʒnaɫɫ).

mac Rait—IV—*M'Craythe,* *M'Craye,* *M'Cragh,* *M'Creagh,* MacRay, MacRea, MacCraith, MacCray, MacCrea, MacWray, Rea, &c. ; 'son of mac Rait' (a common Irish personal name, meaning 'son of grace' or 'prosperity'). V. maʒ Rait, under which the chief families of the name are mentioned.

mac Raois, mac Raosa—IV—*M'Greece,* MacCreesh, MacCreech ; a corruption of mac Aonʒuir, mac Aonʒura, q.v.

mac Reaċtain—IV—*M'Kreaghane,* MacCracken ; a corruption of mac Neaċtain, q.v. I have heard this form as the Gaelic for MacNaughten in Argyleshire. The family had settled in Co. Antrim before the end of the 16th century.

mac Réamoinn—V—*M'Remon,* MacRedmond, Redmond, &c. ; 'son of Redmond' (a personal name introduced by the Normans) ; the name of a branch of the Burkes.

mac Reiórí—V—*M'Reirie, M'Reyry* ; a dialectical var. of mac Ruaióri, q.v.

mac Réiɫɫ—IV—*M'Crell, M'Krell,* MacCrail ; 'son of Ṅiaɫɫ' ; a corruption of mac Néiɫɫ, q.v.

mac Riaḃaiʒ—IV—*M'Creve,* *M'Krevie,* MacReavy, MacCreavy, MacCreevy, MacCrevey ; 'son of Riaḃaċ' (greyish, brindled).

Mac Riada—IV—MacReedy, MacReady, MacCreedy, MacCready, &c. ; ' son of Riada.'

Mac Riagáin—IV—M'Regan, M'Crigan, Creegan, Cregan, Creggan, &c. ; ' son of Riagán.' V. Mac Criagáin and Ó Criagáin.

Mac Riceid—V—Cricket, Ricketson, Rickets ; ' son of Ricket ' (a dim. of Rickard, or Richard).

Mac Riocáird, Mac Riocáird—V.—M'Ricard, M'Richerd, MacRichard, Crickard, Dickson, Dixon, [Sinclair], &c. ; ' son of Rickard ' or ' Richard '; a patronymic surname assumed by the Scottish family of Sinclair.

Mac Risteáird, Mac Risteáird—V—M'Ristard, M'Risterd, MacRichard, Richardson, Richards ; ' son of Richard.'

Mac Ritbeartaig—IV—M'Criffortie, M'Creverty, Mac-Crifferty ; son of Robartac ' ; the name of a Fermanagh family who were poets to the Maguires. Cf. Ó Raitbeartaig.

Mac Rob—V—MacRub, MacCrub, MacRubs, Robson, Robbs ; ' son of Rob ' (short for Robert).

Mac Robuic—V—M'Robuck, M'Crobacke ; ' son of Robuc ' (dim. of Robert) ; probably obsolete.

Mac Robartaig—IV—M'Rortie, MacRoarty ; ' son of Robartac ' ; the name of a Tirconnell family, the head of which lived at Ballymagroarty, near Donegal, and was keeper of the celebrated ' cathach ' of St. Columcille. V. Ó Robartaig.

Mac Rodaig—IV—M'Ruddie, Ruddy ; ' son of Rodac ' (strong) ; a rare Donegal surname.

Mac Rodáin—IV—M'Rudane, M'Roddane, M'Crodane, M'Croddan, MacCrudden, Crudden, Rodden, Roddon, Rudden, Ruddon, &c. ; ' son of Rodán ' (dim. of rod, strong) ; an Ulster surname.

Mac Rogallaig—IV—M'Craly, M'Crawley, M'Crole, Crowley, Croly, Crolly ; ' son of Rogallac ' (a var. of Ragallac, in use among the O'Mahonys of West Cork, and other families). This surname, which is a var. of Mac Ragallaig and Mag Ragallaig (q.v.), is now corrupted in the spoken language, to Ó Cɲoʒaɬ-ᴀɩ̄ʒ, and written Ó Cɲuᴀ́ᴅᴌᴀoɩċ, q.v.

mᴀc ʀoɩbeᴀ́ɩʀᴅ, mᴀc ʀoɩbeᴀ́ɩʀᴅ—V—*M'Robert*, *M'Robart*, MacRoberts, MacCrobarts, Robertson, Roberts; 'son of Robert.'

mᴀc ʀoɩbɩ́n—V—*M'Robyn*, *M'Roben*, MacRobin, Cribbin, Cribbon, Cribbins, Robinson, Robbinson, Robbins; 'son of Robin' (dim. of Robert).

mᴀc ʀoɩbɩʀᴅ, v. mᴀc ʀoɩbeᴀɩʀᴅ.

mᴀc ʀuᴀɩᴅ—IV—*M'Roe*, *M'Croy*, Roe, Rowe, Roy; 'son of ʀuᴀᴅ' (red).

mᴀc ʀuᴀɩᴅʀɩ́—V—*M'Rury*, *M'Roory*, *M'Rowry*, MacRoary, MacRory, MacArory, MacCrory, Rorison, Rogerson, Rogers, Rodgers; 'son of ʀuᴀɩᴅɲi' (the Norse Hrothrekr, Domesday Book Roric, angl. Rory, Roderick and Roger); the name (1) of a family who were anciently chiefs of Tellach Ainbhith and Muinntear Birn, in Co. Tyrone, and erenaghs of Ballynascreen, in Co. Derry; and (2) of a Scoto-Irish family of the same stock as the MacDonnells, who came over to Ireland as gallowglasses about the middle of the 14th century.

mᴀc ʀuᴀɩʀc—V— *M'Rwrcke*, *M'Royrke*; 'son of ʀuᴀɩɲc.' V. mᴀʒ ʀuᴀɩɲc.

*mᴀc ʀuᴀɩʀcɩ́n, *mᴀc ʀuᴀʀcᴀ́ɩn—V—MacCrorken, Croarkien; 'son of ʀuᴀɩɲcɩ́n' or 'ʀuᴀɲcᴀ́n' (dim. of ʀuᴀɲc).

mᴀc ʀuɩᴅʀɩ́—V—*M'Rierie*, MacReery, MacCreery, MacCreary; a dialectical var. of mᴀc ʀuᴀɩᴅɲi, q.v.

mᴀc sᴀmueɬ—V—Samuelson, Samuels; 'son of Samuel.' Cairbre Mac Samuel, chief ollav of Ireland in penmanship, died in 1162 (F. Masters).

mᴀc sᴀnᴅᴀɩʀ—V—Sanderson, Saunderson, Sanders, Saunders; 'son of Sander' (short for Alexander).

mᴀc sᴀoʒᴀɩʀ—V—*M'Sawer*, Searson, Seares, Sears, &c.; 'son of Sigar' (the Anglo-Saxon Saegaer; v. sᴀoʒᴀɲ).

mᴀc scᴀɩċʒɩɬ—IV—Scahill, Skahill, Schaill; 'son of

Scᴀɪᴄ̇ʒeᴀʟ ' (flower-bright) ; an older form of Ó Scᴀᴄ̇-
ʒᴀɪʟ, q.v.

mᴀc Scᴀʟᴀɪʒe—IV—*M'Scally*, *M'Skally*, *M'Skelly*,
Miskelly, Miscella, Miskella, Scally, Skally, Skelly ;
' son of Scᴀʟᴀɪʒe ' (crier) ; an old surname in the midlands. It appears to have been a var. of Ó Scᴀʟᴀɪʒe, q.v.

mᴀc Sceᴀᴄ̇ᴅ́ɪn—IV—MacSkeaghan, MacSkean, Skehan,
and, by translation, Thornton ; ' son of Sceᴀᴄ̇ᴅ́n '
(peevish one, dim. of ɼceᴀᴄ̇, a briar) ; a Monaghan
surname. Cf. Ó Scéᴀᴄ̇ᴅ́ɪn.

mᴀc Scoʟóɪʒe—VII—*M'Scolloige*, *M'Skolog*, Mac-
Scollog, and, by translation, Farmer ; a var. of mᴀc
ᴀn Scoʟóɪʒe, q.v.

mᴀc Seᴀꝼʀᴀɪ́ᴏ—V—*M'Shaffrie*, *M'Shefferie*, *M'Gef-
frey*, MacShaffrey, MacSheffrey, MacShufrey, Shaffery,
Jefferson, Jeffreson, Jeffries, &c. ; ' son of Geoffrey.'
V. Seᴀꝼɼᴀɪ́ᴏ.

mᴀc Seᴀʒᴅ́ɪn, mᴀc Seᴅ́ɪn—V—*M'Sheain*, *M'Sheane*,
M'Shaine, *M'Shaen*, MacShane, MacShan, MacCheyne,
Shane, Cheyne, Johnson, (Johnston, Johnstone) ;
' son of Jean,' the Norman-French form of John.
The MacShanes of Tyrone are a branch of the O'Neills.

mᴀc Seᴅ́muɪs—V—*M'Shemus*, *M'Sheames*, *M'James*,
Jameson, Jemison, &c. ; ' son of James.'

mᴀc Seᴀnᴀᴄ̇ᴅ́ɪn—IV—*M'Shenaghan*, *M'Shincane*, Mac-
Shannon ; ' son of Seᴀnᴀᴄ̇ᴅ́n ' (dim. of Seᴀnᴀᴄ̇, from
ɼeᴀn, old, wise) ; extremely rare.

mᴀc Seᴀnᴅ́ɪn—IV—MacShannon ; ' son of Seᴀnᴅ́n '
(dim. of ɼeᴀn, old, wise) ; the name of a Meath family
who were lords of Gaileanga until about the middle of
the 12th century, when they disappeared from history.

mᴀc Seᴀnᴄ̇ᴀ, mᴀc Seᴀnᴄ̇ᴀɪ́ᴏe—VII—MacShanaghy,
Shanaghy, Shanahy, and, by ' translation,' Fox ; ' son
of the historian,' or ' antiquary ' (Ir. ɼeᴀnᴄ̇ᴀ, ɼeᴀn-
ᴄ̇ᴀɪ́ᴏe) ; the name of a family originally from Co.
Sligo, but now found chiefly in Co. Leitrim. Fox is
an incorrect translation, being founded on the erroneous supposition that the surname is derived from
' ɼɪonnᴀᴄ̇,' a fox.

mac seαnɫαoιċ—VII—*M'Shanlie*, *M'Shanly*, Mac-Shanley, Shanley; 'son of the old hero' (Ir. Seαn-ɫαoċ); the name of an old family in Roscommon and Leitrim. Also mαᵹ Seαnɫαoιċ, q.v.

mac séαꝛɫαιs, mac séαꝛɫuιs—V—Charleson, Charles; 'son of Charles.'

mac seαꝛꝛαιᵹ—IV—*M'Sharrie*, MacSharry, Mac-Sherry, Sharry, Sherry, and, by translation, Feley, Foley; 'son of Seαꝛꝛαċ' (foal, flighty); an old Breifney surname; found in the 16th century in Leitrim, Cavan and Sligo, where it is still common; now also in Armagh and Donegal. There was also a family of the name in Co. Down which cannot now be traced unless changed to Ó Seαꝛꝛαιᵹ (q.v.), which is not improbable. Seαꝛꝛαċ signifies a foal, hence the translated forms Feley (Filly) and Foley, the latter common about the town of Sligo.

mac séαꝛċα, mac séαꝛċαιꝺ—V—*M'Shearhie*, *M'Shearihy*, *M'Shiary*, *M'Shera*, *M'Shire*, Shera, Sheera, Shirra, [Hodnett, Fitzpatrick]; 'son of Geoffrey'; a var. of mac Seαꝛꝛαιꝺ, q.v.; (1) a patronymic surname taken by the Hodnetts of Co. Cork, from whom Courtmacsherry is still called in Irish Cúιꝛc ṁιc Séαꝛċαιꝺ; and (2) a second surname assumed by the Fitzpatricks of Ossory from one of their ancestors named Geoffrey Mac Giolla Phadraig.

mac séαꝛċúιn—V—*M'Sherhown*, *M'Sherone*, Shearhoon, (?) Syron, [Prendergast]; 'son of *Geoffron' (dim. of Geoffrey); a patronymic surname assumed by a branch of the Prendergasts in Kerry.

mac seιmιċín—V—*M'Shinekine*, *M'Jenkine*, Jenkinson, Jenkins, Jinkins, &c.; 'son of Jenkin' (i.e., little Jean, or John).

mac seιnín—V—*M'Shenyn*, Jennens, Jennings; 'son of Jenin' (dim. of Jean, the French form of John). Cf. mac Seóιnín.

mac seóιn—V—*M'Shone*, *M'Jonne*, *M'John*, Johnson, Joneson, Jones, &c.; 'son of John.' (Cf. mac Seáιn, from the French Jean).

Mac Seóinín—V—*M'Sheonin*, *M'Shonyne*, *M'Johnine*, *M'Jonine*, *M'Joning*, (Jennings), O'Keoneen, Keoneen; 'son of Jonin' (dim. of John); a patronymic surname assumed by a branch of the Burkes in Connacht from an ancestor named Seóinín, or little John Burke. The initial S of the second part of the surname is now always aspirated, and the pronunciation is often Ó Ceóinín; hence the angl. forms O'Keoneen, Keoneen. The influence of the Norman-French Jenin (v. Mac Seinín above) has, however, made Jennings almost universal as the angl. form.

Mac Siacais, Mac Siacuis—V—*M'Sekays*, *M'Shekish*, Jackson; 'son of Jaques' (the Norman equivalent of James).

Mac Sim—V—MacKim, Simson, Simpson, Sims, &c.; 'son of Sim' (a pet form of Simon); a Scottish surname.

Mac Simid—V—MacKimmie, [Fraser]; 'son of Simmie' (a pet form of Simon); a patronymic designation of the Frasers of Lovat in Scotland.

Mac Sioda—IV—*M'Shida*, MacSheedy, Sheedy; 'son of Sioda' (silk, silken); the name of a branch of the MacNamaras in Clare, Limerick and Tipperary.

Mac Siofraid—V—MacShufrey; a var. of Mac Seafraid, q.v.

Mac Siogair—V—Sigerson; 'son of Sigarr' (a Norse personal name). A family of Segersons was seated at Ballinskelligs, Co. Kerry, in the 18th century.

Mac Siomóin, Mac Siomoinn—V—*M'Shymon*, *M'Simon*, Fitzsimon, Fitzsimons, Fitzsimmons, Simons, Simmons, Symons, Simonds, Symonds, &c.; 'son of Simon,' or 'son of Sigemund' (a Teutonic personal name); these two names have been confused. The Fitzsimons are an old and respectable family of English origin in Dublin and Westmeath.

Mac Siomóin, Mac Siomoinn—V—MacKimmon, Mac-Keemon, MacKeeman; var. of Mac Siomóin, Mac Siomoinn, q.v.

Mac Sitig—IV—*M'Shihy*, *M'Shiehie*, *M'Shee*, Mac-

Sheehy, Sheehy; 'son of Síteac' (peaceful); a branch of the MacDonnells of Scotland, descended from Síteac, great-grandson of Domnall, the ancestor from whom that family took its name. The Mac-Sheehys were famous as gallowglasses, and as such were employed in various parts of Ireland in the 14th and two succeeding centuries. The name is first mentioned in the Annals of the Four Masters at the year 1367, when they took part in a battle fought between two factions of the O'Connors, near Bally-sodare, Co. Sligo. In the year 1420, they came to Munster, and settled in Co. Limerick, as constables to the Earl of Desmond, where they built the castle of Lisnacolla (or Woodfort) in the parish of Clonagh, about four miles west of Rathkeale. The name is now almost peculiar to Munster.

mac Sítis—IV—MacKeith, MacHeath; 'son of Síteac'; a Scottish var. of mac Sítis, q.v.

mac Sitric—V—MacKittrick, MacKitterick, Mac-Kettrick, MacKetterick, MacKirtrick, Munkittrick, Munkettrick, Kittrick, Kitterick, Setright; 'son of Sitreac' (the Norse Sigtryggr, a well-known name in the Irish Annals); a rare and scattered surname; also in use in Scotland.

mac Siúrtáin—V—M'Shurtayne, M'Shurdan, M'Shor-dane, M'Jordaine, Jourdan, Jordan, Jurdan, &c.; 'son of Jordan' (v. Siúrdán); a patronymic surname assumed by the descendants of Jordan D'Exeter, an Anglo-Norman family who settled in Co. Mayo, but in 1571 were, according to Campion, 'very wild Irish.' The initial S of the second part of the surname is now always aspirated, and the pronunciation is often Ó Ciúrtáin.

mac Sleimne—V—M'Sleyny, MacSliney, Sleyne, Sliney, Sliny; 'son of Stephen' (?); the name taken, according to O'Donovan, by the FitzStephens of Cork. A member of this family, Dr. John Baptist Sleyne, was Bishop of Cork and Cloyne from 1693 to 1712.

Ɱac Sluaʒaȯaiʒ—IV—MacSlowey, MacSloy ; 'son of Sluaʒaȯaċ' (one of a host, or hosting expedition).

Ɱac Soilliʒ—IV—MacSolly, MacSoley, Solly ; 'son of Soilleaċ (?) ' ; the name of a family who, in the 11th century, were erenaghs of Iniskeen, on the borders of Louth and Monaghan. It still survives, but is extremely rare.

Ɱac Solaiṁ—V—Soloman, Solomon, Solmons, &c. ; 'son of Solomon.'

Ɱac Soṁairle—V—M'Sorlie, MacSorely, MacSorley, MacSurley ; 'son of Soṁairle' (a personal name of Scandinavian origin) ; the name of a branch of the MacDonnells of Scotland ; well known in the North of Ireland.

Ɱac Spealáin, Ɱac Spealláin—IV—MacSpallane, MacSpollane, (Spencer, Spenser) ; 'son of Spealán' (dim. of rpeal, a scythe) ; a Leinster surname, said to have been anglicised Spencer and Spenser. I have failed to trace it.

Ɱac Steafáin, Ɱac Steiṁin, Ɱac Stiaȯna, Ɱac Stiaṁna, Ɱac Stiȯin, Ɱac Stín, Ɱac Stiop-áin, Ɱac Stiopáin—V—M'Stephen, M'Stephin, M'Steyny, M'Stine, MacSteen, Fitzstephen, Fitz-stephens, Stephenson, Stevenson, Stevinson, Stenson, Steenson, Steinson, Stinson, Steveson, Stephens, Stevens, &c. ; 'son of Stephen.'

Ɱac Suain—V—MacSwan, Swainson, Swanson ; 'son of Swan ' (v. Suain).

Ɱac Suiȯne—IV—MacSeveney, MacSwiney, Mac-Sweeny, MacSweeney, MacSween, MacSwine, Swiney, Sweeney, &c. ; 'son of Suiȯne' (well-going) ; the name of a great military family, formerly famous throughout Ireland as captains of gallowglasses. They derive their name and descent, according to MacFirbis, from Suiȯne, who was son of Ȯonn-fléiȯe Ó Néill and lord of Knapdale in Argyle, about the beginning of the 13th century. The first of the name to come to Ireland was Murchadh, grandson of Suiȯne, who is mentioned in the Annals at the year

1267. Early in the next century, the MacSweeneys effected a permanent settlement in Tirconnell, where they became captains of gallowglasses to O'Donnell. They branched out into three great septs, viz. : Mac-Sweeny of Fanad who dwelt at Rathmullin Castle and had extensive possessions in the north-east of the barony of Kilmacrenan ; MacSweeney of Baghnagh, now the barony of Banagh, in the west of Co. Donegal ; and MacSweeney na dTuath, lord of Tuatha Toraighe, or the districts of Tory Island, sometimes incorrectly called MacSweeney of the Battleaxes. A branch of the MacSweeneys of Fanaid settled in Desmond as commanders of gallowglasses under the MacCarthys. They had several castles in the barony of Muskerry, and were celebrated for their hospitality. The Irish form of the surname is now sometimes Ó Suibne, q.v. ; in Scotland it is generally Mac Suibne (q.v.), but MacSween still survives as an angl. form.

Mac Suibne—IV—*M'Queyn, M'Quine*, MacQueen, Maqueen, &c. ; a var. of Mac Suibne, q.v. ; a Scottish surname.

*Mac Suigin—V—MacSwigin, MacSwiggin, MacSwiggan ; ' son of Swegen,' or ' Swen ' (a common personal name in Domesday Book).

Mac Taidg—IV—MacTeigue, MacTigue, MacTeague, MacTague, Montague, Teige, Teigue, Teague, Tague, Tigue, Tighe ; ' son of Tadg ' (poet, philosopher) ; a common surname in Ulster and North Connacht. A family of this name were anciently chiefs of Muinntear Siorthachain, in Co. Westmeath ; but there are, doubtless, many distinct families so called. V. Mac Taidg.

Mac Taidg—IV—*M'Heig, M'Keige*, MacAig, MacHaig, MacCaig, MacCaigue, MacKaige, MacKague, Mac-Kage, MacKaigue, MacKeag, MacKeague, Keag, Keague, &c. ; a var. of Mac Taidg, q.v. ; sometimes pronounced Mac Caog.

Mac Tamais—V—MacTavish, Thompson ; ' son of Thomas ' ; a var. of Mac Tomair, q.v. See also Mac Tamair.

Mac Táṁais—V—*M'Cawyshe, M'Cawys*, MacAvish, Mac-
Cavish, Cavish ; a var. of Mac Táṁair, q.v. See also
Mac Tóṁair.

Mac TiġeaRnaiġ—IV—MacTierney ; 'son of Tiġeaṗ-
naċ' (lordly) ; very rare.

Mac TiġeaRnáin—IV—*M'Tiernane, M'Ternane*, Mac-
Tiernan, MacTernan, Tiernan, Ternan ; 'son of
Tiġeaṗnán' (dim. of Tiġeaṗna, a lord) ; a var. of Mac
Tiġeaṗnáin, q.v.

Mac TiġeaRnáin—IV—*M'Kiernane, M'Kernane*, Mac-
Kiernan, MacKernan, MacCarnon, MacHarnon, Kiernan, Kernan, Kernon, and, by translation, Lord ;
'son of Tiġeaṗnán' (dim. of 'Tiġeaṗna,' a lord) ; the
name (1) of a branch of the O'Connors in Co. Roscommon, who are descended from Tiġeaṗnán, grandson of Turlough Mor O'Connor, King of Ireland ;
(2) of a Breifney family, of the same stock as the
O'Rourkes, who were formerly chiefs of Tellach
Dhunchadha, now the barony of Tullyhunco, in the
west of Co. Cavan ; and (3) of a Fermanagh family,
of the same stock as the Maguires, who were formerly
chiefs of Clann Fearghaile. V. Mac Tiġeaṗnáin.

Mac Toimilín, Mac Toimilín—V—*M'Tomilin,
M'Tomylin*, Tomlinson, Tomlin, Tomlyn, Timlin,
Timblin, &c. ; 'son of Tomlin' (a double dim. of
Thomas) ; the name of a Welsh or Anglo-Norman
family long settled in Co. Mayo ; pronounced locally
Ó Cuimlín and Ó Tuimlín, and incorrectly angl.
Timlin and Timblin.

Mac Tóimicín—V—Tomkinson, Tomkins, Tompkins ;
'son of Tomkin' (a dim. of Thomas).

Mac Toimín—V—*M'Tomeen, M'Tomyn, M'Tumyn*,
Timmin, Timmins, Timmons, Tymmins, Tymmons ;
'son of Tomin' (a dim. of Thomas) ; the name of a
branch of the Barretts of Tirawley.

Mac ToiRdealḃaiġ—IV—*M'Torrilogh, M'Turlogh,
M'Terrelly, M'Tirlay, M'Terrens*, Torley, Turley,
Terrence, Terry ; 'son of Toiṗdealḃaċ' (shaped like

the god Thor, the Scandinavian Jupiter; an old Irish personal name, angl. Turlough and Terence). V. mac Coɪ҃ɼ́ⱺeᴀlƄᴀɪ҃ʒ.

mac CoɪɼⱺeᴀlƄᴀɪ҃ʒ—IV—*M'Hurryly*, *M'Curyle*, *M'Kyrrelly*, MacCorley, MacKerley, MacKerlie, Mac-Gorley, Corley, Curley, Kerley, Kerly, Kirley; a var. of mac CoɪɼⱺeᴀlƄᴀɪ҃ʒ, q.v.

mac Cóm—V—*M'Com*, *M'Come*, MacComb, MacCombs, MacCombes, Combes, Homes, Holmes; 'son of Thome' (a short form of Thomas). This surname probably came to us from Scotland, but it was in use in Sligo, Leitrim and Louth before the end of the 16th century. V. mac Cómᴀɪɼ.

mac Cómṁuɪc—V—*M'Tomock*, *M'Camacke*, MacComick; 'son of Thomuc' (a dim. of Thomas).

mac Cómᴀɪs, mac Comáɪs—V—*M'Thomas*, Thomson, Thompson, Thomas, &c.; 'son of Thomas'; the first of these forms, which came to us from Scotland, reflects an older pronunciation of Thomas. In Co. Mayo, it is often made Ó Cómᴀɪɼ.

mac Cómᴀɪs—V—MacComish, MacCombes, MacCombs, Comish, Combes, Homes, (Holmes); a var. of mac Cómᴀɪɼ and mac Cáṁᴀɪɼ, q.v. It is of Scottish origin.

mac Comáɪs—V—(Holmes); a var. of mac Cómᴀɪɼ, q.v. This surname is in use in Co. Cork.

mac Comᴀlᴛᴀɪ҃ʒ —IV— *M'Tomolty*, *M'Tumoltagh*, *M'Tymolty*, Tomilty, Tumalty, Tumilty, Tumelty, Tumiltey, Tumblety, (Timothy); 'son of Comᴀlᴛᴀċ' (formerly a common personal name, especially in Connacht). Cf. Ó Comᴀlᴛᴀɪ҃ʒ.

mac Coɼcᴀⱺᴀɪl—V—MacCorcadale, MacCorcodale, MacCorquodale, MacQuorcodale; 'son of Thorketill' (a Norse personal name).

mac Coɼcᴀɪll—V—Thurkell, Thurkill, Thirkell, Thurkle, &c.; 'son of Thorkell' (a shortened form of Thorketill).

mac Coɼcᴀɪll—V—MacCorkill, MacCorkell, MacCorrikle, MacCorkle, Corkhill; a var. of mac Coɼcᴀɪll, q.v. ṁᴀc Ꞇoꞃcᴀıʟʟ was a common surname among the Danes of Dublin, in the 12th century; but as a present-day surname, it seems to be of Scottish origin.

ṁᴀc Ꞇꞃéınꝼıꞃ—IV—*M'Crenir, M'Kreaner*, MacCreanor, MacCranor, MacCrainor, Treanor, Trenor, Trayner, Trainor, Traynor, Tranor; 'son of Ꞇꞃéᴀnꝼeᴀꞃ' (an Irish personal name, meaning 'champion,' literally, 'strong-man'); a well-known Ulster surname.

ṁᴀc Ꞇuᴀċᴀıʟ—IV—MacToole, Toole; 'son of Ꞇuᴀᴛᴀʟ' (people-mighty); in use in parts of Connacht, but very rare.

ṁᴀc Ꞇuᴀᴛċᴀıꞃ—IV—MacTucker; 'son of Ꞇuᴀᴛċᴀꞃ' (people-dear); very rare.

ṁᴀc Ꞇuıʟe—IV—Tully, Flood; a shortened form of ṁᴀc ṁᴀoʟᴛuıʟe, q.v.

ṁᴀc Ꞇuıꞃc—IV—MacTurk; 'son of Ꞇoꞃc' (boar).

ṁᴀc Ꞇuꞃcᴀıʟʟ, v. ṁᴀc Ꞇoꞃcᴀıʟʟ.

ṁᴀc uᴀıᴅ—V—*M'Coode, M'Cowade, M'Quoid*, Mac-Quaid, MacQuaide, MacQuade, MacQuoid, MacWade, Quaid, Quaide, Quade, Quoid, &c.; 'son of Wat' (?) (a 'pet' form of Walter); a well-known Monaghan surname.

ṁᴀc uᴀıʟᴅꞃín, ṁᴀc uᴀıʟᴛꞃín—V—*M'Waldrin*, Waldron; a var. of ṁᴀc bᴀıʟᴅꞃín, ṁᴀc bᴀıʟᴛꞃín, q.v.

ṁᴀc uᴀıᴛ—V—MacWatt, MacQuatt, Watson, Watts; 'son of Wat.' Cf. ṁᴀc uᴀıᴅ.

ṁᴀc uᴀıᴛéıꞃ—V—*M'Water*, MacWatters, MacQuatters, Waterson, Waters, Watters; 'son of Walter' (often pronounced 'Water').

ṁᴀc uᴀıᴛín—V—*M'Watten*; a var. of ṁᴀc bᴀıᴛín, q.v.

ṁᴀc uᴀʟᴅꞃáın—V—Waldron; a var. of ṁᴀc bᴀʟᴅꞃáın and ṁᴀc uᴀʟꞃonᴛᴀ, q.v.

ṁᴀc uᴀʟᵹᴀıꞃᵹ—IV—*M'Walrick, M'Collrick*, Coldrick; 'son of uᴀʟᵹᴀꞃᵹ' (proud-fierce); a var. of ṁᴀᵹ uᴀʟᵹᴀıꞃᵹ, q.v.

ṁᴀc uᴀʟʟᴀċáın—IV—*M'Coulaghan, M'Wolleghan*, Coulahan, Coulihan, Colahan, Coolahan, &c.; 'son of uᴀʟʟᴀċán' (dim. of uᴀʟʟᴀċ, proud, haughty); the name of an ancient and respectable family in Offaly. They are of the same stock as the O'Maddens, and were at one time chiefs of Siol Anmchadha ; but for many centuries have been seated in the parish of Lusmagh, in Offaly, which originally formed part of Siol Anmchadha.

Mac Uᴀlronᴛᴀ—V—*M'Falronte*, *M'Valronte*, Waldron ; a var. of Mac Ɗᴀlꝑonᴛᴀ, q.v.

Mac Uᴀlᴛᴀir—V—MacWalter, MacQualter, Walters, Qualters, Walter, Qualter ; 'son of Walter.' V. Mac Uᴀiᴛéiꝑ, which is a variant.

Mac Uiɗilín, Maꝗ Uiɗilín, Mac Uiʒilín—V—*M'Uilin*, *M'Cuyllen*, *M'Cuilline*, *M'Quilline*, MacQuillin, MacQuillian, MacQuillan, MacQuillen, MacQuillon, &c., 'son of Hugelin' (a double dim. of Hugh), or 'son of Hudelin' (a double dim. of Hud, a 'pet' form of Richard) ; the name of a family, said to be of Welsh origin, who settled, soon after the Anglo-Norman invasion, in the Route, in the north of Co. Antrim. Towards the close of the 16th century, the MacDonnells wrested from them the greater part of their territory and completely destroyed their power.

Mac Uiɗliɗ—V—*M'Quylly*, *M'Willi*, MacQuilly, MacWillie ; a short form of Mac Uiɗilín, q.v.

Mac Uilcín—V—*M'Cwlkine*, MacQuilkin, MacQuilkan, MacQuilquane, MacWilkin, Kilken, Culkeen, Kulkeen, Culkin, Kulkin, Quilkin, Kilkisson, Kilkison, Wilkinson, Wilkison, Wilkins, Wilkin, &c. ; 'son of Wilkin' (a dim. of William).

Mac Uileᴀʒóiɗ—V—*M'Killegode*, *M'Killigott*, *M'Eligott*, MacElligott ; 'son of Wilecot' (i.e., little Ulick, a double dim. of William) ; the name of an old and respectable Kerry family. They are apparently of Anglo-Norman origin, notwithstanding the statement of Dr. O'Brien in his Irish Dictionary, that they are of the same stock as the MacCarthys. Ballymac-Elligott, near Tralee, was probably the first home of the family in Kerry, but at the beginning of the 17th century, they were seated in the parish of Galey, near

Listowel, where Thomas M'Kilgod, 'chief of his nation,' held considerable property which he forfeited on his attainder. The surname, in the spoken language, is shortened to ṁac Clioġóiṫ.

ṁac uilliaṁ—V—*M'Eleam, M'Quillim,* MacWilliam, MacCullyam, MacWilliams, MacQuilliams, Williamson, Williams, Willison, Wilson, &c.; 'son of William.'

ṁac uilliméiṫ—V—*M'Ullemet, M'Collimet,* Killemeade, Killemet, Killimith, Kilmet, and, by 'translation,' Woods; 'son of Willemet' (Fr. Guillemet, a dim. of William); an old, but rare Westmeath surname; sometimes incorrectly 'translated' Woods because of the supposed identity of the latter portion of the surname with 'aḋṁaṫ,' wood.

ṁac uiscín—IV—*M'Guyskine,* MacCuskin; 'son of uircín' (probably a 'pet' form of Cú-uirce, waterdog).

ṁac úiscin—V—*M'Eustin,* MacQuiston, MacQuestion, MacQueston, MacWhiston, Whiston, Houstin, Houston, Hughston, Huston, &c.; 'son of Hutchin' (a dim. of Hugh); the name probably of a branch of the MacDonnells of Scotland.

ṁac unfraiṫ—V—Humphreys, Humphries; 'son of Hunfrid.'

maḋóc, maḋóġ—VIII—*Madocke, Madoge,* Maddock, Maddocks, Madox, Maddox, &c.; 'son of Madoc' or 'Madog' (a Welsh personal name); an old, but rare, surname in Kilkenny, Tipperary and Waterford.

maġ aḋaiṁ—V—Magaw, Megaw, MacGaw, &c.; a var. of ṁac aḋaim, q.v.

maġ aireacṫaiġ—IV—*M'Garraghtie,* MacGarrity, Magarrity, Megarrity, Magarty, Garity, Garrity, &c.; 'son of aireacṫac' (member of a court or assembly, an old Irish personal name); an older form of maġ Oireacṫaiġ, q.v.

maġ aṁalġaḋa, maġ aṁalġaiṫ—IV—Magawley, MacGawley, MacGawlay, MacGaulay, Gawley; var. of ṁac aṁalġaḋa, ṁac aṁalġaiṫ, q.v.

Mag Annaiḋ—IV—*Maganye, Maganay,* Magan, MacGann ; a var. of Mac Annaiḋ, q.v. ; in use in Co. Roscommon. See also Mag Canna.

Mag Aoḋa, Mag Aoiḋ—IV—*M'Gay, M'Gey, M'Ghy,* Magee, MacGee, MacGhee, MacGhie, Ghee, Gee ; var. of Mac Aoḋa and Mac Aoiḋ, q.v. ; a very common surname in Ulster, where there are, doubtless, several families of distinct origin so called. A family of this name were chiefs of Muinntear Tlamain in Co. Westmeath, where they are still represented. Other families are mentioned under Mac Aoḋa.

Mag Aonguis, Mag Aongusa—IV—Maguiness, Maguinness, Magennis, Maginness, MacGuinnessy, MacGuinness, MacGenniss, Meginniss, &c. ; 'son of Aongus' (one-choice) ; var. of Mac Aonguis, Mac Aongusa ; sometimes corrupted to Mag Naois and Mag Raois, q.v. ; the name of an ancient and powerful family in Co. Down. They were originally dynasts of Clann Aoḋa, a subdivision of Ui Eathach Cobha, but in the course of the 12th century their power greatly increased, and they became chief lords of all Ui Eathach, now the baronies of Upper and Lower Iveagh. Many distinguished chiefs of the name are mentioned in the Irish annals. Towards the close of the 16th century, the name was found in many parts of Leinster and Connacht, and also in Co. Limerick, where the rare angl. form, MacGuinnessy, is now found.

Mag Araċáin, v. Mag Garaċáin.

Mag Ascaill—V—MacGaskell ; a var. of Mac Ascaill, q.v.

Mag Ḃrádaiġ—IV—*M'Gradie, M'Grade,* MacGrady, MacGrade ; a var. of Mac Brádaiġ, q.v.

Mag Ḃradáin—IV—*M'Braddyn,* Graden, Groden ; 'son of Bradán' (salmon). This surname, in the 16th century, was almost peculiar to Co. Down.

Mag Ḃraonáin—IV—*M'Grienan,* Greenan ; 'son of Braonán' (dim. of Braon) ; a rare Sligo surname.

Mag Ḃruadair—V—*M'Broder,* Magroder, MacGrudder ; 'son of Bruadar' (a name of Norse origin) ; very rare.

Mag Cafraiḋ, v. Mac Gafraiḋ.

Mag Cana, v. Mag Canna.

Mag Canann—IV—MacGannon, (Magann, MacGann); a var. of Mac Canann, q.v. ; in use in West Clare.

Mag Canna—IV—*M'Gana*, Magann, Magan, MacGann, MacGan, &c. ; a var. of Mac Canna, q.v. See also Mag Annaiḋ, which is a more correct form.

Mag Carrġaṁna, v. Mac Carrġaṁna.

Mag Cineáiṫ—IV—*M'Gennay*, MacKenna, Gennagh, Ginnaw, Ginna, Guinna, Kennagh, Gna, &c., (Ginnane). This well-known Munster surname is, undoubtedly, a corruption of Mac Cionaoiṫ, q.v. It is popularly angl. Ginnaw, but in official documents MacKenna. Ginnane is the angl. form in parts of Clare.

Mag Coċláin, v. Mac Coċláin.

Mag Coiliḋ, Mag Coilig—VII—Magilly, MacGilly, Cox, Coxe ; a var. of Mac an Ċoilig, q.v.

Mag Congail—IV—MacGonagle, MacGonigle, MacGonegle, MacGonegal, MacGonigal, MacGonnigle, MacGonnell, Gunnigle, Gunnell ; a var. of Mac Congail and Mac Congaile, q.v. ; a well-known Tirconnell surname. Donald MagCongail was Bishop of Raphoe from 1562 to 1589 ; he was one of the few Irish bishops who assisted at the Council of Trent.

Mag Corcráin, v. Mac Corcráin.

Mag Corraiḋín, Mag Corráin, Mag Corraoin—IV—MacGorrin, MacGurran, MacGorrian, MacGurrin, MacGurn, Gurrin, &c. ; 'son of Corrán' or 'Corraiḋín' (dim. of Corra) ; var. of Mac Corraiḋín and Mac Corráin, q.v.

Mag Craiṫ—IV—MacGrath, MacGragh, Magrath, Magragh, Megrath, Magraw, &c. ; 'son of Mac Raiṫ.' This surname is frequently written Mac Craiṫ (q.v.), but the most correct form is Mac Raiṫ or Mag Raiṫ (q.v.), under the latter of which the various families of the name are mentioned.

Mag Cuirc—IV—MacGuirk, MacGurk, MacGurke ; a

var. of ᵹᴀᴄ Cuıᵲc, q.v. ; a well-known Ulster surname.

ᵯᴀᵹ ᴅᴀᵬuc, ᵯᴀᵹ ᴅᴀᵬuıᴄ—V—MacGavick, MacGavock ; a var. of ᵯᴀᴄ ᴅᴀᵬuıᴄ, q.v.

ᵯᴀᵹ ᴅonnᴀᵹᴀın—IV—Gunnigan ; ' son of ᴅonnᴀᵹᴀn' ; extremely rare.

ᵯᴀᵹ ᴅoꞃᴄᴀıᴅ, ᵯᴀᵹ ᴅoꞃᴄᴀıᴅe—IV—*Magorchie, M'Gorche*, MacGourkey, MacGourty, MacGoorty, MacGorty ; a var. of ᵯᴀᴄ ᴅoꞃᴄᴀıᴅ, q.v. ; the name of a family in Connacht who were formerly chiefs of Cinel Luachain, comprising the parish of Oughteragh, in the east of Co. Leitrim. The last chief of the name died, according to the Four Masters, in the year 1403. This appears to be the only form under which the surname survives.

ᵯᴀᵹ ᴅuᵬᴀın—IV—*Magwain, M'Gowane*, Maguane, MacGuane, MacGuone, (MacGowan, Magowan) ; ' son of ᴅuᵬᴀn ' (dim. of ᴅuᵬ, black) ; the name of an ancient family in Tirconnell, who were chiefs of Tir-Enda, in the barony of Raphoe ; also found in Clare and Mayo. In the latter county it is always angl. Magowan or MacGowan, which greatly obscures its origin.

ᵯᴀᵹ ᴅuıᴅ—IV—*Maguffe, M'Guffe, M'Guiff*, MacGuff, MacGiff ; ' son of ᴅuᵬ ' (black) ; a var. of ᵯᴀᴄ ᴅuıᴅ, q.v. ; a scattered surname.

ᵯᴀᵹ ᴅuıᴅᵲınn—IV—*M'Duffyn*, MacGuffin, MacGuffen, MacGiffen, MacGaffin ; ' son of ᴅuᵬᵲıonn ' (black ᵲıonn) ; a rare Ulster surname.

*ᵯᴀᵹ ᴅuıᵬín—IV—Giveen, Givin, Given, Givan ; a var. of ᵯᴀᴄ ᴅuıᵬín, q.v.

ᵯᴀᵹ ᴅuıᵬne—IV—*M'Gewnie, M'Giviny*, MacGivney, MacGivena ; a var. of ᵯᴀᴄ ᴅuıᵬne, q.v.

ᵯᴀᵹ ᴅuıneᴀᴄᴀıꞃ—IV—*M'Donoughor*, Ganagher ; ' son of ᴅuıneᴀᴄᴀᵲ ' ; extremely rare.

ᵯᴀᵹ ᴅuınneᴀᵬᴀın—IV—Guinevan, Ginivan ; ' son of ᴅuınneᴀᵬᴀn ' (an attenuated form of ᴅonnᴀᵬᴀn).

ᵯᴀᵹ eᴀᴄᴀᴅᴀ—IV—MacGeagh, MacGagh, MacGaugh, &c. ; a var. of ᵯᴀᴄ eᴀᴄᴀᴅᴀ, q.v. V. ᵯᴀᵹ eᴀᴄᴀıᴅ.

ᵯᴀᵹ eᴀᴄᴀᵹᴀın—IV—MacGaffigan, Gahagan, Gavagan,

Gavigan, Gavacan, Gaffikan, Gaffikin, Gagan, &c.;
'son of eacaᵹán' (dim. of eacaiᵭ); a var. in Ulster
of maᵹ eocaᵹáin, q.v.

maᵹ eacaiᵭ—IV—MacGahey, MacGahy, MacGaughey,
MacGaughy, MacGaggy, MacGaugie, Gahey, Gaffey,
Gaugy, (Hackett); an Ulster var. of maᵹ eocaᵭa, q.v.
See also maᵹ eacac.

maᵹ eacáin—IV—M'Geaghan, MacGahan, Magahan,
Megahan, (Magan, Magann), Geghan, Gaughan, Gahan;
'son of eacán' (a dim. of eacaiᵭ); a var. of mac
eacáin and maᵹ eocáin, q.v. It appears to have
been sometimes used in the midlands as an alias for
mac eocaᵹáin, q.v.

maᵹ eacRáin—IV—Mageaghrane, MacGaughran, Magaheran, Magahern, MacGahran, (?) MacGawran,
(?) MacGarran, Gaughran; 'son of eacŕán'; a var.
of mac eacŕáin, q.v. This surname, in the 16th
century, was found chiefly in Donegal, Armagh and
Monaghan.

maᵹ eanna—IV—(?) MacGeany; a var. of mac eanna,
q.v.

maᵹ eacac—IV—M'Geaffe, MacGeagh, MacGagh, Mac-
Gaugh, Gaff; a var. of maᵹ eacaiᵭ, &c.

mac eibiR, mac eimiR—IV—MacGaver; a var. of
mac eibiŕ, q.v.

maᵹ eiteaᵹáin, maᵹ eitiᵹein—IV—Magettegane,
Magitegen, Magettigan, MacGettigan; 'son of eitiᵹein' or 'eiteaᵹán.' The Magettigans seem to have
belonged originally to Cinel Eoghain, but have been
for centuries settled in Donegal.

maᵹ eitiᵹ—IV—Magetty, Getty; 'son of eiteac' (?);
an old Derry surname.

maᵹ eocaᵭa—IV—M'Geoghoe, MacGeough, Mageogh,
Magough, MacGough, MacGoff, Gough, Goff; 'son
of eocaiᵭ' (rich in cattle); a var. of mac eocaᵭa
(q.v.), under which the different families of the name
are mentioned. See also maᵹ eacac, maᵹ eacaiᵭ.

maᵹ eocaᵹáin — IV — M'Geoghegaine, M'Goghagan,
Magoughegan, Magowghegan, M'Goigan, Mageoghegan,

MacGeoghegan, MacGoogan, MacGuigan, MacGuiggan, Maguigan, Geoghegan, Gehagan, Gehegan, Geogan, Geagan, Geghan, Gegan, Googan, Gogan, &c. ; ' son of eoċaʒán ' (a dim. of eoċaıꝺ) ; the name of an ancient and highly respectable family in Co. Westmeath. They are a branch of the southern Ui Neill, being descended from Fiacha, son of Niall of the Nine Hostages, from whom they took their clan-name of Cinel Fhiachach. The patrimony of Cinel Fhiachach, in the 16th century, comprised the barony of Moycashel, but was anciently much more extensive. The Mageoghegans retained their rank as lords of Moycashel down to the Cromwellian confiscations, when they lost their estates. A branch of the family was transplanted to Co. Galway, where the name is still common. V. maʒ eaċaʒáın, which is a variant.

maʒ eoċaıꝺ—IV—MacGoey, MacGoggy ; a var. of maʒ eoċaꝺa, q.v.

maʒ eoċaıꝺín—IV—M'Gokiane, MacGuickian, Mac-Gughian, MacGuckian, MacGookin, MacGuckin, Guckeane, Gucken, Guckian, Guigan, Guiken, &c. ; ' son of eoċaıꝺín ' (dim. of eoċaıꝺ) ; an Ulster surname.

maʒ eoċáın—IV—M'Geoghan, M'Gokiane, MacGoogan, MacGuighan, MacGuigan, &c. ; ' son of eoċán ' (a dim. of eoċaıꝺ) ; a var. of maʒ eaċáın, q.v. Cf. maʒ eoċaʒáın.

maʒ eoʒáın—IV—Mageown, MacGeown, Magowen, Mac-Gowen, Magone, Gowen, Geon ; a var. of mac eoʒaın, q.v.

maʒ eoċaċ, v. maʒ eoċaꝺa.

maʒ ꝼaċtna—IV—M'Gaghny, Magaffney, Gaughney, Gaffney ; ' son of ꝼaċtna.'

maʒ ꝼeaꝛaꝺaıʒ—IV—M'Garee, M'Garrye, Magearrye, M'Gerrye, M'Girrie, MacGarry, Magarry, MacGeary, MacGerry, MacGherry, Megarry, O'Garriga, Garahy, Garrahy, Garrihy, Garry, Gerry, Gery, and, by ' translation,' O'Hare, Hare ; ' son of ꝼeaꝛaꝺaċ ' (manly) ; a var. of mac ꝼeaꝛaꝺaıʒ, q.v. ; a not uncommon surname, especially in East Connacht, Tyrone and Antrim ; in the spoken language, sometimes corrupted to Ó Ꝼɪoꞃꞃⱥɪꝺe, and erroneously translated O'Hare and Hare, as if from 'ꞅɪꞃꝼɪⱥꝺ,' a hare; sometimes also to Ó Ꝝeⱥꞃⱥꞟⱥ, angl. O'Garriga.   Cf. mⱥc Ꝼeⱥꞃⱥꝺⱥɪꞟ.

mⱥꞟ Ꝼeⱥꞃċⱥɪꞃ—IV—*M'Garragher*, Garragher ; a var. of mⱥc Ꝼeⱥꞃċⱥɪꞃ, q.v.

mⱥꞟ Ꝼeⱥꞃꞟⱥɪꞁ—IV—MacGarrigal, MacGarrigle ; a var. of mⱥc Ꝼeⱥꞃꞟⱥɪꞁ, q.v.

mⱥꞟ Ꝼeⱥꞃꞟⱥɪꞁ—IV—*M'Garrell, M'Garrile*, MacGarrell, MacCarroll, MacGirl, MacGorl ; a var. of mⱥc Ꝼeⱥꞃꞟⱥɪꞁ, q.v.

mⱥꞟ Ꝼeóꞃⱥɪꞅ, mⱥꞟ Ꝼeóꞃuɪꞅ—V—MacGorish, Mac-Gorisk, Magorisk, Gorish, [Bermingham, Birmingham] ; a var. of mⱥc Ꝼeóꞃⱥɪꞃ, q.v.

mⱥꞟ Ꝼɪbín—V—MacGibbin, MacGibben, Gibbin, Gibben, Gibbins, Gibbings ; ' son of Phippin ' (dim. of Philip).

mⱥꞟ Ꝼɪnn—IV—Maginn, MacGinn, MacGin, MacGing, Megginn, Ginn ; a var. of mⱥc Ꝼɪnn, q.v.   This form of the surname was peculiar to Co. Down.

mⱥꞟ Ꝼɪnneⱥċⱥ, mⱥꞟ Ꝼɪnneⱥċⱥɪꞟ, mⱥꞟ Ꝼɪonn-ⱥċⱥ,   mⱥꞟ   Ꝼɪonnⱥċⱥɪꞟ—IV—*M'Ginaghtie*, Maginnetty, MacGinnitty, MacGinety, MacGinity, MacGinty, Maginty, Ginnity, Ginaty, Ginity, Guin-naty, Ginty ; ' son of Ꝼɪonnⱥċⱥ ' (fair-snow) ; a well-known Ulster surname.   In the 16th century, it was almost peculiar to Armagh.

mⱥꞟ Ꝼɪonnáɪn—IV—*M'Gynnan, M'Gennan, M'Gean-ayne*, MacGannon, Ginnane, Gannon ; ' son of Ꝼɪonn-án ' (dim. of Ꝼɪonn, fair) ; the name of an ancient family, formerly of Erris, Co. Mayo, and still repre-sented in that county.

mⱥꞟ   Ꝼɪonnbⱥɪꞃꞃ—IV—*M'Gynnowar,   Magennure, Magennore, Magenor*, Geanor, Gainer, Gaynor ; ' son of Ꝼɪonnbⱥꞃꞃ ' (fair-head), now angl. Finbar.   This family took its name from an ancestor called Ꝼɪonn-bⱥꞃꞃ Ó Ꝝeⱥꞃⱥꝺáɪn who flourished about the be-ginning of the 12th century.   The head of the family was chief of Muinntear Gearadhain, in the north of the present Co. Longford, down to the 17th century. V. Mag Ḟionnḃarra, which is a variant.

Mag Ḟionnḃarra—IV—*M'Genura, M'Genury, Magenura,* Gaynor, &c.; a var. of Mac Ḟionnḃairr, q.v.

Mag Ḟionnġail—IV—*Magennill, M'Gennell, M'Gindale,* MacGennell, MacGindle, Ginnell, Gennell, Gennel; 'son of Fionnġal' (fair-valour); a var. of Mag Ḟionnġaile, q.v.

Mag Ḟionnġaile—IV—*M'Gennowlie, M'Gynnillye, M'Gennely,* Maginley, MacGinley, MacGinly, Ginnelly, Ginley; 'son of Fionnġal' (fair-valour); the name of a well-known Donegal family, some of whom settled in Westmeath and Longford. V. Mag Ḟionnġail.

Mag Ḟlaiṫiṁín—IV—*M'Glavyne,* Hand; 'son of Flaiṫiṁín' (dim. of Flaiṫeaṁ).

Mag Ḟlaiṫiṁ—IV—*Maglaughy, M'Glaughye, Maglavey, M'Glaweye, M'Glawe,* MacGlave, Glaffey, Glavey, &c.; 'son of Flaiṫeaṁ' (ruler, lord). V. Mag Laiṫiṁ.

Mag Ḟlannċaḋa, Mag Ḟlannċaiḋ—IV—*M'Glanchie, M'Glannaghie,* Maglanchy, MacGlancy, Glancy; a var. of Mac Ḟlannċaḋa, q.v.

Mag Ḟloinn—IV—*Maglen, Maglinne, McGlyn, Maglyne,* MacGlin, MacGlynn, Glinn, Glynn; 'son of Flann' (ruddy); a rather common surname in Connacht and Ulster. V. Mac Ḟloinn.

Mag Ḟógartaiġ, Mag Ḟuagartaiġ—IV—Gogarty, Gogerty, Googarty; 'son of Fógartaċ' (proclaimed, banished); a rare North Leinster surname. Ruaiḋrí Mac Fógartaiġ, lord of South Breagh, died, according to the Four Masters, in 1027.

Mag Gafraiḋ, v. Mac Gafraiḋ.

Mag Gaora, Geary.

Mag Garaċáin—IV—*Magaraghan, M'Garaghan,* MacGarran, Garraghan, Garahan, Garron; 'son of Araċán,' or 'Faraċán'; written Mag Araċáin in the Annals of Ulster; a Fermanagh surname, formerly borne by an ecclesiastical family at Lisgool. Cf. Ó Faraċáin.

Mag Garaidh, MacGarry.

Mag Gathan—IV—MacGahan, Magahan, Gahan; a corruption of Mac Gaoithín, q.v.

Mag Gearachaigh, MacGarahy, Garahy, Garrihy; a corruption of Mag Fhearadhaigh, q.v.

Mag Gormáin, v. Mac Gormáin.

Mag Granna, Granny, Grant; probably a corruption of Mag Raighne, q.v.

Mag Gráinne, Granny; doubtless a corruption of Mag Raighne, q.v.

Mag Guagáin, MacGoogan, MacGuigan, MacGuiggan, Maguigan, &c.; a corruption of Mag Eochagáin, q.v.

Mag Gualraic, Mag Guarlaic, Magolrick, Magorlick, &c.; corruptions of Mag Ualghairg, q.v.

Mag Guarnacháin—IV—*M'Gorneghane*, Magournahan, (Gordon); probably a corruption of Mag Muirneacháin, q.v.

Mag Íomhair—V—*M'Givor*, MacGeevor, MacGeever, MacGaver; a var. of Mac Íomhair, q.v.

Mag Labhradha—IV—*M'Glawrie*, MacGlory; a var. of Mac Labhradha, q.v.; a rare surname; found in different parts of Ulster, and also in Offaly.

Mag Labhraidh—IV—(?) Maglamery; a var. of Mag Labhradha, q.v.

Mag Labhraidhín—IV—*M'Glafferine*, *Maglowrine*, *M'Claverine*; 'son of Labhraidhín' (a dim. of Labhraidh); a rare Ulster surname; now probably obsolete, or replaced by some variant, as Mac Labhráin, q.v.

Mag Labhrainn—V—*Maglarent*, *M'Glarent*; a var. of Mac Labhrainn, q.v.

Mag Lachlainn—V—*M'Glaghlin*, MacGlaughlin, Meglaughlin; a var. of Mac Lachlainn, q.v.; not easily distinguishable from Mac Giolla Sheachlainn, q.v.

Mag Láimh, MacGlave, Hand; a contraction of Mag Laithimh, q.v.

Mag Láimhín, Hand; a contraction of Mag Laithimhín, q.v.

Mag Laithimh, Mag Lathaigh—IV—*Maglavey*, *Maglaghy*, *M'Glawe*, MacGlave, Glaffey, Glavey, and, by 'translation,' Hand ; a var. of ma͇ ꝑlaitiṁ and mac Laitiṁ, q.v. ; in use in Longford, Leitrim and Sligo.

ma͇ Laitiṁín—IV—*M'Glavyne*, Hand ; a var. of ma͇ ꝑlaitiṁín, q.v.

ma͇ leannáin—IV—*Maglanan, M'Glanan, M'Glennan, Maglinane*, Maglennon, Glenane, Glennon ; 'son of leannán' (dim. of leann, a cloak) ; a not uncommon Leinster surname.

ma͇ léio, Maglade, MacGlade ; perhaps a form of mac leóio, q.v.

ma͇ loclainn—V—MacGloughlin, MacGlaughlin ; a var. of mac loclainn, q.v.

ma͇ loin͇si͇—IV—*Maglinchie*, *M'Glinche*, Mac-Glinchy ; var. of mac loin͇ri͇, q.v. ; a Donegal surname.

ma͇ ṁuirneacáin—IV—*M'Gornghane, M'Gornaghan*, Magournahan, (Gordon) ; 'son of muirneacán' (dim. of muirneac, loveable, or one of a troop) ; pronounced ma͇ ͇uarnacáin in the spoken language of Co. Mayo. Cf. mórboirneac which is also angl. Gordon in the same county. Apparently there is some connection.

ma͇ neactáin, v. mac neactain and ma͇ Reactain.

ma͇ néill, v. mac néill and ma͇ Réill.

ma͇ niall- áin, v. ma͇ Riall/áin.

ma͇ niallꝓuis, ma͇ niallꝓusa ; var. of mac niall- ͇uir, mac niall͇ uꝑa. V. ma͇ Riall͇uir, ma͇ Riall͇uꝑa.

ma͇ nuaoao, ma͇ nuaoac, Gonoude ; var. of mac nuaoao, mac nuaoac, q.v.

ma͇. oireactai͇—IV—MacGeraghty, Mageraghty, MacGerety, MacGerrity, Geraghty, Geraty, Gerety, Gerity, Gearty, Gerty, &c. ; 'son of oireactac' (member of a court or assembly) ; a var. of ma͇ aireactai͇, q.v. ; the name of an ancient and re- spectable Connacht family, of the same stock as the O'Connors. They were chiefs of Muinntear Roduibh in Co. Roscommon until dispossessed about the middle of the 16th century. Even as late as 1585, they formed a distinct clan, with a recognised chief of the name, who, however, was then seated in O'Kelly's country of Ui Maine. The name is still common in Connacht, and also in parts of Leinster, where branches of the family are long settled. The original surname was Ó Roṁuiḃ, but towards the end of the 12th century the descendants of Oineaċṫac Ó Roṁuiḃ assumed the present surname. Maʒ Oineaċṫaiʒ is often shortened in the spoken language to Maʒ Oineaċṫ. Cf. Ó hOineaċṫ for Ó hOineaċṫaiʒ.

Maʒ Oisín—IV—MacGushion; 'son of Oinín'; an old Meath surname, now extremely rare.

Maʒomraċ, Montgomery, Gomery. V. Mac Iomaine.

Maʒ Oisṫe, MacGusty; a var. of Mac Oinṫe, q.v.

Maʒ Raʒallaiʒ—IV—Magrawley, M'Grawlie, M'Graly, Magreely, Greally, Grealy, Greely; a var. of Mac Raʒailliʒ and Mac Raʒallaiʒ, q.v.; a not uncommon surname in Mayo and Galway, sometimes pronounced locally Maʒ Raoʒallaiʒ and Maʒ Roiʒeallaiʒ. Cf. Mac Roʒallaiʒ.

Maʒ Raʒnaill, Maʒ Raʒnaill—V—Magranaill, M'Gronnyll, Magrannell, MacGranell, Grannell, Gronel, Reynolds, &c.; a var. of Mac Raʒnaill, q.v.

Maʒ Raʒnainn, MacGronan; a corruption of Maʒ Raʒnaill, q.v.

Maʒ Raiʒne, Maʒ Raiʒne—V—Magrina, Magriny, Magrany, Magreny, Magrene, Magrein, Magrane, Mac-Grane, Magrean, MacGrean, Granny, &c.; 'son of Rayny,' a pet form of Raʒnall, or Reginald.

Maʒ Raiṫ—IV—Magrath, Magragh, MacGrath, Mac-Gragh, Megrath, Magraw, MacGraw, Megraw, MacGra, &c.; 'son of Mac Raiṫ' (son of grace, or prosperity; a not uncommon Irish personal name); also written Mac Craiṫ, Maʒ Craiṫ, Mac Ʒraiṫ, Mac Raiṫ, and Maʒ Raṫa, q.v.; the name (1) of a Donegal family, the head of which was coarb of St. Daveog, or erenagh of Termon Daveog, now Tremon Magrath, at Lough Derg, and resided at the Castle of Termon Magrath at the northern extremity of Lough Erne, about half a mile west of Pettigo; (2) of a Thomond family who

were hereditary poets and chroniclers to the O'Briens ;
(3) of a Scottish family in Kintail (v. Ɱ&c Ʀ&ɩᴄ),
some of whom settled in the north of Ireland. The
Magraths were also at one time an influential family
in Co. Waterford ; and there are, doubtless, many
minor families of the name about which history is
silent. The name is now very common all over
Ireland.

Ɱ&ᴣ Ʀ&ᴏᴣ&ʟʟ&ɩᴣ, v. Ɱ&ᴣ Ʀ&ᴣ&ʟʟ&ɩᴣ.

Ɱ&ᴣ Ʀ&ᴏɩꜱ, Ɱ&ᴣ Ʀ&ᴏꜱ&—IV—*Magroice*, Magreece ; a
corruption of Ɱ&ᴣ ᴀᴏɳᴣᴜɩ⸾, Ɱ&ᴣ ᴀᴏɳᴣᴜ⸾&, q.v.
Cf. Ɱ&c Ɲ&ᴏɩ⸾.

Ɱ&ᴣ Ʀ&ᴄ&—IV—*M'Graha*, *M'Grahy*, (?) *M'Grattie*,
(?) MacGrotty ; ' son of Ɱ&c Ʀ&ᴄ& ' (the same as Ɱ&c
Ʀ&ɩᴄ) ; a var. of Ɱ&ᴣ Ʀ&ɩᴄ, q.v.

Ɱ&ᴣ Ʀᴇ&ᴄᴛ&ɩɳ—IV—(?) MacGrattan, Grattan ; a
corruption of Ɱ&c Ɲᴇ&ᴄᴛ&ɩɳ. Cf. Ɱ&c Ʀᴇ&ᴄᴛ&ɩɳ.

Ɱ&ᴣ Ʀᴇ&ɳɳ&ᴄ&ɩɳ—IV—*Magranchane*, *Magranachan*,
Magranechan, MacGranahan, MacGrenehan ; ' son of
Ʀᴇ&ɳɳ&ᴄ&ɳ ' (dim. of ⸾ᴇ&ɳɳ&ᴄ, sharp, spear-like) ; a
Donegal surname.

Ɱ&ᴣ Ʀᴇɩʟʟ—IV—MacGreal ; a corruption of Ɱ&c Ɲᴇɩʟʟ,
q.v. Cf. Ɱ&c Ʀᴇɩʟʟ.

Ɱ&ᴣ Ʀɩ&ᴠ&ɩᴣ—IV—*M'Grevye*, *M'Greave*, Magreevy,
Magreavy, MacGreevy, MacGrievy, &c. ; a var. of
Ɱ&c Ʀɩ&ᴠ&ɩᴣ, q.v. ; the name of a family who were
anciently chiefs of Moylurg, in Co. Roscommon.

Ɱ&ᴣ Ʀɩ&ᴠ&—IV—Gready. (Grady) ; a var. of Ɱ&c
Ʀɩ&ᴠ&, q.v. ; in use in Galway and Mayo ; often pronounced Ó ᴣ⸾ɩ&ᴠ& in the spoken language, and sometimes incorrectly angl. Grady.

Ɱ&ᴣ Ʀɩ&ᴣ&ɩɳ—IV—MacGregan, Gregan ; a var. of Ɱ&c
Ʀɩ&ᴣ&ɩɳ, q.v.

Ɱ&ᴣ Ʀɩ&ʟʟ&ɩɳ—IV—Magrillan, MacGrillan ; ' son of
Ɲɩ&ʟʟ&ɳ ' (dim. of Ɲɩ&ʟʟ) ; a corruption of Ɱ&c Ɲɩ&ʟʟ-
&ɩɳ.

Ɱ&ᴣ Ʀ&ɩʟʟᴣᴜɩꜱ, Ɱ&ᴣ Ʀɩ&ʟʟᴣᴜꜱ&—IV—*Magriellassy*,
M'Grealis, MacGrillish, Grealish, (Greely, Grealy,
Greally, Griffin) ; corrupt for Ɱ&c Ɲɩ&ʟʟᴣᴜɩ⸾, Ɱ&c

Ríaꞁꞁᵹuꞃᴀ, q.v.; not uncommon in parts of Connacht.

Maᵹ Roᵬ—V—Grubb; a var. of Mac Roᵬ, q.v.

Maᵹ Roᵬᴀꞃᴄᴀɪᵹ—IV—*Magourrtie*, Magroarty; a var. of Mac Roᵬᴀꞃᴄᴀɪᵹ, q.v.

Maᵹ Roᴅᴀɪn—IV—Magrudden, Groden; a var. of Mac Roᴅᴀɪn, q.v.; an old Sligo surname, now extremely rare.

Maᵹ Roɪᵬín—V—Gribbin, Gribben, Gribbon; a var. of Mac Roɪᵬín, q.v.

Maᵹ Ruᴀᴅꞃᴀɪc—V—*Magrowricke*, *Magrorick*, *M'Gro ricke*; 'son of Ruᴀᴅꞃᴀc' (the Norse Hrothrekr); an older form of Maᵹ Ruᴀɪꞃc, q.v. This form of the surname was still in use at the middle of the 17th century.

Maᵹ Ruᴀɪᴅꞃí—V—*Magrowry*, *M'Grorye*, Magrory, Mac-Grory, (Rogers, Rodgers, &c.); a var. of Mac Ruᴀɪᴅꞃí, q.v.

Maᵹ Ruᴀɪꞃc—V—*M'Groirke*, *M'Grorke*, Grourke, Groarke; 'son of Ruᴀɪꞃc' (older Ruᴀᴅꞃᴀc, from Norse Hrothrekr, whence also Ruᴀɪᴅꞃí; cf. eɪnꞃí and eᴀnꞃᴀc); the name of an old Westmeath family, descended from Enna Fionn, son of Niall of the Nine Hostages. Maᵹ Ruᴀɪꞃc was chief of Cinel Enda, a small territory near the Hill of Usnagh. The name is still extant in Co. Westmeath, but is more common in Co. Mayo. V. Maᵹ Ruᴀᴅꞃᴀɪc, an older form of the name.

Maᵹ Ruɪᴅꞃí—V—Magrery, Greery; a dialectical form of Maᵹ Ruᴀɪᴅꞃí, q.v.

Maᵹ Sᴀ́mꞃᴀᴅᴀ́ɪn, Maᵹ Sᴀ́mꞃᴀ́ɪn—IV—Magoveran, Magovern, Magawran, Magauran, Magaurn, Magurn, MacGaveran, MacGovran, MacGovern, MacGowran, MacGouran, MacGauran, MacGaurn, Gooravan, Gorevan, Gorevin, &c.; 'son of Sᴀ́mꞃᴀᴅᴀ́ɪn' (dim. of ꞃᴀ́mꞃᴀᴅ, summer); the name of an old Breifney family, the head of which was chief of Tellach Eachach, now the barony of Tullyhaw, in the north-west of Co. Cavan; still very numerous.

Maᵹ Seᴀnꞁᴀoɪc—VII—*M'Ganleie*, Ganley, Ganly,

Gantley; 'son of the old hero' (Ir. 'ɼeᴀnʟᴀoċ'); a var. of mᴀc Seᴀnʟᴀoιċ, q.v. This family was seated in Corca Achlann, Co. Roscommon, and at Ballymacshanly, in Co. Leitrim.

mᴀ5 Sιᴄʀιc—V—MacGetrick, MacGetterick, &c.; a var. of mᴀc Sιᴄɲιc, q.v.

mᴀ5 ᴄoιʀʊeᴀʟꝋᴀι5—IV—M'Gorlighe, MacGorley, Gorley, Gourley; a var. of mᴀc ᴄoιɼʊeᴀʟꝋᴀι5, q.v.

mᴀ5 ᴄʀéιnɸιʀ—IV—MacGrenor; a var. of mᴀc ᴄɼéιnɸιɼ, q.v.

mᴀ5 uᴀʟ5ᴀιʀ5 — IV — Magowlricke, Magollricke, M'Gworlick, Magolrick, Magorlick, MacGolrick, MacGoldrick, MacGouldrick, MacGorlick, Golrick, Goldrick, Goulrick, Gouldrick, Golderick, Godrick, (Goulding, Golding, Golden); 'son of uᴀʟ5ᴀɼ5' (proudfierce, a favourite personal name among the O'Rourkes); the name of a branch of the O'Rourkes in Co. Leitrim and other parts of Connacht, in which province the name is very common, but generally angl. Golden, Goulding, Golding, which greatly obscures its origin. It is also a very common surname in Fermanagh and Donegal where, however, it probably represents a different family.

mᴀ5 uιꝋιʀ—IV—Maguier, M'Guier, M'Gwire, M'Guiver, Maguire, MacGuire, MacGiver; 'son of Oꝋᴀɼ' (pale, dun-coloured); the name of a great Fermanagh family, formerly one of the most powerful in Ulster. The name is first mentioned in the Annals at the year 956. Towards the end of the 13th century, the Maguires became chiefs of Fermanagh, a position which they held down to the reign of James I, when their country was included in the confiscation of Ulster. The family produced many valiant chiefs and learned ecclesiastics. The name is sometimes pronounced dialectically mᴀc 5uιꝋιɼ.

mᴀ5 uιꝋʀín—IV—Maguirin, M'Gwyrin, M'Guiverin, Magiverin, Magivern, Magiveran, MacGiverin, MacGiveran, MacGivern, Guerin; 'son of uιꝋɼín' (a dim. of Oꝋᴀɼ; v. mᴀ5 uιꝋιɼ); an old Ulster surname.

Early in the 12th century, Eachmarcach Mac Uidhrin was chief of Cinel Fearadhaigh, in the present Co. Tyrone. In the 16th century, the name was peculiar to Co. Down, and even at the present day is confined to that county and the neighbouring counties of Antrim and Armagh. For change of ⱷ to ъ, cf. mᴀᴢ ⴎⱤⱷⱤ, angl. MacGiver.

mᴀᴢ ⴎⱤⱡⱭⱤⱤ—V—*M'Gillkine*, Gilkinson, Gilkison, Gilkisson, Gilkeson, Gilkieson ; a var. of mᴀc ⴎⱤⱡⱭⱤⱤ, q.v.

mᴀᴢ ⴎⱤⱡⱡⱭⱭ, mᴀᴢ ⴎⱤⱡⱭⱭ—*M'Gilleg*, MacGillick, MacGellick, Gillick ; ' son of Willuc,' or ' Ulick ' (a dim. of William).

mᴀᴢ ⴎⱤⱤⱤseᴀⱤⱤᴅⱭⱤ, mᴀᴢ ⴎⱤⱤⱤsⱭⱤⱤⱤᴅⱭⱤ, *M'Gwinshenan*, *M'Gunchenan*, Gilsenan, Gunshinan, (Nugent, Leonard) ; a corruption of mᴀc ᴢⱭⱡⱡᴀ seᴀⱤᴅⱭⱤ, q.v.

mᴅᴢⴎⱤ—VIII—*Mayon*, Maune, Mawne, and probably Maume, Mawme ; ' son of Mayon ' (a Nor. dim. of Matthew) ; an old Co. Limerick surname, still in use, and probably sometimes represented by Mawme.

mᴅⱭᴢⱭⴎ—VIII—*Mayowe, Mao, Mawe*, Mahew, Mayhew, Mayhow, Mayo, May ; ' son of Maheu ' (a Nor. form of Matthew) ; very rare. Cf. mᴀc mᴅⱭᴢⱭⴎ.

mᴀⱤⱤᴢⱤéⱤⱤ—VIII—*Magnel, Magnell*, Mangner, Magner, Magnier, &c. ; probably ' son of Magnel ' (Nor. dim. of Magnus). Castlemagner, Co. Cork, was formerly known as Magnelstown, from William Magnel. The family is an old one in Co. Cork ; now numerous also in Co. Limerick.

mᴅⱭⱤⱤⱤⱤ—VIII—*Martyne*, Martin, Marten, Martyn ; ' son of Martin.' There are many distinct families of this name in Ireland, the most distinguished of which were the Martyns of Galway.

mᴅⱭⱭⱤⱤⴎ—VIII—*Matheu*, Mathew, Matthew, Mathews, Matthews ; ' son of Matthew.' There are several scattered families of this name in Ireland. Of these the most distinguished were the Mathews of Thomastown, Co. Tipperary, to which belonged the celebrated Apostle of Temperance, Father Theobald Mathew.

ṁáló1ṭ—VIII—*Malode, Mallot*, Mellot, Mylott, Mylotte ; probably a corruption of ṁ1olóṭṭ, q.v. ; at least, it has the same angl. forms. Malet was, however, an early Anglo-Norman surname in Ireland, and Malot, the corresponding dim. in -ot, might also have existed.

ṁɑo1l1ṛ—VIII—Meyler, Myler ; 'son of Meyler' (a Norman form of the Welsh Meilyr). The Four Masters, under the year 1205, mention a Maelir mac Maelir, who took forcible possession of Limerick, and give the gen. case of the name as Maoilir, the Irish spelling having been probably influenced by the Welsh word maeliwr, a trader, with which it was supposed to be identical. The Meylers were an old Wexford family. In Co. Waterford, the surname is pronounced ṁ1lé1ṗ.

ṁáp—VIII—*Map*, Mape ; 'son of Mab' (sharpened to Map, a short form of Mabel) ; a rare Meath surname. In 1598, Map of Mapston and Mape of Maperath were two of the chief gentlemen of Meath.

ṁɑṛɑscɑl—XII—Marshall ; Nor. 'le Marescal,' 'le Mareschal' (i.e., the marshal, the servant or official who had charge of the horses ; not the marshal in the sense of military title) ; a very common surname in early Anglo-Irish records.

ṁɑṛcṳs—VIII—*Markys*, Marks ; 'son of Marcus,' or Mark.

ṁɑsṳn—XII—*Masoun*, Mason ; Nor. 'le Macun' (i.e., the mason) ; an old surname in Ireland.

ṁéɑló1ṭ, *Melod*, Mellet, Mylott, Mylotte ; a var. in Co. Mayo of ṁ1olóṭṭ, q.v.

ṁeɑsɑ1ʒ, Massey ; a late English surname, probably of Norman origin, from Massy in Normandy.

ṁe1ḃṛ1c, ṁe1ṛ1c—VIII—*Meuryk, Meryk*, Meyrick, Mayrick, Merrick ; 'son of Merick' (the Norman form of the Welsh Meurug). This family settled at an early period in Co. Mayo. Also ṁɑc ṁe1ḃṗ1c, ṁɑc ṁe1ṗ1c, ṁɑc ṁ1ḃṗ1c, q.v.

ṁ1ċeɑl—VIII—Michael, Michell, Mihell, &c. ; 'son of Michael.'

ⅿⅰ᷄ⷠⷮⷮⷮⷮ—X—*Miache, Meagh, Miagh, Myagh,* Meade;
Ir. 'ⅿⅰⷠⷮⷮⷮ' (i.e., the Meathman, native of, or in
some way connected with, Meath). The Meades were
merchant families who settled at an early period in
Cork, Kinsale, Youghal and Kilmallock. They were
of Anglo-Norman origin and had, as the surname
implies, previously settled in Meath. The anglicised
form of the surname down to the end of the 16th
century was always Meagh or Miagh. The modern
form, Meade, seems to have been intended to represent
'Meath.' The Meades are still numerous in Cork
and Limerick.

ⅿⅰⷲⷵⷵ, Myler, Meyler. V. ⅿⲁoⅰⷵ.

ⅿⅰⷵⷲ—VIII—*Mile, Myle, Moyle,* Miles, Myles, Moyles;
'son of Milo' (a Latin name introduced by the Normans, and later confused with Miles). V. ⅿⅰⷵ.

ⅿⅰⷵⷵ—VIII—*Milys,* Miles, Myles, Moyles; 'son of
Miles' (the Latin 'miles,' a soldier, used in the Middle
Ages as a title, and which became a personal name,
probably by being confused with Milo). V. ⅿⅰⷵⷲ
above.

ⅿⅰⷵⷵⷵⷵ, ⅿⅰⷵⷵⷵⷵ—XII—*Myneter,* Miniter, Myniter;
Nor. 'le Myneter,' 'le Mineter' (i.e., the minter,
maker of money); an old, but extremely rare, surname in Clare and Galway. It occurs frequently in
the Black Book of Limerick.

ⅿⅰⷵⷵⷵⷵ—VIII—*Mylode, Melod,* Mylott, Moylotte,
Mellott, Mellet, Millet, Mylett, Mullet, &c.; 'son of
Milot' (dim. of Milo; v. ⅿⅰⷵⷲ above); formerly a
Tipperary surname, but now most common in Co.
Mayo. In the latter county, ⅿⷠⷮⷵⷵⷵ and ⅿⲁⷵⷵⷵ
(q.v.) are apparently variants and are similarly
anglicised.

ⅿⅰⷵⷠⷵ, Misset. V. ⷣⷠ ⅿⅰⷲⷠⷵ.

ⅿⅰⷵⷵⷠⷵ—VIII—*Mesteil, Misdell,* Michell, Mitchell, &c.,
'son of Michell' (a form of Michael). V. ⅿⅰⷠⷠⷵ.

ⅿⷠⷵⷠⷵⷠⷵ—XII—*Malclerk, Manclerk, Mauclerk, Mau-
clerc, Mauclere, Mowclere,* Mockler, Muckler; Nor.
'Malclerk' (i.e., the unlearned clerk, bad scholar,

opposed to Beauclerk). The family so called settled
in Co. Tipperary, where John Mauclerk, in 1356, was
a person of importance and the owner of extensive
property.

Ⅿóⅰⅎⅾⰱíoⱡ—XI—*Mandevill, Mandefill, Monfield, Mans-
fild, Maunsfield,* Mandeville, and in Co. Waterford
Mansfield; a var. of ⰱe Ⅿóⅰⅎⰱíoⱡ, q.v.; sometimes
pronounced Ⅿúⅰⅎⰱíoⱡ. The assimilation to Mansfield
is old in Waterford.

ⅯóⅰⅎⱾéⅰⱡ—XII—*Monshale, Monsheall, Mounsell, Maun-
cell,* Maunsell, Monsell, Mansell, and incorrectly Mansfield; Nor. ' le Maunsel,' ' le Mansel ' (i.e., the farmer
who cultivated a ' manse,' land sufficient to support
a family, or received its revenues); the name of a
family who settled early in Co. Kilkenny, and thence
passed over into Tipperary and Cork.

ⅯoⅰⱤéⅰⱾ, *Morresh,* Morris, and incorrectly Morrison and
Morrissey. V. ⰱe ⅯoⅰⱤéⅰⱤ.

ⅯoⅰⱤⱦéⅰⱡ—VIII—*Martel, Martell,* Mortell; ' son of
Martel ' (dim. of Martin); an old surname in Meath
and Cork; now also numerous in Co. Limerick.

ⅯóⱤⰱoⅰⱤⅎeⰰċ—X—*Morvornagh, Morvernagh, Morvorny,*
now always Gordon; Ir.' ⅯóⱤⰱoⅰⱤⅎeⰰċ,' i.e., belonging
to ⅯóⱤⰱoⅰⱤeⰰⅎⅎ, a place-name, meaning a rocky hill
or district. This was formerly a Roscommon
surname, but is now found chiefly in Co. Mayo, where
it is not uncommon. It is as old at least as the 16th
century. I can discover no satisfactory explanation
of Gordon as its English equivalent.

ⅯoⱤⰳⰱⅎ—VIII—*Morgane,* Morgan; ' son of Morgan
(a Welsh personal name). This surname, though
fairly common in Ireland, is apparently not older than
the 16th century.

ⅯóⱤⱦúⅎ, *Moretoun,* Moreton, Morton. V. ⰱe ⅯóⱤⱦúⅎ.

ⅯuⅰⱡⱡeóⅰⱤ—XII—Miller, Millar; i.e., the miller.

Ⅿuⅰⅿⅎeⰰċ—X—Moynagh, Moyna, Meenagh, Minnagh,
&c.; Ir. ' Ⅿuⅰⅿⅎeⰰċ ' (i.e., the Munsterman); a
descriptive epithet which supplanted the real surname.
Cf. ⰰéⅰⱤeⰰċ, Ⱡⰰⅰⰳⅎeⰰċ.

múinḃíol, Mandeville, Mansfield. V. móinḃíol.
muiréis, Morris, &c. V. ᴅe moipéiṙ.

na ᴅpaiᴅiʀ—XIII—Beades; Ir. 'na ᴅpaiᴅiṗ' (i.e., of
the prayers, or beads); a rare Roscommon name.
na ᴅʀíᵹᴅe, na ᴅʀíᴅe—XIII—*ny Brydy*, Bride; Ir.
' na ᴅṗiᵹᴅe ' (i.e., of the Bride River, from residence
thereby); a rare East Cork surname.
noiréis, noʀais, nóʀas, Norrish, Norris, &c. V.
ᴅe noipéiṙ.
nuaman—XII—Newman; Nor. ' le Neuman,' ' le
Neweman ' (i.e., the new man, newcomer, the newly
settled stranger); an old surname in Cork and parts
of the midlands.
núinnseann, Nugent. V. ᴅe núnnṙeann.

Ó ainṁiʀe, Ó ainṁiʀeaċ, v. Ó hainṁiṙe, Ó hain-
ṁiṙeaċ.
Ó an Ċáinᴅe—III—*O Encantie, On Conty*, Canty, County;
'des. of the satirist ' (Ir. ' cáinᴅeaċ '); the name of a
bardic family in West Cork. ṙeaṙṙeaṙa Ó an Ċáinᴅe
was a celebrated poet who flourished about the beginning of the 17th century, and took part in the
' Contention of the Bards.' V. Ó Cáinᴅe.
Ó ᴅaċlaiᵹ—III—*O Baghly*, Bockley, (Buckley); ' des.
of the husbandman ' (Ir. ᴅaċlaċ); a rare Mayo surname.
Ó ᴅáiʀe—I—*O Barre*, Barry; ' des. of ᴅáiṙe ' (short
for ᴅaṙṙṙionn or ṙionnᴅaṙṙ, fair-head); the name
of a family of Corca Laoighdhe who anciently possessed the peninsula of miunnᴅeaṙ ᴅáiṙe, or Munter-
vary, in West Cork; said to be still extant in Co. Cork,
angl. Barry.
Ó ᴅaiʀʀ—I—*O Barr*, Barr; ' son of ᴅaṙṙ ' (short for
ᴅaṙṙṙionn or ṙionnᴅaṙṙ); a var. of Ó ᴅáiṙe, q.v.;
formerly in use in Carlow and Donegal, but rare.
Ó ᴅaiscinn—I—Baskin, Buskin; ' des. of ᴅaṙcaoin
(fair-hand); the name of a family who were seated
in Corca Bhaiscinn in West Clare until dispossessed

by the MacMahons early in the 14th century; now very rare.

Ó bALbÁIN—III—*O Ballavane, O Ballevan*, Ballevan; 'des. of the stammerer' (Ir. bALb, dim. bALbÁn); originally a Connacht surname; found at the beginning of the 17th century in Donegal and Tipperary; now very rare and scattered.

Ó bANAZÁIN—I—Banigan, Bannigan; 'des. of bAN-AZÁN' (dim. of bÁn, white); a rare Donegal surname.

Ó bANÁIN—I—*O Banane, O Bannan, O Bynnan*, Banane, Banan, Bannan, Bannon, Banim, &c., and, by translation, White; 'des. of bANÁn' (a dim. of bÁn, white). There are several distinct families of this name, the best-known and most numerous being that of Ely O'Carroll, in the present Offaly. Other families of the name were seated in Mayo and Fermanagh.

Ó b'AObÁIN—I—'des. of bAobÁn' (simpleton, dim. of bAoc); the name of a family formerly seated in the district of Badhna, in the east of Co. Roscommon; now obsolete, or changed into the synonymous form Ó bAoiċín, q.v. O'Donovan erroneously supposed it to be the origin of the surname Boyton.

Ó bAoIZEALLÁIN—I—*O Boylane, O Boylan*, Boylan, Boyland; des. of 'bAoIZEALLÁn' (dim. of bAoIZEALL); the name of a well-known Ulster family who were anciently chiefs of Dartraighe, the present barony of Dartry, in the west of Co. Monaghan, and at one time of all Oriel.

Ó bAoIZILL—I—O'Boyle, Boyle, &c.; 'des. of bAoI-ZEALL' (probably for bAoIc-ZEALL, vain-pledge). The O'Boyles, who are one of the principal families of Cinel Conaill and of the same stock as the O'Donnells and O'Doghertys, were originally chiefs of the Three Tuaths in the north-west of Co. Donegal; but when these territories passed into the possession of the MacSweeneys, O'Boyle became chief Tir-Ainmhireach in the west of the same county, which was thenceforward known as Cṗíoċ bAoIZEALLAċ, or O'Boyle's country, now the barony of Boylagh. During the wars in the reign of Elizabeth, the O'Boyles spread into different parts of Ireland, and towards the close of the 16th century were found in nearly every county. The references to the name in the Annals of the Four Masters and the Fiants of Elizabeth are very numerous.

Ó bᴀoⁱᴛín—I—Boyne; 'des. of bᴀoⁱᴛín' (simpleton, dim. of bᴀoᴛ, foolish); a very rare Connacht surname, probably a substitute for the old Roscommon surname Ó bᴀoᴠáⁱn (q.v.), with which it is synonymous.

Ó bᴀoᴛᴈᴀlᴀⁱᴈ—I—Bohill, (Bowes); 'son of bᴀoᴛ-ᴈᴀlᴀċ' (foolhardy). The head of this family is mentioned by O'Dugan as one of the chiefs of Clan Fergus in Ulster. I have failed to discover any early angl. form of the surname, and am by no means certain that it is still extant. There was also a family surnamed Ó bᴀoᴛᴈᴀⁱl or Ó bᴀoᴛᴈᴀⁱle in the parish of Skreen, Co. Sligo, but that too seems to have disappeared.

Ó báʀᴠáⁱn—III—O Bardane, O Barden, Bardan, Barden, Bardon; 'des. of the little bard' (Ir. báʀᴠ, dim. báʀᴠáⁿ); a rare surname; almost peculiar, in the 16th century, to Wexford and Longford. The O'Bardons of Longford seem to have been at one time professional harpers.

Ó beᴀċáⁱn—I—O Beaghane, O Beghan, O Behan, Beaghan, Beahan, Behane, Behan, Beegan, Beane, Bean; 'des. of beᴀċáⁿ' (dim. of beᴀċ, a bee, a name applied to a child); the name of a literary family in Offaly and Leix, now widely spread through Leinster and Munster.

Ó beᴀᴈᴀċáⁱn—I—O Beggahan, O Begkehan, Begaddon; 'son of beᴀᴈᴀċáⁿ' (dim. of beᴀᴈᴀċ, from beᴀᴈ, small); an old Carlow surname; very rare.

Ó beᴀᴈáⁱn—I—O Begane, O Began, Begane, Biggane, Beggan, and, by translation, Little, Littleton; 'des. of beᴀᴈáⁿ' (dim. of beᴀᴈ, little); a rare and scattered surname. In Co. Limerick, it is pronounced Ó bⁱᴈeáⁱn and sometimes Englished Littleton, a form also in use in parts of Co. Clare.

Ó beaʒlaoıċ—III—*O Beagly, O Begely, O Biggely, O Begley*, Begley, Bagley, Bigly ; 'des. of the little hero' (Ir. beaʒlaoċ), but perhaps the original name was Ó beıʒꝼıle,' des. of the little poet' (cf. the older angl. forms). In the 16th century, this surname was almost peculiar to Donegal and Cork. The O'Begleys of Cork seem to have come southwards with the Mac-Sweeneys, under whom they served as gallowglasses.

Ó beannaċáın—I—*O Benachain, O Benachane, O Benahan*, Banahan ; 'des. of beannaċán' (dim. of beannaċ, pointed, peaked, horned) ; the name of an old Sligo family who, according to O'Flaherty, are of Firbolgic descent.

Ó béara—?—*O Beara, O Berie, O Berry*, Bera, Beary, Berry ; 'des. of béapa (?)' ; the name of an Offaly family of the same race as the O'Connors and O'Dempseys ; also a Mayo surname.

Ó bearáın—I—*O Barrane, O Barran*, Barron, Berrane (Barnes, Barrington) ; 'des. of beapán' (stripling, dim. of beap, a spear, spit, javelin) ; an old surname in Thomond and Tirconnell ; also Ó bıopáın, q.v.

Ó bearʒa—I—*O Barrie, O Barry*, Barrie, Barry ; 'des. of beapʒa' (spear-like) ; the name of a Co. Limerick family who were anciently. lords of Iveross, in the barony of Kenry. There need scarcely be a doubt that many of the Barrys of East Limerick are of this race, and not of Anglo-Norman origin. There was another family of the same name in Tirawley, Co. Mayo, but, according to O'Donovan, it is extinct. It is certainly not the surname which is angl. Berry in that county, the Irish of which is Ó béapa, q.v.

Ó bearnáın—II—Barnane, (Bernard) ; 'des. of beapnán' (dim. of beapn). MacFirbis mentions a Clann beapnáın among the descendants of Colla meann.

Ó béıce—I—*O Beaky*, Beaky, Bakey ; 'des. of béıce' (clamour, weeping). Two persons of this name are mentioned in the Annals of the Four Masters as lords of Ó méıt in the 11th century. O Huidhrin mentions another family of the name as lords of Bantry, Co.

Cork. The name is apparently long extinct in both places. ' O Beaky' was a Co. Wicklow surname at the beginning of the 17th century. O'Donovan gives Beck and Peck as the modern angl. forms of Ó béice, but this I have failed to verify.

Ó beiʒ—I—*O Begg*, Begg, Beggs, Biggs, and, by translation, Little ; ' des. of beaʒ ' (little).

Ó beiʒín—I—*O Beggin*, Beggan, Biggin, Biggins ; ' des. of beiʒin ' (dim. of beaʒ, little) ; a var. of Ó beaʒáin and Ó biʒín, q.v.

Ó beiʒleiʒinn—III—*O Begleyn*, Beglin, Beglan, (Begnall), &c. ; ' des. of the little scholar ' (Ir. beaʒ-léiʒinn) ; the name of a medical family in Longford, Leitrim and Sligo ; also Ó biʒléiʒinn, q.v.

Ó beiRʒin—I—*O Bergin, O Bergen, O Bergan*, Bergin, Berigin, Berrigan, &c. ; a corrupt and shortened form of Ó háiṁeiɲʒin, q.v.

Ó beiRn—II—*O Beirn, O Berne*, O'Beirne, O'Bierne, Beirne, Berne, Beirne, Beirnes, &c. ; a var. of Ó biɲn, q.v.

Ó beólláin—I—*O Beollaine, O Beolane, O Bowlane, O Bolan*, Bolan, Boland, Bowland, &c. ; ' des. of beóll-án ' (Bjolan in Landnamabok) ; the name (1) of an ecclesiastical family in Co. Sligo, the heads of which were for many centuries erenaghs of the Columban church at Drumcliffe, and were noted for their hospitality ; (2) of a Co. Sligo family of the Ui Fiachrach race who were seated at Doonaltan, in the barony of Tireragh, where it is still numerous ; and (3) of a Dalcassian family, who are stated by Keating, but erroneously, to be descended from Mahon, son of Kennedy, and brother of Brian Boru, the real descent being from Mahon, son of Torlough (MacFirbis, Gen. p. 648).

Ó biaóa, Beatagh, Beatty, &c. ; a Connemara surname, doubtless a corruption of biaóṫaċ, q.v.

Ó biasta—I—Beasty, Biesty ; ' son of biarta ' ; an old West Connacht surname, still well known in Mayo. The family derives its descent, according to MacFirbis, from Echean, King of Connacht in the time of St. Patrick.

Ó bıᵹeáın—I—Biggane, Littleton; a var. in Limerick and Clare of Ó beaᵹáın, q.v.

Ó bıᵹıᵹ—I—Biggy; 'son of bıᵹeać' (deriv. of beaᵹ, small); a rare Mayo surname; probably the modern equivalent of the old Mayo surname Ó beacba, which was borne by a Bishop of Tirawley at the beginning of the 13th century.

Ó bıᵹín—I—*O Beggin*, Biggin, Biggins; ' des. of bıᵹín ' (dim. of beaᵹ, small); a var. of Ó beaᵹáın and Ó beıᵹín, q.v.

Ó bıᵹléıᵹınn—III—*O Biglean, O Bigleyn, O Biglene*, Beglin, Beglan, (Bignel, &c.); a var. of Ó beıᵹléıᵹınn, q.v. This seems to have been the more common form of the name.

Ó bıoráın—I—*O Birrain, O Birrane, O Byrran*, Birrane, Byrrane, Byrane, Byran, Brawn, (Byron, Byrne, Barnes, Burns); ' des. of bıoráın ' (stripling, dim. of bıoʀ, a spear, spit); a var. in Tipperary and East Limerick of Ó beapáın, q.v.

Ó bıoráınn, Burns; a rare Kerry surname, perhaps a var. of Ó bıopáın, q.v.

Ó bıʀᵹın—I—*O Birgin, O Birgyn*, Bergin, &c.; ' des. of Aıṁıpᵹın '; a var. of Ó beıpᵹın, q.v.

Ó bıʀín—I—Berreen; a var. of Ó bıopáın, q.v.; a rare Sligo surname.

Ó bıʀn—II—*O Birn, O Birne, O Byrn*, O'Beirne, O'Bierne, O'Byrne, Birne, Beirne, Byrne, Birnes, Byrns, Byrnes, (Byron, Burns); ' des. of bıopn ' (the Norse personal name Bjorn); a var. of Ó beıpn, q.v. The present is the usual form of the name in the Annals; Ó beıpn was apparently more common at a later period. There are two distinct families of the name in Connacht: (1) Ó bıpn of Siol-Muireadhaig. This family first came into prominence as stewards to the O'Connors, Kings of Connacht and sometimes of all Ireland. About the middle of the 13th century, they super-seded the O'Monaghans as chiefs of Tir-Bhriuin, a beautiful district in Co. Roscommon, a position which they continued to hold for more than three hundred years. In the year 1570, Teig Byrne, alias O Byrne, was 'the chiefest of Tirowyne' (Tir-Bhriuin), and several gentlemen of the name are mentioned in the Fiants of Elizabeth. (2) Ó bıᵽn of Ui Fiachrach. This family enjoyed, at the beginning of the 15th century, a considerable estate in Co. Mayo, a little to the north of Ballinrobe, and there were respectable families of the name in that county at the end of the 16th century. O'Donovan found the name, under the angl. form of Byrne, in the very district anciently occupied by the family. O'Beirne and O'Byrne were in use in Lecale, Co. Down, at the beginning of the 17th century, but whether the Irish was Ó bıᵽn, or Ó bᵽoın (q.v.), I am unable to say.

Ó bᴌáčᵯᴀıc—I—Blawick, Blowick, Blouk, (Blake); 'des. of bᴌáčᵯᴀc' (blossom-son); an ancient and beautiful Irish surname; in use in Co. Mayo, but fast becoming merged in the English surname Blake.

Ó bᴌıčín, Bleheen; a rare Galway surname; a var. of Ó ᵯᴀoıᴌᵯín or Ó ᵯᴀoıᴌᵯıčıᴌ, q.v.

Ó bᴌıᵹe—II—O Blie, O Blye, Bly, Bligh, Blighe; 'des. of bᴌıᵹe' (the Norse personal name Bligr). Mac-Firbis mentions two families of this name in Connacht, one of Clann Bhriuin, descended from Echean who was King of Connacht when St. Patrick came to Ireland; and the other of Ui Fiachrach, descended from Aonghus, grandson of Fiachra, from whom the Ui Fiachrach are named. This latter family were hereditary proprietors of Dunfeeny in the barony of Tirawley, Co. Mayo, about nine miles north-west of Killala. The name is still in Mayo.

Ó boᴅᴦáın—III—O Boherane, O Borhane, Boran; 'des. of the deaf-man' (Ir. boᴅᴦán, dim. of boᴅᴀᵹ, deaf); a very rare surname; in use at the beginning of the 17th century in Tyrone and Tipperary; now peculiar to the latter county and the adjoining parts of Co. Limerick.

Ó boʒalʒ—I—*Obuge*, Buggy; 'des. of boʒać' (deriv. of boʒ, soft, tender); a rare surname.

Ó boʒáın—I—*O Bogane*, Bogan, Boggan; 'des. of boʒán' (dim. of boʒ, soft, tender). This surname was peculiar to Wexford and Donegal.

Ó boınne—I—Byrne, (Burns); doubtless a shortened form of Ó Conboınne, an old Mayo surname, which O'Donovan found still extant under the angl. forms of Burns. V. ɱac Conboınne.

Ó bolʒuıóe—I—*O Bolgie, O Boulgye*, (Bolger, Bulger); an apocopated form of Ó bolʒuıóın, q.v.

Ó bolʒuıóın—I—*O Bolgier, O Bolger, O Bulger*, Bolger, Bulger, Boulger; 'des. of bolʒoóan,' (i.e., bolʒ-oóan, perhaps a nickname). The O'Bolgers were the great medical family of South Leinster. The name is still common in Wexford.

Ó bnacáın—I—*O Brahan*, Brahan; 'des. of bnacán' (pottage); an old Tipperary surname; now very rare, if not actually obsolete. It was in use fifty years ago.

Ó bnaóacáın—I—*O Bradekin*, Bradican, (Brady); a var. in Co. Mayo of Ó bnaóacáın, q.v.

Ó bnaóacáın—I—*O Bradaghan*, (Bradagan, Bradican); 'des. of bnaóacán' (dim. of bnáóac, spirited); a var. of Ó bnaóaʒáın, Ó bnaóacáın, q.v.

Ó bnaóaʒáın—I—*O Bradegane, O Bradagan, O Bradigan*, Bradagan, Braddigan, Brodigan, (Bradican); 'des. of bnaóaʒán' (dim. of bnáóac, spirited). This surname, in the 16th century, was almost peculiar to Co. Roscommon. V. Ó bnaóacáın and Ó bnaóacáın.

Ó bnáóaıʒ—I—*O Brady*, Brady; 'des. of bnáóac, (spirited); probably only a var. of ɱac bnáóaıʒ, q.v.; always very rare, but still extant.

Ó bnaóáın—I—*O Bradane, O Bradan, O Bradden*, Bradan, Bradden, and, by 'translation,' Salmon, Sammon, Fisher; 'des. of bnaóán' (dim. of bnáóac, spirited; also a salmon); a rather scattered surname. In Co. Roscommon, it seems to have been an alias for Ó bnaóaʒáın, q.v. Salmon, as an angl. form of this surname, dates back to the year 1555 ; and Salmon, of course, suggested Fisher.

Ó bʀᴀᴅᵹᴀɪʟ, Ó bʀᴀᴅᵹᴀɪʟe—I—*O Bradile*, Braddell ; 'des. of bʀᴀᴅᵹᴀʟ' (spirit-valour) ; a rare Munster surname.

Ó bʀᴀᵹᴀɪn—I—*O Bragane, O Bragan*, Bragan ; 'des. of bʀᴀᵹᴀn.' Three bishops of this name are mentioned in the Annals of the Four Masters.

Ó bʀᴀnᴀᵹᴀɪn—I—*O Branagan, O Branigan, O Brengan*, Branagan, Branigan, Brannigan, Brennigan, Brangan, Brankin ; 'des. of bʀᴀnᴀᵹᴀn' (dim. of bʀᴀn, a raven) ; the name of a family of Cinel Eoghain in Derry. V. Ó bʀᴀnᴀɪn.

Ó bʀᴀnᴀɪn—I—*O Brannan, O Brennan, O Brynan*, Brannan, Brannon, Brennan, Brinan, &c. ; 'des. of bʀᴀnᴀn' (dim. of bʀᴀn, a raven) ; the name of an ecclesiastical family in Ulster, who were erenaghs of the church of Derry and of Derryvullan, Co. Fermanagh. They seem to have been also known by the synonymous surname of Ó bʀᴀnᴀᵹᴀɪn q.v.

Ó bʀᴀnᴅᴜɪb—I—Braniff ; 'des. of bʀᴀnᴅᴜb' (black bʀᴀn, black-raven, an old Irish personal name) ; a rare surname.

Ó bʀᴀnᵹᴀɪʟ, Ó bʀᴀnᵹᴀɪʟe—I—*O Branyll*, Brannelly, Branley ; 'des. of bʀᴀnᵹᴀʟ' (raven-valour) ; a very rare Connacht surname.

Ó bʀᴀoɪn—I—*O Brean, O Breen, O Bruen, O Browne*, (O'Brien), Breen, Bruen, &c. ; 'des. of bʀᴀon' (sadness, sorrow) ; the name of several distinct families, of which the following are the most important : (1) Ó bʀᴀoɪn of Breaghmhaine. The head of this family, which is descended from Maine, son of Niall of the Nine Hostages, was lord of Breaghmhaine, now the barony of Brawney, in Co. Westmeath, adjoining Athlone and the Shannon. The family still flourishes in this ancient territory, but the name has been incorrectly angl. O'Brien, which somewhat obscures its origin. (2) Ó bʀᴀoɪn of Luighne. The head of this family was lord of Luighne, now the barony of

Lune, in the west of Co. Meath. This family disappeared from history at an early period, the last lord of Luighne mentioned in the Annals of the Four Masters having died in the year 1201. (3) Ó Ḃṛaoin of Loch Gealgosa. This family, which is mentioned by O'Dugan, was probably seated in the barony of Costello, Co. Mayo, but its subsequent history cannot be traced. (4) Ó Ḃṛaoin of Roscommon, the head of which was erenagh of the church of St. Coman. To this family belonged the celebrated annalist, Tighearnach Ó Braoin, one of the most learned men of his age. This family may now be represented by the Bruens in Co. Roscommon. O Bruen, O Bruyn, O Bruyen, &c., as angl. forms of Ó Ḃṛaoin in Leix and Carlow, in the 16th century, are a clear indication of the midland origin of the family of Bruen in these counties ; while O Browne in Kerry is equally suggestive of the origin of the Breens in that county and in Limerick.

Ó Ḃṛaonáin—I—*O Brenane, O Brennan, O Brinane,* O'Brennan, Brennan, Brinane, Brinan, &c. ; ' des. of Ḃṛaonán ' (dim. of Ḃṛaon) ; the name of several distinct families, viz. : (1) Ó Ḃṛaonáin of Ossory, the head of which was chief of Ui Duach, in the north of the present Co. Kilkenny, where the name is still very common ; (2) Ó Ḃṛaonáin of Crevagh in Co. Westmeath, a numerous and powerful clan ; (3) Ó Ḃṛaonáin of Siol Anmchadha, of the same race as the O'Maddens, seated in the barony of Longford, in the south-east of Co. Galway, where they were still numerous at the close of the 16th century ; and (4) Ó Ḃṛaonáin of Dunkerron, who were followers of O'Sullivan More, and are still numerous in Kerry. It is almost impossible to distinguish the angl. forms of this surname from those of Ó Ḃṛanáin, q.v. The same angl. forms were to a great extent common to both ; but, generally speaking, Ó Ḃṛanáin is the origin in Ulster, and Ó Ḃṛaonáin in the other provinces.

Ó Ḃṛeacáin—I—*O Breckan, O Brackan,* Bracken ;

' des. of ḃⱤeacán ' (dim. of ḃⱤeac, speckled) ; the name
of an old family in Offaly.

Ó ḃⱤeaᵹaiᵹ—III—*O Bray, O Brye*, Bray, Bree ; ' des.
of the Bregian,' native of Bregia (Ir. ḃⱤeaᵹac) ;
written Ó ḃⱤeaᵹḃa by O Huidhrin ; the name of a
family in the barony of Imokilly, Co. Cork.

Ó ḃⱤeaꞅaiⱡ—I—*O Brassell*, O'Brazil, Brassill, Brazil,
Brazel ; ' des. of ḃⱤeaⱤaⱡ ' (strife, war) ; a somewhat
rare and scattered surname.

Ó ḃⱤeaꞅⱡáin, Ó ḃⱤeiꞅⱡeáin, Ó ḃⱤeiꞅⱡein—I—
O Breslane, Breslane, Breslaun, Breslin, &c. ; ' des. of
ḃⱤeaⱤⱡán ' (dim. of ḃⱤeaⱤaⱡ). The O'Breslins are a
branch of the Cinel Enda, and were originally chiefs
of Fanad, a district in the north-east of the barony
of Kilmacrenan, in Co. Donegal. Some time in the
second half of the 13th century they were driven
from this territory, and settled in Fermanagh, where
they became distinguished as brehons to the Maguires.
They were also erenaghs of the church of Derryvullen,
in the same county, in which office they succeeded
Ó ḃⱤanáin. Ó ḃⱤeaⱤⱡáin was also the name of a
family of the Ui Fiachrach, in Co. Sligo, who were
chiefs of Kilanley, in the barony of Tireragh. The
name is variously corrupted in the spoken language.
V. Ó ḃⱤeiⱤⱡeáin, Ó ḃⱤeiⱤⱡein, Ó ḃⱤioⱤⱡáin, and Ó
ḃⱤiⱤⱡeáin.

Ó ḃⱤeóⱡⱡáin—I—*O Brollan*, Brolan, (Bolan, Boland) ;
possibly the same as Ó ḃeóⱡⱡáin, q.v. MacFirbis
gives the descent of this family from Ainmire, son of
Cormac Caoch, son of Cairbre, son of Niall of the Nine
Hostages. They belong, therefore, to Clann Chairbre
of Co. Sligo, in whose territory the Ui ḃeóⱡⱡáin also
were seated. This, together with the fact that the
name is now almost universally angl. Bolan and
Boland, would seem to point to the identity of the two
names. Ó ḃⱤeóⱡⱡáin is still in use in Co. Mayo, but
is very rare, and there also is angl. Bolan and Boland.

Ó ḃⱤiáin—I—O'Brian, O'Bryan, O'Bryen, O'Brien,
Brien, &c. ; ' des. of ḃⱤian.' This family derives

its name and descent from Brian Boru, King of Ireland, who was slain at Clontarf, in the year 1014. By his victories over the Danish invaders and their Irish allies, Brian raised his clan, the Ui Toirdealbhaigh, to a position of pre-eminence among the Dalcassians, and laid the foundation of the greatness of his posterity, who became not only the ruling family in Thomond, but one of the most powerful in Ireland. Some of them were kings of Munster, and some of all Ireland. Their possessions included the whole of Co. Clare and large portions of the counties of Limerick, Tipperary and Waterford. They divided into several branches, the principal of which were : the O'Briens of Ara, in the north of Co. Tipperary, whose chief was known as Mac I Bhriain Ara ; of Coonagh in the east of Co. Limerick ; of Pobelbrien, now the barony of that name in Co. Limerick, whose chief stronghold was Carrigogonnell, on the Shannon ; of Aherlow, in Co. Tipperary ; and of Cumaragh, in Co. Waterford, who had extensive possessions along the Cummeragh mountains comprising the valley between Dungarvan and the Suir. O'Brien is now one of the most common surnames in Ireland.

Ó ḃRíc—I—*O Brick*, Brick ; ' des. of ḃᵼeac ' (speckled) ; the name of a Waterford family who were anciently lords of the Southern Decies, but sank at an early period under the power of the O'Phelans and disappeared from history. The family is said to be now extinct.

Ó ḃÍoᵴáin—I—*O Brisan*, Briceson, Bryson ; a corruption, in Co. Donegal, of Ó muiᵽᵹeaᵼáin, q.v. It is by no means a late corruption ; O Brisan appears as the angl. form in the Patent Rolls of James I.

Ó ḃÍoᵴláin, Ó ḃrisleáin—I—*O Brislane, O Brissleayn, O Brislan*, Brislane, Brislawn, Brislan, Brislin, Breslin, &c. ; a var. in the spoken language of Ó ḃᵼeaᵼláin, q.v.

Ó ḃroᵹaiḋ—I—*O Brogy*, Broggy ; ' des. of ḃᵼoᵹaiḋ ' (an ancient Irish personal name ; occurs in the Book of Armagh) ; a rare surname in Clare and Limerick.

Ó ႦႰÓჯႠႬႬ—I—*O Brogane, O Brogan,* Brogan; 'des. of
ჃႰóჯჰn' (dim. of ႦႰóჯ, sorrowful); an old surname
in Mayo and Donegal; still common in both counties.
The O'Brogans of Mayo anciently possessed estates
at Breachmaigh and Cnoc Spealain, in the barony of
Carra.

Ó ႦႰ൦ıLeႠჄჄႬ—I—*O Brellighan, O Brilleghane, O
Brilehan,* (Bradley); an attenuated form of Ó ჃႰ൦ւ-
Ⴤჰn, q.v.; apparently the more common form in
popular use.

Ó ႦႰ൦ın—I—*O Birne,* O'Byrne, Byrne, Byrnes, (Burns,
Byron), &c.; 'des. of ჃႰჰn' (raven). This family
derives its name and descent from ჃႰჰn, son of
Ⴋჰ൦ւႫóႰჄჰ, King of Leinster, whose death at Cologne
is recorded by the Four Masters under the year 1052.
The original patrimony of the family was Ui Faolain,
which comprised the northern half of the present Co.
Kildare; but they were driven thence by the Anglo-
Normans soon after the invasion, and forced to take
refuge in the mountain fastnesses of Wicklow, where
they became very powerful and were long the terror
of the invaders of their ancestral homes. At the head
of the Wicklow clans, they maintained for a period of
three hundred years incessant warfare with the
foreigners, whom they defeated in many a fierce
engagement. Their country, which was called CႰí൦Ⴣ-
ႦႰჰnჰჄ, comprised the entire of the barony of New-
castle and portions of those of Arklow and Ballina-
cor. This last belonged to the Gaval-Rannall, or
Ranelagh, a junior branch of the family, which in
time became very powerful and of which the celebrated
Fiach MacHugh O'Byrne was chief in the reign of
Elizabeth. The name is now very common in Leinster, and has spread into many other parts of Ireland.

Ó ႦႰ൦ısneჄჄჄႬ, v. Ó ႦႰ൦ႰnჰჄჄn.

Ó ႦႰ൦ıჄ, *O Brogh, O Broy,* Brophy, (Bray); a var. of
Ó ႦႰ൦ıჄe, q.v.; found in Iveleary, Co. Cork, where it
is sometimes angl. Bray.

Ó ႦႰ൦ıჄe—I—*O Broha, O Brohy, O Broghie,* Brofie,

Brophy; 'des. of ᵇ————'; written Uᴀ ᵇꞃoıꙅᴛe in the Annals of Ulster, A.D. 1165. The original patrimony of this family was Magh Sedna, in the barony of Galmoy, Co. Kilkenny; but they were driven thence into Upper Ossory, soon after the Anglo-Norman invasion, when their chief settled at Bally-brophy, in the present Leix. The family is still numerous in Ossory and the adjoining districts of Tipperary.

Ó ᵇꞃoᴌᴀċáın, v. Ó ᵇꞃoᴌċáın.

Ó ᵇꞃóᴌᴀıꙅ—I—*O Broloe*, Broly, Brolly, Brawley; ' des. of ᵇꞃóᴌᴀċ'; the name of an old Derry family.

Ó ᵇꞃoᴌċáın—I—O'Brollaghan, O'Brallaghan, Broll-laghan, (Bradley); ' des. of ᵇꞃoᴌᴀċán' (dim. of ᵇꞃó-ᴌᴀċ); the name of a famous Ulster family, descended from Suibhne Meann, King of Ireland in the 7th century. They appear to have been seated originally in the barony of Clogher, Co. Tyrone, but removed thence at an early period and settled in the neighbour-hood of Derry, and in Tirconnell. The name is still well known in Ulster and in Co. Mayo, but is often absurdly angl. Bradley, which greatly obscures the origin of this historic family. A branch of the family seem to have also settled in Cork. Ó ᵇꞃoıᴌeᴀċáın (q.v.) is a common variant in the spoken language of Mayo. For an account of the many distinguished bearers of this surname, see Healy's Ancient Schools and Scholars, pp. 352 et seqq.

Ó ᵇꞃoꙅnᴀċáın—I—*O Brosnaghane, O Brosneghan*, Brosnahan, Bresnihan, Brosnan, &c.; ' des. of ᵇꞃoꞃ-nᴀċán' (native of Brosna, in Kerry); the name of an old Kerry family, now also numerous in Co. Limerick.

Ó ᵇꞃuᴀċáın—I—*O Broughan, O Broghan, O Brohan*, Broughan, Brohan, and, by ' translation,' Banks; ' des. of ᵇꞃuᴀċán' (corpulent, or miser); originally a Connacht surname, but in the 16th century common in Westmeath, Kildare and Tipperary, and now also in Co. Clare. V. Ó ᵇꞃuᴀċóꙅ.

Ó ᵇꞃuᴀċóꙅ—I—Banks; in use in Connacht, but ap-

parently only a modern substitution for Ó bṙuaċáin
(q.v.), with which it is synonymous.

Ó bRUAᵭAIR—II—*O Bruadar, O Brouder, O Broder,
O Brother*, Brouder, Broder, Brooder, Bruder, Brother,
Brauders, Brodders, Brothers, (Broderick), &c. ; ' des.
of Bruadar ' (the Norse Broddr) ; the name of at least
five distinct families in Ireland, viz. : (1) Ó bṙuaᵭaiṙ
of Ossory, the head of which was chief of Iverk in the
south of Co. Kilkenny ; (2) Ó bṙuaᵭaiṙ of Galway, a
respectable family in the 16th century, and still
numerous in that county ; (3) Ó bṙuaᵭaiṙ of Carraic
Brachaidhe in Inishowen, Co. Donegal, a family still
in that district at the beginning of the 16th century ;
(4) Ó bṙuaᵭaiṙ of Ui Ceinnsealaigh, Co. Wexford ;
and (5) Ó bṙuaᵭaiṙ of Corca Laoighdhe, Co. Cork.
To this last, which is of the same stock as the O'Driscolls, the O'Brouders of Co. Limerick almost certainly
belong. (See full account of these families by Rev.
John C. MacErlean, S.J., in his Introduction to the
Poems of David O Bruadair, published by the Irish
Texts Society.)

Ó bRUAIᵭeAᵭA—I—*O Briody*, Briody; des. of ' bṙuaiᵭ-
eaᵭ ' ; an old Cavan surname.

Ó bRUᵷAᵭA—III—*O Browe, O Broe*, Broe, Browe,
Brew ; ' des. of the bṙuᵷaiᵭ ' (or farmer) ; an Ossory
surname.

Ó bRUIC—I—*O Bruck, O Brick*, Brick, and, by ' translation,' Badger ; ' des. of bṙoc ' (badger) ; the name
of a Dalcassian family, long settled in Kerry, and still
well known in that county. The ' translated ' form,
Badger, is found in Co. Galway.

Ó bRÚIN, Bruin, Bruen ; v. Ó bṙaoin.

Ó buAᵭALLA—I—*O Buoghelly, O Bowghilly, O Bohelly*,
Boughla, Buhilly, Buckley ; ' des. of buaċaill ' (the
boy, used as a personal name). This surname, in the
16th century, was peculiar to Cork, Tipperary and
Offaly. It is now also common in Kerry, Kilkenny and Dublin. There are very few of the name
in any other county.

Ó buaohacáin—I—*O Boughane, O Boughan, O Boghan,*
Boughan, Bougan, Boohan, Bohane, Bohan, (?) Boy-
han, (Bowen, Bohanan) ; ' des of buaohacán ' (dim.
of buaohac, victorious) ; a rather scattered surname.
In the 16th century it was found chiefly in Cork,
Kerry, Tipperary, Offaly and Kilkenny.

Ó buaohais—I—*O Boey, O Bowe, O Boyc, O Bwoy, O
Bowige,* Bowie, Bowe, Buie, Bwee, Bowes, Boyes,
Boyce, O'Boyce, Bohig, Bogue, &c. ; ' des. of buaohac '
(victorious) ; a very scattered surname, but most
common in Donegal, Kilkenny and Cork.   In the
last-mentioned county, the final ṡ is sounded ; hence
the early angl. form Ó Bowige and the modern Bogue.
The family is a branch of the Corca Laoighdhe, but
was erroneously supposed to be a branch of the
O'Sullivans, on account of the prevalence of the
Christian name buaohac in that family ; and it is not
improbable that some of them have adopted the name
of O'Sullivan or Sullivan.

Ó buaoháin—I—*O Bowdan, O Bodan,* Bodan, Bowden,
Boden ; ' des. of buaohán ' (an ancient Irish personal
name, older form buacán) ; an old Ossory surname.

Ó caoháin—I—*O Cadane,* Cadan, Cadden ; ' des. of
Caohán ' (an Irish personal name, Lat. Catanus) ; a
rare Ulster surname ; possibly the same as Mac
Caoháin, q.v.

Ó caohain—I—*O Coyne, O Kine,* Coyne, Kyne, Kine,
and, by translation, Barnacle ; ' des. of Caohan ' (wild-
goose, barnacle) ; the name of an old family of Partry,
who are still numerous in Connacht.

Ó caohla—I—*O Keyle, O Kealy, O Quealy,* Kiely, Keily,
Kealy, Keely, Keeley, (Kelly), Quealy, &c. ; ' des. of
Caohla ' (beautiful, comely, graceful) ; the name (1)
of a Connacht family who were formerly chiefs of
Connemara ; and (2) of a Thomond family who were
chiefs of Tuath Luimnigh in the neighbourhood of
the city of Limerick.   Both families are still numer-
ously represented in Connacht and Munster.   To be
distinguished from Ó Caollaihe, q.v.

Ó Cároin, Caden, Cadden; a corruption in the spoken language of Connacht of mac Ároin, q.v.

Ó Caingne—I—*O Kangney*, Cangney, Cagney; 'des. of Caingean' (business, compact, dispute, etc.); a Munster surname. The family, which is a branch of the Corca Laoighdhe, was originally seated in the parish of Myros, in the barony of West Carbery, Co. Cork.

Ó Cainín—I—*O Canine, O Canin*, Caning, Canning; 'des. of Cainín'; a var. of Ó Coinín, q.v.; a rare midland surname.

Ó Cáinte—III—*O Canty*, Canty, County; a short form of Ó an Cáinte, q.v. Ó Canntaið is a common pronunciation of this surname in Kerry and Limerick, hence the angl. form County which is sometimes met with.

Ó Cairbre—I—*O Carbery, O Carbry*, Carbry, Carbery, Carberry; 'des. of Cairbre' (charioteer); the name of an old midland family who were anciently chiefs of Tuath Buadha, now Tuaith or Twy, in the barony of Clonlonan, Co. Westmeath.

Ó Cairealláin—I—*O Caralane, O Carlane*, Carellan, Carlan, Carland, Carlin, (Carleton); 'des. of Caireallán' (dim. of Caireall); the name of a branch of the Cinel Eoghain who were formerly chiefs of Clandermot, Co. Derry. William Carleton, the novelist, was of this family. V. Ó Coirealláin.

Ó Cairre, v. Ó Carra.

Ó Cairrín, v. Ó Carraðin.

Ó Cais—I—*O Case*, Cash; 'des. of Car' (bent, curly, &c.); very rare.

Ó Caisealáin—I—*O Cashellan*, Cushlane, Cashlan, Caslin; doubtless a corruption of Ó Caireaðáin, angl. *O Cassidan*; a rare Ulster surname.

Ó Caisiðe—I—*O Cashedy, O Cassidy, O Kesedy*, Cassidy, Cassedy, Kessidy, &c.; 'des. of *Caisiðe*'; the name of a distinguished medical family in Fermanagh who were hereditary physicians to the Maguires. Branches of the family had settled in the midland counties before the end of the 16th century.

Ó Caisil, Ó Caisile—I—*O Cashell, O Cassell, O Cashuly, O Cassely,* Cashel, Cassell, Cassilly, Casley, &c. ; doubtless corruptions of Ó Cairíoe, q.v. Cf. Ó Caireatáin above.

Ó Caisín—I—*O Cashine, O Cassin, O Kessan,* Casheen, Cashin, Cashen, Cashion, Cashon, Cassian, Cassin, Keshin ; 'des. of Cairín' (dim. of car, bent, curly) ; apparently a var. in the south of Ireland of the Ossory surname Mac Cairín, q.v.

Ó Caitniaó—I—*O Cahenney, O Cany,* Caheny, Canny ; 'des of Caitnia' (battle-champion) ; the name of a distinguished family of the Ui Fiachrach, in Co. Mayo, who were lords of Erris, in the north-west of that county, until dispossessed by the Barretts in the 13th century. The family is still in Mayo.

Ó Calgaig—I—*O Colgy, O Calgie, O Kalligie,* Callagy, Kellegy ; 'des. of Calgac' (peevish) ; a scattered surname, nowhere very common.

Ó Callaóa—I—Kelledy ; 'des. of Callaio' (crafty) ; extremely rare The Four Masters under the year 1168 record the death of Maolpáopaig Ua Callaóa, coarb of St. Cronan of Roscrea.

Ó Callanáin—I—*O Callanane, O Callinan,* Callanane, Callanan, Callinan, Calnan, &c. ; 'des. of Callanán' ; the name of a distinguished medical family in South Munster ; also of a Galway family who were coarbs of Kilcahill. The latter family is mentioned by Mac Firbis.

Ó Callaráin—I—*O Calleran,* Colleran ; perhaps a corruption of Mac Allmuráin, q.v. ; a rare Connacht surname.

Ó Caltáin, Culhane ; a metathesised form of Ó Catláin, q.v.

Ó Camta—I—*O Comy,* Cowmey, Coumey, Coomey ; 'des. of Camta' (bent, stooped) ; a Munster surname extremely rare.

Ó Canáin—I—*O Cannane,* Cannan, Cannon, Canning, &c. ; 'des. of Canán' (an old Irish personal name, probably dim. of Cano, a wolf-cub) ; the name of a branch of the Ui Maine, in Co. Galway, of the same stock as the O'Maddens. V. Ó Conáin.

Ó cAnAnn—I—*O Cannan, O Cannon,* Cannan, Cannon, Canning, &c. ; ' des. of CAno ' (wolf-cub, whelp) ; an old Tirconnell surname ; probably a var. of Ó CAnAnnáin, q.v.

Ó cAnAnnáin—I—*O Cananan, O Conanan, O Kannenan,* (?) Cannon ; ' des. of CAnAnnán ' (dim. of CAnAnn) ; the name of a family who were lords of Tirconnell from the beginning of the 10th to the middle of the 13th century, when they were supplanted by the O'Donnells and sank into obscurity. There were still a few scattered families of the name at the end of the 16th century.

Ó cAocáin—I—*O Kieghane, O Keaghan, O Keahan,* Keahan, Keehan ; ' des. of CAocán ' (dim. of CAoc, blind, Lat. caecus) ; a var. of mAc CAocáin, q.v.

Ó cAoováin, Kane, Kean, Keane ; a corruption in the spoken language of Co. Mayo of mAc Aooáin, q.v.

Ó cAogáin, Keegan ; a corruption in the spoken language of Connacht of mAc AooAgáin, q.v.

Ó cAoilte, Ó cAoiltig—I—*O Cailte, O Kiltie, O Kiltagh,* O'Kielty, O'Kielt, Kielty, Kilty, Keelty, Quilty, Queelty, Keeltagh Kieltagh, and, by ' translation,' Small in parts of Ulster, and Woods in parts of Connacht ; ' des. of CAoilte ' (an ancient Irish personal name, probably meaning ' hardness ') ; a rather scattered surname ; found in Ulster, Munster and Connacht.

Ó cAoim—I—*O Keeve,* O'Keeffe, Keeffe, &c. ; ' des. of CAoim ' (beautiful, noble, gentle, loveable). The O'Keeffes, who are of the royal race of Munster and of the same stock as the MacCarthys and O'Callaghans, derive their name and descent from Aic CAoim who was son of Fionghuine, King of Munster, and flourished in the 10th century. ʋonncAʋ Ó CAoim, the first to bear the surname, lived in the reign of Ceallachan of Cashel. The O'Keeffes were originally seated at Glanworth and possessed the district now called Roches' country, in the barony of Fermoy ; but they were driven thence shortly after the Anglo-Norman invasion, when they settled in a district in the north-west of the barony of Duhallow, to which they gave the name of Pobble O'Keeffe, and where they maintained themselves as a distinct clan down to the end of the 16th century.

Ó Cᴀoɪṁín—I—*O Kavine*, Kevin, Cavan ; 'des. of Cᴀoɪṁín' (dim. of Cᴀoṁ) ; extremely rare. V. Ó Cᴀoṁáɪn.

Ó Cᴀoɪnᴅeᴀʟḃáɪn—I—*O Guindelane, O Kennellan, O Kenolan, O Quinelane*, Kindellan, Kennellan, (Connellan), Kinlan, Kinlen, Kenlan, (Conlan), Quinlivan, Quinlan ; ' des. of Cᴀoɪnᴅeᴀʟḃán ' (gracefully shaped) ; the name of a Meath family who were chiefs of Cinel Laoghaire, near Trim, until the Anglo-Norman invasion. They derive their name and descent from Cᴀoɪnᴅeᴀʟḃán (died 925), the lineal descendant of Laoghaire, son of Niall of the Nine Hostages, who was King of Ireland in the time of St. Patrick. The name is still in Meath, but disguised under the angl. forms of Connellan and Conlon ; in other parts of Leinster it is angl. Kinlan, Kinlen, &c. ; and it is found in all the counties of Munster, but shortened to Ó Cᴀoɪnʟeáɪn (q.v.), or metathesised to Ó Cᴀoɪnʟɪoḃáɪn, q.v.

Ó Cᴀoɪnʟeáɪn—I—*O Kenlan, O Quinlan*, Quinlan, &c. V. Ó Cᴀoɪnᴅeᴀʟḃáɪn.

Ó Cᴀoɪnʟɪoḃáɪn—I—*O Keynlewayn*, Quinlivan, &c. V. Ó Cᴀoɪnᴅeᴀʟḃáɪn.

Ó Cᴀoʟáɪn—I—*O Kealain, O Kayllan*, Keelan, Keelin ; ' des. of Cᴀoʟán ' (dim. of cᴀoʟ, slender). It appears to have been a Meath surname.

Ó Cᴀoʟʟᴀɪᴅe—I—*O Coely, O Kuelly, O Keally, O Kealy*, Kealy, Keely, (Kelly), Quealy, Queely, &c. ; ' des. of Cᴀoʟʟᴀɪᴅe ' (an ancient Irish personal name) ; also written Ó Cᴀoʟʟᴀɪ̇ʒe ; the name (1) of a Kilkenny family who were anciently chiefs of Ui Bearchon, in the present barony of Ida ; (2) of a Leix family who were chiefs of Crioch O mBuidhe, in the present barony of Ballyadams ; and (3) of a Tipperary family, anciently chiefs of Aolmhagh. The name appears to have been also in Ulster. It is now almost everywhere disguised under the angl. form of Kelly, for which it is the ordinary Irish in West Limerick and Kerry. In Waterford, it is angl. Queally. Cf. Ó Caōla.

Ó caoṁáɴ—I—*O Keavane, O Kevane,* Kevane, Keevane, Keevan, Cavan, Kevans, (Cavanagh, Kavanagh, Cavendish) ; ' des. of Caoṁán ' (dim. of Caoṁ) ; the name of a branch of the Ui Fiachrach in Sligo and Mayo. They were at one time an important family, and it was their privilege to inaugurate O'Dowd in the chieftaincy of Ui Fiachrach. Some of them seem to have settled, before the end of the 16th century, in Westmeath, Offaly and Kilkenny ; and at the present day, the name is common in West Munster, but angl. Cavanagh and Kavanagh. It is sometimes absurdly made Cavendish in Mayo. There was also a family of the same name in Co. Tyrone, but it seems to be extinct.

Ó caoṁánaiʒ—I—Cavanagh, Kavanagh, Keaveny, Kevany, (Kevane, Kevans) ; ' des. of Caoṁánac ' (der. of Caoṁán). This surname, which is common in the spoken language of Connacht and West Munster, appears everywhere side by side with Ó Caoṁáin (q.v.), of which it seems to be merely a modern variant. Ó Caoṁánaiʒ is also sometimes, but incorrectly, used for the surname Caoṁánac q.v. I have failed to discover any early instance, Irish or English, of this surname.

Ó caoʀcannáin, Rountree ; probably only a ' translation ' of the English surname Rowantree.

Ó caʀʀa—I—*O Carra, O Carr, O Karr,* Carr, Karr, Kerr ; ' des. of Caʀʀa ' (spear) ; a common Ulster surname, the same as that written Ó Caiʀʀe in the Annals of Ulster and Four Masters. Also found in Co. Galway. V. Ó Coʀʀa.

Ó caʀʀaʒáin—I—O'Carrigan, Carrigan, Carigan, Cargin. V. Ó Coʀʀaʒáin.

Ó Cᴀʀʀᴀɪᴅ—I—*O Carrie,* Carry; ' des. of Cᴀᴘᴘᴀᴅ '
(spear) ; a var. of Ó Cᴀᴘᴘᴀ and Ó Coᴘᴘᴀɪᴅ, q.v.

Ó Cᴀʀʀᴀɪᴅɪɴ—I—*O Carrine,* Caren, Carr; ' des. of
Cᴀᴘᴘᴀɪᴅɪɴ ' (dim. of Cᴀᴘᴘᴀᴅ) ; a var. of Ó Coᴘᴘᴀɪᴅɪɴ,
q.v. ; angl. Carr in Mayo and Galway.

Ó Cᴀʀʀᴀɪɴ—I—*O Carrane, O Carrain, O Carran,* Craan,
Crain, Crane, Crean, Creane, (Crahan, Crehan, Creaghan, Carey) ; ' des. of Cᴀᴘᴘᴀɴ ' (dim. of cᴀᴘᴘᴀ, a
spear) ; a var. of Ó Coᴘᴘᴀɪɴ, q.v.

Ó Cᴀʀʀᵹᴀᵯɴᴀ, O'Growney, &c. ; a var. of Mᴀc Cᴀᴘᴘ-
ᵹᴀᵯɴᴀ, q.v. ; so written by Keating.

Ó Cᴀʀᴄᴀ, Carr ; a var. in Co. Galway of Ó Cᴀᴘᴘᴀ, q.v.

Ó Cᴀʀᴄᴀɪᵹ—I—*O Carhy, O Cartie,* O'Carthy, Carthy,
Carty, &c. ; ' des. of Cᴀᴘᴄᴀċ ' (loving). There were
families of this name in Tipperary, Clare and Roscommon. The last-named family ramified into Longford, Sligo and Donegal. Three of the name are
mentioned by the Four Masters as chief poets of
Connacht in the 11th and 12th centuries. The name
is still common in many parts of Ireland. To be
distinguished from Mᴀc Cᴀᴘᴄᴀɪᵹ, q.v.

Ó Cᴀʀᴄᴀɪɴ—I or IV—*O Cartaine, O Cartayne, O Cartan,*
Cartan, Carton, Carten, Cartin, Curtan, Curtayne,
Curtin, &c. ; ' des. of Cᴀᴘᴄᴀɴ,' if not a corruption
of Mᴀc Aᴘᴄᴀɪɴ (q.v.), which seems probable. At the
beginning of the 17th century, it was found chiefly
in the midlands—Westmeath and Longford—but
appears also at Castleisland, Co. Kerry, where it is
now pronounced Ó Cuᴘᴄᴀɪɴ, and angl. Curtin, &c.,
as it is also in West Limerick where it is now very
common. V. Mᴀc Cᴀɪᴘᴄᴇᴀɪɴ.

Ó Cᴀʀᴄᴀɪɴ—I—Cartan, Carten, (Carthy), &c. ; a rare
West Connacht surname, the origin of which I cannot
trace.

Ó Cᴀsᴀɪᴅᴇ—I—*O Cassada,* Cassidy, &c. ; a var. of Ó
Cᴀɪᴘᴅᴇ, q.v.

Ó Cᴀsᴀɪʟᴇ—I—Cassilly, Casley ; a var. of Ó Cᴀɪᴘɪʟᴇ, q.v.

Ó Cᴀsᴀɪɴ—I—*O Cossane, O Kessan, O Kissane,* Cussane,
Kissane, (Cashman, Patterson) ; ' des. of Cᴀᴘᴀɴ ' (dim.

of cᴀ𝐫, bent, curly, &c.) ; the name of a Galway family, formerly seated in Ui Maine, Co. Galway ; still represented in that county, but pronounced Ó Coɼáın, and angl. Cussane and Patterson. It is also a not uncommon surname in Kerry and Cork, where it is corrupted to Ó Cıoɼáın, and angl. Kissane in the former county, and, very corruptly, Cashman in the latter.

Ó Cᴀċᴀıᵹ—I—*O Cahy*, Cahy ; ' des. of Cᴀċᴀċ ' (war-like) ; a rare Offaly surname.

Ó Cᴀċᴀıl—I—*O Cahill*, Cahill ; ' des. of Cᴀċᴀl' (battle-powerful). There are several distinct families of this name, of which the following are the most important : (1) Ó Cᴀċᴀıl of Cinel Aodha, in the south-west of Co. Galway, of the same stock as the O'Shaughnessys ; (2) Ó Cᴀċᴀıl of Crumthann, in the east of Co. Galway ; (3) Ó Cᴀċᴀıl of Corca Thine, now angl. Corke-henny, in the parish of Templemore, Co. Tipperary, who gave its name to Ballycahill ; (4) Ó Cᴀċᴀıl of Loch Lein, who were lords of the Eoghanacht of that district before the O'Donoghues ; and (5) Ó Cᴀċᴀıl of Ui Flaithri, near Corofin, Co. Clare. These families were all well-represented at the end of the 16th century.

Ó Cᴀċáın—I—*O Caghane, O Cahaine, O Cahane, O Kahane, O Kaane*, O'Cahan, O'Caughan, O'Kane, O'Keane, Cahane, Cahan, Cane, Cain, Kane, Keane, &c. ; ' des. of Cᴀċán' (a ' pet ' form of some name commencing with Cᴀċ-) ; the name (1) of a branch of the Cinel Eoghain, who were lords of Keenaght and possessed the greater part of the present Co. Derry until their estates were confiscated at the time of the plantation of Ulster ; and (2) of a branch of the Ui Fiachrach in Co. Galway. A branch of the Derry family is said to have settled at an early period in Thomond. There are no doubt several distinct families of the name which is now a very common one all over Ireland.

Ó Cᴀċᴀláın—I—*O Cahallane, O Cohallan*, Cahallane,

Cahillane, Cahalane, Cohalane, Cohalan, Callan, Culhane, Clahane, Clehane, &c. ; ' des: of Catalán'
(dim. of Catal, battle-mighty) ; also written Ó Catláin, q.v. ; the name (1) of a Roscommon family who
were formerly chiefs of Clann Fogartaigh ; (2) of a
Limerick family, formerly chiefs of Uaitne Cliach,
now the barony of Owneybeg, until dispossessed by
the O'Mulryans ; (3) of an Ulster family, now represented by Callan in Monaghan and Louth ; and,
doubtless, of other families in different parts of Ireland. All the above-mentioned families were well
represented in the 16th century ; and the name was
then also in Offaly, Leix, Kildare, Cork and Kerry.

Ó CACAOIR—I—*O Cahir*, Cahir ; ' des. of Cataoir ' (an
ancient Irish personal name) ; a rare ·Tipperary surname.

Ó CACARNAIƷ—I—O'Caharney, O'Caherney, Carney,
[Fox] ; ' des. of Catarnac ' (warlike) ; the name of
an old Meath family, descended from Maine, son of
Niall of the Nine Hostages. They were originally
chiefs of all Teffia, but their patrimony was afterwards narrowed down to Muinntear Tadhgain, now
the barony of Kilcoursey, in Offaly. They were
also known by the surname of Sionnac (q.v.), from the
cognomen of their ancestor, Catarnac Sionnac (the
fox), who was slain in the year 1084. The head of the
family was known by the title of an Sionnac, or The
Fox.

Ó CACASAIƷ—I—*O Cahessy*, O'Casey, Casey ; ' des. of
Catarac ' (vigilant, watchful) ; the name (1) of a
family in ancient Meath, who were lords of Saithne,
in the north of the present Co. Dublin, until dispossessed by Sir Hugh de Lacy soon after the Anglo-
Norman invasion ; (2) of a Dalcassian family, seated
in the barony of Coshlea, Co. Limerick ; (3) of a Cork
family who possessed a territory called Coillte Mai-
binacha, near Mitchelstown ; (4) of a Tirawley family
who were erenaghs of Kilarduff, in the parish of Dunfeeny, Co. Mayo ; (5) of a Roscommon family, formerly

erenaghs of Cloondara, in the parish of Tisrara ; and
(6) of a Fermanagh family formerly erenaghs of
Devinish. These families are all still well represented.

Ó Catbada—I—*O Caffoo, O Caffoe,* Coffey ; ' des. of
Catbad ' (older Catbot, gen. Catbota, battle-tent,
an ancient Irish personal name) ; a Tipperary surname.
Cf. Aba Ua gCatbada, near Nenagh.

Ó Catbuadaig—I—*O Caphowagh, O Capphowe, O
Caffowe, O Caffoye,* Coffey ; ' des. of Catbuadac '
(battle-victorious) ; a West Munster surname ; very
common in Kerry.

Ó Catláin—I—*O Callaine, O Collhane, O Callan,* Culhane, Callan, Callen, Callin, Cawlin, Clahane, Clehane,
&c. ; ' des. of Catalán ' (dim. of Catal, battle-mighty);
a shortened form of Ó Cataláin, q.v. Culhane is the
usual angl. form in Co. Limerick, but the name is
sometimes metathesised to Ó Clatáin, angl. Clahane
and Clehane. Callan is more commonly the angl.
form in the North.

Ó Catluain—I—*O Collone, O Cullone,* Calhoun, Colhoun, Colhoon, Culhoun, &c. ; ' des. of Catluan '
(battle-hound, battle-hero, or battle-joyful) ; originally
a Breifney surname, now dispersed through Ulster.
The Uí Catluain are mentioned in the Annals at the
year 1145.

Ó Catmoga—I—*O Cowhow,* Coffey ; ' des. of Catmug '
(battle-slave) ; a rare surname in south-west of Co.
Galway ; to be distinguished from Ó Cobtaig of
the same county. The family is of the same stock
as the O'Clerys and O'Heynes.

Ó Céadacáin, Ó Céadagáin—I—*O Kadegane, O
Keadigan,* Cadigan, Cadogan ; ' des. of Céadacán,'
or ' Céadagán ' (dim. of Céadac, possessing hundreds) ;
an old West Cork surname.

Ó Céadaig—I—*O Keddy,* Keady ; ' des. of Céadac '
(possessing hundreds ; a favourite personal name
among the O'Moores and O'Farrells) ; the name of an
old Co. Galway family, of the same stock as the
O'Clerys and O'Heynes.

Ó ceaʟʟaċáın—I—O'Callaghan, O'Callahan, Callaghan, Callahan, Calligan, &c.; 'des. of Ceaʟʟaċán' (dim. of Ceaʟʟaċ); the name of a well-known Munster family descended from Ceaʟʟaċán of Cashel, king of Munster, in the 10th century. The surname was not, however, taken from this Ceaʟʟaċán, but from a namesake of his four generations later. The O'Callaghans were originally chiefs of Cinel Aodha, now the barony of Kinalea, in the south of Co. Cork, but on being driven thence by Robert FitzStephen and Milo de Cogan, soon after the Anglo-Norman invasion, they settled on the banks of the Blackwater, to the west of Mallow, where they continued to enjoy considerable possessions, known as Pobul Ui Cheallachain, comprising the parishes of Kilshannig and Clonmeen, down to the time of the Cromwellian confiscations, when the head of the family was transplanted to Clare. There is also a Mayo family of the name, a branch of the Ui Fiachrach, who were anciently lords of Erris.

Ó ceaʟʟaıᵹ—I—O'Kelly, Kelly, Kelley; 'des. of Ceaʟʟaċ' (war, contention); the name of several distinct families, of which the following are the best known: (1) Ó Ceaʟʟaıᵹ of Ui Maine, a branch of the Oirghialla of Ulster. They were one of the most powerful families in Connacht, and as chiefs of Ui Maine ruled over an extensive territory in the counties of Galway and Roscommon, which they held down to the reign of Elizabeth. This family produced many distinguished chiefs, among them Taᵹᵹ Móp Ó Ceaʟʟaıᵹ who fell at Clontarf in 1014. (2) Ó Ceaʟʟaıᵹ of Breagh, a branch of the southern Ui Neill, who were lords of Breagh, an extensive district embracing a large portion of Meath and the north of Co. Dublin, until after the Anglo-Norman invasion, when they were dispossessed and dispersed throughout Ireland. Conᵹaʟaċ Ó Ceaʟʟaıᵹ, the last lord of Breagh, died in 1292. (3) Ó Ceaʟʟaıᵹ of Cinel Eachach in the barony of Loughinsholin, Co. Derry, where they are

still numerous; (4) Ó Ceallaiġ of Leighe, now Lea,
(5) Ó Ceallaiġ of Magh Druchtain, (6) Ó Ceallaiġ of
Gallen, all three in Leix; (7) Ó Ceallaiġ of Ui Teigh,
in the north of the present Co. Wicklow; (8) Ó Ceallaiġ of Áᵽo Ó ʒCeallaiġ, in the parish of Templeboy,
Co. Sligo; and (9) Ó Ceallaiġ of Corca Laoighdhe,
in the south-west of Co. Cork.

Ó ceanʒlaċáin, Tighe. This form is found in the
spoken language of Mayo, but seems to be merely a
'translation' of the English or angl. surname Tighe.

Ó ceannoubáin—I—*O Cannovane, O Canavan, O
Kennavain,* Cannavan, Canavan, Kinavan, and, by
'translation,' Whitehead; 'des. of Ceannoubán'
(dim. of Ceannoub, i.e., black-head); the name of a
West Connacht family who, according to MacFirbis,
were physicians to Muinntear Murchadha, the clan
of which the O'Flahertys were chiefs. The name was
also in Co. Cork and other parts of Ireland. Though
really meaning black-head, it has been 'translated'
Whitehead, the termination having been mistaken
for bán, white.

Ó ceannoub—I—*O Canyve, O Kannife,* Canniff,
Canniffe; 'des. of Ceannoub' (black-head); a rare
Cork surname; possibly an alias for Ó Ceannoubáin,
q.v.

Ó cearáin—I—Kerrane, Kirrane, Kearon, Kearons,
(Carr, Carey), &c.; a corruption (or older form) of
Ó Ciaráin, q.v.; common in Mayo; also Ó Cioráin,
q.v.

Ó cearbaill—I—*O Carrowill, O Carwell, O Carvill,*
O'Carroll, Carroll, Carvill; 'des. of Cearbáll' (a very
common Irish personal name). There are several
distinct families so named, of which the following
are the best known: (1) Ó Cearbáill of Eile, who
derive their name and descent from Cearbáll, lord of
Eile, who fought at Clontarf. The head of this family
was originally lord of all Eile, which comprised the
baronies of Clonlisk and Ballybritt, in the present
Offaly, and Ikerrin and Eliogarty, in Co. Tipperary;

but after the Anglo-Norman invasion, Ikerrin and
Eliogarty became tributary to the Earl of Ormond,
and only the portion of Eile subsequently called **Ely
O'Carroll**, remained in possession of O'Carroll, who
resided at Birr. This family is now very numerous.
(2) Ó Ceaρṗaill of Oriel. This family is of the same
stock as the MacMahons and Maguires, and were
chiefs of Oriel until about the period of the Anglo-
Norman invasion, when they disappear from history.
They are still numerous in Monaghan and Louth.
(3) Ó Ceaρṗaill of Loch Lein, anciently chiefs of the
Eoghanacht of Loch Lein, the district about Killarney,
until dispossessed by the O'Donoghues. (4) Ó Ceaρṗaill of Ossory who are descended from Ceaρṗall, a
celebrated chieftain of Ossory at the middle of the
9th century. (5) Ó Ceaρṗaill of Tara, a branch of
the southern Ui Neill. This family disappeared from
history at an early period. (6) Ó Ceaρṗaill of Calry,
in Sligo and Leitrim. The MacBradys of Cavan are
said, but erroneously, to be a branch of this family.

Ó ceaRṗáin—I—*O Carvan, O Kervan,* Carvan, Carvin,
Kervan, (Kirwan) ; ' des. of Ceaρṗán ' (probably dim.
of ceaρṗ, a stag, Lat. cervus) ; a rare Leinster surname.

Ó ceaRṗalláin—I—*O Carowlane, O Carolan,* Carolan,
Carrolan, &c. ; ' des. of Ceaρṗallán ' (dim. of Ceaρṗall) ; a well-known Ulster surname ; formerly
common in Donegal, Tyrone, Monaghan and Cavan ;
also in Meath. There are probably several distinct
families of the name. To be distinguished from Ó
Coιρealláin, q.v.

Ó ceaRmaᴅa—I—*O Carmody, O Kermody,* Carmody,
Kermody ; ' des of Ceaρmaιᴅ ' (a very ancient Irish
personal name) ; an old and still well-known Thomond
surname.

Ó ceaRnaċáin—I—*O Kernaghan, O Kernan,* Carnahan,
Kernaghan, Kernahan, Kernan, Kernon, &c. ; ' des.
of Ceaρnaċán ' (dim. of Ceaρnaċ, victorious) ; the name
(I) of a Meath family who were anciently chiefs of
Luighne, now the barony of Lune ; and (2) of a Tir-

connell family who were chiefs of Tuath Bladhach, now angl. Doe, in the barony of Kilmacrenan.

Ó ceᴀꞃnᴀiꞟ—I—*O Carny*, O'Kearney, Carney, Kearney, &c. ; 'des. of Ceᴀꞃnᴀċ' (victorious) ; the name (1) of a Dalcassian family who in later times attained to a high position at Cashel ; (2) of a family of Ui Fiachrach in Co. Mayo who formerly held extensive possessions in the parishes of Moynulla and Balla ; and (3) of an ecclesiastical family who were formerly erenaghs of Derry. The name cannot now always be distinguished from Ó Ceiteᴀꞃnᴀiꞟ, q.v.

Ó céᴀṫꝼᴀᴅᴀ—I—Keaty, (Keating) ; ' des. of Céᴀṫꝼᴀiᴅ' (sense) ; the name of a Dalcassian family who were anciently seated in the neighbourhood of the city of Limerick ; apparently also a Leinster surname.

Ó céile—I—*O Kely*, Kealy, Wisdom ; ' des. of Céile' (servant, friend, companion) ; the name of an ecclesiastical family who were erenaghs of Tullow, Co. Carlow, and of another who were erenaghs of Slaine, Co. Meath. It is said to be now angl. by ' translation,' Wisdom in Co. Louth.

Ó céileᴀċáin—I—*O Kellechan, O Kellichan*, Kelaghan, Keleghan, Kellaghan, Keelaghan, Kelihan, (O'Callaghan, Callaghan), &c. ; ' des of Céileᴀċán' (dim. of Céile) ; the name of an Armagh family who were anciently chiefs of Ui Breasail ; to be distinguished from Ó Ceᴀllᴀċáin, q.v.

Ó céileᴀċᴀiꞃ—I—*O Keallaghir*, O'Kelliher, Kellegher, Kelleher, Kelliher, Keller, &c. ; ' des of Céileᴀċᴀꞃ' (companion-dear, spouse-loving) ; the name of a well-known family in Cork and Kerry. They are of Dalcassian origin, being descended from Donnchuan, brother of Brian Boru.

Ó céin—I—*O Keyne, O Kean*, Kean, Keane ; ' des. of Ciᴀn' (an old Irish personal name) ; the name of a Waterford family who were anciently chiefs of a district bordering on the River Mahon. To this family belonged, according to O'Donovan, the two great tragedians, Edmund Keane and his son, Charles John

Keane. Ó Céin was also the name of a Derry family. It is now very rare and its angl. forms cannot be distinguished from those of Ó Catáin, q.v.

Ó ceinnéiʋiʋ, Ó ceinnéiʋiʒ, v. Ó Cinnéiʋiʋ, Ó Cinnéiʋiʒ.

Ó ceinnsealaiʒ, v. Ó Cinnrealaiʒ.

Ó céiʀín—I—*O Kearin, O Kerine, O Kerrin,* Cairn, Kearin, Kearn, Kereen, Kerin, Kerrin, Cairns, Kearns, Kerins, Kerrins, Kerns, (Carey), &c. ; ' des. of Céiʃín ' (dim. of ciaʃ, black) ; the name of a family who were anciently lords of Ciarraighe Locha na n-airne, in the barony of Costello, Co. Mayo, and doubtless of several other families in different parts of Ireland. In the 16th century, it was very widespread, and is now represented in every province. V. Ó Ciaʃáin, with which it is synnoymous.

Ó ceiʀisc, v. ʍac ʃiaʃaiʃ.

Ó ceit—I—*O Kett,* Kett ; ' des. of Ceat ' ; a rare West Clare surname. The family is probably descended from Ceat, son of Flaithbheartach, lord of Corca Modhruaidh, who flourished early in the 10th century.

Ó ceiteaʀnaiʒ—I—*O Keherne, O Kerny, O Kerne,* Keherny, Kerney, (Kearney, Kerns, Kearns) ; ' des. of Ceiteaʃnac ' (foot-soldier, one of a ceiteaʃn, or company of foot-soldiers) ; the name (1) of a family in Co. Roscommon, also called ʍac Ceiteaʃnaiʒ (q.v.), who were chiefs of Ciarraighe, in the barony of Castlerea ; and (2) of a West Cork family. These are the only families of which there is record, but there were, doubtless, others, as the name in the 16th century was rather widespread, being found in Tipperary, Kilkenny, Westmeath, Offaly, and Donegal, as well as in Roscommon and Cork. Its angl. forms cannot always be distinguished from those of Ó Ceaʃnaiʒ, q.v.

Ó ceocáin—IV—Keoghane, Keohane, &c. ; a corruption, in West Cork, of ʍac Eocáin, q.v. The eo of this surname, as I have heard it, is pronounced short.

Ó ceóinín—IV—O'Keoneen, Keoneen, Jennings. V. ʍac Seóinín.

Ó Ciaḃaiʒ—I—Keavy, Keevey ; ' des. of Ciaḃaċ ' (having long locks of hair) ; very rare.

Ó Ciaḃáin—I—O Kivane, Keevane, Keavan ; 'des. of Ciaḃán ' (dim. of Ciaḃaċ) ; the name of a family of Corca Laoighdhe, in West Cork. It can with difficulty be distinguished from Ó Caoṁáin, q.v.

Ó Cianaiʒ—I—O'Keeney, Keaney, Keany, Keeney, Keeny ; ' des. of *Cianaċ ' (der. of Cian) ; or perhaps more correctly Ó Caoinniʒ, ' des. of Caoinneaċ ' (a var. of Coinneaċ) ; in use in Galway and Donegal.

Ó Cianáin—I—O Kinane, O Keynan, O'Keenan, Keenan, Kinnan ; ' des of. Cianán ' (dim. of cian) ; the name of a literary family in Ulster, who were hereditary historians to the Maguires ; still numerous in that province.

Ó Ciaraʒáin—I—O Kierregain, O Kerigane, Kerigan, Kerrigan, Kergan, and, by ' translation,' Comber, Comer ; ' des. of Ciaraʒán ' (dim. of ciaṟ, black) ; the name of a branch of the Ui Fiachrach, formerly seated at Baile Ui Chiaragain, now angl.˙Ballykerrigan, in the parish of Balla, Co. Mayo. Before the end of the 16th century, the name had ramified into Donegal and Tyrone. In the north of Co. Galway, it is often ' translated ' Comber and Comer, from its supposed connection with ' cíoṟ,' a comb.

Ó Ciaráin—I—O Kearane, O Kirrane, O'Kieran, Kieran, Kearon, Kearn, Keern, Keirans, Kearons, Kerans, Kerons, Kearns, Kerns, Cairns, Comber, Comer, (Carey) ; ' des. of Ciarán ' (dim. of ciaṟ, black) ; the name (1) of a Tirconnell family who were formerly lords of Fearmhaigh in Co. Donegal ; and (2) of a Cork family, originally seated in the barony of Imokilly. Ó Ciaráin is the same surname as Ó Céiṟín (q.v.), which is the more common form, and is also a var. in parts of Connacht of Ó Ciaraʒáin. For explanation of the angl. forms Comber and Comer, see under Ó Ciaraʒáin above.

Ó Ciarḃa—I—O Kerby, Kerby, Kirby ; a corruption, in Limerick and Kerry, of Ó Ciarṁaic, q.v.

Ó Ciarḋa—I—O Kirry, O Kerry, Keery, Keary, Karey,

Carey, &c. ; ' des. of Ciaṙoa ' (der. of ciaṙ, black) ; the name of a family of the southern Ui Neill who were lords of Cairbre, the present barony of Carbury in the north-west of Co. Kildare, until the period of the Anglo-Norman invasion, when they disappear from history. The name is, however, still common in Kildare, Meath, Westmeath, and many parts of the south of Ireland, but generally angl. Carey, which makes it difficult to distinguish it from the many other names similarly anglicised.

Ó Ciaṙoubáin—I—*O Kerevan, O Kerrywane,* O'Kirwan, Kierevan, Kiervan, Kirivan, Kerevan, Kerivan, Kirvan, Kirwan, Kirwin, &c. ; ' des. of Ciaṙoubáin ' (dim. of ciaṙoub, jet-black) ; the name of a family who were anciently erenaghs of Louth, and apparently of another family in Co. Clare. The Kirwans were in later times an important family in the city of Galway. Their claim to be of English origin is rightly denied by O'Donovan, there being no such English family name.

Ó Ciaṙmacáin—I—*O Kerymokyn,* (Irwin, Irwine, Carey); ' des. of Ciaṙmacán ' (dim. of Ciaṙmac, black-son) ; a rare Munster surname.

Ó Ciaṙmaic—I—*O Kervick, O Kerwick, O Kervy, O Kerby,* Kerwick, Keerwick, Kerby, Kirby ; ' des. of Ciaṙmac ' (black-son) ; the name of an ancient family in East Limerick, who were chiefs of Eoghanacht Aine, the district lying around Knockany, until after the Anglo-Norman invasion, and are still numerous not only in Limerick, but throughout Munster. It would appear from the Annals of the Four Masters (A.D. 1087) that there was another family of the same name in Leinster, doubtless that now represented by Kerwick in Co. Kilkenny. Ó Ciaṙmaic has long been corrupted in the spoken language of Limerick and Kerry to Ó Ciaṙba, q.v.

Ó Cibil—I—*O Kiwilla,* Keville, Kiville ; apparently a shortened form of Ó Cibleacáin, q.v. ; in use in Mayo and Galway.

Ó Cıḃleaċáın—I—*O Kiveleghan*, Kevlihan, Kevlean, Keevlin; 'des. of Cıḃleaċán'; the name of a Westmeath family who were coarbs of St. Feichin at Fore; now rare and scattered. V. Ó Cıḃıl and Ó Cıḃlín, which appear to be shortened forms of this surname.

Ó Cıḃlín—I—Keevlin, Kevlean, Keville, Kiville; a var. in parts of Mayo of Ó Cıḃıl (q.v.), and apparently the same as Ó Cıḃleaċáın, q.v.

Ó Cılleáın—I—*O Killane*, Killane, Killan, Killian, Killion; 'des. of Cılleán' (dim. of Ceallaċ); a var. in Clare and Galway of Ó Cıllín, q.v.

Ó Cıllín—I—*O Killine, O Killen*, Killeen, Killen, Killian, Killion; 'des. of Cıllín' (a 'pet' dim. of Ceallaċ, war); the name of several distinct families in different parts of the country, as Clare, Galway, Mayo, Westmeath, Offaly, Kildare and Down, in all of which it is still extant.

Ó Cıneáıċ, Kinna, Kenna, Kennah, &c.; a var. in the spoken language of Ó Cıonaoıċ, q.v.

Ó Cınżeaḃ—I—*O Kinga, O King*, King; 'des. of Cınżeaḃ' (valiant). This surname belonged chiefly to Westmeath, Offaly, Galway and Clare. Also written Ó Cıonża, q.v.

Ó Cınnċnáṁa—I—Kinnavy, Kineavy; 'des. of Ceannċnáṁa' (bone-head); the name of a branch of the Uí Fiachrach, who were anciently proprietors of a district in the barony of Carra, Co. Mayo, where the family is still extant. I have not been able to discover any early angl. form of the name.

Ó Cınnḋearżáın—I—*O Kinregane*, Kindregan, Kinregan; 'des. of Ceannḋeapżán' (dim. of Ceannḋeapż, red-head); a rare Thomond surname.

Ó Cınnéıḋe, Ó Cınnéıḋıḋ, Ó Cınnéıḋıż—I—*O Kinedy*, O'Kennedy, Kennedy; 'des. of Cınnéıḋıḋ' (helmeted-head); the name of at least two families in Ireland: (1) Ó C. of Ormond, a branch of the Ḋál żCaıp, who derive their name and descent from Cınnéıḋıż, son of Donnchuan the brother of Brian

Boru. They were originally seated at Glenomra, co-extensive with the present parish of Killokennedy, in the east of Co. Clare, but on being driven thence at an early period by the O'Briens and MacNamaras, they settled in Tipperary, in the baronies of Upper and Lower Ormond, where they became very numerous and far more powerful than they had ever been in their ancient home in Thomond. From the 12th to the 16th century, they ranked as lords of Ormond, and were divided into three great branches, viz : Ó C. ꝼıonn (the Fair), Ó C. ꝛonn (the Brown), and Ó C. Ruꝛ (the Red). (2) Ó C. of Clann Cear-naigh, a branch of the Ui Maine, in Co. Galway. The name is now very common throughout Ireland.

Ó cınnꝼꝛolꝛıꝛ—I—*O Kenneally, O Kennelly*, O'Kin-nealy, Kinnealy, Kinneally, Kennealy, Kennelly, &c. ; ' des. of Ceꝛnnꝼꝛolꝛ ' (wolf-head, learned man) ; the name of a branch of the Ui Fidhgheinte, in Co, Limerick, who were seated in Ui Conaill Gabhra, now the baronies of Upper and Lower Connello, until dis-possessed by the Fitzgeralds and other Anglo-Norman settlers soon after the invasion. The name is, how-ever, still common in West Limerick and in Kerry. To be distinguished from Ó Coınꝣeꝛllꝛıꝣ, q.v.

Ó cınnseꝛlꝛıꝣ—I—*O Kynsillaghe*, Kinshela, Kinsella, Kinsley, &c. ; ' des. of Cınnꝛeꝛlꝛ ' ; the name of a Wexford family who are descended from Eanna Cinn-sealach, son of Diarmaid MacMurchadha ; usually Cınnꝛeꝛlꝛ, without the Ó. Cf. Cꝛomꝛnꝛ.

Ó cınnseꝛmꝛın, Kingston, Kingstone ; a var. of Mꝛc Oınꝛeꝛmꝛın, q.v.

Ó cıoꝺlꝛꝛın—I—*O Kiveleghan*, Kevlihan, Coolihan ; a var., in parts of Connacht, of Ó Cıꝺleꝛꝛın, q.v.

Ó cıoꝺuın—IV—O'Kibbon ; a corruption of Mꝛc Ꝣıoꝺuın, q.v.

Ó cꝼocꝛꝛın—I—*O Kiereaghan*, Keighron, (Kerrigan) ; ' des. of Cꝼocꝛꝛn ' (hungry) ; the name of a branch of the Siol-Anmchadha in Co. Galway. It seems to have been sometimes metathesised to Ó Cꝼoꝛꝛın, angl. *O Kiereaghan*, Kerrigan. It has always been very rare.

Ó Cionáiṫ, v. Ó Cionaoḋa.

Ó Cionaoḋa, Ó Cionaoiṫ—I—*O Kenaith, O Kenny, O Kenna*, Kinna, Kinney, Kenna, Kenny, &c.; 'des. of Cionaoḋ' (fire-sprung); the name of several distinct families in different parts of Ireland. It was common, in the 16th century, in all parts of Leinster and Munster, and in Galway, Roscommon and Tyrone.

Ó Cionga—I or II—*O Kenga, O Kinga*, King; a var. of Ó Cingeaḋ, q.v.

Ó Cioráin—I—*O Kirrane*, Kirrane, Kerrane, &c.; a corruption of Ó Ciaráin, q.v. See also Ó Ceapáin.

Ó Cíorḋubáin, v. Ó Ciaṙoubáin.

Ó Ciosáin—I—*O Kissaine, O Kissane*, Kissane, (Cashman); a var., in Kerry and Cork, of Ó Caráin, q.v.

Ó Cirṁic—I—*O Kiervicke*, Keerivick, Kerwick; 'des. of Ciarṁac' (black-son); a var. of Ó Ciarṁaic, q.v.; very rare.

Ó Ciseáin—I—*O Kishane*, Keeshan; an attenuated form of Ó Cioráin, q.v.

Ó Clabaiġ—I—*O Clabby*, Clabby; 'des. of Clabaċ' (thick-lipped, wide-mouthed); the name of an old Roscommon family who were erenaghs of the church founded by St. Patrick at Oran, in the barony of Ballymoe, and noted for their hospitality.

Ó Claiṁín, Ó Clamáin—I—*O Clavan*, Clavan, Claveen, Clavin, Swords, &c.; 'des. of Claiṁín' or 'Clamán' (dim. of clam, a sick person, a leper); a not uncommon surname in Mayo, but generally angl. Swords, which is supposed to be a translation. Cf. claiḋeaṁ, a sword.

Ó Claonáin—I—*O Clenan*, Clinane, (Conlon); 'des. of Claonán' (dim. of claon, bent); a rare surname. It appears to have originated in Kildare, but I have found it as the Irish for Conlon in parts of Mayo.

Ó Claċáin—I—Clahane, Clehane; a metathesised form of Ó Caċláin, q.v.

Ó Cléireaċáin, Ó Cléircín—I—*O Clearkane, O*

Clercan, Clerihan, Clerkan, Clerkin, Clarkins, Clarke, &c. ; 'des. of Cléıɼeɑcán,' or 'Cléıɼcín' (dim. of Cléıɼeɑc, cleric, clerk) ; the name (1) of a family of Ui Fidhgheinte who were anciently lords of Ui Cairbre Aebhdha, in the east of Co. Limerick ; now represented by Clerihan in Co. Tipperary ; and (2) of a Meath family who were anciently lords of Coillte Fallamhain. This family probably removed to Monaghan and Cavan, where the name was common at the end of the 16th century.

Ó Cléınıʒ—I—O'Clery, O'Cleary, Clery, Cleary, Clarke, &c. ; 'des. of Cléıɼeɑc' (cleric, clerk). This family derives its name and descent from an ancestor named Cléıɼeɑc who flourished about the middle of the 9th century, and was the seventh in descent from the celebrated Guaire the Hospitable, King of Connacht. They were at one time the ruling family of Aidhne, co-extensive with the diocese of Kilmacduagh, but early in the 11th century they lost their power, and towards the close of the 13th, were finally driven out of Aidhne and dispersed to different parts of Ireland. One branch of the family settled in Tirawley, Co. Mayo, another in Co. Cavan, and a third in the neighbourhood of Kilkenny. From the Tirawley branch sprang the O'Clerys of Tirconnell, who succeeded the O'Scingins as poets and chroniclers to the O'Donnells, and became celebrated in Irish literary history as the compilers of the Annals of the Four Masters and other valuable works on Irish history and antiquities. Besides the patrimony of the O'Scingins which they inherited by marriage, the O'Clerys obtained large grants of land from the O'Donnells. Their residence was at the castle of Kilbarron, near Ballyshannon. The family is now very numerous throughout Ireland, but the name is often disguised, especially in Ulster, under the translated form of Clarke.

Ó Cloċɑnτɑıʒ—I—*O Cloghertie,* Clogherty, Cloherty, and, by 'translation,' Stone ; 'des. of Cloċɑɼτɑc' ; a Galway surname.

Ó clocásais—I—O'Cloghessy, O'Clohessy, **Cloghessy,** Clohessy ; ' des. of clocápac ' ; an old Thomond sur-name, still well known in Clare and Limerick. The O'Cloghessys, in the 16th and early 17th century, owned the townland of Ballynaglearach, in the parish of O'Gonnelloe, Co. Clare.

Ó clocacáin—I—*O Cloghane*, Clogan, (Callaghan) ; ' des. of clocacán ' (dim. of clocac, famous) ; the name of an old ecclesiastical family the head of which was ' steward of St. Patrick ' in Munster, now angl. Clogan in Co. Limerick. It appears to be the same as the name which is pronounced Ó colacáin in West Clare and angl. Callaghan.

Ó cluain, *O Clowne*, Clune ; a shortened form of Ó Cluanais, q.v.

Ó cluanais—I—*O Clony*, Cloney, Cluney, **Clowney,** Clowny, Cloony ; ' des. of cluanac ' (deceitful) ; an old surname in South Leinster.

Ó cluanáin—I—*O Clonan*, Clunan, Cloonan ; ' des. of Cluanán ' (dim. of Cluanac) ; a rare Galway surname.

Ó cluasais—I—*O Closse*, Close ; ' des. of Cluapac ' (having large ears) ; an old surname in Antrim and Tyrone.

Ó clúmáin—I—*O Clufwayne, O Clovane, O Clowan*, Clu-vane, Clovan, Cloven, (Coleman, Clifford) ; ' des of Clúmán ' (dim. of clúmac, hairy, from clúm, down, feathers, Lat. pluma) ; the name of a literary and bardic family in Co. Sligo who were poets and chroni-clers to the O'Haras. Branches of the family settled early in South Leinster and West Munster, where the name is now common, but disguised under the angl. forms of Coleman and Clifford. The fact that these forms are also in use in the original territory is a proof that the families of the name in the south of Ireland are of the Sligo stock. Coleman, as an angl. form, seems to have arisen from confusion of the present surname with Ó Clomáin, a metathesised form current in the spoken language of Ó Colmáin.

Ó cnáimín—I—*O Knavin*, Navin, Nevin, Bowen, (Neville) ; ' des. of Cnáiṁín' (dim. of cnáṁ, a bone, an old Irish personal name) ; the name of a Dalcassian family, descended from Coscrach, son of Lorcan, King of Munster. The name was common, at the end of the 16th century, in many places outside of Thomond. Bowen is intended as a translation (Ir. cnáṁ, a bone). Neville is used as an angl. form in parts of West Clare.

Ó Cnáiṁsiġe—I—*O Cnawsie, O Knawsie, O Crashie*, Kneafsey, Neaphsey, Neecy, Cramsie, Crampsey, &c., and, by ' translation,' Boner, Bonner, &c. ; ' des. of Cnáiṁreaċ' (a woman's name, corresponding to Cnáiṁín) ; a Donegal surname ; now also in Mayo, often corrupted to Ó Cráiṁriġe. It is one of our very few metronymic surnames.

Ó Coḃċaiġ—I—*O Coffie, O Cohy*, Coffey, Cowhey, Cowey, Cowhig, &c. ; ' des. of Coḃċaċ' (victorious) ; the name of several distinct families in different parts of Ireland, viz. : (1) Ó C. of Corca Laoighdhe, an ancient and once powerful family in West Cork, of the same stock as the O'Driscolls. They were seated in the barony of Barryroe, where Dun Ui Chobhthaigh, angl. Dunocowhey, marks the site of their residence. The final ġ is often sounded in South Munster, hence the angl. form Cowhig. (2) Ó C. of Ui Maine, of the same stock as the O'Maddens, who possessed considerable property, down to the 17th century, in the barony of Clonmacnowen, Co. Galway, and had their residence at Tuaim Catraigh, angl. Tomcatry. (3) Ó C. of Umhall, anciently lords of Umhall, Co. Mayo. (4) Ó C. of Westmeath, a celebrated bardic family. (5) Ó C. of Derry, a family which produced many worthy ecclesiastics.

Ó Coċláin—I—*O Coghlaine, O Coughlane*, Coghlan, Coughlan, Coughlin, Coghlin, Colin, &c. ; ' des. of Coċlán' (dim. of coċal, a cape or hood) ; an ancient and still common surname in Co. Cork ; to be distinguished from Ó Caṫaláin, q.v.

Ó Coolaṫa—I—*O Collitie*, Culloty, Cullity ; ' des. of

*Coꞃlaꞅ ' (sleep) ; a rare Kerry surname, pronounced Ó Collaꞇa.

Ó coꞇlaꞇáin—I—*O Colletane*, Colleton, Collotan, Culleton, Culliton, (Cullington) ; ' des. of Coꞇlaꞇán ' (sleeper) ; an alias for Mac Coꞇlaꞇáin, q.v.

Ó coᵹaráin—I—*O Cogran*, Coghran, Caughran, (Cochrane, Cockrane) ; ' des. of Coᵹapán ' (possibly dim. of coᵹap, a confidant) ; an alias for Mac Coᵹapáin, q.v.

Ó coiꞇꞟeanaiᵹ—I—Coveney, Keveny, (?) Keverney ; ' des. of Coiꞇꞟeanaċ ' (leader or member of a troop, Ir. coiꞇꞟean) ; the name of an Ossory family who were anciently chiefs of Magh Airbh, in the barony of Crannagh, Co. Kilkenny ; now very rare.

Ó coiᵹealaiᵹ—I—*O Keagalagh, O Kegelagh, O Kegley*, Kegley ; ' des. of Coiᵹealaċ ' (an untidy person) ; a var. of Ó Coiᵹliᵹ, q.v.

Ó coiᵹliᵹ—I—*O Cogly, O Cwigley, O Quigly, O Kegly*, O'Coigley, O'Quigley, Cogley, Kegley, Quigley, Twigley ; ' des. of Coiᵹleaċ ' (der. of coiᵹeal, a distaff, an untidy person, with unkempt hair) ; the name of a branch of the Ui Fiachrach who were anciently seated in the barony of Carra, Co. Mayo. In the 16th century, the name was common in Sligo, Donegal, Monaghan, Carlow, Wexford and Waterford.

Ó coileáin—I—*O Collaine, O Collan*, Collen, Collins ; ' des. of Coileán ' (whelp) ; the name of a family of the Ui Fidhgheinte in the present Co. Limerick, who are of the same stock as the O'Donovans and were originally lords of Ui Conaill Gabhra, now the baronies of Upper and Lower Connello. In the year 1178, they were expelled from this territory and the main body of the clan settled in West Cork. Those who remained continued to be lords of Claonghlas, a district in the south-west of the county, until towards the end of the 13th century, when they were dispossessed by the Fitzgeralds. The name is now very common in the original territory of the family and throughout

Munster, but is universally angl. Collins. V. Ó
Cuileáin which is a variant.

Ó coil5ín—I—*O Culliggine*, Quiligan, Quilligan; an
attenuated form of Ó Colʒán, q.v.

Ó coiliʒ—I—*O Quilly, O Killie,* Cox, Woods; ' des of
Coileaᴄ' (cock); a rare surname in Donegal and
parts of Connacht.

Ó coimín—I—*O Comyn,* Comyn; ' des. of Coimín' (dim.
of cam, crooked); a var. of Ó Cuimín and Ó Comáin,
q.v.

Ó coineáin—I—*O Kenane,* Kennane; ' des. of Coineán'
(same as Coinín); a var. of Ó Cuineáin. q.v.

Ó coineóil—I—Conole, Connole; ' des of Coineól';
the name of a Sligo family who were anciently coarbs
of Drumcliffe; now represented by Conole and Connole in Co. Clare.

Ó coinʒeallaiʒ—I—*O Cangelly, O Connilla, O Kennelly,* Kangley, Quinnelly, Kennelly, (Connelly), &c.;
' des. of Coinʒeallaᴄ' (pledged, serving under con-
ditions); the name of a West Cork family who were retainers of the O'Donovans, from whom they held at one
time seven ploughlands in the parish of Drinagh, near
Drimoleague. The name was also in Ormond. Mac
Coinʒeallaiʒ was an alias in both places.

Ó coinʒill—I—*O Coniell, O Coinnill, O Kennell,* Quinnell; apparently a shortened form of Ó Coinʒeallaiʒ;
in use in Cork and Tipperary at the end of the 16th
century, but always very rare.

Ó coinín—I—*O Conyne, O Kenyn,* Conyeen, Cuneen,
Cunneen, Cunnien, &c., and, by ' translation,' Rabbit;
' des. of Coinín' (probably a dim. of cano, a whelp,
wolf, if not a var. of Conán); a rare surname; found
chiefly in the midlands.

Ó coinleisc, Ó coinlisc—I—*O Conliske, O Coynliske,*
Cunlisk, Quinlisk, Quinlish, (Grimes); the name of a
literary family in Connacht; now rare, and in West
Mayo strangely angl. Grimes. V. Ó Cuinᴐuir.

Ó coinne—I—*O Cunny, O Quiney,* Conney, Cunny,
Quinny, (Kenny, Quin), &c; ' des. of Coinne' (a var.

of Coinneaċ) ; a not uncommon Ulster surname. The
family was originally seated in Ui Eachach, in Co.
Down, but seems to have afterwards removed to the
neighbourhood of Strabane.

Ó coinneaċáin—I—*O Kenaghan*, Kinaghan, Kinahan,
&c. ; ' des. of Coinneaċán ' (dim. of Coinn) ; a var. of
Ó Cuinneaċáin, q.v.

Ó coirbín—I—*O Corbin*, O'Corrobeen, Coribeen, Corbin,
Kerbin, (Corbett, Kirby), &c. ; ' des. of Coirbín ' ;
var. of Ó Corbáin, q.v. ; in Connacht, often pronounced Ó Croibín, q.v.

Ó coirealláin—I—*O Kerolan*, Curland, Kerlin, Kirlin,
Kirland ; ' des. of Coireallán ' (dim. of Coireall) ;
a var. of Ó Cairealláin q.v.

Ó coirill—I—*O Kirle*, Kirrell ; ' des. of Coireall '
(older Caireall) ; very rare.

Ó coirín, Curreen, Currin, Creen, &c. ; a var. of Ó
Corrairdín, q.v.

Ó coise—I—*O Coishe, O Cushie, O Coshe*, Quish ; the
name of an old Leix family ; now very rare and found
chiefly in Co. Tipperary, where it is angl. Quish.

Ó coistín—V—Costine, Costin, Costen ; a corruption
of Mac Oirtín. q.v.

Ó coitil—II—Cottle ; ' des. of Ketill ' (a Norse personal
name ; cf. Mac Coitil) ; the name of a branch of the
Ui Fiachrach in Co. Sligo, who resided at Baile Ui
Choitil, now angl. Cottlestown, in the parish of Castle-
conor. O'Donovan found it still in the district under
the angl. form of Cottle.

Ó colgan—I—*O Colgan, O Collogan, O Culligan*, Colgan,
Collogan, Culligan, Quilligan, &c. ; ' des. of Colga ' ;
more anciently Mac Colgan ; the name of an old
family in Offaly, of the same stock as the O'Connors,
O'Dempseys and O'Dunnes ; also common in Thomond.

Ó colla—I—*O Collo, O Cully, O Colle*, Cully, Coll ; ' des.
of Colla.'

Ó collata, *O Collitie*, Culloty ; also written Ó Coolata ;
a rare Kerry surname.

Ó Colmáin—I—*O Colman, O Collomayne,* Colman, Coleman ; ' des. of Colmán ' (dim. of Colm, dove, a very common Irish personal name) ; the name of a family of the Ui Fiachrach, who were anciently seated in the townland of Grangemore, in the parish of Templeboy, Co. Sligo ; and doubtless of several others in different parts of the country. It was most common, in the 16th century, in Cork, Tipperary, Waterford, Dublin, Wexford, Meath, Longford, Roscommon and Cavan. It is sometimes metathesised to Ó Clomáin.

Ó Colpa, Ó Colpta—I—*O Colloupy,* Collopy ; ' des. of Colpta ' (calf of the leg, an ancient Irish personal name) ; an old Limerick surname ; very rare.

Ó Coltáir—I—O'Colter, Colter, Coalter, Coulter ; ' des. of Coltap '; seemingly a var. of Ó Coltapáin, q.v.

Ó Coltaráin—I—*O Coultran,* O'Colter, Colter, &c. ; ' des. of Coltapán '; the name of an ancient family in Co. Down, from whom the parish of Ballycolter probably derives its name. It seems to have been shortened to Ó Coltaip, q.v.

Ó Comáin—I—*O Comane, O Comman, O Cowmane,* Coman, Commane, Cowman, Cummane, Commons, &c., and, by ' translation,' Hurley ; ' des. of Comán ' (dim. of cam, bent, crooked) ; formerly a very common surname, and found in all the provinces, especially in Munster. The var. Ó Cuimín (q.v.) seems to have been, in recent times, substituted for it in many instances. It is sometimes ' translated ' Hurley. Cf. ' camán,' a hurly.

Ó Comaltáin—I—*O Cowltayn,* Coulton, Colton ; ' des. of Comaltán ' (dim. of comalta, foster-brother) ; the name of a branch of the O'Clerys in South Galway ; now very rare, if not actually obsolete.

Ó Comhdáin—I—*O Coain, O Coan, O Cowan,* Coan, Coen, Cowan, Cowen, (Coyne), &c. ; ' des. of Comgán ' (cobirth) ; also written Ó Comgáin ; the name of a branch of the Ui Fiachrach, anciently seated in the parish of Dunfeeny, Co. Sligo, but in the 16th century more numerous in Galway and Roscommon. The name is still well known in Connacht, usually angl. Coen.

Ó comRaroe—I—*O Cowrie, O Cory,* O'Curry, Corey, Corry, Curry; 'des. of Comparoe'; the name (1) of a Westmeath family who were anciently chiefs of Ui Mac Uais, now the barony of Moygoish; (2) of a family of Corca Laoighdhe, in South-west Cork; and (3) of a branch of the Dal gCais in Thomond, to which belonged the celebrated Eugene O'Curry.

Ó conaill—I—*O Conaill,* O'Connell, Connell; 'des. of Conall' (high-powerful, an ancient personal name Welsh Cynvall, British Cunovalos, Celtic Kunovalos); the name of at least three distinct families in Ireland, viz.: (1) Ó Conaill of Derry, a branch of the Oirghialla, who were anciently lords of Ui Mac Carthainn, now the barony of Tirkeeran; (2) Ó Conaill of Galway, a branch of the Ui Maine, who anciently possessed a territory in the south of Co. Galway, between the river Grian and the borders of Thomond; and (3) Ó Conaill of Kerry, who were anciently chiefs of Magh O gCoinchin, in the east of that county, until dispossessed by the O'Donoghues about the middle of the 11th century. From the time of the Anglo-Norman invasion down to the 17th century, the O'Connells were followers of MacCarthy More and hereditary castellans of Ballycarbery, near Caherciveen. Maurice O'Connell, the head of the family in Cromwell's time, was transplanted to Brentir, near Lisdoonvarna, in Co. Clare. Several of this family became distinguished in the Irish Brigades in the service of France, among whom may be mentioned Count Daniel O'Connell, uncle of the Liberator, Daniel O'Connell, by whom this surname has been made for ever illustrious. O'Connell is now one of the most numerous of Irish surnames. O'Heerin writes the name of the Kerry family Ó Congaile, but Ó Conaill is the form now universally in use in Munster.

Ó conáin—I—*O Conane, O Conan,* Conan, Cunnane; 'des. of Conán' (dim. of 'con,' high, or the ancient

Celtic personal name, Kunagnos); more commonly
Ó Cuineáin, q.v.

Ó conaing—I—*O Gunning*, Cunning, Gunning; 'des.
of Conaing'; the name of a branch of the Dal gCais
who are descended from Donnchuan, brother of Brian
Boru. Before the Anglo-Norman invasion, they
were lords of Aos Greine, the present barony of Clanwilliam, Co. Limerick, and had their chief seat at
Caislean Ui Chonaing, now Castleconnell, but were
dispossessed, about the beginning of the 13th century,
by a branch of the Burkes. The name has now
entirely disappeared from Co. Limerick.

Ó conairce—I—Conarchy; (?) 'des. of Cú-airce'
(hound of greed). Giolla Chriost Ó Conairce was
Bishop of Lismore and Papal Legate in Ireland about
the middle of the 12th century. The name is now
exceedingly rare.

Ó conaire—I—*O Connery, O Conrey*, Connery, Conry,
(Conroy), &c.; 'des. of Conaire' (probably dog-
keeper, an ancient Irish personal name); an old
Munster surname, common throughout the province;
to be distinguished from Ó Conraoi, q.v.

Ó conalláin—I—*O Connellane, O Conlan*, Connellan,
Conlan, &c.; 'des. of Conallán' (dim. of Conall);
the name of a Roscommon family; but in the 16th
century, it was found in all the provinces. Its angl.
forms cannot always be distinguished from those of
Ó Caoinoealbáin, q.v.

Ó conallta—I—*O Conalty*, Conalty; 'des. of Cú-
allaid' or 'Cú-allta' (wolf); a rare Ulster surname.

Ó conaráin—I—*O Conoran, O Coneran*, Conran, Conron, Condron, Condrin; 'des. of Conarán'; an old
Offaly surname, now scattered through Leinster.

Ó conbáṡa—I—*O Conebaghe, O Conba*, Conba, Conbay,
(Conboy, Conaboy, Corbett); 'des. of Cú-báṡa'
(hound of battle); a rare surname. In the 16th
century, it was found chiefly in Offaly, Tipperary
and Cork; now also in Connacht. In Co. Limerick it
is often disguised under the angl. form of Corbett.

Ó conbáin—I—*O Convane, O Convan,* Cunvane ; ' des. of Cú-bán ' (white-hound) ; very rare.

Ó conboirne—I—Burns ; ' des. of Cú-boirne ' (hound of Burren) ; apparently an alias for mac Conboirne, q.v.

Ó conburde—I—Conboy, Conaboy, Conwy, (Conway) ; ' des. of Cú-burde ' (yellow-hound) ; the name (1) of a family of the Ui Fiachrach who were anciently seated at Dunneill, in the barony of Tireragh, Co. Sligo, and were still numerous in O'Donovan's time in the parish of Easky, in the same county ; and (2) of a family of the Ui Maine, in Co. Galway. I have not been able to discover any early angl. form of the name in either district.

Ó conceanainn, Ó conceannainn—I—*O Concannen,* O'Concannon, O'Concannen, Concannon ; ' des. of Cú-ceanainn ' (fair-headed hound) ; the name of a well-known Galway family who were chiefs of Corca Mogha, angl. Corcamoe, in the north-east of that county. The head of the family resided at Kiltullagh, in the parish of Kilkerrin, or Corcamoe.

Ó concobáir, Ó concubáir—I—*O Conchor, O Connour,* O'Conor, O'Connor, Connor, Connors, &c. ; ' des. of Concobar ' (high-will or desire, an ancient Irish personal name) ; one of the most numerous and widespread of Irish family names. There are, at least, six distinct families so called, viz. : (1) Ó C. of Connacht who derive their name and descent from Concobar, King of Connacht in the latter part of the 10th century, and were long the ruling race in that province, and of whom two became kings of all Ireland. They were divided into three great branches, namely Ó Concobair Donn (the brown O'Connor), Ó Concobair Ruad (the red O'Connor), and Ó Concobair Sligeac (the O'Connor of Sligo). The present head of the family is known as The O'Conor Don. (2) Ó C. of Offaly who derive their descent from Ros Failghe, son of Cathaoir Mor, King of Ireland in the second century, and their surname from Concobar, son of Fionn, lord of Offaly, who died in the year 979. They were a powerful and warlike race, and for more than three hundred years successfully defended their territory against the English of the Pale. Their chief stronghold was Dangan, now Philipstown. They were dispossessed in the reign of Philip and Mary. (3) Ó C. of Kerry. Before the Anglo-Norman invasion, the head of this family was lord of that portion of Kerry lying between Tralee and the Shannon ; but owing to the encroachments of the Fitzmaurices and other Anglo-Norman settlers this territory was narrowed down to the limits of the present barony of Iraghticonor (Oιρeαċτ uí Conċoḃαιρ), which remained in the possession of the family until the close of the reign of Elizabeth, when it was confiscated and given to Trinity College. The chief stronghold of the O'Connors was Carrigafoyle, near Ballylongford. (4) Ó C. of Corcomroe. This family derives its name from Conċoḃαρ, son of Maelseachlainn, lord of Corcomroe, who was slain in the year 1002, and the head of the family was lord of the barony of Corcomroe, in West Clare, down to the close of the 16th century. (5) Ó C. of Keenaght. The head of this family was lord of Cianachta, now the barony of Keenaght, in Co. Derry, until dispossessed by the family of Ó Cατάιn, or O'Kane, shortly before the Anglo-Norman invasion. (6) Ó C. of Ui Breasail, a branch of the Oirghialla.

Ó ConċoḃαιR ꝺonn—I—O'Conor Don ; i.e., ' the brown O'Connor ' ; the designation of the head of a branch of the O'Connors of Connacht, in contradistinction to Ó Conċoḃαιρ Ruαꝺ and Ó Conċoḃαιρ Sliᵹeαċ ; now used as title of distinction.

Ó Conꝺuḃάιn—I—O Condon, Condon ; ' des. of Cú-ꝺuḃάn ' ; the name of an Ulster family who were anciently erenaghs of Derryloran, in Co. Tyrone ; now rare.

Ó Conꝺuιḃ—I—Conniff, Conneff, Cunniffe, Quinniff, (Conliffe), &c. ; ' des. of Cú-ꝺuḃ ' (black-hound) ; a rare Connacht surname.

Ó conᵹᴀɪle—I— Conneely, Cunneely, (Connelly, Kennelly), &c. ; ' des. of Conᵹᴀl ' (high-valour) ; the name
(1) of a family of the Ui Fiachrach, who were anciently
seated at Killarduff, in the parish of Dunfeeny, Co.
Mayo ; (2) of an ecclesiastical family of Loch Erne
who were connected with Devenish, Rossory and
Lisgool ; and (3) of an ecclesiastical family at Clonmacnoise. The angl. forms of this surname cannot
always be distinguished from those of mᴀc Conᵹᴀɪle,
mᴀc Conᵹᴀolᴀ, and Ó Conᵹᴀlᴀɪᵹ, q.v. The last of
these is sometimes substituted in the Annals for Ó
Conᵹᴀɪle.

Ó conᵹᴀlᴀɪᵹ—I—O Connally, O Connolly, O Conely,
Connolly, Connelly, &c. ; ' des. of Conᵹᴀlᴀc ' (valorous, der. of Conᵹᴀl) ; the name (1) of a family of the
southern Ui Neill who were seated in East Meath
until dispossessed soon after the Anglo-Norman invasion, when they settled with the MacMahons in
Co. Monaghan, where they became very numerous ;
(2) of a Dalcassian family in Thomond who are said
to be descended from Mahon, the brother of Brian
Boru ; (3) of a branch of the Ui Maine in Co. Galway,
of the same stock as the O'Maddens ; and (4) of a Roscommon family. The angl. forms of this surname
cannot always be distinguished from those of Ó Conᵹᴀɪle, Ó Coɪnᵹeᴀllᴀɪᵹ, mᴀc Conᵹᴀɪle, &c.

Ó conmeᴀ᷄ᴅᴀ—I—O Convey, O Conwey, Convey, (Conway) ; ' des. of Cú-meᴀ᷄ᴅᴀ ' (hound of Meadh, a place-
name) ; very rare.

Ó connᴀcᴄᴀ́ɪn—I—O Conoghane, O Cunnaghan, Conaghan, (Cunningham) ; ' des. of Connᴀcᴀ́n ' (dim. of
Conn) ; a var. of Ó Connᴀᵹᴀ́ɪn, q.v.

Ó connᴀᴄᴛᴀɪᵹ—I—O Connaghty, Connaghty, Conaghty,
Conaty, Conotty ; ' des. of Connᴀᴄᴛᴀc ' (Connachtman) ; the name of an old Breifney family, still well
represented in Cavan. Flann Ó Connachtaigh was
Bishop of Kilmore in the early part of the 13th century.

Ó connᴀᴄᴛᴀ́ɪn—I—O Connaghtane, Connaghtane, Connaughton, Connorton, Connerton ; ' des. of Connᴀᴄ-

ᴄᴀɴ ' (dim. of Connᴀᴄᴄᴀᴄ) ; the name of a branch of
the Ui Fiachrach, formerly seated in the townland
of Cabragh, parish of Easkey, Co. Sligo, but at the
end of the 16th century very scattered, being found
in Roscommon, Donegal, Limerick and Kerry.

Ó connᴀ**ʒ**ᴀ**ı**n—I—*O Connegaine, O Connigaine, O
Conegan,* Connigan, (Conyngham, Cunningham) ; ' des.
of Connᴀʒᴀn ' (dim. of Conn) ; the name (1) of a
family of Ui Fiachrach, formerly seated in the parish
of Magh Gamhnach, now angl. Moygawnagh, Co.
Sligo ; and (2) of a family of Ui Maine in Co.
Galway, of the same stock as the O'Maddens. At
the end of the 16th century this surname was common
in Clare, Limerick, Kerry, Cork, Offaly, Kildare and
Monaghan, as well as in Mayo and Galway, and is
now nearly everywhere angl. Cunningham.

Ó connṁᴀᴄᴀın—I—*O Conawchane, O Connowghane,
O Conoughan,* Kanavaghan, (Conway) ; ' des. of Conn-
ṁᴀᴄᴀn,' (dim. of Connṁᴀᴄ) ; the name of a Sligo
family who were followers of the O'Haras. At the
beginning of the 17th century it was also found in
West Ulster and in Offaly. It is now generally angl.
Conway in Connacht.

Ó connṁᴀıʒ—I—*O Connowe, O Conway,* Conoo, Cunnoo,
Conway ; ' des. of Connṁᴀᴄ ' ; the name of a Dalcassian
family who were formerly ollaves of music in Thomond.
At the end of the 16th century it was common throughout Munster and South Leinster, and was also found
in Roscommon and Cavan. It is now generally angl.
Conway.

Ó conrᴀ, Ó conrᴀᴄ, *O Conorech, O Conra,* Conry ;
' des. of Conrᴀ ' ; very rare.

Ó conrᴀoı—I—*O Conree, O Conrie,* Conroy ; ' des. of
Cú-rᴀoı ' (hound of the plain) ; the name of a branch
of the Ui Maine in Co. Galway ; but in the 16th century
very scattered.

Ó conrᴀᴄᴀ—I—*O Conrahy,* Conrahy, (Conroy) ; ' des. of
Cú-rᴀᴄᴀ ' (hound of prosperity) ; also mᴀᴄ Conrᴀᴄᴀ ;
written Ó Conrᴇᴄᴇ by MacFirbis ; a Leix surname.

Ó conReiᴄe, v. Ó Conꞃꞓᴄᴅ.

Ó coRbᴅin—I—*O Corbane, O Coribane*, Corbane, Corban, Corbin, (Corbett, Corbitt) ; ' des. of Coꞃbᴅn ' (dim. of coꞃb, a chariot, a pet form of some name commencing with Coꞃb). This surname was formerly found in all the counties of Munster, and in Kilkenny, Carlow and Galway. It is now nearly always disguised under the angl. form of Corbett.

Ó coRcᴅin—I—*O Corkan*, Corken, Corkin, (Coreoran) ; ' des. of Coꞃcᴅn ' (dim. of Coꞃc) ; a rare midland surname.

Ó coRcRᴅ—I—*O Corkery*, Corkery, Corkerry ; ' des. of Coꞃcᴅiꞃ ' (purple) ; a Munster surname ; found chiefly in Cork, Kerry and Limerick.

Ó coRcRᴅin—I—*O Corcrane, O Corkerane, O Corkran*, Corcoran, Corkeran, Corkran, &c. ; ' des. of Coꞃcꞃᴅn ' (dim. of Coꞃcᴅiꞃ, purple) ; the name of an ecclesiastical, literary and bardic family in many parts of Ireland. At the end of the 16th century it was largely represented in every province and, in the southern half of Ireland, almost in every county.

Ó coRmᴅcᴅin—I—*O Cormacan, O Cormakane, O Gormacan*, Cormocan, Cormican, Gormican, (Cormack, Cormick, MacCormack, MacCormick) ; ' des. of Coꞃmᴅcᴅn ' (dim. of Coꞃmᴅc) ; the name of at least four distinct families in different parts of Ireland, viz. : (1) Ó C. of Roscommon. This family appears to have been connected with the church of St. Coman. Fionn O Cormacain was one of the four hostages given by Cahal Crovderg O'Conor, King of Connacht, to King John, when the latter visited Ireland in 1210. (2) Ó C. of Thomond, a branch of the Dal gCais. These appear to have been an ecclesiastical family and erenaghs of the parish of Moynoe, in Co. Clare. Three of them were bishops of Killaloe in the 13th and 14th century. (3) Ó C. of Galway, a family formerly seated in the parish of Abbey-Gormican, in the barony of Longford, where they founded the abbey from which the parish derives its name. (4) Ó C. of Down,

an ecclesiastical family who were erenaghs of Inis-
courcey. The name appears to have been sometimes
corrupted to Ó Ꝣoꝛmacáin, was often shortened to
Ó Coꝛmaic (q.v.), and is now in many places disguised
under the angl. form of MacCormack.

Ó CORMAIC—I—*O Cormack, O Cormick*, Cormac, Cormack, Cormick; ' des. of Coꝛmac ' (son of Coꝛb, or
son of a chariot, charioteer); the name (1) of a branch
of the ·Oirghialla, seated in the barony of Tirkeeran,
Co. Derry, until dispossessed by the O'Kanes; (2) of
a branch of the Corca Laoighdhe, in South-west Cork,
where the name was common in the 16th century;
(3) of a Dalcassian family, probably the same as
Ó Coꝛmacáin, q.v.; and (4) of a Co. Down family,
also probably the same as Ó Coꝛmacáin.

Ó CORRA—I—*O Corry, O Corr*, Corra, Corry, Corr, Curry,
and, by ' translation,' Weir; ' des. of Coꝛꝛa ' (spear);
a var. of Ó Caꝛꝛa (q.v.); a rather common Ulster
surname. V. Ó Coꝛꝛaio, which is also a variant.

Ó CORRADÁIN—I—*O Curridane, O Corridan*, Corridon,
Cordan; doubtless, a var. of Ó Coꝛꝛaꝣáin, q.v.;
apparently originally a Clare surname, but now found
chiefly about Listowel, Co. Kerry.

Ó CORRAꝢÁIN—I—*O Corrigane, O Currigan*, Corrigan,
Currigan, &c.; ' des. of Coꝛꝛaꝣán ' (dim. of Coꝛꝛa);
a rather widespread surname; found in Ulster, Leinster and Connacht.

Ó CORRAIO—I—*O Corrie, O Corry*, Corree, Corrie, Corry,
Curry; ' des. of Coꝛꝛao ' (spear); a var. of Ó Coꝛꝛa
and Ó Caꝛꝛaio, q.v.

Ó CORRAIOIN—I—*O Corrin, O Corren, O Currine*, Curreen, Curren, Currin, (Curran), Creen, Crean; ' des.
of Coꝛꝛaioin ' (dim. of Coꝛꝛao); a var. of Ó Coꝛꝛáin,
q.v.; also written Ó Cuiꝛín: a common surname
throughout Munster and South Leinster, but generally
angl. Curran. Creen is a contracted form of Curreen,

Ó CORRÁIN—I—*O Corraine, O Currane, O Corhane*.
O'Curran, Currain, Currane, Curran, Corran, Craan,
Crain, Crane, Crahan, Creane, Crean, (Crehan, Creaghan,

Carey), &c.; 'des. of Coṗṗán' (dim. of Coṗṗaḋ);
also written Ó Cuṗṗáin; a var. of Ó Caṗṗáin, Ó Caṗ-
ṗaiṙín, Ó Coṗṗaiṙín, with which it was sometimes
used interchangeably; a common Irish surname,
found in all the provinces.

Ó CORROUIṘe—I—*O Corbae*, Corboy, Corby, Curby;
'des. of Coṗṗḃuiṙe' (yellow-crane); an old surname
in West Cork. The family belonged to Corca Laoighdhe.

Ó CORROUIḃ—I—*O Corduffe, O Curduffe*, Corduff; 'des.
of Coṗṙouḃ' (black-crane); a rare West Ulster surname.

Ó CORĊAIṙ, Currid; a Sligo surname. I cannot trace
its origin. The above is the local pronunciation as I
got it from an old Irish speaker at Grange.

Ó COSÁin—I—*O Cossane*, Cussane, (Patterson); 'des. of
Caṙán' (dim. of caṙ, bent, curly); a var. of Ó Caṙáin,
q.v.

Ó COSCAIR—I—*O Cosker, O Coskirr*, Coscor, Cosker,
Cusker, Cuskor, (Cosgrave, Cosgrove); a shortened
form of Ó Coṙcṙaiġ, q.v.

Ó COSCRAĊÁin—I—*O Coschrachan*, Coskeran, Cuskern,
(Cosgrave, Cosgrove); 'des. of Coṙcṙaċán' (dim. of
Coṙcṙaċ); a rare Ulster surname.

Ó COSCRAIġ—I—*O Coskry, O Cosgra*, Cosgry, Coskery,
Coskerry, Cuskery, Cosgriff, Cosgrive, Cosgreve, (Cosgreave, Cosgrave, Cosgrove); 'des. of Coṙcṙaċ'
(victorious); the name (1) of a Wicklow family who
were lords of Feara Cualann, comprising the manor of
Powerscourt, until dispossessed soon after the Anglo-
Norman invasion by the O'Tooles and O'Byrnes;
(2) of a Monaghan family who were anciently chiefs
of Feara Rois, in the neighbourhood of Carrickmacross; and (3) of a Galway family who belonged to
the Ui Maine race, and are of the same stock as the
O'Maddens. The name is now generally angl. Cosgrave and Cosgrove.

Ó COSnAĊÁin—I—*O Cosnechan*, Cusnahan, Cushanan;
'des. of Coṙnaċán' (dim. of Coṙnaċ, or Coṙnaṁaċ,
defender); very rare.

483

Ó cosᴄᴀʒáın, Costigan ; a corruption of mᴀc Oıʀᴄıcín, q.v.

Ó cʀáʋáın, Ó cʀáıʋín—I—Cravane, Craven, Cravin, Creaven ; ' des. of Cʀáʋᴀʋán ' (pious) ; the name of an old family of Ui Maine ; still in use in Co. Galway.

Ó cʀᴀıʋeáın—I—O Kryane, O Kryan, Cryan ; ' des. of Cʀᴀıʋeán ' (dim. of cʀᴀıʋe, a heart) ; a var. of Ó Cʀoıʋeáın, q.v. ; a Roscommon surname.

Ó cʀáıṁsıʒe—I—O Crashie, Cramsie, Crampsie, Crampsey, &c. ; a corruption of Ó Cnáıṁʀıʒe, q.v.

Ó cʀᴀoıʋe—I—O Crevy, Creevy, Creevey ; ' des. of Cʀᴀoıʋeᴀċ ' (branchy, curly, the dim., Cʀᴀoıʋeᴀcán, occurs in the Annals, A.D. 760) ; a family of Cinel Eoghain, mentioned by MacFirbis.

Ó cʀᴀoʋáın—I—O Crevan, Creaven, Creavin ; ' des. of Cʀᴀoʋán ' (dim. of Cʀᴀoıʋeᴀċ) ; a rare Sligo surname.

Ó cʀeᴀcáın, Ó cʀéᴀcáın—I—O Creghan, Creaghan, Crehan, (Creaton), Crean ; ' des. of Cʀeᴀcán ' (dim. of cʀeᴀċ, or cʀéᴀċ, blind) ; sometimes corrupted to Ó ʒʀéᴀcáın ; the name of a branch of the Ui Fiachrach who were formerly seated in Tirawley, Co. Mayo. V. Ó Cʀíocáın.

Ó cʀeᴀcṁᴀoıl, Craughwell ; a rare Co. Galway surname, the origin of which I cannot trace. Croughwell is found in Cork.

Ó cʀıᴀʒáın—IV—Cregan ; a corruption of mᴀc Rıᴀʒáın, q.v.

Ó cʀıocáın, Ó cʀíocáın—I—O Criaghan, O Creghan, Creghan, Creaghan, Creehan, Crehan, Creighan, (Creighton, Creaton), Creen, Crean ; ' des. of Cʀıocán ' (probably a var. of cʀeᴀcán ; also a small person) ; the name of an Oriel family who were lords of Ui Fiachrach of Ardsratha, now Ardstraw, Co. Tyrone. In the 16th century it was found in all the counties of Munster, and in Kilkenny, Carlow and Dublin. V. Ó Cʀeᴀcáın.

Ó cʀíoʋáın—I—O Credane, Creedon, Creed ; ' des. of Cʀíoʋán ' ; also formerly mᴀc Cʀíoʋáın ; an old

Munster surname, still well known, especially in Cork, where the angl. form is often shortened to Creed.

Ó CRIONAȜÁIN—*O Crunegane, O Crinegine*, Crinigan, Crenegan ; ' des. of Cṗıonaȝán ' (dim. of cṗıon, old, worn) ; a rare midland surname.

Ó CRÍONÁIN—I—Crennan, Crinion, Crinneen ; ' des. of Cṗıonán ' (dim. of cṗıon, old, worn out) ; a rare Leix surname.

Ó CROΌLAOIĊ, Ó CROȜALLAIȜ, v. Ó CṗuaΌlaoıċ.

Ó CROIBÍN—I—Cribbin, Cribbon, Cribbins ; a metathesised form of Ó Coıṗbín, q.v.

Ó CROIΌEAȜÁIN—I—*O Cridigan, O Crigane, O Crigan*, Creegan, Creigan, Cregan, Creggan ; ' des. of CṗoıΌeaȝán ' (dim. of cṗoıΌe, heart, a term of endearment) ; also written Ó CṗaıΌeaȝáın and Ó CṗıΌeaȝáın ; a var. of Ó CṗaıΌeáın and Ó CṗoıΌeáın, q.v. ; the name of a family of Cinel Eoghain who, in the 16th century, were seated in Donegal. Some of them later removed to Sligo where they became wealthy merchants and landed proprietors. MacFirbis (p. 140) gives the pedigree of the family.

Ó CROIΌEÁIN—I—*O Criane, O Creane, O Crean*, Crean, Creen, &c. ; ' des. of CṗoıΌeán ' (dim. of cṗoıΌe, heart) ; a var. of Ó CṗaıΌeáın and Ó CṗoıΌeaȝáın, q.v. ; the name of a family of Cinel Eoghain who settled at Sligo in the 16th century, where they became wealthy merchants, and later on acquired a considerable amount of landed property. The pedigree of the family is given by MacFirbis (p. 140).

Ó CROIMÍN—I—*O Cromine*, Cremeen, Cremen, Cremin ; ' des. of Cṗoımín ' (dim. of cṗom, bent). V. Ó Cṗuımín.

Ó CRÓIN—*O Crone*, Crone ; ' des of Cṗón ' (brown, swarthy) ; a rare and scattered surname ; formerly found in Donegal, Kilkenny and Galway.

Ó CRÓINÍN—I—*O Cronine, O Cronyn*, Cronin, Cronyn, Cronan ; ' des. of Cṗóının ' (dim. of cṗón, brown, swarthy) ; the name of a family of Corca Laoighdhe, originally seated in the neighbourhood of Clonakilty, but now numerous throughout Cork, Kerry and Limerick.

*Ó CROMLAOIĊ, Crumley; 'des. of the bent hero' (Ir. Cromlaoċ).

Ó CROMRUISC—I—*O Cromruske, O Crumreske,* (?) Crumlish; 'des. of Cromrorc' (squint-eye, perhaps a nickname); a Donegal surname, now probably represented by the angl. form Crumlish.

Ó CROMĊA—I—*O Cromy,* Crummy; 'des. of Cromċa' (bent); very rare.

Ó CRÓNAȝáIN—I—*O Cronigane,* Cronekan, Croniken; 'des. of Crónaȝán' (dim. of Crón); a rare Munster surname, still extant in Waterford and Limerick.

Ó CRÓNáIN—I—*O Kronane,* Cronan, Cronin; 'des. of Crónán' (dim. of Crón); a rare Leix surname. Cf. Ó Cróinín and Ó Crónaȝáin.

Ó CRÓNȝAIL—I—*O Cronegil, O Cronell,* Crangle; 'des. of Crónȝal'; a var. of Ó Crónȝaile, q.v.

Ó CRÓNȝAILE—I—*O Cronowly, O Cronully,* Cronelly, Cranley; 'des. of Crónȝal' (compound of crón, brown, and ȝal, valour, an old Irish personal name); the name of an old Galway family who were coarbs of St. Grellan, patron of Ui Maine, and keepers of that saint's crozier, which was wont to be carried in battle by the king of Ui Maine. By the end of the 16th century, some of the family had crossed the Shannon into Offaly and Ormond.

Ó CROTAIȝ—I—*O Crotty,* Crotty; 'des. of Crotaċ' (hunch-backed); the name of a Waterford family, said to be a branch of the O'Briens of Thomond, who were formerly seated in the neighbourhood of Lismore and are now found in many parts of Munster.

Ó CRUAÓLAOIĊ—I—*O Crowly, O Croley, O Croly,* O'Crowley, Crowley, Crawley, Croly, Crolly; 'des. of Cruaólaoċ' (hard-hero); the name of a branch of the MacDermotts in Co. Roscommon. MacFirbis, in his Genealogies (p. 228), gives the pedigree of this family, from which it appears that they derive their name and descent from Ⱃⰹⰰⱃⰿⰰⰹⰳ, ' ⰰⱀ ⱄⱃⱛⰰⰳⰲⰰⱁⰳ,' who was fourth in descent from Ⰳⰹⰰⱃⰿⰰⰹⰳ, the eponymous ancestor of the MacDermotts. This family is still represented in Connacht. Ó Ⱄⱃⱛⰰⰳⰲⰰⱁⰹⰳ is also used as the surname of a family originally seated in West Cork, but now numerous throughout Munster and known in English as Crowley and Crawley. The Irish pronunciation of the surname, as I have heard it in different parts of that province, is Ó Ⱄⱃⱁⰳⰰⰱⰱⰰⰹⰼ, evidently a corruption of ⰿⰰⱁ Ⱃⱁⰳⰰⰱⰱⰰⰹⰼ, q.v. The family, which was once a strong one in West Cork, is probably a branch of the O'Mahonys. Croly and Crolly in the northern parts of Ireland are apparently similar corruptions.

Ó ⱆⱃⱆⰹⰿⰹⱀ—I—*O Crumyne*, Crimmeen, Cremeen, Cremin, Cremen, Crimmins ; ' des. of ⱄⱃⱆⰹⰿⰹⱀ ' (dim. of ⱄⱃⱁⰿ, bent) ; the name of a well-known family in Cork, Kerry and Limerick ; of West Cork origin, and said to be a branch of the MacCarthys.

Ó ⱆⱆⰰⰳⱙⰹⱀ—I—*O Coughane, O Cowghane, O Quoghane*, (Gough) ; ' des. of ⱆⱆⰰⰳⱙⰰⱀ ' (dim. of ⱆⱆⰰⰳ, a cuckoo) ; the name of a family of Ui Fiachrach, formerly seated in the barony of Carra, Co. Mayo, where O'Donovan found it still extant under the angl. form of Gough. At the end of the 16th century, it appears in Roscommon, Cavan and Cork, but I have failed to discover any modern angl. form of it in these counties.

Ó ⱆⱆⰰⰷⱙⰹⱀ—I—*O Choogan, O Cowgan, O Cogan*, Coogan, Cogan ; ' des of ⱆⱆⰰⰷⱙⰰⱀ ' ; the name of a family of the Ui Maine in Co. Galway, of the same stock as the O'Maddens. Before the end of the 16th century it had ramified into Offaly, Kildare and Kilkenny. Ó ⱆⱆⰰⰷⱙⰰⱀ was also the name of a Leitrim family who were anciently chiefs of Cinel Duachain, but apparently long extinct.

Ó ⱆⱆⰰⰹⱀ—I—*O Cuayn, O Quane*, Quan, Quann, Quane, Quaine, (Coyne, Quaid) ; ' des. of ⱆⱆⰰⱀ ' (probably a ' pet ' form of ⰳⱁⱀⱀⱆⱆⰰⱀ, lord of harbours ; hardly for ⱆⱛⰰⱀ, dim. of ⱆⱛ, a hound) ; the name of a branch of the Ui Fiachrach, anciently seated at Dun Ui Chobhthaigh, now angl. Doonycoy, in the parish of Templeboy, Co. Sligo. At the end of the 16th century it was very scattered, but found chiefly in Cork and Limerick, in the latter of which counties it is now angl. Quaine and Quaid.

Ó cuᴀɴᴀ, Ó cuᴀɴᴀċ—I—*O Cowna, O Cwony, O Coony,* Cooney ; ' des. of Cuᴀɴᴀ' (handsome, elegant) ; the name of a family who, according to O'Dugan, were chiefs of Clann Fergus in Ulster. At the end of the 16th century it was most common in Sligo and Cork.

Ó cuᴀɴᴀċáɴ—I—*O Coonaghan,* Coonaghan, Coonahan, Coonihan, Counihan, (Cooney) ; ' des. of Cuᴀɴᴀċáɴ' (dim. of Cuᴀɴᴀ) ; a rare surname, now found chiefly in Kerry ; angl. Cooney in some parts of Munster.

Ó cuᴀɴáɴ—I—*O Cownan,* Coonan, (Conan) ; ' des. of Cuᴀɴáɴ' (dim. of Cuᴀɴ) ; the name of a family formerly seated at Dunbeakin in the parish of Kilmacshalgan, Co. Sligo, but no longer found in that district. It is still extant, however, in parts of Leinster. Isaac O Cuanain was Bishop of Ely and Roscrea about the middle of the 12th century.

Ó cuᴀɴᴀʀᴛᴀıᵹ—I—Coonerty ; des. of ' Cuᴀɴᴀʀᴛᴀċ' (having a pack of hounds ; cf. Ráᴛ Ċuᴀɴᴀʀᴛᴀıᵹ) ; a rare surname. I cannot discover any early form, Irish or English.

Ó cuḃʀáıɴ—I—Cowran ; ' des. of *Cuḃʀáɴ ; a Breifney surname. It is mentioned in the Annals at the year 1145. O'Donovan gives the angl. forms as Cowran and Corran. But see Ó Cumpáıɴ.

Ó cuıᴅıᵹᴛıᵹ—I—*O Codihie, O Kuddyhy, O Cuddie,* Cuddihy, Cudihy, Cuddehy, Quiddihy, Cuddy, Cody, &c. ; ' des. of Cuıᴅıᵹᴛeᴀċ' (helper) ; an Ormond surname. Though apparently distinct, it is probably a mere substitution for mᴀc Óᴅᴀ, q.v.

Ó cúıle—I—Cooley ; cf. mᴀc ᵹıoʟʟᴀ Ċúıʟe.

Ó cuıʟeᴀᵹᴀıɴ—I—Quiligan, Quilligan ; an attenuated form of Ó Coʟᵹᴀɴ, q.v.

Ó cuıʟeáıɴ—I—*O Cullaine, O Quillayne,* O'Cullane,

Cullane, Cullan, Cullen, Quillan, Quillen, Collins;
'des. of Cuileán' (whelp); a var. of Ó Coileáin, q.v.
Besides the Uí Coileáin of Ui Conaill Gabhra, there
were distinct families of this name in Galway, Tyrone,
Tipperary and Cork, and perhaps also in Clare and
Sligo. The Galway family was a branch of the Ui
Maine; that of the Cork of the Corca Laoighdhe, and
therefore distinct from the Uí Coileáin of Ui Conaill
Gabhra who settled in the same territory after they
were driven out of their native Ui Fidhgheinte. The
Uí Cuileáin of Tyrone were erenaghs of Clogher.

Ó Cuileaṁáin—I—*O Cullone, O Collone*, Culloon, Culhoun, Colhoon, Colhoun, Cullen; 'des. of Cuileaṁan';
the name of a South Leinster family to which belonged,
according to O'Curry, the late Cardinal Cullen.

Ó Cuileannáin—I—*O Cullanayne, O Cullinan*, Cullinane, Cullinan, Quillinan, Culnane, Quilnan, (Callanane,
Callanan), &c.; 'des. of Cuileannán' (dim. of Cuileann); the name (1) of a Co. Louth family who were
anciently lords of Conaille; and (2) of a family of
Corca Laoighdhe, formerly seated in the barony of
Barryroe, in South Cork. Dr. O'Brien, in his Irish
Dictionary, mentions another family of this name as
lords of Muscraighe-tri-maighe, now the barony of
Orrery, Co. Cork, but I have failed to trace it. There
was also a remarkable family of the name in Tir-
connell, to which belonged Dr. John O'Cullinan,
Bishop of Raphoe at the period of the Confederation.

Ó Cuilín—I—*O Culline*, Cullin, Cullen, &c.; a var., in
South Cork, of Ó Cuileáin, q.v.

Ó Cuilinn—I—*O Cullin, O Quillin*, Cullen, Quillen, &c.;
'des of Cuileann' (holly).

Ó Cuill—I—*O Cwill*, Quill, and, by 'translation,' Woods;
'des. of Coll' (hazel, also head); the name of a
celebrated literary and bardic family in Munster.
They are, according to MacFirbis (p. 622), of the same
stock as the O'Sullivans. The name is now found
chiefly in Cork and Kerry, but is sometimes disguised
under the angl. form of Woods, which is supposed to

be a translation, from its resemblance to 'coıll,' a wood.

Ó cuımín—I—O *Cumyn*, Cumin, Cummin, Cummins, Cummings, &c. ; ' des. of Cuımín ' (dim. of cᴀm, bent, crooked) ; the name of several distinct families in different parts of Ireland. It is a var. of Ó Comᴀın (q.v.) for which, in many instances, it has been substituted. The Sligo family of the name is a branch of the Ui Fiachrach.

Ó cuınᴰlıs—I—Cundlish, Cunlish, Quinlish ; ' des. of Cuınᴰleᴀꞃ ' (an ancient Irish personal name) ; the name of a literary family in Connacht, who had a share in compiling the Book of Lecan. It would seem that this name was changed into Ó Coınleıꞃc, q.v. The same person is called Ó Cuınᴰlıꞃ by Annalists of Loch Cé and Ó Coınleıꞃc by the Four Masters. (See Annals, A.D. 1342.) The latter is the form now in use in Mayo.

o cuıneᴀın—I—O *Kinane*, O *Kynnan*, Cunnane, Kinane, Kinnane, Guinane, Guinnane, Guinan, Quinane, Quenan, Queenane, &c. ; ' des. of Cuıneᴀn ' (an attenuated form of Conᴀn) ; a var. of Ó Coıneᴀın, q.v. ; a common surname in many parts of Ireland. There is also a distinct surname Ó Cuınneᴀın, q.v.

Ó cuıneóᵹ—I—O *Conoge*, Kinnock ; ' des. of Conóᵹ ' (a var. of Conᴀn) ; an exceedingly rare Thomond surname.

Ó cuınín—I—O *Quynnyne*, O *Kynnyne*, Cuneen, Cunion, Cunneen, Cunnien, Cunnion, Kinnian, and, by 'translation,' Rabbit ; a var. of Ó Coınín and Ó Cuıneᴀın, q.v.

Ó cuınn—I—O *Quyn*, O *Quine*, O *Coyne*, O'Quin, Quin, Quinn, Queen, Coyne ; ' des. of Conn ' (head, sense, reason, intelligence ; also a freeman) ; a very common surname in all parts of Ireland. There are several distinct families so called, of which the following are the best known :—(1) Ó Cuınn of Thomond, a branch of the Dal gCais, descended from Conn, lord of Muinntear Ifearnain, who flourished in the latter part of the 10th century. They were originally seated at

Inchiquin, and their territory which, from their clan-name, was designated Muinntear Ifearnain, comprised the country around Corofin, in Co. Clare. The Earl of Dunraven is a member of this family. (2) Ó Cuinn of Annaly, a branch of the Conmaicne and of the same stock as the O'Farrells, who were chiefs of Muinntear Giollagain, an extensive district in Co. Longford, until towards the end of the 14th century when they were supplanted by the O'Farrells. Quin is now a very common surname in Co. Longford. (3) Ó Cuinn of Antrim who were chiefs of Magh Lughadh and Siol Cathasaigh. Conghalach O Cuinn of this family, 'a tower of valour, hospitality, and renown of the North of Ireland,' was slain by the English in the year 1218. (4) Ó Cuinn of Magh Itha, in the barony of Raphoe, now numerous in West Ulster. (5) Ó Cuinn of Clann Cuain, a branch of the Ui Fiachrach, who were chiefs of Clann Chuain, in the neighbourhood of Castlebar, Co. Mayo. About the middle of the 12th century they transferred their allegiance from the Ui Fiachrach to the Siol Muireadhaigh and became tributary to Mac-Dermott of Moylurg. Ó Cuinn is pronounced O'Coyne in the south of Ireland ; hence the angl. form Coyne which is sometimes used.

Ó cuinneaċáin—I—*O Kineghan, O Kynaghan, O Quenahan*, Cunnighan, Cunnahan, Cunihan, Kinaghan, Kinnighan, Kinnan, (Keenan, Cunninghan) &c. ; a var. of Ó Coinneaċáin and Ó Cuinneaġáin, q.v.

Ó cuinneaġáin—I—*O Quinegane*, Cunnigan, Kinnegan, Kinnighan, (Cunningham) ; ' des. of Cuinneaġán ' (dim. of Conn) ; a common surname all over Ireland. Mac Cuinneaġáin (q.v.) was a variant. See also Ó Connaġáin.

Ó cuinneáin—I—*O Kinnane, O Kynnan*, Kinnane, Guinnane, Quinane, &c. ; ' des. of Cuinneán ' (dim. of Conn). This surname was in use in Tipperary, Limerick, Clare, and perhaps other places, but it is now impossible to distinguish it from Ó Cuineáin, q.v.

Ó cuirc—I—*O Cuirk, O Quirke*, Quirk, Quirke, Querk,

Kirk; 'des. of Co�c' (heart); the name of a family who were anciently chiefs of Muscraighe Breogain, also called Muscraighe Cuirc, in the present barony of Clanwilliam, Co. Tipperary; still common in Tipperary, and also in Cork and Kerry.

Ó cuiрín—I—*O Curine, O Quyrrine,* Curreen, Creen, &c.; a var. of Ó Coррaıбín, q.v.

Ó cuiрnín, Ó cúiрnín—I—*O Curnyne,* Corneen, Curneene, Curneen, Curnin, Courneen, (Courtney); 'des. of Cuıрnín' (dim. of coрn, a horn, a drinking cup); the name of a literary family in Breifney who were poets and chroniclers to the O'Rourkes. The head of the family resided in Church Island, in Lough Gill.

Ó cúlaċáin—I—*O Coullaghan, O Couloghan,* O'Colohan, Cuolohan, Coulihan, &c.; 'des. of Cúlaċán' (dim. of cúlaċ, fat); the name of a family of the Ui Fiachrach who were formerly seated in the barony of Carra, Co. Mayo. At the end of the 16th century it was also found in Sligo, Tipperary and Limerick.

Ó cumaрáin, Ó cumрáin—I—Cameron; 'des. of *Cumрán'; apparently the same as Ó Cuбрáin, q.v.; the name of an old Breifney family. It is, no doubt, the surname pronounced Cumaрán (without the Ó) and angl. Cameron, in Co. Mayo.

Ó cuрnáin, Ó cúрnáin—I—*O Kurnane,* Curnane, Cournane, (Courtney); 'des. of Cuрnán' (an ancient Irish personal name, the same as Cuıрnín); a Kerry surname. It is a var. of the Breifney surname Ó Cuıрnín, and there is reason for believing that the families are the same.

Ó cuрráin—I—*O Currane,* O'Curran, Currain, Currane, Curran, &c.; a corrupt spelling of Ó Coрráin, q.v.

Ó cuрtáin—I or IV—Curtayne, Curtin, &c.; a corrupt form of older Ó Caрtáin, q.v.; common in the spoken language of West Limerick and Kerry.

Ó óáбoiрeann—I—*O Davoren, O Daverin, O Davern,* Davoran, Davoren, Davern; 'des. of Ouбóáбoiрeann' (Black of the two Burrens); a shortened form of Ó Ouıбóáбoiрeann; the name of a learned brehon family in Thomond. They belonged originally to Corcomroe, in north-west of Co. Clare, where for successive generations they maintained a great literary and legal school, of which the celebrated Irish antiquary, Duald MacFirbis, was at one time a pupil. The head of the family resided at Lisdoonvarna. The O'Davorans are also numerous in Co. Tipperary, where they seem to have settled before the end of the 16th century.

Ó DAGNÁIN—I—*O Dinan,* Dinan, Dynan; 'des. of Dagnán'; a not uncommon Munster surname.

Ó DAIGRE—I—*O Dyry,* Derry, Deery; 'des. of Daigre'; the name of an ecclesiastical family at Derry, of the church of which they were erenaghs.

Ó DAILBHRE—I—*O Dallarie,* Dollery; 'des. of Dailbhre' (an ancient Irish personal name); a rare old surname in Co. Limerick, and also in Offaly. The Limerick family is almost extinct.

Ó DAIMHÍN—I—*O Davine, O Dovine,* O'Devine, Davine, Devine, Davin, Devin, Deven, Devon, Devins, (Davy, Davis); 'des. of Daimhín' (dim. of damh, bard, poet); the name of an Oriel family, of the same stock as the Maguires, who were chiefs of Tirkennedy, in the east of Co. Fermanagh. It is now generally angl. Devine in Ulster, and Davin in Munster and Connacht. In West Galway, where it is not uncommon, it is sometimes made Davy and Davis. It is to be distinguished from Ó Duibhín, q.v.

Ó DAIRBHRE—I—*O Dwrrero, Derriroe,* Derow, Deroe, &c.; 'des. of Dairbhre' (an ancient Irish personal name); an old, but rare surname in Offaly.

Ó DÁIRE—I—*O Dawry, O Daire,* Adair; 'des. of Dáire' (an ancient Irish personal name).

Ó DAITHGHIL, v. Ó Dathail.

Ó DALACHÁIN—I—*O Dallaghan, O Dolaghan,* Dallaghan, Dolaghan, &c.; 'des. of Dalachán' (dim. of Dálach); the name of an ancient family in Tirconnell who were chiefs of Tuath Bladhach, now angl. Doe, in the north of the barony of Kilmacrenan. In the 16th century, the name was found chiefly in the midlands, especially in Offaly, where the family was numerous and respectable. The castle of Liscloony, in the parish in Tisaran, the ruins of which are still to be seen, was built by Melaghlin O'Dalachain, in the year 1556. The angl. forms of this surname cannot always be distinguished from those of Ó Ɗuƀlacáin or Ó Ɗuiƀleacáin, q.v.

Ó ƊᴀLᴀᴄᴀıᴚ—I—O Dologher, Dallagher, Dolaher, Dooler, Dowler; 'des. of Ɗᴀlᴀᴄᴀᴘ'; always extremely rare.

Ó Ɗᴀ́Lᴀıᵹ—I—O'Daly, Daly, Dawley, &c.; 'des. of Ɗᴀ́lᴀᴄ' (holding assemblies, frequenting assemblies). The O'Dalys derive their descent from Maine, son of Niall of the Nine Hostages, and were originally chiefs of Corca Adain, or Corca Adhaimh, in the present county of Westmeath. In later times they became famous as a bardic family all over Ireland. "There is certainly no family," writes O'Donovan, "to which the bardic literature of Ireland is more deeply indebted than that of O'Daly." The first of the family to become famous for his learning was Cuchonnacht na scoile (C. of the school) who died at Clonard in 1139. He was the ancestor of all the bardic families of the name. "From his time forward," says O'Donovan, "poetry became a profession in the family, and Corca Adain sent forth poetic professors to various parts of Ireland." About the middle of the 13th century, a branch of the family, descended from Donough More O'Daly, a celebrated bard, settled at Finavarra, in Burren, Co. Clare, where they became poets to the O'Loghlens. To this branch belonged the Dalys of Galway, whose ancestor settled in Ui Maine in the latter part of the 15th century. Raghnall O Dalaigh, who settled in Desmond about the middle of the 12th century, and became chief ollave in poetry to MacCarthy, was doubtless the ancestor of the O'Dalys of Muinntear Bhaire and O'Keeffe's country. Another branch settled in Cavan, and became poets

to the O'Reillys; while other branches were poets
to the O'Neills of Ulster and the O'Connors of Connacht. The name is now common all over Ireland.

Ó Ɗᴀʟᴀʀᴜᴀɪ́ꝺ, Delaroe, Dollery; evidently a corruption
of Ó Ɗᴀɪʟᴛꝺ ᴘᴇ, q.v.

Ó Ɗᴀʟʟᴀ́ɪɴ—I—*O Dullane, O Dallan, O Dallon,* Dallon,
Delane, (Delany), &c.; ' des. of Ɗᴀʟʟᴀ́ɴ ' (dim. of
ᴅᴀʟʟ, blind); formerly a not uncommon surname
throughout the south of Ireland; now also in use in
West Connacht, where it is incorrectly angl. Delany.
V. Ó Ɗᴜɪʟʟᴇᴀ́ɪɴ, which is a variant.

Ó Ɗᴀᴍᴀ́ɪɴ—I—*O Davan,* Davane, Devane; ' des. cf
Ɗᴀᴍᴀ́ɴ ' (dim. of ᴅᴀᴍ, a poet). Cf. Ó Ɗᴀɪᴍɪ́ɴ; a
rare Ulster surname. MacFirbis mentions a family
of the name among the Cinel Eoghain.

Ó Ɗᴀᴏᴅᴀ, v. Ó Ɗᴇᴀᴅᴀɪʒ,

Ó Ɗᴀʀᴀ, Ó Ɗᴀʀᴀᴄ—I—Daragh, Darragh, Darrah,
Darrock, Oak, Oakes, Oaks; ' des. of Ɗᴜᴃꝺᴀ ᴘᴀᴄ '
(Black of the Oak); short for Ó Ɗᴜᴃᴅᴀᴘᴀᴄ. Cf. Ó
Ɗᴀ́ᴃᴏɪ ᴘᴇᴀɴɴ.

Ó Ɗᴀᴛᴀɪʟ—I—*O Dahill,* Dahill; ' des. of Ɗᴀɪᴛʒᴇᴀʟ '
(fair complexion); also written Ó Ɗᴀɪᴛʒɪʟ; the name,
according to MacFirbis, of a family of the Siol Muireadhaigh, in Co. Roscommon; now peculiar to Tipperary.

Ó Ɗᴀᴛʟᴀᴏɪᴄ—I—*O Dolly,* Dolly; ' des. of Ɗᴀᴛʟᴀᴏᴄ '
(bright or nimble hero); the name of a Galway family
who were anciently chiefs of Ui Briúin Ratha, to the
east and north-east of the town of Galway, where it
is still represented.

Ó Ɗᴇᴀᴃᴛᴀɪʒ—I—*O Daffie,* Daffy; ' des. of Ɗᴇᴀᴃᴛᴀᴄ '
(quarrelsome); a rare West Clare surname.

Ó Ɗᴇᴀᴅᴀɪʒ, v. Ó Ɗᴇᴀʒᴀɪ́ꝺ.

Ó Ɗᴇᴀᴅᴀɪʒ—I—*O Deadie,* Deady; ' des. of Ɗᴇᴀᴅᴀᴄ '
(der. of ᴅᴇᴀᴅ, a tooth); a rare West Munster surname.
The pronunciation in Limerick and Kerry is Ó Ɗᴀᴏᴅᴀ,
which is apparently corrupt.

Ó Ɗᴇᴀʒᴀɪ́ꝺ—I—*O Daa, O Dawe, O Daye, O Deay,*
O'Dea, Dea, Day, Daw, Dee, Godwin, Goodwin, &c.;
' des. of Ɗᴇᴀʒᴀꝺ '; the name (1) of a Dalcassian

family, still numerous in Thomond, who were chiefs of Ui Fearmaic, which comprised the greater part of the present barony of Inchiquin, Co. Clare, and had their principal strongholds at Tullyodea and Dyserttola ; and (2) of a Tipperary family who were anciently chiefs of Sliabh Ardacha, now angl. Slewardagh, in the east of that county.

Ó Deagáin—III—*O Dyeane, O Deane, O Dane,* Deane, Dean, Deen, Dane ; ' des. of the dean ' (Ir. Deadán or Deagán) ; a scattered surname ; found at the end of the 16th century in many parts of the south of Ireland, and also in Donegal.

Ó Deamáin, v. Ó Diamáin.

Ó Dearáin—I—*O Dearain, O Derane,* Dearan, Derrane, Dirrane ; ' des. of Deapán ' (dim. of Deap, great, large) ; a rare and scattered surname ; found chiefly in the 16th century, in Kildare, Leix and Galway. MacFirbis mentions a Muinntear Dearain among the Cinel Eoghain, in Ulster.

Ó Deargáin—I—*O Dargane, O Dergane, O Darigan,* Dargan, Dergan, Dorgan, Dorrigan ; ' des. of Deapgán ' (dim. of Deapg, red) ; an old surname in Westmeath, Offaly and Cork. In the last-named county, it is now angl. Dorgan, which is not very correct.

Ó Dearmada—I—*O Darmodie,* Darmody ; ' des. of Diapmaid ' ; a var. of Ó Diapmada, q.v.

Ó Deasmumnaig—III—*O Dassuny, O Dasshowne, O Deason, O Desmonde,* Desmond ; ' des. of the Desmonian ' (Ir. Deapmumnac, native of Desmond or South Munster) ; a Cork surname.

Ó Deirbreó, Devereux, Devery, Derow, Deroe ; v. Ó Daipbpe, of which it is apparently a corruption.

Ó Deirg—I—*O Derig, O Derrick,* Derrig, Derrick, Durrig ; ' des. of Deapg ' (red) ; the name of a family of the Ui Fiachrach who were seated in the neighbourhood of Killala ; still extant in Mayo and Sligo.

Ó Deocáin—I—*O Dycane, O Decan,* Deacon ; ' des. of Deocán ' (a personal name).

Ó Deóradáin, Ó Deóraidín, Ó Deórdáin—I—*O*

Dorian, O Dowerine, O Doreane, O Dorrane, Adorian,
O'Doran, Dorian, Dorrian, Doran, Dorran, Durrian ;
' des. of 'Oeópaóán ' or ' 'Oeópaıóín ' (dim. of 'oeópaó,
an exile, stranger) ; the name (1) of a great brehon
family in Leinster, where it is still very common ; and
(2) a Co. Down surname. Ó 'Oeopáın is a shortened
form of Ó 'Oeópaóáın ; Ó 'Oeópaıóín was everywhere
a variant.

Ó 'Oıaʒaıó—I—*O Die,* O'Dea, Dea, Dee, Godwin, Goodwin ; var. of Ó 'Oeaʒaıó, q.v. The angl. form Godwin
was suggested by the similarity of the first syllable
to 'Oıa, God.

Ó 'Oıamáın—I—*O'Diamain,* Diaman, Diamon, Diamond,
Dimond ; ' des. of 'Oıamán ' or ' 'Oéamán ' (more
correctly 'Oíomán, dim. of 'Oíoma, a personal name) ;
the name of an old ecclesiastical family in Ulster who
were erenaghs of Kilrea, in Co. Derry, and are still
numerous in Derry and Antrim.

Ó 'Oıaʀmaóa—I—*Ó Diermoda, O Dermody, O Diermot,*
O'Dermott, Dermody, Darmody, Dermott, Darby,
&c. ; ' des. of 'Oıapmaıó ' (an ancient Irish personal
name signifying freeman) ; a scattered surname ; found
in all the provinces.

Ó 'Oíoċon—I—*O Deachan,* Deehan, Dehan, Deighan ;
' des. of 'Oíoċú ' (great-hound) ; a rare Ulster surname.

Ó 'Oíomáın, v. Ó 'Oıamáın.

Ó 'Oíomasaıʒ—I—*O Dymasa, O Demsy,* O'Dempsey,
Dempsey ; ' des. of 'Oíomapaċ ' (proud). The O'Dempseys, who are of the same stock as the O'Connors of
Offaly, derive their descent from Ros Failghe, eldest
son of Cathaoir Mor, King of Ireland in the second
century, and were long one of the most powerful
families in Leinster. Their territory was Clann
Mhaoilughra, an extensive district on both sides of the
river Barrow, and comprising the baronies of Port-
nahinch in Leix, and Upper Philipstown, in Offaly.
During the reign of Elizabeth, the O'Dempseys were
on friendly terms with the English, and their estates
for a time escaped confiscation ; Terence O'Dempsey

was knighted by Essex in 1599, and in 1631 created Baron of Philipstown and Viscount Clanmalier. They took, however, an honourable part in the Confederation of Kilkenny, and later on were staunch adherents to the cause of James II. For their loyalty on this occasion they suffered the loss of their estates.

Ó Díoráin—I—*O Derran*, Dirrane, Durrane; a var. of Ó Dearáin, q.v.

Ó Díorma, Ó Díormaıȝ—I—*O Dierma, O Dermoe*, Diurmagh, O'Dermott, Dermott, &c.; a shortened form of Ó Duıḃḋíorma, q.v.

Ó Dırín—I—*O Derren*, Direen; a var. of Ó Dıoráın, q.v.; a rare Kilkenny surname.

Ó Díscín—I—*O Duskin*, Diskin; 'des. of Dırcín' (dim. of dıorc, apparently not a personal name); the name of a family of the Ui Fiachrach who were formerly seated in the townland of Baile Ui Dhiscin, angl. Ballyeeskeen, in the parish of Templeboy, Co. Sligo; now not uncommon in Co. Galway and other parts of Connacht.

Ó Doḃaıleın—I—*O Deublinge, O Devlin*, Develin, Devlin, &c.; 'des. of Doḃaıḻen'; the name (1) of a Sligo family who were anciently chiefs of Corca Firthri in that county, and are frequently mentioned in the Annals; and (2) of a Tyrone family who were chiefs of Muintar Devlin, on the west side of Lough Neagh, and now very numerous throughout Ulster. Also written Ó Doıḃıleın and Ó Doıḃılín, q.v.

Ó Doḃaráın—I—Davoran, Davoren, Davern; 'des. of Doḃarán' or 'Doḃrán' (dim. of doḃar, water, perhaps 'pet' dim. of doḃarcú, water-dog, otter); a rare Connacht surname.

Ó Doćartaıȝ—I—*O Doghartie*, O'Dogherty, O'Dougherty, O'Doherty, Dogherty, Dougherty, Doherty, &c.; 'des. of Doćartać' (hurtful, disobliging). The O'Dohertys, who are a branch of the Cinel Conaill and of the same stock as the O'Donnells, were originally chiefs of Cinel Enna and Ard Miodhair, now angl. Ardmire, in the barony of Raphoe, but about the beginning of the 15th century, they became lords of Inishowen and one of the most powerful families of Tirconnell, a position which they retained down to the reign of James I, when, after the rebellion of Sir Cahir O'Dogherty, their possessions were confiscated and granted to Sir Arthur Chichester. The O'Doghertys are now one of the most numerous of Irish families.

Ó DOĊRAIÐ, Ó DOĊRAIᵹ—I—*O Dogrie, O Dockrey,* Dockeray, Dockery, Dockrey, Dockry; 'des. of Doċraᵭ,' or 'Doċraċ' (unfortunate, hurtful, &c.); the name of a branch of the Siol Muireadhaigh in Co. Roscommon.

Ó DOᵹAIR—I—*O Dowar, O Dower, O Dore,* Dower, Dore; 'des. of Doᵹar' (sad, sorrowful); a Munster surname, found chiefly in Co. Limerick.

Ó DOIḂILEIN, Ó DOIḂILÍN—I—*O Devline, O Devlin,* Develin, Devlin, &c.; a var. of Ó DoḃAILEIN, q.v. Ó DOIḂILEIN is the usual form of the name in the Annals of Ulster.

Ó DOIĊEARTAIᵹ—I—*O Dihirtie,* Deherty, Deharty, Doherty; an attenuated form of Ó DoċARTAIᵹ, q.v.; found here and there in Munster.

Ó DOIᵹRE—I—*O Dyry, O Deery,* Deery, Derry; a later form of Ó DAIᵹre, q.v.

Ó DOIṁÍN—I—*O Dovine, O Devine,* Devine, Devin, Deven, Devins, &c.; a var. of Ó DAIṁin, q.v.; so written in Annals of Loch Cé, A.D. 1278.

Ó DOINEANNAIᵹ—I—Denanny, Dennany, Dennan; 'des. of Doineannaċ' (stormy, tempestuous); originally a midland surname. Ruithin Ó Doineannaigh, tanist of Teathbha, was slain, according to the Four Masters, in 1044. I cannot find any early angl. form.

Ó DOIRḂÍN—I—*O Durvin,* Derivin, Derwin; 'des. of Doirḃín' (dim. of Doirḃ, peevish, quarrelsome).

Ó DOIREIᵭ, Ó DOIRIᵭ—I—*O'Derrie,* Derry; 'des. of Doireᵭ'; the name of an ecclesiastical family in Donegal, who were erenaghs of Donoughmore, near Castlefin. O'Donovan seems to have regarded this as the same name as Ó Ɔoᵹᵹe, but, except that their angl. forms are the same, there is apparently no connection.

Ó Ɔoiʀᵹnne—I—*O Dorryny*, *O Dorreny*, *O Dorney*, Dorney, Darney; 'des. of Ɔoᵹᵹeann' (sullen, a woman's name). This is one of our very few Irish metronymic surnames.

Ó Ɔoiʀnín—I—*O Dornine*, Dornin, Durnin, Durnian, Dornan, &c.; a var. of Ó Ɔuᵹᵹnín, ᵹ.v.

Ó Ɔoiᵹe—I—*O Dohie*, O'Diff, (Duffy); an old Mayo surname, still common in that county and in Co. Galway, but always made Duffy in English. Baile Ui Dhoithe, angl. Ballyduffy, in the parish of Addergoole, Co. Mayo, marks the site of the ancient residence of the family.

Ó Ɔomaᵹáin—I—Domigan, Domegan, Dumegan; 'des. of *Ɔomaᵹán*' (dim. of ɔoma, want, scarcity). Cf. *O Domagh*, *O Duma*, for Ó Ɔomaᵹ; *O Demine*, *O Domyn* for *Ó Ɔoimín*.

Ó Ɔoᵹnaill—I—*O Donill*, *O Daniell*, O'Donnell, Donnell, Daniel; 'des. of Ɔoᵹnall' (world-mighty, an ancient and very common Irish personal name, now generally angl. Daniel); the name of several distinct families in Ireland, of which the following were the most important:—(1) Ó Ɔoᵹnaill of Tirconaill. This family is descended from Conall Gulban, son of Niall of the Nine Hostages, and for four centuries was one of the most powerful in Ireland. The original patrimony of this family was Cinel Luighdheach, a mountainous district between the Swilly and the Dobhar, but on the decline of the O'Muldorys and O'Canannains, some time after the Anglo-Norman invasion, they became the ruling family in Tirconnell. Previous to that event, only two of the immediate ancestors of the O'Donnells had been lords of Tirconnell, namely, Dalach, who died in 868 and from whom they derived their later clan-name of Clann Dalaigh, and his son, Eigheachan, who was the father of Domhnall from whom they took the surname of

Ó Ɗoṁnaıll, or O'Donnell. The family produced
many able chieftains who, during the four stormy
centuries that the O'Donnells held sway in Tirconnell,
not only defended their territory against foreign and
native foes, but made their power respected throughout the north and west of Ireland. The most celebrated of all the chieftains of Tirconnell was Red
Hugh O'Donnell, who so often led his clan to victory
in the closing years of the reign of Elizabeth. Many
of the O'Donnells were distinguished military commanders in the service of continental powers, and in
the last century, Leopold O'Donnell became prime
minister of Spain and Duke of Tetuan. The O'Donnells of Limerick and Tipperary are, according to
O'Donovan, descended from Shane Luirg, son of
Turlough O'Donnell of the Wine, lord of Tirconnell
at the beginning of the 15th century. (2) Ó Ɗomnaıll of Corcabaskin, in West Clare. This family
derives its descent from Ɗoṁnall, son of Ɗıaṛmaıɗ,
lord of Corcabaskin, who was slain at the battle of
Clontarf in 1014. The O'Donnells continued to be
lords of Corcabaskin until dispossessed by the Mac-
Mahons early in the 14th century. They are, no
doubt, still numerous in Thomond. (3) Ó Ɗoṁnaıll
of Ui Maine, who were chiefs of Clann Flaitheamhail,
in the present Co. Galway. (4) Ó Ɗoṁnaıll of Carlow,
anciently lords of Ui Drona, now the barony of Idrone.
(5) Ó Ɗoṁnaıll of Cinel Binnigh, a sept of the Cinel
Eoghain. (6) Ó Ɗoṁnaıll of Ui Eathach, a sept of
the Oirghialla, who were seated in the present Co.
Armagh. The O'Donnells are now very numerous,
especially in Ulster and Munster.

Ó Ɗoṁnallaın—I—*O Donellane*, *O Donnellan*, Donelan, Donnellan, Donlan, &c. ; ' des. of Ɗoṁnallán '
(dim. of Ɗoṁnall). The principal family of this
name is that of Ui Maine, in the present Co. Galway.
The head of this family, which is of the same stock as
the O'Kellys, was chief of Clann Bhreasail, a district
lying between Ballinasloe and Loughrea, and had his

residence at Ballydonnellan. This family produced some poets who are referred to in the Annals. Another family of the name, a branch of the Oirghialla, were anciently lords of Ui Tuirtre, comprising the modern baronies of Upper and Lower Toome, in Co. Antrim. There was also a Brehon family of the name in Offaly, and the name was not uncommon in that and the neighbouring districts of Leinster at the end of the 16th century. A family of the name is also mentioned as anciently chiefs of Teallach Ainbhith in Tyrone. Most of the Donnellans in Ireland at present belong to the Ui Maine family.

Ó ᴅonnaᴃáın—I—O'Donovan, Donovan; ' des. of ᴅonnᴅuᴃán ' (brown ᴅuᴃán, or compound of ᴅonn, brown, and ᴅuᴃ, black, with dim. termination). The O'Donovans, who belong to the royal race of Munster, were originally chiefs of Ui Cairbre Aedhbha, a district lying along the banks of the River Maigue, in the present Co. Limerick. Their principal stronghold was at Bruree. About the year 1178, however, they were driven from Ui Cairbre and forced to take refuge in South-west Cork where, with the aid of their old allies, the O'Mahonys, they effected a settlement in O'Driscoll's country of Corca Laoighdhe, to which they gave their clan-name of Ui Cairbre, and where they retained considerable power and extensive possessions down to the close of the Jacobite wars. A branch of the family settled in Co. Wexford; and from another branch, settled in Kilkenny, the celebrated Irish antiquarian and scholar, Dr. John O'Donovan, was descended. There is also a family of O'Donovan in Tipperary, which, however, is not of this stock, but of that of the O'Mahers. See also Ó ᴅonnamáın.

Ó ᴅonnaᴃáır—I—O Downever, O Donowre, O Donnor, Dooner, Dunner, Donor; ' des. of ᴅonnaᴃaᴘ ' (brown-eyebrow); also written Ó ᴅúnaᴃᴘa. This surname appears to have originated in Co. Roscommon. The Annals of the Four Masters at the year 1101 record the death of Ʒıoᴌᴌᴀ nᴀ ᴨᴀoᵯ Ó Ꝺúnᴀḃⱋᴀ, chief poet of Connacht. In the year 1297, Marian O Donnabhair was elected Bishop of Elphin, but died on his way to Rome, to uphold the validity of his election, which was contested. The surname had reached Tipperary before the end of the 16th century.

Ó Ꝺonnᴀċáın—I—*O Donaghan, O Duneghan, O Dunchan,* Doonican, Dunican, Duncan ; ' des. of Ꝺonnᴀċán' (dim. of Ꝺonn, brown) ; apparently a var. of Ó Ꝺonnᴀʒáın, q.v. See also Ó Ꝺuınneᴀċáın.

Ó Ꝺonnᴀʒáın—I—*O Donegaine, O Dunegaine, O Donegan, O Dongane, O Dungan,* Donnegan, Dunnegan, Donegan, Dunigan, Dongan, Dungan, Duncan, &c. ; ' des. of Ꝺonnᴀʒán' (dim. of Ꝺonn, brown) ; the name of several distinct families in Ireland. The O'Donegans of Tipperary and Limerick were in early times a very important family. They were chiefs of the extensive district of Ara, now the barony of Ara (or Duhara) in the north-west of Co. Tipperary, and of Ui Cuanach, now the barony of Coonagh in Co. Limerick. They are frequently mentioned in the Annals during the 11th and 12th century, but after the Anglo-Norman invasion they began to decline and soon disappeared from history. Their territory in later times was occupied by a branch of the O'Briens, the chief of which was styled Mac I Brien Ara. The O'Donegans of Cork were anciently chiefs of Muscraighe-tri-maighe, or Muskerry of the Three Plains, now the barony of Orrery in the neighbourhood of Rathluirc. Their patrimony was granted by King John to William de Barry, under the name of Muskerry-Donegan. There were, in early times, three distinct families of O'Donegans in Ulster, and the name is still extant in that province. The O'Donegans were numerous at the end of the 16th century in the midlands and in North Connacht ; and, though by no means common, the name is at the present day found in all the provinces.

Ó Ꝺonnáın—I—*O Donayne, O Donnane,* Donnan ; ' des.

of 'Oonnán ' (dim. of 'Oonn, brown) ; also written Ó 'Oúnáin, q.v.

Ó ओonnᴀṁáin—I—O'Donovan, Donovan ; ' des. of 'Oonn'oᴀṁán ' (brown 'Oᴀṁán, or compound of 'oonn; brown, and 'oᴀṁ, a poet, with the dim. termination), the name of a family of Corca Laoighdhe, who were seated in Tuath O Feehily, in O'Driscoll's country, before the O'Donovans of Ui Cairbre settled in that district. " It is highly probable," says Dr. O'Donovan, " that a great number of the O'Donovans of the County of Cork are of this family." (Four Masters, p. 2483).

Ó ओonnċᴀṫᴀ, Ó ओonnċᴀıṫ—I—O Donochowe, O Donaghie, O Dunaghy, O'Donoghue, O'Donohue, Donaghoe, Donoghue, Donohoe, Donaghy, Donagh, Dunphy, Dunfy, Dumphy, &c. ; ' des. of 'Oonnċᴀṫ ' (brown-warrior, or strong-warrior, a very common Irish personal name). There are several distinct families of this name in Ireland, of which the following are the best known :—(1) Ó 'Oonnċᴀṫᴀ of Cashel, who are of the same stock as the MacCarthys and O'Callaghans, and derive their name and descent from 'Oonnċᴀṫ, son of Ceallachan, King of Cashel. They were seated in Magh Feimhin, now the barony of Iffa and Offa, in the south-east of Co. Tipperary, and during the greater part of the 11th century were lords of Eoghanacht Caisil ; but towards the close of that century, they were overshadowed by the growing power of the MacCarthys and disappeared from history. (2) Ó 'Oonnċᴀṫᴀ of Desmond, a branch of the Ui Eathach Mumhan and of the same stock as the O'Mahonys, who derive their descent from Eochaidh, son of Cas, son of Corc, King of Munster in the 5th century, and more immediately from Domhnall, the son of Dubhdabhoireann, King of Munster, who commanded, conjointly with Cian, ancestor of the O'Mahonys, the forces of Desmond at the battle of Clontarf. The descendants of Domhnall were at first surnamed Ó 'Ooṁnᴀıll, but afterwards adopted the present surname of Ó Oonncaóa, which they took from Oonncaó, his son. They were known by the clan-names of Cinel Laoghaire and Clann tSealbaigh. The original patrimony of the family lay in West Cork, but about the end of the 12th century or the beginning of the 13th, they were driven out by the MacCarthys and O'Mahonys, and settled in Kerry, where they became lords of all the country about Killarney, to which they gave the name of Eoghanacht Ui Dhonn-chadha, angl. Onaght O'Donoghue. They divided at an early period into two great branches, namely Ó Oonncaóa of Loch Lein, the head of which was known as Ó Oonncaóa Móp, or O'Donoghue More, and resided at Ross Castle, and Ó Oonncaóa of Glenflesk, the head of which was designated Ó Oonn-caóa an Sleanna, or O'Donoghue of the Glen. The estates of O'Donoghue More were confiscated in the reign of Elizabeth, and ultimately passed into the possession of the ancestors of the Earl of Kenmare, but O'Donoghue of the Glen retained considerable property down to modern times. The head of this branch is now known as The O'Donoghue. (3) Ó Oonncaóa of Ossory who are of the same stock as the Fitzpatricks, and were anciently one of the ruling families of Ossory. Oonncaó Ó Oonncaóa, the head of the family in the latter part of the 12th century, was the founder of Jerpoint Abbey. This family now anglicise the name Dunphy. (4) Ó Oonncaóa of Meath, who were chiefs of Teallach Modharain, which, according to O'Donovan, was probably in the barony of South Moyfenrath, but nothing is known of their history. (5) Ó Oonncaóa of Ui Maine, who are of the same stock as the O'Kellys, and were chiefs of Ui Cormaic, in the present Co. Galway. (6) Ó Oonncaóa of Tireragh, a branch of the Ui Fiachrach of the Moy. (7) Ó Oonncaóa of Teallach Dhonn-chadha, who are still numerous in Co. Cavan. This surname, under various angl. forms, is now very com-mon in all parts of Ireland.

Ó Donncaṫaiġ—I—Duncahy. V. Ó Duinncaṫaiġ.

Ó Donndaṁáin, v. Ó Donnaṁáin.

Ó Donnduḃáin, v. Ó Donnaḃáin.

Ó Donnduḃartaiġ—I—*O Donnoartie, O Donorty, O Dunort*, Donarty, Donworth, Dunworth, Dunfort, Dunford, (Davenport); 'des. of Donnduḃartaċ, (brown Duḃartaċ); an old Munster surname, still well represented in the province. It appears to have originated in the neighbourhood of Clonmel.

Ó Donnġaile—I—O'Donnelly, Donnelly, Donneely; 'des. of Donnġal' (brown-valour); the name of a distinguished family of Cinel Eoghain in Ulster who derive their name and descent from Donnġal, the fourth in descent from Doṁnall, King of Aileach and brother of Niall Glúnduḃ, the eponymous ancestor of the O'Neills. The O'Donnellys were originally seated at Druim Lighean, now angl. Drumleen, a short distance to the north of Lifford, Co. Donegal, but were afterwards expelled by the Cinel Conaill, when they settled at Ballydonnelly, now Castlecaulfield, to the west of Dungannon. It was at Ballydonnelly that the celebrated Shane O'Neill was fostered by the O'Donnellys. O'Donnelly was hereditary marshal of O'Neill's forces; and Donnell O'Donelly, who accompanied Hugh O'Neill to Kinsale as 'captain of one hundred men,' fought bravely until he and all his men were slain. Ballydonnelly was granted by James I to Sir Toby Caulfield, ancestor of the Earl of Charlemont. The family is now very numerous in Ulster. There were also families of the name in Sligo and Cork. The former were a branch of the Ui Fiachrach, and were seated at Dun Ui Chobhthaigh, now angl. Doonycoy, in the parish of Templeboy. The latter were a branch of the Corca Laoighdhe, and were seated near Dunmanway.

Ó Donnġalaiġ—I—*O Donnowly*, O'Donnelly, Donnelly, &c.; 'des. of Donnġalaċ' (der. of Donnġal); the name (1) of a Tipperary family who were anciently chiefs of Muscraighe-Thire, now the barony of Lower

Ormond, but disappeared from history towards the end of the 11th century; and (2) of a Galway family, a branch of the Siol Anmchadha, who were numerous in that county at the beginning of the 17th century. This surname is also written Ó Dúnʒaʟaıʒ. Its angl. forms cannot now be distinguished from those of Ó Donnʒaıʟe, q.v.

Ó ᴅoɴɴʒusᴀ—I—*O Dangussa, O Danaisa, O Denisi,* Dennis, Denis, Denison, Dennison, Denson; 'des. of Donnʒuʁ' (brown-choice); the name of an ecclesiastical family in Ulster; also of a Munster family, chiefly in Cork and Waterford.

Ó ᴅoʁaıᴅ—I—*O Durry,* Durry, (?) Dorr, (?) Durr; 'des. of Doʁaᴅ' (perhaps Doʁaıᴅ, strife; cf. Ó ᴍaoʟ-ᴅoʁaıᴅ).

O ᴅoʁᴅáıɴ—I—Derivan, Derivin, ; a var. of Óᴅoıʁᴅin, q.v.

Ó ᴅoʁᴄaıᴅe—I—*O Doroghie, O Dorichie, O Dorchie,* Dorcey, Darkey, Darcy, (D'Arcy); 'des. of Doʁ-ᴄaıᴅe' (dark-man); the name (1) of a branch of the Ui Fiachrach, who were chiefs of the extensive district of Partry, to the west of Lough Mask, Co. Mayo; and (2) of a branch of the Ui Maine in Co. Galway. Both families are still well represented. At the end of the 16th century, the name was also found in nearly every county in Munster, and in Kildare and Carlow. It is now nearly everywhere angl. Darcy or D'Arcy, which disguises the Irish origin of the family.

Ó ᴅoʁᴄáıɴ—I—*O Dorchane,* Dorgan, Dorrigan, (?) Doorigan; 'des. of Doʁᴄán' (dim. of Doʁᴄaıᴅe); a rare surname in Cork and Kerry; probably the same as Ó Doʁᴄaıᴅe, q.v.

Ó ᴅoʁɴáıɴ—I—*O Dornane,* O'Dornan, Dornan, Durnan, &c.; 'des. of Doʁnán' (dim. of ᴅoʁɴ, a fist); a rare surname; found chiefly in Antrim and Down. V. Ó ᴅuıʁnin.

Ó ᴅʁaᴅe—III—*O Drea,* Drea, Drew, (Drewry, Drury); 'des. of the druid' (Ir. ᴅʁaᴅe); apparently the same as the Thomond Ó ᴅʁaoı, q.v.; a rare surname in

Kerry and West Limerick. The family has been located for centuries in the parish of Duagh, near Listowel.

Ó 'ORAᵹnáin, Ó 'ORAIᵹneáin—I—*O Drinane, O Drenan*, Drinane, Drinan, Dreinan, Drennan, and, by translation, Thornton; 'des. of 'Opaiᵹneán' (blackthorn); the name (1) of a branch of the Siol Anmchadha in Co. Galway; and (2) of a Clare family, who were formerly seated in the barony of Corcumroe. The name was also common in Cavan, Westmeath, Leix and Kilkenny.

Ó 'ORAO'OA—I—Drudy, Droody, Draddy; 'des. of 'O_____'; an old, but rare, Connacht surname. ᵹiolla Ciapáin Ó 'Opao'oa, erenagh of Cong, is mentioned by the Four Masters at the year 1128.

Ó 'ORAOI—III—*O Dree*, Drea, Drew, (Drewry, Drury); 'des. of the druid' (Ir. 'opaoi); a rare Thomond surname; also Ó 'Opuai'o, q.v. Cf. Ó 'Opae.

*Ó 'ORAOileáin, Dreelan.

Ó 'OREA'OA—I—*O Dready, O Dradye*, Draddy; 'des. of 'O_____'; a rare Cork surname. Seán Ó 'Opea'oa was a Munster scribe at the beginning of the last century. V. Ó ᵹpea'oa, of which it is possibly a variant.

Ó 'OREáin—I—*O Dreane*, Adrien, Adrian, Drain, Draine; 'des. of 'Opeán' (wren). The O'Dreains were anciently chiefs of Calraidhe in Co. Roscommon, and erenaghs of Ardcarne, near Boyle, but were dispossessed in the 13th or 14th century by the Mac-Dermotts. They appear to have removed to Co. Antrim, which is the only place where the name was found in the 16th century.

Ó 'ORISCEóil—I—*O Driscole*, O'Driscoll, Driscoll, &c.; a corrupt form of Ó he'oippceóil, q.v.

Ó 'ORISleáin—I—*O Drislane*, Drislane; 'des. of 'Opipleán' (brier).

Ó 'OROᴄᴄAiᵹ—I—*O Drughta, O Drought*, Drought; 'des. of 'Opoᴄᴄaᴄ' (from 'opoᴄᴄ, a mill-wheel?). V. Ó 'Opoiᴄi'o.

Ó ᴅᴿoɪċɪᴅ—I—*O Drehitt*, Bridgeman; probably a corruption of *Ó ᴅʀoɪċᴄɪᵹ, des. of ᴅʀoɪċᴅᴇᴀċ (bridge-maker or bridge-keeper); a rare Limerick surname. Cf. Ó ᴅʀoċᴄᴀɪᵹ.

Ó ᴅʀoᴍᴀ—I—*O Drommy*, Dromey, Drummy, Drum, Drumm, (Drummond); 'des. of ᴅʀuɪᴍ' (back); the name of an ecclesiastical family who were erenaghs of the parish of Kinnawley, in the Counties of Fermanagh and Cavan, where they are still numerous. Some of them settled in Munster in the 16th century, Solomon O'Droma was one of the compilers of the Book of Ballymote.

Ó ᴅʀoᴍᴀɪɴ—I—Droman; 'des. of ᴅʀoᴍᴀɴ' (dim. of ᴅʀoᴍ, a back); a rare Waterford surname; also Ó ᴅʀuɪᴍɪɴ, q.v.

Ó ᴅʀóɴᴀ—I—*O Drony*, Droney; 'des. of ᴅʀóɴᴀ'; a rare Clare surname.

Ó ᴅʀuᴀċᴀɪɴ—I—*O Drwoghane, O Droughane, O Droghane*, Droohan, Drohane, Drohan; 'des. of ᴅʀuᴀċᴀɴ'; a rare surname, found chiefly in Waterford and Cork. There was an ecclesiastical family of Ó ᴅʀuᴄᴀɪɴ at Armagh which may possibly be the same.

Ó ᴅʀuᴀɪᴅ—III—Drew, (Drewry, Drury); a var. of Ó ᴅʀᴀoɪ, q.v.

Ó ᴅʀuɪᴍɪɴ—I—*O Dromen*, Drummin; 'des. of ᴅʀuɪᴍɪɴ' (dim. of ᴅʀuɪᴍ, a back). Cf. Ó ᴅʀoᴍᴀɪɴ and Ó ᴅʀoᴍᴀ.

Ó ᴅuᴀċᴀɪɴ—I—*O Doughane*, Doughan, Doohane; 'des. of ᴅuᴀċᴀɴ' (dim. of ᴅuɪ or ᴅuᴀċ); a Donegal surname; to be distinguished from Ó ᴅuᴅᴄoɴ, which is often similarly anglicised.

Ó ᴅuᴅᴀᵹᴀɪɴ—I—*O Doogaine, O Dowgaine*, O'Doogan, Doogan, Dougan, Dugan, Duggan, &c.; 'des of ᴅuᴅᴀᵹᴀɴ' (dim. of ᴅuᴅ, black). There are several distinct families of this name, of which the following are the most important:—(1) Ó ᴅuᴅᴀᵹᴀɪɴ of Fermoy, who before the Anglo-Norman invasion were lords of the northern half of Feara Maighe, which comprised the modern baronies of Fermoy, Condons, and Clan-gibbon ; (2) Ó Ouɓaᵹáιn of Ui Maine, a literary family, who were hereditary historians to the O'Kellys and compilers of the Book of Ui Maine, and had their residence at Ballydugan, near Loughrea ; (3) Ó Ouɓaᵹáιn of Tirawley who are of the same stock as the MacFirbises, and were anciently seated in the parish of Kilmore-Moy, to the north-west of Ballina ; (4) Ó Ouɓaᵹáιn of Corca Laoighdhe, in South-west Cork, where they are still numerous ; and (5) Ó Ouɓaᵹáιn of Aidhne, in South-west Galway.

Ó Ouɓáιn—I—*O Dovayne, O Dwane, O Duan, O Dowane, O Doane, O Downe,* Dewane, Devane, Divane, Divan, Dwane, Duane, Dwan, Duan, Dune, Doane, Dooan, Doon, Down, Downes, (Devine, Devany), &c., and by ' translation ' Kidney ; ' des. of Ouɓán ' (a dim. of ouɓ, black) ; the name of several distinct families, viz. : (1) a Meath family, anciently lords of Cnodhbha, now angl. Knowth, in the parish of Monks-town, but dispossessed at an early period and dis-persed through Leinster ; (2) a family of Corca Laoigh-dhe in South-west Cork, still numerous in that county, but sometimes calling themselves Kidney in English ; (3) a Connemara family, an old family in that district and still well represented, but the name is sometimes made Devany in English, as happens sometimes also in Mayo ; and (4) an old Limerick family who now sometimes anglicise the name Downes. At the end of the 16th century, Ó Ouɓáιn was a common surname throughout the southern half of Ireland. Ó Ouιɓín, which is synonymous, is often used interchangeably with it, especially in Connacht.

Ó Ouɓánaιᵹ—I—*O Douvany, O Dowanie, O Devany,* Duany, Devany ; ' des. of Ouɓánaċ ' (der. of Ouɓán) ; a rare surname in Donegal and Sligo.

Ó Ouɓarcaιᵹ—I—*O Duarty, O Duhartie, O Dowhirty,* Duarty, Doorty, Dooherty, (Doherty) ; ' des. of Ouɓarcaċ ' (black áιtaċ, or compound of ouɓ, black, áιrc, noble, bear, &c., and the adjectival suffix aċ) ; the name of a family of the Corca Laoighdhe, in south-west Cork. The family, which has been long dispersed through Munster, is numerous in the counties of Cork, Kerry, Limerick and Tipperary, but often disguised as Dohertys.

Ó Ⱃⱆⰱⰰⱄⰰ, v. Ó Ⱃⱆⰱⰶⱕⱃⰰ.

Ó Ⱃⱆⰱⰽⰰⰹⱃ — I — *O Duchir, O Dougher,* Doughar, Dougher, Dooher ; ' des. of Ⱃⱆⰱⰽⱕⱃ ' (black-dear) ; a rare and scattered surname. In the 16th century, it was found in Donegal, Tipperary and Wexford.

Ó Ⱃⱆⰱⰽⱁⱀ—I—*O Duchon, O Doghon, O Dughan, O Dohon,* Doughan, Doohan ; ' des. of Ⱃⱆⰱⰽⱙ ' (black-hound) ; the name of a family of the Corca Laoighdhe in South-west Cork, but long peculiar to Tipperary and Clare.

Ó Ⱃⱆⰱⰽⱁⱀⱀⰰ—I—O'Dooghany, Dougheny, Dogheny, Doheny, Deheny, Dahony, Dawney, &c. ; ' des. of Ⱃⱆⰱⰽⱁⱀⱀⰰ ' (black Conna, a man's name) ; the name of a family of the Corca Laoighdhe, in South-west Cork ; now scattered through Munster.

Ó ⰓⱆⰱⰓⰰⰱⱁⰹⱃⱕⰰⱀⱀ—I—Davoran, Davoren, Davern ; ' des. of ⰓⱆⰱⰓⰰⰱⱁⰹⱃⱕⰰⱀⱀ ' (Black of the two Burrens) ; now shortened to Ó Ⰴⰰⰱⱁⰹⱃⱕⰰⱀⱀ, q.v.

Ó ⰓⱆⰱⰓⰰ—I—*O Dowda, O Douda, O Dooda, O Dowdy, O Duda, O Doddie,* O'Dowd, O'Doud, Dowda, Dowdie, Doody, Duddy, Doud, Dowd, &c. ; ' des. of ⰓⱆⰱⰓⰰ ' (black) ; the name (1) of a Connacht family, and (2) of an Ulster family. The first of these derive their descent from the celebrated King Dathi and were the head family of the northern Ui Fiachrach. Before the irruption of the English into Connacht in 1237, they were the ruling family in all Lower Connacht, including the greater part of the present counties of Mayo and Sligo. And their power was great on sea as well as on land. (See Annals, A.D. 1154.) In the 14th century they had in immediate succession three able chieftains who drove the English out of their territory, but they were never able to regain the position of power and dignity which the family enjoyed before the English settlement in Connacht.

The O'Dowd lands were confiscated after the Cromwellian and Jacobite wars. Branches of the family had settled in Munster before the end of the 16th century, where they now anglicise the name Doody. The Ulster family, which is a branch of the Cinel Eoghain, is still numerous in Derry and other parts of that province.

Ó Ɔuḃɔacáin, Ó Ɔuḃɔaᵹáin—I—*O Dowdegane, O Dwdigane*, Dowdican, Dudican; des. of 'Ɔuḃɔacán' or 'Ɔuḃɔaᵹán' (dim. of Ɔuḃɔa); a rare Sligo surname. MacFirbis mentions a family of Ó Ɔuḃɔacáin among the Cinel Eoghain.

Ó Ɔuḃɔáleiᵹe—I—Dudley; 'des. of Ɔuḃɔáleiᵹe' (Black of the two sides); a rare South Cork surname.

Ó Ɔuḃɔúin—I—*O Dughune, O Dwghune, O Dogowyn,* (?) Duggan; 'des. of Ɔuḃɔúin' (Black of the fort); an old Kerry surname, probably still extant, but disguised under the angl. form of Duggan.

Ó Ɔuḃᵹaile—I—*O Dowilly,* (Doyle); 'des. of Ɔuḃᵹal' (black-valour); an old surname in Co. Roscommon, where it is still extant under the angl. form of Doyle. It has always been extremely rare.

Ó Ɔuḃᵹaill—II—*O Dogaill, O Dowill, O Dowell, O Doole,* O'Doyle, Doyle, Dowell, Doole, &c.; 'des. of Ɔuḃᵹall' (the black foreigner); a very common Irish surname, doubtless of Danish origin. It is found in all parts of Ireland, but is most frequent in the maritime counties of Leinster and Munster, and in the neighbourhood of the old Danish settlements.

Ó Ɔuḃᵹusa—I—*O Dwysy,* Doocey, Doocie, Doocy, Ducey; 'des. of Ɔuḃᵹur' (black-choice); an old, but rare, Ormond surname.

Ó Ɔuḃlacáin—I—*O Duelaghane,* Doolaghan, Dullaghan, Dolaghan, Dologhan; 'des. of Ɔuḃlacán'; also Ó Ɔuiḃleacáin, q.v.

Ó Ɔuḃlaɔaiᵹ—I—Doolady, Dooladdy; 'des. of Ɔuḃrlaɔac'; a rare Co. Leitrim surname. I cannot find any early angl. form.

Ó Ɔuḃlaiḃe, Ó Ɔuḃlaiᵹe, v. Ó Ɔuḃlaoic.

Ó ᴅuᴜᴸáɪɴ—I—*O Doelane, O Dowlane, O Dolane,* O'Doolan, Doolan, Dolan, (Dowling, Delaney, Delany) ; ' des. of ᴅuᴜᵽᴸáɴ ' (black defiance, challenge) ; a rather common surname in all parts of Ireland, but its angl. forms cannot always be distinguished from those of Ó ᴅuᴜᴸᴀɪɴɴ and Ó ᴅuɴᴸᴀɪɴɢ, q.v. Felix O Dubhlain was Bishop of Ossory at the beginning of the 13th century.

Ó ᴅuᴜᴸᴀɪɴɴ—I—*O Dowlan, O Dowlin, O Doolen,* O'Doolan, Doolan, Doolin, (Dowling), &c. ; ' des. of ᴅuᴜᵽᴸᴀɴɴ ' (black ᵽᴸᴀɴɴ) ; the name of a family of the Uí Maine, in Co. Galway. Its angl. forms cannot always be distinguished from those of Ó ᴅuᴜᴸáɪɴ and Ó ᴅúɴᴸᴀɪɴɢ, q.v.

Ó ᴅuᴜᴸᴀᴄᴛᴀ, Ó ᴅuᴜᴸᴀᴄᴛɴᴀ—I—Doolaghty, Doo-loughty ; ' des. of ᴅuᴜᴸᴀᴄᴛɴᴀ ' (black ᴸᴀᴄᴛɴᴀ, a man's name) ; a Clare surname.

Ó ᴅuᴜᴸᴀᴏɪᴄ—I—*O Dowlee, O Dowley, O Dooly,* Dowley, Dooley, Dooly ; ' des. of ᴅuᴜᴸᴀᴏᴄ ' (black hero). There are three distinct families of this name, viz. : (1) Ó ᴅuᴜᴸᴀᴏɪᴄ of Feara Tulach who are of the race of Feidlimidh, son of Enna Ceinnsealach, and before the Anglo-Norman invasion were lords of Feara Tulach, now the barony of Fertullagh, in the south-east of Co. Westmeath. They were dispossessed soon after the invasion and their lands given to the Tyrrells. (2) Ó ᴅuᴜᴸᴀᴏɪᴄ of Clann Mhaonaigh, who, according to MacFirbis, are a branch of the O'Melaghlens of Meath, whence they were banished in the 11th century. They settled on the western side of Slieve Bloom, in Ely O'Carroll, where they are still very numerous. The head of the family had the privilege of inaugurating O'Carroll as king of Ely. MacFirbis writes the name of this family Ó ᴅuᴜᴸuɪᵹe (Gen. p. 161). (3) Ó ᴅuᴜᴸᴀᴏɪᴄ of Siol Anmchadha who are of the same stock as the O'Maddens and were originally located in the south-east of the present Co. Galway.

Ó ᴅuᴜᴸuᴀᴄʀᴀ—I—*O Dwlougherie,* Dilloughery, De-loughery, Delooghery, Delouhery, Delohery, Deloorey,

Delury, Deloury, Delacour, (Dilworth, Dillworth);
'des. of 'Oubluacpa' (Black of Luacaip, a place-
name in West Munster); an old surname in Co. Cork.

Ó 'OuÓRAIC—I—*O Duvrick, O Durick, O Dowricke,*
Durack, Durick, Darrick; 'des. of 'Ouópata' (Black
of prosperity); older form Ó 'Ouópata; the name of a
Dalcassian family who were anciently lords of Ui
Conghaile, now the parish of O'Connelloe, near Killaloe.
The family is almost extinct in Clare, but survives
in Tipperary and Offaly. Also Ó 'Ouiópic, q.v.

Ó 'OuÓROSA, Ó 'OuÓRUIS—I—*O Durise,* Dooris,
Doorish, Doris; 'des. of 'Ouópop' (black Rop);
formerly the name of a family in the neighbourhood
of Bruff in Co. Limerick, but it has long since disappeared from that part of the country. It occurs
in Fermanagh early in the 17th century. I find the
modern forms in Longford and Mayo.

Ó 'OuÓSLáine, Ó 'OuÓSLáinᵹe—I—*O Dowlaney, O
Dulany,* Delaney, Delany, Deleany, Laney, &c.·;
'des. of 'Ouópláine' or 'Ouópláinᵹe' (Black of the
Slaney); the name of a numerous family in Leix, who
were formerly chiefs of Coill Uachtarach, now Upper-
woods, at the foot of Slieve Bloom.

Ó 'OuÓCAIᵹ—I—*O Duffie, O Duhie, O Duhig, O Dowhie,
O Dowey,* O'Duffy, Duffy, Duhy, Duhig, Dowey,
Douey, Dooey, Doey, &c., and sometimes, by translation, Black; 'des. of 'Ouócac' (black). This surname is found in all parts of Ireland, and, doubtless,
there are several distinct families so called. The
O'Duffys of Connacht are remarkable for the number
of eminent prelates they formerly gave to the church
in that province. The O'Duffys were also a family
of note in Monaghan. In Munster, the name is
generally anglicised Duhig, owing to the pronunciation of the final ᵹ. The family is, according to Keating,
of Dalcassian origin. In Ulster, where the name is
very common, especially in Monaghan and Donegal,
it is sometimes angl. Dowey and Dooey. V. Ó 'Ouitce.

Ó 'OuÓUIÓe—I—*O Dywoie, O Dyvoye,* Devoy, Deevey,

Deevy; 'des. of Ouḃoḋaṗ' (Black Oḋaṗ); also Ó Ouıḃıḋe, q.v.; an apocopated form of Ó Ouḃuıḋıṗ, q.v.; cf. Ó Ḃolʒuıḋe for Ó Ḃolʒuıḋıṗ; a Leix surname.

Ó OuḃuıḋıR—I—*O Duvire, O Duire,* O'Dwyer, Dwyer, Dwire, &c.; 'des. of Ouḃoḋaṗ' (black Oḋaṗ); also written Ó Ouıḃıḋıṗ, q.v.; the name of a Tipperary family, of Leinster origin, who were chiefs of Coill na manach, now the barony of Kilnamanagh, in the west of that county. Philip O'Dwyer and Owen O'Dwyer were exempted from pardon for life and estate in the Cromwellian Act of 1652. Some of the name held high rank in the service of France, Austria and Russia. The name is now common in all the south of Ireland. Ó Ouıḃıḋıṗ is also a Donegal name, but whether or not the family is a branch of that of Tipperary, I am unable to say.

Ó OuḃuRċuıle—I—*O Dorhilly, O Durley, O Dowrley,* Dufferly, Doorley, Doorly; 'des. of Ouḃuṗċuıle' (black Uṗċuıle); the name of a family of Ui Maine in Co. Galway, who were seated near Loughrea. It is still common in Connacht.

Ó Ouıḃ—I—*O Duff,* O'Diff, Duff, and, by translation, Black; 'des. of Ouḃ' (Black); the name of an old family in Leix who were chiefs of Cinel Criomhthainn, in the present barony of East Maryborough; also apparently of a Connacht family.

Ó Ouıḃcınn, v. Ó Ouıḃʒınn.

Ó OuıḃḋíoRmA, Ó OuıḃḋíoRmAıʒ—I—*O Dughierma,* Dooyearma, Dyermott, Diarmod, Dermott, Dermond, (O'Dermott, MacDermott), &c.; 'des. of OuḃḋıoṗmA(ċ)' (black-trooper); the name of a family of Cinel Eoghain who were anciently lords of Bredach, which comprised the eastern half of Inishowen, and are still numerous in Donegal; often shortened to Ó OíoṗmA, and angl. MacDermott.

Ó OuıḃeAṁnA—I—*O'Doveanna,* Devanny, Devany, &c.; 'des. of OuḃeAṁnA' (Black of EAṁaın, near Armagh); the name of an Ulster family who were anciently chiefs of Ui Breasail, in Co. Armagh. Its angl. forms cannot be distinguished from those of Ó Duibeⱥnnⱥiჳ, q.v.

Ó Duibeⱥnnⱥiჳ—I—*O Doveanna, O Devenie*, Devanny, Devaney, Devany, Devenny, Divenney, &c.; ' des. of Dubeⱥnnⱥiჳ' (perhaps Black of eⱥnⱥc, a place-name); the name of a Co. Down family, to which belonged the Bishop of Down and Connor, Cornelius, or Connor O'Devany, whose martyrdom at Dublin, in 1612, is so touchingly described by the Four Masters. Its angl. forms cannot be distinguished from those of Ó Duibeⱥṁnⱥ, q.v.

Ó Duibfinn—I—*O Duffin*, Duffin, Diffin; ' des. of Dubfionn' (black-fionn); a rare surname; found chiefly in Antrim, Cork and Waterford.

Ó Duibჳeⱥoáin—I—Dugidan, Degidan, (Dixon); ' des. of Dubჳeⱥoán'; a Clare surname.

Ó Duibჳeⱥnnáin—I—*O Duigenain*, Duigenan, Duignan, Dignan, Deignan, Duignam, Dignam, &c.; ' des. of Dubჳeⱥnnán' (dim. of Dubceⱥnn, black-head); the name of a distinguished literary family in Co. Roscommon, who were hereditary chroniclers to the Clann Mulrony and Conmaicne, that is, to the MacDermotts, O'Farrells, Magrannells, &c. Their chief residence was at Kilronan.

Ó Duibჳinn—I—*O Duygin, O Digin*, Digin, Diggin, Deegin, Digan, Deighan, Deegan, Duigan, (Dugan, Duggan, Duggen); ' des. of Dubceⱥnn' (Black-head). There are three distinct families of this name, formerly seated respectively in Galway, Clare and Wexford. It was also common, at the beginning of the 17th century, in Offaly and Leix and also in Kerry. It is now sometimes disguised under the angl. form of Dugan, or Duggan.

Ó Duibჳiollⱥ—I—Duffley, Diffily, Diffely, Diffley, Deffely, Divilly, Devilly, Devily, Deely, Dealy, &c.; ' des. of Dubჳiollⱥ' (black-lad); the name (1) of a family of the southern Ui Fiachrach, who were chiefs of Cinel Cinnghamhna, near Kinvara, in south-west of Co. Galway ; and (2) of a family of Siol Anmchadha, in the south-east of the same county.

Ó Ɒuıȯıȯe—I—*O Divie, O Devy,* Deevey, Deevy, Devoy ; a var. of Ó Ɒuȯuıȯe, q.v.

Ó Ɒuıȯıȯı*R*—I—*O Duire, O Diver, O Dyer,* O'Dwyer, O'Deere, Dwyer, Deere, Dyer, Diver, Divver, Dever, Devers ; a var. of Ó Ɒuȯuıȯıp, q.v.

Ó Ɒuıȯín—I—*O Dovine,* O'Devine, Devine, Deveen, Devon, (Devany, Devaney) ; ' des. of Ɒuıȯín ' (dim. of Ɒuȯ, black) ; a scattered surname ; often an alias for Ó Ɒuȯáın, q.v. It is not possible always to distinguish its angl. forms from those of Ó Ɒaıṁín, q.v.

Ó Ɒuıȯınnʀeᴀċᴛᴀıʒ—I—*O Denrathay,* Dunroche, Denroche ; ' des. of Ɒuȯınnpeᴀċᴛᴀċ ' (Black ınnpeᴀċᴛᴀċ) ; a rare old Sligo surname.

Ó Ɒuıȯleᴀċáın—I—*O Duelaghane,* Delahan, Dillahan, (Dillon) ; an attenuated form of Ó Ɒuȯlᴀċáın, q.v.

Ó Ɒuıȯleᴀʀʒᴀ—I—Delargy, Delargey, De Largey ; ' des. of Ɒuȯleᴀnʒᴀ ' (Black of leᴀnʒᴀ, a place-name) ; an old Tirawley surname ; still survives in Galway and Antrim.

Ó Ɒuıȯluᴀċʀᴀ, v. Ó Ɒuȯluᴀċpᴀ.

Ó Ɒuıȯne—I—*O Dynie,* Deeny, Deeney, Denny, &c. ; ' des. of Ɒuıȯne ' (ill-going, opposed to Suıȯne).

Ó Ɒuıȯʀıc—I—*O Divrick, Diviricke,* (Devereux), Devery, &c. ; a var. of Ó Ɒuȯpᴀıc, q.v.

Ó Ɒuılleáın—I—*O Dullaine, O Dyllane,* Dillane, (Dillon) ; an attenuated form of Ó Ɒᴀlláın, q.v. ; common in Kerry, Limerick, Clare and Galway, but often disguised under the angl. form of Dillon.

Ó Ɒuıllín—I—*O Dulline, O Dilline,* Dilleen ; a var. of Ó Ɒuılleáın, q.v. ; very rare.

Ó Ɒuıneᴀċᴀıʀ—I—*O Dinagher, O Donogher,* Donogher, Danagher, Deneher, Donaher, Danaher, Daniher, Dannaher ; ' des. of Ɒuıneᴀċᴀp ' (man-loving) ; the name of a family who were anciently lords of Crioch Cathbhaidh, in the neighbourhood of Nenagh, but were dispossessed soon after the Anglo-Norman invasion and dispersed through Munster, Leinster and Connacht ; now most numerous in Co. Limerick.

Ó Ouıneáċóá —I—*O Denaghie*, Dennahy, Dennehy, Dannahy, Danihy, Denehy, Denny, &c. ; '.des. of Ouıneáċaıṁ' (humane) ; a well-known Co. Cork surname.

Ó Oúın——, v. Ó Ouınn——, which is often pronounced, and sometimes written, Ó Oúın——.

Ó Oúınín—I—*O Downine*, O *Downyne*, O *Dwnyn*, Dunion, Dunning, Downing, &c. ; ' des. of Oúınín' (dim. of Oonn, brown) ; a var. of Ó Ouınnín, q.v.

Ó Ouınn—I—*O Dunne*, *O Doyne*, Dunne, Dunn, Dun, Doyne, Dyne, &c. ; ' des. of Oonn' (brown). There are two distinct families of this name : (1) Ó Ouınn of Uí Riagaın, a branch of the Uí Faılghe, and one of the chief families of Leinster. The head of this family was lord of Uí Riagaın, now angl. Iregan, which was co-extensive with the present barony of Tinnahinch, in Leix. (2) Ó Ouınn of Tara. This family was dispossessed soon after the Anglo-Norman invasion. The name is now very common in Leinster and Munster.

Ó Ouınnċáċaıg—I—Duncahy ; ' des. of Oonnċáċaċ' ; the name of a Sligo family who were anciently lords of Corann, now the barony of Corran ; now very rare, if not actually obsolete.

Ó Ouınnċınn—I—*O Dingine*, *O Dongyn*, *O Dongen*, Dinkin, Dunkin, (Duncan) ; ' des. of Oonnċeánn' (Brown-head) ; an old Sligo surname ; rare and often disguised as Duncan. Some of the family migrated to Leinster.

Ó Ouınneáḃáın—I—*O Dunivane*, Dingavan, Dennivan ; an attenuated form of Ó Oonnáḃáın, q.v.

Ó Ouınneáċáın—I—*O Duinaghan*, *O Dwynighan*, Dinahan, Dinihan, Denehan, Deenihan ; ' des. of Ouınneáċáın' (dim. of oonn, brown) ; an attenuated form of Ó Oonnáċáın, q.v. ; a rare surname, found chiefly in Limerick and Kerry. The family, according to Dr. O'Brien, belonged originally to Uaıthne, the present barony of Owney, in Limerick and Tipperary.

Ó Ɗuınneᴀʓᴀ́ın—I—*O Dwinagane, O Dinegane,* Dinnegan, Denegan, Denigan ; an attenuated form of Ó
Ɗonnᴀʓᴀ́ın, q.v.

Ó Ɗuınnín—I—*O Dunnyne, O Downine,* Dinneen,
Dineen, Dunion, Dunning, Denning, Downing ; 'des.
of Ɗuınnín' (dim. of Ɗonn, brown) ; the name of a
literary family of Corca Laoighdhe, in South-west
Cork, who became hereditary historians to MacCarthy
More ; also of a midland family. In Munster the
name is generally angl. Dineen and Dinneen, but sometimes Downing, while it is made Dunning and Denning
in Leinster.

Ó Ɗuınnŕléıƀe—I—*O Dunlevy, O Downlay,* Dunlevy,
Dunleavy, Dunlavy, Dunleevy, Dunlea, Dullea, Delea,
Delay, Delee ; 'des. of Ɗonnŕléıƀe' (Brown of the
mountain) ; the name of a branch of the family of Ó
ħeocᴀ́ɒᴀ of Ulidia, who were also known by the surname of Mᴀc Ɗuınnŕléıƀe and, from their place of
origin, Ulcᴀċ and Ulcᴀċᴀ́n. For history of family,
see Mᴀc Ɗuınnŕléıƀe.

Ó Ɗuıꞃnín—I—*O Durnyne,* O'Durnin, Durnin, Durnian,
Durnion, Dornin, and, by 'translation,' Cuffe ; 'des.
of Ɗuıꞃnín' (dim. of ɒoꞃn, a fist) ; an Ulster surname.
In the 16th century it was found chiefly in Donegal,
and Fermanagh. V. Ó Ɗoꞃnᴀ́ın.

Ó Ɗúıċċe—I—*O Dowghie, O Dowchy,* Dooey, Duffy ; a
common corruption of Ó Ɗuƀċᴀıʓ, q.v.

Ó Ɗulċᴀoıncıʓ, Ó Ɗulċoncᴀ—I—*O Dulchenta, O
Dulchienta, O Dologhintye, O Dullechonty, O Dulle-
honty, O Dulchante,* Dolohunty, Delahunty, Delahunt,
Delhunty, Dellunty, Dulanty, Dullenty, Dulinty ;
'des. of Ɗulċᴀoınceᴀċ' (plaintive satirist) ; the name
of an old family of Ely O'Carroll, in the present
Offaly, who are of the same stock as the O'Carrolls.
A branch of the family had settled in Kerry before
the 17th century. Ó Ɗulċoncᴀ is a corruption.

Ó Ɗún——, v. Ó Ɗonn——, which is often pronounced,
and sometimes written, Ó Ɗún——.

Ó Ɗúnᴀɒꞃᴀ, v. Ó Ɗonnᴀɒᴀıꞃ.

Ó ·oúnꙇꙇ́in—I—*O Dúneghan*, Doonican, Dunican; a var. of Ó ·oonnꙇꙇ́in, q.v.

Ó ·oúnꙇ·oꙇꙇ—I—*O Downie*, *O Downy*, *O Duny*, *O Dony*, Dooney, Downey, Doney, Donney, Dunny, (Downing); 'des. of ·oúnꙇ·oꙇꙇ' (belonging to a ·oún, or fort); the name of, at least, three distinct families: (1) Ó ·oúnꙇ·oꙇꙇ of Siol Anmchadha, in Co. Galway, who are of the same stock as the O'Maddens; (2) O ·oúnꙇ·oꙇꙇ of Corca Laoighdhe, in South-west Cork, who are of the same stock as the O'Driscolls; and (3) Ó ·oúnꙇ·oꙇꙇ of Luachair, who were chiefs of Luachair, an extensive district on the borders of Cork, Kerry and Limerick. This family is still numerous in Kerry and Limerick, but in the former county, the name is sometimes incorrectly angl. Downing. The name was also found in Ulster and Leinster.

Ó ·oúnꙇ́in—I—*O Doonan*, Doonan, Donnan; a var. of Ó ·oonnꙇ́in, q.v.; a scattered surname, but now found chiefly in Leitrim and Roscommon. ꙳ꙇꙇꙇꙇꙇ·ꙇꙇ Ó ·oúnꙇ́in was Bishop of Cashel in the early part of the 12th century.

Ó ·oúnꙃꙇꙇꙇ, v. Ó ·oonnꙃꙇꙇꙇ.

Ó ·oúnꙃꙇꙇꙇꙃ, v. Ó ·oonnꙃꙇꙇꙇꙃ.

Ó ·oúnꙃꙇꙇ, v. Ó ·oonnꙃꙇꙇꙇ.

Ó ·oúnꙇꙇꙃ, Ó ·oúnꙇꙇꙃ—I—*O Dowling*, *O Doolin*, Dowling, Dowlin, Dooling, Doolin, Doolen, Doolan, &c.; 'des. of ·oúnꙇꙇꙃ' (an ancient personal name, also written ·oúnꙇꙇꙃ); the name (1) of a numerous family in Leinster, who were at one time lords of Leix; and (2) of a family of Corca Laoighdhe, in South-west Cork, still numerous in Cork and Kerry. This surname is pronounced Ó Dúllaing, and its angl. forms can hardly be distinguished from those of Ó ·oú·ʙꙇꙇꙇ, q.v.

Ó eꙇꙇꙇꙃeꙇꙇꙇꙇ, Ó eꙇꙇꙇꙃeꙇꙇꙇ, Ó eꙇꙇꙇꙃeꙇꙇꙇ—I—*O Aghierny*, *O Aghierin*, Ahearne, Aherne, Ahearn, Aheran, Aheron, Ahern, &c.; 'des. of eꙇꙇꙇꙃeꙇꙇꙇꙇ' (horse-lord); the name of a Dalcassian family who were lords of Ui Cearnaigh, in the neighbourhood of

Six-mile-bridge, until about the year 1318, when they were driven out by the MacNamaras and dispersed through Munster. The name is now common in Limerick and Cork. Also Ó ⁊eᴀᴄᴄıᵹeıⱦn, q.v.

Ó ⱦᴀᴄᴄnᴀ—I—*O Faughny*, Faulkney, (Faulkner); 'des. of ⱦᴀᴄᴄnᴀ' (just, an ancient personal name).

Ó ⱦᴀᴄᴄnᴀ́ın—I—Faughnan; 'des. of ⱦᴀᴄᴄnᴀ́n' (dim. of ⱦᴀᴄᴄnᴀ).

Ó ⱦᴀᵹᴀ́ın—I—*O Fagan*, Fagan, Fagin; a var. of Ó ⁊ᴀᵹᴀ́ın, q.v.; rare.

Ó ⱦᴀᵹᴀⱤᴄᴀıᵹ—I—*O Fayerty*, Fagarty, Fagarthy, Whearty; 'des. of 'ⱦᴀᵹᴀⱤᴄᴀᴄ' (noisy); the name of a family of Ui Fiachrach who were anciently seated at Tulach Spealain, in the barony of Carra, Co. Mayo; now found chiefly in Leinster. It is the same as Ó ⱦᴀᴄᴀⱤᴄᴀıᵹ (q.v.) of Co. Galway, and by the aspiration of the initial ⱦ has in some places become Ó ⁊ᴀᵹᴀⱤᴄᴀıᵹ, q.v.

Ó ⱦᴀ́ılⱱe—I—*O Falvie, O Falvy, O Fallie*, O'Falvey, Falvey, Fealy, Fealey; 'des. of ⱦᴀ́ılⱱe' (lively); the name of an ancient family in Kerry, who before the Anglo-Norman invasion were lords of Corca Dhuibhne, the present barony of Corcaguiny; now rather rare; in parts of North Kerry sometimes pronounced Ó ⱦᴀ́ıle, angl. Fealy.

Ó ⱦᴀıⱤᴄeᴀllᴀıᵹ—I—*O Ferrally*, O'Farrelly, Farrelly, Farley, &c.; 'des. of ⱦᴀıⱤᴄeᴀllᴀᴄ' (super-war); the name of a distinguished ecclesiastical family who, until the suppression of the monastery, were coarbs of St. Mogue, or erenaghs of Drumlane, in Co. Cavan, and are now very numerous throughout the county. There was another family of the name in the neighbourhood of Duntryleague, in the east of Co. Limerick, but it has long since disappeared from that district and is probably extinct.

Ó ⱦᴀıᴄ—I—*O Fagh, O Faye*, Fay, Foy, Fahy, Fahey; a shortened form of Ó ⱦᴀᴄᴀıᵹ, q.v.; common in Connacht.

Ó ḟáLLáṁáin—I—*O Fallowne, O Fallone, O Fallon,*
Falloon, Faloon, Faloona, Fallon, &c. ; ' des. of
ḟáLLáṁán ' (ruler) ; also written Ó ḟoLLáṁáin, and
sometimes, by the aspiration of the initial ḟ, changed
to Ó ṅáLLáṁáin, q.v. ; the name (1) of a Leinster
family who were formerly lords of Crioch na gCeadach,
which comprised the present parish of Castlejordan
in Offaly ; and (2) of a Connacht family who were
lords of Clann Uadach, which comprised the parishes
of Camma and Dysart, in the barony of Athlone.
In 1585, O'Fallon had his residence at Milltown, in
the parish of Dysart, where the ruins of his castle are
still to be seen.

Ó ḟáoḋáġáin—I—*O Fegane, O Fegan,* Feagan, Fegan,
Fagan ; a var. of Ó ṅáoḋáġáin, q.v.

Ó ḟáoileáin—I—*O Foylane, O Fylane,* Whelan, Phelan,
&c. ; an attenuated form of Ó ḟáoLáin, q.v.

Ó ḟáoiLLeáċáin—I—*O Whyleghane, O Philaghane, O
Feylaghan,* Wheleghan, Wheelahan, Whelahan, Whele-
han, (Whelan, Phelan) ; ' des of ḟáoiLLeáċán ' (dim.
of ḟáoiLLeáċ, joyful ; perhaps born in carnival time,
the month of rejoicing, from middle of January to
middle of February) ; an old Westmeath surname.
Ó ṅáoiLLeáċáin (q.v.) is a Munster variant.

Ó ḟáoLáin—I—*O Whealane, O Phelane, O Foelane, O
Folane, O Fylane,* O'Phelan, Phelan, Whelan, Philan,
Fylan, &c. ; ' des. of ḟáoLán ' (dim of faol, a wolf) ;
the name (1) of a numerous and once powerful Mun-
ster family, who before the Anglo-Norman invasion
were lords of the Decies, in the present counties of
Waterford and Tipperary ; and (2) of a numerous
Leinster family who were anciently seated at Magh
Lacha, a plain in the barony of Kells, Co. Kilkenny.
In the 16th century the name was found in nearly all
the counties of Munster and Leinster, and also in
Roscommon and Galway. It was often pronounced
Ó ḟuáLáin, and, by the aspiration of the initial ḟ,
changed to Ó ṅáoLáin and Ó ṅuáLáin, q.v.

Ó ḟáoLċáiḋ—I—*O Fellaghy,* Falahy, Falahee, Falsey ;

'des. of ꝼaolċaꝺ' (wolf-warrior); a rare Thomond surname.

Ó ꝼaolċair—I—Fallaher; 'des. of ꝼaolċaꝛ' (wolf-dear); extremely rare.

Ó ꝼaraċáin—I—O Farraghan, O Farrohan, O Farhan, O Farran, O Faran, Farran, Farron, Farren, Faran, Forran, &c.; probably for Ó hAꝛaċáin, 'des. of Aꝛaċán,' the initial ꝼ being intrusive; a Donegal surname.

Ó ꝼarannáin—I—O Farenane, O Ferrenan, Farnan, Farnon, Farnand, (Farnham); 'des. of ꝼaꝛannán' (an ancient Irish personal name); also written Ó ꝼoꝛannáin, q.v.; the name of an ecclesiastical family in Ulster who were erenaghs of Ardstraw.

Ó ꝼarraiᵹ, Farry, Forry; a rare Mayo surname.

Ó ꝼaċaiᵹ—I—O Faughy, O Faghy, O Fahy, O Faye, Faughy, Faghy, Fahey, Fahy, Fay, Foy, and, by 'translation,' Green; also written Ó ꝼaċaꝺ; 'des. of ꝼaċaꝺ' (older ꝼoċaꝺ, foundation); the name of a family of Ui Maine in Co. Galway, whose patrimony, which was known as Poblewinterfahy, lay in the barony of Loughrea, and a considerable portion of which remained in the possession of the family down to the Cromwellian confiscations. There is also an old and respectable family of the name in Co. Tipperary. The name, according to O'Donovan, was sometimes angl. Green from its resemblance to the Irish word 'ꝼaiċċe,' a green, or field.

Ó ꝼaċarċaiᵹ—I—O Faherty, Faherty, (Flaherty); written Ó ꝼaᵹaꝛċaiᵹ by MacFirbis, and Ó ꝼoᵹaꝛċaiᵹ by the Four Masters; des of 'ꝼaċaꝛċaċ' or 'ꝼaᵹaꝛċaċ,' or 'ꝼoᵹaꝛċaċ' (all variants of the same name); the name of an old Galway family who were formerly chiefs of Dealbhna Cuile Fabhair, on the east side of Lough Corrib. It is still common in Co. Galway, but sometimes disguised under the angl. form of Flaherty; while by the aspiration of the initial ꝼ, it has become changed in Munster to Ó hAċaꝛċaiᵹ, q.v.

Ó ꝼeaꝺaᵹáin—I—O Faddigane, Fedigan; 'des. of

ꞃéᴀꝺᴀɢán '; a rare Ulster surname. The family, according to MacFirbis, is a branch of the Oirghialla.

Ó ꝼeᴀꞃáın—I—*O Feran, O Faran, O Ferran, O Farrane,* Feran, Feron, Ferran, Fearon, Fearen, Fearn, Fern, Farran, Farren, &c.; ' des. of ꝼeᴀꞃán '. (dim. of ꝼeᴀꞃ, a man, or ' pet ' dim. of ꝼeᴀꞃᴀꝺᴀċ); the name of a branch of the Cinel Eoghain in Ulster.

Ó ꝼeᴀꞃᴀꝺᴀıɠ—I—*O Farry,* O'Ferry, Farry, Ferry; ' des. of ꝼeᴀꞃᴀꝺᴀċ ' (manly); a scattered surname, but found chiefly in East Ulster.

Ó ꝼeᴀꞃċᴀıꞃ—I—*Ó Farragher,* Farragher, Faragher, Farraher, Faraher, Fraher; ' des. of ꝼeᴀꞃċᴀꞃ ' (very dear); a Connacht surname. In Munster, where there are a few of the name, it is metathesised to Ó ꝼꞃeᴀċᴀıꞃ, angl. Fraher; while the aspiration of the initial ꝼ gives rise to the further variants Ó ħeᴀꞃċᴀıꞃ and Ó Reᴀċᴀıꞃ, q.v.

Ó ꝼeᴀꞃɠᴀıl—I—*O Ferrall,* O'Farrell, Farrell, Ferrall, Farrahill, Frahill, Fraul; ' des. of ꝼeᴀꞃɠᴀl ' (super-valour); the name of several distinct families, of which the best known are the O'Farrells of Annaly, in the present Co. Longford, of which they were for many centuries the ruling race. The head of the family resided at the town of Longford, which was formerly known as Longphort Ui Fhearghail, or O'Farrell's fortress. In later times, the O'Farrells divided into two great branches, the heads of which were known respectively as O'Farrell Boy, the yellow O'Farrell, and O'Farrell Bane, the fair O'Farrell. The O'Farrells maintained their independence as a clan down to the year 1565, when Annaly was reduced to shire ground by the lord-deputy, Sir Henry Sidney. Though suffering severely from the plantation schemes of James I, the O'Farrells were able to take a prominent part in all the political and military movements of the 17th century, and many of them were afterwards distinguished officers in the Irish brigades in the service of France. This family is now very numerous. Other families of this name were seated in Wicklow and Tyrone. The name is also written Ó ꝼeaꞃᵹaıle and Ó ꝼıꞃᵹıl, q.v., and sometimes, by the aspiration of the initial ꝼ, changed into Ó neaꞃᵹaıl, Ó neaꞃᵹaıle, q.v.

Ó ꝼeaꞃᵹaıle—I—*O Farrialla, O Ferralla*, Farrelly, Frawley, Farrell, &c. ; 'des. of ꝼeaꞃᵹal'; a var. of Ó ꝼeaꞃᵹaıl, q.v. ; sometimes metathesised to Ó ꝼꞃeaᵹaıle, angl. Frawley.

Ó ꝼeaꞃᵹuıs, Ó ꝼeaꞃᵹusa—I—*O Farguise, O Farris, O Ferris, O Farrissa*, Fergus, Ferris, Farris, Farrissy, &c. ; 'des. of ꝼeaꞃᵹuꞃ' (super-choice) ; the name (1) of a medical family in West Connacht who were hereditary physicians to the O'Malleys ; and (2) of an ecclesiastical family in Co. Leitrim who were coarbs of St. Mogue, or erenaghs of Rossinver. At the end of the 16th century, the name was very scattered.

Ó ꝼeaꞃnáın—I—*O Farnane, O Fernan*, Fernane, Fernan ; a shortened form of Ó nıꝼeaꞃnáın, q.v. By the aspiration of the initial ꝼ, it often becomes Ó neaꞃnáın, q.v.

Ó ꝼeıċ—I—*O Fey*, Fey, Fay, and, by 'translation,' Hunt ; 'des. of ꝼıaċ' (raven) ; a var. of Ó ꝼıaıċ, q.v.

Ó ꝼeıċín—I—*O Feahine, O Fehin, O Fein*, Feehin, Fehen, Feen, Feane, Fane ; 'des. of ꝼeıċín' (dim. of ꝼıaċ, a raven) ; a var. of Ó ꝼıaċáın, q.v. ; originally a West Connacht surname. The family is mentioned by MacFirbis.

Ó ꝼeınneaᵭa, v. Ó ꝼıannaıᵭe.

Ó ꝼıaċa, Ó ꝼıaċaċ—I—*O Fiecha, O Fiaghy, O Fyhie*, Fyfee, Fye, Fee, and, by 'translation,' Hunt and Vingin ; 'des. of ꝼıaċa'; a common surname in Waterford and other parts of Munster, where it is now angl. Hunt, by supposed translation. It was also in use in Monaghan and Donegal, but seems to have there been merged in the surname Ó ꝼıaıċ, q.v.

Ó ꝼıaċáın—I—*O Fighane, O Feehan, O Pheane*, Feighan, Feehan, Fehane, Feghan, Fehan, Feane, Fane, (Fegan, Fagan) ; 'des. of ꝼıaċán' (dim. of ꝼıaċ, a raven) ; same as Ó ꝼeıċín, q.v. ; a scattered surname.

Ó ꝼιαċηα, Ó ꝼιαċηαċ—I—*O Fiaghny, O Fieghny, O Feoghny*, Feighney, Feeheny, Feoghney, Feghany, Faheney, (Fenton), and, by 'translation,' Hunt; 'des. of ꝼιαċηα' (an ancient Irish personal name); the name of a family of Sil-Murray in Co. Roscommon; now also in Cork, Limerick and Tipperary. It is 'translated' Hunt, in parts of Sligo, and changed to Fenton in parts of Munster.

Ó ꝼιαċꞃα, Ó ꝼιαċꞃαċ—I—*O Fieghraie, O Fierhie*, Feighry, Feighery, Feehery, Feerey, Feary, Hunt; 'des. of ꝼιαċꞃα' (an ancient Irish personal name); the name of a family in Co. Tyrone, and of another in Co. Wicklow. Both families have been long dispersed and the name is now very rare. It is in some places made Hunt, by supposed translation.

Ó ꝼιαιċ—I—*O Fee, O Fye*, Fye, Foy, Fey, Fay, Hunt; 'des. of ꝼιαċ' (raven); the same as Ó ꝼéιċ, q.v.; the name of an ecclesiastical family in Ulster who were erenaghs of Derrybrusk, near Enniskillen; also found in Munster and Connacht.

Ó ꝼιαλάιη—I—*O Fillan*, Fylan, Fyland, Philan, (Phelan); 'des. of ꝼιαλάη' (dim. of ꝼιαλ, generous); the name of a distinguished bardic family in the north of Ireland. Its angl. forms can hardly be distinguished from those of Ó ꝼαολάιη, q.v.

Ó ꝼιαηᵹαλαιᵹ, v, Ó ꝼιοηηᵹαλαιᵹ.

Ó ꝼιαηηαċτα—I—*O Fianaghta*, Feenaghty, Finnerty, (Fenton); a common form of Ó ꝼιοηηαċτα, q.v.; now generally angl. Fenton in Munster.

Ó ꝼιαηηα, Ó ꝼιαηηαιᵭe—I—*O Fynea, O Finnee*, Feeney, Feeny, Finney, Finny; 'des. of ꝼιαηηαιᵭe' (soldier); a substitution for older Ó ꝼéιηηeαᵭα; the name of a family of the Ui Fiachrach who were formerly seated at Finghid, now angl. Finned, in the parish of Easkey, Co. Sligo, and are still numerous in Connacht. To be distinguished from Ó ꝼιᵭηe, q.v.

Ó ꝼιᵭᵹeαλλαιᵹ—I—*O Fielly, O Filla*, Feely, Feeley, Field; a var. of Ó ꝼιτċeαλλαιᵹ, q.v.

Ó ꝼιᵭηe—I—*O Finny*, Finney, Feeny, Feeney; 'des.

of *ꝼᵻʊne '; the name of a Galway family, still in use in that county. The family is mentioned by Mac-Firbis. Cf. Ó ꝼᵻᴀɴɴᴀᵻʊe.

Ó ꝼᵻᴌᵻbín—V—O'Filbin. V. ᴍᴀc Ᵽᵻᴌᵻbín.

Ó ꝼíne, v. Ó ꝼᵻʊne.

Ó ꝼᵻɴᵹᵻn—I—O Fynine, O Fenine, O Fynninge, O Faninge, Finning, Fenning, (Fannin, Fanning); 'des. of ꝼᵻɴᵹᵻn' (fair offspring); a South Leinster surname.

Ó ꝼᵻɴɴ—I—O Finn, O Finne, Finn, Fynn, Finne; 'des. of ꝼᵻonn' (fair); the name (1) of a Breifney family who were chiefs of Calraighe of Lough Gill, now the parish of Calry, near the town of Sligo; (2) of a Monaghan family who were lords of Feara Rois, in the neighbourhood of Carrickmacross; and (3) of a Galway family who were formerly erenaghs of Kilcolgan. All these families are still well represented in their native districts; and the name is also found in various other parts of Ireland.

Ó ꝼínne, v. Ó ꝼᵻʊne.

Ó ꝼᵻnneᴀċᴛᴀ(ᵹ), v. Ó ꝼᵻonnᴀċᴛᴀ.

Ó ꝼᵻɴɴᴛᵻᵹeᴀꞃɴ—I—O Finaran, Finneran; 'des. of ꝼᵻɴɴᴛᵻᵹeᴀꞃnᴀ' (fair lord); the name of a family who were originally chiefs of Uí Mealla in Leinster, but are now most numerous in Co. Galway.

Ó ꝼᵻoʊᴀbᴀᵻꞃ—I—O Feover, O Feure, O Feore, Feore; 'des. of ꝼᵻoʊᴀbᴀꞃ' (bushy-eyebrows); a var. of Ó ꝼᵻoʊᴀbꞃᴀ, q.v. The present form is found chiefly in the neighbourhood of Kilmallock, in Co. Limerick.

Ó ꝼᵻoʊᴀbꞃᴀ—I—O Fiorie, O Fuery, O Fury, Fury, Furey, (?) Fleury; 'des. of ꝼᵻoʊᴀbꞃᴀ' (bushy-eyebrows, from ꝼᵻoʊ, a wood, and ꞃᴀbꞃᴀ, an eyebrow); also Ó ꝼᵻoʊᴀbᴀᵻꞃ, q.v.; the name of an old Westmeath family who, not improbably, are a branch of the O'Melaghlens. Two of them were bishops, or abbots, of Clonmacnoise in the latter part of the 12th century; and in the next century, Donat O Fiodhabhra, after filling the see of Clogher for nine years, was translated to the primatial see of Armagh. He died in England in 1237, as he was returning from Rome, "with great honour and spiritual glory from the Pope." Before the end of the 16th century the name had spread into Roscommon, Sligo and Cork. It is now most frequently met with in Co. Galway. In Munster the present form is Ó ꝼíoᵹaᵬaíꞃ, angl. Feore.

Ó ꝼionaċꞇa(iᵹ), v. Ó ꝼionnaċꞇa.

Ó ꝼionáin, v. Ó ꝼionnáin.

*Ó ꝼionᵹaꞃᵭaíl, Finnerell.

Ó ꝼionnaċáin—I—*O Finoghane* Fenihan, Fanahan; probably only a var. of Ó ꝼionnaᵹáin, q.v.; extremely rare.

Ó ꝼionnaċꞇa, Ó ꝼionnaċꞇaíᵹ—I—*O Fynaghta, O Fenaghtie, O Finatie,* Finnaghty, Finaghty, Feenaghty, Fenaghty, Fenaughty, (?) Feenaghy, (?) Fanaghey, Finnerty, Finerty, Fannerty, (Fenton); ' des. of ꝼionnaċꞇa' (fair-snow); also written Ó ꝼionaċꞇa, Ó ꝼinneaċꞇa, Ó ꝼianaċꞇa, Ó ꝼionnaċꞇaíᵹ, &c., and, by the aspiration of the initial ꝼ, Ó níonnaċꞇa, q.v.; the name of a Connacht family who are a branch of the Siol Muireadhaigh, or Sil-Murry, and of the same stock as the O'Connors of that province. They seem to have formed two clans, known as Clann Chonnmhaigh and Clann Mhurchadha, seated respectively on the west and east side of the Suck, in the counties of Galway and Roscommon. Ó ꝼionnaċꞇa of Clann Chonnmhaigh, or Clanconoo, had his castle at Dunamon, in Co. Roscommon, and as the representative of the senior branch of the Sil-Murry had the privilege of drinking the first cup at every royal banquet. The family is frequently mentioned in the Annals, but soon after the Anglo-Norman invasion, they were supplanted by a branch of the Burkes, the head of which was known as MacDavid. There was another family of the same name, a branch of the Ui Maine, anciently settled in south-east of Co. Galway. The name is not uncommon in Munster, but is often disguised under the angl. form of Fenton.

Ó ꝼionnaᵹáin—I—*O Finegane, O Fenegane,* Finnigan,

Finnegan, Finigan, Finegan, Fanagan; 'des. of Fionnᴀᵹán' (dim. of Fionn, fair); the name (1) of a family of Ui Fiachrach, in Co. Mayo, and (2) of a Breifney family. At the end of the 16th century there were O'Finegans in all the provinces.

Ó Fionnáin—I—*O Finane, O Fenane, O Fanane,* O'Finan, Finan, Finnan, Fannon, (Fannin, Fanning); 'des. of Fionnán' (dim. of Fionn, fair); also written Ó Fionáin; the name of a Mayo family who were chiefs of Coolcarney, a district which embraced the parishes of Kilgarvan and Attymas, but now long dispersed; also, according to MacFirbis, of a family of Cinel Eoghain in Ulster.

Ó FionnᴀⱢⱢáin—I—*O Fynnolane, O Fennelane,* Fenelon, Fenlon, Fendlon; 'des. of FionnᴀⱢⱢán'; the name of a Leinster family who before the Anglo-Norman invasion were lords of Dealbhna Mor, now the barony of Delvin, in the east of Co. Westmeath. They were dispossessed by Hugh de Lacy, who granted their lands to Gilbert Nugent.

Ó FionnᵹᴀıⱢ, Ó FionnᵹᴀıⱢe—I—*O Fynnull, O Fennell,* Finnell, Fennell; 'des. of FionnᵹᴀⱢ' (fair-valour).

Ó FionnᵹᴀⱢᴀıᵹ—I—*O Fynnola, O Fenellie,* Finnelly, Fennelly, Finley, Fenley, Finlay, Findley, &c.; 'des. of FionnᵹᴀⱢᴀć' (fair-valorous, der. of FionnᵹᴀⱢ); also written Ó FiᴀnᵹᴀⱢᴀıᵹ, and, by the aspiration of the initial F, changed to Ó ɴıonnᵹᴀⱢᴀıᵹ, q.v.; the name of an Ormond family, doubtless descended from FionnᵹᴀⱢᴀć, son of 'ᴅonnćuᴀn, one of the leaders of Brian Boru's hosts at Clontarf.

Ó Fionnᵹusᴀ—I—*O Finisey,* Finnessy, Fennessy; 'des. of Fionnᵹuᵱ' (fair choice); an old, but rare, Munster surname.

Ó FionnᵯᴀcáIn—I—Finnucane, Finucane; 'des. of Fionnᵯᴀcán' (fair little son); a rare, but well-known, Munster surname. I cannot find any early angl. form.

Ó FıRᵹıⱢ—I—*O Ferrill, O Phirell,* O'Freel, Freel, Friel, Freal, &c.; 'des. of FeᴀᵱᵹᴀⱢ' (super-valour); a var.

of Ó Fearġail, q.v.; the name of a family of Cinel Conaill who derive their descent from Eoghan, brother of St. Columcille, and were hereditary erenaghs of Kilmacrenan, in Co. Donegal. The name is still common in that county, but pronounced Ó Friġil, q.v. O'Freel had the privilege of inaugurating O'Donnell as chieftain of Tirconnell.

Ó Firġile, v. Ó Friġile and Ó Friṫile.

Ó Fiṫċeallaiġ—I—*O Fihillie, O Fihily, O Fielly,* Fihelly, Fihily, Fehily, Fehely, Feehely, Feehily, Feely, (Field, Fielding), &c.; 'des. of Fiṫċeallaċ' (chess-player); the name of a family of Corca Laoighdhe, in South-west Cork, where they were chiefs of Tuath O Fithcheallaigh, an extensive district in the neighbourhood of Baltimore. To this family belonged the celebrated Maurice de Portu, Archbishop of Tuam from 1506 to 1513, who on account of his great learning and other accomplishments was called 'Flos Mundi.' Field as an angl. form of this surname dates back to the middle of the 16th century; Fielding is a modern development.

Ó Fiṫċill—I—*O Fihel,* Fehill, (Field); a shortened form of Ó Fiṫċeallaiġ, q.v. This form is still in use in Limerick, where the family has been long settled.

Ó Flainn—I—*O Flayne, O Floyng,* Flang, Flyng, Flynn; 'des. of Flann' (red); usually written Ó Floinn, q.v.

Ó Flaiṫḃeartaiġ—I—*O Flagherty,* O'Flaherty, Flagherty, Flaherty, Flaverty; 'des. of Flaiṫḃeartaċ' (bright ruler); the name of a Connacht family who were originally chiefs of Muinntear Mhurchadha, now angl. Muntermorroghoe, a district on the east side of Lough Corrib, in the barony of Clare, Co. Galway, but on being expelled from there by the English, in the 13th century, settled on the other side of Lough Corrib, where they obtained extensive possessions in the barony of Moycullen, and were styled lords of Iar-Connacht. There is also a family of the name, but of an entirely different stock, in Thomond. In Ulster, owing to the aspiration of the initial ꝼ, the name has been changed to Ó Laitbeaꝛc-aiᵹ, q.v.

Ó ꝼlaiteaṁáin—I—*O Flaghavane, O Flahevane, O Flavane,* Flahavan, Flahevan, Flahavin, Flavahan, Flavin ; 'des. of ꝼlaiteaṁán' (dim. of ꝼlaiteaṁ, lord, ruler) ; an old Munster surname ; often found as Ó ꝼlataṁáin and Ó ꝼlaitiṁín, q.v.

Ó ꝼlaitꝼileaꝺ, v. Ó ꝼlaitile and Ó ꝼlaitiꝛe.

Ó ꝼlaitᵹeasa—I—*O Flahysse, O Flayshe* ; 'des. of ꝼlaitᵹeaꝛ' (dominion-choice) ; an old Wexford surname ; now changed, by the aspiration of the initial ꝼ, into Ó laitᵹeaꝛa, q.v.

Ó ꝼlaitile—I—*O Flatilly,* Flatley, Flattley ; 'des of ꝼlaitꝼile' (prince-poet) ; older form Ó ꝼlaitꝼileaꝺ ; the name of a branch of the Ui Fiachrach in Mayo and Sligo, where it is still well known. V. Ó ꝼlaitiꝛe.

Ó ꝼlaitiṁ—I—*O Flahiff, O Flahie,* Flahive, Flahy ; 'des. of ꝼlaiteaṁ' (lord, ruler) ; a scattered surname. In the 16th century, it was found in Galway, Clare, Tipperary, Kilkenny and Wexford. It is now often changed, by the aspiration of the initial ꝼ, to Ó laitiṁ, q.v. Also Ó ꝼlataiᵹ, q.v.

Ó ꝼlaitiṁín—I—Flahavin, Flavin ; a var. of Ó ꝼlaiteaṁáin, q.v

Ó ꝼlaitiꝛe—I—*O Flattery,* Flattery ; 'des. of ꝼlaitꝼile' (prince-poet) ; a corruption of Ó ꝼlaitꝼileaꝺ ; the name of a family of Dealbhna Eathra, in the barony of Garrycastle, in the present Offaly, where it is still in use. The corruption of this name to its present form had taken place before the end of the 16th century. Cf. Ó ꝼlaitile.

Ó ꝼlannaꝟꝛa—I—*O Flanura, O Flanory,* Flannery ; 'des. of ꝼlannaꝟꝛa' (red-eyebrows) ; the name (1) of a family of the Ui Fidhgheinte, in the present Co. Limerick, but long dispersed through Munster ; and (2) of a family of Ui Fiachrach who were formerly seated in the neighbourhood of Killala, but are now dispersed through Connacht.

Ó ꝼlannacáin—I—*O Flanaghan,* Flanaghan ; ' des. of
ꝼlannacán ' (dim. of ꝼlann, red) ; probably only a
var. of Ó ꝼlannaзáin, q.v. ; extremely rare

Ó ꝼlannaзáin—I—*O Flannagaine,* O'Flanagan,
Flanagan, Flanigan, &c. ; ' des. of ꝼlannaзán ' (dim.
of ꝼlann, red) ; the name of at least five distinct
families in different parts of Ireland, viz. : (1) of
Fermanagh, a branch of the Oirghialla, who were
chiefs of Tuathratha, now angl. Toorah, an extensive
district in the barony of Magheraboy, in the north-
west of Co. Fermanagh, and are still numerous in
Ulster ; (2) of Roscommon, a branch of the Sil-Murry
and of the same stock as the O'Connors, who were
hereditary stewards to the kings of Connacht and
chiefs of Clann Chathail, a district which embraced
several parishes in the neighbourhood of Elphin ;
(3) of Westmeath who were anciently lords of Comair
and sometimes of all Teffia ; (4) of Ely O'Carroll in
the present Offaly, who are of the same stock as the
O'Carrolls, and were chiefs of Cinel Arga, a district
nearly, if not exactly, co-extensive with the present
barony of Ballybrit ; and (5) of Waterford, who were
formerly chiefs of Uachtartire, now the barony of
Upperthird, in the north-west of Co. Waterford, but
were dispossessed by the Powers soon after the Anglo-
Norman invasion.

Ó ꝼlanncaᴅa, Ó ꝼlanncaiᴅ—I—*O Flanchy, O
Flanahee,* Flanahy ; ' des. of ꝼlanncaᴅ ' (red-warrior) ;
a rare Thomond surname.

Ó ꝼlannзail—I—*O Flanhill, O Flanill,* (?) Flavell ;
' des. of ꝼlannзal ' (red-valour) ; a var. of Ó ꝼlannзaile, q.v.

Ó ꝼlannзaile—I—*O Flannylla,* O'Flannelly, Flannelly, (Flannery) ; ' des. of ꝼlannзal ' (red-valour) ;
the name of a family of the Ui Fiachrach who were
originally seated at Loch Glinne, in the parish of
Crossmolina, Co. Mayo, but, on being driven thence
by the English, settled at Finghid, now Finned, in
the parish of Easkey, Co. Sligo. It is still common

in both counties, but often disguised under the angl.
form of Flannery.

Ó Ꞁꞁᴀᴄᴀɪᵹ—I—*O Flaghie, O Flahie,* Flahy ; a common
corruption, in the spoken language, of Ó Ꞁꞁᴀɪᴄɪ́ᵯ,
q.v. ; sometimes, by the aspiration of the initial Ꞁꞁ,
changed to Ó Lᴀᴄᴀɪᵹ, q.v.

Ó Ꞁꞁᴀᴄᴀᵯᴀ́ɪɴ—I—*O Flaghavane,* Flahavan, Flahevan,
Flahavin ; a var. of Ó Ꞁꞁᴀɪᴄᴇᴀᵯᴀ́ɪɴ, q.v.

Ó Ꞁꞁoɪɴɴ—I—*O Floine, O Floinge,* O'Flynn, Flynn,
Flinn, &c. ; ' des. of Ꞁꞁᴀɴɴ ' (red) ; the name of several
distinct families in different parts of Ireland, of which
the following are the best known : (1) Ó Ꞁꞁoɪɴɴ of
Siol Maolruain, a Roscommon family who were chiefs
of Siol Maolruain, a district which embraced the
parish of Kiltulagh and part of that of Kilkeevin, in
the west of Co. Roscommon. Another family of the
name were erenaghs of the church of St. Dachonna,
at Eas Ui Fhloinn, a short distance to the west of the
town of Boyle. (2) Ó Ꞁꞁoɪɴɴ of Tirawley who were
seated in Magh hEleog, in the parish of Crossmolina ;
a branch of the family were hereditary erenaghs of
the church and monastery of St. Tighearnan at Errew,
on Lough Conn. (3) Ó Ꞁꞁoɪɴɴ of Ardagh, a branch
of the Corca Laoighdhe, who were anciently chiefs
of Ui Baghamhna, now the barony of Ibawn, in the
south of Co. Cork. The head of the family resided
at Ardagh Castle between Skibbereen and Baltimore.
(4) Ó Ꞁꞁoɪɴɴ of Muskerry, who were lords of an extensive district called Muscraidhe Ui Fhloinn, angl.
Muskerrylinn, lying between Blarney and Ballyvourney, in the barony of Muskerry, Co. Cork. The
O'Flynns continued to be lords of Muskerrylin until
about the beginning of the 14th century, when they
were dispossessed by the MacCarthys of Blarney.
(5) Ó Ꞁꞁoɪɴɴ of Ui Tuirtre, an account of which is
given under Ó Loɪɴɴ, a form the name has assumed
as a result of the aspiration of the initial Ꞁꞁ. All these
families are still well represented in their native
districts.

Ó ᵹoᴅlᴀᴅᴀ, v. Ó ᵹoᵹlᴀᴅᴀ.

Ó ᵹóᵹᴀᴦᴄᴀιᵹ—I—*O Fogartie, O Fogerty,* Fogerty, Fogarty; 'des. of ᵹóᵹᴀᴩᴄᴀċ' (proclaimed, banished, exiled); the name of a family of Dalcassian origin, according to O'Heerin, who were chiefs of Eile Ui Fhogartaigh, now the barony of Elyogarty, in Co. Tipperary; sometimes changed, by the aspiration of the initial ᵹ, into Ó нóᵹᴀᴩᴄᴀιᵹ, q.v.; in West Kerry Ó ᵹóᵹᴀᴩᴄᴀ.

Ó ᵹoᵹlᴀᴅᴀ—I—*O Folowe,* O'Foley, Foley; 'des. of ᵹoᵹlᴀιᴅ' (plunderer); originally a Waterford surname, but now common throughout Munster and South Leinster. mᴀelíoᴩᴀ Ó ᵹoᵹlᴀᴅᴀ was Archbishop of Cashel early in the 12th century.

Ó ᵹoιᴦᴄċeιᴦn—I—*O Fortyerne, O Fortyn,* Fortin, Fortune; 'des. of ᵹoιᴩᴄċeιᴩn' (an old Irish personal name, meaning 'over-lord,' doubtless the same as the British Vortigern); originally a Carlow surname, but now more numerous in Co. Wexford.

Ó ᵹoⱡⱡᴀṁᴀιn, v. Ó ᵹᴀⱡⱡᴀṁᴀιn.

Ó ᵹoᴦᴀnnᴀιn—I—*O Forenan, O Ferrenan, O Fornan.* V. Ó ᵹᴀᴩᴀnnᴀιn.

Ó ᵹᴦᴀoċᴀιn—I—*O Freaghan,* (French); 'des. of ᵹᴩᴀoċᴀn' (dim. of ᵹᴩᴀoċ, prowess, fury); a rare Connacht surname. O'Donovan gives the angl. form as French, but I cannot verify it. It is found in the form Ó ᵹᴩᴀoιċín, angl. Frehen, in the neighbourhood of Shrule.

Ó ᵹᴦᴀoιċín—I—Frehen. V. Ó ᵹᴩᴀoċᴀιn.

Ó ᵹᴦeᴀċᴀιᴦ—I—Fraher; a metathesised form of Ó ᵹeᴀᴩċᴀιᴩ, q.v.

Ó ᵹᴦeᴀᵹᴀιle—I—Frawley; a metathesised form of Ó ᵹeᴀᴩᵹᴀιle, q.v.

Ó ᵹᴦeᴀᴄᴀιⱡ—I—Frahill, Fraul; a metathesised form of Ó ᵹeᴀᴩᵹᴀιⱡ, q.v.

Ó ᵹᴦιᵹιⱡ—I—*O Friell, O Freele, O Freall,* O'Freel, Friel, Freel, Freal; a metathesised form of Ó ᵹιᴩᵹιⱡ, q.v.

Ó ᵹᴦιᵹιle—I—*O Frealie,* Freely; a metathesised form of Ó ᵹιᴩᵹιle; a var. of Ó ᵹᴩιᵹιⱡ, q.v.

Ó ꝼʀɪᴄɪʟ—I—Frehill, Freehill; a metathesised form of
Ó ꝼɪʀꝼɪʟ, q.v.

Ó ꝼʀɪᴄɪʟe—I—Frehilly, Freehily; a metathesised form
of Ó ꝼɪʀꝼɪʟe, q.v.; a var. of Ó ꝼʀɪꝼɪʟe, q.v.

Ó ꝼuᴀᴅᴀ—I—O Foodie, O Foedy, O'Foody, Foody,
Foudy, Foddy, Swift, Speed; 'des. of ꝼuᴀᴅᴀ,' or
'uᴀᴅᴀ'; also written Ó ɴuᴀᴅᴀ, q.v.; the name of a
family of the Ui Fiachrach, formerly seated in the
barony of Carra, Co. Mayo, but long dispersed. Swift
and Speed are supposed translations.

Ó ꝼuᴀᴅᴀᴄáɪn—I—Fodaghan, Swift; 'des. of ꝼuᴀᴅᴀᴄ-
án' (dim. of ꝼuᴀᴅᴀ); a rare Ulster surname; synonymous with Ó ꝼuᴀᴅᴀ, q.v. Swift is a supposed translation.

Ó ꝼuᴀʟʟᴀᴄáɪn—I—O Foulohan, O Whologhane, Whoolahan, Whoolehan, Wholihane, &c.; 'des. of uᴀʟʟᴀᴄ-
án' (dim. of uᴀʟʟᴀᴄ, proud); a var. of Ó ɴuᴀʟʟᴀᴄáɪn,
q.v. The initial ꝼ is intrusive.

Ó ꝼuᴀʟʟᴀɪꝼ—I—O Fowly, Whooley, Wholey, Wholy;
'des. of uᴀʟʟᴀᴄ' (proud); a var. of Ó ɴuᴀʟʟᴀɪꝼ, q.v.
The initial ꝼ is intrusive, as in the case of Ó ꝼuᴀʟʟᴀᴄáɪn above.

Ó ꝼuᴀʀáɪn, v. Ó ꝼuᴀʀᴄáɪn.

Ó ꝼuᴀʀꝼuɪꝼ—I—O Fworishe; 'des. of ꝼuᴀʀꝼuʀ' (cold-
choice); a Connacht surname, of which Ó ꝼuᴀʀuɪʀᴄe
(q.v.) is probably a corruption. By the aspiration of
the initial ꝼ it has become Ó ɴuᴀʀꝼuɪʀ, q.v.

Ó ꝼuᴀʀʀáɪn, Ó ꝼuᴀʀᴄáɪn—I—O Fuarayne, O Fow-
rane, O Forhane, O Fourhan, O Forehan, O Fordhane,
O Forane, Fourhane, Forehane, Forehan, Forhan,
Foran, (Ford, Forde); 'des. of ꝼuᴀʀʀán' or 'ꝼuᴀʀᴄán'
(dim. of ꝼuᴀʀ, cold); the name of an old Munster
family, still numerous in Waterford, Cork, Kerry and
Limerick, but often, especially in Cork, disguised as
Ford or Forde.

Ó ꝼuᴀʀuɪꝼce—I—O Fworiske, Whoriskey, Whorriskey,
Waters, Watters; an old surname in Sligo and Donegal;
perhaps a corruption of Ó ꝼuᴀʀꝼuɪʀ, q.v. By the
aspiration of the initial ꝼ, it becomes Ó ɴuᴀʀuɪʀce,
q.v. Waters is a 'translation.'

Ó ꝼuᴀᴄᴀɪᵹ—I—Foohy, Fouhy, Fuohy, Fowhey ; ' des.
of ꝼuᴀᴄᴀċ ' ; a rare Co. Cork surname.

Ó ꝼuᴀᴄṁᴀʀᴀ́ɪɴ—I—O Whoheran, (?) Forhan ; ' des.
of ꝼuᴀᴄṁᴀʀᴀ́ɴ ' (dim. of ꝼuᴀᴄṁᴀʀ, hateful) ; also
written Ó ɴuᴀᴄṁᴀʀᴀ́ɪɴ ; the name of a family of the Ui
Fiachrach who were anciently seated in the parish
of Ballintobber, Co. Mayo. In the 16th century, it
was found in Westmeath, but was very rare, and is
probably now obsolete.

Ó ꝼuɪʟʟeᴀċᴀ́ɪɴ, v. Ó ꝼᴀoɪʟʟeᴀċᴀ́ɪɴ.

Ó ᵹᴀ́ḃᴀ́ɪɴ—I—O Gavan, Gavan, Gaven, Gavin ; ' des.
of ᵹᴀ́ḃᴀ́ᴅᴀ́ɴ ' (dim. of ᵹᴀ́ḃᴀᴅ, want, need, danger) ;
the name of at least two distinct families, the one of
Munster, the other of Connacht, origin. The Munster
family is a branch of the Corca Laoighdhe, in South-
west Cork. Also Ó ᵹᴀ́ɪḃɪ́ɴ, q.v.

Ó ᵹᴀḃᴀɴɴ, v. Ó ᵹoḃᴀɴɴ.

Ó ᵹᴀḃᴀʟᴀɪᵹ—I—O Guly, O Gowle, Gooley, Forke ;
' des. of ᵹᴀḃᴀʟᴀċ ' (forked, peaked) ; the name of an
old Westmeath family who, according to MacFirbis,
are descended from Brian, son of Maine, son of Niall
of the Nine Hostages ; now very rare, and changed,
by translation, in some places to Forke. Cf. Ó ᵹᴀḃʟᴀ́ɪɴ.

Ó ᵹᴀḃʟᴀ́ɪɴ—I—O Gowlane, Goolden, Golden, Golding,
Goulding, Forkan, Forkin ; ' des. of ᵹᴀḃʟᴀ́ɴ ' (dim. of
ᵹᴀḃᴀʟ, a fork) ; a rare Donegal surname ; now also
current in Mayo and North Galway, where it is angl.
Forkan and Forkin. Cf. Ó ᵹᴀḃᴀʟᴀɪᵹ.

Ó ᵹᴀḃʀᴀ́ɪɴ—I—O Gawran, Gowran ; ' des. of ᵹᴀḃʀᴀ́ɴ '
(dim. of ᵹᴀḃᴀʀ, a horse, a goat) ; the name of a branch
of the Ui Maine in Co. Galway ; now very rare, if not
obsolete. Ó ᵹᴀḃʀᴀ́ɪɴ, angl. MacGovern, which is
common in the spoken language of Co. Mayo, is
probably not the same, but merely a corruption of
Mᴀᵹ Sᴀṁʀᴀ́ɪɴ, q.v.

Ó ᵹᴀċᴀ́ɪɴ—I—Gaughan, Gahan ; a common contraction, in Co. Mayo, of Ó ᵹᴀɪḃᴄeᴀċᴀ́ɪɴ, q.v.

Ó ᵹᴀᴅᴀ́ɪɴ, v. Ó ᵹoᴅᴀ́ɪɴ.

Ó ᵹᴀḃʀᴀ—I—O Garry, O Garey, O Geary, O Geirie, O

Gwyre, O'Gara, Gara, Garry, Geary, Guiry ; ' des. of
ᵹᴀᴏ̇ᵽᴀ ' (an old Irish personal name, perhaps from
ᵹᴀᴏ̇ᴀᵽ, a dog, mastiff) ; the name of a Connacht
family, of the same stock as the O'Haras. Both
families were supposed to be descended from Lugh,
son of Cormac Gaileng, and had from him the common
clan-name of Luighne, which, in accordance with
Irish custom, was afterwards applied as a designation
of the clan-lands. These embraced not only the
modern baronies of Leyney and Corran, in Co. Sligo,
but also the barony of Gallen, in Co. Mayo, and Sliabh
Lugha, which formed about the northern half of the
present barony of Costello in the same county. When
the two families separated, about the end of the tenth
century, they divided this territory between them,
the O'Haras taking the northern, or Sligo, portion,
and the O'Garas the southern, in Co. Mayo. The
O'Garas were then styled lords of Sliabh Lugha, but
after the English invasion of Connacht they were
driven out of this territory by the Jordans, Costellos,
and other English families, and forced to seek a new
settlement. This they acquired in the district
anciently known as Greagraidhe, and now as the
barony of Coolavin, in Co. Sligo, from which in later
times they were known as lords of Coolavin. There,
at the north-eastern extremity of Lough Gara, they
built their castle of Moygara, in which the head of the
family resided. From the 10th to the 18th century,
the O'Garas held a prominent place in Lower Connacht.
About the middle of latter century, two members of
the family successively filled the archiepiscopal see
of Tuam. It is to the patronage of Fergal O'Gara
that we are indebted for the invaluable Annals of
the Four Masters. Branches of the family had
settled in Munster before the end of the 16th century,
and the name still flourishes in Cork, Kerry and
Limerick, under the angl. forms of Geary and Guiry.

Ó ᵹᴀ̇ɪ̇ḃɪᴨ—I—*O Gawine, O Gawin, O Gawen*, Gavin,
Gaven ; a var. of Ó ᵹᴀ̇ḃᴀɪᴨ, q.v.

Ó ᵹᴀɪʙɴeᴀɪɴ, Guinane, Guinan.

Ó ᵹᴀɪʙᴄeᴀᴄᴀɪɴ—I—Gavaghan, Gavahan, Gavagan, Gavacan, Gavigan, Gaffikan, Gaughan, Gahan ; ' des. of ᵹᴀɪʙᴄeᴀᴄᴀɴ ' (dim. of ᵹᴀɪʙᴄeᴀᴄ, plaintive, querimonious) ; the name of a branch of the Ui Fiachrach who were anciently chiefs of Calraighe Muighe hEleog, a district nearly co-extensive with the parish of Crossmolina, in Co. Mayo ; now pronounced Ó ᵹᴀᴄᴀɪɴ, and very common in Mayo and Sligo.

Ó ᵹᴀɪʟɪɴeᴀᴄ, Gallinagh ; a rare Donegal surname.

Ó ᵹᴀɪʟʟɪɴ—I—O Gallin, Gallin, Gallen ; ' des. of ᵹᴀɪʟʟɪɴ ' (dim. of ᵹᴀʟʟ, a cock) ; a rare Ulster surname ; mentioned by MacFirbis among the families of Cinel Eoghain. Cf. Ó ᵹᴀʟᴀɪɴ.

Ó ᵹᴀɪʀʙꝼéɪᴄ, Ó ᵹᴀɪʀʙꝼɪᴀɪᴄ—I—O Garyveigh, O Garrevey, Garveagh, Garvey ; a Kerry surname, probably not distinct from, but merely a corruption of, Ó ᵹᴀɪʀʙɪᴄ, q.v.

Ó ᵹᴀɪʀʙɪɴ—I—O Garvyne, O Garven, Garvin, Garavin, Garwin, Garven, (?) Girvin, Girvan, (Garvey) ; ' des. of ᵹᴀɪʀʙɪɴ ' (dim. of ᵹᴀʀʙ, rough) ; a var. of Ó ᵹᴀʀʙᴀɪɴ, q.v. In Co. Mayo, where this surname is very common, it is always angl. Garvey, which would seem to indicate that the original form in that county was Ó ᵹᴀɪʀʙɪᴄɪɴ, a dim. of Ó ᵹᴀɪʀʙɪᴄ, q.v.

Ó ᵹᴀɪʀʙeɪᴄ, Ó ᵹᴀɪʀʙɪᴄ—I—O Garvie, O Garvey, Garvey ; ' des. of ᵹᴀɪʀʙɪᴄ ' (rough peace) ; the name (1) of an ancient family in Co. Down, of the same stock as the Maguinnesses, who were chiefs of Ui Eathach Cobha, the present barony of Iveagh ; (2) of an Oriel family who were anciently chiefs of Ui Breasail, in the present barony of Oneilland East, Co. Armagh, but dispossessed at an early period by the MacCanns ; and (3) of a branch of the Ui Ceinnsealaigh who were anciently chiefs of Ui Feilmeadha Thuaidh, in the present barony of Rathvilly, Co. Carlow. The name is now well represented in all parts of Ireland. V. Ó ᵹᴀɪʀʙꝼéɪᴄ and Ó ᵹᴀɪʀʙɪɴ.

Ó ᵹᴀɪʀᴍʟeᴀᵹᴀɪᴅ, v. Ó ᵹoɪʀᴍʟeᴀᵹᴀɪᴅ.

Ó ʒᴀʟáɪn, Ó ʒᴀʟʟáɪn—I—*O Gallane, O Gallon*, Gallen, Gallon, Gollan ; ' des. of ʒᴀʟʟán ' (dim. of ʒᴀʟʟ, a cock), or ' ʒᴀʟán ' (dim. of ʒᴀʟ, valour) ; the name of a Breifney family who were anciently chiefs of Clann Dunghalaigh ; still in Co. Leitrim, angl. Gallon ; also in Donegal.

Ó ʒᴀʟʟċoบᴀɪʀ—I—*O Galleghure*, O'Gallagher, Gallagher, Gallaher, Gallogher, Gollagher, &c. ; ' des. of ʒᴀʟʟċoบᴀʀ ' (foreign help) ; the name of a numerous and once powerful family in Tirconnell, who derive their descent from Maolchobha, King of Ireland in the 7th century. As marshalls of O'Donnell's forces, the O'Gallaghers took a prominent part in all the military movements of Cinel Conaill during the 14th and subsequent centuries. Many of them were distinguished as Bishops of Raphoe and Derry. The name was sometimes shortened to Ó ʒᴀʟʟċú, q.v.

Ó ʒᴀʟʟċú—I—*O Gallchoe, O Galloghoe*, Gallahue ; an apocopated form of Ó ʒᴀʟʟċoบᴀɪʀ, q.v. ; formerly common in all parts of Ireland.

Ó ʒᴀʟʟċuบᴀɪʀ, v. Ó ʒᴀʟʟċoบᴀɪʀ.

Ó ʒᴀṁnᴀ—I—*O Gawny, O Gawney*, Gooney, Gaffney, (Caulfield) ; ' des. of ʒᴀṁᴀɪn ' (calf) ; formerly common in Ormond, South Leinster, and North Connacht ; now generally angl. Gaffney, but sometimes disguised as Caulfield.

Ó ʒᴀṁnáɪn—I—*O Gawnaine, O Gownane*, Goonane, Goonan, (Guning, Gunning, Caulfield) ; ' des. of ʒᴀṁnán ' (dim. of ʒᴀṁᴀɪn, a calf) ; the name, according to MacFirbis, of a family of Clann Mhuirthuile in Connacht ; now very scattered. It is angl. Goonan in the neighbourhood of Limerick, Guning in Clare, and Caulfield in Galway and West Mayo. Cf. Ó ʒᴀṁnᴀ.

Ó ʒᴀṁnᴀɪʀe—I—*O Gownro, O Goonerie*, Goonery, Goonry ; ' des. of ʒᴀṁnᴀɪʀe ' (calf-keeper) ; a rare Westmeath surname.

Ó ʒánᴀɪʀ'ᴅ, Gaynard, Gaynor.

Ó ʒᴀoιcín—I—*O Gighine, O Gihine, O Gehin, O Gahan,*
Guiheen, Gweehin, Guihen, Guighan, Guihan, Geehan,
Gihan, Gihon, Gahan, and, by translation, Wynne,
Wyndham ; ' des. of ʒᴀoιcín ' (dim. of ʒᴀoc, wind, a
' pet ' form probably of mᴀoιʒᴀoιce, chief of the
wind) ; the name (1) of a Leinster family who were
formerly chiefs of Siol Elaigh, now the barony of
Shillelagh, in the south-west of Co. Wicklow, and are
still numerous in the neighbouring county of Wexford,
where the name is angl. Gahan ; and (2) of a Connacht
family who are numerous in that province, but sometimes disguised as Wynnes and Wyndhams.

Ó ʒᴀʀbáιn—I—*O Garvane, O Garvan,* Garvan, Garavin,
Garvin, Garven, Garwin, (?) Girvan ; ' des. of ʒᴀρbáп '
(dim. of ʒᴀρb, rough) ; the name of a family of the
southern Ui Neill, formerly seated in Meath, but now
found chiefly in Sligo and Cork. V. Ó. ʒᴀιρbín which
is a variant.

Ó ʒᴀcιᴀoιc—I—Gately, Keatley, Keitley, Keightly ;
' des. of ʒᴀcιᴀoc '; a Connacht surname.

Ó ʒeᴀιᴀʒáιn—I—*O Gallegane, O Galgan,* Galligan,
White ; ' des. of ʒeᴀιᴀʒáη ' (dim. of ʒeᴀι, bright,
white) ; originally a Sligo surname, but long dispersed
through the south of Ireland.

Ó ʒeᴀιáιn—I—*O Gealane, O Geallane,* Gellan, Gellen,
Gelland ; ' des. of ʒeᴀιáн ' (dim. of ʒeᴀι, bright,
white) ; an old surname in Sligo and Offaly perhaps
the same as Ó ʒeᴀιᴀʒáιn, q.v.

Ó ʒeᴀιbáιn—I—*O Gealwaine, O Gallivain, O Galvane,*
Gallivan, Galvan, Galven, Galvin ; ' des. of ʒeᴀιbáн '
(bright-white) ; the name of a Dalcassian family,
now numerous in Munster, especially in Kerry ; also
found in Co. Roscommon.

Ó ʒeᴀʀᴀʒᴀ, O'Garriga ; a corruption in the spoken
language of Connacht of mᴀʒ ғeᴀρᴀbᴀιʒ, q.v.

Ó ʒéᴀʀáιn—I—*O Gerane, O Gieran,* Geran, Gearon,
Guerin, Gearn, Gearns, Sharpe ; ' des. of ʒéᴀρáн '
(dim. of ʒeᴀρ, sharp) ; the name of a family of the Ui
Fiachrach, originally seated in the barony of Erris,

Co. Mayo, but long dispersed ; also the original name of the family of Ⅿⱥᵹ ᵽᵼoɴɴⱱⱥᵼᵽᵽ, or Gaynor.

Ó ᵹeⱥᵽᵹⱥᵼɴ—I—*O Gargan*, Gargan, Garagan, Garrigan ; ' des. of ᵹeⱥᵽᵹⱥɴ ' (dim. of ᵹeⱥᵽᵹ, fierce) ; a Meath surname ; more frequently Ⅿⱥc ᵹeⱥᵽᵹⱥᵼɴ, q.v.

Ó ᵹéᵼⱱeⱥɴɴⱥᵼᵹ, Ó ᵹeᵼⱱeⱥɴɴⱥᵼᵹ—I—*O Geveney, O Giany, O Geany*, Geaveny, Keaveny, Kevany, Geaney, Geany, Guiney, Guiny ; ' des. of ᵹéᵼⱱeⱥɴɴⱥc,' or ' ᵹeᵼⱱeⱥɴɴⱥc ' (fettered, prisoner) ; the name of a family of Ui Maine in Co. Galway ; still common in Connacht ; also in Munster, where it is sometimes shortened to Ó ᵹéᵼⱱᵼɴɴ, q.v.

Ó ᵹéᵼⱱᵼɴɴ—I—*O Gaine, O Geyne, O Geane*, Gaine, Geane ; short for Ó ᵹéᵼⱱeⱥɴɴⱥᵼᵹ, or Ó ᵹeᵼⱱeⱥɴɴⱥᵼᵹ ; in use in Kerry.

Ó ᵹᵼⱥⱡⱡⱥᵼɴ—I—Geelan, Gealon ; ' des. of ᵹᵼⱥⱡⱡⱥɴ ' (dim. of ᵹᵼⱥⱡⱡ, hostage) ; the name of a Ui Maine family in Co. Galway.

Ó ᵹᵼⱱeⱥⱡⱡⱥᵼɴ—I—*O Gibbellayne, O Gibbelan*, Gibulawn, Giblin, (Gibson, Gibsey, Gipsey) ; ' des. of ᵹᵼⱱeⱥⱡⱡⱥɴ ' ; the name of a distinguished ecclesiastical family in Connacht, where it is still well known, though sometimes disguised under the angl. forms of Gibson and Gipsey.

Ó ᵹᵼⱱɴe—I—*O Gibney, O Gibny*, Gibney, Giboney ; ' des. of ᵹᵼⱱɴe ' (hound) ; a well-known surname in Meath and Cavan.

Ó ᵹᵼⱡᵼɴ—I—Gilleen, Gillen, Gellen, Gillon ; ' des. of ᵹᵼⱡᵼɴ ' (dim. of ᵹeⱥⱡ, bright, white) ; the name of two distinct families in Connacht, one in Tirawley and the other in Partry. Both families have been long dispersed, but the name is still extant in Connacht and in other parts of Ireland.

Ó ᵹᵼɴᵼⱱe, Guinee, Guinea, Guiney. V. Ó ᵹᵿᵼɴᵼⱱe.

Ó ᵹᵼoⱱⱥⱡⱡⱥᵼɴ, v. Ó ᵹᵼⱱeⱥⱡⱡⱥᵼɴ.

Ó ᵹᵼoⱡⱡⱥⱱᵿᵼⱱe—I—*O Gillavoye, O Gilboy*, O'Gilvie, O'Gilbie, Ogilby, Gilbey, Gillbee, Gilboy, Gilvoy, &c. ; ' des. of ᵹᵼoⱡⱡⱥⱱᵿᵼⱱe ' (yellow lad) ; a Donegal surname. Cf. Ⅿⱥc ᵹᵼoⱡⱡⱥⱱᵿᵼⱱe.

Ó ᵹıoᴌᴌᴀᵹᴀ́ın—I—*O Gillegane, O Gilgan*, Gilligan, Gillgan, Gilgan ; des. of ᵹıoᴌᴌᴀᵹᴀ́n ' (dim. of ᵹıoᴌᴌᴀ, servant, youth) ; a var. of Ó ᵹıoᴌᴌᴀ́ın, q.v. ; a scattered surname ; formerly most common in Westmeath, Thomond, Galway, Roscommon and Sligo ; perhaps sometimes substituted for Ó ᵹeᴀᴌᴀᵹᴀ́ın, q.v.

Ó ᵹıoᴌᴌᴀ́ın—I—*O Gillane, O Gillain*, Gillane, Gillan, Gilland, Gillon, Gillen ; ' des. of ᵹıoᴌᴌᴀ́n ' (dim. of ᵹıoᴌᴌᴀ, servant, youth) ; the name of a family of Cinel Eoghain ; given by MacFirbis as an alias for Ó ᵹıoᴌᴌᴀᵹᴀ́ın, q.v.

Ó ᵹıoᴌᴌᴀʀᴀ́ın, Gilleran, Gilrain, Gilrane, Killeran, Kilrain, Kilrane ; a corruption of mᴀc ᵹıoᴌᴌᴀ Éᴀnᴀ́ın, q.v.

Ó ᵹıoᴌᴌᴀʀnᴀ́ᴛ, v. mᴀc ᵹıoᴌᴌᴀ nᴀ nᴀoṁ.

Ó ᵹıonnᴀ́ın—IV—*O Ganon*, Gannon ; a corruption of mᴀᵹ Fıonnᴀ́ın, q.v.

Ó ᵹıoʀʀᴀıᴅe—IV—O'Hare, Hare, Haire ; a corruption of mᴀᵹ Feᴀʀᴀᴅᴀıᵹ, q.v. ; supposed to be derived from ' ᵹıʀʀFıᴀᴅ,' a hare ; hence the angl. forms, O'Hare, &c.

Ó ᵹᴌᴀcᴀ́ın—I—*O Glackane*, Glackan, Glakan ; ' des. of ᵹᴌᴀcᴀ́n ' (dim. of ᵹᴌᴀc, a hand) ; a rare surname, found chiefly in Donegal and Sligo.

Ó ᵹᴌᴀ́ıṁín—I—*O Glavine*, Glavin ; ' des. of ᵹᴌᴀ́ıṁín ' (glutton) ; the name of a family of the Ui Fiachrach, formerly seated in Tirawley, Co. Mayo, but now found chiefly in Cork, Kerry and Waterford.

Ó ᵹᴌᴀısín—I—*O Glassyn, O Glissine*, Glasheen ; ' des. of ᵹᴌᴀıʀín ' (dim. of ᵹᴌᴀʀ, grey) ; the name of a family who were anciently seated in the barony of Imokilly, Co. Cork, but long dispersed through Munster ; now very rare.

Ó ᵹᴌᴀısne—I—*O'Glassnie*, (Giles, Gyles) ; ' des. of ᵹᴌᴀıʀne ' ; a rare Louth surname.

Ó ᵹᴌᴀsᴀ́ın—I—*O Glassane, O Glessaine, O Gleasan*, Glessane, Glissane, Glissawn, Gleason, Gleeson ; ' des. of ᵹᴌᴀʀᴀ́n ' (dim. of ᵹᴌᴀʀ, grey) ; a common surname in all the south of Ireland, especially in Cork, Limerick,

Tipperary and Kilkenny; now generally pronounced Ó Ⴍⴎⴀⵔⴀⵏ.

Ó Ⴍⴎⴄⴀⅅⴑⴀ—I—Gladdery, Gladdry; 'des. of Ⴍⴎⴄⴀⅅⵔⴀ'; an old surname in Ui Maine, Co. Galway; still in use in Connacht, but extremely rare.

Ó Ⴍⴎⴎⴀⵑⴀⵏ, v. Ó Ⴍⴎⴀⵔⴀⵏ.

Ó Ⴍⴎⵎⵕⴀⵕⵑ—I—(?) Glorney; the name of a family formerly seated at Callan, Co. Kilkenny. O'Donovan says it was angl. Glory.

Ó Ⴍⵑⵕⴒ—I—O Gneiffe, O Gnyw, Agnew; 'des. of Ⴍⵑⵕⴒ' (action); the name of a literary and bardic family in Ulster, who were hereditary poets to the O'Neills of Clanaboy.

Ó Ⴍⵔⴒⴀ—III—O Gowe, Gow, Smith; 'des. of the smith'; a var. of Ó Ⴍⵔⴒⴀⵏⵏ, q.v.

Ó Ⴍⵔⴒⴀⵏⵏ—I—O Gobbane, O Gobban, O Gubben, Gobin; 'des. of Ⴍⵔⴒⴀⵏ,' (dim. of Ⴍⵔⴒ, a mouth, snout); a rare Ulster surname; in the 16th century, found chiefly in Tyrone and Donegal; perhaps the origin of Gubbins in Co. Limerick.

Ó Ⴍⵔⴒⴀⵏⵏ—III—O Gowen, O Gowin, O Goen, Ò Goine, O'Gowan, Gowan, Goan, Gowen, Gowing, Going, Smith, Smyth; 'des. of the smith' (Ir. 'Ⴍⵔⴒⴀ'); the name of an old Cavan family who, in the latter part of the 16th century, were one of the most numerous in O'Reilly's country, and were also found in Monaghan, Down, Louth, Meath and Westmeath; still very common in all these counties, but nearly always disguised as Smith or Smyth. To be distinguished from Ⴋⴀⵛ ⴀⵏ Ⴍⵔⴒⴀⵏⵏ, which is often similarly anglicised.

Ó Ⴍⵔⴅⴀⵏⵏ—I—Goddan, (Godwin, Goodwin); 'des. of Ⴍⵔⴅⴀⵏ' (dim. of Ⴍⵔⴅ, stammerer); also Ó Ⴍⴀⴅⴀⵏⵏ; the name of a Mayo family, originally seated in the parish of Moygawnagh, in the barony of Tirawley, but long dispersed. The angl. forms are given on the authority of O'Donovan. I have, however, failed to verify them, and have found the name only in the form of Ó Ⴍⵔⵕⴒⵏ, q.v.

Ó ʒoıbín—I—*O Gubben*, Gubbins; ' des. of ʒoıbín '
(dim. of ʒob, a mouth or snout) ; a var. of Ó ʒobáın,
q.v.

Ó ʒoıʋín—I—Godwin, Goodwin ; ' des. of ʒoıʋín '
(dim. of ʒoʋ, stammerer). This surname, which
appears to be a var. of Ó ʒoʋáın (q.v.), is still in use
in parts of Co. Mayo, angl. Godwin and Goodwin.

Ó ʒoıllıʋe—I—Golden, Golding, Goulding. V. Ó ʒoıllín.

Ó ʒoıllín—I—*O Gullin, O Gullyn*; ' des. of ʒoıllín '
(dim. of ʒoll, one-eyed, or of ʒall, a cock) ; apparently
a var. of Ó ʒaıllín, q.v. ; formerly in use in Cork and
Kerry, and, doubtless, the original form of the surname
now pronounced Ó ʒoıllıʋe, and angl. Golden and
Golding in these counties.

Ó ʒoıRmʒıalla, Ó ʒoıRmʒıallaıʒ, Ó ʒoıRm-
ʒıolla—I—Gormilly, Gormley; ' des. of ʒoıʀm-
ʒıalla ' (blue-hostage) ; or ' ʒoıʀmʒıolla ' (blue
servant or youth) ; the name of a Mayo family who
were formerly lords of Partry, in the west of the
barony of Carra ; possibly a substitution for Ó ʒoʀm-
ʒaıl(e), q.v.

Ó ʒoıRmleaʒaıʒ, Ó ʒoıRmŝleaʒaıʒ—I—*O
Gormeley, O Gorumley, O Grimeley*, Gormilly, O'Gormley, Gormley, Gormilly, Grumley, Grimley, Bloomer ;
' des. of ʒoıʀmŝleaʒaċ ' (blue-spearman) ; the
name of a distinguished Ulster family who were
chiefs of Cinel Moen, a sub-clan of Cinel Eoghain,
and originally seated in the barony of Raphoe, Co.
Donegal. In the 13th century, they were expelled
by the Cinel Conaill, whereupon they settled on the
other side of Lough Foyle, between Strabane and
Derry. They retained considerable property down
to the plantation of Ulster in 1608. The name is
now very common in Ulster.

Ó ʒolláın—I—Gullan, Gulan ; ' des. of ʒollán ' (dim.
of ʒoll, one-eyed).

Ó ʒoRmaʒáın—I—*O Gormegaine*, Gormagan ; (1) ' des.
of ʒoʀmaʒán ' (dim. of ʒoʀm, blue), and (2) a corruption of Ó CoʀmacáIn.

Ó ʒoꞃmáın—I—*O Gormane*, O'Gorman, Gorman ; ' des. of ʒoꞃmán ' (dim. of ʒoꞃm, blue) ; a rare and scattered surname ; to be distinguished from Mac ʒoꞃmáın, which is often angl. O'Gorman, as well as Gorman.

Ó ʒoꞃmʒaıl, Ó ʒoꞃmʒaıle—I—*O Gormowle*, *O Gormoill*, *O Gormaly*, *O Gormooly*, Gormaly, Gormilly, Gormley, (Gorman, Grimes) ; ' des. of ʒoꞃmʒal ' (blue-valour) ; the name (1) of a Mayo family who were anciently lords of the barony of Carra ; and (2) of a Roscommon family who were formerly erenaghs of Elphin. It is still common in Connacht, and has spread into Leinster, but is often disguised under the angl. forms of Gorman and Grimes. Ó ʒoꞃmꞃúıl and Ó ʒoꞃmꞃúılıʒ represent the local pronunciation in Connacht, and the name is so written in the Annals of Loch Cé.

Ó ʒoꞃmóʒ—I—*O Gormoge*, (Gorman) ; ' des. of ʒoꞃmóʒ ' (dim. of ʒoꞃm, blue) ; the name of a Mayo family who were anciently lords of the barony of Carra. O'Donovan found it still extant in that district, but angl. Gorman. It appears to have been an alias for Ó ʒoꞃmʒaıl, q.v.

Ó ʒoꞃmꞃúıl, Ó ʒoꞃmꞃúılıʒ, v. Ó ʒoꞃmʒaıl, Ó ʒoꞃmʒaıle.

Ó ʒoćꞃaıᵬ—IV—*O Gogherie*, *O Goherye*, Geoghery, Gohary, Godfrey ; ' des. of ʒoćꞃaıć ' (God-peace, angl. Godfrey, a name introduced by the Danes and early adopted by the Irish) ; a not uncommon surname in East Limerick and Tipperary. The family, which is old in that district, is probably of Danish descent.

Ó ʒꞃáᴅa—I—*O Grada*, O'Grady, Grady, (Brady) ; ' des. of ʒꞃáᴅa ' (noble, illustrious) ; the name of a distinguished Dalcassian family who were originally seated in the parish of Killonasoolagh, near the river Fergus, in the south of Co. Clare. After the year 1318, they removed to the neighbourhood of Tomgraney, where they obtained from the O'Briens an extensive tract of land, embracing several parishes in the counties of Clare and Galway. In 1543, Donogh

O'Grady, 'Captain of his nation,' was knighted by Henry VIII, and granted by letters patent the lands of his clan. Thenceforward the heads of the O'Grady family were steadily on the side of the English interest. The surname about this time, in some unaccountable way, got anglicised O'Brady and Brady. Hugh Brady, the first Protestant bishop of Meath, was a son of Sir Donogh O'Grady, and the ancestor of the Bradys of Raheen, Co. Clare. Another son, John O'Grady, alias Brady, who settled in Co. Limerick, was the ancestor of the O'Gradys of Kilballyowen. The name is now common in Munster and Connacht. To be distinguished from Ó Ʒᵉᵃᴅᵃ, q.v.

Ó Ʒʀáınne—I—*O Graine, O Granie*, Greany, Greaney; ' des. of Ʒʀáınne ' (a woman's name) ; a rather common surname in Kerry and Galway. It is one of our few Irish metronymics.

Ó Ʒʀálaıʒ, Ó Ʒʀállaıʒ, Greally, Grealy, Greely; a corruption, in the spoken language of Mayo, of Maʒ Raʒallaıʒ, q.v. Also Ó Ʒaolaıʒ or Ó Ʒʀaollaıʒ.

Ó Ʒʀamna—IV—O'Growney. V. Mac Cappʒamna.

Ó Ʒʀeacáın—I—*O Greghane, O Greaghan, O Grahin, O Gryhen, O Gryhme, O Grame*, Greaghan, Greahan, Grehan, Gregan, Greyhan, Grayhan, Greaham, Greham, Graham, Greame, Graeme, Grame, Greames, Grimes ; ' des. of Cpeacáın ' (dim. of cpeac, blind) ; a var. of Ó Cpeacáın (q.v.) owing to the softening of the initial c to Ʒ. It is undoubtedly the name which has been corrupted to Ó Ʒpeıóm (q.v.) in Munster.

Ó Ʒʀeaᴅa—I—*O Greadie, O Graddy*, O'Gready, Gready, Graddy, (O'Grady, Grady) ; ' des. of Ʒpeıc ' (gen. Ʒpeaᴅa, a champion) ; an old Munster surname.

Ó Ʒʀeıóm—I—*O Gryhme, O Grame*, Grimes, Graeme, Graham ; undoubtedly a Munster corruption of Ó Ʒpeacáın, q.v.

Ó Ʒʀıaᴅáın, v. Ó Ʒpíobᴅáın.

Ó Ʒʀıaᴅa—IV—Grady ; a corruption in Connacht of Maʒ Rıaᴅa, q.v.

Ó Ʒʀıalluıs, Grealish, (Greally, Grealy, Greely, Griffin) ;

a corruption, in the spoken language of Galway and Mayo, of Mag Niallguir, q.v.

Ó Grianáin—I—*O Greenane, O Grienan, O Greynan, O Grenan,* Greenan, Grennan, Grannon; 'des. of Grianán' (dim. of grianaċ, sunny, pleasant); a scattered surname.

Ó Griḃín—I—*O Gribbine, O Gribin,* Gribbin, Gribben, Gribbon; 'des. of Griḃín'; a Donegal surname.

Ó Gríḃṫín, Ó Gríḟín—II—*O Griffine,* Guffin; 'des. of Gríḃṫín' or 'Grifin'; a Munster surname; perhaps a var. of Ó Gríoḃṫa, q.v.

Ó Gríoḃṫa—I—*O Greefa, O Griffy, O Grighie,* Griffey, Griffy, Greehy, (Griffith, Griffiths, Griffin); 'des. of Gríoḃṫa' (griffin-like, fierce warrior); the name of a Dalcassian family who were chiefs of Cinel Cuallachta, in the south-east of the barony of Inchiquin, and had their castle at Ballygriffy; common in Thomond, but usually angl. Griffin.

Ó Gríoḃṫáin—I—*O Greffane, O Grevan,* Griffin, Greaven, Greven, (Griffith, Griffiths, Greaves, Grieves); 'des. of Gríoḃṫán' (dim. of Gríoḃṫa); a Connacht surname, found chiefly in Galway and Mayo.

Ó Gríoċa, Greehy; a corruption of Ó Gríoḃṫa, q.v.

Ó Gruagáin, Ó Grúgáin—I—*O Growgane, O Grogaine,* Groogan, Grogan, Groggan; 'des. of Gru(a)gán' (dim. of gruag, hair of the head, or of grúg, fierceness, anger); the name of a Roscommon family who were erenaghs of Elphin; now found in all parts of Ireland.

Ó Guaire—I—Goorey, Gorey; 'des. of Guaire' (noble); the name of a family who were anciently lords of Ui Cuilinn, in Leinster; now very rare.

Ó Guairim, Gorham; a Galway surname; probably a substitution for de Gúram, q.v.

Ó Guallaċta—IV—Goolden, Golden, Goulding; a corruption in Co. Mayo of Mac Cuallaċta, q.v.

Ó Guiḃín—I—*O Gubben,* Gobin, Gubbins; a var. of Ó Goiḃín, q.v.

Ó Guiniḋe—I—*O Guinye,* Guinee, Guinea, Guiney; 'des. of *Guiniḋe'; a common surname in Kerry and North

Cork. Its angl. forms cannot always be distinguished from those of Ó ᵹeıƀeannaıᵹ, of which it is possibly a corruption.

Ó ᵹusáın—I—Gossan, Gosson, Gasson, Gaussen; ' des. of ᵹurán ' (strength, force, action, anger) ; the name, according to MacFirbis, of a family of Sil-Murry, in Connacht. The death of Ruaıóṗı Ua ᵹurán is recorded in the Annals of the Four Masters at the year 992.

Ó náƀartaıᵹ—I—O Havorta, O Haverta, Haverty ; ' des. of Áƀartaċ,' or more probably of ' ṗaᵹartaċ '; v. Ó náᵹartaıᵹ and cf. Ó nOᵹartaıᵹ ; a rare Galway surname.

Ó náótlaıᵹ—I—Addley, Addly ; ' des. of a———'; a rare surname in parts of Mayo and Galway. The Annals of Ulster at the year 947 record the death of 'Anmere Ua Adlai,' coarb of St. Ciaran of Clonmacnoise.

Ó náómaıll—I—O Hammell, O'Hamill, Hamill, Hamell, Hammill, Hammell ; ' des. of Áómaıl ' (quick, ready, active) ; also written Ó náᵹmaıl ; the name of a branch of the Cinel Eoghain, still numerous in Ulster.

Ó náónaıó, Ó náónaıᵹ—I—O Heynee, O Hyneye, Hyney, Hiney ; ' des. of Aónaó ' (old age ; wise) ; also Ó náıóne and Ó neıónıᵹ ; the name (1) of a Galway family who were anciently chiefs of Gno-beg, in the present barony of Moycullen ; and (2) of a West Cork family. In the 16th century, it was very scattered and is now extremely rare.

Ó náᵹáın—I—O Hagane, O'Hagan, Hagan, Haggan, &c. ; ' des. of Óᵹán ' (dim. of óᵹ, young) ; a northern var. of Ó nOᵹáın, q.v. ; the name (1) of a distinguished family of Cinel Eoghain, who were chiefs of Cinel Fearghusa and were seated at Tullaghoge, in Co. Tyrone, where it was O'Hagan's privilege to inaugurate O'Neill ; and (2) of another family of the same race who were chiefs of Cinel Tighearnaigh, in Ulster.

Ó náᵹaırt—I—O Haggart, Heggert ; short for Ó náᵹartaıᵹ, q.v.

Ó háȝaʀᴄaiȝ— I —O Hagirtie, Agarty, Hagarty, Hagerty, Hegarty, Hegerty, Heggerty, &c.; ' des. of ᵽáȝaптac' (same as ᵽóȝaптac); a var. of Ó hÓȝапᴄaiȝ, q.v. Cf. Ó háȝáin for Ó hÓȝáin.

Ó háȝaʀᴄaiȝ—I—O Haerty, Hearty, (Hegarty); ' des. of ᵽáȝaптac' (same as ᵽáȝaптac); a var. of Ó ᵽáȝaптaiȝ (q.v.), owing to the aspiration of the initial ᵽ. Cf. Ó hÓȝaптaiȝ.

Ó háȝmaill, v. Ó háᴐmaill.

Ó haiċiʀ—I—O Haghir, O Hagher, O Hahir, O'Hehir, O'Haire, O'Hare, Hegher, Hehir, Aher, Hair, Hare, Herr, &c.; ' des. of aiceaп' (sharp, bitter, angry); also written Ó haiᴄᴄiп, Ó hOiċiп, &c.; the name of a Thomond family who, at the end of the 11th century, were lords of Magh Adhair, between Ennis and Tulla, but afterwards settled in Ui Cormaic, on the west side of the Fergus, between Ennis and Slieve Callan. Though long settled in Thomond, the family was not of Dalcassian origin, but a branch of the Ui Fidh-gheinte, in the present Co. Limerick. The name is still common in Clare and Limerick.

Ó haioeiᴄ, Ó haioioe, v. Ó háioiᴄ.

Ó haioín—I—O Hidiene, O Hidden, Hadian, Haden, Hayden, Haydin, &c.; ' des. of aioiᴄín' (dim. of aioiᴄ); a var. of Ó heioín, q.v.

Ó haioiᴄ—I—O Hidia, Haidee, Haidy; ' des. of aioiᴄ' (humility); also written Ó haioeiᴄ, Ó haioioe, &c.; the name (1) of an Ulidian family who were lords of Ui Eathach, now the barony of Iveagh, Co. Down, from about the middle of the 10th to the middle of the 12th century, when they were superseded by the Ma-guinnesses; and (2) of a Connacht family, mentioned by MacFirbis. The name, which is now extremely rare, is current about Shrule, Co. Mayo, in the modernised forms of Ó heioio and Ó heaoeaᴐa, q.v.

Ó haioпe, v. Ó háᴐпaiȝ.

Ó haɪlbeaʀᴄaiȝ—I—O Helvertie, O Helfertie, Halverty, Halferty, Hilferty; ' des. of ailbeaптac' (noble-bright); an old, but rare, Donegal surname.

Ó háilċe—II—*O Hallihey, O Hally*, Hally, Halley ; ' des. of áilċe ' (a personal name of Danish origin, meaning ' English ') ; the name of a family, probably of Danish origin, who were seated in the neighbourhood of Templemore, Co. Tipperary. In the 16th century, there were merchant families of the name in Cashel and Kilmallock. It is still common in Tipperary and parts of Limerick.

Ó háilġeanáin—I—*O Hallinaine*, O'Hallinan, Hallinan, Hallanan, Halnan ; ' des. of áilġeanán ' (dim. of áilġean, noble offspring) ; an old Munster surname, found chiefly in Cork and Limerick ; also apparently a Connacht surname, now not uncommon in West Mayo. macbeaċaḋ Ó háilġeanáin was Bishop of Cork at the beginning of the 12th century.

Ó háilġeasa—I—*O Hallyse, O Hallishy*, Hallissy, Hallissey, Hallessy ; ' des. of áilġear ' (desire, request, importunity) ; a Munster surname ; found chiefly in West Cork and South Kerry.

Ó háilín—I—*O Hallyne*, Hallin, Hallion, Allin, Allen ; ' des of áilín ' (dim. of áil, noble, rock, a ' pet ' form of some name commencing with áil-) ; also written Ó háillín ; a rare surname ; found chiefly in Ormond and Offaly.

Ó háille—I—*O Hally*, Hally ; 'des. of áille,' or ' áinle ' (handsome, beautiful ; also a hero or warrior) ; the name of a Thomond family who were seated at baile uí áille, now angl. Ballyally, near Bunratty, in Co. Clare. V. Ó háinuiġe.

Ó háilleaċáin—I—*O Halleghane, O Hallaghan*, Hallaghan, Hallihane, Hallahan, Hallihan ; ' des. of áilleaċán ' (dim. of áille, handsome, beautiful) ; also Ó hallaċáin ; the name of an old Cork family.

Ó háilleaġáin—I—*O Hallegane, O Hallagan*, Halligan, Hilligan ; ' des. of áilleaġán ' (dim. of áille, handsome, beautiful) ; also Ó hallaġáin ; an old Ulster surname ; now common also in Mayo and Roscommon.

Ó háilmic—I—*O Halwick, O Halvie*, (?) Halvey, Han-

wick; ' des. of ⱭⰉⱢⰏⰀⰄ ' (noble-son); the name oɫ a
family of Ui Fiachrach in Connacht, now possibly
represented by the Mayo surname Hanwick. For
the angl. form ' Halvey,' cf. Kirby for Ó ⰄⰋⱃⰏⰉⰄ.

Ó ⱱⰀⰋⱢⱂⰉⱀ—I—*O Halpin, O Halpeny, O Halfpenny,*
Halpin, Halpeny, Halfpenny; ' des. of ⰀⰉⱢⱂⰉⱀ ' (dim.
of ⰀⱢⱂ, a lump, a stout person). This surname appears
to have originated in Co. Monaghan, but for centuries
it has been found also in Co. Limerick. The angl.
forms O Halpeny, Halpeny, &c., represent an older
form, Ó ⱱⰀⰋⱢⱂⰉⱀⰉ.

Ó ⱱⰀⰋⰏⰅⰉⱃⰃⰉⱀ, Ó ⱱⰀⰋⰏⰉⱃⰃⰉⱀ—I—*O Havergan, O
Hemergin,* Mergin, Bergin, Bergen, Bergan, Berrigan,
&c.; ' des. of ⰀⰉⰏⰉⱃⰃⰉⱀ ' (wondrous birth); the name
of an Offaly family who were formerly chiefs of the
barony of Geashill; still common in Leinster, but
long corrupted to Ó ⰏⰅⰉⱃⰃⰉⱀ and Ó ⰱⰅⰉⱃⰃⰉⱀ, q.v.

Ó ⱱⰀⰋⱀⰱⰅⰉⰝ, Ó ⱱⰀⰋⱀⰱⰉⰝ—I—*O Hanfy,* Hanvy, Hanvey,
Hanify, Hanafy, Hannify, Hanway, &c.; ' des. of
ⰀⰉⱀⰱⰉⱁⰝ ' (storm); also written Ó ⱱⰀⰋⱀⱑⰅⰉⰝ, Ó ⱱⰀⰋⱀ-
ⱑⰉⱐ, Ó ⱱⰀⰋⱀⱑⰉⰝ, &c.; the name (1) of a distinguished
Oriel family who were chiefs of Ui Seaghain, sometimes of Ui Meith, and sometimes of all Oriel; (2) of
a Meath family who were chiefs of Fearabile, now the
barony of Farbil, in Co. Westmeath, until dispossessed
by Sir Hugh de Lacy soon after the Anglo-Norman
invasion; (3) of an Ulidian family who were chiefs of
Ui Eathach Cobha, now the barony of Iveagh, Co.
Down; and (4) of a branch of the Corca Laoighdhe,
in South-west Cork. The name is now comparatively
rare, having been corrupted or changed into other
forms. See Ó ⱱⰀⰋⱀⰱⰝⰅⰀⰉⱀ, Ó ⱱⰀⱀⰀⰉⰝⰅ, &c.

Ó ⱱⰀⰋⱀⰱⰝⰅⰀⰉⱀ, Ó ⱱⰀⰋⱀⰱⰝⰉⱀ—I—*O Hanavane, O Hene-
faine, O Hannefean,* Hanefan, Hanifan, Hanafin,
Hanifin, &c.; ' des. of ⰀⰉⱀⰱⰝⰅⰀⱀ ' or ' ⰀⰉⱀⰱⰝⰉⱀ '
(dim. of ⰀⰉⱀⰱⰉⱁⰝ); also written Ó ⱱⰀⰋⱀⱑⰅⰀⰉⱀ, Ó
ⱱⰀⰋⱀⱑⰉⱀ, &c.; a well known surname in Cork and
Kerry, where, not improbably, it represents the old
surname Ó ⱱⰀⰋⱀⰱⰉⰝ, of Corca Laoighdhe. See Ó

 hᴀınȯıꞇ above (4). MacFirbis mentions a family of the name in Roscommon.

Ó hᴀınꞓín—I—*O Hanhine, O Hanhin,* Hanneen, Hannin, Hannen, (Hannan, Hannon) ; ' des. of *ᴀınꞓín ' (perhaps for ᴀınᵹeın, unborn) ; the name of a family of Siol Anmchadha, in south-east of Co. Galway. It was common at the end of the 16th century in many parts of Connacht and Munster. See also Ó hᴀınnín. MacFirbis mentions Ó hᴀınᵹeın as a Connacht surname.

Ó hᴀınꝼeıꞇ, Ó hᴀınꝼıȯ, Ó hᴀınꝼıꞇ, v. Ó hᴀınȯeıꞇ, Ó hᴀınȯıꞇ.

Ó hᴀınꝼeᴀın, Ó hᴀınꝼín, Ó hᴀınıꝼeᴀın, Ó hᴀınıꝼín, v. Ó hᴀınȯꞇeᴀın, Ó hᴀınȯꞓín.

Ó hᴀınle, Ó hᴀınlıᵹe, Ó hᴀınlıᵹe—I—*O Hanlee, O Hanley, O Henly,* Hanley, Handly, Hanly, Henly ; ' des. of ᴀınle ' (beauty, also a hero or warrior) ; the name of a Connacht family who were chiefs of Cinel Dobhtha, also called in later times Tuaohanly and Doohy Hanly, a district in Co. Roscommon, extending along the Shannon and comprising the parishes of Kilglass, Termonbarry, Cloontuskert, and the eastern half of the parish of Lisonuffy. The O'Hanlys continued to hold this territory, as tributaries to O'Conor Don, down to the 17th century. In the year 1568-9, Gillyerneuf O Haly was nominated by Queen Elizabeth to be captain of the country of Towohaly in succession to his father, and in 1582, Fergananym O Hanly, gentleman, was granted the office of seneschal of Tohahohanly. The name is now common in many parts of the South of Ireland. Ó hᴀılle of Thomond is doubtless the same name.

Ó hᴀınṁıꞃe, Ó hᴀınṁıꞃeᴀꞓ—I—*O Hanvirre, O Hanneraghe,* Hanberry, Hanbury, (Ansberry, Ansboro) ; ' des. of ᴀınṁıꞃe ' (compound of ᴀın-, a negative or intensitive particle, and mıꞃe, madness, levity) ; an old Connacht surname, corruptly Ó hᴀınmneᴀꞓ. It still survives in Co. Galway under the English form of Ansboro, Hanbury, &c. Ⓜaelíꞃᴀ Ó hᴀınṁıꞃe was Archbishop of Cashel in the early part of the 12th century.

Ó háinnín—I—*O Hanine, O Haneene,* Hannin, Hanneen, Hannen, (Hannan, Hannon); 'des. of Áinnín'; perhaps the same as Ó háincín, q.v. maelóiriṡoe Uá háinnín, 'noble martyr of Ireland,' died in the year 1133.

Ó háinte—I—*O Hanhie, O Henhie,* Hanify, &c.; also Ó hánaite; a corruption of Ó háinbit, q.v.

Ó háiReáctaiṡ—I—*O Harrati, Harrity,* (Harty, Harrington); 'des. of Áireáctac' (holding assemblies, belonging to an assembly); a var. of Ó hOireáctaiṡ, q.v.

Ó háiRṡeáoáin, v. Ó háriṡaoáin.

Ó háiRṁeáoáiṡ—I—*O Harvey,* Harvey, Hervy; 'des. of Áirṁeáoac' (having a herd of cattle); the name of a family of the Ui Fiachrach, in Connacht; now very rare and scattered.

Ó háiRt—I—*O Hairt,* O'Hart, O'Harte, Hart, Harte; 'des. of Árt' (bear, stone, noble); the name of a Meath family originally seated in the neighbourhood of Tara, but dispossessed soon after the Anglo-Norman invasion, when they settled in the barony of Carbury, in Co. Sligo. The name is still very common in Connacht.

Ó háiRtnéáoá—I—*O Hartnedy, O Harniady, O Harnett,* Harnedy, Hartnett, Harnett; 'des. of *Ártnéáoá' (battle-bear, battle-stone); the name of an old West Munster family who are still numerous in Cork, Kerry and Limerick.

Ó háiRtRí—I—Hartry, Hartery; 'des. of Áirtrí'; a rare and scattered surname. The Four Masters, at the year 1123, record the death of maelíra Ó háirtrí, steward of Connacht.

Ó háiSeáoá—I—*O Hassia, O Hassey, O Hassett,* Hassey Hassett; 'des. of Áirío' (strife, discord); the name of an old Thomond family of the same stock as the MacNamaras, being a branch of Clann Chuileain. The name is still well known in the neighbourhood of the city of Limerick and in other parts of Munster.

Ó hⱭⱠⱲⱱⱤ, v. Ó hⱭⱲⱱⱲ.

Ó hⱭⱣⱲⱲⱭⱱⱭ—I—*O Hahassie, O Hahesy,* O'Hahasy, Hahasy, Hahessy, Ahessy; 'des. of ⱭⱣⱲⱲⱭⱲ' (pain, distress); the name of a family of Siol Anmchadha, in the south-east of Co. Galway. At the end of the 16th century, it was found chiefly in Tipperary and Waterford. It is now very rare.

Ó hⱭⱣⱲⱲⱱⱶ, Ó hⱭⱣⱲⱱⱶⱲⱲ, v. Ó hⱭⱱⱲⱱⱲ.

Ó hⱭⱠⱠⱭⱲⱭⱱⱲ—I—*O Hallaghan,* Hallaghan, Hallahan, Hallihan; a var. of Ó hⱭⱱⱠⱠⱲⱭⱲⱭⱱⱲ, q.v.; the name of an old family in Co. Cork.

Ó hⱭⱠⱠⱭⱱⱶⱲ—I—Halley, Hally; doubtless for Ó hⱲⱭⱠⱭⱱⱶⱲ, q.v.

Ó hⱭⱠⱠⱭⱱⱭⱱⱲ—I—*O Hallagan,* Halligan; a var. of Ó hⱭⱱⱠⱠⱲⱭⱱⱭⱱⱲ, q.v. This is the usual form in Connacht.

Ó hⱭⱠⱠⱭⱱⱶⱭⱱⱲ—I—Hallan, Allan, Allen; a var. of Ó ⱱⱭⱠⱠⱭⱱⱶⱭⱱⱲ (q.v.), owing to the aspiration of the initial ⱱ.

Ó hⱭⱠⱠⱶⱱⱤⱭⱱⱲ—I—*O Halowrane, O Halloraine,* O'Halloran, O'Hallaran, O'Halleran, O'Halleron, Halloran, Holloran, &c.; 'des. of ⱭⱠⱠⱶⱱⱲⱭⱲ' (stranger from beyond the sea); the name (1) of a Galway family who were anciently chiefs of Clann Fearghaile, an extensive district in the neighbourhood of the present city of Galway; and (2) of a Thomond family, of the same stock as the MacNamaras, who, before the year 1641, were seated in the parish of Ogonnelloe, in the east of Co. Clare. The name is still very common in both counties.

Ó hⱭⱱⱶⱤⱭⱱⱲ—I—*O Heveran,* Haveron, Haveren, Havern, Havron, Haffron, Heffron, &c.; 'des. of ⱭⱱⱶⱤⱭⱲ' (dim. of ⱭⱱⱶⱭ, eminent, noble, prosperous); the name of a Co. Down family who were anciently chiefs of Dal Fiatach; still extant in East Ulster.

Ó hⱭⱲⱭⱱⱠⱠⱱⱲ, Hamilton; in use in West Clare.

Ó hⱭⱱⱭⱱⱶⱲ—I—*O Hanhie,* Hanify, Hannify; a corruption of Ó hⱭⱱⱱⱶⱱⱶ, q.v.

Ó h-Ɑⱱ ⱲⱭⱱⱲⱶⱲ—III—*O Hencainteyhe,* Canty; a var. of Ó ⱲⱭⱱⱲⱶⱲ, q.v.

Ó ħⱥngłuınn—I—*O Hanglin,* Anglin, Anglim ; ' des. of Ⱥngłonn ' (herỏ, champion) ; an old Cork surname, almost peculiar to that county ; sometimes corrupted to Ó ħⱥngłuım and angl. Anglim. The Four Masters, under the year 1490, record the death of Ƒıonn Uⱥ ħⱥngłuınn, chief tympanist of Ireland.

Ó ħⱥnłuⱥın—I—*O Hanlowne, O Hanlone, O Handlon,* O'Hanlon, Hanlon, Handlon, Hanlan, &c. ; ' des. of Ⱥnłuⱥn ' (great hero or champion) ; the name of a distinguished Oriel family who were chiefs of Ui Niallain, now the barony of Oneilland in Co. Armagh, and once of Oirthear, now the barony of Orier, in the east of the same county. The O'Hanlons were a powerful clan, and many valiant chiefs of the name are mentioned in the Irish annals. In 1587, Sir Oghie O'Hanlon, the then chief, surrendered his lands to the crown and had them regranted by letters patent in tail male, and the chieftaincy was abolished. O'Hanlon was hereditary royal standard bearer north of the Boyne, as O'Molloy was to the south ; and, owing to his loyalty to the English connection, seems to have retained possession of most of the clan-lands down to the period of the Cromwellian confiscations. The name is still numerous in Armagh, and has spread to many other parts of Ireland ; often written Ó ħⱥnnłuⱥın, and sometimes pronounced Ó ħⱥnnłáın.

Ó ħⱥnnⱥċáın—I—*O Hanaghane, O Hanihane,* Hanihan, Hannahan, Yanahan, (Hannan) ; probably a var. of Ó ħⱥnnⱥɠáın, q.v.

Ó ħⱥnnⱥɠáın—I—*O Hannegan, O Hanigan,* Hannigan, Hanigan ; ' des. of Ⱥnnⱥɠán ' (dim. of Ⱥnnⱥ, delay) ; an old Limerick surname, where it was probably a variant of Ó ħⱥnnáın, q.v.

*Ó ħⱥnnⱥı♉, Hanna ; ' des. of Ⱥnnⱥ.'

Ó ħⱥnnáın—I—*O Hannaine, O Hanain,* Hannan, Hannon, Hanan, Hanon, &c.; ' des. of Ⱥnnán' (dim. of Ⱥnnⱥ, delay); the name of an old family in Co. Limerick, where it is still common. But see Ó ħáınċın and Ó ħáınnín.

Ó ħAnnLuAin, v. Ó ħAnLuAin.

Ó ħAnnRAċÁin—I—O *Hawreghane*, O *Howreghan*, O'Hourihane, Hourihane, Hourahan, Hourihan, Hourican ; a corruption of Ó ħAnpAẋÁin, q.v. This form of the surname is peculiar to Co. Cork.

Ó ħAnnRAʒÁin—I—O *Howrigane*, O *Hourigan*, Hourigan ; a corruption of Ó ħAnpAẋÁin, q.v. But see Ó ħOẋpAʒÁin.

Ó ħAnnRAiċ—II—O *Hanrick*, O *Henricke*, Hanrick, Handrick, &c. ; ' des. of AnnpAc ' (from Norse Heimerkr) ; also Ó ħeAnpAic, q.v. ; a rare and scattered surname, probably of Norse origin.

Ó ħAnnRÁin—I—O *Hawrane*, O *Howrane*, Haran, Haren, Horan ; a corruption of Ó ħAnpAẋÁin, q.v. Cf. Ó ħAppAċÁin.

Ó ħAnRAċÁin—I—O *Hanraghane*, O'Hanrahan, Hanrahan, Handrahan ; a corruption of Ó ħAnpAẋÁin, q.v. This form of the surname is very common in Thomond.

Ó ħAnRAċτAiʒ—I—O *Hanraghty*, O *Hanratty*, Hanratty ; ' des. of AnpAċτAċ ' (unrighteous, unlawful) ; also written Ó ħionpAċτAiʒ, and Ó ħinpeAċτAiʒ, q.v. ; the name of an Oriel family who were chiefs of Ui Meith Macha, now the barony of Monaghan, in Co. Monaghan ; still common in Monaghan, Armagh and Louth.

Ó ħAnRAẋÁin—I—O'Hanrahan, O'Hourihane, O *Harraghan*, O *Horoghane*, O *Hourigan*, O *Harragan*, O *Horigane*, O *Horgane*, O *Hawrane*, O *Howrane*, Hanrahan, Hourihane, Hourigan, Horrigan, Haran, Horan, Horgan, &c. ; ' des. of AnpAẋÁin,' (dim. of AnpAẋ, warrior, champion) ; variously corrupted in different parts of Ireland to O ħAnpAċÁin, Ó ħAnnpAċÁin, Ó ħAnnpAʒÁin, Ó ħAppAċÁin, Ó ħAppAʒÁin, Ó ħApʒÁin, Ó ħAnnpÁin, Ó ħionpÁin, &c. ; the name (1) of a Dalcassian family in Thomond, where it is still very common (v. Ó ħAnpAċÁin) ; (2) of a West Cork family who were anciently erenaghs of Ross (v. Ó ħAnnpAċÁin) ; (3) of a Leix family who were anciently chiefs of Ui Creamhthainn, a district lying

around the rock of Dunamase, in the present Leix
(v. Ó ħⱭⱤⱤⱭᵹáın and Ó ħⱭⱤᵹáın) ; and (4) of a
Meath family who were formerly chiefs of Corca
Raoidhe, now the barony of Corcaree, in Co. Westmeath (v. Ó ħıonⱤáın and Ó ħıonnⱤáın). Ó ħⱭnn-
ⱤⱭᵹáın (q.v.) appears to be a Tipperary form of this
surname. The different forms are now very widely
scattered.

Ó ħⱭoᵭⱭ—I—*O Heaa, O Hay, O Hewe, O Hugh,* O'Hea,
Hay, Hays, Hayes, Hews, Hughes, &c. ; ' des.
of Ɑoᵭ ' (fire) ; the name of several distinct families in
different parts of Ireland, of which the following are
the best known : (1) a Tyrone family, formerly lords
of Ui Fiachrach of Ardstraw ; (2) a Tirconnell family,
chiefs of Eas Ruadh, in the neighbourhood of Ballyshannon ; (3) an Oriel family, chiefs of Fearnmaighe,
now the barony of Farney, in Co. Monaghan ; (4) a
Meath family, lords of Odhbha, in the neighbourhood
of Navan ; (5) a Meath family, chiefs of East Tir
Teathbha ; (6) a Wexford family, chiefs of Ui Deagh-
aidh, a district nearly co-extensive with the barony
of Gorey ; (7) a Cork family, lords of Muscraighe-
Luachra, in the north-west of Co. Cork ; (8) a Cork
family, sub-chiefs of Tuath O Donnghaile, in the south-
west of Co. Cork, where they are still numerous ;
(9) a Dalcassian family in Thomond; (10) a family of
Ui Maine in Co. Galway ; (11) a family of Ui Fiachrach
in Co. Mayo, formerly seated at Ard O nAodha, in the
parish of Templemurray ; (12) another family of the
same race, seated in the parish of Ballintobber ; and
(13) a family of Ui Fiachrach, seated at Tonrego,
in the parish of Dromard, Co. Sligo. This surname,
which is numerically one of the strongest in Ireland,
is generally angl. Hughes in the North and Hayes
in the South. The O' is almost universally rejected,
being retained only by the family of Ó ħⱭoᵭⱭ of Corca
Laoighdhe (8), who anglicise the name O'Hea.

Ó ħⱭoᵭⱭᵹáın—I—*O Hegane, O Higane, O Heagan, O
Heegan, O Heaken, O Hoogan, O Huggain,* O'Hegan,

Hegan, Heagan, Hagan, Hogan, Egan, Eagan, Eakin, Hegans, Hagans, Higgans, Huggins, &c.; 'des. of Aoⱱaʒán' (dim. of Aoⱱ); the name (1) of an Oriel family who, in the 10th and 11th centuries, were lords of Dartraighe, in Co. Monaghan, and of Ui Niallain, in Co. Armagh, and to which belonged Ivor O'Hegan, the tutor of St. Malachy and founder of the church of SS. Peter and Paul at Armagh; and (2) of a family of Ely-O'Carroll, in the present Offaly. This surname, owing to the different dialectical pronunciations of the syllable 'Aoⱱ,' is variously anglicised in different parts of Ireland. In Ulster, it frequently became Ó ꝼaoⱱaʒáin (q.v.), angl. Fegan.

Ó ndoileáin—I—Hylan, Hyland, &c.; a var. of Ó ndoláin, q.v.

Ó ndoilleacáin—I—O Hillichain, O Heleghane, O Helighane, O Hylegane, Hellican, Helehan, Helihan, (O'Higgins, Higgins, Hedigan); a var. of Ó ꝼaoilleacáin, through the loss of the initial ꝼ. It is strangely angl. Higgins in the neighbourhood of Dungarvan and Hedigan about Kilkee.

Ó ndoláin—I—O Healane, O Heyllane, O Helane, O Hilane, O Hillane, O Hylane, O Heolane, O Hoolane, O Holane, O Hollan, O Holland, Heelan, Helen, Hillane, Hillan, Holian, Heyland, Hiland, Hylan, Hyland, Holland, (Whelan), &c.; 'des. of ꝼaolán' (dim. of ꝼaol, a wolf); a var. of Ó ꝼaoláin (q.v.) through the aspiration of the initial ꝼ; a common surname, in the 16th century, in Offaly and Leix, whence it spread into other parts of Ireland. Owing to the different dialectical pronunciations of 'Ao,' it is variously anglicised in the different provinces. In Munster, it is generally angl. Heelan; Hyland is the usual form in Leinster; Holland in Ulster. In Connacht, it is sometimes corrupted to Ó ndioláin, Ó ndoláin, Ó ndoileáin, and Ó ndoileáin, angl. Hillane, Hyland, Holland, &c., but the origin is clearly shown by the fact that these forms are nearly always also angl. Whelan. Cf. Ó ndoⱱaʒáin.

Ó nAonACáin, v. Ó néAnACáin.

Ó nAonᵹuιs—I—*O Henees, O Hennis*, Ennes, Ennis ; 'des. of Aonᵹuр' ; a var. of Ó nAonᵹuрA, q.v.

Ó nAonᵹusA—I—*O Heanesey, O Hennesy, O Hensey*, Hennessy, Hensy, Hinsy, Henchy, Hinchy ; 'des. of Aonᵹuр' (one-choice) ; the name (1) of an Offaly family who were lords of Clann Cholgan, a district co-extensive with the barony of Lower Philipstown ; (2) of a Meath family who were lords of Ui Mac Uais, in the barony of Moyfenrath ; (3) of a Bregian family who were chiefs of Gailenga Beaga, in Meath and the north of the present Co. Dublin ; and (4) of a Dal-cassian family in Thomond. The name is now common throughout Munster and Leinster.

Ó nAORCAιᵹ, Hearty ; a var. in the spoken language of Ó nAᵹAрcAιᵹ, q.v.

Ó nARACáin, v. Ó ғAрACáin.

Ó nARAᵹáin, v. Ó nAррAᵹáin.

Ó nARAιlc—II—*O Harold*, Harold, Harrold ; 'des. of Harold' (Norse Haraldr) ; a Limerick surname, apparently of Norse origin.

Ó nARᵹAᴅáin—I—*O Hargedaine, O Hardagane, O Hargedan*, Hargaden, Hargadon, (Hardiman, Harman, Harmon) ; 'des. of Aрᵹaᴅán' or 'Aιрᵹeaᴅán' (dim. of Aιрᵹeaᴅ, silver, hence white, shining) ; also Ó nAιрᵹeaᴅáin ; a Connacht surname ; now often, but incorrectly, angl. Hardiman, Harman, &c.

Ó nARᵹáin—I—*O Horgaine, O Horgane, O Horgan, O Hargan*, Hargan, Horgan, Organ ; a contracted form of Ó nAррAᵹáin, q.v. This form of the surname is most frequent in Cork and Kerry.

Ó nARRACáin—I—*O Harraghan, O Horoghane, O Horo-han, O Horran*, Horahan, Harran, Haran, Horan, &c. ; a corruption of Ó nAрраᴅáin, q.v. ; common in Leix and Tipperary.

Ó nARRACCáin—I—*O Haraghtane, O Harreghtane, O Harrighton, O Herraghton*, Harroughton, Haroughton, (Harrington, Errington, Irrington), &c. ; 'des. of Aррaccán' (dim. of Aррacca, tall, mighty, brave, heroic); the name of a family of Ui Maine in Co. Galway. In the 16th century, it was scattered through all North Munster. To be distinguished from Ó ḣlonġaiṙoáil and Ó ḣoiﬔeáċcaiġ, which are also angl. Harrington.

Ó ḣaṙṙaġáin—I—*O Harragan, O Horrogan, O Horigane,* Harrigan, Herrigan, Horrigan, Horrogan, Horagan, Horgan, &c.; a corruption of Ó ḣanﬔaṙáin, q.v. This form of the surname originated in Leix.

Ó ḣáﬔca, Ó ḣáﬔcaiġ—I—*O Harta,* Harty; a corrupt form of Ó ḣaġaﬔcaiġ and Ó ḣácaﬔcaiġ, q.v.

Ó ḣaﬔcaġáin—I—*O Hartigan,* Hartigan, Hartican; ' des. of aﬔcaġán ' (dim. of aﬔc); the name of a Dalcassian family in Thomond, still well known in Clare and Limerick. Ṫúnlainġ Ó ḣaﬔcaġáin was one of the heroes of Clontarf.

Ó ḣaﬔcáin—I—*O Hartane, O Hartan,* Hartan, Harton, Harten, Hartin, Horton; ' des. of aﬔcán ' (dim. of aﬔc); a scattered surname, but found chiefly in Derry and Donegal. Cf. Ó ḣaﬔcaġáin.

Ó ḣaﬔcġaile—I—Hartley; ' des. of aﬔcġal ' (noble valour); the name of a South Leinster family who, before the Anglo-Norman invasion, were chiefs of a district near the town of Wexford.

Ó ḣacaiﬔne—I—*O Haherny, O Harney,* Harney, Hartney; ' des. of acaiﬔne ' (fatherly, paternal); a rare and scattered surname.

Ó ḣacaﬔcaiġ—I—*O Haherty, O Harty,* Harty; ' des. of ﬔacaﬔcaċ ' (same as ﬔaġaﬔcaċ); a var. of Ó ﬔacaﬔcaiġ (q.v.), owing to the aspiration of the initial ﬔ; shortened in the spoken language to Ó ḣaﬔcaiġ and Ó ḣaﬔca; the name, according to Mageoghegan, of an Offaly family. At the end of the 16th century, it was common in Tipperary, Limerick, Cork and Kerry.

Ó ḣeaċaċ—I—*O Heagh, O Hagh,* Haugh, Hawe, Hawes; ' des. of eaċaṙ '; a var. of Ó ḣeoċaṙa, q.v.

Ó ḣeaċaṙa, Ó ḣeaċaiṙ—I—*O Haghie, O Haghy,* Haghey, Haughey, Haffy, Hahee, Hawey, Hoey;

'des. of ⲉⲁⲥⲁⲓⲇ' (a var. of ⲉⲟⲥⲁⲓⲇ); an Ulster surname. V. Ó ⲛⲉⲟⲥⲁⲇⲁ.

Ó ⲛⲉⲁⲥⲁⲓⲇⲓⲛ—I—*O Haughine, O Heaghean,* Haughean, Haughian, (Hawkins); 'des. of ⲉⲁⲥⲁⲓⲇⲓⲛ' (dim. of ⲉⲁⲥⲁⲓⲇ); a var. of Ó ⲛⲉⲁⲥⲁⲓⲛ, q.v.

Ó ⲛⲉⲁⲥⲁⲓⲛ—I—*O Heaghane, O Haghaine, O Haghan,* Haughan, Haghan, Haghen, (Hawkins, Haughton); 'des. of ⲉⲁⲥⲁⲛ' (dim. of ⲉⲁⲥⲁⲓⲇ); more anciently Ó ⲛⲉⲁⲥⲁⲇⲁⲓⲛ and Ó ⲛⲉⲟⲥⲁⲅⲁⲓⲛ; the name of an Ulidian family, still well known in Down and Tyrone.

Ó ⲛⲉⲁⲥⲇⲩⲇⲁⲓⲛ—I—Aghoon, Whitesteed; 'des. of ⲉⲁⲥⲇⲩⲇⲁⲛ' (black-steed); a rare Mayo surname. Whitesteed is supposed to be a translation; Blacksteed would be more correct.

Ó ⲛⲉⲁⲥⲣⲁⲓⲛ—I—Haughran, Haran; 'des. of ⲉⲁⲥⲣⲁⲛ.' Cf. ⲙⲁⲅ ⲉⲁⲥⲣⲁⲓⲛ.

Ó ⲛⲉⲁⲥⲧⲁⲓⲣ—II—*O Haghtir,* Hoctor, Hocter; 'des. of Hector'; an old Tipperary surname; still extant in that county.

Ó ⲛⲉⲁⲥⲧⲓⲅⲉⲁⲣⲛⲁ—I—*O Haghierny,* Aherne, &c.; now usually Ó ⲛⲉⲁⲥⲧⲓⲅⲉⲓⲣⲛ, q.v.

Ó ⲛⲉⲁⲥⲧⲓⲅⲉⲓⲣⲛ—I—*O Haghierin, O Hagherne, O Haherne, O Hearne,* Ahearn, Aherin, Aherne, Ahern, Hearne, Hearn, &c.; 'des. of ⲉⲁⲥⲧⲓⲅⲉⲁⲣⲛ' (horselord); also written Ó ⲉⲁⲥⲧⲓⲅⲉⲓⲣⲛ, Ó ⲛⲉⲁⲥⲧⲓⲅⲉⲁⲣⲛⲁ, Ó ⲛⲉⲓⲥⲧⲓⲅⲉⲓⲣⲛ, &c.; a common surname in Cork and Limerick, where it is generally angl. Aherne, and in Waterford, where it is made Hearne. For history of family, see Ó ⲉⲁⲥⲧⲓⲅⲉⲓⲣⲛ.

Ó ⲛⲉⲁⲇⲁⲙⲁⲓⲛ—I—*O Hedevan,* Heduvan, Hedivan; 'des. of ⲉⲁⲇⲁⲙⲁⲛ'; a rare Westmeath surname.

Ó ⲛⲉⲁⲇⲣⲁ, v. ⲛⲉⲁⲅⲣⲁ.

Ó ⲛⲉⲁⲇⲣⲟⲙⲁⲓⲛ—I—*O Hederiman,* Hederman, Hedderman; 'des. of ⲉⲁⲇⲧⲣⲟⲙⲁⲛ' (light, fickle); an old Limerick surname, still well known in that county.

Ó ⲛⲉⲁⲣⲁ—I—*O Heafa,* Heaphy, &c. V. Ó ⲛⲉⲁⲙⲧⲁⲓⲅ.

Ó ⲛⲉⲁⲅⲣⲁ—I—O'Hara, O'Harra, Hara; 'des. of ⲉⲁⲅⲣⲁ'; also written Ó ⲛⲉⲁⲇⲣⲁ. The O'Haras, who are of the same stock as the O'Garas (v. Ó ⲅⲁⲇⲣⲁ), derive their name and descent from eᴀᵹnᴀ, lord of Luighne, who died in the year 926, and were for many centuries lords of Luighne, now the barony of Leyney, in Co. Sligo. Since the 14th century, they were divided into two branches, the heads of which were known respectively as Ó ɦeᴀᵹnᴀ ᴅuiᴅe and Ó ɦeᴀᵹnᴀ Ríᴀᴅᴀċ, i.e., the yellow O'Hara and the speckled or brindled O'Hara. A branch of the family settled early in the Route, Co. Antrim, where they rose to importance and are still well known. The O'Haras of Leyney were all dispossessed at the Cromwellian period, except one family which threw in its lot with the Cromwellians.

Ó ɦeᴀᵹRáɪn—I—*O Harane, O Haran,* Haran, Haren, Harran, Harren, &c. ; ' des. of eᴀᵹnán ' (dim. of eᴀᵹnᴀ) ; an old Galway surname.

Ó ɦeᴀᴌᴀᴅᴀɪᵹ, Ó ɦeᴀᴌᴀɪᴅe, v. Ó ɦeᴀᴌuɪᵹᴄe and Ó ɦeɪᴌɪᴅe.

Ó ɦeᴀᴌuɪᵹᴄe—I—*O Healihie, O Heally, O Healy, O Hely,* Healy, Heally, Hely, Hayles ; ' des. of eᴀᴌᴀᴅᴀċ ' (scientific, ingenious) ; often pronounced Ó ɦeᴀᴌuɪᵹᴄe, but, without doubt, originally Ó ɦeᴀᴌᴀᴅᴀɪᵹ ; the name of an ancient family who, according to Dr. O'Brien, were proprietors of Donoghmore, in the barony of Muskerry, Co. Cork, and are still numerous in that county. See also Ó ɦeɪᴌɪᴅe.

Ó ɦeᴀṁᴀċáɪn, Hevaghan. V. Ó ɦeɪṁeᴀċáɪn.

Ó ɦeᴀṁᴀɪᵹ—I—*O Hevie,* Heavy, Heavey, Havy, Havey, &c. ; a var. of Ó ɦeɪṁɪᵹ, q.v. See also Ó ɦeᴀṁᴄᴀɪᵹ.

Ó ɦeᴀṁáɪn—I—*O Heavane, O Hevane,* Evans, &c. ; a var. of Ó ɦeɪṁɪn, q.v.

Ó ɦeᴀṁᴄᴀɪᵹ—I—*O Heafegh, O Heafa,* Heaphy, Heify ; the same as Ó ɦeᴀṁᴀɪᵹ and Ó ɦeɪṁɪᵹ, q.v. ; a Munster surname, most frequent ɪn Cork and Waterford.

Ó ɦeᴀnᴀċáɪn—I—*O Heneghane,* Heanaghan, Henaghan, Heneghan, Henehan, Henihan, Henekan, Heenan, Bird ; a var., in Co. Mayo, of Ó ɦeɪneᴀċáɪn, q.v. It is sometimes angl. Bird, on the erroneous supposition

562

that it is derived from ' ᴇᴀn,' a bird. No doubt, it
also stands for older Ó ħᴀonᴀċᴀın.

Ó ħᴇᴀnᴀᴅᴀ—I—Heanue, Heaney, Heany; also Ó
ħᴇıneᴀᴅᴀ; a Galway surname, the origin of which
I cannot trace. It is pos. ibly the same as Ó ħᴇᴀnnᴀ,
or Ó ᵹᴇınneᴀᴅᴀ, q.v.

Ó ħᴇᴀnᴀᵹᴀın—I—O Heanagane, O Henegane, O Heni-
gane, Hennigan, Henekan, Bird; a var. of Ó ħᴇᴀn-
ᴀċᴀın, q.v.

Ó ħᴇᴀnᴀıᵹ, Heaney, Heany.

Ó ħᴇᴀnᴀın—I—O Henane, O Hennaine, Henan, Heenan,
Hennan, Heanen, &c.; a var., probably, of Ó ħᴇıᴅ-
neᴀın, q.v.

Ó ħᴇᴀnnᴀ—I—O Heany, O Heney, Heany, Heaney,
Heeny, Heney, &c., Bird; ' des. of ᴇᴀnnᴀ' (Enda);
also written Ó ħᴇınne; the name (1) of a family of Ui
Fiachrach who were formerly proprietors of Imleach-
loisce, in Co. Mayo: (2) of an Eoghanacht family in
the present Co. Limerick; and (3) of a Dalcassian
family in Thomond. This last-named family produced several distinguished ecclesiastics, two of whom,
Donald (1098) and Matthew (1206), filled the see of
Cashel, and one, Connor, that of Killaloe. Connor
died while returning from the Fourth General Council
of Lateran. This surname is to be distinguished from
Ó ħᴇınıᵹ, q.v.

Ó ħᴇᴀnnꞃᴀıc, Ó ħᴇᴀnꞃᴀıc—II—O Henrick, Henrick,
Hanrick, Hendrick, Handrick; a var. of Ó ħᴀnn-
ꞃᴀıc, q.v.

Ó ħᴇᴀꞃᴀın—I—O Harrane, O Haran, O Heron, O'Harran,
O'Haran, O'Hern, Haran, Harran, Heran, Herran,
Heron, Herron, Hearn, Herne; ' des. of ᴇᴀꞃᴀᴅᴀn'
(dim. of ᴇᴀꞃᴀᴅ, fear, dread); older Ó ħᴇᴀꞃᴀᴅᴀın; the
name of an Oriel family who were lords of Ui Breasail
Macha, in the barony of Oneilland, Co. Armagh; still
common in the north of Ireland.

Ó ħᴇᴀꞃᴀıꞃín, Ó ħᴇᴀꞃᴀꞃᴀın—I—O Harreryne, O
Hererane, Herrerin, Herreran; ' des. of ᴇᴀꞃᴀıꞃín,' or
' ᴇᴀꞃᴀꞃᴀn' (dim. of ᴇᴀꞃᴀꞃ); a rare and scattered

surname. It still survives in parts of Ulster and Louth. Ó neᴀpᴀıp, angl. O Herrere, also once existed. In the Annals of Ulster, at the year 1205, it is recorded that mᴀeⱡⱱpıȝⱦe Uᴀ nepᴀpᴀn of Derry was chosen to be successor of St. Brendan, that is, very probably, made Bishop of Clonfert.

Ó neᴀRCᴀ—I—O Herke, Herky ; a var. of Ó neıpc, q.v. ; very rare.

Ó neᴀRĊᴀⱱᴀ, Ó neᴀRĊᴀıⱱ—I—O Harroughow, O Harrochoe, O Horrochoe, O Horchoy, O Hurkoy, O Hurowe, Haraghy, Hiraghy, Harrihy, Harkey, Horohoe, Horahoe, Harroe, Hurroe, (Hore, Hoare, Harris, Harrison) ; ' des. of eᴀpċᴀıⱱ ' (noble warrior) ; an old Connacht surname, now variously anglicised, and in Mayo disguised as Harris and Harrison. It was not uncommon in Tipperary in the 16th and 17th centuries, but I have not been able to trace any modern angl. form in that county.

Ó neᴀRCᴀın—I—O Harkane, O Harkan, Harkan, Harkin, Harkins ; ' des. of eᴀpcᴀn ' (dim. of eᴀpc, red, speckled) ; a common surname in Donegal and Derry. See also Ó nOpcᴀın.

Ó neᴀRĊᴀıR—I—Harragher, Harraher ; a var. of Ó ⱡeᴀpcᴀıp (q.v.), owing to the aspiration of the initial ⱡ ; very rare.

Ó neᴀRȝᴀıl—I—O Herrall, O Herrell, Harrell, Harrel, Herald, &c. ; a var. of Ó ⱡeᴀpȝᴀıl (q.v.), owing to the aspiration of the initial ⱡ.

Ó neᴀRȝᴀıle—I—O Harrily, O Harely, Harrily, Harley, Herley, Herly ; a var. of Ó ⱡeᴀppȝᴀıle, q.v. Cf. Ó neᴀpȝᴀıl.

Ó neᴀRnᴀın—I—O Hernane, O Harnan, O Hortenan, Hernon, Harnon, Hartnane, Hertnan, Hertnon, (Heffernan) ; (1) ' des. of eᴀpnᴀn ' (dim. of eᴀpnᴀ, knowing, experienced) ; and (2) a short form in Munster of Ó nıⱡeᴀpnᴀın, q.v.

Ó neıĊⱦıȝeıRn, v. Ó neᴀċⱦıȝeıpn.

Ó neıⱱeᴀⱱᴀ, v. Ó neıⱱıⱱ.

Ó neıⱱeᴀȝᴀın—I—O Hettigane, O Hedeghan, Hedegan,

Hedigan, Haddigan; 'des. of ᴇ1ᴅᴇᴀᴈᴀ́n'; more anciently Ó ɴᴇ1ᴄᴇᴀᴈᴀ́n and ṁᴀᴄ ᴇ1ᴅᴇᴀᴈᴀ́1n; the name of an ecclesiastical family at Elphin, Co. Roscommon. William O Hetigan was Bishop of Elphin about the middle of the 15th century. The name is now more commonly Ó ɴᴇ1ᴅᴇᴀ́1n, q.v. Ó ɴᴇ1ᴄᴇᴀᴈᴀ́1n was also the name of a family of Cinel Eoghain in Ulster, but in that province it is generally changed to ṁᴀᴈ ᴇ1ᴄᴇᴀᴈᴀ́1n, q.v. MacFirbis also mentions a midland family of the same name.

Ó ɴᴇ1ᴅᴇᴀ́1n, Ó ɴᴇ1ᴅᴇᴀ́1n—I—*O Hedayne, O Hedane, O Heyden,* Heden, Headen, Haden, Hayden, Haydon, &c. ; ' des. of ᴇ1ᴅᴇᴀᴅᴀ́n ' (dim. of ᴇ1ᴅᴇᴀᴅ) ; a var. of Ó ɴᴇ1ᴅ1n and Ó ɴᴇ1ᴅᴇᴀᴈᴀ́1n, q.v. In Roscommon it probably represents the older Ó ɴᴇ1ᴅᴇᴀᴈᴀ́1n or Ó ɴᴇ1ᴄᴇᴀᴈᴀ́1n, q.v.

Ó ɴᴇ1ᴅ1ᴅ—I—*O Hidia,* Haidy, Haidee ; ' des. of ᴇ1ᴅᴇᴀᴅ ' ; also Ó ɴᴇ1ᴅᴇᴀᴅᴀ ; a modern form of Ó ɴᴀ1ᴅ1ᴄ, or Ó ɴᴀ1ᴅ1ᴅᴇ, q.v. ; current in the neighbourhood of Shrule, where it has been long established.

Ó ɴᴇ1ᴅ1n, Ó ɴᴇ1ᴅ1n—I—*O Hedine, O Headyne, O Heden, O Headen, O Hedian, O Heyden,* Heden, Headen, Hadian, Haydin, Hayden, Haydon, &c. ; ' des of ᴇ1ᴅ1ᴅ1n ' (dim. of ᴇ1ᴅᴇᴀᴅ) ; a var. of Ó ɴᴇ1ᴅᴇᴀ́1n, q.v. ; formerly a common surname, especially in Roscommon, Tipperary and South Leinster. See also Ó ɴᴀ1ᴅ1n, and cf. Ó ɴᴇ1ᴅ1ᴅ and Ó ɴᴇ1ᴅᴇᴀᴈᴀ́1n.

Ó ɴᴇ1ᴅ1n—I—*O Heine, O Heyne, O Hine, O Hyne,* Heines, Hynes, Hyndes, &c. ; ' des. of ᴇ1ᴅᴇᴀn ' (ivy) ; the name of a Galway family who derive their descent from the celebrated Guaire Aidhne, King of Connacht in the 7th century, and for the space of six hundred years were the chief family of Ui Fiachrach Aidhne and lords of Aidhne, a district co-extensive with the diocese of Kilmacduagh. ṁᴀᴏʟʀᴜᴀnᴀ1ᴅ Ó ɴᴇ1ᴅ1n, lord of Aidhne, who fell at Clontarf, in 1014, was the first person to bear the surname. There was also a family of the name. formerly of considerable importance seated in the neighbourhood of Caherconlish, Co. Limerick, but it is now almost extinct. The name is however still common in Galway and the adjoining parts of Co. Clare.

Ó ḣéiⱱín—I—*O Heane, O Haine, O Hayne,* Haines, Haynes, Hynes ; a var. of Ó ḣeiⱱin, q.v. ; rare and scattered.

Ó ḣeiⱱiᴿsceóil—I—*O Hederscoll, O Hidirscoll,* O'Driscoll, Driscoll ; ' des. of eiⱱiⱱⱱceóil ' (interpreter); now shortened to Ó Oⱱuⱱceóil, q.v. ; the name of an ancient West Cork family who were chiefs of Corca Laoighdhe, a district which originally embraced the whole of the south-west of Co. Cork, namely, the baronies of Carbery, Beare and Bantry, but shortly after the Anglo-Norman invasion was narrowed down, through the encroachments of the O'Donovans, O'Mahonys and O'Sullivans, to a strip of sea-coast around the bay of Baltimore. The O'Driscolls, however, possessed considerable power and had several strong castles even as late as the beginning of the 17th century. They took an active part in the wars in Munster in the reign of Elizabeth. After the defeat of Kinsale, their property was confiscated and given to Lord Castlehaven.

Ó ḣeiⱱneaċáin, v. Ó ḣéineaċáin.

Ó ḣeiⱱneáin—I—*O Hinane, O Hynane,* Hinan, Hynan ; ' des. of eiⱱⱱneán ' (dim. of eiⱱⱱean, ivy) ; a scattered surname. See also Ó ḣéanáin.

Ó ḣeiⱱníⱱ—I—*O Hynye,* Hyney, Hiney ; ' des. of eiⱱⱱneaċ ' ; a var. of Ó ḣaoⱱnaiⱱ, q.v.

Ó ḣeiⱱceaᴿcaiⱱ, Ó ḣeiⱱⱱeaᴿcaiⱱ—I—*O Heagertie, O Hegertie, O Hagirtie,* O'Hegarty, Hegarty, Hegerty, Hagarty, Higerty, &c., (Hoverty) ; ' des. of eiⱱⱱceaⱱⱱⱱ ' (unjust) ; the name of a family of Cinel Eoghain, in Tyrone, Derry and Donegal. A branch of the family settled in Cork, where the name is now common. Cf. Ó ḣáⱱⱱaⱱⱱaiⱱ.

Ó ḣeiⱱⱱníⱱ, Ó ḣeiⱱⱱníⱱ—I—*O Hicknie, O Hignie,* Hegney, Heagney, Haigney ; ' des. of eiⱱⱱneaċ ' ; the name of an Oriel family who in the 11th and 12th centuries

were lords of Fermanagh and sometimes of all Oriel ;
(2) of another family of the same race who were chiefs
of Clann Chearnaigh, apparently in the east of the
present Co. Armagh ; and (3) of a Mayo family who
were anciently chiefs of Clann Laoghaire, in Tirawley.
The name is now almost universally changed to Ó
ńéiġniż, or Ó ńéiniż, q.v.

Ó neilżeaⱅáın—I—Ellison.

Ó ńéilıⱦe, Ó ńéiliże—I—*O Healie, O Healy, O Hely,*
Healy, Hely, &c. ; ' des. of ealⱶaⱶ ' (scientific,
ingenious) ; sometimes pronounced Ó ńealⱶaıⱦe (or
Ó ńealⱶaⱶaiż) and Ó ńeiliⱦe ; the name of a Sligo
family who formerly possessed the Curlews, Ballina-
fad, and the district lying around the western shore
of Lough Arrow, and had their chief residence at
Ⱶaile Uí éiliⱦe, angl. Ballyhely, in the present
demesne of Hollybrooke. The O'Helys ranked among
the gentry of Co. Sligo down to the Cromwellian period.
The late Most Rev. John Healy, Archbishop of Tuam,
was a scion of this ancient family. In the 16th
century the name was very widely spread in Connacht
and Leinster ; and Ó ńéiliⱦe, it may be remarked,
is quite common in Munster. See Ó ńéaluıżⱶe.

Ó ńéiṁeaċáın—I—Hevaghan ; ' des. of éiṁeaċán '
(dim. of éiṁeaċ, swift) ; the name (1) of a family of
Ui Fiachrach in Co. Mayo ; and (2) of a family of Cinel
Fhiachach, in Co. Westmeath. It is now extremely
rare, having been, most probably, changed to Ó
ńéiṁiż, q.v.

Ó ńéiṁiż—I—*O Hevie,* Hevey, Heavy, Heavey, &c. ;
' des of éiṁeaċ '(swift) ; probably short for Ó ńéiṁeaċáın, q.v.   See also Ó ńéaṁaiż and Ó ńéaṁⱶaiż,
which are variants.

Ó ńéiṁín—I—*O Hevine,* Evins, Evens, Evans ; ' des. of
éiṁín ' (dim. of eiṁ, swift, active) ; also Ó ńéaṁáın,
q.v. ; an old surname in Ormond and Thomond ; still
represented in Munster.

Ó ńéiṁⱤín—I—Heverine, Heveran, Heveron, Hefferin,
&c. ; ' des. of éiṁⱤín ' (dim. of éiṁeaⱤ) ; the name of

a family of Cinel Eoghain, still extant in Mayo. O'Donovan erroneously supposed it to be a corruption of Ó ⁿUacṁaṗáin. It is, however, mentioned by MacFirbis.

Ó ⁿéineacáin—I—*O Henechan, O Heneghane*, Heanaghan, Henaghan, Henehan, Henihan, Henekan, (Heenan), Bird; ' des. of eiṫneacán '; the name of a family of Ui Fiachrach in Co. Mayo, who were formerly proprietors of a large estate in the parishes of Manulla and Balla; still common in that county, sometimes pronounced Ó ⁿéanacáin, and angl. Bird, being erroneously supposed to be derived from ' éan,' a bird.

Ó ⁿéineaṫ́a, v. Ó ⁿéanaṫa.

Ó ⁿéiniⱫ—I—*O Heany, O Heney*, Heany, Heaney, Heeny, &c., Bird; a modernised form of Ó ⁿeiⱫniⱫ, q.v.; often angl. Bird, owing to the erroneous notion that it is derived from ' éan,' a bird.

Ó ⁿéinín—I—*O Heanyne, O Henyne*, Heanen, &c.; a var. of Ó ⁿéanáin, q.v.

Ó ⁿéinne, v. Ó ⁿéanna.

Ó ⁿéiR—I—*O Haer*, O'Hare, Hare, Haire; a popular form of Ó ⁿíṗ, q.v.

Ó ⁿeiRC—I—*O Herke, O Herrick*, Erke, Herrick, Herricks, Harricks; ' des. of eaṗc ' (red, speckled); the name (I) of an Oriel family who were chiefs of Ui Fiachrach Finn, and seated along the river Derg, in the northwest of Co. Tyrone; and (2) of a Tipperary family. The name seems to have disappeared from Ulster, having, most probably, been changed to Ó ⁿeaṗcáin (q.v.), but is still represented in Munster.

Ó ⁿeiReaṁóin—I—*O Hervan*, Ervine, Erwin, Irvine, Irwin; ' des. of eiṗeaṁón '; a rare South of Ireland surname. Aeṫ Ó ⁿeiṗeaṁóin was Bishop of Kildare at the end of the IIth century.

Ó ⁿeisleanáin—I—*O Hislenane*, (Heslin); ' des. of eiṗleanán '; a Breifney surname, now shortened to Ó ⁿeiṗlin, q.v.

Ó ⁿeislin—I—*O Hisclan*, Heslin; a shortened form of Ó ⁿeiṗleanáin, q.v.

Ó ṅeoċaċ—I—Hough; 'des. of eoċaıṫ' (possessing cattle); a var. of Ó ṅeaċaċ and Ó ṅeoċaṫa, q.v.

Ó ṅeoċaṫa—I—O Hoa, Howe, Howes, &c.; 'des. of eoċaıṫ'; also Ó ṅeoċaċ, Ó ṅeoċaıṫ, q.v.; a var. of Ó ṅeaċaṫa, q.v.; the name (1) of an Ulster family who, in the 11th and 12th centuries, were kings of Ulidia, but lost their dignity soon after the Anglo-Norman invasion; still common in Down and Antrim; and (2) of a Meath family who were chiefs of Cinel Aonghusa, and are still numerous in Leinster.

Ó ṅeoċaᵹáın—I—O Hoghegane, Houghegan, (Hogan); 'des. of eoċaᵹán' (dim of eoċaıṫ); an old Ulidian surname, afterwards changed to Ó ṅeaċáın, q.v.; now found only in Co. Galway, where it is sometimes disguised under the angl. form of Hogan.

Ó ṅeoċaıṫ—I—O Hohy, O Hoye, O Huky, Houghy, Hughey, Howie, Howey, Howay, Hoey, Huey, Hoye, Hoy, &c.; 'des. of eoċaıṫ' a var of Ó ṅeoċaṫa, q.v. See also Ó ṅeaċaıṫ.

Ó ṅeoċaıṫín—I—O Houghine, O Hughian; a var. of Ó ṅeaċaṫín, q.v.

Ó ṅeoṫasa, Ó ṅeoṫusa—I—O Hoasy, O Hosey, O Hossy, Hosey, Hussey, (Oswell, Oswald); 'des. of eoṫar'; also written Ó ṅeoᵹara, q.v.; the name of a family of Cinel Eoghain, in Ulster, who were chiefs of Cinel Tighearnaigh, but afterwards migrated to Fermanagh, where they became bards to the Maguires. The family produced several distinguished literary men, among them Eochaidh O hEodhasa and Bonaventure O hEodhasa who flourished at the beginning of the 17th century. The name is now very rare in Ulster, having, according to O'Donovan, been changed to Oswell, which apparently has been more recently further changed to Oswald. Before the end of the 16th century, it had spread to Leinster and Munster, but its angl. forms in these provinces cannot now be distinguished from the Anglo-Irish surname, Hussey.

Ó ṅeoᵹáın—I—O Hoane, O Howen, O Hoyne, Howen, Hone, Hoyne, Owen, Owens, Hoynes, Hoins, (Hynes);

'des. of Eoġan' (well-born); the name (1) of a Dalcassian family in Clare, who, according to Keating, are of the same stock as the O'Neills of Thomond; and (2) of an ecclesiastical family at Lough Erne, in the diocese of Clogher; now very common in Ulster, angl. Owens, and known in every part of Ireland.

Ó hEoġanáin—I—O'Honan, Honan; 'des. of Eoġanán, (dim. of Eoġan); a Thomond surname.

Ó hEoġasa—I—*O Hogasa*, Hosey, Hussey; a var. of Ó hEoḋasa, q.v.

Ó hEóluis, Ó hEólusa—I—Olus; 'des. of Eolus' (knowledge); the name of a Leitrim family who were anciently chiefs of Muinntear Eoluis, in that county. They afterwards changed their name to **Mac Raġnaill**, q.v. O'Donovan, however, writes: "This family name is still in use and anglicised Olus." It must be extremely rare.

Ó hIarḟlaṫa, Ó hIarlaiṫe, Ó hIarlaṫa—I—*O Hierlehy, O Herlehey, O Hurlihie*, O'Herlihy, Herlihy, Herley, (Hurley); 'des. of Iarḟlaiṫ' (under-lord); the name of an ecclesiastical family who were hereditary erenaghs of St. Gobnait's church at Ballyvourny, Co. Cork; still common in Cork and Kerry, but sometimes disguised under the angl. form of Hurley.

Ó hIarnáin—I—*O Hiernan, O Hernane*, Hearnon, Hernon; 'des. of Iarnán'; the same as Ó hEarnáin, q.v.; the name (1) of a family of Ui Fiachrach, in Co. Mayo, and (2) of a family of Corca Laoighdhe, in south-west Cork.

Ó hÍceaḋa, Ó hÍciḋe—III—*O Hickee*, O'Hickey, Hickey, Hickie; 'des. of Íceaḋ' (healer); the name of a medical family of Dalcassian origin who were hereditary physicians to the O'Briens and other families in Thomond. They were seated at Ballyhickey, in the parish of Clooney, Co. Clare. The name is now common all through Munster.

Ó hIfearnáin—I—*O Hiffernane, O Hiffernan, O Hifferan*, Hiffernan, Heffernan, Heffernon, Hefferan, &c.; 'des. of Ifearnán'; the name of an ancient family, who were chiefs of Uaithne-Cliach, now the barony of Owneybeg, in the east of Co. Limerick, until dispossessed by the O'Mulryans in the 14th century; still very common in Limerick and Tipperary, and known all over Munster; sometimes shortened to Ó ꝼeꝛnáin and Ó ꞃeaꞃnáin, q.v.

Ó ꞃinneáċꞇaiᵹ—I—Hinnerty, Hennerty, Hingerty. V. Ó ꞃionnáċꞇaiᵹ.

Ó ꞃinneiꞃᵹe—I—O Hinnerie, O Hennerey, O Henry, Henery, Henry, Hendry; 'des. of inneiꞃᵹe' (the rising, early riser); the name of a family of Cinel Eoghain, who were chiefs of Cuileanntrach, in Co. Tyrone. Cian Ó ꞃinneiꞃᵹe was one of the chiefs who fell at the battle of Down in 1250. The name is very common in Ulster.

Ó ꞃinnꞃeáċꞇaiᵹ, v. Ó ꞃanꞃaċꞇaiᵹ.

Ó ꞃinnꞃeáin, v. Ó ꞃionnꞃáin.

Ó ꞃinꞃeáċꞇaiᵹ, v. Ó ꞃanꞃaċꞇaiᵹ.

Ó ꞃioláin—I—O Hillane, Hillane, Hillan, (Hyland, Holland, Whelan); a var. of Ó ꞃáoláin, q.v., in the spoken language of Connacht. See also Ó ꞃoláin.

Ó ꞃiolꞃaċáin, Eagleton, Eggleton. V. Mac loꞇꞃaċáin.

Ó ꞃiomaiꞃ, Ó ꞃíomaiꞃ—II—O Hyver, O Heiver, O Hewer, O Hiur, O Houre, O Hoare, O Hawrde, O'Hure, Heever, Hever, Hoare, Howard, Ivors, Ivers, Eivers, &c.; 'des. of iomaꞃ' or 'íomaꞃ' (the Norse personal name Ivarr); the name (1) of a Sligo family of the Ui Fiachrach race who were formerly seated at Leacan, now angl. Lackan, on the east side of Killala Bay; and (2) of a Thomond family, now numerous in Clare and Limerick, but generally known in English as Howards.

Ó ꞃiomna, Ellmore.

Ó ꞃionᵹaꞃoail—I—O Hingerdell, O Hungerdell, O Higerdell, (Harrington); 'des. of ionᵹaꞃoal'; now pronounced Ó ꞃúꞃoail; the name of well-known and numerous family in West Cork and South Kerry; also formerly common in Tipperary; now always angl. Harrington.

Ó níonṁáíne—I—Nooney ; ' des. of íonṁáíne ' (love). Cf. Ó níonṁáíneáín.

Ó níonṁáíneáín—I—O Hununane, O Hinownan, Nunan, Noonan ; ' des. of íonṁáíneán ' (dim. of íonṁáín, beloved) ; now shortened to Ó nuánáín ; the name of an ecclesiastical family who were erenaghs of the church of St. Beretchert at Tullylease, in the north-west of Co. Cork, and are now numerous in Cork, Limerick, Tipperary and Clare. The Four Masters at the year 1230 record the death of Ɗonnꞩléíḃe Ua níonṁáíneáín a holy monk of Boyle.

Ó níonnáċċáíꝣ—I—O Hanortye, Hinnerty, Hennerty, Hannerty, Hanaty ; also Ó nínneáċċáíꝣ, q.v. ; a var. of Ó ꝼíonnáċċáíꝣ, through the aspiration of the initial ꝼ.

Ó níonnꝣáíl, Ó níonnꝣáíle—I—O Hannyle, O Henyll, Hannell, Hennelly ; var. of Ó ꝼíonnꝣáíl, Ó ꝼíonnꝣáíle (q.v.) owing to the aspiration of the initial ꝼ.

Ó níonnꞃáḃáín, Ó níonnꞃáín, Ó níonꞃáín—I— O Heneran, Henrion ; a var. of Ó náꞃꝛáḃáín, q.v. This form of the surname was peculiar to Westmeath.

Ó níoꞃuáíɗ—I—O Hiery, O Heyry, Heary, Heery ; ' des. of íoꞃuáɗ ' ; a rare Leinster surname.

Ó níꞃ—I—O Hier, O Hire, O Heere, O'Hear, O'Hare, O'Haire, Hear, Heare, Hare, Hair, Haire ; ' des. of íꞃ ' ; the name of an Oriel family, akin to that of Ó ná nluáín (q.v.), who were chiefs of Oirtheara, now the baronies of Orier in the east of Co. Armagh ; to be distinguished from Ó noíċíꞃ (q.v.) of Thomond, which is similarly anglicised. See also Ó néíꞃ.

Ó níꞃꝣíl—I—O Hirill, O Hirell, Hirill, Hirl ; a var. of Ó ꝼíꞃꝣíl, owing to the aspiration of the initial ꝼ. Cf. Ó neáꞃꝣáíl.

Ó níꞃꝣíle—I—O Hirrely, O Hirley, Hirrely, Hirley, Herley ; a var. of Ó ꝼíꞃꝣíle, or Ó ꝼíꞃꝣíl (q.v.), through the aspiration of the initial ꝼ ; very rare.

Ó níċċeálláíꝣ—I—O Hihilly, O Hilay, Hilly, Hillee ; a var. of Ó ꝼíċċeálláíꝣ (q.v.), owing to the aspiration of the initial ꝼ; extremely rare and found only in Kerry, where it has been in use since the 16th century. The family was located in the neighbourhood of Tralee.

Ó hÓ'ÚRA, O'Hora.

Ó hÓ'ÚRAȝÁIn—I—*O Hourigaine, O Hourigan,* Hourigan; 'des. of O'ópaȝán' (dim. of o'ópa, pale, dark-grey); apparently the name of a family of Corca Laoighdhe, in south-west of Co. Cork, but it cannot now be distinguished in pronunciation from Ó hAnnpa-ȝáin (q.v.), which is most probably the origin in Tipperary and Limerick.

Ó hÓ'ÚRÁIn—I—*O Howrane, O Horane,* Horan; 'des. of O'ópán' (dim. of o'óap, pale, dark-grey); not now distinguishable in pronunciation from Ó hAnnpáin and Ó hUȝpóin, q.v.

Ó hÓȝÁIn—I—*O Hogaine, O Hogane, O Hogan,* Hogan; 'des. of Óȝán' (dim. of óȝ, young); the name (1) of a Dalcassian family who derive their descent from Coscrach, uncle of Brian Boru, and were seated at Ardcrony, about four miles to the north of Nenagh, in Co. Tipperary; and (2) of a family of Corca Laoighdhe, in the south-west of Co. Cork; now very common in Munster, especially in Tipperary, Limerick, Clare and Cork. See Ó hÁȝáin, which is the Ulster form of this surname.

Ó hÓȝAIRC—I—Hogart; short for Ó hÓȝapcaiȝ, q.v. Cf. Ó hÁȝaipc.

Ó hOȝAIRC—I—Howard; short for Ó hOȝapcaiȝ, q.v.

Ó hÓȝARCAIȝ—I—*O Hogertie,* Hogarty, Hogerty, (Hegarty); a var. of Ó ꝼóȝapcaiȝ (q.v.), owing to the aspiration of the initial ꝼ.

Ó hOȝARCAIȝ—I—*O Hoghertie,* Hoverty, (Hegarty); a var. of Ó hÓȝapcaiȝ, q.v. Cf. Ó hAȝapcaiȝ.

Ó hOȝLA'ÚA—I—*O Holowe,* Holey; a var. of Ó ꝼoȝla'úa (q.v.), owing to the aspiration of the initial ꝼ; very rare.

Ó hOȝRÁIn, v. Ó hUȝpóin.

Ó hOIΌICÍn, v. hoiΌicín.

Ó ɳoɩċɩʀ—I—*O Hegher,* O'Hehir, O'Hare, Hegher,
Hehir, Haier, Herr, &c. ; a var. of Ó ɳᴀɩċɩᴩ, q.v.

Ó ɳoɩleᴀɩɳ—I—*O Hilane, O Helane, O Hellan,* Hyland,
(Whelan) ; a corruption of Ó ɳᴀolᴀɩɳ, q.v.

Ó ɳóɩleᴀɩɳ—I—*O Heolane, O Holane,* Holian, (O'Lyons) ;
a corruption of Ó ɳᴀolᴀɩɳ, q.v.

Ó ɳoɩʀeᴀċᴛᴀɩ⁊—I—*O Heraghty, O Heyrity, O Heraght,*
Hearaghty, Heraghty, Heraty, (Harty), Erraught,
Erought, (Geraghty, Harrington, O'Connor) ; ' des. of
Oɩᴩeᴀċᴛᴀċ ' (holding or frequenting assemblies) ; the
name of several distinct families, formerly located in
Galway, Westmeath and Donegal ; now most frequent
in Donegal and Mayo ; often disguised under the angl.
forms of Harty, Geraghty, Harrington, and even
O'Connor. Nearly all the members of this family in
the neighbourhood of Abbeyfeale have, for a peculiar
local reason, now adopted the surname of O'Connor.

Ó ɳoɩsce, v. Ó ɳuɩᴩce.

Ó ɳoɩscíɳ, v. Ó ɳuɩᴩcɩɳ.

Ó ɳoɩseᴀɩɳ—I—*O Hishane,* Hishon ; ' des. of Oɩᴩeᴀɳ '
(dim. of oᴩ, a deer) ; a var. of Ó ɳoɩᴩɩɳ, q.v. ; an old
Tipperary surname.

Ó ɳoɩsíɳ—I—*O Hussine, O Hushin,* Hussian, Hessian,
Hession, Hishon ; ' des. of Oɩᴩɩɳ ' (dim. of oᴩ, a deer) ;
an old surname in Connacht, where it is still common.
Two members of this family filled the see of Tuam in
the 11th and 12th centuries. Ó ɳoɩᴩɩɳ seems to have
been also an alias in Munster for Ó ɳoɩᴩeᴀɩɳ, q.v.

Ó ɳoɩsᴛíɳ—II—*O Hustyne, O Hustin,* Histon, Hestin,
Hestion, Hasting, Hastings, Hestings ; ' des of
Oɩᴩᴛɩɳ ' (a Norse personal name) ; the name of a
Connacht family who were followers of MacDermott
of Moylurg ; still common in Connacht, especially in
Mayo. Some of the family had settled before the end
of the 16th century in Limerick and Kerry, where
their descendants are still to be met with. The name
is now also common in Clare.

Ó ɳoɩsᴛɩʀ, Hester ; a Connacht surname, not uncommon
in Roscommon and Mayo. I cannot trace its origin.

Ó noláin—I—*O Holane, O Hollan, O Holland,* Holland, (Hyland, Whelan) ; a corruption of Ó náoláin, q.v.

Ó nonċon—I—*O Honechan,* Unehan, Ounihan, (Donegan) ; ' des. of Onċú ' (a leopard, warrior) ; the name of a Leinster family who, prior to the Anglo-Norman invasion, were seated in the north of Ui Feilme, in the neighbourhood of the town of Tullow, in Co. Carlow ; now very rare.

Ó nóRᴀ, O'Hora.

Ó noRcáin—I—*O Hurkan,* Horkan, Harkon, Horkin, Harkin, Harkins, Arkins ; ' des. of Opcán ' (dim. of opc, a pig) ; a common surname in Mayo and Clare ; but, not improbably, it is a corruption of Ó neapcáin, q.v.

Ó nosáin—I—*O Hassane, O Hassan,* Hassan, Hasson, Hassin ; ' des. of Opán ' (dim. of op, a deer) ; the name of an old family in Derry and Tyrone.

Ó nuᴀ▯ᴀ—I—Huddy ; ' des. of uᴀ▯ᴀ.'

Ó nuᴀ▯ᴀıᵹ, O'Huadhaigh.

Ó nuᴀını▯e, Ó nuᴀıċne—I—*O Honie, O Howny,* Hooney, (?) Houghney, Green ; ' des. of uᴀıċne ' (green) ; written Ó nuᴀını▯e by Keating and Ó nuᴀıċnıᵹ by the Four Masters ; the name (1) of a Cork family who were followers of O Laoghaire of Corca Laoighdhe ; and (2) of a Thomond family who, however, have long since changed it to Ó nuᴀıċnín, q.v.

Ó nuᴀıċnín—I—*O Hownyn, O Hunnyn,* Houneen, Huneen, Honeen, Oonin, Green, Greene ; ' des. of uᴀıċnín ' (dim. of uᴀıċne, green) ; written Ó nuᴀını▯e by Keating ; the name of a Dalcassian family in Thomond ; now very often anglicised Greene, by translation.

Ó nuᴀllᴀċáin—I—*O Huolighane, O Holeghane, O Holohan,* O'Houlihan, Houlihan, Hoolihan, Holohan, (Holland, Nolan), &c. ; ' des. of uᴀllᴀċán ' (dim. of uᴀllᴀċ, proud) ; the name of several distinct families, the best known being those of Offaly and Thomond. The name was also very common in West Cork,

575

where it is now often angl. Holland ; also common in
Mayo and Roscommon, where it is angl. Nolan. See
Ó Nuallacáin.

Ó hUallaig—I—*O Howley, O Howlig*, Howley ; ' des.
of Uallac ' (proud) ; apparently a var. of Ó hUallacáin, q.v. See also Ó fuallaig.

Ó hUamnacáin—I—*O Honaghane, O Hownighan*,
Honahan ; ' des. of Uamnacán ' (dim. of uamnac,
fearful, dreadful).

Ó hUarguis—I—(*O Fworishe*), Horish ; ' des. of Uar-
gur ' (cold-choice) ; corruptly Ó hUaruirce, q.v. ;
the name of an Ulster family who were anciently lords
of Ui Meith ; now scattered through West Ulster and
North Connacht, where, owing to local corruptions,
it is variously anglicised. See Ó fuarguir, Ó fuar-
uirce, Ó Tuaruir, Ó Tuaruirc, Ó hUirce, &c.

Ó hUaruisce—I—*O Horiske*, Hourisky, Horisky,
Waters, Watters, Coldwell, Caldwell, &c. ; a corruption of Ó hUarguir, q.v. ; popularly supposed to be
derived from ' fuar,' cold, and ' uirce,' water, and so
' translated ' Waters, Coldwell, &c.

Ó hUbáin—I—*O Hubane, O Howbane*, Huban, Hooban,
Hoban ; ' des. of Ubán ' ; a Mayo surname. Mac-
Firbis names ' Clann Ubain ' in Connacht among the
branches of Cinel Eoghain of Ulster.

Ó hUgróin—I—*O Hurrone, O Hurrane, O Horan*, Horan ;
' des. of Ugrón ' ; now corrupted to Ó hOgráin ; the
name (1) of a branch of the Ui Maine who were seated
in the parish of Clonrush, in the south of Co. Galway,
where they were very numerous and possessed considerable property down to the Cromwellian confiscations ; and (2) of an ecclesiastical family who were
coarbs of St. Mochua at Balla, Co. Mayo. Eóin Ó
hUgróin, a member of this family, was appointed
Bishop of Elphin, in 1245, but died the next year.
The name, both in Galway and in Mayo, has long been
corrupted to Ó hOgráin, and in the 16th century was
generally angl. O Horane, or O Horan. Cf. Ó Mugróin, now Ó Mográin.

Ó huıȯ—I—O'Hood, Hood ; ' des. of *uȯ ' ; the name of
an Ulster family who were bards to the O'Neills of
Clanaboy. The Annals of Ulster, at the year 1485,
record the slaying of bⱼⱼⱼⱼⱼ uⱼ huıȯ, " an honoured
poet." Séⱼⱼⱼ Ó huıȯ, another distinguished poet
of this family, flourished in the latter part of the 17th
century. The name is still extant in Antrim and
Derry.

Ó huıȯır—I—Hoar, Hoare, Hore ; ' des. of Oȯⱼⱼ '
(dark-grey) ; a rare Cork surname.

Ó huıȯrín—I—O Heerine, O Herine, O Heverine, O
Heveren, O Hevren, Hearon, Heron, Hearn, Herne,
Heveran, Heveron, Hefferan, Heffron, &c. ; ' des. of
uıȯⱼⱼⱼ ' (dim. of oȯⱼⱼ, pale, dark-grey) ; the name
of an Offaly family, still extant in Leinster and Munster, but its angl. forms can hardly be now distinguished from those of several other surnames, as :
Ó heⱼccⱼ̇ⱼⱼⱼⱼ, Ó hípeⱼⱼⱼⱼⱼ, Ó heⱼⱼⱼⱼ, Ó hⱼⱼ̇-
ⱼⱼⱼⱼ, and Ó heⱼⱼⱼⱼ, q.v. To this family, no doubt,
belonged the learned historian, Giolla na Naomh O
hUidhrin, who completed the celebrated poem on
the families of Ireland which had been commenced
by John O Dubhagain.

Ó huıⱼⱼ, Ó huıⱼⱼⱼ, Ó huıⱼⱼⱼⱼ—I—O Higgin, O
Higgen, O'Higgins, Higgins, Higgens ; ' des. of uıⱼⱼ '
(knowledge, skill, ingenuity) ; the name of a branch
of the southern Ui Neill, in the present Co. Westmeath, and one of the most distinguished literary
families in Ireland. The Four Masters mention no
fewer than eleven poets and professors of poetry of
the name. A branch of the family settled in Co.
Sligo, where they acquired large estates in the parishes
of Achonry and Kilmacteige which they retained
down to the Cromwellian confiscations. The name
is now common in most parts of Ireland. Ó huıⱼⱼ
is still in use in East Cork. Ó huıⱼⱼⱼ probably represents an older form *Ó huıⱼⱼⱼⱼ, angl. O'Higgan,
O'Higan ; while Ó huıⱼⱼ is a dialectical variant.

Ó huırȾuıle, v. Ó huⱼⱼⱼⱼⱼ.

Ó ɦuisce—I—*O Hiskie, O Hesky,* Hiskey, Waters,
Watters ; a Connacht surname ; sometimes pronounced
Ó ɦOirce ; doubtless a corruption of Ó ɦuarᵹuir,
q.v. See also Ó ɦuirin.

Ó ɦuiscín—I—Heskin, Hoskins, Waters, Watters ; a
Galway surname ; generally pronounced Ó ɦOircín ;
probably of same origin as Ó ɦuirce, q.v.

Ó ɦuiseáin, v. Ó ɦOireáin.

Ó ɦuisín, v. Ó ɦOirín.

Ó ɦulᴛacáin—I—*O Holteghan,* Hultaghan, Hultahan,
Haltigan, (Nolan) ; ' des. of ulᴛacán ' (dim. of ' ulᴛac,'
the Ultonian) ; a rare Fermanagh surname ; often
disguised under the angl. form of Nolan.

Ó ɦúRᴅail—I—Harrington ; a phonetic rendering of Ó
ɦlonᵹaroail, q.v.

Ó ɦuRmolᴛaiᵹ—I—Hamilton ; ' des. of urmolᴛac ' or
' Turmolᴛac ' ; a rare surname in South-west Cork.

Ó ɦuRnaiᴅe, *O Hurney,* Hurney ; ' des. of *urnaiᴅe* ' ;
a rare Galway surname. I cannot trace its origin.

Ó ɦuRᴄuile—I—*O Hurrilly,* O'Hurley, Hurley ; ' des.
of urᴄuile ' ; also written Ó ɦurᴄaile, and sometimes
pronounced Ó ɦuirᴄuile ; the name of a Dalcassian
family in Thomond, akin to those of O'Moloney and
O'Kearney ; now dispersed throughout Munster. An
important branch of the family settled at Knocklong,
in the east of Co. Limerick, where the remains of their
castle is still a conspicuous object on the Hill of
Knocklong, and commands a magnificent view of the
Galtee mountains and the plain of Co. Limerick.

OileaᴅaRᴅ, OileaᴅaRᴅ—VIII—Elfred, Elwood,
Ellwood ; ' des. of Ailward ' (v. Aiᵹleanᴛ) ; a rare
Connacht surname.

Oiliᴅéar—VIII—Oliver ; ' des. of Oliver.'

Oisᴛín—VIII—*Austyn,* Austin, Austen ; ' son of Augustine,' formerly popular in England as Austin.

Ó labRaᴅa—I—*O Lowrowe, O Lawry,* Lowroo, Lowery,
Lowry, Lavery ; ' des. of laᴅraiᴅ ' (speaker, spokesman) ; the name of an ancient family in Co. Down,
where it is still common. The different branches of

the family are distinguished by epithets attached to the name, as Ó Lаbрада bán, Ó Lаbрада Ruаd, and Ó Lаbрада Cрéаn, q.v. The Uí Lаbрада of Kilkenny and Galway are most probably migrants from Ulster.

Ó Lаbрада bán—I—Baun-Lavery; i.e. 'White O'Lavery.' V. Ó Lаbрада.

Ó Lаbрада Ruаd—I—Roe-Lavery; i.e. 'Red-O'Lavery.' V. Ó Lаbрада.

Ó Lаbрада Cрéаn—I—Trin-Lavery, Tryn-Lavery, Trim-lavery, Armstrong; i.e., 'Strong O'Lavery'; sometimes angl. Armstrong, on the erroneous supposition that it is derived from 'cрéаn,' strong, and 'lám,' a hand (or arm).

Ó Lаbраιd, Lowry, Lowery, Lavery; a var. of Ó Lаbрада, q.v.

Ó Lасáιn—I—O Laughane, O Laghan, Lahan, Duck; evidently the same as Ó Lосáιn and Ó Leосáιn, q.v. Duck is a 'translation.'

Ó Lасlаιnn—II—O Laghlen, O Laughlen, Lachlin, Laghlin, Laghlen, Laughlin; a var. of Ó Lосlаιnn, q.v.

Ó Lасcnа—I—O Laghna, Loughney; 'des. of Lасcnа' (grey, dun); the name of a family of the Uí Fiachrach, who were chiefs of the Two Bacs and of Glen Nephin, in the barony of Tirawley, Co. Mayo; now very rare, having been almost universally replaced by the diminutive form Ó Lасcnáιn, q.v.

Ó Lасcnáιn—I—O Laghnane, O Loghnane, O Loughnane, O Loughton, Laughnan, Loughnane, Loughnan, Loughrane, Loughran, Lawton, (Loughlan, Loughlin, O'Loughlin, MacLoughlin, Loftus); 'des. of Lасcnán' (dim. of Lасcnа, grey); the name of several distinct families in different parts of Ireland, as :—(1) Ó Lасcnáιn of Mayo, also called Ó Lасcnа (q.v.), who were chiefs of the district called the Two Bacs, now the parish of Bacs, and of Glen Nephin, in the barony of Tirawley, and are still numerous in Connacht; but often disguise their name under the angl. form of Loftus. This family gave bishops to various sees in Connacht in the 13th and 14th centuries. (2) Ó

Lachtnáin of Teffia, a midland family who were anciently chiefs of Teathbha, in the present counties of Longford and Westmeath. (3) Ó Lachtnáin of Oriel, who were anciently chiefs of Mughdorn Breagh, which O'Donovan places in the north of Meath, where it adjoins the county of Monaghan. (4) Ó Lachtnáin of Ui Maine, who were followers of O'Kelly. (5) Ó Lachtnáin of Cinel Eoghain ; and (6) Ó Lachtnáin of Siol Muireadhaigh, both mentioned by MacFirbis. In the 16th century, it was also found in Co. Down, Kilkenny, Tipperary and Cork. It is often corrupted to Ó Lochláin, angl. Loughlin and MacLoughlin, and to Ó Lochráin, angl. Loughrane, Loughran. Lawton is now the angl. form in Co. Cork.

Ó Lachtráin, O'Loughran, Loughrane, Loughran, &c. ; a corruption of Ó Lachtnáin, q.v.

Ó Laideáin—I—Ladden,   V. Ó Loideáin.

Ó Laideanáin, Ó Laidgeanáin, Ó Laidgneáin —I—O Laynan, O Loynen, O Leynen, O Lynan, O Leynam, Lynan, Lynam, Lynham, Lyneham, Lineham, &c. ; ' des. of Laidgneán ' (snow-birth) ; the name of an ecclestiasical family in Leinster, who were erenaghs of Ferns and of St. Mullins, Co. Carlow. Many distinguished ecclesiastics of the name in various parts of Ireland, but probably of this family, are mentioned in the Annals. The name, which is still common in Leinster, is now generally angl. Lynam. The Irish form was also variously written Ó Laidneáin, Ó Laidgeanáin, and Ó Laidgneáin.

Ó Laidigh, v. Ó Loidigh.

Ó Laidigh, v. Ó Laoidigh,

Ó Laidín, v. Ó Laigín.

Ó Laidneáin, Ó Laidgeanáin, v. Ó Laidgneáin.

Ó Laigid, v. Ó Laoidigh.

Ó Laigín—I—O Loyne, O Layne, O Leyne, O Lyne, O Lyen, O Lane, O Leane, O Lien, O Lyan, O'Leyne, O'Lane, O'Lyons, Layne, Leyne, Lyne, Lane, Leane, Lean, Leen, Lyons, &c. ; ' des. of Laigean ' (lance, spear) ; the name (1) of an ancient family in Co.

Galway, who retained considerable property in the barony of Kilconnell down to the end of the 17th century ; (2) of a Kildare family, formerly seated at Cill, now angl. Kill, near Naas ; and (3) of an old Kerry family. The name is now very common all over Ireland. It appears to have been sometimes pronounced Ó Laoiġin. In Kerry at the present day it is generally pronounced Ó Leiġin, and sometimes Ó Liġin.

Ó Laiġneáin, v. Ó Laioġneáin.

Ó Laiġniġ—I—*O Leighnagh, O Leiny,* Leeney, Lyons ; ' des. of Laiġneaċ ' (Leinsterman) ; a very rare surname. For pronunciation, cf. Ó Laiġin.

Ó Láiṁín—I—*O Lavine, O Lavin, O Laven,* Lavin, Laven, Lavan, Hand ; doubtless, a corruption of Ó Flaitiṁín, q.v. ; the name of a family who were originally followers of MacDermottroe in Co. Roscommon ; still common in that county, and also in Co. Mayo. It is supposed to be derived from ' Láṁ,' a hand, hence the angl. form Hand. Also Ó Lámáin, q.v.

Ó Lainn—I—Laing, Layng, Lang ; a var. of Ó Flainn, q.v. Cf. Ó Loinn.

Ó Lairġneáin, v. Ó Loirġneáin.

Ó Laisce, v. Ó Loirce.

Ó Laitbeartaiġ—I—*O Laffertie, O Laghertie, O Laherty,* O'Lafferty, O'Laverty, Lafferty, Laverty, Laherty ; ' des. of Flaitbeaptaċ ' ; a var. of Ó Flaitbeaptaiġ, owing to the aspiration of the initial F ; the name of a distinguished family of the Cinel Eoghain in Ulster, where it is still common, especially in Tyrone, Derry, Antrim and Donegal.

Ó Laiteasa, Ó Laitġeasa—I—*O Lahissa, O Lassy, O Lassie, O Lasy, O Lacy,* Lacy, Lacey, Leacy, (De Lacy) ; ' des. of Flaitear,' or ' Flaitġear ' ; older forms Ó Flaiteara and Ó Flaitġeara, q.v. ; the name of an old Wexford family, still numerous in that county. To be distinguished from the Norman de Lacy (v. De Léir).

Ó Laiṫiṁ—I—O Lahiff, O Laffie, O Lahy, Lahive, Lahiff, Lahiffe, Laffey, Laffy, Lahy, Lahey, &c.; a var. of Ó Flaiṫiṁ, q.v.; also corruptly Ó Laṫaiġ, q.v.

Ó Laiṫiṁín—I—Lavin; a var. of Ó Flaiṫiṁín, q.v.; in use in Co. Kerry. It is doubtless the correct original of Ó Láiṁín, q.v.

Ó Lamáin—I—O Lawan, Lavan; a var., doubtless, of Ó Flaṫamáin, q.v.; rare.

Ó Laocḋa—I—O Leaghy, O Leahy, Leahy, Leehy, &c.; 'des. of Laocḋa' (heroic); an old Munster surname; now very common in Cork, Kerry, Limerick and Tipperary; to be distinguished from Ó Laṫaiġ, which is sometimes similarly anglicised.

Ó Laoḋóġ, v. Ó Laoġóġ.

Ó Laoġaire—I—O'Leary, Leary, &c.; 'des. of Laoġaire' (calf-keeper); the name of a family of Corca Laoighdhe, who were originally chiefs of the country lying around Rosscarberry, in West Cork, but removed from there about the time of the Anglo-Norman invasion and settled in the parish of Inchigeelagh, where they became lords, under the Mac-Carthys, of the country between Macroom and Inchigeelagh. The head of the family resided at Carrignacurra, about a mile to the east of the village of Inchigeelagh. In 1642, Connor O'Leary of Carrignacurra, Auliff O'Leary of Cunnowley, and fourteen others of the name were attainted. The O'Learys are now very numerous throughout Munster.

Ó Laoġóġ—I—O Lioge, Leeogue, Leogue, League, Luogue, Loogue, Logue, (Leech, Molloy, Mulloy); 'des. of Laoġóġ' (dim. of Laoġ, a calf); the name of an old Galway family who were chiefs of Caladh, which is supposed to have been co-extensive with the barony of Kilconnell, but now long dispersed. The name is now found in Longford, Westmeath, Mayo and Donegal, as well as in Galway, where it is sometimes angl. Leech. In Donegal, it may be merely a corruption of Ó Maolṁaoḋóġ, q.v. In that county, and also in Mayo, it is angl. Molloy. Ó Laoʒacáin appears to have been an alias in Galway.

Ó Laoiⷣiʒ—I—*O Loye, O Lye, O Leye, O Lie,* O'Lee, Lee ; ' des. of Laoiⷣeac ' (poetic) ; the name of a West Connacht family, who, according to MacFirbis, were chiefs of Ui Briuin Eola. They were also erenaghs of Annadown, and some of them were distinguished as ecclesiastics ; but they are best known as a medical family, having been for many centuries hereditary physicians to the O'Flahertys. As early as the 15th century, a learned member of the family produced a most complete course of medicine, written in Latin and Irish. The family is now widely dispersed.

Ó Laoiʒill—I—*O Leagail,* Lyle; ' des. of Laoiʒeall.' This is probably the surname which is written Ó Luccail in the Annals of Loch Ce.

Ó Laomⷣa—I—*O Lemagh, O Leamy,* Leamy ; ' des. of Laomⷣa ' (bent, bowed). Keating writes it Ó Léime.

Ó Lapáin—I—*O Lapane, O Lappan,* Lapin, Lappin, Laphin, (De Lapp, Delap) ; ' des. of Lapán ' (dim. of Lapa, a paw, or fist) ; the name of an Ulster family who were anciently chiefs of Cinel Enda, in Co. Donegal, and erenaghs of Derry, but afterwards removed to Co. Armagh. The name is still common in Ulster. In Co. Mayo, it is sometimes made Delap in English.

Oláⷃⷫ, Ellard. V. Aiⷣleaⷫc.

Ó Lacáiʒ—I—*O Lahy,* Lahy, Lahey, Laffy, Laffey, (Leahy) ; a var. of Ó Flacaiʒ and Ó Laicim, q.v.

Ó Léanacáin—I—*O Lenaghan, O Leneghan,* Lenaghan, Leneghan, Lenahan, Lenehan, Lenihan, Lennihan, &c. ; ' des. of Léanacán ' (dim. of Leannac or Léanac, mantled, cloaked) ; the name of a Roscommon family; still numerous, but dispersed through Connacht ; sometimes pronounced Ó Lionacáin.

Ó Leanⷣáin—I—Lenden, Linden, Lindin, Lindon ; a var. of Ó Leannáin, q.v. Also Ó Lionⷣáin, q.v.

Ó Leannáin—I—*O Lennane, O Lennan,* Linnane, Lan-

nan, Lannen, Lannon, Lennon, (Leonard) ; ' des. of
Leannán ' (dim. of Leann, a cloak or mantle) ; the
name of at least three distinct families, seated respectively in the counties of Fermanagh, Mayo and
Galway. The O'Leannains of Fermanagh were an
ecclesiastical family and erenaghs of Lisgoole, near
Enniskillen. Those of Mayo are a branch of the Ui
Fiachrach and were seated in the neighbourhood of
Killala, while the Galway family were followers of
O'Kelly of Ui Maine. All these families are still well
represented, but the name is very often disguised
under the angl. form of Leonard. The pronunciation
is sometimes Ó Lionnáin, sometimes Ó Lionoáin.

Ó leArzusA—I—*O Larryse*, Larrissy, Laracy ; ' des. of
Leanzur ' (sea-choice) ; the name of a family of Ui
Fiachrach, who were formerly seated in the barony of
Carra, Co. Mayo, but are long dispersed.

Ó leAtáin—I—*O Lahan, O Laane*, Laine, Lane ; probably a corruption of Ó liatáin, q.v. ; in use in the
neighbourhood of Shrule, but very rare.

Ó leAtlobAir—I—*O Lalour, O Lawler*, O'Lalor, Lalor,
Lawlor, Lawler ; ' des. of leatlobar ' (half-leper) ; the
name of an Ulidian family, descended from leatlobar, King of Ulidia, who died in the year 871. The
Uí leatlobair are mentioned in the Annals in the
early part of the 10th century as kings of Dalradia
and Ulidia, but after that period they disappear from
history. Another family of the name, kinsmen of
the O'Moores, were one of the ' seven septs of Leix.'
They were seated at Dysart Enos, near the Rock of
Dunamase, from which they were driven by the
English family of Pigott in the reign of Elizabeth,
and dispersed through Leinster. A remnant of them
was transplanted, together with the O'Moores, to
Kerry, in the early part of the 17th century, and their
descendants are now numerous and respectable in
that county. There was also a family of the name
in Co. Monaghan.

Ó leioin, Ó leizin, v. Ó laizin.

Ó Léime, *O Lemagh, O Leamy*, Leamy. V. Ó Laomóa.

Ó Leocáin—I—*O Loughane, O Lochan*, Loghan, Loughan, Duck ; also variously written Ó Lacáin, Ó Lócáin, Ó Lotcáin, Ó Lógáin, Ó Leogáin, &c. ; the name of a famous family in ancient Meath, who were chiefs of Gailenga Móra and Luighne, now the baronies of Morgallion and Lune, in Co. Meath, but were dispossessed, apparently about the time of the Anglo-Norman invasion, and dispersed through Leinster, Ulster and Connacht. The name, according to O'Donovan, was ridiculously translated Duck, on the erroneous supposition that it was derived from ' laca,' a duck.

Ó Leogáin—I—*O Lagane, O Lagan, O Logan*, Logan, Lagan ; a var. of Ó Leocáin, q.v.

Ó Liatáin—I—*O Lyhane, O Leaghan*, O'Lehane, Lyhane, Leehane, Lehane, Leyhane, Lihane, Lyhan, Leehan, Leeane, &c., (O'Lyons, Lyons) ; ' des. of Liatán ' (dim. of liat, grey) ; the name of two distinct families, one seated in Cork, and the other in Sligo. The Uí Liatáin of Cork were, according to O'Donovan, one of the families into which the great old Cork clan of Uí Liathain divided after the establishment of surnames. The surname is not to be confounded with the clan-name, which included several families with distinct surnames. The surname Ó Liatáin is still common in Co. Cork, but is very often angl. Lyons. The Sligo family belonged to the Uí Fiachrach race, and was formerly seated in the parish of Dromard. The name has now disappeared from Co. Sligo, having, as it would seem, removed to Donegal, where it still survives, angl. Lyons.

Ó Lioeaóa—I—*O Lyddie, O Lyddy, O Leddy*, Liddy, Leddy ; ' des. of Lioeaó ' ; the name of a Dalcassian family, formerly seated in the east of Co. Clare. A branch of this family has been long settled in Co. Antrim.

Ó Liooáin, v. Ó Looáin.

Ó Líonacáin, v. Ó Léanacáin.

Ó Lionoáin—I—*O Lyndane*, Lindon, Linden, &c.; a var. of Ó Leannáin, q.v.

Ó Lionnáin, v. Ó Leannáin.

*Ó Liseáin—I—*O Lishane, O Lyshane*, Leeson; perhaps a corruption of Ó Ꙃlaráin, q.v. Cf. *O Glishane* for Ó Ꙃlaireáin.

Ó Lócáin—I—*O Loghane, O Loughane*, Loghan, Loughan, Lohan, Chaff; 'des. of Lócán'; a var. of Ó Leocáin, q.v.; in use in Co. Galway, angl. Chaff by 'translation.'

Ó Loclláin—I—*O Loughlane*, O'Loughlan, O'Loughlin, Loughlan, Loughlin, (Loftus); a corruption of Ó Lactnáin, q.v. To be distinguished from Ó Loclainn, q.v.

Ó Loclainn—II—*O Loghlan, O Laghlan*, O'Loughlan, O'Loughlin, O'Loghlen, Loghlin, Loughlan, Loughlen, Loughlin, Laughlin, &c.; 'des. of Loclainn'; the name (1) of a leading family of Cinel Eoghain, more commonly called Mac Loclainn, q.v.; and (2) of an ancient and distinguished family in Co. Clare, who took their name from Loclainn, lord of Corcomroe, in the 10th century. The O'Loghlins and O'Connors originally formed one clan, and ruled over a district co-extensive with the diocese of Kilfenora. This district, which was called Corcomroe from the clan-name of its inhabitants, the Corca Modhruaidh, was afterwards divided into two nearly equal parts between the two families, O'Loghlen ruling over East Corcomroe, which was also called Burren, and O'Connor over West Corcomroe. The O'Loghlens were a powerful family, and retained their rank as lords of Burren down to the reign of Elizabeth. They are still numerous and respectable in Thomond.

Ó Lógáin—I—*O Logan*, Logan; a var. of Ó Leocáin, q.v.

Ó Lodáin, Ó Loideáin—I—*O Ludan, O Lydan, O Leadon*, Ludden, Liddane, Leddan, Lydden, Lyden, Lydon, Leyden, &c.; 'des. of Lodán,' or 'Loideán'; a common surname in many parts of Connacht, and also in Co. Clare. Ó Lotáin and Ó Laiteáin were probably older forms. See also Ó Luideáin.

Ó Loıoıƀ—I—*O Loddie*, Luddy ; older form Ó Laıoıƀ ;
'des. of Laıoeaƀ' (mighty) ; the name of an old
West Cork family, who were followers of O'Leary.
It still survives in Co. Cork and in South Tipperary,
but is very rare.

Ó Loınȝseaċáın—I—*O Lynseghane*, Lynchahaun,
Lynchahan, Lynchehan, (Lynch) ; 'des. of Loınȝ-
reaċán' (dim. of Loınȝreaċ) ; the name (1) of a family
of the Cinel Eoghain in Ulster, who are descended
from Loınȝreaċ, King of Ireland, and were seated in
the present county of Donegal ; also called Mac
Loınȝreaċáın and Ó Loınȝrıȝ, q.v. ; and (2) of a
family of the Ui Fiachrach, formerly seated in Co.
Sligo. It is now almost always angl. Lynch.

Ó Loınȝsıȝ—I—*O Lynchy, O Lynche, O Lensie*, Linchey,
Linchy, Lynchy, Lynch, Lindsy, (Lindsay) ; 'des. of
Loınȝreaċ' (der. of Loınȝear, a fleet, i.e., having,
or belonging to, a fleet or navy) ; the name of several
distinct families in different parts of Ireland, as :
(1) Ó Loınȝrıȝ of Dalradia, once a very important
family. In the 11th century, they were chiefs of
Dalradia, in the present counties of Antrim and
Down, and are frequently mentioned in the Annals.
They were dispossessed at the time of the Anglo-
Norman invasion of Ulster, but are still numerous
in Antrim and Down. (2) Ó Loınȝrıȝ of Owney, also
a family of note in early times. Before the Anglo-
Norman invasion, they were chiefs of Uaithne-thire, now
the barony of Owney in Tipperary, but were afterwards
dispossessed by the O'Mulryans. (3) Ó Loınȝrıȝ of
Breifney, a strong clan, who were chiefs of Cinel
Bacaid, and are still numerous in Co. Cavan. (4) Ó
Loınȝrıȝ of Thomond. a Dalcassian family, still
numerous in Clare and Limerick. (5) Ó Loınȝrıȝ of
Cork, a branch of the Corca Laoighe, who were
originally seated in West Cork. (6) Ó Loınȝrıȝ of
Sligo, a branch of the Ui Fiachrach. (7) Ó Loınȝrıȝ of
Meath. Ó Loınȝrıȝ is often a shortened form of Ó
Loınȝreaċáın (q.v.), especially in Donegal, Mayo,

and Cork. In Co. Galway, it is sometimes metathecised to Ó Loinrcig, q.v. Lynch is now one of the commonest of Irish surnames, and, as might be expected, is found in every part of Ireland.

Ó Loinn—I—*O Linne, O Linge, O Lynt*, O'Lynn, Lynn, Linn, Lind, (Lindsay) ; ' des. of Flann ' (ruddy) ; a var., owing to the aspiration of the initial F, of Ó Floinn, q.v.; the name of a famous Ulster family who, from about the middle of the 11th until towards the latter part of the 14th century, were chiefs of Ui Tuirtre, a district comprised in the baronies of Upper and Lower Toome, in Co. Antrim, and are frequently mentioned in the Annals. In the year 1177, they defeated John de Courcy when he advanced into their territory, and for two centuries longer they continued to maintain their independence. After the year 1368 they disappear from history. The name, according to O'Donovan, is sometimes angl. Lindsay.

Ó Loinscig—I—Linskey, Lynskey ; a metathesised form, in Co. Galway, of Ó Loingrig, q.v.

Ó Loirgneáin—I—*O'Largan*, Lerkinan, Learhinan, Lerhinan, Largan, (Lardner). This surname is at present in use in Clare and Galway, angl. Lerkinan and Lerhinan in the former county, and Lardner in the latter. It is clearly to be identified with Ó Laiggnen, the name of a family who, in early times, were chiefs of Oriel. O'Dugan writes :—

" To lordship entitled by right,
    Is Ó Laiggnen full king of Oriel."

The family seems to have long since disappeared from Oriel, and is now, so far as I know, represented only in Clare and Galway, and even there by only a few scattered families.

Ó Loiste—I—*O Lastie*, (Leslie, Lesley) ; also Ó Lairte ; a rare Donegal surname, now always angl. Leslie or Lesley.

Ó Lomáin—I—*O Loman, O Lymon*, Loman, Lomand, Lomond, Lemon, Lemmon ; ' des. of Lomán ' (dim. of ʟom, bare, lean) ; the name (1) of an Ulidian family, once a clan of note, but now scarcely known ; and (2) of a branch of the Ui Maine in Co. Galway. This family, though now almost extinct, must have been once powerful, for we learn from the Annals of the Four Masters, at the year 949, that Ó ʟomáın of Gaela (in Co. Galway) in that year defeated the people of Ormond. In the 16th century, the name was most common in Co. Wicklow. It is now everywhere very rare.

Ó ʟomᴀsnᴀ—I—*O Lomasny*, O'Lomasney, Lomosney ; ' des. of ʟomᴀrnᴀ ' (bare rib) ; the name of an old Munster family which apparently originated in S. Tipperary, where bᴀıʟe Uí ʟomᴀrnᴀ, now angl. Bally-nomasna, in the parish of Tubrid, marks its ancient home ; now very rare and scattered, but found chiefly in South Cork. There are a few families of the name in West Limerick.

Ó ʟonᴀzáın—I—*O Lonagan, O Lonegan, O Lanegane, O Lannegan*, Lanigan, Lannigan, &c. ; probably ' des. of ʟonᴀzán ' (dim. of ʟon, a blackbird ; cf. ʟonán), but the origin is not quite clear. O'Donovan thought it might be a corruption of Ó ʟonzᴀcáın ; and Ó fʟᴀnnᴀzáın is not an unlikely origin. Also Ó ʟuıneᴀzáın, q.v.

Ó ʟonáın—I—*O Lonane, O Lonan, O Lonnan, O Lannan, O Lennane*, Lenane, Lanon, Lannan, Lannon, Lannen, Lannin, Lennon, (Leonard) ; ' des. of ʟonán ' (dim. of ʟon, a blackbird) ; the name (1) of a Cork family who were originally settled in the neighbourhood of Ross-carbery, where they were followers of the O'Learys ; and (2) of a Wicklow family who were anciently erenaghs of Kilranelagh ; also, not improbably, (3) of an Ossory family. In Co. Cork, it appears to have been generally pronounced Ó ʟıonáın, and is very often angl. Leonard.

Ó ʟonzᴀcáın, v. Ó ʟuınzeᴀcáın.

Ó ʟonzᴀız—I—*O Longy, O Longe*, Long ; ' des. of ʟonzᴀc ' (der. of ʟonz, a ship, a camp) ; the name of an old family who are still numerous in Cork, Kerry and Limerick.

Ó lonᵹáin—I—*O Longane, O Langane, O Longan, O Langan,* Longan, Langan, Langin, (Long) ; ' des. of loⁿᵹáⁿ ' (dim. of lonᵹ, long, tall) ; the name (1) of an Ulster family who were anciently chiefs of West Ui Breasail, in Co. Armagh, and are now very numerous in Mayo ; and (2) of an ecclesiastical family who were erenaghs of Ardpatrick, in Co. Limerick, and Patrician stewards of Munster. After the destruction of the monastery of Ardpatrick, the family dispersed through Limerick, Kerry and Cork. In the last century, the O'Longans of Cork were a distinguished family of scribes and poets. V. Ó luinᵹeáin.

Ó lonᵹaⁿᵹáin, Ó lonnaⁿᵹáin, Ó lonnⁿaᵹáin —I—*O Lonergane, O Lonregan, O Londregan, O Lorrigane,* Lonnergan, Lonergan, Londregan, Londrigan, Landregan, Ladrigan, Lorrigan, &c. ; ' des. of lonᵹaⁿᵹáⁿ ' (dim. of lonⁿᵹaⁿᵹ, strong-fierce) ; the name of a Dalcassian family who were seated in the east of Thomond until after the year 1318, when they were driven out by the O'Briens and Mac-Namaras, and settled in Co. Tipperary. This family produced several distinguished ecclesiastics. Three of them are mentioned by Ware as Archbishops of Cashel in the 12th and 13th century, two as Bishops of Killaloe, and one as Bishop of Cloyne. The name is now very common in Tipperary, Kilkenny and Waterford

Ó loⁿcáin—I—*O Lurkaine, O Lorkan,* Lorkan, Lorkin, Larkin, Larken, Larkins, &c. ; ' des. of loⁿcáⁿ ' (dim. of loⁿc, fierce) ; the name of several distinct families in different parts of Ireland, of whom the following were in early times the most distinguished : (1) Ó loⁿcáⁿ of Leinster. This family, which is of the royal race of Leinster, was seated in the barony of Forth, in the south-east of Co. Wexford, until dispossessed soon after the Anglo-Norman invasion, and is still numerous in Leinster. (2) Ó loⁿcáⁿ of

Oriel, an important family in early times, and still numerous in Co. Armagh. The head of this family is described at different times as lord of Ui Niallain, Lord of Farney, and lord of West Ui Breasail. (3) Ó Loꞃcáin of Ui Maine, a Galway family of the same stock as the O'Maddens, still numerous and respectable in that county. (4) Ó Loꞃcáin of Meath, the head of which was anciently lord of Caille Follamain. (5) Ó Loꞃcáin of Tipperary, an ecclesiastical family, the head of which was anciently erenagh of Lorrha. All these families are still well represented. Mac-Firbis mentions another family of the name, a branch of the Cinel Eoghain, in Co. Donegal.

Ó LÓROÁ1n—?—*O Lordane*, Lordan ; ' des. of *Lóꞃoán ' ; the name of an old Cork family, still represented in that county. I cannot trace its origin.

Ó LOCCÁ1n, v. Ó Leocáin and Ó Lócáin.

Ó LUAĊA1R, Ó LUAĊRA—I—*O Logher, O Lucry*, Loughry, Loughrey, Lockery, Rush ; ' des. of Luaċán ' (white, pure) ; a corruption, according to O'Donovan, of the old Sligo surname Ó Luaċáin ; the name of a branch of the Ui Fiachrach, formerly seated at Rosslee, in the parish of Easkey. It is now common in Co. Mayo, where it is usually ' translated ' Rush, from an erroneous belief that it is derived from luaċaiꞃ, rushes.

Ó LUA1n—I—*O Loaine, O Loane*, O'Loan, O'Lone, Loane, Lamb, Lambe ; ' des. of Luan' (warrior, champion) ; the name (1) of a Limerick family who were anciently lords of Deisbeg, now the barony of Smallcounty, in the east of Co. Limerick, but have been long dispersed through Limerick, Cork and Kerry ; and (2) of a Monaghan family, now dispersed through Ulster. It is angl. O'Loan, Loane in the north of Ireland, but generally Lambe, by ' translation,' in the south.

Ó LUAnA1ʒ—I—*O Lowny*, O'Looney, Looney, Loony, Lowney ; ' des. of Luanaċ ' (der. of luan, warrior, champion) ; a Munster surname, found chiefly in Cork and Clare.

Ó luanáin—I—*O Loonane, O Lonan*, Lambe; 'des. of luanán' (dim. of luan, warrior, champion); a rare Donegal surname. Cf. Ó luain.

Ó luasaiġ—IV—*O Lwosie*, Lucey, Lucy; undoubtedly a corruption of mac Cluaraiġ; a well-known Co. Cork surname.

Ó lúbaiġ—I—*O Luby, O Looby*, Luby, Looby; 'des. of lúbac' (crooked, deceitful); a rare and scattered surname, now most numerous in Tipperary.

Ó lucaireáin, Ó lucráin—I—*O Lucherin, O Loghrane*, O'Loughran, Lougheran, Loughren, Laugheran, Lochrane, Loughrane, Loughran, O'Loran, Loran; 'des. of lucaipeán' (dim. of lucaip, bright, glittering); the name of a celebrated ecclesiastical family in East Ulster, and especially in the diocese of Armagh.

Ó luiroeáin, v. Ó loiroeáin.

Ó luimbric—I—*O Lymbricke*, Limerick; 'des. of lombpeac' (bare-speckled); a rare Co. Down surname.

Ó luineaġáin—I—*O Lenagan*, Lenagan, Lenegan, Lenigan, Lanigan, Lynegan, &c.; an attenuated form of O lonaġáin, q.v.

Ó luingeacáin—I—*O Lunyghan*, Lunican, Lonican, Linighan, Linahan, Linehan, Lenihan, &c.; 'des. of longacán' (dim. of longac); an attenuated form of Ó longacáin, and apparently a substitution for the old East Limerick or Tipperary surname mac longacáin; common in Cork, Limerick and Kerry.

Ó luingeáin—I—*O Lungane, O Liengan*, Lingane, Linnane, Linane, Lenane, Lynane, (Leonard); an attenuated form of Ó lonġáin, q.v.; now very often disguised under the angl. form of Leonard, especially in Co. Limerick.

Ó luiniġ—I—*O Lonney, O Loney, O Loony*, Luny, Lunny, Lunney, Lonney, Loney, Loony, Looney; 'des. of luineac'; the name of a family of Cinel Moen in Ulster. They were seated orginally in the barony of Raphoe, but were afterwards driven across the Foyle by the O'Donnells, when they settled in

Co. Tyrone, in a district to which they gave the name of Muinter Loony. The name is now very common in Co. Fermanagh.

Ó Luinín—I—*O Luinyn, O Lonine, O Lonin*, Lunneen, Lineen, Linneen, Linnen, Lennon, (Leonard, Linnegar, Lynegar) ; ' des. of Luinín' (dim. of Lon, a blackbird) ; the name of a distinguished Co. Fermanagh family who were erenaghs of Derryvullen, and for many centuries poets, historians, musicians, and physicians to the Maguires. Their chief residence was at Áṙo Uí Luinín, in the parish of Derryvullan. There were also old families of the name in Carlow and Waterford, where they still flourish. Ó Luinín is very often angl. Leonard, and, according to O'Donovan, it was also strangely angl. Linnegar and Lynegar in Co. Fermanagh.

Ó macáin—I—*O Mackane*, Macken, Mackin ; ' des. of macán' (dim. of mac, a son, youth) ; a var. of Ó maicín, q.v.

Ó macáin—I—*O Maghane, O Mauchan, O Mahan*, Maghan, Maughan, Mahon, Mann, (Vaughan) ; a var. of Ó mocáin, q.v.

Ó macasa—II—*O Mackessy*, Macassy, Mackessy, Mac-Kessy, MacAssie, Maxey ; ' des. of macuṙ' (a form of maᵹnuṙ) ; the name of a family of Ui Fidhgheinte who were anciently lords of Corca Oiche in the modern barony of Glenquin, in the west of Co. Limerick, but dispossessed soon after the Anglo-Norman invasion by a branch of the Fitzgeralds and disperesd through Munster and Leinster.

Ó macóa—I—*O Makie, O Macky*, Mackey ; ' des. of macóa' (virile, manly) ; an old Ormond surname, still common in Tipperary, Limerick and Cork ; to be distinguished from mac Aoᵵó (q.v.) which is sometimes similarly anglicised.

Ó maccíre—I—*O Macketyre*, Wolfe ; ' des. of maccíṙe' (wolf) ; the name of a branch of the Ui Liathain in East Cork. Uaṁnacán Ua maccíṙe was Bishop of

Cloyne at the end of the 11th century. The name is
said to be still in East Cork, but now very rare.

Ó mᴀᴅᴀᴈáın—I—*O Madagane, O Madigane,* Madigan,
Maddigan ; the same as Ó mᴀᴅáın or Ó mᴀᴅᴀıᴅín,
q.v. ; an offshoot of the family of O'Madden of Co.
Galway who settled in the 16th century in Clare and
Limerick, where they are still numerous.

Ó mᴀᴅᴀıᴅ—I—*O Maddy,* Maddy ; ' des. of mᴀᴅᴀᴅ '
(dog) ; a var. of Ó mᴀᴅáın, q.v., and an offshoot of
the Galway family of that name ; very rare.

Ó mᴀᴅᴀıᴅín—I—*O Maddine, O Madden,* Madden ;
' des. of mᴀᴅᴀıᴅín ' (dim. of ' mᴀᴅᴀᴅ,' a dog) ; a var.
of Ó mᴀᴅáın, q.v. This seems to have been always
the popular form of the name, and is at the present
day almost universal in the spoken language of Connacht.

Ó mᴀᴅáın—I—*O Maddane, O Madden,* Madden ; ' des.
of mᴀᴅᴀᴅáın ' (dim. of mᴀᴅᴀᴅ, a dog) ; older form
Ó mᴀᴅᴀᴅáın, now generally Ó mᴀᴅᴀıᴅín, q.v., with
variants Ó mᴀᴅᴀıᴅ and Ó mᴀᴅᴀᴈáın, q.v. ; the name
of a distinguished branch of the Ui Maine in Co.
Galway, who derive their descent from mᴀᴅᴀᴅáın
(slain in 1008), who was son of Gadhra Mór, chief of
Ui Maine from 1014 to 1027, and are of the same
stock as the O'Kellys, with whom they originally
formed one clan—the Ui Maine. About the middle
of the 11th century, Siol nAnmchadha, a sub-division
of the Ui Maine, became independent, and from that
period down to the middle of the 17th century the
chieftaincy of Siol nAnmchadha continued in almost
unbroken succession in the family of O'Madden.
The clan-lands, which in accordance with Irish usage
were named from the clan, comprised the barony of
Longford, in the south-east of Co. Galway, and the
parish of Lusnagh, on the other side of the Shannon,
in the present Offaly. Many distinguished chiefs of
the name are mentioned in the Irish annals. In 1612,
Donal O'Madden, ' captain of his nation,' settled his
manor and castle of Longford and all his other estates

in Co. Galway on his son and heir, **Anmchadh**, or Ambrose, O'Madden, in tail male. Ambrose died in 1637, and was succeeded by his son, John O'Madden. John's property was confiscated after the Cromwellian wars, but was in part restored in 1677 by grant under the Act of Settlement. Five of the name were attainted in 1691. The O'Maddens of Co. Antrim (formerly called O Maddegane) are probably a distinct family. On the other hand, there is reason to believe that the Anglo-Irish family of Madden, formerly of Baggotrath, near Dublin, is a branch of the O'Maddens of Siol nAnmchadha.

Ó mᴀeᴌe, v. Ó mᴀ́ıᴌᴌe.

Ó mᴀıᴄín—I—*O Mackine*, Mackin, Macken; des of mᴀıᴄín' (dim. of mᴀᴄ, a son, youth); also Ó mᴀᴄᴀ́ın, q.v.; a scattered surname, now found chiefly in Mayo, Monaghan and Louth. ᴄomᴀ́ᴘ Ó mᴀıᴄín was Bishop of Achonry in the 13th century, (1251-1265).

Ó mᴀᴘóín, O'Madden, Madden. V. Ó mᴀᴅᴀᴘóín.

Ó mᴀ́ıᴌᴌe—I—*O Mailie, O Mallie, O Mally, O Maely*, O'Malley, O'Meally, O'Mealy, Malley, Meally, Mealley, Melly, Melia, &c.; 'des. of mᴀ́ıᴌᴌe' (perhaps Old Celtic Maglios, chief); the name (1) of a Connacht family who were chiefs of the two Umhalls, now the baronies of Burrishoole and Murresk, in the west of Co. Mayo, and were particularly celebrated as naval commanders, being called the Manannans, or sea-gods, of the western ocean, and having a considerable fleet always under their command; and (2) of a Thomond family who were chiefs of Tuath Luimnigh, a district in the neighbourhood of the city of Limerick. Ó mᴀ́ıᴌᴌe is often strangely anglicised Melia in Connacht, which may be explained on the supposition that Ó mᴀeᴌe was formerly a popular variant. Ó mᴀeᴌe was in use in the 10th century in Conmaicne.

Ó mᴀınᴄín—I—*O Manihin*, Manihin, Manihan, Manahan, Mannix; 'des. of mᴀınᴄín' (dim. of mᴀnᴀᴄ, a monk); a var. of Ó mᴀnᴄᴀ́ın, q.v.; the name of a family of Corca Laoighdhe, in South-West Cork; now scattered through Munster, especially Cork, Kerry and Limerick, and generally angl. Mannix.

Ó mᴀ1ne—I—*O Many*, Many, (Meany) ; ' des. of mᴀ1ne ' ; the name of a Dalcassian family in Thomond ; now very rare, and its angl. forms can hardly be distinguished from those of Ó mᴀonᴀ1ᵹ, q.v.

Ó mᴀ1nn1n—I—*O Mannine, O Mannin, O Manynge*, Mannin, Mannion, Manion, Manning, Mangin, (Mangan) ; ' des. of mᴀ1nn1n ' (perhaps the same as mᴀ1n-c1n) ; the name of a Galway family who were formerly chiefs of Sodhan, a district nearly co-extensive with the barony of Tiaquin. Ó mᴀ1nn1n, King of Sodhan, is mentioned in the Chronicon Scotorum as early as the year 1135, and the O Mainnins continued to form a distinct clan down to the time of James I. The chief resided at Menlough Castle, in the parish of Killascobe. In 1617, Hugh O'Mannin surrendered his estates to the king and received them back by letters patent. The whole property was confiscated after the Cromwellian wars, but a small portion of it was restored under the Act of Settlement in 1676. The name is still common in Galway and Roscommon, and has spread into other parts of Ireland. It is sometimes pronounced Ó mᴀ1nᵹ1n and so incorrectly angl. Mangin and Mangan.

Ó mᴀ1ʀⰕ1n—II—*O Martin, O Marten*, Martin ; ' des. of Martin.'

Ó mᴀnᴀċᴀ1n, Ó mᴀnċᴀ1n—I—*O Managhane, O Manahan, O Monaghan*, Monaghan, Monahan, Manahan, etc., Monk, Monks ; ' des. of mᴀnᴀċᴀn ' (dim. of mᴀnᴀċ, a monk) ; the name of a Connacht family who derive their descent from mᴀnᴀċᴀn, a famous warrior mentioned by the Four Masters at the year 866, and were chiefs of Ui Briuin na Sionna, in the barony of Ballintober, Co. Roscommon, until the year 1249, when they were ousted by the O Beirnes. The name at the end of the 16th century was very scattered. It is sometimes pronounced Ó m1onᴀċᴀ1n and Ó mu1neᴀċᴀ1n, q.v.

Ó mⱥnⱥċⱥıR—I—*O Monegher*, Monaher; 'des. of
mⱥnⱥċⱥp' (monk-dear); a rare surname in Offaly,
where it has been in use for more than three hundred
years. It is scarcely found outside that county.

Ó mⱥnⱥʒⱥın—I—*O Monegan*, Monegan, (Mangan);
'des. of mⱥnⱥʒⱥn' (dim. of mⱥnⱥċ, a monk); probably only a var. of Ó mⱥnⱥċⱥın, q.v.

Ó mⱥnⱥnnⱥın—I—*O Manynane, O Mananan*, Marrinan,
Murnane, &c.; 'des. of mⱥnⱥnnⱥn' (the name of an
ancient Irish sea-god); an old Thomond surname;
now found chiefly in East Limerick, Tipperary, Cork,
and parts of Leinster, but long corrupted to Ó mⱥpⱥn-
nⱥın, Ó mⱥpnⱥın, Ó mupnⱥın, and Ó mⱥnⱥpⱥın, q.v.

Ó mⱥnⱥRⱥın—I—*O Mannerane*, Mannering, Manron;
a corruption of Ó mⱥnⱥnnⱥın, q.v.

Ó mⱥnċⱥın—I—*O Manchan, O Monghan*, Monaghan,
Monahan, Manahan, Manghan, (Mangan); a var. of Ó
mⱥnⱥċⱥın, q.v.

Ó mⱥnnⱥⱥın—I—*O Mantane, O Mentane*, Montane,
Montang, Montangue, Mountain, Menton, Mintin;
'des. of mⱥnnⱥⱥn' (dim. of mⱥnnⱥⱥċ, toothless); an
old surname in Ossory and Cork.

Ó mⱥnóʒ—I—*O Monoge*, Manogue, (Mannix); 'des. of
mⱥnóʒ' (dim. of mⱥnⱥċ, a monk); more frequently
Ó muıneóʒ, q.v.

Ó mⱥoılⱥoⱥ, Ó mⱥoılⱥoı—I—*O Mylee, O Miley*,
Millea, Mullee, Miley, Melay, (Malley, Mulloy, Molloy);
a var. of Ó mⱥoⱥoⱥ, q.v. In Connacht, where it
is not uncommon, it is sometimes angl. Mullee, but
generally Mulloy.

Ó mⱥoılⱥeⱥnnⱥċⱥ—I—Mulvanerty, Blessing; 'des.
of mⱥoılⱥeⱥnnⱥċⱥ' (votary of the blessing); a rare
surname. Blessing is a 'translation.'

Ó mⱥoılⱥeⱥnóın—I—*O Mulvanone, O Mulvanon*, Mulvennon; 'des. of mⱥoılⱥeⱥnóın' (servant of St.
Benignus); a rare Meath surname.

Ó mⱥoılⱥeⱥRⱥıʒ—I—*O Mulverie*, Mulberry; 'des.
of mⱥoılⱥeⱥpⱥıʒ' (servant of St. Barry); a rare
Ulster surname.

Ó mᴀoɪꞮͦʀeᴀnᴀɪnn, Ó mᴀoɪꞮͦʀeᴀnᴀɪnn—I—
O Mulrenan, O Mulreanan, O'Mulrennin, Mulrenan,
Mulrenin, Mulrennan, Mulrennin, Mulreany, Renan ;
' des. of mᴀoꞮͦʀeᴀnᴀɪnn ' (servant of St.
Brendan) ; the name (1) of a family of Siol Muireadhaigh who
were chiefs of Clann Choncobhair, or Clan Connor, in
the present Co. Roscommon, and were seated in the
parish of Baslick, near Ballintobber ; and (2) of a
family of Ui Eachach Muaidhe in Tirawley, Co. Mayo.
It has in some places been corrupted to Ó mᴀoɪꞮ-
ͦʀeᴀnᴀɪꞮꞮ and Ó mᴀoɪꞮͦʀeᴀnᴀ.

Ó mᴀoɪꞮͦʀeᴀnnͦᴀɪn, Mulbrandon ; a var. in West
Clare of Ó mᴀoɪꞮͦʀeᴀnᴀɪnn, q.v.

Ó mᴀoɪꞮͦʀɪᵹͦe—I—*O Mulbridy, O Mulridy,* Mulbreedy, Mulbride, Mullbride, Millbride, Mulready,
Murready, Reid ; ' des. of mᴀoꞮͦʀɪᵹͦe ' (servant of
St. Brigid) ; the name of a family of Ui Maine who
were chiefs of Magh Finn, or Bredach, in the barony
of Athlone, Co. Roscommon, but were dispossessed
many centuries ago by the MacKeoghs and dispersed
through the neighbouring districts of Connacht and
Leinster. St. Brigid was patroness of the family,
and Bredach was dedicated to her.

Ó mᴀoɪꞮcéɪʀe—I—*O Mulchery, O Mulkery, O Mulcheir,
O Mulkere,* Mulkerry, Mulcair, Mulhare, Wilhere,
Wilhair ; ' des of mᴀoꞮcéɪꞃe ' (servant of St. Ciar).
This surname probably originated in Co. Galway
where it was most common in the 16th century. It
was current at the same period in Clare, Limerick,
Tipperary and Donegal. For Wilhair, the angl.
form in the last-named county, cf. Vaughan for
Maughan.

Ó mᴀoɪꞮcɪᴀʀᴀɪn—I—*O Mulchieraine, O Mulkerane,*
Mulkieran, Mulkearn, Mulkern, Mulkerrin, Mulheeran,
Mulheran, Mulherrin, Mulherron, Mulhern, Mulkearns,
Mulkerns, &c. ; ' des. of mᴀoꞮcɪᴀꞃᴀɪn ' (servant of
St. Ciaran) ; the name of an ecclesiastical family who
were erenaghs of Eaglais beg, at Clonmacnoise, and
of Ardcarne, in Co. Roscommon. A branch of the

family seems to have settled in Donegal sometime before the end of the 16th century. The name at that period was most frequent in Westmeath, Roscommon and Donegal.

Ó mАОіⱡⱱeіⱤᴢ—I—*O Molderge*, Mulderg, Mulderrig, Reid, (Reddington, Ruthledge) ; ' des. of mАОⱡⱱeАⱤᴢ' (the red chief), or very probably a corruption of the old surname Ó mАОіⱡᴢіⱤіc, q.v. ; an old surname in Donegal, whence it has spread into Mayo, where it is strangely angl. Reddington and Ruthledge. Reid (for Red) is a translation.

Ó mАОіⱡeАċáіn—I—Melican, Millican, Milliken, Millikin, &c. ; a var. of Ó mАОіⱡeАᴢáіn, q.v.

Ó mАОіⱡeАċáіn—I *O Mulleghan*, (Mulligan), Diamond, Diamon ; an attenuated form of Ó mАОⱡАċáіn, q.v. In Co. Galway, it is strangely angl. Diamond and Diamon, being erroneously supposed to be derived from ' muіⱡⱡeАċ,' a diamond (in cards).

Ó mАОіⱡeАċⱡАіnn—I—*O Melaghlin*, (MacLaughlin, MacLoughlin, &c., O'Loughlin, &c.) ; a var. of Ó mАОіⱡⱤeАċⱡАіnn, q.v.

Ó mАОіⱡeАᴢáіn—I—*O Moylegane, O Milligane, O Mellegan*, Milligan, Milligen, Millican, Melican, (Mulligan), &c. ; an attenuated form of Ó mАОⱡАᴢáіn, q.v.

Ó mАОіⱡeáіn—I—*O Moylane, O Melane*, Moylan, Millane, Millan, Miland, Moylin, Mullen, &c. ; an attenuated form of Ó mАОⱡáіn, q.v.

Ó mАОіⱡeАnАіᴢ—I—*O Mullany*, Mullany, Mullaney ; ' des. of mАОⱡⱤeАnАіᴢ,' (servant of St. Seanach) ; a common surname in Connacht, especially in Roscommon (where in 1540 the family was seated in the neighbourhood of Loch Cé), Mayo and Sligo ; also found in Cork and Antrim.

Ó mАОіⱡeАⱤcА—I—*O Moylearky, O Mullarkie*, Melarkey, Mullarkey, Malarky ; ' des. of mАОⱡeАⱤcА' (servant of St. Earc) ; formerly a Tirconnell surname ; now more common in Connacht.

Ó mАОіⱡeАⱤnА—I—(MacLarney) ; ' des. of mАОⱡeАⱤnА ' ; very rare.

Ó mᴀoᴠéᴠoᴠ—I—*O Mulledy, O Mulleadie, O Maledy, O Meledy,* Mulleady, Melledy, Meleady, Meledy, Melody, Malady ; ' des. of mᴀoᴠéᴠoᴠ ' (armoured chief). This surname, in the 16th century, was peculiar to the midlands, especially Westmeath and Offaly, where the family was highly respectable. There appears to have been also a family of the name in early times in Corcumroe, Co. Clare.

Ó mᴀoᴠéᴠmín—I—*O Mulleven, O Mullivine,* Mullavin, Mallavin, M'Lavin ; ' des. of mᴀoᴠéᴠmín ' (servant of St. Evin) ; very rare.

Ó mᴀoᴠᴠeóᴠn—I—*O Mullone, O Melone, O Malone,* Malone ; ' des. of mᴀoᴠᴠeóᴠn ' (servant of St. John) ; the name of a distinguished ecclesiastical family at Clonmacnoise, of which several O'Malones were abbots and bishops. In the 17th century, they rose to power and influence as landed proprietors, and after 1691 seem to have thrown in their lot with the English. Anthony Malone was a celebrated figure in Irish public life about the middle of the 18th century. His nephew, Richard Malone, was in 1785 created Baron Sunderlin ; while another nephew, Edmond Malone, was the celebrated Shakesperian commentator.

Ó mᴀoᴠᴠᴠinn—I—*O Molling, O Mullinn,* Mullin, Mullins ; ' des. of mᴀoᴠᴠᴠonn ' (fair chief) ; a rare South Leinster surname. The Four Masters at the year 1041 record the death of mᴀoᴠᴠᴠᴠᴠoe Uᴀ mᴀoᴠᴠᴠᴠino, Bishop of Glendalough.

Ó mᴀoᴠᴠᴠeᴠᴠc, Ó mᴀoᴠᴠᴠᴠᴠc—I—*O Mulgherick, O Mulhericke, O Mullerick,* Mullerick, Millerick ; ' des. of mᴀoᴠᴠᴠᴠc ' (servant of St. Cyriacus) ; an old Tirconnell surname, formerly not uncommon, but now probably often corrupted to Ó mᴀoᴠᴠᴠeᴠᴠᴠ, q.v. mᴀeᴠᴠᴀ Ó mᴀoᴠᴠᴠᴠc, chief poet and ard-ollav of Ireland, is mentioned in the annals at the year 1088.

Ó mᴀoᴠᴠín—I—*O Moyline, O Mulline, O Myline,* Moylin, Mulleen, Mullin, &c. ; ' des. of mᴀoᴠᴠín ' (dim. of mᴀoᴠ, bald) ; a var. of Ó mᴀoᴠᴠeᴠᴠn and Ó mᴀoᴠᴠᴠn, q.v.

Ó mᴀoιᴌíosᴀ—I—Mellowes; 'des. of mᴀoᴌíopᴀ' (servant of Jesus); apparently modern.

Ó mᴀoιᴌṁeᴀ'ᴅᴀ—I—*O Moylevagh, O Molvay*, Mulvagh, Mulvey; 'des. of mᴀoᴌṁeᴀ'ᴅᴀ' (probably chief of Meadh, a place-name); the name of an old Thomond family who were chiefs of Cinel mBaoith, and seated in the neighbourhood of Milltown-Malbay.

Ó mᴀoιᴌṁeᴀnᴀ—I—*O Mowlvenna, O Mulvany*, Mulvany, Mulvanny, Mulvenna, Mulvenny, Melvenny; 'des. of mᴀoᴌṁeᴀnᴀ' (probably follower of meᴀnᴀ); the name of an Ulster family who were ollavs to O'Kane.

Ó mᴀoιᴌṁiᴀ'ᴅᴀιꞡ—I—*O Mulmee*, Mulvey; 'des. of mᴀoᴌmiᴀ'ᴅᴀċ' (honourable chief); the name of a family of the same stock as the MacRannals and O'Farrells, who were chiefs of muιnnceᴀp Čeᴀpᴅᴀᴌᴌᴀin, in Magh Nisi, a district on the east side of the Shannon, in the barony and county of Leitrim, and sometimes of all muιnnceᴀp eoᴌᴀιp. The family, which was a distinguished one, is frequently mentioned in the Irish annals, and is still well represented in Co. Leitrim.

Ó mᴀoιᴌṁιċιᴌ, ó mᴀoιᴌṁιċíᴌ—I—*O Mulmichell, O Mulvihill, O Mulveill*, Mulvihill, Melville, Mitchell, Michael, &c.; 'des. of mᴀoᴌṁιċιᴌ' (servant of St. Michael); the name of a family of Sιoᴌ muιpeᴀ'ᴅᴀιꞡ, or Sil-Murray, in Co. Roscommon, who derive their descent from mᴀoᴌṁιċιᴌ, chief of Sιoᴌ muιpeᴀ'ᴅᴀιꞡ, who fought at the battle of Cill Ua nDaighre, near Dublin, in 866. They were at one time chiefs of Corca Sheachlainn, a district in the east of Co. Roscommon, but appear to have lost their rank at an early period. The name was, however, common in that county at the end of the 16th century, and branches of the family had about the same time settled in Tipperary, Limerick, Cork and Kerry, where they still flourish.

Ó mᴀoιᴌṁín—I—*O Mullivine*, Mullveen, Mulveen, Mulvin, Molvin, Melvin; 'des. of mᴀoᴌmín' (polished chief). Cf. mᴀc ꞡιoᴌᴌᴀṁín.

Ó mᴀoɪLpeᴀ'oᴀɪʀ—I—*O Mulfadder*, Mullpeters ; ' des.
of mᴀoᴛpeᴀ'oᴀɪp ' (servant of St. Peter) ; the name
of a family of Corca Laoighdhe, in South-West Cork ;
found in Leix at the close of the 16th century ; has
always been exceedingly rare. Father O'Growney
found Mullpeters in the United States of America.

Ó mᴀoɪLʀéᴀnᴀ—I—*O Mulriany, O Mulreany*, Mulreany ; a corruption of Ó mᴀoɪLᴛpéᴀnᴀɪnn, q.v. All
the evidence is in favour of this view.

Ó mᴀoɪLʀɪᴀᴛᴀɪ5—I—*O Mulreigh*, Mulreavy, Milreavy,
&c. ; ' des. of mᴀoᴛpɪᴀᴛᴀᴛ ' (grey or swarthy chief).

Ó mᴀoɪLʀɪᴀ5ᴀɪn, Ó mᴀoɪLʀɪᴀɪn—I—*O Mulrigan,
O Mulryan, O Mulrean*, Mulryan, Mulroyan, Mulryne,
Mulrine, Mulrain, O'Ryan, Ryan ; ' des of mᴀoᴛ-
pɪᴀɪn ' (follower of ʀɪᴀ5ᴀn or ʀɪᴀn) ; the name of a
family of Leinster origin who settled in the 13th or
14th century in Uaithne-tire and Uaithne-cliach,
now the baronies of Owney, in Co. Tipperary, and
Owneybeg, in the east of Co. Limerick, where they
became very numerous and powerful. In 1610,
William Ryan surrendered to the king all his landed
property and all his rights of or in the barony of
Owney O Mulrian, and received them back by letters
patent. The family property was, however, lost in
the confiscations of the 17th century. There are
many very respectable families of the name in Tipperary and Limerick, and the name itself is very
common in these counties. It is to be distinguished
from Ó ʀɪᴀn, q.v.

Ó mᴀoɪLseᴀᴛLᴀɪnn—I—*O Mulshaghlen, O Melaghlin*,
(MacLaughlin, MacLoughlin, &c., O Loughlan,
O Loughlin) ; ' des. of mᴀoᴛpeᴀᴛLᴀɪnn ' (servant of St.
Secundinus) ; the name of a once celebrated Meath
family, of the race of Niall of the Nine Hostages, who
derive their descent from Maelsheachlainn, or Malachy
II, King of Ireland, who was dethroned by Brian
Boru and died in the year 1022. The clan-name of
the O Melaghlins and their co-relatives was Clann
Cholmain. Before the Anglo-Norman invasion they

were kings of Meath, but after that period their
power greatly declined. Meath was granted to Hugh
de Lacy, and for many centuries the O Melaghlens
were confined to the barony of Clonlonan in Westmeath. They were, however, one of the five Irish
families who had the privilege of using English laws.
In the reign of James I they were again stripped of a
considerable portion of what remained of their ancient
patrimony ; and so completely had this ancient and
once powerful family been ruined by the confiscations
of the 17th century that in the attainders of 1691
there appears but one person of the name, Maol-
seachlin O Melaghlin, of Lough Mask, Co. Mayo.
The name is now everywhere disguised under the
angl. forms of MacLaughlin, MacLoughlin, &c.

Ó mᴀoιlꞅⲧéιⲅe—I—*O Mulstegia, O Molstaygh, O Mul-
stey, O Mustey,* Mustay, M'Stay, MacStay ; ' des.
of mᴀoιꞃⲧéιⲅe ' ; the name of an ecclesiastical family
in the diocese of Dromore, Co. Down ; now very rare.

Ó mᴀoιlꞅιonóⲅ—I—Mulshinogue ; ' des. of mᴀoι-
ꞃιonóⲅ.'

Ó mᴀolᴀcáιn—I—*O Molaghan, O Molleghan,* Molohan,
Mallaghan, (Mulligan) ; ' des. of mᴀolᴀcán ' (from
mᴀol, bald) ; a rare surname. In Connacht it is
generally angl. Mulligan. Ó mᴀoιleᴀcáιn, q.v., is
an attenuated form.

Ó mᴀolᴀⲅáιn—I—*O Mollegane, O Mullegan, O Mul-
ghan,* Mullagan, Mulligan, Mulgan, (Molyneux), Baldwin, &c. ; ' des of mᴀolᴀⲅán ' (dim. of mᴀol, bald) ;
the name of a Tirconnell family who were chiefs of
Tir MacCarthainn, in the east of the barony of Boylagh, but seem to have been dispossessed and dispersed at an early period. At the end of the 16th
century, the name, while most frequent in Ulster, was
not uncommon in the other provinces. It is said
to have been anglicised Molyneux and Baldwin in
Donegal, the latter form being intended as a translation, i.e., Bald one. Ó mᴀoιleᴀⲅáιn and Ó mᴀoιleᴀcáιn (q.v.) are attenuated forms.

Ó mАоLáin—I—*O Mollane, O Melane, O Moylane,*
O'Mullane, O'Mullan, Mullane, Mulhane, Melane,
Millane, Millan, Mullan, Mullen, Mullon, Mollan,
Moylan, Mullins, &c. ; ' des. of mАоLán ' (dim. of
mАоL, bald). This surname, which is one of the
commonest in Ireland, is found in almost every part
of the country, but under a great variety of angl.
forms. There are, no doubt, several distinct families
so called, but apparently the only dynastic family
of the name was that of O'Kane's country, in Co.
Derry. Ó mАоiLeáin (q.v.) is a variant.

Ó mАоLАinbte, v. Ó mАоLАnfАib.

Ó mАоLАic—I—(Mulloy) ; a shortened form of Ó
mАоLАicce, q.v.

Ó mАоLАicce—I—Mullahy, (Mulloy) ; ' des. of mАоL-
Аicce ' or ' mАоLАicseiṅ ' (votary of regeneration) ;
the name of a family of Ui Eachach Muaidhe, in Co.
Mayo, where, though very rare, it still survives. It
is sometimes shortened to Ó mАоLАic and angl.
Mulloy. The family was also called Ó mАоLАicseiṅ, q.v.

Ó mАоLАicseiṅ—I—(Mullahy, Mulloy) ; ' des. of
mАоLАicseiṅ ' (votary of regeneration) ; an alias for
Ó mАоLАicce (q.v.), which is probably a corruption
of it. The Four Masters, at the year 1099, mention
an erenagh of bún of this name.

Ó mАоLАLАib—I—*O Mullaly, O Mullally,* Mullally,
Mullaly, Lally ; ' des. of mАоLАLАb ' (speckled chief) ;
the name of a branch of the Ui Maine in Co. Galway.
They are of the same descent as the O'Neachtains, and
both families originally formed one clan, called Ui
Fiachrach Finn from their ancestor, Fiachra Fionn,
grandson of Maine Mór, the common ancestor of all
the Ui Maine. The clan lands comprised the fertile
plain of Maonmhagh, lying around Loughrea, but
about the time of the Anglo-Norman invasion the
O'Mullallys were dispossessed by the Burkes and
forced to retire to the parish of Tuam, where they
settled at Tulach na dála, angl. Tullaghnadaly, or
Tolendal, four miles to the north of the town of Tuam.

604

In the wars of the 17th century, they adhered to the Stuart cause. James Lally of Tullindaly sat as representative of Tuam in King James's Parliament of 1689. He was attainted in 1691 together with his brother, Gerald, whereupon they both retired to France. Gerald married a noble French lady, and their son and grandson, the Counts Lally de Tollendal, made the name celebrated in Europe.

Ó maolanḟaıṫ—I—Mullanphy, Melanphy; ' des. of maolanḟaıṫ ' (chief of the storm).

Ó maol an ṁuaıṫ—I— (Molyneux) ; ' des. of maol an ṁuaıṫ ' (follower of the noble) ; probably a distorted form of Ó maolṁuaıṫ, q.v. ; in use in North Kerry, pronounced Ó mullanua and angl. Molyneux.

Ó maolaoṫa—I—O Mollaye, O Mullae, O Mulley, O Mullye, O Mellawa, O Miley, O Moloy, O'Mealue, (O Malley), Mallew, Melay, Millea, Miley, Mullee, (Mulloy, Molloy, Malley) ; ' des. of maolaoṫa ' (servant of St. Aedh) ; the name of a family of Cinel Aonghusa, a sept of the Cinel Eoghain, in Ulster, Ó maolaoṫa was one of the hostages given by Aodh O Neill to Roderick O'Connor, King of Ireland, in 1167. At the end of the 16th century, the name was very scattered. In the North it seems to have been generally anglicised by assimilation to Malley, but in Connacht, where, under the form of Ó maoılaoṫa (q.v.), it is not uncommon, it is generally angl. Mulloy, sometimes Mullee. See also Ó maolaoṫóᵹ and Ó maolṁaoṫóᵹ.

Ó maolaoṫóᵹ—I—O Mologe, O Molouge Loague, Logue, (Mulloy, Molloy) ; a var. of Ó maolaoṫa and Ó maolṁaoṫóᵹ, q.v. ; a Donegal surname ; also in use in Co. Mayo, angl. Mulloy and Molloy.

Ó maolaoıṫ—I—Mullee, Mulloy. V. Ó maoılaoıṫ and Ó maolaoṫa.

Ó maolaṫarᴄaıᵹ—I—Mulhartagh ; a var. of Ó maolḟaᴄarᴄaıᵹ, q.v.

Ó maolḃáın—I—O Mullowane, Mulvane ; ' des. of maolḃán ' (white chief).

Ó mᴀoʟ́ḃʟoᵹᴀın—I—O *Mollowne*, Mullowne, Malone;
' des. of mᴀoʟ́ḃʟoᵹᴀın'; the name of an old Tipperary
family who were seated in Muscraighe Treitherne, in
the present barony of Clanwilliam. The family is
still extant, but cannot always be distinguished from
that of Ó mᴀoıʟeóın, q.v.

Ó mᴀoʟċᴀısıʟ—I—O *Mulcashell*, Mulcashel, (Mountcashel), Cashel; ' des. of mᴀoʟċᴀıᵱıʟ' (chief of Cashel);
the name of a Thomond family who were seated
originally at Ballymulcashel, near Six-mile-Bridge,
Co. Clare. Coᵱmᴀcᴀ́n Ó mᴀoʟċᴀıᵱıʟ was Bishop of
Killaloe in the early part of the 11th century. The
name is now very rare. In the neighbourhood of
Kilmallock, the angl. form was changed about eighty
years ago by the local registrar to Mountcashel, and
so it remains to the present day.

Ó mᴀoʟċᴀʟʟᴀnn—I—O *Mulchallan*, O *Maghallon*, O
Mohallan, Mulhallen, Mulhollan, Mulholn, Mulholland, Maholland, Holland, &c.; ' des. of mᴀoʟċᴀʟʟᴀnn' (chief of the kalends); the name of three
distinct families in Ireland: (1) of a branch of the Ui
Fidhgheinte, who were chiefs of Caonraidhe, now the
barony of Kenry, in the north of Co. Limerick; (2) of
a Meath family who were chiefs of Dealbhna beg,
now the barony of Demifore; and (3) of an ecclesiastical family in Ulster who from at least the beginning of the 12th down to the end of the 18th
century were keepers of the Bell of St. Patrick, known
as the Bell of the Testament, though it would appear
from the Irish annals that the family of O'Meallain
was at one time associated with them in the guardian-
ship. This is apparently the only family of the name
now extant. They were seated in the barony of
Loghinsholin, in the present county of Derry. A
branch of the family seems to have settled early in
Co. Antrim. The name is common in Ulster, but is
sometimes confused with Ó mᴀoʟċoʟuım, q.v.

Ó mᴀoʟċᴀoın—I—O *Mulchine*, O *Mulkyne*, O *Mulqueen*, O *Mulquin*, Mulkeen, Mulqueen, Mulquin;

' des. of mᴀolcᴀoin ' (gentle chief) ; the name of a
bardic family in Thomond. The Four Masters, under
the year 1096, record the death of Ua Maelcain, ollav
of the Dál gCais. The name is still well known in
Thomond, and is also current in parts of Connacht.
Ó mᴀolcᴀoine (q.v.) is a variant.

Ó mᴀolcᴀoine—I—*O Mulqueeny, O Mulkeiny,* Mulqueeny, Mulqueen ; ' des. of mᴀolcᴀoine ' (servant of
St. Caoine). This has been for centuries an alias for
Ó mᴀolcᴀoin in the spoken language of Thomond.
Thus, among the besiegers of Ballyally castle in 1641
was O'Mulqueen of Ballymulqueeny. It would appear
from the Annals of the Four Masters, A.D. 1096, that
Ó mᴀolcᴀoin is the original and correct form of the
name. Cf. mᴀc ɢiollᴀcᴀoin and mᴀc ɢiollᴀ-
cᴀoine.

Ó mᴀolcᴀtᴀ, Ó mᴀolcᴀtᴀiɢ—I—*O Mulcaha, O
Mulcahy,* Mulcahy ; ' des. of mᴀolcᴀtᴀ' (battle-chief), or
' mᴀolcᴀtᴀc' (warlike chief), or ' mᴀolcᴀtᴀiɢ ' (follower
of Cᴀtᴀc, warlike) ; a well-known Munster surname.
It seems to have originated in South Tipperary, but
is now common also in Waterford, Cork and Limerick.

Ó mᴀolcᴀtᴀil—I—*O Mulcahill, O Molchaill,* Mulhall ;
' des. of mᴀolcᴀtᴀil ' (servant of St. Cathal) ; the
name of an old family in Offaly and Leix ; still
numerous in the latter county and other parts of
Leinster.

Ó mᴀolcᴀtáin—I—*O Mulchathayn, O Mulcayhan,* Mulhatton ; ' des. of mᴀolcᴀtáin ' (servant of St. Catan) ;
very rare.

Ó mᴀolclᴀoin—I—Mulkeen, Mucleen ; ' des. of mᴀol-
clᴀon ' (deceitful chief) ; a rare Connacht surname.

Ó mᴀolcluice—I—*O Molklyhy, O Mulclohy, O Mulclahy, O Mulcloy, O Mucklie, Mulclahy,* (Mulcahy),
Muckley, Stone ; ' des. of mᴀolcluice ' (gamester) ;
the name of a Sligo family who were chiefs of Cairbre,
now the barony of Carbury, in the north of that
county, until dispossessed by the O'Dowds in the
14th century. In the 16th century, the name was

very scattered, but found chiefly in Donegal, West-meath, Offaly and Cork. In the census of 1659, it appears as Mulclahy in Co. Limerick. It is now nearly everywhere angl. Stone owing to an erroneous idea that the latter part of the name is ' cloiċe,' gen. of ' cloċ,' a stone, while really the gen. of ' cluiċe,' a game. In Limerick it has been turned into the more common surname, Mulcahy, while in Co. Cork it has become Muckley. The old form of the name is preserved in Inishmulclohy, also called Coney Island, in Sligo Bay.

Ó mᴀolċolm, Ó mᴀolċoluim—I—O *Molcalm, O Molchalum*, Malcolm, Mulholm, Mulhollum, Maholm, Mahollum ; ' des of mᴀolċolm ' or ' mᴀolċoluim ' (servant of St. Columcille) ; an Antrim surname. The Four Masters, under the year 1061, record the death of muiⱏeᴀᴅᴀċ uᴀ mᴀolċoluim, erenagh of Derry.

Ó mᴀolċomᴀᴅ—I—O *Mollchomy*, Mulumy, Molumby ; ' des. of mᴀol Comᴀᴅ ' ; the name of an ancient family of Corca Laoighdhe, in South-West Cork.

Ó mᴀolċonᴀiⱍe—I—O *Mulchonery, O Mulconry*, Mul-conry, Conry, (Conroy) ; ' des. of mᴀolċonᴀiⱍe ' (follower of Conᴀiⱍe) ; the name of a celebrated literary family who were poets and chroniclers to the Kings of Connacht and other families of Siol Muire-adhaigh. They were seated at Clonahee, near Strokes-town, in Co. Roscommon, where they had consider-able property in right of their profession. Many distinguished poets and historians of the name are mentioned in the Irish annals. A learned branch of this family, to which frequent reference is made in Irish literary history, settled at Ardkyle, in the parish of Feenagh, Co. Clare. John O'Mulconry, a member of this family, who flourished during the first half of the 17th century, was a profound Irish scholar and ' chief teacher in history of all the men of Erin in his own time.' The O'Mulconrys also produced some eminent ecclesiastics among whom may be mentioned Florence O'Mulconry, Archbishop of Tuam and founder of the Irish Franciscan convent of Louvain. The name is now unfortunately too often disguised by being anglicised Conry and Conroy.

Ó MAOLĊRAOIḂE—I—*O Mulcrieve, O Mulchrewe, O Mulcrey,* Mulcreevy, Mulgrievy, Mulgrave, Mulgrew, Mulgroo, Rice; 'des. of Maolċraoiḃe' (chief of Craoḃ, a place-name); the name of an Oriel family who were originally located westward of the Upper Bann, but afterwards settled in Clannaboy, where they were followers of the O'Neills. At the beginning of the 17th century they occupied the west side of Knockbreda, near Belfast, in Co. Down, but the name was even then scattered through Tyrone, Armagh and Antrim. It is still common throughout East Ulster, but generally angl. Rice.

Ó MAOLĊRÓIN—I—Mulchrone, Mulcrone, Mulcroan, Mulcroon; 'des of Maolcrón' (swarthy chief); the name of an old family of Ui Maine; now found chiefly in Mayo, but rare even there.

Ó MAOLĊRÓINE—I—Mulcrowney; 'des of Maol-ċróine' (servant of St. Croine); a rare surname. Cf. Kilcroney for Cill Ċróine, Co. Wicklow.

Ó MAOLDOṀNAIĠ—I—*O Muldowny,* Muldowney, Muldooney, Downey, Dawney; more frequently Ó Maol-doṁnaiġ, q.v.

Ó MAOLḊOṀNAIĠ—I—*O Malowny, O Mollowny, O Mullowny,* Malowny, Molowny, Mullowney, Moloney, Molony, &c.; 'des. of Maoldoṁnaiġ' (devoted to Sunday, or to the Church); the name of a Dalcassian family who were chiefs of a district in the barony of Tulla, Co. Clare; now very numerous throughout Munster. Ó Maoldoṁnaiġ (q.v.) is the same surname, but the family is apparently different.

Ó MAOLDORAIḊ—I—Muldarry, Mulderry, Meelderry; 'des. of Maoldoraiḋ' (contentious chief); the name of a branch of the Cinel Conaill who in the 10th, 11th and 12th centuries were chiefs of Tirconnell; still extant, but very rare.

Ó mᴀoʟᴅuiᴅ—I—Maliffe ; ' des. of mᴀoʟᴅuᴅ ' (black chief) ; the name of a family of Ui Maine ; very rare.

Ó mᴀoʟᴅúın—I—*O Muldoon*, Muldoon, Muldon, Meldon ; ' des. of mᴀoʟᴅúın ' (chief of the fort) ; the name of several distinct families, as : (1) of an Oriel family who until the end of the 14th century were chiefs of Feara Luirg, now the barony of Lurg, in the north of Co. Fermanagh, and are still numerous in that county ; (2) of a branch of the Ui Fiachrach in Co. Sligo ; and (3) of a Thomond family.

Ó mᴀoʟꝼᴀ́ᴅᴀıʟ, Ó mᴀoʟꝼᴀ́ᴅᴀıʟ—I—*O Mowlfoull*, *O Mulfall*, *O Maylawell*, Mulfaal, Mulavill, (Melville), Lawell, Lavelle, (MacFaal, MacFall, MacPaul, Paul) ; ' des. of mᴀoʟꝼᴀ́ᴅᴀıʟ ' (fond of travel) ; the name (1) of a family of Cinel Eoghain who were chiefs of Carraig Brachaidh, angl. Carrickabraghy, in the north-west of the barony of Inishowen, Co. Donegal ; and (2) of a West Connacht family. It is generally angl. Mulfall, or MacFaal, in Ulster, but Lavelle in Connacht, where it is now most numerous.

Ó mᴀoʟꝼᴀᴄᴛnᴀ—I—*Mullaghny*, *Meloughna*, Mulloughney, Mologhney, Mollowney, (Mollony, Moloney) ; ' des. of mᴀoʟꝼᴀᴄᴛnᴀ ' (servant of St. Fachtna) ; an old Tipperary surname, now generally assimilated to Moloney.

Ó mᴀoʟꝼᴀᴄᴀʀᴛᴀıɡ—I—Mulhartagh ; ' des. of mᴀoʟꝼᴀᴄᴀʀᴛᴀıɡ ' (follower of ꝼᴀᴄᴀʀᴛᴀᴄ) ; the name of a family of Cinel Eoghain in Ulster ; now very rare.

Ó mᴀoʟꝼoɡṁᴀıʀ, Ó mᴀoʟꝼoɡṁᴀıʀ—I—*O Mulfover*, *O Mullover*, (Milford, Palmer) ; ' des. of mᴀoʟꝼoɡṁᴀıʀ ' (chief of harvest) ; the name of a distinguished ecclesiastical family who were erenaghs of the church of Killala, and supplied several bishops to that see. O Donovan found the name still in the district, but angl. Milford. According to MacFirbis, the family of mᴀᴄ ᴄéıʟe (q.v.) is a branch of that of Ó mᴀoʟꝼoɡṁᴀıʀ.

Ó mᴀoʟɡᴀoıᴛe—I—*O Mulgehy*, *O Mulgey*, Mulgeehy, (Magee), Wynne ; ' des. of mᴀoʟɡᴀoıᴛe ' (chief of the wind) ; the name of a Tirconnell family who were seated originally in the parish of Clondavaddock, Co. Donegal ; now more common in Connacht, where, however, it is generally disguised under the angl. forms of Magee and Wynne (for Wind).

Ó mᴀoᴌᵹuᴀᴌᴀ—I—O *Mulloly*, Mulooly, Mulhooly ; ' des. of mᴀoᴌᵹuᴀᴌᴀ ' (glutton).

Ó mᴀoᴌṁᴀᵹnᴀ—I—*O Mulvanny*, Mulvany, Mulvanny ; ' des. of mᴀoᴌṁᴀᵹnᴀ ' ; the name of a Tirconnell family who were chiefs of Magh Seiridh, in the north of the barony of Tirhugh, Co. Donegal.

Ó mᴀoᴌṁᴀoᴅóᵹ—I—*O Mulmoge, O Mulvoge*, Mullavogue, (Mulloy, Molloy) ; ' des. of mᴀoᴌṁᴀoᴅóᵹ ' (servant of St. mᴀoᴅóᵹ, or Mogue) ; a var. of Ó mᴀoᴌᴀoᴅóᵹ, q.v. ; a Donegal surname ; now generally disguised under the angl. form of Mulloy or Molloy.

Ó mᴀoᴌṁᴀʀᴛᴀın—I—*O Molmartine*, Martin ; ' des. of mᴀoᴌṁᴀʀᴛᴀın ' (servant of St. Martin).

Ó mᴀoᴌṁoċóıʀ, Ó mᴀoᴌṁoċóıʀᵹe, Ó mᴀoᴌṁoıċeıʀᵹe—I—*O Mulmochore, O Mullmochory, O Molvochory, O Mullucherie*, Early, Earley, Eardley ; ' des. of mᴀoᴌṁoċeıʀᵹe ' (chief of early rising, or fond of early rising). Ó mᴀoᴌṁoıċeıʀᵹe was the original form ; in the spoken language it became Ó mᴀoᴌṁoċóıʀᵹe, or Ó mᴀoᴌṁoċóıʀ, now generally shortened to Ó moċóıʀᵹe and Ó moċóıʀ, q.v. ; the name of an ecclesiastical family in the diocese of Kilmore, the head of which was coarb of Drumreilly, in Co. Leitrim, and of Drumlane, in Co. Cavan. MacFirbis mentions a family of this name among the Siol Muireadhaigh in Co. Roscommon. Before the end of the 16th century, the name had spread into Sligo and Donegal. It is now everywhere angl. Early, Earley or Eardley.

Ó mᴀoᴌmónᴀ—I—Mulmona, Moss ; ' des. of mᴀoᴌmónᴀ ' (chief of the bog) ; a rare Ulster surname. Moss is a ' translation,'

Ó mᴀoᴌmuᴀıᴅ—I—*O Molmoy, O Mulmoy*, Milmo, Milmoe ; a var. of Ó mᴀoᴌṁuᴀıᴅ, q.v. ; a rare Sligo surname.

Ó maolṁuaiṫ—I—*O Molwye, O Meloy, O Molloye, O Mulloye,* O'Molloy, Meloy, Molloy, Mulloy, &c. ; 'des. of maolmuaṫ' (noble chief) ; the name (1) of a distinguished family of the southern Ui Neill, in Meath. They are of the same descent as the Mageoghegans, and both families originally formed one clan, called Cinel Fiachach from their common ancestor, Fiacha, son of Niall of the Nine Hostages. In the 10th or 11th century, Cinel Fiachach and its territory was divided between the two families, Mageoghegan retaining the northern portion under the original clan-name, Cinel Fiachach, and O'Molloy becoming lord of the southern portion, under the name of Feara Ceall. This territory, which comprised the modern baronies of Fircall, Ballycowan and Ballyboy in Offaly, remained in the possession of the O'Molloys down to the beginning of the 17th century. The O'Molloys were hereditary bearers of the British standard in Ireland. (2) MacFirbis mentions another family of the name, a branch of the Siol Muireadhaigh, in Co. Roscommon. They belonged to the sept known as Clann Taidhg na h-oidhche and are now, according to O'Donovan, represented by the Molloys of Oakpark, near Boyle. Ó maolmuaiṫ (q.v.) is a Sligo variant. See also Ó maol an ṁuaiṫ.

Ó maolṁuiʀe—I—*O Moylery,* Mullery, Mulry, (Miles, Myles) ; ' des. of maolṁuiʀe ' (servant of Mary) ; the name of a family of Cinel Eoghain who were at one time chiefs of Cinel Fearadhaigh, in Ulster ; now rare. In Co. Mayo it is angl. Myles.

Ó maolpáḋʀaiʒ—I—*O Mulfadricke, O Mulpatrick,* (?) Fitzpatrick ; ' des. of maolpáḋʀaiʒ ' (servant of St. Patrick) ; once a common surname, especially in Cavan and Cork. In the year 1602, Conor O Molpatrick, ' chief of his name,' was included in a list of pardons for Co. Cavan. Though the name has disappeared, the family was too numerous to have died out, and the probability is that, like the Mac Gillapatricks of Ossory, they have anglicised it to Fitzpatrick.

Ó mᴀoᴌꞃuᴀ́ɽᴓ—I—*O Melrewe*, Mulroe, Mulroy, Mulry, Mulrow, Melroy, Milroy, (Munroe, Monroe) ; ' des. of mᴀoᴌꞃuᴀᴓ ' (red chief) ; ·the name of a family of Ui Fiachrach who were originally seated in the parish of Ardagh, in Tirawley, Co. Mayo. It is still common in Mayo and Galway, but sometimes angl. Monroe.

Ó mᴀoᴌꞃuᴀɪɴ—I—*O Molrone, O Mulrowne*, Mulroon, Meldron ; short for Ó mᴀoᴌꞃuᴀnᴀɽᴓ, q.v.

Ó mᴀoᴌꞃuᴀnᴀɽᴓ—I—*O Mulruony, O Mulrony, O Moronie*, Mulrooney, Mulrony, Murroney, Morooney, Moroney, &c. ; ' des. of mᴀoᴌꞃuᴀnᴀɽᴓ ' (follower of Ꞃuᴀnᴀɽᴓ) ; the name (1) of a Fermanagh family who antecedently to the Maguires were lords of that county ; (2) of a Galway family who were chiefs of Crumhthan, angl. Cruffan, a district comprising the barony of Killyan and part of the adjoining barony of Ballimoe ; (3) of a Dalcassian family who are still numerous in Clare, Limerick and Tipperary, where however, the name is corrupted to Ó muꞃꞃuᴀnᴀɽᴓ and anglicised Moroney, &c. ; and (4) of a Roscommon family who afterwards adopted the surname of mᴀc ᴅɪᴀꞃmᴀᴅᴀ, or MacDermott.

Ó mᴀoᴌꞇuɪᴌe—I—*O Multilly, O Multully*, Tully, Flood ; ' des. of mᴀoᴌꞇuɪᴌe ' (devoted to the will, i.e., of God ; erroneously supposed to mean chief of the flood) ; also mᴀc mᴀoᴌꞇuɪᴌe and mᴀc ṁᴀoᴌꞇuɪᴌe ; the name of a medical family in Connacht and other parts of Ireland. They were hereditary physicians to the O'Connors of Connacht, the O'Reillys of Breifney, &c. The name was not uncommon in Ossory, where, as early as the year 1571, it was angl. Fludd.

Ó mᴀonᴀɪᶃ—I—*O Moeny, O Mooney*, (?) *O Moyney, O Money*, Meany, Meeny, Mooney, Moany, Money ; ' des. of mᴀonᴀċ ' (wealthy) ; the name (1) of a Roscommon family who were anciently chiefs of Clann Murthuile ; (2) of a family of the Ui Fiachrach who were seated on the southern shore of Sligo Bay, in the barony of Tireragh ; and (3) of a branch of the Siol nAnmchadha, in the south-east of Co. Galway. At the end of the 16th century, the name was found in all parts of Ireland.

Ó mᴀonáın—I—*O Monane*, Moonan, Moynan, Monan; 'des. of mᴀonáın' (dim. of mᴀon, dumb).

Ó mᴀonᵹᴀıle—I—*O Monhily, O Monnilly*, Munnelly, Monnelly, Monley, Manley; 'des. of mᴀonᵹᴀl' (gift-valour); found chiefly in Donegal and North Connacht.

Ó mᴀotᴀᵹáın—I—*O Mehegane*, Meehegan, Mehegan, Mehigan; 'des. of mᴀotᴀᵹán' (dim. of mᴀot, soft, tender); an old Cork surname; also found in Kilkenny. Cf. Ó mᴀotáın.

Ó mᴀotáın—I—*O Meawhan*, Meehan; 'des. of mᴀotán' (dim. of mᴀot, soft); a rare surname, still in use in the neighbourhood of Shrule, Co. Mayo. Cf. Ó mᴀotᴀᵹáın.

Ó mᴀRcᴀĊáın—I—*O Markaghaine, O Marcahan*, Markahan, Markan, (Markham), Ryder; 'des. of mᴀpcᴀĊán' (dim. of mᴀpcᴀĊ, a rider); the name of an offshoot of Cinel Guaire, in south-west of Co. Galway. The family has been long settled in Thomond, where the name is now generally angl. Markham. Ryder, which is in use in some places, is a translation.

Ó mᴀRcᴀıᵹ—I—Markey, Ryder; 'des. of mᴀpcᴀĊ' (rider); a Monaghan surname. Cf. Ó mᴀpcᴀĊáın.

Ó mᴀRᴀnnáın, Ó mᴀRnáın—I—*O Marynayne, O Marrinan, O Marnane*, Marrinan, Marinane, Marnane, Marnan, Mornan, (Warren); a corruption of Ó mᴀnᴀnnáın, q.v.; also Ó mᴜpnáın, q.v. It is angl. Warren in the neighbourhood of Kenmare.

Ó mᴀRtᴀın—II—*O Marten, O Martin*, Martin, Marten; 'des. of Martin.' The Four Masters, under the year 1216, record the death of Giollaarnain Ua Martain, chief ollav of law in Ireland. In 1431, Bishop O'Martain of Clogher died.

Ó mᴀtᵹᴀṁnᴀ—I—*O Mahowny, O Mahown*, O'Mahony, Mahony, Mahon, Maughan, (MacMahon); 'des. of mᴀtᵹᴀṁᴀın' (bear); the name of a well-known Cork family who derive their descent from mᴀtᵹᴀṁᴀın (slain in 1014), whose father, Cian, son of Maolmuadh, commanded the forces of Desmond at the battle of Clontarf, and were chiefs of Cinel mBeice, now known as the barony of Kinelmeaky, an extensive district along the River Bandon, in Co. Cork, and at a later period became masters of the district called Fonn Iartharach, that is, the western land, which comprised several parishes in the south-west of Co. Cork, and had previously belonged to Corca Laoighdhe. Another family of the name was very powerful during the 11th and 12th centuries in Ulidia, and is still extant in Co. Down and other parts of East Ulster, but disguised as Mahons and MacMahons.

Ó meᴀċᴀıR—I—O'Meagher, *O Magher, O Maher,* Meagher, Magher, Maher ; ' des. of meᴀċᴀρ ' (hospitable) ; the name of a Tipperary family, of the same stock as the O'Carrolls of Ely-O'Carroll, who were lords of Ui Cairin, now the barony of Ikerrin, in the north of that county. O'Meachair resided at Druim Saileach, where now stands the castle of Moydrum, about five miles south of Roscrea. Shortly after the Anglo-Norman invasion, Ikerrin was added to Ormond, but O'Meachair was left in possession, as tributary, however, to the Earl of Ormond. The O'Meachairs have flourished exceedingly, and are now numerous and respectable, not only in their original territory at the foot of the Devil's Bit, but throughout the counties of Tipperary, Kilkenny and Carlow.

Ó meᴀᴅRᴀ—I—*O Mary,* O'Meara, O'Mara, Meara, Mara ; ' des. of meᴀᴅᴀıρ ' (mirth) ; the name of a Dalcassian family who were chiefs of a district called Rosarguid, in the barony of Upper Ormond, Co. Tipperary. O'Meara had his seat at Toomyvara (Cuᴀım Uı meᴀᴅρᴀ). The family retained considerable property down to the revolution of 1690.

Ó meᴀᴌᴌᴀıᵹ—I—*O Meallie, O Mellie, O Mella,* Melly, (Malley) ; ' des. of meᴀᴌᴌᴀċ ' (from ' meᴀᴌᴌ,' pleasant) ; the name of an old West Connacht family. Three bishops of the name filled the see of Annadown in the 13th and 14th centuries.

Ó meᴀllᴀin—I—*O Meallane, O Mellane, O Mallane*, O'Mellon, Mellan, Mellon, Mallan, Mallen, (Mullen), &c. ' des. of meᴀllᴀn ' (dim. of ' meᴀll,' pleasant) ; the name of an ecclesiastical family in Ulster—a branch of the Cinel Eoghain—who were hereditary keepers of the Bell of St. Patrick, known as the Bell of the Testament, and were seated in the parish of Donaghmore, near Dungannon, Co. Tyrone. The name is still common in Ulster, especially in Tyrone, Armagh and Antrim.

Ó meᴀ́Rᴀ, v. Ó meᴀ́ora.

Ó meᴀRᴀoᴀᴉ5—I—*O Marie, O Merye, O Merehey*, Mariga, Maree, Marry, Merry ; ' des. of meᴀpᴀoᴀċ ' (lively) ; the name of an ancient family who were chiefs of Ui Fathaidh, now the barony of Iffa and Offa West, Co. Tipperary. O'Donovan gives the angl. form as O'Meara or O'Mara, which is incorrect, the pronunciation being that represented by O'Merye and O'Merehey. It is undoubtedly the original form of the Waterford surname Merry, and synonymous with that now pronounced Ó meᴀpoᴀ (q.v.) in Waterford and East Cork. Dr. O'Brien, in his Irish Dictionary, and Dr. MacDermott, in his notes to Connellan's edition of the Annals of the Four Masters, both confound the families of Ó meᴀoᴘᴀ of Rosarguid and Ó meᴀpᴀoᴀᴉ5 of Ui Fathaidh, although their respective territories were separated by nearly the whole length of Tipperary.

Ó meᴀRᴀ́in—I—*O Mearan, O Meran*, Meran, Mearn, Marren, Marron ; ' des. of meᴀpᴀn ' (dim. of ' meᴀp,' lively) ; a scattered surname, now most frequent in Co. Monaghan, where it is angl. Marron.

Ó meᴀRoᴀ—I—*O Merga, O Mergey, O Merye*, Mariga, Maree, Marry, Merry ; ' des. of meᴀpoᴀ ' (lively) ; a variant of Ó meᴀpᴀoᴀᴉ5, q.v. ; a rare and scattered surname. For pronunciation of ending -oᴀ, cf. cpóoᴀ, pronounced cpó5ᴀ.

Ó meᴀRlᴀᴉ5—I—*O Marlie*, Marley ; perhaps a corruption of Ó mᴜp5ᴀᴉle, q.v. ; in use in Mayo.

Ó meıඳıʀ—I—*O Myre, O Mire*, Myres, Myers, Meyers, &c.;
' des. of meıඳıʁ ' (mirth ; cf. Ó meᴀඏʀᴀ) ; a Thomond
surname.

Ó meıʀȝín—I—*O Mergyne, O Mergin, O Merigan*,
Mergin, Merrigan ; a corruption of Ó háıḿeıʀȝın, q.v.

Ó méıʀʟeᴀċáın—I—Merlehan ; ' des. of méıʀʟeᴀċán ' ;
a Westmeath surname. It must have been always
exceedingly rare. The Four Masters, under the year
1001, record the killing of Meirleacan, son of Conn,
King of Gaileng, by Maelsechlainn. He was possibly
the ancestor from whom the family took its name.

(Ó) méıʀnín, Mernin ; a Waterford surname. I cannot
trace its origin.

Ó meıscıʟʟ—I—*O Meskill, O Miskill*, Meskell, Miskell,
Mescall, Mescel, (Maxwell) ; ' des. of meıʀceᴀʟʟ.'

Ó mıᴀඏᴀċáın—I—*O Mighane, O Meaghane, O Meighane,
O Mehane, O Myhane, O Meghan*, O'Meehan, O'Meehon,
Meeghan, Meighan, Meghan, Myhane, Myhan, Mehan,
Meehan, &c. ; ' des. of mıᴀඏᴀċán ' (dim. of ' mıᴀඏᴀċ,'
honourable) ; a common surname in nearly every part
of Ireland. There are, no doubt, several distinct
families so called. Ó míoඏċáın is a frequent, but
incorrect, spelling of the name. See also Ó mıᴀඏ-
ᴀȝáın.

Ó mıᴀඏᴀȝáın—I—*O Miagan, O Megan*, Meegan ; no
doubt, the same as Ó mıᴀඏᴀċáın, q.v. ; found in
Donegal and Monaghan.

Ó mıᴀඏᴀıȝ—I—*O Miey, O Mey*, Mee, Mea, May ; ' des.
of mıᴀඏᴀċ ' (honourable) ; an old Westmeath surname,
still found in the midlands, but now more frequently
in Roscommon and the southern parts of Mayo. It
was an Ó mıᴀඏᴀıȝ that terminated the career of Sir
Hugh de Lacy, ' the profaner and destroyer of many
churches,' by cutting off his head with a blow of an
axe at the castle of Durrow in 1186.

Ó mıᴀnáın—I—*O Minane, O Meanan*, Meenan ; ' des.
of mıᴀnán ' (dim. of mıᴀn, will, desire) ; the name of
an old Tirconnell family ; still common in Donegal
and Tyrone.

Ó mɩcⱴíre—I—Wolfe. V. Ó mⱥcⱴɩpe.

Ó mɩⱷɩr, Ó mír—I—*O Meere*, Meere, Miers, Mears, Meares, &c. ; probably the same as Ó meɩⱷɩp, q.v. ; found in Clare and Galway.

Ó mɩonⱥcáɩn—I—Minahane, Minahan, (Moynihan, Monahan) ; a var. in the spoken language of Ó mⱥnⱥcáɩn, q.v. To be distinguished from Ó muɩⱷneⱥcáɩn which has sometimes the same angl. forms.

Ó mɩrín—I—*O Mirren, O Merren*, Mirreen ; 'des. of mɩpín' (dim. of meⱥp, lively) ; the same as Ó meⱥpáɩn, q.v.

Ó mɩⱴɩⱷín—I—*O Myhiden, O Meehin*, O'Meehin, Meehin, Meehen, Meehan ; 'des. of mɩⱴɩⱷín' or 'mɩⱴɩʒeɩn' (born in June) ; the name (1) of an ecclesiastical family of Ui Maine who were coarbs of Clontuskert, near Ballinasloe ; and (2) of an ecclesiastical family in Co. Leitrim who were coarbs of St. Molaise at Ballaghmeehin, in the parish of Rossinver. About the middle of the last century, the termon lands of Ballaghmeehin were still farmed by a Mr. Meehin, a member of this ancient family. The angl. forms of this surname are apt to be confounded with those of Ó mɩⱥⱷⱥcáɩn, which is an entirely different surname and much more widespread.

Ó mocⱥɩⱷeɩn—I—MacKean ; 'des. of mocⱥɩⱷeɩn' ; the name of an Oriel family who were anciently lords of Cpíoc muʒⱷopn, now the barony of Cremorne in Co. Monaghan ; very rare.

Ó mocáɩn—I—*O Mochane, O Moghane, O Muoghane, O Moughan, O Moone*, Moghan, Mohan, Moughan, Moohan, Moan, Moen, Mowen, Moon, Mahon, Maughan, *Voghane*, Vaughan ; 'des. of mocán' (a 'pet' form of some name commencing with moc-, early) ; also Ó mⱥcáɩn, q.v. ; the name (1) of a family of Cinel Ianna, in the diocese of Kilmacduagh, who are still numerous in Co. Galway, where they generally anglicise the name Mahon ; (v. Ó mⱥcáɩn) ; and (2) of an ecclesiastical family—a branch of the Ui Fiachrach—in Co. Sligo, who were erenaghs of Killaraght, in the barony of Coolavin, and keepers of the cross of St. Attracta. They were great patrons of learning. Many of them were distinguished ecclesiastics. Gregory Ó Mochain was Archbishop of Tuam in the early part of the 14th century. Ó mocáin is now a fairly common surname all through the South of Ireland, as well as in Connacht. In Munster, it is generally angl. Vaughan, a form evidently derived from the gen. case Uí mocáin. Cf. the old angl. form Voghane.

Ó mocóin, Ó mocóinᵹe—I—*O Mucory*, Early, Earley, Eardley ; short forms of Ó maolmocóinᵹe, q.v. ; very common in the spoken language.

Ó mocca—I—*O Moght, O Mought*, Moughty ; ' des. of mocca ' (from ' mocc,' great) ; very rare.

Ó moᵹráin—I—*O Mourane, O Mouran*, O'Moran, Moran ; ' des. of muᵹrón ' (slave-seal) ; a corruption of Ó muᵹróin, q.v.

Ó móirín—I—*O Morine, O Moren, Moreen*, Morin, Moren, (Moran) ; ' des. of móirín ' (dim. of mór, great) ; a var. of Ó móráin, q.v.

Ó moitioe—?—*O Mohedie*, Mahedy, Mahady ; a rare Connacht surname. I cannot trace its origin.

Ó monᵹabáin—I—*O Mongevaine*, Mongavan, Mungavan, Mungavin ; ' des of monᵹbán ' (white hair) ; an old Clare surname.

Ó monᵹaiᵹ—I—Mongey, Mungay, Mungey ; ' des. of monᵹac ' (hairy) ; a Mayo surname. Ó monᵹacáin, its diminutive, occurs in the Four Masters, A.D. 1168.

Ó monᵹáin—I—*O Mongane*, Mongan, Mangan, Mangin, Mongon, (Mannion, Manning), &c. ; ' des. of monᵹán ' (dim. of monᵹac, hairy) ; the name of at least three distinct families, seated respectively in Cork, Mayo and Fermanagh. In the 16th century, it was not uncommon in Galway, Clare, Kerry, Tipperary, Kildare and Wexford. It is now generally angl. Mangan, but Mongan, which is nearer the original, is still preserved in Mayo and other parts of Ireland. Ó muinᵹeáin (q.v.) is an attenuated form.

Ó móráin—I—*O Moraine, O Morane, O Moran*, Moran ;

'des. of mópán' (dim. of móp, great) ; the name of a branch of the Ui Fiachrach, in the present counties of Mayo and Sligo, who ruled over an extensive district on both sides of the river Moy, and were a highly respectable family. The chief resided at Ardnaree, near Ballina. This surname is to be distinguished from Ó muʒpóın (q.v.), which is also angl. Moran. O'Moran was a common surname in the 16th century in all parts of Connacht and Leinster, and also in Ormond and Thomond.

Ó móṟvá—I—*O Mora, O Morey*, O'More, O'Moore, Morey, More, Moore ; ' des. of mópvá ' (majestic) ; the name of a distinguished Leinster family who were chiefs of Leix. Their chief fortress was at Dunamase, near Maryborough, the ruins of which still remain. The O'Mores make a remarkable figure in Irish history, having with conspicuous bravery defied for several centuries all the power of the English invaders to conquer their territory. Rory O'More, a celebrated chieftain in the reigns of Mary and Elizabeth, defeated them in many engagements ; and his son, Owney O'More, was a famous commander in the wars against Elizabeth. Perhaps no Irish family suffered greater cruelties at the hands of the English. In 1609, the remnant of the clan was transplanted to Kerry, where they were settled in the neighbourhood of Tarbert. Many of them, however, returned to their native territory, and the family is now well represented in Leinster.

Ó moṟṟuánáıv—I—*O Moronie*, Murroney, Morooney, Moroney ; a corruption of Ó máoıpuánáıv, q.v. ; common in Clare, Limerick and Tipperary.

Ó motáıṟ—I—*O Mogher, O Moher*, Moher, (Moore) ; ' des. of motáp ' (dark) ; an old Cork surname ; still extant, but extremely rare ; sometimes attenuated to Ó muıtıp.

Ó motlá, Ó motláıʒ—I—*O Mohele*, Mohilly, Moakley ; ' des. of motlác ' (shaggy) ; the name of a family of Corca Laoighdhe who were seated near Dromaleague in South-West Cork.

Ó moᴄʟᴀċᴁ́ın—I—O *Mohilaghane,* ꝛ *Moholane,* (?)
Mullane ; ' des. of moᴄʟᴀċᴁ́n ' (dim. of moᴄʟᴀċ,
shaggy) ; formerly a very common Munster surname.
It was too common to have died out, and must be
disguised under some strange angl. form, perhaps
Mullane.

Ó muᴀᴅᴀıᵹ, Moody.

Ó muᴀnᴁ́ın—I—O *Monane,* Moonan ; a northern pronunciation of Ó mᴀonᴁ́ın, q.v.

Ó muᵹꞃóın—I—O *Morone,* O'Moran, Moran ; ' des. of
muᵹꞃón ' (slave-seal) ; the name (1) of one of the chief
families of Clann Chathail, a branch of the Siol Muireadhaigh, in the present Co. Roscommon ; and (2) of a
branch of the Ui Maine, in Co. Galway, who were
chiefs of Cruffon, an extensive district comprising
the barony of Killyan and part of that of Ballymoe.
The name has been long changed to Ó moᵹꞃᴁ́ın (q.v.)
and is now angl. Moran.

Ó muıᵹe, Moy.

Ó muıċıꞃ, v. Ó moᴄᴀıꞃ.

Ó muıṁneᴀċᴁ́ın—I—O *Moyneghane,* O *Myneghane,*
Mynahan, Minahan, Moynahan, Moynihan, Moynan,
&c., Munster ; ' des. of muıṁneᴀċᴁ́n ' (Munsterman) ;
the name (1) of a family of the Ui Fiachrach in Erris,
Co. Mayo, in which county it is still extant, but sometimes translated Munster ; and (2) a very common
surname in Kerry and West Cork, where it is almost
universally angl. Moynihan. V. Ó muıṁnıᵹ.

Ó muıṁnıᵹ—I—O *Moyney,* O *Moynig,* Moyney, Mooney;
' des. of muıṁneᴀċ ' (Munsterman) ; the name of a
family of Corca Laoighdhe, in South-West Cork. It
is not improbable that it has been changed in most
instances to the dim. Ó muıṁneᴀċᴁ́ın (q.v.) now so
common in West Cork and Kerry.

Ó muıneᴀċᴁ́ın—I—Menehan, Menahan, Meenehan,
(Monahan), &c., Thornton ; an attenuated form of Ó
mᴀnᴀċᴁ́ın, q.v. It is popularly supposed to be
connected with ' muıneᴀċ,' thorny, and is consequently
in some places ' translated ' Thornton.

Ó mµıneóg—I—*O Monoge*, Manogue, Minogue, Minnock, Mannix ; ' des. of Mµıneóg ' (dim. of mɑnɑċ, a monk); an attenuated form of Ó Mɑnóg, q.v. ; a common surname in Clare and Offaly. Cléıɼċen Ó Mµıneóg was Bishop of Leighlin in the 11th century.

Ó mµınȝeáın—I—*O Muynghan*, Mingane, Meenhan, Meenin,(Mangan); an attenuated form of Ó Monȝáın,q.v.

Ó mµıɼċeɑɼcɑıȝ—I—*O Morierty, O Murtagh*, Moriarty, Murtagh, Murtaugh ; ' des. of Mµıɼċeɑɼcɑċ ' (seadirector, expert navigator) ; the name (1) of a Kerry family who were anciently chiefs of Aos Aisde, a district lying probably along the river Mang ; and (2) of a Meath family still numerous in that county and in Monaghan, where it is angl. Murtagh. In Munster it is always angl. Moriarty.

Ó mµıɼeɑ́ɒɑıȝ—I—*O Murrey, O Murry, O Murrihy*, Murry, Murray, Murrihy ; ' des. of Mµıɼeɑɒɑċ ' (seaman, mariner, also a lord) ; the name of several distinct families in different parts of Ireland. Of these, the Uí Mµıɼeɑɒɑıȝ, or O'Murrys, of Mayo, Roscommon, Westmeath and Cork were dynastic families who anciently ruled over extensive districts, but they have all been long dispossessed and dispersed. There were also many distinguished ecclesiastics of the name. Ó Mµıɼıȝce is a common pronunciation. Cf. O Murrihy above.

Ó mµıɼeɑȝáın—I—*O Murrigane, O Moregane, O Morgan*, Murrigan, Murricane, Merrigan, Maragan, Morgan ; ' des. of Mµıɼeɑȝán ' (dim. of some name commencing with Mµıɼ-) ; the name of one of the chief families of Teffia, in the present counties of Westmeath and Longford, and sometimes lords of all that district. About the beginning of the 12th century, they disappeared from history, and apparently dispersed to different parts of Ireland. In the 16th century, the name was most numerous in Down and Armagh. It is still common in many parts of Ireland.

Ó mµıɼeáın—I—*O Murrane, O Murran*, Murrane, Murran, Murrin, Murren, Morrin, (Moran) ; ' des. of

Muiʍeán ' (dim. 3̃ of some name commencing with Muiʍ-) ; possibly a var. of Ó Muiʍeaɠáin, q.v. ; the name of a family of Ui Fiachrach, in the west of Co. Mayo ; also common in many other parts of Ireland.

Ó muiʀɠeasa—I—*O Murrissa, O Morisa, O Morrissy,* Morissy, Morrissey, Morrissy, &c., (Morris, Morrison) ; ' des. of Muiʍɠeaʍ" (sea-choice) ; the name of a branch of the Ui Fiachrach who were formerly chiefs of a district on the southern shore of Sligo Bay, in the barony of Tireragh. It is highly probable that there were several other distinct families so called, as the name, both in the present form and as Ó Muiʍɠiʍ, is common in most parts of Ireland.

Ó muiʀɠeasáin—I—*O Murghesan, O Morrisane, O Morrison, O Brisane,* Morrison, Briceson, Bryson, (Price) ; ' des. of Muiʍɠeaʍán ' (dim. of Muiʍɠeaʍ) ; an old Donegal surname ; pronounced Ó Bʍioʍáin and angl. Briceson and Bryson. In Co. Mayo, the pronunciation is Ó Pʍioʍáin, angl. Price.

Ó muiʀɠis—I—*O Morish, O Morris, O Morice,* Morris, Morice, &c. ; ' des. of Muiʍɠeaʍ ' (sea-choice) ; a var. of Ó Muiʍɠeaʍa, q.v.

Ó muiʀín—I—*O Morrine, O Murrin, O Murren,* Murrin, Murren, Morrin, (Moran) ; ' des. of Muiʍín ' (dim. of some name commencing with Muiʍ-) ; a var. of Muiʍeáin, q.v.

Ó muiʀiɠte—I—*O Murrihey,* Murrihy, Murry, Murray, common in the spoken language for Ó Muiʍeaʋaiɠ, q.v.

Ó muiʀneacáin—I—*O Murnyghan,* Murnaghan ; ' des. of Muiʍneacán ' (dim. of muiʍneac, loveable) ; a rare Ulster surname.

Ó muʀcaʋa—I—*O Morchowe, O Moroghoe, O Morphy,* O'Muracha, O'Murphy, Murchoe, Murphy, Morphy ; ' des. of Muʍcaʋ ' (sea-warrior) ; the name (1) of a family of Cinel Eoghain, who were chiefs of Siol Aodha, in the present Co. Tyrone ; (2) of a family of the Ui Fiachrach who were chiefs of a district on the southern shore of Sligo Bay, now comprised in the parishes of Skreen and Templeboy, but were dispossessed and dispersed in the 13th century ; (3) of a branch of the Ui Ceinnsealaigh, in Co. Wexford, who were chiefs of Ui Feilme, which comprised the barony of Ballaghkeen, in the east of that county, and formed a distinct clan down to the early part of the 17th century. This family is now very numerous throughout Leinster. It is not improbable that, in addition to those mentioned, there are several other families of the name in Ireland.

Ó muꞃcáin—I—*O Murchan, O Morghane, O Moraghan,* Morahan, Morohan, Murchan, Morkan, Morkin, Murkin, (Morgan), Morran, Morrin, (Moran) ; ' des. of muꞃcaoán ' (dim. of muꞃcao, sea-warrior) ; the name (1) of an Offaly family who were formerly chiefs of Magh Aoife, in the barony of East Offaly, and are still numerous in Kildare and Offaly, but often disguised as Morrins and Morans ; and (2) of a family of Ui Maine in Connacht. The name is not uncommon in Co. Leitrim.

Ó muꞃɓail—I—*O Moryle,* Morell ; ' des. of muꞃɓal' (sea-valour) ; a var. of Ó muꞃɓaile, q.v. ; very rare.

Ó muꞃɓaile—I—*O Morchaile, O Moryly, O Morely, O Marlie,* Morrolly, Marrilly, Morley, Marley ; ' des. of muꞃɓal ' (sea-valour) ; a scattered surname ; found chiefly in Donegal and Mayo. See Ó muꞃcuile.

Ó muꞃnáin—I—Murnane, Murnain, Murnan, Mornan, (Warren) ; a corruption of Ó manannáin, q.v. In recent years the angl. form has been absurdly changed to Warren in the neighbourhood of Kenmare.

Ó muꞃcuile—I—*O Murhilly, O Morhelly, O Murrilly, O Murley,* Murhilla, Murley, Morrolly, Morley, (Hurley) ; ' des. of muꞃcuile ' (sea-tide) ; probably the same as Ó muꞃɓaile, q.v. ; a very common surname in Co. Cork where, however, it is now generally disguised under the angl. form of Hurley.

Ó naoioeanáin—I—*O Nenane, O Nynane,* Nynane, Neenan, Neenin, (Nunan, Noonan) ; ' des. of naoioeanán ' (dim. of naoioean, an infant) ; a rare Munster

surname ; sometimes disguised under the angl. form
of Nunan or Noonan.

Ó Náraḃaiᵹ—I—*O Narie, O Nary,* Nary, Neary, Nery ;
' des. of Náṗaḃaċ ' (good, noble) ; a common surname
in Connacht and parts of Leinster.

Ó Náċan—II—*O Nahane, O Nahan, O Nane,* Nawn ;
' des. of Nathan ' ; also written Ó Náan ; the name of
an old ecclesiastical family in Tirconnell. Tomár
Ó Náan was Bishop of Raphoe from 1299 to 1306 ;
and the Four Masters, under the year 1336, record
the death of Tṁonóic Ó Náan, chief ollave of many
sciences, and of civil and canon law. Some of the
family at a later period removed to Cork. The name
is still extant, but exceedingly rare.

Ó neaċcain—I—*O Naghtan, O Neaghten,* O'Naughton,
Naghten, Naghton, Naughtan, Naughten, Naughton,
Nocton, Natton, (Norton), &c. ; ' des. of Neaċcan '
(bright, pure) ; the name (1) of a Dalcassian family,
of the same stock as the O'Quinns and O'Hartigans,
still numerous in Thomond ; and (2) of a branch of
the Ui Maine in Galway and Roscommon. This
family derives its descent from Fiachra Fionn, grandson of Maine Mór, the eponymous ancestor of the Ui
Maine, and was closely akin to that of Ó Maolalaiḃ
(q.v.), both families forming originally one clan under
the common designation of Ui Fiachrach Finn. The
O'Neachtains were chiefs of Maonmhagh, the plain
lying around Loughrea, until about the time of the
Anglo-Norman invasion, when they removed to the
Feadha, or Fews, of Athlone, where they formed a
distinct clan down to the reign of Elizabeth.

Ó néiḃe, v. Ó niaḃ.

Ó neiᵹill—I—*O Nehill, O Nihill, O Nyhill,* O'Nial,
Nehill, Nihill, Nyhill ; ' des. of Nigel ' (a Norse form
of Niall) ; the name of an old Thomond family, still
well known about Limerick. The family is said,
but perhaps erroneously, to be a branch of the O'Neills
of Thomond ; it is more probably of Norse descent.
The name, however, is really the same as Ó néill.

Ó ṅéıɬɬ—I—O'Neill, O'Neal, Neill, Neale, &c. ; ' des.
of ṁıaɬɬ ' (champion) ; the name of several distinct
families in different parts of Ireland, of which the
following are the chief :—(1) Ó ṅéıɬɬ of Ulster. This
family, which is one of the most illustrious in Ireland,
derives its name and descent from ṁıaɬɬ ᵹɬúnᵼᵼoub,
King of Ireland, who fell fighting against the Danes,
near Dublin, in 919. His grandson, ᵼoṁnaɬɬ Ó
ṅéıɬɬ, who is mentioned in the Annals at the year
943, was the first person to bear the surname of
Ó ṅéıɬɬ. The O'Neills were the head family of the
Cinel Eoghain, the most celebrated of all the Irish
clans, whose territory, known as Tir Eoghain, from
Eoghan, son of Niall of the Nine Hostages, ancestor
of the clan, comprised the present counties of Tyrone
and Derry, together with a large portion of Donegal.
As chiefs of Tir Eoghain and Kings of Ulster, they
make a most distinguished figure in Irish history
from the 11th to the 17th century. In the reign of
Henry VIII, Conn Ó ṅéıɬɬ, the then head of the clan,
was created Earl of Tyrone. Shane the Proud and
Hugh, Earl of Tyrone, in the reign of Elizabeth, and
Sir Phelim and Owen Roe, at the period of the Confederation, were the last celebrated bearers of the name.
Several of the O'Neills have been distinguished in the
service of continental powers. A powerful branch
of this family, known as Clann Aodha Bhuidhe,
settled in the 14th century in Antrim and Down.
(2) Ó ṅéıɬɬ of Thomond. The head of this family,
which is of Dalcassian origin and descended, according
to Keating, from Aodh Caomh, King of Cashel (A.D.
571-601), was chief of Clann Dealbhaoith, in the
present barony of Bunratty, in the south of Co. Clare.
The O'Nihills and Creaghs are, according to local
tradition, branches of this family. (3) Ó ṅéıɬɬ of
Leinster, an ancient family in Carlow and Wicklow.
The patrimony of this family was Magh-dá-chon, now
angl. Moyacomb, a parish in the barony of Rathvilly,
Co. Carlow, and extending into the barony of Shil-

lelagh, in Co. Wicklow, also called Farren O'Neill. Ó ᵰéɩᴸ of Magh-dá-chon is mentioned in the Annals of the Four Masters, A D 1088, as having fallen in a battle fought near Dublin, between the men of Munster and Leinster. (4) Ó ᵰéɩᴸ of Deisi. This family was seated in the south of the present Co. Tipperary.

Ó neoċᴀᴸᴸᴀɩᵹ—?—Nohally, Nohilly, Noakley. This surname is in use in the neighbourhood of Shrule, but I have failed to trace its origin.

Ó ᵰɩᴀᴅ—I—*O Nee, O Nea, O Ney,* O'Knee, Nee, Knee, (Needham, Neville) ; ' des. of ᵰɩᴀ ' (champion) ; the name of an ancient Kerry family who were originally seated in the neighbourhood of Tralee, but in later times were erenaghs of Knockpatrick, near Foynes, in Co. Limerick. The name is now most common in West Galway, where it is sometimes angl. Needham. In Kerry and Limerick, where it is now very rare, it is always angl. Neville.

Ó ᵰɩᴀᴅóᵹ—I—(Newcombe) ; probably a var. of Ó ᵰɩᴀᴅ, q.v. ; in use in Co. Mayo. I can find no early instance.

Ó ᵰɩᴀᴸᴸᴀᵹáɩn—I—*O Neligane,* Neligan, Nelligan ; ' des. of ᵰɩᴀᴸᴸᴀᵹán ' (dim. of ᵰɩᴀᴸᴸ) ; a rare surname ; found chiefly in Cork and Kerry.

Ó ᵰɩᴀᴸᴸáɩn—I—*O Nillane, O Neilane, O Nelane, O Neylane,* Nilan, Nelan, Neilan, Nealon, Neylan, Neylon, Nilon, Niland, Neiland, Neyland, Neelan, Neeland, Neelands, &c. ; ' des. of ᵰɩᴀᴸᴸán ' (dim. of ᵰɩᴀᴸᴸ) ; a Thomond surname ; now also common in Connacht.

Ó ᵰɩᴀċáɩn—I—Neehan, Nyhane ; a Co. Cork surname ; probably a var. of Ó ᵰɩᴀᴅ, q.v. Cf. Ó ᵰɩᴀᴅóᵹ. I can find no early instance.

Ó nuᴀᴅᴀn—I—*O Nowan, O Nowne,* Noone, (Noonan), Lambe ; ' des. of ᴺuᴀᴅᴀ ' (the name of an ancient sea divinity) ; the name of a Sligo family of the race of Cairbre, son of Niall of the Nine Hostages. This family anciently possessed the district of Callraighe Laithimh, nearly co-extensive with the present parish of Calry, near the town of Sligo. The name is still veiy common in Connacht. In the spoken language, as I have heard it, the final n is slender.

Ó nuaȯac—I—*O Noude*, Noud, Nowd, Knowd; 'des. of nuaȯa'; the same as Ó nuaȯan, q.v.; a rare Donegal surname.

Ó nuallacáin—I—*O Nolloghaine*, (Nolan); 'des. of Uallacán' (dim. of uallac, proud). The form of this surname is peculiar, being really the gen. plural of Ó nUallacáin, q.v. With names of women it is quite regular, e.g., Ḃríġío Ní Uallacáin.

Ó nuallán—I—*O Nowlane, O Nolane, O Noland*, O'Nowlan, O'Nolan, Nowlan, Nolan, Noland, &c.; 'des. of nuallán' (dim. of nuall, noble, famous); the name (1) of a numerous and respectable family in Leinster, the head of which was chief of Fothart Feadha, now the barony of Forth, in Co. Carlow, and had the privilege of inaugurating MacMurrough as King of Leinster; and (2) of a family of Corca Laoighdhe, in south west Cork.

Ó nuanáin—I—*O Nownan, O Nonan*, Noonane, Noonan, Nunan, Newnan, (Noone); a corruption of Ó nIonṁaineáin, q.v. In Connacht, it may possibly be a dim. of Ó nuaȯan, q.v.

Ó núcáin, Newton; in use in the spoken language of Co. Cork.

Ó páȯín—V—Payton; a corruption in Co. Roscommon of Mac páȯín, q.v.

Ó peacáin—II—*O Petane, O Pettane, O Pattane, O Patten*, Peton, Paton, Patten, Patton, Payton, Peyton; 'des. of peacán' (dim. of Patrick); the name of an old Ulster family, mentioned by MacFirbis among the families of Cinel Eoghain. They belonged to Cinel Moain, a subdivision of Cinel Eoghain, and were apparently seated in the barony of Raphoe, in the present Co. Donegal. The name occurs as early as the year 1178, when the Four Masters record the slaying of Muircheartach O Peatain in revenge for the death of Randal O Cathain. It is now common in

Mayo and North Galway, as well as in Donegal, but the pronunciation is Ó ꝑıoᴄáın or Ó ꝑıᴄeáın.

Ó ꝑıoᴄáın, Ó ꝑıᴄeáın, v. Ó ꝑeaᴄáın.

Ó ꝑᴦéıᴄ—XIII—*O Praye*, O'Pray, O'Prey, Prey, Pray; doubtless a corruption of a' ꝑᴦéıᴄ, i.e., of the cattle-spoil; a rare Co. Down surname.

Ó ꝑᴦíosáın—I—Price; a corruption of Ó mᴜıᴦᵹeaᴦáın, q.v.; current in Co. Mayo. Cf. Ó bᴦíoᴦáın.

Ó ꝑᴦoınnᴄıᵹe—XIII—*O Prenty, O Prontye*, Prunty, Brunty; doubtless a corruption of na ꝑᴦoınnᴄıᵹe, i.e., of the refectory, or dining-room. Cf. Ó ꝑᴦéıᴄ; a rare Ulster surname.

Ó ᴦabaᴦᴄaıᵹ—I—*O Roverty*, O'Rafferty, Rafferty, Raverty, Ravery; a var. of Ó ᴦobaᴦᴄaıᵹ, q.v.; now generally changed to Ó ᴦaıᴄbeaᴦᴄaıᵹ, q.v.

Ó ᴦaᵹaıll—I—*O Raghell, O Reile, O Ryle, O Reale, O Raile*, O'Rahill, Rahill, Reihill, Ryle, Ryall, Rall, Rail, Riall, Real, Reel, &c.; a shortened form of Ó ᴦaᵹallaıᵹ, q.v.; sometimes also pronounced Ó ᴦáᵹaıll, Ó ᴦaıᵹıll, Ó ᴦáıᵹıll, Ó ᴦaoᵹaıll, Ó ᴦeıᵹıll, &c.

Ó ᴦáᵹaıll, v. Ó ᴦaᵹaıll.

Ó ᴦaᵹaıllıᵹ, Ó ᴦaᵹallaıᵹ—I—*O Reyly, O Riellie, O Realy, O Reely*, O'Reilly, O'Reiley, O'Rielly, O'Realley, Reilly, Rielly, Really, Realy, Reely, Riley, &c.; 'des. of ᴦaᵹallaᴄ'; also pronounced Ó ᴦáᵹallaıᵹ, Ó ᴦaıᵹıllıᵹ, Ó ᴦaoᵹallaıᵹ, &c., and sometimes shortened to Ó ᴦaᵹaıll, &c., q.v. The O'Reillys, who are the same stock as the O'Rourkes, were chiefs of Breifney-O'Reilly, which originally comprised the greater part of the present Co. Cavan. In the course of the 13th and 14th centuries they became very powerful and extended their dominion over the whole Co. Cavan and parts of Meath and Westmeath; and they were sometimes chiefs of all Breifney. They maintained their independence as a clan down to the time of James I, and continued in possession of considerable property until the Cromwellian confiscations. Many of the O'Reillys attained to high ecclesiastical rank, no fewer than five of the name having been Primates of Armagh. The name is now one of the most common in Ireland, but owing to its numerous dialectical variations is variously anglicised in different parts of the country.

Ó Ráṡallaiṡ—I—*O Rhawley, O Raly*, Rawley, Rally, (Raleigh, Rawleigh) ; a var. of Ó Raṡallaiṡ, q.v.

Ó Raiṡill, Ó Ráiṡill, v. Ó Raṡaill.

Ó Raiṡill—I—Reckle ; a var. of Ó Raiṡill, q.v.

Ó Raiṡilliṡ, v. Ó Raṡallaiṡ.

Ó Raiṡilliṡ—I—*O Reigly*, Rigley ; a var. of Ó Raṡallaiṡ, q.v. For radical ṡ, cf. Ó Raiṡne ; also Mac Raiṡilliṡ, angl. Crigley.

Ó Raiṡne, Ó Ráiṡne—II—*O Raine, O Ryney*, Ryney, Reyney, Reany, Rainey, Raney, &c. ; ' des. of Rayny ' (a pet form of Reginald or Reynold) ; pronounced Ó Ráiṡne in Co. Mayo. See Ó Raiṡne, wjhch is a variant.

Ó Raiṡne—II—*O Regne, O Regnie, O Rigney*, Rigney ; a var. of Ó Raiṡne, q.v. ; current in Donegal and Offaly. The O'Rigneys of the latter county were followers of Mac Coċláin, in the barony of Garrycastle, where the name is still common.

Ó Raitḃeartaiṡ—I—O'Rafferty, Rafferty, Raverty, Ravery ; a corruption of Ó Raḃaptaiṡ or Ó Roḃaptaiṡ, q.v. The angl. form Ravery is due to the aspiration of the ṫ of the final syllable.

Ó Raitile—I—*O Rathyly, O Rahillie*, O'Rahilly, Rahilly, (O'Reilly, Reilly) ; ' des. of *Raitile ' ; the name of a family of Cinel Eoghain in Ulster, descended, according to MacFirbis, from Echean, son of Eoghan, son of Niall of the Nine Hostages ; but for several centuries it has been almost peculiar to Munster, where it is found chiefly in Cork, Kerry and Limerick. To this family belonged the greatest of our modern Irish poets, Egan O'Rahilly, whose poems have been published by the Irish Texts Society.

*Ó Raitne, Raheny, Ranny ; perhaps a var. of Ó Raiṡne, q.v. ; very rare.

Ó Ꞃᴀᴏᵹᴀɪʟʟ—I—*O Reale*, Real, Reel, Riall. V. Ó Ꞃᴀᵹᴀɪʟʟ.

Ó Ꞃᴀᴏᵹᴀʟʟᴀɪᵹ—I—*O Realy*, *O Reely*, O'Realley, Really, Realy, Reely, &c. V. Ó Ꞃᴀᵹᴀʟʟᴀɪᵹ.

Ó Ꞃᴇᴀᴃᴀċᴀɪn, v. Ó Ꞃoᴃᴀċᴀɪn.

Ó Ꞃᴇᴀċᴀɪꞃ—I—Raher ; a var. of Ó Ꞃꞃᴇᴀċᴀɪꞃ, or Ó Ꞃᴇᴀꞃċᴀɪꞃ (q.v.), owing to the aspiration of the initial ꞃ.

Ó Ꞃᴇᴀċᴛᴀᴃᴀɪꞃ—I—*O Raghtore*, *O Raghter*, Rafter, Wrafter, Raftiss ; a var. of Ó Ꞃᴇᴀċᴛᴀᴃꞃᴀ, q.v. The peculiar Kilkenny pronunciation of slender ꞃ is seen in the angl. form Raftiss.

Ó Ꞃᴇᴀċᴛᴀᴃꞃᴀ—I—*O Raghtoury*, Raftery ; ' des. of Ꞃᴇᴀċᴛᴀᴃꞃᴀ ' (ꞃᴇᴀċᴛ, law, decree, and ᴀᴃꞃᴀ, fringe, border) ; also Ó Ꞃᴇᴀċᴛᴀᴃᴀɪꞃ, q.v. ; sometimes written Ó Ꞃᴇᴀċᴛᴀɪꞃᴇ, and so pronounced in Co. Mayo.

Ó Ꞃᴇᴀċᴛᴀᵹᴀɪn—I—*O Raghtagan*, Raghtigan, Ractigan, Ratican, Ratigan, Rattigan, Rhategan, Rhatigan, &c. ; ' des. of Ꞃᴇᴀċᴛᴀᵹᴀn ' (dim. of ꞃᴇᴀċᴛ, law, decree) ; the name of an ecclesiastical family in Co. Roscommon, who were coarbs of St. Finnen, in the parish of Clooncraff, near Elphin.

Ó Ꞃᴇᴀċᴛᴀɪꞃᴇ—I—Raftery. V. Ó Ꞃᴇᴀċᴛᴀᴃꞃᴀ.

Ó Ꞃᴇᴀċᴛnɪn—I—*O Rachnane*, Raghneen, Rochneen, Roughneen, (Rochford) ; a rare Mayo surname. The older form was probably Ó Ꞃᴇᴀċᴛnᴀɪn.

Ó Ꞃᴇᴀᴅᴀ—I—*O Readie*, Reidy, Ready, Readdy ; a var. in the spoken language of Ó Ꞃɪᴀᴅᴀ, q.v.

Ó Ꞃᴇᴀᵹᴀɪn—I—*O Regaine*, O'Regan, Regan ; a common var. in the spoken language of Ó Ꞃɪᴀᵹᴀɪn, q.v.

Ó Ꞃᴇᴀnnᴀċᴀɪn—I—O'Renahan, Ranaghan, Reneghan, Renihan, Rinaghan, Rinahan, Rinihan, Ranahan, Renehan, Renahan, Ronaghan, &c., Ferns, Ferrons ' des. of Ꞃᴇᴀnnᴀċᴀn ' (dim of ꞃᴇᴀnnᴀċ, spear-like) ; Cf. Mᴀᵹ Ꞃᴇᴀnnᴀċᴀɪn.

Ó Ꞃᴇɪᴅꞃɪ—II—*O Reyrye* ; a var. in the spoken language of Ó Ꞃuᴀɪᴅꞃɪ, q.v.

Ó Ꞃᴇɪᵹɪn—I—*O Reggine*, *O Regin*, O'Regan, Regan ; a var. of Ó Ꞃɪᴀᵹᴀɪn, q.v.

Ó Reiȝill, v. Ó Raȝaill.

Ó Riaḃaiȝ—I—*O Revoay, O Reogh, O Reogh, O Ria, O Ree*, Reavey, Ravy, Reigh, Rea, Ray; 'des. of Riaḃaċ' (brindled).

Ó Riaḋa—I—*O Ryada, O Ryedy, O Readie*, Reidy, Ready, Readdy; 'des. of Riaḋa' (tamed, trained); the name of a Dalcassian family, now numerous in Clare and Kerry; sometimes pronounced Ó Réaḋa.

Ó Riaȝáin—I—*O Riegaine, O Regane*, O'Regan, Regan; 'des. of Riaȝán'; the name of two distinct families, one seated in ancient Meath, and the other in Thomond. The O'Regans of Meath were a branch of the southern Ui Neill and one of the four tribes of Tara. Before the Anglo-Norman invasion, they were lords of South Breagh in Meath and the north of the present Co. Dublin, and appparently a powerful family. They took a leading part in the wars against the Danes. The annalists, under the year 1029, record a notable triumph of Matȝaṁain Ó Riaȝáin, King of Breagh, over the foreigners, when he made prisoner Amhlaoibh, son of Sitric, King of Dublin, and only released him on payment of an enormous ransom, including the celebrated sword of Carlus. The O'Regans were dispossessed soon after the Anglo-Norman invasion and dispersed through Ireland. The O'Regans of Thomond are a Dalcassian family said to be descended from Riaȝán, son of Donncuan, the brother of Brian Boru. The O'Regans are now numerous all over Ireland. The name is often pronounced Ó Réaȝáin.

Ó Riaȝain, Ó Riain—I—*O Rian*, O'Ryan, Ryan; 'des. of Riaȝan,' or 'Rian'; the name of a Carlow family who were lords of Ui Ḋróna, the present barony of Idrone, and are now numerous through Leinster; to be distinguished from Ó Maoilriain of Munster and Ó Ruaiḋín of Connacht, which are both now incorrectly angl. O'Ryan or Ryan.

Ó Ríṁeaḋa—I—*O Rive, O Rives*, Reeves; 'des. of Ríṁeaḋ' (calculator); the name of an ancient family of the Ards of Co. Down; always very rare, and now found chiefly in Co. Limerick. The Four Masters, under the year 1004, record the death of Maelbrigde Ua Rimeada, Abbot of Iona.

Ó Rinn—I—*O Rinne, O Ring*, Rinn, Rynn, Ring, Reen, Wrynn, Wren, Wrenn; ' des. of Reann ' (spear) ; the name (1) of an old Cork family, a branch of the Ui Macaille, from whom the barony of Imokilly got its name ; and (2) of a Roscommon family, still represented in that county.

Ó Ríogbardáin, Ó Ríordáin—I—*O Riverdan, O Riourdane, O Reerdan*, O'Riordan, Riordan, Reardan, Reardon, &c. ; ' des. of Ríogbardán ' (royal-bard) ; written Ó Ríogbradáin by Keating ; the name of a family originally of Ely-O'Corroll, in the present Offaly, and probably a branch of the family of O'Carroll of that district, deriving its name and descent from Ríogbardán, son of Cúcoirne (Ó Cearbaill), lord of Ely, who fell at the battle of Sliabh gCrot, in the Glen of Aherlow, in the year 1058. In 1576, Gaven O Rewrdane was a freeholder in Ely-O'Carroll and one of Sir William O'Carroll's most important followers. The name appears about the same time in Leix and Kilkenny, but the bulk of the family had long before removed to Cork and Limerick. In 1597, Maurice O'Riordan of Croome was attainted and his lands granted to George Sherlocke. The O'Riordans are now very numerous in Cork, Limerick and Kerry.

Ó Robacáin—I—*O Rachaine, O Rawghan, O Rowghane, O Roaghan*, Roughan, Roohan, Ruhan, Rohan, Rowan ; ' des. of Robacán ' (crafty) ; also written Ó Reabacán ; the name of an ecclesiastical family, anciently attached to the monasteries of Swords, Co. Dublin, and Lismore, Co. Waterford. In the 16th and 17th centuries, it was not uncommon in Co. Clare, where members of the family appear to have been stewards to the O'Gradys. In 1641, Donogh oge O'Roughan and Charles O'Roughan were proprietors of the townland of Sunnagh, in the parish of Inchicroman. The name is now rare and scattered, and its angl. forms cannot always be distinguished from those of Ó Ruaʰḃaċáın, q.v.

·Ó Roḃarcaıʒ—I—*O Roverty, O Rowarty,* Roarty; ' des. of Roḃarcaċ '; also written Ó Raḃaρcaıʒ (q.v.), and generally corrupted to Ó Raıċḃeaρcaıʒ, q.v.; the name of at least two distinct families, anciently located respectively in Tirconnell and Sligo. The former family were coarbs of St. Columcille on Tory Island, off the north coast of Donegal; the latter, who are of Ui Fiachrach race, were seated in the parish of Skreen, in the barony of Tireragh, where they had extensive possessions. They are named by MacFirbis among " the pillars of Skrin and the props of the Kings of Ui Fiachrach." They were dispossessed by the Scottish settlers in the early part of the 17th century. There was also a Meath family of the name, but it was probably a branch of that of Tirconnell.

·Ó Roʰḋaċáın—I—*O Rodeghan,* Rodaughan, Rudihan, Rudican, Redahan, Redehan, (Redington, Reddington); ' des. of Roʰḋaċán ' (dim. of Roʰḋaċ); the name of an ecclesiastical family in Co. Leitrim, who were coarbs of St. Caillin at Fenagh; still common in Connacht, but often shortened to Ó Roʰḋaıʒ, and sometimes disguised under the angl. form of Redington or Reddington.

·Ó Roʰḋaıʒ—I—*O Roddy, O Ruddy, O Reddie,* Roddy, Ruddy, Reddy, &c.; ' des. of Roʰḋaċ ' (der. of ρoʰḋ, strong); the name of a branch of the Ui Maine in Co. Galway; also a var. of Ó Roʰḋaċáın (q.v.) in Co. Leitrim.

·Ó Roʰḋáın—I—*O Rodane, O Ruddane, O Rudden,* Rodan, Roden, Rodin, Rodden, Rudden, Ruddon, Reddan, Reddin; ' des. of Roʰḋán ' (dim. of ρoʰḋ, strong); an old surname in Donegal, Monaghan and Clare. The O'Rodains of the last-named county were stewards to the O'Briens and MacNamaras, and held considerable property in the neighbourhood of Six-mile-bridge down to the Cromwellian confiscations.

Ó Roȝállaȝ—I—*O Rwollea, Rolley,* Rowley, Rawley,
(Raleigh) ; ' des. of Roȝallaċ ' ; a var. of Ó Raȝallaȝ,
q.v. Cf. Mac Roȝallaȝ.

Ó Roiꝺeaċáin—I—Redahan, Redehan, (Redington),
&c. ; an attenuated form of Ó Roꝺaċáin, q.v. ;
common in Mayo and Galway.

Ó Roiꝺiȝ—I—*O Reddie,* Reddy ; an attenuated form
of Ó Roꝺaiȝ, q.v.

Ó Roileaċáin—I—*O Rellakan, O Relligan,* Relehan,
Relihan ; probably ' des. of Roȝallaċán ' (dim. of
Roȝallaċ), and an attenuated form of Ó Roȝallaċ-
áin. ' Munter Raulaghan ' appears as a family
name in Inishowen at the beginning of the 17th
century, and about the same time O Rellakan, or
O Relligan, was in use in Co. Antrim. The name is
now peculiar to Co. Kerry, whither, apparently, the
family migrated from Co. Antrim.

Ó Roiċleáin—I—(?) *O Rylan,* Roland, Rowland,
Rowley ; an attenuated form of Ó Roċláin, q.v.

Ó Rónáin—I—*O Ronane, O Ronayne,* Ronane, Ronayne,
Ronan ; ' des. of Rónán ' (dim. of rón, a seal) ; the
name of several distinct families in different parts of
Ireland, as (1) Ó Rónáin of Longford, who were
chiefs of Cairbre Gabhra, in the barony of Granard,
until about the period of the Anglo-Norman invasion,
when they were dispossessed by the O'Farrells and
dispersed through Ireland ; (2) Ó Rónáin of Mayo, a
branch of the Ui Fiachrach ; (3) Ó Rónáin of Dublin,
anciently erenaghs of Clondalkin ; and (4) Ó Rónáin
of Cork, where the name is now most common.

Ó Rosna—I—Rossney ; ' des. of Rorna ' ; the name of
an old family of Corca Laoighdhe, in South-West
Cork ; still extant in West Kerry, but extremely rare.

Ó Roċláin—I—*Roolane,* Roland, Rowland, (Rowley) ;
perhaps originally Ó Roȝalláin, a var. of Ó Roȝallaċ-
áin (v. Ó Roileaċáin above) ; the angl. form Rowley
would go to show that Ó Roȝallaȝ (q.v.) was a
variant ; the name of a Connacht family, formerly
chiefs of Coolcarney, in the barony of Gallen, Co.

Mayo ; still common in Mayo and Sligo, pronounced Ó Roitleáin, q.v.

Ó Ruaḋacáin—I—Roughan, Roohan, Rohan, Rowan, (Rogan), &c. ; 'des. of Ruaḋacán' (dim. of ruaḋ, red) ; a var. of Ó Ruaḋagáin, q.v. ; common in West Ulster and Connacht. Its angl. forms cannot always be distinguished from those of Ó Roḃacáin, q.v.

Ó Ruaḋagáin—I—O Rogane, Rogan ; 'des. of Ruaḋagán' (a dim. of ruaḋ, red) ; also written Ó Ruaḋacáin, q.v. ; the name of an Oriel family who were chiefs of Ui Eathach, or Tuath Eathach, a district embracing the present barony of Armagh ; common in Ulster and Connacht.

Ó Ruaḋáin—I—O Ruane, O Rowane, O Roan, Ruane, Rouane, Roane, Ruan, Roan, Roon, Rowan, Rewan, Royan, (Ryan) ; 'des. of Ruaḋán' (dim. of ruaḋ, red) ; also Ó Ruaiḋín ; the name (1) of an old Mayo family of the Ui Fiachrach, who possessed a district lying between Newbrook and Killeen, to the north of Ballinrobe ; and (2) of an old Galway family of the Ui Maine race. No fewer than seven of the name were bishops of various sees in Connacht, in the 12th and 13th centuries. The name is still very common in that province, generally angl. Ruane, but sometimes disguised as Ryan.

Ó Ruaḋraic—II—O Roreke, O Rorike, Roragh, Rorke, Rourke, &c. ; 'des. of Ruaḋrac' (the Norse Hrothrekr) an older form of Ó Ruairc, q.v. ; the name of a family who were anciently proprietors of Lia Con, in the barony of Tireragh, Co. Sligo, and of another, the head of which was erenagh of Termon Feichin ; now almost completely absorbed in the modern form Ó Ruairc, q.v.

Ó Ruaiḋ—I—O Rowe, O Rewe, Rowe, Roe, (Ormond) ; 'des. of Ruaḋ' (red) ; an old surname on the confines of Cork and Waterford ; now angl. Ormond in the latter county, owing to its similarity in sound to Urṁuṁa, the Irish name of Ormond, or East Munster.

Ó Ruaiḋín—I—O Ruyne, O Royn, O Roen, Rouine,

Royan, Rowen, (Ruane, O'Ryan, Ryan) ; ' des. of
Ruaiḋín ' (dim. of ruaḋ, red) ; the same as Ó Ruaḋáin,
q.v., both forms being used by the same family, and
equally common in Connacht. Some of the name
have been long settled in Leinster.

Ó Ruaiórí—II—O Roury, O Rorie, Rory, (Rogers,
Rodgers) ; ' des. of Ruaiórí ' (Norse Hrothrekr) ; the
name originally of a Meath family, but long dispersed
and now very rare. In Munster, it is pronounced
Ó Reiórí, q.v.

Ó Ruairc—II—O Ruairc, O Rowarke, O'Rourke,
O'Roarke, O'Rorke, Rourke, Roarke, Rorke, &c. ;
' des. of Ruarc ' (older Ruaḋrac, from Norse Hrothrekr) ; the name of several distinct families in different
parts of Ireland. The O'Rourkes of Breifney, one
of the most celebrated families in Irish history, were
chiefs of the great clan of Ui Briuin Breifne, whose
territory comprised the present counties of Leitrim
and Cavan. Three of them, in the 10th and 11th
centuries, were kings of Connacht. As lords of
Breifney, they sometimes ruled over a district extending from Kells in Meath to Drumcliff in Sligo ;
but after the 12th century, their power gradually
declined. O'Reilly became lord of East Breifney,
the present Co. Cavan, and O'Rourke's lordship was
confined to West Breifney, the present Co. Leitrim,
which was known as Breifney-O'Rourke. The
O'Rourkes took a leading part in the Elizabethan
wars, in which they suffered severely, but retained
considerable property down to the Cromwellian
confiscations. Many of them attained to high distinction in the military service of continental powers,
especially of Poland and Russia. A branch of the Ui
Maine, in Co. Galway, also bore this name, but was
never very numerous and, if it survives, cannot now
be distinguished from Ó Ruairc of Breifney. The
same applies to the other families of the name, some
of whom are mentioned above under the form of Ó
Ruaḋrac.

637

Ó ʀuᴀɴᴀᴅᴀ, ó ʀuᴀɴᴀɪ́ᴅ—I—*O Rownoe, O Roney,*
Roonoo, Rowney, Rooney, Roney, &c.; ' des. of
ʀuᴀɴᴀɪ́ᴅ ' (hero) ; a common surname, at the end of
the 16th century, in Ulster, Leinster and Connacht.
The annalists, however, have but comparatively few
notices of the family. Ceᴀllᴀċ Ó ʀuᴀɴᴀᴅᴀ, chief
poet of Ireland, died in 1079 ; eóɪɴ Ó ʀuᴀɴᴀᴅᴀ, who
was chief poet to Magennis, died in 1376. Ó ʀuᴀɴ-
ᴀɪ́ᴅín (q.v.) is a variant.

Ó ʀuᴀɴᴀɪ́ᴅíɴ—I—*O Roynian, O Runynge,* Runian,
Ruineen, Rooneen, (Rooney) ; ' des. of ʀuᴀɴᴀɪ́ᴅín '
(dim. of ʀuᴀɴᴀɪ́ᴅ) ; a var. of Ó ʀuᴀɴᴀᴅᴀ, q.v. ; common
in Sligo and other parts of Connacht ; also Ó ʀuᴀɴᴀᴅáɪɴ, Ó ʀuᴀɴáɪɴ, q.v.

Ó ʀuᴀɴᴀᴅáɪɴ, Ó ʀuᴀɴáɪɴ—I—*O Roynian,* Roynane,
Roonane, Roonan, Ronane, Ronan ; ' des. of ʀuᴀɴ-
ᴀᴅáɴ ' (dim. of ʀuᴀɴᴀɪ́ᴅ) ; a var. of Ó ʀuᴀɴᴀɪ́ᴅín
and Ó ʀuᴀɴᴀᴅᴀ, q.v. ; very rare.

Ó ʀuᴅᵹusᴀ—I—(?) Roughasy ; des. of ʀuᴅᵹuʀ.

Ó ʀuɪᴅíɴ—?—Ribbon ; a rare Connacht surname ;
perhaps for ᴍᴀc ʀoɪᴅíɴ, q.v. Cf. Ó ᴘɪlɪᴅíɴ for
ᴍᴀc ᴘɪlɪᴅíɴ.

Ó ʀuɪs—I—*O Rushe,* Rush ; perhaps for Ó ʀoʀᴀ ; a rare
Leinster surname.

Ó sᴀᴅáɪɴ—I—*O Sawane, O Sawan,* Savin, (Savage) ;
' des. of sᴀᴅáɴ ' (dim. of ʀᴀᴅ, strong, firm ; also a cub,
whelp) ; an old Munster surname, found chiefly in
Cork, Kerry and Tipperary ; now almost always
disguised under the angl. form of Savage.

Ó sᴀ́ᴍʀᴀɪ́ᴅ—I—*O Sawrie, O Sawra,* Summers, Sommers,
Somers ; ' des. of sᴀ́ᴍʀᴀᴅ ' (summer) ; an old South
Leinster surname, still well represented in Carlow
and Wexford ; also now in Waterford, Limerick and
Kerry.

Ó sᴀoʀᴀɪ́ᴅe, Ó sᴀoʀċᴀɪᵹ, Ó sᴀoċʀᴀɪ́ᴅe—II—
O Seyry, O Serie, Seerey, Seery, Freeman, Earner ;
a substitute for the old Westmeath and Tirconnell
surname Ó sɪoᵹʀᴀᴅᴀ, or Ó sɪoᵹʀᴀɪ́ᴅ, q.v. It is

sometimes angl. Freeman, on the erroneous supposition that it is derived from ' ꝛaoꝥaıⱁe,' a freeman. In Mayo and Galway, where it is pronounced Ó Saoꝛᴛaıᵹ, or Ó Saoꝛᴛuıⱁe, as if from ' ꝛaoᴛꝥuıⱁe,' a labourer (earner), the angl. form is Earner.

Ósꝺuꞧ—VIII—*Osbert*, (Osborne) ; ' son of Osbert ' (a common Anglo-Saxon personal name) ; found in parts of Munster, incorrectly re-anglicised Osborne.

Ó scaᴌaıᵹe—I—*O Skallie, O Skelly*, Scally, Skally, Skelly ; ' des of Scaᴌaıᵹe ' (crier) ; also mac Scaᴌaıᵹe, q.v. ; a surname seemingly of midland origin.

Ó scannaıᴌ—I—*O Scandall, O Scannill*, O'Scannell, Scannell ; ' des. of Scannaᴌ ' (scandal) ; the name of a family of the race of Cairbre, son of Niall of the Nine Hostages, who were originally seated in the barony of Carbury, to the north of the town of Sligo. maoᴌꝥáⱁꝥaıᵹ Ó Scannaıᴌ, Bishop of Raphoe, was translated to the primatial See of Armagh in 1261. The name, in the north-west of Ireland, has long been changed to the dim. form Ó Scannᴌáın, q.v. Ó Scannaıᴌ is now found chiefly in Cork and Kerry, whither the family must have migrated from Sligo or Donegal, some time before the end of the 16th century.

Ó scannᴌáın—I—*O Scanlaine, O Scanlan, O Scanlon, O Scandlon*, Scanlan, Scanlon, Scandlon, &c. ; ' des. of Scannᴌán ' (dim. of Scannaᴌ) ; the name of several distinct families in different parts of Ireland, as : (1) of Sligo, who are the present-day representatives of the ancient family of Ó Scannaıᴌ of Carbury (see above) ; (2) of Galway, a branch of the southern Ui Fiachrach and of the same stock as the O'Shaughnessys and O'Heynes ; (3) of Cork, who were formerly erenaghs of Cloyne ; and (4) of Fermanagh, who were erenaghs of Devenish. At the end of the 16th century, the name was found in all the counties of Munster, being specially common in Cork, Limerick and Kerry. It is now common in Munster and Connacht, but is only rarely met with in the other provinces.

Ó scɑᴛꞬɑɪl—I—O *Scahill,* Scahill, Skahill, Schaill; 'des. of ScɑɪᴛꞬeɑl' (flower-fair); more anciently mɑc ScɑɪᴛꞬɪl, q.v.; the name of a Galway family who were chiefs of Corca Mogha, now angl. Corcamoe, which comprised the parish of Kilkerrin, until dispossessed by the O'Concannons soon after the Anglo-Norman invasion. It is now always pronounced Ó Scɑᴛɑɪl in Galway and Mayo.

Ó scéɑcáɪn—I—O *Skeghan,* Skehan, Skeahan, Skeane; 'des. of Ꞅꞅéɑcán' (dim. of ꞃceɑc, a brier); an old Tipperary surname. Cf. mɑc Sceɑcáɪn. *Thornton*

Ó sceɑllɑ́ɪn—I—O *Scalain, O Skallen,* Scallan, Scullane, Scullion; 'des. of Sceɑllán' (kernel); an old surname in Fermanagh and in South Leinster; now very scattered. In Connacht, it is pronounced Ó Scollán, q.v.

Ó scɪnꞬín—I—O *Skynegine, O Skingin, O Skynin,* Skinnion, Delahide, Delahoyde; 'des. of ScɪnꞬín' (probably dim. of ꞃcɪnꞬ, some article of dress); the name of an ecclesiastical and literary family who were originally erenaghs of Ardcarne, near Boyle, Co. Roscommon, but afterwards migrated to Tirconnell, where they became chroniclers to the O'Donnells. Matthew O Scingin, who died in the year 1289, was chief historian of Ireland in his time. The O Scingins of Tirconnell became extinct towards the end of the 14th century and were succeeded by the O'Clerys, whose ancestor married the heiress of the last ollav of the name. The family has, however, survived in other parts of Ireland; but it would appear that some members of it in Co. Cavan now call themselves Delahide, or Delahoyde, doubtless on the erroneous supposition that 'Skin-' of the one name is to be equated with '-hide' of the other.

Ó scoɪꞃeɑ́ᴅ, v. Ó Scuɪꞃe.

Ó scolɑɪᴅe, Ó scolɑɪꞬe—I—O *Scollee, O Scully,* Scully; 'des. of Scolɑɪᴅe' or 'ScolɑɪꞬe' (crier); the name of a Westmeath family who were chiefs of West Delvin until dispersed early in the 12th century,

when they became erenaghs of the church of St.
Ruadhan at Lorrha, in Co. Tipperary. At the end
of the 16th century it was most numerous in Cork,
Dublin, Carlow, Offaly and Tipperary. It is apparently the same name as Ó Scaℓaiξe, q.v.

Ó scoℓℓáin—I—Scullane, Scullion, Skoolin, (Scally,
Skally, Scully) ; a var. in Connacht of Ó Sceaℓℓáin,
q.v. Cf. Ó Spoℓáin for Ó Speaℓáin. It is often incorrectly angl. Scally and Scully.

Ó scuine, Ó scuiniṫ, Ó scurra—I—O Scurry,
Scurry ; ' des. of S———————' ; the name, according
to MacFirbis, of a family of Cinel Eoghain in Ulster.
It was also borne by a family in Ui Maine in Co.
Galway, but is now little known, if at all extant.
MacFirbis writes it Ó Scuine and Ó Scapa. It was
written Ó Scoineaṫ in the title-page of a book pub-
lished by James Scurry at Waterford in 1820.

Ó seaċnais—I—O Shaghnishe. O Shaghnes, Shaughness,
Shaughnessy, &c. ; a shortened form of Ó Seaċnaraiξ,
q.v. ; rather common in the spoken language of
Connacht. I have heard it pronounced Ó Seaċnair
(initial S aspirated) in West Limerick.

Ó seaċnasaiξ—I—O'Shaughnessy, O'Shoughnessy,
O'Shannessy, O'Shanesy, Shaughnessy, Shannessy,
&c. ; ' des. of Seaċnarac ' ; the name of a branch of
the Ui Fiachrach Aidhne, in Co. Galway. On the
decline of the kindred family of O'Cahill in the 13th
century, the O'Shaughnessys became chiefs of Cinel
Aodha, angl. Kinelea, the district lying around the
town of Gort ; but they are only rarely mentioned in
the Irish annals before the reign of Henry VIII. In
1533, Dermot O'Shaughnessy, the then ' chief of his
nation,' was knighted, and ten years later he surrendered all the clan-lands to the crown in order to
receive them back by letters-patent. During the next
two centuries the O'Shaughnessys were one of the most
celebrated families in Ireland. Sir Dermot O'Shaughnessy, the fourth in descent from Sir Dermot of the
time of Henry VIII, joined the Confederation of

Kilkenny and lost his estates in the Cromwellian confiscations, but received back 2,000 acres at the Restoration. This was again forfeited in 1697, and Colonel William O'Shaughnessy, the last chief of the name in the direct line, died in exile in France in 1744. O'Donovan was of opinion that the O'Shaughnessys of Co. Limerick are descended from Lieut.-Colonel William O'Shaughnessy, the uncle of Sir Dermot of the Cromwellian and Restoration period; but this is unlikely, as the O'Shaughnessys were settled at Dromard, near Rathkeale, before the year 1600.

Ó Séaᵭacáin—I—*O Sheahan, O Shaghan,* Sheahan, Shahan, Shean, Shane; a common var. of Ó Síoᵭ-acáin, q.v.

Ó Séaᵹᵭa—I—O'Shea, O'Shee, Shea, Shee, &c.; 'des. of Séaᵹᵭa' (stately, majestic, courteous; also learned, scientific, ingenious); the name of a family of Corca Dhuibhne in West Kerry who until about the period of the Anglo-Norman invasion were lords of Ui Rathach, now the barony of Iveragh. A branch of the family settled, about the beginning of the 15th century, in the city of Kilkenny, where they became wealthy and highly respectable. The name was also borne by a branch of the Ui Fiachrach in the barony of Tirawley, Co. Mayo, but this family, if still extant, is very little known. The O'Sheas are now very numerous, especially in Kerry.

Ó Seaᵴᵭaᵹ—I—*O Shallowe, O Shallie, O Shelly, O Shielly,* Shalvey, Shallow, Shalloe, Shally, Shelloe, Shellew, Shelly, Shealy, Sheily, &c.; 'des. of Seaᵴᵭac' (possessor, proprietor); the name of a branch of the Corca Laoighdhe in South-West Cork, whose seat was probably at ᵬaile Uí Seaᵴᵭaᵹ, about a mile to the east of Dunmanway. The Four Masters, under the year 1140, record the death of ᵭoᵯnall Ua Seaᵴᵭaᵹ, erenagh of Cork, 'pillar of the glory and splendour of Munster.' About the same period, four of the name were bishops of Cork, and one of Lismore. There was probably a distinct family of the name in the north of Ireland. At the end of the 16th century it was found in Cork, Waterford, Tipperary, Kilkenny and Donegal.

Ó Seanacáin—I—*O Sheanaghaine, O Shanahan,* Shanaghan, Shanahan, Shanihan, Shanan, Shannon, &c. ; ' des. of Seanacán ' (dim. of Seanac, old, wise) ; the name of a Dalcassian family who were chiefs of Ui Ronghaile, in the east of Thomond, until the year 1318, when they were expelled by Torlough O'Brien and the MacNamaras. They settled at first in Co. Waterford, but have long been scattered through Munster. See also Ó Sionacáin which is a Westmeath form of the name.

*Ó Seanacair—I -Shanagher ; ' des. of *Seanacar.'

Ó Seanaig—I—*O Shanna, O Shanny,* Shannagh, Shanny ; ' des. of Seanac ' (der. of ʃean, old, wise) ; a rare surname in Co. Clare.

Ó Seanáin—I—*O Shenane, O Shanan, O Shennan,* O'Shannon, Shanan, Shanon, Shannon ; ; 'des. of Seanán ' (dim. of ʃean, old, wise) ; a scattered surname.

Ó Seancáin—I—*O Shenchane, O Shenchan,* Shanahan, &c. ; a var. of Ó Seanacáin, q.v.

Ó Searbáin—I—*O Sharvan,* Sharvin, Sherwin ; ' des. of Searbán ' (dim. of ʃearb, bitter) ; a rare surname which seemingly originated in Co. Roscommon.

Ó Searcaig—I—*O Sharkie, O Sherkie,* Sharkey ; ' des. of Searcac ' (loving) ; a surname which apparently originated in Tyrone, but is now common in many parts of Ulster and Connacht.

Ó Searcói̇d—I—*O Sherkott,* Sharket, Sharkett ; ' des. of Searcoi̇d ' (lover) ; the name of a Roscommon family. ' Sean buiḋe Ó Sergoi̇d, chief priest of Trinity Island, was drowned in Loch Cé, on Easter Sunday, 1578.' The name was never very common, but is still represented in Co. Roscommon.

Ó Searraig—I—*O Sharie,* Sharry, Sherry ; ' des. of Searrac ' (a foal, hence flighty) ; the name of an Ulster family who, according to MacFirbis, are of the race of Eoghan, son of Niall of the Nine Hostages ;

also of a family the head of which was anciently chief of Dal mBuinne, in the present Co. Antrim; still well represented in Ulster and in some of the adjoining counties of Leinster.

Ó seᴀsnáin—I—*O Sesnane, O Shesnan,* Shasnan, (Sexton); 'des. of Seᴀrnán' or ' Seᴀrcnán'; the name of a Dalcassian family in Thomond. At the end of the 16th century it was found in different parts of Munster and also in Longford, Cavan and Monaghan. The angl. form ' Sexten' appears as early as the year 1533 in the city of Limerick, where a respectable branch of the family had settled.

Ó seᴀstᴀ—I—*O Siastie, O Cestie,* Cheasty; 'des. of Seᴀrtᴀ'; a rare Munster surname. It apparently originated in Kerry, where Tuᴀt Ó Siortᴀ, angl. Tuosist, preserves the memory of the family.

Ó seiḃleáin, Ó seiḃlín—I—*O Syvelane, O Shevline,* Shevlin, Shovlin, Shovelin; 'des. of Siḃliᴀn' (quick); older Ó Siḃlen, Ó Siḃliᴀin; the name of a family who were anciently lords of Ui Failghe, or Offaly; also of a branch of the Ui Eachach Muaidhe in Co. Mayo; now found chiefly in Ulster.

Ó seiġin—I—*O Sheine, O Sheyne, O Shyne,* Shine; 'des. of Seiġin' (wild ox); an old Munster surname, still common in that province.

Ó seireᴀᴅáin—I—*O Sheridane, O Sheridan,* Sheridan, Sherridan, &c.; a common form in the spoken language of Ó Siṗroeáin, q.v.

Ó seiteᴀċáin—I—*O Sheheghane,* Hyde; 'des. of Seiteᴀċán'; a rare surname in Co. Cork. Hyde is supposed to be a translation.

Ó siᴀḃᴀil, Ó siᴀġᴀil—I—*O Siegall, O Shiell, O Sheale, O Sheill, O Shill,* O'Shiel, Sheil, Shiels, Sheils, Shields, Sheilds, Sheils, Shiles, Sheals, &c.; 'des. of Siᴀġᴀl' or ' Siᴀḃᴀl' (cf. riᴀḃᴀil, sloth); the name of a family of the race of Maine, son of Niall of the Nine Hostages, who became celebrated as physicians and surgeons in many parts of Ireland, as in Delvin-MacCoghlan, Oriel, Inishowen, &c. Owen O'Sheil, known as the 'Eagle of Doctors,' was physician to the armies of the Confederate Catholics of Ireland from 1642 to 1650.

Ó Síbleáin, Ó Síbliain, v. Ó Seibleáin.

Ó Síveacáin, v. Ó Síovacáin.

Ó Sinoile—XI—Singleton. V. ve Sinʒealtún.

Ó Síocƒnava, Ó Síoċnava,—II—O Shighrowe, Shughrue, Shegrue, Sugrue, Segrue, Sugrew; ' des. of Síocƒnaiv ' (the Norse Sigefrith, victory-peace); an old Kerry surname. The family is said to be a branch of the O'Sullivans.

Ó Síova—I—O Shydie, Sheedy, Silk ; ' des. of Síova ' (silk) ; a rare and scattered surname. In Co. Galway, it is ' translated ' Silk.

Ó Síovacáin—I—O Shieghane, O Shehane, O'Sheehan, O'Sheahan, Sheehan, Sheahan, Sheean, Sheen, Shean, &c. ; ' des. of Síovacán ' (dim. of ríovac, peaceful) ; the name (1) of a Dalcassian family, now very numerous throughout Munster, especially in Cork, Kerry and Limerick ; and (2) of an old Galway family who were followers of O'Kelly of Ui Maine and are still numerous in that county. Ó Síveacáin and Ó Séavacáin (q.v.) are variants. The name is latterly sometimes written Ó Síotcáin.

Ó Síoʒnava, Ó Síoʒnaiv—II—O Shrue, O Shirie, O Shyry ; ' des. of Síoʒnaiv ' (the Norse Sigefrith) ; the same as Ó Síocnava, q.v. ; formerly in use in the midlands and Tirconnell ; now changed to Ó Saonaive or Ó Saotpuive, q.v.

Ó Sionacáin—I—O Shinnaghan, Shinnahan, Fox ; ' des, of Seanacán ' ; a var, of Ó Seanacáin, q.v. ; the name of a Westmeath or Cavan family ; sometimes incorrectly angl. Fox, as if from ' rionnac,' a fox.

Ó Sionaiʒ—I—O Sheny, O Sunny, Shinny, Shunny, Shinnick, Shinwick, Fox, &c. ; ' des. of Seanac (wise, old) ; a var. of Ó Seanaiʒ, q.v. But see Ó Sionnaiʒ

Ó Sionáin—I—O Sinan, Shinane, Shynane, Shinnan, Sheenan, Synan ; ' des. of Seanán ' (dim. of rean,

old, wise) ; a var. of Ó Seanáin, q.v. The Synans
were once an important family in Cork and Limerick.
Ó Sionouile—XI—Singleton. V. ve Singealcún.
Ó Sionnaiġ—I—*O Sheny, O Sunny*, Shunny, Shinagh,
Shinnick, Shinnock, Shinwick, Fox ; ' des. of Sion-
naċ ' (fox) ; probably not distinct from Ó Sionaiġ,
q.v. ; the name of a family of Corca Laoighdhe in
South-West Cork ; also of a Sligo family ; now often
translated Fox.
Ó Siorאדáin—I—Shirdan, Shurdan, Sheridan, &c. ;
a var. of Ó Sipiveáin, q.v.
Ó Síoráin—I—*O Shearane, O Sherane*, Sheeran ; ' des.
of *Siopán ' ; also Ó Sipín. q.v.
Ó Siosnáin—I—*O Sisnane*, (Sexton) ; a var. of Ó
Searnáin, q.v.
Ó Siosta, v. Ó Searta.
Ó Síotċáin, v. Ó Síovaċáin.
Ó Siriveáin—I—*O Shiridane, O Sheridane*, Sheridan,
Sherridan, &c. ; ' des. of Sipiveán ' ; the name of an
ecclesiastical family who were erenaghs of Granard,
in Co. Longford, but appear to have afterwards removed to Co. Cavan, where at the end of the 16th
century they-were followers of O'Reilly and are still
numerous. The family rose to eminence in the 17th
and 18th century by the ability and learning of some
of its members. Thomas Sheridan who was Secretary
of State under James II, Sir Thomas Sheridan, tutor
to Prince Charles Edward, and the Right Hon. Richard
Brinsley Sheridan, orator, statesman, and dramatist,
belonged to this family. MacFirbis mentions a
family of the name among the Siol-Muireadhaigh in
Connacht.
Ó Sirín—I—*O Shirine, O Sherin*, Sherin, Sheeren,
Sheeran, Shirran ; ' des. of *Sipín ' ; a var. of Ó Siop-
áin, q.v.
Ó Síotiġ—I—*O Shihie, O Shehy*, Sheehy ; ' des. of Siteaċ '
(peaceful) ; doubtless, the same as Mac Síotiġ (q.v.),
by substitution of Ó for Mac ; found here and there
in Munster.

Ó SLᴀᴄᴀRRᴀ, Ó SLᴀᴄRᴀ—I—*O Slattra, O Slattery,*
Slattery; 'des. of SLᴀᴄpᴀ' (bold, strong); the name
of a Dalcassian family, formerly seated at Bally-
slattery, in the east of Co. Clare, but now dispersed
through Munster.

Ó SLÉιᴠín—I—*O Slevine, O Slevan,* Slevin, Sleavin,
Sleevin, Slevan, Slavin, (?) Slamon; 'des. of SLÉιᴠín'
(dim. of pιιᴀᴠ, a mountain, a 'pet' dim. of Ꝺonn-
pLÉιᴠe); the name of a branch of the Cinel Eoghain
in Ulster. ꝻιoLLᴀ Ċoṁ́ᴢᴀιLL Ó SLÉιᴠín, chief bard of
Ulster, was the messenger chosen by King Malachy
to rally the forces of the North in defence of Tara
against Brian Boru.

Ó SLuᴀᴢᴀᴠᴀιᴢ—I—*O Slowey,* Slowey, Sloey, Sloy,
(Molloy, Mulloy); 'des. of SLuᴀᴢᴀᴠᴀċ' (belonging to
a host, fit for hosting); the name of a family whicħ
apparently belonged originally to Roscommon, but
is now dispersed through Connacht and Ulster. The
Four Masters, under the year 1015, record the death
of ṁᴀoιpᴀᴅpᴀιᴢ uᴀ SLuᴀᴢᴀᴠᴀιᴢ, sage of Ireland;
and in 1190, ꝻιoLLᴀ ᵫeᴀpᴀιᴢ Ó SLuᴀᴢᴀᴠᴀιᴢ was
slain by Turlough O'Connor. The name is strangely
angl. Molloy, Mulloy, in parts of Ulster.

Ó SLuᴀᴢᴀᴠᴀín, Ó SLuᴀᴢᴀιᴠín, Ó SLuᴀᴢᴀín, Ó
SLuᴀιᴢín—I—*A Sloan,* Sloane, Sloan, Slown, Slone,
Sloyan, Sloyne; 'des. of SLuᴀᴢᴀᴠᴀ́n,' or ' SLuᴀᴢᴀιᴠín'
(dim. of SLuᴀᴢᴀᴠᴀċ); probably a var. of Ó SLuᴀᴢᴀᴠᴀιᴢ, q.v.; a not uncommon surname in Co. Mayo,
where it is angl. Sloyan and Sloyne. The Sloanes
of Antrim and Down are of Scottish origin, but the
Gaelic form of the surname is the same. Sir Hans
Sloan, the founder of the British Museum, was of this
family.

Ó SmeᴀLᴀ́ın, Ó SmoLᴀ́ın—I—Smallen, Smollan,
Smollen, Smullen; a corruption of Ó SpeᴀLᴀ́ın, q.v.
It is apparently a modern corruption, as I can find
no corresponding early angl. forms.

Ó Snιᴀᴠᴀιᴢ—I—Snee; 'des. of Snιᴀᴠᴀċ'; an old
Connacht surname, still extant in Sligo and Mayo.

Clemenᴄ Ó Sꞃιᴀᴆᴀιᵹ was Bishop of Achonry early in the 13th century.

Ó soᴄɭᴀᴄᴀιn—I—*O Soghlaghane*, Soghlahan; ' des. of Soᴄɭᴀᴄᴀn ' (dim. of Soᴄɭᴀᴄ, renowned) ; a rare Connacht surname, borne by a family who were formerly erenaghs of Cong.

Ó soᴄɭᴀιᵹ—I—Soughly, Suckley; ' des. of Soᴄɭᴀᴄ' (famed, renowned). Cf. Ó Soᴄɭᴀᴄᴀιn above.

Ó somᴀᴄᴀιn—I—*O Somaghan, O Summaghan*, O'Summachan, O'Summahan, Somahan, Sumahean, &c., (Sommers, Summers, Somers, Summerly, Somerville, Summerville, &c.) ; ' des. of Somᴀᴄᴀn ' (a soft, innocent person) ; the name of an old Sligo family who were formerly numerous and respectable in the parish of Ballysummaghan ; now generally angl. Somers.

Ó soꞃᴀᴄᴀιn—I—*O Soroghan*, Soraghan Soroghan, Sorahan, Soran ; ' des. of Soꞃᴀᴄᴀn ' (perhaps dim. of ꞃoꞃᴄᴀ, bright, luminous, opposed to ᴆoꞃᴄᴀ) ; an Ulster surname.

Ó speᴀɭᴀιn—I—*O Spallane, O Spillane, O Spollane*, Spalane, Spellane, Spillane, Spollane, Spollan, Splane, Splaine, Smallen, Smollan, Smullen, (Spelman, Spellman), &c. ; ' des. of Speᴀɭᴀn ' (dim. of ꞃpeᴀɭ, a scythe) ; the name (1) of a family, said to be of Dalcassian origin, who were anciently chiefs of Ui Luighdheach, or Ileagh, in the present barony of Eliogarty, Co. Tipperary, but long since dispersed through Munster and Leinster ; and (2) of a family of Ui Fiachrach who were formerly proprietors of Coillin Aodha, now Culleen, in the parish of Kilglas, Co. Sligo, and are still numerous in Connacht, but generally call themselves Spelman in English. The name is usually pronounced Ó Spoɭᴀιn in Munster and Connacht, but sometimes also Ó Smoɭᴀιn in the latter province ; and the angl. forms, Smollan, Smullen, &c., show that it was also sometimes so pronounced in Leinster.

Ó speᴀɭᵹusᴀ, ó spιɭᵹeᴀsᴀ—I—Spelessy, Spellissy

Spillessy, Spilacy ; ' des. of Sₚeₐₗᵹuᵳ ' (scythe-choice) a rare Thomond surname. I can find no early instance.

Ó Sₚıoₗáın, Ó Sₚoₗáın—I—*O Spillane, O Spollane,* Spillane, Spollane, Spollan, &c. ; variants of Ó Sₚeₐₗáın, q.v.

Ó Sᵳáıⱦeáın, Ó Sᵳuıⱦeáın, Ó Sᵳuⱦáın—I—*O Srahane, O Shrihane, O Sreighan, O Shrean, O Streffan,* Shryhane, Sruffaun, Strohane, Strahan, Straghan, Strachan, Strain, Bywater, (Ryan) ; ' des. of Sᵳuⱦáın,' or ' Sᵳuıⱦeáın ' (dim. of ᵳᵳuⱦ, an elder, a sage, a man of letters) ; the name of an old Tirconnell family, the head of which was chief of Clann Snedhgile, a sept of the Cinel Conaill, seated in Glenswilly, to the west of Letterkenny, and also erenagh of Conwall in the same district. Some of the family had come southward before the end of the 16th century, probably as followers of the MacSweenys, and settled in Co. Cork, where the name is still extant, but often ' translated ' Bywater, as if from ' ᵳᵳuⱦáın,' a streamlet. In Co. Mayo, it is sometimes strangely angl. Ryan.

*Ó Sᵳıₐnáın—I—Sreenan. Cf. Cell Srianáin in Hogan's Onomasticon.

Ó Sⱦeₐᵳáın—II—*O Stephane,* Stephens ; ' des. of Stephen ' ; a rare Leix surname.

Ó Sⱦóıᵳín, Storan ; a rare Co. Limerick surname, the origin of which I have failed to trace. The Four Masters, at the year 1098, record the death of Mₐoıₗıᵳₐ Uₐ Sⱦuıₚ, scribe and philosopher of Munster.

Ó Suₐıᵳ𝔡, Ó Suₐıᵳⱦ—II—*O Sworde, O Swerte,* Sword, Seward, Swords ; ' des. of Suₐₚⱦ ' (probably the Norse Sigeweard, Siward) ; the name of an old family in Offaly. The Four Masters record the death of eıⱦne, daughter of Uₐ Suₐıᵳⱦ, abbess of Kildare, in 1016.

Ó Suıꝺne—IV—*O Swynie, O Swenie,* O'Sevnagh, Sweeny, &c. ; a var. of Mₐc Suıꝺne (q.v.), by substitution of Ó for Mₐc ; very rare.

Ó Súıₗeₐꝺáın—I—O'Sullivan, Sullivan, Sullevan, Soolivan, &c. ; ' des. of Súıₗeₐꝺán ' (i.e., Súıₗ-ꝺuꝺ-án, black-eyed) ; also but less correctly written Ó

Súılleaḃáın; the name of a well-known Munster family of the same stock as the MacCarthys and O'Callaghans. The original patrimony of the O'Sullivans lay along the River Suir, in the present Co. Tipperary, and their principal seat was at Knockgraffon, about two miles to the north of Cahir. In the year 1192 they were forced by the progress of the Anglo-Norman invasion to exchange the fertile plains of Tipperary for the mountains of Cork and Kerry. In their new home on the shores of the bays of Kenmare and Bantry they, however, acquired extensive possessions and became one of the most powerful families in Munster and one of the most numerous in all Ireland. They divided into several branches, the heads of which were known respectively as O'Sullivan More, who possessed the barony of Dunkerron and had his castle at Dunkerron, near Kenmare ; O'Sullivan Beare, who owned the territory of Beare, now the baronies of Beare and Bantry ; O'Sullivan Maol ; Mac Finghin Dubh, &c. Notwithstanding the confiscation of their estates in the 17th century, the O'Sullivans are still a respectable family, and the name is everywhere famous. " It has been honoured abroad," writes O'Callaghan, "in Spain, Belgium and Germany, with the titles of Count and Baron. It contributed its proportion of officers to the national regiments of Clare, Dillon, Bulkelely, &c., in France. It was one of note in the service of Naples. It has also attained high military, administrative, and diplomatic positions in the service of the United States of America, and the United Kingdoms of Great Britain and Ireland." (Irish Brigades.)

Ó Súılleaċáın—I—*O Suleghane, O Soolechan, O Solloghan, O Sullaghan*, Sullahan, Sullehan, (Sullivan) ; ' des. of Súılleaċán,' (dim. of Súıleaċ, quick-eyed) ; formerly in use in Longford, Cavan and Louth, but now nearly everywhere incorrectly angl. Sullivan.

Ó Súılıᵹ—I—*O Swally, O Sewell*, Sewell, Suel, &c. ; ' des. of Súıleaċ ' (quick-eyed).

Ó Súilleabáin, v. Ó Súileabáin.

Ó Caożáin—I—O Tagan, Tagan, Teigan, Teegan, Tegan; 'des. of Caożán' (dim. of Caoż); a rare and scattered surname; found chiefly in Leinster.

Ó Caiċliż, v. Ó Caitliż.

Ó Caioż—I—O Teige, Teige, Teigue, Tague, Teague, Tigue, Tighe, Tyghe, Tye, Tee; 'des. of Caoż' (poet); the name (1) of a Leinster family who were anciently chiefs of Ui Mail, now angl. Imail, in Co. Wicklow, but were dispersed soon after the Anglo-Norman invasion; (2) of an Ulster family who were anciently chiefs of Fir Li, in the present Co. Derry; (3) of a Connacht family, of the same stock as the O'Connors, who were chiefs of the household of the Kings of Connacht, and are still numerous in Roscommon and Mayo; and probably (4) of a Thomond family, to which belonged Caoż Ó Caioż, Bishop of Killaloe, in the 11th century.

Ó Cailtiż—I—O Talty, Talty, Taulty; probably a metathesised form of Ó Caitliż, or Ó Caiċliż, q.v.; a Co. Clare surname.

Ó Caitliż—I—O Talheighe, Tally, Tully, Tilly; 'des. of Caitleaċ' (quiet, peaceful); also Ó Caiċliż; the name (1) of a Tyrone family who were chiefs of Ui Laoghaire; and (2) of an ecclesiastical family in Fermanagh.

Ó Calċair—I—O Tolcher, Toler; 'des. of Calċaṗ' (stubborn, obstinate); a rare midland surname.

Ó Calċarán—I—Tolleran; 'des. of Calċaṗán' (dim. of Calċaṗ); the name of a Mayo family who were anciently chiefs of Conmaicne Cuile, now the barony of Kilmaine. O'Donovan found a few families of the name still in the barony.

Ó Canaioeáin—I—Tannian, Tannion; 'des. of Canaioeán' (dim. of canaio, thin, slender); a rare Connacht surname. In 1406, Turlough oge O'Connor, King of Connacht, was slain by Oiaṗmaio Ó Canaioen.

Ó Caráin, v. Ó Coṗáin.

Ó ᴄᴀᴚᴩᴀ, Ó ᴄᴀᴚᴩᴀ1ʋ, Ó ᴄᴀᴚᴩᴀ1ᵹ—I—*O Tarpy*, Tarpey, Torpy; 'des. of ᴄᴀᴩᴩᴀᴄ' (stout, sturdy); the name (1) of a family of Ui Fiachrach who possessed a townland in the parish of Skreen, Co. Sligo, which from them was called Fearann Ui Tharpaigh, now angl. Faranyharpy; long dispersed through Connacht; and (2) of a family of Corca Laoighdhe in South-West Cork, where they were followers of the O'Learys. There are a few households of the name still in Munster; also written Ó ᴄóᴩᴩᴀ, Ó ᴄóᴩᴩᴀ1ᵹ.

Ó ᴄᴀᴚsɴᴀ́1ɴ, Tarsnane.

Ó ᴄéᴀᴄᴀ́1ɴ—I—*O Taughan, O Tauhan*, Teaghan, Teahan, Teehan, Tehane, Tehan; probably a contraction of Ó ᴄᴇ1ᴄᴇᴀᴄᴀ́1ɴ ('des. of ᴄᴇ1ᴄᴇᴀᴄᴀ́ɴ,' fugitive, runaway); the name of a Roscommon family. Ó ᴄéᴀᴄᴀ́1ɴ is an old surname in Kerry, where it is still well represented.

Ó ᴄᴇᴀɴᴣᴀɴᴀ—I—*O Tagney*, Tangney, Tagney; 'des. of ᴄ————'; the name of an old Kerry family; peculiar to that county.

Ó ᴄᴇ1ᴍ1ɴ—I—*O Tine, O Tyne*, Tyne, Tynne; 'des. of ᴄᴇ1ᴍᴇᴀɴ' (dark, grey); a rare Co. Clare surname.

Ó ᴄᴇ1ᴍɴᴇᴀ́1ɴ—I—*O Teynane, O Tyvnane, O Tinan, O Tynnan*, Tynan, Tinan, Tynnan, Tivnane, Tivnan, Tevnane, Tevnan, (?) Tivane, Teevan; 'des. of ᴄᴇ1ᴍɴᴇᴀ́ɴ' (dim. of ᴄᴇ1ᴍᴇᴀɴ, dark, grey); (1) an Ossory surname, now common in Leinster and Munster; and (2) a Sligo surname, still extant in Connacht, angl. Tivnane, Tevnane, &c., but rare.

Ó ᴄᴇ1ᴍɴ1ɴ—I—*O Tynine*, Tinin, Tinan, Tynan; 'des. of ᴄᴇ1ᴍɴ1ɴ' (dim. of ᴄᴇ1ᴍᴇᴀɴ, dark, grey); a var. of Ó ᴄᴇ1ᴍɴᴇᴀ́1ɴ, q.v.; very rare.

Ó ᴄᴇ1ᴄᴇᴀᴄᴀ́1ɴ, v. Ó ᴄéᴀᴄᴀ́1ɴ.

Ó ᴄ1ᵹᴇᴀᴚɴᴀ1ᵹ—I—*O Tierny, O Tearney*, O'Tierney, Tierney, Terney, (Tiernan), Lord; 'des. of ᴄ1ᵹᴇᴀᴩɴᴀᴄ' (lordly); the name (1) of a branch of the Cinel Eoghain who were anciently chiefs of Fearnmaigh, in the present Co. Donegal; (2) of a branch of the Ui Fiachrach who were formerly lords of Ceara, now the barony of Carra, in Co. Mayo, and are still numerous in that county; and (3) of a Westmeath family of the southern Ui Neill race. At the end of the 16th century, the name was common also in Clare and Tipperary. The Mayo family is often called Ó Tiġeaṙnáin (q.v.) in Irish and Tiernan in English; and MacFirbis also gives Ó Tiġeaṙnáin as an alias for Ó Tiġeaṙnaiġ of Westmeath.

Ó TiġeaRnáin—I—*O Ternane, O Tiernan,* Tiernan, Ternan, (Tierney); ' des. of Tiġeaṙnán ' (dim. of Tiġeaṙnać, lordly); an alias, in Mayo and Westmeath, for Ó Tiġeaṙnaiġ, q.v.; but there are probably distinct families of the name, none however numerous, in other parts of Ireland. Of the Mayo family, O'Donovan writes : " They are a stout race of men and very proud of their descent, of which, however, they know nothing, except that their ancestors, a long time ago, had estates in Carra, and were strong men and courageous fighters. They look upon themselves as superior to their neighbours of the same rank, and always use a style of dress, particularly the great coat, by which they are at once distinguished from others of the same neighbourhood. This gave rise to an Irish saying in Carra : ' Iṙ ġeall le móṙġáil ṁuintiṙe Tiġeaṙnáin é '—' It is like the ostentation of the O'Tiernans ' " (Hy Fiachrach, p. 186 n.).

Ó TiobRaioe—I—Tubridy, Tubrit; ' des. of Tiobṙaioe ' (cf. tiobṙaio, a well); a Clare surname.

Ó Tiomáin—I—*O Teman, O Tyman,* Timmin, Timmins, Tymmons, Tymmins; ' des. of Tiomán ' (dim. of tiom, soft, tender, timid); a rare Fermanagh and West Ulster surname; also found in South Leinster.

Ó Tiománaiġ—I—*O Tymonie,* Timony, Tymmany; ' des. of Tiománać '; a rare West Ulster surname; perhaps a var. of Ó Tiomáin, q.v.

Ó Tnútail, Ó Tnútġail—I—*O Knowell,* Newell, Newill, Newells, Knowels, Knowles; ' des. of Tnútġal ' (envy-valour); originally a midland surname, now scattered.

Ó Toġoa—I—*O Toffey,* Towey, Tuffy; ' des. of Toġoa '

(chosen or elected) ; the name of a family of Ui Fiachrach, who were formerly chiefs of Bredagh, a district in the west of the barony of Tirawley, embracing the parish of Moygawnagh and part of the adjoining parish of Kilfian ; still common in Mayo and Roscommon ; generally angl. Towey, but sometimes Tuffy.

Ó ᴛoimín, v. Mac ᴛoimín.

Ó ᴛomáin, v. Ó ᴛuamáin.

Ó ᴛomaʟᴛaiᵹ—I—*O Tomelty*, Tomilty, Tumelty, Tumilty, Tumblety, &c. ; ' des. of ᴛomaʟᴛaċ ' (large, bulky) ; a rare South Leinster surname.

Ó ᴛomnaiʀ—II—*O Toner*, Toner ; ' des. of ᴛompaʀ ' (a Norse personal name) ; older form Ó ᴛompaiʀ ; the name of a family of Cinel Eoghain who were seated near Lough Swilly, in Co. Donegal, where they built the church which was called from them Ciʟʟ Ó ᴅᴛompaiʀ, now angl. Killodonnell ; still common in Ulster. Ó ᴛomnʀa (q.v.) is a variant.

Ó ᴛomnʀa—II—*O Thonery*, Tonra, Tonry ; a var. of Ó ᴛomnaiʀ, q.v. ; found in Mayo and Sligo, but rare. John O Thonery was Bishop of Ossory in the reign of Queen Mary.

Ó ᴛomʀaiʀ, v. Ó ᴛomnaiʀ.

Ó ᴛonnaiᵹ—I—*O Tonney*, Tunny ; ' des. of ᴛonnaċ ' (glittering) ; a rare Sligo surname. The family, according to MacFirbis, is a branch of the Cinel Conaill.

Ó ᴛoʀáin—I—*O Tarrane, O Tarran, O Turran*, Toran, Torran, Thoran, Thorn, Tarrant, Torrans, Torrens, Torrins, Torrance, Torrence, (Thornton), &c. ; ' des. of ᴛoʀán ' (dim. of ᴛoʀ, a lord) ; also written Ó ᴛaʀáin ; originally a Derry surname apparently ; now rare and scattered.

Ó ᴛoʀmaᴅa, Ó ᴛoʀmaiᵹ—II—*O Tormo*, Tormey, Tarmey ; ' des. of Thormodr ' (a common Norse personal name) ; a midland and South Ulster surname.

Ó ᴛóʀna—I—*O Torno*, Torney, Turney ; ' des. of ᴛóʀna ' ; extremely rare. Mainisᴛiʀ Ó ᴅᴛóʀna. now angl. Abbey O'Dorney, in Co. Kerry, is named from the family.

Ó τόRpᴀ, Ó τόRpᴀιξ, v. Ó τᴀppᴀ.

Ó τRᴀιξτιξ—I—*O Trighie, O Trye,* Trahey, Trehy, Troy; an older form of Ó τpoιξτιξ, q.v.

Ó τRеᴀбᴀιR—I—*O Trevir, O Trover,* Trevor, Trower, Trevors, (Travors, Travers); 'des. of τpеᴀбᴀp' (prudent, wise, skilful); the name of an ecclesiastical family in Co. Leitrim, of the same stock as the Mac-Clancys, who were erenaghs of Killarga; still common in Leitrim; now also in parts of Ulster.

Ó τRеᴀṁᴀιn, Troy; a rare West Clare surname.

Ó τRеᴀsᴀιξ—I—*O Trassy, O Tressy, O Trasey,* Trassy, Tressy, Tracy, Tracey, Treacy; ' des. of τpеᴀpᴀċ' (fighter); the name (1) of a Leinster family who were anciently lords of Ui Bairrche, a district embracing the barony of Slievemargy, in Leix, but are long dispersed through Leinster and Munster; and (2) of a Connacht family, of the same stock as the O'Maddens, who were seated in the south-east of Co. Galway, but are long dispersed. The name is now common in many parts of Ireland. The dim. Ó τpеᴀpᴀċᴀιn appears to have been in use in the midlands, but is probably obsolete; at least, it has no distinct angl. form.

Ó τRеоᴅᴀιn—I—*O Tredane,* Trodden, Troddyn; ' des. of τpеоᴅᴀn '; originally a Louth surname; now very rare.

Ó τRоιξτιξ—I—*O Trohie, O Trehie,* Trehy, (Troy), Foote; ' des. of τpоιξτеᴀċ' (a foot-soldier); also Ó τpᴀιξτιξ, q.v. This surname originated in North-West Clare, in or near Corcomroe, where the O'Trehys were a family of some note in the early history of the district. They have, however, been long dispersed, and for centuries have been settled in Offaly, North Tipperary, Limerick and Cork. The name is now generally angl. Troy.

Ó τuᴀιτ—I—*O Toye,* Toy, Toye; a rare Mayo surname; possibly an abbreviated form of Ó τuᴀτᴀιξ, q.v.

Ó τuᴀlτᴀιn—I—Toulhan; a metathesised form of Ó τuᴀτᴀlᴀιn, q.v.

Ó τυαmα—I—O'Twomey, O'Toomey, Twomey, Toomey, Twoomey, Tuomy, Towmey, &c. ; ' des. of τυαιm ' ; the name of a Dalcassian family, still common in Munster, especially in Co. Cork. Seán Ó τυαmα was the most distinguished of the Maigue poets.

Ó τυαmáιn—I—O Tumane, O Tomane, O Toman, Tooman, Tumman, Tummon, Toman, (?) Tumpane, (?) Toompane ; ' des. of τυαmáin ' (dim. of τυαιm) ; originally a Tyrone surname ; now very rare, and family long dispersed.

Ó τυαRυιs, Ó τυαRυιsc—I—Turish, Toorish, Tourisk, (?) Tidins, Waters, Watters ; probably a corruption of Ó hυαргζυιг, q.v. ; a Donegal surname.

Ó τυατάιζ—I—O Twohy, O Towie, Twohy, Twoohy, Tuohy, Touhy, Toohy, Tuhy, Tooey, Towey ; ' des. of τυατάċ ' (rustic ; also a lord) ; the name of a branch of the Ui Maine who were originally seated at Aughrim, in Co. Galway. At the end of the 16th century, it was not uncommon in many parts of Munster, especially in Co. Cork, and also in Offaly and Donegal. In Co. Cork, the final ζ is sometimes pronounced.

Ó τυατάιζ—I—O Towhig, Tuohig, Twohig, Touhig, Towhig, Toohig ; a var. of Ó τυατάιζ (q.v.) in Co. Cork, where the final ζ is sometimes not aspirated. Cf. Ó Coбτάιζ and Ó Ουбτάιζ.

Ó τυατάιζ—I—O Thuoty, Tutty ; a var. of Ó τυατάιζ, q.v. ; very rare.

Ó τυατάιl—I—O Toughill, O Touhill, O Twohill, O Tuale, O Towell, O'Toole, Toughill, Tuohill, Twohill, Toohill, Tohall, Tohill, Towell, Toole, Toal, Toale, &c. ; ' des. of τυατάl ' (people-mighty) ; also written Ó τυατζάιl and Ó τυατζάιle ; the name of at least two distinct families in Ireland, viz. : (1) Ó τυατάιl of Leinster, and (2) Ó τυατάιl of Ulster. The O'Tooles of Leinster, who are one of the most illustrious families of that province, derive their name and descent from τυατάl, son of Ughaire, King of Leinster, who died in the year 956. Their clan-name was Ui

Muireadhaigh. This afterwards became the designation of their territory, which originally comprised the southern half of the present Co. Kildare. Driven thence soon after the Anglo-Norman invasion by Walter de Riddlesford, they settled in the mountain fastnesses of Wicklow, first in Ui Mail and afterwards in Feara Cualann, where in alliance with their kinsmen, the O'Byrnes, they carried on incessant warfare with the English for a period of four hundred years, and preserved their independence as a clan down to the close of the reign of Elizabeth. In the reign of James I, the whole of 'Fercuolen' was confiscated and granted to Sir Richard Wingfield. The O'Tooles, however, retained considerable property down to the Cromwellian and Williamite confiscations. A branch of the family settled at an early period in West Connacht, and are still numerous in Mayo and Galway. The Ulster family of the name is, according to Mac-Firbis, a branch of the Cinel Eoghain.

Ó τυλτλιl—I—*O Thuathayll*, Tuthill, Tothill, Tuttell, Tuttle, &c.; a var. of Ó τυλτλιl, q.v. Cf. Ó τυλτλιξ for Ó τυλτλιξ. I give this form on the authority of O'Mahony (Keating's History), but I have not been able to verify it. Tuthill is apparently an English surname.

Ó τυλτλλáιn—I—*O Twohillane, O Towlane, O Toolane, O Tolane*, Toulhan, Toolan, Toland, Tolan, Tolin, Toolis, Thulis; 'des. of τυλτλλáη' (dim. of τυλτλl, people-mighty); the name of an Ulster family who were originally seated in Inishowen, Co. Donegal. A branch of the family migrated, in the 17th century, with the O'Donnells to Co. Mayo where they still flourish, but strangely anglicise their name Toolis and Thulis.

Ó τυλτċλιr—I—*O Tougher, O Togher*, Tougher, Taugher, Togher, Tooher, Toher, Tooker, Tucker; 'des. of τυλτċλη' (people-dear); the name of at least two distinct families, the one seated originally in Ely-O'Carroll, but now dispersed through the neighbouring counties ; the other in West Ulster, whence the name passed into Mayo, where it is now not uncommon.

Ó cuatȝail, v. Ó cuatail.

Ó cuatȝaile—I—(?) Tooley ; an Ulster var. of Ó cuatail, q.v. ; so written by MacFirbis.

Ó cuile, v. mac maolcuile.

Ó cuinne—I—O Teny, O'Thina, Tunny, Tunney, Flood ; probably a corruption of mac maolcuile. Cf. Ó cuile.

páoraiȝ—VIII—Patryk, Patrick ; 'son of Patrick' (a once popular Christian name in the north of England). The surname came into Ireland about the time of the Anglo-Norman invasion, but has always been rare and confined to a few places in Leinster.

paȝan—VIII—Payen, Poyn, Paine, Payne, Poyne, Pyne, &c. ; 'son of Pagan' (Lat. 'Paganus,' a great Norman name). The surname came into Ireland at the time of the Anglo-Norman invasion.

paȝan—VIII—Fyan, Fyans, Foynes ; a var. of paȝan, q.v. A family of this name settled early at Fyanston in Co. Meath. The name occurs several times in the list of mayors of Limerick in the 13th and 14th centuries. Cf. paȝan.

páoín—VIII—Padyn, Padin, Paden, Padden, Pattin, Patten, Patton, &c. ; 'son of Padin,' or 'Pattin' (dim. of Patrick). It will come as a surprise to most people to learn that our páoín is of English origin. Yet, like Patrick, it was once very common in the north of England. 'Padin Urs' is one of the earliest entries in the Dublin Roll of Names (A.D. 1216), and 'Padyn' is a surname in the English Hundred Rolls.

pailís—XI—Palys, Pallys, Pallice, Palles, Pallas ; i.e., 'at the "palis" or stake-fenced enclosure,' from residence (Fr. 'palis,' a stake. Cf. Ir. 'pailís,' which enters into the composition of several place-names, as Pallaskenry, Pallasgreen, &c.) ; an old surname in Dublin, Louth and Cavan. In 1582, Patrick Palles of Dundalk obtained a grant of pardon from Queen

Elizabeth. In 1642, William Pallys of Dublin and Andrew Pallys of Collatrath, Co. Cavan, were attainted; as were, in 1691, Andrew Pallace of Cloneanat, Co. Cavan, and Christopher Pallas of Dublin.

ṗᴀinín—VIII—*Pannyn, Phanyn, Phannyne,* Panneen, Fannin, Fanning, &c.; · ' son of Panin ' (dim. of Pagan) ; more usually ṗᴀinín, q.v. Panneen is still a Co. Limerick surname.

ṗᴀiṅcéiṙ—XII—Parker ; Nor. ' le Parkere,' i.e., the parker, custodian of a park. Also ṗᴀṅcᴀṅ.

ṗᴀṁᴀṙ—XII—Palmer ; Nor. ' le Palmer,' ' le Paumer,' i.e., the palmer, palm-bearing pilgrim from the Holy Land ; an old surname in Ireland.

ṗᴀol—VI—Powell ; Welsh ' Ap Howel,' i.e., son of Howel.

ṗᴀoṙ Poer, Power. V. ᴅe ṗᴀoṙ.

ṗᴀṙcᴀṙ, Parker ; a late form of ṗᴀiṅcéiṙ, q.v.

ṗᴀṙnᴀil, Parnell. V. ṗeᴀiṙnéil,

ṗᴀtún—VIII—*Patun,* Paton, Patton, Patten ; ' son of Paton ' (a Norman dim. of Patrick). Cf. ṗᴀiᴅín.

ṗéᴀcóc, ṗéᴀcóg—XII—*Pecoc, Pecok,* Peacock, Peacocke ; Mid. Eng. ' pecoc,' ' pecok,' i.e., the peacock, applied to a vain, proud person. The surname, though rare, is old in Ireland.

ṗéᴀgum, Pegum.

ṗeᴀiṙnéil—VIII—*Peronel, Pernel,* Parnell ; ' son of Petronel,' double dim. of Peter.

ṗeᴀṙᴀil—VIII—*Parale, Paral,* Parill, Parle ; probably ' son of Peverel ' (a Norman personal name, Lat. ' Piperellus ' and ' Peverellus ' in early Anglo-Norman documents) ; an old Wexford surname.

ṗeᴀṙóiᴅ—VIII—Parrott, Perrott ; ' son of Perrot,' Nor. dim. of Pierre or Peter.

ṗeitíᴅ, ṗeitíᴅ—XII—Petit, Petite, Pettitt, Petty, and by translation, Little ; Nor. ' le Petit,' ' le Petite,' i.e., the little, small of stature. The Petits settled early in Meath and Westmeath where they obtained large grants of land from de Lacy. They were feudal barons of Dunboyne and of Mullingar.

Piaras—VIII—Pierce, Pierse, Pearse, &c.; 'son of Piers' (an Anglo-Norman form of Petrus, Latin for Peter, very common among the early Anglo-Norman settlers in Ireland). There are, no doubt, several distinct families so called in different parts of the country. The Pierses of Kerry are stated to be a branch of the Fitzmaurices of Lixnaw.

Piaróid, Perrott; a var. of Pearóid, q.v.

Píc—VIII—Pike, Pyke; 'son of Pic' (an Anglo-Saxon and Norse personal name, found in Domesday Book). 'Robert Pic' occurs in the Dublin Roll of Names, A.D. 1216. Cf. Mac Péice.

Pilin, Pillin, Pillon.

Piocóid, **Piogóid**—VIII—*Picot,* Pickett, Pigott, Piggott; 'son of Picot' (dim. of Pic). 'Picot' occurs in Domesday Book as the name of a tenant-in-chief in Hampshire, and 'John Picot' is an early entry in the Dublin Roll of Names, A.D. 1216.

Piombróc, Pembroke. V. de Pionbróc.

Pionndar—XII—Pindar, Pinder, Pender, &c.; Nor. 'le Pinder,' i.e., the pinder or pindar, keeper of a pound. But probably in the great majority of instances Pinder, Pender, &c., are shortened forms of Prendergast. V. Pionndargás.

Pionndargás, **Pionndargrás**, Pendergast, Pindergast, Prendergast; a corruption of de Prionndargrás, q.v.

Piobaire, **Piobar**, **Piobart**, *Pippart, Pipard, Pippard,* Piper, Pyper, Pipper, Pepper, Peppard, &c. This surname came into Ireland about the time of the Anglo-Norman invasion. I can find no satisfactory explanation of its origin.

Pioróid, Perrott, &c.; a var. of Pearóid, q.v.

Ṗiotún, *Phitton,* Fitton, Fetton; a var. of Fiotún, q.v.

Pléamonn, **Pléimeann**—XII—*Flamang,* Flemon, Fleming, &c.; Nor. 'le Fleming,' Lat. 'Flandrensis,' i.e., the Fleming, native of Flanders. Towards the end of the 11th century, an irruption of the sea compelled many Flemings to seek shelter in England. They were at first allowed to settle on the Scottish

borderlands, but later on were removed by Henry I
to the south coast of Wales, where they were granted
a fertile district which had been wrested from the
Welsh. From there they came to Ireland at the
time of the Anglo-Norman invasion. Richard le
Fleming obtained from Hugh de Lacy a grant of the
barony of Slane and other estates in Co. Meath, which
remained in the family down to the Cromwellian and
Williamite confiscations. The name is now common
in many parts of Ireland.

ploingcéiꝺ, pluincéiꝺ, pluingcéiꝺ—XII—
Blounket, Plonket, Plunket, Plunkett ; Nor. ' Blanchet '
(dim. of Fr. ' blanc,' i.e., white, pale, from the complexion). The Plunkets must have come into Ireland
about the time of the Anglo-Norman invasion. They
settled in the north of Co. Dublin, and became in
course of time one of the most distinguished families
of the Pale. In 1403, Sir Christopher Plunket became lord of Killen, in Co. Meath ; and in 1628, Lucas
Plunkett, tenth lord of Killen, was created Earl of
Fingall. Branches of this family were also Barons
of Dunsanny and Earls of Louth. Unlike most of
the great Anglo-Irish families, the Plunketts contrived to retain the greater part of their estates in the
Cromwellian and Williamite confiscations.

póil, Powell, Powel ; perhaps a shortened form of **mac
póil** or **mac Ꝼiolla póil,** q.v. ; in use in Co. Galway.

póiléiꝺ—VIII—Paulett, Powlett, Pollett ; ' son of
Paulet ' (dim. of Paul).

póilín—VIII—*Pawlin, Paulyn, Poleyn,* Polin, Pollen,
and probably Poland ; ' son of Paulin ' (dim. of Paul).
Paulin is a personal name in Domesday Book. Cf.
mac póilín.

póirtéiꝺ—XII—Porter ; Nor. ' le Porter ' (from Fr.
' portier,' Mid. Eng. ' portere '), i.e., the doorkeeper ;
an old Anglo-Norman surname in Dublin, Meath,
Wexford, Waterford, &c. V. **póꝻꜱúꝺ.**

póiꝺcingéil—XI—*Portingale, Portingall,* Portabello.
V. **ꝺe póiꝺcingéil.**

poLáΡρ—VIII or XII—Pollard; 'son of Polard'
(dim. of Paul), or Mid-Eng. 'polard,' 'pollard,' i.e.,
the pollard, one who had his hair cropped short.
poLóc—VIII—Pollock, Pollick, &c.; 'son of Poloc,'
dim. of Paul.
ponns—VIII—*Ponz, Poyns, Poynz, Poyntz, Pounce*
Pointz, Punch; 'son of Ponce' (Lat. Poncius, a not
uncommon Norman personal name); an old, but rare,
surname in Ireland; now found chiefly in Cork and
Limerick, where the modern form is púinre, q.v.
Poynston was the old name of the present Punches-
town in Co. Kildare.
poΡτuιL—XI—Purtell, Purtill, Purtle; Nor. 'de Port-
hull,' i.e. of Porthill; the name of an old family in
Tipperary and Limerick.
póΡτúΡ—XII—Porter; Nor. 'le Portour,' from Fr.
'porteur,' i.e., the porter, carrier. V. póiρτéiρ.
poτáΡ—XII—*Poter*, Potter; Nor. 'le Poter,' i.e., the
potter, maker or seller of earthenware pots. This
surname came into Ireland about the time of the
Anglo-Norman invasion. 'Philys Poter' and 'John le
Poter' occur in the Dublin Roll of Names, A.D. 1216.
pΡáiξeáS, Price; a late form of pρíρ, q.v.
pΡeáSτún, Preston. V. ρe pρeáρτún.
pΡιoρáιL, Pryall, Priall, Priel, Pryle; a Co. Mayo
surname, of which I cannot discover the origin.
pΡιonnSá, pΡιonnSáċ, French; in use in Co. Roscommon; probably only a modern rendering into
Irish of the surname French. V. ρe ρρéιnρ.
pΡιoSτún, Preston. V. ρe pρeáρτún.
pΡíS—VI—*Preece*, Pryse, Price, &c.; Welsh 'Ap-Rhys,'
i.e., son of Rhys (a Welsh personal name). This is,
no doubt, the origin in the great majority of instances,
but such forms as 'le Pryce' and 'de la Prise' in
early Anglo-Irish records show that it is not always
so. Price is an old surname in Ireland.
pΡoιnnbíoL, *Pronevill*, Prendeville, Prindeville, &c.,
and in East Cork, strangely Bransfield. V. ρe pρoιnnbíoL.

pRóinséis—XII—*Fronces*, Francey, Francis ; Nor. 'le Fraunceys,' i.e., the Frenchman ; an early Norman surname, but never very common.

pRuiséil, Purcell ; a metathesised form of puipréil, q.v.

pRúc—XII—*Prut, Prute*, Proud, Prout ; Nor. 'le Prut,' 'le Proute,' 'le Proud,' i.e., the proud (Old Eng. 'prut,' Mid. Eng. 'prout,' proute '). This surname had come into Ireland before the middle of the 13th century. The family settled in Kilkenny and Tipperary, in the latter of which counties, at least, it is still extant.

púinse, *Ponchye, Pounche, Pounce*, Punch ; a later form of ponnp, q.v.

puiRséil—XII—*Porcell, Purshell*, Purcell, Purcill, Pursell ; Nor. 'porcel,' dim. of Old French 'porc,' Lat. 'porcus,' i.e., the little pig, a nickname. This surname is of record in Ireland since about the middle of the 13th century ; at the beginning of the 14th it was already common in Munster. The Purcells were one of the most influential of the Anglo-Norman families of Ormond (Kilkenny and Tipperary), where they had many castles and manors. The head of the family had the title of Baron of Loughmoe, near Thurles, where the ruins of Loughmoe Castle are still to be seen. There was also an important family of the name at Ballyculhane, in Co. Limerick, and another at Crumlin, Co. Dublin.

Rádulb—VIII—*Raulf, Rauf*, Rafe, Ralph ; 'son of Radulf ' or ' Radulph,' a very common Anglo-Norman personal name. As a surname it is inextricably confused with Roðulb, q.v.

Razad, Razac—XII—*Ragid, Raggid, Raggad*, Raggett; Nor. 'le Raggide,' 'le Ragidde,' 'le Ragged,' i.e., the ragged, the shaggy ; the name of an old family in Co. Kilkenny, from whom Ballyragget was so called ; now very rare.

Razaic, Wright ; a phonetic rendering of the English surname Wright.

Rᴀᵹnᴀʟʟ—VIII—*Reynald, Ranell, Reynell, Reynold,*
Randall, Randell, Reynalds, Reynolds, Renolds,
Ranolds, Rannals, &c.; 'son of Reginald' (older
Reginwald, Raginwald, a common Teutonic personal
name); the name of an old Co. Dublin family, of
record since the end of the 13th century. Charles
Reynolds of Dublin, and John Reynolds of Blundels-
town, Co. Dublin, were attainted in 1691.

Rᴀᵹnᴀꞃᴅ—VIII—Raynard, Reynard, Renard, Rynard,
&c., 'son of Reynard,' (older Raginhard, Regen-
heard, &c.), a Teutonic personal name.

Rᴀᵹnóıᴅ—VIII—*Reynaud, Reynott,* Reynolds, &c.;
'son of Reynaud' (a Fr. form of Reginald); a var. of
Rᴀᵹnᴀʟʟ, q.v.

Rᴀıʟéıᵹ, Rawleigh, Raleigh, Rawley, &c. V. ᴅe
Rᴀıʟéıᵹ.

Rᴀ1ncín—VIII—Rankin, Renkin, Renken; 'son of
Rankin,' dim. of Randolf.

Rᴀıꜱᴄꞃıc—XI—Rastrick, Restrick; 'of Rastrick' in
Yorkshire; Rastric in Domesday Book; the name of
a Wexford family.

Rᴀʟᴀıᵹ, Raleigh, &c. V. Rᴀıʟéıᵹ.

Rᴀmꜱᴀıᵹ, *Ramesey,* Ramsey, Ramsay, V. ᴅe Rᴀmꞃᴀıᵹ.

Rᴀnᴅᴀʟ—VIII—*Randulf, Randolf,* Randell, Randall;
'son of Randulf,' a very common Anglo-Norman
personal name. It was Latinised, Rannulfus, Ranul-
fus, Ranulphus, as well as Randulfus, showing that
the older pronunciation in England was Rannulf.
The dropping of the final *f*, which was usual in names
ending in -ulf, caused it to be confused with Rannall,
the English form of Reginald (v. Rᴀᵹnᴀʟʟ above).
Randulph and Randal as Christian names are for this
reason used as equivalents, especially among the
MacDonalds, of Rᴀᵹnᴀʟʟ which is really Reginald.

Réᴀmonn—VIII—*Remund, Reymund,* Raymond, Redmond, &c.; 'son of Remund' (Fr. 'Raimond,'
Frankish 'Raginmund'; not from Anglo-Saxon
'Raedmund,' as I think can be proved); the name
of an old Wexford family. In 1598, Redmond of the

Hooke was one of the principal gentlemen of Co. Wexford, as was, in 1608, Redmond of the Hall. Several gentlemen of the name were attainted in 1691.

Réro—XII—Read, Reade, Reede, Reid, &c. ; Nor. ' le Rede,' i.e., the red, from the complexion of the face or hair. This surname came into Ireland about the time of the Anglo-Norman invasion. It is sometimes incorrectly translated ʒiolcaċ, q.v.

Riaḃaċ—IX—Reagh, Reigh, Rea, &c. ; Ir. ' riaḃaċ,' i.e., grey, brindled ; an epithet which supplanted the real surname.

Riap—VIII—Rafe, Ralph ; ' son of Ralph ' ; a rare Mayo surname.

Riﬅeal, *Ridel, Rydel, Ridall*, Riddell, Riddle. V. ꝺe Rioꝺal.

Rioḃáro—VIII—Robert, Roberts ; ' son of Robert.'

Riocaro, Riocáro—VIII—Rickard ; ' son of Rickard,' or Richard.

Rioꝺal, *Ridall, Rudel, Ruddel*, Ruddell, Ruddle ; an old Co. Limerick surname ; probably the same as Riddell. ' Ridall ' appears as a Co. Limerick surname in the Patent Rolls of James I. V. ꝺe Rioꝺal.

Rís—VIII—*Rys, Reys, Ryse*, Rice, Roice, Royce, Ryce ; ' son of Rhys ' (a Welsh personal name). The Rices, who are of Welsh descent, settled in Ireland in the 14th or 15th century, especially at Limerick and Dingle, where they were wealthy merchants. Walter Ryce was mayor of Limerick in 1520. The Rices of Dingle came much into prominence in the 16th and 17th centuries.

Robuﬅún, Robusún, *Robuston*, Robertson, Robinson. This surname, which is as old at least as the 16th century, seems to be merely a phonetic rendering of the English surname Robertson.

Roꝺlann—VIII—*Roulant*, Rowland ; ' son of Roland,' a personal name of Teutonic origin introduced by the Normans.

Roꝺmonn—VIII—Rodmont, Rodmund, Redmon, Red-

mont ; ' son of Rodmund,' the Teutonic personal name Hrothmund. ' Rodmund ' occurs in Domesday Book.
ROᵹULᵹ—VIII—Rolfe, Rolph; ' son of Rodolf,' or ' Rudolph,' the Teutonic Hrothwulf ; confused with Ráᵹulᵹ, q.v.
ROIᵹeᴀL—VIII—Revel, Revell, Reville ; ' son of Rabel ' or Revel, an old personal name in England, of uncertain origin. Ravelin, its diminutive, occurs in Domesday Book and Searle, and is evidently the origin of the Irish name Raiᵹilin, angl. Revelyn, borne by the Savages of Co. Down. Reville is an old, but rare, Wexford surname.
ROIᵹeáRᵹ—VIII—Robert, Roberts ; ' son of Robert.'
RÓISᴄeᴀċ—XIV—Rostig, Roche, Roache. V. ᵹe Róiᵹce.
RÓS, Roos, Rose. V. ᵹe Rúᵹ.
RÓSᴀiᴄeᴀR—XI—Rowcester, Rawceter, Rossiter, &c. ; ' of Rocester,' a parish in Staffordshire ; the name of an old family in Co. Wexford. Rawceter of Rathmacknee was one of the principal gentlemen of Co. Wexford in 1598. The name is still common in the county.
ROSᴄᴀRᵹ, Rostard, Rochford ; a form in Co. Limerick of ᵹe Roᵹᵹoᵹc, q.v. It was evidently sometimes mistaken for Richard, as in the Patent Rolls of Henry VIII., where we find ' Rochford or Richards of Limerick.' Also Roᵹcún, q.v.
ROSᴄún, Rochford ; an Irish form in Co. Limerick of Rochford. V. Roᵹcaᵹᵹ and ᵹe Roᵹᵹoᵹc.
RUᴀᵹ—IX—Rowe, Roe ; Ir. ' ᵹuᴀᵹ,' i.e., red, red-haired ; an epithet which took the place of the real surname. Roe is often merely the final syllable of such surnames as MacEnroe, &c. Rowe is also an English surname.
RUCSᴄOn, Ruckston, Ruxton.
RUiSéiL—XII—Rushell, Rosel, Rossell, Russell ; Nor. ' russel,' i.e., red-haired, dim. of ' rous.' This surname came into Ireland at the time of the Anglo-Norman invasion and soon became very widespread, being specially common in Dublin, Meath, West-

meath, Limerick, Cork, Waterford, Louth and Down. The Russells of Co. Down came over with Sir John de Courcy. They held extensive property down to the confiscations of the 17th century. The late Lord Russell of Killowen, Lord Chief Justice of England, belonged to this ancient and illustrious family.

Ruitleis, Ruitlis—XI—*Rutlech*, Rutlege, Rutledge, Ruthledge, Routhledge, &c.; 'of Rutledge,' some spot in England.

Rút—VIII—*Route*, Ruth, Routh, Roth, Rothe; 'son of Rot,' Norse Hrutr, red-haired. Rot occurs in Domesday Book. Robert Rot de Kilkudbricht was a member of the Dublin Guild-Merchant, A.D. 1226. In later times, the name was chiefly associated with Kilkenny, of which city the Rothes were one of the chief families. The most illustrious bearer of the name was Dr. David Rothe, Bishop of Ossory, at the time of the Confederation of Kilkenny.

Sabáiste, Savage; a var. in Kilkenny and Waterford of Sábaoir, q.v.

Sabaois, Sábaois—XII—*Sauvage*, Savage; Nor. ' le Salvage,' ' le Sauvage,' i.e., the savage, one of wild, fierce character; the name of an old Anglo-Norman family planted in 1177 by Sir John de Courcy in the Ardes of Co. Down. The Savages are frequently mentioned in the Irish Annals. They possessed considerable property down to the revolution of 1689. Savage is also an old surname in Kilkenny and Waterford; v. Sabáirte.

Sazas—XII—*Says, Seys, Seise,* Size, Seix, Sex; Welsh ' Sais,' i.e., the Saxon, Englishman, stranger; a descriptive surname given by the Welsh to some family of English origin who afterwards settled in Offaly, Leix and Ormond. It is now very rare.

Saileastar, St. Leger, St. Ledger, Ledger, Lister, Lyster, &c.; a later form of Sailigéin, q.v. It was sometimes re-anglicised Lister and Lyster even as early as the 16th century.

Sᴀɪʟɪᵹéɪʀ, Sᴀɪʟɪɴéɪʀ, Sᴀɪʟɪɴᵹéɪʀ, Sallinger, Sellinger, St. Leger, Ledger, &c. V. ᴅe Sᴀɪʟɪᵹéɪʀ.

Sᴀɪɴséɪʟ, Sarsfield ; a var. of Sᴀɪᵹʀéɪʟ, q.v. ; in use in Co. Mayo.

Sᴀɪʀᵹeᴀɴᴄ—XII—*Serjeaunt*, Sergeant, Sargeant, Sargent, &c. ; Nor. ' le Sergant,' i.e., the sergeant, officer (of the law, &c.) ; an early Anglo-Irish surname.

Sᴀɪʀséɪʟ, Sarseil, Sarsfield. V. ᴅe Sᴀɪᵹʀéɪʟ.

Sᴀɪséɪʟ, Sausheil, Sarsfield ; a corruption of Sᴀɪᵹʀéɪʟ, q.v. ; in use in Co. Mayo.

Sᴀʟ, *Saale, Sawle*, Sall, Saul. V. ᴅe Sᴀʟ.

Sᴀᴍsūɴ—VIII—*Samsun*, Samson, Sampson ; ' son of Samson ' (a Biblical name in use among the Anglo-Saxons and Normans) ; the name of an Anglo-Norman family who came to Ireland about the time of the invasion and settled at Naas, in Co. Kildare, and at Callan, in Co. Kilkenny. Since the Cromwellian period, it has been found chiefly in the parish of Galbally, Co. Limerick, but is an old surname in East Limerick.

Sᴀɴᴅᴀɪʀ, Sᴀɴᴅᴀʀ—VIII—*Sandre, Saunder*, Sanders, Saunders ; ' son of Sander ' (short for Alexander) ; an old Anglo-Irish surname in Dublin, Meath, and other parts of Leinster.

Sᴀɴᴅᴀʟ, Sandall, Sandell. V. ᴅe Sᴀɴᴅᴀʟ.

Sᴀᴏʙᴀʟ—VIII—*Sawald, Sewall*, Sewell, Suel, &c. ; ' son of Saeweald,' an Anglo-Saxon personal name.

Sᴀᴏʙᴀʀᴅ—VIII—*Saoward*, Seaward, Seward ; ' son of Saeweard,' an Anglo-Saxon personal name, but it can hardly be distinguished from Sigeweard (Siweard, Siward).

Sᴀᴏᵹᴀʀ—VIII—Sayer, Sear, Sayers, Sears ; ' son of Saegaer,' a common Anglo-Saxon personal name, frequent in early Anglo-Irish records.

Sᴀᴏᴍᴀʀ—VIII—*Seamer*, Semore, Seymore, Semour, Seymour, &c. ; ' son of Saemaer,' an Anglo-Saxon personal name, hardly distinguishable from Sigemaer.

Sᴄᴀᴍᴄūɴ, Sᴄeᴀɪᴍɪᴄíɴ—XI—Scamaton, Scampton ; i.e., ' of Scampton,' a parish in Lincolnshire ; a rare Co. Cork surname.

Sceᴀrᴀᴄ, Skerrett. V. Scipéιᴅ.
Sceιᵐᵉᴀʟᴄûn—XI—Skivington, Skeffington, Skiffington, &c. ; i.e., ' of Skeffington,' a parish in Leicestershire.

Scιᴅιᴣ—VIII—*Skydy, Skiddie*, Skiddy ; ' son of Skithi ' (a Norse personal name, probably the same as ' skyti,' an archer) ; an old Cork surname of Danish origin. The Skiddys formed a clan after the Irish fashion, with a ' chief of the name.' No fewer than thirty-four Skiddys figure on the roll of mayors of Cork.

Scιʟʟιnᴣ, Scιʟʟιnn—VIII—Skilling, Skillen ; ' son of Scilling ' (a Norse personal name, the same as the English ' shilling ' ; cf. ᵽeóιpʟιnᴣ). Mac Scelling was the name of a naval commander from the Hebrides, mentioned by the Four Masters at the year 1154.

Scιnéιr—XII—Skinner ; Nor. ' le Skynnere,' i.e., the skinner, dealer in skins ; an old, but rare, surname in Ireland.

Scιréιᴅ, *Skirret*, Skerrett. This surname, according to Hardiman (History of Galway, p. 19), was originally Huscared, which was shortened to Scared. The Skerrets were an old and respectable Galway family. Richard Scared, or Skeret, was provost of Galway in 1378.

Scoᵽuʟ, Scuffil, Scholefield. V. ᴅe Scoᵽuʟ.

Scoʟᴀᴅᴅ—XII—*Skolard*, Scolard, Scollard ; Eng. ' the Scholar,' i.e., one belonging to a school, a learned man ; an old, but rare, Kerry surname. In the year 1601, Maurice Skolard of Castleisland was the recipient of a pardon from Queen Elizabeth.

Scorʟóᴣ—XII—*Scorloge, Scorloke, Scurlok*, Scurlock, Shirlock, Shearlock, Sherlock ; Ang.-Sax. ' Scortlog,' i.e., short lock, one with shorn locks. This family, which, to judge from the name, is of Anglo-Saxon origin, had settled in Ireland before the beginning of the 13th century, and soon after became very widespread, being found in Dublin, Meath, Louth, Wexford, Waterford, Tipperary, &c.

Scoᴄ—XII—*Scot*, Scott ; Eng. ' the Scot,' i.e., the Scotch-

man, an immigrant from Scotland ; an old surname
in Ireland, but rare until the plantation of Ulster.
Albanac (q.v.) was the corresponding Irish surname.
soonoún, soonnoún, Sdundon. V. Stonoún.

seac—VIII—*Jakes, Jak,* Jack, Jacke, and incorrectly
Jackman ; ' son of Jaques ' (a French name, from
Latin Jacobus, same as the English James) ; an
early Anglo-Norman surname. The family seems to
have settled in Kilkenny and Tipperary.

seaoac, seaξac, Shaw.

seafraio—VIII—Jaffrey, Jeffrey, &c. ; ' son of Geoffrey,'
a Norman personal name, the same as Godfrey.

seambar, seambars, seambrac—XI—*Chamber,*
Chambers, Chamberlain ; Fr. ' de la Chambre,' Lat.
' de Camera,' i.e., of the chamber, the chamberlain.

seamróξ—XI—Shamrock, Hamrogue ; doubtless ' of
Sambrook,' or ' Shambrook,' a parish in Shropshire.
There is some connection between this surname and
ħampóc, q.v.

séamus—VIII—James ; ' son of James.'

searlóξ, Shearlock, Sherlock ; a var. of Scoplóξ, q.v.

séarlus—VIII—*Sharles,* Charles ; ' son of Charles.'

searman—XII—*Shereman,* Sharman, Sherman, Shearman ; Nor. ' le Sherman,' i.e., the shearman, cutter
of cloth. This family had settled in Dublin before
the middle of the 13th century.

seartáin, *Shortaun,* Shorten ; doubtless, a corruption
of Seaptal or Soiptéil, q.v. Richard Shortaun of
Limerick, Co. Wexford, was attainted in 1642. This
form of the name is now peculiar to Co. Cork.

seartal, Shortall ; a var. of Soiptéil, q.v.

seinicín—VIII—Jenkin, Jenkins, Jinkins, &c. ; ' son
of Jenkin,' dim. of John.

seoξ, seoξac, *Sheo, Joye,* Joy, Joyce. V. Seóiξ.

seoξas—VIII—*Sheos, Josse, Joce,* Joyce ; ' son of
Joce,' or ' Josse ' (a Breton personal name). This
surname, which appears to be distinct from Seóiξ
(q.v.), was peculiar to Kilkenny and Cork. In Ireland, it dates back at least to the 13th century.

seóiʒ—VIII or XII—*Sheoye, Shoye, Joie, Joye,* Joy, Joyce ; ' son of Joy ' (probably a Norman personal name—Joie, Joye—corresponding to the Latin Letitia ; but possibly merely a descriptive epithet bestowed on one of a joyous disposition). As a surname, it is of record in Ireland since the end of the 12th century, when the family seems to have come hither from Wales, and by the 16th century had become very widespread. The Joyces of Galway, according to Hardiman (Hist. of Galway, pp. 14-15), came from Wales in the reign of Edward I. They acquired considerable tracts of territory in the mountainous district of Iar-Connacht, called from them Duthaigh Seoghach, or the Joyce Country, now forming the barony of Ross, in Co. Galway, where they are still very numerous. They were, according to Hardiman, a race of men remarkable for their extraordinary stature. The surname is now almost everywhere anglicised Joyce. Joy, the correct rendering, is almost peculiar to Kerry. Cf. Seóʒar above.

seóiʒeac, seóiʒeac—XIV—Joy, Joyce. V. Seóiʒ.

seóirse—VIII—George ; ' son of George.'

seóns—*Johns,* Jones ; ' son of John ' ; a phonetic rendering of the English surname Jones.

seorcús—XII—*Shortus, Shorthose,* Shortis, Shortice ; Ang-Sax. ' Sceorthosa,' i.e., of the short hose ; not an old surname in Ireland.

seósac—XIV—Joyce. V. Seóʒar.

siacus—VIII—Jacques ; ' son of Jacques.' V. Seac.

síbear—XII—*Chiver, Chevere,* Chivers, Chevers, Cheevers ; Nor. ' le Chivere,' ' le Chevere,' i.e., the goat (Fr. chevre), a nickname ; the name of a Norman family who came to Ireland about the time of the invasion and settled in Dublin, Louth, Meath, Kildare and Wexford. They were highly respectable, but lost their property in the Cromwellian and Williamite confiscations. A branch of the family was transplanted to Connacht by Cromwell.

Sıᵹín—VIII—*Sigin, Siggin,* Siggins ; ' son of Sigewine,' an Anglo-Saxon personal name.

Sımıcín—VIII—*Symikine,* Simkin, Simpkin, Simkins Simpkins ; ' son of Simkin ' (dim. of Simon).

Sıncléıр, Sinclair, &c. V. ʋe Sıncléıр.

Sımıcín—VIII—Shinkwin ; ' son of Jenkin ' (dim. of Fr. Jean, or John). V. Seınıcín.

Sıomcóc, Sıomcóᵹ—VIII—*Symcok, Symcock,* Simcox ; ' son of Simcock ' (dim. of Simon).

Sıonnᴀċ—X—Shinnagh, Shinnock, &c., and by translation Fox, Foxe ; Ir. ' Sıonnᴀċ,' i.e., the fox ; an epithet or nickname which supplanted the real surname, especially in the case of the family of Ó Cᴀτᴀрn-ᴀıᵹ (q.v.), anciently chiefs of Teffia.

Sıonórʋ—VIII—*Signot, Synod, Synote, Synot,* Sinott, Synott, Sinnott, Synnott ; ' son of Sigenoth ' (an Anglo-Saxon personal name) ; the name of an English family who came to Ireland at the time of the invasion and settled in Wexford, where they have ever since been both numerous and influential. In the reign of Elizabeth, the Sinnotts were great ' loyalists,' and were rewarded with grants of the confiscated lands of the MacMurroughs. David Sinnott was governor of Wexford when that town was besieged by Cromwell. The Sinnotts lost their estates in the Cromwellian and Williamite confiscations. There were also ancient families of the name in Dublin and Tipperary.

Sıonúıр, Shinnor, Shinnors, and in parts of Connacht incorrectly Sinnott, Synnott ; also Soınıúıр, q.v. V. ʋe Sıonúıр.

Sıosᴀl—XI—Chisholm ; Nor. ' de Cheseholme,' i.e., of Chisholm in Roxburgh ; a Scottish surname.

Sıseᴀl—VIII—*Seysel, Seycel,* Chisel, Chissell, (Chisholm) ; evidently ' son of Cecil.'

Sıúınéıр—XII—Joyner ; i.e., ' the joiner,' or carpenter.

Sıúıτ—XI—*Shute,* Chute ; i.e., ' of Chute,' a parish in Wiltshire ; not a very old surname in Ireland.

Sıúrʋᴀn, Sıúrτᴀn—VIII—*Jurdane, Jordane,* Jurdan,

Jordan, &c.; 'son of Jordan' (a personal name derived from the river Jordan, which became popular in crusading times throughout Western Europe, and nowhere more than in England, owing to flasks of Jordan water being brought home to be used for baptismal purposes). The Jordans were an Anglo-Norman family who settled early in Dublin, Meath, Limerick, &c. Jordan of Hilton was one of the chief gentlemen of Dublin at the end of the 16th century, and at the same period three of the name were mayors of Limerick. This surname is to be distinguished from Mac Ṡiúptáin, q.v.

Slócum—XI—*Sloocume*, Slocum, Slocombe, &c.; i.e., 'of Slocombe,' a place-name in the south-west of England; apparently not a very old surname in Ireland.

Smeárt—XII—*Smert*, Smart, Smartt; Anglo-Saxon 'Smeart,' i.e., quick, sharp; an old, but very rare, surname in Ireland.

Smioic—XI—*Smedick*, Smithwick; i.e., 'of Smethwick' in Staffordshire, written Smedewich in Domesday Book and still pronounced locally Smethick; a rare, and apparently not very old, surname in Ireland.

Smioiᵹ, Smioiᵹe—XI—*Smethy*, Smiddy, Smithwick; very probably 'at the smithy,' from residence thereby, but possibly 'of Smethwick,' as above (v. Smioic), to which the angl. form Smithwick would seem to point; a rare Co. Cork surname.

Smíst—XII or XI—*Smeche, Smyche, Smytche, Smythes*, Smeeth, Smiddy, Smithwick; Mid. Eng. 'Smeche,' apparently for 'Smethe,' i.e., smooth, polished, suave, but Smiṙc has evidently been regarded as in some way connected with Smioiᵹe (q.v.), and so the origin may be 'at the smithies.' It is a not uncommon surname in the neighbourhood of Youghal.

Smísteaċ—XIV—Smithwick. V. Smiṙc.

Soiniúir, *Synur*, Shinnor, Shinnors, and, in parts of Connacht, incorrectly Sinnott, Synnott. Also Sionúir, q.v.

SOIRTÉIL—XII—*Scorthals*, *Schorthals*, *Sertell*, *Sertill*, Shorthall, Shortall, Shortell, Shortle, Surtill ; Ang.-Sax. ' Scort-hals,' i.e., short-neck, a nickname or descriptive name ; Langhals also 'once existed. This family, which, to judge from the name, is of Anglo-Saxon origin, probably came to Ireland early in the reign of Edward I. They settled in Co. Kilkenny where they became very influential. Their chief seat was at Ballylorcan, but they had many other castles in the barony of Iverk.

SPÁINEAC—X—*Spainagh*, Spain ; Ir. ' Spáineac,' i.e., the Spaniard, a descriptive name given to an Irishman who returned from Spain, and which supplanted the real surname.

SPÉIRING, Spearing, Spearin.

SPRAT—VIII—*Sprot*, Spratt ; ' son of Sprot ' (an Anglo-Saxon personal name). This surname can boast of considerable antiquity in Ireland.

STAC—XI—*Stak*, *Stake*, Stack ; Mid. Eng. ' Stak,' ' Stake,' i.e., probably, ' at the stack ' (steep rock or hill), or ' at the stock ' (stump of a tree), from residence thereby. The Stacks are an old family in North Kerry, where they have been settled, at least, since the latter part of the 13th century. In the year 1450, Maurice Stak was appointed Bishop of Adfert ; and thirty years later, John Stak was bishop of the same see. By the end of the 16th century, the Stacks had become very numerous in North Kerry. They were then thoroughly Irish. Garrett Roe Stack was one of the principal leaders in the wars against Queen Elizabeth.

STAFORT, Stafford. V. ƊE STAFORT.

STANCARƊ—XI—*Stanckard*, Stancard, Stanford ; doubtless, Nor. ' de Stanford,' i.e., of Stanford, a parish in Kent ; an old surname in Co. Mayo.

STARCAIƊ—VIII—*Starky*, *Starkye*, Starkie, Starkey ; ' son of Starkie ' (a ' pet ' form of one of the many Anglo-Saxon names beginning with Starc-, as Starcbeorht, Starcfrith, Starchere, Starcwulf). Instances of this surname occur in Irish records since the end of the 13th century..

ꂆꞮbɪɴ—VIII—*Stevyn, Stevene,* Steven, Steen, Steene, Stevens, Stephens ; ' son of Stephen ' ; an old Anglo-Irish surname.

ꂆꞮoꞜꜳꞅꝺ, ꂆꞮoꞜꜳꞅꞇ, ꂆꞮuꞜꜳꞅꝺ—XII—*Stiward,* Steward, Stewart, Stuart ; Nor. ' le Stiward,' i.e., the steward. The royal Stuarts of Scotland derived their name from the office of Lord High Steward which was hereditary in the family for two centuries before they came to the throne. Prior to the plantation of Ulster, there are few traces of any families of the name in Ireland, nearly all our Stewarts being the descendants of late immigrants from Scotland.

ꂆꞇóc, *Stoke,* Stokes, Stoakes. V. ꝺe ꂆꞇóc.

ꂆꞇóɪbɪɴ—XI—*Stobyn,* Stubbin, Stubbins ; Nor. ' de St. Obyn,' i.e., of St. Aubin in Brittany ; an old, but rare, surname in Ireland. Cf. ꞇóɪbɪn.

ꂆꞇonꝺún, ꂆꞇonnꝺún, ꂆꞇúnꝺún, Staunton, Stundon, Sdundun. V. ꝺe ꂆꞇonnꝺún.

ꂆꞇꞅꜳɪnꞅe—XII—L'Estrange, Strange ; Nor. ' le Estrange,' ' le Straunge,' i.e., the foreigner, the stranger, the new-comer ; an old surname in Ireland.

ꂆꞇꞅꜳoɪꞇ, ꂆꞇꞅꜳoɪꞇꞅ—XI—*Strete, Streate, Streete, Stretys, Streytis, Streache, Streech, Stretch, Strytch,* Stritch ; Nor. ' de la Strete,' Old. Eng. ' atte Strete ' i.e., at the street or paved (Roman) road, from residence thereby. (The old forms Streache, Stretch, &c., stand for Streets, monosyllabic surnames of local origin often adding *s* after the manner of patronymics, as Williams, Jones, &c.) Stritch was the name of an old and respectable merchant family in Limerick, of which city Nicholas Stritch was mayor in 1427. Among the twenty exempted from pardon by Ireton when he took possession of Limerick in 1651, was Alderman Thomas Stritch. There are very few of this old name now in Limerick.

ꂆꞇꞅonꝿ, ꂆꞇꞅonnꝿ—XII—Strong, Stronge, Strange ; Old. Eng. ' Strang,' Mid. Eng. ' Stronge,' ' Strange,' i.e., strong, powerful, a descriptive surname. There were old and respectable families of this name in the cities of Kilkenny and Waterford.

Sꞇuꞩꝺᴀꞧꞇ—XII—Studdert.

Suᴀꞑ—VIII—*Suan, Swane,* Swaine, Swayne, &c. ; ' son of Swan ' (a common Anglo-Saxon personal name). This surname appears in Anglo-Irish records soon after the invasion, but never became common in Ireland.

Suᴀꞇmᴀꞑ—VIII—*Swetman, Sweteman,* Sweetman ; ' son of Swetman ' (a not uncommon Anglo-Saxon personal name). This family, which, to judge from the name, is of Anglo-Saxon origin, came to Ireland some time before the middle of the 13th century and settled in Co. Kilkenny, where they were highly respectable

Suꞁꞁꞥ5éꞩꞧ, Sellinger, St. Ledger, &c. ; a var. of Sᴀꞁꞁꞥ5éꞩꞧ, q.v.

Suꞥꞥ5eᴀꞑ—XI—Singen, Singin, St. John ; Nor. ' de St. Jehan,' ' de St. Jean,' i.e., of St. John's, a common French place-name; an early Norman surname in Ireland. The family settled in Wexford, Kilkenny and Tipperary. Thomas de St. John was sheriff of Tipperary in 1296.

Suꞥꝺéꞁ—XI—Suppell, Supple ; Nor. ' de la Chapell,' Lat. ' de Capella,' i.e., of the chapel, from residence thereby ; an old surname in Co. Limerick, where it is of record since the last quarter of the 13th century, and of which the Supples were, in the latter part of the 16th century, one of the chief families. They lost their property after the Desmond wars. The ruins of their castle are still to be seen at Kilmocua, near Croom.

Sꞥꞥꞥꞇe—XI—*Souche,* Suche, Zouche ; Nor. ' de la Zouch,' i.e., of the zouch (an old French word, meaning the stock of a tree), from residence thereby ; an old, but extremely rare, surname in Limerick and Kerry.

Suꞥꞇꞩéꞩꞧ—XII—Switzer ; i.e., ' the Swiss,' immigrant from Switzerland.

Sútar—XII—Soutar, Souter, Sutter, Sutor, &c. ; Nor. 'le Suter,' 'le Souter,' i.e., the shoemaker. The following interesting reference to a member of this family occurs in the Fiants of Elizabeth :—A.D. 1601 —Pardon to Nich. Suter, shoemaker.—F. E. 6517.

Táilliúir—XII—*Taillur, Taillour,* Taylour, Taylor, &c. ; Nor. 'le Tailleur,' i.e., the cutter, the tailor ; an old Norman surname in Dublin, where the family settled about the time of the invasion. The majority of our Taylors are, however, the descendants of more recent immigrants.

Talant—XI—Tallan, Tallen, Tallant, Tallent ; i.e., 'of Talland' in Cornwall ; a rare surname in Limerick and Waterford.

Talbóro—VIII—*Talebot, Talbote,* Talbot ; 'son of Talebot' (a Norman personal name). The Talbots came over to England with William the Conqueror. Richard Talebot is mentioned in Domesday Book. His descendant and namesake, Richard Talbot, accompanied Henry II to Ireland and was granted the lordship of Malahide, Co. Dublin, which has continued in his descendants to the present day. The Talbots have at different times filled many of the highest offices of Church and State in Ireland.

Talún—VIII—*Talun, Talown, Tallone,* Tallon ; 'son of Talon' (a Norman personal name). The Tallons were a Norman family who settled early in Dublin and other parts of the Pale.

Tanncáro—VIII—Tankard, Tancard ; 'son of Tancred' (a Norman personal name, Teutonic Tancrad, Ang.-Sax. Thancred, early corrupted to Tancard and Tankard) ; an old, but now extremely rare, surname in Ireland. In 1598 Tankard or Tancard of Castletown was one of the chief gentlemen of Meath. The name was in use at the same period in Co. Cork.

Tanúir—XII—Tanner ; Nor. 'le Tanur,' 'le Tanour,' 'le Tanner,' i.e., the tanner ; an old, but rare, surname in Ireland.

ᴄᴀᴏɪʟɪɴ͵ᵹ—VIII—*Theling, Teling, Teelin,* Teeling ; apparently Ang.-Sax. ' Taeling,' i.e., son of Tael ; the name of an old family in Co. Meath, where, at the end of the 16th century, the Teelings ranked among the gentry.

ᴄᴀʀᴀɴᴄ—XI—Tarrant ; i.e., ' of Tarrant ' in Dorsetshire and other parts of England ; a rare Co. Cork surname, apparently of late origin ; also ᴄopᴀnᴄᴀ, q.v.

ᴄᴀᴄ—VIII—*Ta, Tath, Taath, Taaf,* Taff, Taaffe ; ' son of David ' ; cf. modern Irish Ɔᴀᴄ and Welsh Taffy ; the name of a distinguished family of Welsh origin who settled at an early period in Co. Louth. Towards the end of the 13th century, flourished Sir Nicholas Taaffe, Justice of the Common Pleas, whose son, John Taaffe, became Archbishop of Armagh. In the reign of Elizabeth, Sir William Taaffe did good service against Hugh O'Neill and subsequently against the Spaniards at Kinsale, for which he was rewarded by James I with large grants of confiscated lands in Co. Sligo. In 1628, his son, John Taaffe, was created Baron of Ballymote and Viscount Corren ; and in 1661, Theobald, son of this John Taaffe, was made Earl of Carlingford. The Taaffes were most zealous supporters of the Stuarts, in whose cause they sacrificed everything. Nicholas, the second Earl of Carlingford, fell at the Boyne, and the family honours devolved on his brother Francis, the celebrated Count Taaffe of the German Empire.

ᴄɪɴcʟᴇɪʀ—XII—Tinckler, Tinkler ; Eng. ' the tinkler,' i.e., the hawker, or other tradesman who made his approach known by a tinkling noise.

ᴄɪʀɪᴀʟ—VIII—*Torel, Turrill, Tyrel, Tirrell,* Tyrrell ; ' son of Tyrel ' or ' Thurold ' (corrupt for Ang.-Sax. Thurwald, Norse Thorvaldr). This family, which is of Norman origin, came to England with William the Conqueror. At the time of the Anglo-Norman invasion, Hugh Tyrrell received from Hugh de Lacy the lordship of Castleknock ; and his descendants were styled Barons of Castleknock until the line became extinct in 1385. In Co. Westmeath, the Tyrrells possessed the barony of Fertullagh down to the 17th century. Captain Richard Tyrrell was a celebrated commander in the Elizabethan wars in Ireland. Also TⱼⱤⱭⱡ.

Tⁱú, *Tywe, Tue,* Tew. V. de ꝺe Tⁱú.

TⁱuⁱT, Tuite. V. ꝺe TⁱúⁱT.

Tóc—VIII—Toke, Tooke, Tuke; 'son of Toke,' a personal name of Norse origin, common in Domesday, where it is variously written Toc, Toke, Toka, &c.

Tóibíⁿ—XI—*Tobine,* Tobyn, Tobin; Nor: 'de St. Aubyn,' 'de St. Obyn,' Lat. 'de Sancto Albino,' i.e., of St. Aubin, a town in Brittany, famous as the scene of a battle between the French and Bretons, aided by the English, in 1488. The Tobins settled early in Tipperary and Kilkenny, whence they spread into the neighbouring counties of Waterford, Cork and Limerick. The head of the family was styled Baron of Comsey, in Co. Tipperary.

Tóimicíⁿ—VIII—*Tomekin,* Tomkin, Tomkins; 'son of Tomkin' (dim. of Thomas).

Toimíⁿ—VIII—*Tomine, Tomen,* Timmin, Timmins, Timmons, &c.; 'son of Tomin' (dim. of Thomas); an old surname in Carlow, Kildare and Wexford.

TóiⱤiꝺ, Terry. V. TuiⱤiꝺ.

Tóm—VIII—*Tome,* Thom; 'son of Thome' (a short form of Thomas).

Tomás—VIII—Thomas; 'son of Thomas,' one of the commonest names in use among the Anglo-Norman settlers in Ireland.

Tóⁿ—VIII—*Toan,* Tone; 'son of Tona' (an Anglo-Saxon personal name, found in Domesday Book as the name of holders of land even in the time of Edward the Confessor). As a surname, it appears in Anglo-Irish records as early as the beginning of the 14th century, but has always been very rare, and is now hardly known except through Theobald Wolfe Tone.

TⱤⱭ⯑Ɑ, Tarrant, and incorrectly Thornton; a var. of TⱭⱤⱭⱡⱤ, q.v.

Coꞃbóꞃ—VIII—*Turbot*, Turbett, Turbit ; 'son of Turbot' (dim. of Turbert, or Torbert, Anglo-Saxon Thurbeorht, Norse Thorbiartr) ; an old, but always extremely rare, surname in Ireland.

Coꞃnóꞃ—XII—*Tornour*, *Tournor*, Turnour, Turnor, Turner ; Nor. 'le Turner,' i.e., the turner, latheworker, once a familiar occupation. Turnor is an old surname in Dublin, Wexford, and parts of Munster. 'Abrid le Turnur' occurs in the Dublin Roll of Names soon after the Anglo-Norman invasion, and in 1226, William and Osbeit Turnur were members of the Dublin Guild-Merchant ; while somewhat later in the same century, Clement le Turnur was one of the Free Citizens of Dublin. The most important family of the name in the 16th century was that of Wexford, where, in 1598, Turnor of Ballyasshin was one of the principal gentlemen.

Cóꞃnuꞁꞁ—XI—Thornhill ; i.e., 'of Thornhill,' in Yorkshire ; 'Tornil' in Domesday Book.

Coꞃꞅcán—VIII—*Trostane*, *Trustane*, and incorrectly Tristan and Tristram ; 'son of Thurstan' (an Anglo-Saxon personal name, corresponding to Norse Thorstein ; hardly from Welsh 'trystan' the old Angl. forms being against this derivation) ; a rare Roscommon surname..

Cꞃáꞁbeaꞃꞅ, Travers, Travors, Trevors. V. ꞃe Cꞃáꞁbeaꞃꞃ.

Cꞃéanꞁámaꞔ, Armstrong ; doubtless a translation of the English Armstrong.

Cꞃeannc, Cꞃeanc, *Traunte*, Trant. V. ꞃe Cꞃeanc.

Cꞃeó, *Treo*, *Troe*, *Troye*, Troy. V. ꞃe Cꞃeó.

Cꞃꞁaꞁ, *Tryal*, Tyrrell ; a syncopated form of Cꞁꞃꞁaꞁ, q.v.

Cꞃꞁnnꞅe, Cꞃꞁnꞅe—XI—Trench ; i.e., 'at the trench,' or cutting ; not a very old surname in Ireland.

Cꞃꞁú—XII—*Trewe*, Trew ; Mid. Eng. 'Trewe,' i.e., the true, faithful, loyal man ; an old, but rare, surname in Kildare, &c.

Cꞃꞁúman—XII—*Treweman*, *Treuman*, Trueman ; Mid. Eng. 'Treweman,' i.e., the true man, same as Cꞃꞁú above ; an old, but rare, surname in Co. Down.

ⅭⓊⒾⓃⓁéⒾⱫ, Townley. V. ⅾe ⒸúⒾⓃⓁéⒾⱫ.

ⒸⓊⒾⓇⒾⓄ—VIII—*Thirry*, *Tyrry*, *Tirry*, Terry; 'son of Tyrry' (a Norman form of the Anglo-Saxon personal name Thuri, short for Thured or Thored, common in Domesday Book). Tyrry occurs as a Christian name in the Black Book of Limerick. As a surname, it is of record in Ireland since the last decade of the 13th century, being then established at Kilkenny and Cork. In the latter city, the Tyrrys or Terrys, became one of the most influential families, and upwards of twenty of the name figure in the list of mayors.

ⒸⓊⓃⓄⒶⓇ—XII—*Tunder*, Thunder; Nor. ' le Thunder,' i.e., the vintner, or the cask-maker; an old Dublin surname.

ⒸúⓃⓁⓊⒾⓄ, Townley. V. ⅾe ⒸúⒾⓃⓁéⒾⱫ.

ⒸⓊⓇⒶⓄⒾⓃ, *Turien*, *Toran*, Torran, Torrans, Torrens, Torry, Terry, &c.; possibly for ' de Torigni,' i.e., of Torigny, a town in France.

ⓊⒶⒸⒶⓃ—XII—*Vachan*, *Vaghan*, Vaughan; Welsh ' vychan,' i.e., little, small of stature; the name of a Welsh family, some of whom settled, prior to the 16th century, in Dublin, Wexford, and perhaps other parts of Leinster. The great majority of our Vaughans are, however, of native origin.

ⓊⒶⓄⒶ—VIII—Wade, Waide, &c.; ' son of Wada' (a common Anglo-Saxon personal name). Thomas Wade was one of the free citizens of Dublin, 1225-1250.

*ⓊⒶⓄⓁóⒸ—XI—*Wodeloc*, *Woodloge*, Woodlock; i.e., ' at the woodlock,' or enclosure in or by a wood, from residence thereby. This surname came into Ireland about the time of the Anglo-Norman invasion. It appears to have been most numerous in Tipperary.

ⓊⱫⒶⓃ—XII—*Ugan*, *Owgan*, *Wogane*, Ougan, Oogan, Ogan, Wogan, Vogan; Welsh ' gwgan,' from ' gwg,' a frown, a scowl. The Wogans settled soon after the Anglo-Norman invasion in Co. Kildare, where their chief seat was at Rathcoffey. The family produced several distinguished men.

uᴀɪᴏín—VIII—*Wadin*, Wadden, Wadding; 'son of Wadin' (a dim. of the Anglo-Saxon Wada or of the Norman Walter, the latter by far the more probable; 'Wadin White' occurs in Grace's Annals, A.D. 1316). The Waddings settled early in Wexford and Waterford. In Wexford their chief seat was at Ballycogly. The Waterford family produced several distinguished ecclesiastics, among them the illustrious Franciscan, Father Luke Wadding.

uᴀısᴌéıᵹ—XI—*Wesleie*, Wesley, Wellesley; Nor. 'de Welleslegh,' i.e., of Wellesley, corruptly Wesley, a spot in Somerset, a short distance from Wells. This family came to Ireland at the time of the Anglo-Norman invasion and settled in Kildare and Meath. They assumed the Irish patronymic surname of ṁᴀc uᴀᴌᵽonᴄᴀ, q.v. To the Meath branch belonged the Duke of Wellington.

uᴀıᴄne—IX—*Woney*, Green; Ir. ' uᴀıᴄne,' i.e., green; a descriptive epithet which supplanted the real surname.

uᴀᴌᴏʀᴀ́n—VIII—*Walerand*, *Waleran*, Waldron; 'son of Walerand,' a Teutonic personal name, found in Domesday Book. V. ṁᴀc uᴀᴌᵽonᴄᴀ.

uᴀsᴏún, uᴀsᴄún—XI—*Westoun*, Weston; Nor. 'de Westun,' i.e., of Weston, or the west-town, in England. 'Aluredus de Westun' occurs in the Dublin Roll of Names, A.D. 1216.

uıcsᴄéɪᴏ—XI—Wixted; i.e., 'of Wickstead' in England; a Tipperary surname.

uıᴏeᴀs, Wise, Wyse. V. ᴏe uıᴏeᴀᵽ.

uıᴌıs, Willis, Wills; a phonetic rendering of the English surname Willis.

uıᴌeᴀmóɪᴏ, uıᴌmıᴄ—VIII—Wilmot, Wilmott, Willmott, Willmit; 'son of Williamot' (dim. of William).

uınᵹıᴌ—XI—Winkle, Windle, Wingfield; i.e., 'of Wincle' in Cheshire, or more probably merely a phonetic representation of the sound of the English name, Windle.

uınᵹséıᴌ—XI—Wingfield; i.e., 'of Wingfield,' in England.

uinnseaoún—XI—*Unsedon, Winsedon, Wynchedon,* (Nugent) ; Nor. ' de Wynchester,' i.e., of Winchester, an ancient episcopal city in Hampshire. Members of the family of Nugent who came from this city and settled early in Cork were known in Irish by the surname Uinnpeaoún, which was intended to represent Winchester. These Nugents formed a clan after the Irish fashion. The chief lived at Aghavarten Castle, near Carrigaline. The original surname, Nugent, has been retained in English. Cf. ſúinnpeann.

uinseann—VIII—Vincent ; ' son of Vincent.'

uiséin—XII—*Usshere,* Ussher, Usher ; Nor. ' le Ussher,' i.e., the doorkeeper. This surname is of considerable antiquity in Ireland.

ulp—VIII—*Ulfe, Wulf,* Woulfe, Wolfe ; ' son of Ulf,' or ' Wolf ' (a common personal name among all the Teutonic races). As a surname, it came into Ireland about the time of the Anglo-Norman invasion, and as such is found in the early Dublin rolls ; but it cannot now be distinguished from oe bulb (q.v.), which was the form in use in Kildare and Limerick.

ultac—X—Ultagh, (Dunleavy, Dunlevy) ; Ir. ' ultac,' i.e., the Ultonian ; a descriptive name given to members of the family of Ó Ouinnpléibe (q.v.) from their place of origin, and which in some instances supplanted the real surname.

ultacán—X—(Dunleavy, Dunlevy) ; Ir. ' ultacán,' a dim. of ultac (q.v.), and similarly applied.

unpraio—VIII—Humfrey, Humphrey, Humphries, &c. ; ' son of Hunfrid ' (a Teutonic personal name, in English corruptly Humphrey).

uptún—XI—Upton ; i.e., ' of Upton ' (Ang.-Sax. Uptún, the upper village or farmstead), a common placename in England.

APPENDIX

CLAN-NAMES

Besides personal names, our Irish ancestors had from an early period, and even from pre-historic times, a complete system of fixed clan-names by which each family-group and its subdivisions had its own distinct name. These clan-names are of great importance in tracing the early history of families. Though long obsolete as people-names, they still survive in many instances as baronial and parochial designations, in the same way as Norfolk and Suffolk, which were originally people-names—north-folk and south-folk —became the names of two English counties. They were generally formed by prefixing certain words to the genitive case of the names of distinguished ancestors, sometimes gods and goddesses, or by the addition of terminations, and in many respects resemble the family names of a later period. Some, however, and probably the very oldest, appear to be plural names, like the names of the Celtic tribes of Gaul in Caesar's time ; while others are formed by prefixing certain words to place-names.

Of words prefixed to the names of ancestors to form clan-names, we have the following :

Cineal (Cinel, Cenel, angl. Kinel), kindred, race, descendants, as Cineal Eoghain, race of Eoghan, Cineal Conaill, race of Conall ;

Clann, children, race, descendants, as Clann Cholmain, race of Colman ;

Corca, race, progeny, as Corca Bhaiscinn, race of Baiscinn, Corca Dhuibhne, race of Duibhne ;

Dal, tribe, progeny, as Dál gCais, race of Cas, whence " Dalcassian " ;

Muintear, family, people, as Muintear Mhaolmordha, family of Maolmordha, Muintear Mhurchadha, family of Murchadh ;

Siol, seed, progeny, as Síol nAnmchadha, seed of Anmchadh, Síol Muireadhaigh, seed of Muireadhach ;

Sliocht, progeny, as Sliocht Aodha Sláine, progeny of Aodh Sláine ;

Teallach, family, household, as Teallach Dhunchadha, household of Dunchadh ;

Ui, grandsons, descendants, as Uí Breasail, descendants of Breasal, Uí Liatháin, descendants of Liathán, Uí Néill, descendants of Niall.

Of terminations used to form clan-names, we have the following :

-acht, as in Cianacht, race of Cian, Eoghanacht, race of Eoghan ;
-na, as in Dealbhna, race of Dealbhaoth ;
-ne, as in Conmhaicne, race of Conmhac ;
-raighe, as in Caonraighe, Calraighe, Muscraighe, &c.

Of words prefixed to place-names, we have the following :
Aes, people, as Aes Aisde, Aes Gréine, Aes-trí-máighe ;
Feara, Fir, men, as Feara Luirg, men of Lurg, Fir Teathbha, men of Teffia ;
Pobul, people, as Pobul Uí Chaoimh, O'Keeffe's people, Pobul Uí Cheallacháin, O'Callaghan's people ;
Tuath, people, clan, state, as Tuath Luimnigh, people of Luimneach.

Some, if not all, of these ancient clan-names were capable of being turned into personal surnames by prefixing Moccu, later Mac U, to the genitive case of the eponym. Thus St. Molua, who belonged to Corca Oiche, is in the Annals of Ulster twice called Lugaid Mac U Ochae, that is, Lughaidh, son of the descendants of Ochae (Fochae, the ancestor of the Corca Oiche). Hence probably such modern forms as ᵐᴀc uí Cᴀoiṁ, ᵐᴀc uí Ḃⱳiᴀin, for persons surnamed O'Keeffe and O'Brien respectively (see page 22).

These ancient clan-names in many instances differ little, if at all, in form from modern family names. Muintear and Clann which occur so frequently in clan-names are also used to form the collective plural of family names, as ᵐuinceᴀⱳ Loinᵹⱳiᵹ, the O'Lynches, Cᴌᴀnn ᴄṠíᴄiᵹ, the MacSheehys, or Sheehys. (See p. 25.) Similarly Uí, of frequent occurrence in clan-names, is also the plural of uᴀ of family names. Hence very often the same form, or nearly the same, is a clan-name and a family name, but the meaning in each case is entirely different. ᵐuinceᴀⱳ ⁱⱳeᴀⱳnáin, for instance, as a family name denotes the O'Heffernans of Owney, but as a clan-name the O'Quins of Thomond. Irish writers have been frequently led into error by this similarity or identity in form of names of widely different meaning.

Only such clan-names as are mentioned in the preceding notes are here explained, and they are taken in their original sense of people-names.

CIANACHT (Keenaght), race of Cian, son of Oilioll Olum, King of Munster in the 3rd century ; the families of Ó Ceᴀⱳḃᴀill, Ó ᵐeᴀċᴀⱳ and Ó Ríoᵹḃᴀⱳⱳⱳáin of Eile, Ó Cᴀᴄᴀⱳᴀiᵹ of Breagh, Ó Conċoḃᴀⱳ of Glen Geimhin, and Ó heᴀᵹⱳᴀ and Ó ᵹᴀḃⱳᴀ of Luighne in Connacht.

CINEAL AODHA (Kinelea), (1) race of Aodh, the sixth in descent from Dahy, King of Ireland ; the name of a branch of Ui Fiachrach Aidhne (q.v.), seated in the barony of Kiltartan, Co. Galway, of which Ó Cᴀᴄᴀil and Ó Seᴀċnᴀⱳᴀiᵹ were chiefs ; and (2) race of Aodh Dubh, father of Failbhe Flann, King of Munster in the 7th century ; clan-name of the O'Callaghans whose ancient territory is now represented by the barony of Kinelea, Co. Cork.

CINEAL AONGHUSA, (1) race of Aonghus, son of Eoghan, son of Niall' of the Nine Hostages ; a branch of Cineal Eoghain (q.v.) ; and (2) a branch of Clann Bhreasail (q.v.), in Co. Armagh, of which the MacCanns were the chief family.

CINEAL BACAID, race of Bacad ; clan-name of the family of Ó Loingrig of Breifney.

CINEAL mBAOITH, race of Baoth, a branch of the Dal gCais (q.v.) descended from Aonghus Ceannathrach, son of Cas.

CINEAL mBEICE, race of Beice, grandson of Feidlimidh, King of Desmond in the 6th century ; the clan-name of the O'Mahonys, whose terÞitory lay around the town of Bandon.

CINEAL mBINNIGH, race of Binneach, son of Eoghan, son of Niall of the Nine Hostages ; a branch of Cineal Eoghain, q.v.

CINEAL CAIRBRE, race of Cairbre, son of Niall of the Nine Hostages, who were seated in the barony of Carbury, in the north of Co. Sligo.

CINEAL CINNGAMHNA, race of Seachnasach, surnamed Ceann-gamhna, son of Eoghan Aidhne, who was grandson of the celebrated King Dahy ; the name of a branch of Ui Fiachrach Aidhne, q.v.

CINEAL CONAILL race of Conall Gulban, son of Niall of the Nine Hostages, who were seated in Tirconaill and included the families of Ó Canannáin, Ó Maoloopaió, Ó Domnaill, Ó Oocaptaig, Ó Daoigill, Ó Gallcobaip, &c.

CINEAL CRIOMHTHAINN, race of Criomhthann ; the clan-name of the O'Duffs of Leix.

CINEAL CUALLACHTA, race of Cuallachta (or Collachtach) ; a branch of the Dal gCais (q.v.) descended from Aonghus Ceannathrach, son of Cas, and seated in the barony of Inchiquin, Co. Clare. Ó Spíobta was the chief family.

CINEAL EACHACH, race of Eochaidh, son of Eoghan, son of Niall of the Nine Hostages ; a branch of Cineal Eoghain (q.v.), seated in the present barony of Loughinsolin, Co. Derry, of which the O'Kellys were chiefs.

CINEAL ENDA, (1) race of Enda, son of Niall of the Nine Hostages, a branch of the southern Ui Neill (q.v.), seated near the Hill of Uisneach, in Westmeath ; and (2) race of Enda, son of Conall Gulban ; a branch of Cineal Conaill (q.v.) seated in the present barony of Raphoe.

CINEAL EOGHAIN, race of Eoghan, son of Niall of the Nine Hostages, whose territory originally comprised the present counties of Tyrone and Derry and the baronies of Raphoe and Inishowen in Donegal. The O'Neills were for many centuries the chief family.

CINEAL FAGHARTAIGH, race of Faghartach, the clan-name of the MacArtans, or MacCartans, and their correlatives in the present barony of Kinelarty, Co. Down.

CINEAL FEARADHAIGH, race of Fearadhach, son of Muireadhach, son of Eoghan, son of Niall of the Nine Hostages ; a branch of Cineal Eoghain (q.v.) whose territory embraced the barony of Clogher and other portions of Co. Tyrone.

CINEAL FIACHACH, race of Fiacha, son of Niall of the Nine Hostages, a branch of the southern Ui Neill (q.v.) whose territory extended from Birr to the Hill of Uisneach in Westmeath, and of which the chief families were the Mageoghegans and O'Molloys.

CINEAL GUAIRE, race of Guaire Aidhne, the celebrated King of Connacht in the 7th century ; the name of a branch of Ui Fiachrach Aidhne, q.v.

CINEAL IANNA, race of Ianna, a branch of Cineal Guaire, q.v.

CINEAL LAOGHAIRE, (1) race of Laoghaire, son of Niall of the Nine Hostages, seated in the baronies of Upper and Lower Navan, Co. Meath ; and (2) race of Laoghaire, the fourth in descent from Corc, king of Munster, the clan-name of the O'Donoghues of Desmond and their correlatives.

CINEAL LUACHAIN, race of Luachan, son of Onchu ; a branch of the Conmaicne Rein (q.v.) in the present Co. Leitrim, of which mᴀ𝔤 'Oo𝑟ċᴀɾ'óe was chief.

CINEAL LUIGHDHEACH, race of Lughaidh, son of Seadna, who was grandson of Conall Gulban ; a branch of Cineal Conaill (q.v.) of which the O'Donnells were the chief family.

CINEAL MOAIN, race of Moan (or Moen), son of Muireadhach, son of Eoghan, son of Niall of the Nine Hostages ; a branch of Cineal Eoghain (q.v.), originally seated in the barony of Raphoe, but afterwards in the barony of Strabane.

CINEAL TIGHEARNAIGH, race of Tighearnach, son of Muireadhach, son of Eoghan, son of Niall of the Nine Hostages ; a branch of Cineal Eoghain, q.v.

CLANN AODHA, race of Aodh, clan-name of the Maguinnesses of Co. Down.

CLANN AODHA BHUIDHE, race of yellow Aodh, clan-name of a branch of the O'Neills in Antrim and Down.

CLANN BHREASAIL, (1) race of Breasal ; also Ui Breasail, q.v.; the clan-name of the MacCanns and their correlatives in Co. Armagh ; and (2) race of Breasal, the clan-name of a branch of the Ui Maine (q.v.) seated between Loughrea and Ballinasloe, of which O'Donnellan was chief.

CLANN CHAIRBRE, v. Cineal Cairbre.

CLANN CHATHAIL, race of Cathal, son of Muireadhach Muilleathan, King of Connacht ; a branch of Siol Muireadhaigh, q.v.

CLANN CHEALLAIGH, race of Ceallach, a branch of the

Oirghialla (q.v.) in the south-east of Fermanagh, of which MacDonnell was chief.

CLANN CHEARNAIGH, race of Cearnach, (1) a branch of Maine, q.v. ; and (2) a branch of the Oirghialla (q.v.) of which Ó heıᵹnıᵹ was chief.

CLANN CHOINLEAGAIN, race of Coinleagan ; clan-name of the family of mac ᵹıolla póıl.

CLANN CHOLGAN, race of Colga, son of Maolduin, of the line of Rossa Failgheach, son of Cathaoir Mor ; an Offaly clan (v. Ui Failghe) of which the chief families were those of Ó hᴀonᵹupᴀ and Ó huᴀllᴀcáın.

CLANN CHOLMAIN, race of Colman Mor, son of Diarmaid, son of Fearghus Cirrbel, son of Conall Cremhthainne, son of Niall of the Nine Hostages ; the chief clan of the southern Ui Neill (q.v.) ; the clan-name of the O'Melaghlens and their correlatives in Meath.

CLANN CHONCHOBHAIR, race of Conchobhar ; a branch of Siol Muireadhaigh (q.v.) ; the clan-name of the O'Mulrennans and their correlatives in Co. Roscommon.

CLANN CHONGHAILE, race of Conghal, a branch of the Oirghialla (q.v.), in Co. Fermanagh, of which mac ᵹıolla mícıl was chief.

CLANN CHONNMHAIGH, son of Connmhach, son of Muireadhach Muilleathan, King of Connacht ; a branch of Siol Muireadhaigh (q.v.), of which the O'Finnaghtys were the chief family.

CLANN CHUAIN, race of Cuan, a branch of the Ui Fiachrach (q.v.) who were seated in the neighbourhood of Castlebar.

CLANN CHUILEAIN, race of Cuilean, a branch of the Dal gCais (q.v.) ; one of the clan-names of the MacNamaras and their correlatives in Thomond.

CLANN DALAIGH, race of Dalach, the eighth in descent from Conall Gulban ; a branch of Cineal Conaill (q.v.) ; the clan-name of the O'Donnells of Tirconnell.

CLANN DOMHNAILL, race of Domhnall, the clan-name of the O'Lavertys.

CLANN DUIBHSIONNAIGH, race of Dubhsionnach, a branch of the Oirghialla, q.v.

CLANN FEARGHAILE, race of Fearghal ; the clan-name (1) of the O'Hallorans of Galway, and (2) of the MacKiernans of Fermanagh.

CLANN LAOGHAIRE, race of Laoghaire, son of Eochaidh Breac, son of Dahy, King of Ireland ; a branch of the Ui Fiachrach, q.v.

CLANN MHAOLRUANAIDH, race of Maolruanaidh (O'Connor), son of Tadhg an eich ghil, King of Connacht, A.D. 1014-1036 ; a branch of Siol Muireadhaigh (q.v.), of which the MacDermotts of Moylurg and the MacDonaghs of Tirerrill were the chief families.

CLANN MHAOLUGHRA, race of Maolughra, a branch of the Ui Failghe (q.v.) ; the clan-name of the O'Dempseys and their correlatives in Offaly.

CLANN MHAONAIGH, race of Maonach, the clan-name of the O'Dooleys of Ely O'Carroll.

CLANN MHURCHADHA, race of Murchadh, the clan-name of a branch of the O'Finnaghtys who were seated on the east side of the Suck, in Co. Roscommon.

CLANN NEILL, race of Niall of the Nine Hostages ; v. Ui Neill.

CLANN tSEALBHAIGH, race of Sealbhach, one of the clannames of the O'Donoghues of Desmond and their correlatives.

CLANN TOMALTAIGH, race of Tomaltach, clan-name of the MacMurroughs of the Magh Aoi, in Co. Roscommon.

CONMHAICNE, race of Conmhac, son of Fergus MacRoigh ; alias Conmhaicne Rein ; the clan-name of the O'Farrells, Magrannals, and their correlatives, whose territory was co-extensive with the Diocese of Ardagh.

CONMHAICNE CUILE, race of Conmhac, son of Ferghus Mac-Roigh, seated in the barony of Kilmaine, Co. Mayo.

CORCA ACHLANN, alias Corca Seachlann, race of Seachlann, the clan-name of the MacBrannains and their correlatives in the east of Co. Roscommon.

CORCA ADHAIMH, alias Corca Adain, race of Adam, a branch of the southern Ui Neill (q.v.) who were seated in the present barony of Magheradernon, Co. Westmeath ; clan-name of the O'Dalys.

CORCA BHAISCINN, race of Cairbre Baschaoin, seated in the south-west of Co. Clare.

CORCA DHUIBNE, race of Duibhne, the name of a great clan in West Kerry, whose territory is now represented by Corcaguiny, Iveragh and Magunihy, and of which the chief families were O'Falvey, O'Shea and O'Connell.

CORCA LAOIGHDHE, race of Lughaidh Laidhe, grandfather of Lughaidh MacCon, monarch of Ireland in the 3rd century ; the name of a great clan in the south-west of Co. Cork, whose territory was co-extensive with the Diocese of Ross, and of which the O'Driscolls and O'Learys were the chief families.

CORCA MODHRUADH, race of Modruadh, son of Fergus Mac-Roigh ; the name of a great clan in the north-west of Co. Clare, whose territory was co-extensive with the Diocese of Kilfenora, and of which the chief families were the O'Connors and O'Loghlens.

CORCA MUICHET, race of Muichet, said to have been son of Brian, son of Eochaidh Muighmheadhoin, King of Ireland, who possessed an extensive district in the south of Co. Limerick, of which in later times MacEniry was chief.

CORCA OICHE, race of Ochae (or Fochae) Beg ; a celebrated Munster clan, whose territory comprised a great portion of the south-west of Co. Limerick, and of which Ó ṁacaṗa was chief.

CORCA RAOIDHE, race of Fiacha Raoidhe, son of Feidlimidh Reachtmhar, seated in the barony of Corcaree, Co. Westmeath.

DLAL ARAIDHE, race of Fiacha Araidhe, a great Ulster clan whose territory stretched from Newry to Slemmish, and of which the O'Lynches and O'Lawlors were the chief families.

DAL mBUINNE, race of Buinne, alias Muinntear Bhranain, an Antrim clan whose territory was co-extensive with the parish of Kiltulagh, and of which Ó Seaṗṗaiġ was chief.

DAL gCAIS, race of Cas, the sixth in descent from Cormac Cas, son of Oilioll Olum, King of Munster in the 3rd century ; the name of the great clan of Thomond, or North Munster, which embraced several distinguished families and of which the O'Briens were the chiefs.

DAL bhFIATACH, race of Fiatach Fionn, king of Ulidia, a warlike clan seated in the present Co. Down, of which, in the 12th century, MacDunlevy was chief.

DEALBHNA, race of Lughaidh Dealbhaodh, said to have been son of Cas, the ancestor of the Dal gCais, q.v. ; divided into several branches seated in Meath and Connacht, as D. Mhor, now .represented by the barony of Delvin, in Westmeath ; D. Bheag, now the barony of Demifore, in Co. Meath ; D. Eathra, or MacCoghlan's country, in the barony of Garrycastle ; D. Cuile Fabhair and D. Tire-da-Locha, in Connacht.

EOGHANACHT, race of Eoghan Mor, son of Oilioll Olum, King of Munster in the 3rd century, which was sub-divided into E. Chaisil, E. Locha Lein, E. Aine, &c., and to which belonged the chief families of South Munster.

EOGHANACHT CHAISIL, a branch of the Eoghanacht, (q.v.) seated in the barony of Middlethird, Co. Tipperary.

EOGHANACHT AINE, a branch of the Eoghanacht (q.v.), seated at Knockany, in Co. Limerick, of which Ó Ciaṗṁaic was chief.

FEARA BILE, men of Bile, in Westmeath, the clan-name of the O'Hanveys.

FEARA CEALL, men of churches, one of the clan-names of the O'Molloys, in the present Offaly.

FEARA CUALANN, men of Cuala, a clan whose territory included a great portion of the present counties of Dublin and Wicklow.

FEARA LUIRG, men of Lurg, the clan-name of the O'Muldoons and their correlatives who were seated in the barony of Lurg, in Co. Monaghan.

FEARA MAIGHE, men of the plain, the clan-name of the

O'Dugans whose territory is represented by the present barony of Fermoy.

FEARA ROIS, men of Ros, whose territory lay in the neighbourhood of the present Carrickmacross.

FEARA TULACH, men of the hills, the clan-name of the O'Dooleys, whose territory is now represented by the barony of Fertullagh, in Co. Westmeath.

FIR LI, men of Li, a famous Ulster clan descended from Colla Uais, monarch of Ireland in the 4th century, and originally seated on the west side of the Bann, until expelled by Ó Caṫáın some time before the Anglo-Norman invasion.

FIR TEATHBHA, men of Teathbha, or Teffia, the clan-name of the descendants of Maine, son of Niall of the Nine Hostages, who were one of the chief clans of the southern Ui Neill, and whose territory embraced a great portion of Westmeath and also the barony of Kilcoursey in the present Offaly.

LUIGHNE, race of Lugh, the clan-name of the O'Haras and O'Garas in Co. Sligo.

MUINTEAR BHIRN, family of Biorn, the clan-name of the MacRorys and their correlatives in the present Co. Tyrone.

MUINTEAR CHEARBHALLAIN, family of Cearbhallan, a branch of Muintear Eoluis (q.v.) of which O'Mulvey was chief.

MUINTEAR CHIONAOITH, family of Cionaoth, the clan-name of the MacAnavas and their correlatives in the barony of Dromahare, Co. Leitrim.

MUINTEAR EOLUIS, family of Eolus, a branch of Conmhaicne Rein in Co. Leitrim ; the clan-name of the MacRannals and their correlatives.

MUINTEAR GHEARADHAIN, family of Gearadhan, the clan-name of the Gaynors in the north of Co. Longford.

MUINTEAR GHIOLLAGAIN, family of Giollagan, the clan-name of the O'Quinns in Co. Longford.

MUINTEAR IFEARNAIN, family of Ifearnan, a branch of the Dal gCais (q.v.), the clan-name of the O'Quins of Thomond who derive their descent from Ifearnan, son of Corc, the 15th in descent from Cormac Cas, the ancestor of the Dal gCais.

MUINTEAR LAOGHACHAIN, family of Laoghachan, the 13th in descent from Maine, son of Niall of the Nine Hostages, a branch of Fir Teathbha q.v.

MUINTEAR MHAOILSIONNA, family of Maolsionna, the 13th in descent from Maine, son of Niall of the Nine Hostages, a branch of Fir Teathbha of which Mac Caṙṙġaṁna was chief.

MUINTEAR MHAOLMORDHA, family of Maolmordha, the 14th in descent from Duach Galach, son of Brion, son of Eochaidh Muighmheadhoin, King of Ireland ; a branch of the Ui Briuin, q.v. ; the clan-name of the O'Reillys in Co. Cavan.

MUINTEAR MHURCHADHA, family of Murchadh, the 10th in descent from Duach Teangumha and 14th from Duach

Galach, son of Brion, son of Eochaidh Muighmheadhoin,
King of Ireland ; the clan-name of the O'Flahertys in Connacht.

MUINTEAR RODHUIBH, family of Rodhubh, the clan-name of
the Mageraghtys in Co. Roscommon.

MUINTEAR tSLAMAIN, family of Slaman, a branch of Fir
Teathbha, q.v.

MUINTEAR TADHGAIN, family of Tadhgan, the eighth in
descent from Brian, son of Maine, son of Niall of the Nine
Hostages ; a branch of Fir Teathbha, q.v, ; the clan-name
of the Foxes of Kilcoursey.

OIRGHIALLA (whence Oriel), the name of a great Ulster clan
descended from the three Collas, who conquered the ancient
Ultonians and wrested from them the greater part of Ulster ;
but in later times their territory was confined to Louth,
Armagh, Monaghan and Fermanagh.

SIOL ANMCHADHA, seed of Anmchadh, a branch of the Ui
Maine (q.v.), descended from Anmchadh, the eighth in
descent from Maine Mor, ancestor of the Ui Maine.

SIOL MAOLRUAIN, seed of Maolruanaidh, the seventh in descent
from Duach Galach, son of Brion, son of Eochoidh Muighmheadhoin, King of Ireland ; a branch of the Ui Briuin, in
Co. Roscommon, of which the O'Flynns were the chief
family.

SIOL MUIREADHAIGH (Silmurray), seed of Muireadhach
Muilleathan, King of Connacht, who died in the year 701 ;
the clan-name of the O'Connors and their correlatives in
Connacht, including the MacDermotts, MacDonoughs,
O'Beirnes, O'Flanagans, Mageraghtys and O'Finnaghtys.

TEALLACH DHUNCHADHA, household of Dunchadh, son of
Maonach, the eighth in descent from Duach Galach, son of
Brion, son of Eochaidh Muighmheadhoin, King of Ireland ;
a branch of the Ui Briuin, q.v. ; the clan-name of the Mac-
Kernans ; now represented by the barony of Tullyhunco, in
the west of Co. Cavan.

TEALLACH EACHACH, household of Eochaidh, son of Maonach
(v. Teallach Dhunchadha) ; a branch of the Ui Briuin, q.v. ;
the clan-name of the Magurans ; now represented by the
barony of Tullyhaw, in the north-west of Co. Cavan.

UI BAIRRCHE, dess. of Daire Barrach, son of Cathaoir Mor, King
of Ireland in the 2nd century ; the clan-name of the
O'Tracys and MacGormans in the barony of Slievemargy
in Leix.

UI BLOID, dess. of Blod, son of Cas, a branch of the Dal gCais
(q.v.), including the families of O'Kennedy, O'Shanahan,
O'Durack and O'Ahern, whose territory lay in the east of
Co. Clare, where the name is still preserved in the deanery
of Omulled.

UI BREASAIL(MACHA), alias Clann Bhreasail (q.v.), dess. of Breasal, son of Eochaidh, son of Feidlimidh, son of Fiachra Casan, son of Colla-da-chrioch; a branch of the Oirghialla(q.v.) who were seated in the barony of Oneilland East, Co. Armagh.

UI BRIUIN, dess. of Brion, King of Connacht, son of Eochaidh Muighmheadhoin, King of Ireland, of whom there were different branches in Connacht and Breifney, as :

UI BRIUIN BREIFNE, a branch of the Ui Briuin seated in Breifney, of which the O'Rourkes and O'Reillys were the chief families.

UI BRIUIN EOLA, a branch of the Ui Briuin seated in West Connacht, of which the O'Lees were chiefs.

UI BRIUIN NA SIONNA, a branch of the Ui Briuin seated in Co. Roscommon, of which Ó mαnαċάin was chief.

UI BRIUIN RATHA, a branch of the Ui Briuin in West Connacht, of which Ó Oαċlαoiċ was chief.

UI CAIRBRE AEDHBHA, dess. of Cairbre Aedhbha, grandson of Fiacha Fidhgheinte, a branch of the Ui Fidhgheinte (q.v.), seated along the Maigue in Co. Limerick, of which Ó Oonn-αḃάin was chief.

UI CAISIN, dess. of Caisin, son of Cas, the name of a branch of the Dal gCais of which mαc Conmαρα was chief.

UI CEARNAIGH, dess. of Cearnach, a branch of the Dal gCais of which the Ahernes were chiefs.

UI CEINNSEALAIGH, dess. of Eanna Ceinnsealach, son of Cathaoir Mor, King of Ireland, whose territory was co-extensive with the Diocese of Ferns.

UI CONAILL GABHRA, dess. of Conall, the fourth in descent from Fiacha Fidhgheinte, a branch of the Ui Fidhgheinte (q.v.), of which the chief families were the O'Collins and O'Kinnealys, and whose territory comprised the baronies of Upper and Lower Connello, Shanid and Glenquin, in Co. Limerick.

UI CORMAIC, dess. of Cormac, the clan-name of the O'Hehirs in Thomond.

UI DRONA, dess. of Drona, the fourth in descent from Cathaoir Mor, King of Leinster and monarch of Ireland in the 2nd century ; the clan-name of the O'Ryans in the barony of Idrone, Co. Carlow.

UI DUACH, dess. of Dui, the clan-name of the O'Brennans of Ossory.

UI EACHACH, dess. of Eochaidh, grandson of Fiacha Casan, son of Colla-da-chrioch, a branch of the Oirghialla (q.v.) who were seated in the present barony of Armagh and of which Ó Oomnαill and Ó Ruαóαξάin were chiefs.

UI EACHACH, alias UI EACHACH COBHA, alias UI EACHACH ULADH, dess. of Eochaidh, the name of a branch of Clann Rudhraighe who were seated in, and gave its name to, the barony of Iveagh, in Co. Down.

UI EACHACH MUAIDHE, i.e., Ui Eachach of the Moy, a branch of the Ui Fiachrach (q.v.), descended from Eochaidh Breac, son of Dahy, King of Ireland.

UI EACHACH MUMHAN, i.e., Ui Eachach of Munster, dess. of Eochaidh, son of Cas, son of Corc, King of Munster, the clan-name of the O'Mahonys and O'Donoghues of Desmond.

UI FAILGHE, dess. of Rossa Failgheach, eldest son of Cathoir Mor King of Ireland in the 2nd century, of whom the chief families were the O'Connors, O'Dempseys and O'Dunnes.

UI FAOLAIN, dess. of Faolan of the race of Cathaoir Mor, King of Ireland; the clan-name of the O'Byrnes and MacKeoghs who, prior to the Anglo-Norman invasion, were seated in the north of the present Co. Kildare.

UI FEARMAIC, dess. of Fearmac, of the race of Aonghus Cean-nathrach, son of Cas ; a branch of the Dal gCais (q.v.), of which the O'Deas were the chief family.

UI FEILMEADHA, dess. of Feidlimidh, son of Eanna Ceinn-sealach, King of Leinster in the 4th century, of whom there were two clans in Leinster, viz : Ui F. Teas and Ui F. Tuaidh, q.v.

UI FEILMEADHA TEAS, i.e., the southern Ui Feilmeadha (q.v.), seated in the present barony of Ballaghkeen, in the east of Co. Wexford, of whom Ó Muŗċaóa was chief.

UI FEILMEADHA TUAIDH, i.e., the northern Ui Feilmeadha (q.v.), who were seated in the present barony of Rathvilly Co. Carlow.

UI FIACHRACH, dess. of Fiachra, son of Eochaidh Muigh-mheadhoin, King of Ireland in the 4th century. Fiachra was a brother of Niall of the Nine Hostages and father of the celebrated King Dahy, the last pagan monarch of Ireland. The Ui Fiachrach were divided into two great branches, viz : Ui Fiachrach Muaidhe and Ui Fiachrach Aidhne, q.v.

UI FIACHRACH AIDHNE, or southern Ui Fiachrach, a branch of the Ui Fiachrach (q.v.), seated in the district of Aidhne, in the south of the present Co. Galway, co-extensive with the Diocese of Kilmacduagh. The Ui Fiachrach Aidhne de-rived their descent from Eoghan Aidhne, grandson of the celebrated King Dahy.

UI FIACHRACH ARDA SRATHA, i.e., Ui F. of Ardstraw, also called Ui F. Finn, dess. of Fiachra, son of Erc, son of Colla Uais ; a branch of the Oirghialla, q.v.

UI FIACHRACH FINN, dess. of Fiachra Fionn, son of Breasal, son of Maine Mor, a branch of the Ui Maine (q.v.) ; the clan-name of the O'Naughtons and O'Mullalys of Connacht.

UI FIACHRACH MUAIDHE, i.e., Ui F. of the Moy, also called the northern Ui Fiachrach, a branch of the Ui Fiachrach (q.v.), descended from Fiachra, son of King Dahy, and seated in the present counties of Mayo and Sligo.

696

UI FIDHGHEINTE, dess. of Fiacha Fidhgheinte who was grandson of Oilioll Flanbeg, King of Munster, and flourished in the 4th century ; the name of a great clan whose territory was co-extensive with the Diocese of Limerick and of which Ó Donnabáin was chief.

UI LIATHAIN, dess. of Eochaidh Liathanach,son of Oilioll Flanbeg, King of Munster, whose territory was co-extensive with the present barony of Barrymore, Co. Cork.

UI MAINE, dess. of Maine Mor, the fourth in descent from Colla-da-chrioch, one of the ancestors of the Oirghialla (q.v.) ; the name of a great Connacht clan, whose territory comprised part of the present counties of Galway, Roscommon, Clare and Offaly, and of which O'Kelly was chief.

UI MEITH(MACHA), alias Ui Meith Tire, dess. of Muireadhach Meith, son of Imchadh, son of Colla-da-chrioch ; a branch of the Oirghialla (q.v.), seated in the barony and county of Monaghan.

UI MUIREADHAIGH, dess. of Muireadhach, of the line of Cathaoir Mor, monarch of Ireland ; clan-name of the O'Tooles, whose territory, prior to the Anglo-Norman invasion, comprised the southern half of the present Co. Kildare.

UI NEILL, dess. of Niall of the Nine Hostages, King of Ireland, A.D. 379-406. They were divided into two great branches called the northern and southern Ui Neill. The chief clans of the northern Ui Neill, whose territory lay in the present counties of Tyrone, Derry, Donegal and the north of Co. Sligo, were Cineal Eoghain, Cineal Conaill and Cineal Cairbre ; while those of the southern Ui Neill, whose territory was co-extensive with the Diocese of Meath, were Clann Cholmain, Cineal Fiachach and Fir Teathbha..

UI NIALLAIN, dess. of Niallan, son of Fiacha, son of Feidlimidh, son of Fiachra Casan, son of Colla-da-chrioch ; a branch of the Oirghialla (q.v.), whose territory is now represented by the baronies of Oneilland in Co. Armagh.

UI RIAGAIN, dess. of Riagan, the tenth in descent from Rossa Failgheach, son of Cathaoir Mor, King of Ireland ; a branch of the Ui Failghe of which the O'Dunnes were the chief family.

UI RONGHAILE, dess. of Ronghal, a branch of the Dal gCais (q.v.) of which the O'Shanahans were the chief family.

UI TOIRDEALBHAIGH, dess. of Toirdealbhach (father of St. Flannan), king of Thomond ; the clan-name of the O'Briens and their correlatives in the east of Co. Clare.

UI TUIRTRE, dess. of Fiacha Tort, grandson of Colla Uais, a branch of the Oirghialla (q.v.) seated to the east of the Bann and Lough Neagh, in Co. Antrim.